Thomas J. Nechyba

INTERMEDIATE MICROECONOMICS

AN INTUITIVE APPROACH
WITH CALCULUS

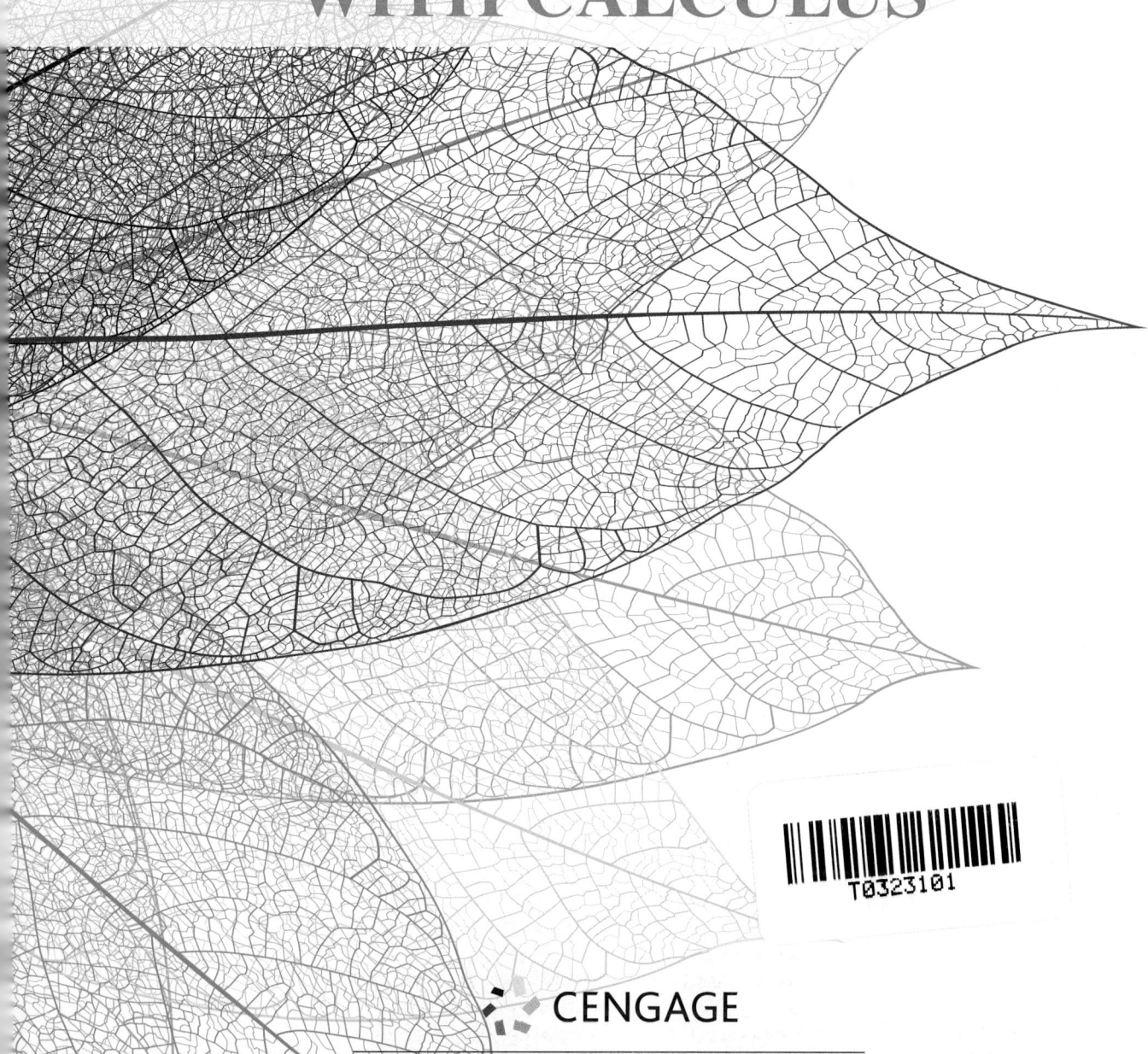

CENGAGE

Australia • Brazil • Mexico • Singapore • United Kingdom • United States

Intermediate Microeconomics: An Intuitive Approach with Calculus, **First EMEA Edition**
Thomas Nechyba

Publisher: Annabel Ainscow

List Manager: Abigail Coppin

Marketing Manager: Sophie Clarke

Content Project Manager: Phillipa Davidson-Blake

Manufacturing Manager: Eyvett Davis

Typesetter: MPS Limited

Cover design: Simon Levy Associates

Cover Image: © Yuliya Koldovska/Shutterstock

For product information and technology assistance, contact us at
emea.info@cengage.com
For permission to use material from this text or product,
and for permission queries,
email **emea.permissions@cengage.com**

British Library Cataloguing-in-Publication Data

A catalogue record for this book is available from the British Library.

ISBN: 978-1-4737-5900-8

Cengage Learning EMEA
Cheriton House, North Way
Andover, Hampshire, SP10 5BE
United Kingdom

Cengage Learning is a leading provider of customized learning solutions with employees residing in nearly 40 different countries and sales in more than 125 countries around the world. Find your local representative at: **www.cengage.co.uk**

Cengage Learning products are represented in Canada by Nelson Education, Ltd.

For your course and learning solutions, visit **www.cengage.co.uk**

Purchase any of our products at your local college store or at our preferred online store **www.cengagebrain.com.**

Printed in China by RR Donnelley
Print Number: 01   Print Year: 2018

Brief Contents

Contents

Preface

To Students

Here are a few points on how best to use this text:

1 You may want to review parts of Chapter 0, which is available on the MindTap to revise some basics before proceeding to Chapter 2.
2 Attempt the *within-chapter exercises* as you read—and check your answers with those in the Study Guide. (Quasi-controlled experiments during the initial drafting of this text with students show that those who use within-chapter exercises and solutions, do considerably better on exams.)
3 Graphs with blue bars at the bottom can be unpacked directly within the MindTap Reader, and almost all graphs are available to view as animated and narrated videos that can be accessed through MindTap. While some of the video animations are long, you can skip ahead and use chapter markers to locate the part of the video you are most interested in.
4 Look for interesting applications in the *end-of-chapter exercises*, but know that some of these are designed to be challenging. Don't get frustrated if they don't make sense at first. It helps to work with others to solve these.
5 The book has an extensive Glossary and Index but develops definitions within a narrative rather than pulling them out within the text. Use the Glossary to remind yourself of the meaning of terms and the Index to find where the associated concepts are discussed in detail. Resist the temptation to memorize too much. The terms aren't as important as the concepts.

To Instructors

This book attempts to build a framework around five primary goals that we believe any microeconomics course should accomplish:

1 It should present microeconomics not as a collection of unrelated models but *as a way of looking at the world*. People respond to incentives because they try to do the best they can given their circumstances. That's microeconomics in a nutshell—and everything—*everything*—flows from it.
2 It should persuade that microeconomics does not just change the way *we think* about the world—it also tells us a lot about *how and why the world works* and sometimes doesn't work.
3 It should not only get us to think more clearly about economics but also *to think more clearly in general*—without relying on memorization. Such *conceptual thinking skills* are the very skills that are most sought after and most rewarded in the modern world.
4 It should directly confront the fact that few of us can move from memorizing to conceptual thinking without *applying concepts directly*, but different students learn differently, and instructors need the *flexibility* to target material to *their* students' needs.
5 Finally, it should provide students with a *roadmap for further studies*—a sense of what the most compelling next courses might be given *their* interests.

Half the text builds up to the most fundamental result in all of economics—that self-interested individuals will—*under certain conditions and without intending to*—give rise to a spontaneous order that has great benefits for society. The second half probes these certain conditions and develops insights into how firms, governments and civil society can contribute to human welfare when markets by themselves fail. Future courses can then be seen as sub-fields that come to terms with these certain conditions.

While the material in the full text is more than enough for a two-semester sequence, the text offers a *variety of flexible paths for a one-semester course*. In each chapter, you can emphasize an intuitive A part or link it to a more mathematical B part; and, while the last part of the text relies heavily on game theory, the underlying narrative can also be developed through a non-game theoretic approach. Substantive paths include some focused on *theory*, others focused on *policy*, and yet others focused on *business*, with all paths including core material as well as optional topics. Throughout, the models build in complexity, with applications woven into the narrative. They are then further developed in an extensive array of exercises that get students to apply concepts to *Everyday*, *Business* and *Policy* settings.

The Instructor's Manual provides more details on how you might use the various parts of the text and its accompanying tools.

While the student study guide includes answers to all odd numbered end-of-chapter exercises (in addition to answers to within-chapter exercises), answers to all end-of-chapter exercises are available to instructors.

Acknowledgements

The publisher wishes to thank the following reviewers for their helpful feedback during the development of this edition:

Sean Byrne, Dublin Institute of Technology, Ireland
Giovanni Ferro-Luzzi, University of Geneva, Switzerland
Alain Kaninda, Monash University, South Africa
Stefan Franz Schubert, Free University of Bozen-Bolzano, Italy
Thomas Wein, Leuphana University, Germany

About the Author

PROFESSOR THOMAS J. NECHYBA who received his PhD from the University of Rochester, USA in 1994, joined the Duke faculty, USA in 1999 after spending five years on the faculty at Stanford University, USA. In addition to his activities in the USA, he has lectured internationally in Europe, Latin America and New Zealand. His teaching has been recognized with numerous awards including the Stanford Dean's Award for Distinguished Teaching (1996), the Southern Economic Association's Ken Elzinga Distinguished Teaching Award (2004) and the Duke University Scholar/Teacher of the Year Award (2007). Dr Nechyba is currently a Research Associate at the National Bureau of Economic Research and has served (or is serving) as Associate Editor for the *American Economic Review, International Tax and Public Finance* and the *Journal of Economic Literature*, among others. At Duke, he has previously served as Director of Undergraduate Studies and as Department Chair and currently directs the Economics Center for Teaching (EcoTeach) as well as Duke's Social Science Research Institute. Dr Nechyba's research on public finance, urban economics and the economics of education has been funded by agencies such as the National Science Foundation and has been published in journals such as the *American Economic Review*, the *Journal of Political Economy*, the *International Journal of Economics* and the *Journal of Public Economics*, among others.

Adapting Author for Europe, Middle East and Africa

ANDREW ASHWIN has over 20 years' experience as a teacher of economics. He has an MBA from the University of Hull and a PhD in assessment and the notion of threshold concepts in economics from the University of Leicester. Andrew is an experienced author, writing a number of texts for students at different levels, and journal publications related to his PhD research. Andrew was Chair of Examiners for a major awarding body for business and economics in England and is a subject specialist consultant in economics for the UK regulator, Ofqual. Andrew has a keen interest in assessment and learning in economics and has received accreditation as a Chartered Assessor with the Chartered Institute of Educational Assessors. He has also edited the journal of the Economics, Business and Enterprise Association (EBEA).

Chapter 1

Introduction

Do safer cars necessarily result in fewer traffic deaths? Is it sensible to subsidize solar energy in an effort to reduce the reliance on fossil fuel energy? Would outlawing live Christmas trees help to reduce deforestation? Should we impose laws against 'price gouging'? Is boycotting companies that use cheap labour abroad a good way to protest about working conditions in those countries? Should we tax the profits of monopolies?

Many people would instinctively answer 'yes' to each of these questions. Many economists would say 'no', or at least 'not necessarily'. Why is that?

By and large, economists are an ideologically diverse group, distributed along the political spectrum much as the rest of the population. Economists do, however, look at the world through a somewhat different lens, a lens that presumes people respond to incentives and that these responses aggregate in ways that are often surprising, frequently humbling and sometimes quite stunning. What we think we know isn't always so, and, as a result, our actions, particularly in the policy realm, often have 'unintended' consequences.

Through the lens of social science, economists see many instances of remarkable social order emerging from millions of seemingly unconnected choices in the marketplace, spontaneous cooperation among individuals on different ends of the globe, the kind of cooperation that propels societies out of the material poverty and despair that has characterized most of human history. At the same time, our lens clarifies when individual incentives run counter to the common good, when private interests unravel social cooperation in the absence of corrective non-market institutions. Markets have given rise to enormous wealth, but we also have to come to terms with issues such as economic inequality, the impact on the environment of human activity, unscrupulous business practices and racial discrimination.

1A   What is Microeconomics?

We will define *microeconomics* as the *science* that investigates the *social consequences* of the interaction of *rational* beings that pursue their *perceived self-interest*. At first glance, this description of human beings as 'rational' and 'self-interested' may sound naive. After all, most people would not characterize their fellow citizens as always 'rational'. It is useful to say a bit more about this definition.

1A.1 Economics as a Science

Economics is not a science in the same way that physics or chemistry are science. Knowledge and understanding through science progresses through the formulation and testing of models that generate hypotheses, and in this sense, economics can be viewed as a science. Economists formulate models that are rooted in economic theory and check to see whether the hypotheses that emerge are rejected by real-world observations. Some economists actually do perform experiments, but most look at data from the real world to see whether their predictions hold.

1A.2 Rationality and Self-Interest

Many economic models are based on an assumption that people are *rational* and in pursuit of their *perceived self-interest*. The term 'rational' is taken to mean that individuals seek to do the best they can given their circumstances, that is, they are deliberative in trying to achieve their goals. Those goals might include improving the welfare of others they care about, and they may include goals that make sense to them but don't make sense to others. Someone who sacrifices personal consumption to improve their children's well-being may be thought of as 'unselfish', but it may still be in the individual's perceived self-interest if, in making their children happy, their own happiness is improved. That seems quite noble, but not everything that one individual finds worthwhile might be worthwhile in some deeper sense. The business person may seek to maximize their own profit when they could be saving starving children instead; the politician may seek to win elections when they could be making a worthwhile difference in people's lives by doing something unpopular; the drug addict may seek to get their next fix when they might be better off checking into a rehab centre. Nevertheless, each of these individuals is directing their actions towards a goal they perceive to be worthwhile and in their own self-interest.

Self-interest is not necessarily the same as selfishness. The latter presumes you care only about yourself; the former leaves open the possibility that others may contribute to your perception of your own well-being. Often, selfishness and self-interest coincide, but not always. In economics, the term rational simply means that we pick the best available course of action to achieve our self-interested goal.

1A.3 Social Consequences, Pencils and Environmental Impact

Part of the goal of economics is understanding the *social consequences* of the interaction of rational, self-interested individual behaviour. We may model how an individual behaves under certain assumptions, but of greater interest is what happens when hundreds, thousands or even millions of rational, self-interested individuals pursue their individual goals *given that everyone else is doing the same*. Economists call the outcome of these interactions an *equilibrium*, and it is in this equilibrium that we find the social consequences of individual behaviour.

Nobel Prize winning economist, Milton Friedman, famously held up a pencil and made the initially preposterous claim that no one in the world knows how to make that pencil. This might seem to be a strange claim, but if we seriously think about the challenge of making a pencil *from scratch it sounds less strange*. One would have to know which trees to harvest for the wood, how to make the tools to harvest the trees, what chemicals to use to treat the wood once it is cut into the right shape, how to drill the hole to make room for the lead and how to make the tools to drill the hole. That does not begin to scratch the surface, because we also have to know everything about where to get the materials to eventually make the lead and how to make it and all the necessary tools required for that, how to create the paint and paintbrushes to coat the outside of the pencil, and so on. When you really think about it, tens of thousands of people somehow cooperated across all the continents in the world to make the pencil Friedman was holding, and few of those tens of thousands of people would be aware that they were participating in a process that would result in a pencil.

Economists are fascinated by the fact that pencils, and many other goods, are produced despite the fact that few individuals know how to produce them and despite the fact that no one is charged with coordinating all these people and materials into the production of pencils. Cooperation on such a massive scale can emerge from the bottom up without the individuals knowing that they are cooperating with one another. This cooperation can emerge purely from the rational, self-interested choices that individuals make along the way, each one trying to earn a living, to do the best they can given the circumstances. This is a *social consequence* of the interaction of rational, self-interested behaviour, one that is guided by the impersonal forces of market prices that tell individuals where to work, what to produce, whom to sell to, etc.

Not all social consequences of rational, self-interested behaviour are desirable. The same economic lens that explains how people cooperate to make pencils also highlights the impact of human activity on the environment, how relative as opposed to absolute poverty persists, how concentrated power distorts markets and how some goods might never get produced unless non-market institutions intervene. Understanding when we can rely on individual self-interest to give rise to cooperation – and when such self-interest impedes cooperation – is one of the key themes of this book and one of the central goals of microeconomics. With such an understanding, we can formulate ways of changing the circumstances in which decisions are made to bring those decisions more in line with social goals: to change the *social consequences* of rational, self-interested behaviour by *altering the incentives* people face along the way.

1A.4 Economics, Incentives and Economic Models

Economics can be seen as an exploration of the premise that *people respond to incentives* because they generally *attempt to do the best they can given their circumstances*. It is a premise that leads to a rich framework through which to analyze many small and large debates in the world in a logical and rigorous manner. However, much of this book is devoted to the building of economic models that, at least initially, seem to be starkly disconnected from reality. One criticism of these models is that they involve *simplistic* and *unrealistic* characterizations of what we are as human beings. In certain ways, this is correct. Nevertheless, the use of such models represents one method through which economists can make some sense of the underlying issues we are concerned about. In the process, we also get an unintended consequence of learning through economic models. We learn to think more conceptually, to move beyond memorization to 'think in the subject'.

1A.4.1 Economic Models and Simplicity In the first section of this book we will assume consumers are individuals who rationally calculate the costs and benefits of different alternatives using a mechanical characterization of tastes as a guide. This is not a full characterization of all the complexity that underlies the human condition, and it omits some of the very aspects of our make-up that make us human.

Economics does not claim to paint a full picture of who we are as human beings. Economics tries to provide a framework for systematically studying aspects of human decision making that relate to our desire to pursue perceived self-interest in different institutional settings, and how such self-interested decision making affects society as a whole. Simplicity in models becomes a virtue as long as the models can predict well what we are trying to predict.

Economic models are constructed to strip away all the complexity, all the noise that gets in the way of an analysis of particular economic problems and leave us with the essence of individual decision making that matters for the questions at hand. They will not tell us whether there is a God or why we like to stare at the stars at night or why we fall in love. But they can be powerful tools that allow us to understand aspects of the world that would remain impenetrable without the use of simplified models. For this reason, resist the temptation of dismissing models – in economics or elsewhere – by suggesting that they are simplistic. A measuring tape is simplistic, but it is a useful tool to the carpenter who attempts to build a piece of furniture, much more useful than the more complex microscopic tools a neurosurgeon might use to do their work. In the same way, it is precisely because they are simple that many economic models become useful tools as we try to build an understanding of how individual decision making impacts the world.

1A.4.2 Economic Models, Realism and Snooker Players Another analogy by Milton Friedman illustrates a slightly different aspect of economic models. Think about snooker players on the professional circuit. These players are typically not expert physicists who can calculate the precise paths of snooker balls under different circumstances, using the latest knowledge of underlying equations that govern the behaviour of snooker balls. Suppose we wanted to arrive at a useful model that could predict the next move of each snooker player, and suppose it was suggested to you that we should model each snooker player as an expert physicist who can instantly access the latest mathematical complexities in physics to predict the best possible next move. The model is absurd in the sense that it is completely unrealistic; many of these players will not have any advanced grounding in physics or maths. It is likely, however, that the model would do pretty well at predicting the next move of the best snooker players, better than virtually any other model we could come up with.

Similarly, consider the problem of predicting the growth of a particular plant. Which branches will grow leaves this season and in which direction? One possible model would assume that the plant consciously calculates, using the latest knowledge of biologists and other scientists, how to distribute the nutrients it gains from the soil to various branches optimally, taking into consideration the path of the sun and thus the distribution of resulting sunlight, the rotation of the earth, etc. The model is once again absurd in the sense that we can be fairly certain that there is no conscious mind in the plant that is capable of accessing all the relevant facts and making the appropriate calculations. Nevertheless, a model that assumes the presence of such a mind within the plant may well be a useful model to help us predict how the plant will grow.

Models, regardless of what they aim to predict, do not have to be realistic. They can be, and it sometimes might help our understanding if they were. Equally, not all aspects of economic models need to be fully realistic. The consumer model we will look at in the next few chapters implies that individuals can map their tastes into complicated graphs or, alternatively, that they use multivariable calculus to analyze choice alternatives using mathematical functions of which few people are aware. This is absurd in the same way as it is absurd to assume that snooker players are expert physicists or plants are expert biologists. In the same way that these assumptions help us predict the next moves of snooker players and the next steps in the growth of a plant, our assumptions about consumers allow us to make predictions about their economic choices. Thus, just as it is hoped you will not dismiss models because of their simplicity, it is also hoped you will not dismiss them if they appear to be unrealistic in certain ways.

1A.4.3 An Unintended Consequence of Learning Through Economic Models Economists often point out unintended consequences, consequences that don't immediately come to mind when we contemplate doing something. The models we'll be using are specialized in some sense, but they are general in the sense that each model can be applied to many different real-world problems. Once you get really comfortable with the way economists model behaviour, it boils down to one single model, or at least one single conceptual approach. As you internalize this conceptual approach to thinking about the world, you will find that your conceptual thinking skills become much sharper, and that has implications that go far beyond economics. There is, thus, an unintended consequence of learning microeconomics.

The modern world expects more than good memorization skills from students. Those who succeed in the modern world have developed higher conceptual thinking skills that have virtually nothing to do with memorization.

What is important, therefore is to train your conceptual muscle, the muscle that allows you to progress beyond viewing each new situation you encounter as a new problem to be solved from scratch and permits you to learn from situations that share some features in common. The framework of economics enables you to develop skills that allow for the translation of knowledge across time and space.

1A.5 *Predicting* Versus *Judging* Behaviour and Social Outcomes

Aside from learning to think in the subject or think more conceptually, the real point of these models is to *predict* behaviour and to predict the social consequences of that behaviour. For the vast majority of economists, a model is good if it predicts well. The self-interested goals individuals pursue matter in the analysis because they help us predict how behaviour will change as circumstances change; to the economist interested in prediction, the deeper philosophical question of whether some goals are inherently more worthwhile than others, is irrelevant. What matters for predicting what you will do if the price of fuel increases, is how much fuel you consume as a result, not whether it is morally good or bad to consume fuel. Whether it might be good or bad to raise the price of fuel is a very different question, one that presumes some deeper philosophical views about how to *judge* what is good and bad.

Economists do, of course, have objective standards for what is ultimately in our best interest. As human beings, almost all of us, explicitly or implicitly, hold to such standards and wish that we and the rest of the world would abide by them more frequently. Most of us believe the drug addict would indeed be better off if they checked into a treatment centre, that the politician ought to care about more than the next election, and that the business person should care about starving children. Most economists, *in their role as economists*, are in the business of predicting how changing incentives will change the actual behaviour of people who may have quite different ideas about what is worthwhile than the economist who is modelling them. What matters for their behaviour is what *they* think is worthwhile, not what the economist thinks *should be* worthwhile.

1A.5.1 Positive Economics: How to Predict Real Outcomes

The branch of economics that concerns itself primarily with such predictions is known as *positive economics*, and it is the branch of economics that is in a real sense value-free. In the economist's pursuit to predict what will actually happen as incentives change, there is not the luxury of making value judgments about what people ought to be like; there is the taking of people's goals as given and attempting to analyze real behaviour that follows from these goals and the incentive structures within which people attempt to translate those goals to real outcomes. If you are a policy maker who is attempting to determine the best way to lower infant mortality or improve low-income housing or provide a more equitable distribution of educational opportunities, it is important to get the best *positive* economic analysis of each of the policy alternatives you are considering. It is important to know what the real impact of each policy will be before we attempt to choose the 'best' policies. The same is true if you are a business person pricing goods; you need to know how people will actually respond to different prices, not just how you would like them to respond.

1A.5.2 Normative Economics: How to *Judge* Outcomes

Normative economics goes beyond a value-free analysis of what will happen as incentives change. Positive economics can provide predictions of what will happen as a result of various possible policy alternatives; normative economics uses tools that capture explicit value judgments about what outcomes are 'good' and what outcomes are 'bad' to determine which of the policies is the best for society. Normative economists thus draw on disciplines such as political philosophy to formalize mechanisms through which to translate particular values into policy recommendations based on a positive analysis of the likely impact of different incentives.

Much of this book concerns itself with positive rather than normative economics by attempting to build a framework through which we can predict the impact of different institutions on individual decision making. We will have to be careful along the way, however, because the positive models we develop are often used for policy analysis in ways that allow particular normative value judgments to slip in.

1A.5.3 Efficiency: Positive or Normative?

You will notice the term *efficient* or *Pareto efficient* appears throughout the text, often with a normative connotation that efficiency is somehow a good thing. We will define a situation as efficient if there is no way, given the resources available, to change the situation so as to make some people better off without making anyone worse off. Within this definition, we find our value-free notion of better off and worse off; that is, we will consider someone to be better off if *they* think they are better off, and we will consider someone as worse off if *they* think themselves worse off. In that sense, the statement 'situation x is efficient' is a positive statement that could be restated to say there is no way to change things so that someone thinks they are better off without making someone else think they are worse off.

Given this definition of efficiency, you can see how one might tend to be concerned about *inefficiencies*. An *in*efficient situation is one where we can see how to make some people better off without making anyone else worse off. We should also be careful not to assume immediately that moving towards greater efficiency is always good in some bigger philosophical sense. A policy that increases the wealth of the rich by a lot while leaving the wealth of the poor unchanged may be a policy that moves us to greater efficiency, as is a policy that makes the poor a lot wealthier while leaving the wealth of the rich unchanged. It is likely that most of us, if pressed, will think one of these policies is better than the other. Some might think that the first policy, because it increases inequality, is actually bad even if it really doesn't make anyone worse off. Similarly, as we will see in Chapter 18, allowing a healthy poor person to sell their kidney to someone who needs it and can pay a lot for it may indeed make both of them better off, and yet there are many who would have moral concerns over such transactions. We will see other examples of this throughout the text.

1A.6 The Non-Dismal Science: Some Basic Lessons

Studying microeconomics has a way of changing how we think about ourselves and those we interact with and the implications for the larger world we occupy. Often economics stands accused of being a 'dismal science', a term that goes back to the 19th century when historian Thomas Carlyle described economics as 'a dreary, desolate and, indeed, quite abject and distressing [science]; what we might call ... the dismal science' in response to Thomas Malthus's admittedly depressing and erroneous theories on population growth and resource use.

Perhaps people think that because we study how people respond to incentives, we are trying to make people selfish. Or perhaps it is because economists engaged in policy discussions often point out that there are trade-offs in life and that politicians too often promise something for nothing. It is also possible that economics provides a rather uplifting or non-dismal view of the world. This is something that can be seen in three very basic insights that run counter to predispositions that many of us share before we study economics.

1A.6.1 Must There Be a Loser for Every Winner? Psychologists suggest that we appear to be 'built in a way that makes us think that whenever there is a winner, there must be a loser'. To the extent that this is true, it colours our view of the world. Economists have developed a fundamentally different mind-set because our study began with the study of voluntary trade where one party chooses to give up something in exchange for something the other party has to offer. In such trades, there is typically no loser; for example, if one person gives up €2 every day to buy a coffee from the campus coffee shop, they do so because it makes them better off since they could just stop doing it if they did not think it was worth it. Similarly, the campus coffee shop owner is better off because they value the cup of coffee at less than €2. They trade, and by trading the world has just become a better place because no one was hurt and both parties are better off. Internalizing the lesson that *there are many situations when everyone can win* is part of thinking like an economist. In fact, much of the unprecedented wealth that now exists in the world has arisen precisely because individuals continuously identify situations in which voluntary interactions make everyone better off. We will also see many situations that involve winners and losers, and situations when non-market institutions are needed to discipline voluntary interactions, but the mere presence of a winner does not imply the offsetting presence of a loser.

1A.6.2 Can 'Good' People Behave 'Badly'? Psychologists also suggest that humans are built to attribute the nature of actions we observe to the inherent character of the person who is acting. When we see someone doing something that is bad, we tend to think that we are dealing with a bad person, and when we see someone doing something good, we tend to think that this implies we are dealing with a good person. No doubt there are bad people who do bad things because of their predispositions, and there are many good people who do good things for the same reason. The economist has another view to add to this: *Often people do what they do because of the incentives they face, not because of any inherent moral predisposition.* For example, if a country's welfare system is designed so that when they find work, their welfare benefits are cut by €1 for every €1 that they earned in the labour market, it may result in individuals not seeing work as worthwhile. Do we imply from this that these individuals are 'lazy' or 'work-shy' or could the explanation be that they are facing perverse incentives that result in this behaviour? Internalizing this basic scepticism of attributing actions too quickly to moral predispositions sets us up to think about behaviour very differently. *Changing behaviour for the better suddenly does not necessarily require a remaking of the soul; sometimes all it takes is identifying some really bad incentives and changing those.*

1A.6.3 Order: Spontaneous or Created? Finally, there is a third way in which we seem to be built that stands contrary to how economists think. Whenever we see something that is working, something that is creating order in an otherwise disorderly setting, we tend to think that there must be *someone* that deliberately created the order. The more complex the order is, the more we tend to think that someone must be in charge of it all. Our study of markets will tell us a different story. Consider the complex order that is any major European city: millions of people interact with one another, getting food, going to work, finding a place to live, etc. If you think about it, it is an enormously complex order, even more complex than the order that gives rise to the unplanned existence of pencils. For instance, in many cities it is likely that there are only two or three days' supply of food at any given point in time. Few people think about this and take it for granted that all sorts of food will always be available at any time we go to a shop. If the press were to publish a large front page headline proclaiming 'Only Two Days of Food Left in City!' we might just see a panic, but that headline would be basically true on any given day.

There is no commissioner of food distribution who makes sure that food continuously flows into a city at the right place and at the right time. The complex order emerges from the individual actions of millions of people. *Under certain circumstances, order can thus emerge spontaneously and without a single planner*, and understanding when this is the case and when it is not, sets economists apart from others.

Saying that order can emerge spontaneously without someone designing it is not, as we will see, the same as saying that the spontaneously emerged order is good. In some cases, we will identify circumstances when this is the case, circumstances when individual incentives are aligned in such a way as to produce socially desirable outcomes. In other circumstances, however, we will raise serious doubts about the social effects of the spontaneous order of the marketplace and thus suggest non-market institutions that are required for this order to produce socially desirable outcomes. We will identify when individual incentives have to be 'nudged' by non-market institutions for the order that emerges spontaneously to be good in some sense.

1A.7 Parts A and B Chapter Structure and Flexibility

Each chapter in this book has two distinct yet closely connecting parts. Part A requires no mathematical sophistication, while part B usually generalizes the intuitions and graphical approach from the A parts using basic calculus, plus a few additional multivariable calculus tools that are developed as needed. The text in the B parts frequently references graphs and intuition from the A parts, and indications are given in the A parts as to how the mathematical B parts can help us generalize what we have learned. It is possible to focus solely on the A parts and leave the more mathematical treatment of the material for another time.

A side benefit of this structure lies in providing flexibility in relation to the type of course you are following. It may be that your course requires you to use only the A parts, providing you with a full intuitive treatment of microeconomics while also giving you a platform to explore the mathematical side of economics either on your own or in future modules. If your course is more mathematical, you may focus more on the B parts, but use the A parts as a supporting resource. In other cases, you may use both A and B parts for some topics but not for others where these parts are outlined in a lecture and followed up in more detail in seminars or tutorials. Whatever way you use this book, do not lose sight of the fact that all the material is rooted in the same underlying conceptual framework, a framework that is supported in a variety of ways not only by the material contained in the text but also by the associated digital resources available with this book.

1A.7.1 Within-Chapter Exercises and the Study Guide

Within-chapter exercises are incorporated throughout the body of the text, and these are intended to get you to confront the concepts immediately rather than simply absorb them through reading. Experiments with students whereby in some years they are provided with the answers to within-chapter exercises so that they can immediately see whether they understand the relevant material, and in other years holding back and not providing the solutions, have yielded dramatic results. When students have access to the solutions to within-chapter exercises as they read the text, their performance on exams is far better. The Study Guide, therefore, has been written around solutions to exercises, giving not just the answer, but also the reasoning behind the answer. The hope is that you will read the chapter and do the exercises along the way. With the solutions available, you can immediately check yourself and focus on those concepts that are most challenging to you.

The nature of the within-chapter exercises mirrors the nature of each part of the chapters, with exercises in the A parts focusing on intuitive and graphical developments of concepts, and exercises in the B parts developing the mathematical techniques and linking them to intuitions. Some exercises are *conceptually* more demanding than others, and these are labelled (*). Others are especially *computationally* demanding, and these are labelled (**). You will find that the material may at first make sense as you read it, but that the exercises are not always as easy as you initially thought. This is because concepts such as those developed in this text can be understood at various levels, and doing these exercises as you read the text leads you to deeper levels of understanding than what you would gain from just reading the explanations within the text.

1A.7.2 End-of-Chapter Exercises The end-of-chapter exercises differ from the within-chapter exercises in that they take the material to an even deeper level, asking you to integrate several concepts you have learned and apply them to new settings. The same is true as we combine concepts within economic models. Just as the text is divided into A and B parts, these exercises have A and B parts, with the A parts not dependent on the B parts but the B parts often benefiting from an initially intuitive way of approaching the problem in the A parts. These exercises will also include different types of applications to real-world issues which require more engagement.

The aim of the exercises is to encourage a sufficiently deep understanding of concepts so that we cannot just apply them to examples we have seen, but also see them operating all around us and to new examples that you might be presented with in an assessment. The applications exercises aim to sharpen that conceptual level of understanding and help develop an understanding of microeconomics that is more than just the sum of its parts. To succeed at these questions, you have to be able to overcome the instinct that you should just know the answer as you read the question and develop the confidence that the question contains the ingredients to reason towards an answer. They are meant to be challenging – so don't be intimidated.

The advice to approaching these questions is to work in groups with other students, talking through the questions and helping each other out along the way. Much of the learning happens in this back-and-forth between students rather than just from reading textbooks or listening to lectures.

PART I

Utility-Maximizing Choice: Consumers, Workers and Savers

Imagine two people go to local supermarkets in their respective towns. Do you think they will come out with the same amount of milk in their baskets? Probably not—but why not?

If one ended up buying more milk, the obvious explanation is that they like milk more than the other person. We all have different likes and dislikes, and we behave differently in all sorts of ways because of that. Maybe their likes and dislikes are quite similar, and they behaved differently because they faced different *circumstances*. Person 2 might already have a refrigerator full of milk while person 1 has none; person 1 might make more money than person 2 and thus has more to spend on everything, including milk; or perhaps milk is expensive where person 1 lives but cheap where person 2 lives. Differences in their behaviour can thus emerge from two very distinct sources: different tastes and different circumstances.

We spend much of our life making choices—little choices about how much milk to buy and big choices about what career to train for, whom (if anyone) to marry, whether to borrow money to go to university, how much to save for retirement and so on. All these choices have one thing in common: They are shaped by our tastes on the one hand and our circumstances on the other. We try to do what is *best* given what is *possible* for us. What is possible is limited by a lot of factors such as our abilities, our income or wealth and the prices that we face in the marketplace. We call these limitations our *economic circumstances* or *constraints*. It is only once we know what is possible that we can ask *what is best*. The answer to that question will depend on our *tastes* or *preferences*. In terms of mathematical language, we choose by *optimizing subject to our constraints*.

This basic method of choosing applies to many different settings and lies at the core of how economists think about the behaviour we observe. *Consumers* choose the best combination of goods and services given their scarce resources and given the prices they face in shops. *Workers* choose where to work and how much to work given their level of skill and expertise and given the wages that employers pay. *Savers* make choices about how much to consume now and how much to put away for the future given their current and expected future resources and given the rates of return their investments can produce. The choices we make as consumers, workers and savers are different, but the underlying method of choosing the best option given what is possible is conceptually the same. For this reason, we will develop our model of consumer, worker and saver choices simultaneously because it really is the same model. In Chapter 2, we begin by modelling the economic circumstances or constraints faced by consumers.

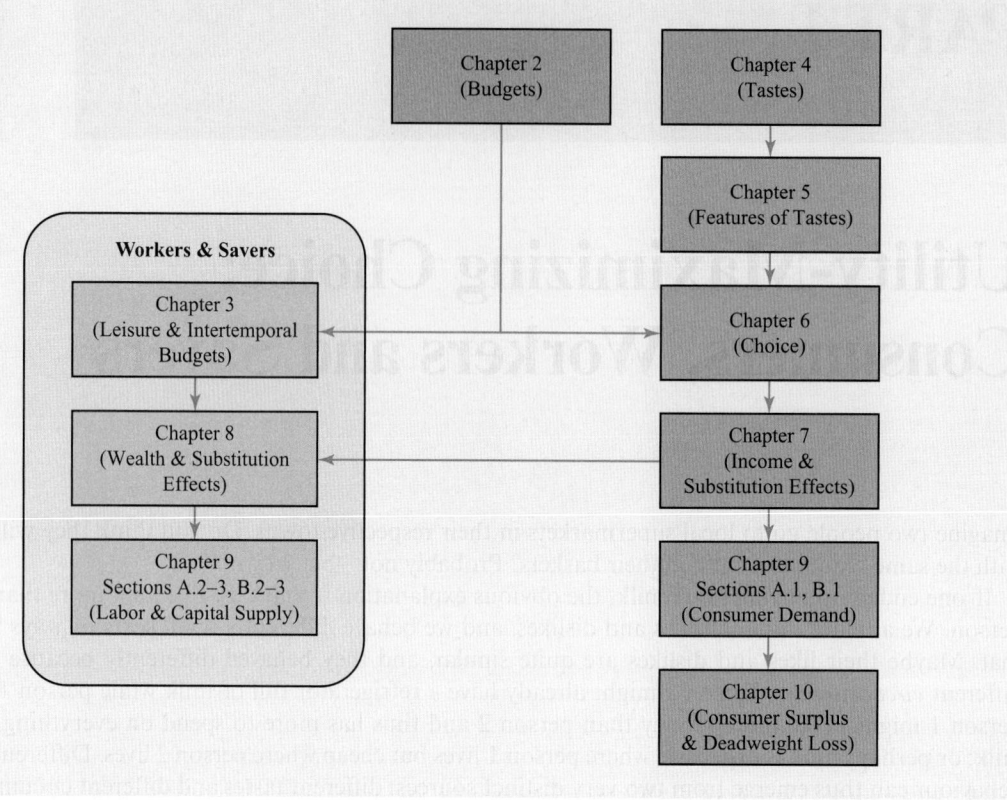

Chapter 2

A Consumer's Economic Circumstances

In this chapter, we will begin to formalize what we mean when we say that people make the best choices they can *given their circumstances*. The logical first step is to find ways of describing how our individual circumstances place limits on the kinds of choices that are available to us. Economists refer to these limits as *constraints*, and we refer to all the options we can choose from, given our constraints, as our *choice set*. Most of us would love, for instance, to go on many exotic holidays, to work only when we feel like it, to retire early, and to forget about constantly worrying about the future. It is simply not possible to do everything we want because our limited resources place constraints on our choice sets. We have to determine what kinds of choices are actually possible for us given who we are, and only once we know what choices are *possible* can we decide which of these choices is *best*.

In the process of focusing on the underlying concepts relevant for thinking about individual circumstances consumers face, we will notice that there are some limits to how easily we can model individual circumstances using only words and graphs. Part B of the chapter will demonstrate how economists use the language of mathematics to generalize intuitions that emerge in the more intuitive and graphical exposition of the material in part A of the chapter.

2A | Consumer Choice Sets and Budget Constraints

Consumers constantly make decisions about how much to consume different goods. They are constrained not only by what financial resources they command, but also by the prices that they face when they make their choices. Typically, they have little control over these prices since most consumers are individually small relative to the market and therefore have no power to influence the prices that are charged within the marketplace. We will therefore assume for now that consumers are *price takers*, or economic agents who cannot influence the prices in the economy. We will also assume that the amount of money we can spend has already been determined by previous decisions.

2A.1 Shopping on a Fixed or Exogenous Income

In our role as consumers, we often have a general idea of what kinds of purchases we would like to make and a fixed income or money budget we can allocate to these purchases. For example, you might begin your year at university with up to €200 to spend on new clothes for the year. This is your fixed income for the purposes of this analysis, and it represents a type of income we will refer to as *exogenous. Income is defined as exogenous if its euro value is unaffected by prices in the economy.* In this case, regardless of the prices of books and equipment, you will always have €200 available.

Assume your clothing choice is divided between hoodies and jeans. In the clothes shop you find that hoodies are priced at €10 and jeans at €20. You can determine the choice set faced given the constraints imposed by your €200 income and the prices of jeans and hoodies. You could, for instance, purchase 10 pairs of jeans and no hoodies, thus spending your total €200 income. Alternatively, you could purchase 20 hoodies and no jeans or any combination of jeans and hoodies such that the total expense does not add up to more than €200.

2A.1.1 Graphing Choice Sets We can depict this graphically in a two-dimensional picture that has the number of pairs of jeans on the horizontal axis and the number of hoodies on the vertical. Point *A* in Graph 2.1 depicts the choice of 10 jeans and no hoodies while point *B* depicts the choice of 20 hoodies and no jeans. The line that connects points *A* and *B* represents other choices that also cost exactly €200. For instance, point *C* represents 5 pairs of jeans and 10 hoodies, which implies a €100 expense on jeans (5 times €20) and another €100 expense on hoodies (10 times €10). Point *D* represents 7 pairs of jeans and 6 hoodies, which again adds up to a €200 total expenditure.

Graph 2.1 Budget Constraint and Choice Set

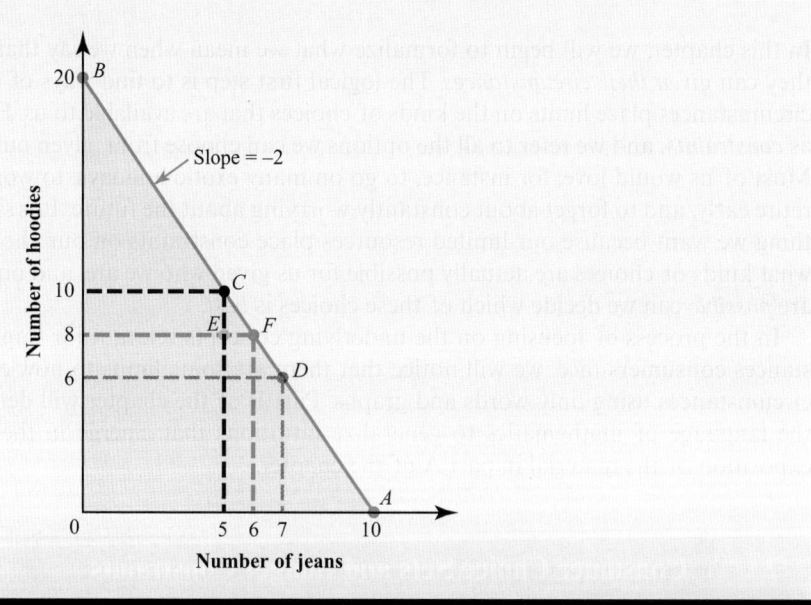

Go to MindTap to interact with this graph

We will refer to the line connecting points *A* and *B* as the *budget line* or the *budget constraint*. The end points, or intercepts, of the budget line are determined by the fixed income divided by the price of the good on each axis: 200 divided by 20 in the case of jeans, and 200 divided by 10 in the case of hoodies. For a particular income and a particular set of prices, this *budget line represents all combinations of goods that if chosen by a particular consumer, would leave no additional money left in their budget*. Points below the budget line, on the other hand, represent combinations of goods that if chosen by the consumer, would still leave some additional unspent money. For instance, point *E* represents 8 hoodies and 5 pairs of jeans, which cost only €180 and would thus leave €20 unspent. Together, the budget line and all shaded points below the budget line represent the choices that are *possible* for a consumer who has a €200 income devoted to spending on jeans and hoodies that are priced at €20 and €10 respectively.

Now suppose that you currently have 10 hoodies and 5 pairs of jeans (point *C*) in your basket, but you decide that you really would like to have 6 instead of 5 new pairs of jeans. Since jeans are twice as expensive as hoodies, you know you will have to put 2 hoodies back on the rack to be able to afford one more pair of jeans. That is exactly what the budget constraint tells you: as you move to 6 pairs of jeans, you can only afford 8 hoodies rather than the 10 you started with in your basket. In going from point C to point F, you traded 2 hoodies on the vertical axis for 1 pair of jeans on the horizontal axis, which implies a slope of -2 since the slope of a line is the change in the variable on the vertical axis (hoodies) divided by the change in the variable on the horizontal axis (jeans). You could equally well have calculated the slope of this line by looking at the end points. In going from point B to point A, you have to give up 20 hoodies to get 10 jeans, giving a slope of -2.

This slope of the budget line arises from the fact that jeans cost twice as much as hoodies, and it represents the trade-off the consumer faces. Economists call this trade-off *opportunity cost. The opportunity cost of any action is the next best alternative one gives up by undertaking this action.* In our example, the opportunity cost of buying one more pair of jeans is the two hoodies you have to give up. We can also talk of the opportunity cost of buying one more unit of the good on the vertical axis. In our example, if you want to buy one more hoodie, you have to give up half a pair of jeans. Given that jeans cannot easily be split into two halves, it might sound silly to say that the opportunity cost of one hoodie is half a pair of jeans, but this statement contains the same information as the statement that the opportunity cost of one pair of jeans is two hoodies: jeans are twice as expensive as hoodies. *In general, the opportunity cost of the good on the horizontal axis in terms of the good on the vertical axis is the slope of the budget line, whereas the opportunity cost of the good on the vertical axis in terms of the good on the horizontal axis is the inverse of the slope of the budget line.*

The slope of the budget constraint can also be determined more directly by simply understanding how the prices a consumer faces translate into opportunity costs. In our example, jeans are €20 and hoodies €10, and the slope of the budget constraint is -2 or, in absolute value, the opportunity cost of one pair of jeans in terms of hoodies. This opportunity cost arises from the fact that jeans are twice as expensive as hoodies, with *the slope of the budget constraint simply being given by the (negative) ratio of the price of the good on the horizontal axis (jeans) divided by the price of the good on the vertical axis (hoodies).*

Exercise 2A.1

Instead of putting jeans on the horizontal axis and hoodies on the vertical, put jeans on the vertical and hoodies on the horizontal. Show how the budget constraint looks and read from the slope what is the opportunity cost of hoodies in terms of jeans, and jeans in terms of hoodies.

2A.1.2 An Increase or Decrease in Fixed Incomes Now suppose that your parents gave you €400 for clothes at the beginning of the academic year. As a result, you could now purchase a maximum of 20 pairs of jeans and no hoodies, or a maximum of 40 hoodies and no jeans. This means that point A shifts to the right by 10 pairs of jeans and point B shifts up by 20 hoodies resulting in a parallel shift of your budget constraint from AB to $A'B'$ in Graph 2.2.

Notice that the set of choices available to you has clearly become larger, but the trade-off you face, the opportunity cost of jeans in terms of hoodies or hoodies in terms of jeans, has not changed. This is because your *opportunity cost is determined by the shop's prices*, not by your parents' generosity. It does not matter whether you, or the richest person in Europe enters the shop to buy hoodies and jeans – each faces the same trade-offs even though their overall budgets may be quite different.

The opportunity cost is determined by the *ratio* of the shop's prices. Suppose, for instance, that instead of giving you an additional €200, your parents gave you a 50 per cent off coupon for hoodies and jeans. In that case, the real price of a hoodie would have dropped to €5 and the real price of jeans would have dropped to €10. This would enable you to buy up to 40 hoodies and no jeans or up to 20 pairs of jeans and no hoodies. Thus, a decline in all prices by the same percentage is equivalent to an increase in income; it merely shifts the budget constraint out without changing its slope. In fact, economists would say that in both scenarios, *real income* has doubled because you could now afford twice as much as before while relative prices remained unchanged, because the trade-off between the goods as expressed in the slope of the budget constraint did not change.

Graph 2.2 An Increase in Exogenous Income

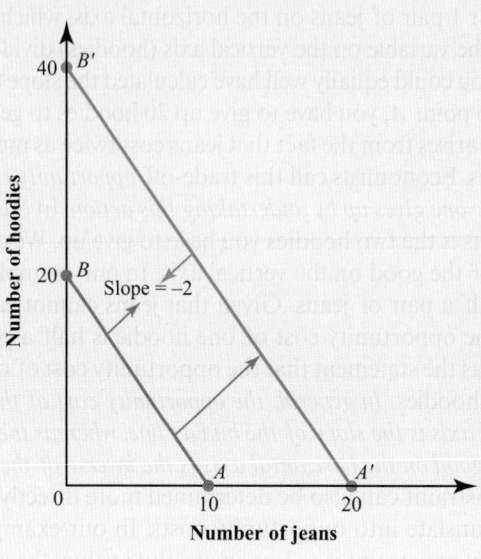

Exercise 2A.2

Demonstrate how your budget constraint would change if, on the way into the shop, you lost €300 of the €400 your parents had given to you. Does your opportunity cost of jeans in terms of hoodies or hoodies in terms of jeans change? What if instead you found that the prices of jeans and hoodies had doubled on arriving at the shop?

2A.1.3 A Change in Price Now suppose that you have a 50 per cent off coupon for jeans but not for hoodies, together with your usual €200 budget. With this coupon, you can purchase any number of jeans and receive half off. As a result, while the posted price for a pair of jeans is €20, each pair only costs you €10 once you present the coupon at the till.

To see how this changes the budget line, we can go through the same exercise as before and find the intercepts of the new budget line by asking how much of each good could be bought if nothing was spent on the other good. This is illustrated in Graph 2.3. Since jeans are now priced at €10 a pair, you can purchase as many as 20 pairs with your €200 money budget assuming you buy no hoodies, and you can similarly buy as many as 20 hoodies at €10 each assuming you buy no jeans. Thus point A shifts from 10 to 20 as a result of the lower price of jeans, but point B does not change since the price of hoodies remains the same and your overall money budget is still €200. The budget line pivots out from the initial budget line, AB to the new budget line $A'B$, with the slope changing from -2 to -1. This slope again reflects the opportunity cost of one pair of jeans in terms of hoodies: since jeans and hoodies are now both priced at €10 each, you have to give up one hoodie for every additional pair of jeans you would like to purchase.

Exercise 2A.3

How would your budget constraint change if instead of a 50 per cent off coupon for jeans, you have a 50 per cent off coupon for hoodies? What would be the opportunity cost of jeans in terms of hoodies?

Graph 2.3 A Decrease in Price

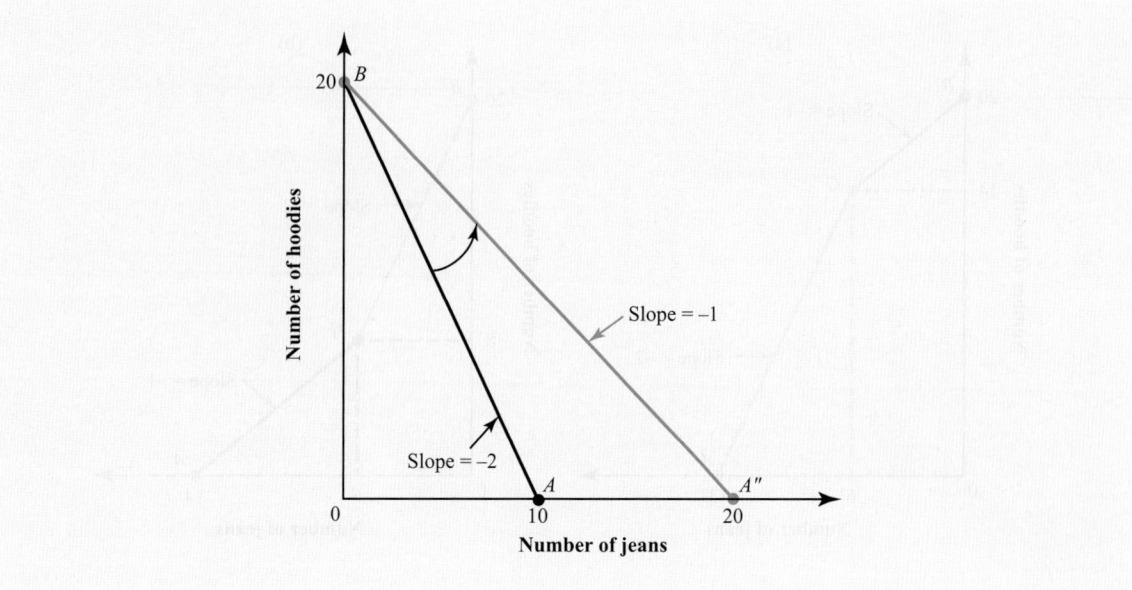

2A.2 Kinked Budgets

Assume that you are directed to the small print on the 50 per cent off coupon that limits the discount to the first 6 pairs of jeans. Thus, rather than facing a price of €10 per pair of jeans for any number of pairs that you buy, the €10 price applies only to the first 6 pairs and that each additional pair is priced at €20. The *marginal price*—the price of one more pair of jeans—changes from €10 to €20 after the 6th pair of jeans.

To see what this does to the budget constraint, we begin by determining where the intercepts of the new budget constraint lie. If you were to purchase only jeans and no hoodies, you would be able to purchase 13 pairs: the first 6 at €10 each for a total of €60 and another 7 at €20 each for an additional €140. Thus, point *A* lies at 13 pairs of jeans on the horizontal axis, as illustrated in panel (a) of Graph 2.4. Point *B* remains unchanged at 20 hoodies on the vertical axis, given that the price of hoodies has not changed. Because the trade-off between hoodies and jeans changes once you have 6 pairs of jeans in your shopping basket, the slope of the budget constraint must change at that point as well. If you purchase exactly 6 pairs of jeans at €10 each with the coupon for a total of €60, you will be able to afford 14 hoodies, also at €10 each, with the remainder of your income (€140). This implies that point *G* is on the budget constraint. Between point *G* and point *B*, if you purchase fewer than 6 pairs of jeans you face a price of €10 for both jeans and hoodies. The line segment connecting point *G* and *B* therefore has a slope of −1, indicating an opportunity cost of one hoodie for each pair of jeans. The line segment connecting *G* and *A*, on the other hand, has a slope of −2, which reflects the higher price of jeans for any pair above 6, and the higher opportunity cost in terms of hoodies you will face once you purchase more than 6 pairs of jeans. The new budget constraint, therefore, starts at point *B* with a shallow slope of −1, has a kink at point *G* where you have exactly 6 pairs of jeans in your shopping basket, and switches to a steeper slope of −2.

Kinked budget constraints of this type occur whenever the price of a good changes as a consumer purchases more of it. This can result in a budget constraint like the one we derived in panel (a) of Graph 2.4, where the kink points out towards the northeast of the graph. Under different circumstances, it could also result in a kink that points in towards the southwest of the graph. Suppose, for instance, that the 50 per cent off coupon was such that you could only get a discount if you purchase more than 6 pairs of jeans, and that this discount applied to each pair of jeans after the initial 6 purchased. This would result in the budget constraint in panel (b) of Graph 2.4.

Graph 2.4 Kinked Budget Constraints

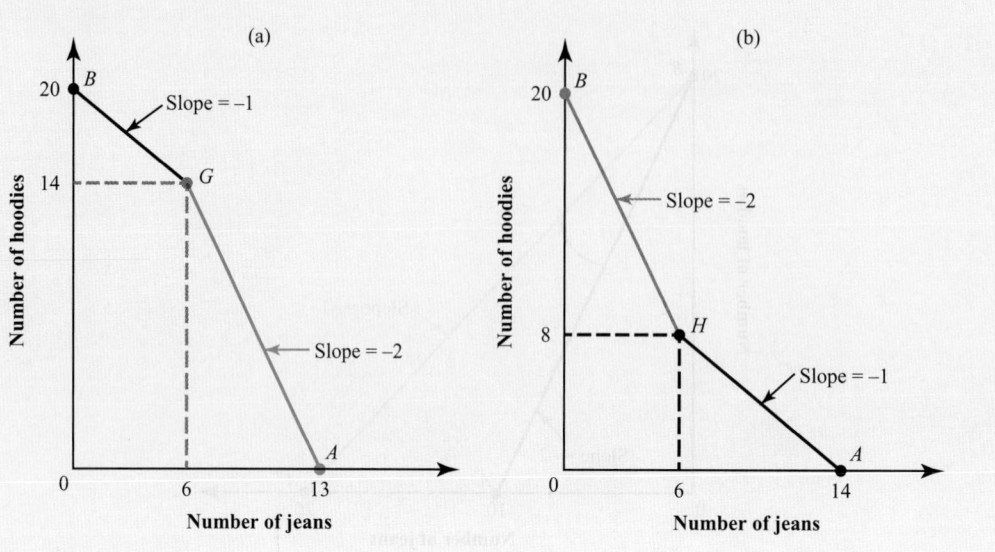

Exercise 2A.4

Suppose that the two coupons analyzed were for hoodies instead of jeans. What would the budget constraints look like?

2A.3 Modelling More General Choices

Although two-good examples like the previous ones are useful because they allow us to easily illustrate budget constraints in a two-dimensional picture, they are of course a little artificial since most consumers face purchasing decisions involving more than two goods. To generalize such examples beyond choices over two goods, we can employ a technique that treats whole categories of goods as if they were a single good.

2A.3.1 Graphing Choice Sets With Three Goods
Assume that in addition to purchasing hoodies and jeans, you also need to purchase new socks. Our illustrations have to become three-dimensional. In Graph 2.5, we plot jeans on one axis, hoodies on another, and socks on yet another axis, and just as in the two-good examples, begin by finding the intercepts on each axis illustrating how much of each good could be purchased if none of the others was purchased. Suppose the price of hoodies and jeans were €10 and €20 and the price of socks were €5, and suppose that exogenous income or money budget is again €200. On the axis labelled number of jeans, the intercept is 10; the number of pairs of jeans you could purchase if you spent all of your money on jeans alone. Similarly, the intercept on the hoodie axis is 20, and the intercept on the socks axis is 40. We can proceed by illustrating what the budget constraint would look like if you purchased no socks but limited yourself to only hoodies and jeans by connecting A and B. This budget constraint is equivalent to the one plotted in Graph 2.1. We can also illustrate the constraint if you limited yourself to only socks and hoodies by connecting points B and C, and the constraint if you limited yourself to only socks and jeans by connecting points A and C. Finally, the full budget constraint is formed by the shaded plane that connects points A, B and C. For instance, point D with 10 pairs of socks, 5 hoodies and 5 pairs of jeans lies on this plane because this combination of goods in your shopping basket costs exactly €200: €50 for socks, €50 for hoodies and €100 for jeans.

Graph 2.5 Budget Constraint with Three Goods

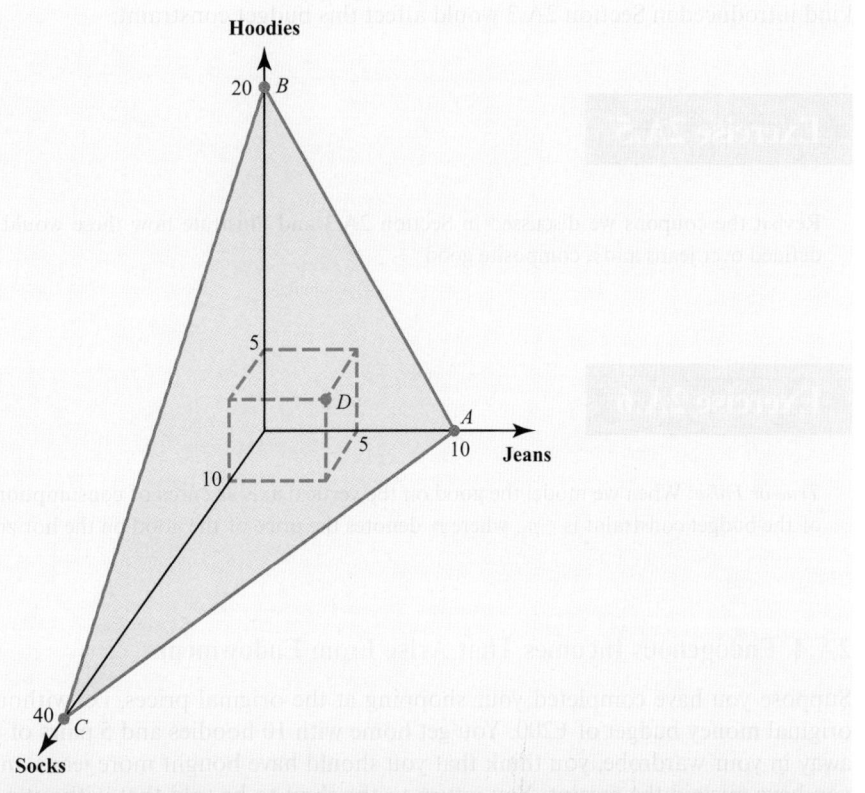

Go to MindTap to interact with this graph

While it is possible to illustrate budget constraints graphically with three goods, it would become increasingly difficult to graph such constraints for more than three goods. Nevertheless, we are able to analyze more general choice sets graphically by focusing on the choice over a good that we are particularly interested in analyzing, and creating, for the purposes of the analysis, a second *composite good* that represents all other goods.

2A.3.2 Modelling Composite Goods Assume you go to the shop with your €200 to purchase not only jeans but also a variety of other goods needed for the academic year, including hoodies and socks but also office supplies, sportswear and equipment, technology and so on. How does the budget constraint change as the price of jeans changes? We could reduce our implicit multi-good model by putting jeans on the horizontal axis and a *composite good representing all other goods you are interested in* on the vertical. We can define this composite good as euros spent on goods other than jeans. This definition of a composite good ensures that €1 spent on goods other than jeans costs you exactly €1. Implicitly, our analysis will have to assume that only the price of jeans changes while all other prices remain the same, or alternatively that all other prices change by the same proportion while the price of jeans remains the same.

With the aid of the modelling assumption of a composite good, we can illustrate your choice set over jeans and other goods exactly as we did in Section 2A.1 when we modelled the choice between jeans and hoodies. On the horizontal axis, point A would again lie at 10 pairs of jeans because that is the most you can afford if your entire income is spent on jeans. Point B on the vertical axis would lie at 200 because you can purchase 200 units of the composite good, i.e. €200 worth of other goods if you do not purchase any jeans. Connecting points A and B gives a budget line with slope −20, indicating that the opportunity cost of a pair of jeans is 20 units of the composite good or €20 worth of other good consumption. We could model how an increase or decrease in your fixed income, a change in the price of jeans, or coupons of the kind introduced in Section 2A.3 would affect this budget constraint.

Exercise 2A.5

Revisit the coupons we discussed in Section 2A.3 and illustrate how these would alter the choice set when defined over jeans and a composite good.

Exercise 2A.6

True or False: When we model the good on the vertical axis as euros of consumption of other goods, the slope of the budget constraint is $-p_1$, where p_1 denotes the price of the good on the horizontal axis.

2A.4 Endogenous Incomes That Arise From Endowments

Suppose you have completed your shopping at the original prices, i.e. without coupons, and with your original money budget of €200. You get home with 10 hoodies and 5 pairs of jeans, but as you put them away in your wardrobe, you think that you should have bought more jeans and fewer hoodies. However, you have mislaid the receipt. You return to the shop to be told that without a receipt all you can get is a credit note for the value of the goods you want to return. You are now at the shop with no money, but with an *endowment* of 10 hoodies and 5 pairs of jeans. *An endowment is a bundle of goods owned by a consumer and tradable for other goods.* A defining feature of endowments is that, because the consumer owns the endowment bundle, *they can always choose to consume that bundle regardless of what the prices of goods in the market happen to be.*

As you stand in line at the customer service desk, you contemplate what your budget constraint looks like now that you have just an endowment bundle of 10 hoodies and 5 pairs of jeans, labelled point E in Graph 2.6. You know that you can always stick with your current hoodies and jeans, so the point 5 jeans, 10 hoodies must lie on your budget constraint. What the rest of the constraint looks like depends on current prices. If jeans are still priced at €20 a pair and hoodies at €10 each, you could return your 5 pairs of jeans, receive €100 in shop credit and use it to buy 10 additional hoodies, thus ending up with 20 hoodies and no jeans. Alternatively, you could trade in your 10 hoodies for €100 shop credit and buy 5 more pairs of jeans, thus ending up with 10 pairs of jeans and no hoodies. Or you could do something in between. If the prices of jeans and hoodies are unchanged from when you originally purchased them, your budget constraint is exactly the same as it was when you first entered the shop with €200 in Graph 2.1 and replicated as line AB in Graph 2.6.

As you approach the customer service representative, however, you notice a member of staff putting up a poster in the window stating: '50% off all Jeans'. This means that jeans are now priced at €10 a pair, rather than the €20 you paid for them. What this now means is that you only get €10 credit for each pair of jeans. How does this change your choice set?

You still have the option of leaving the shop with 5 pairs of jeans and 10 hoodies, so point E remains on the budget constraint. If you now return 5 pairs of jeans, you only receive €50 in credit and thus can only get 5 more hoodies. Point B, therefore, shifts down by 5 hoodies. At the same time, if you return your 10 hoodies, you still get a €100 shop credit, but now, because jeans are cheaper, you can get as many as 10 extra pairs of jeans! Point A shifts out by 5 pairs of jeans, and the new budget constraint $A'B'$, has a slope of -1 that reflects the new opportunity cost of a pair of jeans given that they now cost the same as hoodies. Notice, however, that the budget line now rotates through point E, the endowment point, when the price of jeans changes, not through point B as it did when the price changed and you were on a fixed income (in Section 2A.3). This will always be true for budget constraints that arise from endowment bundles rather than fixed incomes.

Graph 2.6 Price Change With Endowments

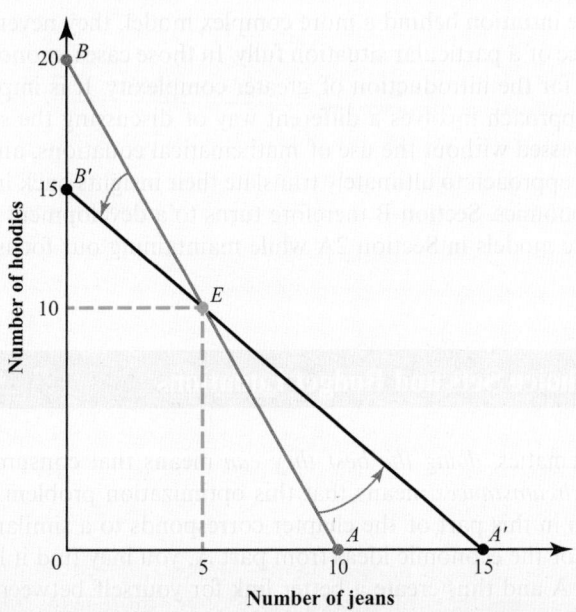

Notice that when budget constraints arise from endowments, the amount of money available to the consumer is *not* fixed. Rather, the money available to you depends on the prices of the goods you are endowed with, since you have to sell some of your endowment in order to get money. We will refer to such incomes as *endogenous* to differentiate them from the fixed or *exogenous* incomes analyzed earlier.

It may not seem all that common that we find ourselves with a basket of goods like jeans and hoodies as an endowment, and so this exercise might look a little contrived. However, as we will see in Chapter 3, our budget constraints are indeed often determined by endowments when we think of our roles in other sectors of the economy such as the labour market or the financial markets. We are, for instance, endowed with a certain amount of time that we can allocate to various purposes including gainful employment. We also often accumulate a set of assets like bank deposits, investment funds, coin or stamp collections, property, etc., which can be treated like an endowment that can be converted into consumption, depending on the value of the endowment.

2A.5 Modelling Constraints Graphically or Mathematically?

We have shown how we can model simple choice sets for consumers facing different circumstances. How much choice a consumer has ultimately depends on (1) the prices of goods and (2) the size of the consumer's available income. The latter can be determined either exogenously by a fixed euro amount that is available to the consumer, or it can arise endogenously from the value of some endowment that the consumer can trade for other consumption. A first step to modelling the circumstances that are most relevant to particular choices is to identify these two elements, prices and incomes, of the consumer's individual circumstances.

However, we have to recognize that our models cannot possibly include all the complexity of the real world when we try to analyze individual decisions that consumers make. Remember that the point of modelling decisions is to draw out the essence of the problem we are investigating in order to better analyze the most essential aspects of the problem. In modelling the circumstances under which consumers make choices, we therefore have to decide which aspects of the complex real world are critical for the particular choices we are modelling and which aspects are, for purposes of our model, 'noise' that we can abstract away from.

Often, we will conclude that a particular situation can be adequately modelled within the graphical framework we have developed so far. Other times, economists will find that while the graphical framework helps them understand the intuition behind a more complex model, they nevertheless require more complexity to model the essence of a particular situation fully. In those cases, economists turn to mathematics as a language that allows for the introduction of greater complexity. It is important to understand that this more mathematical approach involves a different way of discussing the same underlying economic concepts we have just discussed without the use of mathematical equations, and it is important for those who use the mathematical approach to ultimately translate their insights back into words that give expression to the underlying economics. Section B therefore turns to a development of the mathematical tools that can help us generalize models in Section 2A while maintaining our focus on the economic choices made by individuals.

2B   Consumer Choice Sets and Budget Equations

In the language of mathematics, *doing the best they can* means that consumers solve an *optimization problem*, and *given their circumstances* means that this optimization problem is a *constrained optimization problem*. Each section in this part of the chapter corresponds to a similar section in part A. If you find yourself losing track of the economic ideas from part A, you may find it helpful to turn back to the analogous section in part A and thus create a better link for yourself between the mathematics and the underlying economics.

2B.1 Shopping on a Fixed Income

We began our discussion of choice sets in Section 2A by envisioning shopping for jeans and hoodies with a fixed, or exogenous, income. Suppose again that this fixed income is €200 and that the price of jeans is €20 and the price of hoodies is €10. The *choice set* we derived in Graph 2.1 is the set of all combinations of jeans and hoodies that cost no more than €200, and the *budget line* or *budget constraint* is the combination of jeans and hoodies that cost exactly €200.

2B.1.1 Defining Choice Sets and Budget Lines Mathematically Letting jeans be denoted by the variable x_1 and hoodies be denoted by the variable x_2, we can define the choice set formally as:

$$\{(x_1, x_2) \in \mathbb{R}^2_+ \mid 20x_1 + 10x_2 \leq 200\}. \tag{2.1}$$

The curly brackets { } indicate that we are defining a *set* of points. The vertical line '|' is read as *such that*. Everything preceding '|' defines the geometric space within which the points of the set lie, and everything following '|' defines the conditions that must be satisfied in order for a point in that geometric space to lie within the choice set we are defining. The symbol $\mathbb{R}^2_+$ is used to represent the two-dimensional space of non-negative real numbers, and the symbol $\in$ is read as *is an element of*. Thus, the mathematical expression $(x_1, x_2) \in \mathbb{R}^2_+$ says that the set contains points with two components (x_1 and x_2) that are non-negative real numbers. Not all points with two components that are non-negative real numbers are in the choice set – only those points that represent bundles that cost no more than €200. The mathematical statement following '|' indicates precisely that points that lie in the space defined before '|' are part of the set we are defining, only if $20x_1 + 10x_2 \leq 200$. We read the full expression as:

'This set contains all combinations of (x_1, x_2) in which both x_1 and x_2 are non-negative real numbers *such that* 20 times x_1 plus 10 times x_2 is less than or equal to 200'.

There is a logical structure to this formulation of sets that is worth pointing out even more precisely. The statement preceding '|' provides the *necessary condition* for a point to lie in the set we are defining, while the statement following '|' provides the *sufficient conditions*. In order for a point to lie in your choice set under the circumstances described, it is a necessary condition for that point to consist of two non-negative real numbers. That is not sufficient because many points that have two non-negative real numbers represent bundles of goods that are not affordable given an exogenous income of €200. The choice set is fully defined when both necessary and sufficient conditions are stated explicitly.

Exercise 2B.1

What points in Graph 2.1 satisfy the necessary but not the sufficient conditions in expression (2.1)?

To define the set of points that lie *on* the budget line as opposed to *within* the choice set, we start by recognizing that these points lie within the same geometric space as the choice set, and must necessarily consist of points defined by two non-negative real numbers. However, the sufficient condition for such points to be part of the budget line is different from the sufficient condition for such points to be part of the choice set. In particular, the inequality in the constraint $20x_1 + 10x_2 \leq 200$ is replaced with an equality because the budget line represents the set of goods that cost *exactly* €200. We can define the *budget line* as the set of bundles that lie on the boundary of the choice set:

$$\{(x_1, x_2) \in \mathbb{R}^2_+ \mid 20x_1 + 10x_2 = 200\}. \tag{2.2}$$

More generally, we can define choice sets without reference to a particular set of prices or incomes. We can indicate the price of jeans as p_1, the price of hoodies as p_2 and income as I. With these three pieces of information that constitute the consumer's *economic circumstances*, we define a consumer's choice set C as:

$$C(p_1, p_2, I) = \{(x_1, x_2) \in \mathbb{R}^2_+ \mid p_1 x_1 + p_2 x_2 \leq I\}. \tag{2.3}$$

The notation $C(p_1, p_2, I)$ indicates that the precise nature of the choice set depends on what value is taken by the prices of the goods and by the consumer's income level; or, it indicates that the choice set C *is a function of the prices* (p_1, p_2) *and income level I*. If we substitute the values 20, 10 and 200 for the two prices and income, we get precisely the set defined in equation (2.1). Similarly, we can define the budget line B as:

$$B(p_1, p_2, I) = \{(x_1, x_2) \in \mathbb{R}^2_+ \mid p_1 x_1 + p_2 x_2 = I\}, \tag{2.4}$$

where the inequality in equation (2.3) is replaced with an equality.

We can examine the mathematical formulation of a budget line and demonstrate how it relates to the graphical intuitions we built in Section 2A. Beginning with the equation $p_1 x_1 + p_2 x_2 = I$ contained within the set defined in (2.4), we can subtract $p_1 x_1$ from both sides and divide both sides by p_2 to get:

$$x_2 = \frac{I}{p_2} - \frac{p_1}{p_2} x_1. \tag{2.5}$$

Notice that in a graph such as Graph 2.1 with x_1 on the horizontal and x_2 on the vertical axis, this expression of the equation defining a budget line shows an intercept of (I/p_2) on the vertical axis and a slope of $(-p_1/p_2)$, which is what we concluded intuitively in Section 2A. For instance, with the numbers in our example, (I/p_2) is equal to (200/10) or 20, which indicates that you could purchase as many as 20 hoodies with your €200 if all you bought were hoodies. Similarly, the slope $(-p_1/p_2)$ is equal to (−20/10) or (−2), which indicates an opportunity cost of 2 hoodies for 1 pair of jeans.

2B.1.2 An Increase or Decrease in the Fixed Income Our next step in Section 2A was to illustrate what happens as income increases from €200 to €400. Notice that this exogenous income is represented by the variable I in equation (2.5). Thus, when the fixed income changes, only the first term (I/p_2) in equation (2.5) changes. This is the vertical intercept term in the equation, indicating that the intercept on the x_2-axis will shift up as fixed income increases. The second term in equation (2.5) remains unchanged, indicating that the slope of the budget line $(-p_1/p_2)$ remains the same. A change in the x_2-axis intercept without a change in the slope adds up to a parallel shift outward from the budget line, as we concluded intuitively in Graph 2.2. The choice set has become larger, but the trade-off between the goods as represented by the slope of the budget line has remained the same.

Exercise 2B.2

Using equation (2.5), show that the same change in the budget line could happen if both prices simultaneously fell by half while the euro budget remained the same. Does this make intuitive sense?

2B.1.3 A Change in Price Another scenario explored in Section 2A involved a 50 per cent off coupon for jeans, a coupon that effectively lowers the price of jeans (p_1) from €20 to €10. Going back to equation (2.5), notice that p_1 does not appear in the intercept term (I/p_2) but does appear in the slope term $(-p_1/p_2)$. The x_2-axis intercept thus remains unchanged, but the slope becomes shallower as p_1/p_2 becomes smaller in absolute value. This is what we concluded intuitively in Graph 2.3.

Exercise 2B.3

Using the mathematical formulation of a budget line equation (2.5), illustrate how the slope and intercept terms change when p_2 instead of p_1 changes. Relate this to what your intuition would tell you in a graphical model of budget lines.

2B.2 Kinked Budgets

Kinked budget lines of the kind explored in Section 2A.2 are more difficult to describe mathematically. Consider, for instance, the example of a 50 per cent off coupon for only the first 6 pairs of jeans purchased. We graphed the choice set that emerges for someone with an income of €200 facing a before-coupon price of €20 for jeans and €10 for hoodies in panel (a) of Graph 2.4. There, we derived intuitively the result that the budget line would initially be flatter up to 6 pairs of jeans before becoming steeper at the kink point when the effective price of jeans changes from €10 to €20.

Were we to write down this choice set mathematically, we would have to translate the fact that the price of jeans changes after the 6th pair into the set notation we developed earlier. We would need to recognize that if we buy more than 6 pairs of jeans, we in effect have an additional $0.5(6p_1) = 3p_1$ in income because that is how much the coupon gives back. For instance, when $p_1 = 20$, the coupon is worth €60 if we buy 6 or more pairs of jeans. We could define the choice set as:

$$C(p_1, p_2, I) = \{(x_1, x_2) \in \mathbb{R}_+^2 \mid 0.5p_1x_1 + p_2x_2 \le I \text{ for } x_1 \le 6 \text{ and}$$

$$p_1x_1 + p_2x_2 \le I + 3p_1 \text{ for } x_1 > 6\}. \tag{2.6}$$

Graph 2.4a is a graphical depiction of this set when $p_1 = 20$, $p_2 = 10$ and $I = 200$. The budget line itself is defined by two line segments, one for $x_1 \leq 6$ and one for $x_1 > 6$; or, stated formally:

$$B(p_1, p_2, I) = \{(x_1, x_2) \in \mathbb{R}_+^2 \mid 0.5p_1x_1 + p_2x_2 = I \text{ for } x_1 \leq 6, \text{ and}$$

$$p_1x_1 + p_2x_2 = I + 3p_1 \text{ for } x_1 > 6 \}. \tag{2.7}$$

Exercise 2B.4

Convert the two equations contained in the budget set (2.7) into a format that illustrates more clearly the intercept and slope terms as in equation (2.5). Using the numbers for prices and incomes from our example, plot the two lines on a graph. Finally, erase the portions of the lines that are not relevant given that each line applies only for some values of x_1 as indicated in (2.7). Compare your graph with panel (a) of Graph 2.4.

Exercise 2B.5

Now suppose that the 50 per cent off coupon applied to all jeans purchased after you had bought an initial 6 pairs of jeans at regular price. Derive the mathematical formulation of the budget set analogous to equation (2.7) and repeat the previous exercise. Compare your graph with panel (b) of Graph 2.4.

2B.3 Choice Sets With More Than Two Goods

As we discussed in Section 2A, we are often confronted by the fact that realistic models of economic behaviour involve choices over more than two goods. The mathematical formulation of choice sets permits us one way of extending our analysis to settings where choices over many goods can be analyzed. Alternatively, as we noted in Section 2A, we can employ the simplifying assumption that categories of goods can be combined and treated as a composite good.

2B.3.1 Choice Sets With Three or More Goods When faced with three rather than two goods, we illustrated in Graph 2.5 that our choice sets would now have to be plotted in three dimensions. When faced with more than three goods, we no longer have easy graphical techniques to represent choice sets. With the mathematical tools developed here, however, it is possible to extend two-good models to those with many goods.

Returning to the shopping example purchasing jeans, hoodies and socks, let's denote these goods by x_1, x_2 and x_3 and similarly denote their prices by p_1, p_2 and p_3. In order for a particular bundle (x_1, x_2, x_3) to lie within the choice set, it must be true that the total cost of the bundle is no greater than exogenous income I. The cost of each component of the bundle is simply the price of that component times the quantity, and the sum of these is equal to the full cost $p_1x_1 + p_2x_2 + p_3x_3$. Your choice set is an extension of the choice set defined for two goods in equation (2.3):

$$C(p_1, p_2, p_3, I) = \{(x_1, x_2, x_3) \in \mathbb{R}_+^3 \mid p_1x_1 + p_2x_2 + p_3x_3 \leq I \}, \tag{2.8}$$

with the corresponding budget constraint defined by:

$$B(p_1, p_2, p_3, I) = \{(x_1, x_2, x_3) \in \mathbb{R}_+^3 \mid p_1x_1 + p_2x_2 + p_3x_3 = I \}. \tag{2.9}$$

The equation in this definition of the budget constraint defines the triangular plane graphed in Graph 2.5 for the values $p_1 = 20$, $p_2 = 10$, $p_3 = 5$ and $I = 200$.

By now you may be able to see how the definition of choice sets and budget lines extends when faced with choices over more than three goods. For the general case of n different goods with n different prices, we would extend (2.8) and (2.9) to:

$$C(p_1, p_2, \ldots, p_n, I) = \{(x_1, x_2, \ldots, x_n) \in \mathbb{R}_+^n \mid p_1 x_1 + p_2 x_2 + \cdots + p_n x_n \leq I\}, \tag{2.10}$$

and:

$$B(p_1, p_2, \ldots, p_n, I) = \{(x_1, x_2, \ldots, x_n) \in \mathbb{R}_+^n \mid p_1 x_1 + p_2 x_2 + \cdots + p_n x_n = I\}. \tag{2.11}$$

While it is therefore no longer possible to graph these mathematical descriptions of sets, it is nevertheless possible to formulate them using equations. As we explore the consumer model in more detail in the upcoming chapters, you will see how these equations can be used to formulate a quite general model of choice behaviour.

2B.3.2 Choice Sets With Composite Goods We noted in Section 2A that we often find it useful in our graphical models to focus on one good that is of particular interest and to model all other consumption goods as a *composite good* denominated in euros. We will often refer to this composite good as euros of other consumption. One convenient benefit of such a model is that the price of the composite good is by definition 1 ($p_2 = 1$); €1 of consumption of other goods costs €1. This implies that the slope of the budget line becomes the price of the good we are concerned with rather than the ratio of prices that it typically is, and the vertical intercept becomes the exogenous income rather than income divided by the price of good 2.

To see this, we could write down the equation of a budget line with x_2 as the composite good as:

$$p_1 x_1 + x_2 = I, \tag{2.12}$$

leaving out the price for the composite good, which is just 1. Subtracting $p_1 x_1$ from both sides, we get:

$$x_2 = I - p_1 x_1, \tag{2.13}$$

with the equation of a line with vertical intercept I and slope $-p_1$. Note that this is the same equation as equation (2.5) with p_2 set to 1.

2B.4 Choice Sets That Arise From Endowments

So far, we have assumed that the income level or money budget for consumption choices is fixed or exogenous. This is a reasonable assumption when we analyze consumer choices where specific amounts have been budgeted for certain categories of goods like hoodies and jeans, or when we analyze the consumption choices of someone on a fixed income. In other cases, however, the money that can be devoted to consumption is not *exogenous*; rather it arises *endogenously* from the decisions a consumer makes and from the prices they face in the market. Important examples of this include our choices of selling our time in labour markets and our financial assets in capital markets.

In Section 2A.4, we assumed that you had returned to the shop with 10 hoodies and 5 pairs of jeans knowing that you would get a credit note for the value of the returns at the prices the shop was currently charging. How much credit you get now depends on the prices of the hoodies and jeans that the shop charges at the time of your return. Your income can be expressed as:

$$I = 5p_1 + 10p_2, \tag{2.14}$$

since the shop will give you its current price for jeans, p_1, for each of your 5 pairs of jeans and its current price for hoodies, p_2, for each of your 10 hoodies. Your choice set is composed of all combinations of jeans and hoodies such that total spending is no more than this income level; that is:

$$C(p_1, p_2) = \{(x_1, x_2) \in \mathbb{R}_+^2 \mid p_1 x_1 + p_2 x_2 \leq 5p_1 + 10p_2\}. \tag{2.15}$$

Notice that the set C is now a function of only (p_1,p_2) because income is endogenously determined by p_1 and p_2 as described in equation (2.14). When the inequality in (2.15) is replaced with an equality to get the equation for the budget line, we get:

$$p_1 x_1 + p_2 x_2 = 5p_1 + 10p_2. \tag{2.16}$$

Subtracting $p_1 x_1$ from both sides and dividing both sides by p_2, this turns into:

$$x_2 = 5\frac{p_1}{p_2} + 10 - \frac{p_1}{p_2} x_1. \tag{2.17}$$

In Graph 2.6, we plotted this budget set for the case where the shop was charging €10 for both hoodies and jeans. When these prices are substituted into equation (2.17), we get:

$$x_2 = 15 - x_1, \tag{2.18}$$

which represents the equation of a line with vertical intercept 15 and slope -1. This is the budget line $A'B'$ we derived intuitively in Graph 2.6.

More generally, we can denote someone's endowment as the number of goods of each kind a consumer has as they enter the shop. For instance, we might denote your endowment of good 1 as e_1 and of good 2 as e_2. In our example $e_1 = 5$ and $e_2 = 10$. We can define the choice set as a function of your endowment and the prices of the two goods:

$$C(p_1,p_2,e_1,e_2) = \{(x_1,x_2) \mid p_1 x_1 + p_2 x_2 \leq p_1 e_1 + p_2 e_2\}, \tag{2.19}$$

where the left-hand side of the inequality represents spending on the goods you purchase and the right-hand side represents endogenous income from returning your endowment goods to the shop.

Exercise 2B.6

Using the equation in (2.19), derive the general equation of the budget line in terms of prices and endowments. Following steps analogous to those leading to equation (2.17), identify the intercept and slope terms. What would the budget line look like if your endowments are 10 hoodies and 10 pairs of jeans and prices are €5 for jeans and €10 for hoodies? Relate this to both the equation you derived and an intuitive derivation of the same budget line.

End-of-Chapter Exercises

2.1† Suppose the only two goods in the world are marmalade and jam.

A. You have no exogenous income, but you do own 6 jars of marmalade and 2 jars of jam. The price of marmalade is €4 per jar, and the price of jam is €6 per jar.

 a. On a graph with jars of marmalade on the horizontal and jars of jam on the vertical axis, illustrate your budget constraint.

 b. How does your constraint change when the price of marmalade increases to €6? How does this change your opportunity cost of jam?

B. Consider the same economic circumstances described in 2.1A and use x_1 to represent jars of marmalade and x_2 to represent jars of jam.

 a. Write down the equation representing the budget line and relate key components to your graph from 2.1A(a).

 b. Change your equation for your budget line to reflect the change in economic circumstances described in 2.1A(b) and show how this new equation relates to your graph in 2.1A(b).

2.2* Suppose there are three goods in the world: x_1, x_2 and x_3.

A. On a three-dimensional graph, illustrate your budget constraint when your economic circumstances are defined by $p_1 = 2, p_2 = 6, p_3 = 5$ and $I = 120$. Label the intercepts.

 a. What is your opportunity cost of x_1 in terms of x_2? What is your opportunity cost of x_2 in terms of x_3?

 b. Illustrate how your graph changes if I falls to €60. Does your answer to (a) change?

 c. Illustrate how your graph changes if instead p_1 rises to €4. Does your answer to part (a) change?

B. Write down the equation that represents your picture in 2.2A. Suppose that a new good x_4 is invented and priced at €1. How does your equation change? Why is it difficult to represent this new set of economic circumstances graphically?

2.3† **Everyday Application:** *Renting a Car versus Taking Taxis.* Suppose you and a friend go on a week-long holiday to Cyprus and are choosing between renting a car or taking a taxi to tour the island for the week. Renting a car involves a fixed fee of €300 for the week, with each kilometre driven thereafter costing €0.20, which is the price of fuel per kilometre. Taking a taxi involves no fixed fees, but each kilometre driven on the island during the week costs €1 per kilometre.

A. Suppose you have both brought €2000 to spend on 'kilometres driven on the island' and 'other goods'. On a graph with kilometres driven on the horizontal and other consumption on the vertical axis, illustrate your budget constraint assuming you choose to rent a car and your friend's budget constraint assuming they choose to take taxis.

 a. What is the opportunity cost for each kilometre driven that you face?

 b. What is the opportunity cost for each kilometre driven that your friend faces?

B. Derive the mathematical equations for your budget constraint and your friend's budget constraint, and relate elements of these equations to your graphs in part A. Use x_1 to denote kilometres driven and x_2 to denote other consumption.

 a. Where in your budget equation can you locate the opportunity cost of a kilometre driven?

 b. Where in your budget equation for your friend can you locate the opportunity cost of a kilometre driven?

2.4* **Business Application:** *Pricing and Quantity Discounts.* Businesses often give quantity discounts. In the following, you will analyze how such discounts can impact choice sets.

A. The head of your economics department tells you that a photocopier provider charges €0.05 per page or €5 per 100 pages for the first 10 000 copies in any given month but reduces the price per page to €0.035 for each additional page up to 100 000 copies and to €0.02 per page over 100 000. The department has a monthly overall budget of €5000.

a. Putting 'Pages copied in units of 100' on the horizontal axis and 'Euros spent on other goods' on the vertical, illustrate this budget constraint. Label all intercepts and slopes.

b. Suppose the photocopying company changes its pricing policy to €0.05 per page for monthly copying up to 20 000 and €0.025 per page for *all* pages if copying exceeds 20 000 per month. Illustrate this on your graph in part (a). *Hint*: Your budget line will contain a jump.

c. What is the marginal or additional cost of the first page copied after 20 000 in part (b)? What is the marginal cost of the first page copied after 20 001 in part (b)?

B. Write down the mathematical expression for choice sets for each of the scenarios in 2.4A(a) and 2.4A(b) using x_1 to denote 'Pages copied in units of 100', and x_2 to denote 'Euros spent on other goods'.

2.5† **Business Application:** *Frequent Flyer Perks.* Airlines offer frequent flyers different kinds of perks that we will model here as reductions in average prices per kilometre flown.

A. Suppose that an airline charges 20 cents per kilometre flown. However, once a customer reaches 25 000 kilometres in a given year, the price drops to 10 cents per kilometre for each additional kilometre. The alternate way to travel is by train, which costs 16 cents per kilometre.

a. Consider a business person who has a travel budget of €10 000 per year, a budget that can be spent on the cost of getting to places as well as other consumption while travelling. On a graph with 'Kilometres flown' on the horizontal axis and 'Other consumption' on the vertical, illustrate the budget constraint if the person only considers flying and not train travel to their destinations.

b. On a similar graph with 'Kilometres driven' on the horizontal axis, illustrate the budget constraint if the business person considers only using the train and not flying as a means of travel.

c. By overlaying these two budget constraints changing the good on the horizontal axis to 'Kilometres travelled', can you explain how frequent flyer perks might persuade the business person to fly a lot more than they otherwise would?

B. Determine where the air-travel budget from 2.5A(a) intersects the train budget from 2.5A(b).

2.6 **Policy Application:** *Taxing Goods versus Lump Sum Taxes.* In an attempt to reduce the consumption of sugary drinks, a government places a tax on soft drinks which raises the price from €2 per litre to €4 per litre. Subsequent studies show average individual consumption of sugary drinks falls to 10 litres per month compared to 15 litres before the tax.

A. Putting 'Litres of sugary drinks per month' on the horizontal axis and 'Euros of other consumption' on the vertical axis, illustrate the average consumer's budget line before and after the tax is imposed. You can denote income by *I*.

a. How much tax revenue is the government collecting per month from the average consumer? Illustrate this as a vertical distance on your graph. *Hint*: If you know how much they are consuming after the tax and how much in other consumption this leaves them with, and if you know how much in other consumption they would have had if they had consumed that same quantity before the imposition of the tax, the difference between these two other consumption quantities must be equal to how much the average consumer paid in tax.

b. Assume that the tax on sugary drinks has been contested by the drinks industry. The government are being pushed to remove the tax but have to find a way to raise the same tax revenue that was yielded by the tax on sugary drinks. A proposal is made to ask consumers to pay exactly the amount they paid in sugary drinks taxes as a monthly lump sum payment. Ignoring for the moment the difficulty of gathering the necessary information for implementing this proposal, how would this change the average consumer's budget constraint?

B. State the equations for the budget constraints you derived in 2.6A(a) and 2.6A(b), letting sugary drinks be denoted by x_1 and other consumption by x_2.

Chapter 3

Economic Circumstances in Labour and Financial Markets

Before money can be spent on consumer goods, it must first be generated through some form of economic activity. For most of us, this activity involves work, or the giving up of our time in return for pay. Alternatively, we might generate money by borrowing or by cashing in savings from savings accounts, investment funds, property investments or other assets. In each of these scenarios, we are giving up some *endowment*, something whose value is determined by prices in the economy, to receive money for consumption. We are, in effect, trading an endowment in order to generate the money that can be treated as a fixed budget when we go into a shop for hoodies and jeans.

Our economic circumstances in work/leisure and savings/borrowing decisions are shaped by the endowment that we bring to the table as well as the prices that the endowment commands in the market. If the decision involves selling our leisure time for work, the relevant price becomes the wage, and when the decision involves postponing consumption through savings or borrowing on future income through taking out a loan, the relevant price will be the interest rate that we can earn or that we have to pay. Thus, the choice sets that we derive in this chapter are in essence no different from the choice set we thought about in Chapter 2 when you returned to the shop with jeans and hoodies rather than with money; all that is different is that our endowment will not be in terms of jeans and hoodies, and the prices will involve wage rates and interest rates.

3A	Budgets for Workers and Savers

We will begin by analyzing our choice sets as workers and proceed to choice sets that arise as we think about saving and borrowing.

3A.1 Our Choice Sets as Workers

Work involves giving up a precious endowment, our time. Depending on our innate talents and characteristics as well as our educational background and work experience, our time may be worth more or less to employers, or to the market more generally if we are self-employed. Let's assume that you have a summer job while at university which pays €20 per hour. Your employer is trying to determine how many other summer workers they need to hire, and asks you how many hours per week you would like to work over the summer. You now have to determine how much work is best for you given your circumstances. The more you work, the less leisure time you will have but the more consumption goods you will be able to buy with the income. The opportunity cost of taking one hour of leisure time is €20 worth of consumption at the given wage.

3A.1.1 Graphing Leisure/Consumption Choice Sets Illustrating your choice set as you choose between consumption and leisure is no different from illustrating your choice set over jeans and hoodies, except that you begin with a particular endowment of leisure time rather than an exogenous euro income. In Graph 3.1, we put hours of leisure per week on the horizontal axis and euros of consumption per week on the vertical. We make the analysis manageable by combining consumption into one composite consumption good. Let's assume that given your other obligations, such as sleep, you have 60 hours of time available to allocate between work and leisure in any given week. This is your leisure time endowment. The intercept on the leisure axis is at 60 hours (point *E*), indicating that one of your possible choices is to take all 60 hours of leisure endowment and earn no money for consumption. You can consume this endowment bundle *E regardless of what prices, including the wage, in the economy are*, a characteristic shared by all endowment points.

Graph 3.1 A Decrease in Wage

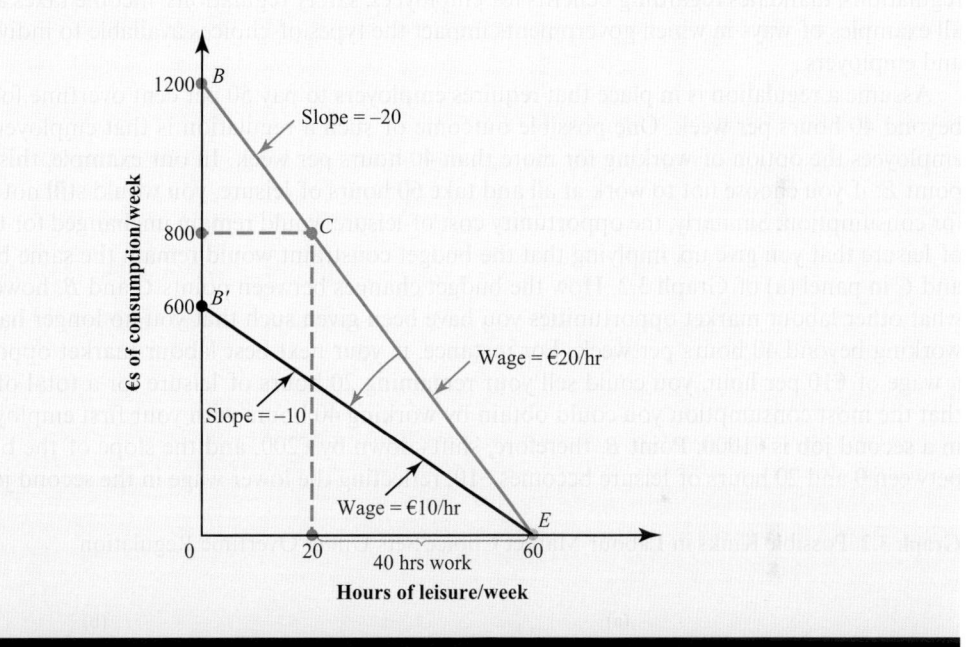

Go to MindTap to interact with this graph

On the other extreme, you could sell your entire time endowment and earn €1200 per week shown as point *B*, the intercept on the consumption axis. More likely would be to do something in between, such as selling 40 hours of leisure leaving you with 20 hours for play and earning €800 per week for consumption (point *C*). Connecting these, we get the budget constraint *BE* that illustrates all the possible combinations of consumption and leisure that are available to you per week given your circumstances. The slope of this line is −20, which is equal to the negative wage identified as the opportunity cost of one hour of leisure in terms of euros of consumption. Assume that the job you are starting is very popular and there are many people seeking work. As a result, the employer can pay a wage of €10 rather than €20 per hour.

When a choice set is derived from an endowment rather than some fixed euro amount, the budget line will pivot around the endowment point when prices change or, in our example here, point *E* illustrates the total amount of discretionary leisure time that you have available per week. Regardless of what the wage rate in the economy turns out to be, this point *E* is *always* available to you since it is your endowment point. Point *E* therefore does not change when the wage rate declines to €10. Point *B*, on the other hand, does change; if you decided to sell all of your available leisure time, you could now only earn €600 rather than €1200 per week. The new budget constraint, $B'E$, contains the endowment point E and has a slope equal to the new opportunity cost of leisure (−10).

Exercise 3A.1

Illustrate what happens to the original budget constraint if your wage increases to €30 per hour. What if you are able to manage with less sleep and take up to 80 hours of leisure time per week?

3A.1.2 Government Policies and Labour Market Choice Sets Government policies on labour market decisions are so vast that entire subfields within economics are devoted to studying their impacts. Overtime regulations, mandates regarding benefits for employees, safety regulations, income taxes and subsidies are all examples of ways in which governments impact the types of choices available to individual employees and employers.

Assume a regulation is in place that requires employers to pay 50 per cent overtime for any work done beyond 40 hours per week. One possible outcome of such a regulation is that employers do not permit employees the option of working for more than 40 hours per week. In our example, this would not alter point E; if you choose not to work at all and take 60 hours of leisure, you would still not earn any money for consumption. Similarly, the opportunity cost of leisure would remain unchanged for the first 40 hours of leisure that you give up, implying that the budget constraint would remain the same between points E and C in panel (a) of Graph 3.2. How the budget changes between points C and B, however, depends on what other labour market opportunities you have been given such that you no longer have the option of working beyond 40 hours per week. For instance, if your next best labour market opportunity involves a wage of €10 per hour, you could sell your remaining 20 hours of leisure for a total of €200, implying that the most consumption you could obtain by working 40 hours with your first employer and 20 hours in a second job is €1000. Point B, therefore, shifts down by €200, and the slope of the budget constraint between 0 and 20 hours of leisure becomes −10, reflecting the lower wage in the second job.

Graph 3.2 Possible Kinks in Labour Market Choice Sets Under Overtime Regulation

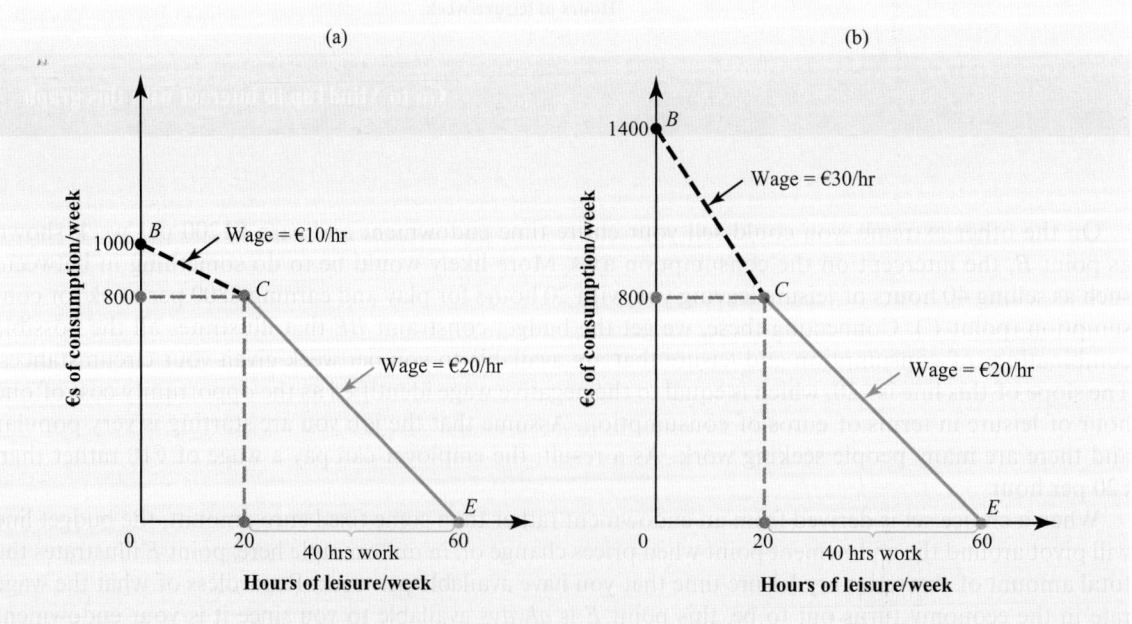

If your employer is willing to meet the overtime pay, your budget constraint would change differently. While the segment between E and C would remain unchanged since it deals with hours of work below 40 per week, the most consumption you could engage in if you worked the full 60 hours would increase to €1400 because your last 20 hours of leisure could now be sold for €30 per hour: the €20 wage plus the required 50 per cent overtime pay. The resulting budget constraint would again be kinked at C but would now point inward rather than outward, as in panel (b) of Graph 3.2.

Different kinds of taxes and subsidies also have important effects on the choice sets that workers face. If wages are subject to a 25 per cent tax and your hourly rate is €20 per hour, your take-home pay will be €15 per hour, and your budget constraint would pivot anti-clockwise around the endowment point E, with a new consumption intercept of €900 instead of €1200. While this is an example of a *proportional tax*, a tax that collects revenues from workers in strict proportion to their wage income, most real-world taxes are significantly more complicated. Often, tax rates imposed on wage income increase as income rises, but sometimes the reverse is true. For example, workers in low-income families in the UK can claim Working Tax Credit which in effect provides a subsidy or negative income tax on wages up to a certain level of income These kinds of tax and subsidy systems can create important kinks in leisure/consumption budget sets.

3A.2 Constraints in Planning for the Future

We now turn to a set of trade-offs which involve planning for the future as we decide whether to delay immediate gratification by saving rather than consuming today, or by limiting the degree to which we borrow against our future income. By saving, we generate an asset that like the time we sell in labour markets, we can later sell in order to consume. Borrowing, on the other hand, is in effect selling a future asset in order to consume today.

3A.2.1 Planning for Next Year: Intertemporal Budget Constraints
Suppose that your summer job is for a total of 500 hours at €20 per hour. This will generate a total of €10 000 this summer. You have plans to spend the next summer travelling. You have full financial aid during the academic year and therefore need money only during the summers.

Your travel plans for next summer are dependent on the income you earn this summer. We can illustrate the trade-offs you face by putting euros of consumption this summer on the horizontal axis and euros of consumption next summer on the vertical axis, as shown in the panels in Graph 3.3. We have chosen to lump all forms of consumption in each summer period together and treat them as a composite good in order to make the analysis manageable in a two-dimensional picture.

You could decide to spend all your income this summer on current consumption, thus obtaining €10 000 worth of consumption, but have no income for next summer as shown by point E in panel (a) of Graph 3.3. At the other extreme, you could forego any consumption this summer, put the €10 000 in the bank and earn interest for a year. Suppose the annual interest rate is 10 per cent. This would permit you a maximum of €11 000 in consumption next year, shown by point B in panel (b) of Graph 3.3. It is also possible to choose any point on the budget constraint $E B$, which has a slope of −1.1 and illustrates the opportunity cost of consuming a euro this summer as €1.10 in foregone consumption next summer. More generally, *the opportunity cost of consuming a euro today is 1 plus the annual interest rate, expressed in decimal form, in foregone consumption one year from now.* Such budget constraints that illustrate trade-offs faced over time are often called *intertemporal budget constraints*.

For the purposes of this model, we are treating this summer's income as your endowment (point E). Regardless of what the prices, or in this case, interest rates are in the economy, you can always choose to consume this endowment; that is, you can always choose to consume all €10 000 now. As the interest rate changes, however, the rest of your budget constraint will pivot around that point. For instance, if the interest rate falls to 5 per cent, the maximum you will be able to consume next summer is €10 500, shown by point B' in panel (a) of Graph 3.3, and the new slope of the budget line (−1.05), illustrates the new opportunity cost of consuming a euro this year.

Now suppose that you decide you want to travel this summer rather than next. Since you have no savings, you can do this only by borrowing against your future income. Your employer agrees to write a note to the bank letting it know that you are guaranteed work next summer with an income of €11 000. Assume the interest rate is still 10 per cent. When plotting your budget constraint across the two summers, you know that one possibility would be for you to borrow nothing and thus have the entire €11 000 for consumption next summer, as shown by point E' in panel (b) of Graph 3.3. Alternatively, you could borrow the maximum amount the bank will lend you and consume all of it this year. Since the bank knows that you can pay back up to €11 000 next summer, it will lend you up to €10 000 now, knowing that this will mean that you will owe €11 000 next year with interest at 10 per cent. Point A therefore lies at €10 000 on the euros of consumption this summer axis in panel (b) of Graph 3.3.

Graph 3.3 Different Types of Intertemporal Budget Constraints

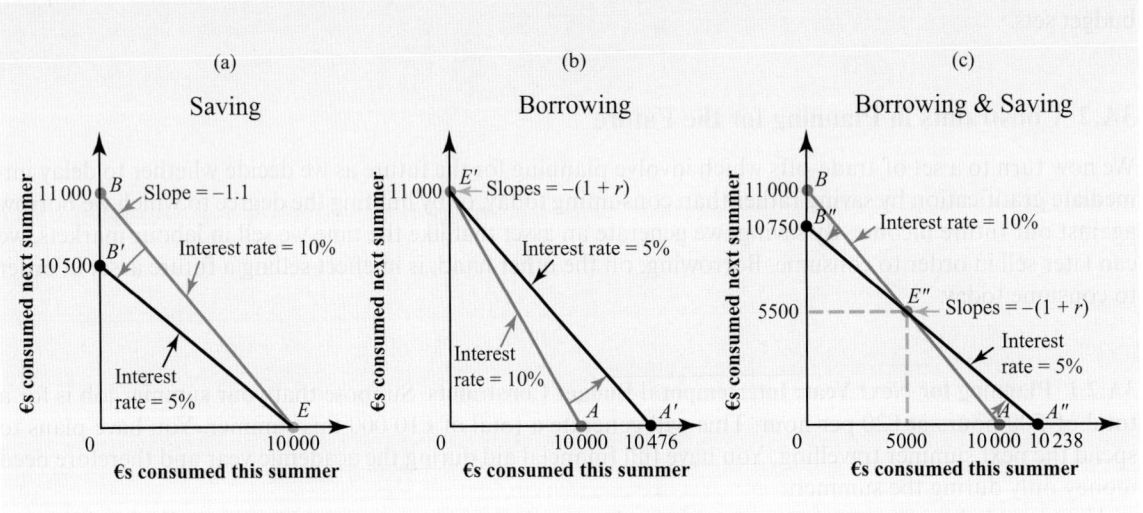

We are now treating income next summer as your endowment that can be consumed regardless of what the interest rate is, which means that your budget line will pivot around point E' as the interest rate changes. For any given interest rate r expressed in decimal form, the budget constraint will run through point E', with slope $-(1 + r)$, which is the opportunity cost of borrowing and consuming a euro and having to pay it back with interest next year. Panel (b) in Graph 3.3 illustrates a decrease in the interest rate from 10 per cent to 5 per cent as the change from $E'A$ to $E'A'$.

On reflection, you decide to split your travelling over two summers and thus to work half of this summer and half of next summer. Your employer is willing to pay you a €5000 summer salary this year and promises a €5500 summer salary next year. In this case, your endowment point – the point that does not depend on the interest rate – is given by a new point E'' in panel (c) of Graph 3.3, where you consume €5000 this year and €5500 next year. At an interest rate of 10 per cent, you could save all of your current summer pay and consume a total of €11 000 next summer, or you could borrow €5000 from the bank and consume as much as €10 000 this summer but have no consumption next summer. As the interest rate changes, your budget line would continue to go through your endowment point E'' since you can always just consume what you earn when you earn it, with a slope $-(1 + r)$. Panel (c) in Graph 3.3 illustrates a change in the interest rate from 10 per cent to 5 per cent as a change in the budget line from BA to $B'A'$.

Exercise 3A.2

In each of the panels of Graph 3.3, how would the choice set change if the interest rate was 20 per cent?

3A.2.2 Planning for Several Years Into the Future The analysis becomes a little more complex as we think of planning beyond a year from now. Suppose, for instance, that you are required to go to a placement next summer in order to complete your degree and thus you won't be able to go travelling until two summers' time. Assume that the placement provides financial support to fully cover your expenses between this summer and two summers from now, but you are responsible for covering this summer and your travel in two years. Again, suppose your summer job this year pays €10 000 and the annual interest rate is 10 per cent.

The budget constraint is now represented as euros of consumption this summer on the horizontal axis and euros of consumption two years from now on the vertical. Point E in panel (a) of Graph 3.3 remains unchanged; you can always just decide to consume everything this summer and nothing two summers from now. But how much could you consume two years from now if you saved everything?

We know that if you put €10 000 in the bank for a year, you will have €11 000 one year from now. In two years from now, you will earn further interest. Since 10 per cent of €11 000 is €1100, you would have a maximum of €12 100 in consumption two summers from now if you consume none of your current summer income.

Keeping €10 000 in the bank for a year will result in a balance of €10 000 $(1 + r)$. Keeping this sum of €10 000$(1 + r)$ in the bank for an additional year will give you a balance of this new amount times $(1 + r)$ two years from now, or:

€10 000$(1 + r)(1 + r)$, or €10 000$(1 + r)^2$. The opportunity cost of €1 of consumption this summer is, therefore, $(1 + r)$. If we think ahead for yet another summer, we would have $(1 + r)$ times the balance after three summers, or:

€10 000$(1 + r)^2(1 + r)$ or €10 000$(1 + r)^3$. If we follow this pattern, a €10 000 deposit in the bank this summer will yield a balance of €10 000$(1 + r)^n$ if we leave the account untouched for n summers.

Exercise 3A.3

So far, we have implicitly assumed that interest compounds yearly; that is, you begin to earn interest on interest only at the end of each year. Often, interest compounds more frequently. Suppose that you put €10 000 in the bank now at an annual interest rate of 10 per cent, but that interest compounds monthly rather than yearly. Your monthly interest rate is 10/12 or 0.833 per cent. Defining n as the number of months and using the information in the previous paragraph, how much would you have in the bank after one year? Compare this to the amount we calculated you would have when interest compounds annually.

Graph 3.4 is a generalized version of the first two panels of Graph 3.3, where instead of thinking about the choice between consuming now and a year from now, we are modelling the choice between consuming now and n years from now. In panel (a) of Graph 3.4, we are assuming that €X is earned this summer and a portion of it potentially saved for use n summers later. Thus, the endowment point E lies on the horizontal axis. In panel (b) of Graph 3.4, on the other hand, we are assuming that €Y will be earned n summers from now, and a portion of this may be borrowed for current consumption. Assuming the interest rate for borrowing and saving is the same, we get two budget constraints with the same slope but with different endowment points.

Graph 3.4 Intertemporal Choice Sets When Planning n Years Ahead

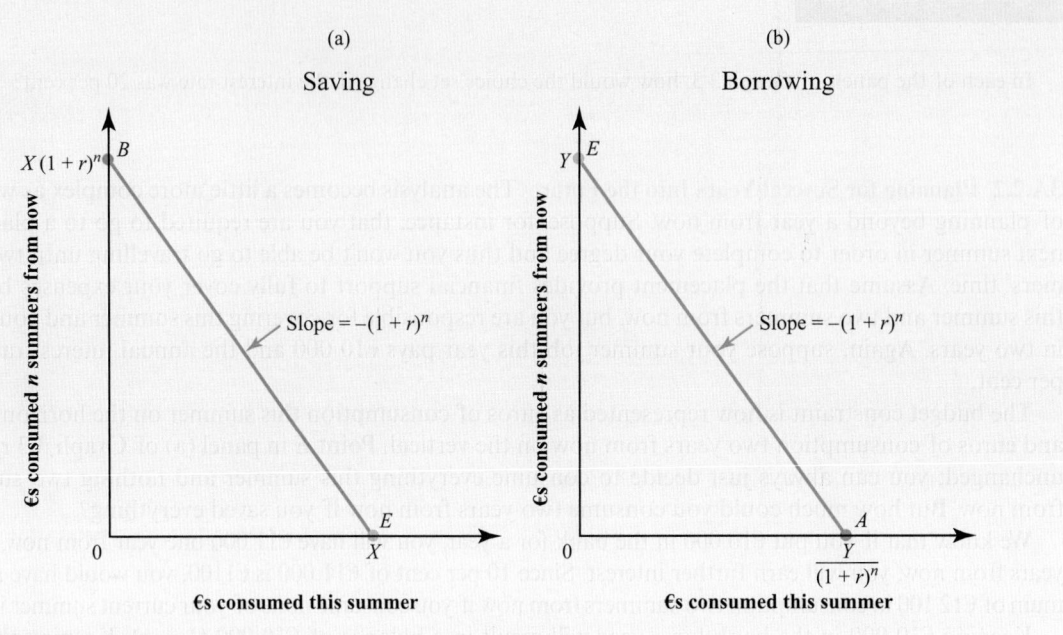

Exercise 3A.4

James inherits €100 000 and is trying to choose how much of this to consume now and how much of it to save for his retirement 20 years from now. Illustrate James' choice set with euros of consumption now and euros of consumption 20 years from now assuming an interest rate of 5 per cent compounded annually. What happens if the interest rate suddenly jumps to 10 per cent compounded annually?

3A.2.3 More Complex Financial Planning Analyzing financial planning is limited using a two-period model because it is difficult to model the full complexity of savings and consumption possibilities as consumers earn income over multiple periods and plan for consumption over those same periods. However, the model does allow substantial intuitions to be developed.

3A.3 Putting It All Into a Single Model

In the real world, economic actors can be consumers, workers and financial planners simultaneously as they work in order to consume and plan for the future by saving or borrowing. It is often useful to model choices as workers, consumers and financial planners separately depending on the type of real-world issue we are trying to address. In principle, it is also possible to merge these separate models into a single framework in order to analyze simultaneously the full choice set faced by an individual who undertakes multiple roles within an economy. This is most easily done with the mathematical tools explored in part B of this chapter, but we can also get a glimpse of how this is accomplished in a somewhat more complex graphical model.

Suppose, for example, we return to your decision regarding how much to work this summer. In Section 3A.1, we analyzed the choice set you face when making this decision, but we assumed that your only two options were consumption or leisure *this summer.* In Section 3A.2, we analyzed your choice set as you are planning for next summer, but we assumed that you had already decided how much you were going to work this summer. Now we can think about what your choice set will look like when you are trying to decide how much to work this summer *and* how you will split your consumption across this and next summer. We thus need a three-dimensional graph such as Graph 3.5, with leisure hours this summer on one axis and consumption this summer and next summer on the other two axes.

Graph 3.5 Consumption/Leisure Choice Set Combined With Intertemporal Choice

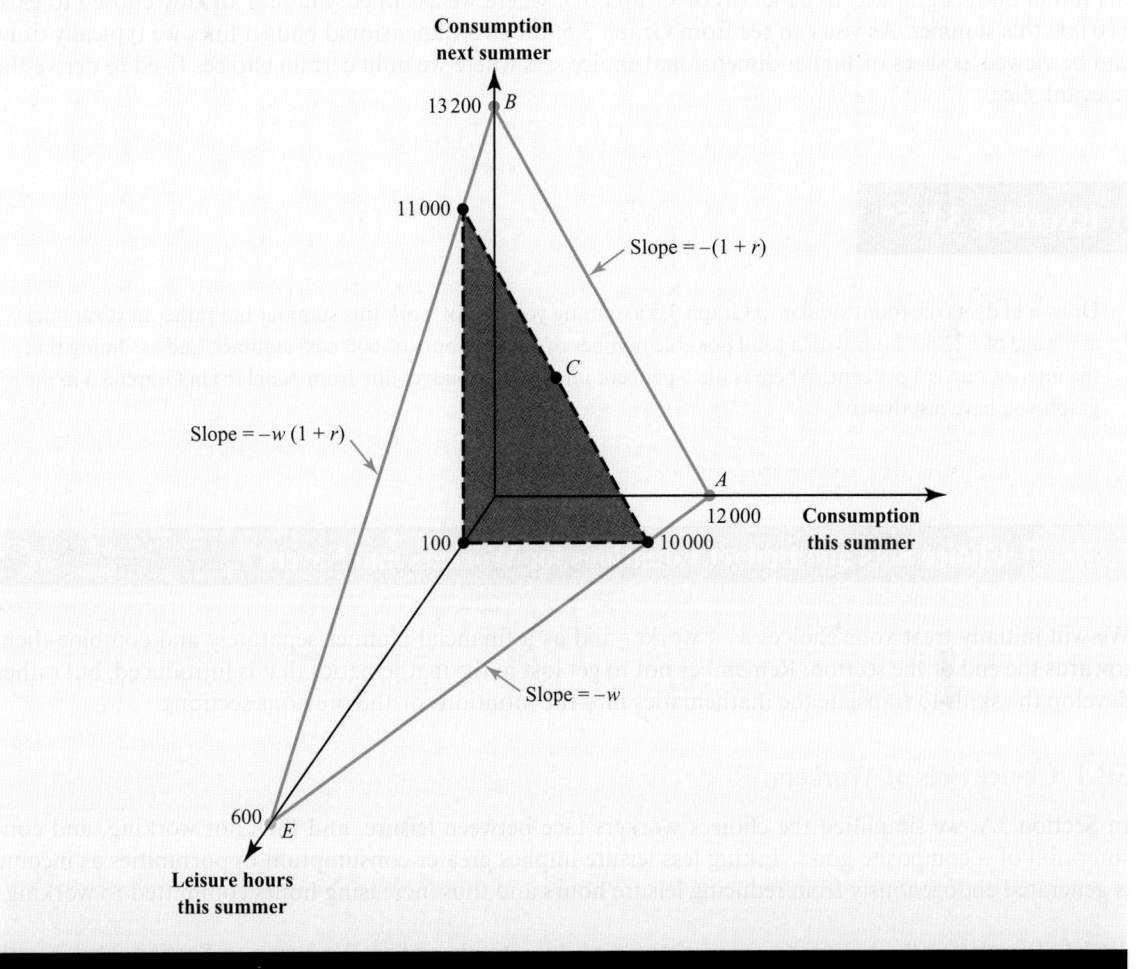

Go to MindTap to interact with this graph

Suppose that you have up to 600 leisure hours this summer, 60 per week for 10 weeks, when you can earn a wage of €20 per hour, and that the annual interest rate is 10 per cent. Your endowment point is point E, at which you consume all of your leisure time leaving you with no goods to consume this summer or next. If you decided to consume nothing next summer, your choice set would lie on the bottom plane of the graph defined by the budget line that connects A and E. This choice set is much like the choice sets we graphed in Section 3A.1 where you considered your trade-off between consumption and leisure *this summer.* Similarly, if you decided to consume no leisure, your choice set would collapse to a two-dimensional picture in the vertical plane that contains the budget line connecting A and B. This is similar to the types of choice sets we analyzed in Section 3A.2 where you were choosing between consuming a given amount now or next year. Finally, in the panel containing E and B, we graph the choice set assuming that you will consume no goods this summer. In that case, for every hour that you work, you will make €20 plus €2 in interest, for a total of €22 of consumption next summer. The opportunity cost of an hour of leisure time is therefore €22 of foregone consumption a year from now, which is your wage w times (1 + r).

Your best choice in a choice set such as this will of course most likely involve some leisure this summer, some consumption now and some consumption a year from now. All points that lie on the interior of the plane connecting A, B and E represent such choices. For instance, if you decided to work for 500 hours, consuming 100 hours of leisure, your remaining choice set would be represented by the slice that contains point C where you spread your consumption between the two summers. This slice is exactly identical to the initial budget graphed in panel (a) of Graph 3.3, where we assumed you had already chosen to earn €10 000 this summer. As you can see from Graph 3.5, the two-dimensional budget lines we typically draw can be viewed as slices of higher dimensional choice sets where we hold certain choices fixed to derive the relevant slice.

Exercise 3A.5*

Draw a budget constraint similar to Graph 3.5 assuming you do not work this summer but rather next summer at a wage of €22 per hour with a total possible number of leisure hours of 600 next summer, and assuming that the interest rate is 5 per cent. Where is the 5 per cent interest rate budget line from panel (b) in Graph 3.3 in the graph you have just drawn?

3B   Choice Sets and Budget Equations for Workers and Savers

We will initially treat your choices as a worker and as a financial planner separately and combine them towards the end of the section. Remember not to get lost in the mathematics that is introduced, but rather develop the skills to translate the mathematics into the intuitions of the previous sections.

3B.1 Choice Sets of Workers

In Section 3A, we simplified the choices workers face between leisure, and thus not working, and consumption of a composite good. Taking less leisure implies greater consumption opportunities as income is generated endogenously from reducing leisure hours and thus increasing hours committed to working.

3B.1.1 Translating the Leisure/Consumption Graph Into Mathematics We began in Section 3A.1.1 with an example in which we assumed you had a leisure endowment of 60 hours per week and could earn an hourly wage of €20. Letting c denote weekly euros of consumption and letting ℓ denote weekly hours of leisure consumption, your choice set was defined as all those combinations of c and ℓ where c is affordable given €20 is earned for each of the 60 hours of leisure endowment that is not consumed. You are constrained to a choice set of combinations of c and ℓ such that:

$$c \leq 20(60 - \ell). \tag{3.1}$$

The budget line is the same equation with the inequality replaced by an equality. Taking this budget line equation and multiplying out the terms, gives:

$$c = 1200 - 20 \ell, \hspace{4cm} (3.2)$$

which is the equation derived intuitively in Graph 3.1.

More generally, we could let our hours of leisure endowment be given by L and the hourly wage by w. Our choice set as a worker would be given by:

$$C(w, L) = \{(c, \ell), \in \mathbb{R}^2_+ \mid c \leq w(L - \ell)\} \hspace{3cm} (3.3)$$

with a budget line given by:

$$B(w, L) = \{(c, \ell), \in \mathbb{R}^2_+ \mid c = w(L - \ell)\}. \hspace{3cm} (3.4)$$

Notice that only a single price appears in the budget line equation $-w$, the price of labour. Implicitly we have again taken the price of c to be 1, since €1 of consumption costs exactly €1.

There may be times when economists would like to model the components of c more specifically, perhaps to investigate how particular public policies towards labour income might influence not only consumption overall, but also our consumption of particular goods that might be more or less complementary to leisure. Suppose, for example, that we are interested in your weekly consumption of n different goods – $x_1, x_2, \ldots, x_n$ – and how your consumption of those goods relates to your decisions in the labour market where you have a weekly leisure endowment L that you can sell at wage w. Your choice set is defined as all those combinations of the n different goods that you can afford at their market prices $(p_1, p_2, \ldots, p_n)$ given how much leisure you sold in the labour market; that is:

$$C(p_1, p_2, \ldots, p_n, w, L)$$
$$= \{(x_1, x_2, \ldots, x_n, \ell) \in \mathbb{R}^{n+1}_+ \mid p_1 x_1 + p_2 x_2 + \cdots + p_n x_n \leq w(L - \ell)\}. \hspace{1.5cm} (3.5)$$

Exercise 3B.1

Graph the choice set in equation (3.5) when $n = 2$, $p_1 = 2$, $w = 20$ and $L = 60$.

3B.1.2 Government Policies and Labour Market Choice Sets Government policies can have a direct impact on labour markets and thus on choice sets of workers, such as potential impacts of overtime legislation and the possible kinks in budget lines within the leisure/consumption graph that might result.

Exercise 3B.2

Translate the choice sets graphed in Graph 3.2 into mathematical notation defining the choice sets.

One particular policy that labour economists often focus on relates to wage taxes. Suppose, for instance, that a government tax on wages results in a tax paid by workers of t per cent expressed in decimal form. Instead of earning w for every hour of leisure that a worker chooses to sell in the labour market, they now only take home $(1-t)w$ because the government collects tw in wage taxes from the worker. This changes the budget line in the leisure/consumption model from the equation that appears in (3.4) to:

$$c = (1-t)w(L-\ell). \tag{3.6}$$

Multiplying out this equation we get:

$$c = (1-t)wL - (1-\ell)w\ell \tag{3.7}$$

with the first term on the right-hand side representing the intercept term and the second term representing the slope. Graphically, this implies that the intercept term falls from wL – the amount of consumption we could have had before taxes had we consumed no leisure – to $(1-t)wL$. Similarly, the slope term falls in absolute value, indicating that the slope of the budget line becomes shallower. Finally, we can verify our intuition that the intercept on the leisure axis remains unchanged by setting c to zero and solving for ℓ. Adding $(1-t)w\ell$ to both sides and dividing by $(1-t)w$ gives us the result that $\ell = L$; our leisure when we have no other consumption is simply equal to our leisure endowment.

Exercise 3B.3

Suppose $w = 20$ and $L = 60$. Graph the budget constraint in the absence of taxes. Suppose a wage tax $t = 0.25$ is introduced. Illustrate how this changes your equation and the graph.

3B.2 Choice Sets as We Plan for the Future

Translating trade-offs we face as we plan current and future consumption into mathematical formulations involves the same techniques applied for consumer and worker choice sets. The more general framework that arises from this opens possibilities for analyzing significantly more complex decisions guided by the same economic intuitions developed with graphical techniques.

3B.2.1 Planning for Next Year: Intertemporal Budgets
We can generalize our discussion on planning between two periods by letting e_1 and e_2 denote the amount of income you expect to earn this summer and next summer and letting r denote the interest rate in decimal form. For simplicity, we will continue to assume that the interest rate for borrowing and saving is the same and that interest compounds annually. In the initial scenario in Section 3A.2.1, we assumed $e_1 = 11\,000$ and $e_1 = 0$, whereas in the other scenarios we assumed first $e_1 = 0$ and $e_2 = 11\,000$ and then $e_1 = 5000$ and $e_2 = 5500$. These are graphed in panels (a), (b) and (c) of Graph 3.3 respectively.

Your consumption set across the two summers is a pair (c_1, c_2), with c_1 representing consumption this summer and c_2 representing consumption next summer. This pair has to be feasible given the endowments you have and the interest rate you face in the market. We can see most easily how this translates to a budget line equation by first determining how much you *could have* available for consumption next summer *if you consumed nothing this summer*, which is the sum of the endowments in the two summers $(e_1 + e_2)$ plus the interest you could have earned between the two summers on the first summer's endowment (re_1)

for a total of $(1 + r)e_1 + e_2$. For every €1 you want to consume this year, you will have to decrease your consumption next year by $(1 + r)$. The most you will actually have for consumption next summer is what you could have had if you had consumed nothing this summer $(1 + r)e_1 + e_2$ minus $(1 + r)$ times your actual consumption this summer (c_1), or:

$$c_2 \leq (1 + r)e_1 + e_2 - (1 + r)c_1, \tag{3.8}$$

which can also be written as:

$$c_2 \leq (1 + r)(e_1 - c_1) + e_2. \tag{3.9}$$

When written in this form, the equation should have particular intuitive appeal. The term $(e_1 - c_1)$ is the difference between your period 1 endowment and your period 1 consumption, or just your savings. When you multiply what's in your savings account by $(1 + r)$, that gives you your savings account balance a year from now $(1 + r)(e_1 - c_1)$. Together with your year 2 endowment, e_2, that's the most you can consume next year.

Using equation (3.8) with $(1 + r)c_1$ added to both sides, we can define your choice set as a function of your endowments and the interest rate:

$$C(e_1, e_2, r) = \{(c_1, c_2) \in \mathbb{R}^2_+ \mid (1 + r)c_1 + c_2 \leq (1 + r)e_1 + e_2\}. \tag{3.10}$$

Note that the budget constraint in equation (3.10) is written in terms of euros *next* summer. It could equivalently be written in terms of euros *this* summer by dividing both sides by $(1 + r)$, giving us:

$$C(e_1, e_2, r) = \left\{(c_1, c_2) \in \mathbb{R}^2_+ \mid c_1 + \frac{c_2}{(1 + r)} \leq e_1 + \frac{e_2}{(1 + r)}\right\}. \tag{3.11}$$

Exercise 3B.4

Using the information behind each of the scenarios graphed in Graph 3.3 to substitute into equation (3.8) that scenario's relevant values for e_1, e_2 and r, demonstrate that the budget lines graphed are consistent with the underlying mathematics of equation (3.8) and, more generally, make intuitive sense of the intercept and slope terms as they appear in equation (3.8).

3B.2.2 Planning for Several Years Into the Future More generally, we demonstrated intuitively in Section 3A.2.2 that planning over multiple time periods is similar to planning over one period, except that the relevant opportunity cost of consuming a euro today changes from $(1 + r)$ to $(1 + r)^n$, where n is the number of time periods over which we plan. For instance, if you plan to allocate income you expect to earn this summer and income you plan to earn n summers from now between consumption this summer and consumption n summers from now, your choice set is an extension of the choice set derived in the expression (3.10), with $(1 + r)$ replaced by $(1 + r)^n$:

$$C(e_1, e_n, r) = \{(c_1, c_n) \in \mathbb{R}^2_+ \mid (1 + r)^n c_1 + c_n \leq (1 + r)^n e_1 + e_n\}. \tag{3.12}$$

3B.2.3 More Complex Financial Planning When looking at the choice set as described in equation (3.12), we might question what happened to all the summers in between the current summer and the summer n years from now? Are we not consuming or earning income in those summers? Should those not be part of our planning as well?

The answer is that we were limited in Section 3A by our graphical tools. We only had room to graph two dimensions and thus could only graph planning over two periods, whether those were 1 or n years apart. With a more mathematical approach, however, we can define much more complex choice sets in which individuals can see their full consumption possibilities across many periods at one time. Suppose, for instance, that you have some expectation about what you will earn not only this year, but also for each of the upcoming $(n - 1)$ years. Thus, you have a total of n different endowments spread across n years, endowments we can denote as $(e_1, e_2, ..., e_n)$. Suppose further that you expect the annual interest rate across the next n years to be constant at r. If you consumed nothing until the last year, you would end up having the last year's endowment e_n plus the next to last year's endowment with one year's worth of interest on that endowment $((1 + r)e_{n-1})$, plus the second to last year's endowment (e_{n-2}) with two years' worth of interest on that endowment $((1 + r)^2 e_{n-1})$, and so on. Thus, if all consumption occurred in the last year, you could consume:

$$c_n = e_n + (1 + r)e_{n-1} + (1 + r)^2 e_{n-2} + \cdots + (1 + r)^{n-1} e_{n-(n-1)}. \tag{3.13}$$

For every euro that you consume in the next to last period, the amount left over for consumption in the last period declines by $(1 + r)$, and for every euro that you consume in the second to last period, the amount left over for consumption in the last period declines by $(1 + r)^2$, and so on. Thus, while you *could* consume in the last period as much as indicated in equation (3.13), the *actual* amount you can consume depends on how much is consumed in the previous periods:

$$c_n = e_n + (1 + r)e_{n-1} + (1 + r)^2 e_{n-2} + \cdots + (1 + r)^{n-1} e_1$$
$$-(1 + r)c_{n-1} - (1 + r)^2 c_{n-2} - \cdots - (1 + r)^{n-1} c_1 \tag{3.14}$$

or, with consumption terms grouped on the left-hand side and two of the subscripts simplified:

$$c_n + (1 + r)c_{n-1} + (1 + r)^2 c_{n-2} + \cdots + (1 + r)^{n-1} c_1$$
$$= e_n + (1 + r)e_{n-1} + (1 + r)^2 e_{n-2} + \cdots + (1 + r)^{n-1} e_1. \tag{3.15}$$

Our two-period graphical simplification is a special case of a more complex choice set, a simplification where the consumption and endowment terms for all but two periods are assumed to net out to zero. In our framework of individuals attempting to do the best they can given their circumstances, translating the graphical model into mathematics thus permits us to specify much richer and more realistic circumstances as we investigate how individuals might plan for the future.

Exercise 3B.5*

Suppose you expect to earn €10 000 this summer, €0 next summer and €15 000 two summers from now. Using c_1, c_2 and c_3 to denote consumption over these three summers, write down your budget constraint assuming an annual and annually compounding interest rate of 10 per cent. Illustrate this constraint on a three-dimensional graph with c_1, c_2 and c_3 on the three axes. How does your equation and graph change if the interest rate increases to 20 per cent?

3B.3 Putting It All in a Single Model

At the conclusion of Section 3A, we briefly explored a three-dimensional graphical example in which a leisure endowment this summer can translate into consumption both this summer and next summer. Specifically, we graphed your choice set under the assumption that you had a particular leisure endowment this summer and you were simultaneously evaluating how much to work this summer and how much to consume over the next two summers, assuming that you would not work anymore next summer.

Your income this summer thus depends on how much leisure ℓ you choose to consume this summer, with your income equal to your hourly wage w times the portion of your time endowment L not consumed as leisure, or $w(L + \ell)$. If you choose not to consume any of this income this summer and you put it all in the bank, you would have a total of:

$$(1 + r)w(L + \ell) \tag{3.16}$$

available for consumption next summer. For each euro you do choose to consume this summer, you will have $(1 + r)$ less in consumption next summer. Thus, your consumption c_2 next summer is equal to the most you could have consumed had you not consumed anything this summer minus $(1 + r)$ times what you actually do consume this summer (c_1), or:

$$c_2 = (1 + r)w(L - \ell) - (1 + r)c_1. \tag{3.17}$$

This, with the consumption terms grouped on one side of the equation, defines the budget constraint as:

$$B(L, w, r) = \{(c_1, c_2, \ell) \in \mathbb{R}^3_+ \mid (1 + r)c_1 + c_2 = (1 + r)w(L - \ell)\}. \tag{3.18}$$

Exercise 3B.6

When $L = 600$, $w = 20$ and $r = 0.1$, show how equation (3.18) translates directly into Graph 3.5.

Recall that whenever we limit ourselves to graphical models in two dimensions, we are essentially holding fixed something in a larger dimensional choice set. For instance, when we graphed your initial choice set between consuming this summer and consuming next summer in panel (a) of Graph 3.3, we assumed that your labour/leisure decision this summer had already been made and had resulted in 500 hours of labour. When analyzing consumption choices over two periods in a two-dimensional model, we are really operating on a slice of a three-dimensional model, a slice where something has been held fixed. In our example, this slice occurs at the fixed leisure consumption of 100 hours, with the 500 remaining hours earning the €10 000 income that makes €10 000 of consumption this summer, or €11 000 in consumption next summer, possible. Mathematically, this slice is:

$$B(r) = \{(c_1, c_2) \in \mathbb{R}^2_+ \mid (1 + r)c_1 + c_2 = (1 + r)(10\,000)\}, \tag{3.19}$$

where we have replaced labour income and time endowments with the exogenous current summer income of €10 000. This slice is depicted graphically in Graph 3.5

In the same way, the three-dimensional Graph 3.5 is also a slice of a yet higher dimensional choice set where something else has been held fixed. For instance, we have assumed in Graph 3.5 that you have decided not to work, i.e. not to sell leisure next summer, thus permitting us to focus on only three dimensions. Adding the possibility of working next summer is easy to handle mathematically, but impossible to graph.

Exercise 3B.7

Define mathematically a generalized version of the budget constraint in expression (3.18) under the assumption that you have both a leisure endowment L_1 this summer and another leisure endowment L_2 next summer. What is the value of L_2 in order for Graph 3.5 to be the correct three-dimensional slice of this four-dimensional choice set?

End-of-Chapter Exercises

3.1† In this chapter, we graphed budget constraints illustrating the trade-off between consumption and leisure.

A. Suppose that your wage is €20 per hour and you have up to 60 hours per week that you could work.

a. Now, instead of putting leisure hours on the horizontal axis as we did in Graph 3.1, put labour hours on the horizontal axis with consumption in euros still on the vertical. What would your choice set and budget constraint look like now?

b. Where on your graph would the endowment point be?

c. What is the interpretation of the slope of the budget constraint you just graphed?

d. If wages fall to €10 per hour, how does your graph change?

e. If you need less sleep and can work up to 80 rather than 60 hours per week, how would your graph change?

B. How would you write the choice set over consumption c and labour l as a function of the wage w and leisure endowment L?

3.2* Suppose you are a farmer whose land produces 50 units of food this year and is expected to produce another 50 units of food next year. Assume that there is no one else in the world to trade with.

A. On a graph with food consumption this year on the horizontal axis and food consumption next year on the vertical, indicate your choice set assuming there is no way for you to store food that you harvest this year for future consumption.

a. Now suppose that you have a barn in which you can store food. However, over the course of a year, half the food that you store spoils. How does this change your choice set?

b. Now suppose that, in addition to the food units you harvest off your land, you also own a cow. You could slaughter the cow this year and eat it for 50 units of food. Or you could let it graze for another year and let it grow fatter, and slaughter it next year for 75 units of food. However, you don't have any means of refrigeration and so cannot store meat over time. How does this alter your budget constraint assuming you still have the barn from part (a)?

B. How would you write the choice set you derived in A(b) mathematically, with c_1 indicating this year's food consumption and c_2 indicating next year's food consumption?

3.3† **Everyday Application:** *Investing for Retirement.* Suppose you were just told that you will receive a year-end bonus of €15 000 from your company. The marginal income tax rate is $33^1/_3$ per cent, which means that you will have to pay €5000 in income tax on this bonus. You expect the average rate of return on an investment account you have set up to be 10 per cent annually and, for the purposes of this example, assume interest compounds annually.

A. Suppose you have decided to save all of this bonus for retirement 30 years from now.

a. In a regular investment account, you will have to pay tax on the interest you earn each year. Thus, even though you earn 10 per cent, you have to pay a third in tax, leaving you with an after-tax return of $6^2/_3$ per cent. Under these circumstances, how much will you have accumulated in your account 30 years from now?

b. An alternative investment strategy is to place your bonus into a pension. Government regulations state that you do not have to pay tax on any income that is put into a pension, and you do not have to pay tax on any interest you earn. Thus, you can put the full €15 000 bonus into the pension, and earn the full 10 per cent return each year for the next 30 years. You do, however, have to pay tax on any amount that you choose to withdraw after you retire. Suppose you plan to withdraw the entire accumulated balance as soon as you retire 30 years from now, and suppose that you expect you will still be paying $33^1/_3$ per cent tax at that time. How much will you have accumulated in your pension, and how much will you have after you pay tax? Compare this with your answer to (a), that is to the amount you would have at retirement if you saved outside the pension.

c. *True or False*: By allowing individuals to defer paying tax into the future, pensions result in a higher rate of return for retirement savings.

B. Suppose more generally that you earn an amount I now, that you face and will face in the future a marginal tax rate of t expressed as a fraction between 0 and 1, that the interest rate now and in the future is r, and that you plan to invest for n periods into the future.

a. How much consumption will you be able to undertake n years from now if you first pay your income tax on the amount I, and place the remainder in a savings account whose interest income is taxed each year? Assume you add nothing further to the savings account between now and n years from now.

b. Now suppose you put the entire amount I into a tax-advantaged retirement account in which interest income can accumulate tax free. Any amount that is taken out of the account is taxed as regular income. Assume you plan to take out the entire balance in the account n years from now but nothing before. How much consumption can you fund from this source n years from now?

c. Compare your answers to (a) and (b) and indicate whether you can tell which will be higher.

3.4** **Business Application:** *Present Value of Winning Lottery Tickets.* The introduction to intertemporal budgeting in this chapter can be applied to thinking about the pricing of basic financial assets. The assets we will consider will differ in terms of when they pay income to the owner of the asset. In order to know how much such assets are worth, we have to determine their *present value*, which is equal to how much *current* consumption such an asset would allow us to undertake.

A. Suppose you just won the lottery and your lottery ticket is transferable to someone else you designate; that is, you can sell your ticket. In each of the following cases, you have won €100 000. Since you can sell your ticket, it is a financial asset, but depending on how exactly the holder of the ticket receives the €100 000, the asset is worth different amounts. Think about what you would be willing to actually sell this asset for by considering how much *current* consumption value the asset contains assuming the annual interest rate is 10 per cent.

a. The holder of the ticket is given a €100 000 government bond that matures in ten years. This means that in ten years, the owner of this bond can cash it for €100 000.

    b. The holder of the ticket will be awarded €50 000 now and €50 000 ten years from now.

    c. The holder of the ticket will receive ten payments of €10 000: one now, and one on the next nine anniversaries of the day they won the lottery.

    d. How does your answer to part (c) change if the first of the ten payments arrived one year from now, with the second arriving two years from now, the third arriving three years from now, and so on?

    e. The holder of the ticket gets €100 000 the moment they present the ticket.

B. More generally, suppose the lottery winnings are paid out in instalments of $x_1, x_2, \ldots, x_{10}$, with payment x_i occurring $(i-1)$ years from now. Suppose the annual interest rate is r.

    a. Determine a formula for how valuable such a stream of income is in present day consumption; that is, how much present consumption could you undertake given that the bank is willing to lend you money based on future income?

    b. Check to make sure that your formula works for each of the scenarios in part A.

    c. The scenario described in part A(c) is an example of a €10 000 payment followed by an annual annuity payment. Consider an annuity that promises to pay out €10 000 every year starting one year from now for n years. How much would you be willing to pay for such an annuity?

    d. How does your answer change if the annuity starts with its first payment now?

    e. What if the annuity from (c) is one that never ends? To give the cleanest possible answer to this, you should note that an infinite series of $1/(1+x) + 1/(1+x)^2 + 1/(1+x)^3 + \cdots = 1/x$. How much would this annuity be worth if the interest rate is 10 per cent?

3.5† **Policy Application:** *Wage Taxes and Budget Constraints.* Suppose you have 60 hours of leisure that you could devote to work per week, and that you can earn an hourly wage of €25.

A. The government imposes a 20 per cent tax on all wage income.

    a. Illustrate your weekly budget constraint before and after the tax on a graph with weekly leisure hours on the horizontal axis and weekly consumption measured in euros on the vertical axis. Label all intercepts and slopes.

    b. You decide to work 40 hours per week after the tax is imposed. How much income tax do you pay per week? Can you illustrate this as a vertical distance in your graph?

    c. Instead of leisure hours on the horizontal axis, put labour hours on this axis. Illustrate your budget constraints that have the same information as the ones you drew in (a).

B. The government imposes a tax rate t expressed as a rate between 0 and 1 on all wage income.

    a. Write down the mathematical equations for the budget constraints and describe how they relate to the constraints you drew in A(a). Assume again that the leisure endowment is 60 per week.

    b. Use your equation to verify your answer to part A(b).

    c. Write down the mathematical equations for the budget constraints you derived in B(a), but now make consumption a function of labour, not leisure hours. Relate this to your graph in A(c).

3.6 **Policy Application:** *Proportional versus Progressive Wage Taxes.* The tax analyzed in exercise 3.5 is a *proportional* wage tax. Most income tax systems, however, are *progressive*. This means that the *average* tax rate paid increases the more wage income is earned.

A. Suppose the government exempts the first €500 of weekly earnings from taxation, taxes the next €500 at 20 per cent and any earnings beyond that at 40 per cent. Suppose that you again have 60 hours of leisure per week and can earn €25 per hour.

    a. Graph your weekly budget constraint illustrating the trade-offs between leisure and consumption.

    b. The *marginal tax rate* is defined as the tax rate you pay for the next euro you earn, while the *average tax rate* is defined as your total tax payment divided by your before-tax income. What is your average and marginal tax rate if you choose to work 20 hours per week?

    c. How does your answer change if you work 30 hours? What if you work 40 hours?

d. On a graph with before-tax weekly income on the horizontal axis and tax rates on the vertical, illustrate how average and marginal tax rates change as income goes up. Will the average tax rate ever reach the top marginal tax rate of 40 per cent?

e. Assume that there is a proposal to switch to a flat tax, a tax with one single marginal tax rate and that some initial portion of income is exempt from taxation. The flat tax therefore imposes two different marginal tax rates: a tax rate of zero for income up to some amount x per year, and a single rate t applied to any income earned above x per year. Is such a tax progressive?

B. Suppose more generally that the government does not tax income below x per week; that it taxes income at t for anything above x and below $2x$; and that it taxes additional income (beyond $2x$) at $2t$. Let I denote income per week.

a. Derive the average tax rate as a function of income and denote that function $a(I,t,x)$, where I represents weekly income.

b. Derive the marginal tax rate function $m(I,t,x)$.

Chapter 4

Tastes and Indifference Curves

Individuals try to do the *best* they can given their circumstances. Choice sets do not tell us what individuals *will* do, only all the possible actions they *could* take. Knowing what our choice sets are is a *necessary* first step to finding what choices are best, but it is not *sufficient*. To determine what an individual will actually do when presented with a given choice set, we need to know more about the individual and about their tastes. Tastes, however, differ enormously across people and can be difficult to observe.

There are, however, some regularities in tastes that we can reasonably assume are shared across most people, and these regularities will lead us to be able to make predictions about behaviour that will be independent of what exact tastes an individual has. Economists have developed ways of observing choices that individuals make and inferring from these choices what kinds of tastes they have. We will be able to say a great deal about behaviour and how behaviour changes as different aspects of an economy change.

4A   The Economic Model of Tastes

Recall that a choice set is a subset of all possible combinations of goods and services that is affordable given an individual's particular circumstances. In our example of purchasing hoodies and jeans, we used the information we had on the money available and the prices for hoodies and jeans to delineate the budget line in the larger space of all combinations of hoodies and jeans. While you were unable to *afford* bundles of hoodies and jeans outside the choice set, you may nevertheless dream about bundles outside that set; you have tastes for bundles outside the choice set. Tastes can be defined not only over bundles of goods that fall in our choice sets but also over bundles that we may never be able to attain.

4A.1 Two Fundamental Rationality Assumptions About Tastes

While individuals vary widely in how they would rank different bundles of goods, we will argue in this section that there are two basic properties of tastes that must be satisfied in order for us to be able to analyze rational choice behaviour. There is some controversy within the broader social sciences regarding these basic properties, but they are nevertheless quite fundamental to much of what we will have to say in the rest of this book.

4A.1.1 Complete Tastes Economists assume that individuals are able to compare any two bundles to one another, and this represents our most fundamental assumption about tastes. Economic actors, whether they are workers, consumers or financial planners, are able to look at any two choice bundles and tell us which they prefer or whether they are indifferent between them. When an economic actor can do this, we say that they have *complete tastes or preferences*, in the sense that the actor is always able to make comparisons between bundles.

4A.1.2 Transitive Tastes It is also assumed that there is an internal consistency to tastes that makes choosing a *best* bundle possible. Consider, for instance, bundles *A*, *B* and *C*, each containing different quantities of jeans and hoodies. If tastes are complete, it should be possible to compare any two of these bundles and state which is preferred or whether you are indifferent between the bundles. It is assumed that *whenever an individual likes A at least as much as B and B at least as much as C, it must be the case that they also like A at least as much as C*. Similarly, if an individual prefers *A* to *B* and *B* to *C*, it must be the case that the individual prefers *A* to *C*. This is referred to as the *axiom of transitivity*.

Psychologists have been critical of the transitivity assumption based on experiments in which people seemed to violate the assumption. Economists, however, continue to find the assumption useful in the sense that it permits us to make predictions about people's choice behaviour, predictions that seem consistent with the data most of the time even if there are instances when the assumption might appear to be violated.

4A.1.3 Rational Tastes When an economic actor's tastes satisfy both completeness and transitivity, we will say that the individual has *rational tastes* or preferences. The term *rational* here does not imply any grand philosophical value judgments. Individuals might have tastes that most of us would consider entirely self-destructive and irrational, as the term is commonly used, but such individuals might still be able to compare any pair of alternatives and always choose the best one or one where none of the other alternatives is worse. Rationality means the ability to make consistent choices.

4A.2 Three More Assumptions

Much of what economists have modelled depends critically only on the validity of the two rationality assumptions discussed earlier. Some additional assumptions about tastes can simplify our models while remaining true to most real-world applications.

4A.2.1 More Is Better, or at Least Not Worse (Monotonicity) In most economic applications, we are interested in situations where individuals make choices involving aspects of life that involve scarcity, whether this involves current consumption, future consumption or leisure. If individuals did not in fact think more is better in such choices, scarcity would not be a problem. Everyone would be content with what they have. It appears that we always seem to want more, and our choices are often aimed at getting more. The economist's recognition of this is not an endorsement of a philosophy of life focused on materialism or consumerism; rather, it is a starting point for better understanding human behaviour in a world characterized by scarcity. If an individual has tastes for goods such that more is better, or at least that more is not worse, we will sometimes call such tastes *monotonic*, or we will say that such tastes satisfy the *monotonicity assumption*.

Consider the five bundles of jeans and hoodies depicted in Graph 4.1. The monotonicity assumption allows us to conclude that *E* must be better than *C* because *E* contains more jeans and hoodies than *C*. In cases where we compare two bundles that are the same in terms of one of the goods but differ in terms of the other, we will interpret more is better as meaning more is at least as good. For instance, bundle *C* contains just as many hoodies as *D*, but it also contains more jeans. Thus, more is better implies that *C* is at least as good as *D*. The more is better assumption does *not* make it clear how *A* and *C* relate to each other because neither contains clearly more; *A* has more hoodies than *C*, but *C* has more jeans than *A*. Similarly, the assumption does not clarify how the pairs *A* and *B*, *C* and *B*, or *B* and *D* are ranked.

Exercise 4A.1

Do we know from the monotonicity assumption how *E* relates to *D*, *A* and *B*? Do we know how *A* relates to *D*?

It is worth noting that monotonicity may hold even in cases where it seems at first glance that it does not. For instance, we might think that we would prefer less work over more and thus cite labour as a good that violates the more is better assumption. We could equivalently model our choices over how much labour to provide as a choice of how much leisure we choose not to consume, as we did when we constructed choice sets for workers in Chapter 3. By reconceptualizing labour as the amount of leisure we do not consume, we have redefined the choice as one between leisure and consumption rather than between labour and consumption, and leisure can be assumed to be a good that we would like to have more of rather than less. Similarly, consider someone who does not like more consumption beyond some basic subsistence level. For such a person, more consumption may not be better than less. At the same time, such an individual might care about the well-being of others whose consumption has not reached subsistence levels. The economic scarcity problem that such a person faces involves choices over what to do with money in excess of their own subsistence needs, perhaps which charitable causes to support. Once the problem has been reconceptualized in this way, more charity is once again better than less. Thus, in many cases we can reconceptualize a choice involving goods we would prefer to have fewer of as a choice involving goods that satisfy the more is better assumption.

Graph 4.1 Ranking Consumption Bundles

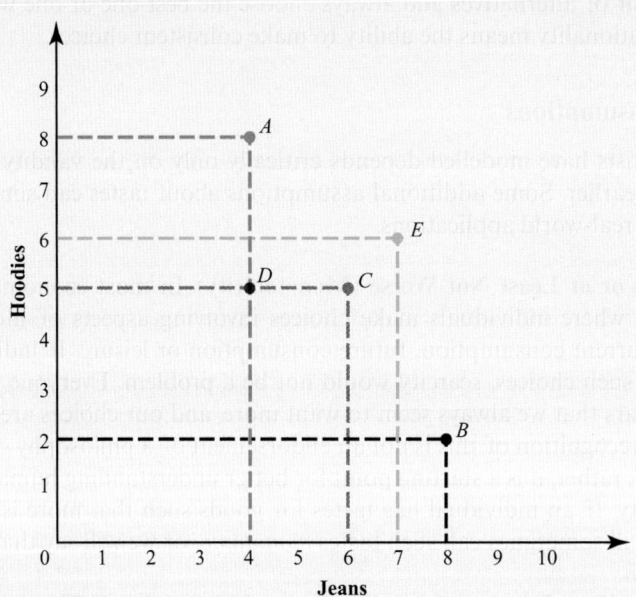

Exercise 4A.2

What other goods are such that we would prefer to have fewer of them than many? How can we reconceptualize choices over such goods so that it becomes reasonable to assume more is better?

4A.2.2 Averages Are Better Than Extremes, or At Least No Worse (Convexity) While it may be obvious that the very nature of economic problems arises from the reality that people believe more is better than less, it is less obvious what we mean by averages are better than extremes or why this should be an assumption that is at all reasonable. Consider, for instance, two baskets of goods: The first contains 9 apples and 1 orange while the second contains 9 oranges and 1 apple. If we mixed the two baskets together and divided them into two identical average baskets, we would get baskets with 5 apples and 5 oranges. It seems plausible that this average basket might be preferred to the more extreme baskets we started with, but one could imagine someone who really likes apples and only sort of likes oranges preferring the more extreme basket with 9 apples. The assumption that averages are better than extremes, when properly defined, does not actually rule out this scenario. Rather, it gives expression to a general tendency by human beings to like variety in consumption choices.

Let's begin by stating what we mean more precisely. We will say that tastes satisfy the assumption that averages are better than extremes whenever it is the case that the average between two baskets *that you are indifferent between* is at least as good as the original two baskets. Thus, *if* you are indifferent between the 9 apples/1 orange basket and the 9 oranges/1 apple basket, you would be willing to trade either of these extreme baskets for a basket with 5 apples and 5 oranges. If someone really likes apples and only sort of likes oranges, they would not be indifferent between the two extreme baskets. If you *are* indifferent between the more extreme baskets, it is reasonable to assume that you would be willing to give up some of the good that you have a lot of for some of the good that you have only a little of, and that you would, therefore, prefer the 5 apples/5 oranges basket or at least not mind taking such a basket instead of one of the extremes. This assumption of averages being better than extremes is often called the *convexity assumption*, and tastes that satisfy it are referred to as *convex tastes*.

Consider again the five bundles graphed in Graph 4.1. There is nothing immediate the convexity assumption allows us to say in addition to what we could conclude from applying the monotonicity assumption in the previous section. However, suppose you are indifferent between bundles A and B. The convexity assumption lets us know that you would be at least as happy with an average between A and B. Bundle C is just that; it contains 5 hoodies and 6 pairs of jeans, which is exactly half of bundles A and B added together. Note that such an average bundle lies halfway between the more extreme bundles on the line segment connecting those bundles. Thus, convexity implies that C is at least as good as A and B.

Exercise 4A.3

Combining the convexity and monotonicity assumptions, can you now conclude something about the relationship between the pairs E and A and E and B if you do not know how A and B are related? What if you are indifferent between A and B?

Exercise 4A.4

Knowing that you are indifferent between A and B, can you now conclude something about how you would rank B and D? To reach this conclusion, do you have to invoke the convexity assumption?

In essence, the averages are better than extremes or convexity assumption gives expression to the general human tendency to seek diversity in consumption. No matter how much we like a particular good, few of us sit down to a meal of only steak, or only salad, only potatoes, only coffee, only dessert or only wine. We might in fact be able to create all sorts of single-item meals that we are indifferent between: a certain quantity of steak, a certain quantity of salad, a certain quantity of potatoes and so on. However, most of us would prefer a meal with some of each of these, or an average of single-item meals. The meal here is just an analogy that we don't want to push too far; certain sets of single-item meals, perhaps cheesecake and caviar, would not average well into one meal. Over the course of a week, however, even single-item meals that we may not want to mix in one meal might create welcome variety.

This analogy gives a sense of what it is that we mean intuitively when we say that often, averages in life are indeed better than extremes. In more life-changing decisions, the same seems to be true. Suppose you are indifferent between, on the one hand, consuming €100 000 a year before retirement and living in poverty afterwards and, on the other, living in poverty now and consuming €150 000 a year after retirement.

It seems reasonable that most of us would prefer an average between these scenarios, one that permits us a comfortable standard of living both before and after retirement. Or suppose that you are equally happy consuming a lot while working almost all the time and consuming very little while working very little. Most of us would probably prefer an average between these two bundles, to work without becoming a workaholic and consume less than we could if we worked all the time.

4A.2.3 No Sudden Jumps (or Continuity) We will usually assume that a consumer's happiness does not change dramatically if the basket they consume changes only slightly. For example, if you like milk in your coffee, our no sudden jumps assumption implies that you will become neither dramatically better off nor dramatically worse off if you add one more drop of milk to the coffee. Starting out with coffee without milk, you may become gradually happier as you add milk and, at some point, gradually worse off as even more milk is added, but it is unlikely that you will switch from agony to ecstasy from just one more drop. Tastes that satisfy this assumption are often called *continuous*, and the no sudden jumps assumption is referred to as the *continuity assumption*.

The continuity assumption is most appealing for goods that can easily be divided into smaller and smaller units such as milk, and less appealing for goods that come in very discrete units, such as jeans and hoodies, or larger goods like cars. For the purposes of our models, however, we will treat these other types of goods just as we treat milk. We will assume that you can consume fractions of jeans and hoodies and cars. We do this not because it is realistic, but rather because it simplifies our models in ways that are not that critical for any of the analysis we will do with our models. If, for instance, we conclude from our analysis that a 10 per cent drop in the price of jeans will result in an increase in consumption of jeans by 3.2, we can simply round this off and know that you will probably end up buying 3 more pairs of jeans.

Furthermore, in cases where the assumption of continuity becomes particularly problematic, there are often other ways of modelling the behaviour such that the assumption once again is reasonable. For instance, we might think of cars or houses as very discrete units; it is, after all, not easy to consume three-quarters of a car or house. At the same time, we could model cars as bundled goods, goods that provide you with varying degrees of speed, safety, comfort and so on. What you are really trying to buy is not a car but rather speed, safety and comfort on the road, and your tastes over these attributes are probably quite immune to sudden jumps. Similarly, in the case of housing, we can think of your choice as one involving size, the age of the house, the quality of the neighbourhood, features of the floorplan and so on, and once again it is likely that your tastes over these attributes of housing are not subject to sudden jumps.

4A.3 Graphing Tastes

In Chapters 2 and 3, we graphically represented the constraints on people's choices given their circumstances. Armed with the assumptions we just introduced, we will now do the same for people's tastes before demonstrating in Chapter 6 how tastes and constraints combine to result in human behaviour we can observe. We will find that it is impossible to graph fully the tastes of any individual, but we will develop ways of graphing the particular portions of individual tastes that are most relevant for the choices that confront us at different times.

4A.3.1 An Indifference Curve The basic building block of our graphs of tastes is an *indifference curve*. Suppose, for instance, that we are back to choosing between jeans and hoodies, and suppose that an individual currently has 8 hoodies and 4 pairs of jeans in their shopping basket. This is represented as point *A* in panel (a) of Graph 4.2. *The indifference curve containing point A* is defined as the set of all other consumption bundles, i.e. the set of all other pairs of hoodies and jeans that would make them exactly as happy as bundle *A*. While it is difficult to know exactly where such bundles lie, our assumptions about tastes allow us to derive the approximate location of this indifference curve.

We can begin by noting some places that could not possibly contain bundles that lie on the indifference curve which contains bundle *A*. Consider, for instance, the shaded area to the northeast of *A*. All bundles in this area contain more jeans and more hoodies. If more is better, bundles that contain more jeans and hoodies *must be* better than *A* and thus could not be indifferent to *A*. Similarly, consider bundles to the southwest of bundle *A*. All bundles represented by this shaded area contain fewer jeans and hoodies than bundle *A* and must therefore be worse. The monotonicity assumption allows us to rule out the shaded areas in panel (a) of Graph 4.2 as bundles that could lie on the indifference curve containing bundle *A*. Bundles that lie in non-shaded areas, on the other hand, are not ruled out by the monotonicity assumption. Those to the northwest of *A*, for instance, all have fewer jeans but more hoodies, while those to the southeast have more jeans and fewer hoodies than bundle *A*. You therefore know from the monotonicity assumption that the indifference curve containing bundle *A* must be downward sloping through bundle *A*, but you can glean nothing further without knowing more about the individual.

Graph 4.2 Tastes and Indifference Curves

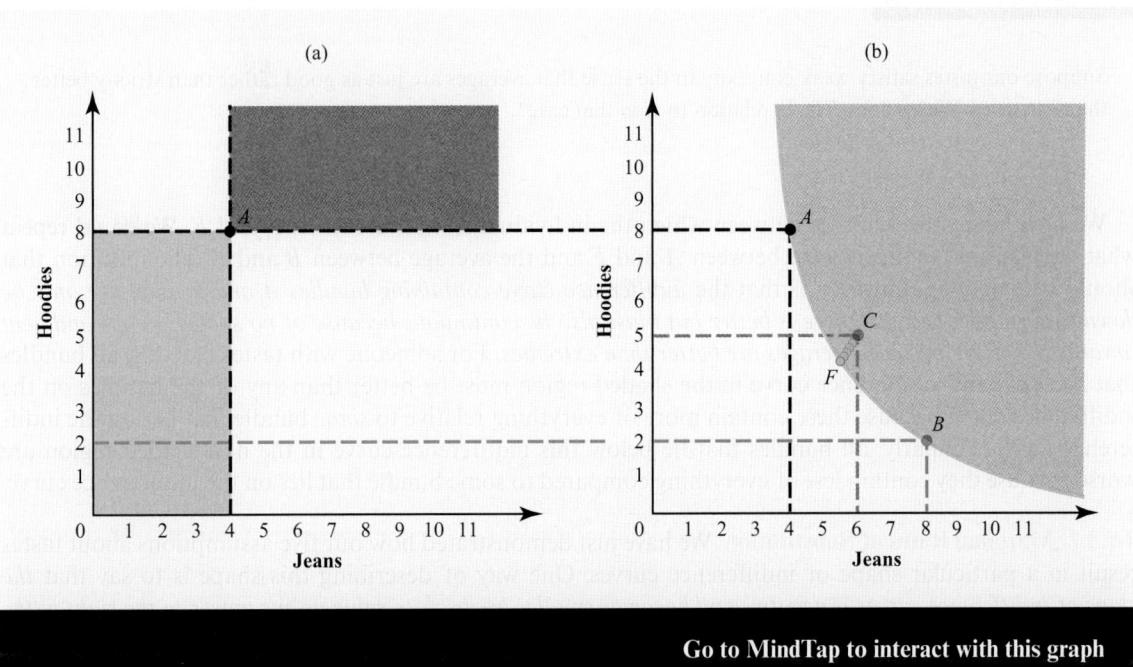

Go to MindTap to interact with this graph

Now suppose we find out that the individual is indifferent between the bundles represented by points *A* (4 pairs of jeans, 8 hoodies) and *B* (2 hoodies, 8 pairs of jeans) in panel (b) of Graph 4.2. This means that bundle *B* lies on the indifference curve that contains bundle *A*. You can also now draw some additional shaded areas to the northeast and southwest of point *B* that could not possibly include further indifferent bundles based on the more is better or monotonicity assumption. More importantly, however, you can now employ the averages are better than extremes or convexity assumption to come to some additional conclusions about the shape of the indifference curve that contains bundles *A* and *B*.

The convexity assumption states that whenever someone is indifferent between two bundles of goods and services, the average bundle that is created by mixing the two original bundles and dividing them into two equal ones is judged to be at least as good as the extreme bundles. In our case, the average bundle would be 5 hoodies and 6 pairs of jeans. Graphically, this average bundle is the midpoint of the line segment connecting points *A* and *B*, labelled *C* in panel (b) of Graph 4.2.

Now notice that any bundle to the southwest of *C* has fewer jeans and fewer hoodies and is thus worse than *C*. Suppose we start at *C* and move a little to the southwest by taking just a tiny bit of each good away, assuming for the moment that it is possible to take away bits of hoodies and jeans. Given our no sudden jumps or continuity assumption, the new bundle is just a little worse than *C*. Suppose we keep doing this, each time creating yet another bundle that's just a little worse and moving a little further southwest. If *C* is strictly better than *A* and *B*, it should be the case that as we inch our way southwest from *C*, we at some point hit a bundle *F* that is indifferent to *A* and *B*. Without knowing more about the individual, you can't tell exactly how far southwest of *C* the new indifferent point *F* will lie. All we know is that it lies to the southwest.

Exercise 4A.5

Illustrate the area in panel (b) of Graph 4.2 in which *F* must lie, keeping in mind the monotonicity assumption.

Exercise 4A.6

Suppose our tastes satisfy weak convexity in the sense that averages are just as good rather than strictly better than extremes. Where does *F* lie in relation to *C* in that case?

We now have three bundles between which the individual is indifferent: *A*, *B* and *F*. We could repeat what we just did for the average between *A* and *F* and the average between *B* and *F*. The intuition that should be emerging, however, is that the *indifference curve containing bundles A and B must not only be downward sloping because more is better but must also be continuous because of no sudden jumps and bent towards the origin because averages are better than extremes.* For someone with tastes like this, all bundles that lie above the indifference curve in the shaded region must be better than any of the bundles on the indifference curve because these contain more of everything relative to *some* bundle that lies on the indifference curve. Similarly, all bundles that lie below this indifference curve in the non-shaded region are worse because they contain less of everything compared to some bundle that lies on the indifference curve.

4A.3.2 Marginal Rates of Substitution We have just demonstrated how our five assumptions about tastes result in a particular shape of indifference curves. One way of describing this shape is to say that *the slope of indifference curves is negative and becomes smaller in absolute value as one moves to the right in the graph.* The slope of the indifference curve at any given point is, however, more than a mere description of what the indifference curve looks like. It has real economic content and is called the *marginal rate of substitution.*

Consider, for instance, the slope of −3 at point *A* in Graph 4.3. This slope tells us that we could go down by 3 hoodies and over to the right by 1 pair of jeans and end up roughly on the same indifference curve as the one that contains bundle *A*. When the individual is consuming bundle *A*, they would be *willing to* trade in 3 hoodies to get 1 more pair of jeans because that would leave them roughly as well off as they currently are. Thus, the slope of the indifference curve at point *A* gives an indication of how much an individual values 1 more pair of jeans in terms of hoodies. This *marginal rate of substitution* is therefore *the willingness to trade hoodies for 1 more additional or marginal pair of jeans given current consumption.*

Since the slope of the indifference curve typically changes as one moves along the indifference curve, the marginal rate of substitution – how much value we place on an additional good on the horizontal axis in terms of the good on the vertical axis – also changes. Consider, for example, the shallower slope of −1/2 at point *B* in Graph 4.3. This slope tells us that the individual would be willing to give up only half a hoodie for 1 more pair of jeans or 1 hoodie for 2 additional jeans when they are already consuming bundle *B*. This makes sense given our discussion about the averages are better than extremes assumption. At bundle *A*, the individual has relatively few jeans and relatively many hoodies, and thus places a high value on additional jeans because that would get them to a less extreme bundle. At bundle *B*, on the other hand, they have relatively many jeans and few hoodies, and thus would not be willing to give up more hoodies very easily given that this would get them to even more extreme bundles.

We concluded in the previous section that the shape of the indifference curve in Graph 4.3 is due to the averages are better than extremes assumption. This shape implies that marginal rates of substitution begin as large numbers in absolute value and decline in absolute value as we move down an indifference curve. This is known as the concept of *diminishing marginal rates of substitution*, and it arises only when averages are indeed better than extremes.

Graph 4.3 Diminishing Marginal Rate of Substitution

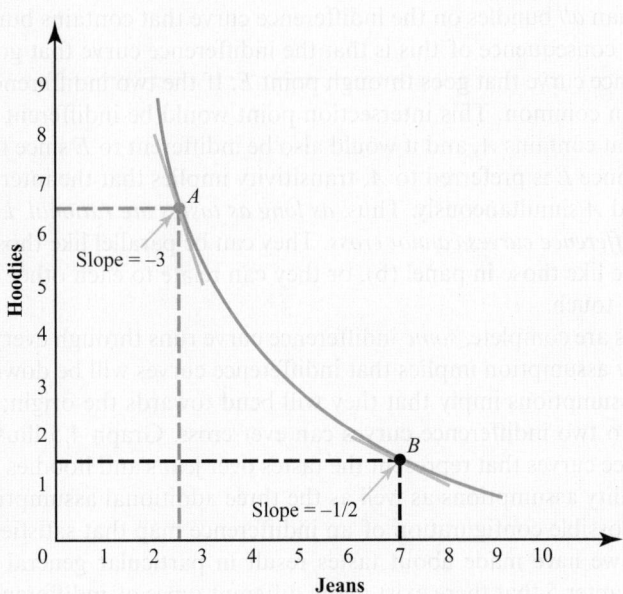

4A.3.3 **Maps of Indifference Curves** In deriving our first indifference curve, we defined it *with respect to one bundle*. We mapped out the indifference curve that contains one arbitrarily selected bundle: bundle A in panel (b) of Graph 4.2. We could have begun with some other arbitrary bundle, for instance bundle E in panel (a) of Graph 4.4. Just as there is an indifference curve that runs through bundle A, there is an indifference curve that runs through bundle E. Notice that E lies to the northeast of the highlighted segment of the indifference curve that contains A in panel (a) of Graph 4.4.

Graph 4.4 Parallel and Converging Indifference Curves

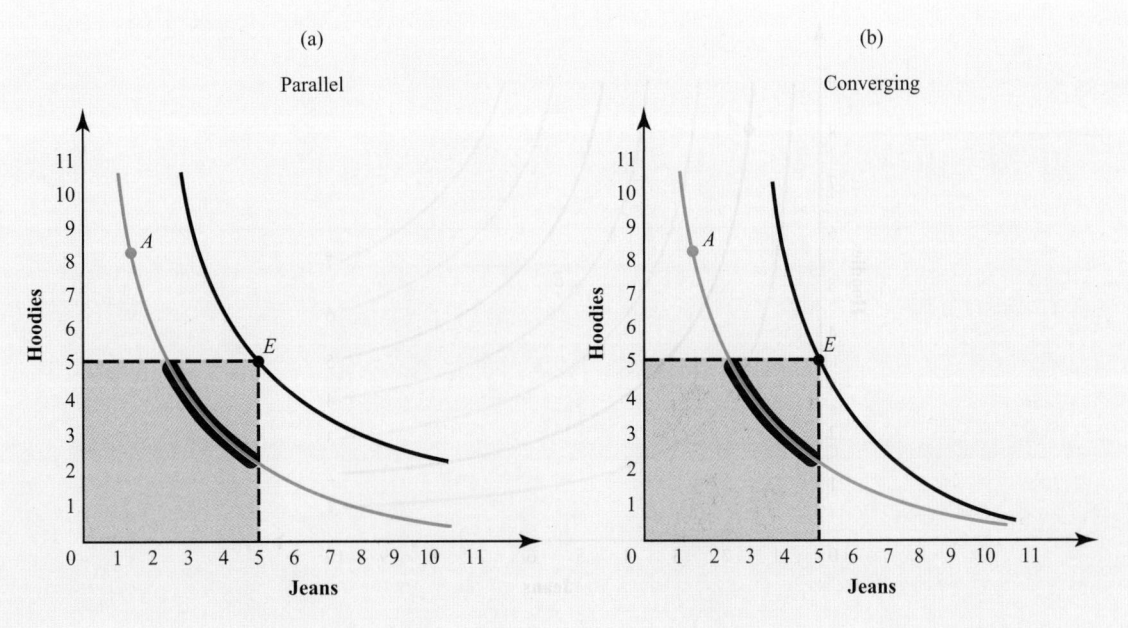

This means that E contains more hoodies and jeans than any of the highlighted bundles, which means that it must be the case that E is better than those bundles because of our more is better assumption. This also means that E is better than *all* bundles on the indifference curve that contains bundle A.

An important logical consequence of this is that the indifference curve that goes through point A can never cross the indifference curve that goes through point E. If the two indifference curves did cross, they would share one point in common. This intersection point would be indifferent to A, because it lies on the indifference curve that contains A, and it would also be indifferent to E since it lies on the indifference curve that contains E. Since E is preferred to A, transitivity implies that the intersection point cannot be indifferent to both E and A simultaneously. Thus, *as long as tastes are rational, i.e. they satisfy completeness and transitivity, indifference curves cannot cross*. They can be parallel like those in panel (a) of Graph 4.4, or they can converge like those in panel (b), or they can relate to each other in any number of other ways, but they can never touch.

Furthermore, if tastes are complete, *some* indifference curve runs through every bundle. As we showed earlier, the monotonicity assumption implies that indifference curves will be downward sloping; the convexity and continuity assumptions imply that they will bend towards the origin; and the transitivity assumption implies that no two indifference curves can ever cross. Graph 4.5 illustrates an example of a whole map of indifference curves that represent the tastes over jeans and hoodies for an individual whose tastes satisfy the rationality assumptions as well as the three additional assumptions outlined in Section 4A.2. This is only one possible configuration of an indifference map that satisfies all these assumptions. While the assumptions we have made about tastes result in particular general shapes for indifference curves, we will see in Chapter 5 that there exist many different types of indifference maps and thus many different tastes that can be modelled using these assumptions.

Finally, to indicate that indifference curves to the northeast of Graph 4.5 represent bundles that yield greater happiness than indifference curves to the southwest of the graph, each indifference curve is accompanied by a number that indicates how bundles on that particular curve compare with bundles on other curves. For instance, when we compare bundle A with bundle E, we can read off the number 2 on the indifference curve containing point A and the number 4 on the indifference curve containing point E, and we can infer from this that bundle E is preferred to bundle A. If less is better than more, the ordering of the numbers attached to these indifference curves would be reversed.

Graph 4.5 Map of Indifference Curves

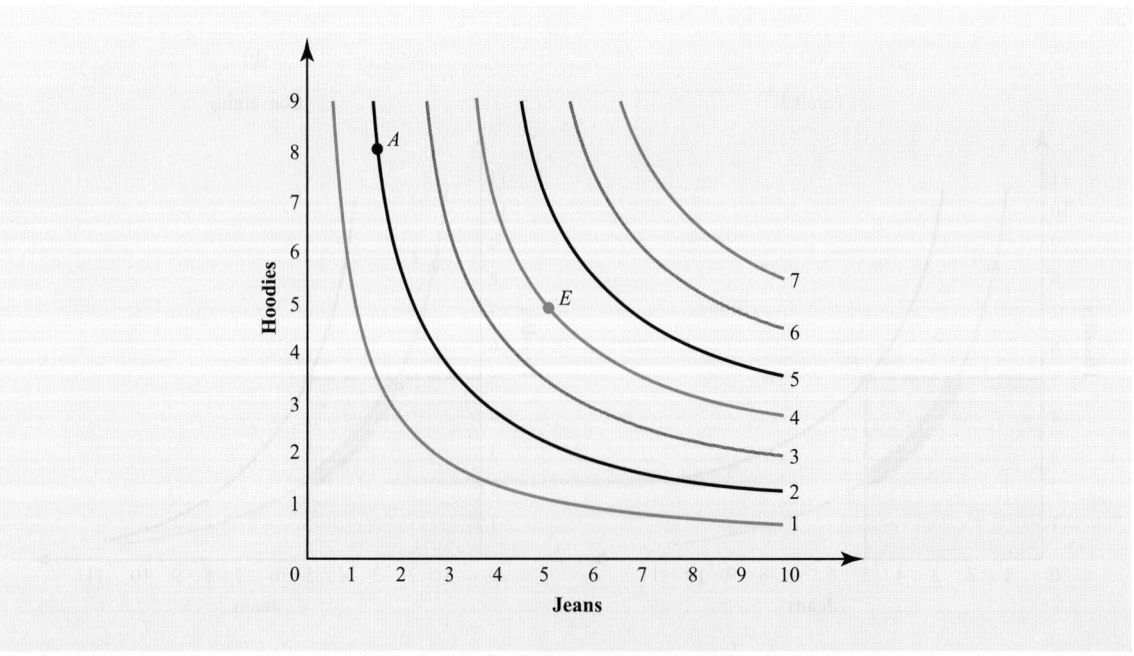

Exercise 4A.7

Suppose less is better than more and averages are better than extremes. Draw three indifference curves with numerical labels that would be consistent with this.

We *cannot*, however, infer from these two numbers that bundles on one indifference curve yield twice as much happiness as bundles on the other indifference curve. *Happiness is not something that is objectively quantifiable*. Economists have used the measure of *utils* as a representation of the amount of satisfaction gained from consumption. The measure is strictly ordinal in that it allows for a ranking but that ranking does not imply degrees of difference between the rankings, i.e. we cannot say that one good is preferred twice as much as another in the ranking. We *can* say that all bundles on a particular indifference curve yield the same level of utility and thus must have the same numerical label, and that different utility numbers associated with different indifference curves tell us which are more preferred and which less. We could change all the numbers in Graph 4.5 by multiplying them by 2 or dividing them by 5 or adding 13 to them because in each case, the *ordering* of indifference curves would remain unchanged. Thus, *as long as the shape of indifference curves and the ordering of the numbers that accompany the curves are unchanged between two graphs, we will say that the maps of indifference curves in the two graphs represent the same tastes*. By changing the numerical labels on indifference curves without changing their order, all we are in effect doing is changing the ruler we use to measure happiness, and since there isn't an agreed upon ruler, any ruler that preserves the ordering of indifference curves will do.

This becomes somewhat clearer if you think of the following analogy. Consider a two-dimensional map of a mountain, a map in which different heights of the mountain are represented by outlines of the shape of the mountain at that height accompanied by a number that indicates the elevation of that outline. In essence, such maps are depictions of horizontal slices of the mountain at different heights drawn on a single two-dimensional surface. Indifference curves are very much like this. Longitude and latitude are replaced with jeans and hoodies, and the height of the mountain is replaced with the level of happiness. While real-world mountains have peaks, our happiness mountains generally do not have peaks because of our more is better assumption. Indifference curves are horizontal slices of our happiness mountain such as the one depicted later in Graph 4.8, with numbers indicating the height of happiness attained at that slice. Just as the outlines of the different elevations of a real-world mountain don't change whether we measure the height of the elevation in feet or metres, the outlines of the slices of our happiness mountain, that is the indifference curves, do not change shape if we use a different ruler to measure happiness.

We will now develop some of the underlying mathematics of the utility mountains through the concept of *utility functions*.

4B   Tastes and Utility Functions

We have shown in Section 4A how certain basic assumptions about our tastes can enable us to generate graphical ways of representing tastes with the tool of indifference curves. The assumptions we introduced in Section 4A.1 and 4A.2 will translate directly into mathematical properties of functions that we can use to represent tastes.

4B.1 Two Fundamental Rationality Assumptions

When we speak of bundles or baskets of two goods, we have already defined these as points with two components, each representing the quantity of one of the goods in the basket. The point labelled A in Graph 4.1, for instance, can be expressed as $(x_1^A, x_2^A) = (4, 8)$, representing a basket with 4 units of good 1 (jeans) and 8 units of good 2 (hoodies). In general, we can express a basket that contains two types of goods as:

$$(x_1, x_2) \in \mathbb{R}^2_+, \tag{4.1}$$

where $\in$ is read as 'is an element of' and $\mathbb{R}^2_+$ denotes the set of all points with two non-negative real number components. Almost all of our graphs of choice sets consist of some subset of points in $\mathbb{R}^2_+$, as do our graphs of indifference curves in Section 4A. When a larger number of different types of goods is included in a basket – hoodies, jeans *and* socks, for instance – we can further generalize this by denoting a basket with n different types of goods by:

$$(x_1, x_2, \ldots, x_n) \in \mathbb{R}^n_+, \tag{4.2}$$

where $\mathbb{R}^n_+$ now represents the set of all points with n non-negative components. In the case of hoodies, jeans and socks, $n = 3$.

Tastes or preferences involve subjective comparisons of different baskets or different points as denoted in (4.1) and (4.2). We will use the following shorthand notation:

$\succsim$ means 'at least as good';
$\succ$ means 'is strictly better than';
$\sim$ means 'is indifferent to'.

Hence, we will use:

$$(x_1^A, x_2^A, \ldots, x_n^A) \succsim (x_1^B, x_2^B, \ldots, x_n^B) \tag{4.3}$$

whenever we want to say that the basket $(x_1^A, x_2^A, \ldots, x_n^A)$ *is at least as good* as the basket $(x_1^B, x_2^B, \ldots, x_n^B)$. Similarly, we read:

$$(x_1^A, x_2^A, \ldots, x_n^A) \succ (x_1^B, x_2^B, \ldots, x_n^B) \tag{4.4}$$

as basket $(x_1^A, x_2^A, \ldots, x_n^A)$ *is strictly better than* basket $(x_1^B, x_2^B, \ldots, x_n^B)$, and we will read:

$$(x_1^A, x_2^A, \ldots, x_n^A) \sim (x_1^B, x_2^B, \ldots, x_n^B) \tag{4.5}$$

as a person being *indifferent* between these two baskets. The objects $\succsim$, $\succ$ and $\sim$ are called *binary relations* because they relate two points to one another.

4B.1.1 Complete Tastes In Section 4A, we defined tastes as *complete* whenever a person with those tastes can unequivocally compare any two baskets, indicating whether one basket is better than the other or whether they are indifferent between the two baskets. We can write this definition formally as follows: *A person has complete tastes over all baskets with n goods if and only if it is true that for all* $(x_1^A, x_2^A, \ldots, x_n^A) \in \mathbb{R}^n_+$ *and for all* $(x_1^B, x_2^B, \ldots, x_n^B) \in \mathbb{R}^n_+$,

$$(x_1^A, x_2^A, \ldots, x_n^A) \succsim (x_1^B, x_2^B, \ldots, x_n^B) \text{ or}$$
$$(x_1^B, x_2^B, \ldots, x_n^B) \succsim (x_1^A, x_2^A, \ldots, x_n^A) \text{ or both.} \tag{4.6}$$

All we are saying is that a person can compare any two bundles in $\mathbb{R}^n_+$. Note that logically it has to be the case that if both of the statements in (4.6) are true for a given set of two bundles, then:

$$(x^A_1, x^A_2, \ldots, x^A_n) \sim (x^B_1, x^B_2, \ldots, x^B_n). \tag{4.7}$$

Exercise 4B.1

True or False: If only one of the statements in (4.6) is true for a given set of bundles, what statements $\succeq$ can be replaced with $\succ$?

4B.1.2 Transitive Tastes We argued in Section 4A that in order for an individual to be able to settle on a best choice, there needs to be a certain internal consistency to the tastes that guide the person's choices. We said that a person's tastes are *transitive* if, whenever the person likes a bundle A at least as much as a bundle B and they like B at least as much as C, it must be the case that the person likes A at least as much as C. We can now define this more formally using the notation we have just developed.

A person's tastes are transitive if and only if it is true that whenever three bundles are evaluated by the person such that:

$$(x^A_1, x^A_2, \ldots, x^A_n) \succeq (x^B_1, x^B_2, \ldots, x^B_n)$$
$$\text{and } (x^B_1, x^B_2, \ldots, x^B_n) \succeq (x^C_1, x^C_2, \ldots, x^C_n), \tag{4.8}$$

we can conclude that:

$$(x^A_1, x^A_2, \ldots, x^A_n) \succeq (x^C_1, x^C_2, \ldots, x^C_n). \tag{4.9}$$

Exercise 4B.2

Does transitivity also imply that (4.8) implies (4.9) when $\succeq$ is replaced with $\succ$?

4B.1.3 Rational Tastes The assumptions of completeness and transitivity of tastes are so fundamental to the economist's modelling of tastes that together they define what we mean by *rational* tastes. An individual's tastes over a particular set of bundles are said to be rational if they are both complete and transitive.

4B.2 Three More Assumptions

The three additional assumptions introduced in Section 4A2 were referred to as *monotonicity*, *convexity* and *continuity*.

4B.2.1 Monotonicity (Or More Is Better Or At Least Not Worse) We argued in Section 4A.2.1 that the fundamental scarcity that underlies economic decision making implies that more is considered better by most individuals in most economic contexts. Given that bundles of goods and services by definition contain many different types of goods, we have to be clear about what we mean by more. In Graph 4.1, for instance, bundle E clearly has more of everything than bundle C, but it has more of some and less of other goods when compared with bundles A and B. By *more* we can mean either more of all goods or more of at least some goods and no less of any of the other goods. When a bundle contains more of all goods than a second bundle, we will generally assume that a consumer strictly prefers that bundle. When a bundle contains more of at least some goods and no less of any of the other goods than a second bundle, on the other hand, we will typically assume that a consumer thinks of this bundle as *at least as good as* the second bundle, thus leaving open the possibility that the consumer might be indifferent between the bundles.

Formally we can define more is better, monotonic tastes, as: *A consumer's tastes are monotonic if and only if:*

$$(x_1^A, x_2^A, \ldots, x_n^A) \succsim (x_1^B, x_2^B, \ldots, x_n^B) \text{ whenever } x_i^A \geq x_i^B \text{ for all } i = 1, 2 \ldots, n; \text{ and}$$

$$(x_1^A, x_2^A, \ldots, x_n^A) \succ (x_1^B, x_2^B, \ldots, x_n^B) \text{ whenever } x_i^A > x_i^B \text{ for all } i = 1, 2 \ldots, n. \tag{4.10}$$

The first line of this definition allows for the possibility that some of the goods in the A and B bundles are the same while others are larger for the A bundle than for the B bundle, whereas the second line applies only to pairs of bundles where one contains more of every good than the other. In Graph 4.1, for instance, bundle A contains more hoodies but the same number of jeans as bundle D, and our definition of monotonic tastes therefore implies that $A \succsim D$, or A is at least as good as D. Bundle E, on the other hand, contains more of all goods than bundle D, implying that $E \succ D$, or E is strictly better than D.

Monotonicity assumptions are sometimes divided into *weak* and *strong* monotonicity, where weak monotonicity requires that each element of a bundle A must be larger than each corresponding element of B for us to be sure that A is strictly preferred to B, while a stronger form of monotonicity would require only some elements of A to be larger than the corresponding elements in B with all remaining elements the same. Our definition corresponds to the weaker of these definitions of monotonicity. Finally, although we will generally maintain our assumption of monotonicity throughout the text, many of the results that we derive actually hold for a much weaker assumption called *local non-satiation*. This assumption simply requires that there exists no bundle of goods for which there isn't another bundle close by that is strictly better.

4B.2.2 Convexity – Averages Are Better Than (Or At Least As Good As) Extremes In Section 4A.2.2 we said that it is often reasonable for us to assume that averages are better than extremes whenever an individual is indifferent between extreme bundles. By an average bundle we simply meant the bundle that emerges if we mix 2 more extreme bundles like bundles A and B in Graph 4.2, and divide them into 2 identical bundles. We could translate this into a more formal statement by saying that:

$$(x_1^A, x_2^A, \ldots, x_n^A) \sim (x_1^B, x_2^B, \ldots, x_n^B) \text{ implies} \tag{4.11}$$

$$\left(\frac{1}{2}\right)(x_1^A, x_2^A, \ldots, x_n^A) + \left(\frac{1}{2}\right)(x_1^B, x_2^B, \ldots, x_n^B) \succsim (x_1^A, x_2^A, \ldots, x_n^A) \text{ and}$$

$$\left(\frac{1}{2}\right)(x_1^A, x_2^A, \ldots, x_n^A) + \left(\frac{1}{2}\right)(x_1^B, x_2^B, \ldots, x_n^B) \succsim (x_1^B, x_2^B, \ldots, x_n^B).$$

As in the case of monotonicity, there exist several stronger and weaker versions of the convexity assumption. *Strict convexity* is usually defined as 'averages are strictly preferred to extremes' while weak convexity is defined as 'averages are at least as good as extremes'.

More generally, if the literal average as opposed to a weighted average with weights different from 0.5 of two more extreme bundles is better than the extremes, the same logic would suggest that *any weighted average* that emerges from mixing two extremes is preferable to the extremes, as long as it is not even more extreme. For instance, suppose an individual is indifferent between bundle A and B in Graph 4.2, where bundle A contains 4 pairs of jeans and 8 hoodies while bundle B contains 8 pairs of jeans and 2 hoodies.

Instead of strictly averaging the bundles to yield a bundle with 6 jeans and 5 hoodies, suppose that we create one bundle that consists of 1/4 of bundle A and 3/4 of bundle B, and a second bundle that consists of 3/4 of A and 1/4 of B. An individual who likes averages better than extremes will also prefer these two bundles to the more extreme original ones, and these bundles would also lie on the line segment connecting A and B.

Bundles that are created as a weighted average of extremes are called *convex combinations* of the extreme bundles. Any bundle that is created by weighting bundle A by α and bundle B by $(1 - \alpha)$ is a convex combination of A and B as long as α lies between 0 and 1. Our averages are better than extremes, or convexity, assumption from Section 4A can be restated in the following way: *Tastes are convex if and only if convex combinations of indifferent bundles are at least as good as the bundles used to create the convex combination.* Or, in terms of the notation we have developed, *tastes over bundles of n goods are convex if and only if, for any α such that $0 \leq \alpha \leq 1$,*

$$(x_1^A, x_2^A, \ldots, x_n^A) \sim (x_1^B, x_2^B, \ldots, x_n^B) \text{ implies}$$

$$\alpha(x_1^A, x_2^A, \ldots, x_n^A) + (1-\alpha)(x_1^B, x_2^B, \ldots, x_n^B) \succsim (x_1^A, x_2^A, \ldots, x_n^A). \tag{4.12}$$

4B.2.3 Continuity – No Sudden Jumps We can formalize the assumption that tastes generally do not have sudden jumps by introducing a mathematical concept called a *converging sequence of points*. This concept is quite intuitive, but it consists of several parts. First, a *sequence of points in* $\mathbb{R}_+^n$ is simply a list of points, each with n different non-negative components. This sequence is *infinite* if and only if the list has an infinite number of points in it. An infinite sequence of points is said to *converge* to a single point in $\mathbb{R}_+^n$ if and only if the distance between the points in the sequence and that single point becomes smaller and smaller beginning at some point in the sequence.

Suppose for instance that we start in Graph 4.6 at a point B in $\mathbb{R}_+^2$.

Graph 4.6 Continuity: Converging Sequence of Points

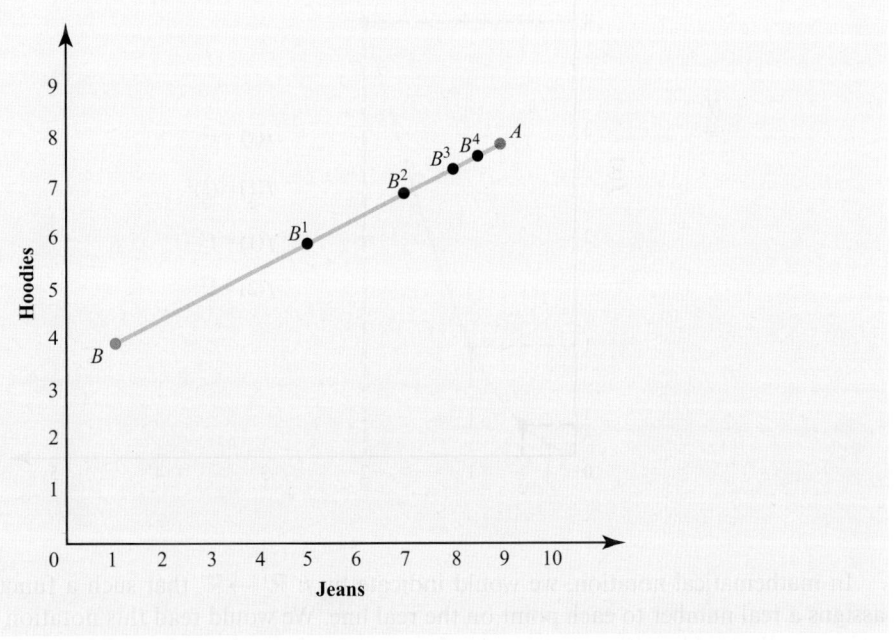

Suppose that point B is the first point in an infinite sequence that continues with B^1 lying halfway between point B and some other point A, with B^2 lying halfway between point B^1 and A, with B^3 lying halfway between B^2 and A, and so forth. An example of the first four points of such a sequence is graphed in Graph 4.6. If we now imagine this sequence of points continuing forever, no point in the sequence will ever quite reach point A, but it will get ever closer. In the language of calculus, the *limit of the sequence* is point A, and the sequence itself *converges* to point A.

Now suppose we have two infinite sequences of points: one denoted $\{B^1, B^2, B^3, \ldots\}$ and the other denoted $\{C^1, C^2, C^3, \ldots\}$, with the first sequence converging to point A and the second sequence converging to point D. *If it is the case that $B^i > C^i$ for all i's, the continuity assumption requires that $A \succsim D$.* Thus, if the B bundles are always preferred to the C bundles as we move along the two sequences and if this continues to hold as we get closer and closer to the bundles A and D to which the two sequences converge, we can't suddenly have a jump at the end of the sequences that reverses the preference relation and causes D to be preferred to A.

4B.3 Representing Tastes With Utility Functions

In Section 4A.3, we demonstrated how the assumptions we have made about people's tastes allow us to graph different types of tastes using indifference curves. We will now see that these indifference curves can be interpreted as parts of mathematical functions that summarize tastes more fully. These functions are called *utility functions*, and are mathematical rules that assign numbers to bundles of goods in such a way that more preferred bundles are assigned higher numbers.

A *mathematical function* is a formula that assigns numbers to points. For instance, the function $f(x) = x^2$ is a way of assigning numbers to different points in the space $\mathbb{R}^1$, the real line, the space consisting of points with only a single component. To the point $x = 1/2$, the function assigns a value of $1/4$; to the point $x = 1$, the function assigns a value of 1; and to the point $x = 2$, the function assigns the value 4. The full function is depicted in Graph 4.7.

Graph 4.7 An Example of a Function $f: \mathbb{R}^1 \rightarrow \mathbb{R}^1$

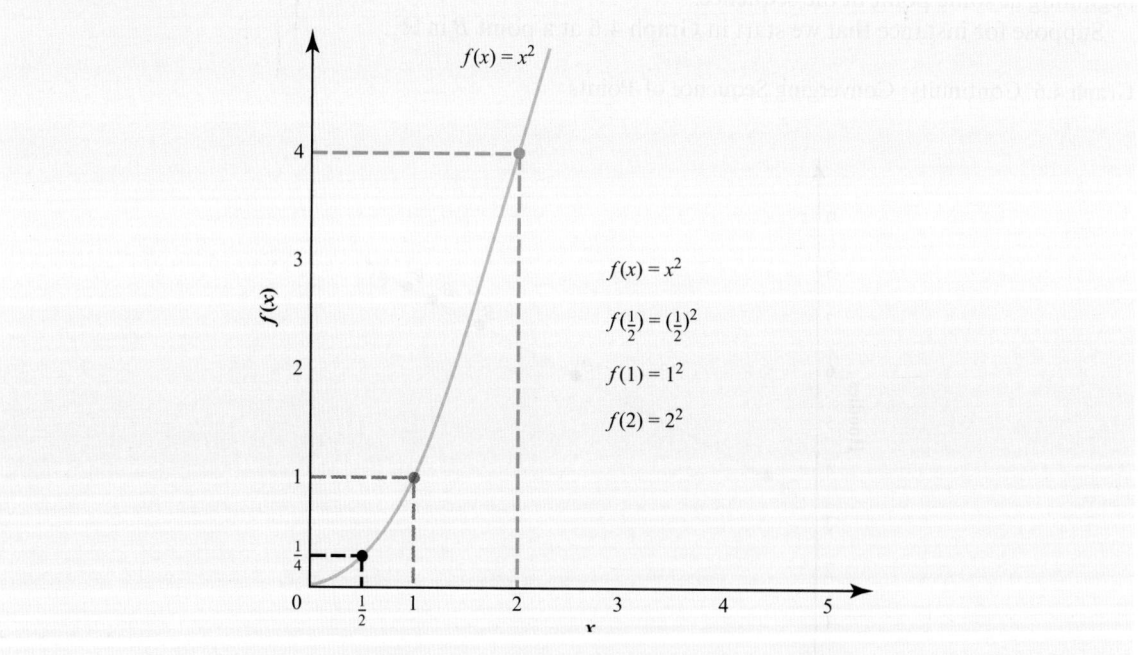

In mathematical notation, we would indicate by $f: \mathbb{R}^1 \rightarrow \mathbb{R}^1$ that such a function f is a formula that assigns a real number to each point on the real line. We would read this notation as 'the function f takes points on the real line $\mathbb{R}^1$ and assigns to them a value from the real line $\mathbb{R}^1$'. Such functions are not, however, of particular use to us as we think about representing tastes because we are generally considering bundles that consist of more than one good, bundles such as those consisting of combinations of hoodies and jeans. Thus, we might be more interested in a function $f: \mathbb{R}^2_+ \rightarrow \mathbb{R}^1$ that assigns to each point made up of two real numbers (i.e. points that lie in $\mathbb{R}^2_+$) a single real number (i.e. a number in $\mathbb{R}^1$). One example of such a function would be $f(x_1, x_2) = x_1 x_2$, a function that assigns the value 1 to the bundle (1,1), the value 4 to the bundle (2,2) and the value 2 to the bundle (2,1).

Assume we are choosing between bundles composed of hoodies and jeans. If you have rational tastes, you can compare any two bundles and state which you prefer or whether you are indifferent between them. If you can find a function $f: \mathbb{R}_+^2 \to \mathbb{R}^1$ that assigns to each bundle of hoodies and jeans represented by points in $\mathbb{R}_+^2$ a value in such a way that more preferred bundles are assigned higher numbers and indifferent bundles are assigned the same number, we will say that you have found a utility function that represents your tastes. More formally, a function $f: \mathbb{R}_+^2 \to \mathbb{R}^1$ represents tastes over jeans (x_1) and hoodies (x_2) if and only if,

$$(x_1^A, x_2^A) > (x_1^B, x_2^B) \text{ implies } f(x_1^A, x_2^A) > f(x_1^B, x_2^B) \text{ and} \tag{4.13}$$
$$(x_1^A, x_2^A) \sim (x_1^B, x_2^B) \text{ implies } f(x_1^A, x_2^A) = f(x_1^B, x_2^B).$$

We will typically use u instead of f to denote such utility functions.

For the more general case of tastes over bundles with n different goods, we can now define a utility function as follows: $u: \mathbb{R}_+^n \to \mathbb{R}^1$ *represents tastes* $\succsim$ *over bundles of n goods if and only if, for any* $(x_1^A, x_2^A, \ldots, x_n^A)$ *and* $(x_1^B, x_2^B, \ldots, x_n^B)$ *in* $\mathbb{R}_+^n$

$$(x_1^A, x_2^A, \ldots, x_n^A) > (x_1^B, x_2^B, \ldots, x_n^B) \text{ implies } u(x_1^A, x_2^A, \ldots, x_n^A) > u(x_1^B, x_2^B, \ldots, x_n^B) \text{ and} \tag{4.14}$$
$$(x_1^A, x_2^A, \ldots, x_n^A) \sim (x_1^B, x_2^B, \ldots, x_n^B) \text{ implies } u(x_1^A, x_2^A, \ldots, x_n^A) = u(x_1^B, x_2^B, \ldots, x_n^B).$$

You might notice how important our rationality assumptions about tastes are in ensuring that we can indeed represent tastes with utility functions. Functions assign values to all points in the space over which they are defined. Thus, we could not use functions to represent tastes unless we indeed were able to evaluate each bundle in relation to others; that is unless our tastes were complete. Similarly, mathematical functions *have to be* logically consistent in the sense that whenever point A is assigned a value greater than point B and point B is assigned a value greater than point C, point A *must be* assigned a value greater than point C. Thus, if tastes were not also logically consistent as required by our transitivity assumption, we could not use mathematical functions to represent them.

4B.3.1 Utility Functions and Indifference Curves Let's return to tastes over bundles of jeans and hoodies, with jeans represented by x_1 and hoodies represented by x_2, and suppose that your tastes can be captured fully by the function $u(x_1, x_2) = x_1^{1/2} x_2^{1/2}$. Panel (a) in Graph 4.8 illustrates this function graphically, with hoodies and jeans measured on the lower axes and the values $u(x_1, x_2)$ plotted on the vertical axis. If we wanted to plot only those bundles that are assigned a value of precisely 4, we would focus on one horizontal slice of this function that occurs at a height of 4 and could plot that slice in a two-dimensional picture with just jeans and hoodies on the axes, as in panels (b) and (c) of Graph 4.8. Since bundles that are assigned the same number are, by the definition of a utility function, valued exactly the same by the individual, these bundles represent one indifference curve, i.e. all those bundles of goods that give a utility of exactly 4 as measured by the utility function u. Similarly, we could focus on all bundles that are assigned a value of 2 by the utility function, thus creating a second indifference curve and continue for all possible values on the vertical axis in panel (a) of Graph 4.8, thus creating an entire map of indifference curves that is represented by this particular utility function.

4B.3.2 Marginal Rates of Substitution In Section 4A.3.2, we defined the slope of the indifference curve as the marginal rate of substitution, or how much has to be given up in terms of one good on the vertical axis to get one more unit of another on the horizontal axis. This slope is a mathematical concept, derived from a utility function that gives rise to particular kinds of indifference curves.

One way to express the definition of a marginal rate of substitution is to say that it is the change in x_2 divided by the change in x_1 such that utility remains unchanged, or

$$\frac{\Delta x_2}{\Delta x_1} \text{ such that } \Delta u = 0. \tag{4.15}$$

Graph 4.8 Indifference Curves and Utility Functions

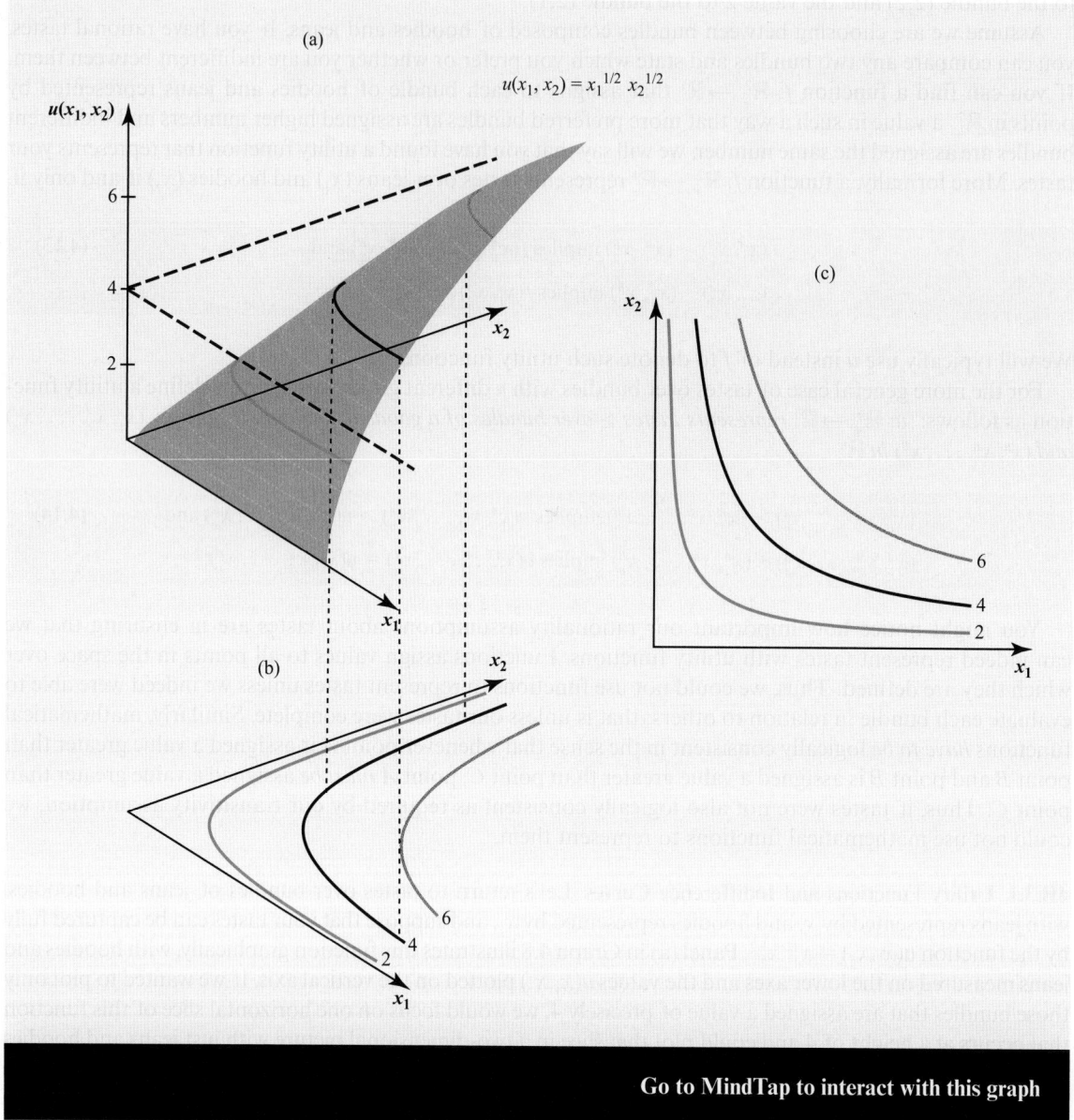

(a)

$$u(x_1, x_2) = x_1^{1/2} x_2^{1/2}$$

Go to MindTap to interact with this graph

Actually, what we mean by a marginal rate of substitution is somewhat more precise; we are not looking for just *any* combination of changes in x_2 and x_1 such that $\Delta u = 0$. Rather, we are looking for small changes that define the slope around a particular point. Such small changes are denoted in calculus by using d instead of Δ. Thus, we can rewrite (4.15) as:

$$\frac{dx_2}{dx_1} \text{ such that } du = 0. \tag{4.16}$$

The following step now requires some knowledge of multivariable calculus. This chapter's appendix provides some background on total and partial differentiation.

Changes in utility arise from the combined change in x_2 and x_1 consumption, and this is expressed as the total differential (du):

$$du = \frac{\partial u}{\partial x_1} dx_1 + \frac{\partial u}{\partial x_2} dx_2. \tag{4.17}$$

Since we are interested in changes in consumption that result in no change in utility (thus leaving us on the same indifference curve), we set expression (4.17) to zero:

$$\frac{\partial u}{\partial x_1} dx_1 + \frac{\partial u}{\partial x_2} dx_2 = 0. \tag{4.18}$$

and solve out for dx_2/dx_1 to get:

$$\frac{dx_2}{dx_1} = -\frac{(\partial u/\partial x_1)}{(\partial u/\partial x_2)}. \tag{4.19}$$

Since this expression for dx_2/dx_1 was derived from the expression $du = 0$, it gives us the equation for small changes in x_2 divided by small changes in x_1 such that utility remains unchanged – the definition of a marginal rate substitution. Thus, if we know that a particular utility function u gives rise to an indifference map that accurately represents someone's tastes, we now know how to calculate the marginal rate of substitution for that person at any consumption bundle (x_1, x_2) with:

$$MRS(x_1, x_2) = -\frac{(\partial u/\partial x_1)}{(\partial u/\partial x_2)}. \tag{4.20}$$

Suppose, for instance, your tastes for jeans (x_1) and hoodies (x_2) can be summarized by the utility function $u(x_1, x_2) = x_1^{1/2} x_2^{1/2}$ represented in panel (a) of Graph 4.8, and suppose that we would like to determine the marginal rate of substitution when you are consuming 4 pairs of jeans and 3 hoodies. We can begin by finding the general expression for your marginal rate of substitution given that you have tastes summarized by this utility function. To do this, we have to take the partial derivative of u with respect to each of the two goods,

$$\frac{\partial u}{\partial x_1} = \left(\frac{1}{2}\right)(x_1^{-1/2} x_2^{1/2}) \text{ and } \frac{\partial u}{\partial x_2} = \left(\frac{1}{2}\right)(x_1^{1/2} x_2^{-1/2}) \tag{4.21}$$

and substitute the results into the formula for MRS in equation (4.20) to get:

$$MRS = -\frac{(1/2)(x_1^{-1/2} x_2^{1/2})}{(1/2)(x_1^{1/2} x_2^{-1/2})} = -\frac{x_2}{x_1}. \tag{4.22}$$

This simplified expression, $MRS = -x_2/x_1$, gives the formula for the slope of all your indifference curves at every possible bundle in $\mathbb{R}_+^2$ assuming that these indifference curves can indeed be represented by the utility function $u(x_1, x_2) = x_1^{1/2} x_2^{1/2}$. For instance, if you are currently consuming 4 pairs of jeans (x_1) and 3 hoodies (x_2), your marginal rate of substitution is equal to $-3/4$. If you are consuming 10 pairs of jeans and 1 hoodie, your marginal rate of substitution is $-1/10$, and if you are consuming 1 pair of jeans and 10 hoodies, it is -10.

Exercise 4B.3

How does the expression for the marginal rate of substitution change if tastes could instead be summarized by the utility function $u(x_1,x_2) = x_1^{1/4}x_2^{3/4}$?

4B.3.3 Interpreting Values Assigned to Indifference Curves by Utility Functions Recall that in Section 4A.3.3, we stated that happiness or utility cannot be measured objectively and yet we seem to be measuring utility here with utility functions. When discussing the numbers next to indifference curves in Graph 4.5, we indicated that the numbers themselves were not important; it was the ordering of the numbers that mattered because we were simply using the numbers to indicate which indifference curves yield more happiness and which yield less. We mentioned that we could just as easily have multiplied the numbers in Graph 4.5 by 2 or divided them by 5 or added 13 to them because in each case, the *ordering* of indifference curves would remain unchanged. We concluded that, *as long as the shape of indifference curves and the ordering of the numbers that accompany the curves are unchanged between the two graphs, the maps of indifference curves in the two graphs represent the same tastes.*

The same is true of utility functions. You can think of these functions as rulers that use some scale to measure utility. We can adjust the scale: *As long as two functions give rise to the same shapes of indifference curves and as long as the ordering of the numbers assigned to these indifference curves is the same, the two functions represent the same underlying tastes.* All we are doing is using a different ruler.

Consider the utility function $u(x_1,x_2) = x_1^{1/2}x_2^{1/2}$ that we graphed in panel (a) of Graph 4.8 that is replicated in panel (a) of Graph 4.9. Now consider the same function squared, that is, $v(x_1,x_2) = (x_1^{1/2}x_2^{1/2})^2 = x_1x_2$, which is graphed in panel (c) of Graph 4.9. The functions certainly look different, but it turns out that they give rise to exactly the same indifference curves in panels (b) and (d). To prove this mathematically, we check whether the two utility functions give rise to the same expression for the marginal rate of substitution because if the slopes of the indifference curves are the same at all points, the shapes of the indifference curves must be the same. First, we find the partial derivatives of v with respect to each good (as we did for u in (4.21)):

$$\frac{\partial v}{\partial x_1} = x_2 \text{ and } \frac{\partial v}{\partial x_2} = x_1. \tag{4.23}$$

These expressions differ from the analogous derivatives for u in equation (4.21). They represent the additional or *marginal utility* you would obtain from one more unit of consumption of each of the two goods, and this additional utility differs depending on what ruler we use to measure utility. It therefore makes sense that the two different utility functions, u and v, have different partial derivatives with respect to each of the two goods. For this reason, we do not think that there is any real content in the concept of marginal utility. When we substitute the results in equation (4.23) into our formula for a marginal rate of substitution in equation (4.20), we find that the marginal rate of substitution implied by the utility function v is again equal to $-x_2/x_1$, just as it was when we calculated the marginal rate of substitution for the utility function u in equation (4.22).

Exercise 4B.4

Can you verify that squaring the utility function in exercise 4B.3 does not also change the underlying indifference curves?

Graph 4.9 Rescaling Panel (a) of Graph 4.8

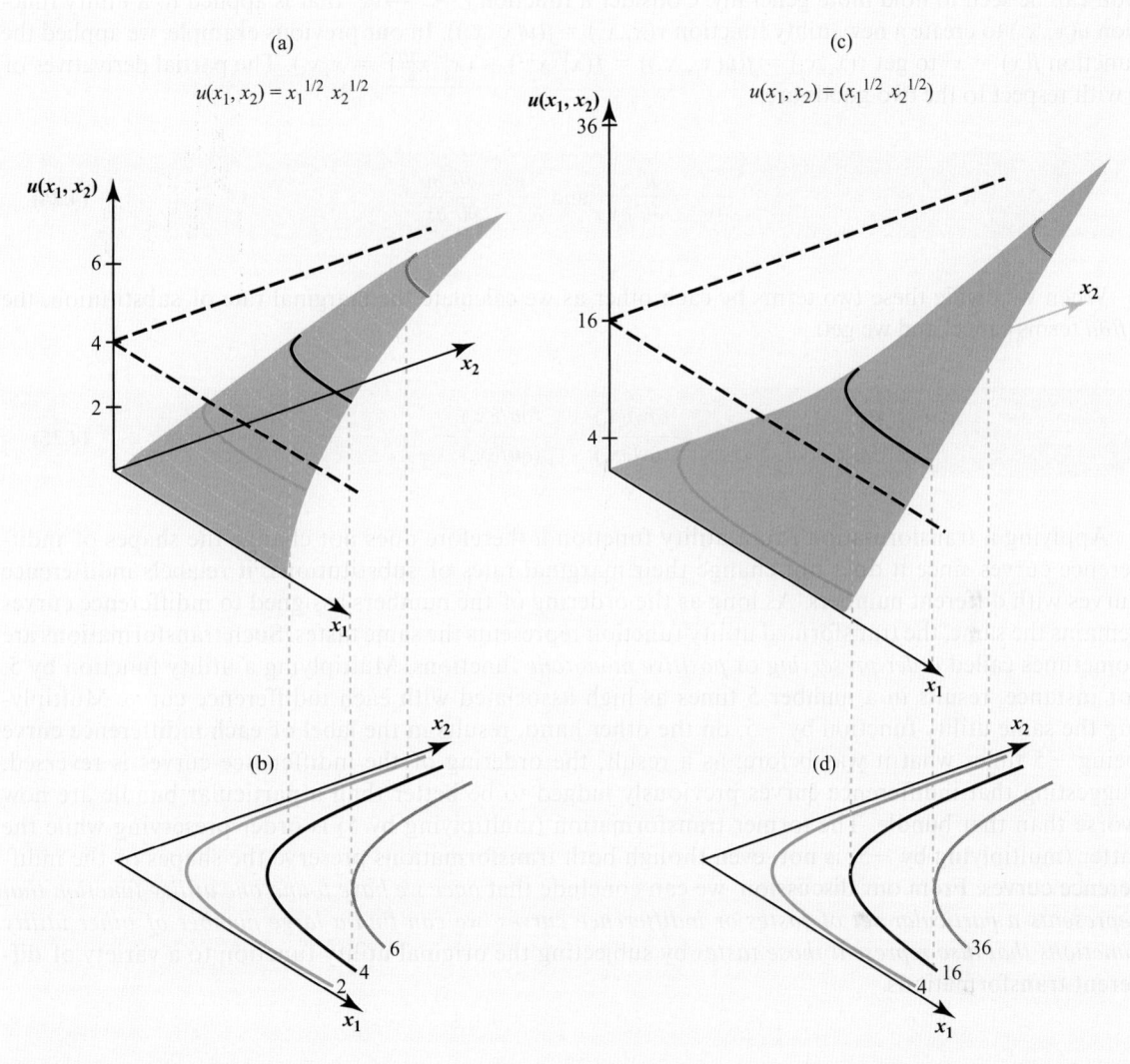

(a)

$u(x_1, x_2) = x_1^{1/2} x_2^{1/2}$

(c)

$u(x_1, x_2) = (x_1^{1/2} x_2^{1/2})$

(b)

(d)

The intuition for what happened by comparing the partial derivatives in equations (4.21) and (4.23) is that while they are different, they are different only in ways that cancel out when we divide one partial derivative by the other as we calculate the marginal rate of substitution. The units that measure marginal utility drop out of the equation when we divide two marginal utilities by each another. Thus, *the concept of a marginal rate of substitution is independent of what scale we use to measure utility*, and is thus meaningful even though we do not think utility itself can be objectively quantified.

Exercise 4B.5

Illustrate that the same conclusion we reached with respect to u and v representing the same indifference curves also holds when we take the square root of u; that is when we consider the function $w(x_1, x_2) = (x_1^{1/2}x_2^{1/2})^{1/2} = x_1^{1/4}x_2^{1/4}$.

The idea that a rescaling of a utility function cancels out when we calculate marginal rates of substitution can be seen to hold more generally. Consider a function $f: \mathbb{R}^1 \to \mathbb{R}^1$ that is applied to a utility function $u(x_1,x_2)$ to create a new utility function $v(x_1,x_2) = f(u(x_1,x_2))$. In our previous example, we applied the function $f(x) = x^2$ to get $v(x_1,x_2) = f(u(x_1, x_2)) = f(x_1^{1/2}x_2^{1/2}) = (x_1^{1/2}x_2^{1/2})^2 = x_1x_2$. The partial derivatives of v with respect to the two goods are:

$$\frac{\partial v}{\partial x_1} = \frac{\partial f}{\partial u}\frac{\partial u}{\partial x_1} \text{ and } \frac{\partial v}{\partial x_2} = \frac{\partial f}{\partial u}\frac{\partial u}{\partial x_2}. \tag{4.24}$$

When we divide these two terms by each other as we calculate the marginal rate of substitution, the $\partial f/\partial u$ terms cancel and we get:

$$-\frac{(\partial v/\partial x_1)}{(\partial v/\partial x_2)} = -\frac{(\partial u/\partial x_1)}{(\partial u/\partial x_2)}. \tag{4.25}$$

Applying a transformation f to a utility function u therefore does not change the shapes of indifference curves since it does not change their marginal rates of substitutions; it relabels indifference curves with different numbers. As long as the ordering of the numbers assigned to indifference curves remains the same, the transformed utility function represents the same tastes. Such transformations are sometimes called *order preserving* or *positive monotone* functions. Multiplying a utility function by 5, for instance, results in a number 5 times as high associated with each indifference curve. Multiplying the same utility function by -5, on the other hand, results in the label of each indifference curve being -5 times what it was before; as a result, the ordering of the indifference curves is reversed, suggesting that indifference curves previously judged to be better than a particular bundle are now worse than that bundle. The former transformation (multiplying by 5) is order preserving while the latter (multiplying by -5) is not, even though both transformations preserve the shapes of the indifference curves. From our discussion, we can conclude that *once we have found one utility function that represents a particular set of tastes or indifference curves, we can find a large number of other utility functions that also represent those tastes* by subjecting the original utility function to a variety of different transformations.

Exercise 4B.6

Consider the utility function $u(x_1, x_2) = (x_1^{1/2}x_2^{1/2})$. Take natural logs of this function and calculate the marginal rate of substitution of the new function. Can the natural log transformation be applied to utility functions such that the new utility function represents the same underlying tastes?

Exercise 4B.7

Consider the utility function $u(x_1, x_2, x_3) = x_1^{1/2}x_2^{1/2}x_3^{1/2}$. Take natural logs of this function and calculate the marginal rates of substitution of each pair of goods. Can the natural log transformation be applied to utility functions of three goods such that the new utility function represents the same underlying tastes?

Appendix   Some Basics of Multivariable Calculus

This appendix is intended to cover the basics of extending single-variable differentiation to functions of multiple variables.

Single-variable functions take the form $y = f(x)$ such as the function graphed in Graph 4.7, which graphs $y = f(x) = x^2$. The derivative or slope of this function is $df/dx = 2x$. Utility functions, however, are typically multivariable functions because we are interested in the trade-offs consumers make between different goods. For instance, we graphed in panel (a) of Graph 4.8 the function $u(x_1,x_2) = x_1^{1/2}x_2^{1/2}$. The difference between a single-variable function and a function of multiple variables is that the former assigns a number to points on the real line $\mathbb{R}^1$ while the latter assigns numbers to points in a higher dimensional space. A single-variable function is therefore denoted as a rule that assigns a real number to elements of the real line, or $f: \mathbb{R}^1 \rightarrow \mathbb{R}^1$. A multivariable function $y = f(x_1,x_2,\ldots,x_n)$, on the other hand, is a formula that assigns a real number to points with n components and is therefore denoted $f: R^n \rightarrow \mathbb{R}^1$.

4B.4 Partial Derivatives

Any multivariable function becomes a single-variable function if we hold all but one variable fixed. Consider, for instance, the utility function $u(x_1,x_2) = x_1^{1/2}x_2^{1/2}$ and suppose that we want to ask how utility as measured by this function changes when x_2 changes while $x_1 = 4$. In that case, we are holding the x_1 variable fixed at 4 and are operating on a slice of the three-dimensional function depicted in panel (a) of Graph 4.10. This slice is just a single-variable function $v(x_2) = u(4,x_2) = 2x_2^{1/2}$ (since the square root of 4 is 2) and is depicted in panel (a) of the graph and separately in panel (b).

Graph 4.10 A Single-Variable Slice of a Multivariable Function

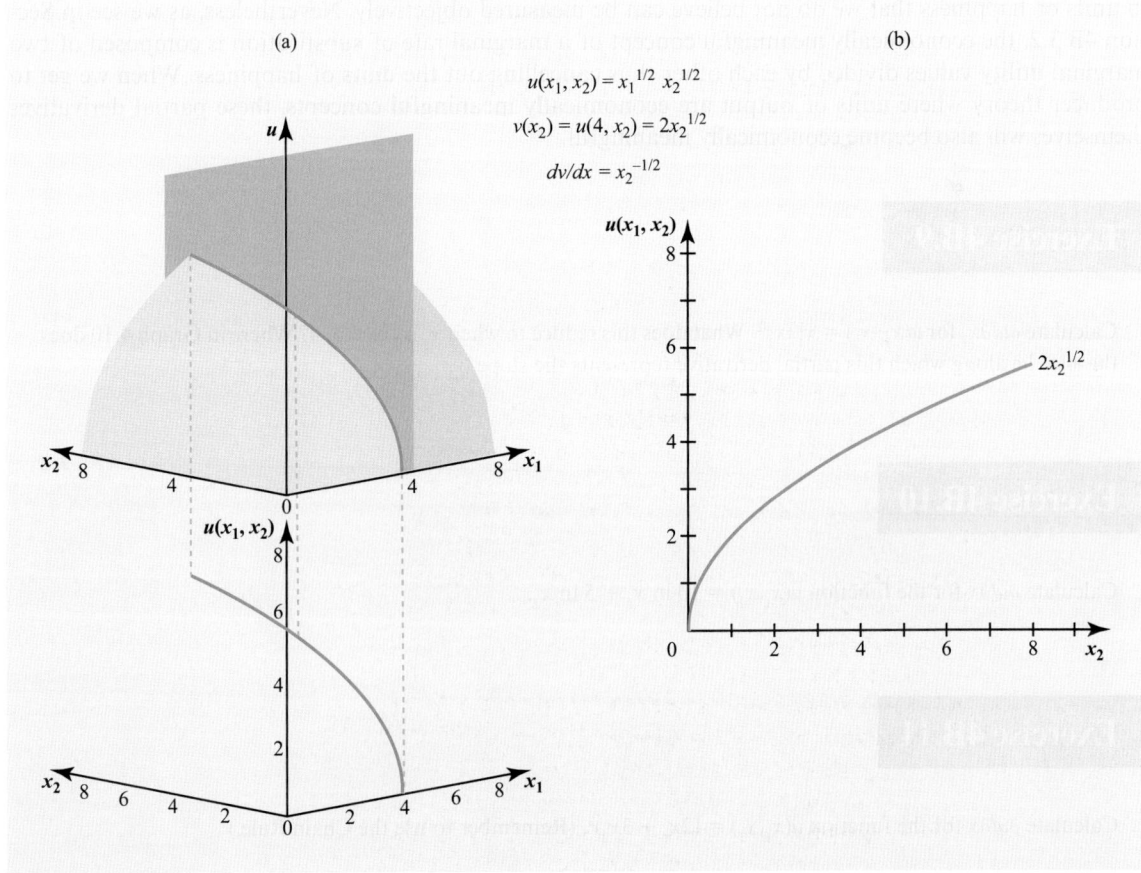

The *derivative* of the function $v(x_2)$ in panel (b) of the graph is $dv/dx = x_2^{-1/2}$ and is the slope of the slice of the two-variable function $u(x_1, x_2)$ depicted in panel (a). It is also called the *partial derivative of u with respect to x_2 when $x_1 = 4$*.

More generally, we can take the partial derivative of u with respect to x_2 by treating the x_1 variable as a constant. This partial derivative is denoted $\partial u / \partial x_2$ and is calculated exactly the same way you would calculate a derivative of a single-variable function in which x_1 is just a constant; that is:

$$\frac{\partial u}{\partial x_2} = \left(\frac{1}{2}\right) x_1^{1/2} x_2^{-1/2}. \tag{4.26}$$

This gives us the derivative of a slice of the utility function $u(x_1, x_2)$ that holds x_1 constant at some value. For instance, when $x_1 = 4$ as we assumed before, the expression reduces to $x_2^{-1/4}$ and represents the slope of the slice in Graph 4.10 at different values of x_2.

Exercise 4B.8

What would be the expression of the slope of the slice of the utility function $u(x_1, x_2) = x_1^{1/2} x_2^{1/2}$ when x_1 is fixed at 9? What is the slope of that slice when $x_2 = 4$?

Such partial derivatives of a utility function give us the *marginal utility* of an additional unit of a consumption good when the quantity of all other consumption goods is held fixed. As we discuss in the main part of the chapter, this concept in and of itself is not economically meaningful because it is expressed in units of happiness that we do not believe can be measured objectively. Nevertheless, as we see in Section 4B.3.2, the economically meaningful concept of a marginal rate of substitution is composed of two marginal utility values divided by each other thus cancelling out the units of happiness. When we get to producer theory where units of output are economically meaningful concepts, these partial derivatives themselves will also become economically meaningful.

Exercise 4B.9

Calculate $\partial u / \partial x_1$ for $u(x_1, x_2) = x_1^{1/2} x_2^{1/2}$. What does this reduce to when x_2 is fixed at 4? Where in Graph 4.10 does the slice lie along which this partial derivative represents the slope?

Exercise 4B.10

Calculate $\partial u / \partial x$ for the function $u(x_1, x_2) = 10 \ln x_1 + 5 \ln x_2$.

Exercise 4B.11

Calculate $\partial u / \partial x$ for the function $u(x_1, x_2) = (2x_1 + 3x_2)^3$. (Remember to use the Chain Rule.)

4B.5 Total Differential of Multivariable Functions

While a partial derivative of a function like $u(x_1,x_2) = x_1^{1/2}x_2^{1/2}$ tells us the rate at which utility will change if the quantity of one of the two goods in a consumption bundle is increased by a small amount as the quantity of the other consumption good stays fixed, we might also be interested in how the utility changes when the quantity of both consumption goods changes by small amounts. The *total differential* of the function u measures the change in utility resulting from small changes in both x_1 and x_2. Letting dx_1 and dx_2 represent such small changes, the total differential du is expressed mathematically as:

$$du = \frac{\partial u}{\partial x_1}dx_1 + \frac{\partial u}{\partial x_2}dx_2 \tag{4.27}$$

which, for the utility function $u(x_1,x_2) = x_1^{1/2}x_2^{1/2}$, is:

$$du = \frac{x_2^{1/2}}{2x_1^{1/2}}dx_1 + \frac{x_1^{1/2}}{2x_2^{1/2}}dx_2. \tag{4.28}$$

Exercise 4B.12

Verify that equation (4.28) is correct.

Notice that if $dx_1 = 0$, that is, if x_1 does not change and only x_2 changes, equation (4.27) reduces to:

$$du = \frac{\partial u}{\partial x_2}dx_2, \tag{4.29}$$

which is called the *partial differential* of u with respect to x_2.

Exercise 4B.13

Calculate the total differential du of $u(x_1,x_2) = 10 \ln x_1 + 5 \ln x_2$.

End-of-Chapter Exercises

4.1† Assume that you are highly allergic to eggs but enjoy bacon at breakfast.

A. In each of the following, put eggs on the horizontal axis and bacon on the vertical. Graph three indifference curves and number them.

a. Assume that your tastes satisfy the convexity and continuity assumptions and otherwise satisfy the previous description.

b. How would your answer change if your tastes were non-convex; that is, if averages were worse than extremes?

    c. How would your answer to (a) change if you disliked both bacon and eggs but we again assume tastes satisfy the convexity assumption?

    d. What if you hated both goods and their tastes were non-convex?

B. Now suppose you like both eggs and bacon, that your tastes satisfy our five basic assumptions, and that they can be represented by the utility function $u(x_1,x_2) = x_1 x_2$.

    a. Consider two bundles, $A = (1,20)$ and $B = (10,2)$. Which one do you prefer?

    b. Use bundles A and B to illustrate that these tastes are convex.

    c. What is the MRS at bundle A? What is it at bundle B?

    d. What is the simplest possible transformation of this function that would represent tastes consistent with those described in A(d)?

    e. Now consider tastes that are instead defined by the function $u(x_1,x_2) = x_1^2 x_2^2$. What is the MRS of this function?

    f. Do these tastes have diminishing marginal rates of substitution? Are they convex?

    g. How could you most easily turn this utility function into one that represents tastes like those described in A(c)?

4.2 Consider an individual's tastes for consumption and leisure.

A. Begin by assuming the individual's tastes over consumption and leisure satisfy our five basic assumptions.

    a. On a graph with leisure hours per week on the horizontal axis and consumption euros per week on the vertical, give an example of 3 indifference curves with associated utility numbers from an indifference map that satisfies our assumptions.

    b. Now redefine the good on the horizontal axis as labour hours rather than leisure hours. How would the same tastes look in this graph?

    c. How would both of your graphs change if tastes over leisure and consumption were non-convex, that is, if averages were worse than extremes?

B. Suppose your tastes over consumption and leisure could be described by the utility function $u(l,c) = l^{1/2}c^{1/2}$.

    a. Do these tastes satisfy our five basic assumptions?

    b. Can you find a utility function that would describe the same tastes when the second good is defined as labour hours instead of leisure hours? *Hint:* Suppose your weekly endowment of leisure time is 60 hours. How does that relate to the sign of the slopes of indifference curves you graphed in part A(b)?

    c. What is the marginal rate of substitution for the function you just derived? How does that relate to your graph from part A(b)?

    d. Do the tastes represented by the utility function in part B(b) satisfy our five basic assumptions?

4.3† In this exercise, we explore further the concept of marginal rates of substitution and, in part B, its relation to utility functions.

A. Suppose person A own 3 bananas and 6 apples, and person B owns 5 bananas and 10 apples.

    a. With bananas on the horizontal axis and apples on the vertical, the slope of A's indifference curve at their current bundle is −2, and the slope of B's indifference curve through their current bundle is −1. Assume that their tastes satisfy our usual five assumptions. Can you suggest a trade to A that would make them both better off? Feel free to assume they can trade fractions of apples and bananas.

    b. After they engage in the trade you suggested, will their MRSs have gone up or down in absolute value?

    c. If the values for our MRSs at current consumption bundles were reversed, how would your answers to (a) and (b) change?

    d. What would have to be true about our MRSs at current bundles in order for B not to be able to come up with a mutually beneficial trade?

e. *True or False*: If A and B have different tastes, they will always be able to trade with both benefiting.

f. *True or False*: If A and B have the same tastes, they will never be able to trade with both benefiting.

B. Consider the following five utility functions and assume that α and β are positive real numbers:

$$1.\ u^A(x_1,x_2) = x_1^\alpha x_2^\beta$$
$$2.\ u^B(x_1,x_2) = \alpha x_1 + \beta x_2$$
$$3.\ u^C(x_1,x_2) = \alpha x_1 + \beta \ln x_2$$
$$4.\ u^D(x_1,x_2) = \left(\frac{\alpha}{\beta}\right)\ln x_1 + \ln x_2 \qquad (4.30)$$
$$5.\ u^E(x_1,x_2) = -\alpha \ln x_1 - \beta \ln x_2$$

a. Calculate the formula for *MRS* for each of these utility functions.

b. Which utility functions represent tastes that have linear indifference curves?

c. Which of these utility functions represent the same underlying tastes?

d. Which of these utility functions represent tastes that do not satisfy the monotonicity assumption?

e. Which of these utility functions represent tastes that do not satisfy the convexity assumption?

f. Which of these utility functions represent tastes that are not rational, i.e. that do not satisfy the completeness and transitivity assumptions?

g. Which of these utility functions represent tastes that are not continuous?

h. Consider the following statement: Benefits from trade emerge because we have different tastes. If individuals had the same tastes, they would not be able to benefit from trading with one another. Is this statement ever true, and if so, are there any tastes represented by the utility functions in this problem for which the statement is true?

4.4 Everyday Application: *Rating Films on a Numerical Scale.* Assume that you and a friend often go to the cinema and afterwards assign a rating ranging from 0 to 10 to the film you have just seen.

A. Suppose you go to see a double feature, first *Terminator Genisys* and an adaptation of Jane Austen's *Emma*. You rate *Terminator Genisys* as an 8 and *Emma* as a 2, and your friend rates *Terminator Genisys* a 5 and *Emma* a 4.

a. Do you and your friend agree on which film is better?

b. How would your answer change if your friend's ratings had been reversed?

c. Can you tell for sure whether you liked *Terminator Genisys* more than your friend did?

d. Assume you both argue about your rankings. *True or False*: It makes little sense for you to argue if you both rank one film higher than the other even if you assign very different numbers.

B. Suppose that the only thing you really care about in evaluating films is the fraction of action time as opposed to thoughtful conversation and let the fraction of screen time devoted to action be denoted x_1. Suppose that the only thing your friend cares about when evaluating films is the fraction of time strong women appear on screen, and let that fraction be denoted x_2. *Terminator Genisys* has $x_1 = 0.8$ and $x_2 = 0.5$, while *Emma* has $x_1 = 0.2$ and $x_2 = 0.4$.

a. Consider the functions $u(x_1) = 10x_1$ and $v(x_2) = 10x_2$ and suppose that you use the function u to determine your film rating and your friend uses the function v. What ratings do you give to the two films?

b. Assume you decide that you will assign ratings differently, using the function $\bar{u}(x_1) = 5.25x_1^{1/6}$. Will you rank any pair of films differently using this function rather than your previous function u? What approximate values do you now assign to *Terminator Genisys* and *Emma*?

c. Your friend also decides to change their way of assigning ratings to films. They now use the function $\bar{v}(x_2) = 590x_2^{6.2}$. Will their rankings of any two films change as a result? What approximate values do they now assign to the two films?

d. Suppose your friend had instead chosen the function $\underline{v}(x_2) = 10(1 - x_2)$. Will they now rank films differently?

4.5† **Everyday Application:** *Tastes of a Cocaine Addict.* Carl is addicted to cocaine. Suppose we want to model his tastes over cocaine and other goods.

A. We propose to model his tastes in the following way: For any two bundles A and B of grammes of cocaine and euros of other consumption, we will assume that Carl always prefers bundle A if it contains more grammes of cocaine than bundle B. If bundles A and B contain the same amount of cocaine, we will assume he prefers A to B if and only if A contains more other consumption than B.

  a. On a graph with grammes of cocaine on the horizontal axis and other consumption denominated in euros on the vertical, denote one arbitrary bundle as A. Indicate all the bundles that are strictly preferred to A.

  b. On a separate graph, indicate all bundles that are strictly less preferred than A.

  c. Looking over your two graphs, is there any bundle that Carl would say gives him exactly as much happiness as A? Are there any two bundles not necessarily involving bundle A that Carl is indifferent between?

  d. In order for this to be a useful model for studying Carl's behaviour, how severe would Carl's addiction have to be?

  e. Are these tastes rational? In other words, are they complete and transitive?

  f. Do these tastes satisfy the monotonicity property?

  g. Do they satisfy the convexity property?

B. The tastes previously defined are called *lexicographic*. Formally, we can define them as follows: For any $A, B \in \mathbb{R}^2_+$, $A > B$ if either $x_1^A > x_1^B$ or $x_1^A = x_1^B$ and $x_2^A > x_2^B$.

  a. In this formal definition, which good is cocaine, x_1 or x_2?

  b. On a graph with x_1 on the horizontal axis and x_2 on the vertical, pick an arbitrary bundle $A = (x_1^A, x_2^A)$. Pick a second bundle $D = (x_1^D, x_2^D)$ such that $x_1^A = x_1^D$ and $x_2^A > x_2^D$.

  c. On your graph, illustrate an infinite sequence of bundles $(B^1, B^2, B^3, \ldots)$ that converges to A from the left. Illustrate an infinite sequence of bundles $(C^1, C^2, C^3, \ldots)$ that converges to D from the right.

  d. *True or False*: Every bundle in the C-sequence is strictly preferred to every bundle in the B-sequence.

  e. *True or False*: Bundle A is strictly preferred to bundle D.

  f. Based on the answers you just gave to (d) and (e), do lexicographic tastes satisfy the continuity property?

  g. Can these tastes be represented by a utility function?

4.6* In this exercise, we will explore some logical relationships between families of tastes that satisfy different assumptions.

A. Suppose we define a strong and a weak version of convexity as follows: Tastes are said to be *strongly convex* if whenever a person with those tastes is indifferent between A and B, the person strictly prefers the average of A and B to A and B. Tastes are said to be *weakly convex* if whenever a person with those tastes is indifferent between A and B, the average of A and B is at least as good as A and B for that person.

  a. Let the set of all tastes that satisfy strong convexity be denoted as SC and the set of all tastes that satisfy weak convexity as WC. Which set is contained in the other? We would, for instance, say that WC is contained in SC if any taste that satisfies weak convexity also automatically satisfies strong convexity.

  b. Consider the set of tastes that are contained in one and only one of the two sets defined previously. What must be true about some indifference curves on any indifference map from this newly defined set of tastes?

  c. Suppose you are told the following about three people: Person 1 strictly prefers bundle A to bundle B whenever A contains more of each and every good than bundle B. If only some goods are represented in greater quantity in A than in B while the remaining goods are represented in equal quantity, A is at least as good as B for this person. Such tastes are often said to be *weakly monotonic*. Person 2 likes bundle A strictly better than B whenever at least some goods are represented in greater quantity in A than in B while others may be represented in equal quantity. Such tastes are said to be *strongly monotonic*. Finally, person 3's tastes are such that for every bundle A, there always exists a bundle B very close to A that is strictly better than A. Such tastes are said to satisfy *local non-satiation*. Call the set of tastes that satisfy strict monotonicity SM, the set of tastes that satisfy weak monotonicity WM, and the set of tastes that satisfy local non-satiation L. Give an example of tastes that fall in one and only one of these three sets.

d. What is true about tastes that are in one and only one of these three sets?

e. What is true of tastes that are in one and only one of the sets SM and WM?

B. Here, we will consider the logical implications of convexity for utility functions. For the following definitions, $0 \leq \alpha \leq 1$. A function $f: \mathbb{R}^2_+ \rightarrow \mathbb{R}^1$ is defined to be *quasiconcave* if and only if the following is true: Whenever $f(x_1^A, x_2^A) \leq f(x_1^B, x_2^B)$, then $f(x_1^A, x_2^A) \leq f(\alpha x_1^A + (1 - \alpha)x_1^B, \alpha x_2^A + (1 - \alpha)x_2^B)$. The same type of function is defined as *concave* if and only if $\alpha f(x_1^A, x_2^A) + (1 - \alpha) f(x_1^B, x_2^B) \leq f(\alpha x_1^A + (1 + \alpha)x_1^B, \alpha x_2^A + (1 - \alpha)x_2^B)$.

a. *True or False*: All concave functions are quasiconcave, but not all quasiconcave functions are concave.

b. Demonstrate that if u is a quasiconcave utility function, the tastes represented by u are convex.

c. Do your conclusions imply that if u is a concave utility function, the tastes represented by u are convex?

d. Demonstrate that if tastes over two goods are convex, any utility functions that represent those tastes must be quasiconcave.

e. Do your conclusions imply that if tastes over two goods are convex, any utility function that represents those tastes must be concave?

f. Do the previous conclusions imply that utility functions that are not quasiconcave represent tastes that are not convex?

*conceptually challenging
†solutions in Study Guide

Chapter 5

Different Types of Tastes

In this chapter, we will analyze how maps of indifference curves can differ in important ways while still satisfying our five basic assumptions. This will tell us much about how different types of tastes can be modelled using our simple graphical framework as well as the more general mathematical framework that builds on our graphically derived intuitions. One of the important insights that should emerge from this chapter is that our basic model of tastes is enormously general and allows us to consider all sorts of tastes that individuals might have.

5A | Different Types of Indifference Maps

Understanding how different tastes can be graphed will be important for understanding how consumer behaviour differs depending on underlying modelling.

5A.1 Substitutability Along an Indifference Curve: Coke, Pepsi and Coffee

The extent to which two goods are substitutes depends on the nature of the goods we are modelling as well as the types of tastes that individuals have. For instance, Coke and Pepsi are similar to one another and as such can be viewed as being very close substitutes.

5A.1.1 Perfect Substitutes
Assume we want to model an individual's tastes for Coke and Pepsi. We could begin by thinking about some arbitrary bundle currently consumed, say, 1 can of Coke and 1 can of Pepsi. We could ask what other bundles might be of equal value assuming the individual cannot tell the difference between the products. For instance, 2 cans of Coke and no cans of Pepsi should be just as good a choice as 2 cans of Pepsi and no cans of Coke. Each of these three bundles must lie on the same indifference curve for this individual, as must any other linear combination, such as 1.5 cans of Coke and 0.5 cans of Pepsi. In Graph 5.1, these bundles are plotted and connected by the light blue line. Each point on this line represents some combination of Coke and Pepsi that adds up to 2 cans, which is after all the only thing that matters to someone who can't tell the difference between the products. We could construct other indifference curves as well, such as those representing quantities of Coke and Pepsi that add up to 1 can or 3 cans, as also depicted in Graph 5.1 by the gold and dark blue lines.

The tastes we have graphed represent tastes over goods that are *perfect substitutes*. Such tastes are unusual in the sense that one of our five basic assumptions is already almost violated. In particular, notice that averages are no longer *better than* extremes; rather, averages are valued *the same as* extremes when two goods are perfect substitutes. 1 can of Coke and 1 can of Pepsi is the average between the more extreme bundles of 2 Cokes or 2 Pepsis, but it is equally valued by a consumer with the tastes we have graphed

74

here. This also implies that the slope of each indifference curve is constant, giving us constant rather than diminishing marginal rates of substitution. It should be noted that marginal rates of substitution are constant in this case; no matter how much or how little Coke the consumer has, they will always be willing to trade 1 Coke for 1 Pepsi.

The defining characteristic of perfect substitutes is not that $MRS = -1$, but rather that the MRS is the same everywhere. Even when $MRS = -1$, the individual could change the units with which we measure quantities of Coke and Pepsi and get a different $MRS = -1$ without changing a person's tastes.

Graph 5.1 Indifference Curves for Perfect Substitutes

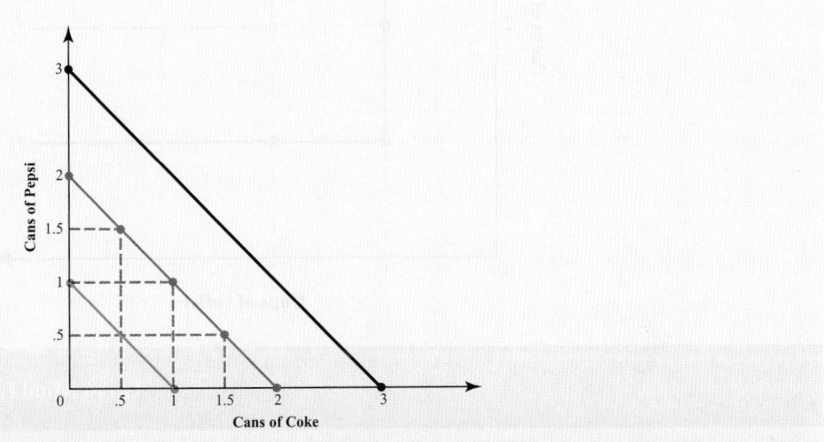

Go to MindTap to interact with this graph

Exercise 5A.1

How would the graph of indifference curves change if Coke came in 330ml cans and Pepsi came in 165ml cans?

5A.1.2 Perfect Complements Assume an individual orders a coffee in a restaurant and adds exactly 1 packet of sugar before drinking it. If there is less than 1 packet of sugar available, the individual will leave the coffee untouched, whereas if there is more than 1 packet of sugar available, the additional sugar will remain unused unless they get more coffee. For this individual, coffee and sugar are *perfect complements*: they complement each other to the point that the individual gets no satisfaction from consuming 1 unit of one without also consuming 1 unit of the other.

We can model this consumer's tastes for coffee and sugar by again starting with an arbitrary point and asking which other bundles will make them indifferent. Suppose we start with 1 pack of sugar and 1 cup of coffee. Together, these two represent the ingredients for 1 acceptable beverage. Suppose we give the individual another pack of sugar without any additional coffee, giving them a bundle of 2 sugar packs and 1 cup of coffee. This would still only give them 1 acceptable beverage, and they would be no better and no worse off; that is, they would be indifferent. The same is true for a bundle containing any number of sugar packs greater than 1 so long as the bundle included only 1 cup of coffee, and it would be true for any number of additional cups of coffee if only 1 sugar pack were available. Indifference curve, I_1 with a right angle at 1 cup of coffee and 1 sugar pack in Graph 5.2 represents all bundles that, given the individual's tastes, result in 1 acceptable beverage for them. Similar indifference curves exist for bundles that add up to 2 or 3 acceptable beverages as indicated by curves I_2 and I_3.

Graph 5.2 Indifference Curves for Perfect Complements

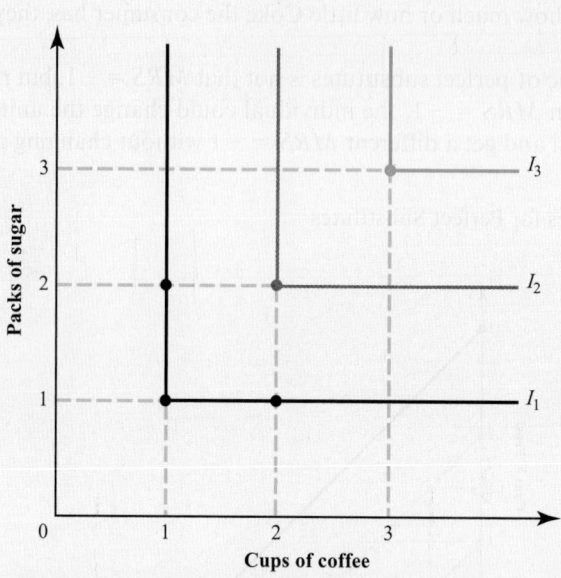

Go to MindTap to interact with this graph

Notice that, as in the case of perfect substitutes, perfect complements represent an extreme case in the sense that some of our five basic assumptions about tastes are almost violated. In particular, more is no longer necessarily better in the case of perfect complements, only more of *both* goods is better. Similarly, averages are not always better than extremes, as for bundles of goods that lie on the linear portions of the indifference curves where averages are just as good as extremes. Tastes that do not allow for substitutability between goods are sometimes referred to as *Leontief* tastes after 1973 Nobel Prize winning economist, Wassily Leontief (1906–1999), who extensively used a similar notion in producer theory.

Exercise 5A.2

What would the individual's indifference curves for packs of sugar and cups of coffee look like if they required 2 packs of sugar instead of 1 for each cup of coffee?

5A.1.3 Less Extreme Cases of Substitutability and Complementarity Rarely do goods fall into either of the two extreme cases of perfect complements or perfect substitutes. Rather, goods tend to be relatively more or less substitutable depending on their inherent characteristics and the underlying tastes of the person whose tastes we are modelling. Such less extreme examples will have shapes falling between the two extremes in Graphs 5.1 and 5.2, as for instance the tastes for goods x_1 and x_2 graphed in panels (a) to (c) in Graph 5.3. Here, unlike for the case of perfect complements, a person is willing to substitute some of x_2 for some of x_1, but not always in the same proportions as would be true for perfect substitutes. In particular, a person with such tastes would be willing to substitute x_2 for x_1 more easily if the current bundle has a lot of x_2 and little x_1, and this willingness to substitute one for the other decreases as the person moves to bundles that contain relatively more x_1 than x_2. This is the case because of the embedded assumption that averages are better than extremes and lead to diminishing marginal rates of substitution.

Graph 5.3 Indifference Curves for Less Extreme Cases of Substitutability and Complementarity

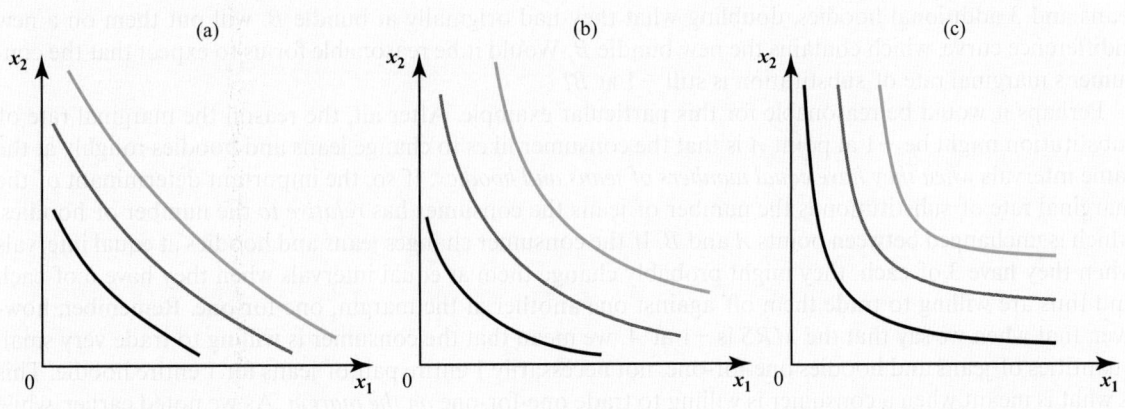

For the tastes modelled in panel (a) of Graph 5.3, this willingness to substitute x_1 for x_2 changes relatively little as the underlying bundle changes, thus giving rise to indifference curves that are relatively flat and close in shape to those of tastes representing perfect substitutes. Tastes modelled in panel (c) of Graph 5.3, on the other hand, are such that the willingness to substitute x_1 for x_2 changes relatively quickly along at least a portion of each indifference curve, thus giving rise to indifference curves whose shape is closer to those of perfect complements. Keeping the extremes of perfect substitutes and perfect complements in mind, it becomes relatively easy to look at particular maps of indifference curves and discern whether they contain a relatively high or a relatively low degree of substitutability. This degree of substitutability decreases as we move from panel (a) to panels (b) and (c) in Graph 5.3.

The degree of substitutability will play an important role in our discussion of consumer behaviour and consumer welfare in the next few chapters. It may at first seem like a trivial concept when applied to simple examples like Coke and Pepsi, but it becomes one of the most crucial concepts in controversies surrounding such issues as tax and retirement policies. In such debates, the degree of substitutability between current and future consumption or between consumption and leisure takes centre stage.

Exercise 5A.3

Suppose each of the indifference maps graphed in Graph 5.3 corresponded to an individual's tastes for one of the following sets of goods. Which pair would you think corresponds to which map? Pair 1: Levi Jeans and Diesel Jeans; Pair 2: Jeans and Hoodies; Pair 3: Jeans and SuperDry trousers.

5A.2 Some Common Indifference Maps

A second important feature of indifference maps centres on *the relationship of indifference curves to one another rather than the shape of individual indifference curves.* How, for instance, do marginal rates of substitution change along a linear ray from the origin? How do they change holding fixed one of the goods? Do indifference curves touch the axes? What do such features of indifference maps tell us about the underlying tastes of individuals? In the following section, we will take each of these questions and define particular types of tastes that represent important special cases that may be relevant for modelling tastes over different kinds of goods.

5A.2.1 Homothetic Tastes
Assume an individual currently consumes bundle A in panel (a) of Graph 5.4: 3 pairs of jeans and 3 hoodies. Further, assume that the indifference curve that contains bundle A

has a marginal rate of substitution of −1 at bundle *A*, which implies the consumer is willing to exchange 1 hoodie for 1 pair of jeans whenever they have 3 of each. If we gave the consumer 3 additional pairs of jeans and 3 additional hoodies, doubling what they had originally at bundle *B*, will put them on a new indifference curve, which contains the new bundle *B*. Would it be reasonable for us to expect that the consumer's marginal rate of substitution is still −1 at *B*?

Perhaps it would be reasonable for this particular example. After all, the reason the marginal rate of substitution might be −1 at point *A* is that the consumer likes to change jeans and hoodies roughly at the same intervals *when they have equal numbers of jeans and hoodies*. If so, the important determinant of the marginal rate of substitution is the number of jeans the consumer has *relative to* the number of hoodies, which is unchanged between points *A* and *B*. If the consumer changes jeans and hoodies at equal intervals when they have 3 of each, they might probably change them at equal intervals when they have 6 of each and thus are willing to trade them off against one another at the margin, one-for-one. Remember, however, that when we say that the *MRS* is −1 at *A*, we mean that the consumer is willing to trade very small quantities of jeans and hoodies one-for-one, not necessarily 1 entire pair of jeans for 1 entire hoodie. This is what is meant when a consumer is willing to trade one-for-one *on the margin*. As we noted earlier, while it is awkward to think of jeans and hoodies as divisible goods, it is a useful modelling simplification and one that usually is not overly restrictive when we talk about bigger examples that matter more than jeans and hoodies.

Graph 5.4 Homothetic Tastes, Marginal Rates of Substitution and Indifference Curves

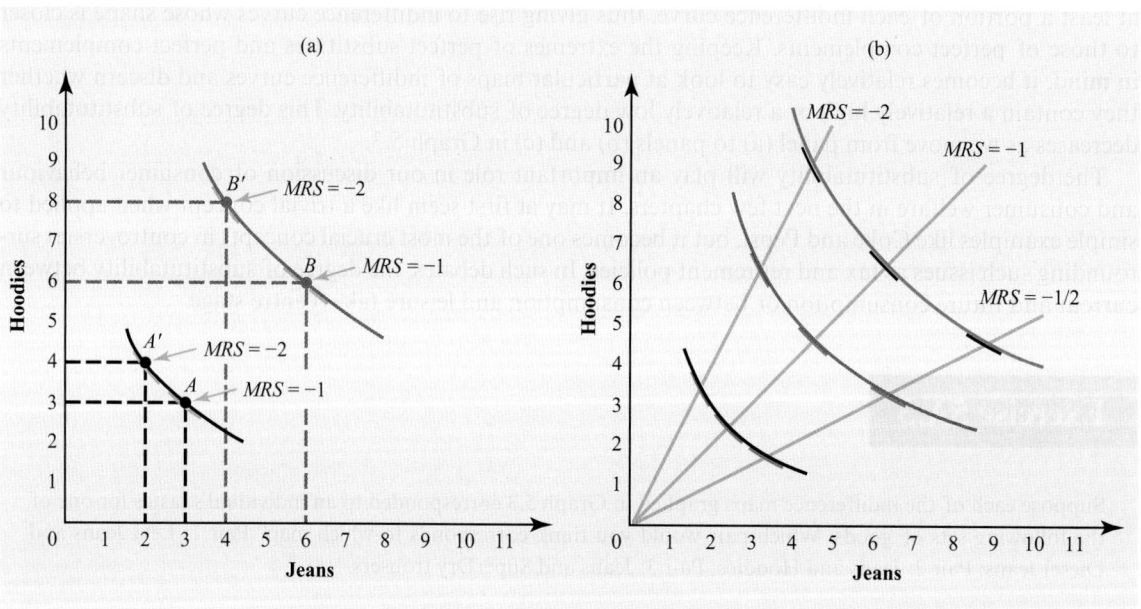

A similar argument could hold for other bundles on the indifference curve that contains bundle *A*. For instance, bundle *A'* contains 4 hoodies and 2 pairs of jeans, and the indifference curve shows a marginal rate of substitution of −7 at *A'*. Thus, the consumer would be willing to give up 2 hoodies to get 1 more pair of jeans if they were currently consuming bundle *A'* because hoodies are not of as much value to the consumer when they have so few pairs of jeans relative to hoodies. It sounds plausible, however, for the marginal rate of substitution to remain the same if the consumer doubled *A'* to *B'*: they still have relatively many hoodies compared with jeans and thus might still be willing to trade 2 hoodies for 1 pair of jeans at *B'*.

Homothetic tastes is the term used whenever tastes exhibit the property that marginal rates of substitution at particular bundles depend only on how much of one good relative to the other is contained in that bundle. This technical term means nothing more than what we have already described for the consumer's tastes for jeans and hoodies. In determining the marginal rate of substitution at one particular bundle, the marginal rate of substitution at all other bundles that lie on a ray connecting the origin and the original bundle is exactly the same. This is true because the amount of one good *relative* to the other is unchanged along this ray. Panel (b) of Graph 5.4 illustrates three indifference curves of such a homothetic indifference map.

In Chapter 6, we will see how consumers with homothetic tastes will choose to double their current consumption basket whenever their income doubles. Tastes for certain big-ticket consumption goods can thus be quite accurately modelled using homothetic tastes because they represent goods that we consume in rough proportion to our income. For many consumers, for instance, the square metreage of housing consumed increases linearly with income. Similarly, as we think of modelling our tastes for consumption across different time periods, it may be reasonable to assume that tastes are homothetic and consumption increases this year and next year by the same proportion if yearly income doubles.

It is important to note that when we say that someone's tastes are homothetic, we are making a statement about how different indifference curves relate to one another; we are *not* saying anything in particular about the shape of individual indifference curves.

Exercise 5A.4

Are tastes over Coke and Pepsi as described in Section 5A.1 homothetic? Are tastes over coffee and sugar homothetic? Why or why not?

5A.2.2 Quasilinear Tastes While the assumption that marginal rates of substitution at different consumption bundles depend only on the relative quantities of goods at those bundles is plausible for many applications, there are also many important instances when the assumption does not seem reasonable. Consider, for instance, a consumer's tastes for weekly soft drink consumption and a composite good representing weekly consumption of all other goods in euros.

Suppose we begin with a bundle A in panel (a) of Graph 5.5, a bundle that contains 25 soft drinks and €500 in other consumption. The indifference curve has a slope of -1 at that bundle, indicating that, given the current consumption bundle A, the consumer is willing to give up €1 in other consumption for 1 additional soft drink. If the consumer doubled current consumption to point B with 50 soft drinks and €1000 in other consumption, is it likely that they would value the 50th soft drink in bundle B the same as they would value the 25th soft drink in bundle A? If so, their tastes would again be homothetic. It is more likely that there is room for only so many soft drinks in the consumer's stomach during any week, and even if they were able to consume a lot more in other goods, they would still not value additional soft drinks very highly. In that case, the marginal rate of substitution at point B would be less than 1 in absolute value; that is, the consumer would be willing to consume additional soft drinks at bundle B only if they had to give up less than €1 in additional consumption.

In many examples like this, a more accurate description of tastes might be that the marginal rate of substitution depends *only* on how many soft drinks are being consumed, not on how much in other consumption the consumer has during the same week. Consider, for instance, point C in panel (a) of Graph 5.5 – a bundle containing €1000 in other consumption and 25 soft drinks. It may well be that the consumer's willingness to trade euros for additional soft drinks does not change at all between points A and C; whether the consumer is consuming €500 or €1000 in other goods, they will still only consume any soft drinks beyond 25 if they can get them for less than €1 in other consumption. If this is the case, tastes will be such that the marginal rate of substitution is *the same along any vertical line* in panel (a) of Graph 5.5. Two examples of indifference maps that satisfy this property are depicted in panels (b) and (c) of Graph 5.5.

Tastes for goods that are valued the same at the margin regardless of how much of the 'other good' is being consumed are called *quasilinear* tastes. Goods that are likely to be modelled well using quasilinear tastes tend to be goods that represent a relatively small fraction of income. They are goods that tend to be consumed at largely the same quantities even if income rises by a large amount. Examples of such goods might include milk, soft drinks, paper clips and so on, but some clearly do not. For instance, we cited tastes for housing as an example better modelled as homothetic because housing is, at the margin, valued more highly as we become better off. More generally, tastes for many big-ticket consumption items are not likely to be well modelled using the quasilinear specification of indifference maps.

Graph 5.5 Quasilinear Tastes, Marginal Rates of Substitution and Indifference Curves

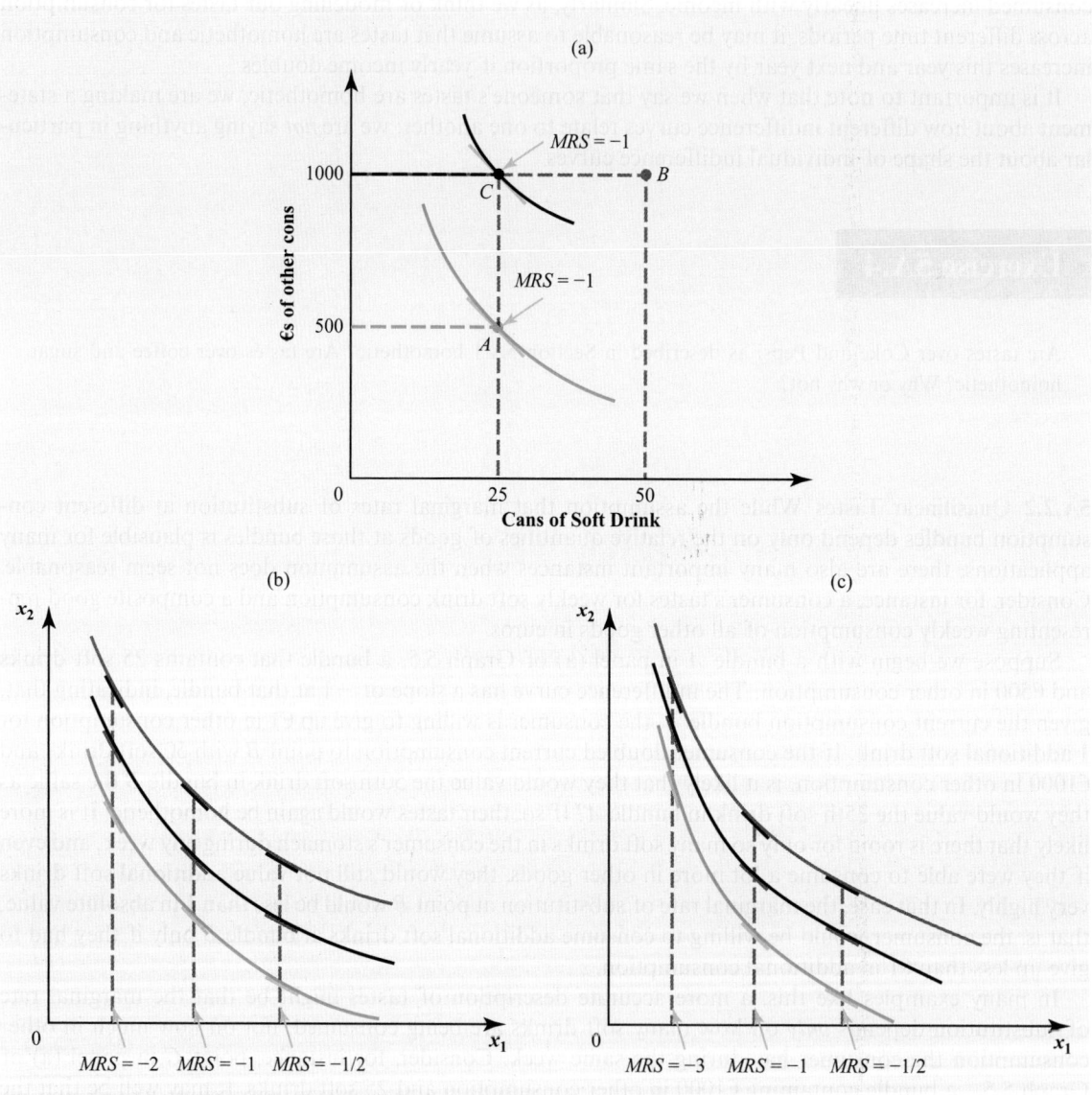

Exercise 5A.5

Are tastes over Coke and Pepsi as described in Section 5A.1 quasilinear? Are tastes over coffee and sugar quasilinear? Why or why not?

5A.2.3 Homothetic Versus Quasilinear Tastes Tastes are quasilinear in a particular good if the marginal rate of substitution between this and the other good depends only on the *absolute quantity* of the quasilinear good, and is thus independent of how much of the other good a consumer has in their consumption bundle. Graphically, this means that the marginal rate of substitution is the same along lines that are perpendicular to the axis on which we model the good that is quasilinear. Tastes are homothetic, on the other hand, if the marginal rate of substitution at any given bundle depends only on the quantity of one good *relative* to the quantity of the other. Graphically, this means that the marginal rates of substitution across indifference curves are the same along rays emanating from the origin of the graph.

Exercise 5A.6

Can you explain why tastes for perfect substitutes are the only tastes that are both quasilinear and homothetic?

5A.3 Essential Goods

There is one final dimension along which we can categorize indifference maps: whether the indifference curves intersect one or both of the axes in our graphs. Many of the indifference maps we have drawn so far have indifference curves that *converge* to the axes of the graphs without ever touching them; they are asymptotic to the axes. Some, such as those representing quasilinear tastes, however, intersect one or both of the axes. The distinction between indifference maps of the first and second kind will become important in the next chapter as we consider what we can say about the 'best' bundle that individuals who are seeking to do the best they can will choose, given their circumstances.

For now, we will say little more about this but indicate that the difference between these two types of tastes has something to do with how essential both goods are to the well-being of an individual. Take, for example, tastes for Coke and Pepsi. When we model such tastes, neither of the goods is in and of itself very essential since the consumer is indifferent between bundles that contain both goods and bundles that contain only one of the two goods. This is not true for the case of perfect complements such as coffee and sugar which we explored earlier. For this consumer, neither coffee nor sugar is of any use unless they have both in their consumption bundle. In that sense, we could say both goods are essential for their well-being, at least so long as our model assumes the consumer consumes only coffee and sugar.

More generally, suppose we compare the indifference map in panel (a) of Graph 5.6 to that in panel (b). In the first graph, the indifference curves converge to the vertical axis without touching it while they *intersect* the horizontal axis. Therefore, there are bundles that contain no quantity of good x_2 such as A and C that are just as good as bundles that contain both x_1 and x_2 such as B and D. In some sense, x_2 is therefore not as essential as x_1. In panel (b), on the other hand, bundles must always contain some of each good in order for the individual to be happier than they are without consuming anything at all at the origin. An individual is indifferent to any bundle that contains both goods like bundle E, *only if* the second bundle (like F) also contains some of both goods. In that sense, both goods are quite essential to the well-being of the individual.

Exercise 5A.7

True or False: Quasilinear goods are never essential.

Graph 5.6 x_2 is Essential in (b) But Not in (a)

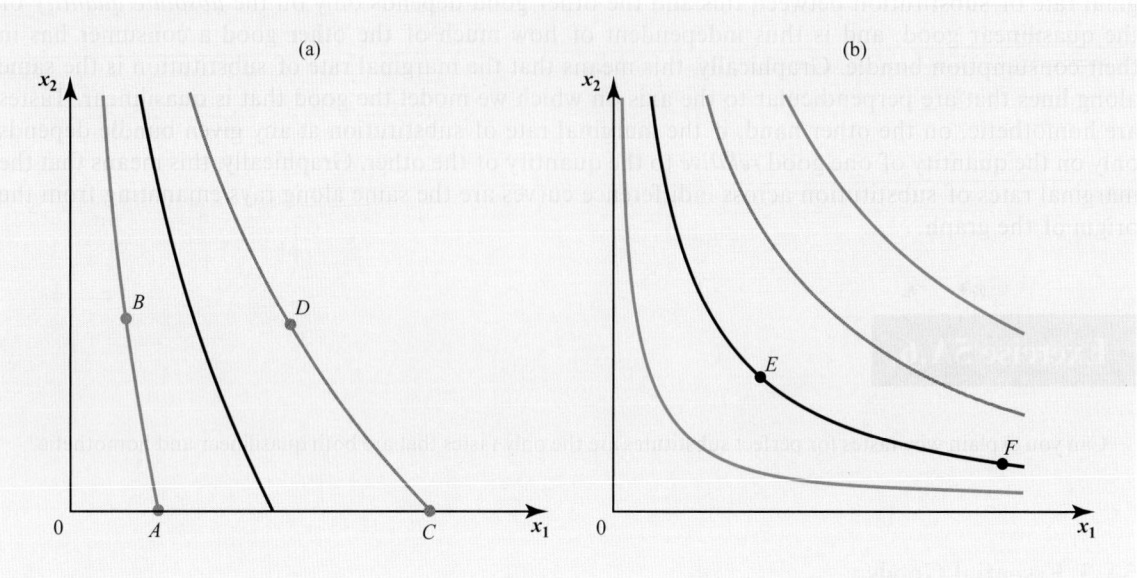

| 5B | Different Types of Utility Functions |

We now take the opportunity to introduce some common types of utility functions that generalize precisely the kinds of intuitive concepts we illustrated graphically in Section 5A.

5B.1 Degrees of Substitutability and the Elasticities of Substitution

In Section 5A.1, we described different shapes of indifference curves that imply different levels of substitutability. Tastes for Coke and Pepsi which indicated perfect substitutability between the two goods were illustrated with linear indifference curves in Graph 5.1. The opposite extreme of no substitutability was illustrated using sugar and coffee with L-shaped indifference curves in Graph 5.2. Less extreme indifference curves ranging from those that implied a relatively large degree of substitutability to a relatively small degree of substitutability were illustrated in a sequence of graphs in Graph 5.3. From this discussion, one quickly walks away with the sense that *the degree of substitutability is directly related to the speed with which the slope of an indifference curve changes as one moves along the indifference curve*. The slope, for instance, changes relatively slowly in panel (a) of Graph 5.3, where two goods are relatively substitutable, and much more quickly in panel (c) where goods are less substitutable.

What we referred to informally as the degree of substitutability in our discussion of these graphs is formalized mathematically through a concept known as the *elasticity of substitution*, a concept introduced independently in the early 1930s by two of the major economists of the 20th century, Sir John Hicks (1904–1989) and Joan Robinson (1903–1983). Hicks was awarded the Nobel Prize in Economics in 1972. *Elasticity* is a measure of responsiveness. We are attempting to formalize how quickly the bundle of goods on an indifference curve changes as the slope or marginal rate of substitution of that indifference curve changes; or, how responsive the bundle of goods along an indifference curve is to the changes in the marginal rate of substitution.

Consider, for instance, point A with marginal rate of substitution of -2 on the indifference curve graphed in panel (a) of Graph 5.7. In order for us to find a point B where the marginal rate of substitution is -1 instead of -2, we have to go from the initial bundle $(2,10)$ to the new bundle $(8,4)$.

In panel (b) of Graph 5.7, a similar change from an initial point A with marginal rate of substitution of -2 to a new point B with marginal rate of substitution of -1 implies a significantly smaller change in the bundle, taking us from $(2,10)$ to $(4,8)$. The ratio of x_2 over x_1 declines quickly from 5 to 1/2 in panel (a) as the marginal rate of substitution falls in absolute value from 2 to 1, while it declines less rapidly from 5 to 2 in panel (b) for the same change in the marginal rate of substitution.

Graph 5.7 Degrees of Substitutability and Marginal Rates of Substitution

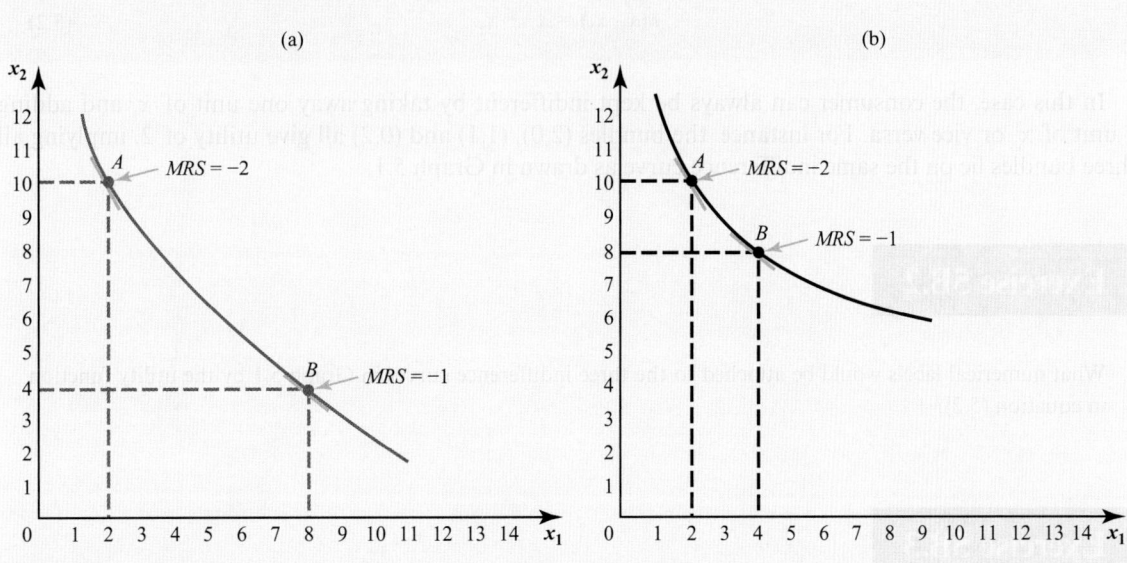

Economists have developed a mathematical way to give expression to the intuition that the degree of substitutability between two goods is related to the speed with which the ratio of the two goods along an indifference curve changes as the marginal rate of substitution changes. This is done by defining the *elasticity of substitution* (denoted by σ – the Greek letter sigma) at a particular bundle of two consumption goods as *the percentage change in the ratio of those two goods that results from a 1 per cent change in the marginal rate of substitution along the indifference curve that contains the bundle*, or, put mathematically:

$$\text{Elasticity of substitution} = \sigma = \left| \frac{\%\Delta(x_2/x_1)}{\%\Delta MRS} \right|. \tag{5.1}$$

where the Greek letter delta (Δ) means 'change'. The percentage change of a variable is the change of the variable divided by the original level of that variable. For instance, if the ratio of the two goods changes from 5 to 1/2 as it does in panel (a) of Graph 5.7, the percentage change in the ratio is given by $-4.5/5$ or -0.9. Similarly, the $\%\Delta MRS$ in panel (a) of Graph 5.7 is 0.5. Dividing -0.9 by 0.5 gives an elasticity of substitution of -1.8 or 1.8 in absolute value. This figure is only approximate because the formula in equation (5.1) evaluates the elasticity of substitution precisely at a point when the changes are very small. The calculus version of the elasticity formula is treated explicitly in the appendix to this chapter.

Exercise 5B.1

Calculate the same approximate elasticity of substitution for the indifference curve in panel (b) of Graph 5.7.

Our definitions of perfect complements and perfect substitutes give rise to extreme values of zero and infinity for this elasticity of substitution, while tastes that lie in between these extremes are associated with values somewhere in between these extreme values.

5B.1.1 Perfect Substitutes The case of perfect substitutes illustrated by the example of Coke and Pepsi in Section 5A.1.1, is one where an additional unit of x_1 a can of Coke, always adds exactly the same amount to happiness as an additional unit of x_2, a can of Pepsi. A way of expressing such tastes in terms of a utility function is to write the utility function as:

$$u(x_1, x_2) = x_1 + x_2. \tag{5.2}$$

In this case, the consumer can always be kept indifferent by taking away one unit of x_1 and adding 1 unit of x_2 or vice versa. For instance, the bundles (2,0), (1,1) and (0,2) all give utility of 2, implying all three bundles lie on the same indifference curve as drawn in Graph 5.1.

Exercise 5B.2

What numerical labels would be attached to the three indifference curves in Graph 5.1 by the utility function in equation (5.2)?

Exercise 5B.3

Suppose you measured Coke in 330ml cans and Pepsi in 165ml cans. Draw indifference curves and find the simplest possible utility function that would give rise to those indifference curves.

Intuitively, it can be seen that the elasticity of substitution in this case is infinity (∞). This is easiest to see if we think of an indifference map that is close to perfect substitutes, such as the indifference map in panel (a) of Graph 5.8 in which indifference curves are almost linear. Beginning at point A, even the very small percentage change in the MRS that gets us to point B is accompanied by a very large change in the ratio of the consumption goods. Considering this in light of equation 5.1, we get an elasticity of substitution that is determined by a large numerator divided by a very small denominator, giving a large value for the elasticity. The closer this indifference map comes to being linear, the larger will be the numerator and the smaller will be the denominator, thus causing the elasticity of substitution to approach ∞ as the indifference map approaches that of perfect substitutes.

Exercise 5B.4

Can you use similar reasoning to determine the elasticity of substitution for the utility function derived in exercise 5B.3?

5B.1.2 Perfect Complements We can also arrive at a utility function that represents the L-shaped indifference curves for goods that represent perfect complements. Since the two goods are of use only when consumed together, happiness from such goods is determined by whichever of the two goods the consumer has less of. For instance, if a consumer has 3 cups of coffee but only 2 packs of sugar, they are just as happy with any other combination of coffee and sugar that contains exactly two units of one of the goods and at least two units of the other. For any bundle, happiness is therefore determined by the smaller quantity of the two goods in the bundle, or:

$$u(x_1, x_2) = \min\{x_1, x_2\}. \tag{5.3}$$

Graph 5.8 Degrees of Substitutability and the Elasticities of Substitution

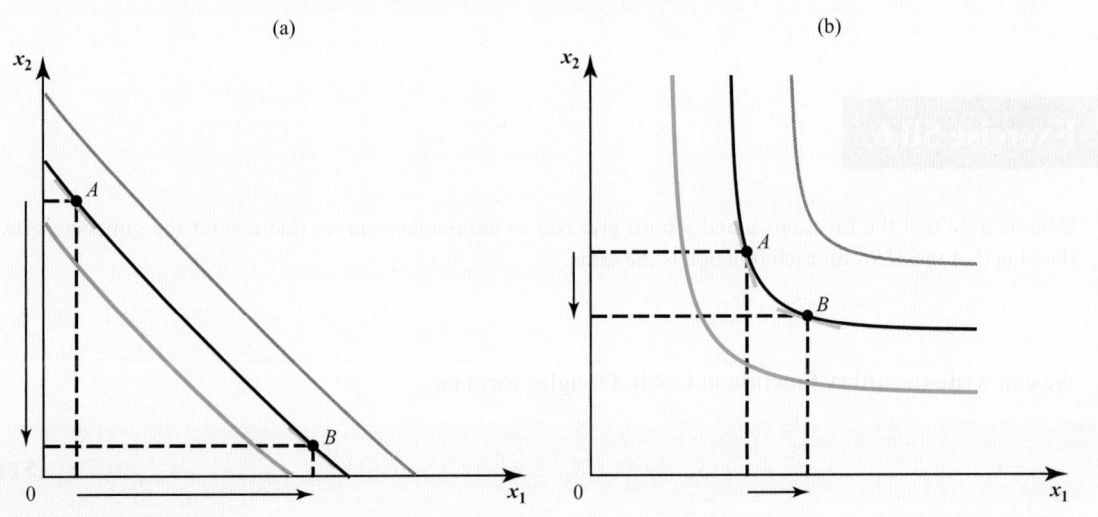

Exercise 5B.5

Substitute the bundles (3,1), (2,1), (1,1), (1,2) and (1,3) into utility function (5.3) and verify that each is shown to give the same utility, thus lying on the same indifference curve as plotted in Graph 5.2. What numerical labels does this indifference curve attach to each of the three indifference curves in Graph 5.2?

Intuition suggests that the elasticity of substitution for goods that are perfect complements will be zero. As in the case of perfect substitutes, this is easiest to see if we begin by considering an indifference map that is close to one representing perfect complements, such as the indifference map drawn in panel (b) of Graph 5.8. Beginning at point A, even the very large percentage change in the MRS that gets us to point B, implies a small percentage change in the ratio of the inputs. Considering this in light of equation 5.1, this implies a small numerator divided by a large denominator, giving a small number for the elasticity of substitution. As this map comes closer and closer to one that represents perfect complements, the numerator becomes smaller and the denominator rises. This leads to an elasticity of substitution that approaches zero as the indifference map approaches that of perfect complements.

5B.1.3 The Cobb–Douglas Function Probably the most widely used utility function in economics is one that gives rise to indifference curves that lie between the extremes of perfect substitutes and perfect complements and that, as we will see, exhibits an elasticity of substitution of 1. It is known as the *Cobb–Douglas* utility function and takes the form:

$$u(x_1, x_2) = x_1^\gamma x_2^\delta \text{ where } \gamma > 0, \delta > 0. \tag{5.4}$$

While the exponents in the Cobb–Douglas function can in principle take any positive values, they are often restricted to exponents that sum to 1. We know from Chapter 4 that we can transform utility functions without changing the underlying indifference map; restricting the exponents to sum to 1 turns out to be no restriction at all. We can, for instance, transform the function u by taking it to the power $1/(\gamma + \delta)$ to get

$$(u(x_1, x_2))^{1/(\gamma+\delta)} = (x_1^\gamma x_2^\gamma)^{1/(\gamma+\delta)} = x_1^{\gamma/(\gamma+\delta)}x_2^{\delta/(\gamma+\delta)} =$$
$$= x_1^\alpha x_2^{(1-\alpha)} \text{(where } \alpha = \gamma/(\gamma+\delta)) =$$
$$= v(x_1, x_2). \tag{5.5}$$

Exercise 5B.6

Demonstrate that the functions u and v both give rise to indifference curves that exhibit the same shape by showing that the MRS for each function is the same.

We can write the utility function in Cobb–Douglas form as:

$$u(x_1, x_2) = x_1^\alpha x_2^{(1-\alpha)} \text{ where } 0 < \alpha < 1. \tag{5.6}$$

In the n-good case, the Cobb–Douglas form extends to:

$$u(x_1, x_2, \ldots, x_n) = x_1^{\alpha_1}x_2^{\alpha_2})\ldots x_n^{\alpha_n} \text{ with } \alpha_1 + \alpha_2 + \cdots + \alpha + \alpha_n = 1. \tag{5.7}$$

We will show in the next section that this Cobb–Douglas function is just a special case of a more general functional form, the special case in which the elasticity of substitution is equal to 1 everywhere. Before doing so, however, we can get some intuition about the variety of tastes that can be represented through Cobb–Douglas functions by illustrating how these functions change as α changes in equation 5.6. The series of graphs in Graph 5.9 provide some examples.

While each of these graphs belongs to the family of Cobb–Douglas utility functions, and thus each represents tastes with elasticity of substitution of 1, you can see how Cobb–Douglas tastes can indeed cover many different types of indifference maps. When $\alpha = 0.5$ as in panel (b) of Graph 5.9, the function places equal weight on x_1 and x_2, resulting in an indifference map that is symmetric around the 45-degree line. Since the two goods enter the utility function symmetrically, the portions of indifference curves that lie below the 45-degree line are mirror images of the corresponding portions that lie above the 45-degree line. This implies that the MRS on the 45-degree line must be equal to -1; when individuals with such tastes have equal quantities of both goods, they are willing to trade them one-for-one.

When $\alpha \neq 0.5$, on the other hand, the two goods do not enter the utility function symmetrically, and so the symmetry around the 45-degree line is lost. If $\alpha > 0.5$ as in panel (c) of Graph 5.9, relatively more weight is put on x_1. Thus, if a consumer with such tastes has equal quantities of x_1 and x_2, they are not willing to trade them one-for-one. Rather, since x_1 plays a more prominent role in the utility function, the consumer would demand more than 1 unit of x_2 to give up 1 unit of x_1 when they start with an equal number of each, i.e. on the 45-degree line, implying an MRS greater than 1 in absolute value along the 45-degree line. As α increases above 0.5, the points where MRS $= -1$, therefore, fall below the 45-degree line. The reverse is, of course, true as α falls below 0.5 when more emphasis is placed on x_2 rather than x_1, as in panel (a) of Graph 5.9.

Graph 5.9 Different Cobb–Douglas Utility Functions

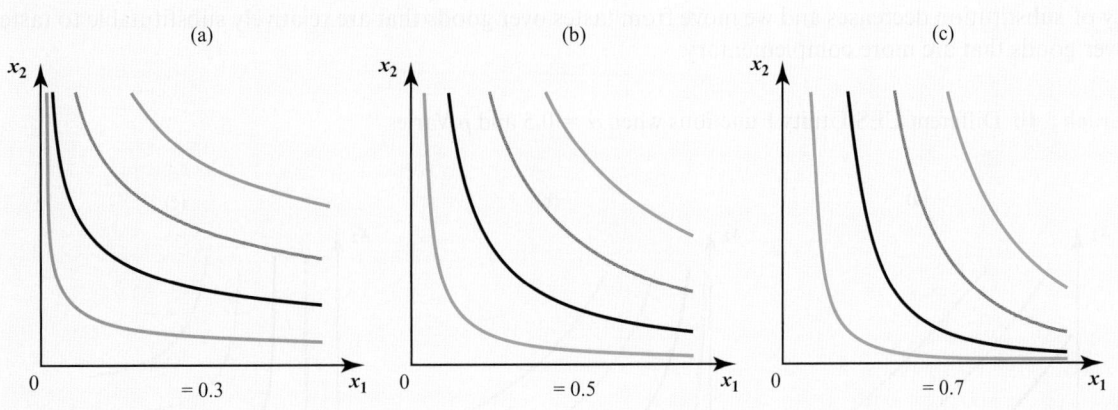

Exercise 5B.7

Derive the *MRS* for the Cobb–Douglas utility function and use it to show what happens to the slope of indifference curves along the 45-degree line as α changes.

5B.1.4 A More General Model: Constant Elasticity of Substitution (CES) Utility So far, we have explored the extremes of perfect substitutes with elasticity of substitution of ∞ and perfect complements with elasticity of substitution of 0, and we have identified the Cobb–Douglas case, which lies in between with an elasticity of substitution of 1. There exist other in-between cases where the elasticity of substitution lies between 0 and 1 or between 1 and ∞. Economists have identified a more general utility function that can capture all of these, including the cases of perfect substitutes, Cobb–Douglas tastes and perfect complements. All utility functions that take this form have one thing in common: the elasticity of substitution is the same at all bundles, and it is for this reason that these functions are called *constant elasticity of substitution utility functions* or just *CES utility functions*.

For bundles that contain two goods, these functions take on the following form:

$$u(x_1, x_2) = (\alpha x_1^{-\rho} + (1 - \alpha)x_2^{-\rho})^{-1/\rho},\tag{5.8}$$

where $0 < \alpha < 1$ and $-1 \le \rho \le \infty$.

It is mathematically intensive to derive explicitly the formula for an elasticity of substitution for utility functions that take this form; if you are curious, you can follow this derivation in the appendix. As it turns out, however, the elasticity of substitution σ takes on the following form for this CES function:

$$\sigma = 1/(1 + \rho).\tag{5.9}$$

Thus, as ρ gets close to ∞, the elasticity of substitution approaches 0, implying that the underlying indifference curves approach those of perfect complements. If, on the other hand, ρ gets close to -1, the elasticity approaches ∞, implying that the underlying indifference curves approach those of perfect substitutes. Thus, as the parameter ρ moves from -1 to ∞, the underlying indifference map changes from that of perfect substitutes to perfect complements. This is illustrated graphically in Graph 5.10 for the case where α is set to 0.5. As we move left across the three panels of the graph, ρ increases, which implies the elasticity of substitution decreases and we move from tastes over goods that are relatively substitutable to tastes over goods that are more complementary.

Graph 5.10 Different CES Utility Functions when $\alpha = 0.5$ and ρ Varies

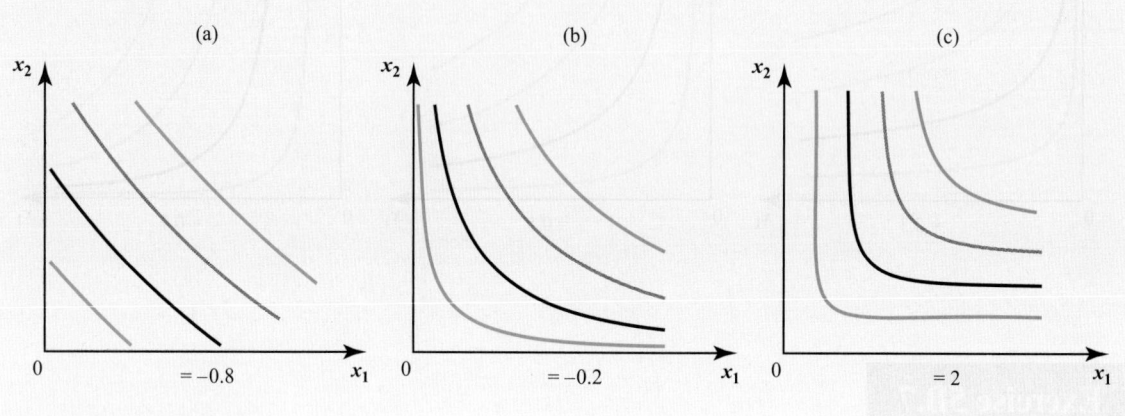

Exercise 5B.8

What is the elasticity of substitution in each panel of Graph 5.10?

The best way to see how the CES function gives rise to different indifference maps is to derive its marginal rate of substitution; that is:

$$
\begin{aligned}
MRS &= -\frac{\partial u/\partial x_1}{\partial u/\partial x_2} \\
&= -\frac{(\alpha x_1^{-\rho} + (1-\alpha)x_2^{-\rho})^{-(\rho+1)/\rho}\alpha x_2^{-(\rho+1)}}{(\alpha x_1^{-\rho} + (1-\alpha)x_2^{-\rho})^{-(\rho+1)/\rho}(1-\alpha)x_2^{-(\rho+1)}} \\
&= -\frac{\alpha x_1^{-(\rho+1)}}{(1-\alpha)x_2^{-(\rho+1)}} = -\left(\frac{\alpha}{1-\alpha}\right)\left(\frac{x_2}{x_1}\right)^{\rho+1}
\end{aligned}
\tag{5.10}
$$

Note, for instance, what happens when $\rho = -1$: The absolute value of the MRS becomes $\alpha/(1-\alpha)$ and no longer depends on the bundle (x_1, x_2). When $\rho = -1$, the slopes of indifference curves are just straight parallel lines indicating that the consumer is willing to substitute perfectly $\alpha/(1-\alpha)$ of x_2 for one more unit of x_1 regardless of how many of each of the two goods the consumer currently has.

We have also indicated that the Cobb–Douglas utility function $u(x_2, x_2) = x_1^{\alpha}x_2^{(1-\alpha)}$ represents a special case of the CES utility function. To see this, consider the MRS for the Cobb–Douglas function, which is:

$$
MRS = -\frac{\partial u/\partial x_1}{\partial u/\partial x_2} = -\frac{\alpha x_1^{(\alpha-1)}x_2^{(1-\alpha)}}{(1-\alpha)x_1^{\alpha}x_2^{-\alpha}} = -\left(\frac{\alpha}{1-\alpha}\right)\left(\frac{x_2}{x_1}\right).
\tag{5.11}
$$

Note that the MRS from the CES function in equation 5.11 reduces to the MRS from the Cobb–Douglas function in equation 5.12 when $\rho = 0$. Thus, when $\rho = 0$, the indifference curves of the CES function take on the same shapes as the indifference curves of the Cobb–Douglas function, implying that the two functions represent exactly the same tastes. This is not easy to see by comparing the actual CES function to the Cobb–Douglas function, because the CES function ceases to be well defined at $\rho = 0$ when the exponent $-1/\rho$ is undefined. By deriving the respective marginal rates of substitution for the two functions, we can see how the CES function in fact does *approach* the Cobb–Douglas function as ρ approaches zero.

Finally, since we know that the elasticity of substitution for the CES utility function is $\sigma = 1/(1 + \rho)$, we know that $\sigma = 1$ when $\rho = 0$. This implies that the elasticity of substitution of the Cobb–Douglas utility function is 1 as we had foreshadowed in our introduction to the Cobb–Douglas function.

Exercise 5B.9*

Can you describe what happens to the slopes of the indifference curves on the 45-degree line, above the 45-degree line and below the 45-degree line as ρ becomes large and as the elasticity of substitution therefore becomes small?

5B.2 Some Common Indifference Maps We now turn towards exploring two special cases of indifference maps: those defined as homothetic and those defined as quasilinear in Section 5A.2.

5B.2.1 Homothetic Tastes and Homogeneous Utility Functions Recall that we defined tastes as homothetic whenever the indifference map has the property that the marginal rate of substitution at a particular bundle depends only on how much of one good *relative* to the other is contained in that bundle. The *MRS* of homothetic tastes is the same along any ray emanating from the origin of our graphs, implying that whenever we increase each of the goods in a particular bundle by the same proportion, the *MRS* will remain unchanged.

Consider, for instance, tastes that can be represented by the Cobb–Douglas utility function in equation 5.6. The *MRS* implied by this function is $-\alpha x_2/(1 - \alpha)x_1$. Suppose we begin at a particular bundle (x_1, x_2) and increase the quantity of each of the goods in the bundle by a factor t to get to the bundle (tx_1, tx_2) that lies on a ray from the origin that also contains (x_1, x_2). This implies that the new *MRS* is $-\alpha tx_2/(1 - \alpha)tx_1$, but this reduces to $-\alpha x_2/(1 - \alpha)x_1$ since the t appears in both the numerator and the denominator and thus cancels out. Cobb–Douglas utility functions therefore represent homothetic tastes because the *MRS* is unchanged along a ray from the origin.

More generally, homothetic tastes can be represented by any utility function that has the mathematical property of being *homogeneous*. A function $f(x_1, x_2)$ is defined as being *homogeneous of degree k* if and only if:

$$f(tx_1, tx_2) = t^k f(x_1, x_2).\tag{5.12}$$

For instance, the Cobb–Douglas function is homogeneous of degree $(\gamma + \delta)$ because:

$$u(tx_1, tx_2) = (tx_1)^\gamma(tx_2)^\delta = t^{(\gamma+\delta)}x_1^\gamma x_2^\delta = t^{(\gamma+\delta)}u(x_1, x_2).\tag{5.13}$$

Exercise 5B.10

Show that when we normalize the exponents of the Cobb–Douglas utility function to sum to 1, the function is homogeneous of degree 1.

Exercise 5B.11

Consider the following variant of the CES function that will play an important role in producer theory: $f(x_1, x_2) = (\alpha x_1^{-\rho} + (1 - \alpha)x_2^{-\rho})^{-\beta/\rho}$. Show that this function is homogeneous of degree β.

We can see how *homogeneous utility functions must represent homothetic tastes*. Suppose $u(x_1, x_2)$ is homogeneous of degree k. The *MRS* at a bundle (tx_1, tx_2) is:

$$MRS(tx_1, tx_2) = -\frac{\partial u(tx_1, tx_2)/\partial x_1}{\partial u(tx_1, tx_2)/\partial x_2} = -\frac{\partial(t^k u(x_1, x_2))/\partial x_1}{\partial(t^k u(x_1, x_2))/\partial x_2} =$$

$$= -\frac{t^k \partial u(x_1, x_2)/\partial x_1}{t^k \partial u(x_1, x_2)/\partial x_2} = -\frac{\partial u(x_1, x_2)/\partial x_1}{\partial u(x_1, x_2))/\partial x_2} = \qquad (5.14)$$

$$= MRS(x_1, x_2).$$

In this derivation, we use the definition of a homogeneous function in the first line in 5.15, and are then able to take the t^k term outside the partial derivative since it is not a function of x_1 or x_2. Finally, we can cancel the t^k that now appears in both the numerator and the denominator to end up at the definition of the *MRS* at bundle (x_1, x_2). Thus, the *MRS* is the same when we increase each good in a bundle by the same proportion t, implying that the underlying tastes are homothetic.

Furthermore, *any function that is homogeneous of degree k can be transformed into a function that is homogeneous of degree 1 by taking that function to the power $(1/k)$*. We already showed in equation 5.5, for instance, that we can transform the Cobb–Douglas utility function $u(x_1, x_2) = x_1^\gamma x_2^\delta$, which is homogeneous of degree $(\gamma + \delta)$, into a utility function that is homogeneous of degree 1 taking the form $v(x_1, x_2) = x_1^\alpha x_2^{(1-\alpha)}$ by taking it to the power $1/(\gamma + \delta)$.

Exercise 5B.12

Can you demonstrate, using the definition of a homogeneous function, that it is generally possible to transform a function that is homogeneous of degree k to one that is homogeneous of degree 1 in the way suggested?

We can conclude that homothetic tastes *can always be represented* by utility functions that are homogeneous, and since homogeneous functions can always be transformed into functions that are homogeneous of degree 1 without altering the underlying indifference curves, we can also conclude that *homothetic tastes can always be represented by utility functions that are homogeneous of degree 1*. Even if a utility function is *not* homogeneous, however, it might still represent homothetic tastes because it is possible to transform a homogeneous function into a non-homogeneous function by, for example, adding a constant term. The function $w(x_1, x_2) = x_1^\alpha x_2^{(1-\alpha)} + 5$, for example, has the same indifference curves as the utility function $u(x_1, x_2) = x_1^\alpha x_2^{(1-\alpha)}$, but w is not homogeneous whereas u is. Given that utility functions are only tools we use to represent tastes (indifference curves), *there is no reason to use non-homogeneous utility functions when we want to model homothetic tastes because no economic content is lost if we simply use utility functions that are homogeneous of degree 1 to model such tastes*.

Many commonly used utility functions are, however, homogeneous and thus represent homothetic tastes, including *all* CES functions we defined in the previous sections.

5B.2.2 Quasilinear Tastes In Section 5A.2.2, we defined tastes as quasilinear in good x_1 *whenever the indifference map has the property that the marginal rate of substitution at a particular bundle depends only on how much of x_1 that bundle contains and thus NOT on how much of x_2 it contains.* Formally, this means that the marginal rate of substitution is a function of only x_1 and not x_2. This is generally not the case. For instance, we derived the *MRS* for a Cobb–Douglas utility function $u(x_1,x_2) = x_1^\alpha x_2^{(1-\alpha)}$ to be $-\alpha x_2/((1-\alpha)x_1)$. Thus, for tastes that can be represented by Cobb–Douglas utility functions, the marginal rate of substitution is a function of both x_1 and x_2, which allows us to conclude immediately that such tastes are not quasilinear in either good.

Consider, however, the class of utility functions that can be written as:

$$u(x_1, x_2) = v(x_1) + x_2, \tag{5.15}$$

where $v: \mathbb{R}_+ \to \mathbb{R}$ is a function of only the level of consumption of good x_1.

The partial derivative of u with respect to x_1 is equal to the derivative of v with respect to x_1, and the partial derivative of u with respect to x_2 is equal to 1. Thus, the marginal rate of substitution implied by this utility function is:

$$MRS = -\frac{\partial u/\partial x_1}{\partial u/\partial x_2} = -\frac{dv}{dx_1}, \tag{5.16}$$

which is a function of x_1 but *NOT* of x_2. We will refer to tastes that can be represented by utility functions of the form given in expression 5.16 as *quasilinear in x_1*. While some advanced textbooks refer to the good x_2 that enters the utility function linearly as the quasilinear good, we are using the term differently here, referring to the good x_1 as the quasilinear good. This convention will make it much easier for us to discuss economically important forces in later chapters.

The simplest possible form of equation 5.16 arises when $v(x_1) = x_1$. This implies $u(x_1, x_2) = x_1 + x_2$, the equation we derived in Section 5B.1.1 as representing perfect substitutes. The function v can, however, take on a variety of other forms, giving utility functions that represent quasilinear tastes that do not have linear indifference curves. The indifference curves in Graph 5.11, for instance, are derived from the function $u(x_1,x_2) = \alpha \ln x_1 + x_2$, and α varies as is indicated in the panels of the graph.

Graph 5.11 The Quasilinear Utility Functions $u(x_1, x_2) = \alpha \ln x_1 + x_2$

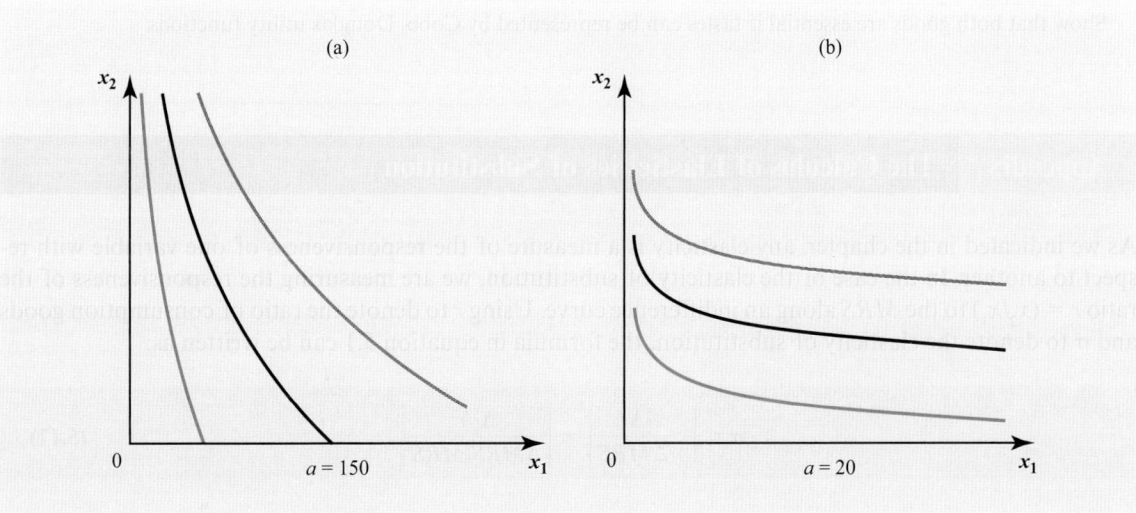

5B.2.3 Homothetic Versus Quasilinear Tastes It can be seen from these graphs of quasilinear tastes that, *in general, quasilinear tastes are not homothetic* because the *MRS* is constant along any vertical line and thus generally not along a ray emanating from the origin. The same intuition arises from our mathematical formulation of utility functions that represent quasilinear tastes. In equation 5.17, we demonstrated that the *MRS* implied by 5.16 is $-(dv/dx_1)$. In order for tastes to be homothetic, the *MRS* evaluated at (tx_1, tx_2) would have to be the same as the *MRS* evaluated at (x_1, x_2), which implies $dv(tx_1)/dx_1$ would have to be equal to $dv(x_1)/dx_1$. The only way that can be true is if v is a linear function of x_1 where x_1 drops out when we take the derivative of v with respect to x_1.

Thus, if $v(x_1) = \alpha x_1$ where α is a real number, the marginal rate of substitution implied by 5.16 is just α, implying that the *MRS* is the same for all values of x_1 regardless of the value of x_2. This means that indifference curves are straight lines, as in the case of perfect substitutes. Perfect substitutes therefore represent the only quasilinear tastes that are also homothetic.

5B.3 Essential Goods

A final distinction between indifference maps that we made in Section 5A is between those that contain essential goods and those in which some goods are not essential. We defined a good as essential if some consumption of that good was required in order for an individual to achieve greater utility than they would by consuming nothing at all, and we concluded that goods are essential so long as indifference curves do not intersect the axis on which those goods are measured. From our various graphs of CES utility functions, it can be seen that most of these functions implicitly assume that all goods are essential, with the exception of perfect substitutes. From our graphs of quasilinear utility functions, on the other hand, we can easily see that such functions implicitly assume that goods are not essential. This distinction will become important in our discussion in the next chapter.

Exercise 5B.13

Use the mathematical expression for quasilinear tastes to illustrate that neither good is essential if tastes are quasilinear in one of the goods.

Exercise 5B.14

Show that both goods are essential if tastes can be represented by Cobb–Douglas utility functions.

Appendix | The Calculus of Elasticities of Substitution

As we indicated in the chapter, any elasticity is a measure of the responsiveness of one variable with respect to another. In the case of the elasticity of substitution, we are measuring the responsiveness of the ratio $r = (x_2/x_1)$ to the *MRS* along an indifference curve. Using r to denote the ratio of consumption goods and σ to denote the elasticity of substitution, the formula in equation 5.1 can be written as:

$$\sigma = \left| \frac{\%\Delta r}{\%\Delta MRS} \right| = \left| \frac{\Delta r/r}{\Delta MRS/MRS} \right|. \tag{5.17}$$

Expressing this for small changes in calculus notation, we can rewrite this as:

$$\sigma = \left| \frac{dr/r}{dMRS/MRS} \right| = \left| \frac{MRS}{r} \frac{dr}{dMRS} \right|. \tag{5.18}$$

Calculating such elasticities is often easiest using the *logarithmic derivative*. To derive this, note that:

$$d \ln r = \frac{1}{r} dr \text{ and}$$
$$d \ln |MRS| = \frac{1}{MRS} dMRS, \tag{5.19}$$

where we have placed *MRS* in absolute values in order for the logarithm to exist. Dividing these by each other, we get:

$$\frac{d \ln r}{d \ln |MRS|} = \frac{MRS}{r} \frac{dr}{dMRS} \tag{5.20}$$

which, aside from the absolute values, is equivalent to the expression for σ in equation 5.19. Expanding out the *r* term, we can write the elasticity of substitution as:

$$\sigma = \frac{d \ln (x_2/x_1)}{d \ln |MRS|}. \tag{5.21}$$

You can now see more directly why the elasticity of substitution of the CES utility function is indeed $1/(1 + \rho)$. We already calculated in equation 5.11 that the *MRS* of the CES function is $-(\alpha/(1 - \alpha))(x_2/x_1)^{\rho+1}$. Taking absolute values and solving for (x_2/x_1), we get:

$$\frac{x_2}{x_1} = \left(\frac{(1 - \alpha)}{\alpha} |MRS| \right)^{\frac{1}{1 + \rho}}, \tag{5.22}$$

and taking logs,

$$\ln \frac{x_2}{x_1} = \frac{1}{1 + \rho} \ln |MRS| + \frac{1}{1 + \rho} \ln \left(\frac{(1 - \alpha)}{\alpha} \right). \tag{5.23}$$

We can apply equation (5.22) to get:

$$\sigma = \frac{1}{1 + \rho}. \tag{5.24}$$

Exercise 5B.15*

Can you demonstrate similarly that $\sigma = 1$ for the Cobb–Douglas utility function $u(x_1, x_2) = x_1^{\alpha} x_2^{(1-\alpha)}$?

End-of-Chapter Exercises

5.1† Consider your tastes for right and left shoes.

   A. Suppose you, like most of us, are the kind of person who expects a pair of shoes to be designed to fit your right foot and your left foot and would never wear a left shoe on your right foot or a right shoe on your left foot, neither would you ever choose not to wear shoes on just one of your feet.

   a. In a graph with the number of right shoes on the horizontal axis and the number of left shoes on the vertical, illustrate three indifference curves that are part of your indifference map.

   b. Now suppose you hurt your left leg and have to wear a cast which means you cannot wear shoes on your left foot for six months. Illustrate how the indifference curves you have drawn would change for this period. Can you think of why goods such as left shoes in this case are called *neutral goods*?

   c. Suppose you hurt your right foot instead. How would this change your answer to part (b).

   d. Are any of the tastes you have graphed homothetic? Are any quasilinear?

   e. In the three different tastes that you graphed, are any of the goods ever essential? Are any not essential?

   B. Continue with the description of your tastes given in part A and let x_1 represent right shoes and let x_2 represent left shoes.

   a. Write down a utility function that represents your tastes as illustrated in A(a). Can you think of a second utility function that also represents these tastes?

   b. Write down a utility function that represents your tastes as graphed in A(b).

   c. Write down a utility function that represents your tastes as drawn in A(c).

   d. Can any of the tastes you have graphed in part A be represented by a utility function that is homogeneous of degree 1? If so, can they also be represented by a utility function that is not homogeneous?

   e. Recall the concepts of strong monotonicity, weak monotonicity and local non-satiation. Which of these is/are satisfied by the tastes you have graphed in this exercise?

   f. Recall the concepts of strong convexity and weak convexity. Which of these is/are satisfied by the tastes you have graphed in this exercise?

5.2 Consider your tastes for €5 notes and €10 notes.

   A. Suppose that all you care about is how much money you have, but you don't care whether a particular amount comes in more or fewer notes and suppose that you could have partial €10 and €5 notes.

   a. With the number of €5 notes on the horizontal axis and the number of €10 notes on the vertical, illustrate three indifference curves from your indifference map.

   b. What is your marginal rate of substitution of €10 notes for €5 notes?

   c. What is the marginal rate of substitution of €5 notes for €10 notes?

   d. Are averages strictly better than extremes? How does this relate to whether your tastes exhibit diminishing marginal rates of substitution?

   e. Are these tastes homothetic? Are they quasilinear?

   f. Are either of the goods on your axes essential?

   B. Continue with the assumption that you care only about the total amount of money in your pocket, and let €5 notes be denoted x_1 and €10 notes be denoted x_2.

   a. Write down a utility function that represents the tastes you graphed in A(a). Can you think of a second utility function that also represents these tastes?

   b. Calculate the marginal rate of substitution from the utility functions you wrote down in B(a) and compare it to your intuitive answer in A(b).

   c. Can these tastes be represented by a utility function that is homogeneous of degree 1? If so, can they also be represented by a utility function that is not homogeneous?

   d. Recall the concepts of strong monotonicity, weak monotonicity and local non-satiation. Which of these is/are satisfied by the tastes you have graphed in this exercise?

e. Recall the concepts of strong convexity and weak convexity. Which of these is/are satisfied by the tastes you have graphed in this exercise?

5.3† Suppose two people want to see if they could benefit from trading with one another in a two-good world.

A. In each of the following cases, determine whether trade might benefit the individuals:

a. As soon as they start talking to one another, they find that they own exactly the same amount of each good as the other does.

b. They discover that they are long-lost twins who have identical tastes.

c. The two goods are perfect substitutes for each of them, with the same *MRS* within and across their indifference maps.

d. They have the same tastes and own different bundles of goods, but are currently located on the same indifference curve.

B. *Suppose that the two individuals have CES utility functions, with individual 1's utility given by $u(x_1, x_2) = (\alpha x_1^{-\rho} + (1 - \alpha)x_2^{-\rho})^{-1/\rho}$ and individual 2's by $v(x_1, x_2) = (\beta x_1^{-\rho} + (1-\beta)x_2^{-\rho})^{-1/\rho}$.

a. For what values of α, β and ρ is it the case that owning the same bundle will always imply that there are no gains from trade for the two individuals?

b. Suppose $\alpha = \beta$ and the two individuals therefore share the same preferences. For what values of $\alpha = \beta$ and ρ is it the case that the two individuals are not able to gain from trade regardless of what current bundles they own?

c. Suppose that person 1 owns twice as much of all goods as person 2. What has to be true about α, β and ρ for them not to be able to trade?

5.4 **Everyday Application:** *Thinking About Old Age.* Consider two individuals who each take a very different view of life, and consider how this shapes their tastes over intertemporal trade-offs.

A. Jess is a 25-year-old athlete who derives most of her pleasure in life from expensive and physically intense activities: mountain climbing in the Himalayas, kayaking in the Amazon, bungee jumping in New Zealand, lion safaris in Africa and skiing in the Alps. She does not look forward to old age when she can no longer be as active and plans on getting as much out of life as early on as she can. Mike is quite different; he shuns physical activity but enjoys reading in comfortable surroundings. The more he reads, the more he wants to read and the more he wants to retreat to luxurious libraries in the comfort of his home. He looks forward to quiet years of retirement when he can do what he loves most.

a. Suppose both Jess and Mike are willing to perfectly substitute current for future consumption, but at different rates. Given the descriptions of them, draw two different indifference maps and indicate which is more likely to be Jess's and which is more likely to be Mike's.

b. Now suppose neither Jess nor Mike is willing to substitute at all across time periods. How would their indifference maps differ now given the descriptions of them provided?

c. Finally, suppose they both allowed for some substitutability across time periods but not as extreme as what you considered in part (a). Again, draw two indifference maps and indicate which refers to Jess and which to Mike.

d. Which of the indifference maps you have drawn could be homothetic?

e. Can you say for sure if the indifference maps of Jess and Mike in part (c) satisfy the single-crossing property?

B. Continue with the descriptions of Jess and Mike as given in part A and let c_1 represent consumption now and let c_2 represent consumption in retirement.

a. Suppose that Jess's and Mike's tastes can be represented by $u^J(c_1, c_2) = \alpha c_1 + c_2$ and $u^m(c_1, c_2) = \beta c_1 + c_2$, respectively. How does α compare with β; that is, which is larger?

b. How would you similarly differentiate, using a constant α for Jess and β for Mike, two utility functions that give rise to tastes as described in A(b)?

c. Now consider the case described in A(c), with their tastes now described by the Cobb–Douglas utility functions $u^J(c_1, c_2) = c_1^{\alpha}c_2^{(1-\alpha)}$ and $u^m(c_1,c_2) = c_1^{\beta}c_2^{(1-\beta)}$. How would α and β in those functions be related to one another?

    d. Are all the tastes described by the given utility functions homothetic? Are any of them quasilinear?

    e. Can you show that the tastes in B(c) satisfy the single-crossing property?

    f. Are all the functions in B(a)–(c) members of the family of CES utility functions?

5.5*† Consider the family of homothetic tastes.

  A. Recall that essential goods are goods that have to be present in positive quantities in a consumption bundle in order for the individual to get utility above what they would get by not consuming anything at all.

    a. Aside from the case of perfect substitutes, is it possible for neither good to be essential but tastes nevertheless to be homothetic? If so, can you give an example?

    b. Can there be homothetic tastes where one of the two goods is essential and the other is not? If so, give an example.

    c. Is it possible for tastes to be non-monotonic (less is better than more) but still homothetic?

    d. Is it possible for tastes to be monotonic (more is better), homothetic but strictly non-convex, i.e. averages are worse than extremes?

  B. Now relate the homotheticity property of indifference maps to utility functions.

    a. Aside from the case of perfect substitutes, are there any CES utility functions that represent tastes for goods that are not essential?

    b. All CES utility functions represent tastes that are homothetic. Is it also true that all homothetic indifference maps can be represented by a CES utility function? *Hint*: Consider your answer to A(a) and ask yourself, in light of your answer to B(a), if it can be represented by a CES function.

    c. *True or False*: The elasticity of substitution can be the same at all bundles only if the underlying tastes are homothetic.

    d. *True or False*: If tastes are homothetic, the elasticity of substitution is the same at all bundles.

    e. What is the simplest possible transformation of the CES utility function that can generate tastes that are homothetic but non-monotonic?

    f. Are the tastes represented by this transformed CES utility function convex?

    g. So far, we have always assumed that the parameter ρ in the CES utility function falls between -1 and ∞. Can you determine what indifference curves would look like when ρ is less than -1?

    h. Are such tastes convex? Are they monotonic?

    i. What is the simplest possible transformation of this utility function that would change both your answers to the previous question?

5.6* In this exercise, we are working with the concept of an elasticity of substitution. This concept was introduced in part B of the chapter. Thus, this entire question relates to material from part B, but the A part of the question can be done by knowing the formula for an elasticity of substitution while the B part of the question requires further material from part B of the chapter. In Section 5B.1, we defined the elasticity of substitution as:

$$\sigma = \left| \frac{\%\Delta(x_2/x_1)}{\%\Delta MRS} \right|. \tag{5.25}$$

  A. Suppose you consume only apples and oranges. Last month, you consumed bundle $A = (100,25)$, 100 apples and 25 oranges, and you were willing to trade at most 4 apples for every orange. Two months ago, oranges were in season and you consumed $B = (25,100)$ and you were willing to trade at most 4 oranges for 1 apple. Suppose your happiness was unchanged over the past two months.

    a. On a graph with apples on the horizontal axis and oranges on the vertical, illustrate the indifference curve on which you have been operating these past two months and label the *MRS* where you know it.

    b. Using the formula for elasticity of substitution, estimate your elasticity of substitution of apples for oranges.

    c. Suppose we know that the elasticity of substitution is the same at every bundle for you and is equal to what you calculated in (b). Suppose the bundle $C = (50, 50)$ is another bundle that makes you just as happy as bundles A and B. What is the *MRS* at bundle C?

d. Consider a bundle $D = (25,25)$. If your tastes are homothetic, what is the MRS at bundle C?

e. Suppose you are consuming 50 apples, you are willing to trade 4 apples for 1 orange, and you are just as happy as you were when you consumed at bundle D. How many oranges are you consuming assuming the same elasticity of substitution?

f. Call the bundle you derived in part (e) E. If the elasticity is as it was before, at what bundle would you be just as happy as at E but would be willing to trade 4 oranges for 1 apple?

B. Suppose your tastes can be summarized by the utility function $u(x_1,x_2) = (\alpha x_1^{-\rho} + (1 - \alpha)x_2^{-\rho})^{-1/\rho}$.

a. In order for these tastes to contain an indifference curve such as the one containing bundle A that you graphed in A(a), what must be the value of ρ? What about α?

b. Suppose you were told that the same tastes can be represented by $u(x_1,x_2) = x_1^{\gamma}x_2^{\delta}$. In light of your answer, is this possible? If so, what has to be true about γ and δ given the symmetry of the indifference curves on the two sides of the 45-degree line?

c. What exact value(s) do the exponents γ and δ take if the label on the indifference curve containing bundle A is 50? What if that label is 2500? What if the label is 6 250 000?

d. Verify that bundles A, B and C, as defined in part A, indeed lie on the same indifference curve when tastes are represented by the three different utility functions you implicitly derived in B(c). Which of these utility functions is homogeneous of degree 1? Which is homogeneous of degree 2? Is the third utility function also homogeneous?

e. What values do each of these utility functions assign to the indifference curve that contains bundle D?

f. *True or False*: Homogeneity of degree 1 implies that a doubling of goods in a consumption basket leads to twice the utility as measured by the homogeneous function, whereas homogeneity greater than 1 implies that a doubling of goods in a consumption bundle leads to more than twice the utility.

g. Demonstrate that the MRS is unchanged regardless of which of the three utility functions derived in B(c) is used.

h. Can you think of representing these tastes with a utility function that assigns the value of 100 to the indifference curve containing bundle A and 75 to the indifference curve containing bundle D? Is the utility function you derived homogeneous?

i. *True or False*: Homothetic tastes can always be represented by functions that are homogeneous of degree k, where k is greater than zero, but even functions that are not homogeneous can represent tastes that are homothetic.

j. *True or False*: The marginal rate of substitution is homogeneous of degree 0, if and only if, the underlying tastes are homothetic.

* conceptually challenging
† solutions in Study Guide

Chapter 6

Doing the Best We Can

We began our introduction of microeconomics with the premise that economic actors try to do the best they can given their circumstances. We now begin the analysis of how individuals in our basic model *optimize*; that is, how they would behave if they are indeed doing the best they can.

6A	Choice: Combining Economic Circumstances With Tastes

We begin by building some intuition about how tastes and choice sets interact to determine optimal choices. In the process, we'll get our first glimpse of the important role market prices play in helping us exploit all the potential *gains from trade* that would be difficult to realize in the absence of such prices. In Section 6A.2, we consider scenarios, referred to as *corner solutions*, under which individuals may choose not to purchase any quantity of a particular good. In Section 6A.3, we will uncover scenarios under which individuals may discover that more than one choice is optimal for them, scenarios that arise when either choice sets or tastes exhibit *non-convexities*.

6A.1 The Best Bundle of Hoodies and Jeans

Recall the story of going to a shop with €200 to spend on hoodies and jeans, with hoodies priced at €10 each and jeans priced at €20 per pair. We know from our work in Chapter 2 that in a graph with jeans on the horizontal axis and hoodies on the vertical, the budget constraint intersects at 20 on the vertical and at 10 on the horizontal. Its slope – the opportunity cost of one more pair of jeans in terms of how many hoodies have to be given up, is −2. Assume further that the marginal rate of substitution is equal to −2 at all bundles where the consumer has twice as many hoodies as jeans, that it is equal to −1 at bundles where they have an equal number of hoodies and jeans, and that it is equal to −1/2 at bundles where they have twice as many jeans as hoodies. This is an example of homothetic tastes. The budget constraint and choice set are graphed in panel (a) of Graph 6.1, and some of the indifference curves from the indifference map that represents the consumer's tastes are graphed in panel (b) of Graph 6.1. To determine which of the available choices is best given the consumer's circumstances, we now have to combine the information from both panels of Graph 6.1.

This is done in panel (c) of Graph 6.1 where panel (b) is laid on top of panel (a). Of the three indifference curves that are graphed, IC_1, IC_2 and IC_3, IC_3 contains only bundles that are not available to the consumer given their circumstances because the entire curve lies outside their choice set. The indifference curve, IC_1, has many bundles that fall within the consumer's choice set, but none of these is best for them because there are bundles in the shaded area to the northeast that all lie within their choice set and above this indifference curve, bundles that are better for someone with the consumer's tastes. We might think of them starting at some low indifference curve like IC_1, and pushing northeast to get to higher and higher indifference curves without leaving the choice set. This process would end at the indifference curve IC_2 in panel (c) of Graph 6.1, an indifference curve that contains 1 bundle that lies in the choice set (bundle A) with no bundles above the indifference curve that also lie in the choice set. Bundle A is the bundle the consumer would choose if they are trying to do the best they can given their circumstances. More precisely, they would consume 5 pairs of jeans and 10 hoodies at their optimal bundle A. This optimal bundle lies at the intersection of the budget line ($x_2 = 20 - 2x_1$) and the ray $x_2 = 2x_1$ representing all the points with MRS of -2. Solving these by substituting the second equation into the first gives us the answer $x_1 = 5$, and putting that into either of the two equations gives us $x_2 = 10$.

Graph 6.1 Graphical Optimization: Budget Constraint and Indifference Curves

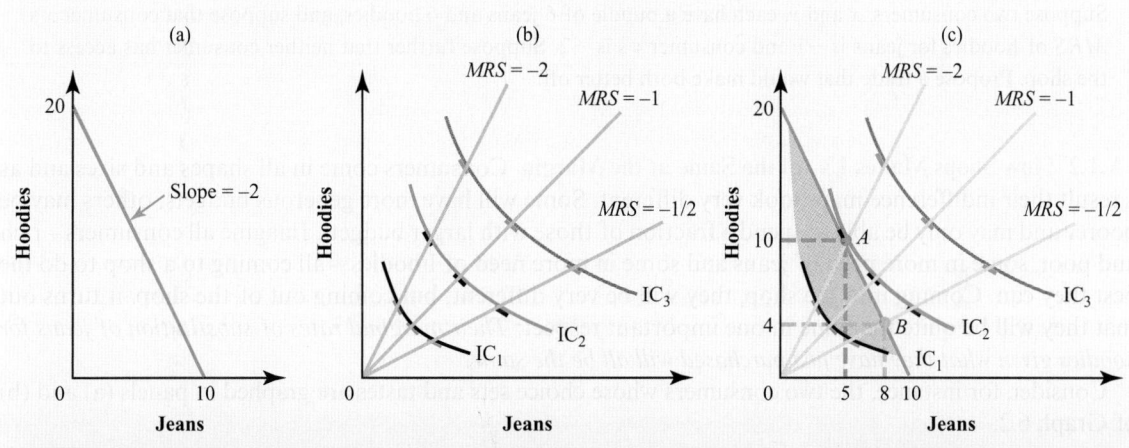

Go to MindTap to interact with this graph

Exercise 6A.1

Assume the consumer has a coupon that reduces the effective price of jeans to €10 per pair. Assuming the same tastes, what would be the consumer's best bundle?

6A.1.1 Opportunity Cost = Marginal Rate of Substitution At bundle A in panel (c) of Graph 6.1, a very particular relationship exists between the slope of the budget constraint and the slope of the indifference curve that contains bundle A: *The two slopes are equal.* This is no accident. The slope of the budget constraint represents the opportunity cost of jeans in terms of hoodies, which is the number of hoodies the consumer would *have* to give up to gain one more pair of jeans given the prices for jeans and hoodies. The slope of the budget constraint represents the rate at which the shop is allowing the consumer to change jeans into hoodies. The slope of the indifference curve, in contrast, represents the marginal rate of substitution, which is the number of hoodies the consumer is *willing* to give up to gain one more pair of jeans. If the consumer has a bundle in their shopping basket at which the value they place on jeans in terms of hoodies differs from the rate at which the shop is allowing them to change jeans into hoodies, the consumer can make themselves better off by choosing a different bundle. Thus, at the optimal bundle, the rate at which the consumer is *willing* to trade jeans for hoodies and the rate at which they *have to* trade them must be equal.

Suppose the consumer chooses B from panel (c) of Graph 6.1, 8 pairs of jeans and 4 hoodies, in their shopping basket. The marginal rate of substitution at B is 1/2. This means that the consumer is *willing* to trade 1 pair of jeans for half a hoodie, but the shop will give the consumer 2 hoodies for every pair of jeans that they put back on the shelf. If the consumer is willing to trade a pair of jeans for half a hoodie and the shop will give them 2 hoodies for a pair of jeans, the consumer can clearly make themselves better off by trading jeans for more hoodies. At choice *B*, the marginal value placed on jeans is lower than the marginal value the shop is placing on those jeans, and the shop is therefore willing to give the consumer more for jeans in terms of hoodies than the consumer thinks they are worth. *B* therefore cannot possibly be a best bundle because the consumer can make themselves better off by exchanging jeans for hoodies.

Exercise 6A.2

Suppose two consumers, *x* and *y*, each have a bundle of 6 jeans and 6 hoodies, and suppose that consumer *x*'s *MRS* of hoodies for jeans is −1 and consumer *y*'s is −2. Suppose further that neither consumer has access to the shop. Propose a trade that would make both better off.

6A.1.2 **How Shops Makes Us All the Same at the Margin** Consumers come in all shapes and sizes and as a result their indifference maps look very different. Some will have more generous budgets; others may be poorer and may only be able to spend a fraction of those with larger budgets. Imagine all consumers – rich and poor, some in more need of jeans and some in more need of hoodies – all coming to a shop to do the best they can. Coming into the shop, they will be very different; but coming out of the shop, it turns out that they will be quite the same in one important respect: *Their marginal rates of substitution of jeans for hoodies given what they have just purchased will all be the same.*

Consider, for instance, the two consumers whose choice sets and tastes are graphed in panels (a) and (b) of Graph 6.2.

Graph 6.2 Different Choice Sets, Different Tastes: But Same Tastes at the Margin

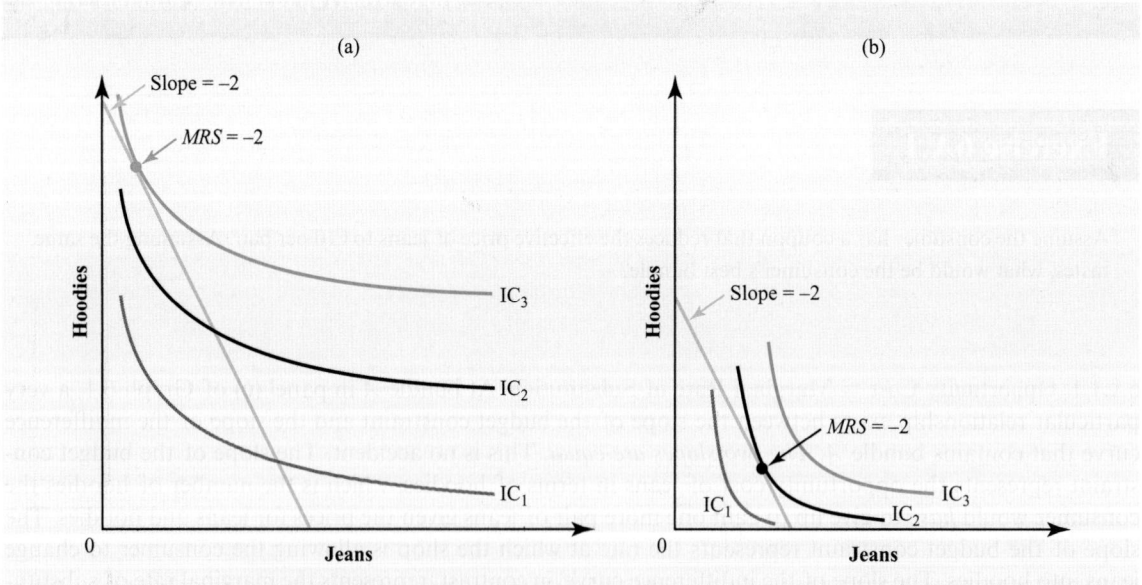

Consumer 1 is rich and thus has a large choice set whereas consumer 2 is poor and thus has a small choice set. Consumer 1 and consumer 2 also have very different indifference maps. In the end, however, they both choose an optimal bundle of hoodies and jeans at which their marginal rate of substitution is equal to the slope of their budget constraint. Since the slope of each consumer's budget constraint is determined by the ratio of prices for hoodies and jeans at the shop, and since the shop charges the same prices to anyone who enters the shop, the marginal rates of substitution for both people is thus equal once they have chosen their best bundle. *While the two consumers enter the shop with very different incomes and tastes, they leave the shop with the same tastes for jeans and hoodies at the margin,* i.e. around the bundle they purchase.

6A.1.3 How Shops Eliminate Any Need for Us to Trade An important and unintended side effect of a shop's policy to charge everyone the same price is that *all gains from trade in jeans and hoodies occur inside the shop,* eliminating any need for consumers to trade with one another once they leave the shop. As all consumers enter the shop, we may have different quantities of jeans and hoodies at home, and they could probably benefit from trading hoodies and jeans between themselves given that some might be willing to trade hoodies for jeans more easily than others. Once consumers leave the shop, they value jeans and hoodies exactly the same at the margin; that is, they all have the same marginal rate of substitution of jeans for hoodies. There is therefore no more possibility for consumers to trade and become better off because they became as well off as they could by simply doing the best they can inside the shop.

This is an important initial insight into a more general result we will develop later on in this book. Whenever two people have bundles of goods at which they value the goods in the bundle differently on the margin, there is the *potential for gains from trade,* the potential for trade to make both people better off. Suppose consumer X is willing to trade 1 can of Coke for 1 can of Pepsi, i.e. their marginal rate of substitution is -1, but consumer Y is willing to trade 1 can of Coke for 2 cans of Pepsi, i.e. their marginal rate of substitution is -2. Both consumers can gain from trading with one another as long as each has both Coke and Pepsi in their bundles. In particular, consumer X could offer Y 2 Cokes for 3 Pepsis. This will make X better off because they would have been willing to take only 2 Pepsis for 2 Cokes, and it will make Y better off because they would have been willing to give X as many as 4 Pepsis for 2 Cokes. The fact that their marginal rates of substitution are different, the fact that they value goods differently at the margin, makes it possible for both to trade in a way that makes both better off.

Economists say that a situation is efficient if there is no way to change the situation so as to make some people better off without making anyone worse off. This is referred to as *Pareto efficient* or *Pareto optimal* after Italian economist, Vilfredo Pareto (1848–1923). A situation is therefore inefficient if there is a way to change the situation and make some people better off without making anyone else worse off. If we find ourselves in a situation where people value goods that they possess differently at the margin, we know there is a way to make everyone better off through trade. Thus, situations where people have different marginal rates of substitution for goods that they possess are inefficient. Since a shop's policy of charging the same prices to everyone results in a situation where everyone leaves the shop with identical marginal rates of substitution between goods in their baskets, *the shop ensures that the distribution of jeans and hoodies is efficient among those that purchase jeans and hoodies at the shop.*

It is doubtful you have ever thought of approaching someone in the shop car park to propose a trade of goods in your shopping basket with goods you see in their basket. It turns out that there is a very good reason for this. It would be an exercise in futility because all gains from trade have been exhausted within the shop, and the distribution of goods is already efficient. Once consumers leave the shop, any trade proposed will either leave them just as well off as they would be without trading or would make at least one of them worse off.

6A.2 To Buy or Not to Buy

With the indifference maps and budget sets used above, 'doing the best you can' led consumers to purchase *both* jeans and hoodies at the shop. Sometimes our tastes and circumstances are such that doing the best we can implies we will choose *not* to consume any of a particular good. This certainly happens for goods that we consider 'bads', goods of which we would prefer less rather than more. Some people are allergic to nuts or eggs, for example, and would not choose to buy these products as a result. There are other instances where consumers may choose not to purchase a good, for example, if Coke and Pepsi are considered perfect substitutes, i.e. an individual cannot tell the difference between the two. If Pepsi is more expensive than Coke, they would not buy Pepsi. A consumer's tastes for goods combine with their economic circumstances to lead to a *best* choice at a *corner* of their budget constraint.

6A.2.1 Corner Solutions Let's consider the case of a consumer choosing between Coke and Pepsi in the context of our model of tastes and circumstances. Assume a consumer goes to a shop which only sells

Coke and Pepsi, with €15 to spend on soft drinks. The price of Coke is €1 per can and the price of Pepsi is €1.50 per can. Panel (a) of Graph 6.3 illustrates the choice set and budget constraint. If we assume that the consumer cannot tell the difference between the two, they are always willing to trade them one for one and the marginal rate of substitution is equal to −1. Such indifference curves, illustrated in panel (b) of Graph 6.3, give expression to this fact.

In panel (c) of Graph 6.3, we overlay the choice set from panel (a) and the indifference map from panel (b). The consumer's goal is to reach the highest indifference curve that contains at least one bundle in the choice set. They could start with the lowest indifference curve, IC_1, where all bundles on that indifference curve lie in the consumer's choice set, and move to the northeast to higher indifference curves. Eventually, the consumer will reach the indifference curve IC_2 in panel (c) of Graph 6.3, which contains one bundle (bundle A) that lies both on the indifference curve and within the consumer's choice set. Since any bundle on an indifference curve higher than this lies outside the consumer's choice set, bundle A is their best bundle. It contains 15 Cokes and no Pepsi and is called a corner solution because it lies on one corner of the consumer's choice set.

Graph 6.3 Corner Solutions

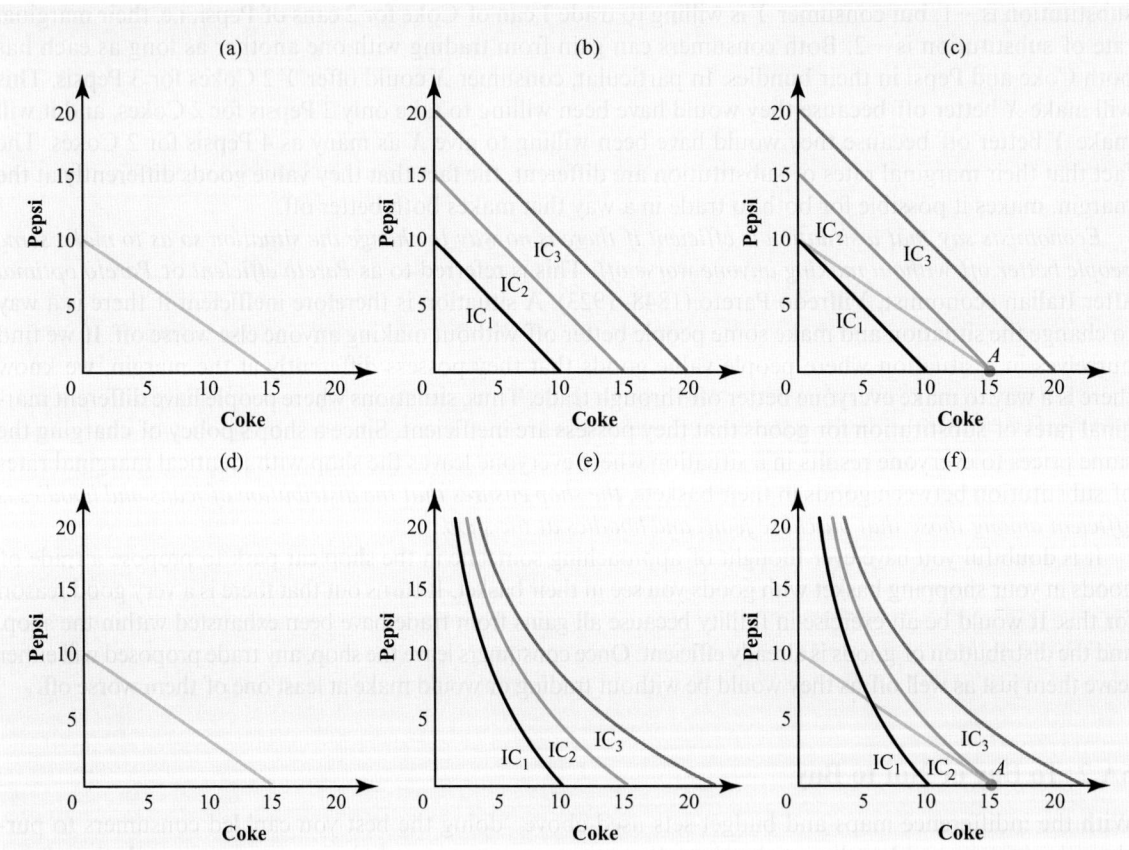

Exercise 6A.3

Suppose the prices of Coke and Pepsi were the same. Illustrate that now there are many optimal bundles for someone with the kind of tastes outlined above. What would be the consumer's best bundle if Pepsi is cheaper than Coke?

Tastes do not have to be as extreme as those for perfect substitutes in order for corner solutions to arise. Panels (d), (e) and (f) of Graph 6.3, for instance, illustrate a less extreme set of indifference curves that nevertheless result in corner solutions for certain economic circumstances.

6A.2.2 Ruling Out Corner Solutions In Chapter 5, we discussed how a good is essential if indifference curves do not intersect the axes on which the other good is measured, essential in the sense that no utility above that of consuming at the origin of the graph can be attained without at least some consumption of such essential goods. If all goods in a particular model of a consumer's tastes are essential, corner solutions are not possible; it can never be optimal to choose a bundle with zero quantity of one of the goods because that would be the same as choosing zero quantity of all goods. *Whenever indifference curves intersect an axis, however, some goods are not essential, and there is thus a potential for a corner solution to be the optimal choice under some economic circumstances.*

Consider, for instance, a consumer's tastes for coffee and sugar. Suppose that sugar is priced at €0.25 per packet and coffee at €0.50 per cup, and suppose the consumer has budgeted €15 for their weekly coffee consumption. This consumer's weekly choice set is illustrated in panel (a) of Graph 6.4, and their tastes for coffee and sugar packets are illustrated with three indifference curves, IC_1, IC_2 and IC_3 in panel (b) of Graph 6.4, given that these are perfect complements for the consumer. Panel (c) of Graph 6.4 illustrates their optimal choice as bundle A, with equal numbers of cups of coffee and sugar packets.

We could now think of changing the prices of coffee and sugar packets, of making sugar packets really cheap and making coffee really expensive, for instance. While the total quantity of coffee and sugar packets that is optimal will be different, it will always be true that the consumer will consume equal numbers of cups of coffee and sugar packets, and there will never be a corner solution.

Graph 6.4 Ruling Out Corner Solutions

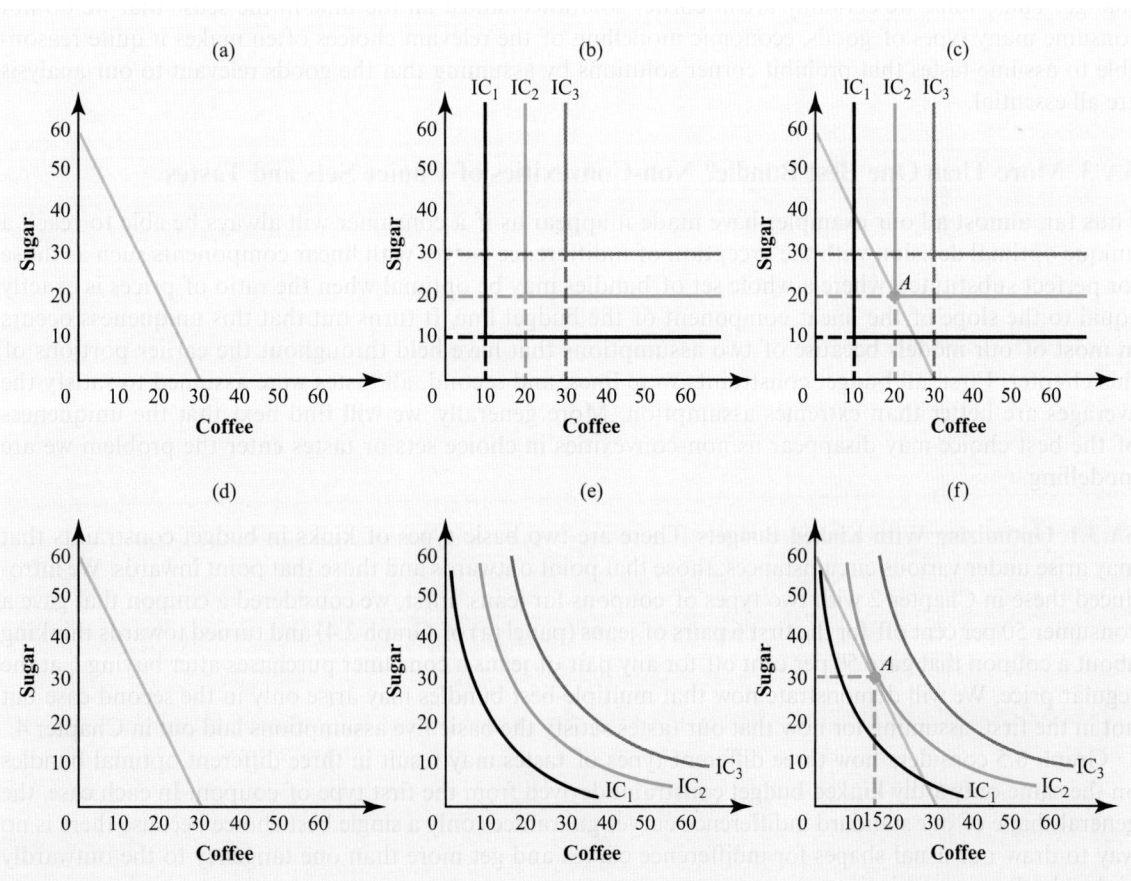

The case of perfect complements is an extreme case that ensures no corner solutions will ever be optimal. The same logic holds for any map of indifference curves that do not intersect either axis, or for any set of goods that are all essential. Panels (d) to (f) of Graph 6.4, for instance, model a consumer's tastes for coffee and sugar as less extreme, with some willingness to trade off some sugar for more coffee and vice versa. The indifference map in panel (e) of the graph is such that no indifference curve ever intersects either axis, ensuring an *interior solution* where the marginal rate of substitution is exactly equal to the slope of the budget constraint.

6A.2.3 Is It Realistic to Rule Out Corner Solutions? In many of our applications throughout this book, we will assume tastes with indifference maps that rule out corner solutions by assuming that all goods are essential. It might be argued that this is highly unrealistic. After all, consumers are at corner solutions because there are many goods in shops that never end up in our shopping baskets. This is certainly true, but remember that we are not trying to model everything that happens in the world when we write down an economic model. Rather, we try to isolate the aspects of the world that are essential for a proper analysis of particular questions, and so it may often make sense to abstract away from the existence of all those goods that we never purchase.

For instance, assume we analyzed how a consumer's housing choices change as their circumstances change. We might therefore abstract away from the consumer's tastes over Coke and Pepsi and jeans and hoodies, and model their tastes for square metres of housing and other consumption. In that case, it makes sense to assume indifference maps that exclude the possibility of corner solutions because the consumer will almost certainly choose to consume some housing and some other goods regardless of how much their circumstances change. Similarly, when analyzing the choice of leisure and consumption, it is likely that the consumer will always choose some leisure and some consumption. The same is probably the case when we model a choice of how much to consume this year versus next year: few people will consciously plan to consume only today or only next year regardless of how much individual circumstances change. Thus, while we certainly are at corner solutions almost all the time in the sense that we do not consume many types of goods, economic modelling of the relevant choices often makes it quite reasonable to assume tastes that prohibit corner solutions by assuming that the goods relevant to our analysis are all essential.

6A.3 More Than One Best Bundle? Non-Convexities of Choice Sets and Tastes

Thus far, almost all our examples have made it appear as if a consumer will always be able to reach a unique optimal decision with the exception of indifference curves with linear components such as those for perfect substitutes, where a whole set of bundles may be optimal when the ratio of prices is exactly equal to the slope of the linear component of the budget line. It turns out that this uniqueness occurs in most of our models because of two assumptions that have held throughout the earlier portions of this chapter. First, all budget constraints were lines, and second, all tastes were assumed to satisfy the averages are better than extremes assumption. More generally, we will find next that the uniqueness of the best choice may disappear as non-convexities in choice sets or tastes enter the problem we are modelling.

6A.3.1 Optimizing With Kinked Budgets There are two basic types of kinks in budget constraints that may arise under various circumstances: those that point outwards and those that point inwards. We introduced these in Chapter 2 with two types of coupons for jeans. First, we considered a coupon that gave a consumer 50 per cent off for the first 6 pairs of jeans (panel (a) of Graph 2.4) and turned towards thinking about a coupon that gave 50 per cent off for any pair of jeans a consumer purchases after buying 6 at the regular price. We will demonstrate now that multiple best bundles may arise only in the second case but not in the first, assuming for now that our tastes satisfy the basic five assumptions laid out in Chapter 4.

Graph 6.5 considers how three different types of tastes may result in three different optimal bundles on the same outwardly kinked budget constraint derived from the first type of coupon. In each case, the general shape of our standard indifference curves guarantees only a single best choice because there is no way to draw our usual shapes for indifference curves and get more than one tangency to the outwardly kinked budget constraint.

Graph 6.5 Optimizing Along Budget With an Outward Kink

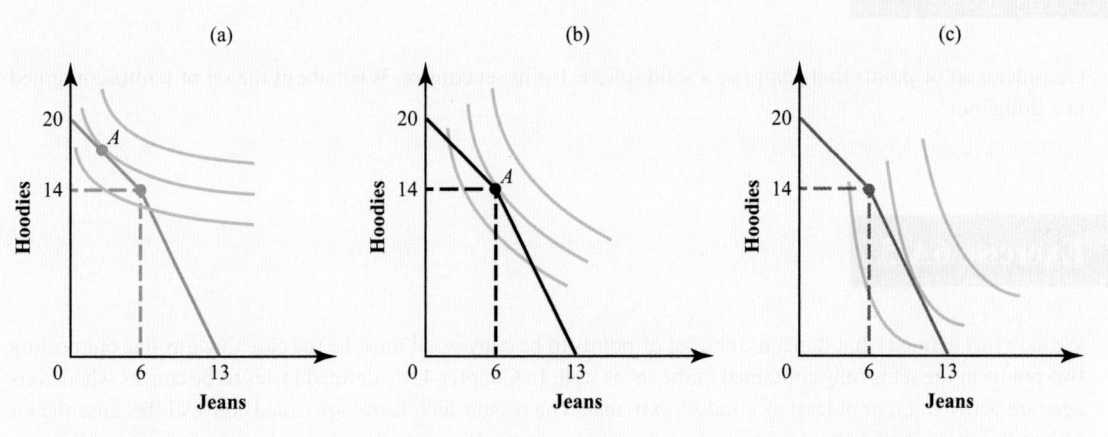

Graph 6.6, in contrast, considers the inwardly kinked budget that arises under the second type of coupon and particularly models tastes that lead to two best bundles: bundles *A* and *B*. This is possible since indifference curves begin steep and become shallower as we move towards the right in the graph. The only way we can have two bundles at which the budget constraint has the same slope at the best indifference curve is for the budget constraint itself also to become shallower as we move to the right. This can happen with an inward kink in the budget, but it cannot happen with an outward kink such as that in Graph 6.5.

6A.3.2 Non-Convexities in Choice Sets In fact, a kink in the budget is, strictly speaking, not necessary for the possibility of multiple best bundles when indifference maps satisfy the averages better than extremes assumption. Rather, what is necessary is a property known as non-convexity of the choice set.

A set of points is said to be *convex* whenever the line connecting any two points in the set is itself contained within the set. Conversely, a set of points is said to be *non-convex* whenever some part of a line connecting two points in the set lies outside the set. No such non-convexity exists in the choice set of Graph 6.5. Regardless of which two points in the set we pick, the line connecting them always also lies within the set. In the choice set of Graph 6.6, it is possible to find pairs of points where the line connecting those points lies outside the set. For instance, both points *A* and *B* in Graph 6.6 lie inside the choice set, but the line connecting the two points lies outside the set. Thus, the choice set in Graph 6.6 is non-convex.

Graph 6.6 Example of Two Optimal Bundles When the Choice Set Is Kinked Inwards

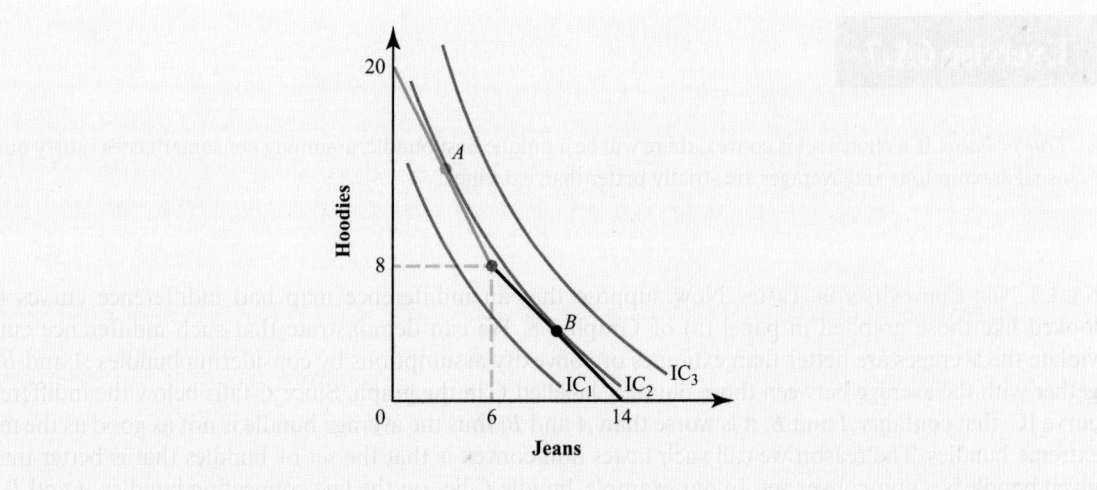

Exercise 6A.4

Consider a set of points that comprise a solid sphere. Is this set convex? What about the set of points contained in a doughnut?

Exercise 6A.5

We have just defined what it means for a set of points to be convex – it must be the case that any line connecting two points in the set is fully contained in the set as well. In Chapter 4, we defined tastes to be convex when averages are better than, or at least as good as, extremes. The reason such tastes are called convex is because the set of bundles that is better than any given bundle is a convex set. Illustrate that this is the case with an indifference curve from an indifference map of convex tastes.

Notice that a regularly shaped indifference curve can be tangential to the boundary of a choice set more than once *only if* the choice set is non-convex. The series of graphs in Graph 6.7 attempts to show this intuitively by beginning with a convex choice set in panel (a), continuing with a linear budget that is still convex in panel (b), and proceeding to two non-convex choice sets in panels (c) and (d). *The important characteristic of a choice set to produce multiple best bundles is therefore not the existence of a kink but rather the existence of a non-convexity which may or may not involve a kink.* While we can think of examples of non-convex choice sets, we will see that convex choice sets are most common in most of the economic applications we will discuss in the remainder of this book.

Exercise 6A.6

True or False: If a choice set is non-convex, there are definitely multiple best bundles for a consumer whose tastes satisfy the usual assumptions.

Exercise 6A.7

True or False: If a choice set is convex, there will be a unique best bundle, assuming consumer tastes satisfy our usual assumptions and averages are strictly better than extremes.

6A.3.3 Non-Convexities in Tastes Now suppose that an indifference map had indifference curves that looked like those graphed in panel (a) of Graph 6.8. We can demonstrate that such indifference curves violate the averages are better than extremes or convexity assumptions by considering bundles A and B together with the average between those bundles, labelled C in the graph. Since C falls below the indifference curve IC_2 that contains A and B, it is worse than A and B; thus the average bundle is not as good as the more extreme bundles. The reason we call such tastes non-convex is that the set of bundles that is better than a given bundle is a non-convex set. In our example, bundle C lies on the line connecting bundles A and B but is worse, not better, than bundles A and B. Thus, the set of bundles that are better than those on the indifference curve IC_2, containing bundle A, the shaded area in panel (a) of Graph 6.8, is non-convex.

Graph 6.7 The Role of Convexity of Choice Sets in Ensuring Unique Optimal Bundles

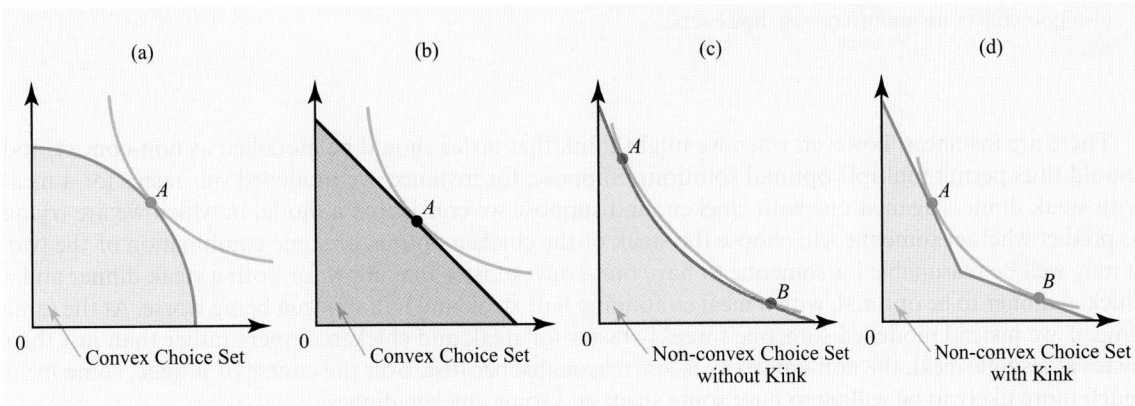

Now suppose we consider an individual with tastes that can be represented by the indifference map in panel (a) in Graph 6.8 trying to do the best they can on the linear and thus convex budget in panel (b) of Graph 6.8. This can result in both A and B in panel (c) of Graph 6.8 being optimal. Our averages are better than extremes assumption rules out this scenario by explicitly ruling out non-convexities in tastes. We have argued in Chapter 4 that assuming averages are better than extremes is reasonable for most economic models. It makes sense that people are more willing to trade hoodies for jeans if they have lots of hoodies and relatively few jeans. In most economic models, we therefore feel comfortable ruling out non-convex tastes and thus ruling out multiple optimal bundles due to non-convexities in tastes.

Graph 6.8 Example of Two Optimal Bundles When Tastes Are Non-Convex

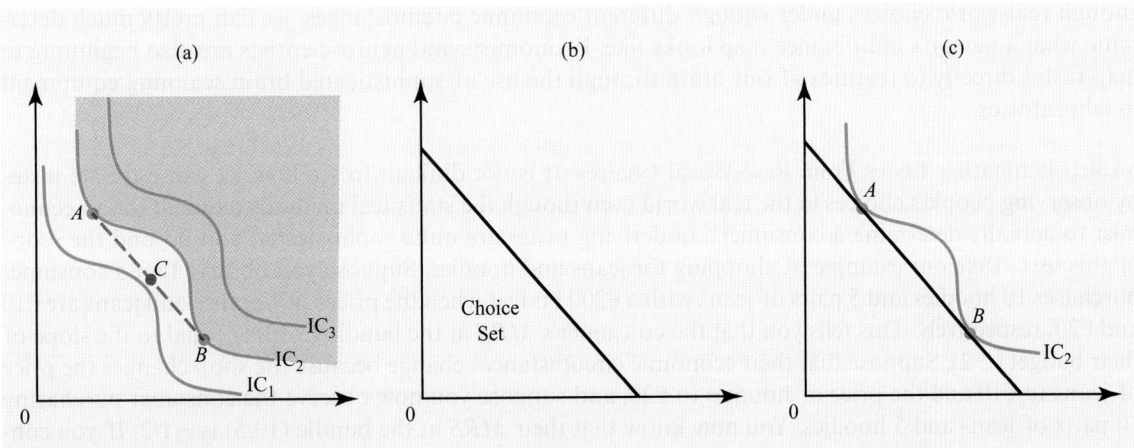

Exercise 6A.8*

Suppose that the choice set is defined by linear budget constraint and tastes satisfy the usual assumptions but contain indifference curves with linear components or flat spots. *True or False*: There might be multiple best bundles, but we can be sure that the set of best bundles is a convex set.

Exercise 6A.9*

True or False: When there are multiple best bundles due to non-convexities in tastes, the set of best bundles is also non-convex assuming convex choice sets.

There are instances, however, when we might think that tastes should be modelled as non-convex, and should thus permit multiple optimal solutions. Suppose, for instance, we modelled our tastes for a meal with steak dinners against one with chicken, and suppose we considered a model in which we are trying to predict whether someone will choose the steak or the chicken option, or some combination of the two. It may well be reasonable for someone to have non-convex tastes that allow for both a steak dinner and a chicken dinner to be optimal, with a meal containing half steak and half chicken being worse. At the same time, if we instead modelled someone's weekly tastes for steak and chicken dinners rather than just their tastes at a single meal, the non-convexity is less reasonable because, over the course of a week, someone is much more likely to be willing to have some steak and some chicken dinners.

Putting the insights from this and the previous section together, we can conclude that *we can be sure an individual has a single, unique best choice given a particular set of economic circumstances only if neither their choice set nor their tastes exhibit non-convexities.* More precisely, we need tastes to be *strictly convex* – averages to be strictly better than, and not just as good as, extremes, because, as we saw in exercise 6A.8, multiple optimal bundles are possible when indifference curves contain linear segments or flat spots.

6A.4 Learning About Tastes by Observing Choices in Supermarkets or Laboratories

Consumers do not carry their tastes around on their sleeves for all the world to see. *Despite the fact that tastes are not directly observable, we are able to observe people's choices under different economic circumstances, and from those choices we can conclude something about their tastes.* In fact, if we observe enough real-world choices under enough different economic circumstances, we can pretty much determine what a person's indifference map looks like. Economists and neuroscientists are also beginning to map tastes directly to features of our brain through the use of sophisticated brain scanning equipment in laboratories.

6A.4.1 Estimating Tastes From Real-World Choices

It is not difficult to see how we can estimate tastes by observing people's choices in the real world even though the statistical methods required for an economist to actually determine a consumer's underlying tastes are quite sophisticated and beyond the scope of this text. Take our example of shopping for jeans and hoodies. Suppose you observe that a consumer purchases 10 hoodies and 5 pairs of jeans with a €200 budget when the prices of hoodies and jeans are €10 and €20, respectively. This tells you that the consumer's *MRS* at the bundle $(5,10)$ is equal to the slope of their budget (-2). Suppose that their economic circumstances change because the shop changes the price of jeans to €10 and the price of hoodies to €20, and suppose you now observe the consumer purchasing 10 pairs of jeans and 5 hoodies. You now know that their *MRS* at the bundle $(10,5)$ is $-1/2$. If you continue to see changes in their economic circumstances and their response to those changes in terms of their choices, you can keep collecting information about the *MRS* at each of the bundles they purchase under each scenario. The more such choices you observe, the easier it is for you to estimate what the consumer's underlying indifference map must look like.

Economists have developed ways to estimate underlying tastes by observing choices under different economic circumstances. Many supermarkets, for instance, provide consumers with cards that can be scanned at the check-out and give consumers some discounts on certain products. The supermarket collects data on consumers' consumption patterns. It knows what they buy when they shop, and how their consumption patterns change with the supermarket's discounts and price changes. Economists can analyze such data to recover underlying tastes for particular consumers or the average consumer.

6A.4.2 Learning About the Link From the Brain to Tastes Over the last few years, a new area has emerged within economics known as *neuroeconomics*. Many neuroeconomists are actually neuroscientists who specialized in understanding how our brain makes decisions, and a small but increasing number have been trained as economists who collaborate with neuroscientists. Their aim is, in part, to understand what determines our tastes and how they change over time, to what extent tastes are 'hard-wired' into our brain, and how our brain uses tastes to make decisions. In doing their work, neuroeconomists rely on both the economic theory of choice as well as experimental evidence gathered from observing individuals making choices within a laboratory, where various aspects of their physiology can be closely monitored. Neuroeconomists can, for instance, see which parts of the brain are active – and how active they are – when individuals confront a variety of choices, and through this they are beginning to be able to infer something about the mapping of features of tastes, such as marginal rates of substitution, to the structure of the brain. They are also able to see how the decision-making process changes when the brain is altered by such factors as substance abuse.

6B   Optimizing Within the Mathematical Model

We now turn towards an exposition of the mathematics that underlies the intuition outlined in part 6A. Specifically, we will see that consumers face what mathematicians call a *constrained optimization problem*, a problem where some variables, the goods in the consumption bundle, are *chosen* so as to *optimize* a function, the utility function, subject to the fact that there are *constraints*, the choice set.

6B.1 Optimizing by Choosing Jeans and Hoodies

Letting x_1 and x_2 denote jeans and hoodies, consider the example of a consumer choosing a consumption bundle (x_1, x_2) in a shop, given that the price of a pair of jeans is €20 and the price of a hoodie is €10, and given that they have a total of €200 to spend. Suppose further that their tastes can be represented by the Cobb – Douglas utility function $u(x_1, x_2) = x_1^{1/2} x_2^{1/2}$, which gives rise to the indifference curves drawn in Graph 6.1. The mathematical problem the consumer faces is that they would like to choose the quantities of x_1 and x_2 so that they are affordable, i.e. they lie within the choice set, and attain the highest possible utility as evaluated by the utility function u. That is, of course, exactly the same problem we were solving graphically in Graph 6.1, where we were finding the best bundle by finding the highest indifference curve and thus the highest level of utility that contains at least one point in the budget set.

The consumer would like to *choose* (x_1, x_2) so as to *maximize* the function $u(x_1, x_2)$ *subject to the constraint* that their expenditures on good x_1 plus expenditures on good x_2 are no larger than €200. Formally, we write this as:

$$\max_{x_1, x_2} u(x_1, x_2) = x_1^{1/2} x_2^{1/2} \text{ subject to } 20x_1 + 10x_2 \leq 200. \tag{6.1}$$

The max notation at the beginning of the expression signifies that we are attempting to *maximize* or get to the highest possible value of a function. The variables that appear immediately below the max notation as subscripts signify those variables that we are choosing, or the *choice variables* in the optimization problem. The consumer is able to choose the quantities of the two goods, but is not able to choose the prices at which they are purchased nor their money budget. Thus, x_1 and x_2 are the only choice variables in this optimization problem. This is followed by the function that we are maximizing, called the *objective function* of the optimization problem. Finally, if there is a constraint to the optimization problem, it appears as the last item of the formal statement of the problem following the words subject to. We will follow this general format for stating optimization problems throughout this text.

Since we know that Cobb – Douglas utility functions represent tastes that satisfy our more is better assumption, we can furthermore rewrite expression (6.1) with the certainty that the bundle (x_1, x_2) that solves the optimization problem is one that lies *on* the budget line, *not inside* the choice set. When such an inequality constraint holds with equality in an optimization problem, we say that the constraint is *binding*. In other words, we know the individual will end up spending all of their allocated money budget, so we might as well write that constraint as an equality rather than as an inequality. Expression (6.1) becomes:

$$\max_{x_1, x_2} u(x_1, x_2) = x_1^{1/2} x_2^{1/2} \text{ subject to } 20x_1 + 10x_2 = 200. \tag{6.2}$$

6B.1.1 Two Ways of Approaching the Problem Mathematically We begin by viewing the problem strictly through the eyes of a mathematician, and we illustrate two equivalent methods to solving the problem defined in equation (6.2).

Method 1: Converting the Constrained Optimization Problem into an Unconstrained Optimization Problem

One way is to turn the problem from a constrained optimization to an *unconstrained* optimization problem by inserting the constraint into the objective function. For example, we can solve the constraint for x_2 by subtracting $20x_1$ from both sides and dividing both sides by 10 to get $x_1 = 20 - 2x_1$. When we insert this into the utility function for x_2, we get a new function that is a function of the variable x_1. We can call this function $f(x_1)$ and rewrite the problem defined in (6.2) as:

$$\max_{x_1} f(x_1) = x_1^{1/2} (20 - 2x_1)^{1/2}. \tag{6.3}$$

Graph 6.9 plots this function, and this graph illustrates that the function f attains a maximum at $x_1 = 5$, which is the same answer we derived graphically in Graph 6.1. Furthermore, the f function attains a value of zero at $x_1 = 10$. Thinking back to the underlying economics, when x_1 (the number of jeans) is 10 the consumer has no money left over for hoodies. Since the tastes are such that both hoodies and jeans are essential, it makes sense that the function returns back to zero when the consumer purchases no hoodies.

Graph 6.9 Unconstrained Optimization: Derivative Is 0 at the Optimum

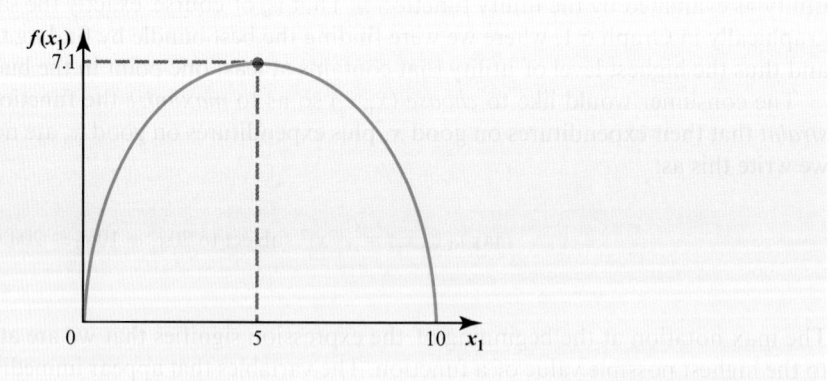

Rather than plotting the whole function and finding the maximum graphically, we can use calculus to find the maximum. More precisely, since the function has a slope of zero when it attains its maximum, we have to find this maximum mathematically where the slope or derivative of the function is zero. Taking the derivative of f with respect to x_1, we get:

$$\frac{df}{dx_1} = \frac{1}{2} x_1^{-1/2} (20 - 2x_1)^{1/2} - x_1^{1/2} (20 - 2x_1)^{-1/2}. \tag{6.4}$$

When we set this expression to zero and solve for x_1, we get $x_1 = 5$ as the maximum of the function, as Graph 6.9 illustrated. Thus, we know that the consumer will purchase 5 pairs of jeans costing a total of €100, leaving €100 to purchase 10 hoodies at a price of €10 each. We have found mathematically what we found graphically in Graph 6.1: the best choice for the consumer given their circumstances.

Method 2: The Lagrange Method for Solving the Constrained Optimization Problem

A second and more general way to solve problems of the type expressed in (6.2) is to use a method that is known as the *Lagrange Method*. The method does essentially what we did in Method 1. It defines a new function and sets derivatives equal to zero to find the maximum of that new function. The function that we define is called the *Lagrange function*, and it is always constructed as a combination of the objective function in the optimization problem plus a term lambda (λ) multiplied by the constraint where the terms in the constraint are all collected to one side, with the other side equal to zero. For instance, expression (6.2) results in the *Lagrange function* $\mathcal{L}$ given by:

$$\mathcal{L}(x_1, x_2, \lambda) = x_1^{1/2}x_2^{1/2} + \lambda(200 - 20x_1 - 10x_2). \tag{6.5}$$

Notice that the function $\mathcal{L}$ is a function of three variables, the two choice variables (x_1, x_2) and λ, which is called the *Lagrange multiplier*. Without explaining exactly why the following solution method works, Lagrange problems of this type are solved by solving the system of three equations that arises when we take the partial derivatives of $\mathcal{L}$ with respect to each of the three variables and set these derivatives to zero; that is, we solve the following system of equations known jointly as the *first-order conditions* of the constrained optimization problem:

$$\frac{\partial \mathcal{L}}{\partial x_1} = \frac{1}{2}x_1^{-1/2}x_2^{1/2} - 20\lambda = 0,$$
$$\frac{\partial \mathcal{L}}{\partial x_2} = \frac{1}{2}x_1^{1/2}x_2^{-1/2} - 10\lambda = 0, \tag{6.6}$$
$$\frac{\partial \mathcal{L}}{\partial \lambda} = 200 - 20x_1 - 10x_2 = 0.$$

One way to solve this system of equations is to rewrite the first two by adding the λ terms to both sides, thus getting:

$$\frac{1}{2}x_1^{-1/2}x_2^{1/2} = 20\lambda$$
$$\frac{1}{2}x_1^{1/2}x_2^{-1/2} = 10\lambda \tag{6.7}$$

and dividing these two equations by each other to get:

$$\frac{x_2}{x_1} = 2. \tag{6.8}$$

Multiplying both sides of (6.8) by x_1 gives us:

$$x_2 = 2x_1 \tag{6.9}$$

which we can insert into the third equation in expression (6.6) to get:

$$200 - 20x_1 - 10(2x_1) = 0. \tag{6.10}$$

Solving this expression for x_1 gives the same answer we calculated using our first method: $x_1 = 5$, and substituting that into expression (6.9) gives us $x_2 = 10$. The consumer doing the best they can, given their circumstances in a shop again means that they will purchase 5 pairs of jeans and 10 hoodies. Intuitively, condition (6.9) tells us that for the type of tastes we are modelling and the prices that we are facing at the shop (€20 and €10), it will be optimal for the consumer to consume twice as many hoodies (x_2) as jeans (x_1); that is, it will be optimal for them to consume on the ray emanating from the origin that contains bundles with twice as many hoodies as jeans. That is exactly the ray containing point A in panel (c) in Graph 6.1, where we modelled the same homothetic tastes graphically. In fact, steps (6.9) and (6.10) above are exactly the same as the steps we used to solve for the optimal solutions when all we had to go on was the graphical information in Section 6A.1!

The Lagrange Method of solving constrained optimization problems is the preferred method for economists because it generalizes most easily to cases where we are choosing more than two goods. For instance, suppose a consumer chooses bundles of jeans (x_1), hoodies (x_2) and socks (x_3) with the price of socks being €5 and all other prices the same as before, and suppose one utility function that can represent their tastes is the Cobb–Douglas function $u(x_1,x_2,x_3)$. The consumer's constrained optimization problem would be written as:

$$\max_{x_1,x_2,x_3} u(x_1, x_2, x_3) = x_1^{1/2}x_2^{1/2}x_3^{1/2} \text{ subject to } 20x_1 + 10x_2 + 5x_3 = 200 \tag{6.11}$$

and the Lagrange function would be written as:

$$\mathcal{L}(x_1, x_2, x_3, \lambda) = x_1^{1/2}x_2^{1/2}x_3^{1/2} + \lambda(200 - 20x_1 - 10x_2 - 5x_3). \tag{6.12}$$

We would solve a system of four equations made up of the partial derivatives of $\mathcal{L}$ with respect to each of the choice variables (x_1,x_2,x_3) and λ.

Exercise 6B.1

Solve for the optimal quantities of x_1, x_2 and x_3 in the problem defined in equation 6.11. *Hint:* The problem will be easier to solve if you take the logarithm of the utility function, which you can do since logarithms are order-preserving transformations that do not alter the shapes of indifference curves.

6B.1.2 Opportunity Cost = Marginal Rate of Substitution: Solving the Problem by Combining Intuition and Maths When we solved the consumer problem graphically in Graph 6.1, we discovered that once they made their best choice given their circumstances, their *MRS* of hoodies for jeans (the slope of their indifference curve at the optimal bundle) was exactly equal to the opportunity cost of jeans given by the slope of the budget constraint, at least as long as their tastes are such that they end up buying at least some of each good. The Lagrange Method we have just learned implicitly confirms this.

Specifically, suppose we just write the general constrained optimization problem for a consumer who chooses a bundle (x_1,x_2) given prices (p_1,p_2), an exogenous income I and tastes that can be summarized by a utility function $u(x_1,x_2)$:

$$\max_{x_1,x_2} u(x_1, x_2) \text{ subject to } p_1x_1 + p_2x_2 = I. \tag{6.13}$$

We write the Lagrange function $\mathcal{L}(x_1,x_2,\lambda)$ as:

$$\mathcal{L}(x_1,x_2, \lambda) = u(x_1,x_2) + \lambda(I - p_1x_1 - p_2x_2) \tag{6.14}$$

and we know that at the optimal bundle, the partial derivatives of $\mathcal{L}$ with respect to each of the three variables is equal to zero. Thus:

$$\frac{\partial \mathcal{L}}{\partial x_1} = \frac{\partial u(x_1, x_2)}{\partial x_1} - \lambda p_1 = 0,$$
$$\frac{\partial \mathcal{L}}{\partial x_2} = \frac{\partial u(x_1, x_2)}{\partial x_2} - \lambda p_2 = 0. \tag{6.15}$$

These first-order conditions can be rewritten as:

$$\frac{\partial u(x_1, x_2)}{\partial x_1} = \lambda p_1$$
$$\frac{\partial u(x_1, x_2)}{\partial x_2} = \lambda p_2 \tag{6.16}$$

and the two equations can be divided by one another and multiplied by -1 to give us:

$$-\left(\frac{\partial u(x_1, x_2)/\partial x_1}{\partial u(x_1, x_2)/\partial x_2}\right) = -\frac{p_1}{p_2}. \tag{6.17}$$

Notice that the left-hand side of equation (6.17) is the definition of the *MRS*, whereas the right-hand side is the definition of the slope of the budget line. Thus, at the optimal bundle:

$$MRS = -\frac{p_1}{p_2} = \text{opportunity cost of } x_1 \text{ (in terms of } x_2). \tag{6.18}$$

Knowing that this condition *has to* hold at the optimum, we can now illustrate a third method for solving the constrained optimization problem defined in (6.2).

Method 3: Using $MRS = -p_1/p_2$ to Solve the Constrained Optimization Problem

Returning to the case of the shop problem, we arrived in the previous section at two equivalent methods of solving for the consumer's best bundle as evaluated by the utility function $u(x_1, x_2) = x_1^{1/2}x_2^{1/2}$, given their circumstances of facing prices of €20 for jeans and €10 for hoodies as well as a budget of €200. In each case, the best option for the consumer was to purchase 5 pairs of jeans and 10 hoodies. We could also, however, use the fact that we know expression (6.17) must hold at the optimum to get the same solution.

In particular, the left-hand side of equation (6.17) for the utility function $u(x_1, x_2) = x_1^{1/2}x_2^{1/2}$ is equal to $-x_2/x_1$ which we previously derived in Chapter 4 when we derived the *MRS* for such a function. Thus, the full equation (6.17) reduces to:

$$-\frac{x_2}{x_1} = -\frac{p_1}{p_2} = -2, \tag{6.19}$$

which can also be written as:

$$x_2 = 2x_1. \tag{6.20}$$

The budget constraint must also hold at the optimum, so we can substitute (6.20) into the budget constraint $20x_1 + 10x_2 = 200$ to get:

$$20x_1 = 10(2x_1) = 200. \tag{6.20}$$

Solving for x_1, we get $x_1 = 5$, and substituting this back into (6.20) we get $x_2 = 10$; that is 5 pairs of jeans and 10 hoodies are once again optimal.

Notice that expressions (6.9) and (6.10) are exactly equivalent to equations (6.20) and (6.21). This is no accident. Method 3 of solving the constrained optimization problem substitutes some of our intuition, i.e. $MRS = -p_1/p_2$, to take a shortcut that is implicitly a part of the Lagrange Method (Method 2). The two methods are rooted in the same underlying logic, with one using only mathematics and the other using the intuition that $MRS = -p_1/p_2$, an intuition that is based on the graphical logic of Graph 6.1.

This also confirms our intuition from Section 6A.1.2 that when all consumers face the same prices, their tastes are the same *at the margin* after they optimize. This is because the equality $MRS = -p_1/p_2$ holds for *all* consumers who consume both goods, regardless of how different their underlying tastes or money budgets are. Thus, tastes can differ even if tastes *at the margin* are the same after consumers choose their optimal bundles. Our discussion of gains from trade and efficiency in Section 6A.1.3 follows from this.

6B.2 To Buy or Not to Buy: How to Find Corner Solutions

Although we have assumed throughout our mathematical discussion in this chapter that optimal choices always involve consumption of each of the goods, we had demonstrated in Section 6A.2 that for certain types of tastes and certain economic circumstances, it is optimal to choose zero consumption of some goods; to choose a *corner solution*. This is important for the three mathematical optimization approaches we have discussed so far because *each of them assumes an interior, not a corner, solution*. We will see in this section what goes wrong with the mathematical approach when there are corner solutions and what assumptions we can make to be certain that the mathematical approach in Section 6B.1 does not run into problems due to the possible existence of corner solutions.

6B.2.1 Corner Solutions and First-Order Conditions
Consider our example of a consumer shopping for jeans(x_1) and hoodies (x_2) when the prices are €20 and €10 and their money budget is €200. Suppose that their tastes are properly summarized by the quasilinear utility function:

$$u(x_1, x_2) = \alpha \ln x_1 + x_2, \tag{6.22}$$

where 'ln' stands for the natural logarithm. Notice that tastes that can be represented by this utility function are such that x_2 is not essential and the indifference curves thus cross the x_1 axis. The *MRS* of good x_1 for x_2 for this function is $-\alpha/x_1$. Using our optimization Method 3, this implies that the optimal bundle must be such that $-\alpha/x_1 = -p_1/p_2 = -2$, which implies $x_1 = -\alpha/2$. Substituting this into the budget constraint and solving for x_2, we get:

$$x_2 = \frac{(200 - 10\alpha)}{10}. \tag{6.23}$$

Exercise 6B.2

Set up the Lagrange function for this problem and solve it to see whether you get the same solution.

Now suppose that $\alpha = 25$ in the utility function (6.22). Our solution for how much of x_2 is best in equation (6.23) would suggest the consumer should consume a negative quantity of hoodies(x_2), minus 5 to be specific. This is of course nonsense, and we can see what went wrong with the mathematics by illustrating the problem graphically.

In panel (a) of Graph 6.10 we illustrate the shape of the optimal indifference curve derived from the utility function (6.22) (when $\alpha = 25$) as well as the budget constraint. The optimal bundle, bundle A, contains no hoodies and 10 pairs of jeans. Our mathematical optimization missed this point because we did not explicitly add the constraint that consumption of neither good can be negative and simply assumed an interior solution where $MRS = -p_1/p_2$. At the actual optimum A, however, $MRS \neq -p_1/p_2$.

Graph 6.10 A Clear Corner Solution (a) With an Economically Nonsensical Interior Solution (b)

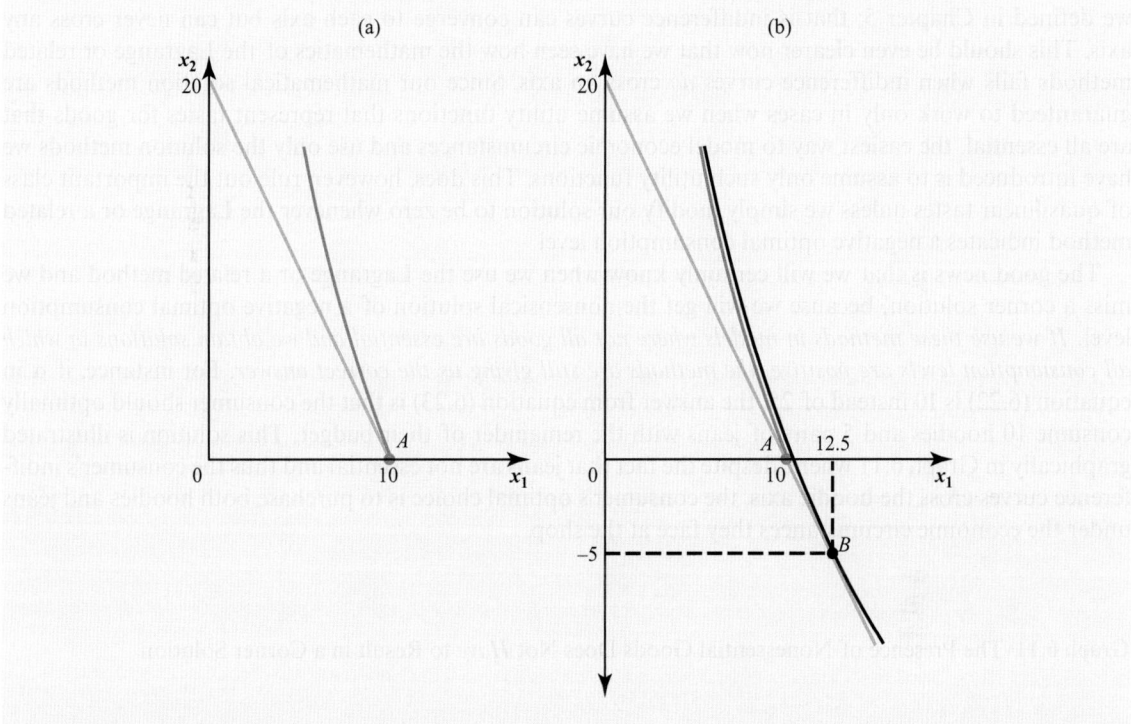

Our mathematical solution method, without the constraint that consumption cannot be negative, pictured the problem as extending into a quadrant of the graph that we usually do not picture, the quadrant in which consumption of x_2 is negative. This is illustrated in panel (b) of Graph 6.10, where indifference curves represented by the utility function (6.22) are allowed to cross into this new quadrant of the graph, as is the budget constraint. The solution found by solving first-order conditions is illustrated as the tangency of the higher indifference curve, IC$_2$, with the extended budget line, where $MRS = -p_1/p_2$, as would be the case if the optimum was an interior solution.

The learning to take from this example is that the mathematical methods of optimization we introduced in this chapter *assume that the actual optimum is an interior solution and thus involves a positive level of consumption of all goods*. When this is not the case, the maths will give us the nonsensical answer unless we employ a more complicated method that explicitly introduces non-negativity constraints for all consumption goods. This more complicated method is a generalization of the Lagrange Method known as the Kuhn Tucker Method, but it goes beyond the scope of this chapter. Instead of resorting to more complex methods, however, we can just use common sense to conclude that the true optimum is a corner solution whenever our solution method suggests a negative level of consumption as optimal.

Exercise 6B.3

Demonstrate how the Lagrange Method, or one of the related methods we introduced earlier in this chapter, fails even more dramatically in the case of perfect substitutes. Can you explain what the Lagrange Method is doing in this case?

6B.2.2 Ruling Out Corner Solutions We have already concluded intuitively in Section 6A.2.2 what assumptions on tastes are required in order for us to be sure that the optimum is an *interior* rather than a *corner* solution. Specifically, we argued that all goods that are modelled must be essential in the sense we defined in Chapter 5; that is indifference curves can converge to each axis but can never cross any axis. This should be even clearer now that we have seen how the mathematics of the Lagrange or related methods fails when indifference curves *do* cross an axis. Since our mathematical solution methods are guaranteed to work only in cases when we assume utility functions that represent tastes for goods that are all essential, the easiest way to model economic circumstances and use only the solution methods we have introduced is to assume only such utility functions. This does, however, rule out the important class of quasilinear tastes unless we simply modify our solution to be zero whenever the Lagrange or a related method indicates a negative optimal consumption level.

The good news is that we will certainly know when we use the Lagrange or a related method and we miss a corner solution, because we will get the nonsensical solution of a negative optimal consumption level. *If we use these methods in models where not all goods are essential and we obtain solutions in which all consumption levels are positive, the methods are still giving us the correct answer.* For instance, if α in equation (6.22) is 10 instead of 25, the answer from equation (6.23) is that the consumer should optimally consume 10 hoodies and 5 pairs of jeans with the remainder of their budget. This solution is illustrated graphically in Graph 6.11 where, despite the fact that jeans are not essential and thus the consumer's indifference curves cross the hoodie axis, the consumer's optimal choice is to purchase both hoodies and jeans under the economic circumstances they face at the shop.

Graph 6.11 The Presence of Nonessential Goods Does Not *Have* to Result in a Corner Solution

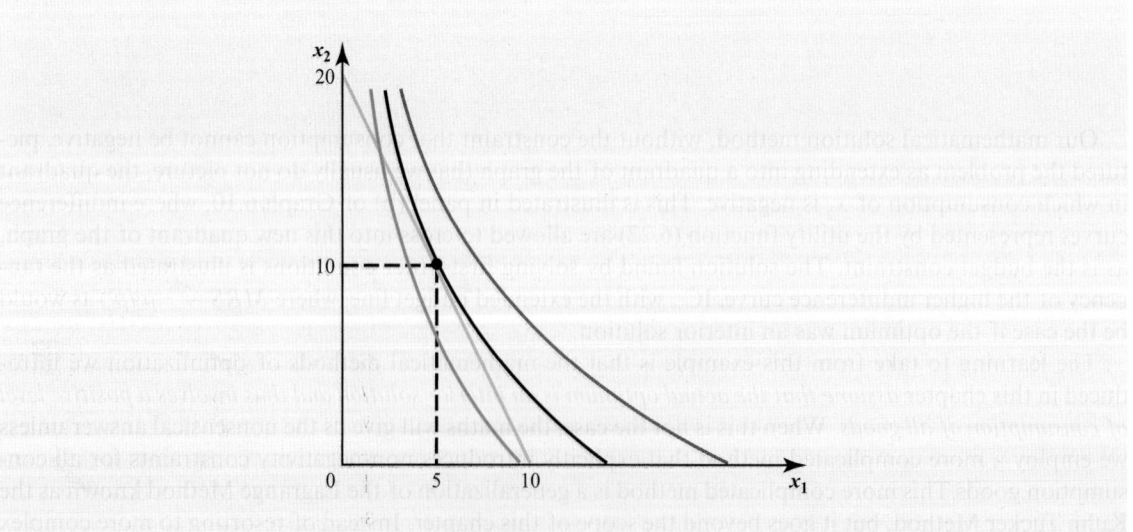

Exercise 6B.4

At what value for α will the Lagrange Method correctly indicate an optimal consumption of zero hoodies? Which of the panels of Graph 6.10 illustrates this?

6B.3 Non-Convexities and First-Order Conditions

When all goods in our optimization problem are essential – that is when indifference curves do not cross the axes – we have shown that any optimum of the problem must satisfy the first-order conditions of the Lagrange problem. In other words, when all goods are essential, the first-order conditions are *necessary conditions* for a point to be optimal. Unless non-convexities are absent from the optimization problem, however, the system of first-order conditions may have multiple solutions as demonstrated in Section 6A.3 of the chapter, and not all of these are true optima, as we will show later. In the presence of non-convexities, the first-order conditions of the constrained optimization problem are necessary but not *sufficient* for a point to be a true optimum.

For this reason, we can solve for the solution of the first-order condition equations and know for sure that the solution will be optimal *only if* we know that the problem has an interior solution *and* that the model has no non-convexities in choice sets or tastes. In the following section, we briefly explore the intuition of how such non-convexities can in fact result in non-optimal solutions to the first-order conditions of the Lagrange problem.

Exercise 6B.5

In the previous section, we concluded that the first-order conditions of the Lagrange problem may be misleading when goods are not essential. Are these conditions either necessary or sufficient in that case?

6B.3.1 Non-Convexities in Choice Sets In Section 6A.3 of the chapter, we motivated the potential for non-convex choice sets by appealing to one of our coupon examples from an earlier chapter, an example in which a kink in the budget constraint emerges. Solving optimizations problems with kinked budgets is a little involved, and so we leave it to be explored in the appendix to this chapter where a problem with an outward kink is solved. The same logic can be used to solve a problem with a non-convex kinked budget, one with an inward kink.

The mathematics of solving for the optimum when a budget is non-convex *without the presence of a kink* is somewhat different. We rarely encounter such budget constraints in microeconomic analysis, so we will not spend much time discussing them here. A problem of this type could be formally written as:

$$\max_{x_1, x_2} u(x_1, x_2) \text{ subject to } f(x_1, x_2) = 0, \tag{6.24}$$

where the function f represents the non-linear budget constraint. Such a problem could be set up exactly as we set up problems with linear budget constraints using a Lagrange function. The intuition of how just using first-order conditions might yield misleading answers is seen relatively clearly with graphical examples. Consider, for instance, the shaded choice set in Graph 6.12 and the indifference curves IC$_1$ and IC$_2$ that are tangent at points A and B. At both points, the *MRS* is equal to the slope of the budget constraint, and thus both points would be solutions to the system of first-derivative equations of the Lagrange function.

Graph 6.12 Non-Convex Budgets: First-Order Conditions Can Hold at a Bundle (*A*) that Is *Not* an Optimum

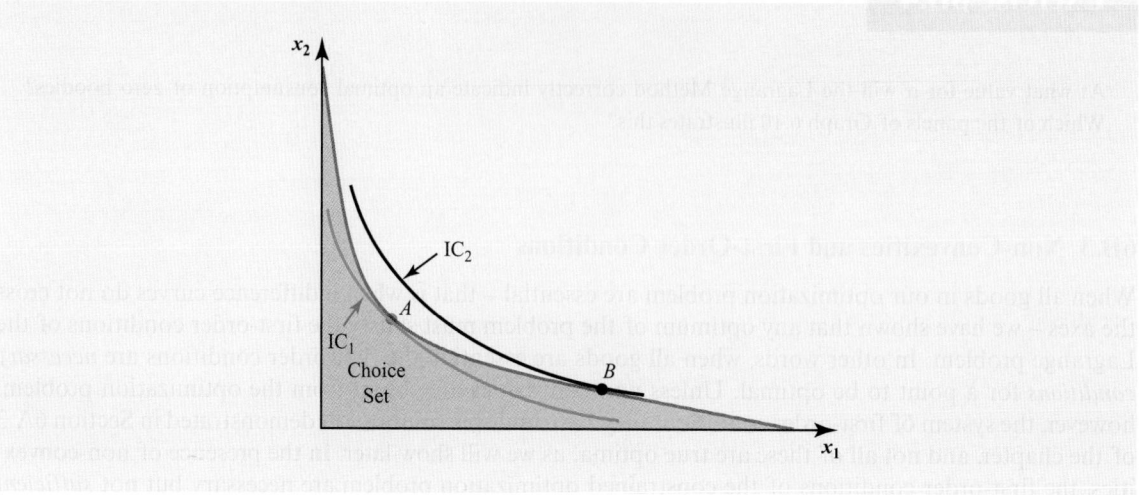

The graph shows that only point *B* is truly optimal since it lies on a higher indifference curve than point *A*. Whenever we solve a problem of this kind, we would therefore have to be careful to identify the true optimum from the possible optima that are produced through the Lagrange Method; first-order conditions are now necessary but not sufficient for identifying an optimal bundle.

6B.3.2 Non-Convexities in Tastes In Section 6A.3.3, we discussed an example in which non-convex tastes result in multiple optimal solutions to an optimization problem (Graph 6.8). In the presence of such non-convexities in tastes, the Lagrange Method will still identify these optimal bundles, but it will once again also identify non-optimal bundles. This is again because when non-convexities appear in constrained optimization problems, the first-order conditions we use to solve for optimal solutions are necessary but not sufficient.

Graph 6.13 expands Graph 6.8 by adding another indifference curve to the picture (IC$_1$), thus giving three points at which the *MRS* is equal to the ratio of prices. We can see in this picture, however, that, while bundles *A* and *B* are optimal, bundle *C* is not since it lies on an indifference curve below that which contains bundles *A* and *B*. The Lagrange Method will offer all three of these points as solutions to the system of first-order conditions, which implies that when we know the underlying tastes are non-convex, we must check to see which of the points the Lagrange Method suggests are actually optimal. One way to do this is to substitute the bundles the Lagrange Method identifies back into the utility function to see which gives the highest utility. In the example of Graph 6.13, bundles *A* and *B* will give the same utility, but bundle *C* will give less. Thus, we could immediately conclude that only *A* and *B* are optimal.

While this method of substituting the candidate optimal points identified by the first-order conditions back into the utility function works, there exists a more general method by which to ensure that the Lagrange Method only yields truly optimal points. This method involves checking second-derivative conditions, known in mathematics as *second-order conditions*. Since we will rarely find a need to model tastes as non-convex, we will not focus on developing this method here. In general, you should simply be aware that we introduce greater complexity to the mathematical approach when we model situations in which non-convexities are important, complexities we do not need to worry about when the optimization problem is convex.

6B.4 Estimating Tastes From Observed Choices

In Section 6A.4, we acknowledged explicitly that tastes in themselves are not observable but also suggested that economists have developed ways of estimating the underlying tastes that are implied by choice behaviour that we can observe. Essentially, we saw that the more choices we observe under different economic circumstances, the more information we can gain regarding the marginal rates of substitutions at different bundles that individuals are choosing. One interesting implication of this, however, is that the tastes that choice behaviour implies are *always* going to satisfy our convexity assumption *even when the true underlying tastes of a consumer are non-convex.*

Graph 6.13 Non-Convex Tastes: First-Order Conditions Can Hold at a Bundle (*C*) That Is *Not* an Optimum

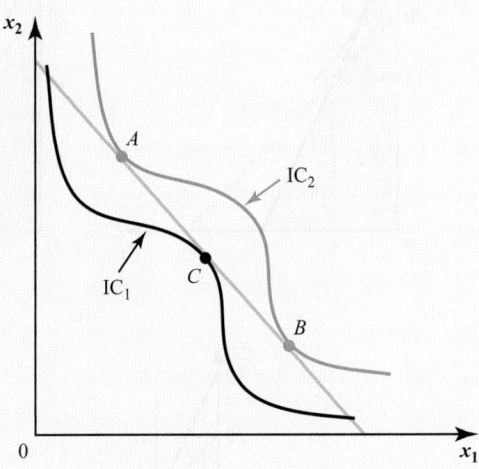

To see the intuition behind this, consider the case of a consumer whose indifference map contains the indifference curves drawn in Graph 6.13. We may observe such a consumer choosing bundles *A* and *B*, but we will never observe them choosing a bundle that lies on the non-convex portion of the indifference curve between *A* and *B* unless the budget sets take on very odd shapes. The reason for this is that tangencies with budget lines that lie on the non-convex portion of an indifference curve are not true optimal choices because they are like the bundle *C* in Graph 6.13. Thus, since we never observe choice behaviour on non-convex portions of indifference maps, we can rarely infer the existence of non-convexities in tastes from choice behaviour. An economist who observes the types of choices an individual makes with indifference curves like the ones in Graph 6.13 could conclude that there might be a flat spot in the indifference curve between *A* and *B*, but such an indifference curve would not contain the underlying non-convexity. The economist might suspect that there is a non-convexity in the indifference curve, but there is no way to identify it from observing consumption behaviour easily.

Appendix | Optimization Problems With Kinked Budgets

The mathematics of solving for optimal bundles when budget constraints have kinks is more complicated because the optimization problem contains a constraint that cannot be captured in a single equation.

Consider the shaded kinked but convex choice set in panel (a) of Graph 6.14, which replicates the coupon example graphed initially in Graph 6.5. The budget constraint of this choice set consists of two line segments, with the dotted extension of each line segment indicating the intercepts. The constrained optimization problem can now be written in two parts as:

$$\max_{x_1, x_2} u(x_1, x_2) \text{ subject to } x_2 = 20 - x_1 \text{ for } 0 \le x_1 \le 6 \text{ and}$$

$$\max_{x_1, x_2} u(x_1, x_2) \text{ subject to } x_2 = 26 - 2x_1 \text{ for } 6 \le x_1, \tag{6.25}$$

with the true optimum represented by the solution that achieves greater utility.

Graph 6.14 Mathematical Optimization on Kinked Budgets

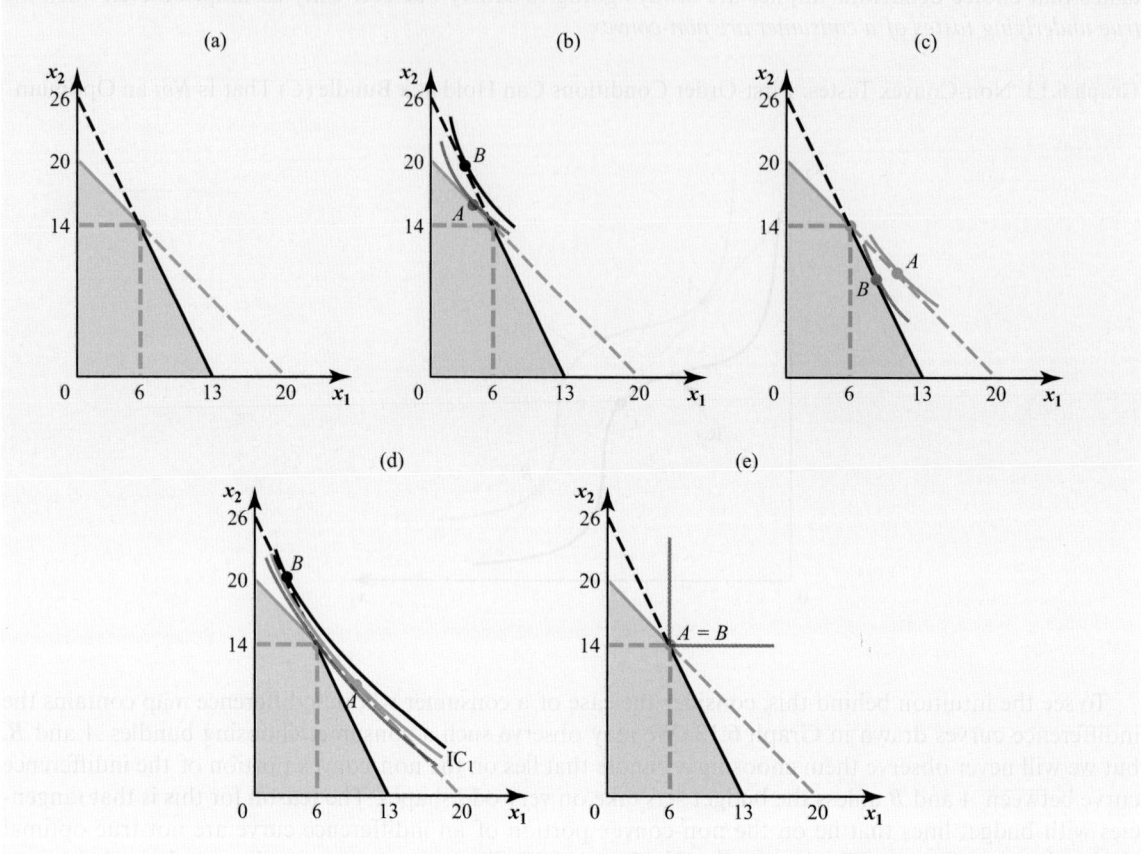

The easiest way to solve such a problem is to solve two separate optimization problems with the extended line segments in panel (a) of Graph 6.14 representing the budget constraints in those problems; that is:

$$\max_{x_1, x_2} u(x_1, x_2) \text{ subject to } x_2 = 20 - x_1 \text{ and}$$
$$\max_{x_1, x_2} u(x_1, x_2) \text{ subject to } x_2 = 26 - 2x_1. \tag{6.26}$$

For the convex budget in panel (a) of Graph 6.14, the true optimal point will occur either *to the left* of the kink as in panel (b) of Graph 6.5, *to the right* of the kink as in panel (c) of Graph 6.5, or *on* the kink as in panel (d) of Graph 6.5. When solving the two separate optimization problems in expression (6.26), we may get one of several corresponding sets of solutions. First, both optimization problems could result in an optimum with $x_1 < 6$, in which case the true optimum is the one resulting from the first optimization problem that is relevant for $x_1 < 6$ represented by A in panel (b) of Graph 6.14. Second, both optimization problems could result in a solution with $x_1 > 6$, in which case the true optimum is the one resulting from the second optimization problem that is relevant when $x_1 > 6$ represented by point B in panel (c) of Graph 6.14. Third, the first optimization problem could result in $x_1 > 6$ while the second optimization problem results in $x_1 < 6$, as represented in panel (d) of Graph 6.14. In this case, both problems give a solution on the dotted extensions of the linear segments of the true budget constraint, with both A and B lying outside the shaded choice set. In this case, the true optimal point is the kink point on indifference curve IC_1. Finally, both optimization problems could result in $x_1 = 6$, thus again indicating that the kink point is optimal as depicted in panel (e) of Graph 6.14.

Exercise 6B.6

Is it necessary for the indifference curve at the kink of the budget constraint to have a kink in order for both problems in (6.26) to result in $x_1 = 6$?

When solving mathematically for optimal bundles when budget constraints are kinked, it is best to combine the mathematics described with the intuition we gain from the graphical analysis. While we have illustrated this here with an outwardly kinked budget, the same is true for inwardly kinked and thus non-convex budgets, which we leave here to the following exercise.

Exercise 6B.7*

Using the intuitions from graphical analysis similar to that in Graph 6.14, illustrate how you might go about solving for the true optimum when a choice set is non-convex due to an inward kink.

End-of-Chapter Exercises

6.1† Assume Coke and Pepsi are perfect substitutes for a consumer, and right and left shoes are perfect complements.

A. Suppose the consumer's income allocated to Coke/Pepsi consumption is €100 per month, and their income allocated to right/left shoe consumption is similarly €100 per month.

a. Suppose Coke is currently priced at €0.50 per can and Pepsi at €0.75 per can. The price of Coke goes up to €1 per can. Illustrate the consumer's original and new optimal bundle with Coke on the horizontal and Pepsi on the vertical axis.

b. Suppose right and left shoes are sold separately. If right and left shoes are originally both priced at €1, illustrate on a graph with right shoes on the horizontal and left shoes on the vertical, the consumer's original and their new optimal bundle when the price of left shoes increases to €2.

c. *True or False*: Perfect complements represent a unique special case of homothetic tastes in the following sense: whether income goes up or whether the price of one of the goods falls, the optimal bundle will always lie on the same ray emerging from the origin.

B. Continue with the assumptions about tastes from part A.

a. Write down two utility functions: one representing the consumer's tastes over Coke and Pepsi, another representing their tastes over right and left shoes.

b. Using the appropriate equation derived in B(a), label the two indifference curves you drew in A(a).

c. Using the appropriate equation derived in B(a), label the two indifference curves you drew in A(b).

d. Consider two different equations representing indifference curves for perfect complements: $u^1(x_1,x_2) = \min\{x_1,x_2\}$ and $u^2(x_1,x_2) = \min\{x_1,2x_2\}$. By inspecting two of the indifference curves for each of these utility functions, determine the equation for the ray along which all optimal bundles will lie for individuals whose tastes these equations can represent.

e. Explain why the Lagrange Method does not seem to work for calculating the optimal consumption bundle when the goods are perfect substitutes.

f. Explain why the Lagrange Method cannot be applied to calculate the optimal bundle when the goods are perfect complements.

6.2 *Pizza and Water*. Sometimes we can infer something about tastes from observing only two choices under two different economic circumstances.

A. Suppose we consume only water and pizza sold at prices p_1 and p_2, respectively, with an exogenously set income I.

a. With the number of waters on the horizontal axis and the number of pizzas on the vertical, illustrate a budget constraint, clearly labelling intercepts and the slope, and some initial optimal interior bundle A.

b. When the consumer's income goes up, you notice that they consume more water and the same amount of pizza. Can you tell whether their tastes might be homothetic? Can you tell whether they might be quasilinear in either pizza or water?

c. How would your answers change if you had observed them decreasing water consumption when income goes up?

d. How would your answers change if both water and pizza consumption increased by the same proportion as income?

B. Suppose the consumer's tastes over water (x_2) and pizza (x_2) can be summarize by the utility function $u(x_1,x_2) = x_1^{2x_2}$ and that $p_1 = 2$, $p_2 = 10$ and weekly income $I = 180$.

a. Calculate the optimal bundle A of weekly water and pizza consumption by using the fact that, at any interior solution, $MRS = -p_1/p_2$.

b. What numerical label does this utility function assign to the indifference curve that contains the consumer's optimal bundle?

c. Set up the more general optimization problem where, instead of using the prices and income given earlier, use p_1, p_2 and I. Derive the consumer's optimal consumption of x_1 and x_2 as a function of p_1, p_2 and I.

d. Substitute the values $p_1 = 2$, $p_2 = 10$ and $I = 180$ into your answer to B(c) and verify that you get the same result originally calculated in B(a).

e. Using your answer to part B(c), verify that the consumer's tastes are homothetic.

f. Which of the scenarios in A(b) through (d) could be generated by the utility function $u(x_1,x_2) = x_1^2 x_2$?

6.3† Everyday Application: *Price Fluctuations in the Housing Market*. Suppose you have €400 000 to spend on a house and other goods denominated in euros.

A. The price of 1 m² of housing is €100, and you choose to purchase your optimally sized house at 2000 m². Assume throughout that you spend money on housing solely for its consumption value and not as part of an investment strategy.

a. On a graph with square metres of housing on the horizontal axis and other goods on the vertical, illustrate your budget constraint and your optimal bundle A.

b. After you bought the house, the price of housing falls to €50 per square metre. Given that you can sell your house from bundle A if you want to, are you better or worse off?

c. Assuming you can easily buy and sell houses, will you now buy a different house? If so, is your new house smaller or larger than your initial house?

d. Does your answer to (c) differ depending on whether you assume tastes are quasilinear in housing or homothetic?

e. How does your answer to (c) change if the price of housing went up to €200 per square metre rather than down to €50?

f. What form would tastes have to take in order for you not to sell your 2000 m² house when the price per square metre goes up or down?

g. *True or False*: As long as housing and other consumption is at least somewhat substitutable, any change in the price per square metre of housing makes homeowners better off assuming it is easy to buy and sell houses.

h. *True or False*: Renters are always better off when the rental price of housing goes down and worse off when it goes up.

B. Suppose your tastes for square metres of housing (x_1) and other goods (x_2) can be represented by the utility function $u(x_1, x_2) = x_1 x_2$.

   a. Calculate your optimal housing consumption as a function of the price of housing (p_1) and your exogenous income I, assuming that p_2 is by definition equal to 1.

   b. Using your answer, verify that you will purchase a 2000 m² house when your income is €400 000 and the price per square metre is €100.

   c. Now suppose the price of housing falls to €50 per square metre and you choose to sell your 2000 m² house. How big a house would you now buy?

   d. Calculate your utility as measured by your utility function at your initial 2000 m² house and your new utility after you bought your new house. Did the price decline make you better off?

   e. How would your answers to B(c) and B(d) change if, instead of falling, the price of housing had increased to €200 per square metre?

6.4* **Business Application:** *Quantity Discounts and Optimal Choices.* Assume a university economics department has an overall monthly photocopying budget of €5000. In this exercise, assume the department's tastes do not change with time. When we ask whether someone is respecting the department's tastes, we mean whether that person is using the department's tastes to make optimal decisions for the department, given the circumstances the department faces. Assume throughout that the department's tastes are convex.

   A. a. *True or False*: If copies and other expenditures are very substitutable for the department, you should observe either very little or a great deal of photocopying by the department at the local copy shop.

   b. Suppose that the head of department (HOD) had approximately 5000 copies per month made last academic year. This year, the HOD is on a study sabbatical and a temporary HOD has taken their place. That person has chosen to make 150 000 copies per month. Given that the department's tastes are not changing over time, can you say that either the past HOD or the current temporary HOD is not respecting the department's tastes?

   c. The temporary HOD goes to an important academic conference for a month, and a 'temporary temporary' HOD has been named for that month. They have decided to purchase 75 000 copies per month. If the original HOD was respecting the department's tastes, is this 'temporary temporary' HOD necessarily violating them?

   d. If both the temporary HOD and the original HOD were respecting the department's tastes, is the new 'temporary temporary' HOD necessarily violating them?

   B. Consider the decisions made by the three HODs as previously described.

   a. If the 'temporary temporary' HOD and the original HOD both respected the department's tastes, can you approximate the elasticity of substitution of the department's tastes?

   b. If the first and second temporary HODs both respected the department's tastes, can you approximate the elasticity of substitution for the department?

   c. Could the underlying tastes under which all three HODs respect the department's tastes be represented by a CES utility function?

6.5† **Policy Application:** *Fuel Duties and Tax Rebates.* To counter the concerns about environmental damage from car pollution, some environmentalists have proposed increasing duties on petrol and diesel. Here we look at the impact on a single consumer.

   A. Suppose a consumer has annual income of €50 000 and suppose the price of a litre of fuel is currently €1.25.

   a. Illustrate the consumer's budget constraint with litres of fuel per year on the horizontal axis and euros spent on other goods on the vertical. Illustrate how this changes if the government imposes a duty on fuel that raises the price per litre to €2.50.

   b. Pick some bundle A on the after tax budget constraint and assume that bundle is the optimal bundle for our consumer. Illustrate in your graph how much in fuel duties this consumer is paying, and call this amount T.

   c. One of the concerns about using fuel duties to combat pollution is that it will impose hardship on consumers. Some have therefore suggested that the government should rebate all revenues from fuel duty to taxpayers. Suppose that our consumer receives a rebate of exactly T. Illustrate how this alters the budget of our consumer.

d. Suppose our consumer's tastes are quasilinear in fuel. How much fuel will they consume after getting the rebate?

e. Can you tell whether the duty/rebate policy is successful at getting our consumer to consume less fuel than they would were there neither the duty nor the rebate?

f. *True or False*: Because the government is giving back in the form of a rebate exactly the same amount as it collected in fuel duties from our consumer, the consumer is made no better or worse off from the duty/rebate policy.

B. Suppose our consumer's tastes can be captured by the quasilinear utility function $u(x_1,x_2) = 200x_1^{0.5} + x_2$, where x_1 denotes litres of fuel and x_2 denotes euros of other goods.

a. Calculate how much fuel this consumer consumes as a function of the price of fuel (p_1) and income I. Because other consumption is denominated in euros, you can set its price (p_2) to 1.

b. After the tax increases the price of fuel to €2.50, how much fuel does our consumer purchase this year?

c. How much duty do they pay?

d. Can you verify that their fuel consumption will not change when the government sends them a rebate equal to the duty payments they have made?

e. How does annual fuel consumption for our consumer differ under the duty/rebate programme from what it would be in the absence of either a duty or rebate?

f. Illustrate that our consumer would prefer no duty/rebate programme but, if there is to be a duty on fuel, they would prefer to have the rebate rather than no rebate.

6.6 **Policy Application:** *Cost of Living Adjustments of Pension Benefits.* Assume pension payments to the elderly are adjusted every year in the following way. The government has in the past determined some average bundle of goods consumed by an average elderly person. Each year, the government takes a look at changes in the prices of all the goods in that bundle and raises pension payments by the percentage required to allow the hypothetical elderly person to continue consuming that same bundle. This is referred to as a cost of living adjustment or COLA.

A. Consider the impact on an average pensioner's budget constraint as cost of living adjustments are put in place. Analyze this in a two-good model where the goods are x_1 and x_2.

a. Begin by drawing such a budget constraint in a graph where you indicate the average bundle the government has identified as A and assume that initially this average bundle is the one our average pensioner would have chosen from their budget.

b. Suppose the prices of both goods went up by exactly the same proportion. After the government implements the COLA, has anything changed for the average pensioner? Is behaviour likely to change?

c. Now suppose that the price of x_1 went up but the price of x_2 stayed the same. Illustrate how the government will change the average pensioner's budget constraint when it calculates and passes along the COLA. Will the pensioner alter their behaviour? Are they better off, worse off or unaffected?

d. How would your answers change if the price of x_2 increased and the price of x_1 stayed the same?

e. Suppose the government's goal in paying COLAs to pensioners is to ensure that pensioners become neither better nor worse off from price changes. Is the current policy successful if all price changes come in the form of general inflation; that is, if all prices always change together by the same proportion? What if inflation hits some categories of goods more than others?

f. If you could choose your tastes under this system, would you choose tastes for which goods are highly substitutable, or would you choose tastes for which goods are highly complementary?

B. ** Suppose the average pensioner has tastes that can be captured by the utility function $u(x_1,x_2) = (x_1^{-\rho} + x_2^{-\rho})^{-1/\rho}$.

a. Suppose the average pensioner has income from all sources equal to €40 000 per year, and suppose that prices are given by p_1 and p_2. How much will our pensioner consume of x_1 and x_2? *Hint:* It may be easiest to use what you know about the *MRS* of CES utility functions to solve this problem.

b. If $p_1 = p_2 = 1$ initially, how much of each good will the pensioner consume? Does your answer depend on the elasticity of substitution?

c. Now suppose that the price of x_1 increases to $p_1 = 1.25$. By how much does the government have to increase the pensioner's pension payment in order for the pensioner to still be able to purchase the same bundle as they purchased prior to the price change?

d. Assuming the government adjusts the pension payment to allow the pensioner to continue to purchase the same bundle as before the price increase, how much x_1 and x_2 will the pensioner actually end up buying if $p = 0$?

e. How does your answer change if $p = -0.5$ and if $p = -0.95$? What happens as p approaches -1?

f. How does your answer change when $p = 1$ and when $p = 10$? What happens as p approaches infinity?

g. Can you come to a conclusion about the relationship between how much a pensioner benefits from the way the government calculates COLAs and the elasticity of substitution that the pensioner's tastes exhibit? Can you explain intuitively how this makes sense, particularly in light of your answer to A(f)?

h. Finally, show how COLAs affect consumption decisions by pensioners under general inflation that raises all prices simultaneously and in proportion to one another as, for instance, when both p_1 and p_2 increase from 1.00 to 1.25 simultaneously.

Chapter 7

Income and Substitution Effects in Consumer Goods Markets

In this chapter, we turn to the question of how optimal decisions change when economic circumstances change; specifically, how optimal choices change when income, endowments or prices change.

As we proceed, it is important for us to keep in mind the difference between *tastes* and *behaviour*. Behaviour, or what we have been calling *choice*, emerges when tastes confront circumstances as individuals try to do the best they can given those circumstances. If an individual were to buy less cheese because the price of cheese has increased, their *behaviour* has changed but their *tastes* have not. Cheese still tastes the same as it did before; it just costs more. In terms of the tools we have developed, the indifference map remains exactly as it was. The individual moves to a different indifference curve as their circumstances, that is the price of cheese, change.

In the process of thinking about how *behaviour* changes with economic circumstances, we will identify two conceptually distinct causes, known as *income* and *substitution* effects. This distinction was fully introduced into neoclassical economics by Sir John Hicks in his influential book *Value and Capital* originally published in 1939. Hicks was awarded the Nobel Prize in Economics in 1972 together with Ken Arrow. Understanding income and substitution effects help provide answers to deep questions related to the efficiency of tax policy, the effectiveness of welfare benefits and health policy, and the desirability of different types of antipoverty programmes.

An initial example will help whet the appetite; there is increasing concern about carbon-based emissions from vehicles, and an increased desire by policy makers to find ways of reducing such emissions. Many economists have long recommended the simple policy of taxing fuel heavily in order to encourage consumers to find ways of reducing vehicle use and/or buying more fuel-efficient cars. The concern with such a policy is that it can impose hardship on households that rely heavily on their cars, particularly poorer households. Some economists have therefore proposed sending all tax revenues from such a fuel tax back to taxpayers in the form of a tax refund. This has been queried by some editorial writers who note that if we send money back to the consumers, wouldn't they just buy the same amount of fuel as before since, at least on average, they would still be able to afford it? Our analysis will suggest that such a policy has some merits and could lead to a change in behaviour because of the influence of substitution effects.

7A   Graphical Exposition of Income and Substitution Effects

There are two primary ways in which choice sets and thus our economic circumstances can change. First, a change in income or wealth might shift budget constraints without changing their slopes, and thus without changing the opportunity costs of the various goods we consume. Second, individual prices in the economy – whether in the form of prices of goods, wages or interest rates – may change and thus alter the slopes of budget constraints and the opportunity costs faced. These two types of changes in choice sets result in different types of effects on behaviour, and we will discuss them separately in what follows.

7A.1 The Impact of Changing Income on Behaviour

What happens to our consumption when our income increases because of a pay rise at work or when our wealth endowment increases because of an unexpected inheritance or when our leisure endowment rises due to the invention of some time-saving technology? Would we consume more hoodies, pairs of jeans, Coke, housing and jewellery? Would we consume more of some goods and fewer of others, work more or less, save more or less? Would our consumption of all goods go up by the same proportion as our income or wealth?

The answer depends entirely on the nature of our tastes and the indifference map that represents our tastes. For most of us, it is likely that our consumption of some goods will go up by a lot while our consumption of other goods will increase by less, stay the same or even decline. *The impact of changes in our income or wealth on our consumption decisions in the absence of changes in opportunity costs is known as the income or wealth effect.*

Whenever we are analyzing a model where the size of the choice set is determined by exogenously given income, and for the remainder of this chapter, we will refer to the impact of a change in income as an *income effect*. In models where the size of the choice set is determined by the value of an endowment, we will refer to the impact of changes in that endowment as a *wealth effect*. What should be understood throughout, is that by both income and wealth effect we mean *an impact on consumer decisions that arises from a parallel shift in the budget constraint*, a shift that does *not* include a change in opportunity costs as captured by a change in the slope of the budget line.

7A.1.1 Normal and Inferior Goods
It may be that as a student you have to be careful in managing your money. You may find that many of your meals are based on relatively cheap foods such as potatoes and pasta. When you leave university and get employment, you are likely to find that your income increases and you may consume less pasta and potatoes and eat more expensive foods such as salmon or steak instead.

Consider a simple model in which we put monthly consumption of packets of pasta on the horizontal axis and the monthly consumption of kilos of steak on the vertical. As a consumer's income increases, the budget constraint will shift outwards as shown in the move from BC_1 to BC_2 in each of the panels of Graph 7.1. If we add the indifference curves that contain the consumer's optimal choices under the two budget constraints, pasta consumption is only lower at the higher income if the tangency on BC_2 occurs to the left of the tangency on BC_1 as illustrated in panel (a) of Graph 7.1. Panel (b), on the other hand, illustrates the relationship between the two indifference curves if pasta consumption had remained unchanged with the increase in income, while panel (c) illustrates the case where pasta consumption increased with income. This change in consumer behaviour as exogenous income changes is called the *income effect*.

If consumption of pasta *declines* with an increase in income, the consumer's preferences must look more like those in panel (a), where increased income has a negative impact on pasta consumption. *The income effect is negative whenever an increase in exogenous income without a change in opportunity cost results in less consumption*, and goods whose consumption is characterized by negative income effects are called *inferior goods*. In contrast, *the income effect is positive whenever an increase in exogenous income without a change in opportunity cost, results in more consumption*, and goods whose consumption is characterized by positive income effects are called *normal goods*. Panel (c) of Graph 7.1 illustrates an example of what our preferences could look like if pasta were a normal good for the consumer.

Finally, panel (b) of Graph 7.1 illustrates an indifference map that gives rise to *no* income effect on pasta consumption. Notice the following defining characteristic of this indifference map: the marginal rate of substitution is constant along the vertical line that connects points *A* and *B*. In Chapter 5, we called tastes that are represented by indifference curves whose marginal rates of substitution are constant in this way *quasilinear (in pasta)*. The sequence of panels in Graph 7.1 illustrates how *quasilinear tastes are the only kinds of tastes that do not give rise to income effects for some good, and as such they represent the borderline case between normal and inferior goods.*

Graph 7.1 Income Effects for Inferior and Normal Goods

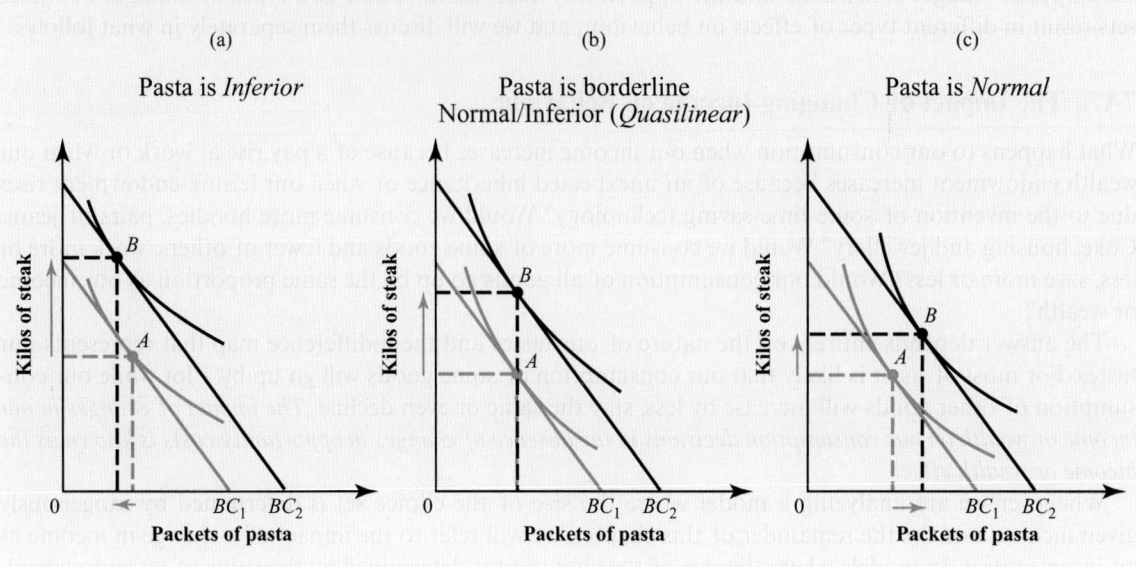

It is worthwhile noting that *whenever we observe a negative income effect on our consumption of one good, there must be a positive income effect on our consumption of a different good*. After all, the increased income must be going somewhere, whether it is increased consumption of some good today or increased savings for consumption in the future. In panel (a) of Graph 7.1, for instance, we observe a negative income effect on consumption of pasta on the horizontal axis; at the same time, on the vertical axis we observe a positive income effect on consumption of steak.

Exercise 7A.1

Is it also the case that whenever there is a positive income effect on consumption of one good, there must be a negative income effect on consumption of a different good?

Exercise 7A.2

Can a good be an inferior good at all income levels? *Hint:* Consider the bundle (0,0).

7A.1.2 Luxuries and Necessities As we have just seen, quasilinear tastes represent one special case that divides two types of goods: normal goods whose consumption increases with income and inferior goods whose consumption decreases with income. The defining difference between these two types of goods is how consumption changes in an *absolute* sense as our income changes. A different way of dividing goods into two sets is to ask how *relative* consumption of different goods changes as income changes. Instead of asking whether *total* consumption of a particular good increases or decreases with an increase in income, we could ask whether the *fraction of our income spent* on a particular good increases or decreases as our income goes up, that is, whether our consumption increases *relative to income*.

Consider the consumption of housing. In each panel of Graph 7.2, we model choices between square metreage of housing and euros of other goods. As in Graph 7.1, we consider how choices will change as income doubles, with bundle A representing the optimal choice at the lower income represented by the budget constraint BC_1 and bundle B representing the optimal choice at the higher income represented by the budget constraint BC_2. Suppose that in each panel, the individual spends 25 per cent of their income on housing at bundle A. If housing remains a constant fraction of consumption as income increases, the optimal consumption bundle B when income doubles would involve twice as much housing and twice as much other good consumption. This bundle would lie on a ray emanating from the origin and passing through point A, as pictured in panel (b) of Graph 7.2. If, on the other hand, the fraction of income allocated to housing declines as income rises, B would lie to the left of this ray as in panel (a) of Graph 7.2, and if the fraction of income allocated to housing increases as income rises, B would lie to the right of the ray as in panel (c). It turns out that on average, people spend approximately 25 per cent of their income on housing regardless of the level of their income, which implies that tastes for housing typically look most like those in panel (b) of Graph 7.2.

Graph 7.2 Income Effects for Necessities and Luxuries

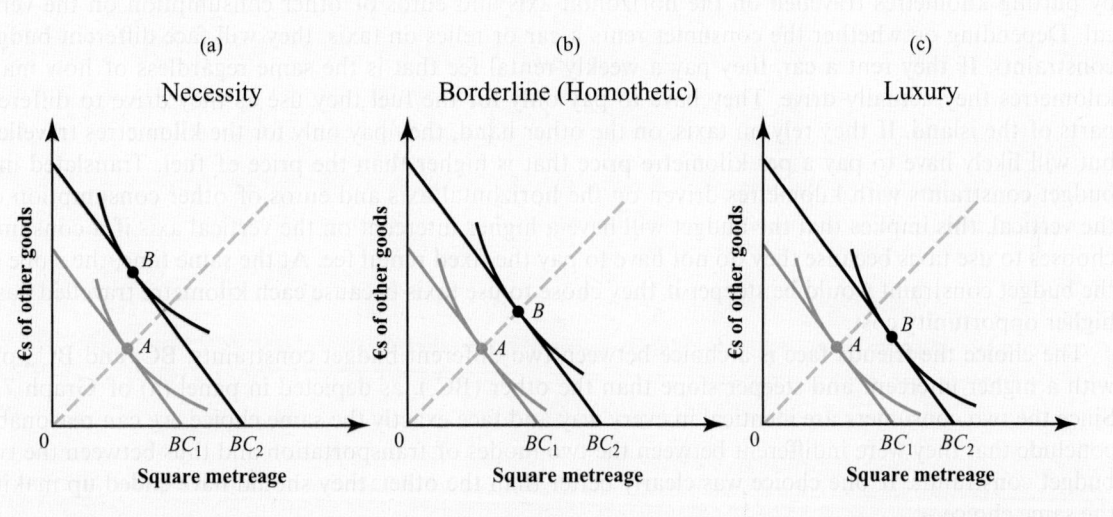

Economists have come to refer to goods as necessities where their consumption as a fraction of income declines as income rises, while referring to goods as luxuries where their consumption as a fraction of income increases as income rises. The borderline tastes that divide these two classes of goods are tastes of the kind represented in panel (b) of Graph 7.2, tastes that we defined as *homothetic* in Chapter 5, where the marginal rates of substitution are constant along any ray emanating from the origin. Thus, just as quasilinear tastes represent the borderline tastes between normal and inferior goods, *homothetic tastes represent the borderline tastes between necessary and luxury goods.*

Exercise 7A.3

All inferior goods are necessities, but not all necessities are inferior goods. Explain.

Exercise 7A.4

At a particular consumption bundle, can both goods in a two-good model be luxuries? Can they both be necessities?

7A.2 The Impact of Changing Opportunity Costs on Behaviour

Assume two friends go for a week-long holiday to the Cayman Islands during different weeks. Both are identical in every way, same income, same tastes. Since there is no public transportation on the Cayman Islands, they only have two choices of what to do once they step off the plane. They can either rent a car for the week, or take a taxi to their hotel and rely on taxis for any additional transportation needs. After the two friends return home,they compare notes and discover that although they had stayed at the same hotel, one had rented a car whereas the other had used only taxis. Which one of the two do you think went on more trips away from the hotel? The difference between the number of car journeys one takes and what the other took is the substitution effect.

7A.2.1 Renting a Car Versus Taking Taxis on Holiday
The answer is revealed if we model the relevant aspects of the choice problem that the two were facing when they arrived at the airport. The two consumers had to choose the best way to travel by car during their holiday. We can model this choice by putting kilometres travelled on the horizontal axis and euros of other consumption on the vertical. Depending on whether the consumer rents a car or relies on taxis, they will face different budget constraints. If they rent a car, they pay a weekly rental fee that is the same regardless of how many kilometres they actually drive. They have to pay only for the fuel they use as they drive to different parts of the island. If they rely on taxis, on the other hand, they pay only for the kilometres travelled, but will likely have to pay a per kilometre price that is higher than the price of fuel. Translated into budget constraints with kilometres driven on the horizontal axis and euros of other consumption on the vertical, this implies that the budget will have a higher intercept on the vertical axis if a consumer chooses to use taxis because they do not have to pay the fixed rental fee. At the same time, the slope of the budget constraint would be steeper if they chose to use taxis because each kilometre travelled has a higher opportunity cost.

The choice the friends face is a choice between two different budget constraints, BC_1 and BC_2, one with a higher intercept and steeper slope than the other (BC_1), as depicted in panel (a) of Graph 7.3. Since the two consumers are identical in every way and face exactly the same choice, we can reasonably conclude that they were indifferent between the two modes of transportation and thus between the two budget constraints. If one choice was clearly better than the other, they should have ended up making the same choice.

Graph 7.3 Substitution Effects in the Cayman Islands

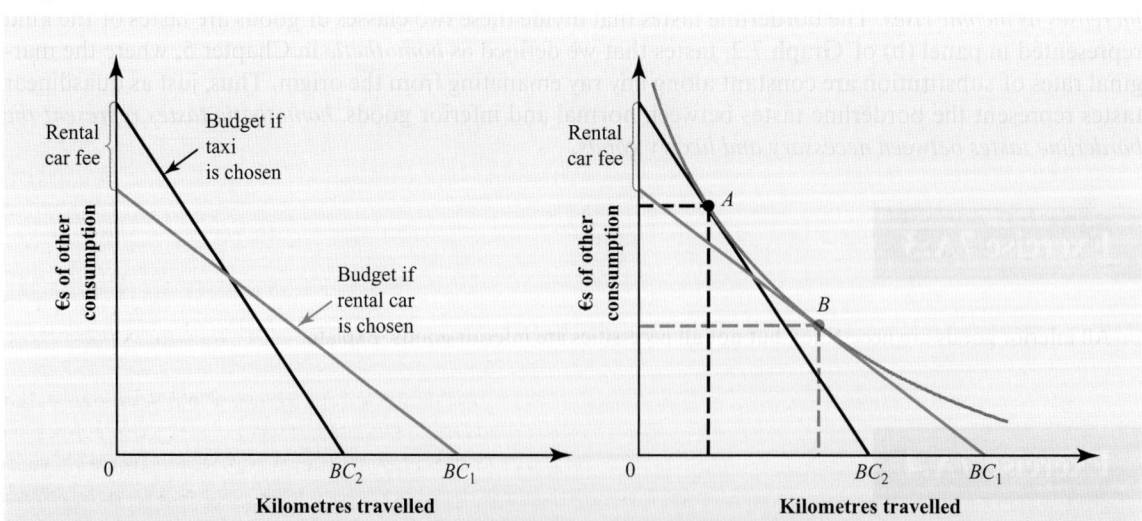

Go to MindTap to interact with this graph

Even if both consumers made different choices, they must have ended up on the same indifference curve because the two have the same tastes, the same map of indifference curves and the same exogenous income. Panel (b) of Graph 7.3, therefore, fits a single indifference curve tangent to the two budget constraints, illustrating that their optimal choices on the two different budget constraints result in the same level of satisfaction. One consumer's optimal choice *A* indicates fewer kilometres travelled than the other's optimal choice *B*.

The intuition behind the model's prediction is that if one consumer pays for the rental car at the airport, they would be unable to get the fee back no matter what else they did for the week. The opportunity cost or price of driving a kilometre once the consumer decides to rent a car, was only the cost of fuel. The other consumer faces a much higher opportunity cost since they had to pay taxi prices for every kilometre travelled. Even though their choices made both equally well off, the lower opportunity cost of driving leads one consumer to travel more kilometres and consume less of other goods than the other.

Exercise 7A.5

If you knew only that both consumers had the same income but not necessarily the same tastes, could you tell which one drove more kilometres: the one that rented or the one that took taxis?

Economists note that the flat weekly rental fee becomes a *sunk cost* as soon as the consumer choses to rent a car, as the fee is non-refundable. The rental fee, therefore, is never an opportunity cost of anything the consumer does once they have rented the car. Such sunk costs, once they have been incurred, therefore do not affect economic decisions because our economic decisions are shaped by the trade-offs inherent in opportunity costs. We will return to the concept of sunk costs more extensively when we discuss producer behaviour, and we will note in Chapter 29 that some psychologists quarrel with the economist's conclusion that such costs should have no impact on behaviour.

7A.2.2 Substitution Effects Substitution effects arise whenever opportunity costs or prices change. In our example, for instance, we analyzed the difference in consumer behaviour when the price of driving changes, but the general intuition behind the substitution effect will be important for many more general applications throughout this book.

We will define a substitution effect more precisely as follows: *The substitution effect of a price change is the change in behaviour that results purely from the change in opportunity costs and not from a change in real income.* By *real income*, we mean *real welfare*, so no change in real income should be taken to mean no change in satisfaction or no change in indifference curves. The Cayman Island example was constructed so that we could isolate a substitution effect clearly by focusing our attention on a single indifference curve, or a single level of real income.

The fact that bundle *B must* lie to the right of bundle *A* is a matter of geometry. A steeper budget line tangential to an indifference curve *must* lie to the left of a shallower budget line that is tangential to the same indifference curve. *The direction of a substitution effect is therefore always towards more consumption of the good that has become relatively cheaper and away from the good that has become relatively more expensive.* Note that this differs from what we concluded about income effects whose direction depends on whether a good is normal or inferior.

7A.2.3 How Large Are Substitution Effects? While the *direction* of substitution effects is unambiguous, the *size* of the effect is dependent entirely on the kinds of underlying tastes a consumer has. Panel (b) in Graph 7.3 suggests a pretty clear and sizable difference between the number of kilometres one consumer drives and the number of kilometres the other drives given that they faced different opportunity costs for driving, while having the same level of satisfaction or welfare. We could have equally well drawn the indifference curve with more curvature, and thus with less substitutability between kilometres driven and other consumption. *The less substitutability that is built into a consumer's tastes, the smaller will be the substitution effects arising from changes in opportunity costs.*

For instance, consider the indifference curve in panel (b) in Graph 7.4, an indifference curve with more curvature than that in panel (a) and thus less built-in substitutability along the portion on which the two consumers are making their choices. Notice that although the substitution effect points in the same direction as before, the effect is considerably smaller. Panel (c) of Graph 7.4 illustrates this even more clearly by focusing on the extreme case of perfect complements. Such tastes give rise to indifference curves that permit no substitutability between goods, leading to bundles *A* and *B* overlapping and a consequent disappearance of the substitution effect.

Exercise 7A.6

True or False: If you observed the two consumers consuming the same number of kilometres driven during their holiday, their tastes must be those of perfect complements between kilometres driven and other consumption.

Graph 7.4 The Degree of Substitutability and the Size of Substitution Effects

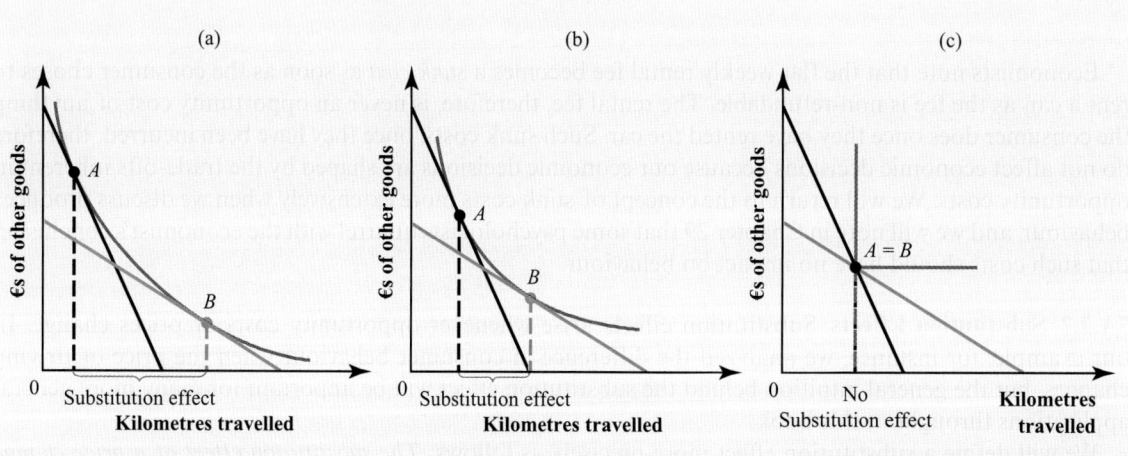

7A.2.4 Hicks Versus Slutsky Substitution

The substitution effect is defined as the change in consumption that is due to a change in opportunity cost without a change in real income, that is, without a change in the indifference curve. This is sometimes called *Hicksian* substitution. A slightly different concept of a substitution effect arises when we ask how a change in opportunity costs alters a consumer's behaviour assuming that their ability to purchase the original bundle remains intact. This is called *Slutsky* substitution.

7A.3 Price Changes: Income and Substitution Effects Combined

The Cayman Island example was used to focus our discussion of *pure* income effects, which occur in the absence of changes in opportunity costs, in Section 7A.1 with a discussion of *pure* substitution effects, which occur in the absence of any changes in real income or wealth, in Section 7A.2. Most real-world changes in opportunity costs, however, implicitly also give rise to changes in real income, causing the simultaneous operation of both income and substitution effects.

To broaden the discussion, consider what happens when the price of a good that most of us consumes goes up, as, for instance, the price of fuel. When this happens, the consumer can no longer afford to reach the same indifference curve as before if their exogenous income remains the same. Not only do they face a different opportunity cost for fuel but they also have to face the prospect of ending up with less satisfaction – or what we have called less real income – because they are doomed to operate on a lower indifference curve than before the price increase. Similarly, if the price of fuel falls, they not only face a different opportunity cost for fuel but will also end up on a higher indifference curve, and thus experience an increase in real income. *A price change therefore typically results in both an income effect and a substitution effect.* These can be conceptually disentangled even though they occur simultaneously, and it will become quite important for many policy applications to know the relative sizes of these conceptually different effects. You will see how this is important more clearly in later chapters. For now, we will focus on conceptually disentangling the two effects of price changes.

7A.3.1 An Increase in the Price of Fuel To model the impact of an increase in the price of fuel on consumer behaviour, we again put kilometres driven on the horizontal axis and euros of other consumption on the vertical. An increase in the price of fuel causes an inward rotation of the budget line around the vertical intercept, as illustrated in panel (a) of Graph 7.5. The consumer's optimal bundle prior to the price increase is illustrated by the tangency of the indifference curve at point *A*.

Graph 7.5 Income and Substitution Effects When Fuel Is a Normal Good

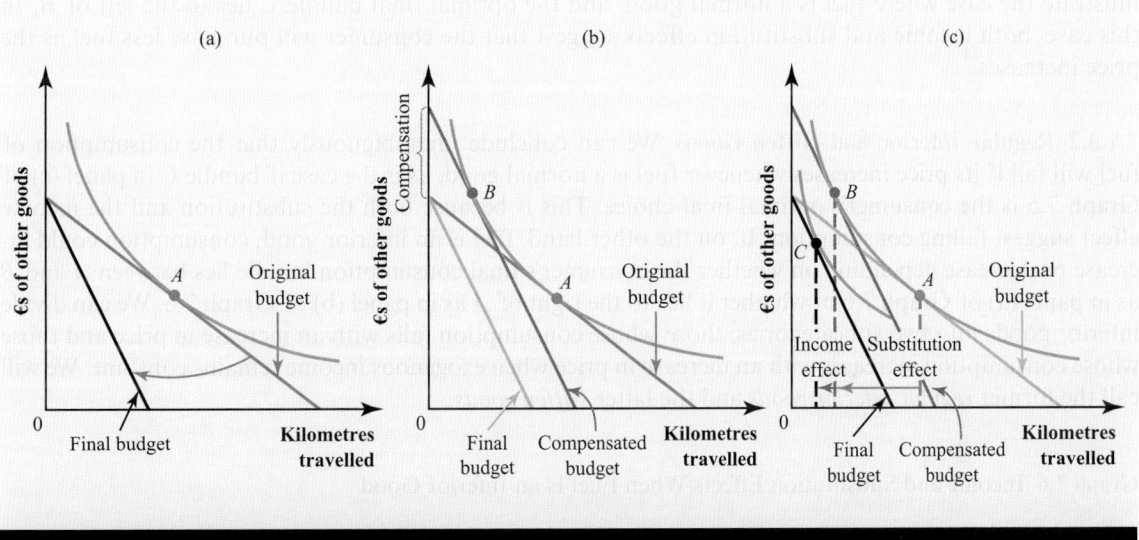

Go to MindTap to interact with this graph

We can now begin our disentangling of income and substitution effects by asking how the consumption bundle would have changed had the consumer only experienced the change in opportunity costs without a change in real income. How would the consumption decision change if the consumer faced a new budget that incorporated the steeper slope implied by the price change but was large enough to permit them to be as satisfied as they were before the price change, large enough to keep them on their original indifference curve? This budget is illustrated tangentially to the indifference curve containing bundle *A* in panel (b) of Graph 7.5 and is called the *compensated budget*. *A compensated budget for a price change is the budget that incorporates the new price but includes sufficient monetary compensation to make the consumer as well off as they were before the price change.* If income is exogenous as it is in our example, the compensated budget requires positive compensation when prices increase and negative compensation when prices decrease.

Panel (b) of Graph 7.5 looks very much like panel (b) of Graph 7.4 that illustrated a pure substitution effect for our Cayman Islands example. This is because we have imagined that the consumer was provided with sufficient compensation at the higher fuel price to keep their real income constant in order to focus only on the change in consumption that is due to the change in opportunity costs along a single indifference curve. As in the Cayman Islands example, we can see that consumption of fuel is less at point *B* than at point *A*. When real income is unchanged, the substitution effect tells us that they will consume less fuel because it has become more expensive relative to other goods.

Rarely, however, will someone offer consumers compensation for a price change in real life. Rather, they will have to settle for a decrease in real income when prices go up. In panel (c) of Graph 7.5, we start with the compensated budget and ask how the actual consumption decision will differ from the hypothetical outcome *B*. Notice that the compensated budget and the final budget in panel (c) of Graph 7.5, have the same slope and thus differ only by the hypothetical compensation we have assumed when plotting the compensated budget. Thus when going from the compensated budget line to the final budget line, we are analyzing the impact of a change in exogenous money income, or what we called a pure income effect in Section 7A.1.

Whether the optimal consumption of fuel on the consumer's final budget line is larger or smaller than at point *B* depends entirely on whether fuel is a normal or an inferior good for the consumer. We defined a normal good as one whose consumption moves in the same direction as changes in exogenous income, while we defined an inferior good as one whose consumption moved in the opposite direction of changes in exogenous income. Thus, the optimal bundle on the final budget line might lie to the left of point *B* if fuel is a normal good, and to the right of *B* if an inferior good. In the latter case, it could lie in between *A* and *B* if the income effect is smaller than the substitution effect, or it might lie to the right of point *A* if the income effect is larger than the substitution effect. In panel (c) of Graph 7.5, we illustrate the case where fuel is a normal good, and the optimal final bundle *C* lies to the left of *B*. In this case, both income and substitution effects suggest that the consumer will purchase less fuel as the price increases.

7A.3.2 Regular Inferior and Giffen Goods

We can conclude unambiguously that the consumption of fuel will fall if its price increases whenever fuel is a normal good, as is the case if bundle *C* in panel (c) of Graph 7.5 is the consumer's optimal final choice. This is because both the substitution and the income effect suggest falling consumption. If, on the other hand, fuel is an inferior good, consumption could increase or decrease depending on whether the consumer's final consumption bundle lies between *A* and *B* as in panel (a) of Graph 7.6 or whether it lies to the right of *A* as in panel (b) of Graph 7.6. We can divide inferior goods into two subcategories: those whose consumption falls with an increase in price and those whose consumption increases with an increase in price when exogenous income remains constant. We will call the former *regular inferior goods* and the latter *Giffen goods*.

Graph 7.6 Income and Substitution Effects When Fuel Is an Inferior Good

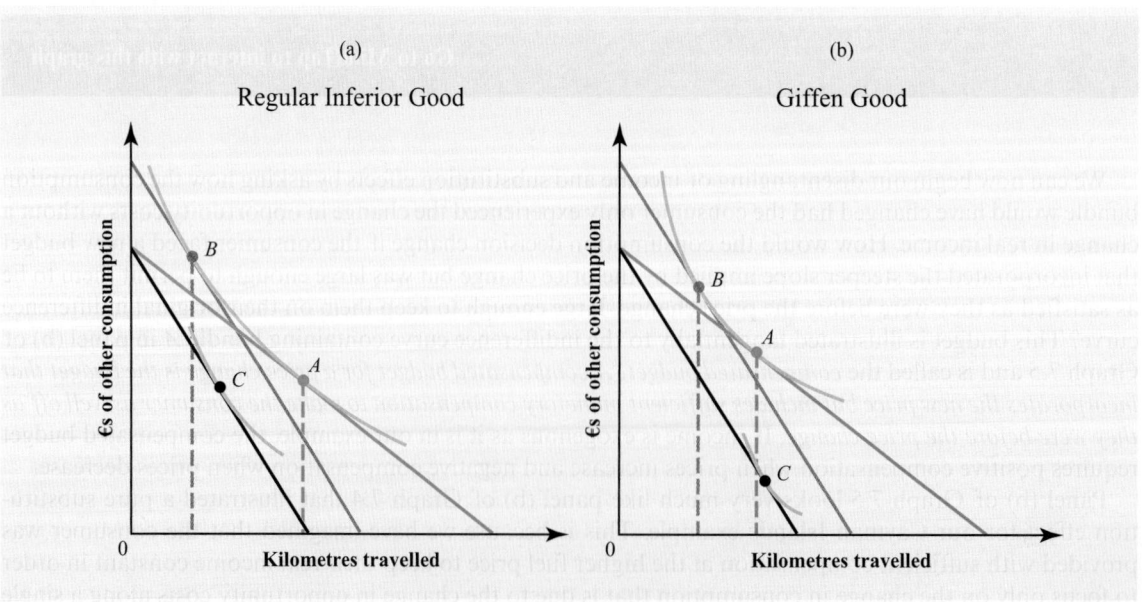

A Giffen good seems to defy the law of demand – a consumer would choose to *consume more of it when the price increases*. Giffen goods are not to be confused with certain goods that carry a high level of prestige precisely because everyone knows they are expensive, such as luxury cars. Some consumers who care about the prestige value of a BMW may be more likely to purchase a BMW as the price, and thus the prestige value, increases. This is *not*, however, the kind of behaviour we have in mind when we think of Giffen goods. The person who attaches a prestige value to the price of a BMW is really buying two different goods when they buy this car: the car itself *and* its prestige value. As the price of the BMW goes up, the car remains the same but the quantity of prestige value rises. When the same consumer's income falls and the price of BMWs remains the same, the consumer would almost certainly be less likely to buy BMWs, which indicates that the car itself with the prestige value held constant is a normal good. While an increase in the price still causes an increase in the consumption of the physical good we observe, such goods are examples of what are known as *Veblen goods* after Thorstein Veblen (1857–1929) who hypothesized that preferences for certain goods intensify as price increases, which can cause what appear to be increases in consumption as price goes up.

Real Giffen goods are quite different and are rarely observed in the real-world. There is disagreement amongst economists as to whether they exist at all. At the end of the 19th century, Alfred Marshall (1842–1924), one of the great economists of that century, included a hypothetical example in his economics textbook and attributed it to Robert Giffen, a contemporary of his. To quote from his text:

> As Mr. Giffen has pointed out, a rise in the price of bread makes so large a drain on the resources of the poorer labouring families ... that they are forced to curtail their consumption of meat and the more expensive farinaceous foods: and bread being still the cheapest food which they can get and will take, they consume more, and not less of it.
>
> (A. Marshall, *Principles of Economics,* London: Macmillan, 1895, p. 208)

While Robert Giffen (1837–1910) was a highly regarded economist and statistician, it appears no one has located a reference to the kinds of goods that are named after him in any of his own writings, only in Marshall's. Over the years, a variety of attempts to find credible historical examples that are not hypothetical have been discredited, although a 2007 paper by Jensen and Miller (Jensen, R. and Miller, N. (2007). *Giffen Behavior: Theory and Evidence*. NBER Working Paper No. 13243) demonstrates that rice in poor areas of China may indeed be a Giffen good there.

Jensen and Miller's research on rice in China suggests that in order to find the Giffen behaviour of increasing consumption with an increase in price, it must be that the good in question represents a large portion of a person's income to begin with, and as a result, a change in price causes a large income effect. It furthermore must be the case that there are no very good substitutes for the good in order for the substitution effect to remain small. Given the variety of substitutable goods in the modern world and the historically high standard of living, it therefore seems very unlikely that we will find much Giffen behaviour in the part of the world that has risen above subsistence income levels.

7A.3.3 Income and Substitution Effects for Jeans and Hoodies Returning to our example of purchasing jeans and hoodies from a shop with a fixed budget, because the consumer knows how much the shop charges for jeans and hoodies, they enter the shop already having solved for their optimal bundle. Now suppose that one of the staff at the shop hands the consumer a 50 per cent off voucher for jeans, effectively decreasing the price of jeans the consumer faces. We already know that this will lead to an outward rotation of the budget line as shown in panel (a) of Graph 7.7. Armed with the new information presented in this chapter, however, we can now predict how the consumption of jeans and hoodies will change depending on whether jeans and hoodies are normal, regular inferior, or Giffen goods.

First, we isolate the substitution effect by drawing the compensated budget line BC_2 under the new price in panel (b) of Graph 7.7. Notice that the compensation in this case is negative. In order to keep real income – that is, the indifference curve – constant and concentrate only on the impact of the change in opportunity costs, we would have to take away some of the consumer's income. The substitution effect, the shift from A to B, indicates that the consumer will switch away from the good that has become relatively more expensive (hoodies) and towards the good that has become relatively cheaper (jeans).

Graph 7.7 Inferring the Type of Good From Observed Choices

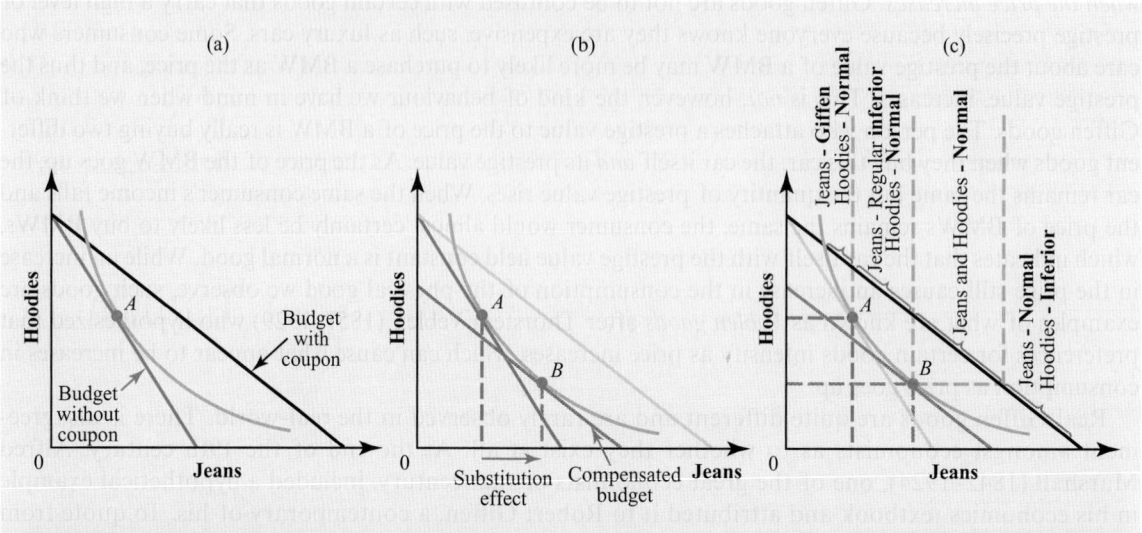

Go to MindTap to interact with this graph

In panel (c) of Graph 7.7, we focus on what happens when we switch from the hypothetical optimum on the compensated budget constraint to the new optimum on the final budget constraint. Since this involves no change in opportunity costs, we are left with a pure income effect as we jump from the optimal point B on the compensated budget constraint to the final optimum on the final budget constraint. Suppose we know that both hoodies and jeans are normal goods for the consumer. This implies that:

- When they experience an increase in income from the compensated to the final budget constraint, they will choose to consume more jeans and hoodies than they did at point B.
- If hoodies are inferior and jeans are normal, the consumer will consume more jeans and fewer hoodies than at B.
- If jeans are inferior and hoodies are normal, they will consume fewer jeans and more hoodies.

Given that the consumer is restricted in this example to consuming only hoodies and jeans, it cannot be the case that both goods are inferior because this would imply that they would consume fewer jeans and fewer hoodies on their final budget constraint than at point B, which would put them at a bundle to the southwest of B. Since more is better, the consumer would not be at an optimum given that they can move to a higher indifference curve from there.

Assume that jeans are an inferior good and that they are also a Giffen good. The definition of a Giffen good implies that the consumer will consume less of the good as its price decreases when exogenous income remains unchanged. Thus, they would end up consuming not just fewer jeans than at point B but also fewer than at point A. Notice that this is the only scenario under which we would not even have to first find the substitution effect; if we know something is a Giffen good and we know its price has decreased, we know that consumption will decrease as well. In each of the other scenarios, however, we needed to find the compensated optimum B before being able to apply the definition of normal or inferior goods.

Exercise 7A.8

In panel (c) of Graph 7.7, where would the final optimal bundle on the budget constraint with voucher lie if tastes were homothetic? What if they were quasilinear?

Finally, suppose you know that hoodies rather than jeans are a Giffen good. In order to observe a Giffen good, we must observe a price change for that good with exogenous income constant since Giffen goods are goods whose consumption moves in the same direction as *price* when income is exogenous and unchanged. In this example, we did not observe a price change for hoodies, which means that we cannot usefully apply the definition of a Giffen good to predict how consumption will change. Rather, we can note that since all Giffen goods are also inferior goods, the consumer will consume fewer hoodies as their income increases from the compensated budget constraint to the final budget constraint. Thus, knowing that hoodies are Giffen goods tells us nothing more in this example than knowing that hoodies are inferior goods.

Exercise 7A.9

Replicate Graph 7.7 for an increase in the price of jeans rather than a decrease.

Exercise 7A.10

Can you explain the following Venn diagram?

7B   The Mathematics of Income and Substitution Effects

In this section, we will begin to explore income and substitution effects mathematically, and our exploration of these effects will become deeper as we move through the next few chapters. As you read through this section, you are advised to follow the calculations we undertake closely on your own. In doing so, you will begin to get a feel for how we can use the various mathematical concepts introduced thus far to identify precisely the points *A*, *B* and *C* that appear in the graphs of this chapter. It might help you even more to re-read the chapter and construct spreadsheets in a programme like Microsoft Excel. Setting up such spreadsheets will give you a good feel for how the mathematics of consumer choice works for specific examples.

7B.1 The Impact of Changing Income on Behaviour

In Section 7A.1, we looked at how consumer behaviour changes when exogenous income changes, and we discovered that the answer depends on the nature of the underlying map of indifference curves. We will now translate some of this analysis from Section 7A.1 into the mathematical optimization language we developed in Chapter 6.

7B.1.1 Inferior and Normal Goods Consider, for instance, the example of pasta and steak introduced in Section 7A.1.1, and suppose the consumers discovered that consumption of pasta remained unchanged as their income increased as depicted in panel (b) of Graph 7.1. Suppose that the price of a box of pasta is €2 and the price of a kilo of steak is €10, and suppose we let boxes of pasta be denoted by x_1 and kilos of steak by x_2. We know from our discussion in Section 7A.1.1 that pasta consumption can remain constant as income increases only if the underlying tastes are quasilinear in pasta, that is, when utility functions can be written as $u(x_1,x_2) = v(x_1)+x_2$. For an income level I and for tastes that can be described by a utility function $u(x_1,x_2) = v(x_1)+x_2$, the constrained optimization problem can be written as:

$$\max_{x_1, x_2} u(x_1, x_2) = v(x_1) + x_2 \text{ subject to } 2x_1 + 10x_2 = I, \tag{7.1}$$

with a corresponding Lagrange function:

$$\mathcal{L}(x_1, x_2, \lambda) = v(x_1) + x_2 + \lambda(I - 2x_1 - 10x_2). \tag{7.2}$$

Taking the first two first-order conditions, we get:

$$\frac{\partial \mathcal{L}}{\partial x_1} = \frac{dv(x_1)}{dx_1} - 2\lambda = 0,$$

$$\frac{\partial \mathcal{L}}{\partial x_2} = 1 - 10\lambda = 0. \tag{7.3}$$

The second of the expressions in (7.3) can be rewritten as $\lambda = 1/10$, which, when substituted into the first expression in (7.3), gives:

$$\frac{dv(x_1)}{dx_1} = \frac{1}{5}. \tag{7.4}$$

The left-hand side of expression (7.4) is a function of x_1, whereas the right-hand side is a real number, which implies that when we have a specific functional form for the function v, we can solve for x_1 as just a real number. For instance, if $u(x_1,x_2) = \ln x_1 + x_2$ (implying $v(x_1) = \ln x_1$), expression (7.4) becomes:

$$\frac{1}{x_1} = \frac{1}{5} \quad \text{or} \quad x_1 = 5. \tag{7.5}$$

When the underlying tastes are quasilinear, the optimal quantity of pasta (x_1) is therefore 5 when prices of pasta and steak are €2 and €10, and is thus always the same regardless of what value the exogenous income I takes in the optimization problem (7.1). The variable I drops out of the analysis as we solve for x_1. Thus, quasilinear – or borderline normal/inferior – goods have no income effects.

This is not true for tastes that cannot be represented by quasilinear utility functions. Consider, for instance, the same problem but with underlying tastes that can be represented by the Cobb–Douglas utility function $u(x_1,x_2) = x_1^{\alpha l} x_2^{(1-\alpha)}$. The Lagrange function is:

$$\mathcal{L}(x_1, x_2, \lambda) = x_1^{\alpha}x_2^{(1-\alpha)} + \lambda(I - 2x_1 - 10x_2), \qquad (7.6)$$

and the first-order conditions for this problem are:

$$\frac{\partial\mathcal{L}}{\partial x_1} = \alpha x_1^{(\alpha-1)}x_2^{(1-\alpha)} - 2\lambda = 0,$$

$$\frac{\partial\mathcal{L}}{\partial x_2} = (1-\alpha)x_1^{\alpha}x_2^{-\alpha} - 10\lambda = 0, \qquad (7.7)$$

$$\frac{\partial\mathcal{L}}{\partial\lambda} = I - 2x_1 - 10x_2 = 0.$$

Adding 2λ to both sides of the first equation and 10λ to both sides of the second equation, and dividing these equations by each other, we get $\alpha x_2/(1-\alpha)x_1 = 1/5$ or $x_2 = (1-\alpha)x_1/5\alpha$. Substituting this into the third equation of expression (7.7) and solving for x_1, we get:

$$x_1 = \frac{\alpha I}{2}. \qquad (7.8)$$

Thus, for the underlying Cobb–Douglas tastes specified here, the optimal consumption of pasta (x_1) depends on income, with higher income leading to greater consumption of pasta. Cobb–Douglas tastes as well as all other homothetic tastes therefore, represent tastes for normal goods as depicted in panel (c) of Graph 7.1.

Finally, none of the utility functions we have discussed thus far represent tastes for inferior goods. This is because such tastes are difficult to capture in simple mathematical functions, in part because *there are no tastes such that a particular good is always an inferior good*. To see this, imagine beginning with zero income, thus consuming the origin (0,0) in our graphs. Now suppose you are given €10. Since we cannot consume negative amounts of goods, it is not possible for you to consume less pasta than you did before you were given €10, and it is therefore not possible to have tastes that represent inferior goods around the origin of our graphs. *All goods are therefore normal or borderline normal/inferior goods at least around the bundle* (0,0). Goods can be inferior only for some portion of an indifference map, and this logical conclusion makes it difficult to represent such tastes in simple utility functions.

7B.1.2 Luxury Goods and Necessities We defined the terms *luxury goods* and *necessities* in Section 7A.1.2, with borderline goods between the two represented by homothetic tastes. Homothetic tastes have the feature that the marginal rates of substitution stay constant along linear rays emanating from the origin, and it is this feature of such tastes that ensures that when exogenous income is increased by k per cent without a change in opportunity costs, consumption of each good also increases by k per cent, leaving the ratio of consumption of one good relative to the other unchanged.

For instance, in equation (7.8), we discovered that the optimal consumption of pasta is equal to $\alpha I/2$ when the consumer's tastes are captured by the Cobb–Douglas function $u(x_1,x_2) = x_1^{\alpha}x_2^{(1-\alpha)}$, when the price of pasta is €2, the price of steak is €10 and when income is given by I. When substituting this value into the budget constraint for x_1 and solving for x_2, we can also determine that the optimal consumption of steak is $(1-\alpha)I/10$. Thus, the ratio (x_1/x_2) of pasta consumption to steak consumption under these economic circumstances is $5\alpha/(1-\alpha)$; consumption of pasta relative to steak is *independent of income*. Since we know that Cobb–Douglas utility functions represent homothetic tastes, this simply confirms what our intuition already tells us: both pasta and steak are borderline luxury/necessity goods when the underlying tastes can be represented by Cobb–Douglas utility functions.

Again, this is not true for all types of tastes. If tastes could be represented by the quasilinear utility function $u(x_1,x_2) = \ln x_1 + x_2$, we concluded in expression (7.5) that optimal consumption of pasta would be equal to 5 boxes *regardless of income level* assuming that the consumer had at least enough income to cover that much pasta consumption. Substituting this into the budget constraint for x_1 and solving for x_2, we also get optimal steak consumption as $(I - 10)/10$; that is, the consumer's optimal steak consumption is a function of their income whereas their optimal pasta consumption is not. Consumption of pasta *relative* to the consumption of steak declines with income, making pasta a necessity and steak a luxury good.

7B.2 The Impact of Changing Opportunity Costs on Behaviour

We introduced the concept of a *substitution effect* in Section 7A.2 by focusing on a particular example of two friends visiting the Cayman Islands. Panel (a) of Graph 7.3 illustrated the choice sets of the friends based on the assumptions made, and panel (b) illustrated a substitution effect from the different opportunity costs arising from those choice sets.

7B.2.1 Renting a Car Versus Taking a Taxi
Assume that the two friends arrived at the Cayman Islands with €2000 to spend on their holiday and that taxi rides cost €1 per kilometre. Letting x_1 denote kilometres driven and x_2 euros of other consumption in the Cayman Islands, we can infer that the budget constraint is $2000 = x_1 + x_2$ given that the price of euros of other consumption is by definition also 1. Assume also that the friends' tastes can be summarized by the Cobb–Douglas utility function $u(x_1,x_2) = x_1^{0.1}x_2^{0.9}$. The constrained optimization problem, allows us to determine that the optimal consumption bundle is $x_1 = 200$ and $x_2 = 1800$.

Exercise 7B.1

Set up one of the friend's constrained optimization problem and solve it to check that their optimal consumption bundle is indeed equal to this.

Now suppose that the consumer who chose to rent the car lost their receipt and no longer remembers how much of a fixed fee they were charged to drive it for the week. All they remember is that fuel cost €0.20 per kilometre. From the information we have, we can calculate what the fixed rental car fee must have been in order for them to be just as well off renting a car as the other friend was using taxis.

Specifically, we can calculate the value associated with the consumer's optimal indifference curve by substituting $x_1 = 200$ and $x_2 = 1800$ into the utility function $u(x_1,x_2) = x_1^{0.1}x_2^{0.9}$ to get a value of approximately 1445. While this number has no inherent meaning since we cannot quantify utility objectively, we do know from our analysis in Section 7A.2.1 and Graph 7.3, that the two friends ended up on the same indifference curve, and thus with the same utility level as measured by the utility function that both share. This gives us enough information to find bundle B – the consumer's optimal bundle of kilometres driven and other consumption in panel (b) of Graph 7.3 using a method that builds on the intuition that comes out of the graph. We have to find the smallest possible choice set with a budget constraint that has the slope reflecting the lower opportunity cost for kilometres driven and is tangential to the indifference curve that the other friend has achieved, that is, the indifference curve associated with the utility value 1445.

This can be formulated mathematically as the following problem: we would like to find the minimum expenditure necessary for achieving a utility value of 1445, as measured by the utility function $u(x_1,x_2) = x_1^{0.1}x_2^{0.9}$, given that the price for kilometres driven is 0.2 while the price for other consumption remains at 1. Letting E stand for expenditure, we can state this formally as a *constrained minimization problem*:

$$\min_{x_1, x_2} E = 0.2x_1 + x_2 \text{ subject to } x_1^{0.1}x_2^{0.9} = 1445. \tag{7.9}$$

Constrained minimization problems have the same basic structure as constrained maximization problems. The first part of (7.9) lets us know that we are trying to minimize a function by choosing the values for x_1 and x_2. The function we are trying to minimize, or what we call our *objective function*, follows and is the equation for the budget constraint that we will end up with, which reflects the new opportunity cost of driving kilometres given that the consumer paid a fixed fee for their rental car and now faces a lower opportunity cost for driving each kilometre. Finally, the last part of (7.9) tells us the *constraint* of our minimization problem: we are trying to reach the indifference curve associated with the value 1445.

Finding the solution to a minimization problem is quite similar to finding the solution to a maximization problem. The reason for this similarity is most easily seen within the economic examples with which we are working. In our utility maximization problem, for instance, we are taking the budget line as fixed and trying to find the indifference curve that is tangential to that line. This is illustrated graphically in panel (a) of Graph 7.8 where a consumer faces a fixed budget constraint and tries to get to the highest possible indifference curve that still contains a bundle within the choice set defined by the fixed budget constraint. In the expenditure minimization problem defined in expression (7.9), on the other hand, we are taking the indifference curve as fixed and trying to find the smallest possible choice set given the opportunity costs of the goods. This is illustrated in panel (b) of Graph 7.8 where we are trying to reach a fixed indifference curve with the smallest possible choice set. In both cases, we are therefore trying to find a solution, a combination of x_1 and x_2, where an indifference curve is tangential to a budget constraint assuming the problem does not have non-convexities or corner solutions.

Graph 7.8 Maximizing Utility with Budgets Fixed (a) Versus Minimizing Expenditure with Utility Fixed (b)

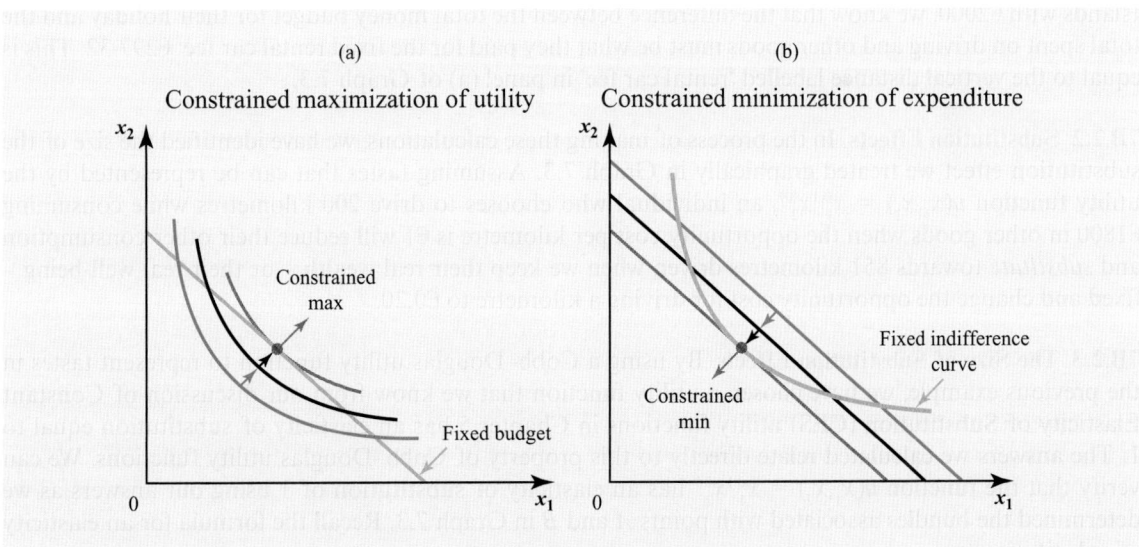

For this reason, the same Lagrange method that we have employed in solving maximization problems can be employed to solve our minimization problem. We create the Lagrange function by combining the *objective function* with a second term that is equal to 1 times the *constraint* set to zero, only now the objective function is the budget constraint and the constraint is the indifference curve:

$$\mathcal{L}(x_1, x_2, \lambda) = 0.2x_1 + x_2 + \lambda(1445 - x_1^{0.1}x_2^{0.9}). \tag{7.10}$$

We take the first derivatives of $\mathcal{L}$ with respect to the choice variables (x_1 and x_2) and λ to get the first-order conditions:

$$\frac{\partial \mathcal{L}}{\partial x_1} = 0.2 - 0.1\lambda x_1^{-0.9}x_2^{0.9} = 0,$$

$$\frac{\partial \mathcal{L}}{\partial x_2} = 1 - 0.9\lambda x_1^{0.1}x_2^{-0.1} = 0, \qquad\qquad (7.11)$$

$$1445 - x_1^{0.1}x_2^{0.9} = 0.$$

Solving the first two equations for x_2 we get:

$$x_2 = \frac{0.9(0.2x_1)}{0.1} = 1.8x_1 \qquad\qquad (7.12)$$

and substituting this into the third equation and solving for x_1, we get $x_1 = 851.34$. Finally, substituting this back into expression (7.12), we get $x_2 = 1532.41$. This is point B in Graph 7.3, which implies that the consumer chose to drive approximately 851 kilometres in their rental car during their Cayman Islands holiday while consuming approximately €1532 in other goods.

We can now see how much the bundle B costs by multiplying the optimal levels of x_1 and x_2 by the prices of those goods, 0.2 for x_1 and 1 for x_2, and adding these expenditures together:

$$E = 0.2(851.34) + 1(1532.41) = 1702.68 \qquad\qquad (7.13)$$

Thus, bundle B costs a total of €1702.68. Since we know that the consumer arrived in the Cayman Islands with €2000, we know that the difference between the total money budget for their holiday and the total spent on driving and other goods must be what they paid for the fixed rental car fee: €297.32. This is equal to the vertical distance labelled 'rental car fee' in panel (a) of Graph 7.3.

7B.2.2 Substitution Effects In the process of making these calculations, we have identified the size of the substitution effect we treated graphically in Graph 7.3. Assuming tastes that can be represented by the utility function $u(x_1,x_2) = x_1^{0.1}x_2^{0.9}$, an individual who chooses to drive 200 kilometres while consuming €1800 in other goods when the opportunity cost per kilometre is €1 will reduce their other consumption and *substitute* towards 851 kilometres driven when we keep their real wealth – or their real well-being – fixed and change the opportunity cost for driving a kilometre to €0.20.

7B.2.3 The Size of Substitution Effects By using a Cobb–Douglas utility function to represent tastes in the previous example, we have chosen a utility function that we know from our discussion of Constant Elasticity of Substitution (CES) utility functions in Chapter 5 has an elasticity of substitution equal to 1. The answers we calculated relate directly to this property of Cobb–Douglas utility functions. We can verify that the function $u(x_1,x_2) = x_1^{0.1}x_2^{0.9}$ has an elasticity of substitution of 1 using our answers as we determined the bundles associated with points A and B in Graph 7.3. Recall the formula for an elasticity of substitution:

$$\text{Elasticity of substitution} = \left| \frac{\%\Delta(x_2/x_1)}{\%\Delta MRS} \right|. \qquad\qquad (7.14)$$

Bundle A, one friend's (Friend X) optimal bundle, is (200, 1800), while bundle B, the other friend's (Friend Y) optimal bundle, is (851.34, 1532.41). Friend X's ratio of x_2/x_1 is therefore equal to 1800/200, or 9, while Friend Y's ratio of x_2/x_1 is 1532.41/851.34 or 1.8. In going from A to B on the same indifference curve, the change in the ratio x_2/x_1, $\Delta (x_2/x_1)$, is therefore equal to 27.2. The $\%\Delta (x_2/x_1)$ is just the change in the ratio (x_2/x_1) divided by the original level of (x_2/x_1) at bundle A, that is:

$$\%\Delta\left(\frac{x_2}{x_1}\right) = \frac{\Delta(x_2/x_1)}{x_2^A/x_1^A} = \frac{-7.2}{9} = -0.8. \tag{7.15}$$

Similarly, the MRS at bundle A is equal to the slope of Friend X's budget constraint, which is equal to -1, given that they face a cost per kilometre of €1. Friend Y's MRS at bundle B, on the other hand, is equal to the slope of their budget constraint, which is equal to 0.2 given that they face a cost per kilometre of only €0.20. The $\%\Delta MRS$ as we go from A to B is therefore the change in the MRS divided by the original MRS at bundle A, that is:

$$\%\Delta MRS = \frac{\Delta MRS}{MRS^A} = 0.8. \tag{7.16}$$

Substituting (7.15) and (7.16) into the equation for an elasticity of substitution in expression (7.14), we get an elasticity of substitution equal to 1. Thus, when the marginal rate of substitution of the indifference curve in Graph 7.3 changed by 80 per cent (from -1 to -0.2), the ratio of other consumption (x_2) to kilometres driven (x_1) also changed by 80 per cent (from 9 to 1.8). *It is the elasticity of substitution in the utility function that determined the size of the substitution effect we calculated.*

This relates directly to the intuition we built in Graph 7.4, where we showed how substitution effects get larger as the degree of substitutability, or the elasticity of substitution in our more mathematical language, changes. Were we to use utility functions with elasticities of substitution different from those in Cobb–Douglas utility functions, we would therefore calculate substitution effects that were larger or smaller depending on whether the elasticity of substitution embedded into those utility functions was greater or smaller.

Consider, for instance, the CES utility function with $\rho = -0.5$, which implies an elasticity of substitution of 2 rather than 1 as in the Cobb–Douglas case where $\rho = 0$. Suppose that the utility function the two friends share is:

$$u(x_1, x_2) = (0.25x_1^{0.5} + 0.75x_2^{0.5})^2, \tag{7.17}$$

and suppose again that their money budget for their Cayman Islands holiday is €2000 and the per kilometre cost is €1 for taxis and €0.20 for rental cars. The exponents in equation (7.17) are positive because ρ is negative and each exponent in the CES utility function has a negative sign in front of it. Friend X's optimization problem is:

$$\max_{x_1, x_2}(0.25x_1^{0.5} + 0.75x_2^{0.5})^2 \text{ subject to } x_1 + x_2 = 2000, \tag{7.18}$$

the results of which you can verify in an optimal consumption bundle of $x_1 = 200$ and $x_2 = 1800$, just as in our previous example. Thus, point A remains unchanged. The indifference curve on which point A lies, however, differs substantially from that in the previous example because of the different elasticity of substitution embedded in equation (7.17). Substituting the optimal bundle for Friend X back into the utility function (7.17), we can calculate that they operate on an indifference curve giving them utility of 1250 as measured by this utility function. We can repeat our analysis of calculating bundle B by solving the problem analogous to the one we stated in expression (7.9) but adapted to the model we are now working with:

$$\min_{x_1, x_2} E = 0.2x_1 + x_2 \text{ subject to } (0.25x_1^{0.5} + 0.75x_2^{0.5})^2 = 1250. \tag{7.19}$$

You can verify on your own that this results in an optimal bundle B of $x_1 = 2551.02$ and $x_2 = 918.37$, which implies a substitution effect much larger than the one we found with the Cobb–Douglas utility function. This is because we have built a greater elasticity of substitution into the utility function of equation (7.17) than we had in our previous Cobb–Douglas utility function. The difference between the two scenarios is illustrated graphically in Graph 7.9.

Exercise 7B.2

How much did Friend Y pay in a fixed rental car fee in order for them to be indifferent to taking taxis in this example? Why is this amount larger than in the Cobb–Douglas case we calculated earlier?

Graph 7.9 Different Elasticities of Substitution

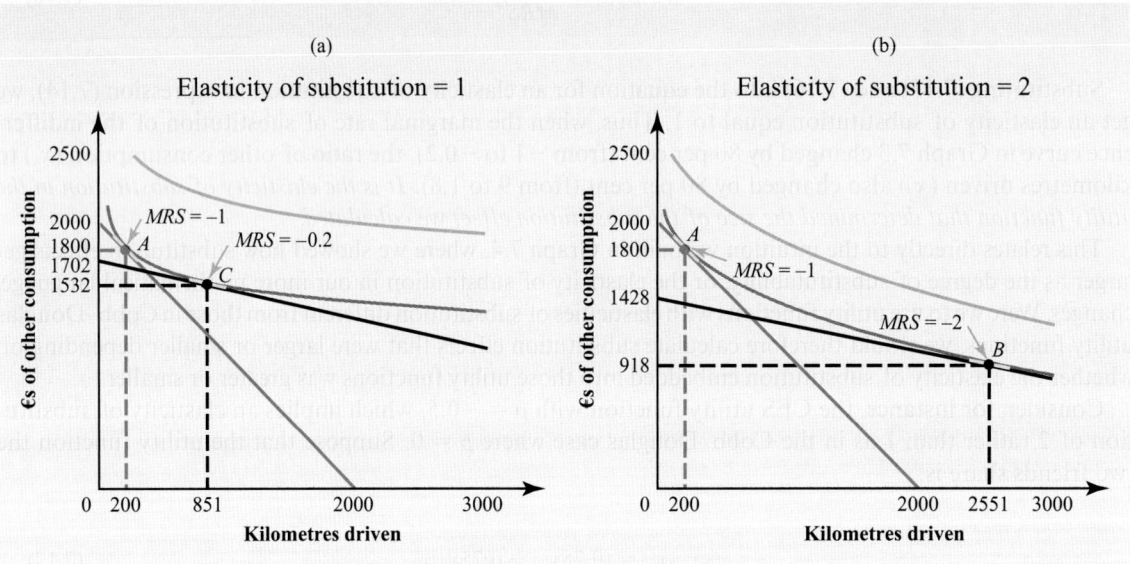

Table 7.1 summarizes the outcome of similar calculations for CES utility functions with different elasticities of substitution. In each case, the remaining parameters of the CES utility function are set to ensure that Friend X's optimal choice remains the same: 200 kilometres driven and €1800 in other consumption. More precisely, the utility function $u(x_1, x_2) = (\alpha x_1^{-\rho} + (1 - \alpha)x_2^{-\rho})^{-1/\rho}$ was used for these calculations, with ρ set as indicated in the first column of the table and α adjusted to ensure that point A remains at $(200, 1800)$.

Table 7.1 $u(x_1, x_2) = (ax_1^{-\rho} + (1 - \alpha)x_2^{-\rho})^{-1/\rho}$

	Substitution Effects as Elasticity of Substitution Changes	
ρ	Elasticity of Substitution	Substitution Effect
−0.5	2	2351.02 more kilometres driven at B than at A
0.0	1	651.34 more kilometres driven at B than at A
0.5	0.67	337.28 more kilometres driven at B than at A
1.0	0.50	222.53 more kilometres driven at B than at A
5.0	0.167	57.55 more kilometres driven at B than at A
10.0	0.091	29.67 more kilometres driven at B than at A
∞	0.000	0.00 more kilometres driven at B than A

7B.3 Price Changes: Income and Substitution Effects Combined

We concluded in Section 7A.3 that most price changes involve both income and substitution effects because they involve both a change in our real wealth or our optimal indifference curve, and a change in opportunity costs. We can employ all the mathematical tools we have built thus far to identify income and substitution effects when prices change. In the following, we will consider once again the case of shopping for jeans (x_1) and hoodies (x_2) to demonstrate how we can identify these effects separately. Throughout, we will assume that the consumer has €200 to spend and that the price of hoodies is €10. We will focus on what happens when the price of jeans, p_1, changes. We will assume (unrealistically) in this section that it is possible to consume fractions of hoodies and jeans.

Suppose first that the consumer's tastes can once again be represented by a Cobb–Douglas utility function:

$$u(x_1, x_2) = x_1^{0.5}x_2^{0.5}. \tag{7.20}$$

The constrained maximization problem at the shop is:

$$\max_{x_1,x_2} x_1^{0.5}x_2^{0.5} \text{ subject to } p_1x_1 + 10x_2 = 200. \tag{7.21}$$

Solving this in the usual way gives us the optimal bundle:

$$x_1 = \frac{100}{p_1} \text{ and } x_2 = 10. \tag{7.22}$$

Exercise 7B.3

Check to see that this solution is correct.

Initially, the consumer faces a price of €20 per pair of jeans, which implies (according to equation 7.22) that their optimal bundle is 5 pairs of jeans and 10 hoodies. The consumer discovers that they have a 50 per cent off voucher for jeans, effectively reducing the price of jeans from €20 to €10. As a result of this decrease in the price of jeans, the optimal consumption bundle changes from (5,10) to (10,10). This is illustrated in panel (a) of Graph 7.10, with bundle A representing the original optimal bundle and bundle C representing the new optimal bundle.

In order to decompose this change in behaviour into income and substitution effects, we have to calculate how consumption would have changed had the consumer faced the same change in opportunity costs without experiencing an increase in real wealth, that is, without having shifted to a higher indifference curve. Thus, we need to employ the method we developed in the previous section to identify how much money they would have to give up when they received the coupon to be able to be just as well off as they were originally without the coupon. Notice that this is analogous to our example involving the two friends in the Cayman Islands, where they wanted to identify how much the fixed rental car fee must have been in order for one of them to be just as well off as the other was using taxis. In both cases, there is a fixed indifference curve, and we are trying to find the smallest possible choice set that will give the consumer a fixed utility level when their opportunity costs change.

In panel (b) of Graph 7.10, we illustrate the problem of finding the substitution effect graphically. We begin by drawing the indifference curve IC^A that contains bundle A and the budget constraint labelled 'original budget' that the consumer has with the voucher. We shift this budget constraint inwards, keeping the slope and thus the new opportunity cost fixed, until only a single point on the indifference curve remains within the choice set. This process identifies bundle B on the compensated budget, the bundle they would choose if they faced the opportunity costs under the voucher but had lost just enough money to be just as well off as they were originally when they consumed bundle A.

Graph 7.10 Income and Substitution Effects When Tastes Are Cobb–Douglas

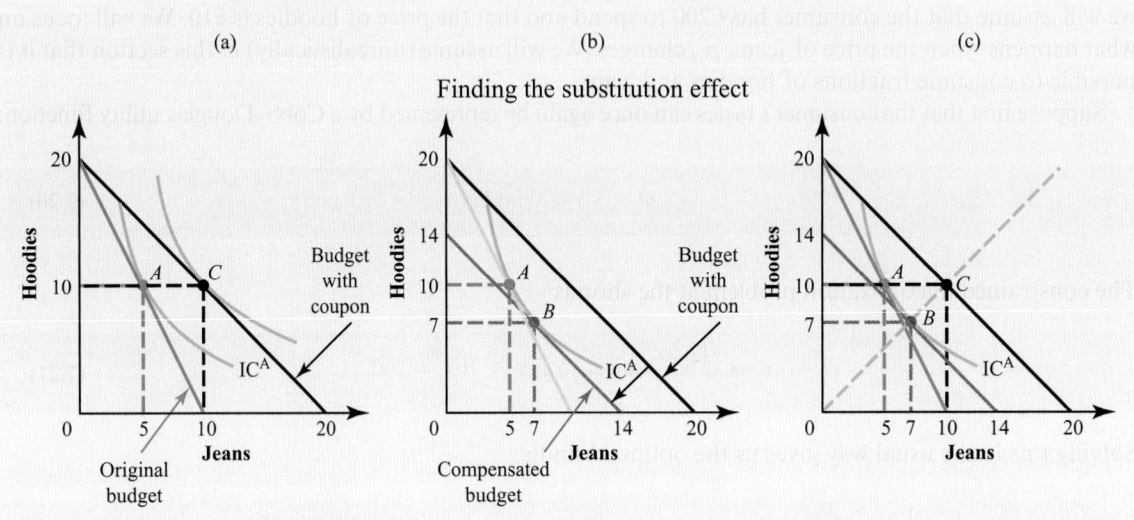

Mathematically, we state the process graphed in panel (b) of Graph 7.10 as a constrained minimization problem in which we are trying to minimize total expenditures or money budget, subject to the constraint that the consumer would like to consume on the indifference curve that contains bundle A.

We can write this as follows:

$$\min_{x_1, x_2} E = 10x_1 + 10x_2 \text{ subject to } x_1^{0.5}x_2^{0.5} = U^A, \tag{7.23}$$

where U^A represents the level of utility attained at bundle A. This level of utility can be calculated using the utility function $x_1^{0.5}x_2^{0.5}$ by substituting the bundle $A(x_1 = 5, x_2 = 10)$ into the function, which gives us $U^A \approx 7.071$. Solving this *minimization* problem using the Lagrange method illustrated in our Cayman Islands in the previous section, we get:

$$x_1 = x_2 \approx 7.071. \tag{7.24}$$

Exercise 7B.4

Verify the solutions to the minimization problem.

The total expenditure required to consume this bundle at prices $p_1 = p_2 = 10$ is €141.42, which implies that you could take €58.58 out of the consumer's initial €200 and give them a 50 per cent off voucher and they would be just as well off as they were without the voucher and with their initial €200. The consumer's real income is €58.58 higher when they get the coupon because that is how much could be taken from them once they get the voucher without changing their well-being. The compensated budget, which keeps utility constant, is therefore €141.42.

Combining panels (a) and (b) in Graph 7.10 into a single graph, we get panel (c) of Graph 7.10 showing bundles A, B and C with the values we have calculated for each of these bundles. The substitution effect is the movement from A to B, while the income effect, reflecting the change in behaviour that is solely due to the fact that the consumer is €58.58 richer when they receive the voucher, is the movement from B to C.

Exercise 7B.5

Notice that the ratio of jeans to hoodies consumption is the same ($= 1$) at bundles B and C. What feature of Cobb–Douglas tastes is responsible for this result?

Just as was true for the substitution effects we identified in the Cayman Islands example, the size of the substitution effect here once again arises from the degree of substitutability of the goods as captured by the shape of indifference curves and the form of the utility function. Similarly, the size of the income effect depends on the underlying nature of tastes and the degree to which jeans and hoodies represent normal or inferior goods.

Suppose, for instance, that a consumer's tastes could be represented by the quasilinear utility function:

$$u(x_1, x_2) = 6x_1^{0.5} + x_2. \tag{7.25}$$

Setting up the maximization problem analogous to (7.21) gives:

$$\max_{x_1, x_2} \; 6x_1^{0.5} + x_2 \text{ subject to } p_1 x_1 + 10 x_2 = 200, \tag{7.26}$$

which you can verify solves to:

$$x_1 = \frac{900}{p_1^2} \text{ and } x_2 = \frac{20p_1 - 90}{p_1}. \tag{7.27}$$

Thus, when the price of jeans is €20, we get an optimal bundle (2.25,15.5), and when the price falls to €10 due to the coupon, we get an optimal bundle (9,11). Total utility without the coupon is found by substituting $x_1 = 2.25$ and $x_2 = 15.5$ into equation (7.25), which gives utility equal to 24.5. This permits us to find the substitution effect by solving the constrained minimization problem:

$$\min_{x_1, x_2} \; E = 10x_1 + 10x_2 \text{ subject to } 6x_1^{0.5} + x_2 = 24.5, \tag{7.28}$$

which gives $x_1 = 9$ and $x_2 = 6.5$. Thus, ignoring the fact that it is difficult to consume fractions of jeans, the substitution effect changes consumption of jeans from the original 2.25 to 9, and the income effect causes no additional change in consumption for jeans. This lack of an income effect arises because tastes that are quasilinear in a particular good, in this case jeans, do not exhibit income effects for that good; such goods are borderline normal/inferior goods.

Exercise 7B.6

Using the previous calculations, plot graphs similar to Graph 7.10 illustrating income and substitution effects when tastes can be represented by the utility function $u(x_1,x_2) = 6x_1^{0.5} + x_2$.

End-of-Chapter Exercises

7.1† Here, we consider some logical relationships between preferences and types of goods.

A. Suppose you consider all the goods that you might potentially want to consume.

a. Is it possible for all these goods to be luxury goods at every consumption bundle? Is it possible for all of them to be necessities?

b. Is it possible for all goods to be inferior goods at every consumption bundle? Is it possible for all of them to be normal goods?

c. *True or False*: When tastes are homothetic, all goods are normal goods.

d. *True or False*: When tastes are homothetic, some goods could be luxuries while others could be necessities.

e. *True or False*: When tastes are quasilinear, one of the goods is a necessity.

f. *True or False*: In a two-good model, if the two goods are perfect complements, they must both be normal goods.

g. *True or False*: In a three-good model, if two of the goods are perfect complements, they must both be normal goods.

B. In each of the following cases, suppose that a person whose tastes can be characterized by the given utility function has income I and faces prices that are all equal to 1. Illustrate mathematically how their consumption of each good changes with income, and use your answer to determine whether the goods are normal or inferior, luxuries or necessities.

a. $u(x_1,x_2) = x_1 x_2$

b. $u(x_1,x_2) = x_1 + \ln x_2$

c. $u(x_1,x_2) = \ln x_1 + \ln x_2$

d. $u(x_1,x_2,x_3) = 2\ln x_1 + \ln x_2 + 4\ln x_3$

e. *$u(x_1,x_2) = 2x_1^{0.5} + \ln x_2$

7.2 Suppose you have an income of €24 and the only two goods you consume are apples (x_1) and peaches (x_2). The price of apples is €4 each and the price of peaches is €3 each.

A. Suppose that your optimal consumption is 4 peaches and 3 apples.

a. Illustrate this in a graph using indifference curves and budget lines.

b. Assume that the price of apples falls to €2 and enough money is taken away from you to make you as happy as you were originally. Will you buy more or fewer peaches?

c. In reality, no income is taken away from you as described in (b), but your income stays at €24 after the price of apples falls. It is observed that after the price of apples fell, you did not change your consumption of peaches. Can you conclude whether peaches are an inferior or normal good for you?

B. Suppose that your tastes can be characterized by the function $u(x_1,x_2) = x_1^\alpha x_2^{(1-\alpha)}$.

a. What value must α take in order for you to choose 3 apples and 4 peaches at the original prices?

b. What bundle would you consume under the scenario described in A(b)?

c. How much income can be taken away from you and still keep you as happy as you were before the price change?

d. What will you actually consume after the price increase?

7.3† **Everyday Application:** *Housing Price Fluctuations: Part 2.* Suppose, as in end-of-chapter exercise 6.3, you have €400 000 to spend on square metres of housing and all other goods. Assume the same is true for another individual.

A. Suppose that you initially face a €100 per square metre price for housing, and you choose to buy a 2000 m² house.

a. Illustrate this on a graph with square metreage of housing on the horizontal axis and other consumption on the vertical. Suppose that the price of housing falls to €50 per square metre after you bought your 2000 m² house. Denote the square metreage of the house you would switch to as h_B.

b. Is h_B smaller or larger than 2000 m²? Does your answer depend on whether housing is normal, regular inferior or Giffen?

c. Now suppose that the price of housing had fallen to €50 per square metre *before* you bought your initial 2000 m² house. Denote the size of house you would have bought h_C and illustrate it in your graph.

d. Is h_C larger than h_B? Is it larger than 2000 m²? Does your answer depend on whether housing is a normal, regular inferior, or Giffen good?

e. Now consider the second individual. They did not buy a house until the price of housing was €50 per square metre, at which time they bought a 4000 m² house. The price of housing rises to €100 per square metre. Would this person sell their house and buy a new one? If so, is the new house size h_B larger or smaller than 4000 m²? Does your answer depend on whether housing is normal, regular inferior or Giffen for the individual?

f. Are they better or worse off?

g. Suppose they had not purchased at the low price, but rather purchased a house of size h_C after the price had risen to €100 per square metres. Is h_C larger or smaller than h_B? Is it larger or smaller than 4000 m²? Does your answer depend on whether housing is normal, regular inferior or Giffen for the individual?

B. Suppose both have tastes that can be represented by the utility function $u(x_1,x_2) = x_1^{0.5}x_2^{0.5}$, where x_1 is square metres of housing and x_2 is euros of other goods.

a. Calculate the optimal level of housing consumption x_1 as a function of per square metre housing prices p_1 and income I.

b. Verify that your initial choice of a 2000 m² house and the other individual's initial choice of a 4000 m² house were optimal under the circumstances faced assuming both started with €400 000.

c. Calculate the values of h_B and h_C as they are described in A(a) and (c).

d. Calculate h_B and h_C as they are described in A(e) and (g).

e. Verify your answer to A(f).

7.4* **Business Application:** *Are Gucci Products Giffen Goods?* We defined a Giffen good as a good that consumers with exogenous incomes buy more of when the price increases. Giffen goods can be mistaken for luxury goods such as expensive Gucci purses and accessories. If the marketing departments for firms like Gucci are very successful, they may find a way of associating price with 'prestige' in the minds of consumers, and this may allow them to raise the price *and* sell more products. Would that make Gucci products Giffen goods? The answer, as you will see in this exercise, is no.

A. Suppose we model a consumer who cares about the practical value and style of Gucci products, euros of other consumption and the prestige value of being seen with Gucci products. Denote these as x_1, x_2 and x_3, respectively.

a. The consumer only has to buy x_1 and x_2 – the prestige value x_3 comes with the Gucci products. Let p_1 denote the price of Gucci products and $p_2 = 1$ be the price of euros of other consumption. Illustrate the consumer's budget constraint assuming an exogenous income I.

b. The prestige value of Gucci purchases, x_3, is something an individual consumer has no control over. If x_3 is fixed at a particular level $\bar{x}_3$, the consumer therefore operates on a two-dimensional slice of their three-dimensional indifference map over x_1, x_2 and x_3. Draw such a slice for the indifference curve that contains the consumer's optimal bundle A on the budget from part (a).

    c. Now suppose that Gucci manages to raise the prestige value of its products and thus x_3 that comes with the purchase of Gucci products. For now, suppose they do this without changing p_1. This implies you will shift to a different two-dimensional slice of your three-dimensional indifference map. Illustrate the new two-dimensional indifference curve that contains A. Is the new *MRS* at A greater or smaller in absolute value than it was before?

    d. *Would the consumer consume more or fewer Gucci products after the increase in prestige value?

    e. Now suppose that Gucci manages to convince consumers Gucci products become more desirable the more expensive they are. The prestige value x_3 is linked to p_1, the price of the Gucci products. On a new graph, illustrate the change in the consumer's budget as a result of an increase in p_1.

    f. Suppose that our consumer increases their purchases of Gucci products as a result of the increase in the price p_1. Illustrate two indifference curves, one that gives rise to the original optimum A and another that gives rise to the new optimum C. Can these indifference curves cross?

    g. Explain why, even though the behaviour is consistent with what we would expect if Gucci products were a Giffen good, Gucci products are not a Giffen good in this case.

    h. In the chapter, we defined the following: A good is a *Veblen good* if *preferences* for the good change as price increases, with this change in preferences possibly leading to an increase in consumption as price increases. Are Gucci products a Veblen good in this exercise?

B. Consider the same definition of x_1, x_2 and x_3 as in part A. Suppose that the tastes for our consumer can be captured by the utility function $u(x_1,x_2,x_3) = ax_3^2 \ln x_1 + x_2$.

    a. Set up the consumer's utility maximization problem, keeping in mind that x_3 is not a choice variable.

    b. Solve for the optimal consumption of x_1, which will be a function of the prestige value x_3.

    c. Is x_1 normal or inferior? Is it Giffen?

    d. Now suppose that prestige value is a function of p_1. In particular, suppose that $x_3 = p_1$. Substitute this into your solution for x_1. Will consumption increase or decrease as p_1 increases?

    e. How would you explain that x_1 is not a Giffen good despite the fact that its consumption increases as p_1 goes up?

7.5† **Policy Application:** *Fuel Efficiency, Fuel Consumption and Fuel Prices.* Policy makers frequently search for ways to reduce consumption of fuel. One straightforward option is to tax petrol and diesel, thereby encouraging consumers to drive less and switch to more fuel-efficient cars.

A. *Suppose that you have tastes for driving and for other consumption, and assume throughout that your tastes are homothetic.

    a. On a graph with monthly kilometres driven on the horizontal and monthly other consumption on the vertical axis, illustrate two budget lines: one in which you own a fuel-inefficient car, which has a low monthly payment that has to be made regardless of how much the car is driven but high fuel use per kilometre the other in which you own a fuel-efficient car, which has a high monthly payment that has to be made regardless of how much the car is driven but uses less fuel per kilometre. Draw this in such a way that it is possible for you to be indifferent between owning the fuel-inefficient and the fuel-efficient car.

    b. Suppose you are indeed indifferent. Which car will you drive more?

    c. Can you tell with which car you will use more fuel? What does your answer depend on?

    d. Now suppose that the government imposes a tax on fuel, and this doubles the opportunity cost of driving both types of cars. If you were indifferent before the tax was imposed, can you now say whether you will definitively buy one car or the other assuming you waited to buy a car until after the tax is imposed? What does your answer depend on? *Hint:* It may be helpful to consider the extreme cases of perfect substitutes and perfect complements before deriving your general conclusion to this question.

    e. The empirical evidence suggests that consumers shift towards more fuel-efficient cars when the price of fuel increases. *True or False*: This would tend to suggest that driving and other good consumption are relatively complementary.

    f. Suppose an increase in fuel taxes raises the opportunity cost of driving a kilometre with a fuel-efficient car to the opportunity cost of driving a fuel-inefficient vehicle *before* the tax increase. Will someone who was previously indifferent between a fuel-efficient and a fuel-inefficient car now drive more or less in a fuel-efficient car than they did in a fuel-inefficient vehicle prior to the tax increase? Continue with the assumption that tastes are homothetic.

B. Suppose your tastes were captured by the utility function $u(x_1,x_2) = x_1^{0.5}x_2^{0.5}$, where x_1 stands for kilometres driven and x_2 stands for other consumption. Suppose you have €600 per month of discretionary income to devote to your transportation and other consumption needs and that the monthly payment on a fuel-inefficient vehicle is €200. Furthermore, suppose the initial price of fuel is €0.10 per kilometre in the fuel-efficient car and €0.20 per kilometre in the fuel-inefficient vehicle.

   a. Calculate the number of monthly kilometres driven if you own a fuel-inefficient vehicle.

   b. Suppose you are indifferent between the fuel-inefficient vehicle and the fuel-efficient car. How much must the monthly payment for the fuel-efficient car be?

   c. Now suppose that the government imposes a tax on fuel that doubles the price per kilometre driven of each of the two cars. Calculate the optimal consumption bundle under each of the new budget constraints.

   d. Do you now switch to the fuel-efficient car?

   e. Consider the utility function you have worked with so far as a special case of the CES family $u(x_1,x_2) = (0.5x_1^{-\rho} + 0.5x_2^{-\rho})^{-1/\rho}$. Given what you concluded in A(d) of this question, how would your answer to B(d) change as ρ changes?

7.6 **Policy Application:** *Social Housing and Housing Subsidies.* Consider two different social housing programmes, one where a family is offered a particular flat for a below-market rent and another where the government provides a housing price subsidy that the family can use anywhere in the private rental market.

A. Suppose we consider a family that earns €1500 per month and either pays €0.50 per square metre in monthly rent for a flat in the private market or accepts a 1500 m² social housing unit at the government's price of €500 per month.

   a. On a graph with square metres of housing and euros of other consumption, illustrate two cases where the family accepts the social housing unit, one where this leads them to consume less housing than they otherwise would and another where it leads them to consume more housing than they otherwise would.

   b. If we use the members of the household's own judgment about the household's well-being, is it always the case that the option of social housing makes the participating households better off?

   c. If the policy goal behind social housing is to increase the housing consumption of the poor, is it more or less likely to succeed the less substitutable housing and other goods are?

   d. What is the government's opportunity cost of owning a social housing unit of 1500 m²? How much does it therefore cost the government to provide the social housing unit to this family?

   e. Now consider instead a housing price subsidy under which the government tells qualified families that it will pay some fraction of their rental bills in the private housing market. If this rental subsidy is set so as to make the household just as well off as it was under social housing, will it lead to more or less consumption of housing than if the household chooses social housing?

   f. Will giving such a rental subsidy cost more or less than providing the social housing unit? What does your answer depend on?

   g. Suppose instead that the government simply gave cash to the household. If it gave sufficient cash to make the household as well off as it is under the social housing programme, would it cost the government more or less than €250? Can you tell whether under such a subsidy the household consumes more or less housing than under social housing?

B. Assume that household tastes regarding square metres of housing (x_1) and euros of other consumption (x_2) can be represented by $u(x_1,x_2) = \alpha \ln x_1 + (1-\alpha) \ln x_2$.

   a. Suppose that empirical studies show we spend about a quarter of our income on housing. What does that imply about α?

   b. Consider a family with an income of €1500 per month facing a per square metre price of $p_1 = 0.50$. For what value of α would the family not change its housing consumption when offered the 1500 m² social housing flat for €500?

   c. Suppose that this family has α as derived in B(a). How much of a rental price subsidy would the government have to give to this family in order to make it as well off as the family is with the social housing unit?

d. How much housing will the family rent under this subsidy? How much will it cost the government to provide this subsidy?

e. Suppose the government instead gave the family cash without changing the price of housing. How much cash would it have to give the family in order to make it as happy?

f. If you are a policy maker whose aim is to make this household happier at the least cost to the taxpayer, how would you rank the three policies? What if your goal were to increase the household's housing consumption?

Chapter 8

Wealth and Substitution Effects in Labour and Capital Markets

In Chapter 7, we introduced the concepts of income and substitution effects in models where income enters the consumer's optimization problem exogenously; that is, where consumers are choosing to allocate a fixed money budget across consumption goods. We now turn to cases where income is endogenous; that is, where our consumption is funded not by a fixed money budget but rather by the sale of something that we own. This can happen, in most cases, in labour markets where we sell our leisure time and in capital markets where we buy and sell financial assets as we plan for the future.

The analysis in this chapter in one sense is no different than that in Chapter 7. We will again look at changes in behaviour that result from changes in opportunity costs, i.e. substitution effects and changes that happen as a result of real income having changed. At the same time, some important differences emerge, differences in the analysis that are in the end quite intuitive. When the price of fuel increases, we would always expect the substitution effect to indicate that we will consume less fuel. Whether the price increase makes us better off and thus increases our real income or whether it makes us worse off and thus decreases our real income depends on whether we own an oil well. Most of us don't, and thus most of us become worse off when fuel prices increase. In the language of Chapter 7, we experience a negative income effect that will lead to a further decrease in our fuel consumption if fuel is a normal good. If you own an oil well, the increase in fuel prices probably makes you better off because what you own just became more valuable. Thus, you would experience a positive income effect, one that will lead you to increase your consumption of fuel if fuel is a normal good.

8A   Wealth Effects, Substitution Effects and Endowments

In this chapter, a change in the price of a good has a different effect from the income effect because it changes the value of something we own and thus alters our budget constraint in a different way. We will call the new effect that emerges a *wealth effect* because it captures the change in wealth a consumer experiences when prices change and thus affects the value of what the consumer owns. As we will see, the substitution effect remains exactly the same for endogenous choice sets, but the wealth effect can point in different directions depending on what the consumer owns.

8A.1 An Increase in the Price of Fuel for George Shell

We will investigate the wealth effect using a fictional example of George Shell who owns large reserves of oil. In our following example, we assume that he finances his entire consumption by selling oil. George's income is thus modelled as arising *endogenously* from the value of his oil endowment.

8A.1.1 The Substitution Effect Revisited Panel (a) of Graph 8.1 illustrates the impact of an increase in the price of oil on George's budget. Point *E* is George's endowment point – the amount of oil he owns and can choose to consume if he would like to consume only oil and no other consumption. In this case an increase in price causes George's budget constraint to rotate *outwards* around his endowment point until its slope reflects the new opportunity cost. Point *A* denotes George's optimal consumption bundle prior to the increase in price.

We can now divide George's behavioural response to the price change into two distinct parts. First, we ask how his behaviour would have changed if his real income as measured by the indifference curve he can reach were held constant and he only faced a change in the opportunity cost reflected in the steeper slope. Panel (b) in Graph 8.1 introduces the compensated budget constraint that has the new budget's slope and its tangent to the original indifference curve reflecting no change in real welfare. The resulting substitution effect from bundle *A* to bundle *B* indicates that George would reduce his consumption of the good that has become relatively more expensive (oil) in favour of other goods that have become relatively cheaper.

Graph 8.1 Substitution and Wealth Effects When Income Is Derived Endogenously From Selling Oil

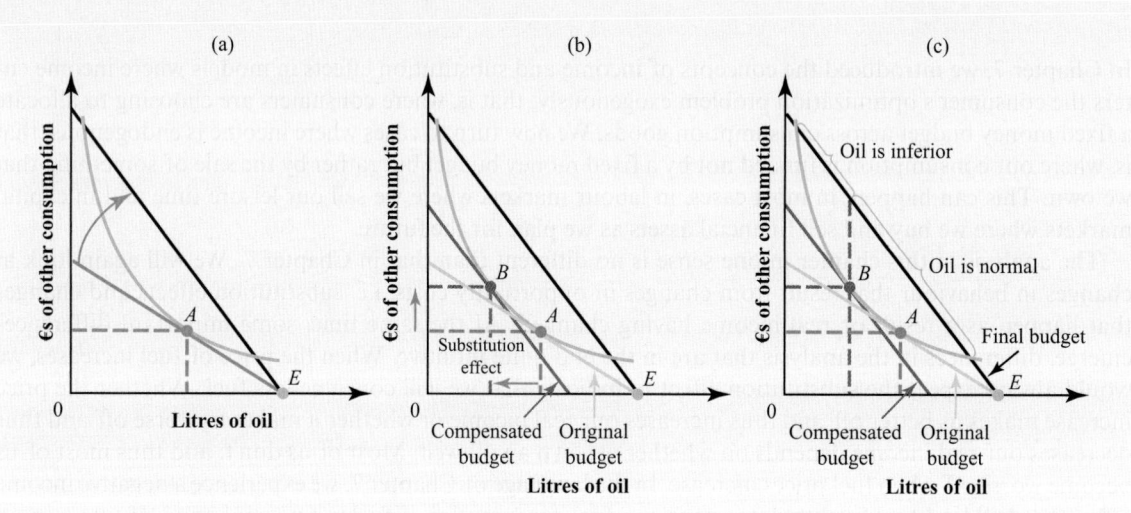

8A.1.2 The Wealth Effect and How an Increase in the Price of One Good Can *Look Like* a Decrease in the Price of Another In panel (c) of Graph 8.1, we determine where on the final budget line George might consume relative to point *B*. Notice that the compensated budget constraint and the final budget constraint are parallel; the only difference is that in going from the compensated to the final, George receives additional income to spend. George is *richer* as a result of the price change because the value of his wealth goes up with an increased price of oil. If oil is a normal good, an increase in income from the compensated to the final budget constraint should imply an increased level of oil consumption, causing the new optimal point on the final budget constraint to lie to the right of *B* and possibly to the right of *A*. If, on the other hand, oil is an inferior good, George will consume less oil as his income rises from the compensated budget, implying a new optimal point to the left of point *B*. Since we are dealing with a model in which income is determined *endogenously*, we will call the change from *B* to the new optimal point a *wealth effect*. This is analogous to the *income effect* we identified in a model with fixed exogenous income.

In Chapter 7, when the price of fuel changed, we concluded that consumption of fuel would decline from the original bundle *A* to the final bundle *C* as long as fuel was a normal good, but we could not be certain whether it would increase or decline if fuel was an inferior good because of offsetting income and substitution effects. The opposite is true in George Shell's case. We know his consumption of oil will definitely decline if oil is an inferior good for him, but we cannot be sure whether his oil consumption will increase or decrease if oil is a normal good. Despite the fact that in both cases price increased, George's situation is different from our consumer in Chapter 7 because his income is derived from oil, unlike the consumer in Chapter 7. Looking at the change in choice sets like the one graphed in panel (a) of Graph 8.1, you might conclude that this individual had experienced *a decrease in the price of other consumption* (the good on the vertical axis), not an increase in the price of oil. That is how we could treat the price change George experienced. George would feel exactly the same about such a price change with his income being exogenous as the one we have analyzed with income being endogenous, because it would alter his budget constraint in exactly the same way. This is also why we cannot identify in George's case any behaviour that would lead us to conclude that oil is a Giffen good for him, because for him it is effectively the price of other consumption that has changed. To identify oil as a Giffen good, we would have to observe an effective change in the price of oil, as we did in Chapter 7.

Exercise 8A.1

Since George's situation is equivalent to a decrease in the price of other goods with exogenous income, illustrate where on his final budget George would consume, if other goods were normal, regular inferior and Giffen.

8A.2 A Change in Wages

Our analysis of wealth and substitution effects can now be extended from models of consumer choices in goods markets to models of worker choices between leisure and consumption in labour markets. Leisure time is an endowment, much like oil was for George Shell. Its value in the labour market depends on the wages that a worker can earn, which in turn determines how easily a worker can turn leisure hours into goods consumption. We will model these choices by putting hours of leisure on the horizontal axis and euros of consumption on the vertical.

8A.2.1 Do Higher Wages Make Us Work More or Less?
Assume you are choosing how many hours you will work per week, and that you have a total of 60 leisure hours per week that you could devote to work. You have no other income, which implies that you will not be able to consume anything other than leisure if you do not work. Your endowment point *E* in panel (a) of Graph 8.2 falls at 60 hours of leisure and no consumption. Assume that the wage rate is €20 per hour, and it is optimal for you to work for 40 hours per week under these circumstances. This choice is illustrated as bundle *A* in panel (a) of Graph 8.2.

Now assume you are offered a wage increase of €5 per hour, which rotates your budget out through point *E* as shown in panel (a) of Graph 8.2. Will you work more or less as you face this new choice set? On the one hand, you might think that work is really paying off now and therefore you should work more. On the other, you are making more every hour you work, so why not work a little less and still end up with more consumption than before? It is not immediately clear which way you might decide to go because there are *competing wealth and substitution effects.*

To see this, we begin by drawing your compensated budget, the budget that keeps your real income the same but has the final budget line's opportunity cost or slope. This indicates that you would consume more of the good that has become relatively cheaper (consumption) and less of the good that has become relatively more expensive (leisure) if all you faced was the new opportunity costs with no change in real income and is illustrated in panel (b) of Graph 8.2. This is the pure substitution effect, the effect that makes you think that work is really paying off now and you should thus work more.

In panel (c) of Graph 8.2, we isolate the wealth effect, which is the impact of going from bundle *B* under the compensated budget constraint to the final budget constraint. The graph looks identical to panel (c) of Graph 8.1, and the conclusion is the same for you as a worker as it was for George as an owner of oil. If leisure is an inferior good, the wealth effect will reinforce the substitution effect as you consume less leisure when your real income goes up. You would end at a point like *C* to the left of *B*. It seems, however, unlikely that leisure is really an inferior good; it is probably a normal good for most of us. This implies that you would consume more of it as your real income rises from the compensated budget to the final budget constraint, formalizing our intuition that you are making more every hour, so why not work a little less.

Graph 8.2 Substitution and Wealth Effects in Leisure/Consumption Choices

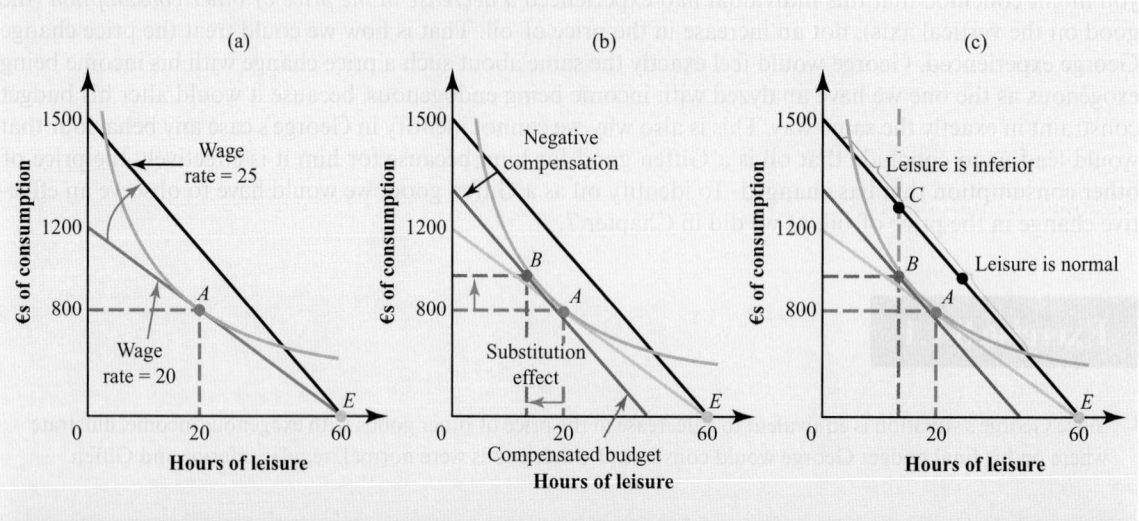

Go to MindTap to interact with this graph

If leisure is a normal good, it is therefore not clear whether an increase in your wage will cause you to work more or less. The substitution and wealth effects point in opposite directions, leaving us guessing, unless we know more about your tastes. Suppose, for instance, that the only way you can enjoy your leisure time is by paying to go parasailing. If your tastes are really that extreme, there is little substitutability in your tastes between leisure hours and consumption – you *must* consume (parasail) to enjoy leisure. Your indifference curves would be those of perfect complements. By doing the following exercise, you can see that this would eliminate the substitution effect and leave you only with the wealth effect, leading to an unambiguous conclusion that you will work less (consume more leisure) as your wages go up.

Exercise 8A.2

Illustrate substitution and wealth effects; that is, the initial bundle, the bundle that incorporates a substitution effect from a wage increase, and the final bundle chosen under the wage increase, assuming that your tastes for consumption and leisure are properly modelled as perfect complements.

On the other hand, suppose that your tastes were properly modelled as quasilinear in leisure. In that case, the only effect of a wage change on your labour supply decision is the substitution effect because quasilinear tastes do not have income or wealth effects. This would imply that an increase in your wages would cause you to unambiguously work more (consume less leisure).

Exercise 8A.3

Replicate the previous exercise under the assumption that your tastes are quasilinear in leisure.

Labour economists who estimate the relationship between labour supply from a worker and that worker's wages, have concluded that an average worker responds to wage increases by working more when their current wage is relatively low. As wages increase, however, the same average worker will eventually tend to work less as wages increase even further.

Exercise 8A.4

Illustrate a set of indifference curves that gives rise to the kind of response to wage changes as described.

8A.2.2 Taxes on Labour Income Politicians like to convince us that their policies help everyone and hurt no one. Those who propose to cut taxes on wages, for instance, often argue that such tax cuts will not only benefit workers but will also cause an *increase* in government revenue as workers work harder when they get to keep more of their money and thus will pay more in overall taxes even though the tax rates have come down. Is this true?

Our analysis of labour/leisure choices suggests that it all depends on what we assume about wealth and substitution effects. For workers, a cut in wage taxes is equivalent to an increase in their take-home wages. Thus, our analysis of a wage increase in the previous section applies directly. We have concluded that substitution effects will cause workers to increase their hours when wages go up, while wealth effects are likely to cause workers to decrease their work hours as their wages rise, assuming that leisure is a normal good. Thus, the politician is more likely to be correct the larger the substitution effect and the smaller the wealth effect. Politicians who make this argument are assuming: (1) that our tastes allow for a great deal of substitutability between consumption and leisure, implying that our indifference curves are relatively flat making substitution effects large, and/or (2) that leisure is an inferior good, which causes wealth effects for wage changes to point in the same direction as the substitution effect. Were they to believe that leisure and consumption are very complementary and that leisure is a normal good, their prediction would almost certainly be false.

Even the combination of substitution and wealth effects leading workers to work more when their after-tax wages increase, however, is not sufficient for the government to increase tax revenue by cutting taxes. To see this, we first have to see how to illustrate tax revenues from a single worker in our leisure/consumption graphs. Consider Graph 8.3 that contains one budget line without taxes and another that shows an effective lower wage because of a wage tax. The worker's optimal choice under the tax is determined on their after-tax budget constraint and is denoted by A in the graph. From point A, we can read off directly how much in euros of other goods this worker is consuming after paying taxes: €800. Since the only difference between the two budget lines in Graph 8.3 is the wage tax, we also know that this same worker could have consumed €1300 in other goods had he not had to pay any taxes and had they worked exactly the same number of hours (40) as they did at bundle A. Thus, the vertical difference between bundle A and bundle a is how much the government collected in tax revenue: €500. Note that this does *not* mean that we are assuming this worker would have consumed bundle a in the absence of taxes. We are using bundle a to identify this worker's before-tax income when they are choosing bundle A on their after-tax budget line.

Now consider the case where the government can choose between two different wage taxes, say one of 20 per cent and another of 40 per cent. Suppose further that we are considering two different workers for whom wealth and substitution effects combine to increase the amount they work when they face a higher after-tax wage. Panels (a) and (b) in Graph 8.4 illustrate two different possibilities, with A representing the workers' optimal bundles at a 20 per cent wage tax and A' representing their optimal bundles at the 40 per cent wage tax. In the first graph, a decrease in the wage tax from 40 per cent to 20 per cent results in a decrease in tax revenue from the worker because the distance between A and a is smaller than the distance between A' and a', while in the second graph it results in an increase in tax revenues because the distance between A and a is larger than the distance between A' and a'.

Graph 8.3 Finding a Wage Tax Payment When Observing After-Tax Behaviour

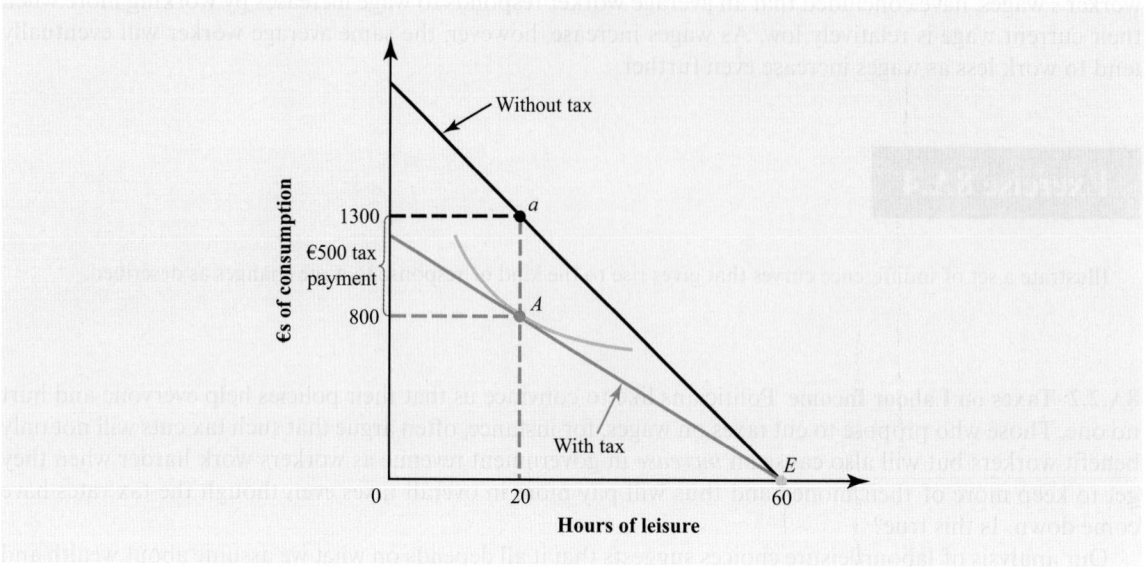

Graph 8.4 Tax Revenue Can Rise (a) or Fall (b) With an Increase in Tax Rates

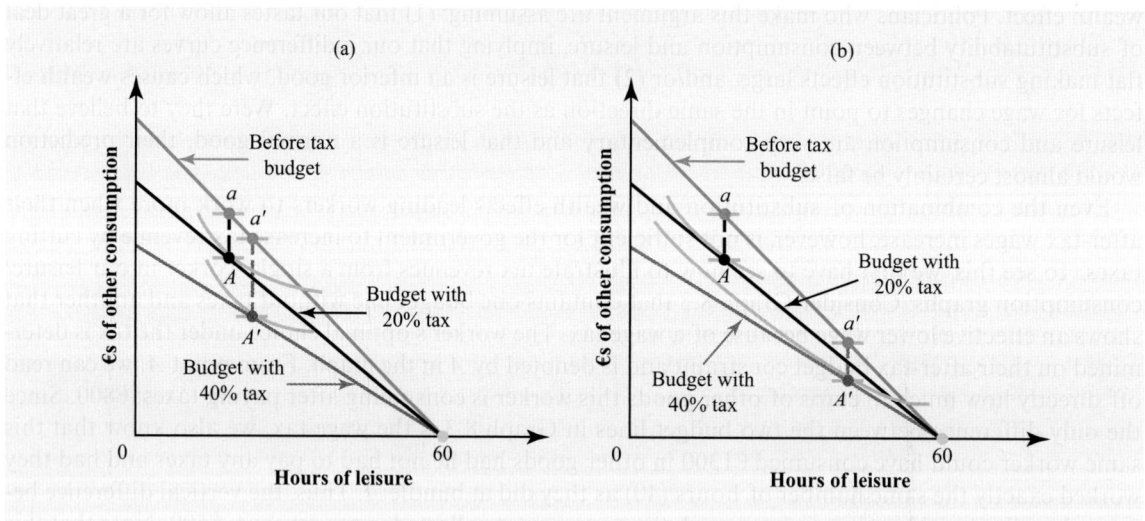

For now, it is worth noting one final lesson from understanding substitution and wealth effects in a labour market that is taxed. While it may not always be the case that tax revenues will rise as tax rates fall or vice versa, the presence of substitution effects in labour markets does suggest that we may over-predict how much tax revenue we are likely to get from a given tax increase. This is because substitution effects in the labour market suggest that workers will work less as wage taxes increase. Unless leisure is not only a normal good but also produces a wealth effect sufficiently large to out-weigh the substitution effect, workers will work less as taxes increase, which means they will pay less in additional tax revenues than we would predict if we did not take this substitution change in behaviour into account.

Exercise 8A.5

True or False: For decreases in wage taxes, substitution effects put positive pressure on tax revenues while wealth effects typically put negative pressure on revenues.

8A.3 A Change in Real Interest Rates

Just as our choices over consumption and leisure are impacted by the size of the wage we can earn, so our financial planning for the future is impacted by the size of the financial return we receive from saving or the financial cost we incur from borrowing – the real interest rate. It is worth emphasizing that we always mean the *real* interest rate, or the interest rate adjusted for inflation.

8A.3.1 Do Higher Interest Rates Make Us Save More? Wealth and substitution effects play important roles in the choices consumers make regarding their financial planning just as they do in their choices in labour and consumer goods markets. When we asked in the previous section whether an increase in wages will cause us to work more, we were unsure of the answer even before we discussed the relevant wealth and substitution effects. Similarly, it is not immediately clear whether higher interest rates lead to increased savings. On the one hand, you might think that saving now really pays off and thus you might be inclined to save more. On the other, you might decide that since you are getting more in the future for every euro you put in your savings account, you might as well consume a little more now knowing that the somewhat smaller savings account will grow faster. The first temptation is an informal statement of the substitution effect, while the latter gives expression to the wealth effect.

Let's return to our example from Chapter 3 of an individual choosing to use €10 000 income from this summer to plan for consumption now and next summer. Their endowment point in this example is point E in Graph 8.5 because this is the bundle that is always available for them regardless of what the interest rate is. Suppose that their initial planning is based on earning interest at an annual rate of 10 per cent, and consuming €5000 this summer and €5500 next summer as indicated by point A in panel (a) of Graph 8.5. Now assume a new investment opportunity arises that will give a 20 per cent annual return, yielding the larger choice set with different opportunity costs depicted in the same graph.

Panel (b) of Graph 8.5 begins by isolating the substitution effect with the hypothetical compensated budget constraint tangential to the original optimal indifference curve.

Graph 8.5 The Impact of an Increase in Interest Rates on Savers

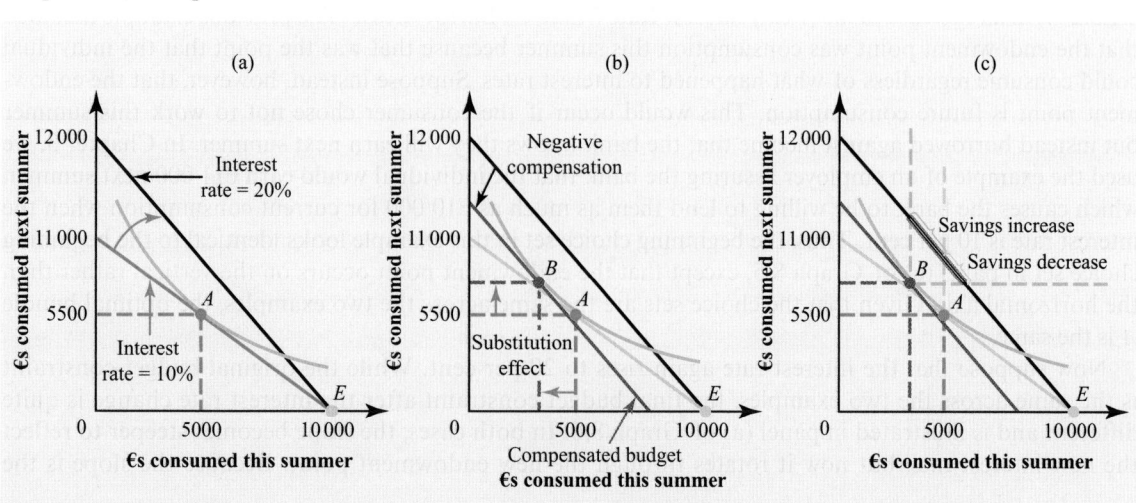

The movement from A to B results in less consumption of the good that has become relatively more expensive (consumption this summer) and more of the good that has become relatively cheaper (consumption next summer). This substitution effect suggests the individual will tend to save more because consuming now as opposed to later has just become more expensive.

Whether or how much the wealth effect will counteract this substitution effect depends on whether consumption this summer and consumption next summer are normal or inferior goods. It seems reasonable to assume that consumption is a normal good in both periods, and so we will restrict ourselves to this assumption in this example. Starting from the optimal point B on the compensated budget, we would expect the individual to increase consumption this and next summer as income rises from the compensated to the final budget constraint in panel (c) of Graph 8.5.

The new optimal bundle will therefore likely lie somewhere in the darkened segment of the final budget line. All bundles on this segment have higher consumption next summer than the €5500 originally planned, but this does not mean that the increase in the interest rate has led to more saving in the sense of putting more money into a savings account now. Notice that the darkened segment of the final budget contains some bundles with more consumption *this* summer than at point A and some with less. Since savings – the amount put away in a savings account – is the amount not consumed *this summer*, we cannot tell whether the individual will *save* more or less, only that they will consume more next summer. The increased consumption next summer *may* happen despite lower saving this summer because each euro in their savings account now earns more than before. This happens if the optimal bundle lies on the darkened segment to the right of point A. It may also be the case that higher consumption next summer happens in part because of additional savings this summer, if the optimal bundle ends up to the left of point A.

Without more information about the individual's tastes, we cannot tell precisely which of these scenarios will happen. All we know for now is that the more substitutable consumption is across time periods, i.e. the flatter the indifference curves, the more likely it is that the substitution effect will outweigh the wealth effect and lead to an increase in savings. The opposite is true as consumption becomes more complementary across periods.

Exercise 8A.6

Illustrate that savings will decline with an increase in the interest rate if consumption this summer and next summer are perfect complements.

8A.3.2 Will an Increase in the (Real) Interest Rate Make Us Borrow Less? The previous example assumed that the endowment point was consumption this summer because that was the point that the individual could consume regardless of what happened to interest rates. Suppose instead, however, that the endowment point is future consumption. This would occur if the consumer chose not to work this summer but instead borrowed against income that the bank knows they will earn next summer. In Chapter 3, we used the example of an employer assuring the bank that the individual would earn €11 000 next summer, which causes the bank to be willing to lend them as much as €10 000 for current consumption when the interest rate is 10 per cent. Thus, the beginning choice set in this example looks identical to the beginning choice set in panel (a) of Graph 8.5, except that the endowment point occurs on the vertical rather than the horizontal axis. Given that the choice sets are the same across the two examples, the optimal bundle A is the same.

Now suppose that the interest rate again rises to 20 per cent. While the original budget constraint is the same across the two examples, the final budget constraint after the interest rate change is quite different and is illustrated in panel (a) of Graph 8.6. In both cases, the slope becomes steeper to reflect the new interest rate, but now it rotates through the new endowment point. Because the slope is the same across the two examples, however, the compensated budget constraint will also be the same since it assumes a constant real income under the new interest rate. The difference is that the compensated budget now requires *positive* compensation while previously it required *negative* compensation. If the interest rate rises and you are a saver, you are made better off and thus need less money to be just as well off as you were originally. If, on the other hand, you are a borrower, an increase in the interest rate makes you worse off, requiring that you are given additional money to make you just as well off as you were originally.

Graph 8.6 The Impact of an Increase in Interest Rates on Borrowers

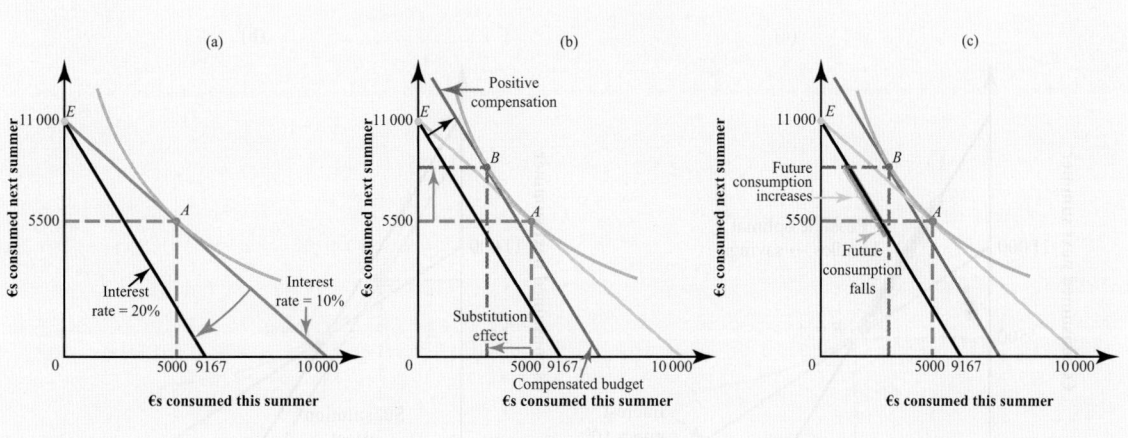

Since the indifference curve that contains point *A* is the same across the two examples and since the original as well as the compensated budgets are the same, it follows that point *B* will be the same. The individual experiences a substitution effect that tells us they should consume less now and more later when the interest rate and thus the cost of consuming now goes up. The wealth effect, however, now points in the opposite direction from the previous example because, in going from the compensated to the final budget constraint, they now lose rather than gain income. If consumption in both periods is a normal good, as we have assumed throughout, the individual will consume less than at point *B* during both summers as their income falls from the compensated to the final budget constraint. In panel (c) of Graph 8.6, the consumer will end up somewhere on the highlighted portion of the final budget line.

Since both wealth and substitution effects suggest that the individual will consume less this summer, we can unambiguously conclude that their consumption this summer will decline and they will borrow less. On the vertical axis of panel (c) of Graph 8.6, the substitution and wealth effects point in opposite directions, leaving us uncertain about whether consumption next summer will be higher or lower as the interest rate for borrowing increases. Whether the individual consumes more or less next summer depends on the degree to which consumption this period and next period are substitutable, and thus whether or not the substitution effect outweighs the wealth effect.

Exercise 8A.7

Illustrate how consumption next summer changes with an increase in the interest rate if consumption this summer and next summer are perfect complements and all income occurs next summer.

8A.3.3 Neither a Borrower Nor a Lender Be... Let us assume that the individual decides to arrange their work plans over the next two summers so that they can consume €5000 this summer and €5500 next summer without borrowing or saving, which is equivalent to lending to the bank. This is accomplished by finding an employer who is willing to employ them for half the time this summer for €5000 and half the time again next summer for €5500. This implies that we have a new endowment bundle in our model, which is labelled E in Graph 8.7. This is the new endowment bundle because it is the bundle that can be consumed regardless of what happens to the interest rate.

Graph 8.7 From No Saving to Positive Saving When Interest Rates Rise

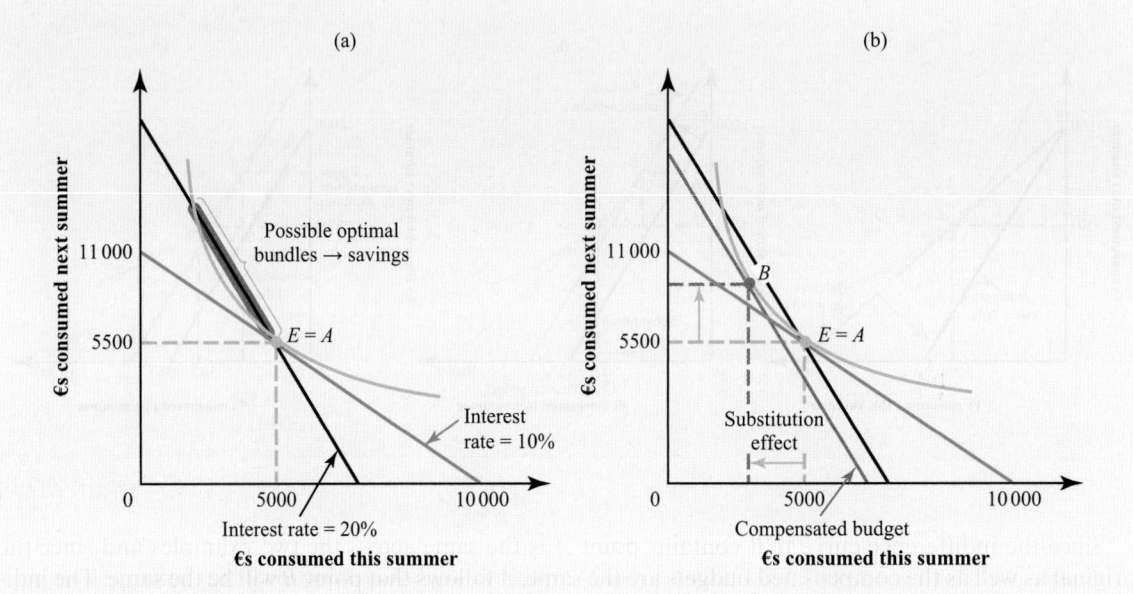

Suppose that the interest rate was 10 per cent when the individual made their work arrangements and changed to 20 per cent afterwards. The initial choice set looks precisely the way it did in the previous two examples, but the final budget constraint now rotates through the new endowment point.

This is one case where it is not necessary to decompose the behavioural change into substitution and wealth effects. We can observe in panel (a) of Graph 8.7 that all the bundles in the final choice set that lie above the original indifference curve, and are thus preferred, lie to the left of bundle E. The new optimal choice involves less consumption this period, and this implies the individual will start saving. The change in the interest rate causes them to violate the advice in Shakespeare's Hamlet of 'neither a borrower nor a lender be' as they open a savings account and become a lender of money to the bank. To see why this is the case, notice in panel (b) of Graph 8.7 that the compensated budget constraint is quite close to the final budget constraint, implying that almost the entire behavioural change is a substitution effect. The small wealth effect that remains is not sufficient to overcome the substitution effect *regardless* of how much substitutability is built into the indifference map. In fact, the entire effect is a Slutsky substitution effect as discussed in Section 7A.2.4.

Exercise 8A.8

Demonstrate that the only way the individual will not violate Shakespeare's advice as the interest rate goes up is if consumption this summer and next are perfect complements.

Exercise 8A.9

Illustrate that unless consumption this summer and consumption next summer are perfect complements, the individual will violate the first part of Shakespeare's advice – not to be a borrower – if the interest rate were to fall instead of rise.

8B   Constrained Optimization With Wealth Effects

Fundamentally, the mathematics underlying models with endowments is not different from what we have already introduced for models with exogenous fixed incomes. We treat consumers or workers or investors as maximizing utility subject to a budget constraint, but now the income term in the budget constraint will be replaced with a wealth term that depends on the prices in the economy. We illustrated in detail how such budgets can be written in Chapter 3, and we will now merge that treatment of budgets into our mathematical optimization framework.

8B.1 George Shell and the Price of Oil

In Section 8A.1, we introduced George Shell, who owns large reserves of oil and derives all his income from selling oil. Letting the number of litres of oil he gets out of the ground each week be denoted by e_1, George's weekly income depends on the price p_1 he can get for his oil. Thus, weekly income from oil extractions is $p_1 e_1$. How much oil he is able to extract per week, e_1, is different from how much oil he *consumes* each week. Letting litres of weekly oil consumption be denoted by x_1 and euros of other weekly consumption be represented by x_2, we can write George's weekly budget constraint as:

$$p_1 x_1 + x_2 = p_1 e_1 \text{ or } x_2 = p_1(e_1 - x_1). \tag{8.1}$$

Notice that the second formulation in (8.1) has non-oil consumption on the left-hand side and income from the sale of oil that is not directly consumed by George on the right-hand side. This budget constraint is just the more general budget constraint we derived in Chapter 3 for someone with endowment income:

$$p_1 x_1 + p_2 x_2 = p_1 e_1 + p_2 e_2, \tag{8.2}$$

except that the price of Euros of Other Weekly Consumption in our example is by definition equal to 1 thus making $p_2 = 1$, and George has no endowment of euros of other weekly consumption thus making $e_2 = 0$.

Suppose George's tastes could be captured by the Cobb–Douglas utility function $u(x_1, x_2) = x_1^{0.1} x_2^{0.9}$. We can write his constrained optimization problem as:

$$\max_{x_1, x_2} u(x_1, x_2) = x_1^{0.1} x_2^{0.9} \text{ subject to } x_2 = p_1(e_1 - x_1). \tag{8.3}$$

The Lagrange function used to calculate the optimal consumption bundle is:

$$\mathcal{L}(x_1, x_2, \lambda) = x_1^{0.1} x_2^{0.9} + \lambda (x_2 - p_1(e_1 - x_1)). \tag{8.4}$$

Solving this we get:

$$x_1 = 0.1e_1 \text{ and } x_2 = 0.9(p_1e_1). \qquad (8.5)$$

Suppose, that the price of oil p_1 is €2 per litre and that George's weekly litres of oil extraction e_1 is 1000. Expression (8.5) tells us that George's optimal consumption bundle is $x_1 = 100$ and $x_2 = 1800$; that is, 100 litres of oil and €1800 in other consumption.

Exercise 8B.1

With the numbers in the previous paragraph, George's income is €2000 per week. Verify that you would get the same optimal consumption bundle if you modelled this as a constrained optimization problem in which income was exogenously set at €2000 per week.

8B.1.1 Revisiting the Substitution Effect

Suppose the price of oil rises to €4 per litre. We can see from expression (8.5) what the impact on George's consumption will be. He will continue to consume 100 litres of oil each week, but his other consumption will rise from €1800 to €3600. This is illustrated in panel (a) of Graph 8.8, where bundle A represents George's initial optimal consumption under the €2 oil price and bundle C represents his new optimal consumption under the €4 price.

This change in behaviour from A to C, however, bundles the substitution and wealth effects. To isolate the substitution effect from the wealth effect, we first need to calculate how George's consumption would have changed when the price of oil increased from €2 to €4 per litre if we took enough money away from George to make him just as well off as he was originally; that is, if only his opportunity costs change without a change in real income as measured by his indifference curve.

To find this effect, we use the expenditure minimization problem that aims to find the lowest possible exogenous money income that George could have at the new €4 price of oil and still reach the same indifference curve that contained his original optimal bundle (100,1800). By substituting this optimal bundle into the utility function $u(x_1, x_2) = x_1^{0.1}x_2^{0.9}$, we find that this indifference curve was assigned a value of approximately 1348 by George's utility function. We can therefore state the expenditure minimization problem used to identify the substitution effect as:

$$\min_{x_1, x_2} E = 4x_1 + x_2 \text{ subject to } x_1^{0.1}x_2^{0.9} = 1348. \qquad (8.6)$$

Notice that this problem makes no reference to George's endowment because that endowment is irrelevant for finding the substitution effect. Once we know the indifference curve we would like George to reach, identifying the level of exogenous income that it would take to get there has nothing to do with how much 'stuff' George actually owns.

Setting up the Lagrange function and solving for x_1 and x_2, you can verify for yourself that:

$$x_1 = 53.59 \text{ and } x_2 = 1929.19, \qquad (8.7)$$

implying that George would consume 53.59 litres of oil and €1929.19 of other consumption each week.

Graph 8.8 Wealth and Substitution Effects for George Shell: From Maths Back to Graphs

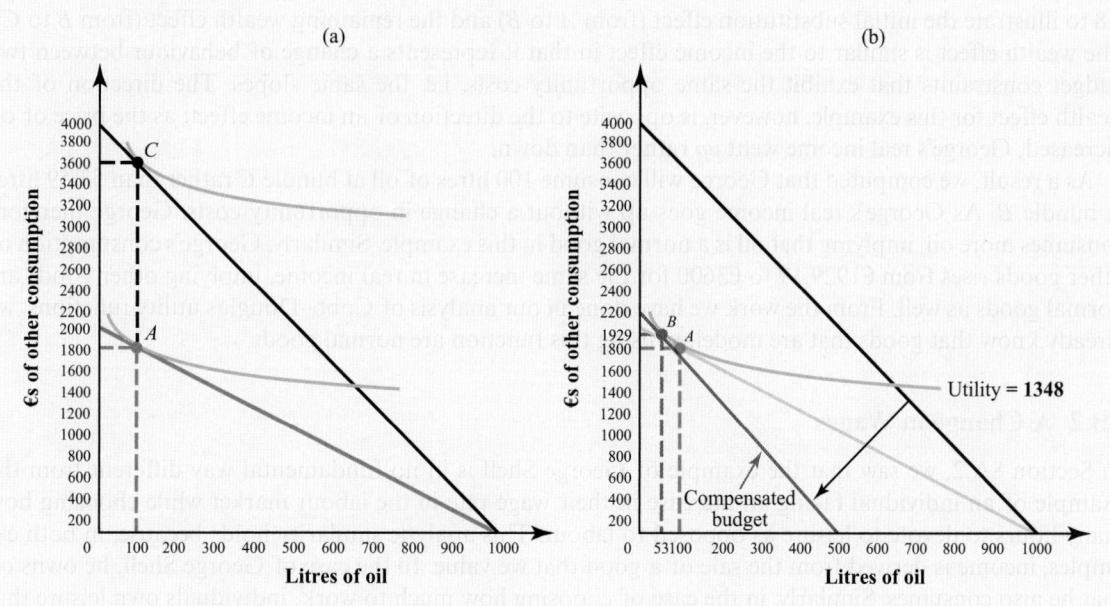

Verify that the solutions in the previous paragraph are correct.

Panel (b) of Graph 8.8 illustrates what we have just done. Beginning with the optimal bundle *A* before the price change, we have identified the smallest possible new budget (compensated budget) constraint that incorporates the new price of oil and will still permit George to reach the indifference curve that contains bundle *A*. The impact of the change in opportunity costs is thus isolated from the impact of the change in wealth that arises from the price change, giving rise to a pure substitution effect. This substitution effect, the change in behaviour that takes George from bundle *A* to bundle *B*, tells us that the change in opportunity costs causes our consumer to reduce their consumption of the good that has become relatively more expensive (oil) in favour of increased consumption of the good that has become relatively cheaper (other consumption).

How much negative compensation was required to get George to be equally well off when the price of oil increased?

8B.1.2 The Wealth Effect Given that we have already identified George's final consumption bundle at the €4 oil price, and graphed it in panel (a) of Graph 8.8, we could now combine panels (a) and (b) of Graph 8.8 to illustrate the initial substitution effect (from A to B) and the remaining wealth effect (from B to C). The wealth effect is similar to the income effect in that it represents a change of behaviour between two budget constraints that exhibit the same opportunity costs, i.e. the same slopes. The direction of the wealth effect for this example, however, is opposite to the direction of an income effect; as the price of oil increased, George's real income went *up* rather than down.

As a result, we computed that George will consume 100 litres of oil at bundle C rather than 53.59 litres at bundle B. As George's real income goes up without a change in opportunity costs, George therefore consumes more oil, implying that oil is a normal good in this example. Similarly, George's consumption of other goods rises from €1929.19 to €3600 for the same increase in real income, implying other goods are normal goods as well. From the work we have done in our analysis of Cobb–Douglas utility functions, we already know that goods that are modelled using this function are normal goods.

8B.2 A Change in Wages

In Section 8A.2, we saw that the example of George Shell is in no fundamental way different from the example of an individual facing an increase in their wage rate in the labour market while choosing how many hours to devote to leisure as opposed to labour. This analytic similarity holds because, in both examples, income is derived from the sale of a good that we value. In the case of George Shell, he owns oil that he also consumes. Similarly, in the case of choosing how much to work, individuals own leisure that they consume is just how George consumes oil. When the price of oil is €2 per litre, the opportunity cost of consuming one more litre of oil is €2 of other consumption. When the hourly wage rate is €20, the opportunity cost of consuming one more hour of leisure is similarly €20 of other consumption. The price of oil in the George Shell example is analogous to the wage rate in the example of an individual choosing how much to work.

8B.2.1 Will an Increase in Your Wage Lead to More Work or Less? We have already demonstrated in panels (a), (b) and (c) in Graph 8.2 how substitution and wealth effects work intuitively in the labour market. Since these effects are analogous to the effects already identified mathematically in the George Shell example, we have in a sense already demonstrated how we would use our mathematical framework to solve for substitution and wealth effects when wages change in the labour market. We begin by setting up the constrained optimization problem. Assume the individual has 60 hours per week to devote to leisure or labour, that the wage rate is w, and that tastes over consumption (c) and leisure (ℓ) can be represented by a utility function $u(c,\ell)$. The mathematical formulation of the problem is:

$$\max_{c,\, \ell} u(c,\, \ell) \text{ subject to } c = w(60 - \ell). \qquad (8.8)$$

The budget constraint in expression (8.8) states that total spending on consumption goods c is equal to the wage rate w times the hours worked; that is, the hours not taken as leisure = $(60 - \ell)$.

Suppose that tastes over consumption and leisure can be modelled using the quasilinear utility function:

$$u(c,\ell) = c + 400 \ln \ell. \qquad (8.9)$$

Using the Lagrange method, we can compute that the optimal bundle of consumption and leisure is:

$$c = 60w - 400 \quad \text{and} \quad \ell = \frac{400}{w}. \qquad (8.10)$$

Thus, we know that the optimal bundle A in panel (a) of Graph 8.9 when the wage rate is €20 per hour is €800 of weekly consumption and 20 hours of leisure, or, equivalently, 40 hours of labour. If the wage rate rises to €25 per hour, the optimal leisure consumption declines to 16 hours, implying 44 hours of work, while other good consumption increases to €1100 per week. For tastes that can be represented by the utility function (8.9), an increase in the wage thus causes the individual to work more.

Graph 8.9 Wealth and Substitution Effects in Labour Choices: From Maths Back to Graphs

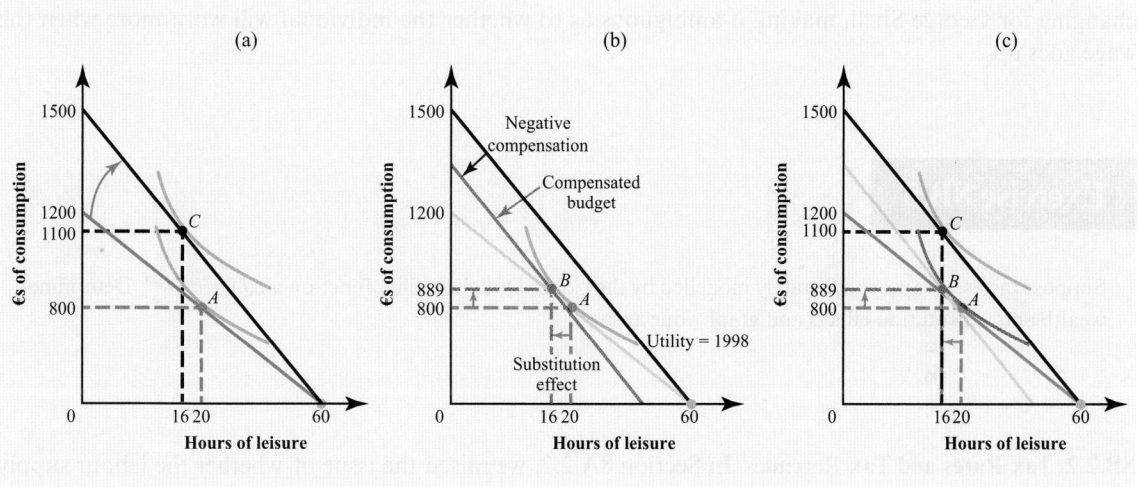

To see why, we can decompose the total move from A to C in panel (a) of Graph 8.9 into substitution and wealth effects. To find the substitution effect, we follow our previous method by specifying a minimization problem that seeks to find the minimum expenditure necessary to achieve the utility level originally attained at A when the wage rate is €25 (rather than the initial €20) per hour. Substituting the leisure and consumption values at bundle A into the utility function in (8.9), we get a utility level of approximately 1998. The relevant minimization problem is:

$$\min_{c, \ell} E = c + 25\ell \text{ subject to } c + 400 \ln\ell = 1998. \tag{8.11}$$

Notice that we are treating the goods consumption and leisure as we have always treated goods in such minimization problems. We are asking how much we would have to spend on these two goods at the market prices to reach the indifference curve that contains bundle A. The market price of consumption is €1 while the market price of leisure is the market wage or €25 in our example.

Exercise 8B.4

Solve the problem defined in equation (8.11).

The solution to this minimization problem is $c \approx 889$ and $\ell \approx 16$. Thus, at bundle B in panel (b) of Graph 8.9, the individual would consume 16 hours of leisure per week, or work for 44 hours. Just as our graphical approach suggested in Section 8A.2, the substitution effect from an increase in the wage leads to less consumption of leisure because consuming leisure has just become more expensive.

Putting panels (a) and (b) of Graph 8.9 together in panel (c), we can depict graphically what we have just calculated mathematically. In terms of its effect on leisure and labour supply, an increase in the wage from €20 per hour to €25 per hour results in a four-hour substitution effect away from leisure and towards labour, and no wealth effect. This arises from the fact that the underlying utility function (8.9) is quasilinear in leisure, which eliminates income or wealth effects in the consumption of leisure and leaves us with only the substitution effect. For utility functions that model leisure as normal, the wealth effect will point in the opposite direction of the substitution effect much as was the case in the example of the price of oil changing for George Shell, making it ambiguous as to whether the individual will work more when the wage goes up.

Exercise 8B.5

Suppose tastes were more accurately modelled by the Cobb–Douglas utility function $u(c,\ell) = c^{0.5}\ell^{0.5}$. Determine wealth and substitution effects and graph your answer.

8B.2.2 Tax Rates and Tax Revenues In Section 8A.2.2, we raised the issue of whether the labour supply response to a wage tax would ever be sufficiently strong to ensure that tax revenues would actually increase as taxes on wages declined. The intuition of the graphical approach in Graph 8.4 tells us that in order for tax revenues to increase with a decrease in the tax rate, it must at a minimum be the case that either leisure is an inferior good or the substitution effect outweighs the wealth effect if leisure is a normal good. These are, however, only necessary conditions; that is, we showed in Graph 8.4 that it is logically possible for work effort to increase as labour taxes decrease but for tax revenue nevertheless to fall. Continuing with our example can shed some further clarity on this.

In particular, suppose that tastes can be described as in equation (8.9), that the individual is earning a €25 per hour pre-tax wage, and that they have up to 60 hours per week to devote to working. Now suppose that you find out that the government will reduce their take-home pay by t per cent through a wage tax. The effective wage becomes €25$(1 - t)$ instead of €25. Replacing w by $25(1 - t)$ in expression (8.10), we get the optimal leisure choice as:

$$\ell = \frac{400}{25(1 - t)}, \tag{8.12}$$

with the optimal labour choice $(60 - \ell)$. Government tax revenue from this worker is the tax rate t times the worker's before-tax income, $25(60 - \ell)$. Table 8.1 calculates the number of hours worked (column 2) under different tax rates (column 1), as well as the tax revenue the government receives (column 3). In addition, column 4 of the table indicates the tax revenue one would expect to receive if the individual were not going to adjust their labour supply to changing tax rates and thus always worked 44 hours per week regardless of the tax rate. Column 5 indicates the difference in the predicted tax revenue from the economic analysis of column 3 as opposed to the more naive analysis of column 4.

By specifying tastes as quasilinear in leisure, we have eliminated any wealth effect from the analysis and are thus left with a pure substitution effect. As a result, the work effort represented by the number of hours worked declines as the after-tax wage declines (see column 2). This results in tax revenues initially increasing with the tax rate because, although the individual works less as the tax increases, each euro earned is taxed more heavily. Eventually, however, work hours decline sufficiently such that tax revenues decline when the tax rate increases further. This happens in the table when the tax rate increases from 50 per cent to 60 per cent, but if you were to fill in tax rates in between those in the table, the actual turning point occurs at a tax rate of 48.4 per cent. Thus, if the government were to try to maximize tax revenue, it would levy a 48.4 per cent tax rate. Notice, however, that well before this turning point, the tax revenue actually collected (column 3) diverges rather dramatically from the tax revenue predicted without taking the substitution effect into account.

Table 8.1 $u(c,\ell) = c + 400 \ln \ell$, $L = 60$, $w = 25$				
Impact of Wage Tax on Labour Supply and Tax Revenue				
Tax Rate t	Labour Hours $(60 - \ell)$	Tax Revenue $t(25(60 - \ell))$	Tax Rev. w/o Subst. Effect	Difference
0.00	44.00	€0.00	€0.00	€0.00
0.05	43.16	€53.95	€55.00	−€1.05
0.10	42.22	€105.56	€110.00	−€4.44
0.15	41.18	€154.41	€165.00	−€10.59
0.20	40.00	€200.00	€220.00	−€20.00
0.25	38.67	€241.67	€275.00	−€33.33
0.30	37.14	€278.57	€330.00	−€51.43
0.35	35.38	€309.62	€385.00	−€75.38
0.40	33.33	€333.33	€440.00	−€106.67
0.45	30.91	€347.73	€495.00	−€147.27
0.50	28.00	€350.00	€550.00	−€200.00
0.55	24.44	€336.11	€605.00	−€268.89
0.60	20.00	€300.00	€660.00	−€360.00
0.65	14.29	€232.14	€715.00	−€482.86
0.70	6.67	€116.67	€770.00	−€653.33
0.75	0.00	€0.00	€825.00	−€825.00

One further thing to note is that were you to solve the maximization problem the usual way when the tax rate equals 75 per cent, the solution would actually indicate 64 hours of leisure and −€25 of consumption. Since such a bundle is not possible – the individual cannot, after all, take more than 60 hours of leisure or consume negative amounts of goods – we know that the actual solution to the problem is a corner solution where the individual chooses to consume nothing and only take leisure. This happens for any tax rate higher than 73.34 per cent.

The relationship between tax rates and tax revenue that emerges from this table is plotted in panel (a) of Graph 8.10 with the tax rate on the horizontal and tax revenue on the vertical. It is known as the *Laffer Curve* named after Arthur Laffer (1940–), an economist who was influential in policy circles during the 1970s and 1980s. Laffer himself admits that the basic idea is not original to him. Jude Wanniski, a writer for the *Wall Street Journal*, appears to be the first to name the curve after Laffer following a 1974 meeting during which Laffer reportedly sketched the curve on a napkin. It illustrates that when tax rates become sufficiently high, tax revenue will eventually drop as individuals choose to avoid the tax by consuming less of the taxed good. Furthermore, as illustrated in panel (b) of Graph 8.10, this Laffer Curve relationship suggests that the difference between actual tax revenues and those predicted without taking changes in economic behaviour into account widens as the tax rate increases.

Exercise 8B.6*

What is the equation for the Laffer Curve in Graph 8.10?

Exercise 8B.7**

Solve for the peak of the Laffer Curve using the equation you derived in the previous exercise and verify that it occurs at a tax rate of approximately 48.4 per cent.

Graph 8.10 The Laffer Curve: Substitution Effects When Tastes Are Quasilinear in Leisure

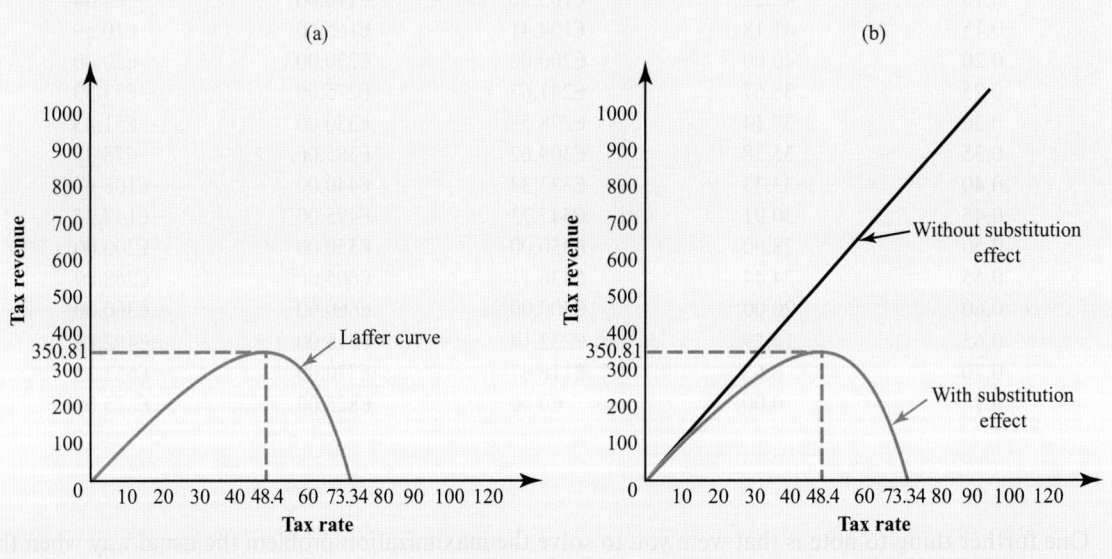

8B.3 A Change in Real Interest Rates

In Section 8A.3, we turned to the question of how changes in real interest rates affect consumption, savings and borrowing decisions under different scenarios. We referred to an example first raised in Chapter 3, in which the consumer chose how to allocate income between consumption this summer and next summer. While the mathematics developed in Chapter 3 allows us to model more complicated savings and borrowing decisions, we will illustrate the basics of substitution and wealth effects in regard to savings and borrowing with just this two-period example. In such a setting, we had denoted the amount of income or wealth received this summer as e_1 and the amount of income or wealth received next summer as e_2. We wrote the intertemporal or across-time budget constraint as:

$$(1 + r)c_1 + c_2 = (1 + r)e_1 + e_2, \tag{8.13}$$

where c_1 stands for consumption this summer, c_2 for consumption next summer and r for the real interest rate.

8B.3.1 Do Higher Interest Rates Make Us Save More We begin with the example of an individual earning €10 000 this summer and choosing how much of it to allocate between consumption this summer and consumption next summer. In Graph 8.5, we illustrated that without knowing more about tastes, it is unclear whether an increase in the real interest rate from 10 per cent to 20 per cent will cause the individual to save more or less this summer, although we concluded that they will unambiguously choose to consume more next summer.

In terms of equation (8.13), $e_1 = 10\ 000$ and $e_2 = 0$ in this example. Thus, equation (8.13) can be written as:

$$(1 + r)c_1 + c_2 = 10\ 000(1 + r). \tag{8.14}$$

Now suppose that your tastes can be described by the Cobb–Douglas utility function $u(c_1, c_2) = c_1^{0.5}c_2^{0.5}$. The utility maximization problem is:

$$\max_{c1,\ c2} c_1^{0.5}c_2^{0.5} \text{ subject to } (1 + r)c_1 + c_2 = 10\,000(1 + r). \tag{8.15}$$

Solving this we get that the optimal consumption levels this summer and next summer as:

$$c_1 = 5000 \text{ and } c_2 = 5000(1 + r). \tag{8.16}$$

Exercise 8B.8

Verify that the answer given in (8.16) is indeed the solution to the problem defined in (8.15).

Thus, at the initial interest rate of 10 per cent the individual will choose to consume €5000 this summer and €5500 next summer, and at the new interest rate of 20 per cent they will continue to consume €5000 this summer but will raise consumption next summer to €6000. This corresponds to our usual bundles A and C, and we can already tell that the substitution and wealth effects must have exactly offset one another since savings – the amount the individual chooses not to consume this summer – remained constant.

For many interesting policy questions, however, it will be important to know just how large the substitution effect is. We can calculate this effect using our expenditure minimization approach in which we simply ask how much we would have to give the individual instead of the €10 000 they are earning this summer, in order for them to remain just as happy under the new interest rate as they were under the old interest rate when they earned €10 000 this summer. Substituting bundle A – €5000 this summer and €5500 next summer – into the utility function, we can calculate that they attained a utility level of 5244 as measured by the Cobb–Douglas function used to represent their tastes. Thus, to calculate our usual bundle B, we need to solve:

$$\min_{c_1,\ c_2} E = (1 + r)c_1 + c_2 \text{ subject to } c_1^{0.5}c_2^{0.5} = 5244, \tag{8.17}$$

with r set to the new interest rate 0.2. Solving this, we get that:

$$c_1 = 4787.14 \text{ and } c_2 = 5744.56. \tag{8.18}$$

Exercise 8B.9

Verify that the answer given in (8.18) is indeed the solution to the problem defined in (8.17).

Thus, the substitution effect in this example indicates that the individual would increase savings this summer by €212.86 if they only faced a change in opportunity costs without a change in real income as indicated by the initial indifference curve. But this temptation to increase savings is undone by the wealth effect, by the fact that they are richer as a result of the increase in the interest rate. As we will show in more detail in Chapter 9, the result that substitution and wealth effects will exactly offset each other is a special case for Cobb–Douglas tastes and is due to the built-in assumption of an elasticity of substitution equal to 1. In the more general class of constant elasticity of substitution (CES) utility functions, of which the Cobb–Douglas function is a special case, we will see that the substitution effect is outweighed by the wealth effect when the elasticity of substitution falls below 1, leading to a decline in savings with an increase in the real interest rate. Analogously, the wealth effect is outweighed by the substitution effect when the elasticity of substitution is greater than 1, leading to an increase in savings when the real interest rate increases.

Exercise 8B.10

Using a set of graphs similar to those depicted in Graph 8.5, label the bundles that we have just calculated.

8B.3.2 Will an Increase in the (Real) Interest Rate Make Us Borrow Less? We next considered in Section 8A.3.2 how the situation changes if, instead of having a €10 000 income this summer and no income next summer, the individual had an €11 000 income next summer and no income this summer. In this case, they would have to borrow against future income to consume anything this summer, and the example is structured in such a way that the intertemporal budget across the two summers is the same as it was in our previous example when the interest rate was 10 per cent. The intuition for how choices are now affected as the interest rate rises to 20 per cent was illustrated in Graph 8.6 where we showed that while such an increase in the interest rate will certainly make an individual consume less and thus borrow less this summer because of the increased cost of borrowing, it is unclear without knowing more about their tastes whether they will consume more or less next summer.

Suppose that the individual's tastes can continue to be described by the Cobb–Douglas utility function $u(c_1, c_2) = c_1^{0.5}c_2^{0.5}$. The only change in the mathematical analysis from the previous section is that the budget constraint differs. In terms of equation (8.13), we now have $e_1 = 0$ and $e_2 = 11\,000$, giving us a new budget constraint of:

$$(1 + r)c_1 + c_2 = 11\,000. \tag{8.19}$$

You should now be able to verify, following exactly the same steps as in the previous section, that bundles A and B will be exactly the same as before as already indicated by the intuition emerging from Graphs 8.5 and 8.6, but that the new bundle C will be:

$$c_1 = 4583.33 \quad \text{and} \quad c_2 = 5500. \tag{8.20}$$

Thus, for tastes described by the Cobb–Douglas function in this example, the individual's consumption next summer will remain unchanged from their original consumption, indicating that substitution and wealth effects exactly offset one another on that dimension. Since consumption this summer declines from €5000 at bundle A to €4583.33 at bundle C, the individual has chosen to borrow €416.67 less as a result of the increase in the interest rate, with €212.86 of that accounted for by the substitution effect and the remainder by the wealth effect.

Exercise 8B.11

Illustrate what we have just calculated in a graph.

Exercise 8B.12

We calculated that consumption next summer is unchanged as the interest rate rises when tastes can be represented by the Cobb–Douglas utility function we used. This is because this function assumes an elasticity of substitution of 1. How would this result change if the elasticity of substitution is larger or smaller than 1?

8B.3.3 Neither a Borrower Nor a Lender Be … Finally, we considered in Section 8A.3.3 the case where an individual had put in place plans to earn €5000 this summer and €5500 next summer knowing that, at an interest rate of 10 per cent, this implied they would have to neither borrow nor lend to consume their optimal bundle: €5000 this summer and €5500 next summer. Continuing with the Cobb–Douglas tastes from the previous section, we can verify that this is indeed the optimal bundle given a summer income of €5000 this summer and €5500 next summer by recognizing that we are once again solving the same maximization problem, except that now $e_1 = 5000$ and $e_2 = 5500$. Thus, the budget constraint (8.13) becomes:

$$(1 + r)c_1 + c_2 = 5000(1 + r) + 5500. \tag{8.21}$$

Going through the same steps as before, you will find that the new optimal bundle when the interest rate rises to 20 per cent is:

$$c_1 = 4791.67 \text{ and } c_2 = 5750, \tag{8.22}$$

with the substitution effect accounting for most of the change in behaviour as suggested by the intuition gained from panels (a) and (b) in Graph 8.7 in Section 8A.3.3. Specifically, point B, the bundle representing just the substitution effect, is:

$$c_1 = 4787.14 \text{ and } c_2 = 5744.56, \tag{8.23}$$

just a few euros off the bundle C of expression (8.22).

Exercise 8B.13

Verify that (8.22) and (8.23) are correct.

End-of-Chapter Exercises

8.1† As we have suggested in the chapter, it is often important to know whether workers will work more or less as their wage increases.

   A. In each of the following cases, can you tell whether a worker will work more or less as their wage increases?

   a. The worker's tastes over consumption and leisure are quasilinear in leisure.
   b. The worker's tastes over consumption and leisure are homothetic.
   c. Leisure is a luxury good.
   d. Leisure is a necessity.
   e. The worker's tastes over consumption and leisure are quasilinear in consumption.

   B. Suppose that tastes take the form $u(c,\ell) = (0.5c^{-p} + 0.5\ell^{-p})^{-1/p}$.

   a. Set up the worker's optimization problem assuming their leisure endowment is L and wage is w.
   b. Set up the Lagrange function corresponding to your maximization problem.
   c. Solve for the optimal amount of leisure.
   d. *Does leisure consumption increase or decrease as w increases? What does your answer depend on?
   e. Relate this to what you know about substitution and wealth effects in this type of problem.

8.2 Assume that an invention has just resulted in everyone being able to cut their sleep requirement by 10 hours per week, thus providing an increase in their weekly leisure endowment.

   A. For each of the following cases, can you tell whether a worker will work more or less?

   a. The worker's tastes over consumption and leisure are quasilinear in leisure.
   b. The worker's tastes over consumption and leisure are homothetic.
   c. Leisure is a luxury good.
   d. Leisure is a necessity.
   e. The worker's tastes over consumption and leisure are quasilinear in consumption.
   f. Do any of your answers have anything to do with how substitutable consumption and leisure are? Why or why not?

   B. Suppose that a worker's tastes for consumption c and leisure ℓ can be represented by the utility function $u(c,\ell) = c^\alpha \ell^{(1-\alpha)}$.

   a. Write down the worker's constrained optimization problem and the Lagrange function used to solve it, using w to denote the wage and L to denote the leisure endowment.

b. Solve the problem to determine leisure consumption as a function of w, α and L. Will an increase in L result in more or less leisure consumption?

c. Can you determine whether an increase in leisure will cause the worker to work more?

d. Repeat parts (a) through (c) using the utility function $u(c,\ell) = c + \alpha \ln \ell$ instead.

e. **Can you show that if tastes can be represented by the CES utility function $u(c,\ell) = (\alpha c^{-\rho}(1 - \alpha)\ell^{-\rho})^{-1/\rho}$, the worker will choose to consume more leisure as well as work more when there is an increase in the leisure endowment L? *Warning*: The algebra gets a little messy. You can occasionally check your answers by substituting $\rho = 0$ and checking that this matches what you know to be true for the Cobb–Douglas function $u(c,\ell) = c^{0.5}\ell^{0.5}$.

8.3† **Business Application:** *Merchandise Exchange Policies.* Suppose you have €200 in discretionary income that you would like to spend on t-shirts and science fiction DVDs.

A. On the way to university, you take your €200 to a shop and buy 10 t-shirts and 5 DVDs at t-shirt prices of €10 and DVD prices of €20.

a. On a graph with DVDs on the horizontal and t-shirts on the vertical, illustrate your budget constraint and your optimal bundle A.

b. On the way home, you drive by the same shop and see a big sign: All DVDs half price – only €10! You also know that the shop has a policy of either refunding returned items for the price at which they were bought if you provide them with a receipt or, alternatively, giving shop credit in the amount that those items are currently priced in the shop if you have lost your receipt. What is the most in shop credit that you could get?

c. Given that you have no more cash and only a bag full of DVDs and t-shirts, will you go back into the shop and buy anything else?

d. On the way to university the next day, you again drive by the shop and notice that the sale sign is gone. You assume that the price of DVDs is back to €20 with the price of t-shirts still unchanged, and you notice you forgot to take your bag of t-shirts and DVDs out of the car last night and have it sitting right there next to you. Will you go back into the shop assuming you still have no cash?

e. Finally, you pass the shop again on the way home and this time see a sign: Big Sale – All t-shirts only €5, All DVDs only €10! With your bag of merchandise still sitting next to you and no cash, will you go back into the shop?

f. If you are the manager of a shop with this shop credit policy, would you tend to favour – all else being equal – across the board price changes or sales on selective items?

g. *True or False*: If it were not for substitution effects, the shop would not have to worry about people gaming their shop credit policies as you did in this example.

B. Suppose your tastes for DVDs (x_1) and t-shirts (x_2) can be characterized by the utility function $u(x_1, x_2) = x_1^{0.5}x_2^{0.5}$. Throughout, assume that it is possible to buy fractions of t-shirts and DVDs.

a. Calculate the bundle you initially buy on your first trip to the shop.

b. Calculate the bundle you buy on your way home from work on the first day when p_1 falls to 10.

c. If you had to pay the shop some fixed fee for letting you get shop credit, what's the most you would be willing to pay on that visit?

d. What bundle will you eventually end up with if you follow all the steps in part A?

e. **Suppose that your tastes were instead characterized by the function $u(x_1, x_2) = (0.5x_1^{-\rho} + 0.5x_2^{-\rho})^{-1/\rho}$. Can you show that your ability to exploit the shop credit policy diminishes as the elasticity of substitution goes to zero (i.e. as ρ goes to ∞)?

8.4* **Policy Application:** *Savings Behaviour and Tax Policy.* Suppose you consider the savings decisions of three households: households 1, 2 and 3. Each household plans for this year's consumption and next year's consumption, and each household anticipates earning €100 000 this year and nothing next year. The real interest rate is 10 per cent. Assume throughout that consumption is always a normal good.

A. Suppose the government does not impose any tax on interest income below €5000 but taxes any interest income above €5000 at 50 per cent.

a. On a graph with Consumption this period (c_1) on the horizontal axis and Consumption next period (c_2) on the vertical, illustrate the choice set each of the three households faces.

b. Suppose you observe that household 1 saves €25 000, household 2 saves €50 000 and household 3 saves €75 000. Illustrate indifference curves for each household that would make these rational choices.

c. Now suppose the government changes the tax system by exempting the first €7500 rather than the first €5000 from taxation. Thus, under the new tax, the first €7500 in interest income is not taxed, but any interest income above €7500 is taxed at 50 per cent. Given what you know about each household's savings decisions before the tax change, can you tell whether each of these households will now save more? *Note*: It is extremely difficult to draw the scenarios in this question to scale, and when not drawn to scale, the graphs can become confusing. It is easier to worry about the general shapes of the budget constraints around the relevant decision points of the households that are described.

d. Instead of the tax change in part (c), suppose the government had proposed to subsidize interest income at 100 per cent for the first €2500 in interest income while raising the tax on any interest income above €2500 to 80 per cent. Thus, if someone earns €2500 in interest, they would receive an additional €2500 in cash from the government. If someone earns €3500, on the other hand, they would receive the same €2500 cash subsidy but would also have to pay €800 in tax. One of the households is overheard saying: 'I actually don't care whether the old policy, i.e. the policy described in part A or this new policy goes into effect'. Which of the three households could have said this, and will that household save more or less than under the old policy if this new policy goes into effect?

B. Now suppose that our three households had tastes that can be represented by the utility function $(c_1, c_2) = c_1^\alpha c_2^{(1-\alpha)}$, where c_1 is consumption now and c_2 is consumption a year from now.

a. Suppose there were no tax on savings income. Write down the intertemporal budget constraint with the real interest rate denoted r and current income denoted I and assume that the consumer anticipates no income next period.

b. Write down the constrained optimization problem and the accompanying Lagrange function. Solve for c_1, current consumption as a function of α, and solve for the implied level of savings as a function of α, I and r. Does savings depend on the interest rate?

c. Determine the α value for consumer 1 as described in part A.

d. Now suppose the initial 50 per cent tax described in part A is introduced. Write down the budget constraint assuming current income I and before-tax interest rate r that is now relevant for consumers who end up saving more than €50 000. *Note*: Don't write down the equation for the kinked budget; write down the equation for the linear budget on which such a consumer would optimize.

e. Use this budget constraint to write down the constrained optimization problem that can be solved for the optimal choice given that households save more than €50 000. Solve for c_1 and for the implied level of savings as a function of α, I and r.

f. What value must α take for household 3 as described in part A?

g. With the values of α that you have determined for households 1 and 3, determine the impact that the tax reform described in (c) of part A would have.

h. What range of values can α take for household 2 as described in part A?

8.5† **Policy Application:** *International Trade and Child Labour.* The economist Jagdish Bhagwati explained in one of his public lectures that international trade causes the wage for child labour to increase in developing countries. He discussed informally that this might lead to more child labour if parents are 'bad' and less child labour if parents are 'good'.

A. Suppose that households in developing countries value two goods: Leisure time for Children in the Household and Household Consumption. Assume that the adults in a household are earning €y in weekly income regardless of how many hours their children work. Assume that child wages are w per hour and that the maximum leisure time for children in a household is E hours per week.

a. On a graph with weekly leisure time for children in the household on the horizontal axis and weekly household consumption on the vertical, illustrate the budget constraint for a household and label the slopes and intercepts.

b. Now suppose that international trade expands and, as a result, child wages increase to w'. Illustrate how this will change the household budget.

c. Suppose that household tastes are homothetic and that households require their children to work during some but not all the time they have available. Can you tell whether children will be asked to work more or less as a result of the expansion of international trade?

d. In the context of the model with homothetic tastes, what distinguishes 'good' parents from 'bad' parents?

e. When international trade increases the wages of children, it is likely that it also increases the wages of other members of the household. Thus, in the context of our model, y – the amount brought to the household by others – would also be expected to go up. If this is so, will we observe more or less behaviour that is consistent with what we have defined as good parent behaviour?

f. In some developing countries with high child labour rates, governments have instituted the following policy: if the parents agree to send a child to school instead of work, the government pays the family an amount x. Assume the government can verify that the child is in fact sent to school and does in fact not work, and assume that the household views time at school as leisure time for the child. How does that alter the choice set for parents? Is the policy more or less likely to succeed the more substitutable the household tastes treat child leisure and household consumption?

B. Suppose parental tastes can be captured by the utility function $u(c,\ell) = c^{0.5}\ell^{0.5}$. For simplicity, suppose further that $y = 0$.

a. Specify the parents' constrained optimization problem and set up the appropriate Lagrange function.

b. Solve the problem you have set up to determine the level of leisure the parents will choose for their children. Does ρ have any impact on this decision?

c. Explain intuitively what you have just found. Consider the CES utility function that has the Cobb–Douglas function you just worked with as a special case. For what ranges of ρ would you expect us to be able to call parents 'good' in the way that Bhagwati informally defined the term?

d. Can parents for whom household consumption is a quasilinear good ever be good?

e. Now suppose with the original Cobb–Douglas tastes that $y > 0$. If international trade pushes up the earnings of other household members thus raising y, what happens to child leisure?

f. Suppose again that $y = 0$ and the government introduces the policy described in part A(f). How large does x have to be to cause our household to send its child to school assuming again that the household views the child's time at school as leisure time for the child?

g. Using your answer to the previous part, put into words what fraction of the market value of the child's time the government has to provide in x in order for the family to choose schooling over work for its child?

8.6 **Policy Application:** *Tax Revenues and the Laffer Curve.* In this exercise, we will consider how the tax rate on wages relates to the amount of tax revenue collected.

A. As introduced in Section B, the *Laffer Curve* depicts the relationship between the tax rate on the horizontal axis and tax revenues on the vertical. Because people's decision on how much to work may be affected by the tax rate, deriving this relationship is not as straightforward as many think.

a. Consider first the extreme case in which leisure and consumption are perfect complements. On a graph with leisure hours on the horizontal and consumption euros on the vertical, illustrate how increases in the tax on wages affect the consumer's optimal choice of leisure and thus labour.

b. Next, consider the less extreme case where a change in after-tax wages gives rise to substitution and wealth effects that exactly offset one another on the leisure axis. In which of these cases does tax revenue rise faster as the tax rate increases?

c. On a graph with the tax rate ranging from 0 to 1 on the horizontal and tax revenues on the vertical, how does this relationship differ for tastes in (a) and (b)?

d. Now suppose that the substitution effect outweighs the wealth effect on the leisure axis as after-tax wages change. Illustrate this and determine how it changes the relationship between tax rates and tax revenue.

e. Laffer suggested that the curve relating tax revenue on the vertical axis to tax rates on the horizontal is initially upward sloping but eventually slopes down, reaching the horizontal axis by the time the tax rate goes to 1. Which of the preferences we described in this problem can give rise to this shape?

f. *True or False*: If leisure is a normal good, the Laffer Curve can have an inverted U-shape only if leisure and consumption are at least at some point sufficiently substitutable such that the substitution effect on leisure outweighs the wealth effect on leisure.

B. **In Section 8B.2.2, we derived a Laffer Curve for the case where tastes were quasilinear in leisure. Now consider the case where tastes are Cobb–Douglas, taking the form $u(c,\ell) = c^\alpha \ell^{(1-\alpha)}$. Assume that a worker has 60 hours of weekly leisure endowment that they can sell in the labour market for wage w.

a. Suppose the worker's wages are taxed at a rate t. Derive the worker's optimal leisure choice.

b. For someone with these tastes, does the Laffer Curve take the inverted U-shape described in Section 8B.2.2? Why or why not? Which of the cases described in A does this represent?

c. Now consider the more general CES function $(\alpha c^{-\rho} + (1-\alpha)\ell^{-\rho})^{-1/\rho}$. Again, derive the optimal leisure consumption.

d. Does your answer simplify to what you would expect when $\rho = 0$?

e. Determine the range of values of ρ such that leisure consumption increases with t.

f. When ρ falls in the range you have just derived, what happens to leisure consumption as t approaches 1? What does this imply for the shape of the Laffer Curve?

g. Suppose $\alpha = 0.25$, $w = 20$ and $\rho = -0.5$ Calculate the amount of leisure a worker would choose as a function of t. Derive an expression for this worker's Laffer Curve and graph it.

Chapter 9

Demand for Goods and Supply of Labour and Capital

To date you may have noticed an absence of supply and demand in our discussions. The reason we have not covered these concepts up to now is that it is difficult to know what they tell us and what they do not tell us, without first understanding how demand and supply arise from individual optimizing behaviour. Having taken a close look at how economists think about individuals doing the best they can given their circumstances, we are now ready to see how such individual decision making leads to some types of demand and supply curves.

We have analyzed how individuals make choices in three different roles within the economy: as consumers choosing between various goods, as workers choosing between consumption and leisure, and as savers/borrowers choosing how to plan for the future. In their role as consumers, individuals become *demanders of goods and services*, while in their role as workers they become *suppliers of labour*. Finally, as savers they become *suppliers of financial capital*, while as borrowers they become *demanders of financial capital*. From what we have modelled so far, we can derive demand curves for goods and supply curves for labour. Depending on whether an individual borrows or saves, we will also be able to derive demand and supply curves for financial capital. In later chapters, we will complete the picture of goods and services markets, labour markets and capital markets by adding the role played by producers, who supply goods and demand labour and capital.

9A | Deriving Demand and Supply Curves

We will begin with demand relationships for goods and services, while later sections extend the analysis to similar relationships in labour and capital markets.

9A.1 Demand for Goods and Services

We have analyzed how the quantity of a good that is demanded may change with changes in underlying economic circumstances, such as income, wealth or prices. Our answer has depended on the underlying tastes that gave rise to sometimes competing income (or wealth) and substitution effects. It became important to know whether, for the particular individual in question, a good was normal or inferior, regular inferior or Giffen. Such distinctions between different types of tastes become similarly important for understanding demand relationships more generally.

We will distinguish between three different kinds of demand relationships or curves: *income–demand curves*, *own-price demand curves* and *cross-price demand curves*. An income–demand curve is the relationship between exogenously given income and the quantity of a good that is demanded; an own-price demand curve is the relationship between the price of a good and the quantity demanded of *that same* good; and a cross-price demand curve is the relationship between one good's price and the quantity demanded of a *different* good. In each of these cases, we will plot demand curves relating the quantity of a good demanded on the horizontal axis and the variable of interest – to income, the good's own price or some other good's price – on the vertical.

9A.1.1 Income–Demand Relationships Of the three types of demand relationships we are interested in, the relationship between income and the quantity of a good demanded is the most straightforward. These income–demand relationships are sometime referred to as *Engel curves*, named after Ernst Engel (1821–1896), a German statistician and economist who studied how consumption behaviour changes with income. He is particularly known for what has become known as 'Engel's Law', which states that the proportion of income spent on food falls as income increases, i.e. food is a necessity as we have defined it even though the overall expenditures on food increase, i.e. food is a normal good as we have defined it.

Let us return to an example from Chapter 7, where pasta is an inferior good and steak is a normal good for a consumer. In Graph 9.1, we derive the income–demand curves for these two goods. In panel (a) of Graph 9.1 we model an income of €100 and a choice between packets of pasta per week and euros of other consumption per week. Since the good on the vertical axis is denominated in euros, its price is 1 and the slope of the budget is minus the price of pasta – for example, if the price is €4 and the optimal bundle *A* contains 10 packets of pasta per week this gives us one point on the income–demand graph directly below: at an income of €100 on the vertical axis, the consumer consumes 10 packets of pasta.

Now suppose the consumer's income goes up to €200, but the price of pasta is unchanged. Since pasta is an inferior good for the consumer, we know that pasta consumption will now decline, perhaps to 5 packets as indicated in the new optimal bundle *B*. This gives us a second point on the income–demand graph: at an income of €200, 5 packets of pasta are consumed. We can go through these same steps for different levels of income, each time finding the optimal point in the top graph and translating it to the lower graph. The curve connecting these points forms the complete income-demand curve. For our particular example, the curve has a negative slope because we have assumed pasta is an inferior good, implying a negative relationship between income and consumption. Panel (b) of Graph 9.1 replicates the same analysis for steak when the price of steak is €10 per kilo. This results in a positive income–demand relationship because steak is assumed to be a normal good.

Exercise 9A.1

In an earlier chapter, we mentioned that it is not possible for a good to be inferior for all income levels. Can you see in the lower diagram of panel (a) of Graph 9.1 why this is true?

The graphical translation of optimizing choices in the top graphs to income–demand curves in the lower graphs is an intuitive way of accomplishing what can be done with mathematical equations. Economists use the techniques developed in the B parts of our chapters. Nevertheless, the graphical technique provides us with the intuition of what the mathematics can accomplish.

The income–demand curves derived in Graph 9.1 are valid for the prices used in the top portions of the graphs: €4 for pasta and €10 for steak. If these prices change, the resulting new optimal bundles in the top portion of the graphs will translate to different points, and thus to different income–demand curves in the lower portion of the graphs. In particular, for normal and regular inferior goods, an increase in the price of a good will result in less consumption of that good for any given income level. This implies that *for normal or regular inferior goods, the income-demand curve will shift inwards for an increase in the price of the good and outwards for a decrease in price*. For Giffen goods, on the other hand, an increase in price results in increased consumption for any given income level, while a decrease in the price will result in decreased consumption. Thus, *for Giffen goods, an increase in price results in an outward shift of the income–demand curve, while a decrease in price results in an inward shift*.

Graph 9.1 Income–Demand Curves when Pasta Is Inferior (a) and Steak Is Normal (b)

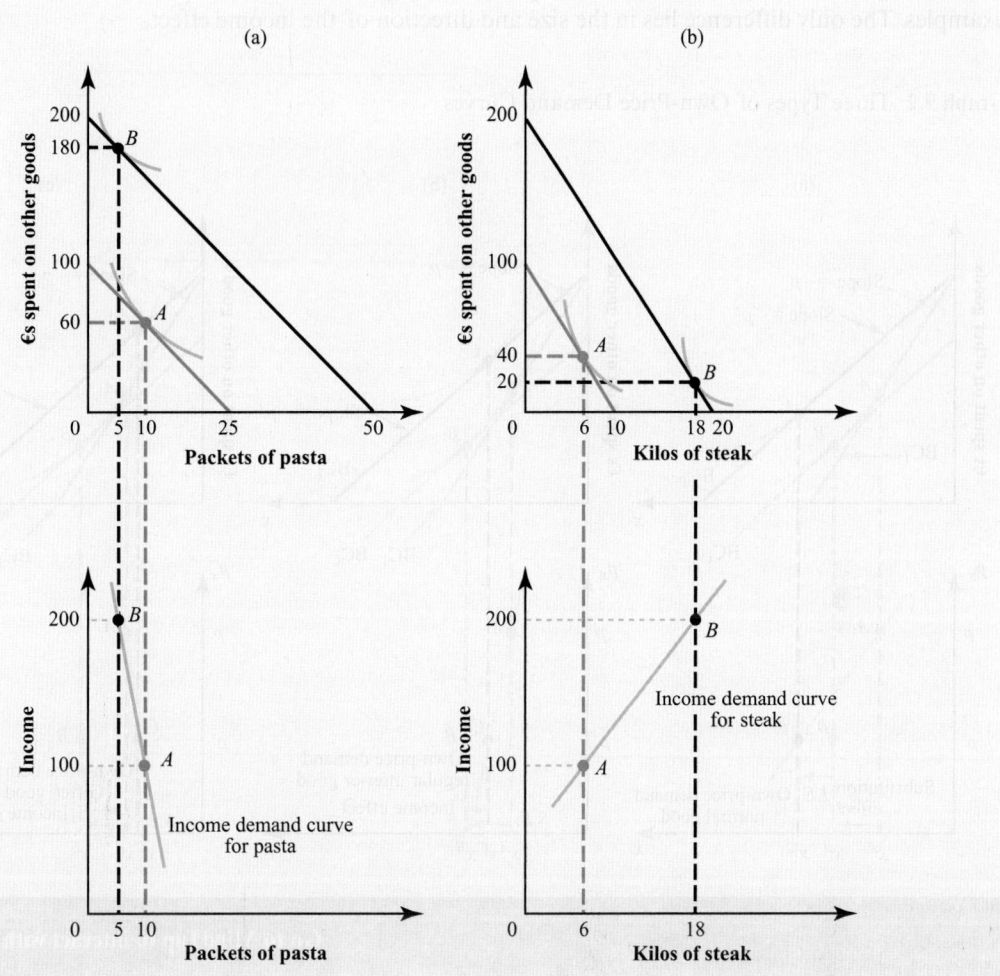

Exercise 9A.2

Suppose good x is an inferior good for an individual. Derive the income–demand curve as in panel (a) of Graph 9.1. Graph (a) decrease in the price for x for both income levels in the top panel and show how this affects the income-demand curve in the lower panel depending on whether x is Giffen or regular inferior.

9A.1.2 Own-Price Demand Relationships We can derive own-price demand curves in much the same way that we derived the income-demand curves in Graph 9.1, except that we now have to change prices, which will be on the vertical axis in the lower graph, rather than incomes in the top portion of the graphs.

In Graph 9.2, we derive the own-price demand curves for a normal good, a regular inferior good and a Giffen good. In each case, we model the good of interest on the horizontal axis and analyze the choices faced by a consumer between that good and a composite good denominated in euros. We begin in the top panel of each graph with the same initial budget constraint BC_1 and the same initial optimal point A, and in each case, we analyze a decrease in the price of the good on the horizontal axis from p to p'. To make the illustration as clean as possible, we also assume in each case that the degree of substitutability built into the indifference curve at point A is the same across the three examples, which implies that the substitution effect that gives rise to point B on the compensated budget constraint, BC_C, is the same across the three examples. The only difference lies in the size and direction of the income effect.

Graph 9.2 Three Types of Own-Price Demand Curves

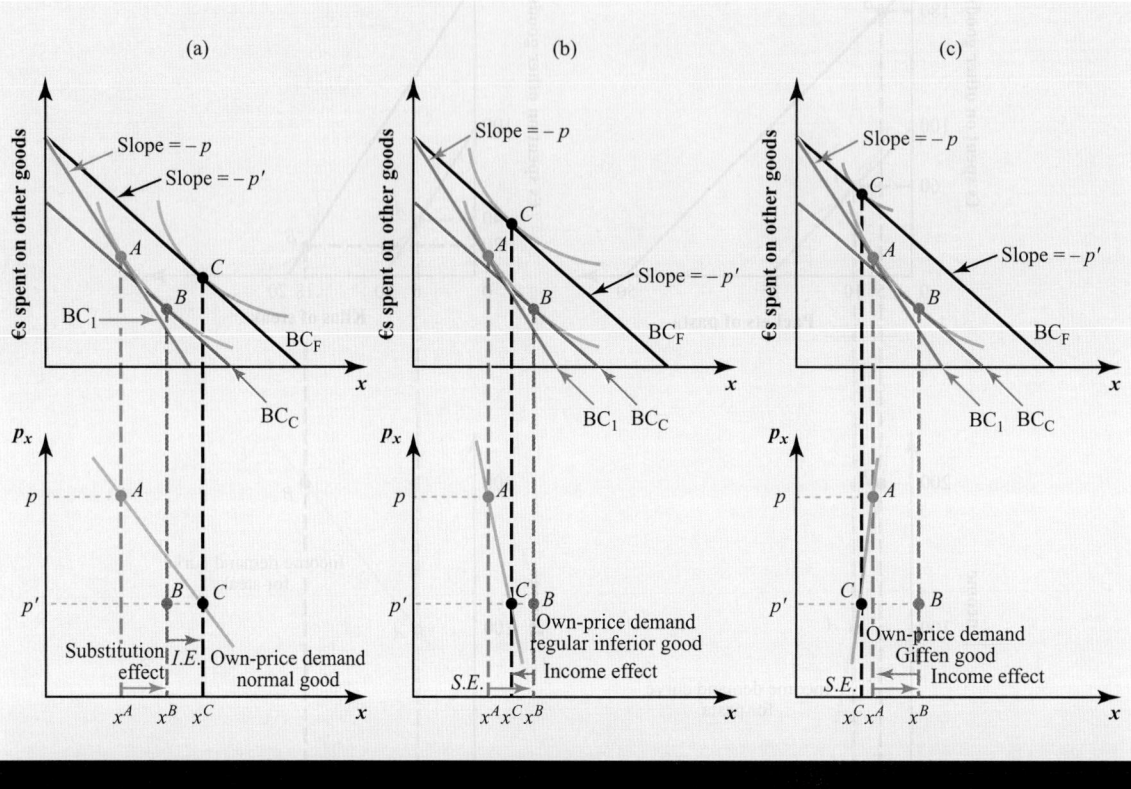

Go to MindTap to interact with this graph

Consider first the derivation of the own-price demand curve for a normal good in panel (a) of Graph 9.2. At the initial price p, the consumer consumes x^A in the top graph, a quantity that is translated to the lower graph and placed at the vertical height p. Bundle B, the optimal choice under the compensated budget, is chosen at the lower price p'. Thus, we could translate the quantity x^B to the lower graph and place it at the vertical height p'. This is not, however, a point on the own-price demand curve since it is the hypothetical consumption level at the compensated budget, BC_C. This will turn out to be an important point in a different relationship we introduce in Chapter 10.

For now, we want to focus on bundle C in the top graph, the bundle that is chosen on the actual final budget constraint. Because we are assuming in panel (a) of this graph that x is a normal good, C falls on the final budget BC_F to the right of B. As income rises from the compensated to the final budget, more of the normal good x is *consumed*. The quantity x^C that is chosen at the final price p' can be translated to the lower graph and placed at the height p'. We can repeat this exercise many times to plot the optimal consumption of x at different prices and fully trace out the relationship between the price of good x and the quantity of x demanded. For our purposes, it is good enough simply to estimate the remaining points on the own-price demand curve by connecting points A and C on the lower graph.

We can see in panel (b) of Graph 9.2 how this analysis differs when x is a regular inferior rather than a normal good. Since bundles A and B are identical to those in panel (a) of the graph, these points translate to the lower graph in exactly the same way as they did for a normal good. This reiterates that substitution effects have nothing to do with whether a good is normal or inferior. As income rises from the compensated to the final budget in the top portion of the graph, the consumer ends up consuming less x rather than more, because x is inferior. The quantity x^C, therefore, now falls to the left of x^B. Because we are assuming that the good is a regular inferior rather than a Giffen good, we know that the size of the income effect is smaller than the size of the substitution effect, causing C to fall in between A and B. When we connect A and C in the lower portion of the graph, we get a demand curve that is steeper for the inferior good than it was for the normal good. The reason for this is that income and substitution effects now point in opposite directions.

Exercise 9A.3

Repeat the derivation of own-price demand curves for the case of quasilinear tastes and explain in this context again how quasilinear tastes are borderline tastes between normal and inferior goods.

Finally, we can compare this to the own-price demand curve for a Giffen good in panel (c) of Graph 9.2. The difference now is that the income effect not only points in the opposite direction of the substitution effect but now it is also larger in size. As a result, point C in both the top and bottom portions of the graph falls not only to the left of B but also to the left of A. This leads to an own-price demand curve that is upward rather than downward sloping, giving expression to the definition of a Giffen good as a good whose consumption moves in the same direction as its own price.

Exercise 9A.4*

How would the own-price demand curves in panels (a), (b) and (c) of Graph 9.2 change with a decrease in income? *Hint:* Your answer for panel (a) should be different from your answers for panels (b) and (c).

Exercise 9A.5

What kind of good would x have to be in order for the demand curve not to shift as income changes?

9A.1.3 Cross-Price Demand Relationships Producers of goods that are used together such as razors and razor blades, or printers and toner cartridges, have to think about how the two goods should be priced, how consumption of each good varies with its own price and also how consumption of one varies with the price of the other. Just as we could derive own-price demand curves in the previous section, we can also derive cross-price demand curves under different scenarios.

Suppose, for instance, that you consume goods x_1 and x_2, that your tastes are quasilinear in good x_1, and that we are interested in the cross-price demand curve for good x_1 as the price of good x_2 varies. We would therefore begin in Graph 9.3 by modelling how choices change as the price of good x_2 decreases from p_2 to p_2'. The optimal bundle A at the original price p_2 could be translated to the lower portion of the graph, where we plot optimal consumption x_1^A at the initial price p_2. We can similarly translate bundle B but are ultimately interested in where bundle C will fall. Since we have assumed in this example that tastes are quasilinear in good x_1, we know that consumption of good x_1 is unchanged as income changes and thus is the same on the compensated and the final budget constraint. Bundle C lies directly above bundle B

in the top portion of the graph and exactly on top of the translated B point on the lower portion. The cross-price demand curve that connects A and C is upward sloping. As the price of good x_2 increases, so does consumption of good x_1.

Graph 9.3 Cross-Price Demand Curve When Tastes Are Quasilinear in x_1

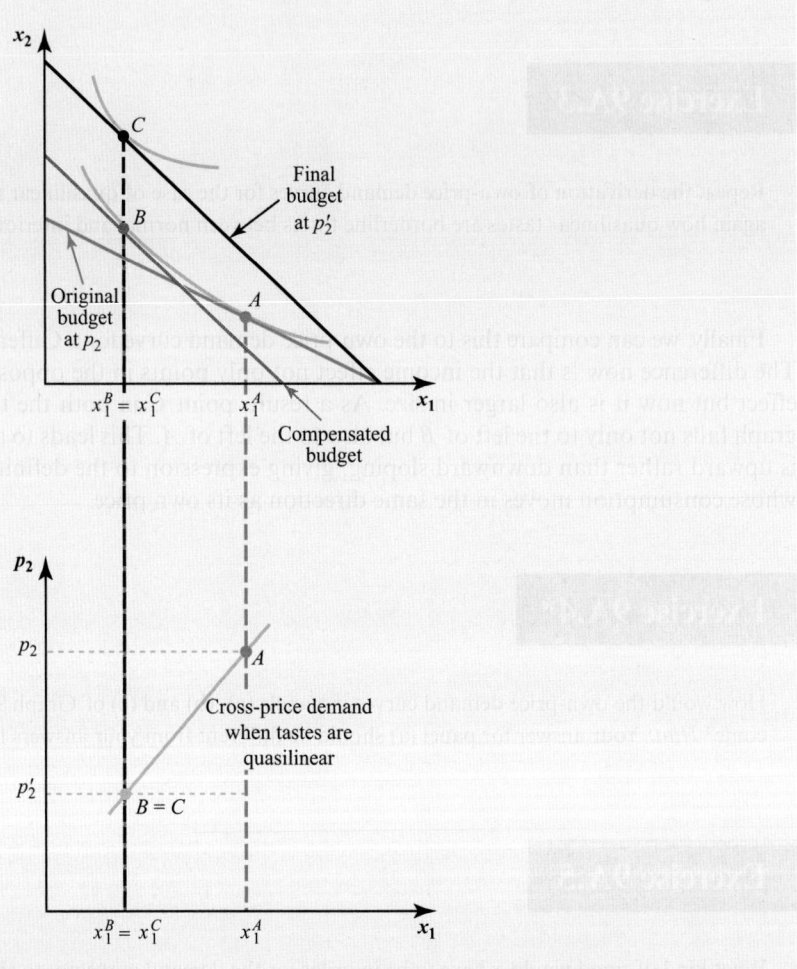

Exercise 9A.6

What kind of good would x_1 have to be in order for this cross-price demand curve to slope down?

9A.2 Labour Supply

Economists and policy makers alike are often interested in how the supply of labour will respond to changes in the wages that workers can earn. Enormous effort has been devoted to determining how different types of workers respond differently to changes in wages, whether women respond differently than men, whether older workers respond differently than younger workers, or high-wage workers differently than low-wage workers. How responsive workers are to changes in their take-home pay impacts the way we think about tax policy as well as labour issues like the minimum wage. At the root of these issues is the question of the direction and relative size of income (or wealth) and substitution effects.

Labour supply curves plot the amount of labour an individual chooses to supply to the market at different wage rates. This choice emerges from an individual's choice of how to spend their leisure endowment; that is, how much of it to consume as leisure and how much of it to convert into consumption of other goods by selling leisure, i.e. by working. The wage itself is like any other price in the economy, and, while individuals can in the long run affect the wage they command in the market by gaining skills and earning higher levels of education, they typically must accept the wage offered by the market for a given set of skills and education.

Consider again the choice of an individual about how much labour to supply this summer given 60 hours of leisure time per week and an initial wage of €20 per hour. We have previously modelled the choice graphically with weekly hours of leisure on the horizontal axis and euros of weekly consumption on the vertical. This is done once again in each of the three cases in the top row of Graph 9.4, where in each case we assume that tastes are such that the optimal level of leisure at the initial €20 wage is equal to 20 hours per week, implying 40 hours of labour supplied.

Graph 9.4 Leisure Demand (Middle Row) and Labour Supply (Bottom Row) Curves

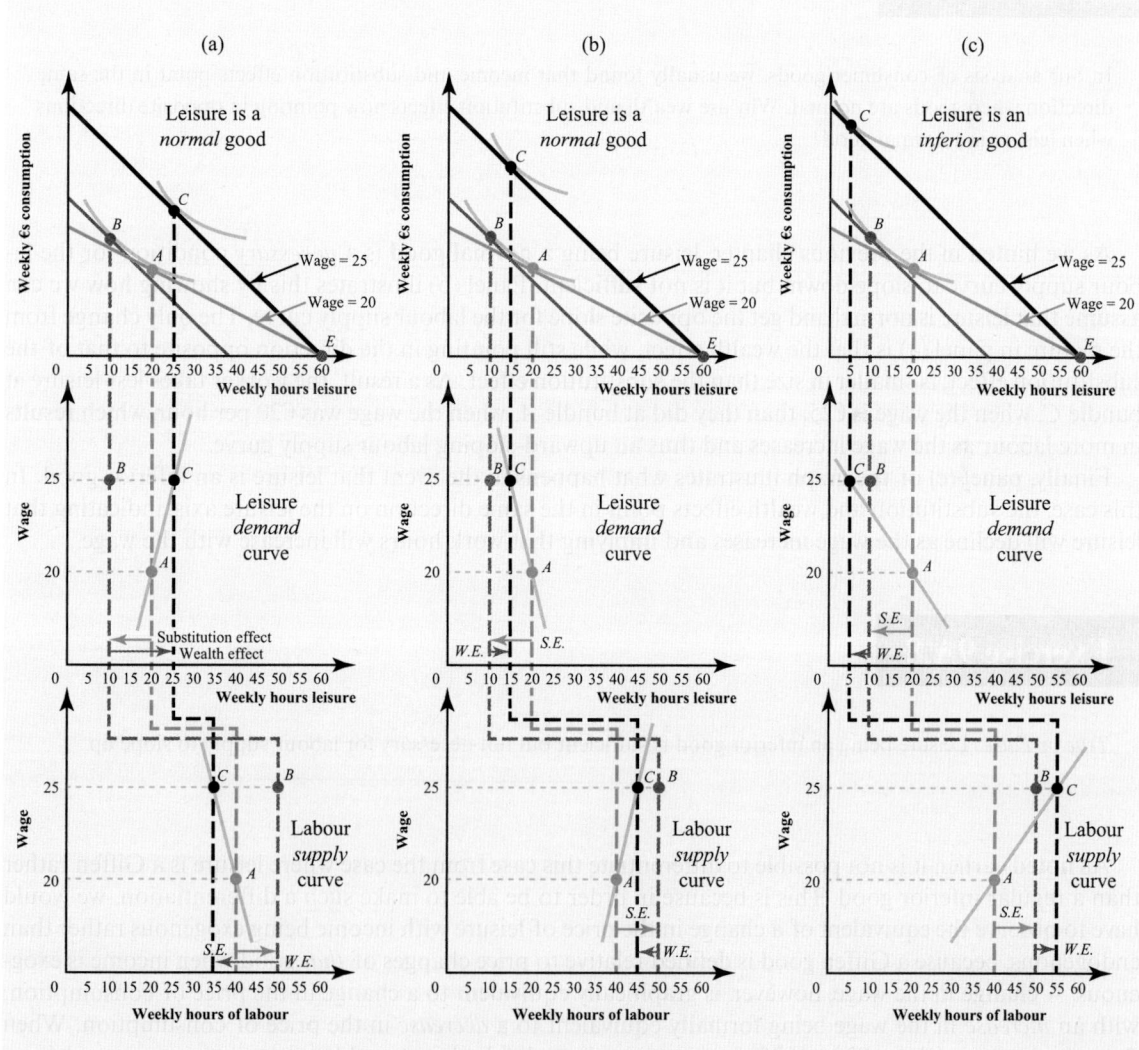

In each of the three bottom panels of Graph 9.4, point *A* indicates a supply of 40 hours of work per week at an hourly wage of €20 per hour. This is one point on the labour supply curve. Note, however, that unlike in the

graphs of the previous section, we are not able to translate the horizontal axis of the top graph to the horizontal axis of the bottom graph because the bottom graph in each panel contains a different good (labour) on the horizontal axis than the top graph (leisure). Rather, we proceed in two steps. In the middle row of Graph 9.4, we derive the leisure demand curve in much the same way as we derived demand curves in the previous section. We proceed to the lowest graph for each case to derive the corresponding *labour supply curve*, which follows from the leisure demand curve given that labour is equal to 60 minus leisure.

Now suppose a labour union is able to negotiate an increase in the market wage to €25 per hour. Several scenarios are now possible depending on which direction and what size the wealth effect assumes. In panel (a) of Graph 9.4, leisure is assumed to be normal, implying a wealth effect that points in the direction opposite to that of the substitution effect. In addition, this wealth effect is assumed in panel (a) of the graph to be larger in size than the substitution effect, thus causing an increase in the wage to result in an *increase* in leisure in the top and middle graph and thus a *decrease* in work hours on the bottom graph. As a result, the labour supply curve, estimated by connecting *A* and *C* in the bottom panel, is downward sloping.

Exercise 9A.7

In our analysis of consumer goods, we usually found that income and substitution effects point in the same direction when goods are normal. Why are wealth and substitution effects now pointing in opposite directions when leisure is a normal good?

As we hinted in the previous chapter, leisure being a normal good is a *necessary* condition for the labour supply curve to slope down, but it is not sufficient. Panel (b) illustrates this by showing how we can assume that leisure is normal and get the opposite slope for the labour supply curve. The only change from the picture in panel (a) is that the wealth effect, while still pointing in the direction opposite to that of the substitution effect, is smaller in size than the substitution effect. As a result, the worker takes less leisure at bundle *C*, when the wage is €25, than they did at bundle *A*, when the wage was €20 per hour, which results in more labour as the wage increases and thus an upward-sloping labour supply curve.

Finally, panel (c) of the graph illustrates what happens in the event that leisure is an inferior good. In this case, the substitution and wealth effects point in the same direction on the leisure axis, indicating that leisure will decline as the wage increases and implying that work hours will increase with the wage.

Exercise 9A.8

True or False: Leisure being an inferior good is sufficient but not necessary for labour supply to slope up.

As noted earlier, it is not possible to differentiate this case from the case where leisure is a Giffen rather than a regular inferior good. This is because in order to be able to make such a differentiation, we would have to observe the equivalent of a change in the price of leisure with income being exogenous rather than endogenous, because a Giffen good is defined relative to price changes of *that* good when income is exogenous. A change in the wage, however, is graphically equivalent to a change in the price of consumption, with an *increase* in the wage being formally equivalent to a *decrease* in the price of consumption. When the wage increased from €20 to €25, for instance, the individual was unable to consume any more leisure on the horizontal axis but was able to consume more of other goods on the vertical. This is exactly what a decrease in the price of the good consumption would look like in a model with exogenous income in which leisure is treated like any other good.

Exercise 9A.9

Can you tell which way the labour supply curve will slope in the unlikely event that other consumption is a Giffen good?

9A.3 Demand and Supply Curves for Financial Capital

Finally, we introduced in Chapter 3 a way of modelling the choices faced as people plan for the future by using graphs of budget constraints known as intertemporal budgets that illustrate the trade-offs between consuming now or at some point in the future. We demonstrated in Chapter 8 how we can combine such intertemporal choice sets with graphs of indifference curves to illustrate how income and substitution effects operate in our savings and borrowing decisions. We now proceed to show how this analysis can be extended to permit us to derive graphically supply and demand curves for financial capital, curves that illustrate how behaviour in financial markets changes as the real interest rate changes.

9A.3.1 Saving and the Supply of Capital Whenever people save money for the future, they are implicitly supplying financial capital to the market. Typically, they do this by putting savings into a bank account or some other financial institution, which either lends the bulk of this money to someone else or uses it directly to finance some operation; saving is equivalent to supplying capital in the economy.

Consider the case where an individual decides how much to save for next summer given that they earn €10 000 this summer and expect to have no earnings next summer. Let us further assume that consumption is always a normal good, whether it happens this summer or next summer, and that the annual interest rate is 10 per cent. At this interest rate, the individual finds it optimal to save €5000 for next summer. This optimum is illustrated as point A in the top of panels (a) and (b) of Graphs 9.5, and this bundle is translated to a lower graph in which we plot the interest rate against the amount of savings undertaken under this interest rate. On the lower graphs, point A occurs at the vertical height of the interest rate, 0.1, and indicates savings of €5000 at that interest rate. Notice that in this case, the quantity on the horizontal axis of the top graph is the same as the quantity on the horizontal axis of the lower graph because the individual is consuming €5000, the quantity on the top graph, which implies savings of €5000 because they started out with a €10 000 income. In general, however, the good on the horizontal axis in the lower panel is different from the good on the horizontal axis in the top panel, much as it was when we had leisure in the consumer diagram and put labour on the horizontal axis when graphing the labour supply curve. Compared to what we did in Graph 9.4, we are in effect skipping the intermediate step of illustrating the consumption now demand curve before illustrating the savings curve.

Next, suppose the interest rate rises to 20 per cent. As in the previous chapter, the top graph in both panels of Graph 9.5 illustrates the substitution effect to bundle B, an effect that causes less consumption this summer and more saving. When translated to the lower graphs, point B appears at the higher interest rate and to the right of point A where savings have increased. Notice that point B occurs at less than €5000 on the horizontal axis of the top graph because consumption this summer has fallen, but it occurs at greater than €5000 in the lower graph because saving is now more than €5000.

Finally, panels (a) and (b) of Graph 9.5 illustrate two differently sized wealth effects while assuming that consumption in both summers is a normal good. In panel (a), the wealth effect on this summer's consumption is larger than the substitution effect, thus causing bundle C to lie to the right of bundle A in the top graph, indicating that the increase in the interest rate causes more consumption this summer. Since this implies less savings, point C on the lower panel (a) of Graph 9.5 falls to the left of point A, giving a negative relationship between savings and the interest rate. Panel (b) of the graph, however, shows that a smaller wealth effect may lead to the opposite conclusion, with savings and the interest rate exhibiting a positive relationship. The underlying question is whether consumption this summer is relatively substitutable with consumption next summer, which would give rise to a large substitution effect and cause the positive interest rate/savings relationship in panel (b) of the graph. Alternatively, if consumption across the two time periods is relatively complementary, the substitution effect would be small, giving rise to the negative interest rate/savings relationship in panel (a) of Graph 9.5.

Exercise 9A.10

Would the interest rate/savings curve slope up or down if consumption during this period were an inferior good?

Graph 9.5 Supply Curves for Capital From Savers

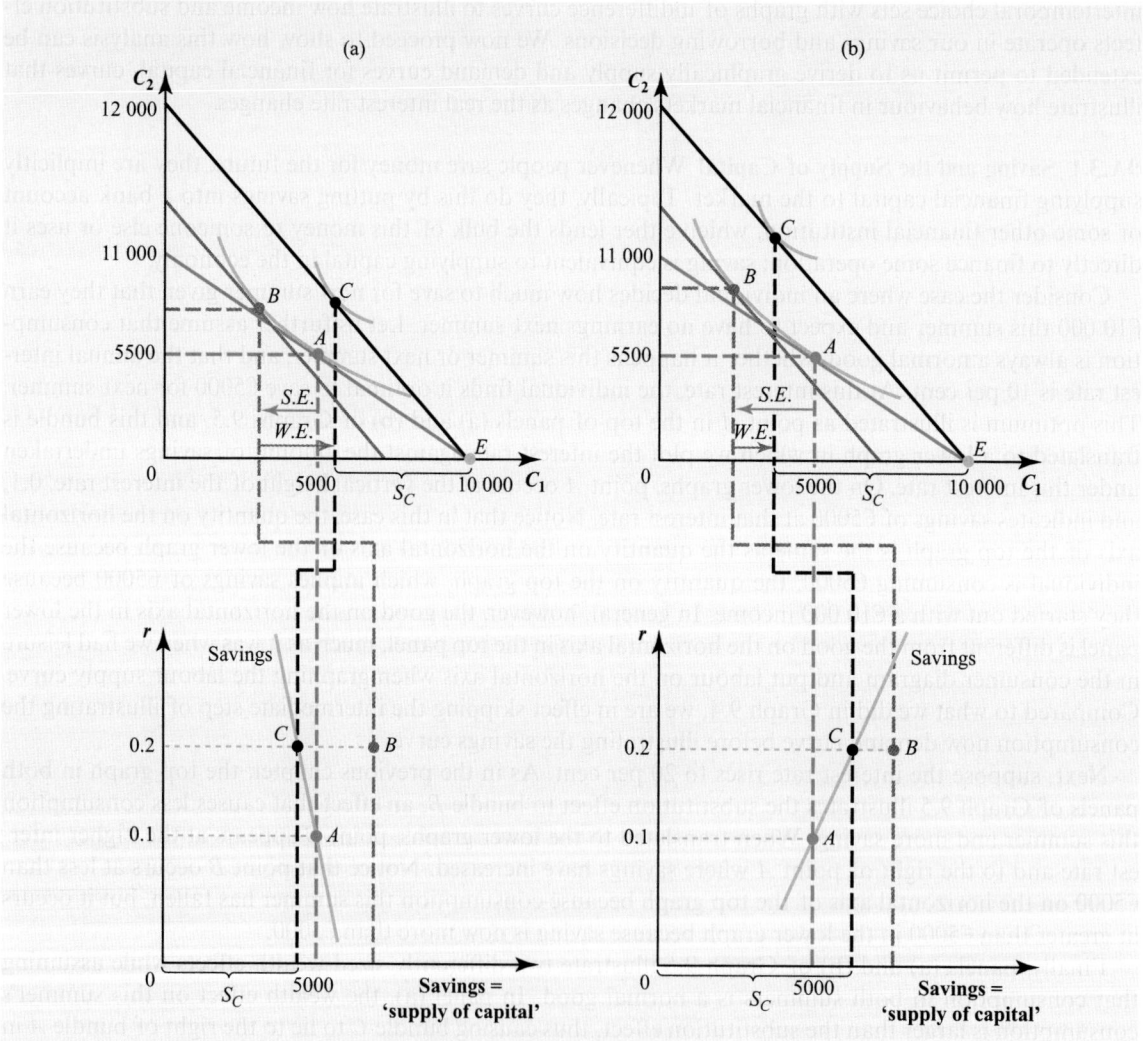

9A.3.2 Borrowing and the Demand for Capital Just as savings is equivalent to supplying capital to the economy, borrowing is equivalent to demanding capital. When you borrow money to purchase a car or to finance a holiday, you are demanding capital that someone else is supplying. We can analyze how borrowers will respond to changes in the interest rate and how demand for capital changes with the interest rate.

Consider an individual who expects to earn €11 000 next summer and needs to decide how much of it to borrow against in order to finance consumption this summer. Assume an initial annual interest rate of 10 per cent and that at this rate, it is optimal for them to borrow €5000 for consumption this summer. This is illustrated as bundle A in both panels of Graph 9.6, and this information is translated to a lower graph relating the interest rate to the amount of borrowing undertaken. Since in this case the amount borrowed is equal to the amount consumed this summer, we can translate horizontal quantities from the top graphs to horizontal quantities on the lower graphs.

Graph 9.6 Demand Curves for Capital From Borrowers

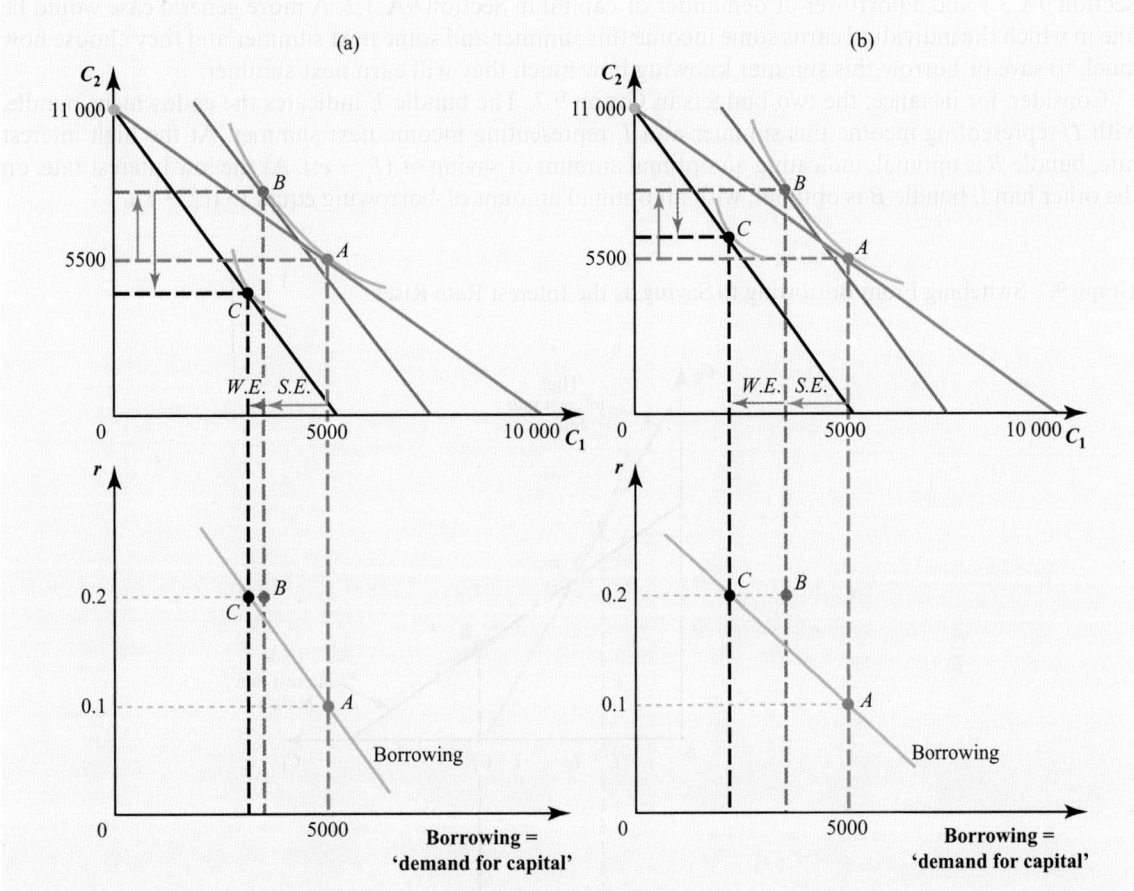

Suppose that the interest rate rises to 20 per cent. As in the previous chapter, we can now draw two possible scenarios given the assumption that consumption is always a normal good. Under the first scenario, in panel (a) of Graph 9.6, consumption next summer, on the vertical axis, declines because the wealth effect outweighs the substitution effect, while under the second scenario, consumption next summer rises because the substitution effect outweighs the wealth effect. In both cases, however, the wealth and substitution effects point in the same direction on the horizontal axis, indicating that the consumer will unambiguously consume less this summer and borrow less as the interest rate rises. Therefore, the relationship between borrowing and the interest rate is negative regardless of which scenario the consumer faces; that is, regardless of how substitutable consumption is across the two time periods. The only impact of having greater substitutability built into the indifference curve that contains bundle A is that it will make the interest rate/borrowing curve in the lower panel shallower.

Exercise 9A.11

What kind of good would consumption this summer have to be in order for the interest rate/borrowing relationship to be positive in Graph 9.6?

9A.3.3 Switching Between Borrowing and Saving In the previous two sections, we have considered the extreme cases when all the individual's income falls either in this summer (Section 9A.3.1) or next summer (Section 9A.3.2). This has allowed us to definitively label them a saver or a supplier of capital in Section 9A.3.1 and a borrower or demander of capital in Section 9A.3.2. A more general case would be one in which the individual earns some income this summer and some next summer and they choose how much to save or borrow this summer knowing how much they will earn next summer.

Consider, for instance, the two budgets in Graph 9.7. The bundle E indicates the endowment bundle, with I_1 representing income this summer and I_2 representing income next summer. At the high interest rate, bundle B is optimal, indicating an optimal amount of saving of $(I_1 - c_1^s)$. At the low interest rate, on the other hand, bundle B is optimal, with an optimal amount of borrowing equal to $(c_1^B - I_1)$.

Graph 9.7 Switching From Borrowing to Saving as the Interest Rate Rises

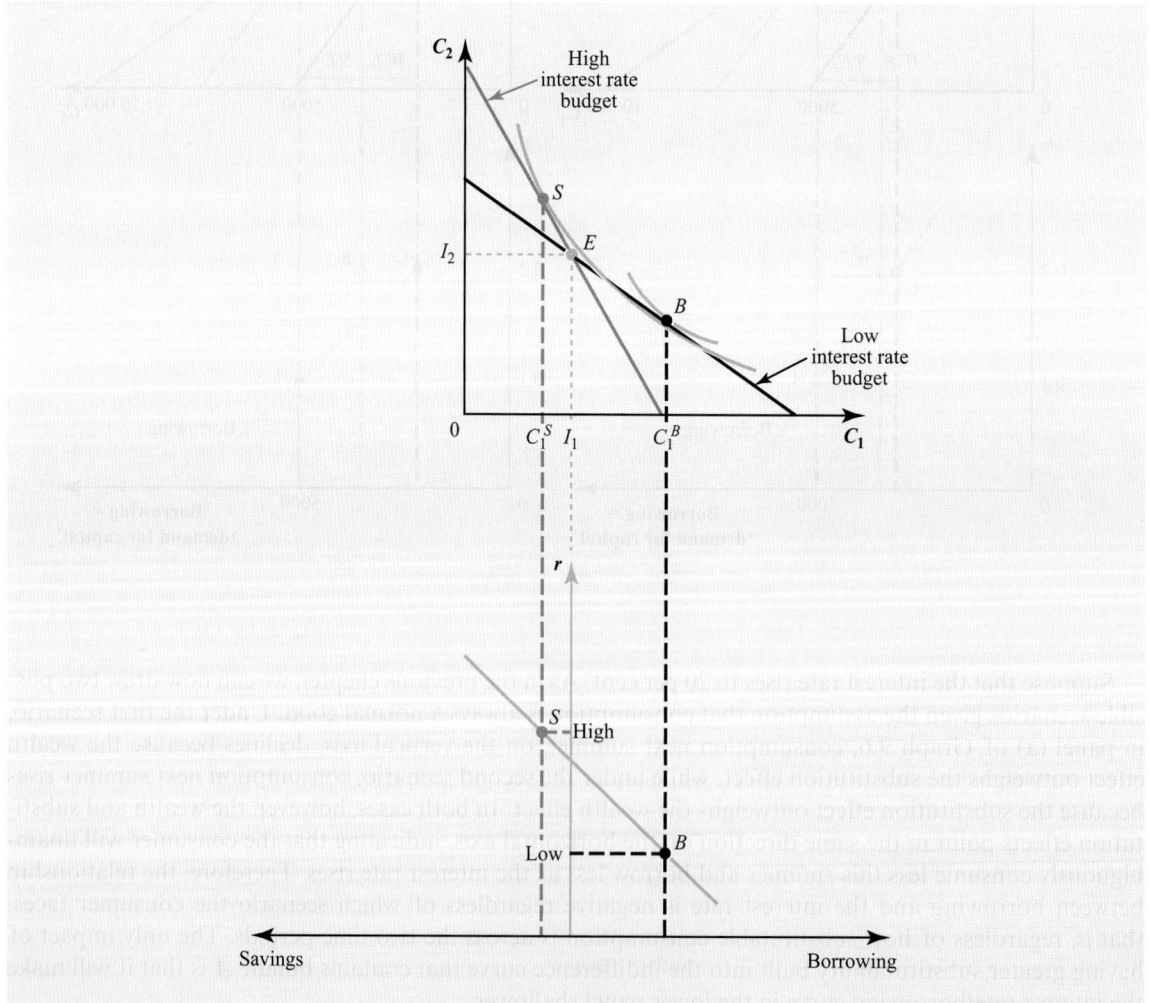

In this case, the consumer will switch between borrowing and saving as the interest rate increases. This is indicated on the lower graph where the interest rate is plotted on the vertical axis, and the vertical axis is placed right underneath the endowment bundle E in the top graph. When the optimal bundle occurs to the right of bundle E in the top graph, the resulting borrowing is plotted in the positive quadrant of the lower graph. When the optimal bundle occurs to the left of bundle E, on the other hand, the resulting savings or negative borrowing is plotted in the negative quadrant of the lower graph.

Exercise 9A.12

Is it possible for someone to begin as a saver at low interest rates and switch to becoming a borrower as the interest rate rises?

Exercise 9A.13

The technique of placing the axis below the endowment point E developed in Graph 9.7 could also be applied to the previous two graphs, Graph 9.5 and Graph 9.6. How would those graphs change?

9B   Demand and Supply Functions

In this section, we will demonstrate that the curves we have graphed are in fact just special cases of more general demand and supply *functions*, cases where all but one of the variables of these functions are held fixed. In that sense, we can think of the curves we derived graphically as two-dimensional slices of multi-dimensional functions.

It should be noted that in these graphs the independent variable like income or price is placed on the vertical axis and the dependent variable like the quantity demanded or supplied on the horizontal. Mathematically, this is the wrong way round. The number of goods bought may depend on exogenous income, but exogenous income is certainly *not* dependent on the number of goods bought. In the case of own-price demand curves, the number of goods demanded depends on the price of those goods, but the price of goods in shops does not depend on how many goods are bought. *When we are graphing demand curves with price on the vertical axis, we are therefore graphing the inverse of the demand functions we will be calculating mathematically.*

This tradition of graphing demand curves as *inverse* demand functions dates back to Alfred Marshall's *Principles of Economics* published in 1890. Marshall's treatment has become the norm even though the discipline became more mathematical in the second half of the 20th century. This requires us to be careful at certain stages when we map properties of demand functions into graphs from our intuitive treatment of the material. In particular, slopes that we calculate for demand *functions* will take on the inverse value in our graphs of demand *curves*, with a slope of 1/2 becoming a slope of 2, a slope of −3 becoming −1/3 and so on.

Exercise 9B.1

Consider the function $f(x) = x/3$. Graph this as you usually would with x on the horizontal axis and $f(x)$ on the vertical. Graph the inverse of the function, with $f(x)$ on the horizontal and x on the vertical.

Exercise 9B.2

Repeat the previous exercise for the function $f(x) = 10$.

9B.1 Demand For Goods and Services

In all the optimization problems that we have computed in the past few chapters, we always restricted ourselves to quite particular examples of tastes and economic circumstances in order to relate particular intuitive concepts to particular mathematical examples. In the process, however, we have set up a much more general approach that gives rise to all of the demand relationships we introduced in Section 9A. We now move towards a more general specification of our optimization problem by letting the economic circumstances of the consumer be represented by I, p_1 and p_2 – income, the price of good 1 and the price of good 2 – without specifying exact values for these.

Suppose, for instance, that tastes can be represented by the Cobb–Douglas utility function $u(x_1, x_2) = x_1^\alpha x_2^{(1-\alpha)}$. The consumer's utility maximization problem can be written as:

$$\max_{x_1,x_2} x_1^\alpha x_2^{(1-\alpha)} \text{ subject to } p_1 x_1 + p_2 x_2 = I, \tag{9.1}$$

with a corresponding Lagrange function:

$$\mathcal{L}(x_1, x_2, \lambda) = x_1^\alpha x_2^{(1-\alpha)} + \lambda(I - p_1 x_1 - p_2 x_2). \tag{9.2}$$

The terms p_1, p_2 and I – the combination of variables that represents an individual's economic circumstances that they take as given and have no control over – are treated as parameters as we solve for the first order conditions, as is the term α which describes tastes that the person also cannot control. The first order conditions, or the first partial derivatives of $\mathcal{L}$ with respect to x_1, x_2 and λ, can be written as:

$$\frac{\partial \mathcal{L}}{\partial x_1} = \alpha x_1^{\alpha-1} x_2^{(1-\alpha)} - \lambda p_1 = 0,$$

$$\frac{\partial \mathcal{L}}{\partial x_2} = (1-\alpha)x_1^\alpha x_2^{-\alpha} - \lambda p_2 = 0, \tag{9.3}$$

$$\frac{\partial \mathcal{L}}{\partial \lambda} = I - p_1 x_1 - p_2 x_2 = 0.$$

Solving these, we get:

$$x_1 = \frac{\alpha I}{p_1} \quad \text{and} \quad x_2 = \frac{(1-\alpha)I}{p_2}. \tag{9.4}$$

These functions are called *demand functions* for tastes that can be represented by the Cobb–Douglas utility function $u(x_1, x_2) = x_1^\alpha x_2^{(1-\alpha)}$. More generally, we can leave the functional form of the utility function unspecified, writing the optimization problem as:

$$\max_{x_1,x_2} u(x_1, x_2) \text{ subject to } p_1 x_1 + p_2 x_2 = I. \tag{9.5}$$

Solving this, we would get general expressions for the optimal values of x_1 and x_2 as simply functions of the consumer's economic circumstances; that is:

$$x_1 = x_1(p_1, p_2, I) \quad \text{and} \quad x_2 = x_2(p_1, p_2, I). \tag{9.6}$$

9B.1.1 Income–Demand Relationships Income–demand curves such as those we derived graphically in Graph 9.1 are inverse slices of the more general functions we derive mathematically. For instance, for the Cobb–Douglas utility function used to derive the demand functions in expression (9.4), we can now hold fixed the price terms and see how the function changes as income changes. Taking the first derivative of each of the two demand functions, we get:

$$\frac{\partial x_1}{\partial I} = \frac{\alpha}{p_1} \quad \text{and} \quad \frac{\partial x_2}{\partial I} = \frac{1-\alpha}{p_2}, \tag{9.7}$$

since both $0 < \alpha < 1$ and the price terms are positive, so we know that for the underlying Cobb–Douglas tastes, the income–demand relationship for each of the two goods is positive. Furthermore, holding prices fixed, this relationship is constant, implying income–demand curves that are straight lines with positive slope and zero intercept. The second partial derivative of each income–demand function with respect to income is zero, implying no change in the slope.

To map these into the income–demand *curves* from part A of the chapter, we begin by solving the demand functions in expression (9.4) for I to get:

$$I_1 = \frac{p_1 x_1}{\alpha} \quad \text{and} \quad I_2 = \frac{p_2 x_2}{(1-\alpha)} \tag{9.8}$$

and note that the partial derivatives with respect to x_1 and x_2 are:

$$\frac{\partial I_1}{\partial x_1} = \frac{p_1}{\alpha} \quad \text{and} \quad \frac{\partial I_2}{\partial x_2} = \frac{p_2}{(1-\alpha)}. \tag{9.9}$$

These slopes of our income–demand *curves* are the inverse of the slopes of the demand functions in expression (9.7).

For instance, suppose that prices are equal to $p_1 = 1$ and $p_2 = 1$, and suppose that $\alpha = 0.75$. The slope of the income–demand curve for x_1 is 4/3 while the slope of the income–demand curve for x_2 is 4. When $p_1 = 1/2$ and $p_2 = 1/2$, on the other hand, the slopes of the two income–demand curves are 2/3 and 2, and when $p_1 = 1/4$ and $p_2 = 1/4$, the slopes become 1/3 and 1. Thus, for each set of prices, we get a different slice of the inverse demand function that becomes an income–demand curve for that particular set of prices. Panels (a) and (b) of Graph 9.8 graph these different income–demand curves for the two goods.

The fact that the income–demand curves for Cobb–Douglas tastes have positive slopes should not be surprising. We know from the previous chapters that such tastes represent tastes for normal goods, and normal goods are defined as goods that consumers consume more of as income rises. Beyond that, the fact that the income–demand curves in Graph 9.8 depend only on the price of one good is a special case that arises from the Cobb–Douglas specification of tastes. Other types of tastes will have the property indicated in the functions in expression (9.6) that demand for each good depends on the prices of both goods.

Exercise 9B.3*

Another special case of tastes that we have emphasized throughout is the case of quasilinear tastes. Consider, for instance, the utility function $u(x_1, x_2) = 100(\ln x_1) + x_2$. Calculate the demand function for x_1 and derive some sample income-demand curves for different prices.

Graph 9.8 Income–Demand Curves when $u(x_1,x_2) = x_1^{0.75}x_2^{0.25}$

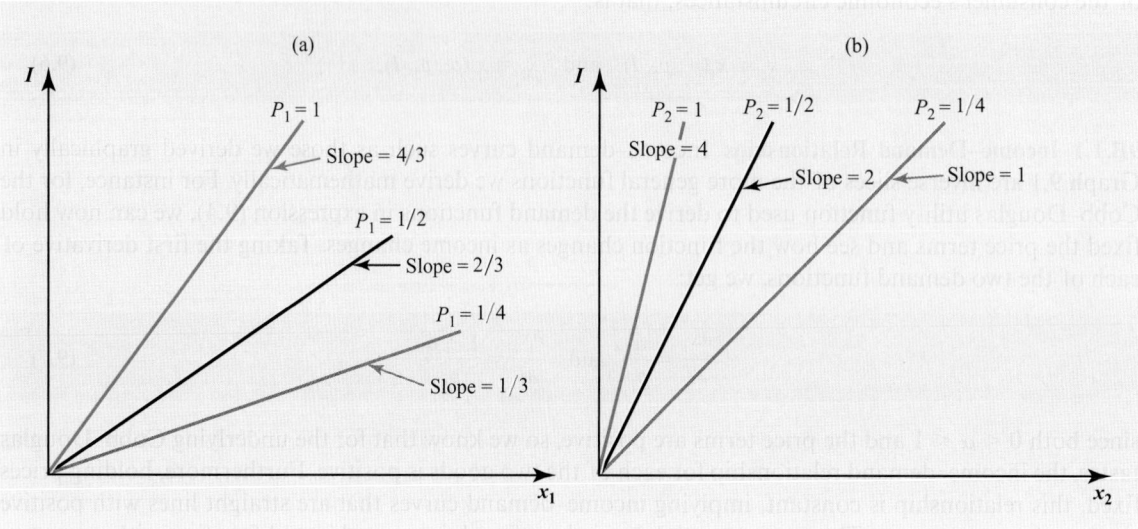

9B.1.2 Own-Price Demand Relationships The own-price demand curves of the kind derived in Graph 9.2 are similarly inverse slices of the more general demand functions in expression (9.6). This time, however, we are interested in the relationship between the quantity demanded and that good's price. The slices of the inverse demand functions that we graph when we graph own-price demand curves take the form:

$$p_1 = p_1(x_1,p_2,I) \quad \text{and} \quad p_2 = p_2(x_2,p_1,I), \tag{9.10}$$

which involves solving the demand functions for prices. In the case of the Cobb–Douglas demand functions from expression (9.4), these are:

$$p_1 = \frac{\alpha I}{x_1} \quad \text{and} \quad p_2 = \frac{(1 - \alpha)}{x_2}. \tag{9.11}$$

The demand *curves* are slices of these inverse demand functions that hold income and the price of the other good fixed. In the special case of Cobb–Douglas tastes, however, each good's demand is independent of the other good's price, so we only have to hold income fixed as we graph the demand curves. This is done in panel (a) of Graph 9.9 for x_1 and in panel (b) for x_2 for three different income levels. Note that for relatively standard tastes such as those represented by Cobb–Douglas utility functions, these demand curves tend to have relatively non-linear shapes. This gives us some sense of what is lost when we derive such demand curves graphically by estimating them from just two points as we did in Graph 9.2. Note also that, in each of the panels of Graph 9.9, the demand curve shifts outwards as income increases. Holding p_1 fixed, the quantity demanded increases as income rises, implying again that the tastes are such that each good is a normal good as we know is the case for Cobb–Douglas tastes. Were one of the underlying goods an inferior good, the demand curve for that good would shift inwards as income goes up. When tastes are quasilinear in one of the goods, the demand curve for that good would be unchanged as income rises, since such a good would be borderline normal/inferior.

The derivatives of the demand functions from expression (9.4) with respect to own prices are:

$$\frac{\partial x_1}{\partial p_1} = -\frac{\alpha I}{p_1^2} \quad \text{and} \quad \frac{\partial x_2}{\partial p_2} = -\frac{(1 - \alpha)I}{p_2^2}, \tag{9.12}$$

and the derivatives of the *inverse* demand functions in expression (9.11) with respect to quantities are:

$$\frac{\partial p_1}{\partial x_1} = -\frac{\alpha I}{x_1^2} \quad \text{and} \quad \frac{\partial p_2}{\partial x_2} = -\frac{(1-\alpha)I}{x_2^2}. \tag{9.13}$$

Graph 9.9 Own-Price Demand Curves when $u(x_1,x_2) = x_1^{0.75}x_2^{0.25}$

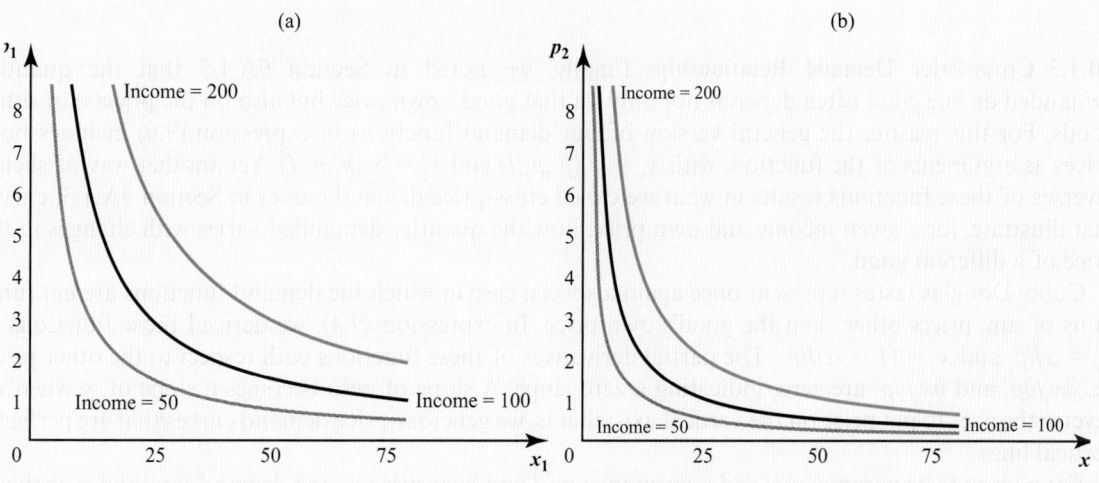

(a)

(b)

Suppose, for instance, that $\alpha = 0.75$ as it is in the graphs, that $I = 100$, and that $p_1 = p_2 = 1$. The first equation in expression (9.12) tells us that when $p_1 = 1$, the slope of the demand function as p_1 changes is $-\alpha I/p_1^2 = -75$. The demand function $x_1 = \alpha I/p_1$ also tells us that $x_1 = 75$ when $p_1 = 1$. Substituting $x_1 = 75$ into the first equation in (9.13) gives the slope of the demand *curve* as $-\alpha I/x_1^2 = -1/75$, which is the inverse of what we got from taking the derivative of the demand *function*. More generally, the same steps allow us to write:

$$\frac{\partial p_1}{\partial x_1} = -\frac{\alpha I}{x_1^2} = -\frac{\alpha I}{(\alpha I/p_1)^2} = -\frac{p_1^2}{\alpha I} = \left(\frac{\partial x_1}{\partial p_1}\right)^{-1}, \tag{9.14}$$

where we use the fact that $x_1 = \alpha I/p_1$ from equation (9.4) in the middle of the expression. Our demand *curves* that treat quantities as if they were the independent variable have slopes at every point that are inverses of the slopes of the corresponding slices of the demand *functions* that treat price as the independent variable.

Exercise 9B.4

Can you derive the same result for x_2?

Exercise 9B.5

As in exercise 9B.3, consider again tastes that can be represented by the utility function $u(x_1,x_2) = 100(\ln x_1) + x_2$. Using the demand function for x_1 that you derived in the previous exercise, plot the own-price demand curve when income is 100 and when $p_2 = 1$. Plot the demand curve again when income rises to 200. Keep in mind that you are actually plotting inverse functions as you are doing this.

Exercise 9B.6

Knowing that own-price demand curves are inverse slices of own-price demand functions, how would the lower panels of Graph 9.2 look if you graphed slices of the actual functions rather than the inverses; that is, when you put price on the horizontal and the quantities of goods on the vertical axis?

9B.1.3 Cross-Price Demand Relationships Finally, we noted in Section 9A.1.3 that the quantity demanded of one good often depends not only on that good's own price but also on the price(s) of other goods. For this reason, the general version of our demand functions in expression (9.6) includes both prices as arguments of the function, with $x_1 = x_1(p_1, p_2, I)$ and $x_2 = x_2(p_1, p_2, I)$. Yet another way of slicing inverses of these functions results in what we called cross-price demand curves in Section 9A.1.3, curves that illustrate, for a given income and own price, how the quantity demanded varies with changes in the price of a different good.

Cobb–Douglas tastes represent once again a special case in which the demand functions are *not* functions of any prices other than the good's own price. In expression (9.4), we derived those functions as $x_1 = \alpha I/p_1$ and $x_2 = (1 - \alpha)I/p_2$. The partial derivatives of these functions with respect to the other price, i.e. $\partial x_1/\partial p_2$ and $\partial x_2/\partial p_1$, are zero, indicating a zero slope. A slope of zero becomes a slope of ∞ when we reverse the axes to put price on the vertical axis; that is, we get cross-price demand curves that are perfectly vertical lines.

For a given taste parameter α and a given income I and own-price p_1, the demand for good x_1 is therefore constant. Take, for example, the case when $\alpha = 0.75$, $I = 100$ and $p_1 = 1$. Substituting these values into the demand function for x_1, we get $x_1 = 75$. Similarly, if the price of good x_1 is 3, we get $x_1 = 25$, and if $p_1 = 5$, $x_1 = 15$. The resulting cross-price demand curves are vertical lines at these respective quantities, as illustrated in panel (a) of Graph 9.10. Similarly, you could derive vertical cross-price demand curves for different levels of income.

Exercise 9B.7

What would the slices of the demand function rather than the inverse slices in panel (a) of Graph 9.10 look like?

The reason for this shape of cross-price demand curves in the Cobb–Douglas case lies in the fact that income and substitution effects are exactly offsetting. In Graph 9.3 of Section 9A.1.3, we illustrated a cross-price demand curve for quasilinear tastes, tastes in which the income effect was zero and thus only the substitution effect operated. This substitution effect implied that whenever p_2 decreases, a consumer would tend to consume more of x_2 and less of x_1, which, in the absence of an income effect, gives rise to the positive slope of the cross-price demand curve. For Cobb–Douglas tastes, however, x_1 is a normal good, implying a positive income effect on x_1 consumption from a decrease in the price of x_2. For a normal good, bundle C in Graph 9.3 would lie to the right of bundle B and possibly to the right of bundle A, and our analysis of Cobb–Douglas demand functions tells us that it would lie exactly above A when tastes can be represented by Cobb–Douglas utility functions.

Recall from our discussion of tastes in Chapter 5, however, that Cobb–Douglas tastes are a special case of a more general class of constant elasticity of substitution (CES) tastes, a case in which the elasticity of substitution is equal to 1. The elasticity of substitution determines the size of the substitution effect, which implies that as that elasticity decreases, the substitution effect will fall and will thus be more than offset by the income effect. Similarly, it should be the case that when the elasticity of substitution is greater than 1, the size of the substitution effect increases and will thus no longer be offset by the income effect.

Graph 9.10 Cross-Price Demand Curves for CES Utility With Different Elasticities of Substitution

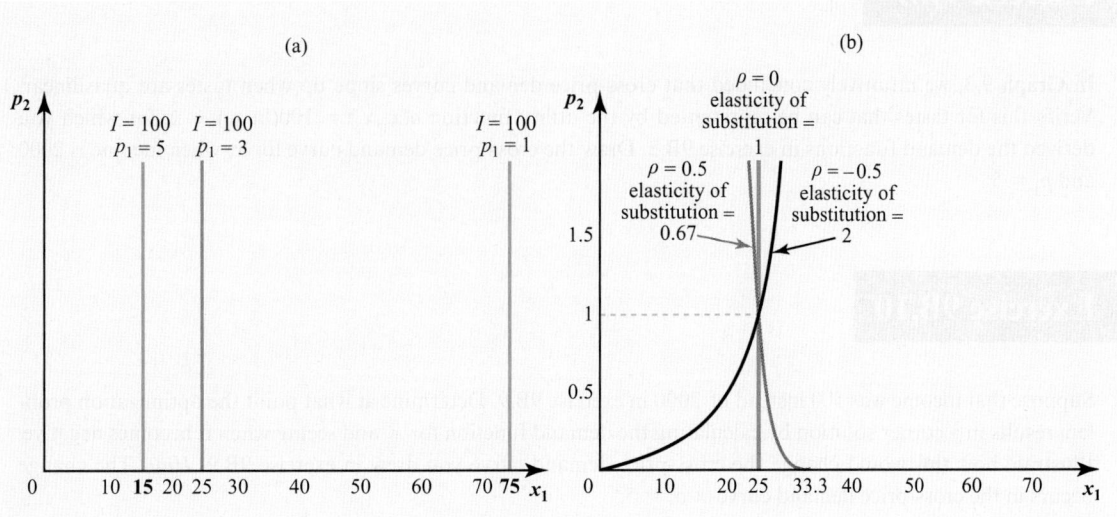

We can check this intuition by calculating the demand functions for the more general class of CES utility functions $u(x_1, x_2) = (\alpha x_1^{-\rho} + (1-\alpha)x_2^{-\rho})^{-1/\rho}$, where the elasticity of substitution is equal to $1/(1+\rho)$. Solving the maximization problem in expression (9.5) using this utility function we get:

$$x_1 = \frac{\alpha^{1/(1+\rho)}I}{(\alpha^{1/(1+\rho)}p_1) + ((1-\alpha)p_1p_2^\rho)^{1/(1+\rho)}} \quad \text{and}$$

$$x_2 = \frac{(1-\alpha)^{1/(1+\rho)}I}{((1-\alpha)^{1/(1+\rho)}p_2) + (\alpha p_1^\rho p_2)^{1/(1+\rho)}}. \tag{9.15}$$

Exercise 9B.8**

Verify that these are in fact the right demand functions for tastes represented by the CES utility function.

Notice that when $\rho = 0$, these functions collapse down to those in expression (9.4), because when $\rho = 0$, CES utility functions are Cobb–Douglas. We can graph different inverse cross-price demand slices of this function by fixing all parameters and variables other than p_2. Suppose, for instance, we set $\alpha = 0.75$, $p_1 = 3$ and $I = 100$. Panel (b) of Graph 9.10 graphs the resulting function for x_1 as it varies with p_2 for three different values of $\rho(0.5, 0 \text{ and } -0.5)$ corresponding to the elasticities of substitution of 0.67, 1 and 2. The middle curve represents the Cobb–Douglas tastes graphed in panel (a) of Graph 9.10. Notice that an elasticity of substitution below that of Cobb–Douglas tastes leads to a downward-sloping cross-price demand curve, while an elasticity greater than that of Cobb–Douglas tastes leads to an upward slope. You could confirm this by showing that $\partial x_1/\partial p_2 < 0$ when $\rho > 0$, and $\partial x_1/\partial p_2 > 0$ when $\rho < 0$, recalling again how this translates to inverse slopes. This confirms our intuition that the greater the elasticity of substitution, the larger will be the substitution effect that suggests a positive cross-price relationship. Cobb–Douglas tastes with an elasticity of substitution of 1 represent the boundary case where this substitution effect is just large enough to exactly offset the income effect.

Exercise 9B.9

In Graph 9.3, we intuitively concluded that cross-price demand curves slope up when tastes are quasilinear. Verify this for tastes that can be represented by the utility function $u(x_1,x_2) = 100(\ln x_1) + x_2$ for which you derived the demand functions in exercise 9B.3. Draw the cross-price demand curve for x_1 when income is 2000 and $p_1 = 5$.

Exercise 9B.10

Suppose that income was 500 instead of 2000 in exercise 9B.9. Determine at what point the optimization problem results in a corner solution by calculating the demand function for x_2 and seeing when it becomes negative. Illustrate how this would change the cross-price demand curve you drew in exercise 9B.9. *Hint:* The change occurs in the cross-price demand curve at $p_2 = 5$.

9B.2 Labour Supply

As in the case of demand relationships in goods markets, we have already developed the basic technique of deriving labour supply curves of the kind drawn in Graph 9.4. The relevant budget constraint now arises from the fact that the amount spent on consumption c has to be equal to the value of the labour sold by the individual at the market wage w. Given that the individual starts with some particular leisure endowment L, the hours spent working is equivalent to the hours *not* spent in leisure, or $(L - \ell)$. Thus, along the budget constraint, $c = w(L - \ell)$, or written differently:

$$wL = c + w\ell. \tag{9.16}$$

When written in this form, the budget constraint most closely resembles the form we are used to seeing in the goods market, with wL being equal to the wealth endowment rather than exogenous income, the price of the c good equal to 1, and the price or opportunity cost of leisure equal to w. The general form of the utility maximization problem that gives rise to labour supply can be written as:

$$\max_{c,\ell} u(c,\ell) \quad \text{subject to } wL = c + w\ell. \tag{9.17}$$

The solutions to this maximization problem are of the form:

$$\ell = \ell(w,L) \quad \text{and} \quad c = c(w,L), \tag{9.18}$$

with both the optimal amount of leisure and the optimal amount of consumption a function of the wage rate and the leisure endowment. Implicitly, these functions are also a function of the price of consumption, but since that is equal to 1 given that we defined consumption as a euro's worth of consumption, it does not formally enter into the previous equations. Were we to use a price for consumption that can vary, this price would become an argument in the functions in expression (9.18) and would appear in front of the c term in expression (9.17).

Once we have derived the function that tells us for any wage w and leisure endowment L the amount of leisure an individual will choose, we are one small step from having derived the labour supply functions.

This is because the quantity of labour supplied is equal to the quantity of the leisure endowment that is not consumed as leisure, or $(L - \ell)$. Using the equation for optimal leisure consumption in expression (9.18), we can write the labour supply function as:

$$l(w,L) = L - \ell(w,L). \tag{9.19}$$

When we hold the leisure endowment fixed, this labour supply function becomes a slice of the more general function, a slice in which labour supply is a function of only the wage rate and can thus be represented in a two-dimensional graph as a labour supply curve when we take its inverse. Notice how the mathematics behind this exactly mirrors the graphical derivation in Graph 9.4. First, holding L fixed at 60, we graphically maximized utility over the budget constraint between consumption and leisure in order to translate our findings into points on labour supply curves; we then subtracted the optimal leisure level from the fixed leisure endowment to plot the labour supply on the lower graphs.

Exercise 9B.11

What function is graphed in the middle portion of each panel of Graph 9.4? What function is graphed in the bottom portion of each panel of Graph 9.4?

As in the section on consumer demand, we can see how specific tastes now translate into labour supply functions. First, consider tastes that are quasilinear in leisure and can be represented by the utility function $u(c,\ell) = c + \alpha \ln \ell$. Solving the maximization problem defined in expression (9.17) for these tastes, we get:

$$\ell = \frac{\alpha}{w} \quad \text{and} \quad c = wL - \alpha, \tag{9.20}$$

with the resulting labour supply function equal to:

$$l(w,L) = L - \frac{\alpha}{w}. \tag{9.21}$$

Exercise 9B.12

Verify these results.

Suppose, for instance, that we hold L fixed at 60 hours per week, as we did in Section 9A.2, and suppose tastes are such that $\alpha = 400$. The labour supply function becomes $l(w) = 60 - (400/w)$, the inverse of which is graphed as a labour supply curve in panel (a) of Graph 9.11 and is labelled $L = 60$, indicating we have assumed a leisure endowment of 60. Similarly, a second labour supply curve corresponding to a leisure endowment of 40 hours per week is graphed for comparison. In each case, the labour supply curve asymptotically approaches the leisure endowment as the wage approaches infinity.

The fact that labour supply is upward sloping for tastes that are quasilinear in leisure should not surprise us given the intuition regarding substitution and wealth effects we built in Section 9A.2. We know that the substitution effect will always suggest that an individual will work more as the wage rises because leisure has become relatively more expensive. When tastes are quasilinear in leisure, we also know that there is no counteracting wealth effect. Thus, the substitution effect is the only effect on the leisure axis, causing consumption of leisure to decline, and work hours to increase, as wages go up.

Graph 9.11 Labour Supply With Tastes That Are (a) Quasilinear, (b) Cobb–Douglas and (c) CES

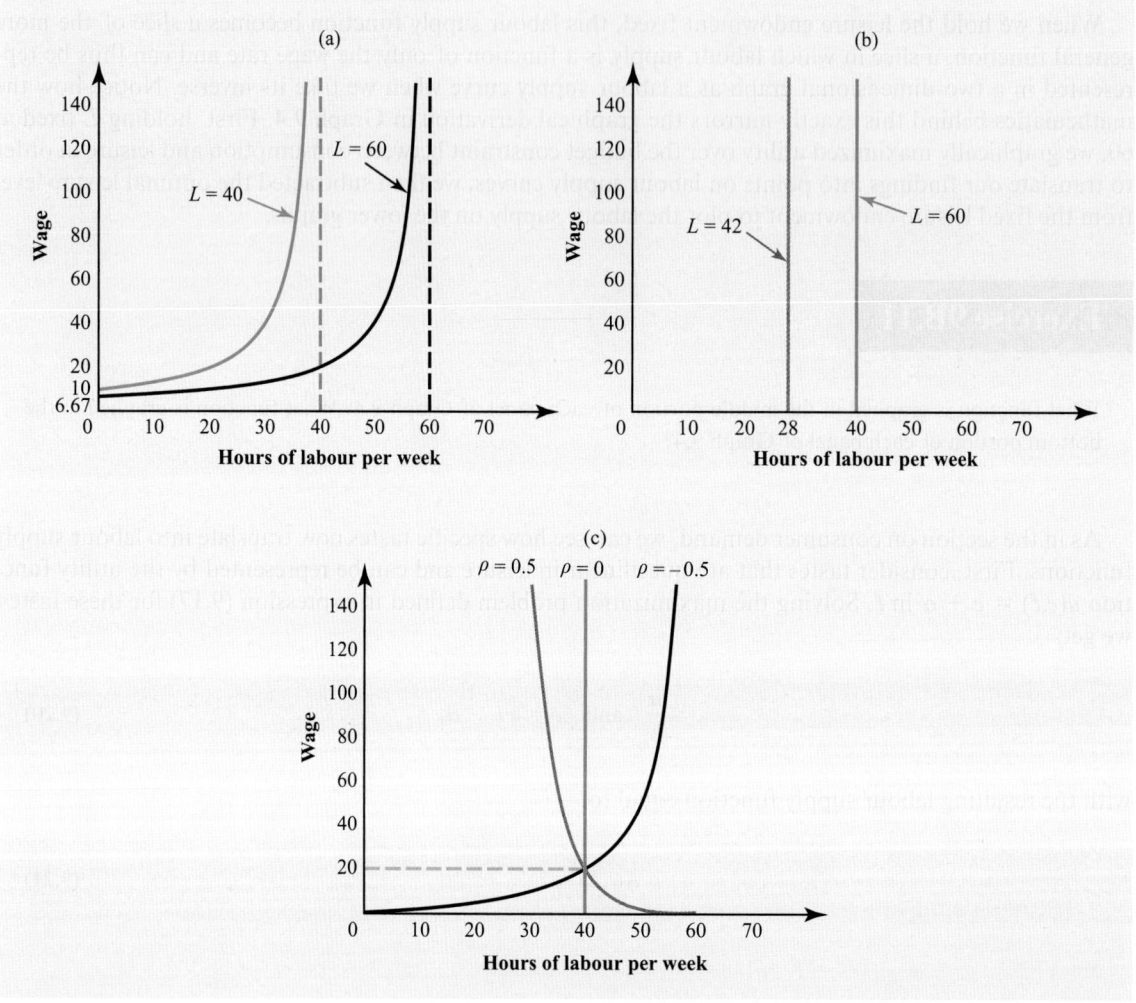

Next, consider Cobb–Douglas tastes that can be represented by the utility function $u(c,\ell) = c^{\alpha}\ell^{(1-\alpha)}$ Solving the maximization problem in expression (9.17) for this utility function, we get:

$$\ell = (1-\alpha)L \quad \text{and} \quad c = \alpha w L, \tag{9.22}$$

with the resulting labour supply function equal to:

$$l(w,L) = L - (1-\alpha)L = \alpha L. \tag{9.23}$$

In this special Cobb–Douglas case, the labour supply function does *not* depend on the wage, which implies that the labour supply curves are vertical lines because $\partial l/\partial w = 0$, with substitution and wealth effects exactly offsetting one another. For instance, suppose that $\alpha = 2/3$ and the leisure endowment L is equal to 60 hours per week. Weekly labour supply is 40 hours regardless of the wage rate. Similarly, if the leisure endowment were 42 hours instead of 60, the number of hours of labour supplied per week would be 28 regardless of the wage. These different labour supply curves are depicted in panel (b) of Graph 9.11.

Finally, consider the more general CES utility specification $u(c,l) = (\alpha c^{-\rho} + (1 - \alpha)\ell^{-\rho})^{-1/\rho}$. Solving the maximization problem in expression (9.17) with this utility function, and doing some algebra, we get:

$$\ell = \frac{L(1 - \alpha)^{1/(\rho+1)}}{(\alpha w^{-\rho})^{1/(\rho+1)} + (1 - \alpha)^{1/(\rho+1)}} \tag{9.24}$$

with corresponding labour supply function:

$$l(w,L) = L - \frac{L(1 - \alpha)^{1/(\rho+1)}}{(\alpha w^{-\rho})^{1/(\rho+1)} + (1 - \alpha)^{1/(\rho+1)}}. \tag{9.25}$$

Exercise 9B.13**

Verify this leisure demand and labour supply function for the CES function that is given.

From our work in Chapter 5, we know that the elasticity of substitution, and thus the size of the substitution effect, is decreasing in the parameter ρ. More specifically, as ρ approaches -1, indifference curves approach those of perfect substitutes; when $\rho = 0$, the tastes are Cobb–Douglas; and as ρ approaches positive infinity, indifference curves approach those of perfect complements. From equation (9.23), we also know that substitution and wealth effects are exactly offsetting on the leisure dimension when tastes are Cobb–Douglas, that is, when $\rho = 0$. This suggests that when $\rho > 0$, the wealth effect will outweigh the substitution effect and will thus result in a negatively sloped labour supply curve, while the opposite holds when $\rho < 0$.

Suppose, for instance, that the weekly leisure endowment L is again set to 60. Panel (c) of Graph 9.11 plots the labour supply curves for different levels of ρ, in each case setting α equal to the level required in order to make the optimal labour supply at a wage of €20 equal to 40 hours per week. This is done so that the resulting labour supply curves have a common labour supply at $w = 20$ – the resulting values of α are 0.24025 when $\rho = -0.5$, 2/3 when $\rho = 0$, and 0.9267 when $\rho = 0.5$. Our intuition regarding the relative sizes of substitution and wealth effects is confirmed, with tastes that exhibit a high level of substitutability between leisure and consumption ($\rho < 0$) generating substitution effects that outweigh wealth effects, and tastes that exhibit low substitutability between leisure and consumption generating substitution effects that are outweighed by wealth effects. You can formally check that this holds by taking the partial derivative of expression (9.25) and showing that $\partial l/\partial w < 0$ when $\rho > 0$ and that $\partial l/\partial w > 0$ when $\rho < 0$.

9B.3 Demand for and Supply of Financial Capital

Finally, we can show again that the supply and demand curves for financial capital, or the demand curves for savings and borrowing, we derived in Section 9A.3 are inverse slices of more general functions that arise from general intertemporal optimization problems. In Chapters 3 and 8, we already demonstrated that two-period versions of intertemporal budget constraints can be written as:

$$(1 + r)c_1 + c_2 = (1 + r)e_1 + e_2, \tag{9.26}$$

where e_1 and e_2 represent period 1 and 2 endowments or income, r represents the relevant interest rate over the intervening period, and c_1 and c_2 represent consumption in the two periods. A consumer thus faces the optimization problem:

$$\max_{c_1,c_2} u(c_1,c_2) \text{ subject to } (1 + r)c_1 + c_2 = (1 + r)e_1 + e_2. \tag{9.27}$$

Solving this, we get general demand functions for c_1 and c_2 of the form:

$$c_1 = c_1(r,e_1,e_2) \quad \text{and} \quad c_2 = c_2(r,e_1,e_2). \tag{9.28}$$

These functions tell us, for any set of economic circumstances faced by the consumer, how much they will consume this period and next period. Subtracting $c_1(r,e_1,e_2)$ from e_1, furthermore, gives us the difference in period 1 consumption and period 1 income, or the amount of savings the consumer will choose to undertake under different economic circumstances. Thus, we can calculate the savings supply function:

$$s(r,e_1,e_2) = e_1 - c_1(r,e_1,e_2). \tag{9.29}$$

When $s(r,e_1,e_2) > 0$, the consumer chooses to save this period or supply financial capital, whereas when $s(r,e_1,e_2) < 0$, they choose to borrow or demand financial capital. A consumer will, of course, switch between saving and borrowing depending on the economic circumstances they face. As we already showed intuitively in Section 9A.3, the consumer will save if $e_1 > 0$ and $e_2 = 0$ (Section 9A.3.1); they will borrow if $e_1 = 0$ and $e_2 > 0$ (Section 9A.3.2); and they may switch between borrowing and saving as the interest rate changes when $e_1 > 0$ and $e_2 > 0$ (Section 9A.3.3).

Solving the optimization problem in expression (9.27) for Cobb–Douglas tastes represented by the utility function $u(c_1,c_2) = c_1^\alpha c_2^{(1-\alpha)}$, for instance, we get:

$$c_1(r,e_1,e_2) = \alpha\left(\frac{(1 + r)e_1 + e_2}{(1 + r)}\right) \text{ and}$$
$$c_2(r,e_1,e_2) = (1 - \alpha)((1 + r)e_1 + e_2). \tag{9.30}$$

with a resulting savings function of:

$$s(r,e_1,e_2) = e_1 - \alpha\left(\frac{(1 + r)e_1 + e_2}{(1 + r)}\right). \tag{9.31}$$

Exercise 9B.14

Verify that equations 9.29. 9.20 and 9.31 are correct.

9B.3.1 Saving and the Supply of Capital Suppose that we return to the example of an individual earning €10 000 this summer and expecting to earn nothing next summer. Suppose further that they place equal value on consumption in both summers, with $\alpha = 0.5$. Our savings function (9.31) becomes:

$$s(r) = 5000. \tag{9.32}$$

Savings are independent of the interest rate in the Cobb–Douglas case, leading to a vertical relationship between savings and the interest rate when the interest rate appears on the vertical axis and savings appears on the horizontal. We know from our intuitive analysis in Section 9A.3.1 that the substitution effect suggests savings will increase with the interest rate, and that the wealth effect suggests the opposite when consumption in period 1 is a normal good as it is under Cobb–Douglas tastes. Thus, the substitution and wealth effects are exactly offsetting for these tastes.

Once again, the key to whether the relationship between savings and the interest rate is positive or negative lies in the relative weights of substitution and wealth effects. Thus, as consumption in periods 1 and 2 becomes more substitutable, leading to a greater substitution effect, the relationship becomes positive, whereas when consumption across the periods becomes more complementary, leading to a smaller substitution effect, the relationship becomes negative.

Exercise 9B.15**

Consider the more general CES utility function $u(c_1,c_2) = (0.5c_1^{-\rho} + 0.5c_2^{-\rho})^{-1/\rho}$ and solve for the savings supply function when an individual earns €10 000 this period and nothing in the future. Verify that they obtain the vertical relationship between savings and the interest rate when $\rho = 0$, and determine how this slope changes when $\rho > 0$, implying relatively low elasticity of substitution, and when $\rho < 0$ implying relatively high elasticity of substitution.

9B.3.2 Borrowing and the Demand for Capital Similarly, we can consider the case in which all income is earned next summer, with any consumption this summer financed through borrowing against next summer's earnings. Suppose that the individual's tastes are Cobb–Douglas with $\alpha = 0.5$, and suppose further that earnings next summer will be €11 000. We can use expression (9.31) to determine savings this summer by substituting in $e_1 = 0$ and $e_2 = 11\,000$ to get:

$$s(r) = -\frac{5500}{(1 + r)}. \tag{9.33}$$

Since income this summer is zero, the individual will naturally have to borrow in order to consume this summer, and the amount that they will borrow, unlike the amount saved in the previous example, will depend on the interest rate. In particular, note that $\partial s/\partial r > 0$, which means that negative savings become smaller as the interest rate rises. Alternatively, we could phrase behaviour in terms of borrowing instead of negative saving, in which case we would consider the negative of the savings function in expression (9.33). The partial derivative of that negative savings function with respect to the interest rate would be negative, implying that borrowing declines as the interest rate rises. These conclusions are once again consistent with our intuition from Section 9A.3.2 in which we demonstrated that the impact of both the substitution and the wealth effect causes the borrower to lower their borrowing as the interest rate rises.

Exercise 9B.16**

Using the CES utility function from exercise 9B.15, verify that the negative relationship between borrowing and the interest rate arises regardless of the value that ρ takes whenever $e_1 = 0$ and $e_2 > 0$.

9B.3.3 Switching Between Borrowing and Saving We concluded Section 9A.3 with an example in which a consumer earns income in both periods and chooses to borrow or save depending on the interest rate. This type of savings function is also implicitly possible in our mathematical setup whenever e_1 and e_2 are both positive. In the Cobb–Douglas case, for instance, suppose that $e_1 = 4600$ and $e_2 = 5400$, and suppose again that $\alpha = 0.5$. Substituting these values into the savings function (9.31), we get:

$$s(r) = 2300 - \frac{2700}{(1 + r)}, \tag{9.34}$$

which is -400 at an interest rate of 0 per cent but has positive slope ($\partial s/\partial r = 2700/(1 + r)^2$) and becomes positive at an interest rate of 17.39 per cent.

Exercise 9B.17

Graph this function in a graph similar to Graph 9.7, which is the graph of an inverse borrowing rather than saving function.

End-of-Chapter Exercises

9.1† The following are intended to explore what kinds of income–demand relationships are logically possible.

A. For each of the following, indicate whether the relationship is possible or not and explain your answer:

a. A good is a necessity and has a positive income–demand relationship.
b. A good is a necessity and has a negative income–demand relationship.
c. A good is a luxury and has a negative income–demand relationship.
d. A good is quasilinear and has a negative income–demand relationship.
e. Tastes are homothetic and one of the goods has a negative income–demand relationship.

B. Derive the income–demand relationships for each good for the following tastes:

a. $u(x_1,x_2,x_3) = x_1^\alpha x_2^\beta x_3^{(1-\alpha-\beta)}$ where α and β lie between zero and 1 and sum to less than 1.
b. $u(x_1,x_2) = \alpha \ln x_1 + x_2$. *Note*: To specify fully the income–demand relationship in this case, you need to watch out for corner solutions. Graph the income–demand curves for x_1 and x_2, carefully labelling slopes and intercepts.

9.2 The following are intended to explore what kinds of own-price demand relationships are logically possible in a two-good model with exogenous income unless otherwise specified.

A. For each of the following, indicate whether the relationship is possible or not and explain your answer:

a. Tastes are homothetic and the own-price demand relationship is positive.
b. A good is inferior and its own-price relationship is negative.
c. In a model with endogenous income, a good is normal and its own-price demand relationship is negative.
d. In a model with endogenous income, a good is normal and its own-price demand relationship is positive.

B. Suppose that tastes can be represented by the Cobb–Douglas utility function $u(x_1,x_2) = x_1^\alpha x_2^{(1-\alpha)}$.

a. Derive the demand functions when income is exogenous and illustrate that own-price demand curves slope down.
b. Now suppose that all income is derived from an endowment (e_1,e_2). If $e_2 = 0$, what is the shape of the own-price demand curve for x_1?
c. Continuing with part (b), what is the shape of the own-price demand curve for x_1 when $e_2 > 0$?

d. Suppose tastes were instead represented by the more general CES utility function. Without doing any additional maths, can you guess what would have to be true about ρ in order for the own-price demand for x_1 to slope up when $e_1 > 0$ and $e_2 = 0$?

9.3† The following are intended to explore what kinds of cross-price demand relationships are logically possible in a two-good model with exogenous income.

A. For each of the following, indicate whether the relationship is possible or not and explain your answer:

   a. A good is normal and its cross-price demand relationship is positive.
   b. A good is normal and its cross-price relationship is negative.
   c. A good is inferior and its cross-price relationship is negative.
   d. Tastes are homothetic and one of the good's cross-price relationship is negative.
   e. Tastes are homothetic and one of the good's cross-price relationship is positive.

B. Now consider specific tastes represented by particular utility functions.

   a. Suppose tastes are represented by the function $u(x_1,x_2) = \alpha \ln x_1 + x_2$. What is the shape of the cross-price demand curves for x_1 and x_2?
   b. Suppose instead tastes are Cobb–Douglas. What do cross-price demand curves look like?
   c. Now suppose tastes can be represented by a CES utility function. Without doing any maths, can you determine for what values of ρ the cross-price demand relationship is upward sloping?
   d. **Suppose tastes can be represented by the CES function $u(x_1,x_2) = (0.5x_1^{-\rho} + 0.5x_2^{-\rho})^{-1/\rho}$. Verify your intuitive answer from part (c).

9.4 Everyday Application: *Backward-Bending Labour Supply Curve*. Some labour economists assert that labour supply curves typically slope up when wages are low and down when wages are high. This is sometimes referred to as a *backward-bending labour supply curve*.

A. Which of the following statements is inconsistent with the empirical finding of a backward-bending labour supply curve?

   a. For the typical worker, leisure is an inferior good when wages are low and a normal good when wages are high.
   b. For the typical worker, leisure is a normal good when wages are low and an inferior good when wages are high.
   c. For the typical worker, leisure is always a normal good.
   d. For the typical worker, leisure is always an inferior good.

B. Suppose that tastes over consumption and leisure are described by a CES utility function: $u(c,\ell) = (0.5c^{-\rho} + 0.5\ell^{-\rho})^{-1/\rho}$

   a. Derive the labour supply curve assuming a leisure endowment L.
   b. **Illustrate for which values of ρ this curve is upward sloping and for which it is downward sloping.
   c. Is it possible for the backward-bending labour supply curve to emerge from tastes captured by a CES utility function?
   d. For practical purposes, we typically only have to worry about modelling tastes accurately at the margin; that is, around the current bundles that consumers/workers are consuming. This is because low-wage workers, for instance, may experience some increases in wages but not so much that they are suddenly high-wage workers, and vice versa. If you were modelling worker behaviour for a group of workers and you modelled each worker's tastes as CES over leisure and consumption, how would you assume ρ differs for low-wage and high-wage workers assuming you are persuaded of the empirical validity of the backward-bending labour supply curve?

9.5† Business Application: *Price Discounts, Substitutes and Complements*. A business might worry that the pricing of one product might impact demand for another product that is also sold by the same business. Here, we'll explore conditions under which such worries are more or less important before turning to some specific examples.

A. Suppose first that we label the two goods that a firm sells as x_1 and x_2. The firm considers putting a discount of δ on the price of x_1, a discount that would lower the price from p_1 to $(1 - \delta)p_1$.

   a. For a consumer who budgets I for consumption of x_1 and x_2, illustrate the budget before and after the discount is put in place.

b. Assuming that tastes are homothetic, derive the relationship between δ on the vertical axis and x_1 on the horizontal axis.

c. Now derive the relationship between δ and x_2; can you tell if it slopes up or down? What does your answer depend on?

d. Suppose that x_1 is printers and x_2 is printer cartridges produced by the same company. Compare this to the case where x_1 is Diet Coke and x_2 is Zero Coke. In which case is there a more compelling case for discounts on x_1?

B. Suppose that tastes are defined by $u(x_1,x_2) = x_1^\alpha x_2^{(1-\alpha)}$.

a. Derive the demand functions for x_1 and x_2 as a function of prices, I and δ.

b. Are these upward or downward sloping in δ?

c. Under the more general specification of tastes as CES, that is, $u(x_1,x_2) = (ax_1^{-\rho} + (1-\alpha)x_2^{-\rho})^{-1/\rho}$, how would your answer change as ρ changes?

9.6 **Policy Application:** *Tax and Retirement Policy.* In Chapter 3, we illustrated budgets in which a consumer faced trade-offs between work and leisure now as well as between consuming now and consuming in the future. We can use a model of this kind to think about tax and retirement policy.

A. Suppose period 1 represents the period over which a worker is productive in the labour force and period 2 represents the period during which the worker expects to be retired. The worker earns a wage w and has L hours of leisure time that could be devoted to work l or leisure consumption ℓ. Earnings in this period can be consumed as current consumption c_1 or saved for retirement consumption c_2 at an interest rate r. Suppose throughout that consumption in both periods is a normal good, as is leisure this period.

a. Illustrate this worker's budget constraint in a three-dimensional graph with c_1, c_2 and ℓ on the axes.

b. For certain types of tastes, as for those used in part B of this question, the optimal labour decision does not vary with the wage or the interest rate in this problem. Suppose this implies that taking ℓ^* in leisure is always optimal for this worker. Illustrate how this puts the worker's decision on a slice of the three-dimensional budget you graphed in part (a).

c. Assume that optimal choices always occur on the two-dimensional slice you have identified. Illustrate how you could derive a demand curve for c_1, that is, a curve that shows the relationship between c_1 on the horizontal axis and the interest rate r on the vertical. Does this curve slope up or down? What does your answer depend on?

d. Can you derive a similar economic relationship except this time with w rather than r on the vertical axis? Can you be certain about whether this relationship is upward sloping given that consumption in both periods is a normal good?

e. Suppose that the government introduces a programme that raises taxes on wages and uses the revenues to subsidize savings. Indicate first how each part of this policy – the tax on wages and the subsidy for savings which raises the effective interest rate – impacts current and retirement consumption.

f. Suppose the tax revenue is exactly enough to pay for the subsidy. Without drawing any further graphs, what do you think will happen to current and retirement consumption?

g. There are two ways that programmes such as this can be structured: Method 1 puts the tax revenues collected from the individual into a personal savings account that is used to finance the savings subsidy when the worker retires; Method 2 uses current tax revenues to support current retirees and uses tax revenues from future workers to subsidize current workers when they retire. The latter is often referred to as pay-as-you-go financing. By knowing what happens to current and retirement consumption of workers under such programmes, can you speculate what will happen to overall savings under Method 1 and Method 2 given that tax revenues become savings under Method 1 but not under Method 2?

B. Suppose the worker's tastes can be summarized by the utility function $u(c_1, c_2, \ell) = (c_1^\alpha \ell^{(1-\alpha)})^\beta c_2^{(1-\beta)}$.

a. Set up the budget equation that takes into account the trade-offs this worker faces between consumption and leisure now as well as between consuming now and consuming in the future.

b. Set up this worker's optimization problem and solve for the optimal consumption levels in each period as well as the optimal leisure consumption this period. Using the natural log transformation of the utility function will make this algebraically easier to solve.

c. In part A, we assumed that the worker would choose the same amount of work effort regardless of the wage and interest rate. Is this true for the tastes used in this part of the exercise?

d. How does consumption before retirement change with w and r? Can you make sense of this in light of your graphical answers in part A?

e. In A(e), we described a policy that imposes a tax t on wages and a subsidy s on savings. Suppose that the tax lowers the wage retained by the worker to $(1 - t)$ and the subsidy raises the effective interest rate for the worker to $(r + s)$. Without necessarily redoing the optimization problem, how will the equations for the optimal levels of c_1, c_2 and ℓ change under such a policy?

f. Are the effects of t and s individually as you concluded in A(e)?

g. For a given t, how much tax revenue does the government raise? For a given s, how much of a cost does the government incur? What do your answers imply about the relationship between s and t if the revenues raised now are exactly offset by the expenditures incurred next period, taking into account that the revenues can earn interest until they need to be spent?

h. Can you now verify your conclusion from A(f)?

i. What happens to the size of personal savings that the individual worker puts away under this policy? If we consider the tax revenue the government collects on behalf of the worker, which will be returned in the form of the savings subsidy when the worker retires, what happens to the worker's overall savings – their personal savings plus the forced savings from the tax?

j. How would your answer about the increase in actual overall savings change if the government, instead of actually saving the tax revenue on behalf of the worker, were to spend current tax revenues on current retirees? This, as mentioned in part A, is sometimes referred to as a pay-as-you-go policy.

Chapter 10

Consumer Surplus and Deadweight Loss

Economists and policy makers may want to know whether particular policies make people better off or worse off, but sometimes they also need to quantify *how much* better off or worse off different consumers are. The tools we have developed will allow us to measure consumer welfare in objective terms rather than trying to measure 'happiness'. We will find ways of quantifying how much better off or worse off consumers are in different economic circumstances by asking how much they are willing to pay to avoid particular circumstances or how much compensation would be required to make it up to them when circumstances change.

This way of thinking about welfare effects from institutional or policy changes allows us to address the following question: Is it at least in principle possible to compensate those who lose from the policy with part of the gains accruing to those who gain from the policy? If the answer is yes, at least in principle, there is a way to make some people better off without making anyone worse off, which we will say enhances *efficiency*. If the answer is no, on the other hand, we know that the new situation will be less *efficient*. If the winners from a policy gain more than the losers lose, the policy could *in principle* be accompanied by a compensation scheme that would result in unanimous approval of the policy.

Just because it is *in principle* possible to come up with such a compensation scheme does not mean it is possible *in practice*. Real-world policies come, at best, with imperfect compensation schemes, and thus, they rarely enjoy unanimous approval. As a result, it is not immediately obvious that we should favour all policies that create more benefits than costs, because in some instances we may place more weight on the decline in welfare of those who lose than on the gains in welfare of those who win. For instance, suppose a group of wealthy citizens would be willing to pay €100 million to have a certain policy implemented, and a group of poor citizens would lose €1 million as a result. If we can't figure out a way to accompany this policy with compensation to those who would otherwise lose, we might decide that the policy is not worth it, that we in essence place more weight on the €1 million loss than on the €100 million gain because the loss would be borne by the most vulnerable.

Before we can even begin to think about such trade-offs, however, we need to be able to quantify gains and losses, which is what we will do for the rest of this chapter.

We will begin our analysis of this measurement of consumer welfare by quantifying how much better off or worse off consumers are for being able to purchase goods voluntarily at given market prices. We will ask how much better off a consumer is for being able to participate in a market rather than be excluded from it. This will lead us to define *marginal willingness to pay, total willingness to pay* and *consumer surplus*. We will proceed to demonstrate how policy makers might analyze the impact of particular proposals on consumers when those proposals change the relative prices in an economy. In the process, we will see the importance of recognizing the difference between income and substitution effects and how the substitution effect contributes to *deadweight losses* for society while the income effect does not.

10A.1 Consumer Surplus

We will use the example of a consumer's choices between fuel and a composite good denominated in euros. In Graph 10.1, we begin with a particular set of economic circumstances: a choice set determined by the price of fuel and current exogenous income. The optimal choice A falls on the indifference curve that is tangential to the choice set assuming the consumer is not at a corner solution.

Now let's ask the following question: How much better off is the consumer for being able to purchase fuel at its current price rather than being excluded from the market for fuels? Or, to be more precise, how much would the consumer be willing to pay for the opportunity to participate in the current market for fuel?

Graph 10.1 Deriving $MWTP$ from MRS of Indifference Curve Containing Bundle A

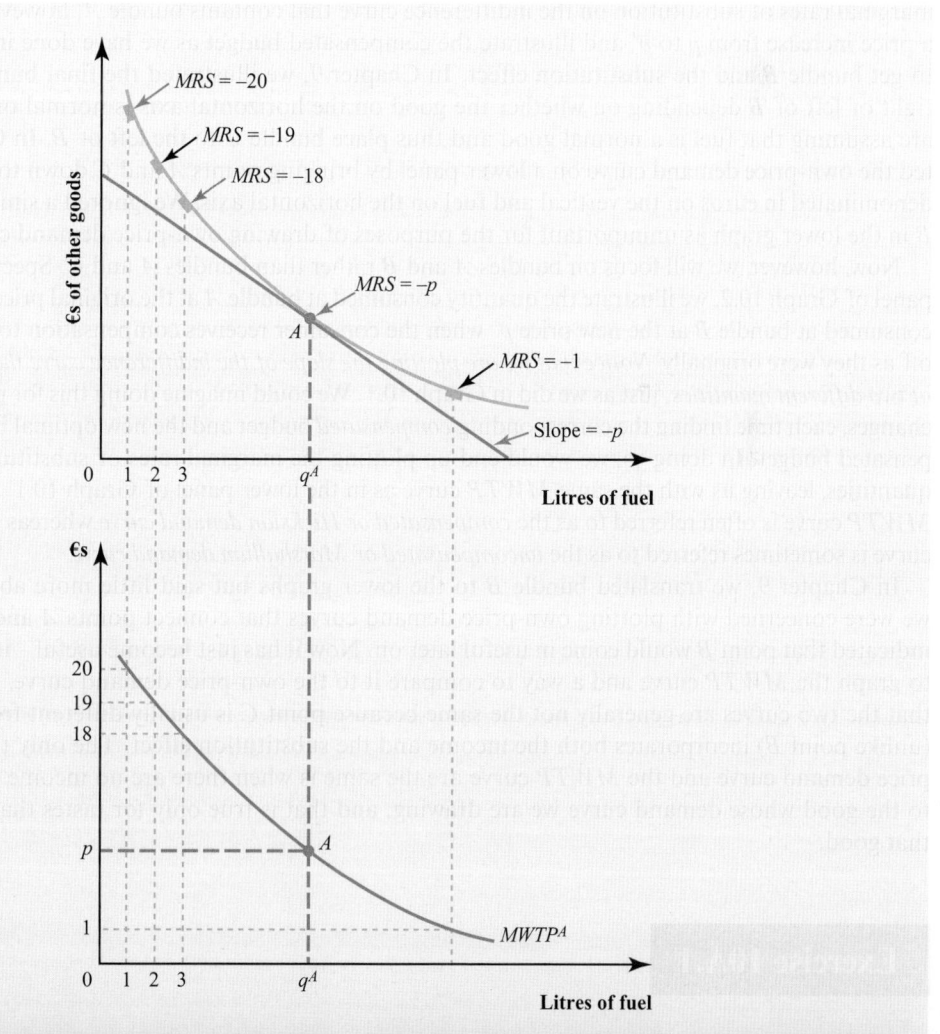

Go to MindTap to interact with this graph

10A.1.1 Marginal Willingness to Pay To formulate an answer to this question, we could look at each litre of fuel consumed and ask how much the consumer would have been willing to pay for that litre given that they ended up at their optimal bundle *A*. For the first litre, we can measure this willingness to pay by finding the slope of the indifference curve – the marginal rate of substitution – at 1 litre. Suppose that this slope is −20. This tells us that the consumer was willing to trade €20 worth of other consumption for the first litre of fuel. We can proceed to the second litre and find the marginal rate of substitution at 2 litres. Suppose that it is −19. This tells us that the consumer would have been willing to give up €19 of other consumption to get the *second* litre of fuel. We could keep doing this for each litre of fuel, with the marginal rate of substitution at bundle *A* being equal to the price of fuel. At the end of this exercise, we will have identified the consumer's *marginal willingness to pay* (*MWTP*) for each of the litres of fuel consumed and all the additional litres that they chose not to consume. In the lower panel of Graph 10.1, we plot litres of fuel on the horizontal axis and euros on the vertical. The *MWTP curve* for a consumer who ends up on the indifference curve containing bundle *A* is generated by plotting the euro values of the *MRS* at each litre of fuel.

10A.1.2 *MWTP* Curves and Substitution Effects There is, however, a slightly different way of deriving *MWTP* curves that builds more directly on material covered in previous chapters and is similar to the way we derived own-price demand curves in Chapter 9. The top panel of Graph 10.2 begins with the same initial budget and optimal bundle *A* as we started with in Graph 10.1. Instead of directly identifying the marginal rates of substitution on the indifference curve that contains bundle *A*, however, we now imagine a price increase from *p* to *p'* and illustrate the compensated budget as we have done in previous chapters to get bundle *B* and the substitution effect. In Chapter 9, we illustrated the final bundle *C* either to the right or left of *B* depending on whether the good on the horizontal axis is normal or inferior. Here, we are assuming that fuel is a normal good and thus place bundle *C* to the left of *B*. In Chapter 9, we plotted the own-price demand curve on a lower panel by bringing points *A* and *C* down to a graph with price denominated in euros on the vertical and fuel on the horizontal axis. We ignored a similarly derived point *B* in the lower graph as unimportant for the purposes of drawing own-price demand curves.

Now, however, we will focus on bundles *A* and *B* rather than bundles *A* and *C*. Specifically, in the lower panel of Graph 10.2, we illustrate the quantity consumed at bundle *A* at the original price *p* and the quantity consumed at bundle *B* at the new price *p'* when the consumer receives compensation to make them as well off as they were originally. *Notice that we are plotting the slope of the indifference curve that contains bundle A at two different quantities*, just as we did in Graph 10.1. We could imagine doing this for many different price changes, each time finding the corresponding *compensated* budget and the new optimal bundle on that compensated budget. In doing so, we would end up plotting the marginal rates of substitution at the different quantities, leaving us with the same *MWTP* curve as in the lower panel of Graph 10.1. For this reason, the *MWTP* curve is often referred to as the *compensated or Hicksian demand curve* whereas the regular demand curve is sometimes referred to as the *uncompensated or Marshallian demand curve*.

In Chapter 9, we translated bundle *B* to the lower graphs but said little more about it. At the time we were concerned with plotting own-price demand curves that connect points *A* and *C*, and we merely indicated that point *B* would come in useful later on. Now it has just become useful – it has given us a way to graph the *MWTP* curve and a way to compare it to the own-price demand curve. It is also now clear that the two curves are generally not the same because point *C* is usually different from point *B* since it (unlike point *B*) incorporates both the income and the substitution effect. The only time when the own-price demand curve and the *MWTP* curve are the same is when there are no income effects with respect to the good whose demand curve we are drawing, and that is true only for tastes that are quasilinear in that good.

Exercise 10A.1

Demonstrate that own-price demand curves are the same as *MWTP* curves for goods that can be represented by quasilinear tastes.

Graph 10.2 Deriving *MWTP* From Compensated Budgets

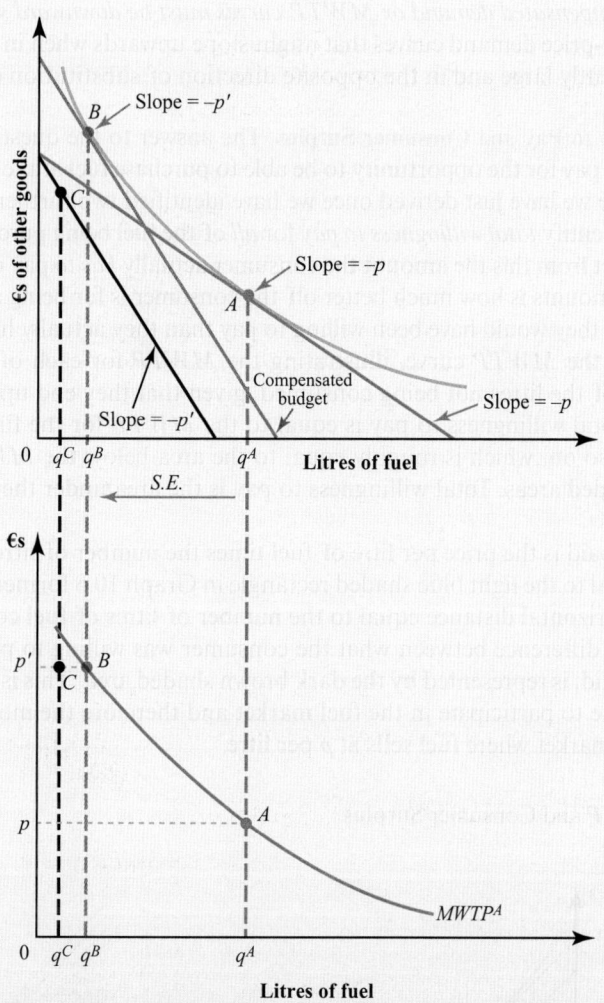

Go to MindTap to interact with this graph

Exercise 10A.2

Using the graphs in Graph 9.2 of the previous chapter, determine under what condition own-price demand curves are steeper and under what conditions they are shallower than *MWTP* curves.

Exercise 10A.3

What does the *MWTP* or compensated demand curve look like if the two goods are perfect complements?

Finally, note that since compensated demand curves only include substitution and not income effects, and since the direction of the substitution effect is always unambiguously away from the good that has become more expensive, *compensated demand or MWTP curves must be downward sloping.* This is at least in principle not true for own-price demand curves that might slope upwards when in the very rare cases when income effects are sufficiently large and in the opposite direction of substitution effects for Giffen goods.

10A.1.3 Total Willingness to Pay and Consumer Surplus The answer to the question of how much a consumer would be willing to pay for the opportunity to be able to purchase fuel at the market price can now be read off the *MWTP* curve we have just derived once we have identified two further concepts in the *MWTP* graph. First, we need to identify *total willingness to pay* for *all* of the fuel being purchased in the market, and second we need to subtract from this the amount the consumer actually *has to* pay in the market. The difference between these two amounts is how much better off the consumer is for being able to participate in this market – how much more they would have been willing to pay than they actually had to pay.

Graph 10.3 replicates the *MWTP* curve, illustrating the *MWTP* for each of the litres of fuel being consumed and for each of the litres not being consumed, given that they end up consuming at bundle *A* facing market price *p*. Total willingness to pay is equal to the *MWTP* for the first litre plus the *MWTP* for the second litre, and so on, which is roughly equal to the area below the *MWTP* curve, i.e. the dark brown and light blue shaded areas. Total willingness to pay is the area under the *MWTP* curve up to the quantity consumed.

The amount *actually* paid is the price per litre of fuel times the number of litres the consumer chooses to consume, which is equal to the light blue shaded rectangle in Graph 10.3 formed by the vertical distance equal to price and the horizontal distance equal to the number of litres of fuel consumed.

Consumer surplus, the difference between what the consumer was willing to pay for fuel consumption and what they actually paid, is represented by the dark brown shaded area. This is how much better off the consumer is for being able to participate in the fuel market and therefore the most they would be willing to pay to get access to a market where fuel sells at *p* per litre.

Graph 10.3 *MWTP, TWTP* and Consumer Surplus

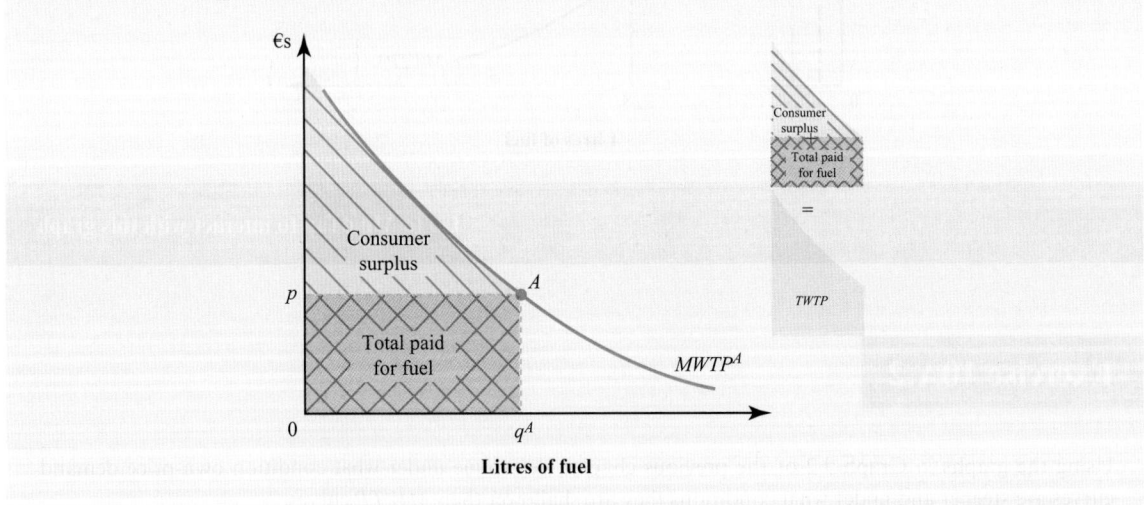

Many introductory texts in economics typically graph consumer surplus along own-price uncompensated demand curves, not along the *MWTP* or compensated demand curves. Strictly, it is correct to use the own-price demand curve to find consumer surplus only in one specific case: when tastes are quasilinear. In all other cases, consumer surplus as we have defined it cannot be identified on own-price demand curves, and policy analysis that uses such curves to identify changes in consumer surplus can give very misleading and incorrect answers. In this section, we will explore in more detail the relationship between demand curves and *MWTP* curves.

10A.2.1 Many *MWTP* and Demand Curves for Any Individual The *MWTP* curves that we derived in Graphs 10.1 and 10.2 are labelled with the superscript *A* indicating that the curve was derived from the indifference curve that contains bundle *A*. We picked this as the indifference curve that was relevant for the exercise of deriving *MWTP* in our example because the consumer was assumed to be consuming at *A*. Had the consumer been consuming at some other bundle, we would have used a different indifference curve to derive *MWTP* and thus would have derived a curve different from *MWTP*^{A}.

There generally exists a different *MWTP* curve for each indifference curve. This is analogous to the case of own-price demand curves. When we derive an own-price demand curve, we hold income fixed; when we derive *MWTP* curves, we hold the indifference curve (or utility) fixed. If income changes, own-price demand curves shift, just as *MWTP* curves shift if utility changes.

Consider, for instance, Graph 10.4. In the top panels of parts (a) and (b), we illustrate the same bundles *A* and *B* with the same indifference curves. On the left, we indicate two income levels at which *A* and *B* are optimal bundles, and on the lower part of panel (a), we illustrate how these two bundles translate to two points on different uncompensated demand curves, one for the higher level of income and one for the lower level.

Graph 10.4 Multiple Demand Curves for Different Incomes and Multiple *MWTP* Curves for Different Utility Levels

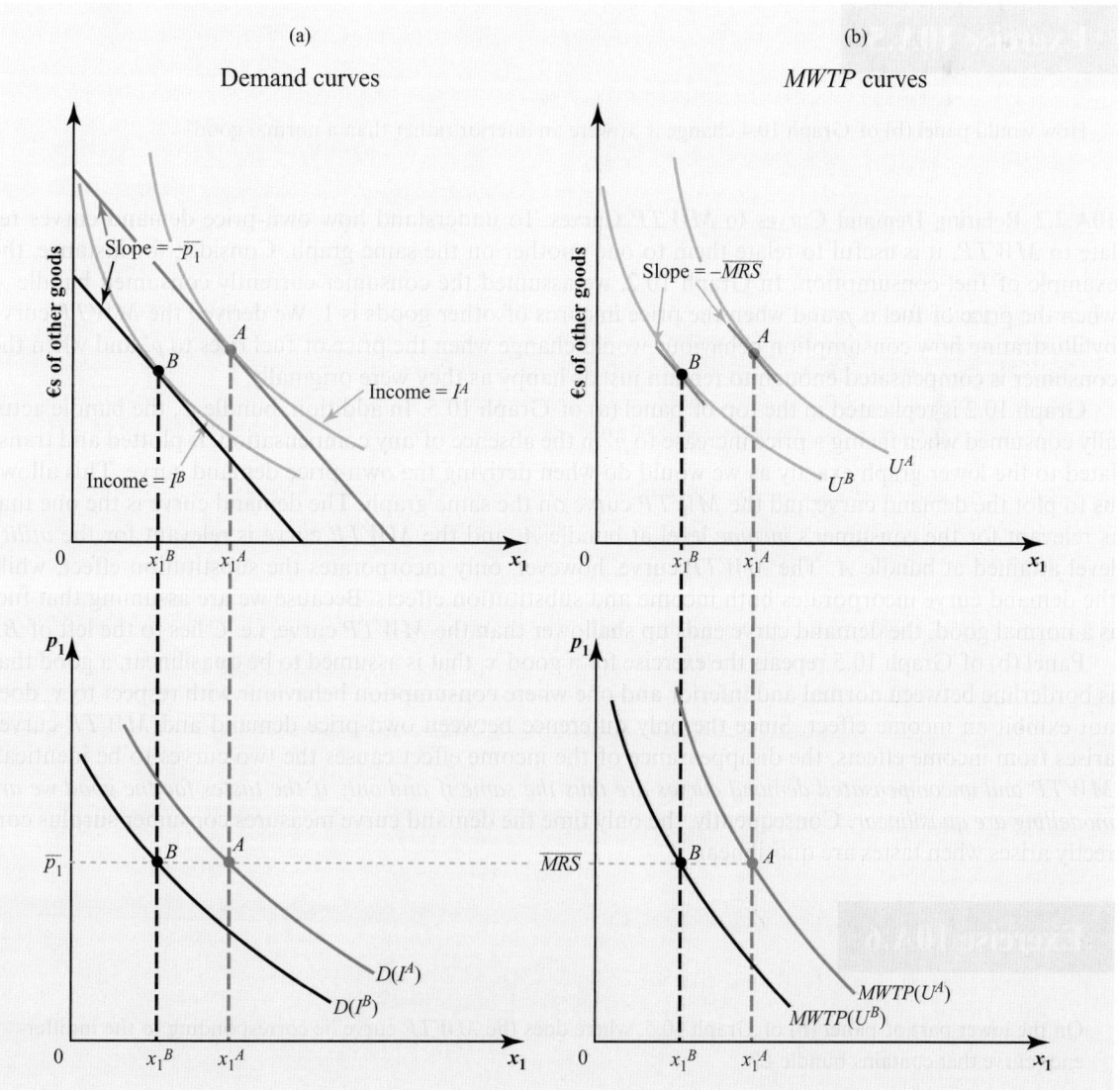

Notice that we are implicitly assuming that x_1 is a normal good, with consumption falling when income falls. Of course, we are guessing what the rest of the demand curves look like and would have to change the price of x_1 in the top graph to derive the rest of the demand curves formally.

Exercise 10A.4

How would panel (a) of Graph 10.4 change if x_1 were an inferior rather than a normal good?

In part (b) of Graph 10.4, we use points A and B in the top graph to plot the $MWTP$, or the negative MRS, at two different consumption levels. Since the MRS is the same at bundle A and B in the top graph, the derived points on the lower graph happen at the same height. As in the case of the uncompensated demand curves in panel (a) of Graph 10.4, we guess the shape of the rest of the $MWTP$ curves but could formally derive these using either of the methods developed in Graphs 10.1 and 10.2. The lower part of panel (b) demonstrates shifts in the $MWTP$ curve as utility changes, just as the lower portion of panel (a) demonstrates shifts in the own-price demand curve as income changes.

Exercise 10A.5

How would panel (b) of Graph 10.4 change if x_1 were an inferior rather than a normal good?

10A.2.2 Relating Demand Curves to $MWTP$ Curves To understand how own-price demand curves relate to $MWTP$, it is useful to relate them to one another on the same graph. Consider, for instance, the example of fuel consumption. In Graph 10.2, we assumed the consumer currently consumed bundle A when the price of fuel is p and when the price in euros of other goods is 1. We derived the $MWTP$ curve by illustrating how consumption behaviour would change when the price of fuel rises to p' and when the consumer is compensated enough to remain just as happy as they were originally.

Graph 10.2 is replicated in the top of panel (a) of Graph 10.5. In addition, bundle C, the bundle actually consumed when facing a price increase to p' in the absence of any compensation, is plotted and translated to the lower graph exactly as we would do when deriving the own-price demand curve. This allows us to plot the demand curve and the $MWTP$ curve on the same graph. The demand curve is the one that is relevant for the consumer's *income* level at bundle A, and the $MWTP$ curve is relevant for the *utility* level attained at bundle A. The $MWTP$ curve, however, only incorporates the substitution effect, while the demand curve incorporates both income and substitution effects. Because we are assuming that fuel is a normal good, the demand curve ends up shallower than the $MWTP$ curve, i.e. C lies to the left of B.

Panel (b) of Graph 10.5 repeats the exercise for a good x_1 that is assumed to be quasilinear, a good that is borderline between normal and inferior and one where consumption behaviour with respect to x_1 does not exhibit an income effect. Since the only difference between own-price demand and $MWTP$ curves arises from income effects, the disappearance of the income effect causes the two curves to be identical. *MWTP and uncompensated demand curves are thus the same if and only if the tastes for the good we are modelling are quasilinear.* Consequently, the only time the demand curve measures consumer surplus correctly arises when tastes are quasilinear.

Exercise 10A.6

On the lower part of panel (b) of Graph 10.5, where does the $MWTP$ curve lie corresponding to the indifference curve that contains bundle C?

Graph 10.5 Relationship of Demand and *MWTP* Curves

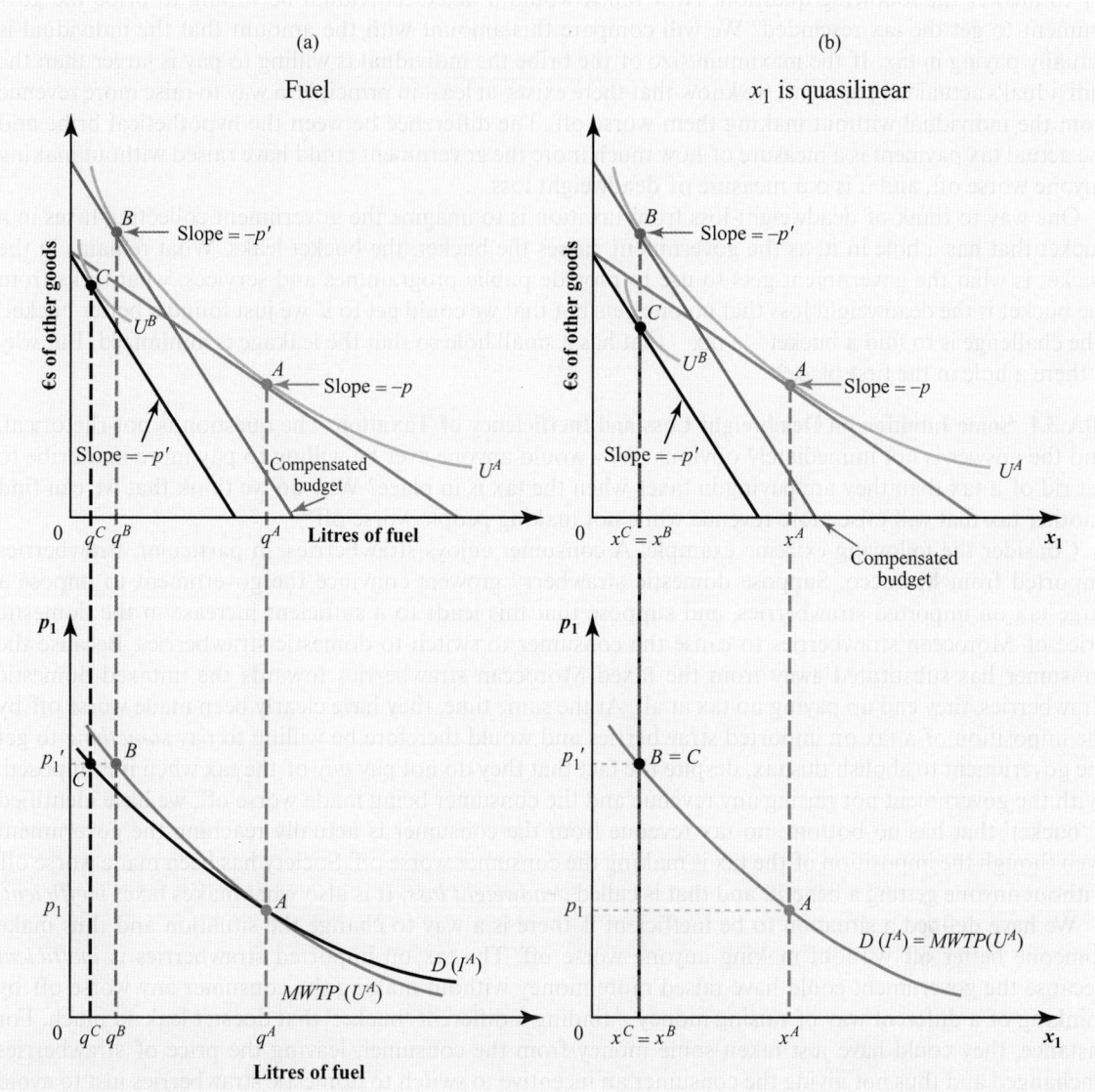

Exercise 10A.7

How do the upper and lower parts of panel (a) of Graph 10.5 change when fuel is an inferior good?

10A.3 What's So Bad About Taxes? Or, Why Is the Bucket Leaking?

Governments use taxes to raise revenues that in turn fund expenditures on a variety of government programmes. These programmes may have enormous benefits, but, to the extent that they are funded through taxes, they come at an economic cost that economists refer to as the *deadweight loss from taxation*. Recognizing an economic cost of taxation does not mean taxes are 'bad' but does lead us to think more carefully about the relative cost of different kinds of taxes, and we can now use the tools we have developed to illustrate how such costs can be measured.

To see what makes a particular tax costly and to see how we can measure this cost objectively, we will try to answer the following question: How much would a taxed individual be willing to bribe the government to get the tax rescinded? We will compare this amount with the amount that the individual is actually paying in tax. If the maximum size of the bribe the individual is willing to pay is larger than the individual's actual tax payment, we know that there exists, at least in principle, a way to raise more revenue from the individual without making them worse off. The difference between the hypothetical bribe and the actual tax payment is a measure of how much more the government could have raised without making anyone worse off, and it is our measure of deadweight loss.

One way to think of deadweight loss from taxation is to imagine the government collecting taxes in a bucket that has a hole in it; as the government passes the bucket, the bucket leaks. What remains in the bucket is what the government gets to use to provide public programmes and services; what leaks from the bucket is the deadweight loss that no one gets but that we could get to if we just found a better bucket. The challenge is to find a bucket – a tax – that has a small hole so that the leakage is minimized. But why is there a hole in the first place?

10A.3.1 Some Intuition on Deadweight Loss and Inefficiency of Taxation The question is not rhetorical, and the answer is not immediately obvious. Why would anyone ever be willing to pay more in a bribe to get rid of a tax than they are paying in taxes when the tax is in place? Why do we think that we can find another tax that will raise more revenue while not making people worse off?

Consider the following extreme example. A consumer enjoys strawberries, in particular, strawberries imported from Morocco. Suppose domestic strawberry growers convince the government to impose a large tax on imported strawberries, and suppose that this leads to a sufficient increase in the domestic price of Moroccan strawberries to cause the consumer to switch to domestic strawberries. Because the consumer has substituted away from the taxed Moroccan strawberries towards the untaxed domestic strawberries, they end up paying no tax at all. At the same time, they have clearly been made worse off by the imposition of a tax on imported strawberries and would therefore be willing to pay *something* to get the government to abolish this tax, despite the fact that they do not pay *any* of the tax when it is imposed. With the government not raising any revenue and the consumer being made worse off, we have identified a 'bucket' that has no bottom; no tax revenue from the consumer is actually reaching the government even though the imposition of the tax is making the consumer worse off. Society has been made worse off without anyone getting a benefit, and that is called *deadweight loss*. It is also what makes taxes *inefficient*.

We have defined a situation to be inefficient if there is a way to change the situation and thus make someone better off without making anyone worse off. The tax on imported strawberries is *inefficient* because the government could have raised more money without making the consumer any worse off by thinking of a different way of raising money – finding a different 'bucket' that doesn't leak so much. For instance, they could have just taken some money from the consumer, leaving the price of strawberries unchanged and thus not giving the consumer an incentive to switch to domestic strawberries just to avoid a tax. The example, though extreme, gives us an initial insight into what it is about taxes that makes taxes costly. *By altering the relative prices in an economy, taxes cause consumers, workers and savers to substitute away from taxed goods and services and towards untaxed goods and services.* To the extent that this substitution activity happens solely because of a change in opportunity costs, to the extent to which taxes give rise to substitution effects, taxes are distortionary and inefficient ways of raising revenues.

Many real-world examples may be less extreme – they may lead us to consume less of the taxed good and more of other goods without causing us to eliminate our consumption of particular taxed goods entirely, but the basic intuition remains: To the extent to which taxes change opportunity costs and thus cause us to alter our consumption plans solely because of those changed opportunity costs, we are worse off without contributing to the government's effort to raise revenues, and society has incurred a deadweight loss. We can now use the tools we have developed to show more formally that this entire deadweight loss happens because of substitution effects, which are therefore the underlying cause of the leak in the 'bucket'.

10A.3.2 Identifying Deadweight Losses in a Consumer Diagram Suppose that instead of a tax on strawberries we considered a tax on housing. We can model such a tax in our usual two-good framework as resulting in an increase in the price of each square metre of housing consumed. Alternatively, we can model removal of such a tax as a decrease in the price of housing. Panel (a) of Graph 10.6 illustrates the change in the choice set resulting from such a tax, with bundle A representing a consumer's optimal after-tax choice.

In Graph 8.3, we illustrated how one can identify the total tax paid by a consumer in a situation where the good modelled on the horizontal axis is taxed. In particular, we can first identify c^A as the euros of 'other goods consumption' the consumer is able to afford *after tax* given that they are consuming h^A. Second, we can identify c^α as the euros of 'other goods consumption' had they consumed the same amount of housing in the absence of the tax. The difference between these amounts, labelled T in panel (a) of Graph 10.6, is the total tax payment the consumer makes under the tax. As explained in Chapter 8, this does not presume that the consumer's optimal consumption bundle without the tax is α. Rather, the bundle α simply helps us identify the magnitude of T.

Panel (b) of Graph 10.6 replicates panel (a) but gives the answer to our second question: How much of this consumer's income could we have taken *without changing opportunity costs* to make the consumer just as well off as they are under the tax on housing? How much can we shift the before-tax budget constraint without changing its slope and still end up on the indifference curve labelled u^A? The answer is that we could shift this budget inwards until we get to the budget line BC_1 that is tangential to u^A at B. The euro value of this parallel shift can be measured on the vertical axis which is denominated in euro units, and since the two budget lines are parallel, this distance can equivalently be measured as a vertical distance between the two lines anywhere. In particular, we can measure it as a distance below the bundle α, a distance labelled L in panel (b) of Graph 10.6.

Graph 10.6 Distortionary Tax on Housing

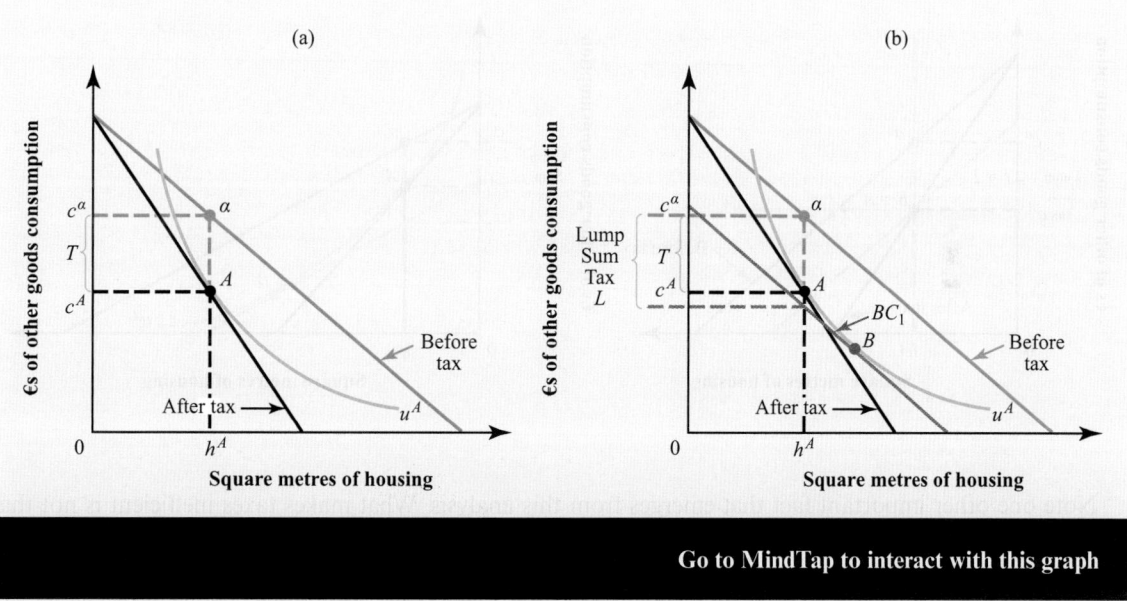

The distance L is how much we could have taxed this consumer using what is called a *lump sum tax*. *A lump sum tax is a tax that does not change opportunity costs,* i.e. slopes of budget constraints. Panel (b) of Graph 10.6 indicates that this consumer would have been willing to pay a larger amount L in a lump sum tax than the amount L they are paying under the tax on housing, with each tax leaving the consumer exactly on the same indifference curve and thus equally happy. The difference between T and L is the deadweight loss from the tax on housing. Since, beginning with a housing tax the lump sum tax represents a way to make someone better off (government revenue is higher) without making anyone worse off (our consumer has the same utility in either case), we can equivalently say that the housing tax is *inefficient*.

10A.3.3 Deadweight Losses and Substitution Effects Consider the same tax on housing modelled in Graph 10.6, but now assume that the consumer views housing and 'other goods' as perfect complements. Panel (a) of Graph 10.7 illustrates such tastes, with A representing the consumer's optimal bundle after the tax is imposed and with u^A representing the consumer's indifference curve at bundle A. We can identify the amount of tax they pay under the housing tax as T just as we did in panel (a) of Graph 10.6. When we now ask how much we could have taken from the consumer in a lump sum tax and still ensured that the consumer reaches the indifference curve u^A, we find that the consumer would end up at exactly the same consumption bundle, i.e. $B = A$. Thus, the amount we could have extracted from the consumer in a lump sum tax is exactly equal to the amount we received from the consumer under the tax on housing, i.e. $L = T$. We have therefore identified a case where a tax on housing does *not* produce a deadweight loss and is therefore efficient.

The reason why $B = A$ in panel (a) of Graph 10.7 is that we have given the consumer tastes that eliminate substitution effects. As the substitution effect disappears, so does the deadweight loss from a tax that changes the opportunity cost of housing. Panel (b) of Graph 10.7, on the other hand, assumes tastes that incorporate a great deal of substitutability, with bundles A and B far from each other. As a result, L is significantly larger than T, implying a large deadweight loss. As the degree of substitutability between housing and other goods consumption increases from zero in panel (a) of Graph 10.7 to some substitutability in panel (b) of Graph 10.6 to a large amount of substitutability in panel (b) of Graph 10.7, the deadweight loss increases as well. As the degree of substitutability shrinks, the leak in our tax 'bucket' disappears.

Graph 10.7 Distortionary Taxes and Substitution Effects

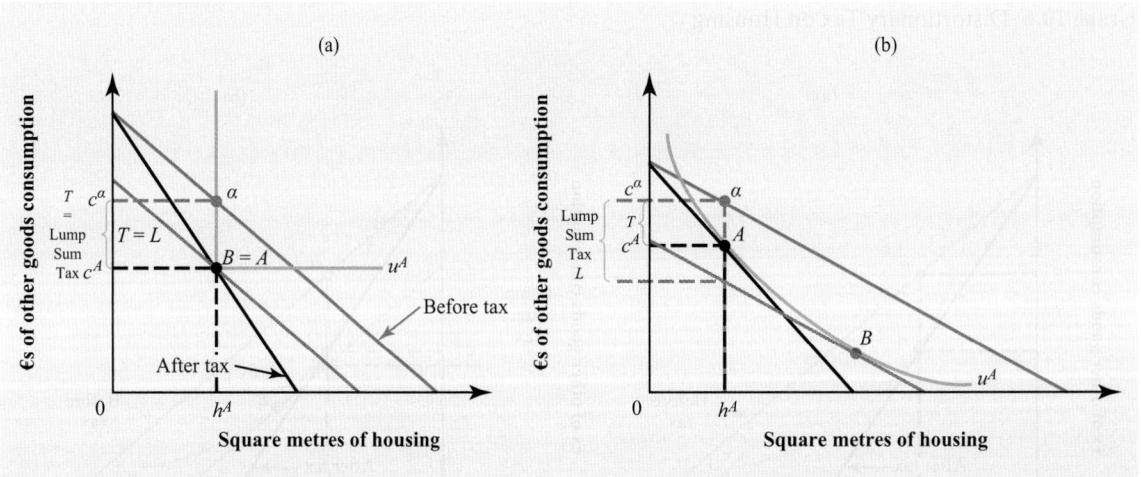

Note one other important fact that emerges from this analysis. What makes taxes inefficient is not that consumers respond by consuming less of the taxed good. The consumer responds to the tax in panel (a) of Graph 10.7 by consuming less than they would at the before-tax budget constraint, but there is no inefficiency. The inefficiency emerges to the extent to which a substitution effect lies behind the change in behaviour. As demonstrated in some of the end-of-chapter exercises, this is particularly important in labour markets where income and substitution effects tend to point in the opposite direction with respect to the good leisure.

Exercise 10A.8

Can you think of a scenario under which a consumer does not change their consumption of a good when it is taxed but there still exists an inefficiency from taxation?

Consider the following statement: 'People hate taxes because of income effects; economists hate taxes because of substitution effects'. Few taxpayers think about income and substitution effects when they pay the tax authorities – they don't like paying taxes because they'd rather have the money for themselves. Economists who care about efficiency, on the other hand, may have no problem with money going from some people to other people through the government *as long as wealth does not get lost in the process*, or as long as someone does not get hurt without someone else at least benefiting. That is precisely what happens when taxes result in changes of opportunity costs that result in substitution effects. It is what is causing the 'bucket' to leak. While individual taxpayers may not easily identify a tax that results in panel (a) of Graph 10.7 as better than a tax that results in panel (b) of Graph 10.7, economists would, all else being equal, tend to have a clear preference for the tax that results in no substitution effects and thus no deadweight losses to society. We may disagree on how big the bucket should be, but we generally agree that it should not have big leaks if we can help it.

10A.3.4 Almost All Real-World Taxes Are Inefficient From our discussion thus far, we can identify two scenarios under which a tax may be efficient: (1) if the tax does not change opportunity costs and is thus a lump sum tax; or (2) if the tax does not give rise to substitution effects even though it causes changes in opportunity costs. Scenario (2) is difficult to count on since we have little control over what kinds of tastes consumers have, although it is possible to identify certain combinations of goods that are less substitutable than others. The first scenario, lump sum taxes, rarely represents real-world policy options. As a result, almost all real-world taxes give rise to deadweight losses and are thus inefficient, at least until we get to the topic of externalities in Chapter 21.

Why are lump sum taxes so hard to come by? In order for a tax to truly represent a lump sum tax, it must be such that the consumer cannot engage in any substituting behaviour that allows them to avoid at least part of the tax. As soon as taxes are imposed differentially on different goods, the possibility of such substituting behaviour arises as opportunity costs of different goods are altered. If you think carefully about the implications of this, it is easier to appreciate how difficult it is in practice to come up with a true lump sum tax. In our example of the tax on housing, for instance, it might be thought we could eliminate the distortionary, or deadweight loss-inducing, aspects of the tax by taxing all other consumption by the same amount, thus keeping the slope of the budget constraint from changing and not causing changes in the opportunity cost of anything. All other goods include, for instance, savings, so why not tax savings at the same rate, thus again keeping opportunity costs unchanged. Yet another good that we have not modelled in our two-good diagram is leisure. Can we think of easy ways to tax leisure at the same rate? If not, the 'bucket' has sprung a leak.

Exercise 10A.9

On a graph with consumption on the vertical axis and leisure on the horizontal, illustrate the deadweight loss of a tax on all consumption other than the consumption of leisure.

The most common taxes are taxes on different forms of consumption (sales taxes, value added taxes) or taxes on different forms of income (income taxes, capital gains taxes, National Insurance Contributions, etc.). Each of these can be avoided in part through a change in behaviour. To truly be a lump sum tax, a tax must be such that consumers can do *nothing* to avoid the tax. In 1990, for instance, UK Prime Minister Margaret Thatcher attempted to introduce such a tax – the poll tax. A poll or head tax is a fixed tax payment (say, €2000 per year) that consumers have to pay as long as they have a head. It is not easy for someone to change the fact that they have a head, and so the tax cannot be avoided by changes in behaviour and thus is truly a lump sum tax without substitution effects. Despite the efficiency argument in favour of such a tax, the opposition to the tax was considerable and ultimately led to Thatcher leaving office.

The poll tax example illustrates why lump sum taxes are rarely considered in the real world and why, as a result, almost all real-world taxes are inefficient to some degree. Because they must be based on something other than changeable behaviour, lump sum taxes usually offend our sense of fairness. It does not seem fair to send everyone the same tax bill, neither does it seem right to base people's tax payments on other unchangeable characteristics such as age, race, sex or other genetic traits. Something like that is usually necessary in order for a tax not to give rise to substitution effects and the resulting inefficiencies. Sometimes the 'bucket' does not leak, but we don't like it for other reasons.

While our analysis thus suggests that virtually any tax we might advocate is inefficient and produces dead-weight loss, it also suggests that different types of taxes will have different magnitudes of deadweight losses depending on just how big the substitution effects – the leaks in the 'bucket' – are that these taxes produce. We will say more about how this might impact tax policy at the end of the next section and again in later chapters.

10A.4 Deadweight Loss Measured on $MWTP$ Curves

We will now show that deadweight loss can be measured along $MWTP$ and, when tastes are quasilinear, own-price demand curves. We will do this within the context of the example of a housing tax discussed in the previous section.

10A.4.1 T, L and Deadweight Loss on $MWTP$ Curves The top part of panel (a) in Graph 10.8 is identical to panel (b) of Graph 10.6 and derives, within the consumer diagram, the tax payment T made by a consumer with indifference curve u^A, the largest possible lump sum tax payment L the consumer would have been willing to make to not incur the tax on housing, and the deadweight loss $DWL = (L - T)$ from the tax on housing. The lower part of panel (a) of Graph 10.8 derives the $MWTP$ curve that corresponds to the indifference curve that includes bundle A. This is done by the same process as the derivation of $MWTP$ in Graph 10.2, except that we are now deriving the $MWTP$ curve corresponding to the optimal indifference curve at the higher tax-inclusive price.

Graph 10.8 Translating DWL to $MWTP$ Curves

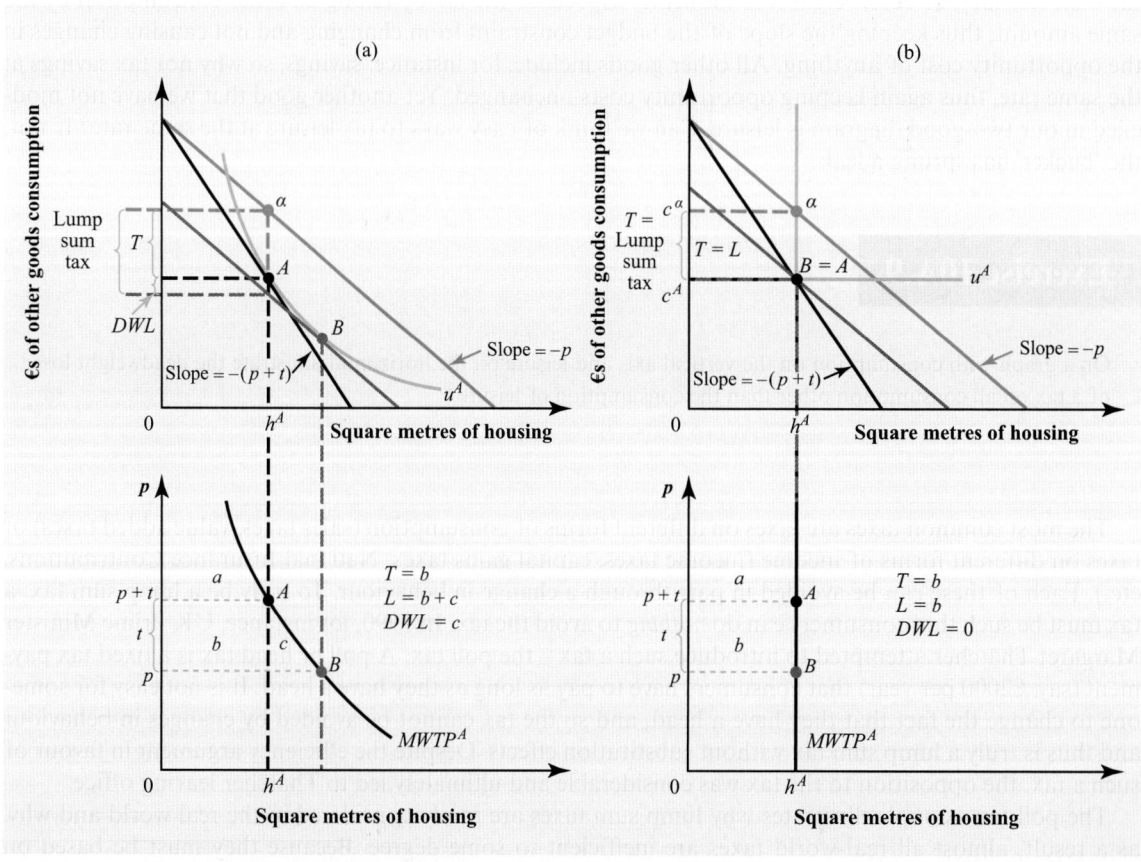

We can now identify the distances T, L and $(L - T)$ from the top graph as areas on the lower graph by carefully thinking about what A and B represent on the lower graph. Point A represents the actual housing consumption this consumer undertakes after a housing tax has been implemented. The difference between the price level $(p + t)$ and the price level p on the vertical axis is just t, or the per square metre tax rate on housing paid by the consumer. Thus, if we multiply the tax paid per square metre of housing t by the square metreage of housing (h^A) consumed under the tax, we get the total tax payment this consumer makes under the housing tax. Area (b) in the lower part of panel (a) of Graph 10.8 is exactly that, which implies that area (b) is equal to distance T in the top graph.

We know that area (a) is equal to the consumer surplus received in the housing market after the consumer paid the tax-inclusive price $(p + t)$ for housing and chose to consume h^A square metres of housing. Similarly, the area $(a + b + c)$ is the consumer surplus the consumer would attain in the housing market if they faced the budget constraint that makes bundle B optimal in the top part of the graph; $(a + b + c)$ is the consumer surplus in the housing market when the consumer pays the before-tax price (p) for housing but also pays the lump sum tax L that produces the relevant budget constraint in the top graph.

Consumer surplus is thus greater at point B than it is at point A. We also know that the consumer is equally happy at A and B; after all, both these points correspond to bundles on the same indifference curve u^A. That the reason the consumer gets more consumer surplus at point B than at point A but is equally happy is that the consumer had to pay a lump sum tax at point B but not at point A. The consumer surplus at point A already takes into account the fact that the consumer is paying a tax on housing that raised the price of housing to $(p + t)$, while the consumer surplus at point B does not reflect any tax payments. Since the consumer is equally happy at the two points but gets a higher consumer surplus at point B than at point A, it must logically be true that the lump sum tax they are implicitly paying to get to point B is the difference between the two consumer surpluses, that is, $(b + c)$. Thus, the distance L in the top panel of the graph is equal to the area $(b + c)$ in the lower panel. Since T is equal to area (b), and since the deadweight loss is the difference between L and T, the area (c) is the deadweight loss from the tax.

10A.4.2 Substitution Effects Once Again We have already shown in Section 10A.3.3 that the size of the deadweight loss is closely related to the size of the substitution effects that are produced by the imposition of a tax. We can see the same to be true once again when we measure deadweight loss on $MWTP$ curves.

Panel (b) of Graph 10.8 repeats the analysis in panel (a) with the exception that we now assume the consumer's tastes do not give rise to substitution effects; that is, they can be represented by indifference curves that treat housing and other goods as perfect complements. It begins with a top panel identical to what we already derived in panel (a) of Graph 10.7, illustrating that $T = L$ and thus there is no deadweight loss from a tax on housing. The lower part of panel (b) of Graph 10.8 illustrates how the $MWTP$ curve corresponding to the indifference curve u^A in the top panel is a vertical line: A and B happen at different prices but at the same quantities because of the absence of substitution effects that moved B to the right of A in panel (a) of Graph 10.8. As a result, area (c) in panel (a) disappears and with it the deadweight loss. By comparing the lower panels in Graph 10.8, we can again see how deadweight losses get larger the further B lies to the right of A on the $MWTP$ curve. The only force that moves B away from A is the substitution effect in the top panel of the graphs.

10A.4.3 Measuring Deadweight Loss on Demand Curves As noted, introductory analysis of consumer surplus tends to implicitly assume that underlying tastes are quasilinear, which represents the only case under which it is truly legitimate to use own-price demand curves to measure consumer welfare and deadweight loss. We can approximate the deadweight loss on own-price demand curves as long as we think income effects are small, which is the same as saying that tastes are close to quasilinear. In cases where income effects are likely to be large, it will be misleading to use the own-price demand curve to approximate consumer surplus and deadweight loss.

In Graph 10.9, we extend the lower part of panel (a) of Graph 10.8 slightly by adding a point C that represents the level of housing consumption if the consumer faced neither a housing tax nor a lump sum tax. Panel (a) does this for the case where housing is a normal good, panel (b) does it for the case where housing is a quasilinear good, and panel (c) does it for the unlikely case where housing is an inferior good.

Graph 10.9 *DWL* from Taxation for Different Types of Goods

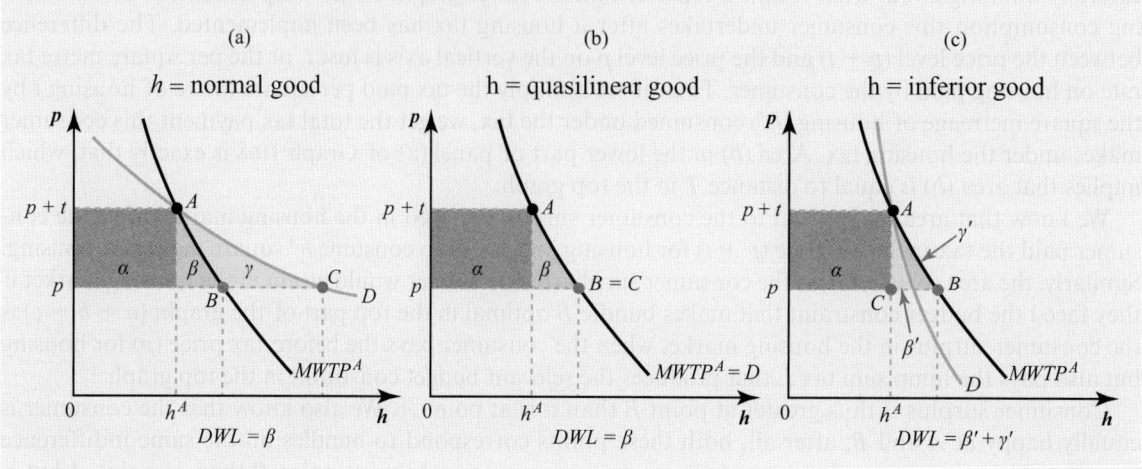

Exercise 10A.10

Using panel (a) of Graph 10.8, verify that the relationship between own-price demand and *MWTP* is as depicted in panels (a) to (c) of Graph 10.9.

It is now possible to read on these graphs whether a measurement of *DWL* approximated on own-price demand curves would over- or understate the true *DWL* from the tax on housing. There is no difference between using the *MWTP* and using the demand curve to measure deadweight loss when housing is a quasilinear good (panel (b) of Graph 10.9). In this case, the demand curve is exactly equal to the *MWTP* curve, and either can be used for consumer welfare analysis. When housing is a normal good, however, a *DWL* measurement on the demand curve will *overstate* the true *DWL* by γ in panel (a) of Graph 10.9, and when housing is an inferior good, it will *understate* it by γ' in panel (c) of Graph 10.9. We will see in Chapter 19 that the problem of using uncompensated curves to approximate *DWL* will become much more severe when we discuss taxes on labour or capital, where wealth effects usually mask the very substitution effects that lie at the heart of tax inefficiency.

10A.4.4 Geometric Increases in Deadweight Loss and the Case for Broad Tax Bases One lesson for tax policy that has emerged from our analysis of taxes and deadweight loss is that taxes give rise to greater deadweight losses the more they give rise to substitution effects. Now that we know how to measure *DWL* along *MWTP* curves, we are ready to derive a second lesson: As tax rates on any given good increase, *DWL* from the tax increases substantially faster; that is, as tax rates increase, the leak in our 'bucket' grows at an increasing rate.

We can see the intuition behind this result in our housing tax example in which we assume that tastes for housing are quasilinear, and the *MWTP* curve is therefore equal to the own-price demand curve. Graph 10.10 depicts a special case of this where the demand and *MWTP* curve is linear. Tax-inclusive housing prices for five different levels of housing taxes are indicated on the vertical axis, from no tax (p) going through tax increases starting with t, $2t$, $3t$ and finally $4t$. For each level of the housing tax, we can identify the corresponding *DWL*. For instance, when the tax rate is t, the *DWL* is a. When it is $2t$, the *DWL* becomes ($a + b + c + d$). Since each letter corresponds to a triangle with the same area, we can conclude that *doubling the tax led to a quadrupling of the DWL*. When the tax is raised to $3t$, the deadweight loss becomes ($a + b + c + d + e + f + g + h + i$). Thus, *multiplying the tax rate by 3 leads to a DWL 9 times as large.* You can verify for yourself that multiplying the tax rate by 4 leads to a *DWL* 16 times as great. While this is a special case since we assumed quasilinear tastes and linear demand curves, the example has led tax economists to use the rule of thumb that *multiplying tax rates by a factor of x leads to an increase of DWL by a factor of approximately x^2!* As tax rates go up linearly, *DWL* increases geometrically.

Graph 10.10 Geometrically Increasing *DWL* When Tastes Are Quasilinear and Demand Is Linear

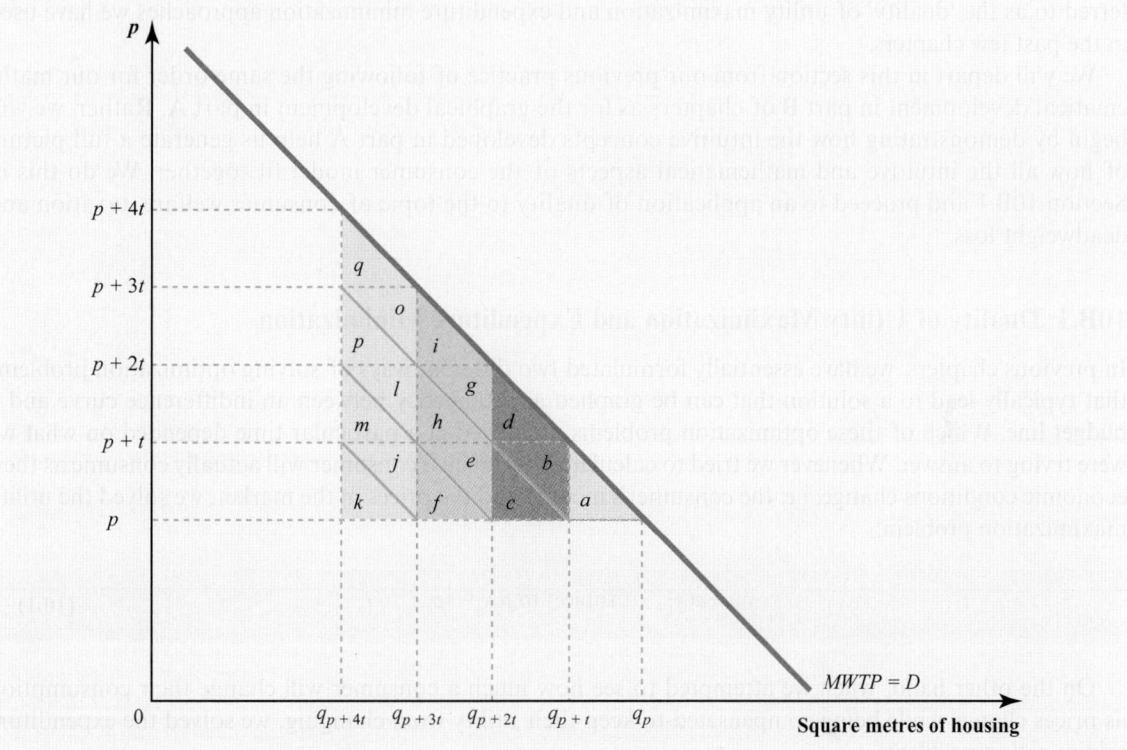

This has led to the commonly given advice to policy makers that *it is better from an efficiency perspective to have low tax rates on large tax bases rather than high tax rates on small tax bases.* The *tax base* is the set of goods that are taxed, whereas the tax rate is the rate at which goods are taxed. Suppose, for instance, that there are two markets, single-family housing and flats, and suppose that consumer tastes in both markets lead to exactly the same demand and *MWTP* curves and that these are furthermore as depicted in Graph 10.10. Assume a policy maker has to choose between two tax proposals. One imposes a tax of 2*t* on the single-family housing market and no tax on the market for flats; the other imposes a tax of *t* on both markets. The first proposal imposes a high tax rate (2*t*) on a small base (single-family housing), and the second proposal imposes a low tax rate (*t*) on a large tax base (single-family and the market for flats). The *DWL* of the first proposal is (*a* + *b* + *c* + *d*) while the *DWL* from the second proposal is (*a* + *a*), which is half the *DWL* of the first proposal. Thus, *because DWL goes up geometrically as tax rates rise, imposing low tax rates on broader bases typically results in less DWL.*

Exercise 10A.11

The two proposals also result in different levels of tax revenue. Which proposal actually results in higher revenue for the government? Does this strengthen or weaken the policy proposal to broaden the base and lower the rates?

| 10B | The Mathematics of Consumer Welfare and Duality |

The mathematical generalization of consumer welfare serves two purposes. First, it allows us to see how the mathematics of the consumer model can help us generalize the graphical analysis and the intuitions that emerge from it. Second, it provides us with a forum in which to bring together all the mathematical techniques introduced so far to paint a full picture of consumer theory, a picture that is commonly referred to as the 'duality' of utility maximization and expenditure minimization approaches we have used in the past few chapters.

We will depart in this section from our previous practice of following the same order for our mathematical development in part B of chapters as for the graphical development in part A. Rather, we will begin by demonstrating how the intuitive concepts developed in part A help us generate a full picture of how all the intuitive and mathematical aspects of the consumer model fit together. We do this in Section 10B.1 and proceed to an application of duality to the topic of consumer welfare, taxation and deadweight loss.

10B.1 Duality of Utility Maximization and Expenditure Minimization

In previous chapters, we have essentially formulated two different ways of solving optimization problems that typically lead to a solution that can be graphed as a tangency between an indifference curve and a budget line. Which of these optimization problems we solved at a particular time depended on what we were trying to answer. Whenever we tried to calculate how much a consumer will actually consume as their economic conditions change, i.e. the consumer's income and the prices in the market, we solved the utility maximization problem:

$$\max_{x_1,x_2} u(x_1, x_2) \text{ subject to } p_1x_1 + p_2x_2 = I. \tag{10.1}$$

On the other hand, when we attempted to see how much a consumer will change their consumption as prices change while being compensated to keep their utility from changing, we solved the expenditure minimization problem:

$$\min_{x_1,x_2} E = p_1x_1 + p_2x_2 \text{ subject to } u(x_1, x_2) = u \tag{10.2}$$

that gave us the least expenditure necessary for the consumer to reach the same indifference curve u as prices change.

We showed in Chapter 9 how the solution to problem (10.1) can be written as the uncompensated *demand functions:*

$$x_1 = x_1(p_1, p_2, I) \text{ and } x_2 = x_2(p_1, p_2, I) \tag{10.3}$$

and how inverse slices of these demand functions are related to the various demand curves we derived graphically. Now consider the solution to problem (10.2), which can be written as:

$$x_1 = h_1(p_1, p_2, u) \quad \text{and} \quad x_2 = h_2(p_1, p_2, u). \tag{10.4}$$

These functions tell us, for any set of prices, how much a consumer will consume of each good *assuming that the consumer is given just enough money to be able to reach utility level u*. For this reason, the functions given in expression (10.4) are often referred to as *compensated demand functions*. They are also known as *Hicksian demand functions* after the economist John Hicks whose work originally identified them, and it is in his honour that we denote the functions in expression (10.4) with '*h*' to distinguish them from the uncompensated demand functions in expression (10.3).

10B.1.1 Compensated or Hicksian Demand and *MWTP* In Graph 10.2, we demonstrated how we can derive *MWTP* curves by tracing out the quantity of a good that a consumer would consume at different prices *assuming the consumer gets sufficient compensation to always reach the same indifference curve*. This is exactly what problem (10.2) formalizes mathematically, and the compensated demand functions in expression (10.4) are therefore a generalization of the *MWTP* curve derived in Graph 10.2.

Note that *MWTP* curves are sometimes referred to as compensated demand curves. More precisely, note that compensated demand functions are functions of prices and utility. Consider the function $h_1(p_1,p_2',u^A)$ with p_2' set to 1 as we do if good x_2 represents other consumption denominated in euros, and utility is fixed at the quantity associated with indifference curve u^A. With the other arguments of the function held fixed, this leaves a function of only p_1, a function that tells us how the consumer will change their consumption of x_1 as p_1 changes, assuming the consumer is compensated sufficiently to permit them to reach indifference curve u^A. The inverse of this function is what is derived graphically in the lower panel of Graph 10.2, the *MWTP* curve associated with the indifference curve u^A. The fact that there exist many *MWTP* curves as demonstrated in panel (b) of Graph 10.4, one corresponding to each indifference curve, falls straight out of the underlying mathematics. As different utility levels are substituted into the compensated demand function instead of u^A, different *MWTP* or compensated demand curves emerge.

Exercise 10B.1

In panel (b) of Graph 10.5, we illustrated that *MWTP* curves and own-price demand curves are the same when tastes are quasilinear. Suppose tastes can be modelled with the quasilinear utility function $u(x,x) = \alpha \ln x + x$. Verify a generalization of the intuition from the graph that demand functions and compensated demand functions are identical for x_1 in this case.

10B.1.2 Linking Indirect Utility and Expenditure Functions in the Duality Picture Once we have solved for demand functions using utility maximization, and compensated demand functions using expenditure minimization, we can formally define two further functions that we have already used in previous chapters without naming them: the *indirect utility function*, which tells us for any set of economic circumstances, i.e. prices and income, how much utility the consumer will achieve if they do the best they can; and the *expenditure function*, which tells us for any price and utility level how big a money budget is required for the consumer to reach that utility level.

To find the utility level a consumer can attain under different economic circumstances, we have to substitute the demand functions which tell us how much the consumer will consume of each of the goods under different circumstances into the utility function. The indirect utility function $V(p_1,p_2,I)$ can be written as:

$$V(p_1, p_2, I) = u(x_1(p_1, p_2, I), x_2(p_1, p_2, I)). \tag{10.5}$$

Similarly, the money required to reach a particular utility level u under different prices is found by multiplying the compensated demands for the goods, which tell us how much of each good a person will consume if the person always gets just enough money to reach the utility level u, by the prices and adding them up; that is, the expenditure function $E(p_1, p_2, u)$ can be written as:

$$E(p_1, p_2, u) = p_1 h_1(p_1, p_2, u) + p_2 h_2(p_1, p_2, u). \tag{10.6}$$

Consider, for example, the case of a Cobb–Douglas utility function $u(x_1, x_2) = x_1^\alpha x_2^{(1-\alpha)}$. The utility maximization and expenditure minimization problems yield demand functions:

$$x_1(p_1, p_2, I) = \frac{\alpha I}{p_1} \text{ and } x_2(p_1, p_2, I) = \frac{(1-\alpha)I}{p_2} \tag{10.7}$$

and compensated demand functions:

$$h_1(p_1, p_2, u) = \left(\frac{\alpha p_2}{(1-\alpha)p_1}\right)^{(1-\alpha)} u$$

$$h_2(p_1, p_2, u) = \left(\frac{(1-\alpha)p_1}{\alpha p_2}\right)^{\alpha} u. \tag{10.8}$$

Exercise 10B.2

Verify the solutions given in equations (10.8).

Substituting (10.7) into the Cobb–Douglas utility function, we get the indirect utility function:

$$V(p_1, p_2, I) = \frac{I\alpha^\alpha(1-\alpha)^{(1-\alpha)}}{p_1^\alpha p_2^{(1-\alpha)}}. \tag{10.9}$$

and multiplying the equations in (10.8) by the relevant prices and adding, we get the expenditure function:

$$E(p_1, p_2, u) = \frac{u p_1^\alpha p_2^{(1-\alpha)}}{\alpha^\alpha(1-\alpha)^{(1-\alpha)}}. \tag{10.10}$$

Exercise 10B.3

Verify the solutions given in equations (10.9) and (10.10).

Notice the following: If we set the left-hand side of (10.9) equal to u and solve for I, we get the right-hand side of (10.10). Similarly, if we set the left-hand side of (10.10) equal to I and solve for u, we get the right-hand side of (10.9). That is because *the indirect utility function is the inverse of the expenditure function and vice versa*. Graph 10.11 shows the intuition behind this by graphing first the indirect utility as a function of income when $p_1 = 4$, $p_2 = 1$ and $\alpha = 0.5$, and graphing the expenditure function evaluated at the same prices and the same α as a function of utility. The only difference between the two graphs is that we have inverted the first graph to get the second, switching the utility and euro axes in the process.

Other linkages between the utility maximization and the expenditure minimization results can also be identified and should make intuitive sense once you have fully internalized what these functions represent. For instance, suppose we substitute the expenditure function for the income variable I in demand functions. Rather than letting income be fixed, we have constructed a new demand function that always provides the consumer with sufficient income to reach utility level u – precisely the definition of a compensated demand function. As a result, we can establish the following logical relationship:

$$x_i(p_1, p_2, E(p_1, p_2, u)) = h_i(p_1, p_2, u). \tag{10.11}$$

Graph 10.11 Indirect Utility and Expenditure Function

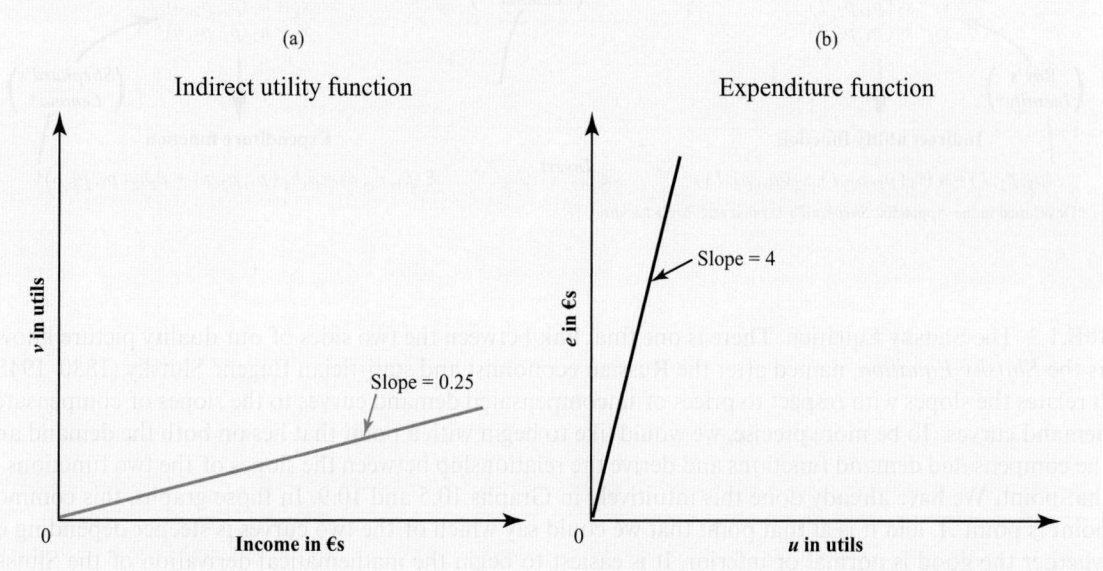

Similarly, suppose we substitute the indirect utility function for the utility term u in compensated demands. Rather than letting utility be fixed, the compensated demand function would give us the optimal consumption level assuming the consumer has enough income to reach the level of utility they would reach with just income I. In other words, the compensated demand function would tell us the optimal bundle assuming the consumer's income rather than utility is fixed, which is the definition of a regular or uncompensated demand function:

$$h_i(p_1, p_2, V(p_1, p_2, I)) = x_i(p_1, p_2, I). \tag{10.12}$$

Exercise 10B.4

Verify that (10.11) and (10.12) are true for the functions that emerge from utility maximization and expenditure minimization when tastes can be modelled by the Cobb–Douglas function $u(x_1, x_2) = x_1^\alpha x_2^{(1-\alpha)}$.

Graph 10.12 summarizes the duality picture as we have developed it in this section, and indicates through arrows the linkages between the utility maximization and expenditure minimization problems that we have developed thus far. The arrows labelled 'Roy's Identity' and 'Shephard's Lemma' are developed in the appendix, and the dotted line labelled 'Slutsky Equation' is developed next.

Graph 10.12 'Duality' of Utility Maximization and Expenditure Minimization

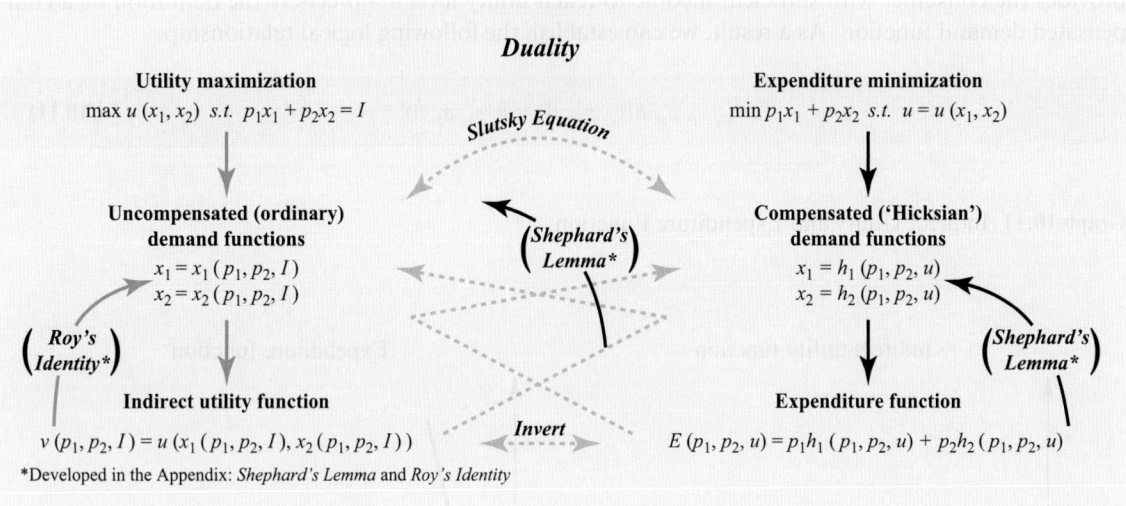

*Developed in the Appendix: *Shephard's Lemma* and *Roy's Identity*

10B.1.3 The Slutsky Equation There is one final link between the two sides of our duality picture known as the *Slutsky Equation*, named after the Russian economist and statistician Eugene Slutsky (1880–1948). It relates the slopes with respect to prices of uncompensated demand curves to the slopes of compensated demand curves. To be more precise, we would like to begin with a point that lies on both the demand and the compensated demand functions and derive the relationship between the slopes of the two functions at that point. We have already done this intuitively in Graphs 10.5 and 10.9. In those graphs, this common point is point A, and it is at that point that we could say which of the two curves is steeper depending on whether the good is normal or inferior. It is easiest to begin the mathematical derivation of the Slutsky Equation with expression (10.11), which already relates demand functions to compensated demand functions but does not relate their slopes to one another. To identify the relationship of the slopes, we take the partial derivative with respect to one of the prices of each side of equation (10.11). This requires us to invoke the chain rule from calculus since the function on the left-hand side contains the expenditure function E that is itself a function of prices:

$$\frac{\partial x_i}{\partial p_j} + \left(\frac{\partial x_i}{\partial E}\right)\left(\frac{\partial E}{\partial p_j}\right) = \frac{\partial h_i}{\partial p_j}. \tag{10.13}$$

Rearranging terms and replacing the E term in $(\partial x_i/\partial E)$ with I, since expenditure is the same as income in the consumer model, we can write this equation as:

$$\frac{\partial x_i}{\partial p_j} = \frac{\partial h_i}{\partial p_j} - \left(\frac{\partial x_i}{\partial I}\right)\left(\frac{\partial E}{\partial p_j}\right). \tag{10.14}$$

Equation (10.14) is written in terms of good x_i and price p_j. To help us investigate precisely how this equation relates to the intuitions we have developed so far, suppose that we focus on good x_1 and a change in p_1. Equation (10.14) can be written as:

$$\frac{\partial x_1}{\partial p_1} = \frac{\partial h_1}{\partial p_1} - \left(\frac{\partial x_1}{\partial I}\right)\left(\frac{\partial E}{\partial p_1}\right). \tag{10.15}$$

The left-hand side of equation (10.15) is the change in the actual quantity demanded of good x_1 when p_1 changes marginally. This is analogous to the move from A to C in Graphs 10.5 and 10.8, although the calculus here corresponds to marginal or very small changes. The first term on the right-hand side of equation (10.15) is the change in the quantity of x_1 demanded assuming the consumer has been compensated to keep their utility constant. It is analogous to the move from A to B in Graphs 10.5 and 10.9, or the substitution effect. This must mean that the final term in equation (10.15) is analogous to the move from B to C in Graphs 10.5 and 10.9, or the income effect. Indeed, that is precisely what the final term suggests: $(\partial x_1/\partial I)$ is the change in the quantity of x_1 demanded when income changes, and $(\partial E/\partial p_1)$ is the size of the required compensation given that p_1 changes.

Note that $\partial h_1/\partial p_1 < 0$; when price increases; the substitution effect always suggests the consumer will purchase less of that good when they are compensated. If we know that a consumer's tastes are quasilinear in x_1; that is, x_1 is borderline between a normal and an inferior good, this implies that consumption of x_1 does not change as income changes, or $\partial x_1/\partial xI = 0$, reducing equation (10.15) to:

$$\frac{\partial x_1}{\partial p_1} = \frac{\partial h_1}{\partial p_1}. \qquad (10.16)$$

This is what is illustrated intuitively in panel (b) of Graph 10.5, where we demonstrated that demand curves and $MWTP$ or compensated demand curves are the same for quasilinear goods. The reason for this is that the income effect disappears in this special case, leaving us with only the substitution effect.

Suppose we knew instead that x_1 was a normal good. In that case, $\partial x_1/\partial I > 0$. Whenever the price of a good we are consuming goes up, it must be true that the expenditure required to reach the same utility level increases, thus $\partial E/\partial p_1 > 0$. Together, these two statements imply that the second term in equation (10.15) is negative – two positive terms multiplied by each other and preceded by a negative sign. Thus, when x_1 is a normal good, the quantity demanded falls first because of the substitution effect ($\partial h_1/\partial p_1 < 0$) and because of the income effect ($-(\partial x_1/\partial I)(\partial E/\partial p_1) < 0$). When x_1 is an inferior good, on the other hand, $\partial x_1/\partial I < 0$, which implies that the second term on the right-hand side of equation (10.15) is positive. Thus, income and substitution effects point in opposite directions. All this reflects what has been concluded in our graphs of consumer choices.

10B.1.4 Graphs and Inverse Graphs It can be confusing when looking at a graph like the lower panel of Graph 10.5 and attempting to relate the slopes of the demand and $MWTP$ curves in the graph to the slopes represented by partial derivatives in equation (10.15). For instance, suppose that x_1 is a normal good. It appears that the slope of the demand curve ($\partial x_1/\partial p_1$) is negative because of the negative slope of the $MWTP$ curve ($\partial h_1/\partial p_1$) and because of an additional negative component implicit in the second term of equation (10.15), the income effect. This would mean that the slope of the demand curve at any point is a negative number that is larger in absolute value than the slope of the $MWTP$ curve at that same point. It means that the demand curve is downward sloping and steeper than the $MWTP$ curve, which is also downward sloping. Panel (a) of Graph 10.5 suggests the opposite, that the demand curve is downward sloping and *shallower* than the $MWTP$ curve for a normal good.

The reason for the appearance of a discrepancy between the intuition developed in panel (a) and the maths implicit in equation (10.15) can be found in the fact that economists graph demand curves as slices of *inverse* demand functions. Thus, the slopes derived from the mathematics represent the inverse of the slopes derived in our graphs. Taking an inverse of a slope does not change the sign of that slope, i.e. downward-sloping curves remain downward sloping, but it does change whether one curve is relatively steeper than the other, i.e. steep slopes become shallow slopes and vice versa. Graph 10.13 illustrates this relationship by plotting demand curves as inverse slices of demand functions in panel (a), which illustrate demand and $MWTP$ curves as depicted in Graph 10.9, and as simple slices of the same demand functions with the axes reversed in panel (b). The arrows in each graph begin with the demand curve representing a normal good and end with the demand curve representing a Giffen good. The slopes in the Slutsky Equation correspond to the slopes in the second graph.

Graph 10.13 Inverse Demand and Demand for Different Types of Goods

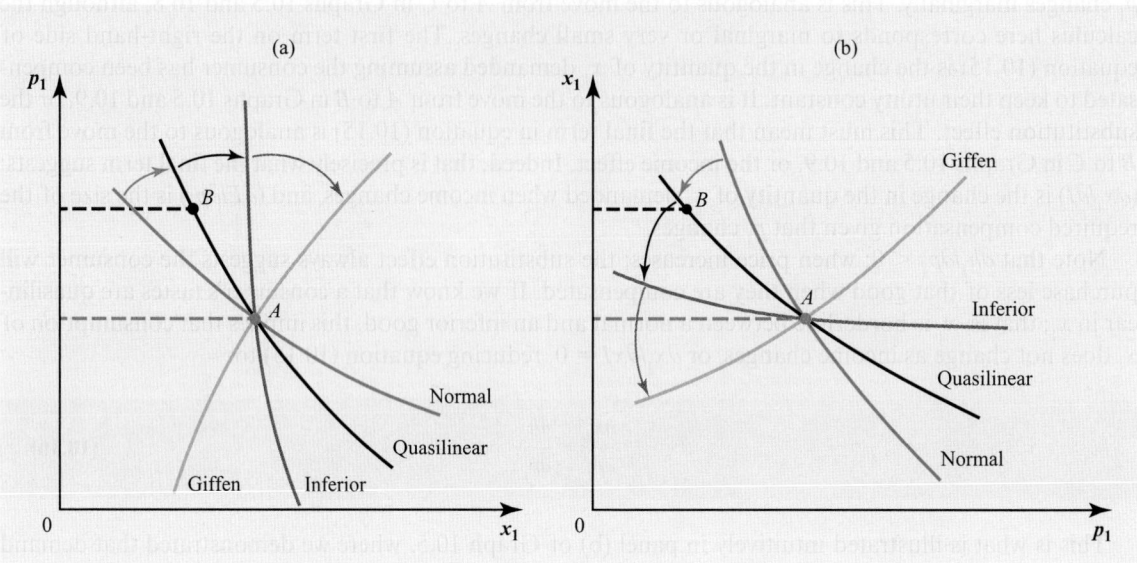

10B.2 Taxes, Deadweight Losses and Consumer Welfare

As suggested in Section 10A, concepts like consumer surplus and deadweight loss can be read off as distances in the consumer diagram or as areas below $MWTP$ curves. Areas under curves can be calculated mathematically as integrals; this section uses the same example of a housing tax discussed throughout Section A to demonstrate how the relevant concepts can be calculated without any additional calculus and using the various parts of our duality picture. The appendix explains how areas along compensated demand curves correspond to distances in the consumer diagram.

10B.2.1 Using Duality Concepts to Calculate Deadweight Loss We concluded in Section 10A.3 that taxes are inefficient because of substitution effects. We furthermore defined the size of the inefficiency through a measure of deadweight loss – the difference between actual tax revenue T and the tax revenue L that could have been raised, without making the consumer worse off, had a lump sum tax been imposed instead.

Suppose that x_1 represents square metres of housing, and t is the tax rate paid by consumers of housing. The tax revenue T raised from a consumer is equal to the tax rate t times the square metreage $x_1(p_1 + t, p_2, I)$ of housing consumed when the tax is in place, where x_1 is the demand function for housing and $(p_1 + t)$ is the price of housing faced by consumers under the housing tax. Put in terms of the mathematical functions in our duality picture:

$$T = tx_1(p_1 + t_1, p_2, I). \tag{10.17}$$

The lump sum tax we could have imposed instead without making the consumer worse off is slightly more challenging to calculate and easiest derived using our graphical intuition from panel (b) of Graph 10.6. First, we have to determine the value (u^A) associated with the indifference curve the consumer ends up on under the housing tax. This is the utility the consumer receives when they have income I and faces the tax-inclusive price $(p_1 + t)$ for housing. The indirect utility function evaluated at the relevant prices and income gives us precisely that utility level; u^A in panel (b) of Graph 10.6 is equivalent to $V(p_1 + t, p_2, I)$.

Next, we have to determine the minimum expenditure or income necessary for the consumer to reach their after-tax utility level $V(p_1 + t, p_2, I)$ if the price of housing is p_1 instead of $(p_1 + t)$. This is given by the expenditure function evaluated at the relevant prices and utility level; that is, $E(p_1, p_2, u^A)$ or

$E(p_1, p_2, V(p_1 + t, p_2, I))$. The lump sum tax we could have taken from the consumer is the difference between the income they start out with and this expenditure level; that is:

$$L = I - E(p_1, p_2, V(p_1 + t, p_2, I)). \tag{10.18}$$

If the underlying utility function is $u(x_1, x_2) = x_1^\alpha x_2^{(1-\alpha)}$, for instance, we calculated demand, compensated demand, indirect utility and expenditure functions in Section 10B.1.2 in equations (10.7) to (10.10). Using these and gathering terms, we can get the following expressions for T and L:

$$T = \frac{t\alpha I}{p_1 + t}$$
$$L = I - I\left(\frac{p_1}{p_1 + t}\right)^\alpha = I\left[1 - \left(\frac{p_1}{p_1 + t}\right)^\alpha\right]. \tag{10.19}$$

Exercise 10B.5

Verify that the equations in (10.19) are correct for the Cobb–Douglas utility function $u(x_1, x_2) = x_1^\alpha x_2^{(1-\alpha)}$.

Using these equations and knowing that $DWL = L - T$, we could calculate the deadweight losses under a variety of taste parameters (α), prices and incomes, and for a variety of possible tax rates. For instance, suppose the rental price of a square metre of housing is €10; the price of other goods is, by definition, €1; the taste parameter α is 0.25; and the housing tax raises the price of housing by €2.50. A consumer whose income is €100 000 will reduce their consumption of housing from 2500 square metres to 2000 square metres, and, while the consumer pays a total housing tax of €5000, they would have been willing to pay €5425.84 in a lump sum tax to avoid the housing tax. Thus, the tax gives rise to a deadweight loss of roughly €426, or roughly 8.5 per cent of total tax revenue from the housing tax; €426 of wealth is lost in society because of the substitution effect of the housing tax for this one consumer.

Exercise 10B.6

Verify that the numbers calculated in the previous paragraph are correct.

10B.2.2 Deadweight Loss and Substitution Effects All our work in Section 10A suggested that deadweight losses from taxation arise from substitution effects, and when tastes are such that substitution effects do not arise, as in panel (b) of Graph 10.8, there is no deadweight loss from taxation. With the underlying mathematics developed, we can now see how this intuition plays out as elasticities of substitution, and thus substitution effects, get larger.

Suppose, for instance, that tastes can be summarized by the CES utility function:

$$u(x_1, x_2) = (\alpha x_1^{-\rho} + (1 - \alpha)x_2^{-\rho})^{1/\rho}, \tag{10.20}$$

where the elasticity of substitution σ, as introduced in Chapter 5, is given by $1/(1 + \rho)$. Suppose further that, as in our example, the rental price of a square metre of housing is €10, the price of other goods is by definition €1, and income is €100 000. Now we can consider the impact of a tax that raises the price of housing from €10 to €12.50 under different assumptions about the underlying elasticity of substitution σ.

Table 10.1 does precisely that, with the column labelled σ varying the elasticity of substitution and with α in the right-most column set to ensure that in each case the consumer rents 2500 square metres of housing in the absence of a tax. The third column in the table indicates the square metreage consumed after the imposition of the tax, and the remaining columns give the resulting values for tax revenue (T), a utility-equivalent lump sum tax (L), the resulting deadweight loss (DWL), and the deadweight loss as a fraction of tax revenue (DWL/T).

Table 10.1 Housing Taxes and the Elasticity of Substitution

			Effects of Housing Taxes as the Elasticity of Substitution Rises				
σ	$x(p_1, ...)$	$x(p_1 + t,...)$	T	L	DWL	DWL/T	α
0.50	2500	2172	€5430	€5650	€220	0.041	0.01098900
0.75	2500	2085	€5212	€5537	€325	0.062	0.09688500
1.00	2500	2000	€5000	€5426	€426	0.085	0.25000000
1.25	2500	1917	€4794	€5316	€523	0.109	0.39690600
1.50	2500	1837	€4593	€5209	€616	0.134	0.50878000
1.75	2500	1760	€4399	€5103	€705	0.160	0.58881600
2.00	2500	1684	€4211	€5000	€789	0.188	0.64611070
2.50	2500	1541	€3852	€4799	€947	0.246	0.71952500
3.00	2500	1407	€3516	€4606	€1090	0.310	0.76293800
4.00	2500	1166	€2916	€4244	€1329	0.456	0.81034997
5.00	2500	961	€2403	€3914	€1511	0.629	0.83511837
7.50	2500	580	€1450	€3215	€1766	1.218	0.86402047
10.00	2500	343	€856	€2674	€1817	2.122	0.87679951

The figures in the table provide potential magnitudes for the distortionary effects of a relatively modest tax on housing. When the elasticity of substitution is low, so is the deadweight loss, but the deadweight loss can rise dramatically as the elasticity of substitution and thus the substitution effect increases. For the case of housing, empirical estimates of likely elasticities of substitution lie around 1, suggesting that our Cobb–Douglas example in the previous section, which is equivalent to the CES utility example with $\sigma = 1$, may be most relevant. Other goods that we commonly tax, however, may have significantly higher or lower elasticities of substitution.

10B.2.3 Deadweight Loss Rising Faster Than Tax Rates A second lesson from our work in Section 10A relates to the change in DWL as tax rates increase. We can now use the Cobb–Douglas example where $\sigma = 1$, to calculate the changing impact of housing tax as the tax increases. Table 10.2 presents the impact of a tax that raises the price of housing from 10 to $(10 + t)$ as t increases. Notice that the DWL of the tax increases much faster than the tax itself, almost quadrupling, for instance, when the tax is doubled from 0.5 to 1.0 and increasing almost ninefold when the tax is tripled from 0.5 to 1.5. This is in line with the rule of thumb we developed when we used a linear demand curve in Graph 10.10 to conclude that, as the level of a tax is increased by a factor of x, the DWL from the tax increases by a factor of x^2. The increase in DWL in Table 10.2 is slightly below what this rule of thumb predicts because compensated demand curves derived from Cobb–Douglas tastes contain some curvature that is not accounted for in Graph 10.10.

In the last column of Table 10.2, the geometric growth in DWL results in a steady increase of DWL as a fraction of tax revenue. This is a common measure of just how inefficient a particular tax is, because it tells us how much of the revenue that is raised society has lost in wealth along the way.

			Effects of Housing Taxes as Tax Rate Increases			
t	$x_1(p_1, \ldots)$	$x_1(p_1, +t, \ldots)$	T	L	DWL	DWL/T
0.50	2500	2381	€1 190	€1 212	€22	0.018
1.00	2500	2273	€2 272	€2 355	€82	0.036
1.50	2500	2174	€3 261	€3 434	€173	0.053
2.00	2500	2083	€4 167	€4 456	€289	0.069
2.50	2500	2000	€5 000	€5 426	€426	0.085
3.00	2500	1923	€5 769	€6 349	€579	0.101
4.00	2500	1786	€7 143	€8 068	€925	0.130
5.00	2500	1667	€8 333	€9 640	€1 306	0.157
10.00	2500	1250	€12 500	€15 910	€3 410	0.273
25.00	2500	714	€17 857	€26 889	€9 032	0.506
50.00	2500	417	€20 833	€36 106	€15 272	0.733
100.00	2500	227	€22 727	€45 090	€22 363	0.984

Table 10.2 Housing Tax Increases Under Cobb–Douglas Tastes (with $\alpha = 0.25$)

Appendix	Shephard's Lemma and Roy's Identity

Two further relationships indicated in parentheses in the duality picture of Graph 10.12 are frequently highlighted in more advanced treatments of duality and deserve some supplemental treatment here. The first and more important of these is known as *Shephard's Lemma* which states:

$$\frac{\partial E(p_1, p_2, u)}{\partial p_i} = h_i(p_1, p_2, u). \tag{10.21}$$

This relationship, while expressed for the two-good case here, holds more generally for the n-good case as well. The same is true for *Roy's Identity*, which states:

$$-\frac{\partial V(p_1, p_2, I)/\partial p_i}{\partial V(p_1, p_2, I)/\partial I} = x_i(p_1, p_2, I). \tag{10.22}$$

Both of these results are a direct application of the *Envelope Theorem* from mathematics. We will briefly state this theorem and apply it to derive Shephard's Lemma and Roy's Identity. Shephard's Lemma is named after Ronald Shephard who formally proved the result in 1953 after it had already been used in work by others over the previous two decades. Rene Roy, a French economist, is credited with the proof for Roy's Identity in a paper in 1947.

Finally, we show that these insights let us demonstrate quickly how consumer welfare translates into areas on *MWTP* curves.

The Envelope Theorem

Take a maximization or minimization problem that can be written as one of the following:

$$\max_{x_1, x_2, \ldots, x_n} f(x_1, x_2, \ldots, x_n; \alpha_1, \alpha_2, \ldots, \alpha_m) \text{ subject to } g(x_1, x_2, \ldots, x_n; \alpha_1, \alpha_2, \ldots, \alpha_m) = 0$$

$$\min_{x_1, x_2, \ldots, x_n} f(x_1, x_2, \ldots, x_n; \alpha_1, \alpha_2, \ldots, \alpha_m) \text{ subject to } g(x_1, x_2, \ldots, x_n; \alpha_1, \alpha_2, \ldots, \alpha_m) = 0 \tag{10.23}$$

where $(x_1, x_2, \ldots, x_n)$ are the choice variables analogous to the consumption bundle in utility maximization and expenditure minimization problems and $(\alpha_1, \alpha_2, \ldots, \alpha_m)$ are parameters such as utility function parameters or prices and income. The Lagrange function for this problem is:

$$\mathcal{L}(x_1, x_2, \ldots, x_n, \lambda) = f(x_1, x_2, \ldots, x_n; \alpha_1, \alpha_2, \ldots, \alpha_m) + \lambda g(x_1, x_2, \ldots, x_n; \alpha_1, \alpha_2, \ldots, \alpha_m) \qquad \textbf{(10.24)}$$

and the solution to the first-order conditions takes the form:

$$x_i^* = x_i(\alpha_1, \alpha_2, \ldots, \alpha_m) \text{ for all } i = 1, 2, \ldots, n, \qquad \textbf{(10.25)}$$

which is analogous to the uncompensated or compensated demand functions. Finally, suppose we call the function that arises when we substitute these solutions into the objective function in (10.23) to get:

$$F(\alpha_1, \alpha_2, \ldots, \alpha_m) = f(x_1^*, x_2^*, \ldots, x_n^*). \qquad \textbf{(10.26)}$$

the Envelope Theorem states that, for all $j = 1, 2, \ldots, m$:

$$\frac{\partial F}{\partial \alpha_j} = \frac{\partial \mathcal{L}}{\partial \alpha_j}\Bigg|_{(x_1^*, x_2^*, \ldots, x_n^*)} = \left(\frac{\partial f}{\partial \alpha_j} + \lambda \frac{\partial g}{\partial \alpha_j}\right)\Bigg|_{(x_1^*, x_2^*, \ldots, x_n^*)} \qquad \textbf{(10.27)}$$

where the $(x_1^*, x_2^*, \ldots, x_n^*)$ following the vertical lines is read as 'evaluated at $(x_1^*, x_2^*, \ldots, x_n^*)$' or 'with the derivatives evaluated at the optimum of the choice variables'.

The Envelope Theorem Applied to Expenditure Minimization and Utility Maximization

Consider the expenditure minimization problem on the right side of the duality Graph 10.12. In terms of the notation of our definition of the Envelope Theorem, the problem is written with:

$$
\begin{aligned}
&(x_1, x_2, \ldots, x_n) \text{ represented by the goods } (x_1, x_2) \\
&(\alpha_1, \alpha_2, \ldots, \alpha_m) \text{ represented by the parameters } (p_1, p_2, u) \\
&f(x_1, x_2, \ldots, x_n; \alpha_1, \alpha_2, \ldots, \alpha_m) \text{ represented by } E = p_1 x_1 + p_2 x_2 \\
&g(x_1, x_2, \ldots, x_n; \alpha_1, \alpha_2, \ldots, \alpha_m) = 0 \text{ represented by } u - u(x_1, x_2) = 0 \\
&x_i^* = x_i(\alpha_1, \alpha_2, \ldots, \alpha_m) \text{ represented by } x_i^* = h_i(p_1, p_2, u) \text{ and} \\
&F(\alpha_1, \alpha_2, \ldots, \alpha_m) \text{ represented by } E(p_1, p_2, u).
\end{aligned}
\qquad \textbf{(10.28)}
$$

We can apply the Envelope Theorem in equation (10.27) directly to get:

$$\frac{\partial E(p_1, p_2, u)}{\partial p_i} = \left(\frac{\partial(p_1 x_1 + p_2 x_2)}{\partial p_i}\right)\Bigg|_{(x_1^*, x_2^*)} + \lambda \left(\frac{\partial(u - u(x_1, x_2))}{\partial p_i}\right)\Bigg|_{(x_1^*, x_2^*)}. \qquad \textbf{(10.29)}$$

Since p_i does not appear in the equation $u - u(x_1, x_2)$, the term following λ is zero. This simplifies the expression in (10.29) to:

$$\frac{\partial E(p_1, p_2, u)}{\partial p_i} = x_i\big|_{(x_1^*, x_2^*)} = h_i(p_1, p_2, u), \qquad \textbf{(10.30)}$$

which is Shephard's Lemma, and can be extended to an expenditure minimization problem with more than two goods. In the utility maximization problem on the left side of the duality in Graph 10.12, on the other hand, we have:

$(x_1, x_2, \ldots, x_n)$ represented by the goods (x_1, x_2)

$(\alpha_1, \alpha_2, \ldots, \alpha_m)$ represented by the parameters (p_1, p_2, I)

$f(x_1, x_2, \ldots, x_n; \alpha_1, \alpha_2, \ldots, \alpha_m)$ represented by $u(x_1, x_2)$

$g(x_1, x_2, \ldots, x_n; \alpha_1, \alpha_2, \ldots, \alpha_m) = 0$ represented by $I - p_1 x_1 - p_2 x_2 = 0$

$x_i^* = x_i(\alpha_1, \alpha_2, \ldots, \alpha_m)$ represented by $x_i^* = x_i(p_1, p_2, I)$ and

$F(\alpha_1, \alpha_2, \ldots, \alpha_m)$ represented by $V(p_1, p_2, I)$.

$$\text{(10.31)}$$

The Envelope Theorem implies:

$$\frac{\partial V(p_1, p_2, I)}{\partial p_i} = \left(\frac{\partial u(x_1, x_2)}{\partial p_i}\right)\bigg|_{(x_1^*, x_2^*)} + \lambda\left(\frac{\partial(I - p_1 x_1 - p_2 x_2)}{\partial p_i}\right)\bigg|_{(x_1^*, x_2^*)}. \qquad \text{(10.32)}$$

Since $(\partial u(x_1, x_2)/\partial p_i) = 0$, equation (10.32) reduces to:

$$\frac{\partial V(p_1, p_2, I)}{\partial p_i} = -\lambda x_i\big|_{(x_1^*, x_2^*)} = -\lambda x_i(p_1, p_2, I). \qquad \text{(10.33)}$$

The Envelope Theorem also implies:

$$\frac{\partial V(p_1, p_2, I)}{\partial I} = \left(\frac{\partial u(x_1, x_2)}{\partial I}\right)\bigg|_{(x_1^*, x_2^*)} + \lambda\left(\frac{\partial(I - p_1 x_1 - p_2 x_2)}{\partial I}\right)\bigg|_{(x_1^*, x_2^*)} = \lambda. \qquad \text{(10.34)}$$

Dividing equations (10.33) by (10.34) and multiplying both sides by -1, we get Roy's Identity:

$$-\frac{\partial V(p_1, p_2, I)/\partial p_i}{\partial V(p_1, p_2, I)/\partial I} = x_i(p_1, p_2, I). \qquad \text{(10.35)}$$

Intuition Behind Shephard's Lemma and the Concavity of the Expenditure Function

Suppose that a consumer initially consumes bundle A when prices of x_1 and x_2 are p_1^A and p_2^A and suppose that the consumer attains utility level u^A as a result. This is illustrated in panel (a) of Graph 10.14 with the tangency between the indifference curve and the budget line BC_1, which involves an overall expenditure level of $E^A = p_1^A x_1^A + p_2^A x_2^A$. This is one point on the expenditure function $E(p_1, p_2, u)$, in particular the point $E(p_1^A, p_2^A, u^A)$.

Now suppose we wanted to graph the 'slice' of the expenditure function that holds the price of x_2 fixed at p_2^A and utility fixed at u^A; that is, the slice $E(p_1, p_2^A, u^A)$ that illustrates how expenditure varies with changes in p_1. The point A' in panel (b) of Graph 10.14 is one point on this slice of the expenditure function, the point $E(p_1^A, p_2^A, u^A)$.

Without knowing about substitution effects, we could naively assume that a consumer would always have to consume bundle A in order to remain equally happy as p_1 changes. If this were the case, the slice of the expenditure function would be $E = p_1 x_1^A + p_2^A x_2^A$, an equation of a line with intercept $p_2^A x_2^A$ and slope x_1^A when expenditure is graphed on the vertical axis and p_1 on the horizontal. This is illustrated as the dark brown line in panel (b) of Graph 10.14.

The real expenditure function, however, takes account of the fact that individuals substitute away from goods that become more expensive and towards goods that become cheaper. For instance, suppose the price of x_1 rises from the initial p_1^A to p_1^B, represented in panel (a) of Graph 10.14 in the slope of the budget line BC_2 tangential to the indifference curve u^A at bundle B. The actual expenditure required to have this individual reach utility level u^A under the prices (p_1^B, p_2^A) is $p_1^B x_1^B + p_2^A x_2^B$, not $p_1^B x_1^A + p_2^A x_2^A$ as suggested by the dark brown line in panel (b), and the former amount is smaller than the latter, which you can see in the fact that when the budget line BC_2 has the steeper slope, bundle A lies outside the budget set that contains bundle B. The actual point $E(p_1^B, p_2^A, u^A)$ in panel (b) of the graph therefore lies somewhere below the dark brown line and is graphed as point B'. The same is true for a decrease in p_1 to p_1^C, which is represented in the slope of the budget line BC_3, tangential to the indifference curve u^A at bundle C; the actual expenditure $E(p_1^C, p_2^A, u^A)$ at bundle C is below the expenditure $p_1^C x_1^A + p_2^A x_2^A$ graphed on the dark brown line in panel (b).

Graph 10.14 Substitution Effects, Shephard's Lemma and the Concavity of $E(p_1, p_2, u)$ in Prices

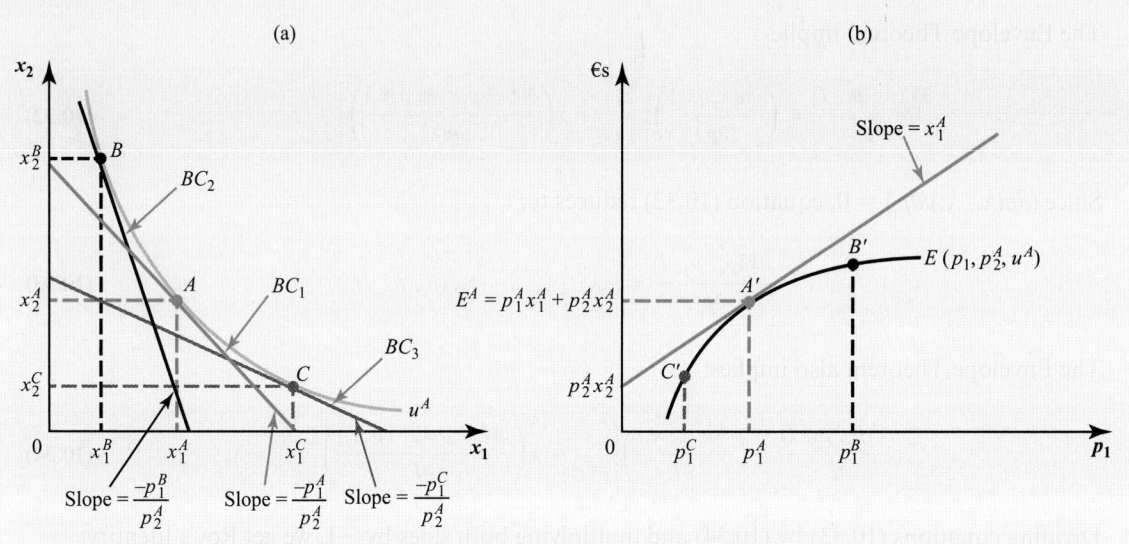

The presence of substitution effects therefore implies that the 'slices' of the expenditure function with a price change on the horizontal axis are *concave* with:

$$\frac{\partial E(p_1, p_2, u)}{\partial p_i} > 0 \quad \text{and} \quad \frac{\partial^2 E(p_1, p_2, u)}{dp_i^2} \leq 0. \tag{10.36}$$

Exercise 10B.7

What shape must the indifference curves have in order for the second derivative of the expenditure function with respect to price to be equal to zero and for the 'slice' of the expenditure function in panel (b) of Graph 10.14 to be equal to the dark brown line?

Panel (b) of Graph 10.14 furthermore is a graphical depiction of Shephard's Lemma and of the intuition behind the Envelope Theorem. The slope of the actual expenditure function, E, at p_1^A is x_1^A, and x_1^A is the expenditure minimizing level of consumption of good 1 to reach the indifference curve u^A when prices are (p_1^A, p_2^A); that is:

$$x_1^A = h_1(p_1^A, p_2^A, u^A). \tag{10.37}$$

The fact that the slope of the slice of the actual expenditure function at A' is equal to x_1^A can therefore be expressed as:

$$\frac{\partial E(p_1^A, p_2^A, u^A)}{\partial p_1} = h_1(p_1^A, p_2^A, u^A), \tag{10.38}$$

which is precisely what Shephard's Lemma tells us. Since we derived this intuition for an arbitrary initial set of prices and utility level, the same intuition applies for any combination of prices and utility levels.

Concavity of the Expenditure Function and the Slope of Compensated Demand Curves

The combination of Shephard's Lemma and the concavity of expenditure functions that implies the conditions in equation (10.36) allows us to conclude:

$$\frac{\partial h_i(p_1, p_2, u)}{\partial p_i} = \frac{\partial^2 E(p_1, p_2, u)}{dp_i^2} \leq 0, \tag{10.39}$$

which states that the slope of compensated demand curves is always negative; that is, compensated demand curves that isolate only substitution effects must be downward sloping. This is something we have concluded to be true intuitively already, and it has become mathematically possible to demonstrate given the additional material developed in this appendix.

Exercise 10B.8

In a two-panel graph with the top panel containing an indifference curve and the lower panel containing a compensated demand curve for x_1 derived from that indifference curve, illustrate the case when the inequality in equation (10.39) becomes an equality. *Hint*: Remember that our graphs of compensated demand curves are graphs of the inverse of a slice of the compensated demand functions, with a slope of 0 turning into a slope of infinity.

Using Shephard's Lemma to Illustrate Consumer Welfare Changes as Areas on Compensated Demand Curves

At the beginning of Section 10B.2 and in Section 10A.4 before that, we indicated that we can use integral calculus to calculate deadweight loss. Now that we have derived Shephard's Lemma, we can demonstrate this mathematically in the context of our example of a tax on housing. In particular, consider the measurement of the lump sum tax L that is equivalent in terms of utility for the consumer to a housing tax that raises the price of housing by t. The amount L is the difference between the consumer's actual income and the hypothetical income required to get the consumer to their after-tax utility level without changing any of the prices. One way to express a consumer's income is to note that it is equivalent to the consumer's expenditures after the housing tax is put in place; that is, $I = E(p_1 + t, p_2, u^A)$ where u^A represents the after-tax utility level. The compensated budget that gets the consumer to the same utility level at the pre-tax prices, on the other hand, is $E(p_1, p_2, u^A)$. Thus:

$$L = E(p_1 + t, p_2, u^A) - E(p_1, p_2, u^A). \tag{10.40}$$

Now note that Shephard's Lemma implies:

$$\frac{\partial E(p_1, p_2, u)}{\partial p_1} = h_1(p_1, p_2, u). \tag{10.41}$$

We can use this directly to expand equation (10.40):

$$L = E(p_1 + t, p_2, u^A) - E(p_1, p_2, u^A) = \int_{p_1}^{p_1 + t} h_1(p_1, p_2, u^A)dp. \tag{10.42}$$

In other words, the amount L needed to calculate the DWL from a tax can be measured as an integral on the compensated demand function that corresponds to the after-tax utility level u^A, exactly as indicated in panel (a) of Graph 10.8.

End-of-Chapter Exercises

10.1† Consider a good x_1 in a model where a consumer chooses between x_1 and a composite good x_2.

A. Explain why the following either cannot happen or, if you think it can happen, how:

  a. Own-price demand for a good is perfectly vertical but taxing the good produces a deadweight loss.
  b. Own-price demand is downward sloping not vertical, and there is no deadweight loss from taxing the good.

B. Now suppose that the consumer's tastes can be summarized by the CES utility function $u(x_1, x_2) = (0.5x_1^{-\rho} + 0.5x_2^{-\rho})^{-1/\rho}$.

  a. Are there values for ρ that would result in the scenario described in A(a)?
  b. Are there values for ρ that would result in the scenario described in A(b)?
  c. Would either of these scenarios work with tastes that are quasilinear in x_1?

10.2 Suppose that both consumption and leisure are always normal goods. Keep in mind the underlying cause for deadweight losses from wage-distorting taxation as you answer the following questions.

A. Explain why the following either cannot happen or, if you think it can happen, how:

  a. Labour supply is perfectly vertical, but there is a significant deadweight loss from taxing wages.
  b. Labour supply is perfectly vertical, and there is no deadweight loss from taxing wages.
  c. Labour supply is downward sloping, and there is a deadweight loss from taxation of wages.
  d. Labour supply is upward sloping, and there is a deadweight loss from taxing wages.
  e. Labour supply is downward sloping, and there is no deadweight loss from taxing wages.
  f. Labour supply is upward sloping, and there is no deadweight loss from taxing wages.

B. *Now suppose that tastes can be summarized by the CES utility function $u(c, \ell) = (0.5c^{-\rho} + 0.5\ell^{-\rho})^{-1/\rho}$, where c is consumption and ℓ is leisure.
Are there values for ρ that would result in the scenario/s in:

  a. A(a)?
  b. A(b)?
  c. A(c)?
  d. A(d)?
  e. A(e) and A(f)?

10.3† Everyday Application: *To Trade or Not to Trade Pizza Vouchers: Exploring the Difference between Willingness to Pay and Willingness to Accept.* Two friends, Lauren and Jenny, are identical in every way, same exogenous income, same tastes on pizza and other goods. The only difference between them is that Lauren has a voucher that allows the owner to buy as much pizza as they want at 50 per cent off.

A. Jenny approaches Lauren to see if there was any way a deal could be made under which Lauren would sell Jenny her voucher. In the following, you will explore under what conditions such a deal is possible.

   a. On a graph with pizza on the horizontal axis and 'other goods' on the vertical, illustrate as a vertical distance the most Jenny would be willing to pay Lauren for her voucher. Call this amount P.

   b. On a separate but similar graph, illustrate as a vertical distance the least Lauren would be willing to accept in cash to give up her voucher. Call this amount R.

   c. Below each of the graphs you have drawn in (a) and (b), illustrate the same amounts P and R as areas along the appropriate marginal willingness to pay curves.

   d. Is P larger or smaller than R? What does your answer depend on? *Hint*: By overlaying your lower graphs that illustrate P and R as areas along marginal willingness to pay curves, you should be able to tell whether one is bigger than the other or whether they are the same size depending on what kind of good pizza is.

   e. *True or False*: Jenny and Lauren will be able to make a deal as long as pizza is not a normal good. Explain your answer intuitively.

B. Suppose Jenny and Lauren's tastes can be represented by the Cobb–Douglas utility function $u(x_1, x_2) = x_1^{0.5}x_2^{0.5}$, and suppose they both have income $I = 100$. Let pizza be denoted by x_1 and other goods by x_2, and let the price of pizza be denoted by p. Since other goods are denominated in euros, the price of x_2 is implicitly set to 1.

   a. Calculate their demand functions for pizza and other goods as a function of p.

   b. Calculate the compensated demand for pizza (x_1) and other goods (x_2) as a function of p ignoring for now the existence of the coupon.

   c. Suppose $p = 10$ and the coupon reduces this price by half to 5. Assume again that Lauren has the coupon but Jenny does not. How much utility do both get when they make optimal decisions?

   d. How much pizza will Jenny consume if she pays Lauren the most she is willing to pay for the voucher? How much will Lauren consume if Jenny pays her the least she is willing to accept?

   e. Calculate the expenditure function for Jenny and Lauren.

   f. Using your answers so far, determine R – the least Lauren is willing to accept to give up her voucher. Determine P – the most Jenny is willing to pay to get a voucher. *Hint*: Use your graphs from A(a) to determine the appropriate values to substitute into the expenditure function to determine how much income Lauren would have to have in order to give up her voucher. Once you have done this, you can subtract Lauren's actual income $I = 100$ to determine how much Jenny has to give Lauren to be willing to give up the voucher. Do the analogous to determine how much Jenny would be willing to pay, this time using your graph from A(b).

   g. Is a deal under which Lauren sells Jenny her voucher possible? Make sense of this given what you found intuitively in part A and given what you know about Cobb–Douglas tastes.

   h. Now suppose their tastes could instead be represented by the utility function $u(x_1, x_2) = 50 \ln x_1 + x_2$. Using steps similar to what you have just done, calculate again the least Lauren is willing to accept and the most Jenny is willing to pay for the voucher. Explain the intuition behind your answer given what you know about quasilinear tastes.

   i. **Can you demonstrate, using the compensated demand functions you calculated for the two types of tastes, that the values for P and R are areas under these functions as you described in your answer to A(c)? *Note*: This part requires you to use integral calculus.

10.4 Everyday Application: *To Take, or not to Take, the Bus.* After you graduate, you get a job in a small town where you have taken your sister's offer of living in her flat. Your job pays you €20 per hour and you have up to 60 hours per week available. The problem is you also have to get to work.

A. Your sister's flat is relatively close to work, so you could lease a car and pay a total, including insurance and fuel, of €100 per week to get to work, spending essentially no time commuting. Alternatively, you could use public transport, but unfortunately there is no direct bus to your place of work and you would have to change buses a few times to get there. This would take approximately 5 hours per week.

   a. Now suppose that you do not consider time spent commuting as leisure, and you don't consider money spent on transportation as consumption. On a graph with 'leisure net of commuting time' on the horizontal axis and 'consumption euros net of commuting costs' on the vertical, illustrate your budget constraint if you choose the bus and a separate budget constraint if you choose to lease the car.

b. Do you prefer the bus to the car?

c. Suppose that before you get to town you find out that a typo had been made in your offer letter and your actual wage is €10 per hour instead of €20 per hour. How does your answer change?

d. After a few weeks, your employer discovers just how good you are and gives you a raise to €25 per hour. What mode of transportation do you take now?

e. Illustrate in a graph, not directly derived from what you have done so far, the relationship between wage on the horizontal axis and the most you'd be willing to pay for the leased car.

f. If the government taxes fuel and thus increases the cost of driving a leased car while keeping buses running for free, predict what will happen to the demand for bus services and indicate what types of workers will be the source of the change in demand.

g. What happens if the government improves bus services by reducing the time one needs to spend to get from one place to the other?

B. Now suppose your tastes were given by $u(c, \ell) = c^{\alpha} \ell^{(1-\alpha)}$, where c is consumption euros net of commuting expenses and ℓ is leisure consumption net of time spent commuting. Suppose your leisure endowment is L and your wage is w.

a. Derive consumption and leisure demand assuming you lease a car that costs you €Y per week, which therefore implies no commuting time.

b. Next, derive your demand for consumption and leisure assuming you take the bus instead, with the bus costing no money but taking T hours per week from your leisure time.

c. Express the indirect utility of leasing the car as a function of Y.

d. Express your indirect utility of taking the bus as a function of T.

e. Using the indirect utility functions, determine the relationship between Y and T that would keep you indifferent between taking the bus and leasing the car. Is your answer consistent with the relationship you illustrated in A(e) and your conclusions in A(f) and A(g)?

f. Could you have skipped all these steps and derived this relationship directly from the budget constraints? Why or why not?

10.5† **Business Application:** *Pricing at a Theme Park.* Suppose you own an amusement park with many rides and assume, for the sake of simplicity, that all rides cost the same to operate. Suppose further that the maximum number of rides a customer can take on any given day is 25, given how long rides take and how long the average wait times are. Your typical visitor has some exogenous daily budget I to allocate between rides at your park and other forms of entertainment that are, for purposes of this problem, bought from vendors other than you. Finally, suppose tastes are quasilinear in amusement park rides.

A. a. Draw a demand curve for rides in your park. Suppose you charge no entrance fee and only charge your visitors per ride. Indicate the maximum price per ride you could charge while ensuring that your visitor will in fact spend all their day riding rides, i.e. ride 25 times.

b. On your graph, indicate the total amount that the visitor will spend.

c. Now suppose that you decide you want to keep the price per ride you have been using but you'd also like to charge a separate entrance fee to the park. What is the most you can charge your visitor?

d. Suppose you decide that it is just too much trouble to collect fees for each ride, so you eliminate the price per ride and switch to a system where you only charge an entrance fee to the park. How high an entrance fee can you charge?

e. How would your analysis change if x_1, amusement park rides, is a normal good rather than being quasilinear?

B. Consider a visitor who visits your amusement park for the day. Suppose the consumer's tastes can be summarized by the utility function $u(x_1, x_2) = 10x_1^{0.5} + x_2$ where x_1 represents daily rides in the amusement park and x_2 represents euros of other entertainment spending. Suppose further that the visitor's exogenous daily budget for entertainment is €100.

a. Derive the uncompensated and compensated demand functions for x_1 and x_2.

b. Suppose again there is only enough time for a visitor to ride 25 rides a day in your amusement park. Suppose further that you'd like your visitor to ride as much as possible so they can spread the word on how great your rides are. What price will you set per ride?

c. How much utility will your visitor attain under your pricing?

d. **Suppose you can charge an entrance fee to your park in addition to charging the price per ride you calculated. How high an entrance fee would you charge? *Hint*: You should be evaluating an integral, which draws on some of the material from the appendix.

e. **Now suppose you decide to make all rides free knowing that the most rides the consumer can squeeze into a day is 25, and you simply charge an entrance fee to your park. How high an entrance fee will you now charge to your park? *Note*: This part is not computationally difficult. It is designated with ** only because you have to use information from the previous part.

f. **How does your analysis change if the visitor's tastes instead were given by $u(x_1, x_2) = (3^{-0.5})x_1^{0.5} + x_2^{0.5}$?

10.6 **Policy Application:** *Taxing Interest on Savings.* Suppose an individual cares only about consumption this year and consumption next year, and suppose they earn an income this year but do not expect to earn an income next year.

A. The government announces an increase in the tax on interest income. Illustrate the individual's before- and after-tax intertemporal budget constraint.

a. Suppose the individual saves 50 per cent of their income after the new tax is imposed. Illustrate the amount of the tax the government will collect from them next year. Call this T.

b. Illustrate the most they would be willing to pay next year to keep the government from imposing this tax on interest income. Call this amount L.

c. Is L larger or smaller than T? What does your answer depend on?

d. If consumption is always a normal good, will the individual consume more or less next year if the tax on interest income is removed?

e. If consumption is always a normal good, will they consume more or less *this* year if the tax on interest income is eliminated?

f. Can you redraw your graph but this time indicate how much T' the individual is paying in tax in terms of *this* year's consumption, and how much L' they would be willing to pay to avoid the tax in terms of *this* year's consumption?

B. Now suppose that their tastes over consumption now, c_1, and consumption next period, c_2, can be captured by the utility function $u(c_1, c_2) = c_1^{\alpha} c_2^{(1-\alpha)}$.

a. Suppose the interest rate is r. What does α have to be in order for the individual to optimally save 50 per cent of their income this year?

b. Assume from now on that α is as you calculated and suppose that the individual's current income is €200 000. Suppose the interest rate before the tax increase was 10 per cent and the after-tax interest rate after the tax increase is 5 per cent. How much tax revenue T does the government collect from the individual? What is the present value of that this period?

c. What is the most (L) they would be willing to pay to avoid this tax increase in either today's euros or in next period's euros?

d. Does the amount that they save today change as a result of the tax increase?

e. Is the tax efficient? If not, how big is the deadweight loss?

* conceptually challenging
** computationally challenging
† solutions in Study Guide

PART II

Profit-Maximizing Choice: Producers or Firms

In Part 1, we modelled individual choice when the chooser's objective is to maximize 'happiness'. This model applied to consumers and resulted in the demand curve for goods, but it also applied to workers and savers to give us labour and capital supply curves. We now turn to the case where the chooser's objective is instead to maximize something more specific: profit. We will refer to the individuals in an economy whose goal is to maximize profit as *producers* or *firms*, and their decisions will lead to supply curves for goods as well as demand curves for labour and capital. Once we have completed this Part, we will be ready to think about the interaction of supply and demand in goods, labour and capital markets.

The basic logic of choice that underlies our model of Part 1 applies also for producers. Firms choose *inputs like labour and capital* and we make an assumption that they aim to maximize *profit—the difference between revenue and cost*. In doing so, they face *technological constraints* that limit how easy it is to convert inputs into outputs and *economic constraints* that emerge from the prices of inputs and outputs. We begin in Chapter 11 with a simple model of producers, where a single output is produced from a *single input* given a particular technology available to the producer. We see how the technology that tells us how easy it is to convert the input into the output serves as the constraint for the firm. We can also see in this model that the tastes for profit are shaped by the prices of the output and input, with more profit possible when output price is high and input price is low. Combining these, we can show how the firm chooses its optimal or profit-maximizing level of output using the lowest possible input level under which it is technologically feasible to produce the desired output. From this choice process, we can illustrate *output supply* and *input demand* relationships, or how output and input decisions are affected by changes in prices in the economy.

The unrealistic simplification in Chapter 11 involves the assumption that only a single input is needed for production. In reality, goods can typically be produced in multiple different ways by combining a little labour with lots of capital or lots of labour with a little capital, and this implies that profit-maximizing producers will typically have to choose the optimal bundle of inputs with which to produce. Producers have to decide not only *how much* to produce but also *how* to produce the goods, that is how much to rely on labour versus capital or some other input.

Chapter 12 expands the model of Chapter 11 to include multiple inputs and thus multiple ways of producing any level of output. This allows us to distinguish between *technologically efficient* production that involves not wasting any inputs and *economically efficient* production that involves producing output at the least cost possible given the input prices in the marketplace.

In this expanded model with multiple inputs, we will see that it is often useful to separate the producer's problem into two separate stages. First, we can think of producers as looking only at their technology and the prices of inputs, and using this information to determine the least costly way of producing different levels of output. We will refer to this part of the problem as the firm's *cost minimization* problem. After solving this problem, firms will know how much it costs to produce any level of output, but they will not yet know what level of output is profit maximizing. They need to compare the cost of producing different levels of output from their cost minimization problem to the revenue they can get from different levels of output. Finding the level of output where the gap between revenue and cost is the largest is equivalent to finding the profit-maximizing level of output and the accompanying profit-maximizing levels of inputs.

In Chapter 13 we introduce a distinction between *short-run* and *long-run* decisions by producers. This distinction arises because firms often face short-run constraints that are more binding than long-run constraints. In the short run, for instance, a firm might already have committed to a certain factory space and thus a certain level of the input 'capital'. While this factory space might have been optimal given the circumstances that the producer faced when committing to the space, it may no longer be optimal when prices change. In the short run, the producer is locked into the space and is able to decide only how intensively to use the space. In the two-input model, this implies that one input might be fixed in the short run but the other can be changed, so that effectively the short run is characterized by a single-input production process like the one we began with in Chapter 11. When it becomes possible to change the factory space, however, the firm will typically re-evaluate its short-run response to changing circumstances and respond some more.

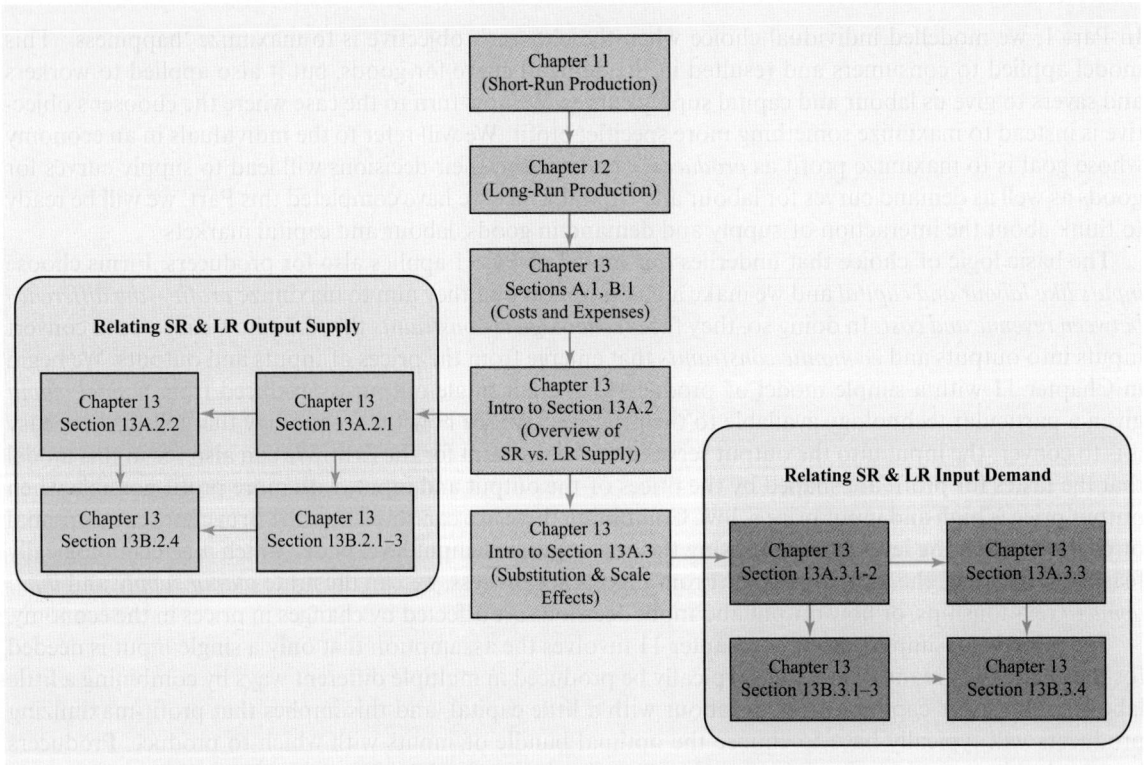

Chapter 11

One Input and One Output: A Short-Run Producer Model

We will begin our exploration of producers as economic actors in a 'non-strategic' environment, where their actions have no impact on the larger economy and where they are price takers.

In some ways, the models of competitive producers and consumers are not all that different. Both producers and consumers make choices that are under their control in an attempt to do the best they can given their economic circumstances that they cannot control. Producers will be a bit more transparent than consumers because we model them under the assumption of caring only about profit, i.e. they are profit maximizers. We will start in this chapter with a simple case of a producer who uses a single input to produce a single output. This will permit us to illustrate the idea of profit maximization in two different ways. First, we will show directly how producers maximize profits by choosing the production plan that puts them on their highest 'indifference curve', and second, we will show that we can split the profit-maximization problem into two steps that will form the basis for our analysis of more complex producers in Chapter 12. This latter approach is fairly intuitive. We will suppose that producers first analyze their costs, and once they have a good picture of the costs of different production plans, they look at how much revenue can be generated to see which plan results in the most profit. In the end, the two approaches to profit maximization result in the same solution for the producer, but sometimes it will be more convenient to use one and sometimes the other.

11A   A Short-Run One-Input/One-Output Model

The assumption of a producer converting a single input into a single output is not meant to be realistic although it is possible to think of realistic production processes in which some of the inputs simply cannot be varied *in the short run*. Perhaps a certain factory space has been leased for a one-year period, and the lease has to be paid regardless of how much or how little is produced. In that case, a producer might be locked into a particular level of the input factory space over the next year even though the producer can choose a smaller or larger space after the current lease runs out. However, while it might not be possible for the producer to vary the factory space in the short run, they might well be able to vary the intensity with which the space is utilized; that is, the number of work hours that go into actually using the space for production. In such a scenario, we would say that this producer's input of factory space is *fixed in the short run* while their labour input is *variable in the short run*.

To frame our discussion, let us assume that a producer is able to secure free factory space on the site of a former steel works, and that the equipment in this factory is appropriate for making handles for exterior doors and there is a supply of metal which can be used to make the handles. The producer, therefore has the factory space, the machines and the raw material for their product without cost, and what they have to do is decide how many workers to employ to start producing.

11A.1 Technological Constraints Faced by Producers

The producer might wish to produce an endless supply of door handles and sell them to every consumer, but just as consumers can't consume without end because they have *finite resources which limit their consumer choice set*, so producers cannot produce without end because *the technology available to them as a producer constrains their producer choice set*.

11A.1.1 Production Plans, Producer Choice Sets and Production Frontiers Let's begin by defining a *production plan* as *a proposed bundle of inputs and outputs*. We can model production plans as a single input and a single output. In modelling all possible production plans for door handles, we put 'hours of labour per day' on the horizontal axis and 'door handles per day' on the vertical, and each point in the resulting two-dimensional space is a production plan that proposes to use a certain number of labour hours to produce a certain number of door handles per day. Not all of these production plans are, however, technologically feasible given the technology the producer has available.

The *producer choice set is defined as the set of all production plans that are feasible given the technology available to the producer*.

Panel (a) of Graph 11.1 illustrates one such possible producer choice set for door handles as the shaded area under the dark brown line. It assumes a very particular underlying technology under which every labour hour can always be turned into *at most* four pairs of door handles. For instance, production plan A calls for 10 labour hours to be transformed into 40 pairs of door handles, and plan B calls for 20 labour hours to be transformed into 80 pairs. This logically implies that plan C is feasible as well. At C, output would be 40 pairs with 20 labour hours. Since the producer can produce that many pairs with 10 labour hours under production plan A, it should not be hard to employ 10 additional labour hours and still produce 40 pairs. Thus the production plan C lies *inside* the producer choice set, indicating that more could be produced with the labour input called for in production plan C. The production plan D, on the other hand, is not feasible under this technology; the producer needs at least 30 worker hours to produce 120 pairs of handles under plan E, and it is not possible given the available technology to produce that many handles with only 20 worker hours. Thus, plan D lies *outside* the producer choice set.

Graph 11.1 Two Types of Producer Choice Sets and Associated Production Frontiers

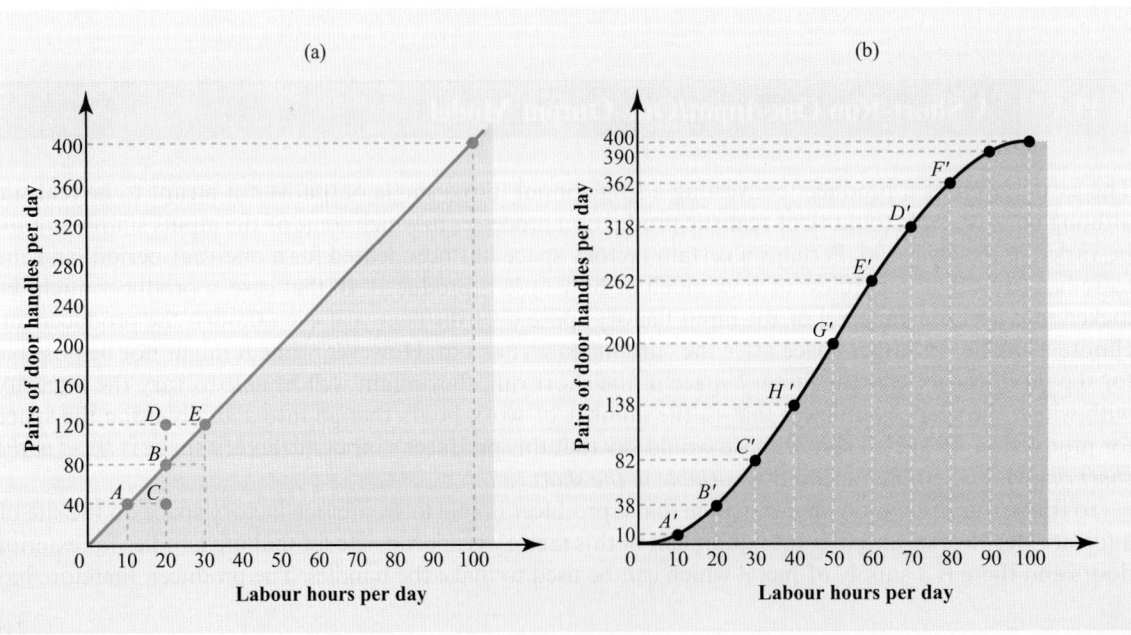

Production plans that lie *inside* the producer choice set are plans under which some input stands idle, implying the producer can produce more with the same level of input. We can *define the boundary of the producer choice set as the production frontier*. Only plans along this production frontier represent plans that do not waste inputs. As a result, producers doing the best they can will pick production plans along the production frontier.

Exercise 11A.1

Can you model a worker as a 'producer of consumption' and interpret their choice set within the context of the single-input, single-output producer model?

The technology graphed in panel (a) of Graph 11.1 does not, however, seem very realistic. It is unlikely that production can continue at the same rate given the current factory space regardless of how much is being produced. When the producer first employs workers for the factory, they would not be able to specialize and probably could not produce as much per worker as when more workers are employed. It would seem more realistic to assume a production frontier along which workers initially become more and more productive as they specialize. At the same time, there is only so much factory floor space and machinery to work with, and adding workers endlessly would eventually lead to lower and lower increases in output as the workers begin to run into each other on the factory floor.

Panel (b) of Graph 11.1 therefore illustrates a more realistic technology for this example. It begins with initial workers not producing nearly as much as initial workers did in the technology represented in panel (a), but as more worker hours are added, each worker hour initially becomes more productive than the last as workers can begin to specialize in particular tasks. The first 10 worker hours, for instance, result in an output of 10 handles per day (A'), while 20 worker hours can produce as many as 38 handles per day (B'). The second 10 worker hours add as much as 28 handles per day, 18 more than the first 10 workers. Similarly, the next 10 worker hours add up to 44 more handles to daily production, allowing the producer to produce at the production plan C'. Eventually, however, this increasing productivity per additional worker hour declines as factory workers begin to run into each other on the factory floor. For instance, 70 worker hours can produce as many as 318 handles per day (D'), 56 more than at E' with just 60 worker hours. The next 10 worker hours, however, can produce only 44 more handles to get to production plan F'.

Exercise 11A.2

Which of the producer choice sets in Graph 11.1 is non-convex? What makes it non-convex?

Exercise 11A.3

Suppose the technology was such that each additional worker hour, beginning with the second one, is less productive than the previous. Would the producer choice set be convex? What if technology was such that each additional worker hour, beginning with the second one, is more productive than the previous?

11A.1.2 Slopes of Production Frontiers: The Marginal Product of Labour Consider the production frontier in panel (a) of Graph 11.1. The slope of this frontier is 4, indicating that every additional hour of labour results in 4 additional pairs of door handles. In other words, the slope of the production frontier in panel (a) of Graph 11.1 is the *marginal benefit of one more worker hour in terms of increased production*. Turning to panel (b) of Graph 11.1, we can now see how this same interpretation of the slope of the production frontier continues to hold, except that now the marginal benefit of hiring additional workers initially increases but eventually decreases. The slope between production plans A' and B', for instance, is approximately 2.8, indicating that the marginal benefit of 1 additional worker hour is approximately 2.8 pairs of door handles when there are between 10 and 20 labour hours employed already. The approximate slope between G' and E', on the other hand, is 6.2, indicating a marginal benefit of approximately 6.2 additional pairs of door handles for every additional labour hour when there are already 50 to 60 labour hours employed.

Exercise 11A.4

Under the production technology in panel (b) of Graph 11.1, what is the approximate marginal benefit of employing an additional labour hour when there are already 95 labour hours employed?

The slope of the production frontier, or the marginal benefit of hiring additional inputs in terms of increased production, is of such economic interest to producers that it is frequently graphed separately from the production frontier and called the *marginal product* curve. The *marginal product of an hour of labour, denoted MP_ℓ is the increase in total production that results from employing one additional labour hour when all other inputs remain fixed*, and it is the slope of the single-input production frontier of the type graphed in Graph 11.1, when all other possible inputs, such as factory space, are fixed. Panels (a) and (b) of Graph 11.2 plot the marginal product of labour curves for the production frontiers in both panels. While the marginal product curve in panel (a) is correct, in panel (b) we have plotted the 'approximate' marginal product curve by plotting the slope between each of the production plans on the frontier of panel (b) for the input level that occurs halfway in between the input levels of the two relevant production plans. For instance, given that production increases by 28 when labour input rises from 10 to 20, we have plotted a marginal product of 2.8 for the 15th labour hour.

Exercise 11A.5

Relate your answer from exercise 11A.4 to a point on the MP_ℓ curve plotted in panel (b) of Graph 11.2.

Exercise 11A.6

What would the MP_ℓ curves look like for the technologies described in exercise 11A.3?

11A.1.3 The Law of Diminishing Marginal Product Notice that the marginal product curve derived from the more realistic production frontier in panel (b) of Graph 11.1 is eventually downward sloping. This downward slope is the direct result of the assumption of a production frontier on which each additional labour hour will *eventually* add less to our total output than the previous labour hour. This is known as the *Law of Diminishing Marginal Product*.

Consider a case where the marginal product of an input never declines. Marginal product is the *additional* output produced from adding one more unit of the input *assuming all other inputs are held fixed*. Suppose the marginal product of labour in the production process for door handles never declines in the fixed factory space available. This would mean the producer could keep squeezing more and more workers into the factory and have them use the same amount of raw materials, and each additional worker employed will increase output by at least as much as the previous worker did. Suppose the factory space is 1000 square metres. How many human beings can fit into 1000 square metres and still be able to produce? If the marginal product of labour never declines, it would be possible to fit the population of the entire world into the 1000 square metre space, and the last person fitted in would have added at least as much to output of door handles as any person employed previously. Not only would the producer be able to fit all of these people into the 1000 square metres but they would also be able to produce more and more door handles out of the same quantity of raw materials. This situation is not characterized by the scarcity that governs the world we live in, and as a result it *must* be the case that the marginal product of an input like labour at some point declines.

Graph 11.2 The MP_ℓ Associated With the Production Frontiers in Graph 11.1

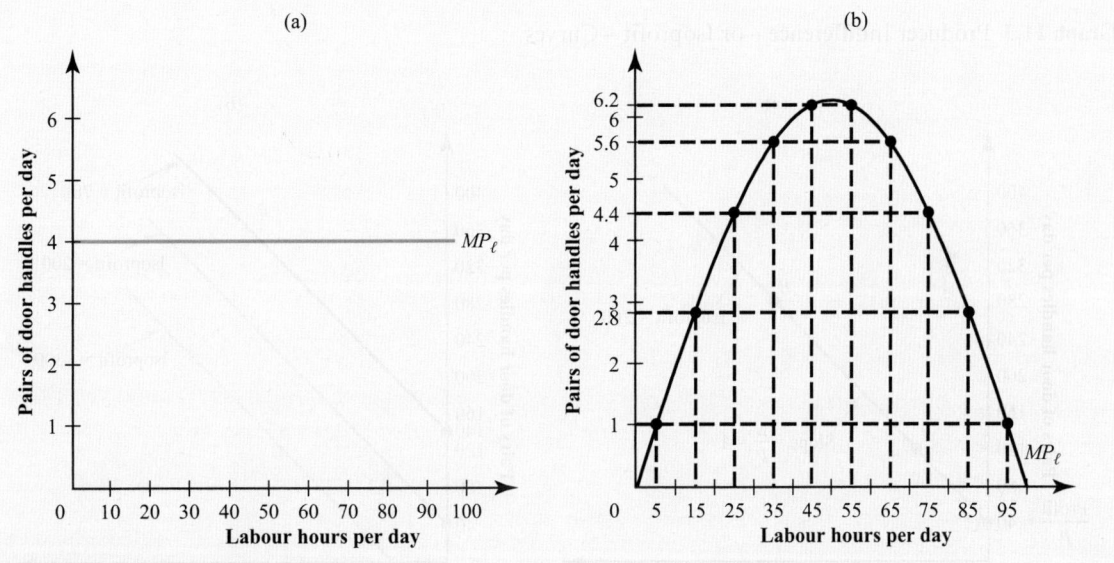

Exercise 11A.7

True or False: The Law of Diminishing Marginal Product implies that producer choice sets in single-input models must be convex beginning at some input level.

Exercise 11A.8

True or False: If the Law of Diminishing Marginal Product did not hold in the dairy industry, the entire world could be fed milk from a single cow. *Hint*: Think of the cow as a fixed input and feed for the cow as the variable input for which you consider the marginal product in terms of milk produced per day.

11A.2 'Tastes' for Profits

Producer 'tastes' are defined in a particular way. It is assumed that producers – in their role as producers – prefer production plans that generate greater profit over those that generate less, and they are indifferent between production plans that generate the same profit. *Profit* is defined as *all economic revenue generated from the sale of outputs, minus all economic cost incurred from the purchase of inputs.*

11A.2.1 Isoprofit Curves: The Producer's 'Indifference Curves' In our single-input/single-output model of door handle production, we can illustrate 'producer indifference curves' as sets of production plans that all yield the same amount of profit, with production plans that yield greater profit valued more than production plans that yield less profit. Consider, for instance, the production plans A and B in panel (a) of Graph 11.3. Plan A calls for 20 daily hours of labour to be converted into 120 daily pairs of door handles, while plan B calls for 60 daily hours of labour to be converted into 280 daily pairs of door handles. Suppose that the market wage for the type of labour the producer needs to employ is €20 per hour, and that the per pair price of handles being produced is €5. Revenues will be €600 under plan A and €1400 under plan B, while costs will be €400 under plan A and €1200 under plan B. Subtracting costs from revenues, both plans result in a daily profit of exactly €200. For producers who care only about profits, A and B are equally desirable production plans whenever a pair of handles sells for €5 and an hour of labour costs €20.

Graph 11.3 Producer Indifference – or Isoprofit – Curves

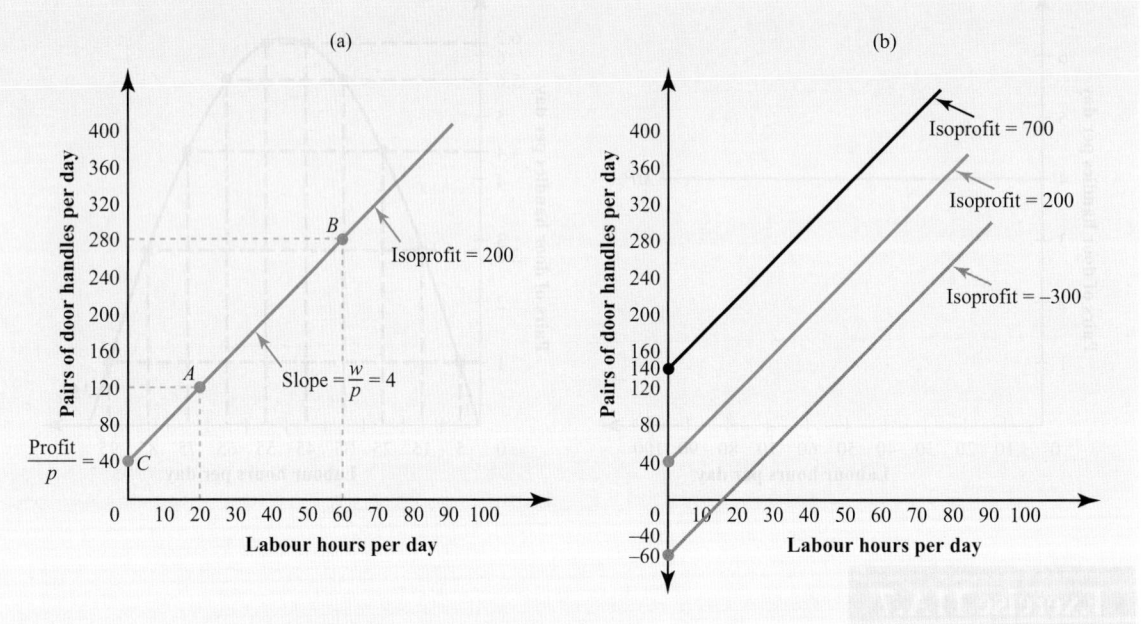

These are not the only production plans that would yield a profit of €200 per day under the assumed price and wage. For instance, production plan C suggests producing 40 pairs of handles without using *any* inputs, would also result in exactly €200 in profit per day (albeit very implausible). Since inputs cost four times as much as outputs, we can start at production plan C and find a production plan for any level of input that will yield €200 per day in profit so long as we include four times as much additional output in the production plan. Plan A, for instance, has 20 more labour hours than plan C *and* 80 more output units, thus keeping profit constant at €200 per day. When we plot the level of output required for each level of input to keep profit at €200, we get the dark brown line in panel (a) of Graph 11.3. The line has a vertical intercept of 40 because it takes 40 pairs of handles to make a €200 profit if there are no costs and has a slope equal to 4, the wage rate w divided by the price of the output p. Assuming the producer only cares about profits, they must be indifferent between all of the production plans on this dark brown line. An indifference curve such as this for a price-taking producer is called an *isoprofit curve* or, more specifically, the dark brown indifference curve is the *isoprofit curve corresponding to €200 in daily profit when the wage rate is €20 per hour and the output price is €5*.

As with consumer indifference curves, the full tastes of producers are not characterized by a single indifference or isoprofit curve. Each profit level carries with it a different isoprofit curve, with the dark blue and light blue isoprofit curves in panel (b) of Graph 11.3 representing production plans that result in €700 and −€300 profit respectively. Since the slope of isoprofit curves is w/p, all isoprofit lines have the same slope when wages and prices are fixed from the perspective of the producer. The vertical intercept is the profit associated with the particular isoprofit curve divided by the price of the output.

Exercise 11A.9

Without knowing what prices and wages are in the economy, can you tell by looking at a single isoprofit curve whether profits for production plans along this curve are positive or negative? What has to be true about an isoprofit curve in order for profit to be zero?

Exercise 11A.10

What would have to be true in order for an isoprofit curve to have a negative slope?

11A.2.2 The Role of Prices in Consumer and Producer Models There are a number of similarities between the consumer and the producer model. For instance, only some consumption bundles are available to consumers because of the budget constraint they face, just as only some production plans are technologically feasible because of production frontiers. Both consumers and producers have tastes that can be represented by points over which they are indifferent: consumption bundles that lie on the same indifference curve in the consumer model, and production plans that lie on the same isoprofit curve in the producer model. As we will see in the next section, both consumers and producers generally find their 'best' point on the boundary of their choice set.

While these similarities are conceptually important, it is equally worthwhile to point out some of the significant conceptual differences. Most important, the prices in the economy affect indifference curves and choice sets differently in the two models. In our consumer model, prices including wages and interest rates affected the size and shape of the consumer choice set, but prices have *nothing* whatsoever to do with consumer tastes and the indifference curves that represent them. Whether the consumer likes apples, how much they like to work rather than take leisure and whether they can tell the difference between Coke and Pepsi, these are internal features that define who they are, features that have arisen in some process that can perhaps be explained by psychologists and biologists but remain outside the area of expertise of most economists. Economists usually just take tastes as given and recognize that, while optimal consumer choices have a lot to do with prices, how a consumer *feels* about the trade-off between different types of goods is a matter of taste, not prices.

In the producer model, on the other hand, things are exactly the reverse. Prices have no impact on the producer choice set, but have everything to do with what the indifference curves—or isoprofit curves—look like. The producer choice set is the set of production plans that are *technologically* feasible, which implies that the size and shape of the producer choice set is driven by technology. Whether a worker is *physically able to* produce 200 door handles with 10 hours of labour has nothing to do with prices and wages; it is a matter for engineers and factory managers to figure out. The producer's indifference curves, on the other hand, are determined entirely by the prices in the economy, with the intercept a function of prices and the slope a function of both wages and prices. We can see this distinction most clearly by asking the question: What will change in our graphs of producer choice sets and isoprofit curves if prices and wages in the economy change? Since neither prices nor wages entered our development of producer choice sets in Graph 11.1, nothing would change in those graphs or in the accompanying graphs of marginal product curves. Our graph of isoprofits in Graph 11.3, on the other hand, will change.

Consider for instance a change in the hourly wage rate from €20 to €10. Since the vertical intercept of each isoprofit curve is profit divided by the output price p, a change in the wage w does not change the intercept. Intuitively, the production plans on the intercept give the output level required to attain a particular profit level *assuming the production plan does not envision employing any labour*. Since labour is not part of the production plan at the vertical intercept of an isoprofit curve, profits for such production plans are therefore unaffected by the wage rate in the economy. The wage rate does become relevant, however, at any other production plan on an isoprofit curve since all production plans other than those located on the vertical axis contain some positive labour input. For a decline in wages from €20 to €10, the slope w/p falls from 4 to 2, assuming a fixed output price of $p = 5$, leading to a shallower slope for each isoprofit curve. Such an impact of a change in wages is illustrated graphically in panel (a) of Graph 11.4.

In panel (b) of Graph 11.4, on the other hand, the impact of a change in the output price p is illustrated. Suppose, for instance, that p rises from €5 per pair of door handles to €10 per pair, with the wage rate holding constant at €20. Since the intercept of an isoprofit curve is profit divided by p, the intercept must now fall. Furthermore, given that the slope of each isoprofit curve is w/p, an increase in p will result in a decline in the slope from 4 when $p = 5$, to 2 when $p = 10$. For a particular profit level such as €200, the isoprofit curve falls at the intercept and becomes shallower as the output price increases. This, too, should make intuitive sense. If the producer can sell handles for more, they should be able to make the same profit as before using production plans that contain less output for each level of input. In both panels of the graph, we illustrate only what happens to one of the infinite number of isoprofit curves that compose the isoprofit map, with similar changes happening for each of the other isoprofits.

Exercise 11A.11

How would the dark brown isoprofit curve in panel (a) of Graph 11.4 change if the wage rises to €30? What if instead the output price falls to €2?

Graph 11.4 Isoprofit Curve for €200 Profit as Wages and Prices Change

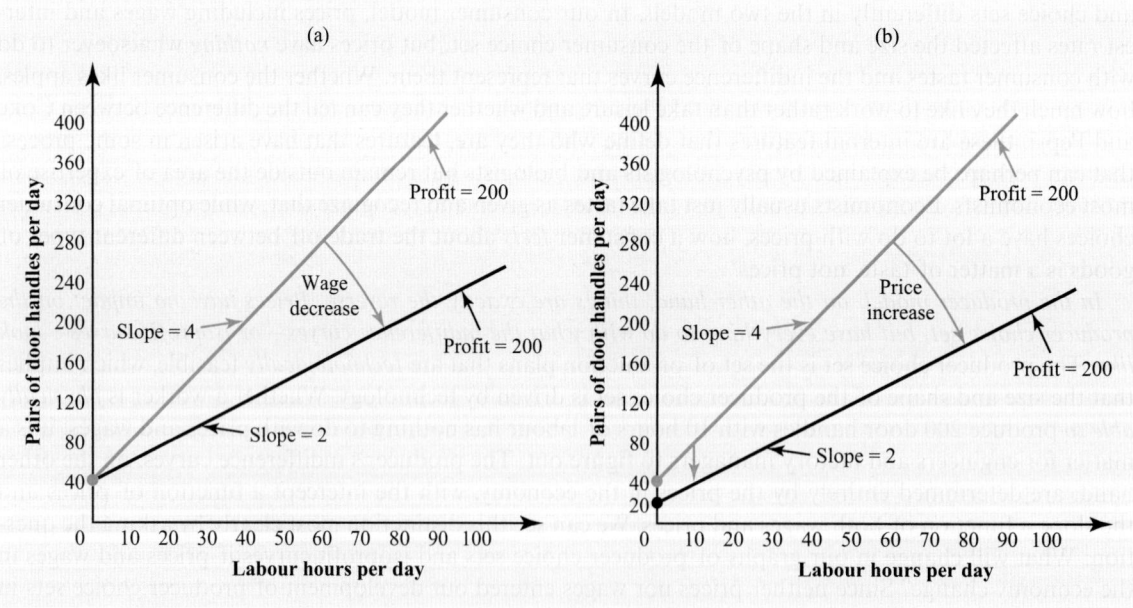

11A.3 Choosing the Production Plan That Maximizes Profit

In the last two sections we explored both producer choice set and tastes *independently*, and we can now proceed directly to analyzing how choice sets and producer tastes *jointly* result in profit-maximizing producer behaviour.

11A.3.1 Combining Production Frontiers With Isoprofit Curves Panel (a) of Graph 11.5 begins by replicating the 'realistic' producer choice set from panel (b) of Graph 11.1, while panel (b) of Graph 11.5 replicates the three isoprofit curves developed in panel (b) of Graph 11.3 under the assumption that the producer has to purchase labour in the labour market at €20 per hour and can sell door handles at €5 per pair. Panel (c) of Graph 11.5 combines the previous two panels into a single graph.

Beginning on the lowest (light blue) isoprofit curve, we can notice that many production plans that result in a profit of −€300 are technically feasible given that they lie within the shaded choice set. However, the producer becomes better off as they move to isoprofit curves that lie to the northwest. Since there are production plans that lie both within the choice set and above, i.e. to the northwest of the light blue isoprofit curve, the producer can do better than a daily profit of −€300. Looking at panel (c) of Graph 11.5, we see that certain levels of profit are not feasible within the current economic and technological environment. For instance, the (dark blue) isoprofit curve of production plans that yield €700 in daily profit lies fully outside the choice set, indicating that no production plan that could yield €700 in daily profits is technologically feasible.

Graph 11.5 Maximizing Profit

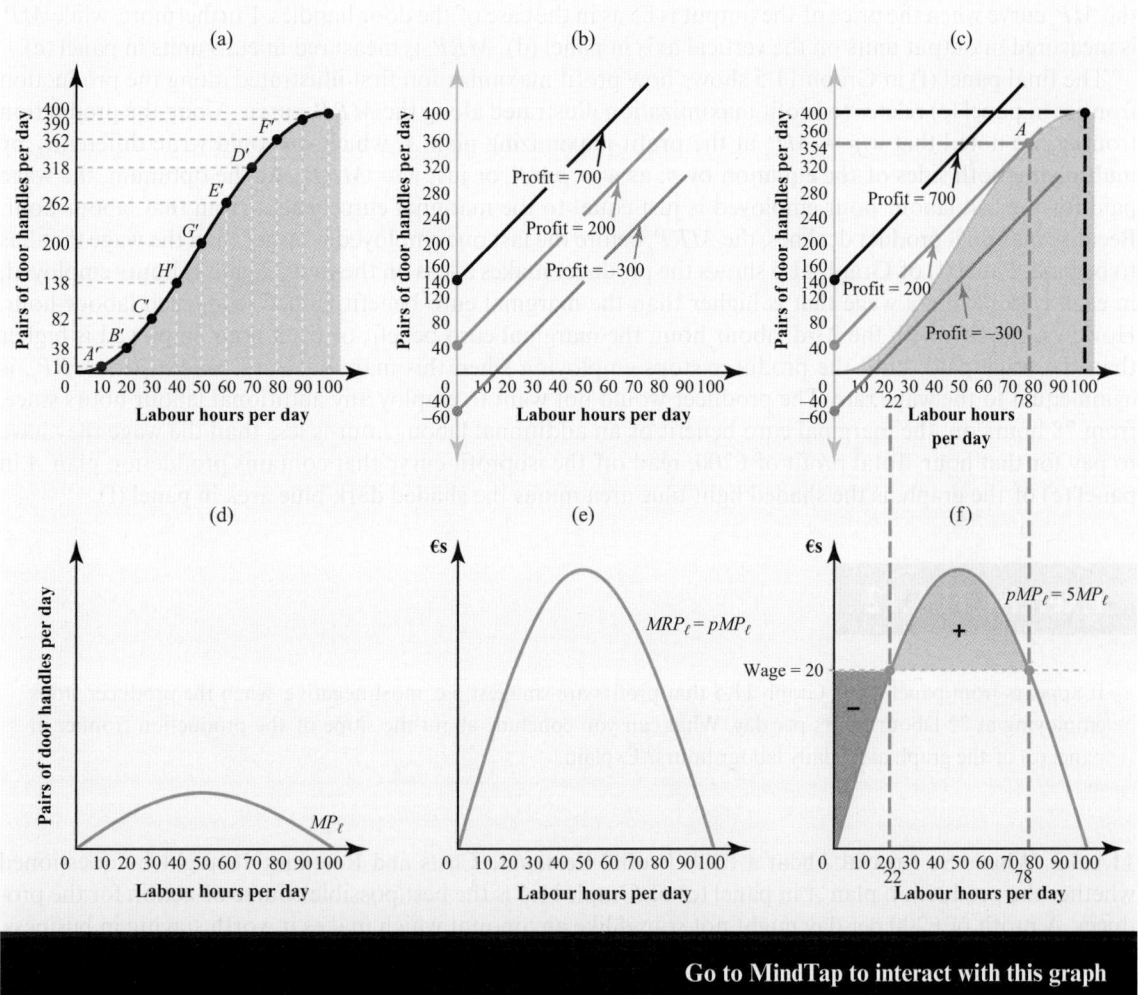

Go to MindTap to interact with this graph

The goal of a profit-maximizing producer of door handles is to find the highest isoprofit curve that contains at least one technologically feasible production plan. Beginning on the light blue isoprofit curve in panel (c) of Graph 11.5 and moving northwest in the direction of the dark blue isoprofit curve, we reach this highest possible profit at the production plan A where the (dark brown) isoprofit curve corresponding to a profit of €200 is tangential to the frontier of the producer choice set. Thus, production plan A is the profit-maximizing plan in this case.

11A.3.2 Marginal Product = w/p (or Marginal Revenue Product = w) From panel (c) of Graph 11.5, at the profit-maximizing production plan A, the slope of the isoprofit curve (w/p) is equal to the slope of the production frontier, which is just the marginal product of labour MP_ℓ. To see how this makes intuitive sense, it is useful for us to see the same profit-maximizing behaviour play out in a variant of the marginal product of labour graph that we derived from the production frontier in panel (b) of Graph 11.2.

Panel (d) of Graph 11.5 begins by replicating the MP_ℓ curve from panel (b) of Graph 11.2 with the vertical axis rescaled for graphing convenience, which makes it appear that the curve creates a hill that is 'less steep' than before. Recall that this is a graph of the slope of the production frontier in panel (a). Panel (e) of the graph plots a slight variant of the marginal product curve known as the *marginal revenue product* curve. While the marginal product of labour (MP_ℓ) tells us the increase in *output* resulting from one more hour of labour being employed, the marginal revenue product of labour (MRP_ℓ) tells us the increase in *revenue* resulting from one more hour of labour. Since revenue is output times the price of the output p, $MRP_\ell = pMP_\ell$, the MRP_ℓ curve is identical to the MP_ℓ curve when the output price is €1 but is five times the MP_ℓ curve when the price of the output is €5 as in the case of the door handles. Furthermore, while MP_ℓ is measured in output units on the vertical axis in panel (d), MRP_ℓ is measured in euro units in panel (e).

The final panel (f) in Graph 11.5 shows how profit maximization first illustrated along the production frontier in panel (c) relates to profit maximization illustrated along the MRP_ℓ curve. Along the production frontier, we noted that $w/p = MP_\ell$ at the profit-maximizing plan A, which we could write differently by multiplying both sides of the equation by p, as $w = pMP_\ell$ or just $w = MRP_\ell$. At the optimum, the wage paid for the last labour hour employed is just equal to the marginal euro benefit from that labour hour. Because marginal product declines, the MRP_ℓ before the last one employed is larger than the wage that has to be paid. Panel (f) of Graph 11.5 shows the producer makes a loss on the first 22 labour hours employed, in each case paying a wage that is higher than the marginal euro benefit gained from each labour hour. However, starting with the 23rd labour hour, the marginal euro benefit of each hour employed is higher than the wage paid, until the producer stops employing when this marginal euro benefit, the MRP_ℓ, is again equal to the wage rate. The producer would not want to employ any additional labour hours since, from 78 hours on, the marginal euro benefit of an additional labour hour is less than the wage they have to pay for that hour. Total profit of €200, read off the isoprofit curve that contains production plan A in panel (c) of the graph, is the shaded light blue area minus the shaded dark blue area in panel (f).

Exercise 11A.12

It appears from panel (f) of Graph 11.5 that profits are smallest, i.e. most negative, when the producer stops employing at 22 labour hours per day. What can you conclude about the slope of the production frontier in panel (c) of the graph at 22 daily labour hours? Explain.

11A.3.3 What's So Special About a €200 Profit? Economic Costs and Revenues It might be questioned whether the production plan A in panel (c) of Graph 11.5 is the best possible course of action for the producer. A profit of €200 per day might not sound like an amount which makes it worth staying in business. Maybe there are better opportunities outside the door handle business. It turns out, however, that this is not the case, *assuming we have defined all the variables correctly*.

In defining the term *profit*, it was noted that this is equal to all economic revenues from sales of the output minus all economic costs from hiring inputs. The key words in this definition are 'all' and 'economic'. Revenue is considered *economic revenue from production* if and only if it is generated from ongoing production and would not exist were the producer to stop production. Similarly, a cost is considered an economic cost incurred in production if and only if it is directly linked to ongoing production and would not arise if the producer chose to discontinue production. These statements may seem trivial at first, but two examples will illustrate how we might understand costs and revenues differently if we talked to accountants instead of economists.

Assume the business has been running for a while and has paid taxes in the past. This year, the government has a budget surplus and decides to return the surplus in the form of tax rebates to businesses, with the amount each business receives proportional to the tax it paid last year. Should this rebate be classed as 'revenue' for the business? In an accounting sense, it is – the money is deposited into the business's account. However, the money is not an *economic* revenue from producing door handles. It is not associated with ongoing production of door handles, and is revenue that would not materialize if the business ceased production. The amount of the funds will be no different whether the business produces 10, 100, 1000 or no door handles per day this year. Since this 'revenue' has nothing to do with current economic decisions in the factory, it is not a relevant or economic revenue for those decisions.

Suppose the factory had a faulty exhaust valve last year which caused illegal pollution to escape into the environment. Suppose further that the producer became aware of the problem at the beginning of the year and quietly fixed it, breathing a sigh of relief that they had not been caught. However, the producer gets a letter from the environmental regulators noting that satellite images taken last year reveal excessive pollution emanating from the factory. As a result, the producer is fined €10 000 and ordered to fix the problem. Since they have already fixed the problem, they just have to pay the fine, which the accountant says is considered a current cost for the business. To determine whether it is an economic cost of producing, we have to consider whether the fine depends on the current production decisions. The answer is again no; regardless of whether or how much the producer produces now and in the future, the fine is based on something that happened in the past. It is no more an economic cost of producing door handles than an increase in the producer's private car insurance premiums, because neither has anything to do with the economic choices the producer currently faces in their business. From the perspective of the business, both are what are called *sunk costs*, not economic costs.

Exercise 11A.13

Suppose the producer has already signed a contract with an agent who is providing the factory space, machinery and raw materials for the business, and suppose that the producer agreed in that contract to pay the owner €100 per month for the coming year. Is this an economic cost with respect to a decision of whether and how much to produce this year?

In terms of whether it is worth staying in business for €200 a day, and whether it would be optimal for the producer to put their energies into something else that will make more profit, the key is taking into consideration the opportunity cost of their time and what the next best alternative to running a door handles business would be. The opportunity cost of time, unlike the fine for last year's pollution, *is* an economic cost of producing door handles; to the extent that the business takes time away from the producer, that is an economic cost that must be included in any calculation of economic profit. By not explicitly including it in the model so far, we have assumed either (1) that the opportunity cost of the producer's time is the market wage of €20 per hour, and the worker hours are part of what is employed to produce the handles, or (2) that this business actually takes no time for the producer at all and will run itself. In the first case, if they spend 8 hours a day at the factory they are already including in the profit calculations that they are paying themselves a wage of €20 per hour, for a total of €160 per day. If that is the opportunity cost of their time, it is the best they could do working anywhere else. In this business, the producer ends up bringing home €360 per day – the €160 wage *plus* €200 profit – and they are, therefore, doing €200 better in the business than they could be doing anything else. In the second case, the business takes no time away from the producer, which implies that there is no time cost on their part, and the €200 is a return they would otherwise not have.

When we conclude that someone is making economic profits above zero, we are by definition assuming we have included everything that should be included in the calculation, concluding that the individual does better in this economic activity than they could in any known alternative.

11A.4 Changing the Economic Environment

We have concluded that the producer should produce 354 handles using 78 labour hours per day when the hourly wage is €20 and the output price is €5. We can now ask how the profit-maximizing choice will change as either output prices or wages change in the economy. The producer's response to such changes could be: (1) to produce more, (2) to produce the same, (3) to produce less or (4) to shut down and stop producing door handles.

11A.4.1 A Change in the Market Wage Suppose first that hourly wages fall from €20 to €10. We have already seen in panel (a) of Graph 11.4 that a change in wages alters the slopes of each isoprofit curve (w/p) from 4 to 2 without altering the intercepts (Profit/p). This implies that the new optimal production plan B *must* lie to the right of the original optimal plan A because a shallower isoprofit line must now be tangential to the production frontier, *which becomes shallower to the right of A*. In the top part of panel (a) of Graph 11.6, the new optimal production plan requires 90 daily labour hours to produce 390 rather than the original 354 pairs of door handles. The intercept of the new optimal isoprofit curve is 209, which implies a profit at production plan B of €1045. At first, it may appear that because there is a new intercept on the optimal isoprofit curve, the graph is contradicting the notion that a change in wages changes the slopes but not the intercepts of isoprofit curves. The statement that intercepts do not change when wages change, however, applies to *any particular isoprofit curve corresponding to a particular amount of profit*. In panel (a) of the graph, for instance, the original isoprofit curve will indeed change slope without changing the intercept. However, at the new wage, this isoprofit curve is *no longer the optimal isoprofit curve*, and so the producer moves to a higher isoprofit that is tangential at B.

Exercise 11A.14

There are also production plans to the left of A where the slope of the production frontier is shallower. Why are we not considering these?

The lower part of panel (a) of Graph 11.6 illustrates the same profit-maximization exercise in the marginal revenue product graph that is derived from the production frontier in the top panel.

Exercise 11A.15

Which areas in the lower part of panel (a) of Graph 11.6 add up to the €200 profit made before wages fell? Which areas add up to the €1045 profit made after wages fall?

Next, suppose the hourly wage rate in the labour market rises to €30. This increases the slope of iso-profit curves (w/p) to 6, implying that the new tangency with the production frontier will lie to the left of A. This is illustrated in the top part of panel (b) of Graph 11.6 where that tangency occurs at the production plan C, which employs 59 daily labour hours to produce 254 daily pairs of door handles. Notice how this looks on the lower part of panel (b) of Graph 11.6 along the marginal revenue product curve. According to the production plan C, the producer would incur losses on each worker employed up to the 42nd worker hour and only begin to generate marginal benefits above the wage when employing workers from the 43rd to the 59th worker hour. If the producer employs 59 hours of labour, as called for in the production plan C, their profit is the tiny shaded light blue area in the lower right panel of the graph minus the large shaded dark blue area, which appears to sum to a negative number. Going back to the top panel, we can see that this is indeed the case because the intercept of the isoprofit curve tangent at production plan C is -100.

Graph 11.6 The Impact of Changing Wages on Profit-Maximizing Choices

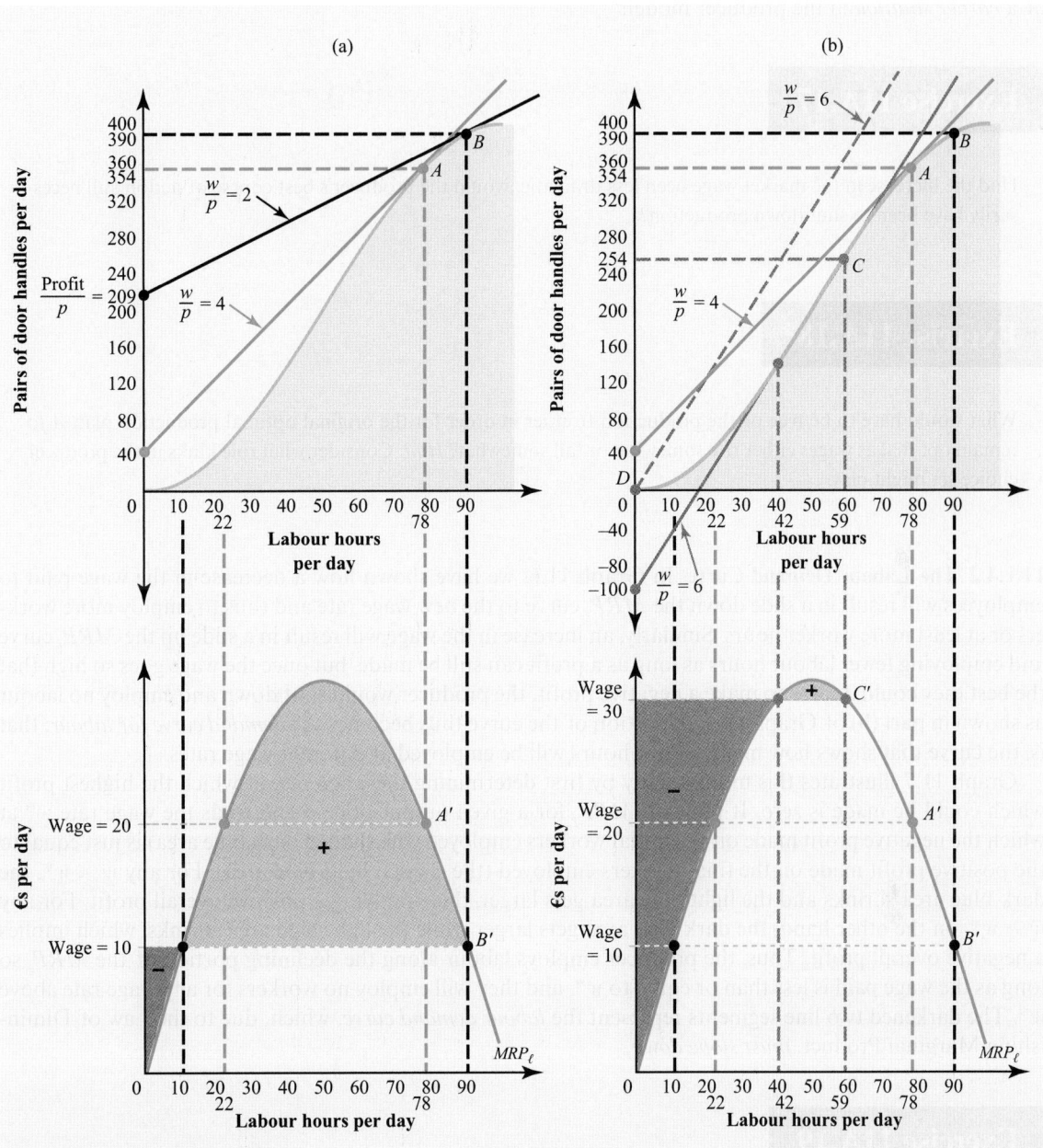

Exercise 11A.16

Given an intercept of −100 of this isoprofit curve, what is the value of profit indicated by the shaded light blue minus the shaded dark blue area in the lower part of panel (b) of Graph 11.6?

Thus, for an increase in the wage to €30 per hour, the best course of action is actually not to implement production plan C, but rather to implement production plan D, which calls for no labour and no production of output and thus zero profit along the dashed light blue isoprofit curve in panel (b) of Graph 11.6.

The producer would be better to engage in the next best alternative economic activity. This is an example of a *corner solution* in the producer model.

Exercise 11A.17

Had the increase in the market wage been less dramatic, would the producer's best course of action still necessarily have been to shut down production?

Exercise 11A.18*

What would have to be true of the production frontier in order for the original optimal production plan *A* to remain optimal as wages either rise somewhat or fall somewhat? *Hint*: Consider what role kinks in the producer choice set might play.

11A.4.2 The Labour Demand Curve In Graph 11.6, we have shown how a decrease in the wage paid to employees will result in a slide down the MRP_ℓ curve to the new wage rate and thus to employ more workers or at least more worker hours. Similarly, an increase in the wage will result in a slide up the MRP_ℓ curve and employing fewer labour hours as long as a profit can still be made, but once the wage goes so high that the best they could do was to make a negative profit, the producer would shut down and employ no labour as shown in part (b) of Graph 11.6. A portion of the curve thus becomes the *demand curve for labour*; that is, the curve that shows how many labour hours will be employed at different wage rates.

Graph 11.7 illustrates this more exactly by first determining the wage rate at which the highest profit which could be made is zero. It plots an MRP_ℓ for a given output price p and finds the wage rate w^* at which the negative profit made on the initial workers employed (the shaded dark blue area) is just equal to the positive profit made on the final workers employed (the shaded light blue area). For any $w < w^*$, the dark blue area shrinks and the light blue area gets larger, thus implying a positive overall profit. For any $w > w^*$, on the other hand, the dark blue area gets larger while the light blue area shrinks, which implies a negative overall profit. Thus, the producer employs labour along the declining portion of the MRP_ℓ so long as the wage paid is less than or equal to w^*, and they will employ no workers for any wage rate above w^*. The darkened two line segments represent the *labour demand curve*, which, due to the Law of Diminishing Marginal Product, *must slope down*.

Exercise 11A.19

Why would it be economically rational for the producer to still stay open for business when $w = w^*$ where the profit is zero?

Exercise 11A.20

If the producer had signed a contract and agreed to make monthly payments for the next year to the agent who provided the factory space, would w^* – the highest wage at which they will still produce – be any different?

Graph 11.7 MRP_{ℓ} and Labour Demand

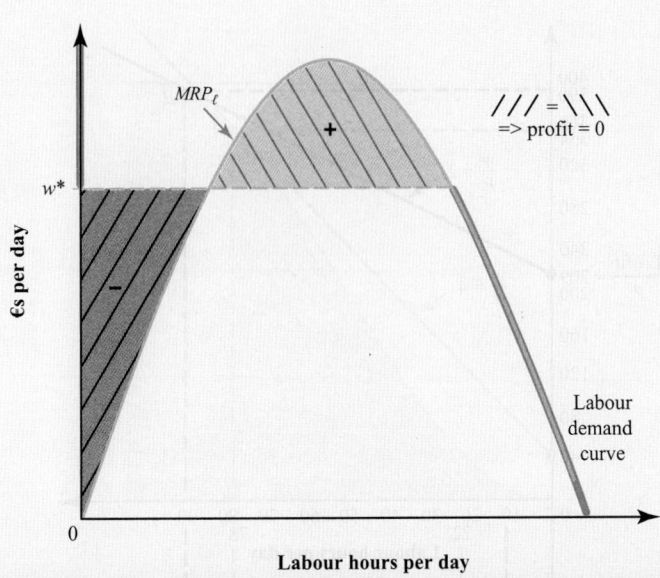

11A.4.3 A Change in the Output Price Now suppose that the wage was unchanged at €20 per hour but the market price of door handles increases to €10 per pair. We have seen in panel (b) of Graph 11.4 how such an increase in price alters the shape of isoprofit curves. The slope of isoprofit curves is now 2 instead of 4, just as it was when wages fell to €10 in panel (a) of Graph 11.6. If the isoprofits now have a slope of 2, the tangency of the highest isoprofit curve must fall exactly at the same production plan B as when wages fell to €10! For this reason, the top panel of Graph 11.8, illustrating the change in profit maximization along the production frontier when price increases to €10, *looks exactly the same as the top part of panel (a) of Graph 11.6*. It is optimal to produce 390 pairs of door handles per day using 90 labour hours.

Despite the fact that the profit maximization along the production frontier *looks* exactly identical for an increase in the price from €5 to €10 as it does for a decrease in the hourly wage from €20 to €10, there are underlying differences that emerge in the lower panels of the graphs. First, note that the marginal revenue product curve did not change when the wage changed because MRP_{ℓ} is just pMP_{ℓ}. Since p is by definition a part of MRP_{ℓ}, however, the marginal revenue product curve *does move when price changes*. In particular, since each pair of door handles now sells for twice what they did before, each worker hour has just become twice as productive in euro terms, even though it remains unchanged in output terms. Thus, each point on the new (dark blue) marginal revenue product curve is twice as high as the corresponding point on the original (dark brown) marginal revenue product curve. While the optimal production plan is the same when the price of pairs of door handles increases to €10 as it is when the wage rate falls to €10, profit is clearly higher under the former scenario than under the latter.

Exercise 11A.21

What areas in the lower panel of Graph 11.8 add up to the new profit? What is the euro value of this new profit, which you can calculate from the intercept of the isoprofit curve in the top panel of the graph?

Graph 11.8 The Impact of Changing Prices on Profit-Maximizing Choices

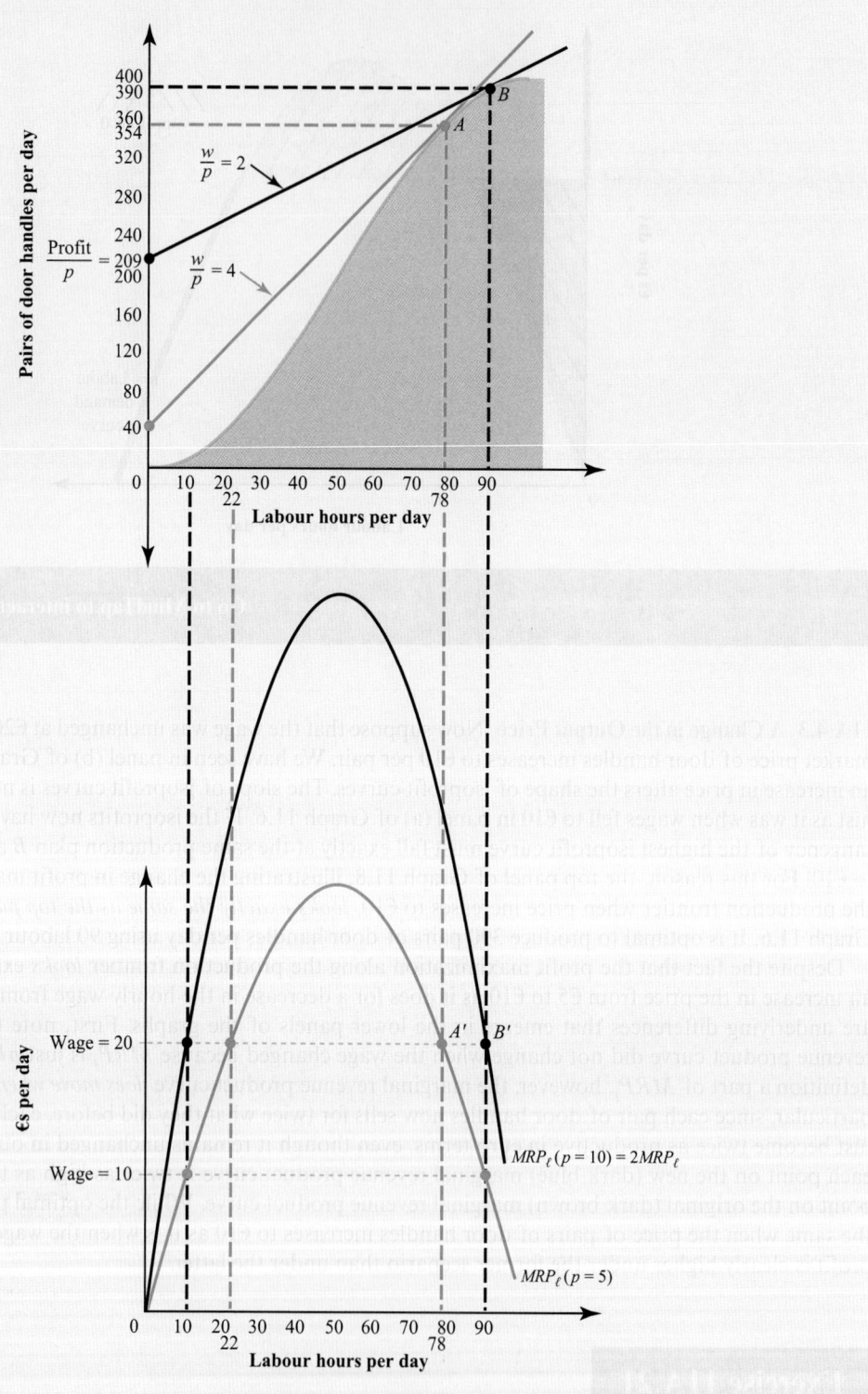

Exercise 11A.22

Can you tell from Graph 11.8 how the labour demand curve will change when p changes?

Exercise 11A.23

What value would p have to take in order for isoprofits to have the same slope as when wages increased to €30 per hour as in panel (b) of Graph 11.6? What would be the optimal course of action in that case?

11A.4.4 The Output Supply Curve From Graph 11.8, we can see that an increase in the price of the output, without a change in price of the input, will lead the producer to produce more output as a flatter isoprofit curve is fitted to the production frontier that becomes flatter as production increases. Panel (a) of Graph 11.9 begins with a slight variant of the top panel of Graph 11.8 by plotting two isoprofit curves tangential to the production frontier. The blue isoprofit curve has a slope (w/p^*) where p^* is set to ensure that the intercept of the tangential isoprofit is exactly zero. This implies that profit for all production plans located along the dark brown isoprofit in panel (a) of Graph 11.9 is zero, and the optimal production plan when price is p^* is the plan A, which uses ℓ^* in labour hours to produce x^* in output.

For any price higher than p^*, the isoprofit curves become shallower, implying optimal production plans that lie to the right of A. For price p', for instance, the plan B, which uses ℓ' hours of labour input to produce x' in output, is optimal. For any price lower than p^*, on the other hand, isoprofits become steeper, and the tangency of such isoprofit curves would result in a production plan that lies to the left of A with negative intercept. Profit at such tangencies is negative, and the producer could do better by shutting down and producing nothing. Therefore, if the price of door handles falls below p^*, the factory will stand idle.

Graph 11.9 The Output Supply Curve

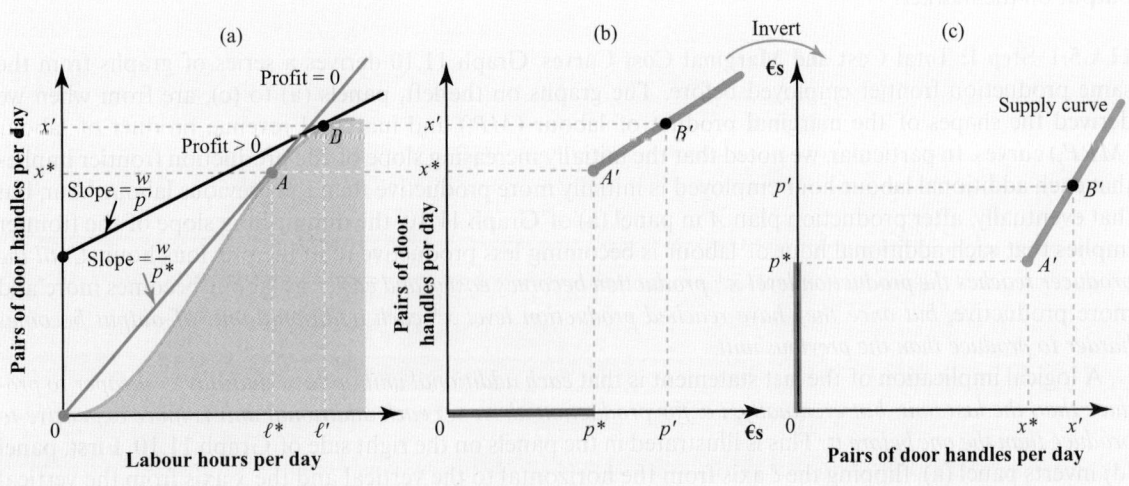

Panel (b) of Graph 11.9 translates the output levels at production plans A and B onto the vertical axis and plots the output prices (p^* and p') at which these production plans are optimal on the horizontal axis. By connecting A' and B' in this new graph, we are approximating how the output of door handles on the vertical axis responds to changes in prices above p^* on the horizontal axis. In addition, the line connecting A' and B' is supplemented by the dark brown line on the horizontal axis below p^*, which indicates that the optimal output at such prices is zero. Panel (c) of the graph inverts panel (b) by flipping the axes, putting output on the horizontal and price on the vertical as we have come to get used to when graphing demand curves. The resulting two line segments in panel (c) represent the *supply curve* for the factory, which is the curve *illustrating the relationship between the price the producer can charge for their output and the amount of output produced.* Just as the labour demand curve slopes down, *the output supply curve slopes up.*

Exercise 11A.24

In Graph 11.9, we implicitly held wages fixed. What happens to the supply curve when wages decrease?

11A.5 Two-Step Profit Maximization

So far, we have explored the direct implications of a firm choosing a profit-maximizing production plan in one step. While this is straightforward to graph in the context of the one-input/one-output model, we will see in the next chapter that this one-step approach becomes considerably more difficult when we have two inputs, i.e. labour *and* capital, rather than one, i.e. just labour. Fortunately, there is a second way to conceptualize the firm's profit-maximization decision. It proceeds in two steps but gives exactly the same answer, and it generalizes more easily to a graphical treatment when the number of inputs goes to two. We will therefore illustrate this alternative conceptual approach here for the one-input model so that we can begin to get used to some of the underlying ideas as we prepare to expand our discussion to models with multiple inputs.

The approach will begin with the assumption that *any profit-maximizing producer will choose to produce whatever quantity they produce at minimum cost.* The assumption allows us to split the profit-maximization problem into two parts. First, how much in terms of costs will the firm incur for all possible quantities of output it might choose to produce? This will permit us to derive *cost curves* that depend on *input prices* but not on the price of the output. We can proceed to the second step and ask how much should the producer produce in order to maximize the difference between costs derived in step 1 and revenues from selling the output on the market?

11A.5.1 Step 1: Total Cost and Marginal Cost Curves Graph 11.10 derives a series of graphs from the same production frontier employed before. The graphs on the left, panels (a) to (c), are from when we derived the shapes of the marginal product of labour (MP_ℓ) and marginal revenue product of labour (MRP_ℓ) curves. In particular, we noted that the initially increasing slope of the production frontier implies that each additional labour hour employed is initially more productive than the previous labour hour, but that eventually, after production plan A in panel (a) of Graph 11.10, the diminishing slope of the frontier implies that each additional hour of labour is becoming less productive than the previous hour. *Until the producer reaches the production level x^A, production becomes easier and easier* as labour becomes more and more productive, *but once they have reached production level x^A, each additional unit of output becomes harder to produce than the previous unit.*

A logical implication of the last statement is that *each additional unit up to x^A initially is cheaper to produce than the last unit, but eventually, i.e. for production above x^A, each additional unit is more expensive to produce than the one before it.* This is illustrated in the panels on the right side of Graph 11.10. First, panel (d) inverts panel (a), flipping the ℓ axis from the horizontal to the vertical and the x axis from the vertical to the horizontal. As a result, the inverse production frontier graphed in panel (d) has the inverse shape of the production frontier in panel (a), with steep slopes becoming shallow and vice versa. For any quantity of output x, this inverse frontier tells us the minimum number of labour hours required to produce this output level.

Graph 11.10 Deriving Total and Marginal Cost From Production Frontiers

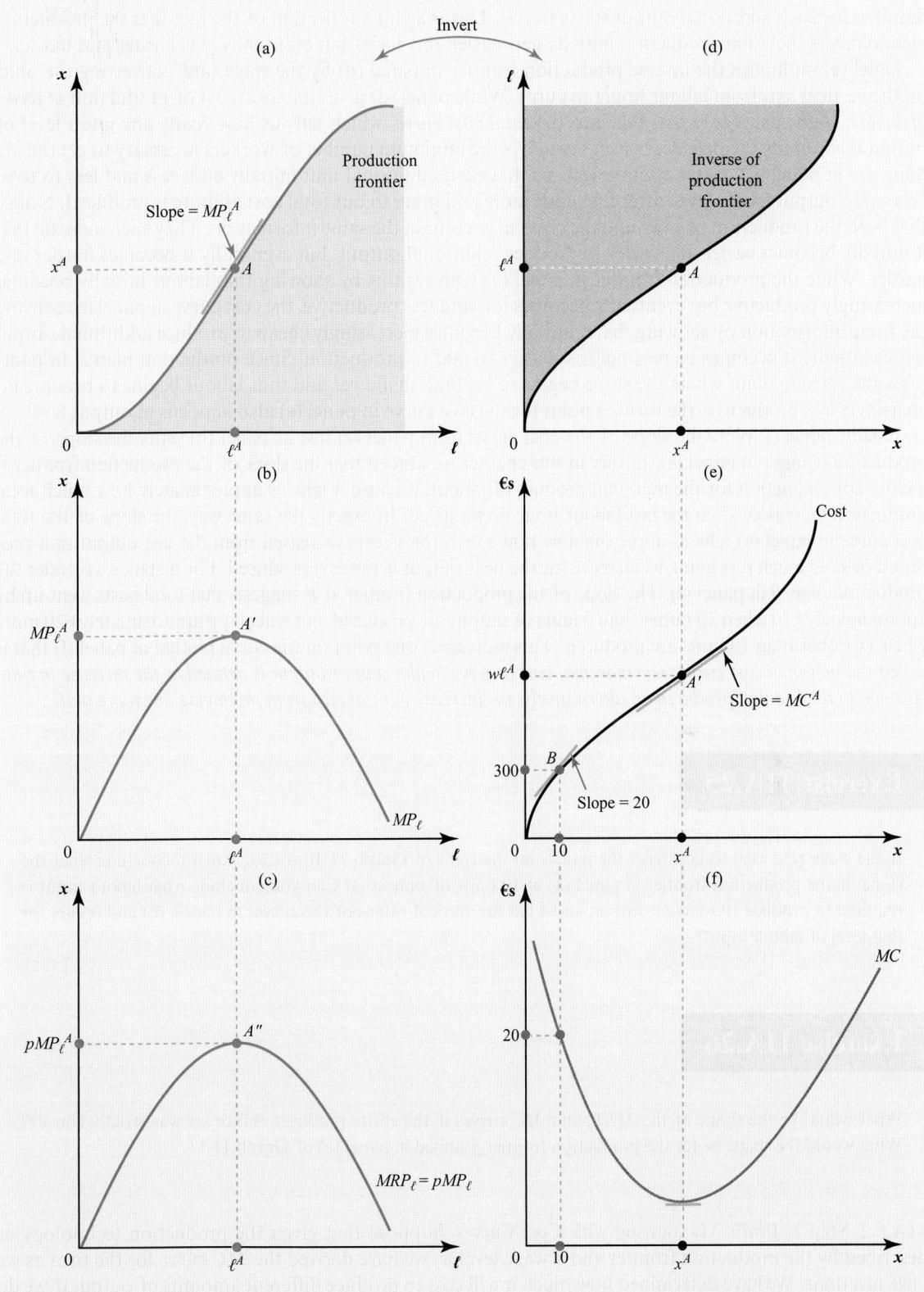

For the first unit of output, a lot of labour is necessary, but the additional labour necessary for each additional unit of output gets less and less until we reach output level x^A, when the additional labour required for each additional output starts to rise. This is again a reflection of the fact that the production technology is such that production initially gets easier and easier but eventually gets harder and harder.

Panel (e) multiplies the inverse production frontier in panel (d) by the wage rate, converting the units on the vertical axis from labour hours to euros. While panel (d) gives the total cost of production *in terms of labour hours*, panel (e) turns this into the *total cost curve*, which tells us how costly any given level of output is assuming the producer always employs the minimum number of workers necessary to get the job done. As in panel (d), this cost curve tells us that each additional unit initially adds less and less to total cost up to output level x^A, but after that adds more and more to our total cost as more is produced. Notice that both the production frontier and the cost curve contain the same information. They each indicate that it initially becomes easier and easier to produce additional output, but eventually it becomes harder and harder. While the production frontier in panel (a) conveys this by showing that labour initially becomes increasingly productive but eventually becomes less and less productive, the cost curve in panel (e) conveys the same information by showing that it initially becomes increasingly cheap to produce additional output but eventually it becomes increasingly expensive to add to production. Since production plan A in panel (a) is the turning point where the slope begins to become shallower and thus labour begins to become increasingly less productive, the turning point for the cost curve in panel (e) also happens at output level x^A.

Finally, panel (f) plots the slope of the cost curve from panel (e) just as panel (b) plots the slope of the production frontier in panel (a). Earlier in this chapter we argued that the slope of the production frontier is a close approximation for the marginal product of labour, because it tells us approximately how much total production increased when the last labour hour is employed. In exactly the same way, the slope of the total cost curve in panel (e) tells us approximately how much total costs increased from the last output unit produced or how much it is going to increase for the next output if more is produced. For instance, consider the production plan B in panel (e). The slope of the production frontier at B suggests that total costs went up by approximately €20 when 10 rather than 9 units of output are produced and will go up approximately €20 more when 11 rather than 10 units are produced. This represents one point on the curve plotted in panel (f) that is called the *marginal cost curve*. *The marginal cost of a particular unit of output is defined as the increase in total cost due to the last unit produced or, alternatively, the increase in total cost from producing one more unit.*

Exercise 11A.25

If the wage rate used to construct the panels on the right of Graph 11.10 is €20, can you conclude what the slope of the production frontier in panel (a) at 10 units of output is? Can you conclude what labour input is required to produce 10 units of output, and what the vertical values of the curves in panels (b) and (c) are for that level of labour input?

Exercise 11A.26

What would be the shape of the MRP_ℓ and MC curves if the entire producer choice set was strictly convex? What would the shape be for the production frontier graphed in panel (a) of Graph 11.1?

11A.5.2 Step 2: Profit Maximizing with Cost Curves Suppose that given the production technology as described by the production frontier and a wage level w, we have derived the MC curve for the firm as we have just done. We have determined how much it will cost to produce different amounts of output if we do so without wasting inputs. None of this had anything to do with the *output* price; what the producer can sell their output for which has nothing to do with what it costs to produce the output. To complete profit maximization in this two-step approach, we now need to ask how much we should produce *given* we know what it costs us and given that the market has set an output price at which goods can be sold.

Panel (a) of Graph 11.11 begins by replicating the *MC* curve from panel (f) of Graph 11.10. Assume the producer faces the output price p^* at which they can sell each unit of output. Since p^* lies below the beginning of the *MC* curve, they will incur a cost for the first unit of output that exceeds the revenue they are able to make from selling that first unit, known as the *marginal revenue* of the first unit. The same is true for the second unit, with the *MC* for that unit indicating the increase in total costs when two rather than one units are produced. Similarly, the producer will incur additional losses equal to the vertical distance between the dotted line at p^* and the *MC* curve for each additional unit produced until the output level x^C where $MC = p^*$. If the producer stopped producing at x^C, they would have incurred losses equal to the dark blue area in panel (a) of Graph 11.11. However, if they continue to produce, they will now be able to sell each additional unit that is produced at a price p^* that is higher than the additional cost incurred from producing that unit, until output level x^D. Thus, if x^D units of output are produced, the producer will have incurred losses summing to the dark blue area and gains summing to the light blue area in panel (a) of Graph 11.11. Producing any more than that would not make any sense since *MC* again rises above the price the producer is able to charge.

Exercise 11A.27

True or False: On a graph with output on the horizontal and euros on the vertical, the marginal revenue curve must always be a flat line so long as the producer is a price taker.

Graph 11.11 Deriving the Output Supply Curve From *MC*

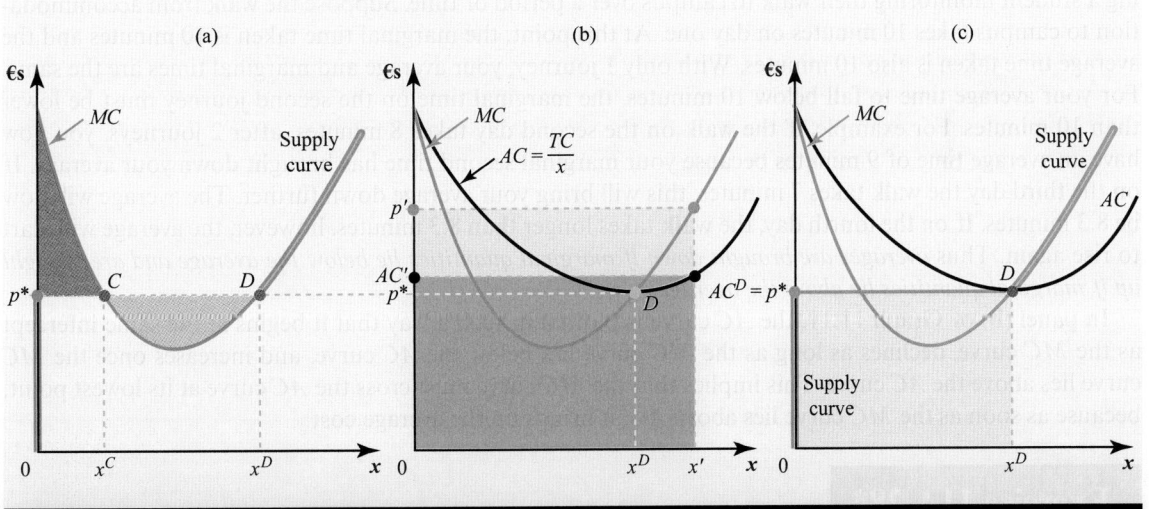

Go to MindTap to interact with this graph

For the price p^* depicted in the graph, the dark blue area is just equal to the light blue area, indicating that the overall profit from producing x^D units of output is equal to zero. If the price of the output falls below p^*, the dark blue area increases and the light blue area decreases, implying that overall negative profits would be incurred by producing, and the producer would choose to shut down production thereby making zero profit instead. This is indicated by the dark brown line segment on the vertical axis below p^*. If, on the other hand, the output price rises above p^*, the dark blue area shrinks and the light blue area increases, implying that overall profit from producing wherever the price intersects MC is positive. The dark brown portion of the MC curve that lies above the 'break-even' price $p*$ therefore indicates how much output the producer will choose to supply to the market when price rises above $p*$. The combination of the two dark blue line segments represents the output supply curve, which has *exactly the same shape as the output supply curve derived in panel (c) of Graph 11.9 when we derived the curve directly using isoprofit curves and the production frontier*. That's because it is exactly the same curve. All we have done here is split the profit-maximization problem into two parts. First, we asked how much it *costs* to produce all possible output levels, and we asked which of these output levels creates the largest difference between total revenues from selling the output, and total production costs which we identified in step 1.

11A.5.3 Using Average Cost Curves to Locate $p*$

There is an easier way than adding dark blue and light blue areas along the MC curve to find the point on the MC curve at which the profit-maximizing producer will choose to shut down. For this, we need to introduce the *average cost curve*.

   Average Cost is defined as total cost divided by output. At the production plan B in panel (e) of Graph 11.10, for instance, the total cost curve indicates that 10 units of the output can be produced at a total cost of €300. This implies that the average cost of producing 1 unit of output when producing an overall quantity of 10 units is €30. This is different from the marginal cost, which is the cost of producing the last unit or the cost of producing 1 additional unit. The *average cost (AC) curve* plots the average cost for each quantity of production by dividing the total cost by that quantity. This curve has a U-shape for the same reason as the marginal cost curve, because we have assumed a production technology under which it initially becomes easier and easier to produce additional output thus causing the average cost to fall, while eventually it becomes harder and harder causing average cost at some point to rise again. In addition, however, the AC curve has a more precise logical relationship to the MC curve in the following two ways. First, *the AC curve begins at essentially the same vertical intercept as the marginal cost curve (although it is not exactly the same since average costs are not defined with quantity equal to zero), and second, it attains its lowest point where the marginal cost curve crosses it*. This is depicted in panel (b) of Graph 11.11.

   We can develop the intuition for this relationship between average and marginal cost curves by imagining a student monitoring their walk to campus over a period of time. Suppose the walk from accommodation to campus takes 10 minutes on day one. At this point, the marginal time taken is 10 minutes and the average time taken is also 10 minutes. With only 1 journey, your average and marginal times are the same. For your average time to fall below 10 minutes, the marginal time on the second journey must be lower than 10 minutes. For example, if the walk on the second day takes 8 minutes, after 2 journeys, you now have an average time of 9 minutes because your marginal second time has brought down your average. If on the third day the walk takes 7 minutes, this will bring your average down further. The average will now be 8.3 minutes. If on the fourth day, the walk takes longer than 8.3 minutes, however, the average will start to rise again. Thus *averages are brought down if marginal quantities lie below the average and are brought up if marginal quantities lie above the average.*

   In panel (b) of Graph 11.11, the AC curve is plotted in such a way that it begins at the same intercept as the MC curve, declines as long as the MC curve lies below the AC curve, and increases once the MC curve lies above the AC curve. This implies that the MC curve must cross the AC curve at its lowest point, because as soon as the MC curve lies above AC, it brings up the average cost.

Exercise 11A.28*

MC can fall while *AC* rises. Can you give an analogous example of marginal test grades falling while the average grade rises at the same time?

   In addition, the lowest point of the AC curve is plotted at point D, which lies at the break-even price $p*$. This is not an arbitrary choice; *it is logically necessary that this is precisely where the AC curve reaches its lowest point because overall profits are zero when the output price is exactly equal to the lowest point of the average cost curve.*

This is not immediately obvious, but we can reason to the conclusion. Suppose the price faced is not p^* but rather p' in panel (b) of Graph 11.11. The producer would choose to produce the quantity x' on the output supply curve, which implies that the average cost per unit of output incurred is AC'. If the average cost is AC' and a total output of x' *is produced*, *total cost* is AC' times x', or the very dark brown shaded area. You can also see this from the definition of AC as $AC = TC/x$, which directly implies that $TC = x(AC)$. *Total revenue*, on the other hand, is equal to the quantity produced (x') times the price charged for each unit of output (p'), which is equal to the very dark brown area plus the less dark brown area in panel (b) of Graph 11.11. This implies that profit is the difference between these two areas, or just the less dark brown area.

We can do the same calculation when the price of the output is p^* in panel (c) of Graph 11.11. In this case, the quantity x^D is produced at average cost AC^D. This implies total cost is the dark brown area. Since the output price is p^*, the producer can sell each of the x^D goods produced at p^*, which implies that total revenue is also equal to the dark brown area in panel (c). Because $p^* = AC^D$, total revenue and total cost are therefore equal and overall profit is zero just as we concluded was true in panel (a) of the graph. The break-even price must therefore lie exactly at the lowest point of the AC curve where MC crosses AC. As a result, *if we have a graph with both the average and the marginal cost curves, we can locate the output supply curve as the portion of the MC curve that lies above AC, with zero supply at prices below.*

Exercise 11A.29

How do the marginal and average cost curves look if the producer choice set is convex?

11B   The Mathematics of the Short-Run Model

For this section, we will continue with the example of a producer producing pairs of door handles denoted x by using the input labour hours denoted by ℓ.

11B.1 Technological Constraints Faced by Producers

When we introduced consumer choice sets in Chapter 2, we did so by defining mathematical notation used to describe sets of points, with the first portion of the definition of a set indicating what geometric space the points occupy, i.e. are they an element of $\mathbb{R}^2_+$, $\mathbb{R}^3_+$, etc., and the latter part of the definition indicating conditions that such points must satisfy in the form of an equation, i.e. the budget equation. The first portion of the definition gave the *necessary* conditions that points must satisfy while the second portion gave the *sufficient* conditions for those points to lie in the set we were describing. We will follow the same practice here when we define producer choice sets and will work directly with the equations that define producer choice sets to illustrate their mathematical properties.

11B.1.1 Production Plans, Producer Choice Sets and Production Frontiers
Production plans for single-input/single-output production processes are points in a two-dimensional space. The producer choice set is given by all production plans that lie below the production frontier that is defined by a *production function*. Defined formally, the producer choice set C defined by the production function $f: \mathbb{R}^1_+ \to \mathbb{R}^1_+$, can be written as:

$$C(f: \mathbb{R}^1_+ \to \mathbb{R}^1_+) = \{(x, \ell) \in \mathbb{R}^2 \mid x \le f(\ell)\}. \tag{11.1}$$

In principle, this producer choice set could take on all sorts of shapes, but in part A of the chapter we emphasized a particular kind of 'sigmoid' shape. There are a number of ways we can derive such a shape of a production function that initially has an increasing but eventually decreasing marginal product of labour. For instance, consider the function:

$$f(\ell) = \alpha(1 - \cos(\beta\ell)) \quad \text{for } 0 \le \ell \le \frac{\pi}{\beta} \approx \frac{3.1416}{\beta}$$

$$2\alpha \quad \text{for } \ell > \frac{\pi}{\beta} \approx \frac{3.1416}{\beta}. \tag{11.2}$$

Since $\cos(0) = 1$, this function begins with zero output for zero labour input, i.e. $f(0) = 0$; and, since $\cos(\pi) = -1$, output reaches 2α when $\ell = \pi/\beta$. In between $\ell = 0$ and $\ell = \pi/\beta$, the function is upward sloping, with initially increasing slope and thus increasing marginal product of labour, but eventually decreasing slope and thus decreasing marginal product of labour. Note that here we are using π to denote the mathematical value of pi. Elsewhere we use the same Greek letter to denote profit.

Exercise 11B.1

How would this production function look differently if we did not specify that output levels off at 2α?

The production function graphed in panel (b) of Graph 11.1, and implicitly used throughout Section A, was derived from this general form, with $\alpha = 200$ and $\beta = 0.031416$ (or $\pi/100$); that is, we used the production function:

$$f(\ell) = 200\left(1 - \cos\left(\frac{3.1416\ell}{100}\right)\right) \quad \text{for } 0 \le \ell \le 100 \text{ and}$$

$$400 \quad \text{for } \ell > 100. \tag{11.3}$$

Exercise 11B.2

Define the production function generating the production frontier in panel (a) of Graph 11.1 and define the corresponding producer choice set formally.

11B.1.2 Slopes of Production Functions: The Marginal Product of Labour The definition of the marginal product of labour (MP_ℓ) is the increase in total output from hiring one more unit of the input. Once we have defined a production function f, we can restate this definition as the derivative of the production function with respect to the input; that is:

$$MP_\ell = \frac{df}{d\ell}. \tag{11.4}$$

Recalling that the derivative of $(\cos x)$ is $(-\sin x)$, the marginal product of labour for the production function defined in (11.3) becomes:

$$MP_\ell = 200\left(\frac{3.1416}{100}\right)\sin\left(\frac{3.1416\ell}{100}\right) = 6.2832\sin\left(\frac{3.1416\ell}{100}\right), \tag{11.5}$$

which is what is graphed in panel (b) of Graph 11.2.

Exercise 11B.3

Given that f is really defined as in equation (11.3), how should equation (11.5) be modified to reflect accurately the marginal product of labour for labour hours above 100?

Exercise 11B.4

Derive the marginal product of labour from the production function you derived in exercise 11B.2. Compare this to the graphical derivation in panel (a) of Graph 11.2.

11B.1.3 Diminishing Marginal Product of Labour In Section 11A.1.3, we argued that in a world of scarcity, the marginal product of any input must eventually decline. Knowing that the marginal product is just the derivative of the production function, we can now see how this Law of Diminishing Marginal Product relates directly to the mathematical properties of the production function f. In particular, we can translate the Law of Diminishing Marginal Product into the mathematical statement that 'the slope, or the derivative, of MP_ℓ is negative for sufficiently high levels of labour'. Since the MP_ℓ is the derivative of f, the Law of Diminishing Marginal Product can furthermore be stated as 'the second derivative of the production function must be negative for sufficiently high levels of labour', or:

$$\text{There exists } \ell^* < \infty \text{ such that } \frac{dMP_\ell}{d\ell} = \frac{d^2f}{d\ell^2} < 0 \text{ for all } \ell > \ell^*. \tag{11.6}$$

This means that the production function must at some point begin to get shallower and shallower.

Exercise 11B.5

Check to see that the Law of Diminishing Marginal Product of labour is satisfied for the production function in equation (11.3).

11B.2 'Tastes' for Profits

Having defined the technology constraint through producer choice sets, Section 11A.2 proceeded to argue that indifference curves for profit-maximizing and price-taking producers must be straight lines of production plans with each yielding the same amount of profit. The intercept of such an indifference curve, or isoprofit, corresponding to the profit level π was derived as (π/p) and the slope as w/p.

More formally, an isoprofit curve p containing all production plans that result in a particular profit level π when the output price is p and the wage rate is w can be defined as a set:

$$P(\pi, w, p) = \{(x, \ell) \in \mathbb{R}^2 | \pi = px - w\ell\}, \tag{11.7}$$

where the equation contained in the definition of this set is that derived intuitively in Section 11A.2. The equation $\pi = px - w\ell$ can be rewritten by adding $w\ell$ to both sides and dividing by p as:

$$x = \left(\frac{\pi}{p}\right) + \left(\frac{w}{p}\right)\ell, \tag{11.8}$$

an equation with intercept (π/p) and slope (w/p). The isoprofit curves in Graphs 11.3 and 11.4 are depictions of equation (11.8) with different values substituted for π, w and p.

11B.3 Choosing the Production Plan That Maximizes Profits

In our development of the consumer model, we ultimately set up a constrained optimization problem, with the utility function as the objective function to be maximized and the budget line as the constraint over which the maximization would happen. In the producer model, on the other hand, we defined profit π as the objective to be maximized over the technological constraint imposed by a production function that limits the set of production plans that are feasible.

11B.3.1 Setting up the Producer's Optimization Problem The producer chooses the production plan (x,ℓ) that will maximize their profit $\pi = px - w\ell$ subject to the constraint that (x,ℓ) is technologically feasible. Stated more formally, the producer solves the problem:

$$\max_{x,\ell} \pi = px - w\ell \text{ subject to } x = f(\ell). \tag{11.9}$$

In Chapter 6, we described several ways of solving such constrained optimization problems, with Method 1 substituting the constraint into the objective function and Method 2 setting up a Lagrange function to differentiate. In the case of the single-input/single-output model, Method 1 is often the simplest method, allowing us to convert the constrained optimization problem described in equation (11.9) into an unconstrained optimization problem:

$$\max_{\ell} \pi = pf(\ell) - w\ell. \tag{11.10}$$

11B.3.2 Marginal Product $= w/p$ or Marginal Revenue Product $= w$ Solving the unconstrained optimization problem (11.10) requires taking the first derivative of the function π and setting it to zero; that is, the first-order condition for the profit-maximization problem (11.10) is:

$$\frac{d\pi}{d\ell} = p\left(\frac{df(\ell)}{d\ell}\right) - w = 0, \tag{11.11}$$

or, with terms rearranged and substituting MP_ℓ for $df(\ell)/d\ell$:

$$MP_\ell = \frac{w}{p} \text{ or equivalently } pMP_\ell = MRP_\ell = w. \tag{11.12}$$

Thus, for our example of a production process defined by equation (11.3), this implies that the optimal production plan has to satisfy the condition that:

$$MP_\ell = 6.2832 \sin\left(\frac{3.1416\ell}{100}\right) = \frac{w}{p}. \tag{11.13}$$

What we concluded from panels (c) and (f) in Graph 11.5 falls out of the mathematics behind the graphs. At the optimum, the marginal product of labour is equal to w/p and the marginal revenue product of labour is equal to w. In terms of the language used in part A, this means that the producer will employ labour along the declining marginal revenue product curve so long as the marginal benefit of an additional labour hour in terms of revenue is greater than its marginal cost in terms of the wage. When $w = 20$ and $p = 5$ as in Graph 11.5, for instance, equation (11.13) simplifies to $\sin(0.031416\ell) = 0.6366$, which is satisfied for $\ell = 22$ and $\ell = 78$. The first of these solutions represents the first point at which wage crosses the marginal revenue product curve in panel (f) of Graph 11.5 and therefore represents a profit 'minimum' rather than a maximum. The second solution, $\ell = 78$, represents the true solution on the downward-sloping part of the marginal revenue product curve.

11B.4 Labour Demand, Output Supply and 'Real Optima'

The optimal solutions in Graphs 11.6 and 11.8 all depict profit-maximizing optima as either w or p changes. Each of these was calculated using the production function (11.3), as the optimization problem (11.10) was solved for these different economic conditions. In fact, the solution to the optimization problem (11.10) implicitly defines a *labour demand function* that gives the quantity of labour ℓ demanded for any wage rate w and price p; that is:

$$\ell = \ell(p, w). \tag{11.14}$$

The initial *labour demand curve* derived in Graph 11.7 is a 'slice' of the *labour demand function*, with p held fixed at €5, i.e. $\ell(5.w)$. To be more precise, just as in the case of consumer demand curves, economists graph slices of *inverse* functions, and the labour demand *curve* in Graph 11.7 is the inverse of $\ell(5.w)$. We noted in panel (b) of Graph 11.8 that as p changes, the MRP_ℓ curve shifts up for an increase in p and down for a decrease in p. Since the labour demand curve is a part of the MRP_ℓ curve, an outward shift with an increase in p from €5 to €10 results in a shift in the labour demand curve, going from the slice $\ell(5.w)$ to $\ell(10.w)$. The labour demand function $\ell(p,w)$ can be similarly sliced, holding w fixed and allowing p to vary providing a curve relating output price to labour demand.

Exercise 11B.6

Without doing the maths, can you tell if the curve $\ell(p,20)$ slopes up or down? How does it relate to $\ell(p,10)$?

Once we have a function $\ell(p,w)$ that tells us for each output price and wage rate how many labour hours the producer will employ, we can also derive the *output supply function* because the production function f shows the output produced for any level of labour input. The supply of x is a function of p and w given by:

$$x(p, w) = f(\ell(p, w)). \tag{11.15}$$

In Graph 11.6, for instance, the output quantity $x = 354$ can be derived by substituting the optimal labour demand of approximately 78 into the production function.

The graph of the supply curve that relates the output price to the quantity produced is again an inverse slice of the supply function in equation (11.15) with wage held fixed. In particular, panel (b) of Graph 11.9 depicts the function $x(p, 20)$ where wage is fixed at €20 per hour, and the graph in panel (c) of Graph 11.9 depicts its inverse, called the supply curve.

Finally, with expressions for output supply and labour demand, a function can be derived that tells us, for any price and wage rate, the amount of profit the producer will earn. This function is known as the *profit function, π*, and is written as:

$$\pi = \pi(p, w) = px(w, p) - w\ell(p, w). \tag{11.16}$$

11B.4.1 Corner Solutions We have noted in our graphs that for certain combinations of wages and prices, it is optimal for producers to shut down and produce nothing. The calculus method of finding optimal solutions, however, implicitly assumes a positive level of output is optimal and searches for a tangency between isoprofit curves and the production function. Just as in the consumer model, it will be the case that *if the true optimal solution involves an 'interior solution'*, i.e. a positive level of production, the calculus previously described will indeed find that solution.

Consider, however, the production function depicted in panel (a) of Graph 11.12 with price p and wage w forming isoprofit curves with slopes as depicted in the graph. If we set up the optimization problem as in expression (11.9) or (11.10) and use any of the calculus-based solution methods we have introduced in this text, the production plan ℓ^A will be offered as the optimal solution, suggesting production of x^A using labour input ℓ^A. If we calculate profit $\pi = px^A - w\ell^A$, however, we would discover that $\pi < 0$ as indicated in the graph by the negative vertical intercept. Thus, the corner solution B, which yields zero profit, is better than the production plan A as indicated by the fact that B lies on a higher isoprofit curve.

Graph 11.12 Non-Convexities in Producer Choice Sets and Negative Profits at Tangencies

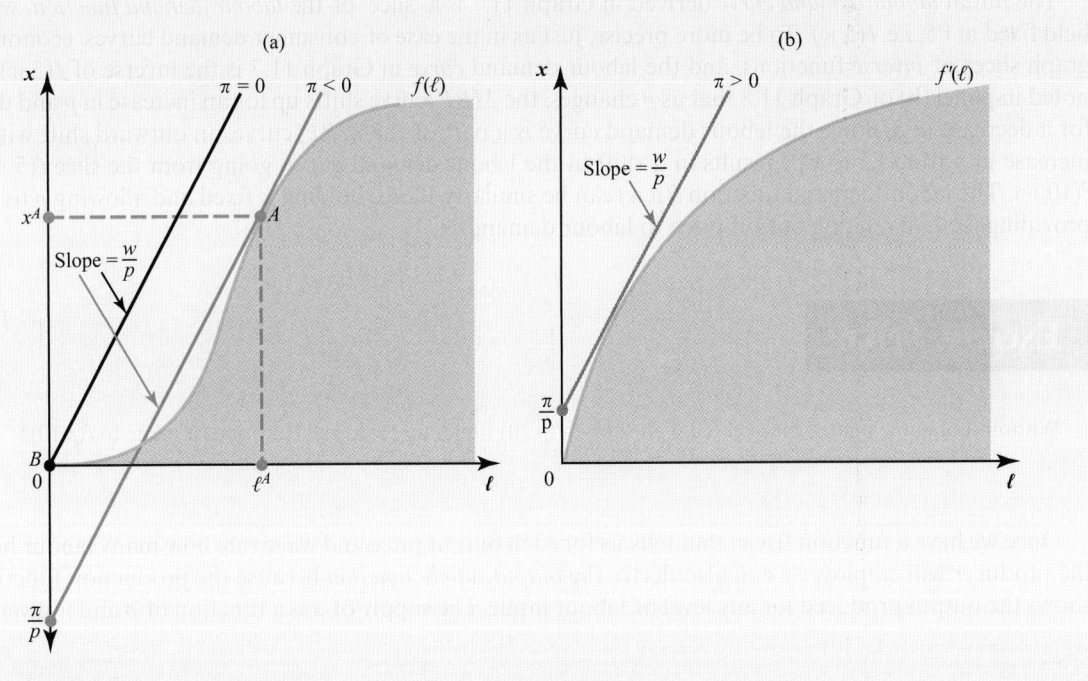

When calculating solutions to profit-maximization problems, it is important to be sure that the solutions suggested are not dominated by corner solutions, especially by the corner solution that implies shutting down. Before claiming that a particular production plan is profit maximizing, we should check to make sure that profits under that production plan are at least zero. Otherwise, we know that shutting down dominates producing. However, one case in which we do not have to check whether profit for a solution emerging from a tangency between isoprofit and the production function arises, is when the producer choice set is convex as in panel (b) of Graph 11.12.

Exercise 11B.7

Consider a production function that gives rise to increasing marginal product of labour throughout, beginning with the first labour hour. *True or False*: In this case, the mathematical optimization problem will unambiguously lead to a 'solution' for which profit is negative.

11B.4.2 Distinguishing a Minimum from Maximum Profit A second technical problem that could emerge from using our calculus-based solution methods to profit maximization involves the appearance of multiple candidate optimal solutions. Consider for instance the production function and isoprofit curves depicted in panel (a) of Graph 11.13. Recall that calculus methods identify production plans where the slopes of isoprofit curves w/p are tangent to the production function. In the case depicted here, this method would identify two such plans, A and B, but it is clear from the picture that A is the true optimal production plan, and B generates negative profits.

Graph 11.13 Non-Convexities in Production Sets and Multiple Solutions

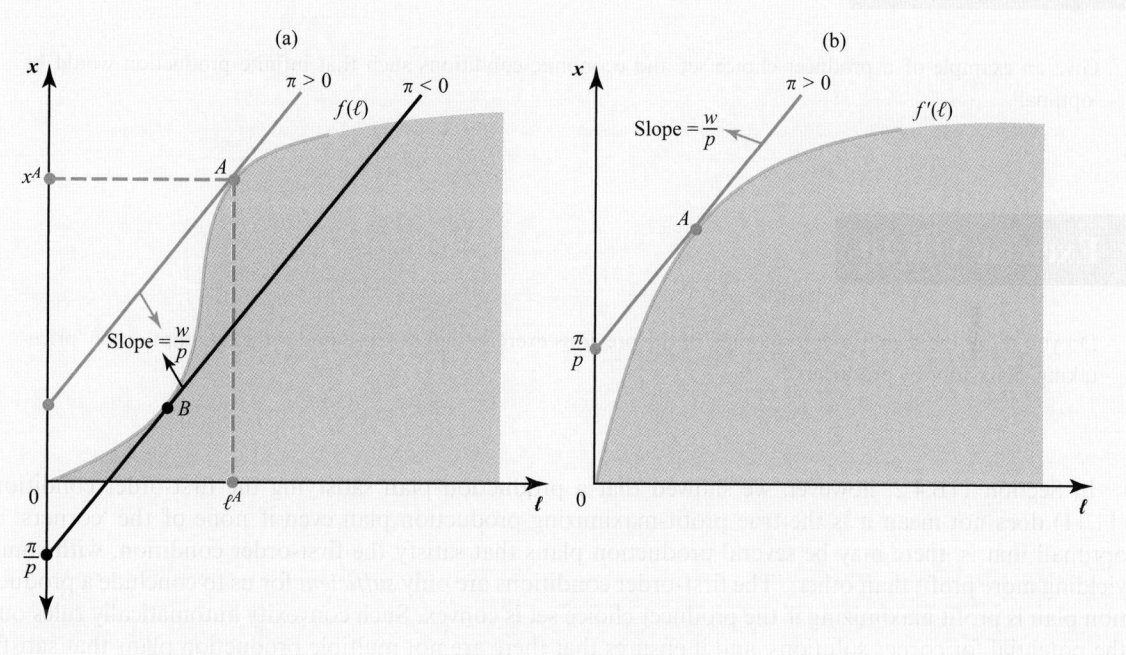

The reasons for this multiplicity of tangencies lies in the non-convexity of the producer choice set, and when such non-convexities disappear, as in panel (b) of Graph 11.13, the calculus-based optimization methods we use in this text yields a single optimal solution. While more complicated methods for calculating the true optimum in profit-maximization problems exist, we can navigate around such methods by being aware of exactly what type of problem we are dealing with, i.e. where the non-convexities are, and checking to make sure our calculated optima are truly optimal. Using equation (11.13), for instance, we derived 'optimal' labour demand for the production function in equation (11.3) when $w = 20$ and $p = 5$ as $\ell = 22$ and $\ell = 78$. Using Graph 11.6, we realized that the maths gave us one incorrect solution because it gave the level of labour where w intersects MRP_ℓ on the upward-sloping portion as well as when it intersects on the downward-sloping part. This is exactly analogous to point B in panel (a) of Graph 11.13, with the real optimum lying at A.

Exercise 11B.8

Consider a production function that gives rise to increasing marginal product of labour throughout, beginning with the first labour hour. *True or False*: In this case, the mathematical optimization problem will give a single solution, albeit one that minimizes rather than maximizes profit.

11B.4.3 Necessary and Sufficient Conditions for Profit Maximization The general point illustrated in Section 11B.4.1 is that the *first-order condition* in equation (11.11) is a *necessary condition* that must be satisfied for profit-maximizing producers so long as the true profit-maximizing plan does not lie at a corner of the producer choice set. There are two such 'corners' – one at which production is zero and another at which it is infinite. As long as the true profit-maximizing plan does not lie at one of these corners, the actual profit-maximizing plan must *necessarily* satisfy the first-order condition (11.11).

Exercise 11B.9

Give an example of a producer choice set and economic conditions such that infinite production would be 'optimal'.

Exercise 11B.10

Do you think the scenario you outlined in the previous exercise makes sense under the assumption of 'price-taking' behaviour by producers?

In Section 11B.4.2, however, we showed that a production plan satisfying the first-order condition (11.11) does not mean it is the true profit-maximizing production plan even if none of the 'corners' is optimal; that is, there may be several production plans that satisfy the first-order condition, with some yielding more profit than others. The first-order conditions are only *sufficient* for us to conclude a production plan is profit maximizing if the producer choice set is convex. Such convexity automatically rules out the potential for corner solutions, and it ensures that there are not multiple production plans that satisfy the first-order conditions. Thus, the first-order condition from which we derive labour demand and output supply functions is *both* necessary *and* sufficient for profit maximization so long as the underlying producer choice set is convex.

11B.5 Two-Step Profit Maximization

There is a second way to derive the profit-maximizing plan for producers: by splitting profit maximizing into two parts. The first part is concerned with how much it costs to produce different output levels; the second part asks how much we should produce given the costs and given the price at which we can sell the goods in the market.

Cost minimization in a single-input production process is trivial because there exists only one technologically efficient way of producing any level of output: by using the input level that lies on the production frontier for the desired level of output. In considering two inputs, this problem will not be nearly as trivial because we will have many different ways in which we can combine labour and capital to produce the same level of output. We illustrated this one-input cost minimization in Graph 11.10 where the cost of producing x^A of the output required ℓ^A input and thus cost $w\ell^A$. More formally, in going from panel (a) to panel (d) of the graph, we took the inverse of the production function $f(x)$ to get:

$$\ell(x) = f^{-1}(x). \tag{11.17}$$

This tells us how many units of labour are required for each level of output. In going from panel (d) to (e), we multiplied this function by the cost of labour w to get a cost function:

$$C(w, x) = w\ell(x). \quad (11.18)$$

This tells us the total cost of production for any level of output. Panel (e) of Graph 11.10 is a slice of the cost function $C(w, x)$ that holds w fixed. From this, we can derive marginal cost and average cost functions:

$$MC(w, x) = \frac{\partial C(w, x)}{\partial x} \quad \text{and} \quad AC(w, x) = \frac{C(w, x)}{x} \quad (11.19)$$

and derive the output supply curve as the portion of the MC curve above the AC curve. The supply curve derived is an inverse slice of the more general supply function $x(p, w)$ that tells us how much a producer supplies in any economic environment characterized by some output price p and wage w. To derive this supply function, we recognize that so long as price is above the lowest point on the C curve, a price-taking producer will produce until price equals marginal cost; that is, they will produce such that:

$$p = MC(w, x) \text{ if } p \geq \min_x \{AC(w, x)\}. \quad (11.20)$$

We can solve the equation $p = MC(w, x)$ for x to get the supply function $x(p, w)$ that lies above AC, with supply equal to zero below that:

$$x(p, w) = \begin{array}{ll} MC^{-1}(p, w) & \text{if } p \geq \min_x \{AC(w, x)\} \\ 0 & \text{if } p < \min_x \{AC(w, x)\} \end{array} \quad (11.21)$$

where MC^{-1} signifies the inverse of the MC function with respect to price. We can furthermore derive the input demand function for labour $\ell(p, w)$ by substituting $x(p, w)$ into the inverse production function $\ell(x)$ from equation (11.17).

11B.5.1 **Relationship Between MC and AC** Having derived mathematical expressions for total, marginal and average cost, we can demonstrate mathematically what we concluded intuitively about the relationship between average and marginal costs. In particular, we concluded that the MC curve crosses the AC curve at its lowest point; that is, where the derivative of the AC curve with respect to x is equal to zero. Using the expression for AC from equation (11.19) and taking the derivative with respect to x, we get:

$$\frac{\partial AC(w, x)}{\partial x} = \frac{\partial C(w, x)/\partial x}{x} - \frac{C(w, x)}{x^2} = \frac{MC(w, x)}{x} - \frac{C(w, x)}{x^2}. \quad (11.22)$$

Multiplying by x, this gives:

$$\frac{\partial AC(w, x)}{\partial x}x = MC(w, x) - \frac{C(w, x)}{x} = MC(w, x) - AC(w, x). \quad (11.23)$$

When the derivative of AC with respect to x is zero, this can be written as:

$$MC(w, x) - AC(w, x) = 0 \text{ or just } MC(w, x) = AC(w, x). \quad (11.24)$$

Thus, when AC reaches its minimum, $MC(w, x) - AC(w, x)$.

11B.5.2 Two Ways of Profit Maximizing: An Example With Strictly Diminishing MP_ℓ Because of the complexity of production functions with initially increasing and eventually decreasing MP_ℓ, such as the one in equation (11.3), we have thus far foregone calculating the exact supply and demand functions but have indicated the two methods by which these can be calculated. To provide an illustration of these methods in a setting where calculations are more manageable, we will now conclude the chapter by offering an example in which we do not have to worry about corner solutions or multiple potential solutions, because we assume from the outset a producer choice set that is strictly convex. Suppose the producer choice set and the production frontier are defined by the production function:

$$f(\ell) = A\ell^\alpha. \tag{11.25}$$

Exercise 11B.11

What has to be true about α in order for this production function to exhibit diminishing marginal product of labour?

Setting up the profit-maximization problem, our first way of calculating input demands and output supplies, we get:

$$\max_{x,\,\ell} \pi = px - w\ell \text{ subject to } x = A\ell^\alpha, \tag{11.26}$$

or, with the constraint placed into the objective function:

$$\max_{\ell} \pi = pA\ell^\alpha - w\ell. \tag{11.27}$$

Taking the first derivative with respect to ℓ, we get the first-order condition:

$$\alpha Ap\ell^{\alpha-1} - w = 0, \tag{11.28}$$

and solving this for ℓ, we find the labour demand function:

$$\ell(p,\,w) = \left(\frac{w}{\alpha Ap}\right)^{1/(\alpha-1)}. \tag{11.29}$$

Exercise 11B.12

Suppose $0 < \alpha < 1$ and $A > 0$. Holding price fixed, is the labour demand function downward sloping in the wage? Holding wage fixed, is it upward or downward sloping in price? Can you graphically illustrate why your answers hold?

The output supply function is the production function evaluated at $\ell(p, w)$:

$$x(p, w) = f(\ell(p, w)) = A\left(\frac{w}{\alpha Ap}\right)^{\alpha/(\alpha-1)}. \tag{11.30}$$

Exercise 11B.13

Suppose $0 < \alpha < 1$ and $A > 0$. Holding wage fixed, is the supply function upward sloping in price? Holding price fixed, is the supply function upward sloping in wage? Can you graphically illustrate why your answers hold?

Exercise 11B.14*

How do your answers to the previous two exercises change when $\alpha > 1$? Can you make sense of what is going on? *Hint*: Graph the production function and illustrate the tangencies of isoprofits for different wages and prices.

Now consider the two-step method: cost minimization on the way to profit maximization. We begin by taking the inverse of the production function to get $\ell(x)$ as in equation (11.17) and multiply it by w to get the cost function as in equation (11.18). This gives us:

$$\ell(x) = \left(\frac{x}{A}\right)^{1/\alpha} \quad \text{and} \quad C(w, x) = w\left(\frac{x}{A}\right)^{1/\alpha}. \tag{11.31}$$

The marginal and average cost functions become:

$$MC(w, x) = \frac{\partial C(x, c)}{\partial x} = \left(\frac{w}{\alpha A^{1/\alpha}}\right)x^{(1-\alpha)/\alpha} \quad \text{and}$$

$$AC(w, x) = \frac{C(w, x)}{x} = \left(\frac{w}{A^{1/\alpha}}\right)x^{(1-\alpha)/\alpha}. \tag{11.32}$$

Notice that, in this case, $MC(w, x) = AC(w, x)$ when $x = 0$, and, whenever $0 < \alpha < 1$, $MC(w,x) > AC(w, x)$ for all $x > 0$. Thus, the lowest point of the AC curve occurs at $x = 0$ for this production function when α lies between zero and 1. As a result, we can set price equal to MC and solve for x to get, as in equation (11.21):

$$x(p, w) = \left(\frac{\alpha A^{1/\alpha}p}{w}\right)^{\alpha/(1-\alpha)} A\left(\frac{\alpha Ap}{w}\right)^{\alpha/(1-\alpha)} = A\left(\frac{w}{\alpha Ap}\right)^{\alpha/(\alpha-1)}. \tag{11.33}$$

Note that this is the supply function calculated in equation (11.30) when we solved the profit-maximization problem for the same production function directly rather than solving first for the cost function and finding the profit-maximizing supply function by setting price equal to marginal cost. Similarly, if we now substitute $x(p, w)$ into the function $\ell(x)$ in equation (11.31), we get:

$$\ell(p, w) = \left(\frac{w}{\alpha A p} \right)^{1/(\alpha - 1)}, \qquad (11.34)$$

just as we did in the profit-maximization problem that resulted in equation (11.29).

Exercise 11B.15

Graphically illustrate the way we have just derived the output supply function assuming α lies between 0 and 1. What changes when $\alpha > 1$?

End-of-Chapter Exercises

11.1† Consider a profit-maximizing firm.

  A. Explain whether the following statements are true or false:

   a. For price-taking, profit-maximizing producers, the 'constraint' is determined by the technological environment in which the producer finds themselves, whereas the 'tastes' are formed by the economic environment in which the producer operates.
   b. Every profit-maximizing producer is automatically cost minimizing.
   c. Every cost-minimizing producer is automatically profit maximizing.
   d. Price-taking behaviour makes sense only when marginal product diminishes at least at some point.

  B. Consider the production function $x = f(\ell) = \alpha \ln (\ell + 1)$.

   a. Does this production function have increasing or decreasing marginal product of labour?
   b. Set up the profit-maximization problem and solve for the labour demand and output supply functions.
   c. Recalling that $x = y$ implies $e^y = x$, where $e \approx 2.7183$ is the base of the natural log, invert the production function and derive from this the cost function $C(w, x)$.
   d. Determine the marginal and average cost functions.
   e. Derive from this the output supply and labour demand functions. Compare them to what you derived directly from the profit-maximization problem in part (b).
   f. In your mathematical derivations, what is required for a producer to be cost minimizing? What, in addition, is required for them to be profit maximizing?

11.2 This exercise explores in some more detail the relationship between production technologies and marginal product of labour.

  A. We often work with production technologies that give rise to initially increasing marginal product of labour that eventually decreases.

   a. *True or False*: For such production technologies, the marginal product of labour is increasing so long as the slope of the production frontier becomes steeper as we move towards more labour input.
   b. *True or False*: The marginal product of labour becomes negative when the slope of the production frontier begins to get shallower as we move towards more labour input.
   c. *True or False*: The marginal product of labour is positive so long as the slope of the production frontier is positive.
   d. *True or False*: If the marginal product of labour ever becomes zero, we know that the production frontier becomes perfectly flat at that point.

e. *True or False*: A negative marginal product of labour necessarily implies a downward-sloping production frontier at that level of labour input.

B. We have thus far introduced two general forms for production functions that give rise to initially increasing and eventually decreasing marginal product.

a. **The first of these was given as an example in the text and took the general form $f(\ell) = \alpha(1 - \cos(\beta\ell))$ for all $\ell \leq \pi/\beta \approx 3.1416/\beta$ and $f(\ell) = 2\alpha$ for all $\ell > \pi/\beta \approx 3.1416/\beta$, with α and β assumed to be greater than 0. Determine the labour input level at which the marginal product of labour begins to decline. *Hint*: Recall that the cosine of $\pi/2 \approx 1.5708$ is equal to zero.

b. Does the marginal product of labour ever become negative? If so, at what labour input level?

c. In light of what you have just learned, can you sketch the production function given in (a)? What does the marginal product of labour for this function look like?

d. The second general form for such a production function was given in exercise 11.5 and took the form $f(\ell) = \beta\ell^2 - \gamma\ell^3$. Determine the labour input level at which the marginal product of labour begins to decline.

e. Does the marginal product of labour ever become negative? If so, at what labour input level?

f. Given what you have learned about the function $f(\ell) = \beta\ell^2 - \gamma\ell^3$, illustrate the production function when $\beta = 150$ and $\gamma = 1$. What does the marginal product of labour look like?

g. In each of the two previous cases, you should have concluded that the marginal product of labour eventually becomes zero and/or negative. Now consider the following new production technology: $f(\ell) = \alpha/(1 + e^{-(\ell-\beta)})$ where $e \approx 2.7183$ is the base of the natural logarithm. Determine the labour input level at which the marginal product of labour begins to decline.

h. Does the marginal product of labour ever become negative? If so, at what labour input level?

i. Given what you have discovered about the production function $f(\ell) = \alpha/(1 + e^{-(\ell-\beta)})$, can you sketch the shape of this function when $\alpha = 150$ and $\beta = 5$? What does the marginal product of labour function look like?

11.3† We have shown that there are two ways in which we can think of the producer as maximizing profits: either directly, or in a two-step process that begins with cost minimization.

A. This exercise reviews this equivalence for the case where the production process initially has increasing marginal product of labour but eventually reaches decreasing marginal product. Assume such a production process throughout.

a. Begin by plotting the production frontier with labour on the horizontal and output on the vertical axis. Identify in your graph the production plan $A = (\ell^A, x^A)$ at which increasing returns turn to decreasing returns.

b. Suppose wage is $w = 1$. Illustrate in your graph the price p_0 at which the firm obtains zero profit by using a profit-maximizing production plan B. Does this necessarily lie above or below A on the production frontier?

c. Draw a second graph next to the one you have just drawn. With price on the vertical axis and output on the horizontal, illustrate the amount the firm produces at p_0.

d. Suppose price rises above p_0. What changes on your graph with the production frontier, and how does that translate to points on the supply curve in your second graph?

e. What if price falls below p_0?

f. Illustrate the cost curve on a graph below your production frontier graph. What is similar about the two graphs – and what is different – around the point that corresponds to production plan A.

g. Next to your cost curve graph, illustrate the marginal and average cost curves. Which of these reaches its lowest point at the output quantity x^A? Which reaches its lowest point at x^B?

h. Illustrate the supply curve on your graph and compare it with the one you derived in parts (c) and (d).

B. **Suppose that you face a production technology characterized by the function $x = f(\ell) = \alpha/(1 + e^{-(\ell-\beta)})$.

a. Assuming labour l costs w and the output x can be sold at p, set up the profit-maximization problem.

b. Derive the first-order condition for this problem.

c. Substitute $y = e^{-(\ell-\beta)}$ into your first-order condition and, using the quadratic formula, solve for y. Recognizing that $y = e^{-(\ell-\beta)}$ implies $\ln y = -(\ell - \beta)$, solve for the two implied labour inputs and identify which is profit maximizing assuming that an interior production plan is optimal.

    d. Use your answer to solve for the supply function assuming an interior solution is optimal.

    e. Now use the two-step method to verify your answer. Begin by solving the production function for ℓ to determine how much labour is required for each output level, assuming none is wasted.

    f. Use your answer to derive the cost function and the marginal cost function.

    g. Set price equal to marginal cost and solve for the output supply function assuming an interior solution is optimal. Can you get your answer into the same form as the supply function from your direct profit-maximization problem?

    h. Use the supply function and your answer from part (e) to derive the labour input demand function, assuming an interior solution is optimal. Is it the same as what you derived through direct profit maximization in part (c)?

11.4 Everyday Application: *Workers as Producers of Consumption.* We can see some of the connections between consumer and producer theory by reframing models from consumer theory in producer language.

    A. Suppose we modelled a worker as a 'producer of consumption' who can sell leisure of up to 60 hours per week at a wage w.

      a. On a graph with 'labour' as the input on the horizontal axis and 'consumption' as the output on the vertical, illustrate what the producer choice set faced by such a 'producer' would look like.

      b. How is this fundamentally different from the usual producer case where the producer choice set has nothing to do with prices in the economy?

      c. What does the marginal product of labour curve look like for this 'producer'?

      d. On the graph you drew for part (a), illustrate what 'producer tastes' for this producer would look like assuming the worker's tastes over consumption and leisure satisfy the usual five assumptions for tastes we developed in Chapter 4. How is this fundamentally different from the usual producer case where the producer's indifference curves are formed by prices in the economy?

    B. Suppose the worker's tastes over consumption and leisure are Cobb–Douglas with equal weights on the two variables in the utility function.

      a. Derive an expression for the production function in this model.

      b. Set up the worker's optimization problem similar to a profit-maximization problem for producers.

      c. Derive the output supply function; that is, the function that tells us how much consumption the worker will produce for different economic conditions.

11.5† Business Application: *Optimal Response to Labour Regulations.* Governments often impose costs on businesses in direct relation to how much labour they employ. They may, for instance, require that businesses provide certain benefits like life insurance or pension schemes.

    A. Suppose we model such government regulations as a cost c per worker hour in addition to the wage w that is paid directly to the worker. Assume that you face a production technology that has the typical property of initially increasing marginal product of labour that eventually diminishes.

      a. Illustrate the isoprofits for this firm and include both the explicit labour cost w as well as the implicit cost c of the regulation.

      b. Illustrate the profit-maximizing production plan.

      c. Assuming that it continues to be optimal for your firm to produce, how does your optimal production plan change as c increases?

      d. Illustrate a case where an increase in c is sufficiently large to cause your firm to stop producing.

      e. *True or False*: For firms that make close to zero profit, additional labour regulations might cause large changes in behaviour.

    B. Suppose that your production technology can be represented by the production function $x = 100/(1 + e^{-(\ell-5)})$ where e is the base of the natural logarithm.

      a. Suppose $w = 10$ and $p = 1$. Set up your profit-maximization problem and explicitly include the cost of regulation.

      b. **Calculate the optimal labour demand and output supply as a function of c. *Hint*: Solving the first-order condition becomes considerably easier if you substitute $y = e^{-(\ell-5)}$ and solve for y using the quadratic formula. Once you have a solution for y, this is equal to $e^{-(\ell-5)}$. You can take natural logs of both sides, recalling that $\ln e^{-(\ell-5)} = -(\ell - 5)$. This follows the steps in exercise 11.3 where an almost identical production function was used.

 c. What is the profit-maximizing production plan when $c = 0$?

 d. How does your answer change when $c = 2$?

 e. What if $c = 3$? *Hint*: Check to see what happens to profit.

11.6* **Policy Application:** *Determining Optimal Class Size.* Policy makers are often pressured to reduce class sizes in schools in order to improve student achievement.

 A. One way to model the production process for student achievement is to view the teacher/student ratio as the input. For the purposes of this problem, let t be defined as the number of teachers per 1000 students; that is, $t = 20$ means there are 20 teachers per 1000 students. Class size in a school of 1000 students is equal to $1000/t$.

  a. Most education scholars believe that the increase in student achievement from reducing class size is high when class size is high, but diminishes as class size falls. Illustrate how this translates into a production frontier with t on the horizontal axis and average student achievement a on the vertical.

  b. Consider a school with 1000 students. If the annual salary of a teacher is given by w, what is the cost of raising the input t by 1; that is, what is the cost per unit of the input t?

  c. Suppose a is the average score on an examination by students in the school, and suppose that the voting public is willing to pay p for each unit increase in a. Illustrate the production plan that the school will choose if it behaves analogously to a profit-maximizing firm.

  d. What happens to class size if teacher salaries increase?

  e. How would your graph change if the voting public's willingness to pay per unit of a decreases as a increases?

  f. Now suppose that you are analyzing two separate countries that fund their equally sized schools from tax contributions by voters in each country. They face the same production technology, but the willingness to pay for marginal improvements in a is lower in country 1 than in country 2 at every production plan. Illustrate how the isoprofit maps differ for the two countries.

  g. Illustrate how this will result in different choices of class size in the two countries.

  h. Suppose that the citizens in each of the two countries were identical in every way except that those in country 1 have a different average income level than those in country 2. Can you hypothesize which of the two countries has the greater average income?

  i. National governments often subsidize local government contributions to education, particularly for poorer communities. What changes in your picture of a country's optimal class size setting when such subsidies are introduced?

 B. Suppose the production technology for average student achievement is given by $a = 100t^{0.75}$, and suppose again that we are dealing with a school that has 1000 students.

  a. Let w denote the annual teacher salary in thousands of euros and let p denote the country's marginal willingness to pay for an increase in student achievement. Calculate the profit-maximizing class size.

  b. What is the optimal class size when $w = 60$ and $p = 2$?

  c. What happens to class size as teacher salaries change?

  d. What happens to class size as the country's marginal willingness to pay for student achievement changes?

  e. What would change if the national government subsidizes the local contribution to school spending?

  f. Now suppose that the country's marginal willingness to pay for additional student achievement is a function of the achievement level. In particular, suppose that $p(a) = Ba^{(\beta-1)}$ where $\beta \leq 1$. For what values of β and B is the problem identical to the one you just solved?

  g. Solve for the optimal t given the marginal willingness to pay of $p(a)$. What is the optimal class size when $B = 3$ and $\beta = 0.95$ assuming again that $w = 60$?

  h. Under the parameter values just specified, does class size respond to changes in teacher salaries as it did before?

*conceptually challenging
**computationally challenging
† solutions in Study Guide

Chapter 12

Production With Multiple Inputs

In this chapter, we will extend the model of a single input and single output developed in Chapter 11 to multiple inputs. This will allow us to ask not just how much a competitive firm will produce at different prices but also what *mix of inputs* it will employ. When the firm is using multiple inputs like workers *and* machines, there are typically many different ways of combining these inputs without wasting any to produce a particular output level. Once we know how to model production processes with such multiple inputs, we can think of how an economist might advise on the choice between these options.

We will find out that the direct profit maximization method first employed in Chapter 11 becomes graphically cumbersome. It is in part for this reason that we will move on to implementing the two-step approach to profit maximization, the approach that starts by first looking at just costs and only afterwards brings revenues into the picture. As you will see, this approach, even with multiple inputs, ends up looking a lot like the approach developed at the end of Chapter 11. It is an approach that lends itself to a more manageable graphical exposition for thinking about competitive firms, but it also provides a series of *cost curves* that can be used for *all* firms whether they are competitive or not. This is because cost curves are the result of firms thinking about how to produce different levels of output in the least costly way, and that part of the producer problem does not depend on whether the firm is a perfectly competitive price taker in the output market. *All* profit-maximizing firms, whether competitive or not, seek to minimize their costs, and the development of cost curves and functions builds a basis for our current thinking about price-taking firms as well as our later thinking about firms that exercise market power.

12A	An Intuitive Development of the Two-Input Model

The basic building block of the producer model extends straightforwardly from the single input to the two-input case. *Production plans*, previously defined as points in two dimensions that indicate how much labour ℓ the plan calls for to produce a certain level of output x, are now defined as points in three dimensions, indicating how much of each of the *two* inputs the plan proposes to use in the production of a certain level of output x. For convenience, we will once again call one input labour, denoted ℓ, and we will usually call the other input capital, denoted k. We are still simplifying the real world a lot, leaving out such important inputs as land or entrepreneurial talent and neglecting to distinguish between different types of labour and capital.

A production plan A, previously defined as a point (ℓ^A), is now defined as a point (ℓ^A, k^A, x^A). We will continue to talk about the labour input ℓ as expressed in hours of labour input and can continue to express its price in the labour market as the hourly wage rate w. Similarly, we can express the output x in terms of those units in which the output is sold, whether as pairs of door handles or bags of oranges or computers. This allows us to interpret the output price p as the price of a unit of the good that is sold to customers in the output market. Finally, we are left with the input k referred to as capital. In some ways, it is harder to clearly identify a natural unit of measurement for this input, partly because the nature of capital will differ across different firms and industries. In some contexts, capital will simply refer to machines such as copiers, as if for instance, we were to analyze the production of photocopiers by Ricoh. In other cases, capital might lump together all types of non-labour investments the firm makes in plant and equipment, and might therefore best be thought of as euros of capital employed in production. In either case, we will denote the price of a unit of capital as the rental rate r.

This *rental rate* of capital is defined as the *opportunity cost of using capital in current production*. To understand what it means intuitively, we have to ask what is the producer giving up by employing a particular form of capital? For example, if a firm enters into an agreement to lease photocopiers, the rental rate is the amount per week, per day, per hour, or whatever time interval we are trying to model, that the firm has to pay for each copier because this is what it is giving up by employing a photocopier. It gets a little more complicated if we assume that the firm purchases its own photocopiers outright. In this case, the firm gives up the opportunity to lease the copiers to other users in the same rental market, and the rental rate is exactly the same as if the firm were leasing the photocopier from someone else. If, on the other hand, capital represents non-labour investments in current production, the rental rate of the financial capital required to make these investments is the interest rate the firm has to pay in order to make use of the capital during the period over which we are studying the firm's production.

Exercise 12A.1

Suppose we are modelling all non-labour investments as capital. Is the rental rate any different depending on whether the firm uses money it already has or chooses to borrow money to make its investments?

12A.1 Profit Maximization With Two-Input Producer Choice Sets

Panels (a) to (c) of Graph 12.1 replicate the three steps employed in Chapter 11 for a convex producer choice set, with the notation π used to denote profit. Panels (d) to (f) illustrate the same steps for a similarly convex producer choice set in the more complicated two-input case.

12A.1.1 Producer Choice Sets and Production Frontiers With Two Inputs Since production plans with two inputs are points with the three components ℓ, k and x, the set of technologically feasible production plans is now a three-dimensional set such as the set of points that lie underneath the production frontier graphed in panel (d) of Graph 12.1. The particular production frontier in this graph is analogous to the two-dimensional production frontier in panel (a) in the sense that it too gives rise to a convex production set because the line connecting any two production plans in the set is fully contained in the same set. Furthermore, when we hold capital fixed at some level such as k, the two-dimensional slice of the three-dimensional production set becomes a two-dimensional producer choice set such as the one depicted in panel (a). If capital is fixed at k in the short run, this slice becomes a one-input production model that can be used to analyze short-run labour demand and output supply decisions by a producer.

12A.1.2 Isoprofit Curves (or Planes) With Two Inputs Next, consider what the set of production plans that all yield the same level of profit would look like in this three-dimensional space. Suppose, for instance, we wanted to find all production plans that would generate zero profit when the output price is p and the input prices are w and r. In the one-input model, such production plans lie on a line emanating from the origin with slope w/p depicted as the lowest of the three isoprofit curves in panel (b). When we restrict ourselves to production plans that make use of no capital in panel (e), we end up with precisely the same isoprofit curve. The line that contains production plan B lies on the two-dimensional plane that holds k fixed at zero and has a slope w/p for precisely the same reasons as in panel (b). It contains all zero profit production plans that make no use of capital. The line emanating from the origin and containing plan C, on the other hand, lies in the two-dimensional plane that holds labour input fixed at zero and represents all zero profit production plans that make no use of labour. This is analogous to the isoprofit curves in the single-input model, except that now the slope of the line is r/p since the price of capital is r. Finally, imagine forming a three-dimensional plane that contains these two line segments and that contains those production plans that make use of both capital and labour and yield zero profit at wage rate w, rental rate r and output price p. This plane represents the three-dimensional isoprofit curve of zero profit production plans. The plane has a vertical intercept at the origin indicating zero profit when no capital and no labour are used to produce no output, a slope of w/p on any slice that holds capital fixed, and a slope of r/p on any slice that holds labour fixed.

Graph 12.1 Profit Maximization in the Single-Input and Two-Input Models

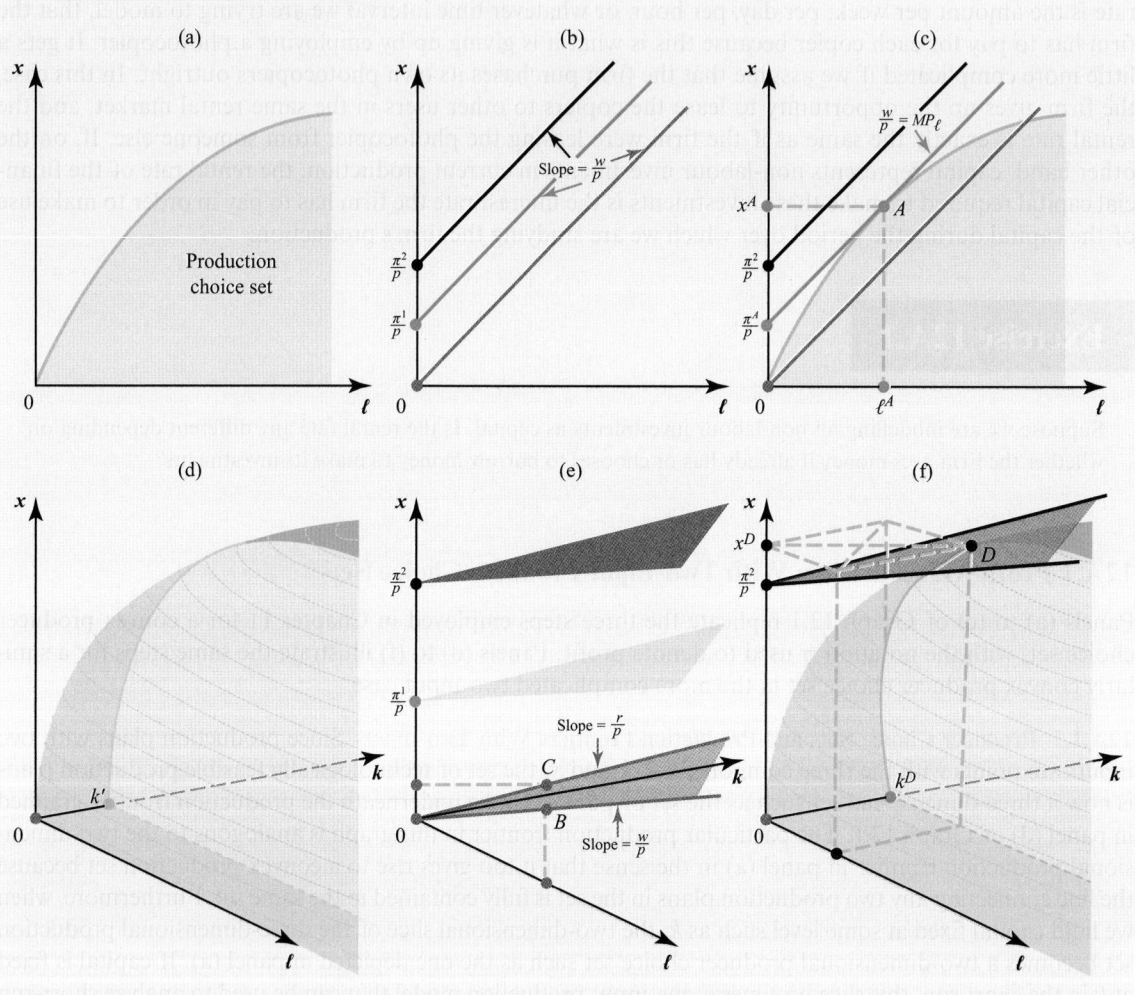

Just as in the single-input case, we can think of planes parallel to the zero profit isoprofit plane. When such a parallel plane of production plans lies above the zero profit plane, it results in positive profit; when it lies below, it represents production plans that give rise to negative profits.

Exercise 12A.2

Explain why the vertical intercept on a three-dimensional isoprofit plane is π/p where π represents the profit associated with that isoprofit plane.

12A.1.3 Profit Maximization In Graph 12.1, the production frontier in panel (d) and the isoprofits of panel (e) are combined in panel (f), which graphs the highest possible isoprofit plane that contains at least one production plan (D) that is technologically feasible. The profit-maximizing production plan D lies at a point where an isoprofit plane is tangential to the three-dimensional frontier. If we look at the slice of panel (f) that holds capital input fixed at its optimal level k^D, we notice that this slice is a two-dimensional picture that looks just like panel (c); that is, we get a two-dimensional graph in which the slope of the line from the isoprofit plane is tangential to the slope of the short-run single-input production frontier that fixes capital at k^D. The slope of the tangent is w/p, and the slope of the slice of the production frontier is the marginal product of labour *given that capital is k^D and given that we are currently employing ℓ^D hours of labour*. Just as in the single-input case, $w/p = MP_\ell$ at the profit-maximizing production plan. Similarly, if we were to look at the slice of the picture with labour held fixed at ℓ^D, we would conclude that the *marginal product of capital MP_k* is exactly equal to r/p at the profit-maximizing production plan. We can conclude that:

$$\text{Profit maximization implies } MP_\ell = \frac{w}{p} \text{ and } MP_k = \frac{r}{p}. \tag{12.1}$$

Exercise 12A.3

We have just concluded that $MP_k = r/p$ at the profit-maximizing bundle. Another way to write this is that the marginal revenue product of capital $MRP_k = pMP_k$ is equal to the rental rate. Can you explain intuitively why this makes sense?

Exercise 12A.4

Suppose capital is fixed in the short run but not in the long run. *True or False*: If the firm has its long-run optimal level of capital k^D in panel (f) of Graph 12.1, it will choose ℓ^D labour in the short run. And if ℓ^D in panel (c) is not equal to ℓ^D in panel (f), it must mean that the firm does not have the long-run optimal level of capital as it is making its short-run labour input decision.

We can also write the expression (12.1) in terms of the marginal revenue products of labour and capital:

$$\text{Profit maximization implies } MRP_\ell = pMP_\ell = w \text{ and } MRP_k = pMP_k = r, \tag{12.2}$$

an extension of the conclusion that $MRP_\ell = pMP_\ell = w$ in the single-input model of Chapter 11 and panel (c) of Graph 12.1. The result from the admittedly complicated lower panels of the graph is that the profit-maximizing conditions from the single-input production model fully generalize to the multi-input production model. The drawback of this depiction of profit maximization is that it is not easy to draw three-dimensional graphs in a way that leads to sound economic analysis.

As an alternative, we can develop a graphical approach to profit maximization analogous to the two-step process that begins with cost minimization first introduced in Chapter 11. This will enable us to picture the process more easily in two dimensions. First, we need to do a little more work in exploring what the different shapes of production choice sets tell us about the underlying technology a firm is using when it employs two inputs.

12A.2 Two-Input Production Sets: Isoquants and Returns to Scale

When firms use both labour and capital, production frontiers are three-dimensional. We became familiar with graphing three-dimensional objects in two dimensions when we learned how to graph indifference curves for consumers.

In the case of producer theory, we can now do the same with the three-dimensional production frontier in panel (d) of Graph 12.1. Panel (a) of Graph 12.2 begins by drawing some of the levels of such a three-dimensional production frontier. These levels are mapped into two dimensions in panel (b), with the axes turned into the usual position in panel (c). The final picture looks a lot like indifference curves, but each curve, now called an *isoquant*, is interpreted in the context of production. *An isoquant for some output level x is the set of all combinations of input levels (k and ℓ) that result in this output level, assuming no input is wasted in the process.* Points in the two-dimensional isoquant graph can be interpreted as *input bundles* or, together with the number associated with the isoquant output, as a production plan. Point A in panel (c) of Graph 12.3, for instance, represents the input bundle $(\ell, k) = (20, 10)$, and it also represents the production plan $(x, \ell, k) = (40, 20, 10)$.

Graph 12.2 Deriving Two-Dimensional Isoquants From a Three-Dimensional Production Frontier

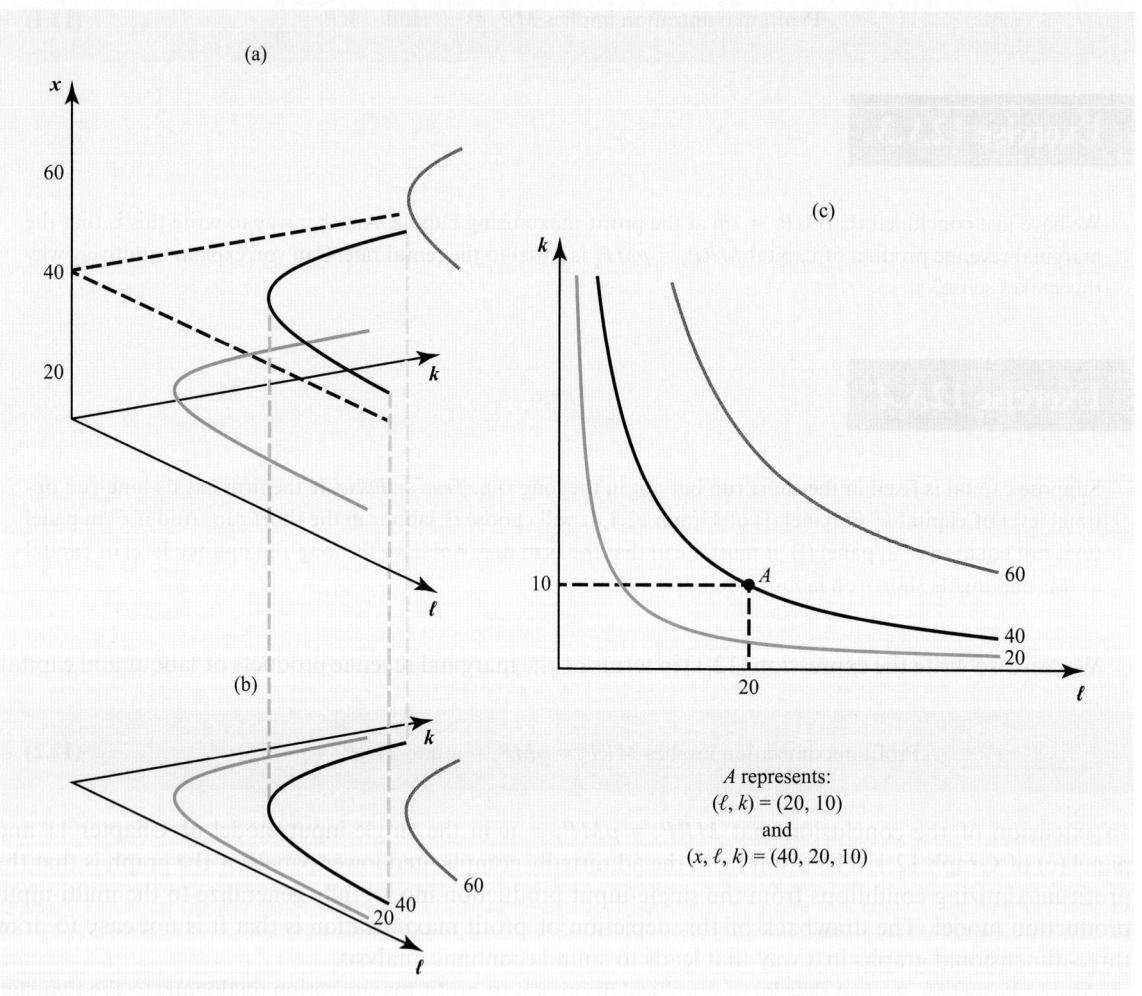

Exercise 12A.5

Apply the definition of an isoquant to the single-input producer model. What does the isoquant look like there? *Hint:* Each isoquant is typically a single point.

Isoquants arise from production frontiers, which are the technological *constraints* faced by producers. Unlike an indifference curve, which had no objective measurement for 'happiness', isoquants do have an objective measurement in that they represent input bundles that yield a particular level of *output*. Because output is something we can objectively measure, we can take an isoquant map and re-label the isoquants as changes in three-dimensional production technology in economically meaningful ways. For instance, while doubling all the values associated with a consumer indifference map leaves us with the same tastes as before, doubling the values associated with isoquants alters the production technology, with the new technology producing twice as much output from any bundle of inputs.

Exercise 12A.6

Why do you think we have emphasized the concept of marginal product of an input in producer theory but not the analogous concept of marginal utility of a consumption good in consumer theory?

12A.2.1 *TRS* and Marginal Product While the economic interpretation of isoquants is in many ways different from the economic interpretation of indifference curves, there is much that we have learned in our study of indifference curves that is directly applicable to our understanding of isoquants. We begin with the interpretation of the slope of isoquants, known as the *marginal technical rate of substitution* or just the *technical rate of substitution*. A slope of -3 on an isoquant as, for instance, in panel (b) of Graph 12.3, indicates that 3 units of capital could be traded for 1 unit of labour with overall production remaining roughly constant. The technical rate of substitution thus tells us at each input bundle how many units of the input on the vertical axis could be substituted for 1 unit of the input on the horizontal axis and maintain a constant level of output. Since it is a mouthful to say marginal technical rate of substitution, we will generally stick with just technical rate of substitution and abbreviate it to *TRS*. Furthermore, since we have adopted the convention of always putting labour on the horizontal and capital on the vertical axis in our isoquant graphs, we will call the slope of an isoquant the *TRS* without always having to add the phrase 'of labour with respect to capital'.

Graph 12.3 Relatively More or Less Substitutability of Capital for Labour

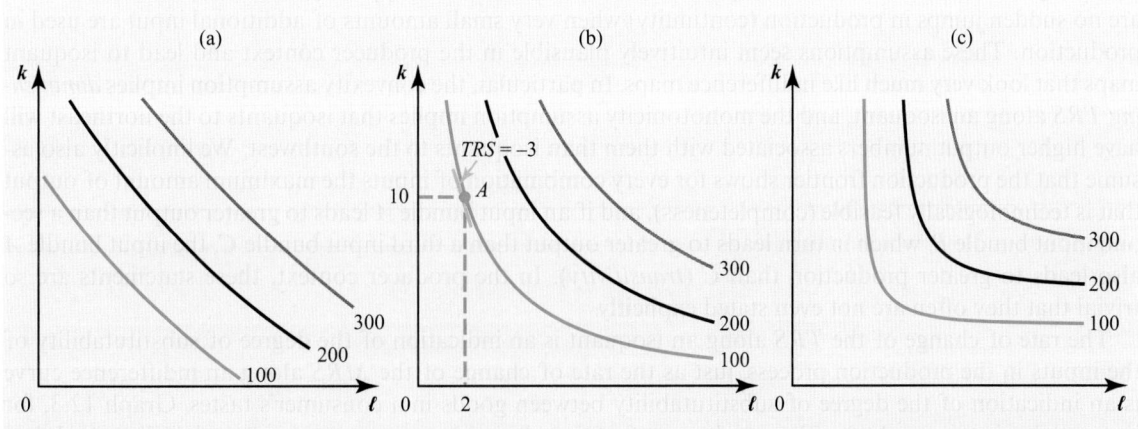

We can now identify a property of isoquants that we did not emphasize for indifference curves: the relationship between the *TRS* and the marginal products of inputs. We have thus far defined these terms separately, with marginal product representing the slope of a slice of the production frontier along which *one of the inputs* is held fixed and the *TRS* representing the slope of an isoquant along which *output* is held fixed. We will make use later of the following relationship, which is not an assumption but rather a logical implication of the definitions of these concepts:

$$TRS = -\frac{MP_\ell}{MP_k}. \qquad (12.3)$$

Suppose, for instance, the firm was using the input bundle (ℓ, k) to produce $x = 100$ on the isoquant for 100 units of output, and suppose that $MP_\ell = 4$ and $MP_k = 2$ at that input bundle. This implies that at this input bundle, a unit of labour is twice as productive as a unit of capital. If the firm employed one additional unit of labour, it could release approximately two units of capital and keep total output roughly constant at 100 units. This is just the definition of $TRS = -2$ at this input bundle; we can replace two units of capital on the vertical axis with one additional unit of labour on the horizontal while keeping production constant. Thus, $TRS = (-MP_\ell/MP_k) = -4/2 = -2$.

Exercise 12A.7

Repeat this reasoning for the case where $MP_\ell = 2$ and $MP_k = 3$.

Exercise 12A.8

Is there a relationship analogous to equation (12.3) that exists in consumer theory and, if so, why do you think we did not highlight it in our development of consumer theory?

12A.2.2 Technical Similarities Between Isoquants and Consumer Indifference Curves We can point out a few more technical similarities between isoquants and consumer indifference curves. First, we assume that (1) more is better (monotonicity) in the sense that more inputs yield more outputs; (2) averages are better than extremes (convexity) in the sense that when two extreme input bundles result in the same output level, an average of these extreme bundles produces at least as much but typically more output; and (3) there are no sudden jumps in production (continuity) when very small amounts of additional input are used in production. These assumptions seem intuitively plausible in the producer context and lead to isoquant maps that look very much like indifference maps. In particular, the convexity assumption implies *diminishing TRS* along an isoquant, and the monotonicity assumption implies that isoquants to the northeast will have higher output numbers associated with them than isoquants to the southwest. We implicitly also assume that the production frontier shows for every combination of inputs the maximum amount of output that is technologically feasible (completeness), and if an input bundle A leads to greater output than a second input bundle B, which in turn leads to greater output than a third input bundle C, the input bundle A also leads to greater production than C (*transitivity*). In the producer context, these statements are so trivial that they often are not even stated explicitly.

The rate of change of the TRS along an isoquant is an indication of the degree of substitutability of the inputs in the production process, just as the rate of change of the MRS along an indifference curve is an indication of the degree of substitutability between goods in a consumer's tastes. Graph 12.3, for instance, begins in panel (a) with a production frontier whose isoquants are almost straight lines and thus indicate that capital and labour can easily be substituted for one another. It continues in panel (b) with isoquants representing a production process in which labour and capital are less substitutable, and ends in panel (c) with a production process in which the inputs are almost perfect complements in production.

We can define the concepts of quasilinear and homothetic tastes for maps of isoquants in analogous ways to those in indifference curves, although homothetic maps of isoquants are more commonly used by economists in producer theory than are quasilinear ones. The homotheticity property allows for production processes that range from having no substitutability between inputs to those allowing perfect substitutability and thus allows for a wide range of different types of production processes as illustrated by the three homothetic production processes in Graph 12.3. We will assume throughout that production processes are homothetic because this allows us to most easily define the very useful new concept known as *returns to scale*, a concept we turn to next.

Exercise 12A.9

What would isoquant maps with no substitutability and perfect substitutability between inputs look like? Why are they homothetic?

12A.2.3 Returns to Scale: A Third Way of Slicing Production Frontiers In panel (d) of Graph 12.1, we illustrated a vertical slice of the three-dimensional production frontier – the *vertical* slice that holds capital fixed at a certain level k'. This, in essence, gives us a short-run production frontier along which only labour can vary, with the slope of this short-run production frontier equal to the marginal product of labour. We could similarly hold labour fixed at some level and create a vertical slice along which only capital varies, and the slope of that slice would be the marginal product of capital. In Graph 12.2 we illustrated a second way of slicing three-dimensional production frontiers, this time holding output fixed and slicing the frontier *horizontally* to obtain isoquants. The shape of these horizontal slices tells us something about the degree of substitutability between capital and labour. We now turn to a third way of slicing the three-dimensional production frontier where the shape of this slice will tell us something about the *returns to scale* of the production process.

Exercise 12A.10

Consider a three-dimensional frontier similar to the one graphed in Graph 12.1 but with two goods on the horizontal axes and utility on the vertical. Why would we not think that vertical slices like the one in panel (d) of Graph 12.1 are meaningful in this case?

Exercise 12A.11

Consider the same utility frontier described in the previous exercise. What would the horizontal slices analogous to those in Graph 12.2 be in consumer theory? Why are they meaningful when the vertical slices in Graph 12.1 are not?

We are looking at *vertical* slices of the production frontier that hold the ratio of capital to labour fixed. Graphically, this implies slicing the production frontier along rays from the origin in the lower plane that measures the inputs capital and labour. Graph 12.4 illustrates such slices along the 45-degree line for two different three-dimensional production frontiers, with the shaded slice in panel (a) forming a convex set while that in panel (b) forms a non-convex set. An alternative and equivalent way of saying this is that the darkened boundary of the slice in panel (a) is a concave function giving rise to a convex set underneath, while the darkened boundary of the slice in panel (b) is a convex function that gives rise to a non-convex set underneath.

Graph 12.4 Producer Choice Sets with (a) Decreasing and (b) Increasing Returns to Scale

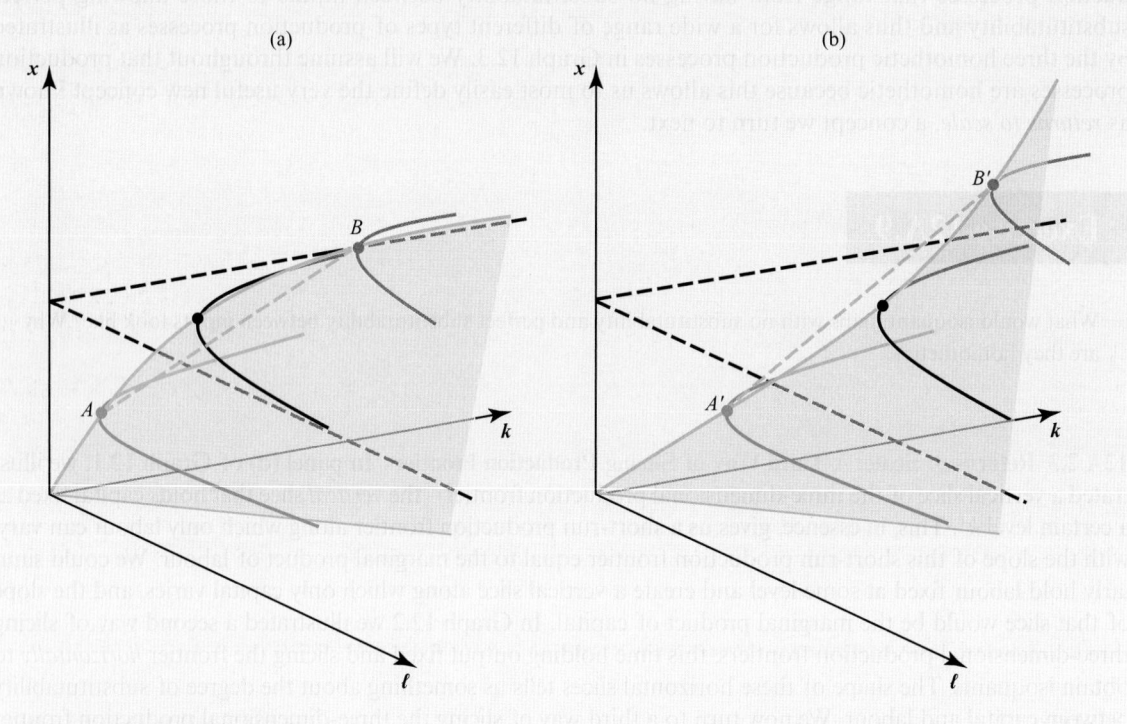

Exercise 12A.12*

Consider a mountain and suppose that the shape of any horizontal slice of this mountain is a perfect filled in circle. We can climb the mountain from every direction, and find that the climb typically starts off easy but gets harder and harder as we approach the top because the mountain gets increasingly steep. If we take a vertical slice of this mountain, will the outer boundary of that slice be a concave or convex function?

Exercise 12A.13*

Is the vertical slice described in the previous section including all the points inside the mountain that lie on the slice, a convex set?

Graph 12.4 shows that as capital and labour is increased by the same proportion holding the ratio of capital to labour fixed along the ray of the slice in panel (a), production is increasing at a slower and slower rate. In panel (a) it is getting harder and harder to produce more as both capital and labour are increased proportionately. This is what is meant by *decreasing returns to scale*. In panel (b), on the other hand, production is increasing at a faster and faster rate as capital and labour are increased by the same proportion along the ray, and represents *increasing returns to scale*. A *constant returns to scale* production process would be the borderline case between these two – with the boundary of the slice taking on the shape of a straight line.

Consider the homothetic isoquant map graphed three times in the upper three panels of Graph 12.5. The only difference between the three panels lies in the labels of the dark blue and light blue isoquants, labels that indicate the height of the isoquant in the underlying three-dimensional production frontier. In the middle panel (b), for instance, doubling the input levels, that is, moving out twice the distance from the origin, results in an exact doubling of the output level, and a tripling of all input levels results in a tripling of the output level. This is the *constant returns to scale* case. In panel (a), on the other hand, a doubling of the inputs leads to less than double the output, the *decreasing returns to scale* case, and in panel (c) a doubling of inputs leads to more than twice the output, the *increasing returns to scale* case. More generally, we will define a homothetic production process as constant returns to scale whenever multiplying inputs by a factor t results in a t-fold change in output, as decreasing returns to scale whenever multiplying inputs by a factor t results in less than a t-fold change in output, and as increasing returns to scale whenever multiplying inputs by a factor t results in more than a t-fold change in output.

Graph 12.5 Homothetic Isoquant Maps Can Represent Increasing, Constant or Decreasing Returns to Scale Production Processes

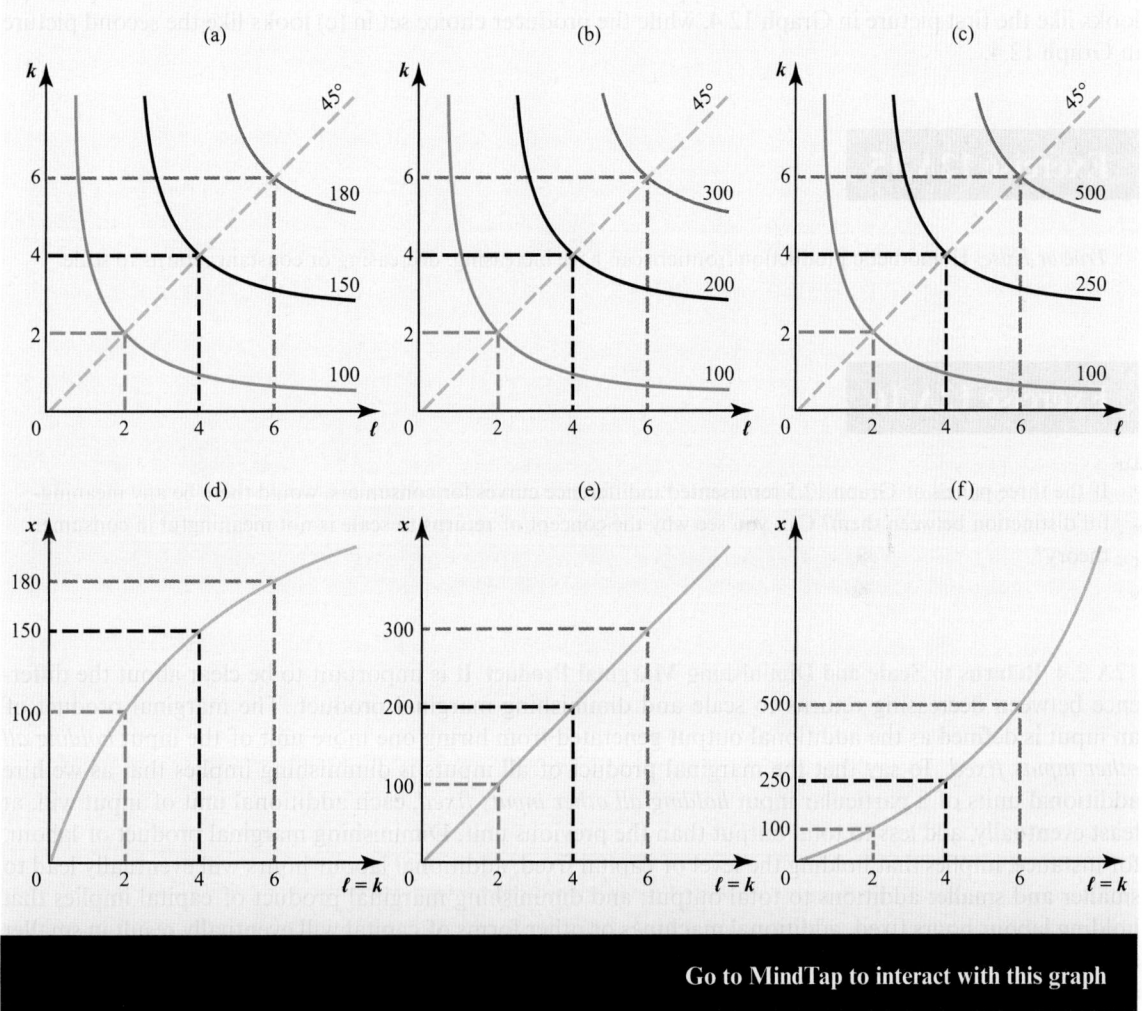

Go to MindTap to interact with this graph

Exercise 12A.14

Consider a single-input production process with increasing marginal product. Does this production process exhibit increasing returns to scale? What about the production process in Graph 11.10?

The upper three panels of Graph 12.5 show what the three-dimensional producer choice sets look like. Consider first panel (b), where the production frontier has constant returns to scale. Imagine taking a vertical slice of the three-dimensional production frontier from which these isoquants are derived along the 45-degree line in the isoquant picture of panel (b). This slice is graphed in panel (e) immediately below panel (b) with ℓ and k both represented on the horizontal axis since they are equal to one another on the 45-degree line in panel (b). Because this production frontier has the feature that multiplying inputs along the 45-degree line by a factor t results in a t-fold increase in output no matter where we start, this lower panel indicates that production increases along a straight line on this slice. The same would be true for any other vertical slice of the production frontier along a ray from the origin. In panel (a), on the other hand, the same slice would have the concave shape in panel (d). The reverse is true in panel (f) for the production frontier from panel (c). If you imagine these producer choice sets as three-dimensional mountains, the first would be a mountain that is initially hard to climb but that becomes easier and easier to climb as we walk up the mountain, while the last producer choice set is a mountain that is initially easy to climb but becomes harder and harder to scale as we approach the top. The underlying producer choice set in panel (a) looks like the first picture in Graph 12.4, while the producer choice set in (c) looks like the second picture in Graph 12.4.

Exercise 12A.15

True or False: Homothetic production frontiers can have increasing, decreasing or constant returns to scale.

Exercise 12A.16

If the three panels of Graph 12.5 represented indifference curves for consumers, would there be any meaningful distinction between them? Can you see why the concept of returns to scale is not meaningful in consumer theory?

12A.2.4 Returns to Scale and Diminishing Marginal Product It is important to be clear about the difference between decreasing returns to scale and diminishing marginal product. The marginal product of an input is defined as the additional output generated from hiring one more unit of the input *holding all other inputs fixed*. To say that the marginal product of all inputs is diminishing implies that as we hire additional units of a particular input *holding all other inputs fixed*, each additional unit of input will, at least eventually, add less to total output than the previous unit. Diminishing marginal product of labour, for instance, implies that holding the level of capital fixed, additional labour hours will eventually lead to smaller and smaller additions to total output; and diminishing marginal product of capital implies that holding labour hours fixed, additional machines or other forms of capital will eventually result in smaller and smaller additions to output. Because all other inputs are held fixed as we define marginal product of a particular input, *marginal product is measured as the slope of a slice of the production frontier that holds all other inputs constant, and diminishing marginal product implies that this slice eventually has diminishing slope*. Panel (f) of Graph 12.1 illustrates such a slice as it holds k fixed at k^D.

This is quite different from the property of decreasing returns to scale, which is a property of slices of the production frontier that emanate from the origin and keep the ratio of ℓ and k fixed as in Graph 12.4 and the lower panels of Graph 12.5. This is because, for a production process to satisfy decreasing returns to scale, we have said that a t-fold increase in *all inputs* must lead to a less than t-fold increase in output. Unlike the definition of diminishing marginal product, the definition of decreasing returns to scale does not hold any input fixed but explicitly defines what happens to output when *all* input levels are adjusted in proportion to one another. While there is a logical relationship between returns to scale and marginal product in the single-input model where increasing *all* inputs is the same as increasing one input, that relationship becomes more complex in the two-input model.

Would it be possible, for instance, to have decreasing marginal product of all inputs and increasing returns to scale? The first reaction might be 'no'. Let's pose the same question differently: If it's *not* possible to double output by *just* doubling the amount of labour employed, and it's *not* possible to double output by *just* doubling the amount of capital employed – does that preclude the possibility that it might be possible to double or more than double output by doubling *both labour and capital*? It might just be possible to more than double output by doubling both labour and capital even though we can't double it by doubling only labour or only capital. This is exactly the same as saying that we can have decreasing marginal product of both labour and capital and still have increasing returns to scale.

Exercise 12A.17

True or False: If you have decreasing marginal product of all inputs, you might have decreasing, constant or increasing returns to scale.

Suppose we have a production process with many inputs, and only one of those inputs has increasing marginal product and all the others have decreasing marginal product. Does this necessarily imply that the production process has increasing returns to scale? Again, the initial reaction might be 'no, not necessarily'. If we rephrase the question again: Suppose that you can more than double output by doubling *just one* input. Does that mean that we will necessarily be able to more than double output by doubling *all inputs?* Of course it does – if we can more than double output by doubling just one input, we can surely do it by doubling all inputs! This is equivalent to saying that increasing marginal product of just one input implies increasing returns to scale.

Exercise 12A.18

True or False: In the two-input model, decreasing returns to scale implies decreasing marginal product of all inputs.

Exercise 12A.19*

True or False: In the two-input model, increasing returns to scale implies increasing marginal product of at least one input.

With the tools developed in this section, we are now ready to illustrate how to identify the economically efficient production plans along an isoquant of many technologically efficient plans, and to show how we can infer profit-maximizing choices from resulting cost curves.

12A.3 Cost Minimization on the Way to Profit Maximization

When we derived the total cost curve in the single-input model in Section 11A.5, we were graphically solving a relatively trivial problem. In essence, we identified the cheapest possible or *economically most efficient* way to produce each output level given the input price *w*, as the one production plan on the production frontier that produces this output level in the *technologically efficient way*; that is, without wasting any resources. In the two-input model, finding the economically efficient way to produce a given output level is not that trivial because *now there are many ways of producing a given output level in a technologically efficient way* as indicated by the many possible input bundles that lie on an isoquant that represents all the ways this output level can be produced without wasting inputs.

12A.3.1 Isocosts and Cost Minimization Suppose, for instance, we are interested in finding the cheapest possible way of producing 100 units of output in panel (a) of Graph 12.6. The isoquant in the graph gives us all the technologically efficient input bundles that can result in 100 units of output with no input going to waste. Given that different inputs are associated with different prices, however, it is not sufficient for a production plan to be *technologically efficient* in the sense of not wasting inputs to conclude that the production plan is *economically efficient* in the sense of being the cheapest.

Graph 12.6 Finding the Cheapest Way of Producing Different Units of Output

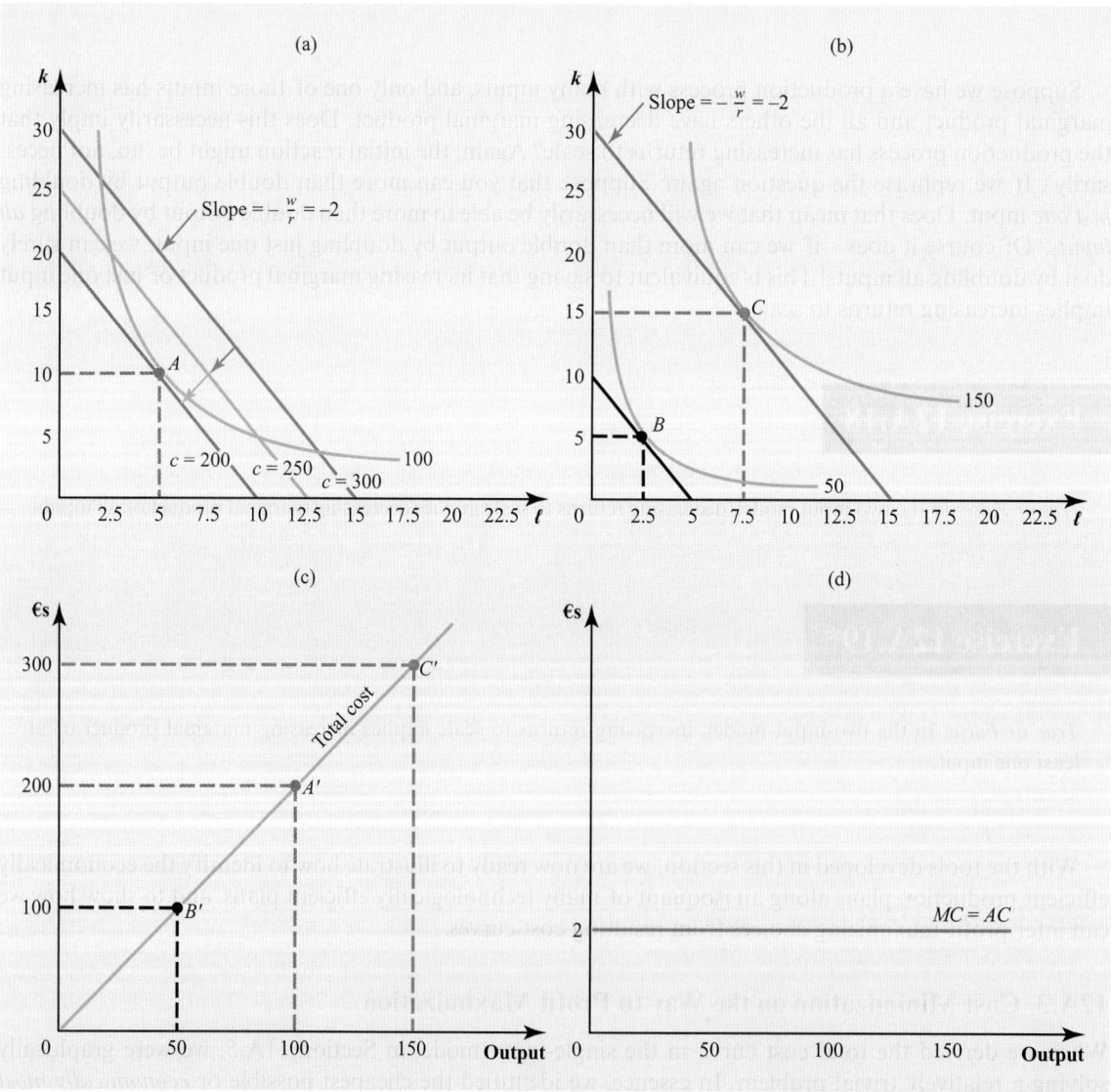

Exercise 12A.20

True or False: In the single-input model, each isoquant is composed of a single point, which implies that all technologically efficient production plans are also economically efficient.

Exercise 12A.21

True or False: In the two-input model, every economically efficient production plan must be technologically efficient but not every technologically efficient production plan is necessarily economically efficient.

We can imagine giving the producer a budget to work with, a budget with which to buy labour (ℓ) and capital (k) at an hourly wage rate w and a rental rate r. If, for instance, the wage rate is €20 per hour and the rental rate is €10 per unit of capital, the producer's hypothetical budget could be represented by the dark brown line in panel (a) of Graph 12.6 if we give the producer a total of €300 to work with.

This type of hypothetical budget for producers is called an *isocost curve*, which *represents all the combinations of inputs that cost the same at input prices* (w, r). While this isocost curve makes it possible for this producer to produce 100 units of output, we could reduce the amount of money given to the producer, moving the isocost curve inwards. For instance, we could give the producer only €250 to work with, which would put us on the light brown isocost curve, but this would still be more than the producer needs to produce 100 units of output. We could keep reducing the producers hypothetical budget until we get to the light blue isocost curve that represents all input combinations that cost exactly €200. This isocost curve contains exactly 1 input bundle – bundle A with 5 hours of labour and 10 units of capital – that can produce 100 units of output. Any less of a hypothetical budget would imply that the producer would not be able to buy sufficiently many inputs to produce 100 units of output. The input bundle A represents *the least cost way of producing 100 units of output when input prices are €20 for labour and €10 for capital*. The production plan (ℓ, k, x) = (5, 10, 100) represented by A is the economically efficient way to produce 100 output units given these input prices. Since the slope of the isoquant must equal the slope of the isocost at this cost-minimizing input bundle, we can conclude that:

$$\text{Cost minimization implies} -TRS = \frac{MP_\ell}{MP_k} = \frac{w}{r}. \tag{12.4}$$

Exercise 12A.22

True or False: We have to know nothing about prices, wages or rental rates to determine the technologically efficient ways of producing different output levels, but we cannot generally find the economically efficient ways of producing any output level without knowing these.

12A.3.2 Cost Curves With Multiple Inputs We can imagine doing this for each possible isoquant; that is, for each possible output level. For instance, in panel (b) of Graph 12.6, we illustrate the least cost input bundle B for producing 50 units of output as well as the least cost input bundle C for producing 150 units of output. Finally, panel (c) of the graph translates the three production plans represented by the input bundles A, B and C and their respective isoquants into a new graph illustrating the cost of producing 50, 100 and 150 units of output with output on the horizontal axis and euros on the vertical. For example, since the least cost input bundle for producing 100 units of output at input prices $w = 20$ and $r = 10$ involves using 5 labour hours costing a total of €100, and 10 units of capital costing an additional €100, the total cost of producing 100 units of output is €200 (point A'). Similarly, the total cost of producing 50 units is €100 (point B') and the total cost of producing 150 units is €300 (point C'). Connecting these points in panel (c) gives an estimate of the *total cost curve, which is the curve illustrating the cost of producing different quantities of output in the economically most efficient way given w = 20 and r = 10.*

Notice that the underlying technology here has constant returns to scale; that is, it has the characteristic that multiplying inputs by a factor t leads to a t-fold increase in output. It is for this reason that each additional unit of output always adds exactly the same additional cost to our total cost of production, causing the marginal cost of production to be constant and equal to €2 per unit of output and exactly equal to the average cost of producing. Panel (d) of Graph 12.6 illustrates this with constant MC at €2 that is equal to AC.

Exercise 12A.23

Suppose the numbers associated with the isoquants in panels (a) and (b) of Graph 12.6 had been 50, 80 and 100 instead of 50, 100 and 150. What would the total cost, MC and AC curves look like? Would this be an increasing or decreasing returns to scale production process, and how does this relate to the shape of the cost curves?

Exercise 12A.24

How would your answer to the previous question change if the numbers associated with the isoquants were 50, 150 and 300 instead?

We implicitly assumed in Graph 12.6 that the underlying production technology is homothetic. If we are faced with a particular wage w and rental rate r, we know where *all* the economically efficient production plans are as soon as we know where *one* such production plan is because all such cost-minimizing production plans will lie on the same vertical ray from the origin. This is true regardless of whether the production technology has constant returns to scale as in Graph 12.6 or whether it has some other returns to scale. For instance, consider the homothetic isoquant map in panel (a) of Graph 12.7 and suppose again that $w = 20$ and $r = 10$. If we know that an isocost with slope $-w/r = -2$ is tangent at D, we know that using 20 units of capital and 10 units of labour is the economically efficient way of producing 140 units of output. We also know that the slope of *all* the isoquants is -2 along the ray that emanates from the origin and passes through D, and thus we know that *all* the tangencies of isocosts with slope -2 will occur along this ray. Thus, A is the economically efficient input bundle for producing 10 output units, B is the economically efficient input bundle for producing 40 output units, and so on.

Exercise 12A.25

If w increases, will the economically efficient production plans lie on a steeper or shallower ray from the origin in the isoquant graph? What if r increases?

The production technology represented by the isoquant map in Graph 12.7 differs from the constant returns to scale technology in Graph 12.6 in that it has one additional feature we often think holds in real-world firms: it initially has increasing returns to scale but eventually assumes decreasing returns. You can tell that this is the case by looking at how quickly the labels on the isoquants increase; initially they increase at an increasing rate but eventually they increase at a decreasing rate. Just as for the typical single-input production process illustrated in Chapter 11, we have an example of a production technology where increased production initially becomes easier and easier but eventually becomes harder and harder.

Graph 12.7 Cost Curves of Typical Production Processes

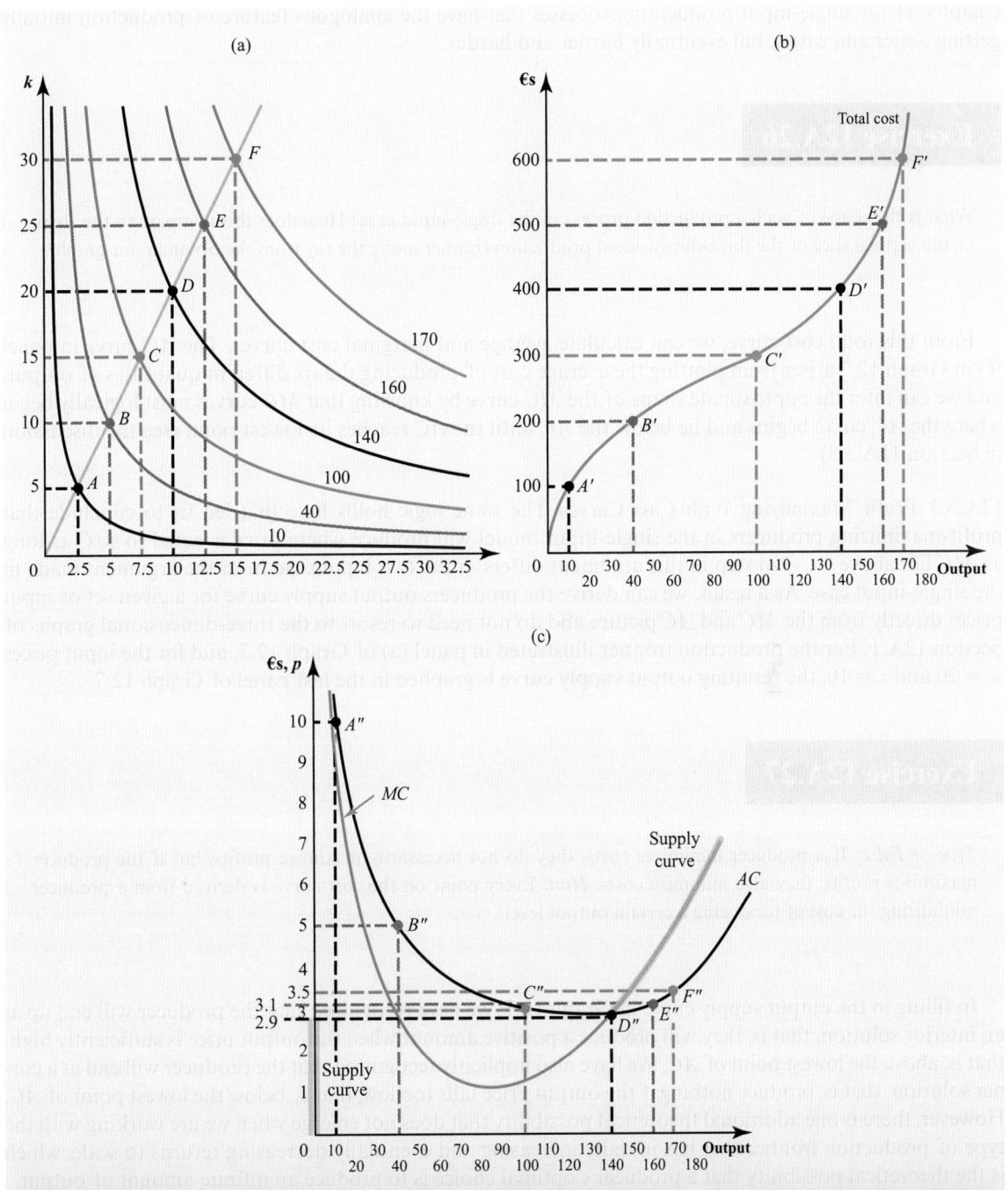

We can now derive the shape of the total cost curve from the points A to F in panel (a) of Graph 12.7 by calculating the cost of the inputs required to reach each of the isoquants, just as we did in Graph 12.6. For instance, panel (a) of the graph tells us that the least cost way of producing 140 units of output when $w = 20$ and $r = 10$ is to use the input bundle D that contains 20 units of capital and 10 units of labour. The cost of that input bundle is $10w + 20r = 10(20) + 20(10) = 400$. In panel (b) of the graph, we plot D with 140 units of output measured on the horizontal axis costing €400 measured on the vertical. Repeating this for each of the isoquants in panel (a), we can derive the shape of the total cost curve as one that initially increases at a decreasing rate but eventually increases at an increasing rate. This is the shape derived in Chapter 11 for single-input production processes that have the analogous feature of production initially getting easier and easier, but eventually harder and harder.

Exercise 12A.26

What is the shape of such a production process in the single-input case? How does this compare to the shape of the vertical slice of the three-dimensional production frontier along the ray from the origin in our graph?

From this total cost curve, we can calculate average and marginal cost curves. The AC curve in panel (c) in Graph 12.7 arises from plotting the average cost of producing the six different quantities of output, and we can infer the approximate shape of the MC curve by knowing that MC curves must logically begin where the AC curve begins and lie below the AC until the AC reaches its lowest point (see the discussion in Section 11A.5.3).

12A.3.3 Profit Maximizing With Cost Curves The same logic holds here that led us to conclude that profit-maximizing producers in the single-input model will produce where price is equal to MC as long as MC lies above AC. No step in this argument differs in the two-input case from the argument made in the single-input case. As a result, we can derive the producers output supply curve for a given set of input prices directly from the MC and AC picture and do not need to resort to the three-dimensional graphs of Section 12A.1. For the production frontier illustrated in panel (a) of Graph 12.7, and for the input prices $w = 20$ and $r = 10$, the resulting output supply curve is graphed in the last panel of Graph 12.7.

Exercise 12A.27

True or False: If a producer minimizes costs, they do not necessarily maximize profits, but if the producer maximizes profits, they also minimize costs. *Hint*: Every point on the cost curve is derived from a producer minimizing the cost of producing a certain output level.

In filling in the output supply curve in Graph 12.7, we have recognized that the producer will end up at an interior solution, that is, they will produce a positive amount when the output price is sufficiently high, that is, above the lowest point of AC. We have also implicitly recognized that the producer will end at a corner solution, that is, produce nothing if the output price falls too low, that is, below the lowest point of AC. However, there is one additional theoretical possibility that does not emerge when we are working with the type of production frontier that has initially increasing and eventually decreasing returns to scale, which is the theoretical possibility that a producer's optimal choice is to produce an infinite amount of output.

Suppose we have a production frontier that has increasing returns throughout. You can verify for yourself that the resulting MC curve will always lie below the AC curve, which implies that the part of the MC curve that lies above AC, and usually becomes the output supply curve, does not exist. Does this mean that a producer for whom it is getting easier and easier to produce should never produce? The answer is no, the producer's optimal choice is to produce either nothing or an infinite amount of the good. This is shown in Graph 12.8 where the MC and AC curves for a production process that has increasing returns to scale is graphed. Here, both the MC and AC curves approach but never quite reach p^*. If the output price is below p^*, the price always lies below AC regardless of how much the producer sends to the market, implying a negative profit no matter how much is produced. In this case, the producer would simply not produce. If the price rises above p^*, although they will make a loss on the initial output produced, the producer can make a positive profit by producing an infinite amount.

Graph 12.8 MC and AC Under Increasing Returns to Scale Production

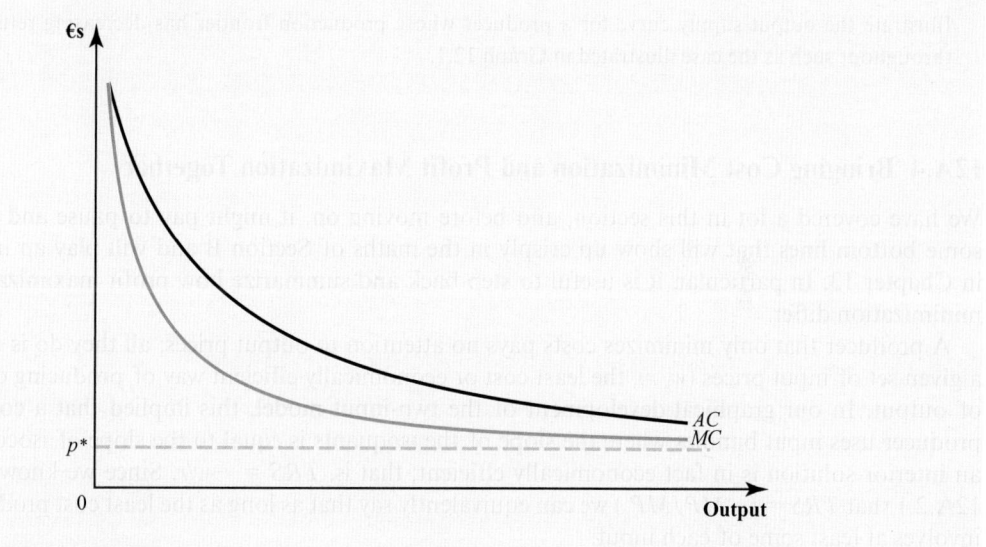

Exercise 12A.28*

Suppose a production process begins initially with increasing returns to scale and eventually assumes constant returns to scale, but never has decreasing returns. Would the MC curve ever cross the AC curve?

Do production processes like this exist? Consider the production of operating systems for personal computers. An enormous amount of effort goes into just producing the first operating system and into getting all the bugs out as one learns where they are. Eventually, producing additional operating systems is just a matter of burning a CD or putting it on a website for people to download, which is virtually costless. Such a production process would give rise to MC and AC curves similar to those in Graph 12.8, perhaps with MC actually reaching p^*, the cost of burning a CD, at some point. So yes, such production processes do exist. However, the decisions by producers that face such production processes are not properly modelled with the assumption that such producers are price takers. Examples of such producers include firms like Microsoft that have substantial market power and can influence price. We will therefore postpone further discussion of the profit-maximizing behaviour of such producers to Chapter 23 where we will relax the price-taking assumption. It is worth noting here, however, that the cost-minimization part of profit maximization will be exactly the same for such producers; it is only the second step of profit maximization that will differ when producers have market power and no longer take price as given.

Exercise 12A.29

Another special case is the one graphed in Graph 12.6. What are the profit-maximizing supply choices for such a producer as the output price changes?

Exercise 12A.30

Illustrate the output supply curve for a producer whose production frontier has decreasing returns to scale throughout such as the case illustrated in Graph 12.1.

12A.4 Bringing Cost Minimization and Profit Maximization Together

We have covered a lot in this section, and before moving on, it might pay to pause and take stock of some bottom lines that will show up crisply in the maths of Section B and will play an important role in Chapter 13. In particular, it is useful to step back and summarize how profit maximization and cost minimization differ.

A producer that only minimizes costs pays no attention to output prices; all they do is determine, for a given set of input prices (w, r), the least cost or economically efficient way of producing different levels of output. In our graphical development of the two-input model, this implied that a cost-minimizing producer uses input bundles where the slope of the isoquants is equal to the slope of isocosts, assuming an interior solution is in fact economically efficient; that is, $TRS = -w/r$. Since we know from Section 12A.2.1 that $TRS = (-MP_\ell/MP_k)$ we can equivalently say that as long as the least cost production bundle involves at least some of each input:

$$\text{Cost minimization implies } -TRS = \frac{MP_\ell}{MP_k} = \frac{w}{r}. \tag{12.5}$$

A *profit-maximizing* producer, on the other hand, also thinks about output price and produces where the marginal revenue product of each input is equal to that input's price. In the two-step profit maximization method that begins with cost minimization, this involves comparing marginal costs to marginal revenues, with the latter simply equal to the output price when producers are price takers. Competitive profit-maximizing firms therefore (1) minimize costs and (2) produce where $p = MC$. This is equivalent to the one-step profit maximization we discussed in Section 12A.1 where we argued that profit-maximizing firms will produce where the isoprofit planes are tangential to the production frontier, which implied that $MP_\ell = w/p$ and $MP_k = r/p$; that is:

$$\text{Profit maximization implies } MRP_\ell = pMP_\ell = w \quad \text{and} \quad MRP_k = pMP_k = r \tag{12.6}$$

as long as the true profit maximum occurs at an interior solution and not at an output of zero or infinity.

Dividing the equations in expression (12.6) by one another, profit maximization implies that $MP_\ell/MP_k = w/r$, which is what cost minimization implies. Thus *profit-maximizing producers are implicitly cost minimizing*. The reverse, however, is not true because $MP_\ell/MP_k = w/r$ does *not* imply that $pMP_\ell = w$ and $pMP_k = r$. For instance, if $pMP_\ell > w$ and $pMP_k > r$, MP_ℓ/MP_k could still be equal to w/r, $p = 1$, $MP_\ell = 20$, $MP_k = 10$, $w = 10$ and $r = 5$.

$$\frac{w}{r} = 2 = \frac{pMP_\ell}{pMP_k} = \frac{MP_\ell}{MP_k} \tag{12.7}$$

but $pMP_\ell = 20 > 10 = w$ and $pMP_k = 10 > 5 = r$. Thus, cost-minimizing producers become profit maximizers only when they set output level such that $p = MC$ as long as MC is greater than or equal to AC, which turns out to be the same as saying that profit maximizers produce where marginal revenue products are equal to input prices.

12B The Mathematics Behind the Multiple-Input Model

Section A began with an illustration of the technical complexity of graphing profit maximization when production technologies have more than one input and set up an alternative graphical method that uses cost minimization as a first step to finding the profit-maximizing choices made by price-taking producers. When we take a more mathematical approach, the complexity of solving for profit-maximizing choices directly is not as overwhelming and thus the need for an alternative approach is less compelling. However, we will find that the alternative cost-minimization approach provides us with a method that is almost identical to the expenditure minimization problem in consumer theory, and it allows us ultimately to derive a duality picture such as the one we derived in consumer theory. Cost minimization furthermore builds the basis for deriving the cost functions that apply to *all* producers, whether they are competitive price takers or whether they can in fact exercise market power.

12B.1 Producer Choice Sets and Production Functions

In the single-input case, we represented production frontiers mathematically with production functions of the form $f: \mathbb{R}^1_+ \to \mathbb{R}^1_+$. Production functions in the multiple-input case are extensions, with a production process that uses n inputs represented by a function $f: \mathbb{R}^n_+ \to \mathbb{R}^1_+$. For the case in which labour ℓ and capital k represent the only two inputs, for instance, the function $f: \mathbb{R}^2_+ \to \mathbb{R}^1_+$ tells us the quantity of output $f(\ell, k)$ that can be produced from any input bundle (ℓ, k) assuming no inputs are wasted. The producer choice set is defined as the set of production plans (x, ℓ, k) that are technologically feasible; that is:

$$C(f: \mathbb{R}^2_+ \to \mathbb{R}^1_+) = \{(x, \ell, k) \in \mathbb{R}^3 | x \leq f(\ell, k)\}. \tag{12.8}$$

In principle, not only could such a choice set contain some arbitrary number n of inputs but it could also result in a number m of different outputs $(x_1, x_2, ..., x_m)$, with a function $f: \mathbb{R}^n_+ \to \mathbb{R}^m_+$ generating the relevant production frontier. Production processes with multiple outputs may be of two different types. First, it may be the case that a producer *intentionally* uses a given set of inputs to *jointly* produce several different outputs to sell on the market. For instance, the owner of an apple orchard might use the inputs apple trees and bees (required for cross-pollination) to produce outputs apples and honey to be sold in the output market. Second, a producer might *unintentionally* produce goods that they do not or are not able to sell on the market but that impact the lives of others. The apple orchard owner might, for instance, unintentionally provide cross-pollination services to a neighbouring plum orchard, or the processing of honey might produce the output water pollution in a neighbouring river. Such unintentionally produced outputs will be referred to as production externalities in later chapters. For now, however, we will restrict ourselves to production processes that yield a single, intentionally produced output x.

12B.1.1 Marginal Product and *TRS* Consider the definition of the marginal product of an input, which is the increase in total output from hiring one more unit of the input while holding all other inputs fixed.

This translates directly into the mathematical definition of marginal product as *the partial derivative of the production function with respect to the input*, or:

$$MP_\ell = \frac{\partial f(\ell, k)}{\partial \ell} \quad \text{and} \quad MP_k = \frac{\partial f(\ell, k)}{\partial k} \tag{12.9}$$

for the case where the inputs are labour ℓ and capital k. Since k is held fixed in the partial derivative that defines MP_ℓ, this implies that the marginal product of labour is the slope of the slice of the production function that holds k fixed, while the marginal product of capital is the slope of the slice that holds labour input fixed. Examples of such slices are depicted graphically in Graph 12.1.

Exercise 12B.1

Just as we can take the partial derivative of a production function with respect to one of the inputs and call it the marginal product of the input, we could take the partial derivative of a utility function with respect to one of the consumption goods and call it the marginal utility from that good. Why is the first of these concepts economically meaningful but the second is not?

As already discussed extensively in Section A, we can also explore the properties of production functions by considering the horizontal slices of these functions, slices that are known as *isoquants*. In Section A, we argued that it is reasonable to assume that such isoquants will have properties similar to consumer indifference curves, which are just horizontal slices of utility rather than production functions. The slope of an isoquant derived from a production function $f(\ell, k)$, the marginal *technical rate of substitution* (*TRS*), is given by:

$$TRS = -\left(\frac{\partial f(\ell, k)/\partial \ell}{\partial f(\ell, k)/\partial k}\right), \tag{12.10}$$

which can be derived in exactly the same way as the formula for MRS in Chapter 4 was derived.

Exercise 12B.2*

Using the same method employed to derive the formula for MRS from a utility function, derive the formula for TRS from a production function $f(l, k)$.

Given the expressions for marginal product in equation (12.9), the TRS can also be expressed as the fraction of the marginal products of the inputs:

$$TRS = -\frac{MP_\ell}{MP_k}, \tag{12.11}$$

as we already derived intuitively in Section 12A.2.1.

12B.1.2 Averages Are Better Than Extremes and Quasiconcavity A particularly important assumption we typically make about producer choice sets is that averages are better than extremes in the sense that an input bundle formed as the average of two input bundles on the same isoquant will produce at least as much but typically more than the more extreme bundles. When we made the same assumption in consumer theory, we called it convexity because it gives rise to convex upper contour sets of indifference curves. As it turns out, assuming convexity of upper contour sets is equivalent to assuming that the underlying production function is *quasiconcave*. Consider the definition of quasiconcavity of a function: A function $f: \mathbb{R}^2_+ \to \mathbb{R}^1_+$ is *quasiconcave* if and only if, for any two points $A = (x^A_1, x^A_2)$ and $B = (x^B_1, x^B_2)$ in $\mathbb{R}^2_+$ and any $\alpha \in (0, 1)$,

$$\min \{f(x^A_1, x^A_2), f(x^B_1, x^B_2)\} \le f(\alpha x^A_1 + (1 - \alpha)x^B_1, \alpha^A_2 + (1 - \alpha)x^B_2). \qquad \text{(12.12)x}$$

Suppose we pick two input bundles $A = (\ell^A, k^A)$ and $B = (\ell^B, k^B)$ on an isoquant of the quasiconcave production function $f(\ell, k)$. Since they lie on the same isoquant, we know that $f(\ell^A, k^A) = f(\ell^B, k^B)$, and from our definition of quasiconcavity, we can infer that the output of any weighted average of input bundles A and B will be at least as much as is produced on the isoquant from which A and B were drawn. Thus, quasiconcave production functions represent production processes under which average input bundles produce more than extremes. Similarly, whenever averages are better than extremes in the sense we have defined this, only quasiconcave functions can represent such production processes. As a result, we can conclude that *quasiconcave production functions give rise to isoquants with convex upper contour sets, and production processes in which isoquants have convex upper contour sets must arise from quasiconcave production functions.* Since all the utility functions we worked with in our development of consumer theory had the averages are better than extremes feature, we know that all these utility functions were also quasiconcave.

Exercise 12B.3

True or False: Producer choice sets whose frontiers are characterized by quasiconcave functions have the following property: all horizontal slices of the choice sets are convex sets.

We can note, however, that this does not imply that production or utility functions that have the averages are better than extremes feature must be *concave*, only that they must be *quasiconcave*. We can clarify this by first stating the definition of a concave function with two inputs. A function $f: \mathbb{R}^2_+ \to \mathbb{R}^1$ is *concave* if and only if, for any two points, $A = (x^A_1, x^A_2)$ and $B = (x^B_1, x^B_2)$ in $\mathbb{R}^2_+$ and any $\alpha \in (0, 1)$,

$$\alpha f(x^A_1, x^A_2) + (1 - \alpha)f(x^B_1, x^B_2) \le f(a x^A_1 + (1 - \alpha)x^B_1, \alpha x^A_2 + (1 - \alpha)x^B_2). \qquad \text{(12.13)}$$

It can be seen that every concave function is also quasiconcave by noting that, for any $A = (x^A_1, x^A_2)$ and $B = (x^B_1, x^B_2)$ and any $\alpha \in (0, 1)$, it is always true that:

$$\min \{f(x^A_1, x^A_2), f(x^B_1, x^B_2)\} \le \alpha f(x^A_1, x^A_2) + (1 - \alpha)f(x^B_1, x^B_2). \qquad \text{(12.14)}$$

as long as f satisfies (12.13). If f is concave, equations (12.13) and (12.14) together imply that equation (12.12) holds; that is, f being concave implies f is quasiconcave.

The reverse, however, does not hold. It is in exploring this through an example that we can get some intuition for the difference between quasiconcavity and concavity of a function. Consider, for instance, the Cobb–Douglas production function $f(\ell, k) = \ell^{1/3}k^{1/3}$, which is graphed in panel (a) of Graph 12.9.

The production plans A and B fall on the vertical slice of this function that lies on the 45-degree line in the (ℓ, k) plane. Since the slope on this slice of the function starts out large and declines, the dotted line connecting

A and *B* lies below the function. Points on this dotted line correspond to the left-hand side of equation (12.13), while points on the boundary of the slice correspond to the right-hand side of equation (12.13). The fact that the former falls below the latter formally satisfies the definition of concavity. Panel (b) of Graph 12.9, on the other hand, illustrates the same function squared; that is, $f(\ell, k) = \ell^{2/3}k^{2/3}$, but this time the dotted line connecting *A* and *B* lies *above* the function, which implies that the definition of concavity is not satisfied.

Graph 12.9 Quasiconcave Functions Can Be Concave (a) But Don't Have to Be (b)

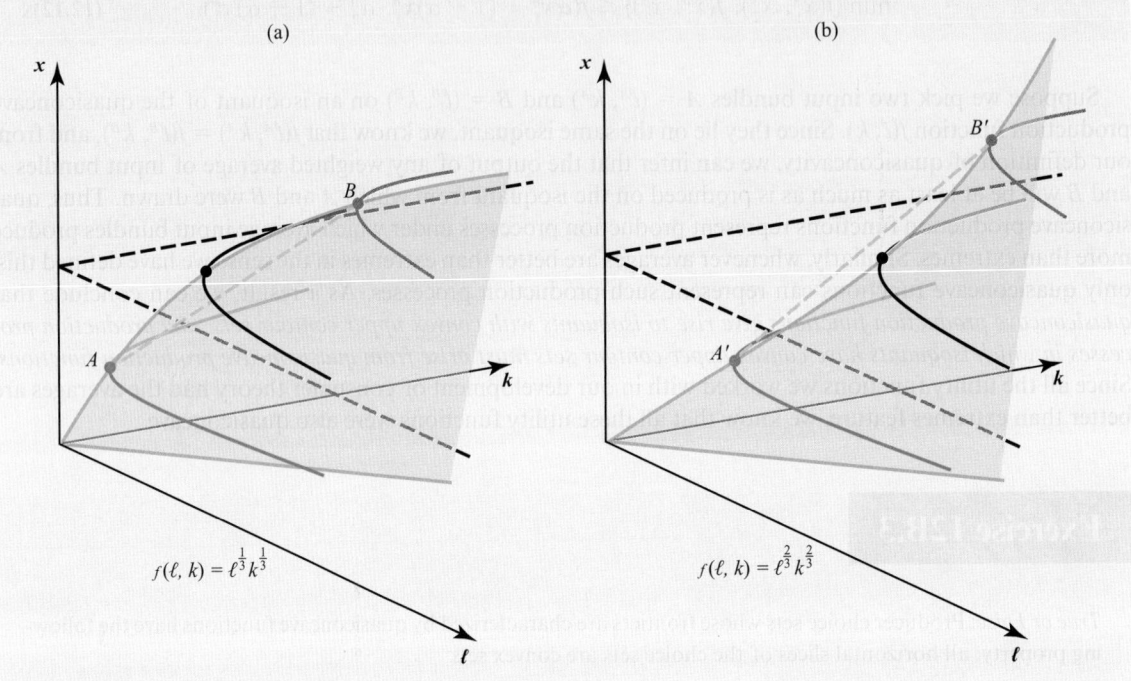

Therefore, panel (a) of Graph 12.9 represents a production function that is concave while panel (b) represents a production function that is not concave. You might see that this is the equivalent to saying that the producer choice set in panel (a) is a convex set, while the producer choice set in panel (b) is a non-convex set. Concave production functions therefore represent convex producer choice sets. At the same time, the shape of the same-coloured isoquants in the two panels is identical since, as we learned in the development of consumer theory, a transformation of a function such as squaring it, does not change the shape of the levels projected into two dimensions, even though it does change the three-dimensional function. These shapes of isoquants give rise to convex upper contour sets, indicating that both functions are quasiconcave.

Exercise 12B.4

True or False: All quasiconcave production functions, but not all concave production functions, give rise to convex producer choice sets.

Exercise 12B.5

True or False: Both quasiconcave and concave production functions represent production processes for which the averages are better than extremes property holds.

12B.1.3 Returns to Scale and Concavity Our discussion of concavity of production functions relates directly to the concept of returns to scale. In Section A, we defined a homothetic production process as having *decreasing returns to scale* if multiplying inputs by a factor t leads to less than t times as much output, *constant returns to scale* if it leads to t times as much output, and *increasing returns to scale* if it leads to more than t times as much output. Notice that the production function graphed in panel (a) of Graph 12.9 has the feature that any vertical slice of the function along a ray from the origin such as the one that is pictured has a slope that gets shallower and shallower, implying that multiplying inputs along the ray by a factor t will result in less than t times as much output. The reverse is true for the production function in panel (b), where the slope of the function along any vertical slice emanating from the origin becomes steeper and steeper. Thus, the same feature of homothetic production functions that makes them either concave or not concave determines whether they have decreasing returns to scale. When isoquant maps are homothetic, *the boundary of convex producer choice sets is represented by a concave production function that has decreasing returns to scale*. Increasing returns to scale, on the other hand, imply a non-convexity in the producer choice set and thus a non-concavity in the production function.

We can be even more precise about what returns to scale means mathematically for the production function if the function is homogeneous. First, recall that all homogeneous functions are homothetic, and a function is homogeneous of degree k if and only if:

$$f(t\ell, tk) = t^k f(\ell, k).$$ (12.15)

Since a production function is defined to have constant returns to scale when a t-fold increase in inputs causes a t-fold increase in outputs, it follows that *constant returns to scale production functions are homogeneous of degree 1*. Similarly, *decreasing returns to scale production functions that are homogeneous are homogeneous of degree less than 1*, and *increasing returns to scale production functions that are homogeneous are homogeneous of degree greater than 1*. In the case of two-input Cobb–Douglas production functions, for instance, this implies that the production function is decreasing returns to scale if the exponents sum to less than 1, constant returns to scale if the exponents sum to 1, and increasing returns to scale if they sum to greater than 1. Note, however, that not all homothetic production functions are homogeneous. You could, for instance, have a homothetic production function that has initially increasing and eventually decreasing returns to scale.

Exercise 12B.6

Verify the last statement regarding two-input Cobb–Douglas production functions.

12B.1.4 Returns to Scale and Diminishing Marginal Product Finally, we can return to our discussion from Section 12A.2.4 in which we argued intuitively that diminishing marginal product of inputs is conceptually quite different from decreasing returns to scale because the first concept holds all inputs but one fixed, while the latter varies all inputs in proportion to one another. We can get some further intuition by illustrating the concepts using the homothetic and homogeneous Cobb–Douglas production function $f(\ell, k) = \ell^\alpha k^\beta$, which has marginal product of labour and capital equal to:

$$MP_\ell = \alpha \ell^{(\alpha-1)} k^\beta \quad \text{and} \quad MP_k = \beta \ell^\alpha k^{(\beta-1)}.$$ (12.16)

The production function has diminishing MP if and only if the derivative of MP is negative, where:

$$\frac{\partial MP_\ell}{\partial \ell} = \alpha(\alpha - 1)\ell^{(\alpha-2)} k^\beta \quad \text{and} \quad \frac{\partial MP_k}{\partial k} = \beta(\beta - 1)\ell^\alpha k^{(\beta-2)}.$$ (12.17)

As long as the exponents α and β are positive, as they always are in Cobb–Douglas production functions, this implies that marginal product of labour and capital will be diminishing only if each exponent is less than 1. That's because only when the exponent on the input is less than 1 will the derivative of marginal product in (12.17) be negative.

Graph 12.10 illustrates two increasing returns to scale Cobb–Douglas production functions, one with diminishing marginal product and the other with increasing marginal product. In particular, panel (a) replicates the production function $f(\ell, k) = \ell^{2/3}k^{2/3}$ from panel (b) of Graph 12.9 but now illustrates the shape of the slice of the production function that holds labour fixed at ℓ^A. Panel (b) of Graph 12.10 does the same for the production function $f(\ell, k) = \ell^{4/3}k^{4/3}$. From equation (12.17), we would expect the production function in panel (a) to exhibit diminishing marginal product of each input, since the exponents on each input in the production function are less than 1, and we would expect the production function in panel (b) to exhibit increasing marginal product, since the same exponents are larger than 1. This is precisely what the shapes of the slices of these functions indicate, with $f(\ell^A, k)$ exhibiting a diminishing slope in panel (a), and thus diminishing MP_k, and an increasingly steep slope in panel (b), and thus increasing MP_k.

Graph 12.10 Increasing Returns to Scale with (a) Diminishing MP and (b) Increasing MP

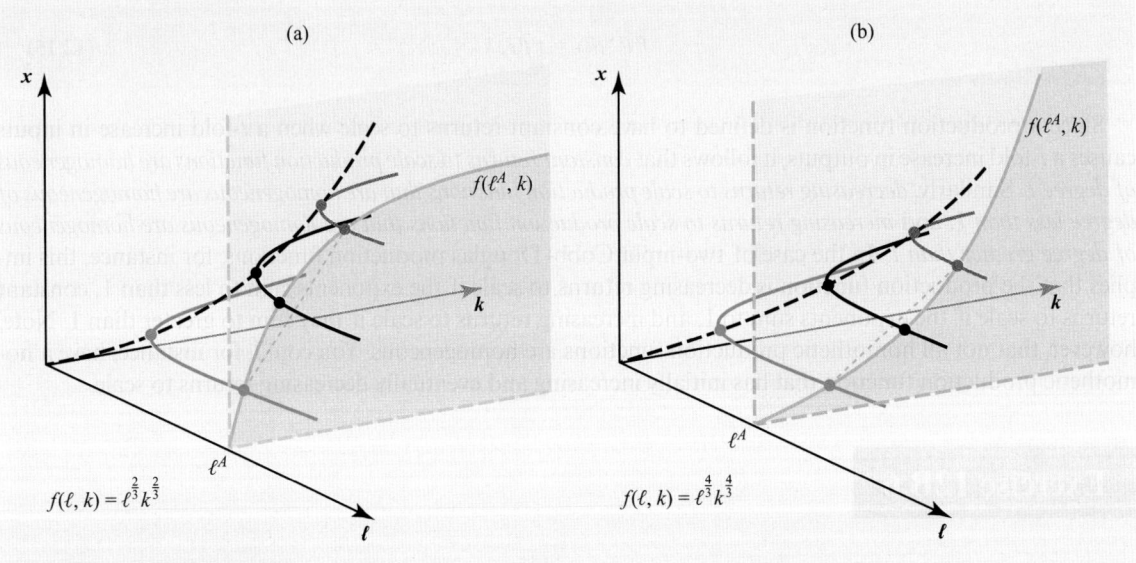

Exercise 12B.7

Can you give an example of a Cobb–Douglas production function that has increasing marginal product of capital and decreasing marginal product of labour? Does this production function have increasing, constant or decreasing returns to scale?

Exercise 12B.8

True or False: It is not possible for a Cobb–Douglas production process to have decreasing returns to scale and increasing marginal product of one of its inputs.

12B.2 Isoprofit Planes and Profit Maximization

In Graph 12.1, we briefly illustrated profit maximization with two-input production frontiers as the tangency of an isoprofit plane with the production frontier. The production frontier represents the technological constraint faced by producers, and the isoprofit curves represent the tastes for profit that arise from the economic environment that the producer takes as given. We will now illustrate the graphical profit maximization of Graph 12.1 mathematically by first defining isoprofits formally and setting up and solving the full profit maximization problem.

12B.2.1 Isoprofit Curves with Multiple Inputs As we have already discussed extensively in Chapter 11, we assume that tastes for producers are generally quantified straightforwardly in terms of profit. Profit, in turn, is expressed as the difference between economic revenue generated from the sale of goods and services, and economic costs incurred as inputs are purchased for producing outputs. In the two-input case with labour ℓ and capital k, profit π at a production plan (x, ℓ, k) is:

$$\pi = px - w\ell - rk, \tag{12.18}$$

where the economic environment is characterized by the output price p and the input prices (w, r), all of which our price-taking producer takes as given. The isoprofit curve P was defined in Chapter 11 as the set of production plans that yield the same amount of profit in a given economic environment (p, w, r). This can be defined more formally as:

$$P(\pi, p, w, r) = \{(x, \ell, k) \in \mathbb{R}^3 \mid \pi = px - w\ell - rk\}. \tag{12.19}$$

Exercise 12B.9

In a three-dimensional graph with x on the vertical axis, can you use equation (12.18) to determine the vertical intercept of an isoprofit curve $P(\pi, p, w, r)$? What about the slope when k is held fixed?

Exercise 12B.10

Define profit and isoprofit curves for the case where land L is a third input and can be rented at a price r_L.

12B.2.2 Profit Maximization with Multiple Inputs The movement to the highest possible isoprofit plane on the three-dimensional production function graphed in panel (f) of Graph 12.1 is formalized mathematically as the solution to the profit maximization problem:

$$\max_{x,\ell,k} \pi = px - w\ell - rk \text{ subject to } x = f(\ell, k). \tag{12.20}$$

This problem could be read as 'pick the production plan that lies on the highest isoprofit plane while remaining technologically feasible'. It can also be written as an unconstrained maximization problem by substituting the constraint into the objective function and writing:

$$\max_{\ell,k} \pi = pf(\ell, k) - w\ell - rk. \tag{12.21}$$

The first-order conditions are the partial derivatives of π with respect to the two choice variables set to zero; that is:

$$\frac{\partial \pi}{\partial \ell} = p\frac{\partial f(\ell, k)}{\partial \ell} - w = 0,$$

$$\frac{\partial \pi}{\partial k} = p\frac{\partial f(\ell, k)}{\partial k} - r = 0, \tag{12.22}$$

which can also be written as:

$$w = p\frac{\partial f(\ell, k)}{\partial \ell} \quad \text{and} \quad r = p\frac{\partial f(\ell, k)}{\partial k}, \tag{12.23}$$

or:

$$w = pMP_{\ell} = MRP_{\ell} \quad \text{and} \quad r = pMP_{k} = MRP_{k}. \tag{12.24}$$

These are the conditions that emerge in panel (f) of Graph 12.1. At the profit-maximizing production plan A, the slope of the slice of the production frontier that holds capital fixed at k^D is equal to the slope of the corresponding slice of the isoprofit plane that also holds capital fixed at k^D ($w/p = MP_{\ell}$); and the slope of the slice of the production frontier that holds labour fixed at ℓ^D is equal to the corresponding slice of the isoprofit plane that also holds labour fixed at ℓ^D ($r/p = MP_{k}$).

Exercise 12B.11

Demonstrate that the problem as written in (12.20) gives the same answer.

The two equations in (12.22) can be solved to give the input demand functions that tell us how much labour and capital the producer will employ in any economic environment (p, w, r) that they might face; that is:

$$\ell(p, w, r) \quad \text{and} \quad k(p, w, r) \tag{12.25}$$

are the *labour and capital demand functions* for this producer. Substituting these into the production function, we can derive the *output supply function:*

$$x(p, w, r) = f((\ell(p, w, r), k(p, w, r)) \tag{12.26}$$

that shows how much output the producer will supply in any economic environment (p, w, r) they might face.

12B.2.3 An Example of Profit Maximization Suppose, for instance, that the technology available to a producer can be represented by the function $f(\ell, k) = 20\ell^{2/5}k^{2/5}$. We can set up the profit maximization problem:

$$\max_{x,\ell,k} \pi = px - w\ell - rk \text{ subject to } x = 20\ell^{2/5}k^{2/5}, \tag{12.27}$$

which can also be written as:

$$\max_{\ell,k} \pi = p(20\ell^{2/5}k^{2/5}) - w\ell - rk. \tag{12.28}$$

The first-order conditions are:

$$\frac{\partial \pi}{\partial \ell} = 8p\ell^{-3/5}k^{2/5} - w = 0,$$

$$\frac{\partial \pi}{\partial k} = 8p\ell^{2/5}k^{-3/5} - r = 0, \tag{12.29}$$

which can be written as:

$$w = 8p\ell^{-3/5}k^{2/5} \quad \text{and} \quad r = 8p\ell^{2/5}k^{-3/5}. \tag{12.30}$$

Solving the second of these two equations for k and substituting it into the first, we get the labour demand function:

$$\ell(p, w, r) = \frac{(8p)^5}{r^2w^3}, \tag{12.31}$$

and substituting this for ℓ in the second equation, we get the capital demand function:

$$k(p, w, r) = \frac{(8p)^5}{w^2r^3}. \tag{12.32}$$

Finally, we can derive the output supply function by substituting equations (12.31) and (12.32) into the production function $f(\ell, k) = 20\ell^{2/5}k^{2/5}$ to get:

$$x(p, w, r) = 20\frac{(8p)^4}{(wr)^2} = 81\,920\frac{p^4}{(wr)^2}. \tag{12.33}$$

Exercise 12B.12

Demonstrate that solving the problem as defined in equation (12.27) results in the same solution.

Suppose, for instance, the economic environment is characterized by an output price of €5 for each good produced, and that the producer pays €20 per hour for labour and €10 per hour for the capital equipment. Substituting these values into equations (12.31), (12.32) and (12.33), the producer chooses a production plan that employs 128 worker hours and 256 units of capital to produce 1280 units of the output. We could illustrate different slices of these functions by varying one price at a time and plotting the resulting economic relationships. For instance, we might be interested to know how output supply responds to output price, in which case we could hold w and r fixed at €20 and €10 and plot the function $x(p, 20, 10)$. Or we might be interested in how labour demand responds to changes in the wage rate and plot $\ell(5, w, 10)$, or how labour demand responds to output price changes ($\ell(p, 20, 10)$ or changes in the rental rate ($\ell(5, 20, r)$. The relationships between output supply and price as well as input demand and each inputs price are graphed in Graph 12.11. These are commonly known as output supply and input demand curves, and they represent the inverse of the slices $x(p, 20, 10)$, $\ell(5, w, 10)$, and $k(5, 20, r)$.

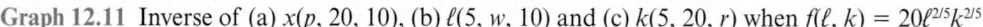

Graph 12.11 Inverse of (a) $x(p, 20, 10)$, (b) $\ell(5, w, 10)$ and (c) $k(5, 20, r)$ when $f(\ell, k) = 20\ell^{2/5}k^{2/5}$

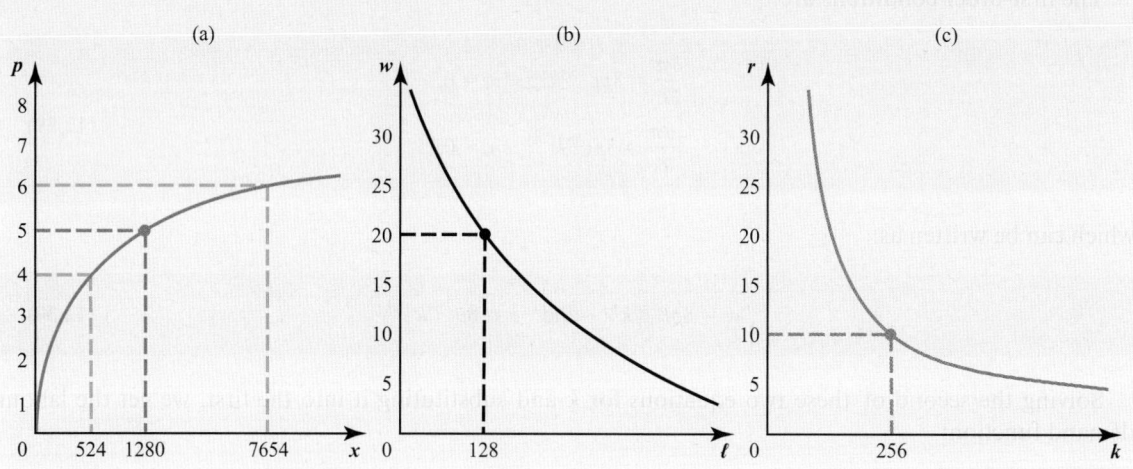

Exercise 12B.13*

Each panel of Graph 12.11 illustrates one of three inverse slices of the respective function through the production plan ($x = 1280$, $\ell = 128$, $k = 256$). What are the other two slices for each of the three functions? Do they slope up or down?

12B.3 Cost Minimization on the Way to Profit Maximization

So far, we have treated the mathematics of the producer's problem by solving it in one shot as a single profit maximization problem. In deriving the cost curves we used in Section A to illustrate profit maximization, however, we instead imagined that a producer first determines how much it would cost to produce each output level in an economically efficient way and uses this information to find the profit-maximizing output quantity by setting price equal to marginal cost. We first illustrated this two-step method of profit maximizing in Section 11A.5 for the single-input case and showed in part A of this chapter how to extend the logic to the two-input case. The defining difference between the single-input and two-input cases was found in the fact that technologically efficient production plans are by default economically efficient in the single-input model but not in the two-input model, because when there are two inputs, there are typically many technologically efficient ways of producing each output level, only one of which is usually economically efficient given the relevant prices for labour and capital. We will now show this mathematically.

12B.3.1 Extending Cost Minimization to Multiple Inputs For the single-input case, we illustrated the steps involved in calculating the output supply function in equations (11.17) to (11.21). The sequence of steps for accomplishing the same in the multiple-input case differs only up to the derivation of the cost function in equation (11.18), with the remaining steps essentially the same. This is analogous to what we concluded graphically in Graph 12.7 where we developed a new way of deriving the (total) cost curve in panel (b) but derived the supply curve in panel (c) exactly as we would have had the cost curve represented a single-input production process.

Since there are now many different technologically efficient ways of producing any output level, the derivation of the cost function now requires us to determine the economically most efficient input bundle on each isoquant rather than simply inverting the production function as we did in Chapter 11 for the single-input case. The process we described in Section A for accomplishing this graphically had us imagine that we try to determine the smallest possible budget under which a producer could produce each level of output; or, in the language of our graphical development, the lowest isocost to reach each isoquant. Put into mathematical language, we can express this process as a constrained minimization problem in which we are attempting to ascertain the minimum cost necessary to reach each of the isoquants from our production function; that is:

$$\min_{\ell,k} C = w\ell + rk \text{ subject to } x = f(\ell, k). \tag{12.34}$$

The Lagrange function is given by:

$$\mathcal{L}(\ell, k, \lambda) = w\ell + rk + \lambda(x - f(\ell, k)), \tag{12.35}$$

with first-order conditions:

$$\frac{\partial \mathcal{L}}{\partial \ell} = w - \lambda \frac{\partial f(\ell, k)}{\partial \ell} = 0,$$

$$\frac{\partial \mathcal{L}}{\partial k} = r - \lambda \frac{\partial f(\ell, k)}{\partial k} = 0, \tag{12.36}$$

$$\frac{\partial \mathcal{L}}{\partial \lambda} = x - f(\ell, k) = 0.$$

Taking the negative terms in the first two equations to the other side and dividing the two equations by each other, we get:

$$\frac{w}{r} = \frac{\partial f(\ell, k)/\partial \ell}{\partial f(\ell, k)/\partial k} = -TRS \text{ or } TRS = -\frac{w}{r}, \tag{12.37}$$

which is what we concluded intuitively in panel (a) of Graph 12.7 where we graphically illustrated the process of minimizing the cost of producing 100 units of output and concluded that the economically efficient input bundle A had the property that the slope of the isoquant or the TRS, is equal to the slope of the isocost $(-w/r)$.

From the three equations in (12.36), we can now calculate the amount of labour and capital input that a cost-minimizing producer will purchase under different economic environments in the input market (w, r) *conditional on* the level of output x the producer wants to reach. We can derive the functions:

$$\ell(w, r, x) \text{ and } k(w, r, x) \tag{12.38}$$

that are known as *conditional input demand functions*. The name derives from the fact that these functions tell us how much labour and capital a producer will employ at prevailing wage and rental rates *conditional on producing x units of the output*. In panel (a) of Graph 12.7, for instance, the conditional labour and capital input demands for producing 40 units of the output when $w = 20$ and $r = 10$ are given by the input bundle B: 5 labour hours and 10 units of capital.

Exercise 12B.14*

Did we calculate a conditional labour demand function when we did cost minimization in the single-input model?

Exercise 12B.15

Why are the conditional input demand functions not a function of output price p?

To calculate the lowest possible cost at which a producer can produce 40 units of output at these input prices, we multiply the input quantities demanded by their respective prices and add up the total expenses for labour and capital. This gives us a cost of €200 and one point on the cost curve in panel (b) of Graph 12.7. More generally, if we know the conditional input demand functions, we can similarly derive the total cost function $C(w, r, x)$ that tells us the minimum cost of producing any output level for any set of input prices:

$$C(w, r, x) = w\ell(w, r, x) + rk(w, r, x). \tag{12.39}$$

Once we know the cost function, we can proceed as in the single-input case to calculate the marginal cost function $MC(w, r, x)$ and the average cost function $AC(w, r, x)$ and derive the output supply $x(p, w, r)$ by setting price equal to marginal cost when price is above average cost. Finally, by substituting this supply function back into the conditional input demands, we can derive the actual rather than the conditional input demand functions.

12B.3.2 An Example Continued Consider, for example, the same production function $f(\ell, k) = 20\ell^{2/5}k^{2/5}$ used in Section 12B.2.3 to derive output supply and input demand directly from the profit maximization problem. Using the cost-minimization approach, we first define the problem as in equation (12.34):

$$\min_{\ell,k} c = w\ell + rk \text{ subject to } x = 20\ell^{2/5}k^{2/5}. \tag{12.40}$$

The Lagrange function is given by:

$$\mathcal{L}(\ell, k, \lambda) = w\ell + rk + \lambda(x - 20\ell^{2/5}k^{2/5}), \tag{12.41}$$

with first-order conditions:

$$\frac{\partial \mathcal{L}}{\partial \ell} = w - 8\lambda \ell^{-3/5} k^{2/5} = 0,$$

$$\frac{\partial \mathcal{L}}{\partial k} = r - 8\lambda \ell^{2/5} k^{-3/5} = 0,$$

$$\frac{\partial \mathcal{L}}{\partial \lambda} = x - 20\ell^{2/5} k^{2/5} = 0. \tag{12.42}$$

Taking the negative terms in the first two equations to the other side and dividing the equations by one another, we get:

$$\frac{w}{r} = \frac{k}{\ell} \text{ or just } k = \frac{w}{r}\ell. \tag{12.43}$$

Substituting the latter into the third first-order condition and solving for ℓ, we get the conditional labour demand function:

$$\ell(w, r, x) = \left(\frac{r}{w}\right)^{1/2}\left(\frac{x}{20}\right)^{5/4}, \tag{12.44}$$

and substituting this back into (12.43), we can solve for the conditional capital demand function:

$$k(w, r, x) = \left(\frac{w}{r}\right)^{1/2}\left(\frac{x}{20}\right)^{5/4}. \tag{12.45}$$

The cost function is the sum of the conditional input demands multiplied by input prices, or:

$$C(w, r, x) = w\ell(w, r, x) + rk(w, r, x) = 2(wr)^{1/2}\left(\frac{x}{20}\right)^{5/4}. \tag{12.46}$$

Once we have a cost function, we can calculate marginal and average costs as:

$$MC(w, r, x) = \frac{\partial C(w, r, x)}{\partial x} = \frac{(wr)^{1/2}}{8}\left(\frac{x}{20}\right)^{1/4} \text{ and}$$

$$AC(w, r, x) = \frac{C(w, r, x)}{x} = \frac{(wr)^{1/2}}{10}\left(\frac{x}{20}\right)^{1/4}. \tag{12.47}$$

Since the Cobb–Douglas production function we used has decreasing returns to scale, $MC = AC$ when $x = 0$ and $AC < MC$ for all $x > 0$, which implies that both MC and AC curves emanate from the origin and slope up, with MC always lying above AC. Setting MC equal to price and solving for x, we get:

$$x(p, w, r) = 20\frac{(8p)^4}{(wr)^2} = 81\,920\frac{p^4}{(wr)^2} \tag{12.48}$$

just as we did in equation (12.33) from the direct profit maximization problem. Similarly, when we now substitute $x(p, w, r)$ from equation (12.48) into the conditional input demands in equations (12.44) and (12.45), we get:

$$\ell(p, w, r) = \frac{(8p)^5}{r^2 w^3} \quad \text{and} \quad k(p, w, r) = \frac{(8p)^5}{w^2 r^3}, \tag{12.49}$$

which we had previously derived as the actual input demand functions in equations (12.31) and (12.32). The two-step approach that first minimizes costs and sets price equal to marginal cost yields the same output supply and input demand functions as the one-step profit maximization problem.

Exercise 12B.16

A producer plans to produce a certain output quantity $\bar{x}$. If the wage rate goes up, how will their production plan change? What if the rental rate goes up?

12B.4 Duality in Producer Theory

There is a duality picture that emerges in producer theory just as there was in consumer theory in Chapter 10. In the case of consumers, Graph 10.12 had the utility maximization problem on the left-hand side and the expenditure minimization problem on the right. In the producer case, the duality picture presented in Graph 12.12 has profit maximization on the left-hand side and cost minimization on the right.

Graph 12.12 Duality of Profit Maximization and Cost Minimization

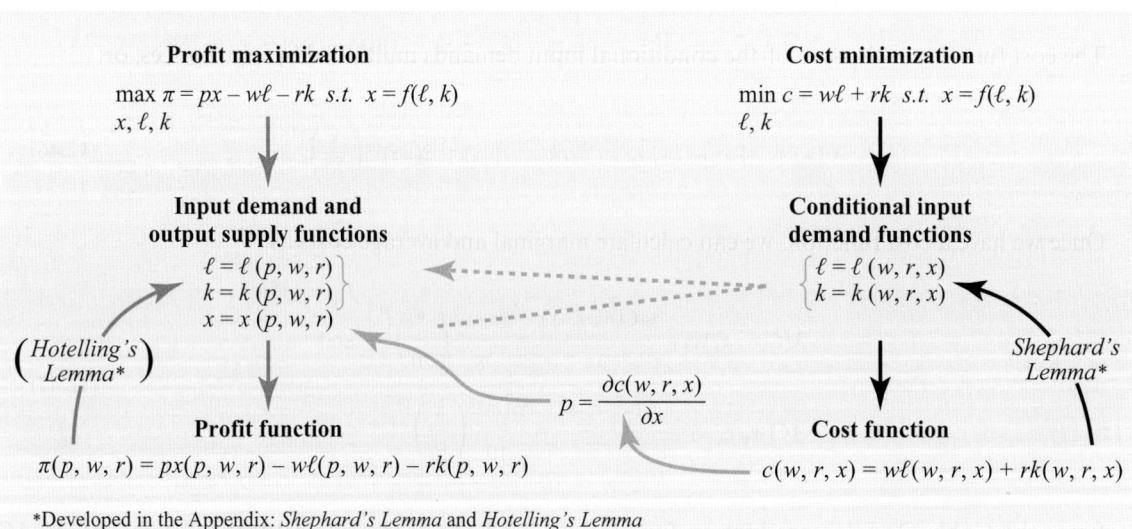

*Developed in the Appendix: *Shephard's Lemma* and *Hotelling's Lemma*

In comparing the consumer duality picture with the producer duality picture, a striking similarity emerges on the right-hand side: *the consumer expenditure minimization problem is identical to the producer cost-minimization problem*, with goods prices (p_1, p_2) replaced by input prices (w, r), the consumer goods bundle (x_1, x_2) replaced by the producer input bundle (ℓ, k) and the utility function u replaced by the production function f. Notice that the compensated or Hicksian demand functions in consumer theory are analogous to conditional input demand functions in producer theory, with the former telling us the consumption bundle a consumer would buy at different output prices assuming they always have just enough money to reach a given indifference curve or utility level, and the latter telling us the input bundle a producer would buy at different input prices assuming they always have just enough money to reach a given isoquant or output level. Similarly, the expenditure function in consumer theory is analogous to the cost function in producer theory, with the former telling us the minimum expenditure necessary at different output prices for a consumer always to reach utility level u and the latter telling us the minimum cost necessary at different input prices for a producer always to reach output level x.

The left-hand side of the duality picture for producers differs, however, from what we developed for consumers. The utility function in consumer theory is the objective function under utility maximization while the production function in producer theory is the constraint under profit maximization. On the right-hand side of the picture, we demonstrated in our development of consumer theory that compensated demand curves incorporated only substitution effects. Since the right-hand side is identical for producers, we will see in the next chapter similar substitution effects for conditional input demands. In addition, consumer theory is complicated by income effects on the left-hand side of the picture, but these only arise because the utility function is maximized subject to a budget constraint. Producers face no such budget constraints; if they can make a profit by producing, the revenues pay for the costs. Thus, income effects will not appear in our discussion of producer theory as these do not emerge on the left-hand side of the producer duality picture.

Appendix | Properties of Expenditure and Profit Functions

In our development of the duality picture for producers in Graph 12.12, we have already noted that the right-hand side of this picture is identical, aside from notation, to the right-hand side of the consumer duality picture in Graph 10.12. As a result, the properties of compensated demand functions in consumer theory are identical to the properties of conditional input demand functions in producer theory, and the properties of the expenditure function in consumer theory are identical to the properties of the cost function in producer theory. Thus, the application of the Envelope Theorem to expenditure minimization in the Appendix to Chapter 10 could be repeated almost verbatim here. We can note that *Shephard's Lemma* holds in producer theory and can be expressed as:

$$\frac{\partial C(w, r, x)}{\partial w} = \ell(w, r, x) \quad \text{and} \quad \frac{\partial C(w, r, x)}{\partial r} = k(w, r, x). \tag{12.50}$$

We furthermore know by analogy to the consumer expenditure minimization problem that the cost function $C(w, r, x)$ is concave in w and r. As a result, we know that conditional input demands always slope down; that is:

$$\frac{\partial \ell(w, r, x)}{\partial w} \leq 0 \quad \text{and} \quad \frac{\partial k(w, r, x)}{\partial r} \leq 0. \tag{12.51}$$

The left-hand sides of the duality pictures for consumers and producers, however, are different, which means we cannot apply what we know from utility maximization to profit maximization.

Exercise 12B.17*

Can you replicate the graphical proof of the concavity of the expenditure function in the Appendix to Chapter 10 to prove that the cost function is concave in w and r?

Exercise 12B.18*

What is the elasticity of substitution between capital and labour if the relationships in equation (12.51) hold with equality?

The Profit Function and Hotelling's Lemma

We can apply the Envelope Theorem once again to prove a relationship analogous to Roy's Identity from the consumer duality picture. Applying this theorem to the profit maximization problem on the left side of Graph 12.12 leads to the following, known as *Hotelling's Lemma*:

$$\frac{\partial \pi(p, w, r)}{\partial p} = x(p, w, r), \quad \frac{\partial \pi(p, w, r)}{\partial w} = -\ell(p, w, r) \quad \text{and} \quad \frac{\partial \pi(p, w, r)}{\partial r} = -k(p, w, r), \tag{12.52}$$

where $\pi(p, w, r)$ is the *profit function* that tells us, for any set of prices, how much profit will be made by a profit-maximizing price taker. This profit function, as the one defined in Chapter 11, is $\pi = px(p, w, r) - w\ell(p, w, r) - rk(p, w, r)$.

Exercise 12B.19*

Demonstrate how these indeed result from an application of the Envelope Theorem.

As we did in the case of expenditure functions, we can get some of the intuition for why these equations hold from some graphical development. It is easiest to do this in the context of the single-input model, but the same logic holds when there are multiple inputs.

Suppose, for instance, we know that when a producer faces the economic environment (p^A, w^A), their optimal production plan is (x^A, ℓ^A), giving profit $\pi(p^A, w^A) = p^A x^A - w^A \ell^A$. In panel (a) of Graph 12.13, we illustrate this using an underlying production function $f(\ell)$, with the optimal production plan A illustrated as the tangency of the (dark brown) isoprofit containing price p^A and wage w^A with the production function. In panel (b) of the graph, the point A represents one point on the slice of the profit function $\pi(p, w^A)$ that holds wage fixed at w^A.

Now suppose that the price rises to p^B. If the producer does not alter their production plan and sticks with the plan (x^A, ℓ^A), profit will be $\pi' = p^B x^A - w^A \ell^A$, which lies on a line represented by the light blue line in panel (b) of the graph, with intercept $(-w^A \ell^A)$ and slope x^A. As a producer who is not responding to the changes in their economic environment, they experience an increase in profit from $\pi(p^A, w^A)$ to π' by being able to sell output at a higher price than before. In addition, however, panel (a) of the graph shows that the profit-maximizing production plan does *not* stay the same when the output price rises from p^A to p^B — it changes from (x^A, ℓ^A) to (x^B, ℓ^B), which results in profit $\pi(p^B, w^A) > \pi'$. Thus, at p^B, $\pi(p^B, w^A)$ lies above the light blue line in panel (b) of Graph 12.13.

Exercise 12B.20*

How can you tell from panel (a) of the graph that $\pi(x^B, \ell^B) > \pi' > \pi(x^A, \ell^A)$?

Graph 12.13 Convexity in Output Price of the Profit Function and Hotelling's Lemma

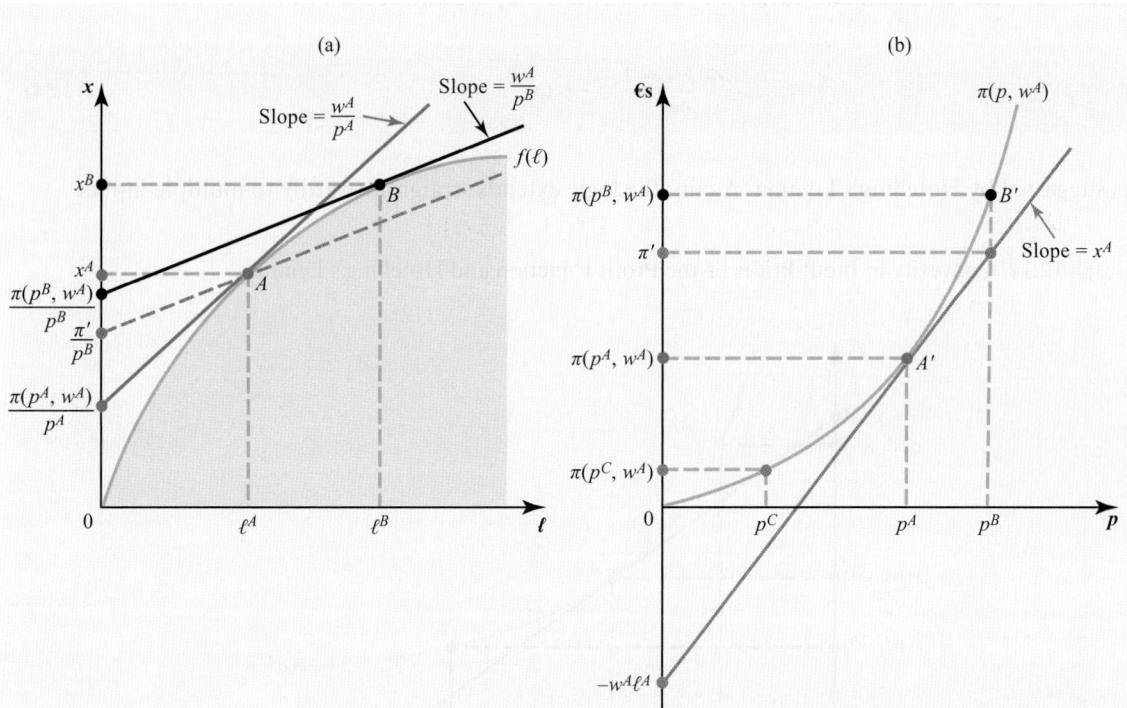

You can similarly show that when price falls to p^C, $\pi(x^C, \ell^C)$ is greater than the profit indicated by the light blue line in panel (b) of Graph 12.13, which represents a producer who does not respond to the price change but continues to produce at the original production plan (x^A, ℓ^A).

The shape of the slice of the profit function $\pi(p, w^A)$ (which holds wage fixed at w^A) that emerges from this analysis is that of a convex function, letting us conclude that *the profit function is convex in the output price*. Furthermore, the slope of this function at p^A is $x^A = x(p^A, w^A)$, or:

$$\frac{\partial \pi(p^A, w^A)}{\partial p} = x(p^A, w^A), \tag{12.53}$$

consistent with Hotelling's Lemma. The same argument holds more generally for multi-input production processes where we can show that the slice $\pi(p, w^A, r^A)$ must be convex in p because producers who respond to changes in price will always make more profit than producers who do not and whose profit can be illustrated on a line such as the light blue line in panel (b) of Graph 12.13.

You can furthermore demonstrate that slices of the profit function $\pi(p^A, w)$ that hold output price constant and vary w are also convex, although, unlike the slice that varies output price (as in panel (b) of Graph 12.13), $\pi(p^A, w)$ is downward sloping. Suppose again that the economic environment is described by (p^A, w^A) and that the optimal production plan in this environment is (x^A, ℓ^A), giving a profit of $\pi(p^A, w^A) = p^A x^A - w^A \ell^A$. In Graph 12.14, point A' is the same point as A' in panel (b) of Graph 12.13 but viewed from a different angle with w rather than p on the horizontal axis. Now suppose that wage increases to w^B and the producer does not change behaviour. Profit will be $\pi'' = p^A x^A - w^B \ell^A$, which lies on the dark brown line in the graph, a line with intercept $p^A x^A$ and slope $-\ell^A$. A producer who responds to changes in the economic environment will make at least as much profit as one who does not but typically will make more profit. Thus, $\pi(p^A, w^B) \geq \pi''$. The same logic applied to a wage decrease to w^C

suggests that $\pi(p^A, w^C)$ will also lie above the dark brown line. As a result, the slice of the profit function that holds price constant and varies w is a downward-sloping and convex function, with:

$$\frac{\partial \pi(p^A, w^A)}{\partial w} = -\ell\ (p^A, w^A), \tag{12.54}$$

as suggested by Hotelling's Lemma. Again, the logic extends straightforwardly to multiple inputs.

Graph 12.14 Convexity in Input Prices of the Profit Function and Hotelling's Lemma

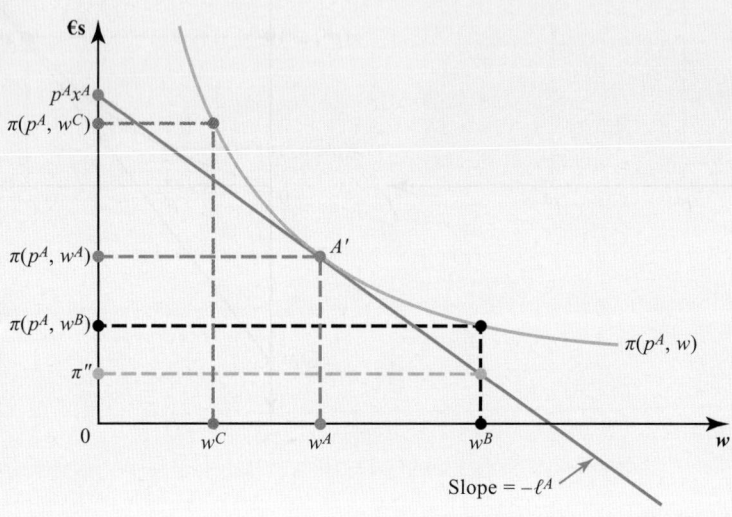

Exercise 12B.21*

Use a graph similar to that in panel (a) of Graph 12.13 to motivate Graph 12.14.

End-of-Chapter Exercises

12.1† A. In each of the following, assume that the production technology faced is homothetic. Suppose further that you currently face input prices (w^A, r^A) and output price p^A, and that, at these prices, your profit-maximizing production plan is $A = (\ell^A, k^A, x^A)$.

    a. On a graph with ℓ on the horizontal and k on the vertical, illustrate an isoquant through the input bundle (ℓ^A, k^A). Indicate where all cost-minimizing input bundles lie given the input prices (w^A, r^A).

    b. Can you tell from what you know whether the shape of the production frontier exhibits increasing or decreasing returns to scale along the ray indicated in (a)?

    c. Can you tell whether the production frontier has increasing or decreasing returns to scale around the production plan $A = (\ell^A, k^A, x^A)$?

    d. Now suppose that wage increases to w. Where will your new profit-maximizing production plan lie relative to the ray identified in (a)?

e. In light of the fact that supply curves shift to the left as input prices increase, where will your new profit-maximizing input bundle lie relative to the isoquant for x^A?

f. Combining your insights from (d) and (e), can you identify the region in which your new profit-maximizing bundle will lie when wage increases to w?

g. How would your answer to (f) change if wage fell instead?

h. Next, suppose that instead of wage changing, the output price increases to p. Where in your graph might your new profit-maximizing production plan lie? What if p decreases?

i. Can you identify the region in your graph where the new profit-maximizing plan would lie if instead the rental rate r fell?

B. Consider the Cobb–Douglas production function $f(\ell, k) = A\ell^\alpha k^\beta$ with $\alpha, \beta > 0$ and $\alpha + \beta < 1$.

a. **Derive the demand functions $\ell(w, r, p)$ and $k(w, r, p)$ as well as the output supply function $x(w, r, p)$.

b. **Derive the conditional demand functions $\ell(w, r, x)$ and $k(w, r, x)$.

c. Given some initial prices (w^A, r^A, p^A), verify that all cost-minimizing bundles lie on the same ray from the origin in the isoquant graph.

d. If w increases, what happens to the ray on which all cost-minimizing bundles lie?

e. What happens to the profit-maximizing input bundles?

f. How do your answers change if w instead decreases?

g. If instead p increases, does the ray along which all cost-minimizing bundles lie change?

h. Where on that ray will the profit-maximizing production plan lie?

i. What happens to the ray on which all cost-minimizing input bundles lie if r falls? What happens to the profit-maximizing input bundle?

12.2 Economic profit is equal to economic revenue minus economic cost, where cash inflows or outflows are not real economic revenues or costs unless they are in fact impacted by the economic decisions of the firm. Suppose that a firm uses both labour l and capital k in its production of x, and that no output can be produced without at least some of each input.

A. In the short run, however, it can only change the level of labour input because it has already committed to a particular capital input level for the coming months. Assume that the firm's homothetic production process is one that has initially increasing but eventually decreasing returns to scale, and that the marginal product of each input is initially increasing but eventually decreasing. The full production frontier would look something like that in Graph 12.15.

a. Suppose the firm is currently implementing the profit-maximizing production plan $A = (l^A, k^A, x^A)$. Given input prices w and r and output price p, what is the expression for the profit this firm earns?

Graph 12.15 Production Frontier with Two Inputs

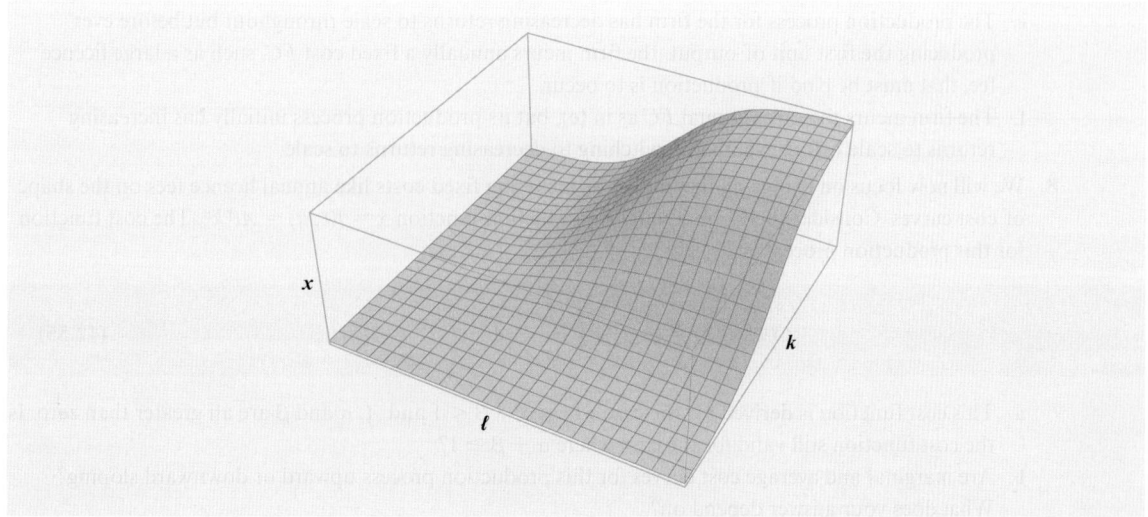

    b. Now consider the short run where capital is fixed at k^A. Graph the short-run production function for this firm.

    c. Add to this graph the slice of the isoprofit plane that is tangential to the production frontier at A. Indicate its slope and vertical intercept.

    d. Given that the vertical intercept of the isoprofit is equal to profit along that isoprofit divided by output price, what does the vertical intercept in your graph suggest is the profit for this firm when viewed from the short-run perspective?

    e. Explain why the short-run perspective of economic profit differs in this case from the long-run perspective.

    f. *True or False*: It is possible for a firm to be earning zero profit in the long run but positive profit when viewed from a short-run perspective.

  B. Suppose that, instead of the production process described in part A, the production frontier is characterized by the Cobb–Douglas production function $x = f(\ell, k) = A\ell^\alpha k^\beta$ with $\alpha + \beta < 1$ and A, α and β all greater than zero.

    a. Does this production process have increasing, decreasing or constant returns to scale?

    b. Set up the profit maximization problem.

    c. **Solve this for the optimal production plan.

    d. Now consider the short-run profit maximization problem for the firm that is currently employing employing $\bar{k}$ of capital. Write down the firm's short-run production function and its short-run profit maximization problem.

    e. *Solve for the short-run labour demand and output supply functions.

    f. *Suppose that the short-run fixed capital is equal to the long-run optimal quantity you calculated in part (c). Demonstrate that the firm would choose the same amount of labour in the short run as it does in the long run.

    g. Finally, illustrate that profit is larger from the short-run perspective than the long-run perspective.

12.3† In upcoming chapters, we will often assume that the average cost curve is U-shaped.

  A. Indicate for each of the following statements whether you believe that the description of the firm's situation would lead to a U-shaped average cost curve.

    a. The firm's production frontier initially exhibits increasing returns to scale but, beginning at some output quantity $\bar{x}$, it exhibits decreasing returns to scale.

    b. The firm's production frontier initially exhibits decreasing returns to scale but, beginning at some output quantity $\bar{x}$, it exhibits increasing returns to scale.

    c. The firm's production process initially has increasing returns to scale, in some interval from $\underline{x}$ to $\bar{x}$, it has constant returns to scale, followed by decreasing returns to scale.

    d. The firm's production process initially has increasing returns to scale, in some interval from $\underline{x}$ to $\bar{x}$, it has constant returns to scale, followed by once again increasing returns to scale.

    e. The production process for the firm has decreasing returns to scale throughout but before ever producing the first unit of output, the firm incurs annually a fixed cost FC, such as a large licence fee, that must be paid if production is to occur.

    f. The firm incurs the same annual FC as in (e), but its production process initially has increasing returns to scale before eventually switching to decreasing returns to scale.

  B. We will now focus on exploring the impact of recurring fixed costs like annual licence fees on the shape of cost curves. Consider the Cobb–Douglas production function $x = f(\ell, k) = A\ell^\alpha k^\beta$. The cost function for this production process is:

$$C(w, r, x) = (\alpha + \beta)\left(\frac{xw^\alpha r^\beta}{A\alpha^\alpha \beta^\beta}\right)^{1/(\alpha + \beta)}. \tag{12.55}$$

    a. This cost function is derived for the case where $\alpha + \beta < 1$ and A, α and β are all greater than zero. Is the cost function still valid for the case where $\alpha + \beta \geq 1$?

    b. Are marginal and average cost curves for this production process upward or downward sloping? What does your answer depend on?

c. Suppose that the firm incurs a fixed cost FC that has to be paid each period before production starts. How does this change the total cost function, the marginal cost function and the average cost function?

d. Suppose that $\alpha + \beta < 1$. What is the relationship between MC and AC now?

e. How does your answer differ if $\alpha + \beta \geq 1$? What if $\alpha + \beta = 1$?

12.4 Everyday Application: *To Study or to Sleep?* Research suggests that successful performance in exams requires preparation, that is, studying, and rest, that is, sleep. Neither by itself produces good exam grades, but in the right combination they maximize exam performance.

A. We can model exam grades as emerging from a production process that takes hours of studying and hours of sleep as inputs. Suppose this production process is homothetic and has decreasing returns to scale.

a. On a graph with hours of sleep on the horizontal axis and hours of studying on the vertical, illustrate an isoquant that represents a particular exam performance level x^A.

b. Suppose you are always willing to pay €5 to get back an hour of sleep and €20 to get back an hour of studying. Illustrate on your graph the least cost way to get to the exam grade x^A.

c. Since the production process is homothetic, where in your graph are the cost-minimizing ways to get to the other exam grade isoquants?

d. Using your answer to (c), can you graph a vertical slice of the production frontier that contains all the cost-minimizing sleep/study input bundles?

e. Suppose you are willing to pay €p for every additional point on your exam. Can you illustrate on your graph from (d) the slice of the isoprofit that gives you your optimal exam grade? Is this necessarily the same as the exam grade x^A from your previous graph?

f. What would change if you placed a higher value on each exam point?

g. Suppose a new caffeine/ginseng drink comes on the market, and you find it makes you twice as productive when you study. What in your graphs will change?

B. Suppose that the production technology described in part A can be captured by the production function $x = 40\ell^{0.25}s^{0.25}$, where x is your exam grade, ℓ is the number of hours spent studying and s is the number of hours spent sleeping.

a. Assume again that you'd be willing to pay €5 to get back an hour of sleep and €20 to get back an hour of studying. If you value each exam point at p, what is your optimal production plan?

b. Can you arrive at the same answer using the Cobb–Douglas cost function given in question 12.3?

c. What is your optimal production plan when you value each exam point at €2?

d. How much would you have to value each exam point in order for you to put in the effort and sleep to get a 100% on the exam.

e. What happens to your optimal production plan as the value you place on each exam point increases?

f. What changes if the caffeine/ginseng drink described in A(g) is factored into the problem?

12.5*† Business and Policy Application: *Investing in Smokestack Filters under Cap-and-Trade.* On their own, firms have little incentive to invest in pollution-abating technologies such as smokestack filters. As a result, governments have increasingly turned to cap-and-trade programmes. Under these programmes, the government puts an overall cap on the amount of permissible pollution and firms are permitted to pollute only to the extent to which they own sufficient numbers of pollution permits or vouchers. If a firm does not need all of its vouchers, it can sell them at a market price p_v to firms that require more.

A. Suppose a firm produces x using a technology that emits pollution through smokestacks. The firm must ensure that it has sufficient pollution vouchers v to emit the level of pollution that escapes the smokestacks, but it can reduce the pollution by installing increasingly sophisticated smokestack filters s.

a. Suppose that the technology for producing x requires capital and labour and, without considering pollution, has constant returns to scale. For a given set of input prices (w, r), what does the marginal cost curve look like?

b. Now suppose that relatively little pollution is emitted initially in the production process, but as the factory is used more intensively, pollution per unit of output increases, and thus more pollution vouchers have to be purchased per unit absent any pollution-abating smokestack filters. What does this do to the marginal cost curve assuming some price p_v per pollution voucher and assuming the firm does not install smokestack filters?

    c. Considering carefully the meaning of economic cost, does your answer to (b) depend on whether the government gives the firm a certain number of vouchers or whether the firm starts out with no vouchers and has to purchase whatever quantity is necessary for its production plan?

    d. Suppose that smokestack filters are such that initial investments in filters yield high reductions in pollution, but as additional filters are added, the marginal reduction in pollution declines. You can now think of the firm as using two additional inputs, pollution vouchers and smokestack filters, to produce output x legally. Does the overall production technology now have increasing, constant or decreasing returns to scale?

    e. Next, consider a graph with smokestack filters s on the horizontal and pollution vouchers v on the vertical axis. Illustrate an isoquant that shows different ways of reaching a particular output level $\bar{x}$ legally; that is, without polluting illegally. Illustrate the least cost way of reaching this output level, not counting the cost of labour and capital, given p_v and p_s.

    f. If the government imposes additional limits on pollution by removing some of the pollution vouchers from the market, p_v will increase. How much will this affect the number of smokestack filters used in any given firm assuming output does not change? What does your answer depend on?

    g. What happens to the overall marginal cost curve for the firm including all costs of production as p_v increases? Will output increase or decrease?

    h. Can you tell whether the firm will buy more or fewer smokestack filters as p_v increases? Do you think it will produce more or less pollution?

    i. *True or False*: The cap-and-trade system reduces overall pollution by getting firms to use smokestack filters more intensively and by causing firms to reduce how much output they produce.

B. Suppose the cost function not considering pollution for a firm is given by $C(w, r, x) = 0.5w^{0.5}r^{0.5}x$, and suppose that the trade-off between using smokestack filters s and pollution vouchers v to achieve legal production is given by the Cobb–Douglas production technology $x = f(s, v) = 50s^{0.25}v^{0.25}$.

    a. In the absence of cap-and-trade policies, does the production process have increasing, decreasing or constant returns to scale?

    b. Ignoring for now the cost of capital and labour, derive the cost function for producing different output levels as a function of p_s and p_v, the price of a smokestack filter and a pollution voucher. You can derive this directly or use the fact that we know the general form of cost functions for Cobb–Douglas production functions from what is given in question 12.3.

    c. What is the full cost function $C(w, r, p_s, p_v, x)$? What is the marginal cost function?

    d. For a given output price p, derive the supply function.

    e. Using Shephard's Lemma, can you derive the conditional smokestack filter demand function?

    f. Using your answers, can you derive the unconditional smokestack filter demand function?

    g. Use your answers to illustrate the effect of an increase in p_v on the demand for smokestack filters holding output fixed as well as the effect of an increase in p_v on the profit-maximizing demand for smokestack filters.

12.6 Policy Application: *Taxes on Firms.* There are several ways in which governments tax firms, including taxes on labour, capital and profits. It is not at all immediately clear whether taxes on labour or capital are paid by firms even when tax laws specify that firms will pay them. We will assume that we know some share of taxes on inputs are real costs to firms. It is also not clear that governments can easily identify the economic profit of firms, or that price-taking firms usually make such profits. Again, we will assume these issues for now.

A. Suppose a firm employs labour ℓ and capital k to produce output x using a homothetic, decreasing returns to scale technology.

    a. Suppose that, at the current wage w, rental rate r and output price p, the firm has identified $A = (x^A, \ell^A, k^A)$ as its profit-maximizing production plan. Illustrate an isoquant corresponding to x^A and show how (ℓ^A, k^A) must satisfy the conditions of cost minimization.

    b. Translate this to a graph of the cost curve that holds w and r fixed, indicating where in your isoquant graph the underlying input bundles lie for this cost curve.

c. Show how x^A emerges as the profit-maximizing production level on the marginal cost curve that is derived from the cost curve you illustrated in (b).

d. Now suppose that the government taxes labour, causing the cost of labour for the firm to increase to $(1 + t)w$. What changes in your pictures, and how will this affect the profit-maximizing production plan?

e. What happens if the government instead imposes a tax on capital that raises the real cost of capital to $(1 + t)r$?

f. What happens if instead the government imposes a tax on both capital and labour, causing the cost of capital and labour to increase by the same proportion, that is, to $(1 + t)w$ and $(1 + t)r$?

g. Now suppose the government instead taxes economic profit at some rate $t < 1$. Thus, if the firm makes pre-tax profit π, the firm gets to keep only $(1 - t)\pi$. What happens to the firm's profit-maximizing production plan?

B. Suppose your firm has a decreasing returns to scale, Cobb–Douglas production function of the form $x = A\ell^\alpha k^\beta$ for which you may have previously calculated input, and output demands as well as the cost function. The latter is also given in problem 12.3.

a. If you have not already done so, calculate input demand and output supply functions. You can do so directly using the profit maximization problem, or you can use the cost function given in problem 12.3 to derive these.

b. Derive the profit function for this firm and check that it is correct by checking whether Hotelling's Lemma works.

c. If you have not already done so, derive the conditional input demand functions. You can do so directly by setting up the cost-minimization problem, or you can employ Shephard's Lemma and use the cost function given in question 12.3.

d. Consider a tax on labour that raises the labour costs for firms to $(1 + t)w$. How does this affect the various functions in the duality picture for the firm?

e. Repeat for a tax on capital that raises the capital cost for the firm to $(1 + t)r$.

f. Repeat for simultaneous taxes on labour and capital that raise the cost of labour and capital to $(1 + t)w$ and $(1 + t)r$.

g. Repeat for a tax on profits as described in part A(g).

Chapter 13

Production Decisions in the Short and Long Run

We continue with the example of a profit-maximizing producer producing door handles using labour and capital. A new government announces a new regulation which will increase the cost of employing workers. If capital is fixed in the short run, the producer now has to make decisions along a short-run production frontier that has output changing solely with the number of workers employed. As we have seen in Chapter 11, the producer will now employ fewer workers and produce fewer door handles. As time passes, the firm has a chance to make some more decisions because it will have the opportunity to change the amount of capital it is using and to re-evaluate whether it wants to employ more or fewer workers. Now both labour and capital can be adjusted to meet the new economic conditions in the labour market. The firm's short-run problem is a slice of the more complex long-run problem they eventually face as time passes. Our focus now turns to how the firm will transition from the short run to the long run as underlying conditions change.

We will ask how changes in the *economic* environment will affect the decisions by producers over time. By the economic environment, we will continue to mean the output and input prices that price-taking producers take as given as they try to do the best they can. In the short run, we will typically assume that capital is fixed and labour is variable, which mirrors an analysis where labour is fixed in the short run and capital is variable. We will begin to introduce a new type of fixed cost for firms, a cost that is not associated with an input like labour or capital. Our main focus in this chapter, however, remains on a firm's economic response to changing input and output prices, whereas the next chapter will consider the underlying causes of such changes in prices within a competitive industry.

13A   Changes in Producer Behaviour as Conditions Change

As we begin to consider how price-taking firms adapt to changing circumstances in both the short and long run, we will consider how such changes impact the cost curves of firms. We will look at how cost curves are affected in changing environments. In the remainder of the chapter, we will illustrate how changes in prices impact decisions. Upcoming chapters build primarily on the material in Section 13A.1.

13A.1 Different Types of Costs and Expenses in the Short and Long Run

Since we will often use changes in cost curves to arrive at conclusions about a firm's supply responses, it is essential to understand what affects these cost curves in the short and the long run. *If we define costs correctly, it will always be the case that a price-taking firm's supply curve is that part of the marginal cost curve that lies above its average cost curve, regardless of whether we are talking about the short run or the long run*. The most important insight we will have to keep in mind, however, is that only true *economic* costs can affect a firm's behaviour, even if we are tempted to call something a cost when it really isn't one. What counts as a cost will differ depending on whether we are thinking about the short or long run. Section 13A.1.1 explores the distinction between costs and expenditures and how this distinction relates to short- and long-run cost curves for firms. We can explore the different types of costs and expenditures, and the impact that changing costs and expenditures have on the firm's short- and long-run supply of output.

13A.1.1 Costs Versus Expenses Consider the producer of door handles facing increased labour costs from some new labour regulation. Suppose we would like to use the picture of short-run cost curves to determine what they will do immediately in response to the increased labour costs. Assume a commitment to $k = 100$ *capital* in the short run, for which the producer has to pay €100r. Is this a cost? The question is whether paying this sum is at all impacted by the decision of whether to produce more or less, or not at all. The answer is that once the producer has committed to rent the 100 units of capital in the short run, the payment €100r has to be made *regardless* of what decisions they make in the firm, even if they decide not to use any of the capital. This means that the expense on the 100 units of capital is *not* a real cost of doing business in the short run; it is not an *economic* cost that affects short-run decisions in any way. For this reason, it is often called a '*sunk* cost'; 'sunk' in the sense that you have to pay it no matter what you do.

There is much confusion that arises in microeconomics courses because we often slip into the bad habit of using the term cost when we don't actually mean economic cost. We will try to avoid this confusion by adopting the following convention: Whenever the expenses we refer to are 100 per cent true economics costs, we will call them 'costs'. If the expenses include sunk costs, we will call them 'expenditures' or 'expenses' even if some fraction of them represents real costs. Some textbooks differentiate between economic and accounting costs, with accounting costs being similar to expenses that are not economic costs.

Let's return to the example where current capital is fixed at $k = 100$ but labour can be adjusted as you are free to employ and release workers in the short run. Panel (a) of Graph 13.1 illustrates the short-run *cost* curve $C_{k=100}$ that is relevant for the short-run decisions the firm makes when it cannot vary the level of capital it is using. If we want to illustrate the total amount paid, including the wages paid to workers as well as the expense of renting the capital, we can show the fixed expense on capital $FE_{k=100} = €100r$ on the vertical axis. Even if the firm produces nothing, it will incur this expense, and the expense does not change as production begins. The rest of the total expenditure curve $TE_{k=100}$ lies exactly €100r above the $C_{k=100}$ curve, and it includes real economic costs as well as sunk expenditures. For this reason, we call it an expenditure curve because it is polluted by expenses that are not real economic costs in the short run and are therefore sunk or irrelevant as you make short-run decisions. Other textbooks refer to the fixed expenditures as fixed costs even though they are sunk in the short run, and the TE expenditure curve as total cost even though it includes sunk costs. To differentiate total costs from the real economic costs, the real cost curve is referred to as a variable cost curve €.

Panel (b) of Graph 13.1 translates these curves into marginal and average cost and expenditure curves. Since the fixed expenditures have to be paid even if no output is produced, they are never an *additional* cost or expense incurred from producing one more unit of the output. The marginal cost curve $MC_{k=100}$, defined as the *additional* cost incurred from producing additional units of output when capital is fixed at 100, thus does *not* include the fixed expenditure of renting the 100 units of capital. It is the slope of the $C_{k=100}$ curve. Similarly, the *average cost curve* $(AC_{k=100})$ that begins at roughly the intercept of the marginal cost curve (but not exactly since average costs are not defined with quantity equal to zero) represents only true economic costs given that capital is fixed at 100. Finally, the *average expenditure curve* $(AE_{k=100})$, derived from the $TE_{k=100}$ curve in panel (a), has an intercept that lies $FE_{k=100}$ above the intercept of the other two curves because at the first unit of output, the difference between the average cost and the average expenditure is equal to the difference between true cost and total expenditure. As production increases, however, the $AE_{k=100}$ curve gets closer and closer to the $AC_{k=100}$ curve because the *average* fixed expenditure declines as output increases. At the output level x^A, for instance, the *average* fixed expenditure per unit of output is equal to the vertical distance between point A and A' and can be mathematically represented as $FE_{k=100}/x^A = €100r/x^A$. When we multiply this average fixed expenditure by the output level x^A, the shaded area in the graph is equal to $FE_{k=100} = €100r$ just as the similarly labelled distance at the intercept.

Graph 13.1 Short-Run Expenditure and Cost Curves

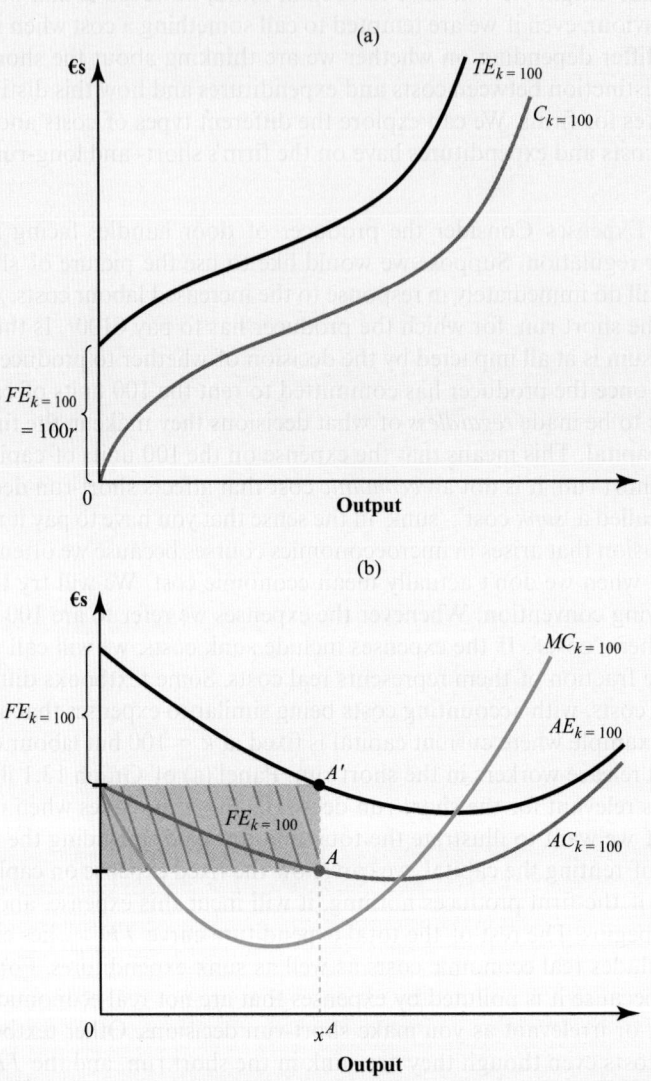

Exercise 13A.1

Can you find similar rectangular areas that are equal to $FE_{k=100}$ for other output levels? Given that these rectangular areas have to be equal to one another, can you see why the AC and AE curves must be getting closer and closer as output rises?

Exercise 13A.2

Can you explain why the MC curve intersects both the AC and the AE curves at their lowest points?

Exercise 13A.3

Where in the graph would you locate the marginal expenditure curve derived from the total expenditure curve?

13A.1.2 Short-Run Expenditure and Long-Run Cost Curves Since the difference between the short run and the long run is that firms have more opportunities to adjust the input bundles in the long run, it would seem intuitive that costs might be higher in the short run due to less flexibility in choosing the right mix of inputs. This is true in the sense that the total *expenditures* on inputs will indeed never be lower in the short run than the long-run *cost* of production.

To see this, consider a producer facing the production technology represented by the isoquants in panel (a) of Graph 13.2 and that capital is the fixed input in the short run while labour hours can be varied. Further assume that the producer has signed a lease for $k^A = 100$ units of capital equipment, committing them to pay a weekly rental rate of $r = 10$ per unit for the next year. At the time the lease was signed, the producer intended to produce 200 units of output per week, and they picked the units of capital they are renting to give them the least cost input bundle (together with $\ell^A = 50$ labour hours) for producing 200 output units assuming a wage rate of $w = 20$. This is graphed in panel (a) of Graph 13.2 as the input bundle A on the (dark brown) isoquant for 200 units of output.

Graph 13.2 Short-Run Expenditure Versus Long-Run Cost Curves

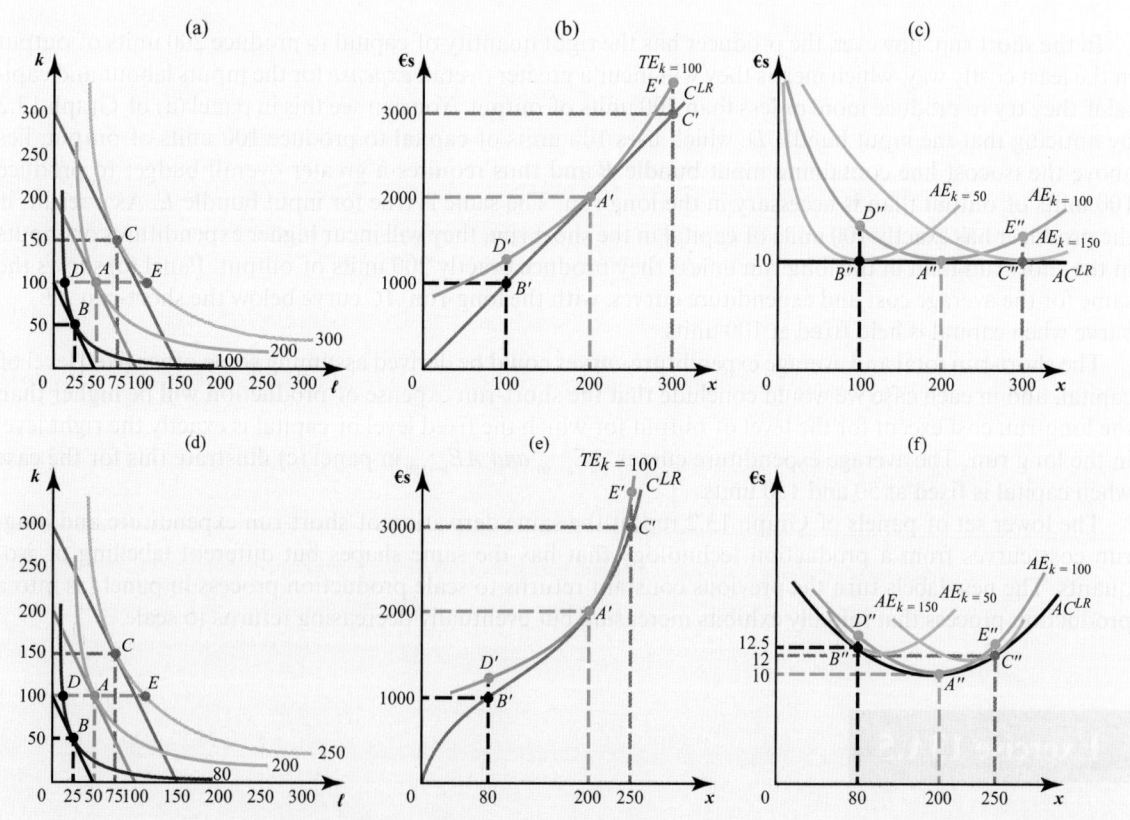

If the producer wants to produce 100 instead of 200 units of output, they would like to reduce both labour and capital inputs to reach the least cost way of producing 100 units of output as represented by

input bundle *B*, and in the long run that is what they will do. In the short run, they have already committed to rent 100 units of capital, which implies they will use the input bundle *D* instead of *B* in the short run. Similarly, if the producer wants to produce 300 units of the output instead, they will choose input bundle *E* in the short run even though they will choose input bundle *C* in the long run. Notice the producer is constrained in the short run to operate on the slice of the isoquant that keeps capital fixed at 100 units.

In panel (b) of the graph, we plot the costs and expenditures necessary to pay for the input bundles labelled in panel (a) while continuing to assume that the rental rate of capital is €10 and the wage rate is €20. The input bundle *A*, for instance, employs 50 hours of labour and 100 units of capital costing a total of €2000. Since the input bundle *A* results in output of 200, panel (b) of the graph plots the total long-run cost of producing 200 units of output as €2000. We can similarly derive the total long-run cost of producing 100 units of output using the input bundle *B* and 300 units of output using the input bundle *C*. Since the input bundles *A*, *B* and *C* all represent the least cost ways of producing different quantities of the output *assuming we can adjust both labour and capital*, the corresponding points *A'*, *B'* and *C'* in panel (b) represent points on the long-run (total) cost curve.

Exercise 13A.4

Can you tell from the shape of the long-run total cost curve whether the production process has increasing, decreasing or constant returns to scale?

In the short run, however, the producer has the right quantity of capital to produce 200 units of output in the least costly way, which means they will incur a greater overall *expense* for the inputs labour and capital if they try to produce more or less than 200 units of output. You can see this in panel (a) of Graph 13.2 by noticing that the input bundle *D*, which uses 100 units of capital to produce 100 units of output, lies above the isocost line containing input bundle *B* and thus requires a greater overall budget to produce 100 units of output than is necessary in the long run. The same is true for input bundle *E*. As a result, if the producer has exactly 100 units of capital in the short run, they will incur higher expenditures on inputs in the short run than in the long run unless they produce exactly 200 units of output. Panel (c) shows the same for the average cost and expenditure curves, with the long-run *AC* curve below the short-run $AE_{k=100}$ curve when capital is held fixed at 100 units.

The short-run total and average expenditure curves could be derived assuming some other fixed level of capital, and in each case we would conclude that the short-run expense of production will be higher than the long-run cost except for the level of output for which the fixed level of capital is exactly the right level in the long run. The average expenditure curves $AE_{k=50}$ and $AE_{k=150}$ in panel (c) illustrate this for the case when capital is fixed at 50 and 150 units.

The lower set of panels of Graph 13.2 repeat the same derivation of short-run expenditure and long-run cost curves from a production technology that has the same shapes but different labelling of isoquants. The new labels turn the previous constant returns to scale production process in panel (a) into a production process that initially exhibits increasing but eventually decreasing returns to scale.

Exercise 13A.5

Verify the derivation of cost curves in panels (e) and (f) in Graph 13.2. In what sense is the relationship between short-run expenditure and long-run cost curves similar in this case to the case we derived in the top panels of the graph for constant returns to scale production processes?

Exercise 13A.6

Where would you find the long-run marginal cost curve in panel (f) of Graph 13.2?

13A.1.3 To Be or Not to Be: Shutting Down Versus Exiting the Industry Using the graphs developed so far, we can now determine how low an output price a firm is willing to tolerate and still produce, and at what point the price has just fallen so far that it is not worth going on because profit would be negative. The answer will differ depending on whether we are thinking about the short or the long run because a firm cannot actually disappear entirely in the short run since it is stuck for some period with a fixed level of capital. We will therefore say that a firm shuts down production if it stops producing in the short run, and it exits the industry if it ceases production in the long run.

We will see that a firm's 'shut-down price' is lower than the 'exit price' because the firm can more easily cover its economic costs in the short run since these don't include the fixed expense of capital that has to be paid regardless of what the firm does. The producer may already know that they won't renew the lease to the factory once the lease comes up for renewal, but it may still be worth it to produce in the meantime until they get a chance to off-load the factory by not renewing the lease. You'll often see this with new restaurants that try to break into the local restaurant market. Within a few weeks of opening, some restaurants are buzzing with activity and others attract few customers. You can tell pretty quickly which restaurants won't be around a year from now, but often the restaurants continue to stay open for some period even though it is clear that not enough people show up for the restaurant to remain viable. Do the restaurant owners not see that their restaurant isn't going to make it? Probably not; rather, the owner probably had to sign a lease for six months or a year and can't get out of the lease, which makes the lease an expense the owner does not have to cover in the short run in order to justify staying open. Short-run profit may be positive even though long-run profit is negative, which implies that it is economically rational to remain open in the short run but not to renew the lease in the long run.

In terms of our graphs, we can identify the shut-down and exit prices by locating the lowest point of the average cost curves in the short and long run because it is *always* the case that a firm produces as long as price is not below its average cost curve, assuming we have not included expenses that aren't really costs. In the short-run picture of Graph 13.1, this lowest point lies on the $AC_{k=100}$ curve; in our long-run picture of Graph 13.2, it lies on the AC^{LR} curves of panels (c) and (f). We can combine the insights of the short-run picture (Graph 13.1) and the long-run curves (of Graph 13.2) to see the relationship between the short-run shut-down price and the long-run exit price.

In Graph 13.3, we assume that the firm is currently producing 200 units of output using the input bundle A from panel (d) of Graph 13.2, precisely the cost-minimizing input bundle for this output level. This implies that the short-run average expenditure curve $AE_{k=100}$ touches the long-run average cost curve AC^{LR} at the output level 200 but exceeds it at every other output level as first derived in panel (f) of Graph 13.2. From our short-run picture in Graph 13.1, we also know that the short-run average cost curve $AC_{k=100}$ lies below the short-run $AE_{k=100}$ curve because it does not include the fixed expenditure on capital, and we can now include this short-run average *cost* curve as well as the short-run marginal cost ($MC_{k=100}$) curve in Graph 13.3. The emboldened portion of the $MC_{k=100}$ curve is the short-run supply curve, which clearly extends below the lowest point of the AC^{LR} curve. Thus, the short-run shut-down price $\bar{p}$ lies below the long-run exit price, which is €10 in the graph. If the output price falls into the range from $\bar{p}$ to €10, the firm will therefore stay open in the short run but will exit in the long run.

Exercise 13A.7

Demonstrate that the firm's long-run profit is zero when $p = 10$.

Graph 13.3 Shut-Down Versus Exit Price

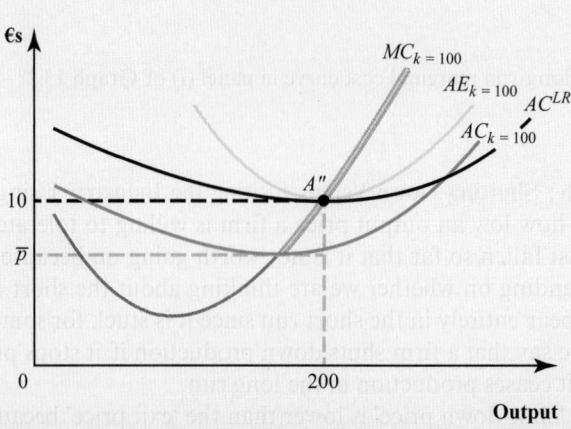

Go to MindTap to interact with this graph

To see how a firm can stay open in the short run but exit in the long run, consider Graph 13.4, which largely replicates the short-run cost and expenditure curves we derived in panel (b) of Graph 13.1 and that are contained in Graph 13.3.

Graph 13.4 Output Supply in the Short Run

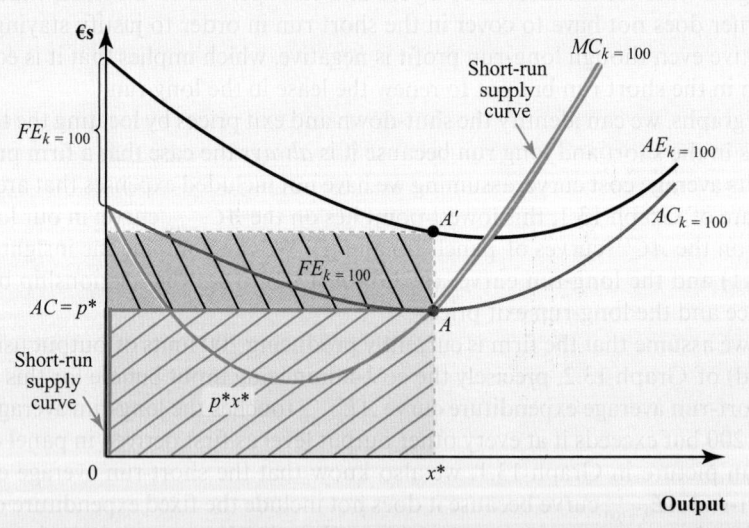

Go to MindTap to interact with this graph

Suppose that the price of the output is p^*. If this firm produces at all, it will produce x^* where the additional cost of producing one more unit of output is just equal to the additional revenue from selling that unit. This would generate total revenue of p^*x^*, the shaded dark brown rectangle in the graph. At the output level x^*, the firm would incur average costs exactly equal to p^*, giving total short-run costs equal to the same dark brown rectangle. Thus, the firm is making enough revenues to cover its short-run economic costs. It does not, however, make enough to cover its fixed expenditure $FE_{k=100}$, represented by the dark blue area, for the fixed amount of capital it has to rent in the short run. Because the firm has to pay $FE_{k=100}$ regardless of whether or not it produces, it does not have to recover $FE_{k=100}$ in the short run in order to produce; the firm has to pay $FE_{k=100}$ whether it produces or not, and so it's no more necessary that the producer covers this expense with short-run revenues than it is that they cover their food bill with those revenues. It is for this reason that we have said the fixed expenditures associated with inputs that are fixed in the short run are not economic costs. They do not impact economic decisions of the firm in the short run. Since *economic profit* is defined as the difference between economic revenues and economic costs, economic profit is equal to exactly zero in the short run when the output price falls to the lowest point of the short-run $AC_{k=100}$ curve.

Exercise 13A.8

Can you illustrate that short-run economic profits will be positive when price falls between the lowest points of the $AC_{K=100}$ and the AC^{LR} curves in Graph 13.4 even though total expenditures exceed total revenues? What will long-run economic profits be in that price range?

Exercise 13A.9

In many seaside towns, business is brisk in the summer but slow in the winter. In the summer, bed and breakfast accommodation can be sold out at high weekly rates, but in the winter they are only partially rented at much lower rates. If you were to calculate expenses and revenues on a monthly basis, you would almost certainly find accommodation with revenues greater than expenses in the summer and expenses greater than revenues in the winter. How come this accommodation doesn't just shut down in the winter?

13A.1.4 (Long-Run) Recurring Fixed Costs In the short run, we have used the term fixed expenditures (*FE*) for the cost of fixed inputs that become variable in the long run. Such *FE* are not true economic costs as long as they have to be paid regardless of any choices the firm makes and thus have no impact on short-run economic behaviour. Since they arise from inputs that can be varied as time goes by, these expenses cease to be fixed when they become real economic costs in the long run. Thus, fixed *expenditures* on inputs that cannot be varied in the short run do not become fixed *costs* in the long run as long as these inputs can in fact be varied in the long run. Such costs are referred to as long-run *variable costs* since they vary with output in the long run. All the economic costs we have dealt with so far, including the costs associated with variable labour input, have been of this type. As such, changes in such costs affect both the long-run marginal and average cost curves. There are, however, certain expenses a firm might incur that are fixed in the sense that they do not vary with the level of output but represent real economic costs that could be avoided in the long run if the firm chose not to produce at all. We will call such costs *fixed costs that are avoidable only by exiting the industry* or simply *long-run or recurring fixed costs*, and it is because they are avoidable by exiting the industry that they are real economic costs in the long run.

Suppose, for instance, the government requires an annual payment for a licence to produce some output. The licence allows the firm to produce, but the amount charged for the licence does not depend on how much is produced. A taxi driver, for example, may need to have a licence to operate. Such licences are typically renewable on an annual basis, with a licence fee charged on, for instance, 1 January of each year. In some instances, the cost of such licences can be quite substantial.

Once paid for or committed to pay for, the expense of the licence becomes a sunk cost. As 1 January approaches each year, the producer has a real economic decision to make. Will they renew the licence and stay in business next year, or will they exit the business and stop producing? In making this decision, the producer will look at all economic costs including the cost of the licence. The only way to avoid paying the licence is to stop producing, thus we have a *recurring fixed cost avoidable only by exiting*. As the decision of whether to renew the licence approaches, the producer will face cost curves for the coming year that look like those in Graph 13.5, with the *AC* curve having a different intercept than the *MC* curve because of the fixed licence fee. The dashed light blue curve is the average cost curve *excluding* the fixed cost of the licence fee, labelled *AVC* for average variable cost. It is dashed in the graph because it is not a curve of any real relevance for the firm's long-run decision, because the firm will produce as always along *MC* as long as the output price lies above the lowest point of its true average cost curve, which is *AC* in this case.

Exercise 13A.10

Compare Graphs 13.4 and 13.5. Why is the supply curve beginning at the higher average curve in 13.5 and on the lower one in 13.4?

Another example of a recurring fixed cost in the real world is the cost associated with an input that always remains fixed in both the short and long run. Different entrepreneurs may, for instance, possess different levels of entrepreneurial skill as they manage the various inputs in their firm. Facing the same technology, some producers are better at motivating workers or getting other organizational objectives accomplished. That entrepreneurial skill, unlike the number of labour hours or units of capital employed by the producer, is in fixed supply within the firm. Successful entrepreneurs can double the number of workers and the equipment and facility space as they increase production, but they cannot replicate themselves. Their leadership or entrepreneurial skill is a fixed input, and the opportunity cost of hiring this fixed input is a recurring fixed cost. If there is such an input that is always fixed as long as the firm is in production, it thus becomes a recurring fixed cost just like the licence fee, with the entrepreneur having to decide each year whether to stay in production or to close shop and employ their talents elsewhere. Most real-world production processes probably have some such fixed input, and it is for this reason that it is usually, although not always, not possible for a firm simply to keep doubling all its inputs to produce twice as much output.

Graph 13.5 Long-Run Output Supply With Fixed Cost

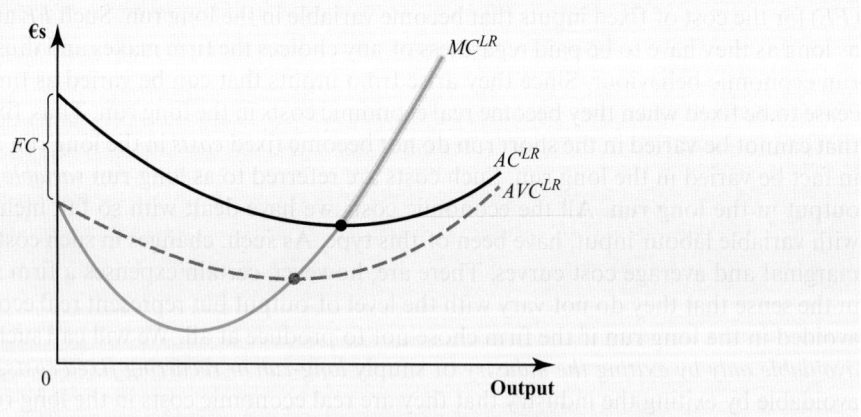

13A.1.5 Overview of Cost and Expense Types Keeping track of the different types of cost and expenditure changes that might impact firm behaviour can get confusing, but in essence, we have really identified only three types of costs that will change what firms do. Table 13.1 identifies examples of each. The first example is the annual licence fee that we discussed in the previous section. It is a fixed *expense* in the short run because there is nothing the firm can do to avoid paying it right now, but it becomes a recurring fixed *cost* in the long run as the firm gets to decide whether to stay in business and renew the licence or to exit the industry. Thus, the only cost curves that can possibly be affected by the licence fee are those in the long run, but among those, the *MC* curve does not change because the licence fee does not actually change the cost of producing additional output, only the cost of staying in business and beginning production. This is illustrated in panel (a) of Graph 13.6; an increase in the licence fee raises the long-run average cost curve from AC to AC' without impacting the long-run marginal cost curve. As a result, the long-run supply curve for the firm does not move; it becomes shorter as the dashed portion disappears.

Table 13.1 Examples of Costs and Expenses				
	Impact on Firm		**Effect on MC and AC**	
Example	**Short Run**	**Long Run**	**Short Run**	**Long Run**
Annual licence fee	Fixed expense	Fixed cost	None	AC
Cost of capital	Fixed expense	Variable cost	None	AC, MC
Cost of labour	Variable cost	Variable cost	AC, MC	AC, MC

Graph 13.6 Three Types of Cost Changes

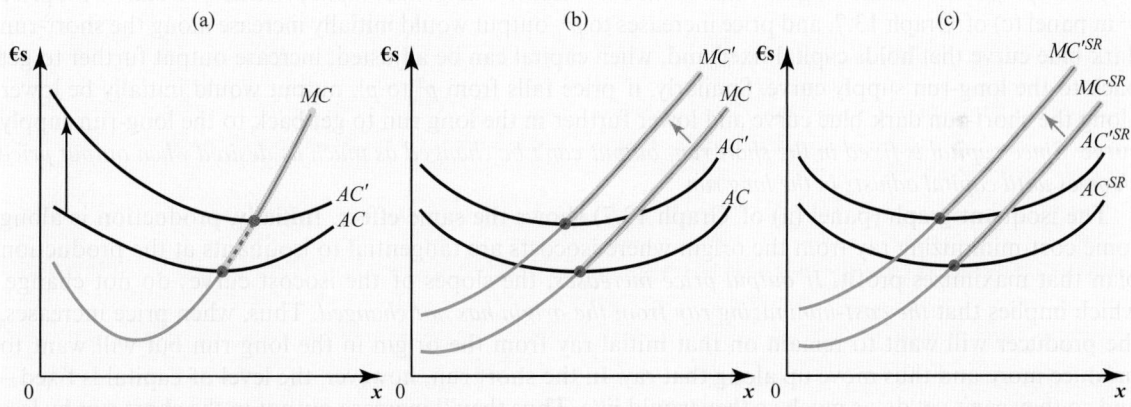

The second type of cost listed in Table 13.1 is the cost of capital, an input we are assuming is fixed in the short run. As we argued in Section 13A.1.1, this is not a real cost in the short run. The only cost curves that can be affected are therefore those in the long run, but this time the MC curve is affected in addition to the total cost curve C and the average cost curve AC. This is because, unlike the licence fee, the amount paid for capital will increase as output increases when capital is variable in the long run. An increase in the cost of capital is illustrated in panel (b) of Graph 13.6, with the long-run AC curve shifting up and the MC curve shifting as well.

Finally, the Table 13.1 lists the cost of labour, an input that is assumed to be variable in both the short and long run. Since the amount paid for labour depends on how much is produced in both the short and long run, it is always a real cost, with all the cost curves affected in the short and long run. This is illustrated for the short run in panel (c) of Graph 13.6 for an increase in labour costs. The long-run cost curves are similarly changed. Whether the lowest point of the long-run AC curve shifts to the left or the right will depend on the underlying technology and the degree to which the firm can substitute capital and labour.

Exercise 13A.11

Can we say for sure that the lowest point of the long-run AC curve in Graph 13.6 will shift to the right when the licence fee increases?

13A.2 Output Supply in the Short and Long Run

In our discussion of short- and long-run cost curves, we illustrated how changes in input and output prices affect output supply across time by focusing on the difference between shutting down and exiting. We'll now investigate the short- and long-run impact of changes in output prices on supply and turn towards the impact of input prices on supply in the short and long run. In Sections 13A.2.1 and 13A.2.2, we will work through some of the details of this.

In panel (f) of Graph 13.2, we illustrated the relationship between short-run average expenditure curves and long-run AC curves. Because the picture was already cluttered enough, we did not include the short-run MC curves corresponding to each fixed level of capital nor the long-run MC. Looking back at the picture, each short-run MC curve for a fixed level of capital would have an upward-sloping part that passes through the lowest point of the AE curve that has the same level of fixed capital, and the long-run MC curve would have an upward-sloping part that passes through the lowest point of the long-run AC curve. This would result in one long-run MC curve that has lots of short-run MC curves crossing for different levels of fixed capital – and those would form the basis for short- and long-run supply curves that end up looking exactly like panel (c) of Graph 13.7 in the next section. The conclusion from that graph is that *output responds more in the long run than in the short run to changes in output price.* If you start with price p^2 in panel (c) of Graph 13.7, and price increases to p^3, output would initially increase along the short-run dark blue curve that holds capital fixed and, when capital can be adjusted, increase output further to get back to the long-run supply curve. Similarly, if price falls from p^2 to p^1, output would initially be lower along the short-run dark blue curve and lower further in the long run to get back to the long-run supply curve. *Since capital is fixed in the short run, output can't be changed as much as desired when output price changes until capital adjusts in the long run.*

The isoquant graph (panel (a) of Graph 13.7) shows the same effect. Initially, production is along some cost-minimizing ray from the origin where isocosts are tangential to isoquants at the production plan that maximizes profit. *If output price increases*, the slopes of the isocost curves do not change, which implies that *the cost-minimizing ray from the origin has not changed.* Thus, when price increases, the producer will want to remain on that initial ray from the origin in the long run but will want to produce more and thus move up along that ray. In the short run, however, the level of capital is fixed – and so they can't yet do as much as they would like. Thus they'll increase output in the short run by less than in the long run.

When input prices change, on the other hand, the slopes of the isocost curves do change – which implies that the new cost-minimizing ray that has isocosts tangential to isoquants will change. When the input price change makes isocosts shallower because either wage falls or the rental rate increases, the new cost-minimizing ray will become shallower; and when the input price change makes isocosts steeper because either wage increases or the rental rate falls, the new cost-minimizing ray will become steeper. This is entirely due to a *substitution effect away from the input that has become more expensive and towards the input that has become cheaper.* For instance, if the wage increases, the producer will substitute away from labour and towards capital in order to lessen the increase in costs incurred for any level of output that they might choose to produce. As a result, the long-run MC curve – and thus the long-run supply curve, will shift up by less than it would have had they not substituted away from labour and towards capital.

The next two sections illustrate all of this more precisely.

13A.2.1 Output Price and Supply Over Time Suppose that a producer is currently facing the economic environment (w^A, r^A, p^A) and is producing at their long-run profit-maximizing production plan $A = (\ell^A, k^A, x^A)$. This is illustrated in panel (a) of Graph 13.7 as point A on the isoquant x^A with the slope of the isocost $(-w^A/r^A)$ equal to the TRS^A. Suppose that the output price rises to p'. We know from our previous work that this will cause *an increase in output* and thus a movement to a higher isoquant, both in the short and long run. In the short run, the producer cannot vary capital away from its current input level k^A and must therefore operate with input bundles lying on the horizontal line emanating from k^A on the vertical axis of the graph. Suppose that it is optimal for the producer to pick the input bundle B in the short run.

Graph 13.7 Short-Run Versus Long-Run Supply Curves

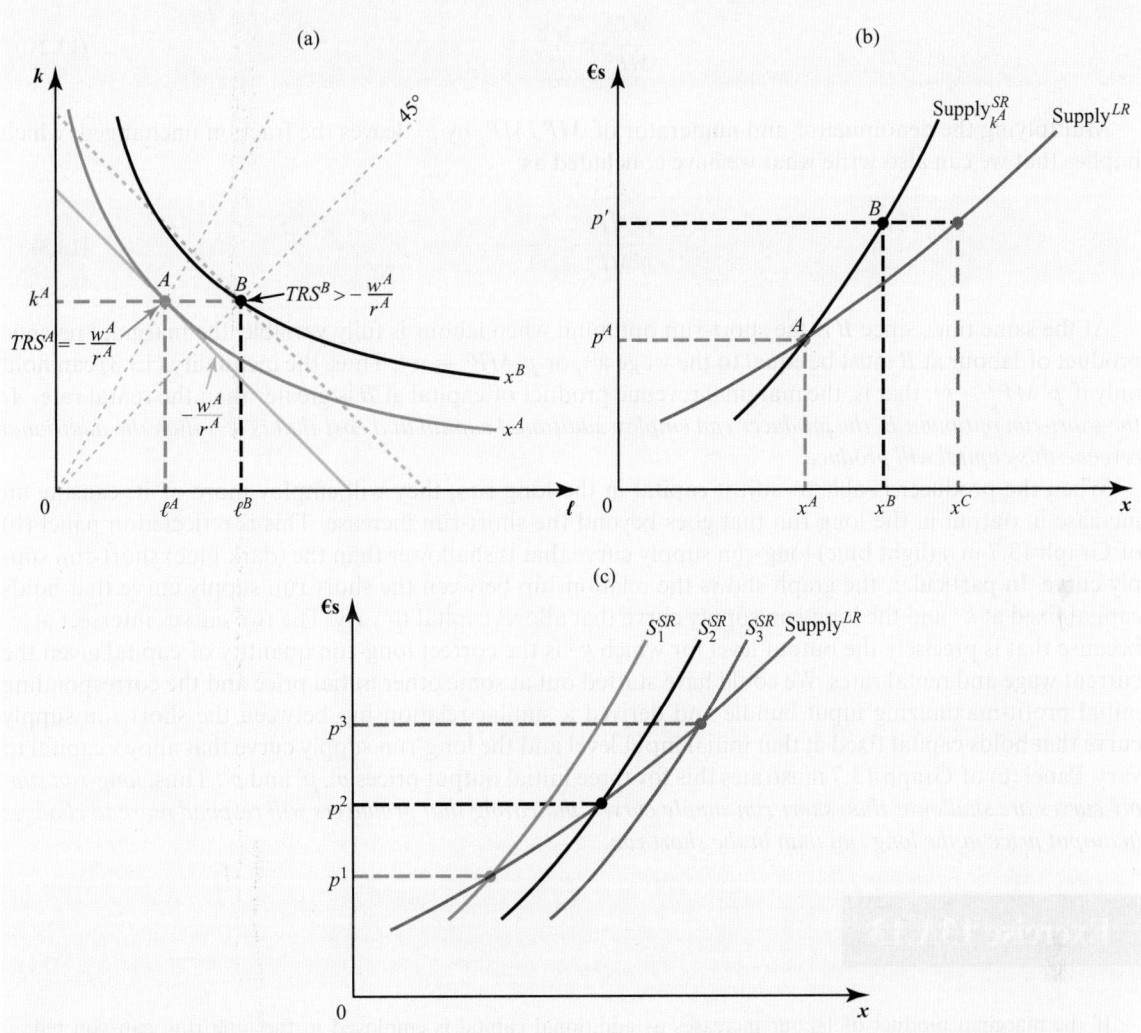

Exercise 13A.12

True or False: $p' MP_\ell^B = w^A$.

Since we are assuming that the underlying production technology is homothetic, any input bundle to the right of the diagonal connecting to the origin has a shallower isoquant slope than the slope of the isoquant at A, which is equal to $(-w^A/r^A)$. Thus:

$$TRS^B > -\frac{w^A}{r^A}. \qquad (13.1)$$

or, given that $-TRS = (MP_\ell/MP_k)$:

$$\frac{MP_\ell^B}{MP_k^B} < \frac{w^A}{r^A}. \tag{13.2}$$

Multiplying the denominator and numerator of MP_ℓ/MP_k by p' leaves the fraction unchanged, which implies that we can also write what we have concluded as:

$$\frac{p'MP_\ell^B}{p'MP_k^B} < \frac{w^A}{r^A}. \tag{13.3}$$

At the same time, since B is the short-run optimum when labour is fully variable, the marginal revenue product of labour at B must be equal to the wage w^A, or $p'MP_\ell^B = w^A$. Thus, the inequality (13.3) can hold only if $p'MP_k^B > r^A$, that is, the marginal revenue product of capital at B is greater than the rental rate. *At the short-run optimum B, the producer can employ additional capital at a cost that is less than the additional revenue this capital will produce.*

When the producer is able to adjust capital in the long run, they will employ more of it, causing an increase in output in the long run that goes beyond the short-run increase. This is reflected in panel (b) of Graph 13.7 in a (light blue) long-run supply curve that is shallower than the (dark blue) short-run supply curve. In particular, the graph shows the relationship between the short-run supply curve that holds capital fixed at k^A and the long-run supply curve that allows capital to vary. The two curves intersect at x^A because that is precisely the output level for which k^A is the correct long-run quantity of capital given the current wage and rental rates. We could have started out at some other initial price and the corresponding initial profit-maximizing input bundle and derived a similar relationship between the short-run supply curve that holds capital fixed at that initial input level and the long-run supply curve that allows capital to vary. Panel (c) of Graph 13.7 illustrates this for three initial output prices p^1, p^2 and p^3. Thus, *long-run supply curves are shallower than short-run supply curves, indicating that producers will respond more to changes in output price in the long run than in the short run.*

Exercise 13A.13

If the marginal product of labour increases as additional capital is employed in the long run, can you tell whether the producer will employ additional labour beyond ℓ^B in the long run? Can you identify the minimum distance above A on the ray through A the long-run optimal isoquant in panel (a) of Graph 13.7 will lie?

13A.2.2 Long-Run Supply and Input Prices: Substitution Effects in Production While changes in output prices will cause producers to alter their production behaviour *along supply curves*, changes in input prices will *shift supply curves* because such changes cause shifts in cost curves. These shifts are complicated by the fact that as the relative prices of inputs change, producers will, at least in the long run, adjust the ratio of capital to labour that they use to produce any given level of output. This was an issue that did not arise in the single-input model since there was only a single technologically efficient way of producing any level of output without wasting inputs. Now, however, we have a whole isoquant of possible input combinations that all represent technologically efficient ways of producing a given output level. Which of these technologically efficient input bundles is economically efficient depends on the relative prices of the inputs, and this implies that the economically efficient input bundle for producing any given level of output will typically change as input prices change.

Suppose, for instance, that we initially face the input prices $w = 20$ and $r = 10$ and the production frontier is represented by the isoquant map in panel (a) of Graph 13.8, which is the same map first introduced in panel (a) of Graph 12.8. Since the isoquant map is homothetic, the economically efficient ratio of inputs will be the same for any output level and can be located along a ray from the origin where isocosts with slope $-w/r = -2$ are tangential to each isoquant. Now suppose that the wage rate falls to $w' = 10$. The new economically efficient input bundles on each of the isoquants in the graph would lie at tangencies with isocosts that have a slope of -1 rather than -2, causing us to slide down to a new input bundle on each of the isoquants with economically efficient input bundles again lying on a ray from the origin. A change in input prices will result in a *substitution away from the input that has become relatively more expensive and towards the input bundle that has become relatively cheaper*.

The change in isocosts when w falls from €20 to €10 is represented in panel (a) of Graph 13.8 along the isoquant labelled 100 as a change in the tangency at the initial isocost at input bundle C to the tangency at the new isocost at bundle C', with all other economically efficient input bundles for other isoquants lying on the ray connecting the origin with bundle C'. Each of the new input bundles is now cheaper, both because the wage has fallen *and* because we have substituted away from capital and towards the cheaper labour. This is represented in a change in the total long-run cost curve in panel (b) from the initial dark brown curve, which is identical to the one derived in panel (b) of Graph 12.8, to the final light blue cost curve. The dotted dark blue curve in between represents the change in total costs that would have occurred had the producer not changed input bundles but experienced lower costs because the wage had fallen, with the remaining drop in total costs due to the substituting behaviour induced by the change in relative input prices.

Graph 13.8 Costs and Input Substitution Effects

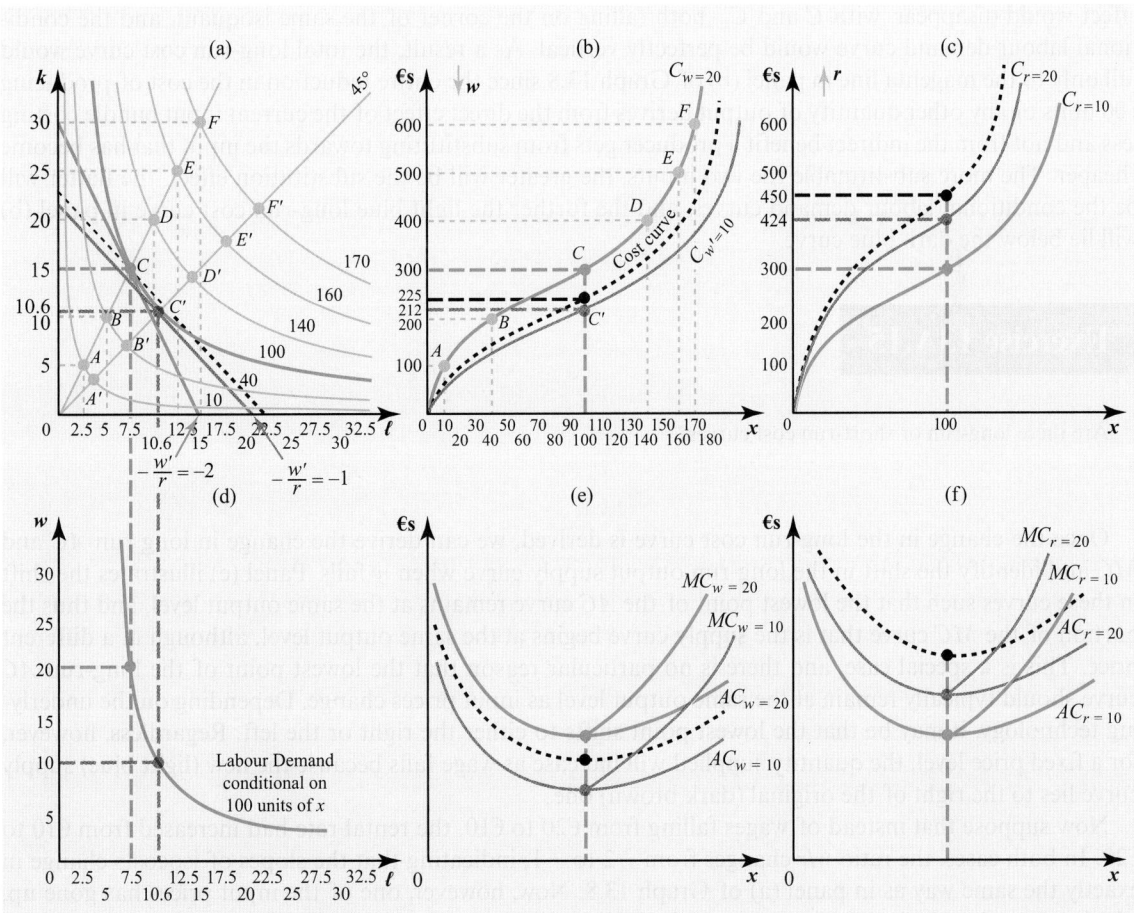

Exercise 13A.14

Can you see in panel (a) of Graph 13.8 the cost of not substituting from C to C'? Can you verify that the numbers in panel (b) are correct?

The size of the input substitution effect depends on the degree of substitutability of the two inputs in the production process. One way to represent this is in what is called a *conditional input demand curve that tells us, conditional on a given level of output, how the producer's demand for the input changes with the input price*. We already derived the mathematical counterpart to this – the conditional labour demand curve – in part B of Chapter 12. Panel (d) of the graph, for example, illustrates the conditional labour demand curve given an output level of 100 units. It shows that as the wage drops from €20 to €10, the producer substitutes away from capital and towards labour when they produce 100 units of x. This conditional labour demand curve is, therefore, derived solely from the isoquant representing 100 units of output and the tangencies of isocosts as w changes. It incorporates a pure substitution effect induced solely by the change in the opportunity cost of labour, just as the compensated demand curve in consumer theory illustrates a pure substitution effect from changes in the opportunity costs of goods. As the slope of compensated demand curves depends on the substitutability of goods in consumption along an indifference curve, the slope of the conditional labour demand curve depends on the substitutability of inputs in production along an isoquant.

Suppose, for instance, that the two inputs were perfect complements in production. The substitution effect would disappear, with C and C' both falling on the corner of the same isoquant, and the conditional labour demand curve would be perfectly vertical. As a result, the total long-run cost curve would fall only to the magenta line in panel (b) of Graph 13.8 since the entire reduction in the cost of producing 100 units or any other quantity of output derives from the direct effect of the current input bundle costing less and not from the indirect benefit a producer gets from substituting towards the input that has become cheaper. The more substitutable the two inputs, the greater will be the substitution effect, the flatter will be the conditional labour demand curves, and the further the light blue long-run cost curve in panel (b) will lie below the dark blue curve.

Exercise 13A.15

Are these long-run or short-run cost curves?

Once the change in the long-run cost curve is derived, we can derive the change in long run AC and MC and identify the shift in the long-run output supply curve when w falls. Panel (e) illustrates the shift in these curves such that the lowest point of the AC curve remains at the same output level, and thus the portion of the MC curve that is the supply curve begins at the same output level, although at a different price. This is a special case, and there is no particular reason that the lowest point of the long-run AC curve should typically remain at the same output level as input prices change. Depending on the underlying technology, it may be that the lowest point shifts to either the right or the left. Regardless, however, for a fixed price level, the quantity supplied will increase as wage falls because the new (light blue) supply curve lies to the right of the original (dark brown) one.

Now suppose that instead of wages falling from €20 to €10, the rental rate had increased from €10 to €20. In both cases, the ratio w/r changes from -2 to -1, indicating that the slopes of isocosts change in exactly the same way as in panel (a) of Graph 13.8. Now, however, one of the input prices has gone up, which means that the long-run total cost of producing any quantity of output must be higher than it was originally. This is graphed in panels (c) and (f) of Graph 13.8 as a change in the total cost, the AC and the

MC curves from the initial dark brown to the final light blue curve. The dotted dark blue curves represent how much total and average costs would have increased had the producer not substituted away from capital and towards labour. The conclusion in panel (f) is that *as the rental rate increases, output supply decreases.*

Exercise 13A.16

Can you verify that the numbers in panel (c) of Graph 13.8 are correct?

Exercise 13A.17*

Assuming the original cost-minimizing input bundle remains C, which of the three curves graphed in panel (c) of Graph 13.8 would be different, and how, if the inputs in panel (a) of the graph were more substitutable? How would the graph change if the two inputs were perfect complements in productions?

In the short run, the substitution effects in Graph 13.8 will not occur when capital is held fixed. The short-run supply curve appears as the MC curve above short-run average cost as in Graph 13.4, and a change in the price of the variable input shifts the short-run MC and short-run AC as production of any given output level is undertaken with production plans that hold capital constant. It can be shown, however, that *output responses for changes in input prices are at least as large in the long run as in the short run.*

13A.3 Input Demand and Changes in the Economic Environment

Since the distinguishing characteristic of the short run in the two-input model is that one of the inputs is fixed, it must be true that the *short-run* labour demand decision occurs along the marginal revenue product of labour curve as wage changes. As we discussed in detail in Chapter 11, *some portion of the declining part of the MRP_ℓ curve with capital held fixed at its short-run quantity is the short-run labour demand curve.* Similarly, short-run labour demand varies with output price as described for the single-input model in Chapter 11, with changes in p causing the labour demand curve to shift just as changes in p shift the MRP_ℓ curve (see Graph 11.8). In the long run, however, both ℓ and k can be adjusted, which implies that the long-run labour demand curve will be different from the short-run labour demand curve that lies on the MRP_ℓ curve. In the following, we explore how labour demand changes in the long run as input and output prices change.

Exercise 13A.18*

In panel (d) of Graph 13.8, we already derived conditional labour demand curves along which capital is allowed to adjust. Explain why these are not long-run labour demand curves.

We will again develop the ideas in this section under the assumption that production technologies are homothetic. As demonstrated in part B of the chapter, these ideas hold more generally, but the homotheticity assumption simplifies the graphical approach a bit by giving us a convenient way to narrow the region within the isoquant space where new *cost-minimizing* input bundles will lie as relative input prices change. Suppose, for instance, that the input bundle $A = (\ell^A, k^A)$ in Graph 13.9 is the cost-minimizing way of producing x^A at input prices (w^A, r^A). If input prices change such that isocosts become steeper, the new cost-minimizing input bundles must lie on a steeper ray to the *left* of the ray connecting A to the origin, because only in that region could there be a tangency between an isoquant and one of the new steeper isocosts. Similarly, if input prices change such that isocosts become shallower, the new cost-minimizing input bundles must lie on a shallower ray to the *right* of the same ray. This is entirely due to the substitution effect discussed in the previous section.

Graph 13.9 Changes in Input Prices and New Long-Run Profit-Maximizing Input Bundles

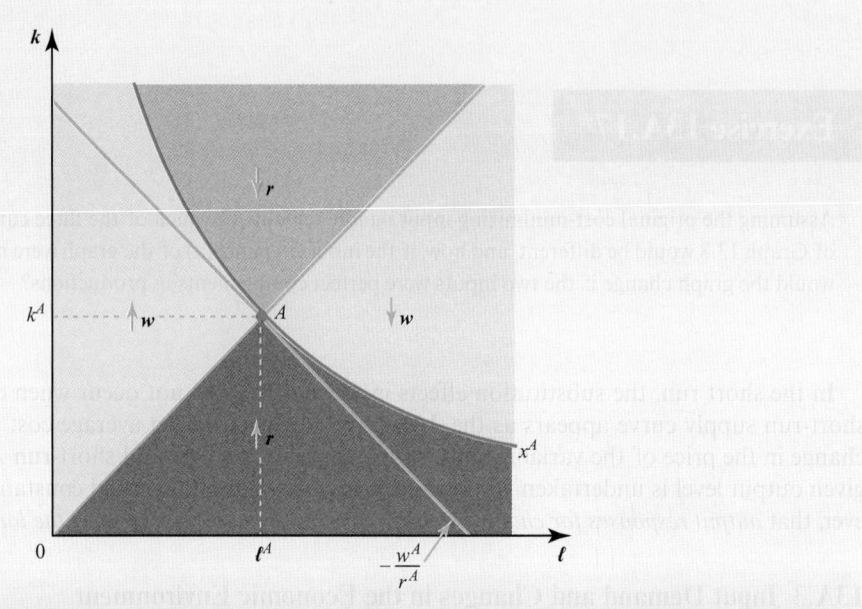

Go to MindTap to interact with this graph

Exercise 13A.19

Can you tell from just seeing the tangency at (ℓ^A, k^A) of the isocost with the isoquant in Graph 13.9 whether the production plan $A = (\ell^A, k^A, x^A)$ is profit-maximizing at prices (w^A, r^A, p^A)?

Identifying where the new profit-maximizing production plan lies in this isoquant picture when input prices change, however, requires more than identifying where the substitution effect has placed the new cost-minimizing ray. In addition, we have to know whether the input price change causes the profit-maximizing firm to produce more or less on that ray – an effect we will call the *scale effect*. Suppose, for instance, that the production plan $A = (\ell^A, k^A, x^A)$ is not only cost-minimizing at input prices (w^A, r^A) but is also long-run profit-maximizing given the output price p^A. If w decreases, this implies that the long-run MC curve will shift down, resulting in an *increase* in the profit-maximizing output level where p^A intersects MC. The scale effect is, therefore, positive. Output will increase above the isoquant x^A in addition to lying on the shallower cost-minimizing ray from the substitution effect towards the input that has become relatively cheaper. Putting the substitution effect together with the scale effect, we can conclude that the new profit-maximizing production plan will lie in the shaded dark brown region when wage falls – that is, the intersection of the region that contains bundles on a shallower ray from the origin with the region that contains more output than was originally produced. If instead the rental rate r increased, the substitution effect would again suggest a more labour-intensive production process along a shallower cost-minimizing ray from the origin, but this time the long-run MC curve shifts up. This implies that p^A intersects MC at a lower output level than x^A – giving us a negative scale effect. As a result, we can conclude that the new profit-maximizing production plan when r increases will lie in the shaded dark blue region of Graph 13.9.

Similarly, we can conclude that an increase in w or a decrease in r, both of which cause isocosts to become steeper, will lead to substitution effects that result in a steeper cost-minimizing ray from the origin to the left of the original ray through A. An increase in w will furthermore cause an upward shift in long-run MC and therefore a negative scale effect, placing the new profit-maximizing plan in the shaded light blue region of Graph 13.9. A decrease in r, on the other hand, will cause a downward shift in long-run MC and therefore a positive scale effect, placing the new profit-maximizing plan in the shaded light brown region.

Exercise 13A.20*

Do you see from Graph 13.9 that long-run demand curves for labour with respect to wage must slope down, as must long-run demand curves for capital with respect to the rental rate?

Exercise 13A.21*

Does Graph 13.9 tell us anything about whether the cross-price demand curve for labour with the rental rate on the vertical axis slopes up or down in the long run?

The shaded regions in Graph 13.9 thus tell us where our new long-run production plan might lie as different input prices change, assuming that A was the profit-maximizing plan prior to the change in input prices. In the short run, however, we are constrained to keep capital at its current level k^A – which raises the question of how short-run firm choices relate to long-run firm choices as these input prices change. A lot will depend on the degree of substitutability between capital and labour, as we will see next.

Suppose, for instance, a firm employs labour and capital, and the wage paid to workers goes up. In the short run when capital is fixed, the firm employs fewer workers, which moves it up the MRP_ℓ curve. Thus, once the new short-run optimal number of workers is chosen, the marginal product of labour (MP_ℓ) will be higher than it was before the wage increase. Since labour has become more expensive, the firm will only employ workers as long as output justifies the higher cost. What will the firm do once it can adjust capital? Will it employ more capital or less? The shaded light blue area in Graph 13.9 suggests both are possible. What does that in turn imply for whether the firm will let even more workers go in the long run? The answers, it turns out, depend on whether the capital employed in our firm is more like robots or more like computers.

Exercise 13A.22*

Where in Graph 13.9 will the new production plan fall after the firm has made its short-run labour adjustment?

First, suppose our firm is one that employs both robots and workers to produce cars. In this case, it may be that capital and labour are very substitutable if robots can do many of the same tasks as workers. Since we know that the MP_ℓ has gone up as a result of the decision to have fewer workers in the short run, it would also be the case that the MP_k has increased. If workers are a lot like robots in this firm, what happens to the marginal product of one should be roughly equal to what happens to the marginal product of the other. If the MP_k has increased, that means it will want to employ more robots that have *not* become any more expensive, and it should let go of more workers that *have* become more expensive once it can replace them with robots in the long run. Thus, it is because robots and workers are substitutable that we know the MP_k must have increased when the firm employed fewer workers in the short run, which in turn means it will want to employ more robots and replace additional workers with robots in the long run. The labour demand response is, therefore, greater in the long run than in the short run, all because the firm will *increase* capital in the long run due to its substitutability with labour.

Exercise 13A.23*

We know that output will decrease in the short run as w increases because the firm employs fewer workers. In the case of robots and workers, do you think that it will increase or decrease output once it can employ more robots in the long run?

Next, suppose that capital and labour were instead quite complementary in production, as perhaps in the case of a computer animations firm that employs computers as capital and computer graphics artists as labour. If the firm is of that type, an increase in w will initially cause a decrease in labour for the same reasons as before. Now labour and capital are more complementary and less substitutable, because the computer is not of much use without a computer graphics artist. Thus, when labour is decreased in the short run, the MP_k *falls* even as the MP_ℓ increases. When the firm can adjust capital in the long run, it will let go of some of the computers, which will reduce the marginal product of workers further and result in the firm letting go of even more of them. It is because computers and graphic artists are relatively complementary that we know the MP_k *falls* as graphics artists are let go in response to an increase in their wage, which in turn causes a reduction in the number of computers and with it a further reduction in the number of workers. As in the case where labour and capital were substitutable, we again conclude that the long-run reduction in labour exceeds the short-run reduction, but this time it is accompanied by a long-run *reduction* of capital.

The two examples illustrate that regardless of how substitutable capital and labour are in production, the long-run labour demand response to wage changes is always greater than the short-run response. The long-run capital demand response to a wage change, on the other hand, depends on the substitutability of capital and labour. An inbetween special case also exists: the case where capital and labour are neither too substitutable nor too complementary, and, as a result, the firm does not change its capital as w increases even when it can in the long run. In that special case, as we will see, the firm's long-run labour demand response is equal to its short-run labour demand response. It is therefore more accurate to restate the conclusion about the long-run labour demand response slightly: *Regardless of how substitutable or complementary capital and labour are in production, the long-run labour response to wage changes will be at least as large as the short-run response.*

13A.3.1 **Demand for Labour and Capital as w Changes** We can now demonstrate this a little more formally by applying the fact that two main conditions must hold in order for a producer to be maximizing profits in the short and long run. First, each input's marginal revenue product must equal its price, and second, the negative TRS, which is equal to MP_ℓ/MP_k, must equal the ratio of input prices (w/r) in the long run thus getting us to a new tangency between isocost and isoquant. Note that the second condition follows logically from the first, but we will proceed in this section as if they were distinct conditions. Suppose again as we did in Graph 13.9 that a producer is currently operating at a production plan $A = (\ell^A, k^A, x^A)$ that is their long-run profit-maximizing production plan in the economic environment (w^A, r^A, p^A). We know that:

$$p^A MP_\ell^A = w^A, \, p^A MP_k^A = r^A \quad \text{and} \quad -TRS^A \left(= \frac{MP_\ell^A}{MP_k^A} \right) = \frac{w^A}{r^A}. \tag{13.4}$$

This production plan is depicted as point A in panels (a), (b) and (c) of Graph 13.10.

Now suppose the wage rises to w', thus causing all isocosts to become steeper and implying that the new long-run optimal input bundle C will lie to the left of the ray connecting the origin to A and below the isoquant containing A as illustrated in Graph 13.9. In the short run, however, the producer cannot adjust capital and therefore must operate with an input bundle B that lies on the horizontal line that holds capital at k^A.

Panel (b) of Graph 13.10 illustrates the special case where the new long-run optimal input bundle C has exactly the same level of capital input as the original input bundle A. In this case, there is nothing to keep the producer from implementing the new long-run optimum even in the short run, which implies that the short-run optimal input bundle B is the same as the long-run optimal bundle C, and the long-run labour and capital demand responses are exactly the same as the short-run responses. Since labour is variable in the short run, $p^A MP_\ell^B = w'$ as the firm adjusts its labour input in exactly the way described in the single-input model of Chapter 11. Since the new isocost happens to be tangential to the isoquant at B:

$$\frac{MP_\ell^B}{MP_k^B} = \frac{w'}{r^A} \quad \text{or, equivalently,} \quad \frac{p^A MP_\ell^B}{p^A MP_k^B} = \frac{w'}{r^A}. \tag{13.5}$$

Since $p^A MP_\ell^B = w'$, this implies $p^A MP_k^B = r^A$, which, given that $p^A MP_k^A = r^A$, implies $MP_k^A = MP_k^B$. The fact that we have graphed the new isocost tangential to the isoquant at B, implies that we have graphed a technology where the short-run reduction in labour input has left the marginal product of capital unchanged. This in turn implies that the producer reaches their long-run optimum in the short run, causing the short- and long-run labour demand curves to coincide in panel (e) and the cross-price relationship between w and k to be vertical as in panel (h).

Now consider the technology graphed in panel (a). Here, the new optimal input bundle C contains more capital input than the original bundle A, which implies that the producer cannot immediately switch to the long-run optimum when capital is fixed in the short run. Rather, in the short run, the producer switches to input bundle B, which has the characteristic that the isocost containing B cuts the isoquant containing B from above; that is, $TRS^B > -w'/r^A$ or equivalently:

$$\frac{MP_\ell^B}{MP_k^B} < \frac{w'}{r^A}, \quad \text{which implies} \quad \frac{p^A MP_\ell^B}{p^A MP_k^B} < \frac{w'}{r^A}. \tag{13.6}$$

In the short run the firm will adjust labour until $p^A MP_\ell^B = w'$. The previous equation implies that $p^A MP_k^B > r^A$ and thus (since $p^A MP_k^A = r^A$) that $MP_k^B > MP_k^A$. Capital is therefore more productive at the margin at B than at A, which causes producers to substitute away from labour and towards capital, causing a decline in labour input beyond the initial decline from ℓ^A to ℓ^B all the way to ℓ^C. This leads the labour demand curve in panel (d) to be shallower in the long run than in the short run and the cross-price relationship between w and k to be upward sloping. As suggested by the relatively flat shape of isoquants in panel (a), this occurs when capital and labour are relatively substitutable in production as in the example of robots and workers, and when an increase in the cost of labour leads to a lot of substitution into capital.

Panel (c) of Graph 13.10 illustrates the opposite case where the producer adjusts to less capital in the long run as wage increases from w^A to w'. Since the producer finds it optimal to adjust capital that is fixed in the short run, their long-run response to the wage increase will differ from their short-run response. In the short run, they switch to input bundle B where the isocost containing B cuts the isoquant containing B from below. Using steps analogous to those in the previous paragraph, this allows us to conclude that $MP_k^B < MP_k^A$; that is, capital has become less productive at the margin when labour input is adjusted in the short run. As a result, the producer reduces the capital input in the long run and further reduces labour input as well, which leads again to a long-run labour demand curve that is shallower than in the short run (panel (f)) but a cross-price relationship between w and k that is downward sloping (panel (i)). Notice that this is derived from panel (c) where isoquants represent inputs that are relatively complementary as in the example of computers and workers, and an increase in the cost of labour results in less use of both labour and its complementary input capital.

Graph 13.10 Short- and Long-Run Input Demand Responses When w Increases

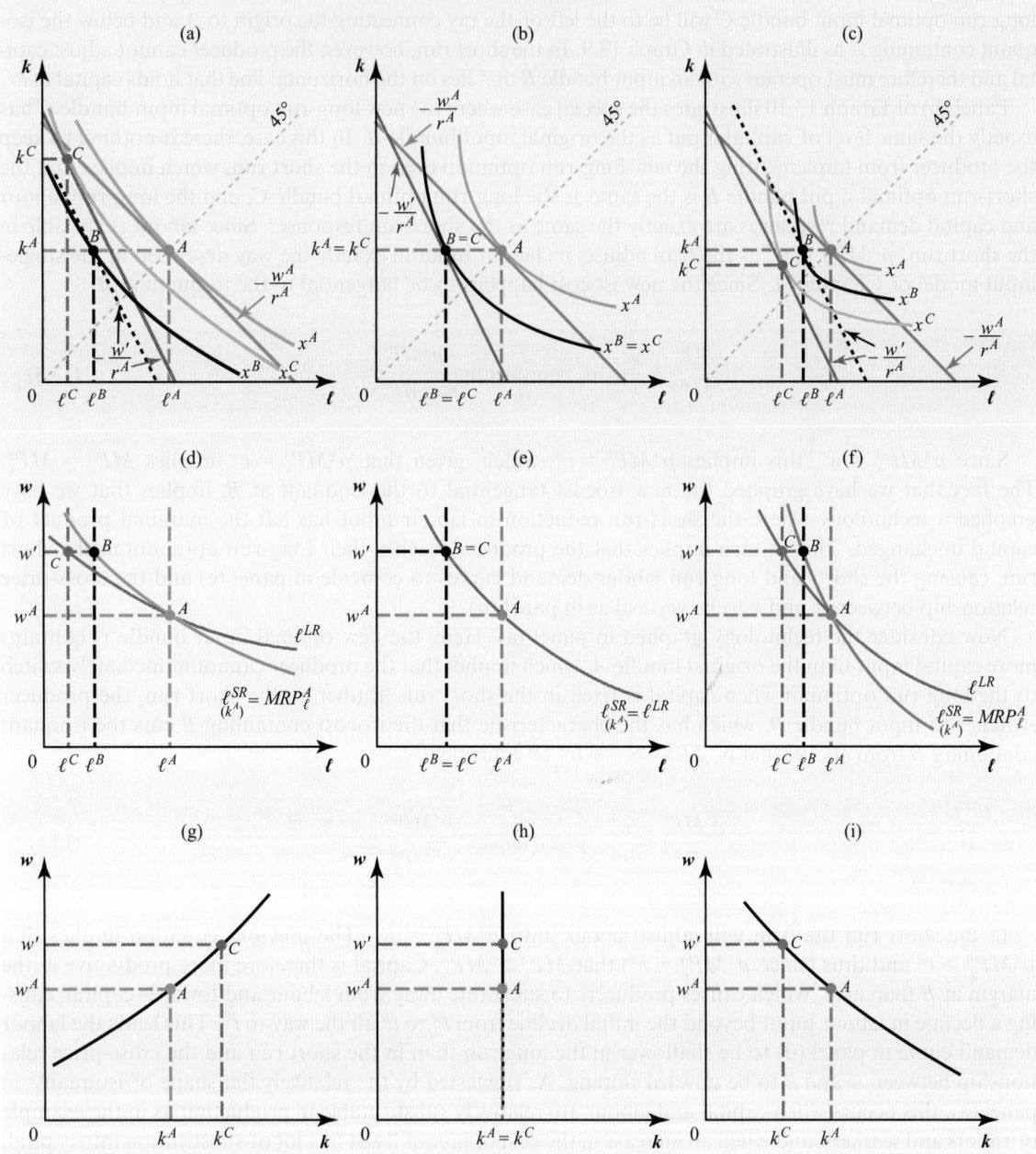

Exercise 13A.24*

Suppose labour and capital were perfect complements in production. What would the analogous graph for an increase in w look like?

Exercise 13A.25*

Demonstrate that $MP_k^B < MP_k^A$ in panel (c) of Graph 13.10.

Exercise 13A.26*

How is the long-run response in output related to the short-run response in output as w increases? What does your answer depend on? *Hint*: You should be able to see the answer in Graph 13.10.

We can conclude that except for the special case in panel (b) of the graph, *the long-run labour demand response to changes in w is larger than the short-run labour demand response* just as we concluded earlier in the chapter that the long-run output supply response to a change in output price is larger in the long run than in the short run. The underlying reasoning is somewhat subtle. In the case where labour and capital are relatively substitutable in production in panel (a) analogous to our example of capital as robots, the marginal product of capital *increases* because of the short-run drop in labour when w increases. As a result, the firm will employ more capital when it can and reduce labour further because capital and labour are relatively substitutable. In the case where labour and capital are relatively complementary in production in panel (c) analogous to our example of capital as computers, the marginal product of capital *falls* as a result of the short-run drop in labour when w increases. This causes the firm to reduce its capital when it can in the long run, and, because labour and capital are relatively complementary, it will reduce the labour it employs beyond the short-run reduction. Whether labour and capital are relatively substitutable or relatively complementary, the long-run labour demand response exceeds the short-run response – albeit for somewhat different reasons – and the demand for capital either increases or decreases depending on the degree of substitutability between capital and labour.

13A.3.2 Demand for Labour and Capital as *r* Changes An analogous set of steps can lead us to an analogous set of conclusions regarding the long-run change in the demand for labour and capital when r rather than w rises. Since we are assuming throughout that capital is fixed in the short run, however, an increase in the cost of capital is a sunk cost in the short run and thus does not affect production decisions with respect to labour, capital or output in the short run.

Suppose again that a producer is currently operating at a production plan $A = (\ell^A, k^A, x^A)$, that is their long-run profit-maximizing production plan in the economic environment (w^A, r^A, p^A). If r increases, which makes isocosts shallower, we know from Graph 13.9 that this will lead to a new profit-maximizing input bundle that lies below the isoquant containing A and to the right of the ray connecting A to the origin. Graph 13.11 illustrates three possibilities, with panel (a) once again representing a production process in which capital and labour are relatively substitutable and panel (c) representing the case where capital and labour are relatively complementary in production.

Since capital falls in all three scenarios as r increases, we can conclude that *the long-run demand curve for capital is downward sloping with respect to r*. The cross-price relationship between r and ℓ, however, may slope up when labour and capital are relatively substitutable or down when labour and capital are relatively complementary in production as demonstrated by panels (d) to (f) in Graph 13.11. This happens for reasons analogous to those cited for the potentially upward- or downward-sloping cross-price relationship between w and k in Graph 13.10.

Graph 13.11 Long-Run Labour Demand Responses When r Increases

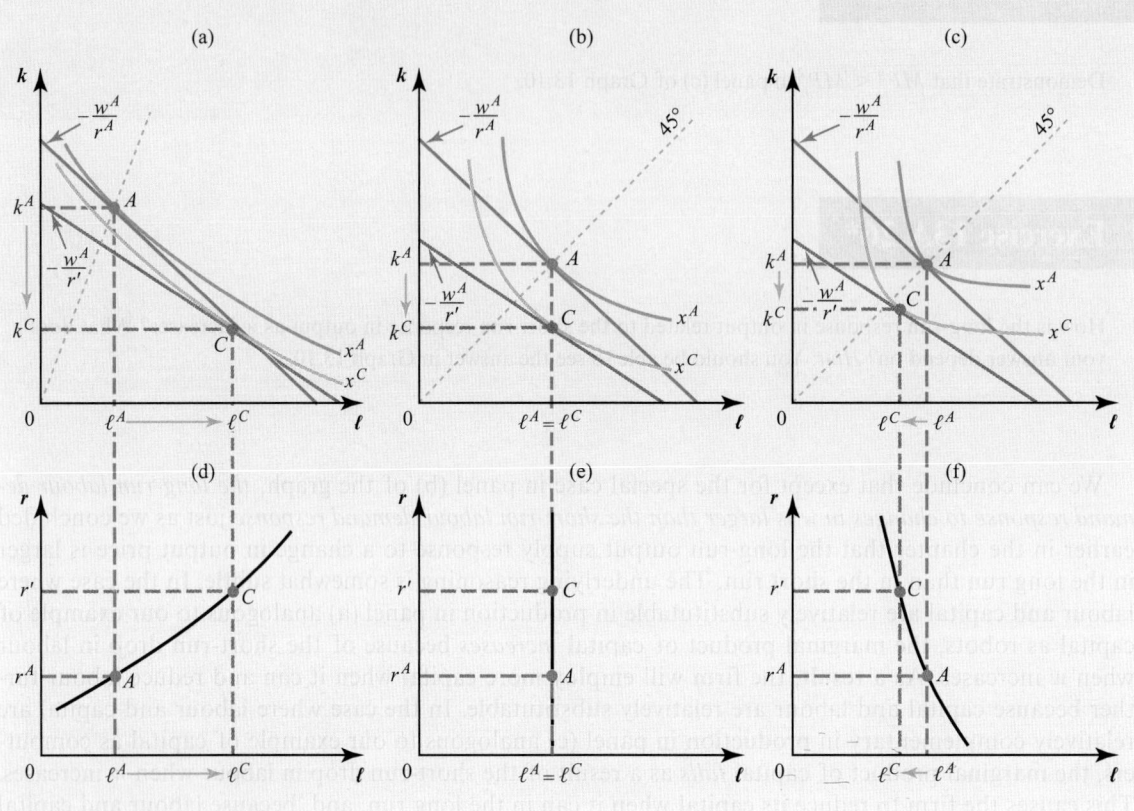

Exercise 13A.27

Can you arrive at these conclusions intuitively using the examples of robots and computers?

13A.3.3 Demand for Labour and Capital as p Changes We know from our previous work that output supply curves slope up because the relevant portion of MC curves slope up, which implies that output increases when the output price p rises. Since a change in output price by itself does not alter the slope of isocosts which is equal to $-w/r$, this implies that increases in output price do not give rise to substitution effects. They do, however, give rise to a positive scale effect, implying that the new profit-maximizing production plan will lie on the original cost-minimizing ray but on a higher isoquant.

In the short run, however, capital may be fixed, implying that the increase in output in the short run results entirely from additional labour being employed. Whether the increase in labour demand is higher or lower in the short run depends on the relative substitutability of capital and labour in production. Consider, for instance, the case of capital and labour being perfect complements in production, as illustrated in panel (a) of Graph 13.12, where again A is the initial profit-maximizing input bundle before the price of the output rises. Since it is impossible in this case to produce additional output without adjusting both capital and labour, the producer would have no choice but to keep output unchanged in the short run as long as capital is fixed, resulting in $A = B$. Thus, when capital and labour are very complementary in production, there will be little or no change in labour demand in the short run as output price rises, and the bulk of the increase in production happens in the long run as both labour and capital can be adjusted in the same proportion.

Graph 13.12 Input Demand Responses When p Increases

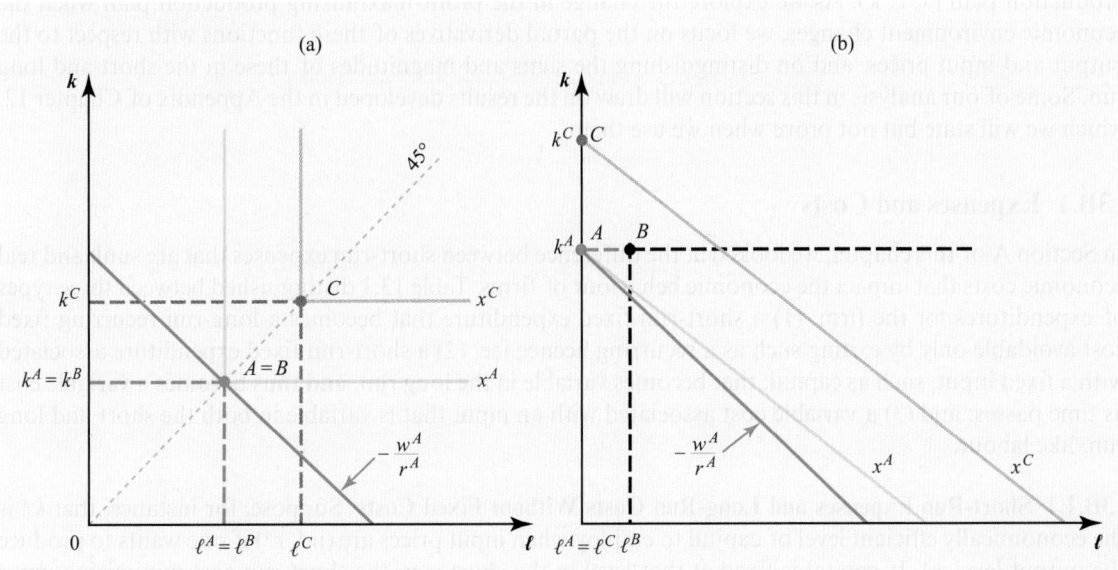

Now consider the case where capital and labour are perfect substitutes in production as illustrated in panel (b) of Graph 13.12. Suppose that capital is relatively cheaper than labour, which implies that the producer is using only capital and no labour at the original input bundle A. When output price increases without a change in input prices, the producer will end up producing more output with an increase in capital in the long run (bundle C), but in the short run they cannot change the level of capital in production. As a result, the producer may well employ some labour in the short run taking them to input bundle B before being able to adjust capital. In this case there is a temporary increase in labour demand in the short run as output price increases, but this increase vanishes in the long run.

From these extremes, we can conclude that *the short-run labour demand response from a change in output price might be larger or smaller than the long-run response depending on the degree of substitutability between capital and labour in production.* We will illustrate this more mathematically in Section B.

Exercise 13A.28*

In panel (a) of Graph 13.7, we determined that the firm will once again end up on the steeper ray once it can adjust capital. Call the new long-run input bundle at the higher output price C. Can you now tell what will determine whether C lies to the right or left of B?

13B Transitioning from Short Run to Long Run Mathematically

In the duality picture in Graph 12.13, the profit-maximization problem on the left-hand side yields output supply and input demand functions:

$$x(p, w, r), \ell(p, w, r) \text{ and } k(p, w, r). \tag{13.7}$$

These functions tell us, purely as a function of the economic environment (p, w, r), the profit-maximizing production plan (x, ℓ, k). As we explore the change in the profit-maximizing production plan when the economic environment changes, we focus on the partial derivatives of these functions with respect to the output and input prices, and on distinguishing the signs and magnitudes of these in the short and long run. Some of our analysis in this section will draw on the results developed in the Appendix of Chapter 12, which we will state but not prove when we use them.

13B.1 Expenses and Costs

In Section A of this chapter, we looked at the difference between short-run expenses that are sunk and real economic costs that impact the economic behaviour of firms. Table 13.1 distinguished between three types of expenditures for the firm: (1) a short-run fixed expenditure that becomes a long-run recurring fixed cost avoidable only by exiting such as a recurring licence fee; (2) a short-run fixed expenditure associated with a fixed input, such as capital, that becomes variable in the long run, and thus becomes a variable cost as time passes; and (3) a variable cost associated with an input that is variable in both the short and long run, like labour.

13B.1.1 Short-Run Expenses and Long-Run Costs Without Fixed Costs

Suppose, for instance, that k^A is the economically efficient level of capital to employ when input prices are (w^A, r^A) if one wants to produce the output level x^A. If capital is fixed at that level in the short run, the short-run cost-minimizing input bundle for producing any given level of output x is $(\ell_{k^A}(x), k^A)$, where $\ell_{k^A}(x)$ is the minimum amount of labour necessary to produce output x given that capital is fixed at k^A. We would arrive at this in exactly the same way as we did in Chapter 11, with the relevant production function in the short run being the slice of the long-run production function that holds capital fixed at k^A. We can denote this slice as $f_{k^A}(\ell)$. For instance, if the full (long-run) production function is $f(\ell, k) = A\ell^\alpha k^\beta$, the short-run production function when the firm is restricted to keep capital at k^A is $x = f_{k^A} = [A(k^A)^\beta]\ell^\alpha$, with the term in brackets being treated as a constant. To find the cost-minimizing labour input level for producing x in the short run, we would invert this to get:

$$\ell_{k^A}(x) = \left(\frac{x}{[A(k^A)^\beta]} \right)^{1/\alpha}. \tag{13.8}$$

Exercise 13B.1

Suppose the long-run production function were a function of three inputs, labour, capital and land, and suppose that both labour and capital were variable in the short run but land is only variable in the long run. How would we now calculate the short-run cost-minimizing labour and capital input levels conditional on some short-run fixed level of land?

When input prices are (w^A, r^A), the short-run *expense* associated with producing x is:

$$E_{k^A}(x, w^A, r^A) = w^A \ell_{k^A}(x) + r^A k^A \tag{13.9}$$

while the short run *cost* is:

$$C_{k^A}(x, w^A) = w^A \ell_{k^A}(x). \tag{13.10}$$

Exercise 13B.2

Can you use these expressions to justify the difference in the total cost and total expenditure curves in panel (a) of Graph 13.1 as well as the difference between AC and AE in panel (b) of that graph?

The long-run cost, however, is derived from solving the cost minimization problem:

$$\min_{\ell,k} w\ell + rk \quad \text{subject to } x = f(\ell, k) \tag{13.11}$$

with the underlying assumption that both capital and labour can be adjusted. This results in conditional input demands $\ell(x, w, r)$ and $k(x, w, r)$ and the long-run cost function $C(x, w, r) = w\ell(x, w, r) + rk(x, w, r)$. When input prices are (w^A, r^A) the long-run cost is, therefore:

$$C(x, w^A, r^A) = w^A \ell(x, w^A, r^A) + r^A k(x, w^A, r^A). \tag{13.12}$$

Saying that x^A is the output level for which k^A is the long-run optimal quantity of capital is the same as saying $k^A = k(x^A, w^A, r^A)$. If the firm starts with k^A in the short run and decides to produce x^A, it can set labour (which is variable in the short run) to its (long-run) cost-minimizing level, resulting in $\ell_{k^A}(x^A) = \ell(x^A, w^A, r^A)$ which implies that the firm's short-run expenses are equal to its long-run costs; that is, $E_{k^A}(x^A, w^A, r^A) = C(x^A, w^A, r^A)$. For any other output level, however, k^A is not generally the long-run optimal level, which implies that:

$$E_{k^A}(x, w^A, r^A) \geq C(x, w^A, r^A) \tag{13.13}$$

with the expression holding with equality only when $x = x^A$. This is what we showed graphically in Graph 13.2.

Exercise 13B.3

Can you derive from this the relationship between long-run average cost and short-run average expenses as illustrated graphically in Graph 13.2?

The short-run supply curve would be calculated by setting price equal to short-run marginal cost derived from $C_{k^A}(x, w^A)$ while the long-run supply curve would be calculated by setting price equal to long-run marginal cost derived from $C(x, w^A, r^A)$.

Exercise 13B.4

In the case of U-shaped average cost curves, how can you use the previous mathematical expressions to argue that the short-run shut-down price is lower than the long-run exit price?

13B.1.2 An Example Consider, for instance, our example of a decreasing returns to scale production process modelled by the production function $f(\ell, k) = 20\ell^{2/5}k^{2/5}$. In Chapter 12 (equations (12.44) and (12.45)), we derived the conditional input demands for this production function as:

$$\ell(w, r, x) = \left(\frac{r}{w}\right)^{1/2}\left(\frac{x}{20}\right)^{5/4} \quad \text{and} \quad k(w, r, x) = \left(\frac{w}{r}\right)^{1/2}\left(\frac{x}{20}\right)^{5/4}, \tag{13.14}$$

and the long-run cost function (in equation (12.46)) as:

$$C(w, r, x) = w\ell(w, r, x) + rk(w, r, x) = 2(wr)^{1/2}\left(\frac{x}{20}\right)^{5/4}. \tag{13.15}$$

If the firm produced 1280 units of output at input prices $(w, r) = (20, 10)$, for instance, these functions imply that the firm would choose the cost-minimizing input bundle $(\ell, k) = (128, 256)$ incurring a long-run cost of €5120.

Exercise 13B.5

Verify that these numbers are correct.

Suppose this is the current input bundle employed by a producer facing input prices $(w, r) = (20, 10)$, and the producer now considers producing a different level of output. In the long run, the cost of producing other levels of output at these input prices is given by the cost function in equation (13.15) with $w = 20$ and $r = 10$ substituted into the equation, which results in:

$$C(x, 20, 10) = 0.66874x^{5/4}. \tag{13.16}$$

In the short run, however, demand for labour is given by the inverse of the short-run production function $f^{kA=256} = [20(256)^{2/5}]\ell^{2/5}$, which is:

$$\ell_{k^A=256}(x) = \left(\frac{x}{20(256)^{2/5}}\right)^{5/2} = \frac{x^{5/2}}{20^{5/2}(256)}. \tag{13.17}$$

This gives a short-run expenditure function of:

$$E_{k^A=256}(x, 20, 10) = 20\ell_{k^A=256}(x) + (10)256 = \frac{x^{5/2}}{20^{3/2}256} + 2560. \tag{13.18}$$

Exercise 13B.6

What is the short-run cost as opposed to expenditure function?

The cost function in equation (13.16) and the short-run expense function in equation (13.18) are graphed in panel (a) of Graph 13.13, with panel (b) graphing the corresponding average cost and expense functions. As we concluded intuitively, these functions are related in that average short-run expenses are never lower than average long-run costs.

Graph 13.13 Long-Run Cost and Short-Run Expense Curves when $f(\ell, k) = 20\ell^{2/5}k^{2/5}$ and $k^A = 256$

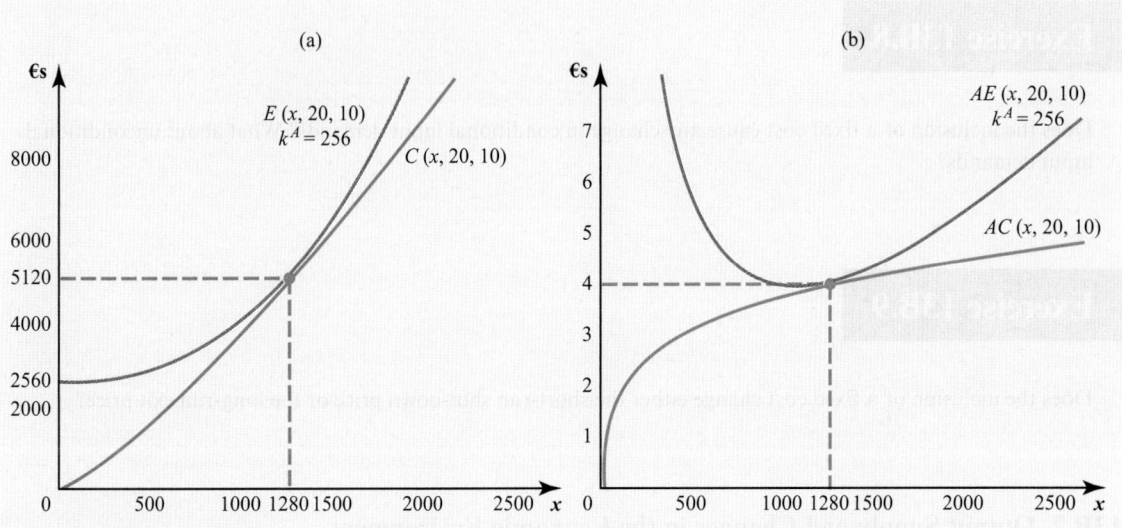

Exercise 13B.7

Verify that when $x = 1280$, the short-run expense is equal to the long-run cost.

13B.1.3 Adding a Long-Run Recurring Fixed Cost So far, we have included in our analysis the expenses and costs associated with inputs, with the expense on fixed inputs not showing up as an economic cost in the short run and showing up as a variable cost in the long run. In part A of the chapter, we introduced a fixed cost avoidable only by exiting, or a recurring fixed cost. We gave two examples of such a cost: the cost associated with recurring licence fees that do not vary with the level of output and the cost associated with an input, such as the management skills of the firm's CEO, that remains fixed even in the long run. These are fixed expenses in the short run and therefore do not affect short-run costs and thus short-run supply decisions, but they are real economic costs in the long run. We can include them in our usual cost function $C(x, w, r)$ by adding them as a fixed cost FC term. The new cost function becomes:

$$\overline{C}(x, w, r) = C(x, w, r) + FC = w\ell(x, w, r) + rk(x, w, r) + FC. \qquad \textbf{(13.19)}$$

The addition of such a fixed cost has no impact on the marginal cost function because, when we take the derivative of $\overline{C}(x, w, r)$ with respect to x, the FC term drops out. The average cost function, however, changes to:

$$AC(x, w, r) = \frac{C(x, w, r)}{x} + \frac{FC}{x} = AVC(x, w, r) + \frac{FC}{x}, \qquad \textbf{(13.20)}$$

where *AVC* denotes the average *variable* cost associated with the variable inputs of capital and labour. Since the term *FC/x* declines as *x* increases, the new average cost *AC* converges to the average variable cost as illustrated in Graph 13.5. This implies that the long-run supply curve is not shifted by the addition of such a fixed cost; it becomes 'shorter' because its starting point at the lowest point of *AC* moves up with an upward shift in the *AC* curve.

Exercise 13B.8

Does the inclusion of a fixed cost cause any change in conditional input demands? What about unconditional input demands?

Exercise 13B.9

Does the inclusion of a fixed cost change either the short-run shut-down price or the long-run exit price?

13B.2 Output Supply and Changes in the Economic Environment

We now turn more directly to the output supply function $x(p, w, r)$, asking why it slopes up and how short- and long-run supply curves relate to one another as in Graph 13.7. We investigate how changes in input prices shift these supply curves. Note that a supply curve is an inverse slice of the supply function $x(p, w, r)$ that holds the input prices (w, r) fixed and illustrates how output supply changes with output price p.

13B.2.1 Supply Curves Always Slope Up In the Appendix to Chapter 12, we developed two concepts relating to output supply that are taken as given in this chapter. First, part of Hotelling's Lemma in equation (12.52) states that:

$$\frac{\partial \pi(p, w, r)}{\partial p} = x(p, w, r), \tag{13.21}$$

and one of our conclusions from Graph 12.14 was that the profit function $\pi(p, w, r)$ in our duality picture is convex in p; that is:

$$\frac{\partial^2 \pi(p, w, r)}{\partial p^2} \geq 0. \tag{13.22}$$

Combining these two equations, we get:

$$\frac{\partial \pi(p, w, r)}{\partial p} = \frac{\partial^2 \pi(p, w, r)}{\partial p^2} \geq 0; \tag{13.23}$$

that is, the output supply curve is upward sloping in price. Since Hotelling's Lemma holds for production functions of any number of inputs, it also holds for short-run production functions in which some inputs are held fixed; thus *all output supply curves, both in the short and long run, slope upwards*. Notice furthermore that none of this requires assumptions like homotheticity, which we used in part A of the chapter for convenience.

13B.2.2 Short-Run Supply Curves Are Steeper Than Long-Run Supply Curves

Next, suppose that capital is fixed at quantity k^A in the short run as it was in Graph 13.7. While the long-run supply function is $x(p, w, r)$, the short-run supply function $x_{k^A}(p, w)$ is derived from the single-input production function that is given by the slice of the two-input production function which holds capital fixed at k^A. For instance, as discussed in the example of Section 13B.1.2, if the long-run production function is $f(\ell, k) = 20\ell^{2/5}k^{2/5}$, the short-run production function with capital fixed at k^A is $f_{k^A}(\ell) = [20(k^A)^{2/5}]\ell^{2/5}$ where the bracketed term is a constant parameter. While $x(p, w, r)$ is derived from the profit-maximization problem using the function $f(\ell, k)$, $x_{k^A}(p, w)$ is derived from the profit-maximization problem using $f_{k^A}(\ell)$. The short-run supply function will not be a function of r because the expense on the fixed amount of capital k^A is not an economic cost in the short run.

The short-run profit-maximization problem is:

$$\max_{x, \ell} px - w\ell \text{ such that } x = f_{k^A}(\ell) \tag{13.24}$$

which can be written as the unconstrained optimization problem:

$$\max_{\ell} pf_{k^A}(\ell) - w\ell. \tag{13.25}$$

Exercise 13B.10

Would including the fixed expense rk^A in the short-run profit-maximization problem so that the objective function becomes $px - wl - rk^A$, make any difference as the problem is solved?

Solving this as we solved the single-input profit-maximization problem in Chapter 11, we get the short-run labour demand function $\ell_{k^A}(p, w)$, and substituting this back into the short-run production function, we get the short-run output supply function $x_{k^A}(p, w)$. At this short-run optimum, the marginal revenue product of labour is equal to the wage, but the marginal revenue product of capital is not typically equal to the rental rate because we are unable to adjust capital away from its fixed quantity k^A in the short run. The short-run profit function is equal to $\pi_{k^A}(p, w) = px_{k^A}(p, w) - w\ell_{k^A}(p, w)$, which does not include a term rk^A for the expense on capital because this expense is a sunk cost in the short run.

If input and output prices are such that k^A happens to be equal to the long-run optimal quantity of capital, that is, we happen to have just the right quantity of capital that results in the marginal revenue product of capital being equal to the rental rate, then the short-run profit *minus* the expense on fixed capital is exactly equal to the long-run profit, which takes the cost of capital as a real economic cost; that is, $\pi(p, w, r) = \pi_{k^A}(p, w) - rk^A$. This emerges directly from the insight that the short-run total *expenditure* is exactly equal to the total *cost* in the long run when capital is at its long-run optimum, an insight we first developed in Graph 13.2 and developed mathematically in Section 13B.1.1. If k^A is not equal to the long-run optimal level of capital, the short-run profit *minus* rk^A must be less than the long-run profit, because in the long run we would adjust capital to the optimal quantity. This emerges directly from Graph 13.2 and from equation (13.13) where we showed that the short-run total *expenditure* exceeds the long-run total cost whenever capital is not at its long-run optimal level. We can therefore conclude that:

$$\pi(p, w, r) \geq \pi_{k^A}(p, w) - rk^A, \tag{13.26}$$

with this equation holding with equality only when k^A is in fact at its long-run optimal level.

Suppose next that the input prices are currently fixed at (w^A, r^A). We can define $g(p)$ as the difference between long-run profit and short-run profit adjusted for the expense on capital; that is:

$$g(p) = \pi(p, w^A, r^A) - \pi_{k^A}(p, w^A) + r^A k^A, \tag{13.27}$$

and we know from what we have concluded so far that $g(p)$ will be equal to zero when k^A is the long-run optimal level of capital for the output price p, but $g(p)$ is greater than zero when this is not the case. This function is sketched out in Graph 13.14 where p^A is the price at which k^A is the long-run optimal quantity of capital when input prices are held at (w^A, r^A).

Graph 13.14 Graph of $g(p) = \pi(p, w^A, r^A) - \pi_{k^A}(p, w^A) + r^A k^A$

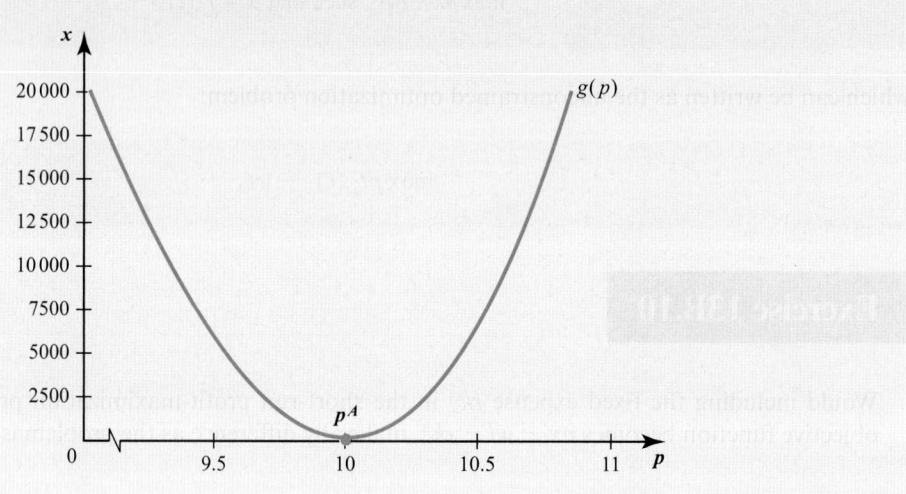

As is apparent from this graph, $g(p)$ attains its minimum at p^A, which implies that the second derivative of g is positive at p^A. Thus,

$$\frac{\partial^2 g(p^A)}{\partial p^2} = \frac{\partial^2 \pi(p^A, w^A, r^A)}{\partial p^2} - \frac{\partial^2 \pi_{k^A}(p^A, w^A)}{\partial p^2} \geq 0. \tag{13.28}$$

Hotelling's Lemma is valid for both short-run and long-run profit functions, so, when applying Hotelling's Lemma to both these profit functions in equation (13.28), we can rewrite the equation as:

$$\frac{\partial x(p^A, w^A, r^A)}{\partial p} - \frac{\partial x_{k^A}(p^A, w^A)}{\partial p} \geq 0, \tag{13.29}$$

or:

$$\frac{\partial x(p^A, w^A, r^A)}{\partial p} \geq \frac{\partial x_{k^A}(p^A, w^A)}{\partial p}. \tag{13.30}$$

This states what we showed graphically in Graph 13.7: the long-run supply response is larger than the short-run supply response from a change in output price. Note that while we showed this for homothetic production processes in our graphical development, the mathematical proof again required no such restrictions on production. Thus, the result holds generally for all production processes.

Exercise 13B.11

Equation (13.30) can also be read as 'the slope of the long-run output supply function is larger than the slope of the short-run output supply function with respect to price'. The long-run supply curve in Graph 13.7 appears to have a shallower and thus smaller slope than that of the short-run supply curve. How can you reconcile what the maths and the graphs seem to be telling us?

13B.2.3 An Example Continued In our example of the long-run production function $f(\ell, k) = 20\ell^{2/5}k^{2/5}$, for instance, we determined in Chapter 12 that the long-run output supply and input demand functions are:

$$x(p, w, r) = 81\,920\,\frac{p^4}{(wr)^2}, \quad \ell(p, w, r) = 32\,768\,\frac{p^5}{r^2w^3} \quad \text{and} \quad k(p, w, r) = 32\,768\,\frac{p^5}{r^2w} \tag{13.31}$$

Suppose the economic environment is given by $(p, \ell, r) = (5, 20, 10)$ for which we concluded in Chapter 12 that the long-run optimal production plan is $(x, \ell, k) = (1280, 128, 256)$. Now suppose capital is fixed at 256 in the short run. The short-run production function is given by $f_{k=256}(\ell) = 20(256^{2/5})\ell^{2/5} = 183.79\ell^{2/5}$. When this production function is used to define the short-run profit-maximization problem:

$$\max_{\ell} p(183.79\ell^{2/5}) - w\ell, \tag{13.32}$$

the resulting short-run output supply and input demand functions are:

$$x_{k=256}(p, w) = 3225\left(\frac{p}{w}\right)^{2/3} \quad \text{and} \quad \ell_{k=256}(p, w) = 1290\left(\frac{p}{w}\right)^{5/3}. \tag{13.33}$$

Exercise 13B.12

Verify that these are truly the short-run output supply and input demand functions by checking to see if the short-run functions give the same answers as the long-run functions when $(p, w, r) = (5, 20, 10)$.

Taking derivatives of the long-run and short-run output supply functions with respect to p, we get:

$$\frac{\partial x(p, w, r)}{\partial p} = 327\,680\,\frac{p^3}{(wr)^2} \quad \text{and} \quad \frac{\partial x_{k=256}(p, w)}{\partial p} = \frac{2150}{p^{1/3}w^{2/3}}. \tag{13.34}$$

Evaluated at the $(p, w, r) = (5, 20, 10)$, this gives a partial derivative of the long-run supply function of 1024 and a partial derivative of the short-run supply function of 170.67, indicating the predicted larger change in output in the long run than in the short run when we begin at a production plan that is long-run profit-maximizing and experience a change in output price. If p, for instance, were to rise from €5.00 to €7.50, the long-run profit-maximizing production plan given by equations (13.31) would go from $(x, \ell, k) = (1280, 128, 256)$ to $(x, \ell, k) = (6480, 972, 1944)$, but the new short-run production plan (holding k fixed at 256) would be given by equations (13.33) as $(x, \ell, k) = (1677, 252, 256)$, implying that production will rise from 1280 to 1677 output units in the short run and to 6480 in the long run when capital can be adjusted.

13B.2.4 Substitution Effects in Production In Graph 13.8, we illustrated that as input prices fall, the cost of production falls both because of the *direct effect* of current cost-minimizing input bundles becoming cheaper and because of the *substitution effect* leading to less intensive use of relatively more expensive inputs. We can illustrate this with our example of a production process represented by the production function $f(\ell, k) = 20\ell^{2/5}k^{2/5}$ for which we have calculated the various functions in our producer duality picture. In particular, we recall again the conditional input demands (from equation (13.14)):

$$\ell(w, r, x) = \left(\frac{r}{w}\right)^{1/2}\left(\frac{x}{20}\right)^{5/4} \quad \text{and} \quad k(w, r, x) = \left(\frac{w}{r}\right)^{1/2}\left(\frac{x}{20}\right)^{5/4}, \tag{13.35}$$

which explicitly incorporate the substitution effect, with the slice of the conditional labour demand curve in panel (d) of Graph 13.8 derived explicitly from a single isoquant. The corresponding cost function, previously given in equation (13.15), incorporates both the direct and the substitution effect from input price changes and is given by:

$$C(w, x) = 2(wr)^{1/2}\left(\frac{x}{20}\right)^{5/4}. \tag{13.36}$$

Suppose we begin with input prices of $(w, r) = (20, 10)$ and w falls to €10. The slice of the cost function at the original input prices is $C(x, 20, 10) = 0.66874x^{5/4}$ while the slice at the new input prices becomes $C(x, 10, 10) = 0.47287x^{5/4}$. Thus the (total) long-run cost curve shifts down by $0.19587x^{5/4}$. Taking the derivative of these functions with respect to x, we can also calculate the corresponding marginal cost curves $MC(x, 20, 10) = 0.83593x^{1/4}$ and $MC(x, 10, 10) = 0.59109x^{1/4}$, and dividing the total cost curves by x we can calculate the average cost curves $AC(x, 20, 10) = 0.66874x^{1/4}$ and $AC(x, 10, 10) = 0.47287x^{1/4}$. The shift in the total and marginal cost curves are illustrated in Graph 13.15 as a shift from dark brown to light blue curves.

Let's suppose we isolate the direct effect of an input price change by assuming that the producer does not substitute away from capital and into labour when w falls from €20 to €10. When input prices are $(20, 10)$, the conditional labour demand for different output levels x is given by $\ell(20, 10, x) = 0.01672x^{5/4}$ and $k(20, 10, x) = 0.03344x^{5/4}$. If the producer does not alter their behaviour as a result of a decline in the wage to €10, this would imply that total costs are given by $10\ell(20, 10, x) + 10k(20, 10, x) = 0.5016x^{5/4}$, which is higher than the total cost including the substitution effect ($C(x, 10, 10) = 0.47287x^{5/4}$) we calculated. The dark blue curves in Graph 13.15 represent the change in cost curves that is due to this direct effect, with the remainder due to the substitution effect.

Exercise 13B.13

Panels (a) and (b) of Graph 13.15 are analogous to panels (b) and (e) of Graph 13.8. Calculate the relevant curves and graph them for the case that is analogous to panels (c) and (f) of Graph 13.8 where, instead of wage falling from €20 to €10, the rental rate of capital rises from €10 to €20.

Graph 13.15 Change in Cost Curves as w Falls When $f(\ell, k) = 20\ell^{2/5}k^{2/5}$

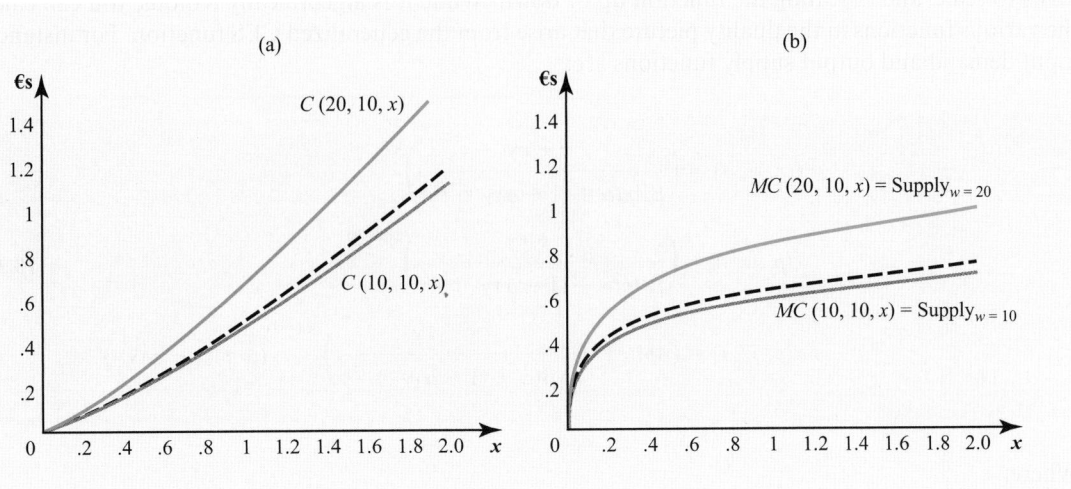

Table 13.2 Declining Substitution Effects With Declining Substitutability as w Falls from 10 to 5

Producing 5000 Units of Output When w Falls and $f(\ell, k) = 100(0.5\ell^{-\rho} + 0.5k^{-\rho})^{-0.5/\rho}$

ρ	$\ell(5, 10, 5000)$	$k(5, 10, 5000)$	Change in Cost	Direct Effect	Substitution Effect
−1.00	5000	0	−€25 000	−€12 500	−€12 500
−0.90	5388	5	−€23 004	−€12 500	−€10 504
−0.75	5384	336	−€19 715	−€12 500	−€7 215
−0.50	4444	1111	−€16 667	−€12 500	−€4 167
0.00	3536	1768	−€14 645	−€12 500	−€2 145
1.00	3018	2134	−€13 572	−€12 500	−€1 072
5.00	2617	2379	−€12 855	−€12 500	−€365
25.00	2538	2472	−€12 582	−€12 500	−€82
∞	2500	2500	−€12 500	−€12 500	€0

It should be clear by this point that the size of the substitution effect is captured in the downward slope of the conditional input demands. As the elasticity of substitution in production increases, the input demand curves become flatter causing the substitution effect to become relatively more important. Table 13.2 illustrates this with an example in which the production function is a generalized CES production function with decreasing returns to scale. The general form of this function is:

$$f(\ell, k) = A(\alpha\ell^{-\rho} + (1 - \alpha)k^{-\rho})^{-\beta/\rho}, \tag{13.37}$$

where, as in the case of CES utility functions, ρ can take on values between −1 and ∞ with the elasticity of substitution given by $1(1 + \rho)$. Thus, when $\rho = -1$, the isoquants are straight lines with perfect substitutability between labour and capital, while when $\rho = \infty$, labour and capital are perfect complements in production. The only difference between this family of CES production functions and the family of CES utility functions we defined in Chapter 5, is that we have included the additional β and A terms in the producer version, terms we will see used later in this chapter. For now, we note that β indicates the returns to scale of the function, with $\beta < 1$ indicating decreasing returns to scale, $\beta > 1$ indicating increasing returns to scale, and A scaling the function up or down. While it is algebraically tedious, you can calculate the various functions in the duality picture that arise from the generalized CES function. For instance, the input demand and output supply functions are:

$$\ell(p, w, r) = \left(\frac{w + r\gamma}{\beta A p (\alpha + (1 - \alpha)\gamma^{-\rho})^{-(\beta/\rho)}} \right)^{1/(\beta - 1)},$$

$$k(p, w, r) = \left(\frac{w + r\gamma}{\beta A p (\alpha + (1 - \alpha)\gamma^{-\rho})^{-(\beta/\rho)}} \right)^{1/(\beta - 1)}, \qquad \textbf{(10.38)}$$

$$x(p, w, r) = (Ap)^{-1/(\beta - 1)} \left(\frac{w + r\gamma}{\beta (\alpha + (1 - \alpha)\gamma^{-\rho})^{-(\beta/\rho)}} \right)^{\beta/(\beta - 1)} (\alpha + (1 - \alpha)\gamma^{-\rho})^{-(\beta/\rho)},$$

Where:

$$\gamma = \left(\frac{(1 - \alpha)w}{\alpha r} \right)^{1/(\rho + 1)}. \qquad \textbf{(13.39)}$$

Exercise 13B.14

If the generalized CES function were used as a utility function instead of the version where A and β are set to 1, would the underlying tastes represented by that function be changed?

The particular version of this production function selected for the derivation of results in Table 13.2 has the property that when w and r are set to €10 and p is set to €20, the profit-maximizing production plan is $(x, \ell, k) = (5000, 2500, 2500)$ regardless of what value ρ takes. Table 13.2 presents the conditional input demand for labour and capital when wage drops to €5 and production remains at 5000 units of output, and it reports the overall change in the cost of producing 5000 units of output as well as the portion of the overall drop in costs that is due to the direct effect and the portion that is due to the substitution effect. As the production process becomes one of declining substitutability between capital and labour as one goes down Table 13.2, the direct effect of the drop in w on cost equivalent to moving from the dark brown to the dark blue curves in our graphs, remains constant while the effect due to the substitution effect equivalent to moving from the dark blue to the light blue curves in our graphs declines dramatically.

Exercise 13B.15

Explain why the direct effect in Table 13.2 does not depend on the degree of substitutability between capital and labour in production.

13B.3 Input Demand and Changes in the Economic Environment

In Section A, we demonstrated that input demand curves slope down and that short-run input demand curves are steeper than long-run input demand curves. We also showed that the cross-price relationship between one input's price and demand for another input is ambiguous and depends on the relative substitutability of the inputs in production. Similarly, we showed that short-run and long-run labour responses to output price changes may differ with the relative substitutability of the inputs. In this section, we will demonstrate some of these results mathematically and illustrate others by using specific production functions.

13B.3.1 Input Demand Curves Slope Down In Graph 13.10, and implicitly in Graphs 13.9 and 13.11, we illustrated the impact of input price changes on input demand, and for both labour and capital found that the *own price input demand curves slope down*; that is, the quantity of labour demanded falls with increases in w and the quantity of capital demanded falls with increases in r. While our graphical illustrations were for the case of homothetic production processes, the result turns out to hold more generally, with no possibility of upward-sloping input demand curves unlike in consumer theory where a sufficiently large income effect – absent from producer theory – could lead to upward-sloping consumer demand curves. Like our proof that output supply curves slope down in Section 13B.2.1, this can be illustrated from Hotelling's Lemma and the fact that profit functions are convex. First, Hotelling's Lemma states that:

$$\frac{\partial \pi(p,\,w,\,r)}{\partial w} = -\ell(p,\,w,\,r) \quad \text{and} \quad \frac{\partial \pi(p,\,w,\,r)}{\partial r} = -k(p,\,w,\,r). \tag{13.40}$$

The convexity of the profit function implies that:

$$\frac{\partial^2 \pi(p,\,w,\,r)}{\partial w^2} \geq 0 \quad \text{and} \quad \frac{\partial^2 \pi(p,\,w,\,r)}{\partial r^2} \geq 0. \tag{13.41}$$

Combining these, we can conclude that:

$$\frac{\partial \ell(p,\,w,\,r)}{\partial w} = -\frac{\partial^2 \pi(p,\,w,\,r)}{\partial w^2} \leq 0 \quad \text{and} \quad \frac{\partial k(p,\,w,\,r)}{\partial r} = -\frac{\partial^2 \pi(p,\,w,\,r)}{\partial r^2} \leq 0; \tag{13.42}$$

that is, labour and capital demand curves slope down with respect to their own prices. Since the properties of profit functions and Hotelling's Lemma apply regardless of how many inputs a production function has when the optimization problem is solved, this implies that the result holds for both short-run and long-run input demand curves since short-run supply curves are derived from smaller-dimensional slices of larger-dimensional production frontiers.

Exercise 13B.16

Show that the short- and long-run input demand curves calculated for the production function $f(\ell, k) = 20\ell^{2/5}k^{2/5}$ in equations (13.33) and (13.31) are downward sloping.

13B.3.2 Labour Demand Curves Are Steeper in the Long Run Than in the Short Run Next, we illustrated in Graph 13.10 that short-run labour demand curves are steeper than long-run labour demand curves; or, as wage changes, the quantity of labour adjusts more in the long run than in the short run. This result is similar to the result in Section 13B.2.2 in that output supply is more responsive in the long run than in the short run. The steps are virtually identical to those in equations (13.26) to (13.30), except that derivatives are with respect to w rather than p. It will be a useful exercise for you to demonstrate that labour demand responses to wage changes are stronger in the long run than in the short run.

13B.3.3 Substitutability of ℓ and k and Slopes of Cross-Price Input Demand In some of the same graphs (particularly Graphs 13.10 and 13.11), we demonstrated that cross-price input demand relationships may be upward or downward sloping depending on the substitutability of capital and labour in production. We showed that demand for capital may increase or decrease with the wage rate, and demand for labour may increase or decrease with the rental rate of capital. We demonstrated that *a positive cross-price input demand relationship emerges when inputs are relatively substitutable, while a negative relationship emerges when they are relatively complementary.*

We will forego demonstrating this formally but will return to our example of a generalized CES production function $f(\ell, k) = A(\alpha\ell^{-\rho} + (1 - \alpha)k^{-\rho})^{-\beta/\rho}$ We will let $A = 100$, $\alpha = 0.5$ and $\beta = 0.5$ and Table 13.3 shows how input demands change as the substitutability of the inputs, captured by the parameter ρ, changes. As in the previous table, we begin in the economic environment $(p, w, r) = (20, 10, 10)$. For this particular configuration of economic and technological parameters, the profit-maximizing production plan is invariant to changes in ρ, with $(x, \ell, r) = (5000, 2500, 2500)$ optimal for all degrees of substitutability of inputs.

Beginning with the economic environment $(p, w, r) = (20, 10, 10)$, we ask how the behaviour of the producer changes in the short and long run as w increases from 10 to 11. Table 13.3 reports the new short- and long-run labour demand, the new long-run demand for capital, and the new short- and long-run output supply for this wage increase as the input substitutability varies, as captured by ρ, beginning with virtually perfect substitutes in the first row to virtually perfect complements in the final row. Notice that labour demand falls from the initial 2500, both in the short run and the long run, for all rows, and it always falls more in the long run than in the short run. This is consistent with our conclusions about labour demand thus far.

Table 13.3 Cross-Price Input Demands When w Increases From 10 to 11 and $\bar{k} = 2500$

	SR and LR Production Plans When w Increases and $f(\ell, k) = 100(0.5\ell^{-\rho} + 0.5k^{-\rho})^{-0.5/\rho}$					
ρ	$\ell(20, 10, 10)$	$\ell_{\bar{k}}(20, 11, 10)$	$\ell(20, 11, 10)$	$k(20, 11, 10)$	$X_{\bar{k}}(20, 11, 10)$	$x(20, 11, 10)$
−0.99	2500	1652	0.36	4965	4556	4965
−0.80	2500	1891	1767	2845	4681	4789
−0.60	2500	2021	2016	2558	4749	4775
−0.50	2500	2066	2066	2500	4773	4773
−0.25	2500	2147	2133	2422	4815	4769
0.00	2500	2201	2167	2384	4843	4767
0.50	2500	2271	2200	2345	4880	4766
1.00	2500	2314	2217	2326	4902	4765
5.00	2500	2425	2250	2287	4961	4763
50.00	2500	2490	2266	2270	4995	4762

Exercise 13B.17

Can you make sense of the fact that the demand for labour falls less both in the short and long run the more complementary labour and capital are in production?

Second, consider the column that illustrates demand for capital at the higher wage ($k(20, 11, 10)$) and recall that the optimal production plan before w increased contained 2500 units of capital. When ρ lies between -1 and -0.5 and the inputs are therefore relatively substitutable, demand for capital increases as wage increases, whereas when ρ rises above -0.5 and inputs become less substitutable, demand for capital falls when wage increases. This is precisely the result we derived intuitively in Graph 13.10 where the relationship between capital and wage was upward sloping in panel (g) when it was derived from relatively flat isoquants in panel (a), while the relationship was downward sloping in panel (i) when it was derived from isoquants with relatively little substitutability in panel (c). Panel (h) of Graph 13.10 gives the inbetween case where the quantity of capital demanded as the wage changes is the same as the original quantity at the initial wage. In this special case, the producer is therefore able to go immediately to the long-run profit-maximizing production plan because there is no need to change how much capital is used.

Exercise 13B.18

What value of ρ and what implied elasticity of substitution between capital and labour correspond to the inbetween case?

Notice one other feature of Table 13.3. While output always falls, both in the short and long run, from the 5000 units of output before the wage increased, it *increases* from the short to the long run when labour and capital are relatively substitutable and *decreases* from the short to the long run when labour and capital are relatively complementary. This, too, is consistent with Graph 13.10 where long-run output x^C falls on a higher isoquant than short-run output x^B in panel (a) but not in panel (c). The dividing line between these two cases is the case where capital input remains unchanged as w rises, with short-run and long-run production plans coinciding in panel (b).

13B.3.4 Demand for Labour as p Changes Finally, we used two extreme sets of isoquants in Graph 13.12 to argue that the relationship between the short- and long-run labour demand response to changes in output price also depends on the relative substitutability of labour and capital. The intuition behind this result is relatively straightforward. Whenever output price rises, we know from results on output supply curves that producers will want to produce more in the short run and even more in the long run. Suppose capital and labour are relatively substitutable and capital is relatively cheap compared to labour. Producers would rely primarily on capital in their production processes, but if capital is fixed in the short run, they might initially employ additional labour to increase production in response to an output price increase. In the long run, however, they would substitute away from this additional labour and into more capital. Thus, it may well be the case that labour demand increases in the short run with an increase in output price, but that some of that increased labour is laid off as the producer enters the long run. If capital and labour are relatively more complementary, short-run increases in labour may be supplemented with additional increases as capital is adjusted in the long run.

We illustrate this with the CES production function we previously used in Table 13.3 and with an initial economic environment $(p, w, r) = (20, 10, 10)$. Table 13.4 varies ρ in the first column, going from virtually perfect substitutes in the first row to virtually perfect complements in the last row. Table 13.4 differs from Table 13.3 in that now we are changing the output price from 20 to 25 rather than changing the wage. Note that since the ratio of wage to rental rate therefore does not change in Table 13.4, the long-run profit-maximizing input bundle will have the same ratio of labour to capital at any output price, but in the short run this ratio changes as we hold capital fixed.

Exercise 13B.19

Can you identify in Table 13.4 the relationship between the substitutability of capital and labour to the degree of short- versus long-run response in labour demand from an increase in output price? Is this consistent with what emerges in Graph 13.12?

Table 13.4 Substitutability and Responses to a Change in p (from 20 to 25) When $\bar{k} = 2500$

	SR and LR Production Plans When p Increases and $f(\ell, k) = 100(0.5\ell^{-\rho} + 0.5k^{-\rho})^{-0.5/\rho}$					
ρ	$\ell(20, 10, 10)$	$\ell_{\bar{k}}(25, 10, 10)$	$\ell(25, 10, 10)$	$k(25, 10, 10)$	$X_{\bar{k}}(25, 10, 10)$	$x(25, 10, 10)$
-0.99	2500	5270	3906	3906	6230	6250
-0.80	2500	4584	3906	3906	5925	6250
-0.60	2500	4088	3906	3906	5707	6250
-0.50	2500	3906	3906	3906	5625	6250
-0.25	2500	3579	3906	3906	5480	6250
0.00	2500	3366	3906	3906	5386	6250
0.50	2500	3116	3906	3906	5275	6250
1.00	2500	2975	3906	3906	5212	6250
5.00	2500	2666	3906	3906	5074	6250
50.00	2500	2520	3906	3906	5009	6250

End-of-Chapter Exercises

13.1† The following problem explores the relationship between maximizing profit in the short and long run when capital is fixed in the short run.

   A. Assume a homothetic production technology and output price p and input prices (w, r).

   a. On a graph with labour ℓ on the horizontal and capital k on the vertical axis, draw an isoquant and label a point on that isoquant as $(\bar{\ell}, \bar{k})$.

   b. Suppose that the point in your graph represents a profit-maximizing production plan. What has to be true at this point?

   c. In your graph, illustrate the slice along which the firm must operate in the short run.

   d. Suppose that the production technology has decreasing returns to scale throughout. If p falls, illustrate all the possible points in your graph where the new profit-maximizing production plan might lie in the long run? What about the short run?

   e. What condition that is satisfied in the long run will typically not be satisfied in the short run?

   f. What qualification would you have to make to your answer in (d) if the production process had initially increasing but eventually decreasing returns to scale?

   B. Consider the Cobb–Douglas production function $x = f(\ell, k) = A\ell^{-\alpha}k^{-\beta}$.

   ** For input prices (w, r) and output price p, calculate the long-run input demand and output supply functions assuming $0 < \alpha, \beta \leq 1$ and $\alpha + \beta < 1$.

   a. How would your answer change if $\alpha + \beta \geq 1$?

   b. Suppose that capital is fixed at $\bar{k}$ in the short run. Calculate the short-run input demand and output supply functions.

   c. What has to be true about α and β for these short-run functions to be correct?

   d. Suppose $\bar{k} = k(w, r, p)$ (where $k(w, r, p)$ is the long-run capital demand function you calculated in part (a)). What is the optimal short-run labour demand and output supply in that case?

   e. How do your answers compare to the long-run labour demand function $\ell(w, r, p)$ and the long-run supply function $x(w, r, p)$ calculated in part (a)? Can you make intuitive sense of this?

13.2 The following problem explores issues similar to those in exercise 13.1, but instead of thinking directly about profit maximization, we will think about cost minimization on the way to profit maximization.

   A. Assume a homothetic production technology and input prices (w, r).

a. On a graph with labour ℓ on the horizontal and capital k on the vertical axis, illustrate a ray along which all cost-minimizing production plans might lie for a given set of input prices. Does your answer depend on whether the production technology has increasing or decreasing returns to scale or some combination of these?

b. Illustrate in your graph an isoquant corresponding to some output level $\bar{x}$. What has to be true at the intersection of the ray and the isoquant?

c. Show what happens to the ray of cost-minimizing input bundles if w increases to w'. Illustrate how you would derive the conditional labour demand curve for producing $\bar{x}$.

d. From this point forward, assume that the production technology has decreasing returns to scale. Illustrate how you would derive the firm's long-run cost curve for the original input prices.

e. What happens to the cost curve when w increases to w'?

f. Output is initially at the intersection of the original isoquant corresponding to $\bar{x}$. and the original ray. If w remained unchanged, where would the short-run *expenditure* curve fall on your graph with the long-run cost curve?

g. Translate your cost/expenditure curve graph to a graph with the average long-run cost and average short-run expenditure curves.

h. How does the average long-run cost curve change when w increases to w'? If you also graphed a cost curve that removed the substitution effect, where would it generally lie relative to the original and final cost curve? What would its precise location depend on?

i. Suppose that instead of wage increasing, the rental rate on capital r fell to r'. What happens to the conditional labour demand curve that you graphed in part (c)?

j. Repeat (h) for the change in the rental rate.

B. Suppose that the production process is defined by the Cobb–Douglas production function $x = f(\ell, k) = A\ell^\alpha k^\beta$.

a. **For input prices (w, r), calculate the long-run conditional input demand functions.

b. Do you need to assume $0 < \alpha, \beta \leq 1$ and $\alpha + \beta < 1$ in order for these to be valid?

c. Derive the long-run total, marginal and average cost functions.

d. Suppose output price is p. Use your answer to derive the firm's long-run profit-maximizing output supply function. Do you need to assume $0 < \alpha, \beta \leq 1$ and $\alpha + \beta < 1$ for this to be valid? If you have done exercise 13.1, check to make sure your answer agrees with what you concluded in part (a) of that exercise. From your answer, derive the firm's profit-maximizing long-run labour and capital demand functions. Check your answers with those you derived through direct profit maximization in exercise 13.1.

e. Now suppose capital is fixed in the short run at $\bar{k}$. Derive the short-run conditional input demand for labour.

f. Derive the short-run total cost function as well as the short-run marginal and average cost functions.

g. Derive the short-run supply curve.

h. *True or False*: As long as the production function has decreasing returns the scale, the short-run average *expenditure* curve will be U-shaped even though the short-run average cost curve is not.

i. What is the shape of the long-run average cost curve? Can the Cobb–Douglas production function yield U-shaped long-run average cost curves?

13.3† In this exercise, we add a long-run fixed cost to the analysis.

A. Suppose the production process for a firm is homothetic and has decreasing returns to scale.

a. On a graph with labour ℓ on the horizontal and capital k on the vertical axis, draw an isoquant corresponding to output level $\bar{x}$. For some wage rate w and rental rate r, indicate the cost-minimizing input bundle for producing $\bar{x}$.

b. Indicate in your graph the slice of the production frontier along which all cost-minimizing input bundles lie for this wage and rental rate.

c. In two separate graphs, draw the total cost curve and the average cost curve with the marginal cost curve.

d. Suppose that in addition to paying for labour and capital, the firm has to pay a recurring fixed cost such as a licence fee. What changes in your graphs?

    e. What is the firm's exit price in the absence of fixed costs? What happens to that exit price when a fixed cost is added?

    f. Does the firm's supply curve shift as a fixed cost is added?

    g. Suppose that the cost-minimizing input bundle for producing $\bar{x}$ graphed in part (a) is also the profit-maximizing production plan before a fixed cost is considered. Will it still be the profit-maximizing production plan after the fixed cost is included in our analysis?

B. As in exercises 13.1 and 13.2, suppose the production process is again characterized by the production function $x = f(\ell, k) = A\ell^{\alpha}k^{\beta}$ with $0 < \alpha, \beta \leq 1$ and $\alpha + \beta < 1$.

    a. If you have not already done so in a previous exercise, derive the long-run cost function for this firm.

    b. Now suppose that in addition to the cost associated with inputs, the firm has to pay a recurring fixed cost of FC. Write down the cost minimization problem that includes this FC. Will the conditional input demand functions change as a result of the FC being included?

    c. Write down the new cost function and derive the marginal and average cost functions from it.

    d. What is the shape of the average cost curve? How does its lowest point change with changes in the FC?

    e. Does the addition of an FC term change the long-run marginal cost curve? Does it change the long-run supply curve?

    f. How would you write out the profit-maximization problem for this firm including fixed costs? If you were to solve this problem, what role would the FC term play?

    g. Considering not just the maths but also the underlying economics, does the addition of the FC have any implications for the input demand and output supply functions?

13.4 We will often assume that a firm's long-run average cost curve is U-shaped. This shape may arise for two different reasons that we explore in this exercise.

A. Assume that the production technology uses labour ℓ and capital k as inputs, and assume throughout this problem that the firm is currently long-run profit-maximizing and employing a production plan that is placing it at the lowest point of its long-run AC curve.

    a. Suppose first that the technology has decreasing returns to scale but that in order to begin producing each year, the firm has to pay a fixed licence fee F. Explain why this causes the long-run AC curve to be U-shaped.

    b. Draw a graph with the U-shaped AC curve from the production process described in part (a). Add to this the short-run MC and AC curves. Is the short-run AC curve also U-shaped?

    c. Suppose that there are no fixed costs in the long run. Instead, the production process is such that the marginal product of each input was initially increasing but eventually decreasing, and the production process as a whole was initially increasing but eventually decreasing returns to scale. A picture of such a production process was given in Graph 12.16 of the previous chapter. Explain why the long-run AC curve is U-shaped in this case.

    d. Draw another graph with the U-shaped AC curve. Add the short-run MC and AC curves. Are they also U-shaped?

    e. *Is it possible for short-run AC curves to *not* be U-shaped if the production process has initially increasing but eventually decreasing returns to scale?

B. Suppose first that the production process is Cobb–Douglas, characterized by the production function $x = f(\ell, k) = A\ell^{\alpha}k^{\beta}$ with $\alpha, \beta > 0$ and $\alpha + \beta < 1$.

    a. In the absence of fixed costs, you should have derived in exercise 13.2 that the long-run cost function for this technology is given by:

$$C(w, r, x) = (\alpha + \beta)\left(\frac{w^{\alpha}r^{\beta}x}{A\alpha^{\alpha}\beta^{\beta}}\right)^{1/(\alpha+\beta)}. \tag{13.43}$$

If the firm has long-run fixed costs F, what is its long-run average cost function? Is the average cost curve U-shaped?

b. What is the short-run cost curve for a fixed level of capital $\bar{k}$? Is the short-run average cost curve U-shaped?

c. Now suppose that the production function is still $f(\ell, k) = A\ell^\alpha k^\beta$ but now $\alpha + \beta < 1$. Are long-run average and marginal cost curves upward or downward sloping? Are short-run average cost curves upward or downward sloping? What does your answer depend on?

d. *Next, suppose that the production technology was given by the equation:

$$x = f(\ell, k) = \frac{\alpha}{1 + e^{-(\ell-\beta)} + e^{-(k-\gamma)}}, \qquad (13.44)$$

where e is the base of the natural logarithm. If capital is fixed at $\bar{k}$, what is the short-run production function and what is the short-run cost function?

e. **What is the short-run marginal cost function?

f. The long-run MC function is $MC(w, r, x) = \alpha(w + r)/(x(\alpha - x))$ and the MC curve and thus the long-run AC curve is U-shaped for the parameters $\alpha = 100, \beta = 5 = \gamma$ when $w = r = 20$. Now suppose capital is fixed at $\bar{k} = 8$. Graph the short-run MC curve and use the information to conclude whether the short-run AC curve is also U-shaped.

g. What characteristic of this production function is responsible for your answer in part (f)?

13.5*† **Business Application:** *Switching Technologies.* Suppose that a firm has two different homothetic, decreasing returns to scale technologies it could use, but one of these is patented and requires recurring licence payments F to the owner of the patent. In this exercise, assume that all inputs, including the choice of which technology is used, are viewed from a long-run perspective.

A. Suppose further that both technologies take capital k and labour ℓ as inputs but that the patented technology is more capital intensive.

a. Draw two isoquants, one from the technology representing the less capital intensive and one representing the more capital intensive technology. Illustrate the slice of each map that a firm will choose to operate on assuming the wage w and rental rate r are the same in each case.

b. Suppose that the patented technology is sufficiently advanced such that, for any set of input prices, there always exists an output level $\bar{x}$ at which it is long-run cost effective to switch to this technology. On a graph with output x on the horizontal and euros on the vertical, illustrate two cost curves corresponding to the two technologies and locate $\bar{x}$. Illustrate the cost curve that takes into account that a firm will switch to the patented technology at $\bar{x}$.

c. What happens to $\bar{x}$ if the licence cost F for using the patented technology increases? Is it possible to tell what happens if the capital rental rate r increases?

d. At $\bar{x}$, which technology must have a higher marginal cost of production? On a separate graph, illustrate the marginal cost curves for the two technologies.

e. At $\bar{x}$, the firm is cost-indifferent between using the two technologies. Recognizing that the marginal cost curves capture all costs that are not fixed and that total costs excluding fixed costs can be represented as areas under marginal cost curves, can you identify an area in your graph that represents the recurring fixed licence fee F?

f. Suppose output price p is such that it is profit-maximizing *under the non-patented technology* to produce $\bar{x}$. Denote this as $\bar{p}$. Can you use marginal cost curves to illustrate whether you would produce more or less if you switched to the patented technology?

g. Would profit be higher if you used the patented or non-patented technology when output price is $\bar{p}$? *Hint*: Identify the total revenues if the firm produces at $\bar{p}$ under each of the technologies. Identify the total cost of using the non-patented technology as an area under the appropriate marginal cost curve and compare it to the total costs of using the patented technology as an area under the other marginal cost curve and add to it the fixed fee F.

h. *True or False*: Although the total cost of production is the same under both technologies at output level $\bar{x}$, a profit-maximizing firm will choose the patented technology if price is such that $\bar{x}$ is profit-maximizing under the non-patented technology.

i. Illustrate the firm's supply curve. *Hint*: The supply curve is not continuous, and the discontinuity occurs at a price below $\bar{p}$.

B. Suppose that the two technologies available can be represented by the production functions $f(\ell, k) = 19.125\ell^{0.4}k^{0.4}$ and $g(\ell, k) = 30\ell^{0.2}k^{0.6}$, but technology g carries with it a recurring fee of F.

a. In exercise 13.2, if you derived the general form for the two-input Cobb–Douglas conditional input demands and cost function for the Cobb–Douglas production function $x = f(\ell, k) = A\ell^\alpha k^\beta$, you should have derived the conditional input demands:

$$\ell(w, r, x) = \left(\frac{\alpha r}{\beta w}\right)^{\beta/(\alpha + \beta)}\left(\frac{x}{A}\right)^{1/(\alpha + \beta)} \quad \text{and} \quad k(w, r, x) = \left(\frac{\beta w}{\alpha r}\right)^{\alpha/(\alpha + \beta)}\left(\frac{x}{A}\right)^{1/(\alpha + \beta)}. \quad (13.45)$$

The cost function was previously provided in equation (13.43). Use this to determine the ratio of capital to labour as a function of w and r used under these two technologies. Which technology is more capital intensive?

b. Determine the cost functions for the two technologies and be sure to include F where appropriate.

c. Determine the output level $\bar{x}$ as a function of w, r and F at which it becomes cost effective to switch from the technology f to the technology g. If F increases, is it possible to tell whether $\bar{x}$ increases or decreases? What if r increases?

d. Suppose $w = 20$ and $r = 10$. Determine the price $\bar{p}$ as a function of F at which a firm using technology f would produce $\bar{x}$.

e. How much would the firm produce with technology g if it faces $\bar{p}$? Can you tell whether, regardless of the size of F, this is larger or smaller than $\bar{x}$ which is the profit-maximizing quantity when the firm uses technology f and faces $\bar{p}$?

f. The long-run profit function for a Cobb–Douglas production function $f(\ell, k) = A\ell^\alpha k^\beta$ is:

$$\pi(w, r, p) = (1 - \alpha - \beta)\left(\frac{Ap\alpha^\alpha\beta^\beta}{w^\alpha r^\beta}\right)^{1/(1 - \alpha - \beta)}. \quad (13.46)$$

Can you use this to determine, as a function of p, w and r, the highest level of F at which a profit-maximizing firm will switch from f to g? Call this $\overline{F}(w, r, p)$.

g. From your answer to (f), determine as a function of w, r and F the price p^* at which a profit-maximizing firm will switch from technology f to technology g.

h. Suppose again that $w = 20$, $r = 10$. What is p^* as a function of F? Compare this to $\bar{p}$ you calculated in part (d) and interpret your answer in light of what you did in A(i).

i. Suppose in addition to the values for parameters specified so far that $F = 1000$. What are $\bar{p}$ and p^*? At the price at which the profit-maximizing firm is indifferent between using technology f and technology g, how much does it produce when it uses f and how much does it produce when it uses g? Recall from your previous work in exercise 13.1 that the supply function for a Cobb–Douglas production process $f(\ell, k) = A\ell^\alpha k^\beta$ is:

$$x(w, r, p) = \left(\frac{Ap^{(\alpha+\beta)}\alpha^\alpha\beta^\beta}{w^\alpha r^\beta}\right)^{1/(1-\alpha-\beta)}.$$

j. Continuing with the values we have been using including $F = 1000$, can you use your answer to (a) to determine how much labour and capital the firm employs at p^* under the two technologies? How else could you have calculated this?

k. Use what you have calculated in (i) and (j) to verify that profit is indeed the same for a firm whether it uses the f or the g technology when price is p^* and the rest of the parameters of the problem are as we have specified them in (i) and (j). *Note*: If you rounded some of your previous numbers, you will not get exactly the same profit in both cases, but if the difference is small, it is almost certainly just a rounding error.

13.6 Policy and Business Application: *Minimum Wage Labour Subsidy.* Suppose you run your business by using a homothetic, decreasing returns to scale production process that requires minimum wage labour ℓ and capital k where the minimum wage is w and the rental rate on capital is r.

A. The government, concerned over the lack of minimum wage jobs, agrees to subsidize your employment of minimum wage workers, effectively reducing the wage you have to pay to $(1 - s)$, where $0 < s < 1$. Suppose your long-run profit-maximizing production plan before the subsidy was (ℓ^*, k^*, x^*).

  a. Begin with an isoquant graph that contains the isoquant corresponding to x^* and indicate on it the cost-minimizing input bundle as A. What region in the graph encompasses all possible production plans that could potentially be long-run profit-maximizing when the effective wage falls to $(1 - s)w$?

  b. On your graph, illustrate the slice of the production frontier to which you are constrained in the short run when capital is fixed. Choose a plausible point on that slice as your new short-run profit-maximizing production plan B. What has to be true at this point?

  c. Can you conclude anything about how the marginal product of capital changes as you switch to its new short-run profit-maximizing production plan?

  d. Will you employ more workers in the long run than in the short run?

  e. Will you employ more capital in the long run than in the short run?

  f. Once you have located B in part (b), can you now use this to narrow down the region that you initially indicated in part (a), where the long-run profit-maximizing production plan must lie?

B. Suppose, as in previous exercises, that your production function is $f(\ell, k) = 30\ell^{0.2}k^{0.6}$.

  a. Suppose that $w = 10 = r$ and $p = 5$. What is your profit-maximizing production plan before the labour subsidy?

  b. What is the short-run profit-maximizing plan after a subsidy of $s = 0.5$ is implemented?

  c. What is the new long-run profit-maximizing plan once capital can be adjusted?

  d. For any Cobb–Douglas function $f(\ell, k) = A\ell^{\beta\alpha}k^{\beta(1-\alpha)}$, the CES production function $g(\ell, k) = A(\alpha\ell^{-\rho} + (1-\alpha)k^{-\rho})^{-\beta\rho}$ converges to f as ρ approaches 0. What values of A, α and β will do this for the production function $x = 30\ell^{0.2}k^{0.6}$?

  e. **Using a spreadsheet to programme the output supply and input demand equations for a CES production function given in equation (13.38), verify that your long-run production plans mirror those you calculated for the Cobb–Douglas function when ρ approaches 0, and α and β are set appropriately.

  f. **Finally, derive the first-order condition for the short-run profit-maximization problem with fixed capital using the CES production function. Using your spreadsheet, check to see whether those first-order conditions hold when you plug in the short-run profit-maximizing quantity of labour that you calculated in (b).

* conceptually challenging
** computationally challenging
† solutions in Study Guide

PART III

Competitive Markets and the Invisible Hand

In Part 1, we derived demand and supply curves and functions for goods and labour and capital from an underlying model of individual choice aimed at maximizing happiness. In Part 2, we derived supply and demand curves and functions for goods, and labour and capital from an underlying model of firm choice aimed at maximizing profit. We are now ready to combine them to analyze an entire market. This will allow us to talk about the concept of *equilibrium* for the first time, and it will enable us to analyze *how prices form* rather than taking prices as given as we have thus far. It will allow us to illustrate more fully how, under certain conditions, competitive markets lead to a *spontaneous order* in which millions of individual choices combine to form prices that guide behaviour in such a way as to allocate resources efficiently. We will refer to this result as the *first welfare theorem*.

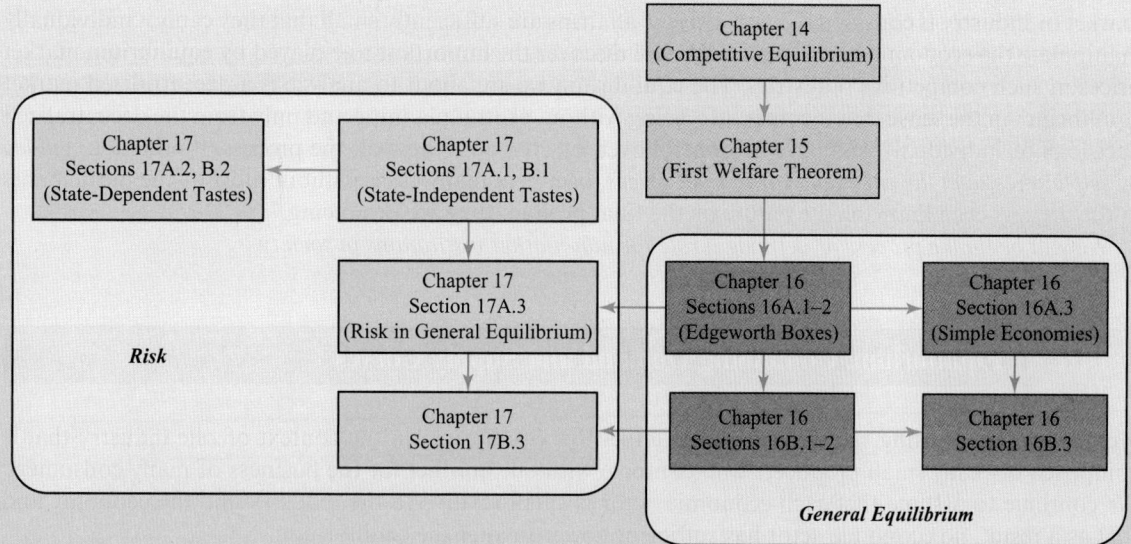

Chapter 14

Competitive Market Equilibrium

We have spent the bulk of our time up to now developing relationships between economic variables and the behaviour of actors such as consumers, workers and producers. We began by developing models, simplified versions of reality, in which we assumed that economic actors do the best they can given their economic circumstances. This process of optimizing results in the relationships between prices and behaviour, such as demand curves, supply curves and cross-price demand and supply curves. It is these relationships we can now use to take the economic analysis to its final step: describing how the economic environment that actors take as given arises within the model as many individuals optimize. This economic environment is called a *competitive equilibrium*.

In this and the next chapter, we will focus on a market or an industry, terms we will use interchangeably. Firms are considered to operate in the same market or industry if they produce the same goods, and the market or industry is considered competitive if all firms are sufficiently small that they cannot individually manipulate the economic environment. We will discover the important role played by equilibrium market prices in such competitive industries. The equilibrium we are about to analyze is a decentralized market equilibrium in the sense that it comes into being without central planning and only from the decentralized decisions of individuals who have no control over, or even awareness of, the process. Production, *guided by self-interest and the emergence of market prices*, occurs in many cases without most of the participants in the process even knowing the nature of the final product they are producing.

We will *begin the process of defining a role for non-market institutions in society*.

14A   Equilibrium: Combining Demand and Supply Curves

We begin by illustrating the concept of a competitive equilibrium in the context of one industry that is composed of many small producers who compete with one another for the business of many consumers. We continue to assume that each economic actor is small relative to the industry and the economy and that as a result, no economic actor has sufficient power to alter the equilibrium.

14A.1 Equilibrium in the Short Run

An equilibrium in an industry is defined by the intersection of market or industry demand and supply curves. Deriving these curves for a particular industry *in the short run* involves adding up the individual demand and supply curves that are generated from individual optimization problems. For instance, in panel (a) of Graph 14.1, we plot two individual demand curves D^1 and D^2 and a third *market demand curve* D^M

that would result if these were the only two consumers in the market. At a price above €90, individual 2 demands none of the output x_1, which implies that individual 1 is the only consumer in the market, and this individual's demand curve therefore represents the market demand curve for $p > 90$. For prices below €90, however, both consumers demand some of the output. For instance, at a price of €80, consumer 1 demands 20 units of x_1 while consumer 2 demands 10 units, for an overall market demand of 30 units. A similar process for adding up individual supply curves to get a *short-run market supply curve* S^M is illustrated in panel (b) of Graph 14.1, with only firm 2 supplying output for prices below €40 and both firms supplying output for prices above €40. The process of adding up more than two demand or supply curves is an extension of this.

Graph 14.1 Adding Up Demand and Supply Curves

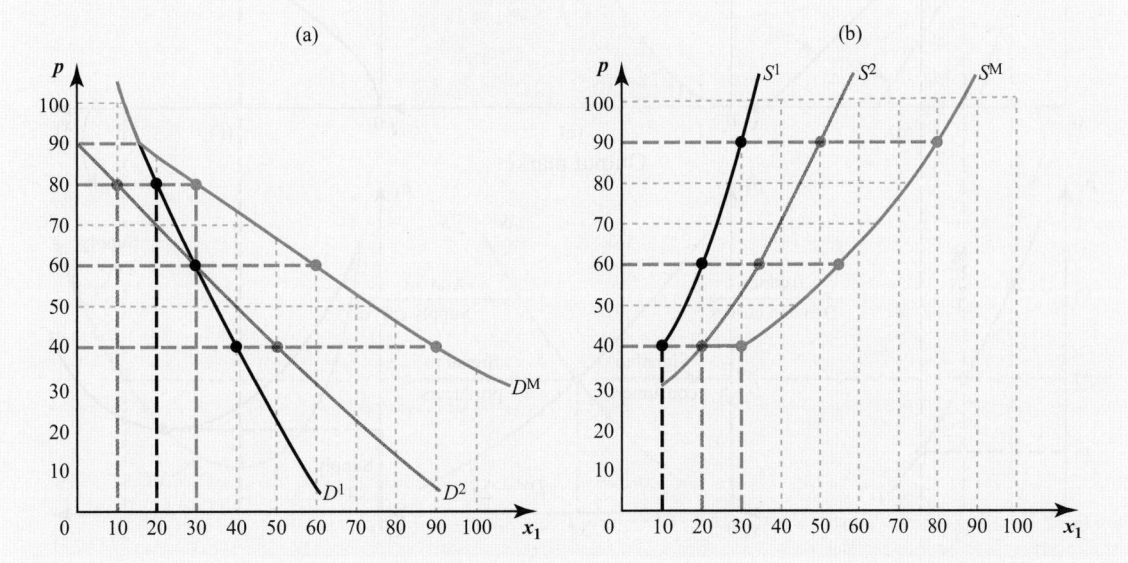

Market supply is derived somewhat differently in the long run; adding up supply curves is the correct way of finding market supply curves only in the short run. Hence we investigate the short-run equilibrium.

14A.1.1 Short-Run Equilibrium in the Goods Market Market or industry demand and supply curves are powerful tools that help us predict the terms under which consumers and producers will interact in a competitive world, and how these terms will change as underlying institutional and technological constraints change.

Consider the sequence of graphs in Graph 14.2. In panel (a), we begin with the basic building blocks of the consumer model: indifference curves representing tastes and budgets representing different economic environments as the price for good x_1 changes. From the budgets and indifference curves in (a), we can derive the consumer's demand curve D^i for x_1 in panel (d), as we did in Chapter 9. If we were to conduct the same analysis for all consumers in the market, we would be deriving many different demand curves, which we could add up to arrive at the market demand curve D^M in panel (e) with ΣD^i in the graph read as the sum of all individual D^i demand curves.

On the producer side, we are similarly starting with the fundamentals of the producer model in panel (b): the technological constraint represented by the short-run producer choice set. Panel (c) derives the total cost curve assuming a particular input price from the short-run production frontier as we did in Chapter 11, allowing us to derive the average and marginal cost curves for a single firm in panel (f). The portion of the marginal cost curve above AC is a profit-maximizing firm's supply short-run curve S^i. We could repeat this analysis for each of the firms in the industry that produces output x_1, thus arriving at many individual supply curves that we can add up to derive the market supply curve S^M in panel (e).

Graph 14.2 Equilibrium and What's Behind It

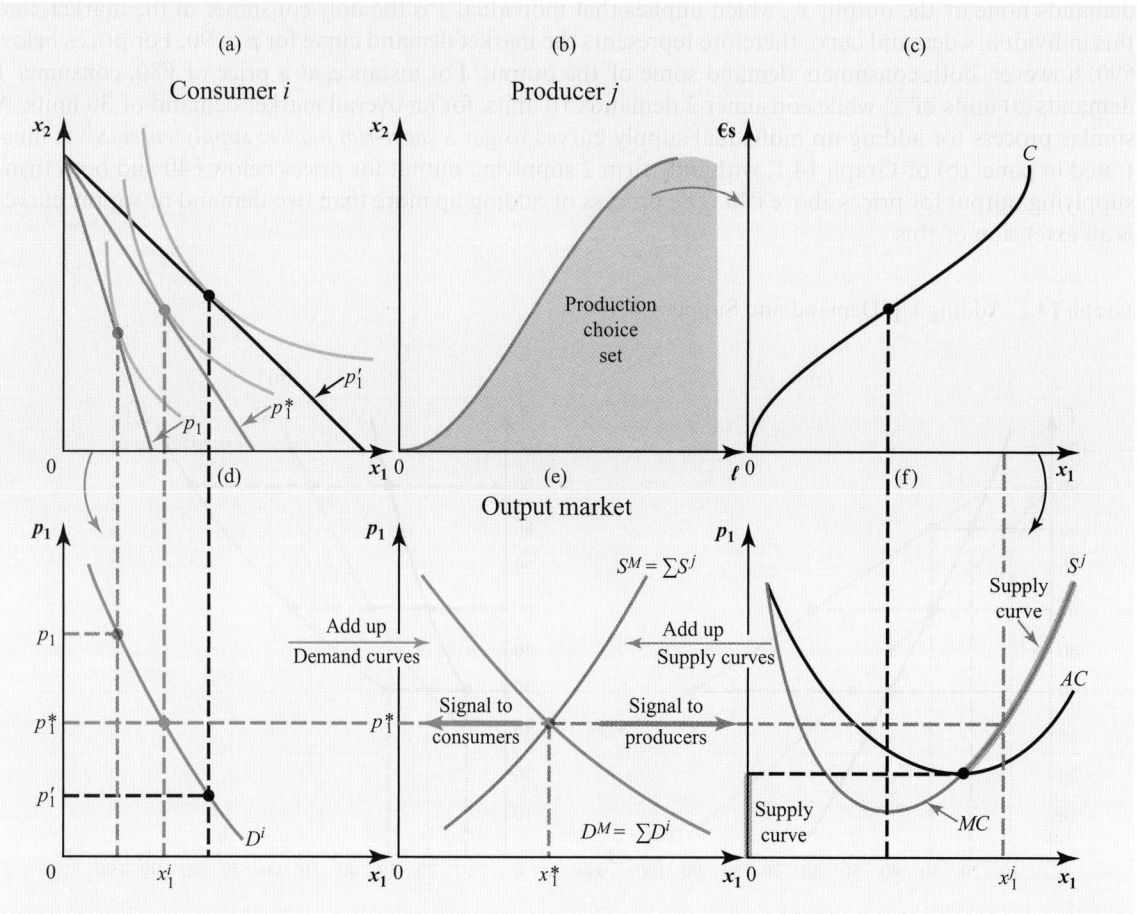

Focusing on panel (e), we have a simple demand and supply picture of the market for good x_1, with the intersection of the two curves representing the market equilibrium that results in equilibrium price p^* and equilibrium output quantity X_1^*. If price were to rise above this equilibrium, more of x_1 would be supplied than demanded, which would cause producers who are seeing their stocks build up to lower prices to sell their goods and make themselves better off. Thus, price would drop. Similarly, if price were ever below p^*, consumers would demand more than producers are willing to supply, giving an incentive to each producer to raise price.

Without any particular individual intentionally directing the formation of p^*, the natural tendency is in place for p^* to emerge as individual consumers and producers simply try to do the best for themselves. Once p^* is formed, it provides a signal to consumers and producers, coordinating their actions in a decentralized way that is efficient under some circumstances. In the case graphed here, the signal p^* tells the consumer we modelled to consume x_1^i and the producer we modelled to produce x_1^j, with the market as a whole producing X_1^*.

14A.1.2 Short-Run Equilibrium in Input Markets In an analogous way, a decentralized market equilibrium also emerges in the labour market when different producers in many different industries compete for workers. Graph 14.3 illustrates this, with producers facing short-run producer choice sets in panel (a) that result in marginal revenue product curves in panel (d), and with a portion of this marginal revenue product curve composing the short-run labour demand curve for each producer. Workers, on the other hand, begin with preferences over leisure and consumption in panel (b), with different wages resulting in different optimal leisure choices. Panel (c) illustrates a typical leisure demand curve, with panel (f) representing the implied labour supply curve for this consumer. Adding up the individual labour demand curves of firms and labour supply curves of workers, we arrive at a market demand and supply curve for the particular type of labour modelled here, with the intersection of the two resulting in an *equilibrium wage rate w** that sends a signal back to workers and producers. This signal causes the producer we modelled to hire ℓ^j worker hours and the worker we modelled to sell ℓ^i labour hours, with the market as a whole trading L^* labour hours across the many industries that hire the types of workers modelled in the series of graphs.

Graph 14.3 Labour Market Equilibrium

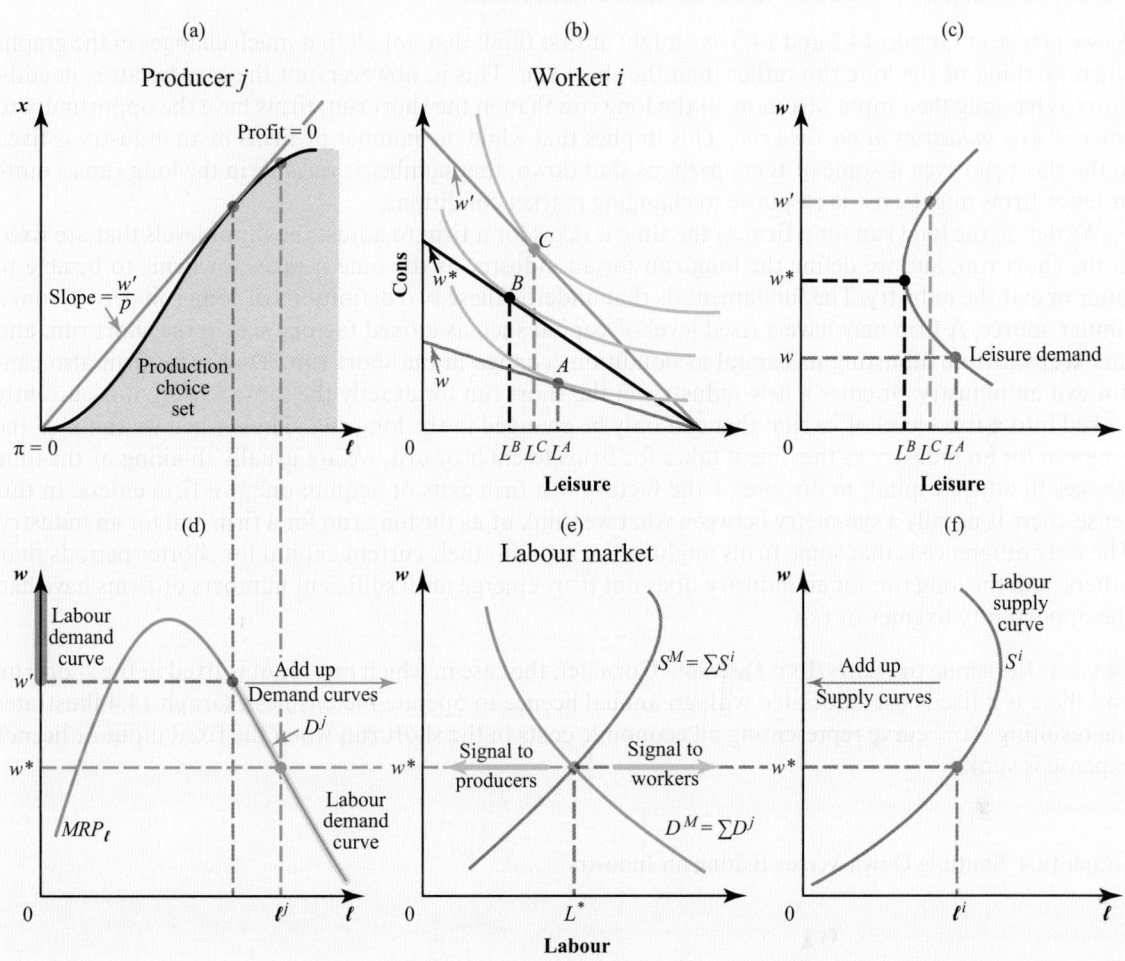

Note that while the demand curve in output markets comes from all those *consumers* who consume the output we are modelling, the demand curve in labour markets comes from all those *producers* who hire the kind of labour we are modelling. In our labour market graph, we are adding up labour demand curves from firms that could potentially be producing very different outputs but are all demanding the same kind of labour input. On the supply side, we considered in our output market only those firms that produce the particular output we are modelling, just as in the labour market we only consider those workers who supply the type of labour we are modelling.

Exercise 14A.1

Can you explain why there is always a natural tendency for wage to move towards the equilibrium wage if all individuals try to do the best they can?

In the capital market, we could similarly derive a demand curve for capital by producers except that it would be a more long-run demand curve if capital for firms were fixed in the short run. The supply curve would emerge from consumers making trade-offs between consuming now or consuming in the future – and thus saving for future consumption – and the equilibrium price that emerges in the market is the equilibrium interest rate.

14A.2 A Market or Industry in Long-Run Equilibrium

As we glance at Graphs 14.2 and 14.3, we might at first think that not all that much changes in the graphs when we think of the long run rather than the short run. This is, however, not the case because, in addition to changing their input mix more in the long run than in the short run, firms have the opportunity to *enter or exit industries in the long run.* This implies that while the number of firms in an industry is fixed in the short run even if some of them perhaps shut down, that number is *variable* in the long run as more or fewer firms might exist in response to changing market conditions.

We define the long run for a firm as the time it takes for a firm to adjust the input levels that are fixed in the short run, and we define the long run for an industry as the time it takes for firms to be able to enter or exit the industry. The fundamentals that underlie these two definitions of long run derive from a similar source. A firm may have a fixed level of capital such as a fixed factory size in the short run, and this keeps it from adjusting its capital as conditions change in the short run. That same firm also cannot exit an industry, or enter a new industry, in the short run for exactly the same reason: it is currently locked into a fixed level of capital that can only be changed in the long run. Thus, when we think of the long run for an industry as the time it takes for firms to enter or exit, we are usually thinking of the time it takes to adjust capital, to dispose of the factory if a firm exits or acquire one if a firm enters. In this sense, there is usually a symmetry between what we think of as the long run for a firm and for an industry. The only difference is that some firms might be locked into their current capital for shorter periods than others, and the long run for an industry does not truly emerge until sufficient numbers of firms have had the opportunity to enter or exit.

14A.2.1 Revisiting the Entry/Exit Decision Consider, the case in which one input is fixed in the short run and there is a fixed cost associated with an annual licence to operate the business. Graph 14.4 illustrates the resulting AC^{SR} curve representing all economic costs in the short run when the fixed input or licence expense is sunk.

Graph 14.4 Shutting Down Versus Exiting an Industry

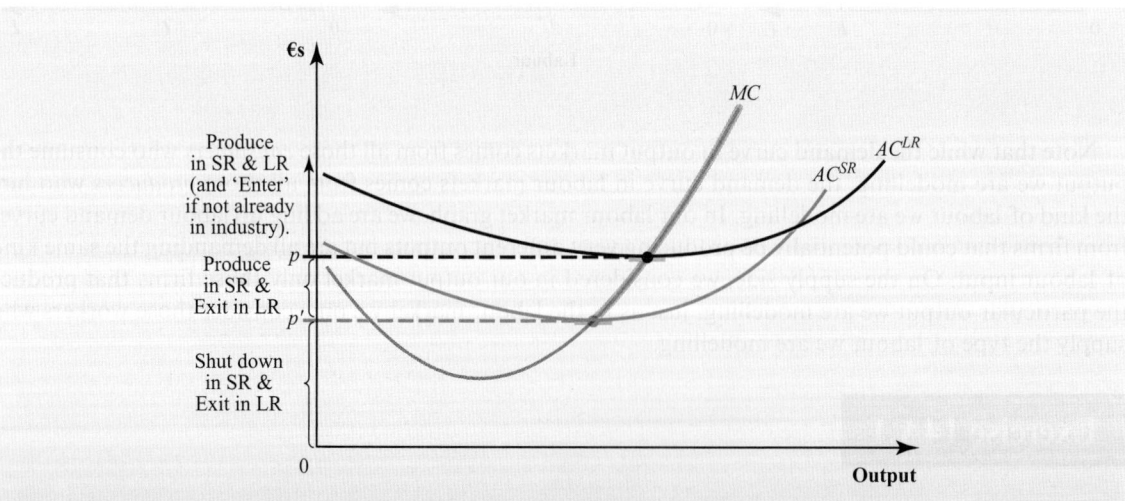

Go to MindTap to interact with this graph

The AC^{LR} curve that represents long-run economic costs that take into account the cost of all inputs and of renewing the annual licence. In the short run, the firm operates as long as price is not below p', the lowest point of the short-run AC curve, while in the long run it will exit if price falls below p, the lowest point of the long-run AC curve. In between these prices, there exists a range of prices that allow the firm to cover short-run costs but not fixed expenses, sufficient to keep it open in the short run but not sufficient to keep it from exiting in the long run. If price is above p, on the other hand, the firm can make long-run positive profits, implying that it will produce and will enter the industry if not already in it.

Exercise 14A.2

Suppose a firm only used labour inputs and not capital and that labour is always a variable input. If the firm had to renew an annual licence fee, would the AC^{SR} and the long-run AC curves ever cross in this case?

Exercise 14A.3

Why might the AC^{SR} and the long-run AC curves cross when the difference emerges because of an input like capital that is fixed in the short run? *Hint:* Review Graphs 13.2 and 13.3.

Exercise 14A.4

Explain why the MC curve in Graph 14.4 would be the same in the long and short run in the scenario of exercise 14A.2 but not in the scenario of exercise 14A.3.

14A.2.2 Long-Run Equilibrium Price When All Producers Are Identical Assume there are many producers of door handles, each of which wants to make as much profit as possible, and constantly look around for the best opportunities. In the short run, the producers are stuck in the particular industries in which they are currently producing, but in the long run some can switch if new opportunities open up. Producers can keep track of the AC curves in many different industries, and when they notice that AC is below output price in some industry, they know there is profit to be made, and enter. Some might be a little faster at doing this than others, or some might notice opportunities a bit sooner than others. Whatever determines the sequence by which one producer pounces on new opportunities first, the fact that all will eventually pounce on these opportunities means that together they shift the market supply curve as they enter, and keep shifting it as long as there are profits to be made.

Suppose that the market for good x is in the short-run equilibrium represented by the intersection of the market demand and supply curves, D^M and S^M, with equilibrium price p' in panel (a) of Graph 14.5. This price signal tells each producer to produce x' of output along their supply curve, S in panel (b), which generates a long-run profit equal to the shaded dark brown area in panel (b) for each firm, assuming we have included all the costs relevant for the long run in the AC curve. Positive or abnormal profit, no matter how small, means that a producer is doing better here than they could do anywhere else. Since we are assuming that all producers are identical, there are producers who currently operate in a different industry and see that they could make positive profits in the industry that produces x, which logically implies that they are making a negative profit in their current industry.

Graph 14.5 Moving From Short-Run to Long-Run Equilibrium

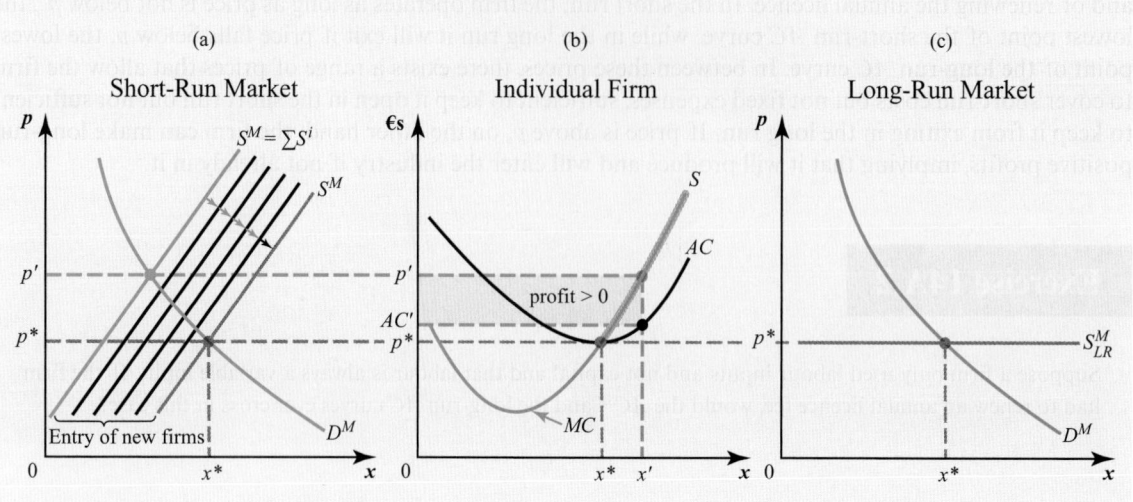

Given the current price p', there is thus an incentive in place for additional firms to enter the industry, with each entry shifting the short-run market supply curve just a little bit in panel (a). The incentive for firms to enter remains as long as long-run profits in the industry are positive and thus as long as price remains above p^*. Thus, the shift in short-run market supply curves in panel (a) of the graph will not stop until we arrive at the short-run market supply curve S^M when the price has reached the lowest point of each individual producer's long-run AC curve. Once we have reached this new short-run equilibrium, each producer in the industry makes zero or normal long-run profit, eliminating any incentive for any new producers to enter and stopping short of giving an incentive to current producers to exit.

We could have drawn a similar sequence of shifts in short-run supply curves, but in the opposite direction, if we had drawn the original intersection of the supply and demand curves in panel (a) at an equilibrium price below p^*. In that case, the shift in short-run supply curves would have resulted from the exiting of firms from the industry in which firms were experiencing negative profits; that is, where firms could be doing better elsewhere. Thus, *whenever producers face identical costs and the short-run equilibrium output price lies anywhere other than the lowest point of long-run AC, entry and exit of firms will drive the long-run price of output to that lowest point.* In panel (c) of the graph, *the long-run market supply curve, S^M_{LR} is horizontal and lies at the lowest point of AC.* The market will, in the long run when firms can enter and exit, supply any quantity that is demanded at the price p^* that falls at the lowest point for AC. This implies that the long-run market or industry supply curve arises not from adding up individual supply curves, but rather from the entry and exit decision of firms that will drive price to the point where long-run profit is equal to zero; that is, where price settles at the lowest point of the long-run AC curve for individual firms.

Exercise 14A.5

Draw the analogous sequence of graphs for the case when the short-run equilibrium price falls below p^*.

Exercise 14A.6

How does the full picture of equilibrium in Graph 14.2 look different in the long run?

14A.2.3 Long-Run Equilibrium in Labour Markets While entry and exit of firms shape the difference between long- and short-run equilibrium in the output market for a particular industry's good, the same is generally not true of labour market equilibria, at least not when a particular industry is small relative to the whole economy. This is because the labour market in Graph 14.3 is composed of firms from many different industries, and conditions that affect one particular industry will tend not to have an impact on the economy-wide labour market when an industry is small relative to the economy as a whole. Thus, whether some firms are entering or exiting a particular industry will not be perceptible as causing a shift in labour demand.

Entry and exit may play a role on the labour supply curve if an increase or decrease of wages for a particular type of labour alters perceptions sufficiently to cause workers to retrain or new workers to choose training differently from in the past. For instance, over the past 20 years, there has been a substantial increase in salaries paid to young PhD economists. While it is not easy to simply retrain from being a non-economist to being an economist, one would expect that in the long run, more graduates might choose to get a PhD in economics when salaries for young economists have risen, thus increasing the supply of economists and driving down wages in the long run. Long-run wages in each labour market thus have to have a relationship with the relevant opportunity costs of workers.

Exercise 14A.7

How would you think the time-lag between short- and long-run changes in labour markets is related to the barriers to entry that workers face, where the barrier to entry into the PhD economist market, for instance, lies in the cost of obtaining a PhD?

14A.2.4 Long-Run Market Supply When Producers Differ In deriving the flat long-run industry supply curve in panel (c) of Graph 14.5, we explicitly assumed that all producers had access to the same technology and thus faced the same AC and MC curves. For the argument that the long-run market supply curve is horizontal to hold, it is only necessary to assume that all firms have technologies that give rise to long-run AC curves that reach their minimum at the same euro value, regardless of what the remainder of the curves look like.

Exercise 14A.8

Can you explain why the previous sentence is true?

If different producers have access to very different technologies, it might be true that at a given output price, some producers are able to make a profit while others are not. This in turn has implications for who will enter and who will exit an industry as market conditions change, and it has implications for the shape of the long-run market supply curve.

Consider, for instance, the short-run market equilibrium pictured in panel (a) of Graph 14.6 as the intersection of the demand and supply curves D^M and S^M at point A, with p^* as the equilibrium price. Assume that there are many potential firms for this industry, and to keep the graph manageable, suppose that each of these firms has a long-run AC curve that reaches its minimum at output level x^*, but some AC curves are lower everywhere than others. Six such AC curves are pictured in panel (b) of the graph, and we can imagine that there are many firms whose similarly shaped AC curves fall in between these. At the price p^*, firms 1, 2 and 3 all make at least zero profit, while firms 4, 5 and 6 would make negative long-run profit if they produced. Those firms with lower average cost curves – those that are better at producing x – will choose to be in the industry while those with higher cost curves will not.

Graph 14.6 Long-Run Market Supply When Firms Differ

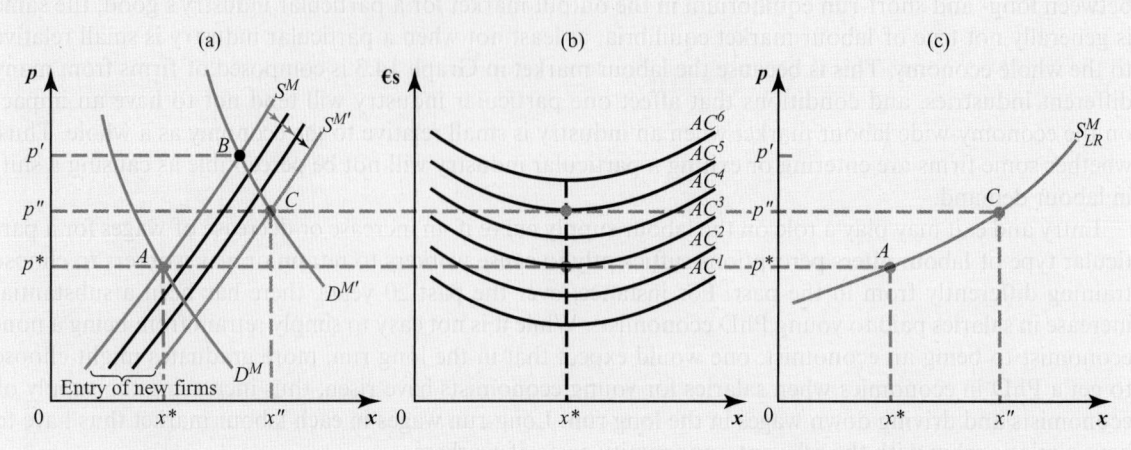

Suppose that there is a shift in market demand from D^M to $D^{M'}$ that causes the short-run equilibrium price in panel (a) to rise above p^* to p'. Producer 4 would notice that they are now able to make a positive profit in this industry, and would therefore have an incentive to enter the industry, as would other firms that previously would have made negative profit. This entry of new firms shifts the short-run supply curve in panel (a) as new firms enter the market, but the process will stop *before* the price falls back to the original p^* because the firms that are entering have higher costs than the firms that originally composed the industry. Producer 5 is the last one to enter, with all producers whose costs fall below p'' also entering, but no producer whose costs are higher than those of producer 5 entering. The shift in market demand from D^M to $D^{M'}$ causes a short-run shift in the equilibrium from p^* to p' and a long-run shift to C in panel (a) of the graph, with a short-run increase in the price from p^* to p' and a long-run change to p''. Panel (c) graphs the long-run market supply relationship from A to C, indicating an upward-sloping long-run market supply curve when producers have different cost curves. Once again, the long-run market supply curve is not determined by the shape of individual firm supply curves, only by the distribution of the lowest point of the AC curves for firms. Industries like this, with upward-sloping long-run industry supply curves, are called *increasing cost industries*.

Exercise 14A.9

Suppose market demand shifts inwards instead of outwards. Illustrate what would happen in graphs similar to those of Graph 14.6?

Exercise 14A.10

True or False: The entry and exit of firms in the long run ensures that the long-run market supply curve is always shallower than the short-run market supply curve.

It is in principle possible for long-run market supply curves to slope downwards in industries where firm costs fall as the industry expands. This may occur if, for instance, the expansion of an industry leads to greater competition in one of the input markets unique to that industry, and thus to a decline in costs for all firms. Such industries are called *decreasing cost industries*. Since this is relatively rare for industries that are appropriately modelled as perfectly competitive, we will not focus on this case here and only mention it for the sake of completeness.

Exercise 14A.11*

True or False: While long-run industry supply curves slope upwards in increasing cost industries because firms have different cost curves, long-run industry supply curves in decreasing cost industries slope downwards even if firms have identical cost curves.

14A.2.5 Zero Profit for Marginal Firms in the Long Run Entry and exit of firms into markets always continues until the *marginal producer makes zero long-run profit*. The marginal producer is the producer who has the highest costs within an industry. In the case where all producers have the same costs, as in Graph 14.5, all producers are marginal, and thus all producers make zero long-run profit. In the case where producers have access to different technologies and thus face different cost curves as in Graph 14.6, on the other hand, all producers other than the marginal producer make positive long-run profit. If all potential producers have the same costs as all those within the industry, all producers who are not in the industry are also marginal and would make zero long-run profit if they entered. When producers face different costs, however, those who are outside the industry in long-run equilibrium would make negative profits if they entered because their costs are greater than the costs of the marginal producer in the industry who is making zero profit.

Exercise 14A.12

True or False: In the presence of fixed costs or fixed expenditures, short-run profit is always greater than zero in long-run equilibrium.

14A.3 Changing Conditions and Changing Equilibria

In the real world, conditions facing particular industries change constantly as new competing products enter the larger market, labour and capital input prices change, and government tax and regulatory policies are altered. The concepts of short- and long-run equilibria are useful, however, not only for those industries that find themselves in relatively stable economic environments for long periods but also for those industries that experience constantly changing conditions. Whether equilibrium is maintained for a period or whether a static equilibrium is even reached before conditions change once again, knowing what the ultimate equilibrium in an economy is indicates the direction of an economy, which is useful in its own right. It is a bit like predicting the weather: it is never quite in equilibrium, but the forces of nature are constantly aiming to get towards an equilibrium. Thus, if we know that a new high pressure system is moving into our area, we can predict what will happen to the weather because we understand how the weather will adjust in an attempt to head towards a new equilibrium. So it is with an economy. When a new force is introduced, we can predict which way things are headed by knowing the equilibrium the economy is aiming for.

In our model of a competitive industry, a change in conditions translates in some way into a change in demand or supply curves, and thus a change in short-run and/or long-run equilibrium. On the producer side, changing conditions might result from (1) a change in variable costs like those associated with labour, (2) a change in fixed expenditures associated with an input that is fixed in the short run, or (3) a change in a fixed cost that is avoidable only by exiting the industry. On the consumer side, changes in consumer tastes or the appearance of new products on the market may cause shifts in market demand. For each of these cases, we will begin our analysis with the assumption that the market was in long-run equilibrium prior to the change in underlying conditions faced by the industry.

14A.3.1 Short-Run Equilibrium Within a Long-Run Equilibrium Assume an industry is currently in long-run equilibrium, and the marginal producer is making normal profits and thus producing at a price that falls at the lowest point of the producer's long-run *AC* curve. This is illustrated in Graph 14.7 where the market demand and market supply curves, both consisting simply of individual demand and short-run supply curves added up, cross in panel (a) at price p^*, which falls at the lowest point of the long-run AC curve of the marginal firm in the industry in panel (b). Since panel (b) illustrates the marginal firm in the industry, all firms outside the industry have costs that are at least as high as this firm's. All firms outside the industry would make normal profit or less if they entered the industry. Firms inside the industry have costs that are no higher than the marginal firms. All the firms inside the industry make at least normal profit. The industry finds itself in long-run equilibrium because no firm has an incentive to enter or exit this industry unless conditions change. Entry and exit have led to just the right number of firms such that demand and short-run supply intersect at the long-run equilibrium price.

Graph 14.7 An Industry in Both Short- and Long-Run Equilibrium

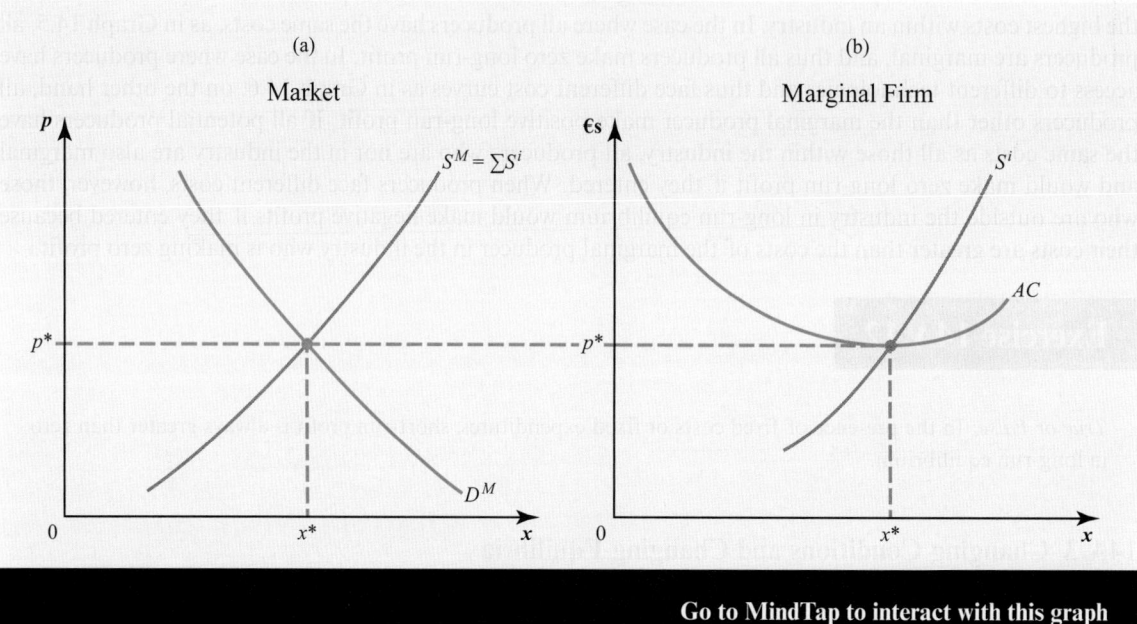

Go to MindTap to interact with this graph

At the same time, each firm in the industry makes positive short-run profits, because short-run economic costs are fully contained in the short-run average cost curve whose lowest point lies below the lowest point of the long-run AC curve. It is for this reason that the light brown short-run supply curve in panel (b) of the graph extends below the lowest point of the long-run AC curve as illustrated in Graph 14.4.

Exercise 14A.13

Illustrate graphically the short- and long-run profits of the marginal firm in long-run equilibrium? *Hint:* You can do this by inserting into the graph the AC^{SR} curve as previously pictured in Graph 14.4.

This will be the starting point for our analysis of the impact of changing conditions on short- and long-run equilibrium. In each case, we will need to ask ourselves which curves in our graph are affected by the change, and this will permit us to come to a conclusion about how changing firm behaviour results in changes in the equilibrium. For the purposes of illustration, we will also assume for the remainder of this chapter that all firms face the same cost curves, and all firms are therefore marginal firms. We have stripped the firm side of our pictures to only those curves that actually matter for our analysis: the short-run supply curve and the long-run AC curve, with the short-run supply curve extending below AC. Keep in mind throughout, however, that the short-run supply curve is a portion of the short-run MC curve and is thus moved by changes in short-run marginal costs.

14A.3.2 A Change in a Recurring Fixed Cost Suppose that producers in an industry incur some annual fixed cost that is not associated with an input, for example, an annual licence fee charged by the government or annual insurance premiums that might insure the firm against damage to its property or its consumer or employee liabilities. Once paid, such fees are sunk costs in the short run and do not enter the short-run cost curves. In the long run, however, such fees are a real economic cost of staying in the industry and become part of the long-run cost curve AC.

Assume that this fee goes up, a scenario shown in Graph 14.8. Since it is not a part of the short-run average or marginal curves, it is not part of any of the cost curves that are relevant for the firm's short-run decisions. Thus the firm's short-run supply curve which is not pictured in panel (b) remains unchanged. Since the short-run market supply curve S^M is composed of the sum of all firm supply curves, this also implies that the market supply curve does not change in the short run. This further implies that the equilibrium price in the market remains at p^* in the short run. As a result, the increase in the fee causes no changes in the industry in the short run.

Graph 14.8 An Increase in a Long-Run Fixed Cost

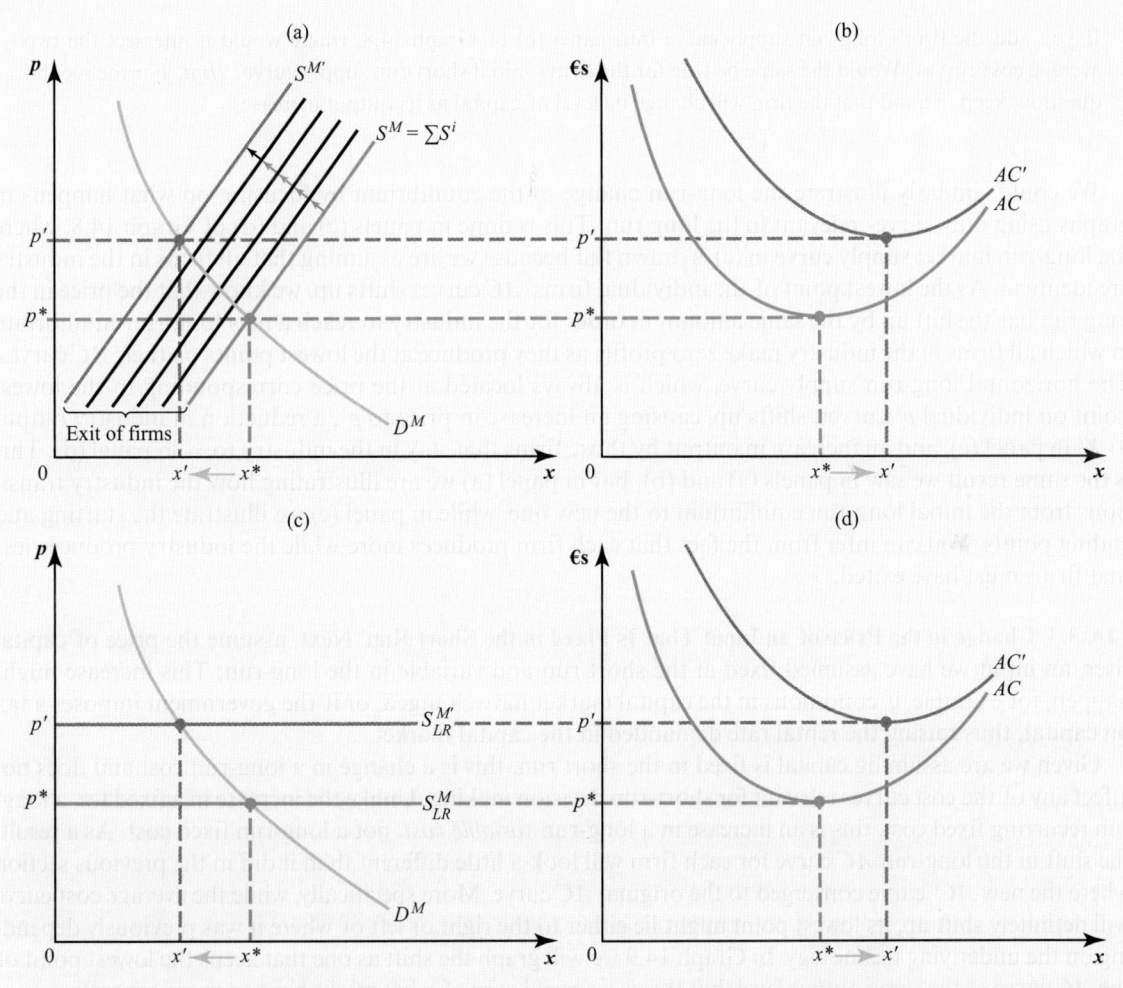

The increased fee does, however, cause the long-run AC curve to move up to AC' as in panel (b) of Graph 14.8. While short-run profit is unchanged, long-run profit falls and, since it was normal in the initial equilibrium, it now becomes negative or sub-normal. This causes some firms to exit the market in the long run, which in turn causes the short-run market supply curve S^M to shift inwards. As individual firms exit, the dark blue market supply curves in panel (a) drive up the market price, and firms will continue to exit as long as the market price remains below the new lowest point of the light blue AC' curve in panel (b). Only when the market price has increased all the way to p' will the firms that remain in the industry make normal profits again, eliminating any further incentive for firms to exit or enter. The short-run market supply curve stops shifting as firms stop exiting when it has reached $S^{M'}$ in panel (a). The firms that remain in the industry produce x', which is more than they produced initially (x^*), but the industry as a whole produces less, X' rather than X^* in panel (a).

Exercise 14A.14

Why does the increase in the fee result in a new AC' curve that converges to the original AC curve in Graph 14.8?

Exercise 14A.15

If you add the firm's long-run supply curve into panel (b) of Graph 14.8, where would it intersect the two average cost curves? Would the same be true for the firm's initial short-run supply curve? *Hint:* For the second question, keep in mind that the firm will change its level of capital as its output increases.

We could similarly illustrate the long-run change in the equilibrium by focusing on what happens in graphs using only curves relevant in the long run. This is done in panels (c) and (d) of Graph 14.8, where the long-run market supply curve in (c) is drawn flat because we are assuming that all firms in the industry are identical. As the lowest point of the individual firms' AC curves shifts up, we know that the price in the long run has to shift up by the same amount in order for the industry to reach a new long-run equilibrium in which all firms in the industry make zero profits as they produce at the lowest points on their AC curves. The horizontal long-run supply curve, which is always located at the price corresponding to the lowest point on individual p' curves, shifts up, causing an increase in price to p', a reduction in industry output to X' in panel (c), and an increase in output by those firms that stay in the industry to x' in panel (d). This is the same result we saw in panels (a) and (b), but in panel (a) we are illustrating how the industry transitions from the initial long-run equilibrium to the new one, while in panel (c) we illustrate the starting and ending points. You can infer from the fact that each firm produces more while the industry produces less that firms must have exited.

14A.3.3 Change in the Price of an Input That Is Fixed in the Short Run Next, assume the price of capital rises, an input we have assumed fixed in the short run and variable in the long run. This increase might happen, for example, if conditions in the capital market have changed, or if the government imposes a tax on capital, thus raising the rental rate demanded in the capital market.

Given we are assuming capital is fixed in the short run, this is a change in a long-run cost and does not affect any of the cost curves relevant for short-run decision making. Unlike the increase in a fixed fee, a long-run recurring fixed cost, this is an increase in a long-run *variable cost*, not a long-run fixed cost. As a result, the shift in the long-run AC curve for each firm will look a little different than it did in the previous section where the new AC' curve converged to the original AC curve. More specifically, while the average cost curve will definitely shift up, its lowest point might lie either to the right or left of where it was previously depending on the underlying technology. In Graph 14.9 we will graph the shift as one that keeps the lowest point of the AC curve at the same output level, but this is a special case of what might happen more generally.

Exercise 14A.16

Could the AC curve shift similarly in the case where the increase in cost was that of a long-run fixed cost?

Graph 14.9 An Increase in the Rental Rate of Capital

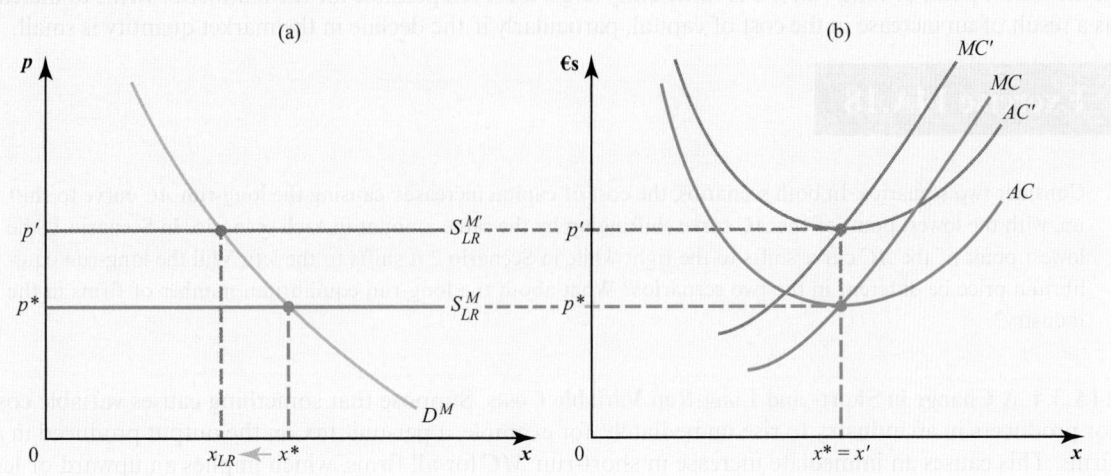

This can be confusing because it seems to involve a logical contradiction: how can it be that the lowest point of the long-run AC curve can remain at the same output quantity when we know that the short-run MC curve has to cross the long-run AC curve at its lowest point in the new long-run equilibrium? After all, doesn't the short-run MC curve include only the cost of labour and not the cost of capital that has just increased? The apparent contradiction is resolved if we recognize that the firm will shift away from capital and towards labour when r increases. This implies that from a short-run perspective, in the new long-run equilibrium, costs will be higher since more labour will be involved in producing each unit of output. It is for this reason that the short-run MC curve shifts as a result of moving to the new long-run equilibrium, but that shift only happens in the long run when firms substitute away from capital and towards labour. This is illustrated in panel (b) of Graph 14.9 where the dark brown curves represent the original long-run AC and short-run MC curves and the light blue curves represent the new long-run AC and short-run MC.

The rest of the story of how the equilibrium changes is similar to that discussed in the previous section for an increase in a fixed fee. Nothing changes in the short run since none of the short-run curves is affected *in the short run* by an increase in the cost of an input that is fixed in the short run. However, each firm in the industry now makes negative profits, which means that the industry is no longer in long-run equilibrium. The new long-run industry supply curve must shift up to the lowest point of the new long-run AC, the price at which all firms will once again be making normal profit. Industry output falls to X_{LR} in panel (a), with each firm in the industry continuing to produce the same as it did before. The fact that individual firms do not change how much they produce, but the industry produces less at the higher long-run price, necessarily implies that in this case, firms must have exited.

Exercise 14A.17

How would you illustrate the transition from the short run to the long run using graphs similar to those in panels (a) and (b) in Graph 14.8?

However, the case in Graph 14.9 where an increase in the cost of capital causes the lowest point of long-run AC to shift up but remain at the same output level is a special case. It is logically possible that the underlying production technology for firms is such that an increase in the cost of capital causes the lowest point of long-run AC to instead shift to the right as it did for an increase in recurring fixed costs. This would imply that more firms will exit as there is room for fewer firms to produce the new market quantity X' when each firm that remains in the industry produces more than it did originally. It is also logically possible, however, for the underlying production technology to give rise to a leftward shift of the lowest point of long-run AC when the cost of capital increases. In such a case, fewer firms would exit as relatively more firms would be needed to produce the new long-run market quantity X' when each firm produces less. If the leftward shift in the lowest point of long-run AC is sufficiently large, it is even possible for the number of firms to increase as a result of an increase in the cost of capital, particularly if the decline in the market quantity is small.

Exercise 14A.18

Consider two scenarios. In both scenarios, the cost of capital increases, causing the long-run AC curve to shift up, with the lowest point of the AC curve shifting up by the same amount in each scenario. In Scenario 1, the lowest point of the AC curve shifts to the right while in Scenario 2 it shifts to the left. Will the long-run equilibrium price be different in the two scenarios? What about the long-run equilibrium number of firms in the industry?

14A.3.4 A Change in Short- and Long-Run Variable Costs Suppose that something causes variable costs for producers in an industry to rise immediately, for example, a per-unit tax on the output produced in all firms. This causes an immediate increase in short-run MC for all firms, which implies an upward or leftward shift in each firm's short-run supply curve in panel (b) of Graph 14.10. Since this is happening to all firms in the industry, the same shift will happen to the short-run market supply curve in panel (a) – leading to an immediate increase in output price from p to p'.

Graph 14.10 An Increase in Short-Run Variable Cost

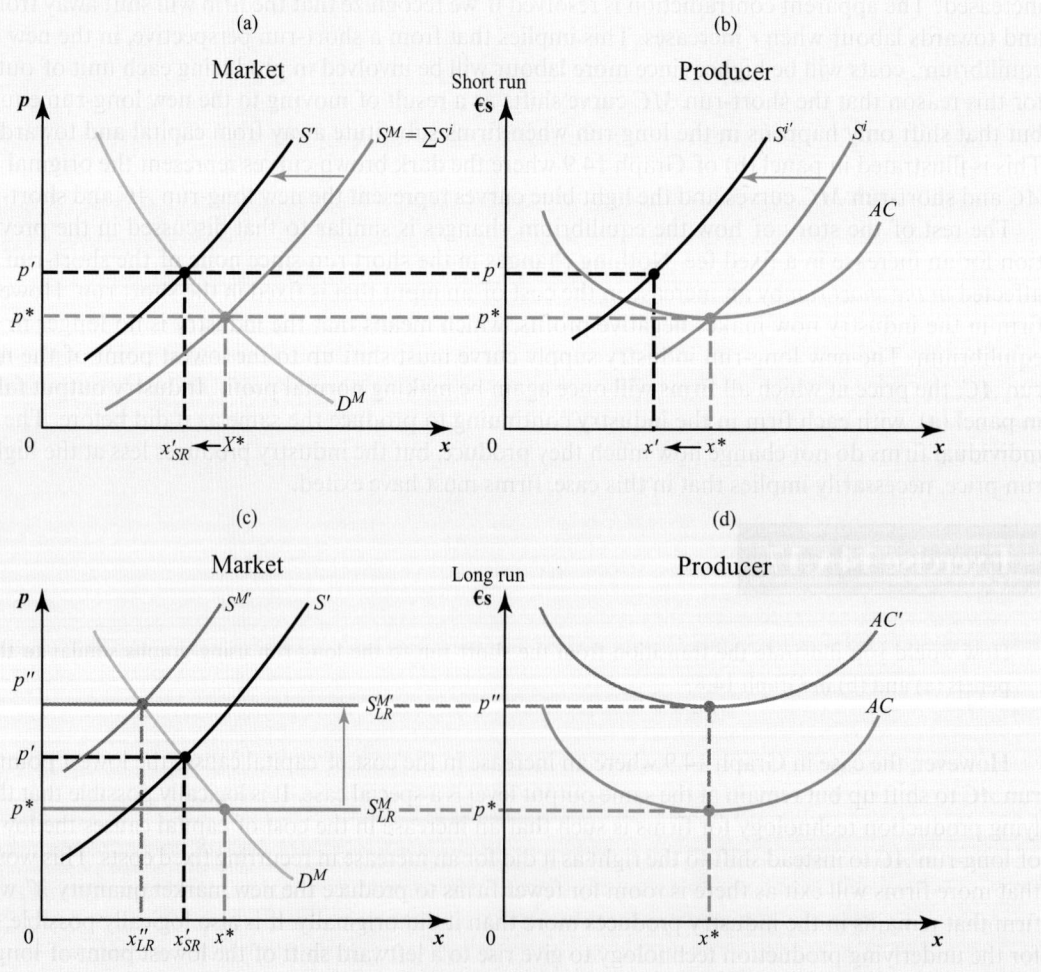

In the short run, the industry as a whole will therefore produce less, X'_{SR} instead of X^*, with the number of firms staying the same as no firms can enter or exit in the short run. Since all firms are assumed to be identical, each firm will continue to produce in the short run, which implies each firm produces less, x' rather than x^* in panel (b). Thus, price in the short run rises sufficiently to p' to ensure that short-run profit remains above zero. If we assumed instead that some firms had lower cost curves than others, some higher cost firms might shut down in the short run if they can no longer make non-negative short-run profits.

In the long run, however, price has to adjust to the new lowest point of long-run AC', which implies that the long-run market supply curve in panel (c) rises from the initial dark brown horizontal line to the new light blue line at price p''. Since the per-unit tax applies the same to all units that are produced, the long-run AC shifts up as shown in the graph, with each point shifting up by the amount of the tax. The lowest point of the average cost curve remains at the same output quantity x^* in panel (d). In the long run, each firm that remains in the industry will produce as much as it did before costs increased in panel (d), but since the overall market output falls at higher prices, some firms must have exited in the transition from the short run to the long run. It is for this reason that we can place the dark blue short-run shift in the market supply curve that resulted from an increase in short-run MC for all firms in panel (c) intersecting the demand curve at a price below the long-run price p'', with the shift from this dark blue curve to the new (light blue) final short-run supply curve resulting from the exit of firms that experienced negative long-run profits at the price p'. Even though each firm that remains in the industry will end up producing as much as it did before costs increased, the market produces less X''_{LR} as the industry has shrunk.

Assume instead that the increased variable cost came from a higher cost of labour from an increase in the market wage or because the government imposed a tax on wages, for example. It is possible that the same analysis for the per-unit output tax holds, but only if the lowest point of the long-run AC curve shifts up without shifting to the left or right. While in the case of the per-unit output tax we knew this to be the case, with an increase in labour costs this lowest point of AC might shift to the left or right instead, depending on the nature of the underlying production technology. If it shifted to the right, we could conclude that the number of firms in the industry has fallen as a result of the increase in the wage just as when the lowest point of AC shifts vertically up. This is because the industry produces less at the higher price and *each firm* produces more when the lowest point of the long-run AC curve shifts to the right. In fact, the further to the right this lowest point shifts, the more exiting of firms we must observe. If that lowest point shifts to the left instead, it is no longer as clear whether the number of firms in the industry will increase or decrease. While the total industry output would fall just as before because consumers demand less when prices are higher, it may still take more firms to produce that lower industry output if each firm produces sufficiently less than before, and the market quantity at the new price does not fall too much. In this case, p and p' in panel (c) of Graph 14.10 would be reversed, with the short-run increase in price being sufficiently high to attract new firms into the industry. The short-run (dark blue) shift in market supply would be larger than the long-run (light blue) shift, thus causing the short-run price to overshoot the long-run price – leading to the entry of new firms.

Exercise 14A.19

If an increase in the wage causes an increase in the number of firms in an industry, does this give you enough information to know whether the lowest point of long-run AC for firms shifted to the left or right? What if an increase in the wage causes a decrease in the number of firms in the industry?

14A.3.5 A Change in Demand An industry may be impacted not only by changing costs but also by changing market demand. The market may be affected by changing tastes as new, substitute products come onto the market, for example the increase in streaming music which has affected the demand for music on CD. Such shifts in market demand may change individual demand curves that compose the market demand curve, from the introduction of new products in a related market, or from new consumers entering a market. Such shifts in demand have no impact on the cost curves of firms, which implies that we will not need to change any of the firm cost curves.

Consider, for instance, the increase in demand for the good x graphed in panel (a) of Graph 14.11, with the assumption that all firms are identical in terms of their cost structure. We begin at the initial industry equilibrium, with the industry producing X^* at the equilibrium price p^*. When demand shifts from D^M to $D^{M'}$, there is an immediate increase in price to p' as existing firms in the industry meet the new demand along the existing individual supply curves that sum to the market supply curve. Since firms were initially making zero long-run profits, the increase in price now allows them to earn positive long-run profits. This provides new firms with an incentive to enter the industry, and the short-run market supply curve shifts out with each new entrant. This puts downward pressure on price, continuing for as long as firms in the industry are making positive long-run profits. Thus, entry into the industry will stop, assuming all firms have identical costs, only when price falls back to the original p^* where all firms once again make zero or normal long-run profits. The final short-run market supply curve therefore settles at $S^{M'}$.

Graph 14.11 An Increase in Market Demand

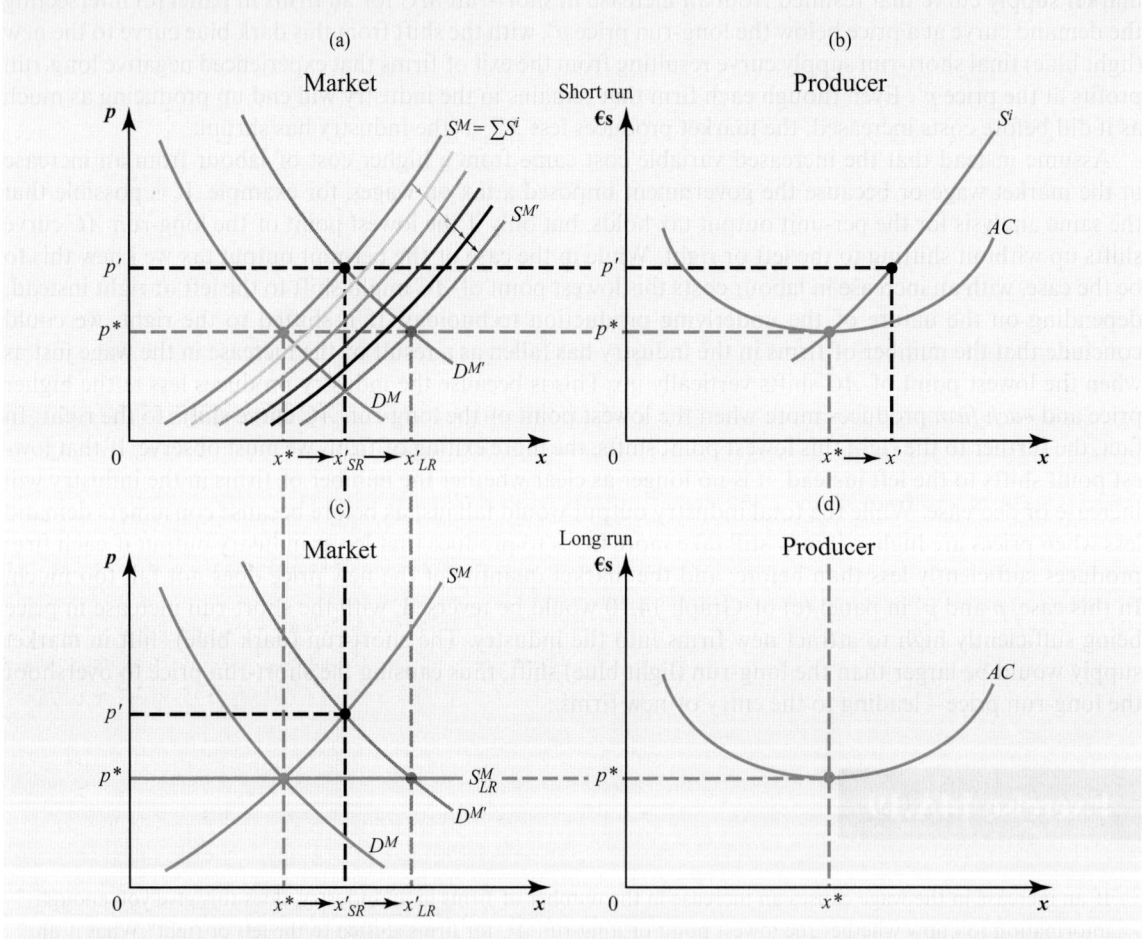

While panel (a) of the graph illustrates the transition from the initial change in the short-run equilibrium to the final long-run equilibrium by showing the shifting (dark blue) supply curves as new firms enter, panel (c) illustrates the change from the initial long-run equilibrium to the final long-run equilibrium by focusing on the long-run supply curve S^M_{LR} that does not shift, because the lowest point of the long-run AC curve for firms does not shift. In both panels (a) and (c), we see that industry output rises to X'_{SR} in the short run and ultimately settles at the larger industry output X'_{LR}. In panel (b), each firm in the industry initially increases its production, but panel (d) illustrates that each firm will ultimately end up producing the same as it did before the increase in demand. The larger industry output therefore arises solely from the fact that the industry as a whole has expanded through the entry of new firms.

14A.3.6 Changes Affecting a Single Firm Versus Changes Affecting the Industry We have assumed so far that the change we are analyzing affects every firm in the industry. Sometimes, however, only a single firm in the industry might experience a change. Recall that each firm in a competitive industry is sufficiently small so that any change in behaviour by that firm will not affect the short- or long-run market equilibrium.

If a producer of door handles is one of many producers who produce door handles, what they do has no impact on the market. If, for some reason, that producer faced an increase in an annual licence fee for operating in the market but no other firm is similarly affected, the producer will continue to produce in the short run as if nothing has happened until the licence fee for next year becomes due. Since the producer like every other firm in the industry was initially making zero profits, they now make negative long-run profits if they pay the licence fee again and continue to produce. The firm therefore exits the industry, leaving the market equilibrium unchanged since the firm is one of many producers and therefore can't by itself shift the market supply curve.

Sometimes, the change in costs that affect a single firm are less obvious than the simple example above. Suppose, for instance, the door handle factory sits on land that contains substantial oil reserves beneath. This new information would imply that the value of the land under the factory is considerably higher than initially thought, and thus the opportunity cost of using this land has gone up. The producer's long-run *AC* shifts upwards, implying that they will now make negative profits if they continue to produce door handles. They will therefore exit the industry and either go into the oil business or sell the land to an oil company. The increase in costs has driven the producer out of the door handle business, even though they are better off since they get to make more money in the oil business or make more money by selling the land. If, on the other hand, the producer rented the land rather than owned it, the rent for the land would have increased, again raising long-run *AC* and driving them out of business. Now the owner of the land would have benefited rather than the producer. In either case, though, the increase in opportunity costs increased and drove them out of the industry.

Exercise 14A.20

True or False: Regardless of what cost it is, if it increases for only one firm in a competitive industry, that firm will exit in the long run but it might not shut down in the short run.

14A.4 An Overview of Changes Affecting Firms and Industries

In this chapter, we have aggregated the consumer and producer sides of a competitive market. By understanding what moves the supply side of the goods market, we have traced the short- and long-run impacts of changes in several types of market conditions on prices and output levels within affected industries. Table 14.1 summarizes our main conclusions.

Table 14.1 The Impact of Changing Conditions of Firms and Industries Assuming Identical Firms						
	Affected Costs		Market	Industry	Firm	LR No. of
Example	SR	LR	Price	Output	Output	Firms
↑Licence Fee	None	AC	_SR↑LR	_SR↓LR	_SR↑LR	↓
↑r	None	AC, MC	_SR↑LR	_SR↓LR	_SR?LR	?
↑w	AC, MC	AC, MC	↑SR↑LR	↓SR↓LR	↓SR?LR	?
↑Demand	None	None	↑SR_LR	↓SR↑↑LR	↓SR_LR	↑

Table 14.1 gives an example for four general market conditions: (1) changes in recurring fixed costs, e.g. licence fees; (2) changes in costs associated with inputs that are fixed in the short run but variable in the long run, e.g. the price r of capital; (3) changes in costs associated with inputs that are immediately variable, e.g. the price w of labour; and (4) changes in consumer demand for the product produced in the industry. For each of these, Table 14.1 first indicates which of the key cost curves are affected in firms in both the short and long run. It indicates short- and long-run movements in equilibrium prices, industry output levels and individual firm output levels. Single arrows (such as ↑) indicate a smaller change than a double arrow (such as ⇑) when variables are expected to move in the same direction in both the short and long run; a horizontal line (–) indicates no change from the initial equilibrium; and a question mark (?) indicates that the theory, without additional assumptions, allows for changes in either direction. Finally, the last column indicates whether the change causes the overall number of firms in the industry to increase or decrease in the long run, indicating whether firms are expected to enter or exit the industry as a result of the change.

Exercise 14A.21*

What would a fifth row for an increase in per-unit taxes on output look like? Can you also replicate Table 14.1 for the cases where the demand and the various cost examples decrease rather than increase?

14B The Mathematics of Industry or Market Equilibrium

Section B of this chapter will run through an example illustrating how we use all we have learned so far to calculate an industry equilibrium from knowing some basics about an economy. This is obviously going to be a stylized example, not one meant in any way to approximate any real-world industry. Nevertheless, it is often the case that understanding the full implications of what one learns is more than understanding the sum of all the parts. It is for this reason that we benefit from fully developing an industry equilibrium from the ground up.

We will begin with consumers who all have tastes over the good x and all other goods y that can be represented by the quasilinear utility function:

$$u(x, y) = 50x^{1/2} + y. \tag{14.1}$$

Such consumers have the demand function:

$$x^d(p) = \left(\frac{25}{p}\right)^2 = \frac{625}{p^2}, \tag{14.2}$$

where we assume a price of 1 for the composite good y and p denotes the price of good x.

Exercise 14B.1

Why is the demand function not a function of income?

Suppose that producers operate in competitive input markets in which labour costs $w = 20$ and capital costs $r = 10$, and all producers and potential producers for the good x face the same technology that can be captured by the production function:

$$f(\ell, k) = 20\ell^{2/5}k^{2/5}. \tag{14.3}$$

This is the same decreasing returns to scale technology for which we calculated the various functions in the duality picture in Chapter 12. Suppose that in addition to the inputs ℓ and k, however, the firm must purchase a recurring operating licence from the government that costs €1280. An addition of a recurring fixed cost such as this to a decreasing returns to scale production process results in a U-shaped long-run average cost curve for the producer.

In Chapter 12, equation (12.46), we derived the cost function for the production function (14.3) as $C(w, r, x) = 2(wr)^{1/2}(x/20)^{5/4}$. With the additional recurring fixed cost of 1280, this implies a long-run cost function for the production process in equation (14.3) of:

$$C(w, r, x) = 2(wr)^{1/2}\left(\frac{x}{20}\right)^{5/4} + 1280 \tag{14.4}$$

or, when $w = 20$ and $r = 10$:

$$C(x) = 0.66874x^{5/4} + 1280. \tag{14.5}$$

This implies an AC function when $w = 20$ and $r = 10$ of:

$$AC(x) = 0.66874x^{1/4} + \frac{1280}{x}, \tag{14.6}$$

which is U-shaped and attains its minimum at $x = 1280$ at an average cost of €5 per unit.

Exercise 14B.2

Demonstrate that the average cost of production is U-shaped and reaches its lowest point at $x = 1280$ where $AC = 5$. *Hint:* You can illustrate the U-shape by showing that the derivative of AC is zero at 1280, negative for output less than 1280 and positive for output greater than 1280.

14B.1 Industry Equilibrium in the Short Run

Short-run industry equilibrium is determined solely by the intersection of market demand and supply curves, where demand and supply curves are represented by the sum of all individual demand curves from consumers and supply curves from producers who are currently operating in the industry. Adding up demand curves in our example is straightforward because the demand functions (equation (14.2)) of *all* consumers are identical since they share the same quasilinear tastes and thus their income does not matter for demand. Adding up demand curves for all consumers means multiplying equation (14.2) by the number of consumers in the market for good x. If the total number of consumers in the market is 64 000, the market demand function $D^M(p)$ is:

$$D^M(p) = 64\,000x^d(p) = 64\,000\left(\frac{625}{p^2}\right) = \frac{40\,000\,000}{p^2}. \tag{14.7}$$

14B.1.1 Short-Run Industry Supply To calculate the short-run market supply curve, we need to know the individual short-run supply function for each producer and add up these functions. In equation (11.33) of Chapter 11, we concluded that the supply function for a producer with technology $f(\ell) = A\ell^\alpha$ is:

$$x(p, w) = A\left(\frac{w}{\alpha Ap}\right)^{\alpha/(\alpha-1)}. \tag{14.8}$$

If capital is fixed at k^A in the short run, our production function from equation (14.3) is:

$$f(\ell) = A\ell^\alpha \quad \text{where} \quad A = 20(k^A)^{2/5} \quad \text{and} \quad \alpha = 2/5. \tag{14.9}$$

If $k^A = 256$, which we will show shortly in Section 14B.2 is the case in long-run equilibrium, using the values for A and α specified in equation (14.9) and substituting them into equation (14.8), we get a short-run supply function:

$$x(p, w) = 3\,225.398\left(\frac{p}{w}\right)^{2/3} \quad \text{or} \quad x^s(p) = 437.754p^{2/3} \text{ when } w = 20. \tag{14.10}$$

Since we are assuming all producers are identical, adding up these supply functions to get short-run market supply is equivalent to multiplying them by the number of firms *that are currently operating in the industry*. If the number is 1250, which we will shortly show is the correct number of firms in long-run equilibrium, the short-run industry supply function $S^M(p)$ is:

$$S^M(p) = 1250x^s(p) = 1250(437.754)p^{2/3} = 547\,192p^{2/3}. \tag{14.11}$$

14B.1.2 Short-Run Industry Equilibrium With market demand and market supply given by equations (14.7) and (14.11) respectively, we calculate the short-run equilibrium by setting the two equations equal to one another and solving for the equilibrium price:

$$S^M(p) = 547\,192p^{2/3} = \frac{40\,000\,000}{p^2} = D^M(p), \tag{14.12}$$

which gives $p = 5$. With 64 000 consumers and 1250 producers, with tastes and technologies described by equations (14.1) and (14.3), with short-run capital k^A fixed at 256 units and with the wage rate given by $w = 20$, market demand and supply intersect at an equilibrium price $p^* = 5$. Substituting this back into the individual consumer and producer equations, each consumer in the market consumes 25 units of x, and each producer produces 1280 units of output by employing 128 labour hours.

Exercise 14B.3

Verify these individual production and consumption quantities.

To make sure that each firm is making non-negative short-run profits, we compare total revenues to total short-run economic costs. Total revenues are given by the output quantity (1280) times price (€5), for a total of €6400. Short-run economic costs in this case include only labour costs: 128 labour hours at a wage of €20, or €2560. Thus, short-run profit for each producer is €3840. At the same time, the producer also incurs fixed short-run *expenses* of €10 for each of the 256 units of capital that are fixed in the short run *and* the recurring fixed licence fee of €1280, for a total of €3840 in total expenditures that are not costs in the short run.

Exercise 14B.4

We have indicated that $k = 256$ is the optimal long-run quantity of capital when $(p, w, r) = (5, 20, 10)$. Can you conclude that the industry is in long-run equilibrium from the information in the previous paragraph? *Hint:* This can only be true if no firm has an incentive to enter or exit the industry.

14B.2 An Industry in Long-Run Equilibrium

We concluded after equation (14.6) that the long-run AC curve for each of the firms assuming $w = 20$ and $r = 10$ is U-shaped and attains its lowest point of €5 at output quantity 1280. We also know that *in the long run, the number of firms in the market will adjust to keep the equilibrium price at this lowest point of the long-run AC curve*; in the long run, equilibrium price is €5. With market demand given by equation (14.7), this implies that the industry will produce a total of 1 600 000 units of x, which is the quantity demanded by the market when price is €5. Since each firm will produce at the lowest point of its AC curve in long-run equilibrium, we know that each individual firm will produce 1280 units of x, implying that there will be 1250 producers in the industry.

The short-run equilibrium calculated in the previous section is, therefore, also the long-run equilibrium, with the short-run fixed quantity of capital (256 units per firm) equal to how much capital each firm wishes to utilize given the current prices. The industry equilibrium is pictured in Graph 14.12, with panel (b) illustrating the short-run industry demand curves whose intersection signals prices to the typical consumer in panel (a) and the typical producer in panel (c).

Graph 14.12 A Graphical Representation of the Industry Equilibrium

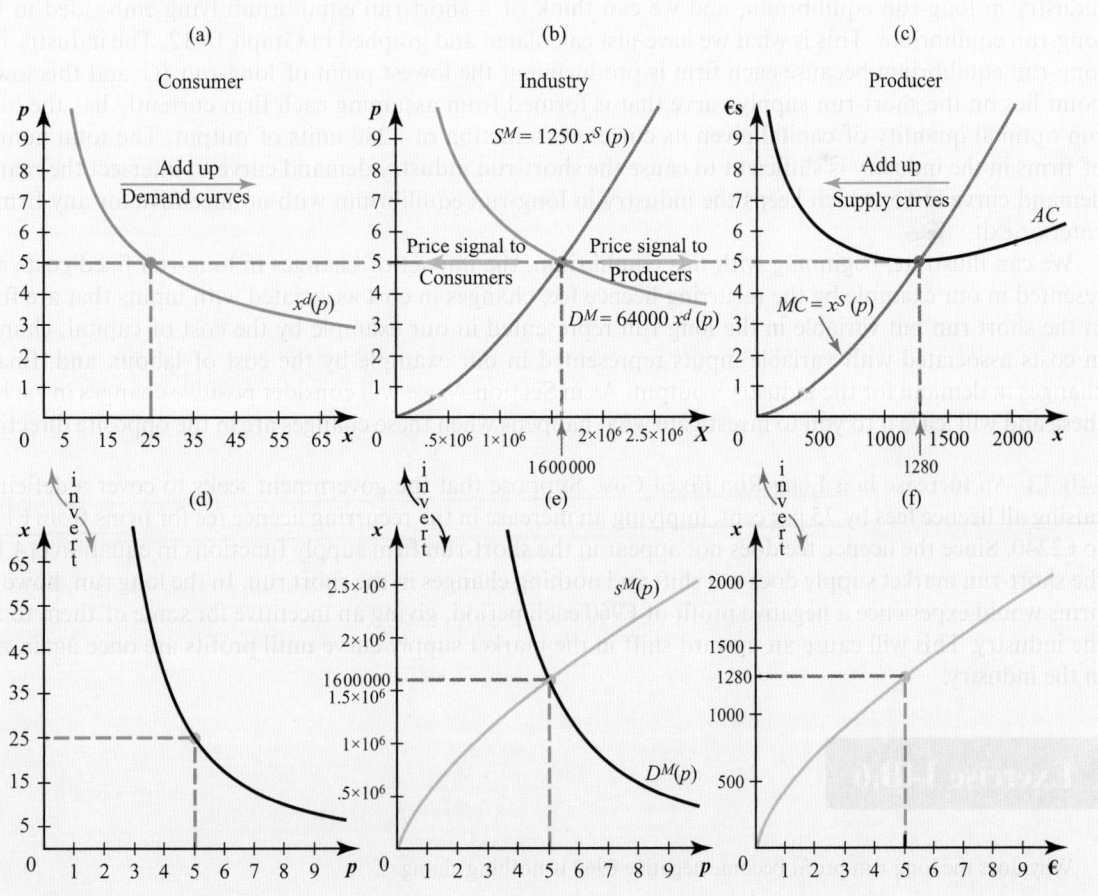

Note that the supply and demand curves are plotted as inverse supply and demand functions given that they are functions of prices, but prices appear on the vertical axes.

The graph looks similar to those in Section A except for the fact that short-run firm supply curves begin at the origin in panel (b) whereas we drew them as beginning at the lowest point of short-run average cost AC^{SR} in the graphs in Section A. When you think about the underlying assumptions in Graph 14.12, however, the reasons for this difference should become apparent. The short-run production function given in equation (14.9) has decreasing returns to scale throughout, implying increasing MC throughout. In the graphs in Section A, we implicitly assumed a sigmoid shaped short-run production function of the type introduced in Chapter 11, with an initial portion that has increasing marginal product of labour before eventually exhibiting diminishing marginal product of labour. This assumption led to a U-shaped AC^{SR}, with the portion of the MC above AC^{SR} forming the short-run firm supply curve. In the case of the short-run production function that has diminishing marginal product of labour throughout, however, the AC^{SR} is not U-shaped and has its lowest point at the origin.

Exercise 14B.5

Can you graph the AC^{SR} into panel (c) of Graph 14.12?

14B.3 Changing Conditions and Changing Equilibrium

At this point in Section A, we demonstrated how the short- and long-run equilibrium change as different parts of the economic environment change. We began by noting that our starting point will always be an industry in long-run equilibrium, and we can think of a short-run equilibrium lying embedded in this long-run equilibrium. This is what we have just calculated and graphed in Graph 14.12. The industry is in long-run equilibrium because each firm is producing at the lowest point of long-run AC, and this lowest point lies on the short-run supply curve that is formed from assuming each firm currently has the long-run optimal quantity of capital given its current production of 1280 units of output. The total number of firms in the industry is sufficient to cause the short-run industry demand curve to intersect the market demand curve at €5, which keeps the industry in long-run equilibrium with no incentive for any firm to enter or exit.

We can illustrate, beginning with this equilibrium, the impact of changes in long-run fixed costs represented in our example by the recurring licence fee, changes in cost associated with inputs that are fixed in the short run but variable in the long run represented in our example by the cost of capital, changes in costs associated with variable inputs represented in our example by the cost of labour, and, finally, changes in demand for the industry's output. As in Section A, we will consider positive changes in each of these and will leave it to you to investigate what happens when these changes are in the opposite direction.

14B.3.1 An Increase in a Long-Run Fixed Cost Suppose that the government seeks to cover a deficit by raising all licence fees by 75 per cent, implying an increase in the recurring licence fee for firms from €1280 to €2240. Since the licence fee does not appear in the short-run firm supply functions in equation (14.10), the short-run market supply does not shift and nothing changes in the short run. In the long run, however, firms would experience a negative profit of €960 each period, giving an incentive for some of them to exit the industry. This will cause an upward shift in the market supply curve until profits are once again zero in the industry.

Exercise 14B.6

Why does the long-run profit become negative €960 if nothing changes?

To see at what output price profits will be zero, we have to see where the new lowest point of each producer's long-run AC curve lies. Instead of the AC in equation (14.6), the increase in the licence fee causes the new long-run AC' curve to be:

$$AC'(x) = 0.66874x^{1/4} + \frac{2240}{x}, \tag{14.13}$$

which is once again U-shaped but now has its lowest point at approximately $x = 2000$ where average cost is approximately €5.59 per unit. We therefore know that the new long-run equilibrium will have an output price of approximately €5.59, up from the previous price of €5.00 per unit, with each firm that remains in the industry producing approximately 2000 units of output each period, up from the previous 1280 units produced by each firm in the industry. Substituting this new price into the market demand function in equation (14.7), we find that consumers will demand approximately 1 280 000 units of output each period at this new long-run equilibrium price. With each firm in the industry producing approximately 2000 units, this implies that the new long-run equilibrium will have approximately 640 firms, down from 1250 before the increase in the licence fee. Finally, we can insert the new price into the individual demand functions in equation (14.2) to conclude that each consumer will lower their consumption from 25 to approximately 20 units of x each period.

Exercise 14B.7

Verify these calculations.

Exercise 14B.8

Compare the changes set off by an increase in the licence fee to those predicted in Graph 14.8.

14B.3.2 An Increase in the Cost of Capital Now assume the cost of capital r increases from €10 per unit to €15 per unit. Since capital is a fixed input in the short run, this change once again does not alter the short-run supply curve of firms (equation (14.10)) and thus has no impact on the short-run market equilibrium. However, as capital becomes a variable input in the long run, it becomes an economic cost, and profit for each firm becomes negative unless output price rises.

How high the price rises again depends on how far up the lowest point of the producers' long-run AC curve has shifted. Substituting in the wage $w = 20$ and the new rental rate $r' = 15$ into the general cost function in equation (14.5), we get cost as a function of output given by:

$$C(x) = 0.819036x^{5/4} + 1280, \tag{14.14}$$

with accompanying average cost given by:

$$AC'(x) = 0.819036x^{1/4} + \frac{1280}{x}. \tag{14.15}$$

This new AC' curve reaches its lowest point at approximately $x = 1088$ where average cost is approximately €5.88 per unit, up from €5.00 per unit before the increase in r. Thus, the new long-run equilibrium price has to be approximately €5.88, with each firm that remains in the industry producing 1088 units of x each period. At this price, the market demand function tells us that consumers will demand approximately

1 156 925 units of x, which implies that the new long-run equilibrium will have approximately 1063 producers, down from the initial 1250.

Exercise 14B.9

Verify these calculations.

Exercise 14B.10

Are these results consistent with Graph 14.9?

Exercise 14B.11

How much capital and labour are employed in the industry before and after the increase in r?

Notice that in this example, the lowest point of the long-run AC curve has shifted to the left from 1280 to 1088. Each firm is producing less in the new long-run equilibrium, but because industry demand has fallen sufficiently much due to the long-run increase in price from €5 to €5.88, this has still required some firms to exit. Were the industry demand curve steeper and thus less responsive to the price increase, this result could have gone in the opposite direction, with more rather than fewer firms in the new long-run equilibrium.

14B.3.3 An Increase in the Cost of Labour The most complicated cost change we analyzed in Section A was that of an increase in the wage rate w because labour can be adjusted in both the short and long run. Suppose that the wage rate increases from €20 to €30 with the cost of capital remaining at €10 and the licence fee remaining at €1280. From equation (14.10), we know that the short-run supply function for each producer is $x(p, w) = 3225.398(p/w)^{2/3}$, which implies that the supply function shifts from $x^s(p) = 437.754p^{2/3}$ when $w = 20$ to:

$$x^{s'}(p) = 334.069p^{2/3}. \tag{14.16}$$

With 1250 producers in the industry, this implies that short-run industry supply shifts from $S^M(p) = 547\,192p^{2/3}$ to:

$$S^{M'}(p) = 417\,586p^{2/3}. \tag{14.17}$$

When set equal to the unchanged market demand $D^M(p) = 40\,000\,000/p^2$, we get a short-run equilibrium price of approximately €5.53, up from the initial equilibrium price of €5.00 before the wage increase. At this price, each firm produces approximately 1045 units of output, down from 1280, earning revenue of approximately €5782 each period.

Exercise 14B.12

Verify these calculations.

In the short run, expenses associated with capital and licence fees are not economic costs, and labour costs are the only short-run economic costs. With each firm's capital fixed at 256 units, approximately 77 units of labour are employed by each firm to produce the 1045 units of output, implying that short-run economic costs are approximately €2310. Given €5782 in revenue, this leaves a short-run economic profit of €3472.

Exercise 14B.13

How much does the industry production change in the short run?

In the long run, licence costs and costs associated with capital become economic costs. Were each firm to continue to produce as it does in short-run equilibrium, total costs would therefore include €2560 for capital inputs and €1280 for the licence to operate, implying that each firm would earn a long-run economic profit of $-€367$ each period. Thus, firms have an incentive to exit until long-run profit is once again zero for all firms that remain in the industry. This will occur when price reaches the lowest point of the new long-run AC' curve, which happens when long-run output price settles at approximately €5.88, up from €5.53 in the short run. At this long-run equilibrium price, each producer that remains in the market will produce approximately 1088 units of output, up from 1045 in the short run, while the market demand for output falls to approximately 1 156 925 from 1 306 395 in the short run. This leaves room for approximately 1063 producers in the industry, down from 1250.

Exercise 14B.14

Verify these calculations and compare the results with our graphical analysis of an increase in the wage rate in Graph 14.10.

As in the case of an increase in the rental rate in the previous section, note again that the lowest point of the long-run AC curve has shifted to the left from 1280 to 1088. Each firm is again producing less in the new long-run equilibrium, but because industry demand fell sufficiently due to the long-run increase in price from €5 to €5.53, this still required some firms to exit. Were the industry demand curve steeper and thus less responsive to the price increase, this could again result in more rather than fewer firms in the new long-run equilibrium. Were that the case, the short-run increase in price would have over-shot the long-run zero-profit price.

14B.3.4 An Increase in Market Demand We concluded Section A with a brief analysis of how the industry changes in the short and long run when there is an increase in market demand. Suppose, for instance, that some unexpected news coverage of the health benefits of consuming x good increases the number of consumers in our market from 64 000 to 100 000. Market demand, initially equal to $D^M(p) = 64 000x^d(p) = 40 000 000/p^2$ shifts to the new $(D)^{M'}(p)$ given by:

$$D^M(p) = 100 000x^d(p) = 100 000 \left(\frac{625}{p^2} \right) = \frac{62\,500\,000}{p^2}. \tag{14.18}$$

The short-run market supply function $S^M(p) = 547\,192p^{2/3}$ remains unchanged since each firm's cost curves remain unchanged. Setting this equal to the new demand function, we get a new short-run equilibrium price of approximately €5.91, up from €5.00. At this price, each of the 1250 existing firms produce, given their short-run supply curves from equation (14.10), approximately 1431 units of output, up from 1280, with industry supply rising to approximately 1 789 234 from 1 600 000.

Exercise 14B.15

How much does individual consumption by consumers who were originally in the market change in the short run?

At the new short-run equilibrium price, each firm earns positive economic profits, thus providing an incentive for new firms to enter the industry until price is driven back to €5 when all firms in the industry make zero profits. At €5, the new market demand curve tells us that consumers demand 2 500 000 units of x. With each firm once again producing at the lowest point of its long-run average cost curve where $x = 1280$, this implies that there will be approximately 1953 producers in the new long-run equilibrium, up from 1250.

Exercise 14B.16

Verify these calculations and compare the results with Graph 14.11, where we graphically illustrated the impact of an increase in market demand.

End-of-Chapter Exercises

14.1† In Table 14.1, the last column indicates the predicted change in the number of firms within an industry when economic conditions change.

A. In two cases, Table 14.1 makes a definitive prediction, whereas in two other cases it does not.

a. Explain why we can say definitively that the number of firms falls as a recurring fixed cost increases. Relate your answer to what we know about firm output and price in the long run.

b. Repeat (a) for the case of an increase in demand.

c. Now consider an increase in the wage rate and suppose first that this causes the long-run AC curve to shift upwards without changing the output level at which the curve reaches its lowest point. In this case, can you predict whether the number of firms increases or decreases?

d. Repeat (c) but assume that the lowest point of the AC curve shifts up and to the right.

e. Repeat (c) again but this time assume that the lowest point of the AC curve shifts up and to the left.

f. Is the analysis regarding the new equilibrium number of firms any different for a change in r?

g. Which way would the lowest point of the AC curve have to shift in order for us not to be sure whether the number of firms increases or decreases when w falls?

B. Consider the case of a firm that operates with a Cobb–Douglas production function $f(\ell, k) = A\ell^\alpha k^\beta$ where $\alpha, \beta > 0$ and $\alpha + \beta < 1$.

a. The cost function for such a production process, assuming no fixed costs, was given in equation (13.43). Assuming an additional recurring fixed cost F, what is the average cost function for this firm?

b. **Derive the equation for the output level x^* at which the long-run AC curve reaches its lowest point.

c. How does x^* change with F, w and r?

d. *True or False*: For industries in which firms face Cobb–Douglas production processes with recurring fixed costs, we can predict that the number of firms in the industry increases with F but we cannot predict whether the number of firms will increase or decrease with w or r.

14.2 Table 14.1 was constructed under the assumption that all firms in the industry are identical.

A. Suppose that all firms in an industry have U-shaped long-run average cost curves.

a. Leaving aside the column in Table 14.1 labelled 'Firm Output', what would change if firms have different cost structures; that is, some firms have lower marginal and average costs than others?

b. Industries such as those described in (a) are sometimes called *increasing cost industries* compared with *constant cost industries* where all firms are identical. Can you derive a rationale for these terms?

c. It has been argued that in some industries, the average and marginal costs of *all* firms decline as more firms enter the market. For instance, such industries might make use of an unusual labour market skill that becomes more plentiful in the market as more workers train for this skill when many firms demand it. How would the long-run industry supply curve differ in this case from that discussed in the text as well as that described in (a)?

d. Industries such as those described in (c) are sometimes referred to as *decreasing cost industries*. Can you explain why?

14.3† **Business Application:** *Economic Rent and Profiting from Entrepreneurial Skill.* Assume you are the owner-operator of a sandwich bar that is part of a competitive industry. Despite being the owner, you are also one of the workers in the restaurant and collect the same wage as other workers for the time you put into the business each week. In addition, you keep any weekly profits.

A. Assume that all the sandwich bars are using the same homothetic decreasing returns to scale technology, but now the inputs include the level of entrepreneurial capital c in addition to weekly labour ℓ and capital k. Assume also that all restaurants are required to pay a recurring weekly fixed cost F.

a. All sandwich bar owners possess the same level of entrepreneurial skill c. Draw the long-run AC curve for weekly sandwich production and indicate how many sandwiches per week the firm will sell and at what price assuming that the industry is in long-run equilibrium.

b. Suppose that you are special and possess more entrepreneurial and management skill than all other sandwich bar owners. As a result of your higher level of c, the marginal product of labour and capital is 20 per cent greater for any bundle of ℓ and k than it is for any of your competitors. Will the long-run equilibrium price be any different as a result?

c. If your entrepreneurial skill causes the marginal product of capital and labour to be 20 per cent greater for any combination of MC and AC than for your competitors, how does your isoquant map differ from theirs? For a given wage and rental rate, will you employ the same labour to capital ratio as your competitors?

d. Will you produce more or less than your competitors? Illustrate this on your graph by determining where the long-run MC and AC curves for your firm will lie relative to the AC curve of your competitors.

e. Illustrate in your graph how much weekly profit you will earn from your unusually high entrepreneurial skill.

f. Suppose the owner of MacroSoft, a new computer firm, is interested in employing you as the manager of one of its branches. How high a weekly salary would it have to offer you in order for you to leave the sandwich business, assuming you would work for 36 hours per week in either case and assuming the wage rate in the sandwich business is €15 per hour?

g. The benefit that an entrepreneur receives from their skill is sometimes referred to as the *economic rent* of that skill because the entrepreneur could be renting that skill out to someone like MacroSoft instead of using it in their own business. If the economic rent of entrepreneurial skill is included as a cost to the sandwich business you run, how much profit are you making in the sandwich business?

h. Would counting this economic rent on your skill as a cost in the sandwich business affect how many sandwiches you produce? How would it change the AC curve in your graph?

B. Suppose that all sandwich bars are employing the production function $f(\ell, k, c) = 30\ell^{0.4}k^{0.4}c$ where ℓ stands for weekly labour hours, k stands for weekly hours of rented capital and c stands for the entrepreneurial skill of the owner. The weekly demand for sandwiches in your region is $x(p) = 100040 - 1000p$

a. Suppose that $c = 1$ for all owners, that $w = 15$ and $r = 20$, that there is a fixed weekly cost €4320 of operating a sandwich bar, and the industry is in long-run equilibrium. Determine the number of sandwiches per week sold by each firm, the price at which sandwiches sell, and the number of sandwich bars that are operating.

b. Suppose that you are the only sandwich bar owner who is different from all the others in that you are a better manager and entrepreneur and that this is reflected in $c = 1.24573$ for you. Determine your long-run AC and MC functions. Use the cost function derived for Cobb–Douglas technologies given in equation (13.43) in exercise 13.4 and remember to add the fixed cost.

c. How many sandwiches will you produce in long-run equilibrium?

d. How many restaurants will there be in long-run equilibrium given your higher level of c?

e. How many workers including yourself and units of capital are you employing in your business compared with those employed by your competitors? Recall that the average worker is assumed to work 36 hours per week.

f. How does your bar's weekly long-run profit differ from that of the other sandwich bars?

g. Suppose MacroSoft is interested in employing you as described in part A(f). How high a weekly salary would MacroSoft have to offer you in order for you to exit the sandwich bar business and accept the MacroSoft offer?

h. If you decide to accept the MacroSoft offer and you exit the sandwich business, will total employment in the sandwich business go up or down?

14.4 **Business and Policy Application:** *Capital Gains Taxes.* Taxes on capital gains are applied to income earned on investments that return a profit or capital gain and not on income derived from labour. We will investigate the impact of a capital-gains-tax-induced increase in the rental price of capital on firms within an industry.

A. Suppose you are running a fuel station in a competitive market where all firms are identical. You employ weekly labour ℓ and capital k using a homothetic decreasing returns to scale production function, and incur a weekly fixed cost of F.

a. Begin with your firm's long-run weekly average cost curve and relate it to the weekly demand curve for fuel in your region as well as the short-run weekly aggregate supply curve assuming the industry is in long-run equilibrium. Indicate by x^* how much weekly fuel you sell, by p^* the price at which you sell it, and by X^* the total number of litres of fuel sold in the region per week.

b. Now suppose that an increase in the capital gains tax raises the rental rate on capital k, which is fixed for each fuel station in the short run. Does anything change in the short run?

c. What happens to x^*, p^* and X^* in the long run? Explain how this emerges from your graph.

d. Is it possible for you to tell whether you will employ more or fewer workers as a result of the capital-gains-tax-induced increase in the rental rate? To the extent that it is not possible, what information could help clarify this?

e. Is it possible for you to be able to tell whether the number of fuel stations in the region increases or decreases as a result of the increase in the rental rate? What factors might your answer depend on?

f. Can you tell whether employment of labour in fuel stations increases or decreases? What about employment of capital?

B. Suppose that your production function is given by $f(\ell, k) = 30\ell^{0.4}k^{0.4}$, $F = 1080$ and the weekly region-wide demand for litres of fuel is $x(p) = 100040 - 1000p$. Furthermore, suppose that the wage is $w = 15$ and the current rental rate is 32.1568. Fuel prices are typically in terms of tenths of cents, so express your answer accordingly.

a. Suppose the industry is in long-run equilibrium in the absence of capital gains taxes. Assuming that you can employ fractions of hours of capital and produce fractions of litres of fuel, how much fuel will you produce and at what price will you sell fuel? Use the cost function derived for Cobb–Douglas technologies given in equation (13.43) and remember to add the fixed cost.

b. How many fuel stations are there in your region?

c. Now suppose the government's capital gains tax increases the rental rate of capital by 24.39 per cent to €40. How will your sales of fuel be affected in the new long-run equilibrium?

d. What is the new price of fuel?

e. Will you change the number of workers you employ? How about the hours of capital you rent?

f. Will there be more or fewer fuel stations in the city? How is your answer consistent with the change in the total sales of fuel in the region?

g. What happens to total employment at fuel stations as a result of the capital gains tax? Explain intuitively how this can happen.

h. *Which of your conclusions do you think is qualitatively independent of the production function used as long as it is decreasing returns to scale, and which do you think is not?

i. *Which of your conclusions do you think is qualitatively independent of the demand function, and which do you think is not?

14.5† **Policy and Business Application:** *Minimum Wage Labour Subsidy.* In exercise 13.6, we investigated the firm's decisions in the presence of a government subsidy for employing minimum wage workers. Implicitly, we assumed that the policy has no impact on the prices faced by the firm in question.

A. Suppose that you operate a business that uses minimum wage workers ℓ and capital k. The minimum wage is w, the rental rate for capital is r and you are one of many identical businesses in the industry, each using a homothetic, decreasing returns to scale production process and each facing a recurring fixed cost F.

a. Begin by drawing the average cost curve of one firm and relating it to the short-run supply and demand in the industry assuming it is in long-run equilibrium.

b. Now the government introduces a wage subsidy s that lowers the effective cost of employing minimum wage workers from w to $(1 - s)w$. What happens in the firm and in the industry in the short run?

c. What happens to price and output in the firm and the market in the long run compared with the original quantities?

d. Is it possible to tell whether there will be more or fewer firms in the new long-run equilibrium?

e. Is it possible to tell whether the long-run price will be higher or lower than the short-run price? How does this relate to your answer to part (d)?

B. Suppose that the firms in the industry use the production technology $x = f(\ell, k) = 100\ell^{0.25}k^{0.25}$ and pay a recurring fixed cost of $F = 2210$. Suppose further that the minimum wage is €10 and the rental rate of capital is $r = 20$.

a. What is the initial long-run equilibrium price and firm output level?

b. Suppose that $s = 0.5$, implying that the cost of employing minimum wage labour falls to €5. How does your answer to (a) change?

c. How much more or less of each input does the firm buy in the new long-run equilibrium compared with the original one? For a Cobb–Douglas production process of the form $f(\ell, k) = A\ell^\alpha k^\beta$, the input demand functions are:

$$\ell(w, r, p) = \left(\frac{pA\alpha^{(1-\beta)}\beta^\beta}{w^{(1-\beta)}r^\beta}\right)^{1/(1-\alpha-\beta)} \quad \text{and} \quad k(w, r, p) = \left(\frac{pA\alpha^\alpha\beta^{(1-\alpha)\alpha}}{w^\alpha r^{(1-\alpha)\alpha}}\right)^{1/(1-\alpha-\beta)} \tag{13.47}$$

d. If price does not affect the quantity of x demanded very much, will the number of firms increase or decrease in the long run?

e. Suppose that demand is given by $x(p) = 200\,048 - 2000p$. How many firms are there in the initial long-run equilibrium?

f. Derive the short-run market supply function and illustrate that it results in the initial long-run equilibrium price.

g. Verify that the short-run equilibrium price falls to approximately €2.69 when the wage is subsidized.

h. How much does each firm's output change in the short run?

i. Determine the change in the long-run equilibrium number of firms when the wage is subsidized and make sense of this in light of the short-run equilibrium results.

14.6 **Policy Application:** *Pollution Taxes on Output.* Suppose you are one of many firms that refine crude oil into petrol. This process creates pollution. The government announces a new tax of €t on each litre of petrol that leaves a refinery, to be paid by the refinery.

   A. For purposes of this exercise, assume that the refinement process of crude oil into petrol has decreasing returns to scale but entails a recurring fixed cost.

      a. Begin by illustrating the industry in pre-tax equilibrium, showing one firm's average cost curve as well as the short-run market supply and demand that supports an industry in long-run equilibrium.
      b. What changes for each firm and in the industry in the short run when the tax is introduced?
      c. What changes in the long run?
      d. *True or False:* While refineries bear some of the burden of this tax in the short run, they will pass all of the tax on to consumers in the long run.
      e. Consider the statement: 'Regulators are particularly concerned about reports that companies in the industry managed to pass the pollution tax fully onto consumers and view this as a sign that the industry is not competitive but is rather engaged in strategic manipulation of petrol prices'. Comment on this statement.
      f. Will refineries change the mix of labour and capital in the long run assuming they continue operating?
      g. Consider this statement: 'In talking to this refinery's owner, it seems that there are no plans in place to lay off any workers in response to the pollution tax on refined petrol. Jobs in the industry therefore appear to be safe for now'. Do you agree?

   B. Suppose that the production function used by firms in the petrol refinery industry is $f(\ell, k) = A\ell^\alpha k^\beta$ with $\alpha, \beta > 0$ and $\alpha + \beta < 1$, and suppose that each refinery pays a recurring fixed cost F.

      a. If you did not already do so in exercise 14.1, derive the expression for the output level x^* at which the long-run AC curve reaches its lowest point. This should be a function of A, α, β, w and r.
      b. How does x^* change under the per-litre tax on petrol leaving the refinery?
      c. Can you use your answer to determine whether the number of petrol refineries will increase or decrease as a result of the tax?
      d. If you have not already done so in exercise 14.1, determine the long-run equilibrium price p^* before the tax as a function of A, α, β, w and r. How does this change under the tax?
      e. Can you use your answer to determine who actually pays the tax?
      f. Will the tax result in less pollution? If so, why?

*conceptually challenging
**computationally challenging
†solutions in Study Guide

Chapter 15

The Invisible Hand and the First Welfare Theorem

The insight that order can emerge without anyone planning it is quite remarkable in and of itself. What is even more remarkable, however, is that under certain conditions, the spontaneous order generated in a decentralized market mimics what a central planner might wish to implement if they knew everything there was to know about the individuals in the market. Not only do the incentives in a decentralized market generate a predictable equilibrium but also, under certain conditions, there is no way that the resulting situation could be altered to make some people better off without making anyone worse off. The spontaneous order of the decentralized market is, under certain conditions, fully efficient. This chapter, and much of the remainder of the book, is devoted to demonstrating this important result. We will demonstrate the conditions necessary for the result to hold as well as the real-world conditions that might cause the result to break down, making room for civil society or government institutions to improve on the spontaneous order of the market.

15A	Welfare Analysis in Equilibrium

In order to demonstrate the welfare properties of markets, we will need to measure the benefit each economic actor derives from being able to participate in markets. In output markets, this is the benefit to consumers and producers, whereas in input markets it is the benefit to workers, to firms and to those supplying capital. The suppliers of capital are often individuals who are lending financial capital by saving, and the demanders of capital are often firms that invest in order to produce goods and services.

We have already defined the basic building blocks for conducting this analysis through the concepts of consumer surplus. We can extend this concept to workers, with worker surplus defined as the benefit workers derive from being able to sell their labour in labour markets, and we can similarly define the surplus that is derived from being able to plan for the future by those who provide capital to the market. On the producer side, producer surplus is the relevant measure for producers. We will discuss each of these in turn before illustrating how markets, under certain conditions, maximize the sum of producer and consumer surplus – which is another way of saying that the equilibrium is efficient.

15A.1 Consumer and Worker Surplus

Individual consumer surplus can be measured as the area underneath the compensated demand or marginal willingness to pay curve, and above the price at which a consumer consumes. However, unless consumer tastes for the good that we are analyzing are borderline between normal and inferior, and tastes are thus quasilinear in the good of interest, the compensated demand curves for individual consumers are different from their regular demand curves that we added up in Chapter 14 to derive market demand. This tells us that we cannot, in general, illustrate the total consumer surplus for all the consumers in a market along the market demand curve that we use to derive the equilibrium. While the market demand curve allows us to predict behaviour, it is not typically the right curve on which to measure consumer surplus.

To simplify thinking about market demand curves, we may be tempted to think of them as if they had emerged from a single choice problem the way individual demand curves do. When we think this way, we are implicitly assuming that we can treat the demand side in the goods market as if it emerges from a single representative consumer, and if we assume a certain indifference map for that representative consumer, we can derive not only the observable market demand curve but also the compensated market demand curve on which we measure consumer surplus, just as we did in Chapter 10. This sounds strange at first since we have made a big point of the fact that the equilibrium that arises in a competitive market results from the decentralized actions of many individuals that simply take the economic environment as given. Nevertheless, we will see that there exist circumstances under which we can in fact simply think of all these individuals as a single individual who also takes the economic environment as given. Microeconomists may do this when they lump individuals into groups such as households, and treat their aggregate demand curves as if they emerged from one individual's decision.

15A.1.1 Representative Consumers

What has to be true about individuals in a group that would allow us to treat the group is if it were a single individual with well-defined tastes? To develop some intuition, suppose first that the group is composed of only two people, 'A' and 'B', with the market demand curve being a household demand curve that results from summing the two individual demand curves. To be even more specific, suppose that A is the higher income earner and has exogenous disposable income $I^1 = 800$ and has permitted B to have exogenous disposable income $I^2 = 400$ as they go to buy clothes, denoted x_1, and other goods, denoted x_2. Within the shop they face the same prices (p_1 and p_2) and end up at two different checkouts with two different baskets of goods (A^1 and A^2) that emerged from both of them doing the best they can, given their individual circumstances at the shop. The composition of these individual baskets thus depends on their individual tastes, individual incomes and the common prices they face.

We could think that this household demand really is as if it had arisen from a single consumer doing the best they can, given their total household budget. If the household jointly behaves like a single individual, it should not matter how the household's exogenous income is divided between B and A. If a streak of righteous indignation at the inequity of the exogenous incomes led you to take €200 out of A's pocket and put it into B's pocket so that each now has €600 as they walk into the shop, they would jointly come out of the store with the same number of clothes and other goods as if they had gone in with their original budgets. The individual baskets at the checkout counters would be different, but when they put it in the boot of their car, they would end up having exactly the same items as if you had never interfered. Only if this is true do A and B really behave as if they were the single unit.

This does not, however, have to imply that A and B have exactly the same tastes. Suppose, for instance, that A and B initially faced the dark brown and dark blue budget lines in Graph 15.1. A arrives at the checkout counter with bundle A^1 as their optimal basket, and B arrives with bundle A^2 in their basket. Let's imagine that you had pulled off your righteous transfer of €200 from A's pocket into B's pocket before they entered the shop, causing both to face the light blue budget rather than the initial dark brown and dark blue. In order for them to end up putting the same overall basket into the car's boot, it must be that the change in A's optimal basket from their initial dark brown to their new light blue budget is exactly offset by the change in B's optimal basket as they move from their initial dark blue to their new light blue budget. The dark brown arrow linking A's original optimum A^1 to their new optimum B^1 must be exactly parallel to the dark blue arrow from B's original optimum A^2 to their new optimum B^2. Their individual tastes may be quite different, but the change in individual behaviour as income is redistributed between them keeps their overall consumption bundle constant. As long as this holds over the relevant range of economic environments that is of interest to us, they behave as a single representative actor. This implies that they behave in the aggregate as if they were a single individual with rational tastes, tastes that give rise to demand and compensated demand curves that have exactly the interpretation we developed in Part 1 of the text for a single consumer.

Graph 15.1 Two Consumers Behaving as One Unit

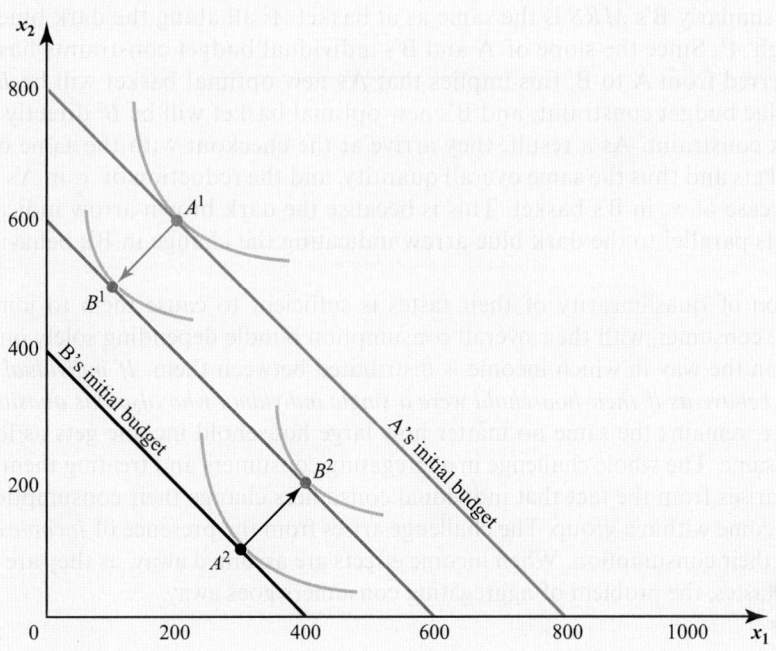

Exercise 15A.1

Suppose that A's and B's tastes are exactly identical. If their tastes are also homothetic, does their household behave like a single representative actor? What if their tastes are quasilinear and neither individual is at a corner solution?

Exercise 15A.2

Can you illustrate a case where their tastes are identical but they do not behave as a representative actor?

Exercise 15A.3

Suppose A and B have homothetic tastes but they are not identical. Does this still imply that they behave like a single representative actor?

15A.1.2 Consumer Surplus and the Special Case of Quasilinear Tastes Consider the same budget lines for consumers A and B as we did in Graph 15.1 with the same initially optimal baskets for A (A^1) and B (A^2) when their incomes are €800 and €400. If you succeed in redistributing €200 of A's income to B both, therefore, now face the light blue budget constraint. If A and B's tastes are quasilinear in x_1, we know that A's MRS is the same as it is at basket A^1 all along the (dark brown) dashed vertical line going through A^1, and similarly B's MRS is the same as at basket A^2 all along the dark blue dashed vertical line going through A^2. Since the slope of A and B's individual budget constraints has not changed as income is transferred from A to B, this implies that A's new optimal basket will be B^1 directly below A^1 on the light blue budget constraint, and B's new optimal basket will be B^2 directly above A^2 on the light blue budget constraint. As a result, they arrive at the checkout with the same quantity of x_1 in each of their baskets and thus the same overall quantity, and the reduction of x_2 in A's basket is exactly offset by the increase of x_2 in B's basket. This is because the dark brown arrow indicating the change in A's behaviour is parallel to the dark blue arrow indicating the change in B's behaviour as shown in Graph 15.2.

The assumption of quasilinearity of their tastes is sufficient to cause them to jointly behave *as if* they were a single consumer, with their overall consumption bundle depending solely on their household income and not on the way in which income is distributed between them. *If individual tastes are quasilinear, consumers behave as if their household were a single individual who also has quasilinear tastes* since consumption of x_1 remains the same no matter how large household income gets as long as the prices faced remain the same. The whole challenge in aggregating consumers and treating them as if they were a single consumer arises from the fact that individual consumers change their consumption bundles when we redistribute income within a group. The challenge arises from the presence of *income effects* that cause people to change their consumption. When income effects are assumed away, as they are when we assume quasilinearity of tastes, the problem of aggregating consumers goes away.

Graph 15.2 Aggregating Consumers With Quasilinear Tastes

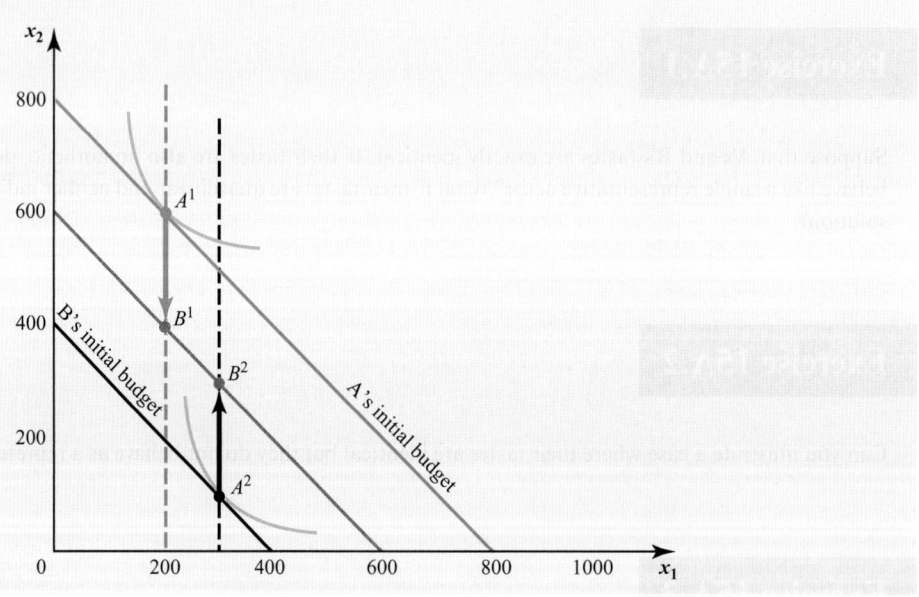

Exercise 15A.4

True or False: As long as everyone has quasilinear tastes, the group will behave like a representative actor even if all the individuals do not share the same tastes assuming no one is at a corner solution. The same is also true if everyone has homothetic tastes.

Let us move beyond the simple example of a household and consider all the consumers in a particular output market. If we assume that all consumers have tastes that are quasilinear in the output, we can, by the same logic we outlined, treat the market demand curve that sums all the individual demand curves as if it had arisen from a single representative consumer who also has quasilinear tastes. Since the only difference between compensated and regular demand curves arises from income effects, and since quasilinear tastes do not give rise to income effects, we can furthermore assume that the regular demand curve is also the compensated demand curve, and that this demand curve therefore also represents the marginal willingness to pay curve along which we can measure consumer surplus. We have therefore identified the conditions that individual tastes have to satisfy in order to use the uncompensated market demand curve for measuring aggregate consumer surplus.

Exercise 15A.5

Suppose that A and B share identical homothetic tastes that are not over perfect substitutes. Will their household demand curve be identical to their marginal willingness to pay curve?

15A.1.3 Worker and Saver Surplus Measuring the surplus that workers attain in labour markets is analogous to measuring consumer surplus in output markets because worker behaviour arises from the same underlying consumer model in which we replace goods x_1 and x_2 with leisure L and consumption c. The important difference is that the two-good consumer model produces output *demand* curves when x_1 and x_2 are the goods that are modelled, but results in labour *supply* curves when L and c are the goods we model, with the difference between leisure endowment and leisure consumption resulting in labour supply. Compensated and regular curves overlap when tastes are quasilinear. When tastes for leisure are quasilinear for all workers, each worker's labour supply curve is equal to their *compensated* labour supply curve, and the market labour supply curve can be treated as if it had arisen from a single worker's choices, with that worker's tastes themselves also being quasilinear in leisure.

Graph 15.3 depicts consumer and worker surplus in two graphs of output and labour markets that are in equilibrium.

Graph 15.3 Aggregate Consumer and Worker Surplus When Tastes Are Quasilinear

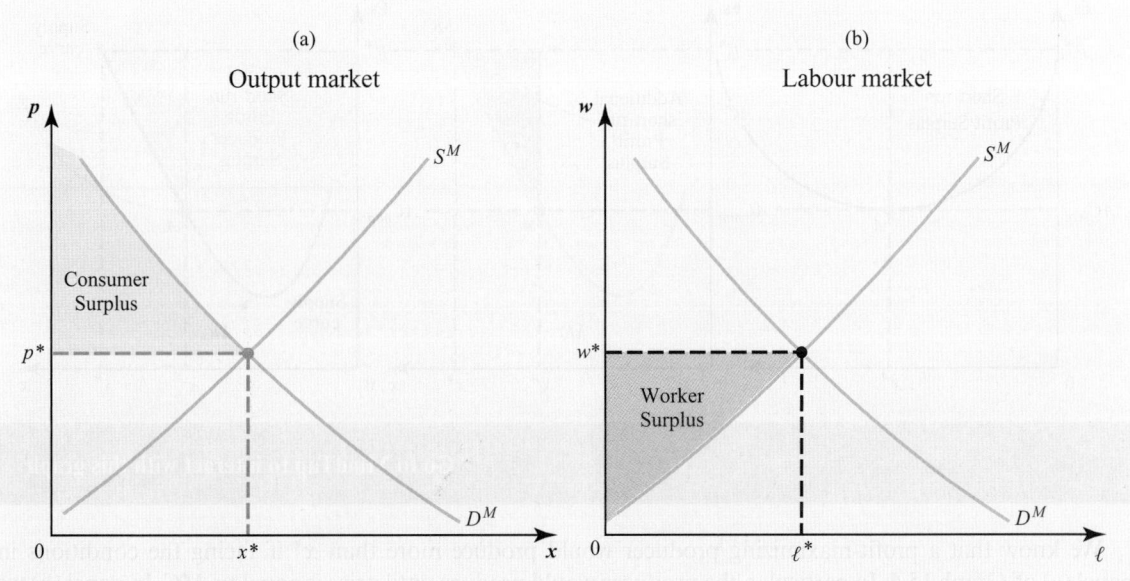

Our analysis of the underlying consumer model shows that the surplus areas in these graphs are correct only for the special case where consumers and workers can be modelled as representative actors who have quasilinear tastes in x_1 in panel (a) and in leisure in panel (b). While the description of the equilibrium prices and quantities is correct regardless of underlying assumptions about tastes, the depiction of consumer and producer surplus areas is correct only in the special case of quasilinear tastes.

Finally, we could draw an analogous graph representing the surplus attained by those who save financial capital and therefore lend it to others at the market interest rate. It becomes particularly problematic, however, to assume that the underlying tastes that result in capital supply curves are quasilinear. Recall that these curves arise from choices in the consumer model where consumption this period is put on the horizontal axis and consumption in some future period is put on the vertical. It seems implausible that tastes are quasilinear in consumption in either period, with consumption in that period being neither a normal nor an inferior good but consumption in the other period being normal. Consumption, one would think, is likely to be a normal good regardless of when it takes place. We will therefore need to be particularly cautious with welfare analysis involving those who plan for the future by saving in financial markets.

15A.2 Producer Surplus or Profit

Producers, it is assumed, are in business to make profit, and if a producer is able to earn positive economic profit, the producer has, by definition, been made better off by the amount of that profit by being able to participate in this market rather than pursue their next best alternative. Economic profit is our measure of the surplus producers derive from being able to participate in markets. We will use the terms *producer surplus* and *economic profit* interchangeably.

15A.2.1 Measuring Producer Surplus on the Supply Curve In our development of producer theory, we covered two ways of illustrating profit in the absence of fixed costs graphically, using either the MC curve or the AC curve. We can combine these methods of illustrating profit to demonstrate that profit can also be measured as an area above the producer's supply curve.

Consider first the AC curve pictured in panel (a) of Graph 15.4. Suppose that the equilibrium price was p^* and that the producer is initially producing quantity x^A corresponding to the lowest point of the AC curve. In that case, total revenues would be p^* times x^A while total costs would be AC_{min} times x^A, and the difference between those two areas in the graph would be equal to the shaded dark brown area.

Graph 15.4 Three Ways of Illustrating Short-Run Profit or Short-Run Producer Surplus

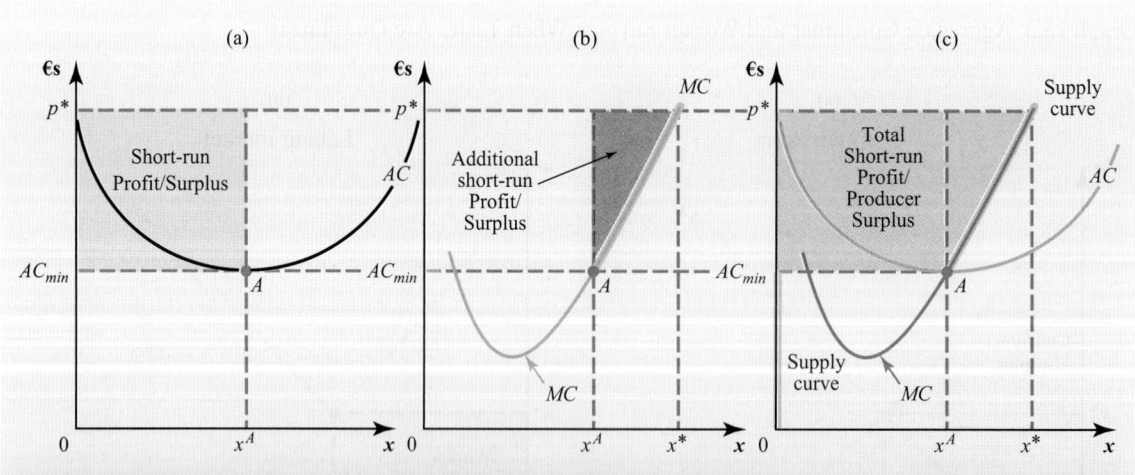

Go to MindTap to interact with this graph

We know that a profit-maximizing producer would produce more than x^A if facing the conditions in panel (a) of Graph 15.4. In particular, the producer would produce until price is equal to MC. In panel (b) we therefore graph the MC curve, with the portion of the MC that lies above AC, and thus above point A from panel (a), highlighted. We know that we can measure the profit a producer makes by producing x^A units of output as the dark brown area in panel (a), and so we are now interested in how much *additional* profit the producer will make by producing x^* rather than x^A. This *additional* profit is equal to the difference between the *additional* revenue and the *additional* cost the producer incurs. The additional revenue is represented by the area formed by the vertical distance p^* times the horizontal distance $(x^* - x^A)$ while the additional cost is represented as the area below the MC curve in the interval between x^A and x^*. The difference between these areas, representing the additional profit from producing x^* rather than x^A, is the shaded dark blue area in panel (b).

Since the dark brown area in panel (a) is the profit the producer makes when producing x^A and the dark blue area in panel (b) is the *additional* profit the producer makes when producing x^* rather than just x^A, the two areas summed together are equal to total profit from producing x^* at price p^*. This is depicted as the light blue area in panel (c) of the graph, and you can see that this light blue area is the area to the left or above the firm's supply curve up to the equilibrium price.

The argument that *profit can be measured as the area above the producer's supply curve* applies to both short-run and long-run profit. In the case of short-run profit, the dark brown area in panel (a) is measured along the short-run AC curve, while in the case of long-run profit it is measured along the long-run AC curve. Similarly, the dark blue area in panel (b) is measured along the short-run MC curve for short-run profit and along the long-run MC curve for long-run profit. In panel (c), profit is measured either along the short-run or the long-run firm supply curve depending on whether we want to measure short-run or long-run profit.

Exercise 15A.6

Does this measure of long-run profit apply also when the firm encounters long-run recurring fixed costs?

15A.2.2 Treating Producers in an Industry as a Single Representative Producer In our discussion of representative consumers, we noted the difficulty in treating groups of consumers as if they were a single consumer resulted from the presence of income effects.

In the case of producers, there are no analogous income effects to cause any difficulty in aggregating producers and treating them as a single representative producer. Therefore, when we add individual producer supply curves into market supply curves, the area above the market supply curve is the sum of the areas above individual supply curves, and *producer surplus as measured on the market supply curve is the sum of the individual producer surpluses of the firms in the industry*; we can treat the market supply curve as if it were the supply curve of a single representative producer.

15A.2.3 Producer Surplus in Labour Markets We can make a similar argument about the area *under* a firm's demand curve for labour. The short-run demand for labour arises from the downward-sloping part of the marginal revenue product of labour curve pictured in panel (a) of Graph 15.5. There exists a break-even wage W^A at which the producer will make zero profit by employing ℓ^A labour hours. At that wage, the loss incurred for hiring the first ℓ' workers is offset by the gain from hiring the remaining workers. If the equilibrium wage falls below this break-even wage, the firm will employ along the dark brown portion of the MRP_ℓ curve in panel (a) of Graph 15.5, which corresponds to the firm's short-run labour demand curve D^i.

Suppose that the market wage is w^* and that the firm stopped hiring at ℓ^A. We can ask how much additional profit the firm makes from what it would have made had the wage been the break-even wage w^A where profit was zero. Since the firm has to pay $(w^A - w^*)$ *less* per worker hour, this becomes surplus or profit for the firm for each of the ℓ^A worker hours. Summing up all ℓ^A worker hours, the total surplus from being able to employ ℓ^A worker hours at the market wage w^* is equal to the shaded dark brown area in panel (a) of Graph 15.5.

The producer would not stop employing at ℓ^A if the market wage was W^* but would employ ℓ^* worker hours instead. For each *additional* worker hour the firm employs beyond ℓ^A, the *additional* surplus would be the difference between the MRP_ℓ for that worker hour and the wage w^*. The *additional* profit made on the worker hours employed beyond ℓ^A is equal to the shaded dark blue area in panel (a) of the graph, and the *total* surplus for the producer is the sum of the dark brown and dark blue areas.

Graph 15.5 Producer Surplus in Labour Markets

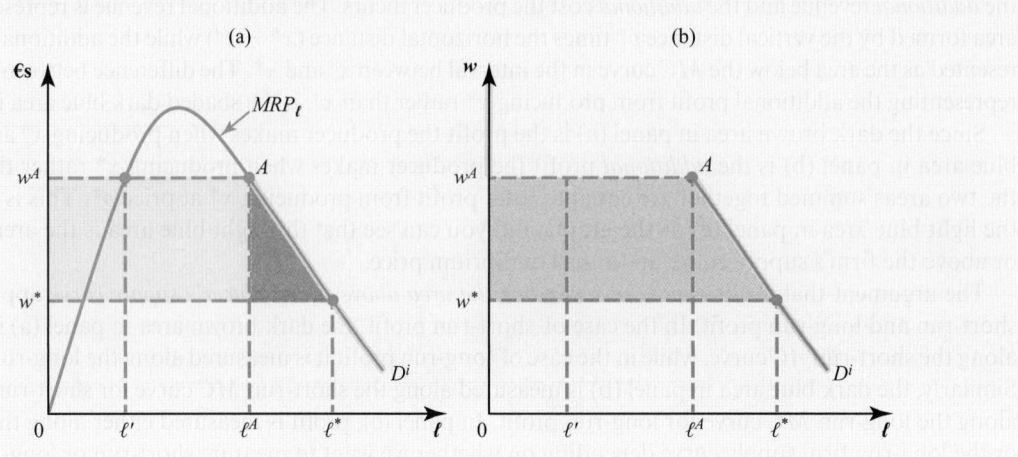

In panel (b) of the graph, we graph the entire short-run labour demand curve for the producer, which includes the bold segment from the MRP_ℓ curve in panel (a) and the vertical dark brown line segment at $\ell = 0$ for wages above the break-even wage w^A. The light blue area in panel (b) is equal to the sum of the dark brown and dark blue areas in panel (a) and represents short-run producer surplus. Note that this *producer surplus is equal to the area below the firm's labour demand curve down to the market wage*. The treatment of long-run labour demand curves and firm surpluses is somewhat more complicated and we will therefore not get into it here.

15A.2.4 Putting All Surpluses Together Graph 15.6 completes what we started in Graph 15.3. Panel (a) depicts the output market in equilibrium, with the industry producing X^* output and selling it at price P^*. Under the assumption of quasilinear tastes on the part of consumers, we previously concluded that the dark brown area represents aggregate consumer surplus. From our work in this section, we have concluded that we can measure producer surplus or profit as the area above the industry supply curve up to the equilibrium price. Thus, the light blue area represents producer surplus, and the two areas together represent the total surplus gained by producers and consumers from the existence of the market for good X.

Graph 15.6 Surpluses in Output and Labour Markets When Tastes Are Quasilinear

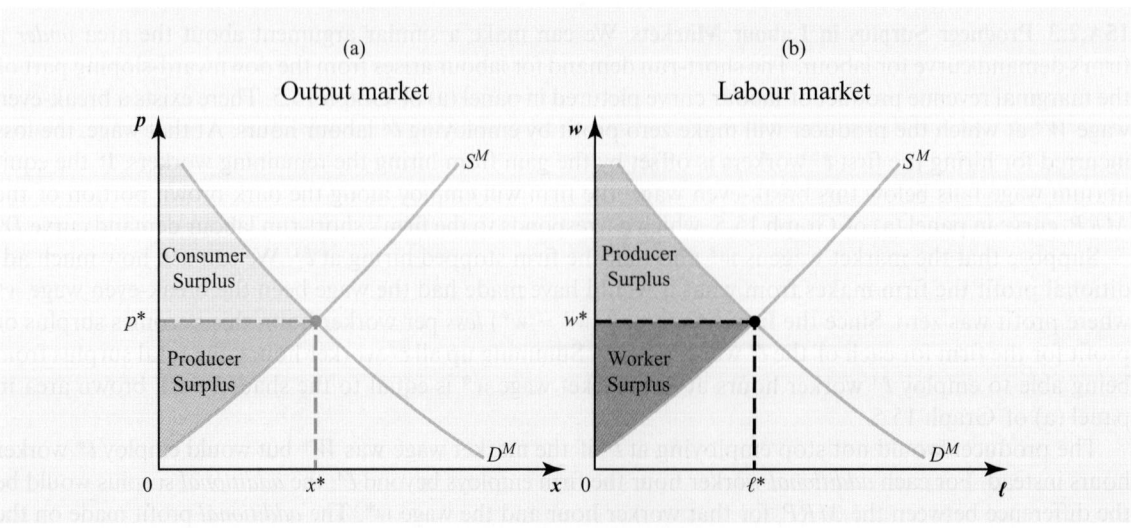

Exercise 15A.7

How would the picture be different if we were depicting an industry in long-run equilibrium with all firms facing the same costs? What would long-run producer surplus be in that case?

In panel (b) of Graph 15.6 we previously concluded that the dark blue area above the market supply curve for labour up to the equilibrium wage is the aggregate worker surplus under the assumption that tastes are quasilinear in leisure. We can now conclude that the area below the market demand curve for labour down to the equilibrium wage is equal to the producer surplus. The dark brown area in panel (a) and the dark blue area in panel (b) are derived from the consumer model while the light blue areas are derived from the producer model. The dark brown and dark blue areas require our assumption of quasilinearity in tastes to be able to treat the market curves as if they depicted an economic relationship derived from a single representative actor doing the best they can in the absence of income effects. The light blue areas, on the other hand, do not require any particular assumptions since they are derived from the producer model that is not subject to the income effects that make aggregating individual economic relationships and interpreting welfare measures along them problematic.

Exercise 15A.8

Suppose we were not concerned about identifying producer and worker surplus but instead wanted to only predict the equilibrium wage and the number of workers employed. Would we also have to assume that leisure is quasilinear for workers?

15A.3 The Invisible Hand and the First Welfare Theorem

We can now consider the question of how well decentralized market forces do in maximizing the total surplus for society. We have to come up with some ideal benchmark of what could be accomplished for society and compare this benchmark to how the market measures up. Economists establish this ideal by imagining that instead of market forces determining how much is produced in each industry, a fictional all-knowing and benevolent 'social planner' was in charge and dictated how much of each good is produced in the economy, which firms produce what and how much each consumer gets to consume.

15A.3.1 The Benevolent Social Planner We assume that the benevolent social planner (BSP) knows all our desires and dreams, knows all the different production technologies of all the possible firms in the world and desires to create the greatest possible surplus for the world. What would this benevolent and omniscient BSP do?

Let's begin with the simplest possible world in which the BSP wants to maximize overall surplus and knows that all our tastes for good x are quasilinear and thus does not have to consider income effects. The BSP would try to calculate how much of x should be produced by finding those firms that can produce x at the lowest possible cost and try to match what these firms produce with those consumers who value x the most. In particular, the BSP would try to begin by finding the consumer who values the first good x more than anyone else, and is thus willing to pay more than anyone else for it. Similarly, they would try to find the producer who can produce that first good at the lowest possible cost. Suppose that this first consumer has a marginal willingness to pay $MWTP^A$ and this first producer has a marginal cost MC^B for that first unit of x. These quantities are graphed for the first x in Graph 15.7. After getting this first unit produced and channelling it to the right consumer, the BSP would move to the next unit, finding the consumer who has the highest marginal willingness to pay for the next unit and matching the consumer with the producer who can produce this unit at the lowest marginal cost. By continuing to do this for each additional unit of output, the BSP would slowly plot the *marginal social benefit* (*MSB*) and the *marginal social cost* (*MSC*) for all levels of output as depicted in Graph 15.7.

Graph 15.7 A Social Planner Finding the Optimal Output x^*

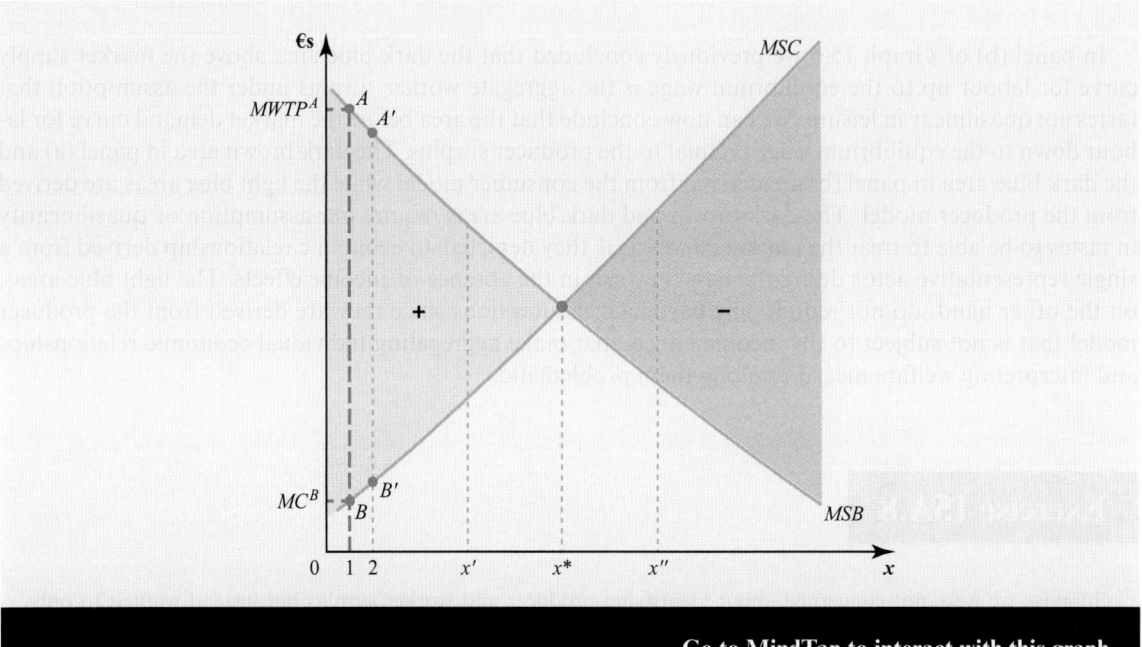

Go to MindTap to interact with this graph

For the first unit of x, the total surplus for society, would be the difference between how much society has benefited from this unit of x and how much it has cost society. As long as the only beneficiary of a unit of x is the person who consumes that unit, $MWTP^A$ is a measure of the MSB, and as long as the only costs society incurs are those incurred by the producer of x, MC^B is a measure of the MSC because the value of the resources employed in production could have been used elsewhere in society. The dashed dark brown line connecting A to B is society's surplus from the first unit of output. The same is true for each additional unit of output, with society's surplus for each *additional* output represented by the vertical difference between the MSB and the MSC curves. As long as that difference is positive, the BSP would decide it is worth continuing production. This difference remains positive as long as the BSP produces less than x^*, the output level at which MSB and MSC intersect, but the difference becomes negative for any output level beyond x^*.

The *total surplus for society is maximized at the output level* x^*, with the dark brown area representing this maximum level of surplus. For instance, were the BSP to stop producing at x' before x^* is reached, society would be left with only the portion of the dark brown area to the left of x' and would therefore give up the dark brown area to the right of x'. Similarly, were the BSP to produce x'' above x^*, society would get all of the dark brown area but would *lose* the dark blue area to the left of x''.

15A.3.2 The Market Versus the BSP As long as consumers gain all the benefits of consuming the output, the MSB curve in Graph 15.7 is the aggregate $MWTP$ curve for all the consumers in the market, and if all the consumers have tastes that are quasilinear in x, the aggregate $MWTP$ curve is the market demand curve. Similarly, as long as producers bear all of the costs of producing, the MSC curve in Graph 15.7 is the industry supply curve. The decentralized market, in which consumers and producers just selfishly try to do the best they can given their circumstances, produces where market demand and supply intersect, which is, under the assumptions we have made, exactly the same intersection as that of the *MSB* and *MSC* curves in Graph 15.7. *The decentralized market therefore produces exactly the quantity the social planner would have chosen to produce if the planner's objective was to maximize the total surplus for society.*

This result is known in its most general form as the First Welfare Theorem, and it is a result that is considerably more general than might be apparent at this point. It states that *under certain conditions, decentralized markets maximize total surplus for society, leaving no possible way for anyone, even an omniscient social planner, to change the situation and make someone better off without making anyone else worse off.* The first welfare theorem states that, *under certain conditions, markets are efficient.* The social planner could decide to distribute the overall surplus differently than the market does, giving more to consumers or more to producers than the market does, but the omniscient BSP *cannot increase the total pie.*

Exercise 15A.9

Imagine that you are the BSP and that you would like consumers to get a bigger share of the total pie than they would get in a decentralized market. How might you accomplish this? *Hint:* Given your omnipotence, you are not restricted to charging the same price to everyone.

Exercise 15A.10

Suppose the social marginal cost curve is perfectly flat, as it would be in the case of identical producers in the long run. Would the BSP be able to give producers a share of the surplus?

To appreciate this result, imagine for a minute how much information the BSP would have to have and process in order to achieve what the decentralized market achieves by itself. They would have to know everyone's tastes and every potential producer's costs in every market for every good in the world. They would have to calculate everyone's demand and supply curves and aggregate these. As conditions in the world change, they would constantly have to recalculate. It is a task that is impossible; no one in the world can ever come close to obtaining the necessary information required for the BSP's task, and no supercomputer could ever be fast enough to continually process this information as it continually changes.

Consider even the simplest task, ensuring that consumers who value pencils sufficiently much have access to pencils when they need them. Pencils, as we have seen are not that easy to make from scratch. The right trees have to be grown and harvested for wood; the wood has to be cut just right and treated with chemicals; the lead has to be mined and refined, cut into just the right shape; the rubber has to be manufactured from various raw materials; the metal holding the rubber on the pencil has to be produced and shaped; the paint and the black lettering on the paint indicating what kind of pencil it is, have to be produced and applied, coated with a finish to make them stick. Literally hundreds of thousands of steps are involved, with each step requiring different expertise, and raw materials from literally all corners of the world have to come together in just the right way. Thousands of individuals are coordinated in just the right way, motivated at each turn by their own desire to do the best they can given their circumstances, and somehow, almost *as if guided by an invisible hand*, their actions result in pencils being available in abundance. Most of these individuals have no idea that they are participating in a sequence of events that leads to the availability of pencils, and yet it happens. Because of the complexity of the process involved in getting it to happen, the world has seen in centrally planned economies that when a single individual is put in charge of planning the process, it almost always results in shortages.

15A.3.3 **The Crucial Role of Information Contained in Prices** How a decentralized and unplanned market can do what no planner in the world could ever accomplish is answered in the information contained in market prices. Prices, whether in input or output markets, signal to consumers and producers what they need to do in order to do the best they can. If milk in Belgium is running low, prices will rise, signalling to suppliers of milk that they can make a profit by shipping milk to Belgium. Lead for pencils running short drives up the price of lead, signalling to mining companies across the world that profit can be made by increasing production. Miners themselves may be needed to get to more lead, causing wages for miners to go up as mining companies compete with other firms for labour, which signals to workers that they might want to switch to mining lead. Prices capture the information the BSP so desperately needs and coordinate the actions of millions across thousands of different markets around the world.

It is because of the information implicitly contained in prices that individuals do not need to know anything beyond their individual circumstances to determine what their next step should be as they try to do the best they can. It is not necessary for any individual actor in the market to know how their actions fit into the bigger picture because prices ensure that their actions fit together. This is one of the great advantages of decentralized markets: Markets do not require anyone to have information that is not easily available at their fingertips. Relying on central planning, on the other hand, requires us to rely on the central planner to gather and process vast amounts of information. The success of decentralized market economies in their competition with centrally planned economies in the 20th century has much to do with this insight.

15A.3.4 The Crucial Role of Self-Interest

A second advantage in decentralized markets is that the emergence of efficient market equilibria does not presume any benevolence on anyone's part as the implementation of the BSP's social planning does. Markets explicitly rely on individuals, consumers, workers and producers alike, to be guided purely by their own perceptions of what is in their self-interest.

Adam Smith (1723–1790), who was one of the earliest economists to focus sharply on the spontaneous order generated by decentralized market forces, gives the example of a consumer purchasing bread from a baker. He asks rhetorically: 'Do we appeal to the baker's benevolence when we come to get his bread? Do we present our need for bread and ask him to consider this carefully in deciding whether to give us bread? Or do we instead rely on his self-interest, proposing to pay him an amount that is larger than the value he places on the bread? Does he in turn ask for our benevolence when he appeals to us to pay him? Does he give us a list of all the reasons why he needs or deserves some money so that he can buy clothing and shelter for his family? Or does he simply appeal to our self-interest as he agrees to accept payment that is lower than the value we place on the bread but higher than the value he places on it?' The answer is that we interact in markets with a clear understanding that each of us is trying to do the best we can for ourselves, and it is from this self-interested behaviour that market demand and supply curves emerge and generate the equilibrium that maximizes the social surplus.

Decentralized markets, therefore, generate outcomes that maximize social surplus not only because they process information efficiently but because they rely on the aspect of human nature that governs most of our actions. Centralized planning runs into difficulty because it faces enormous hurdles in gathering and processing the required information, and because it relies on powerful central planners to be benevolent in ways that appear not to happen when such planners are put in place. While there are many real-world limits to this result, it remains central to an understanding of much the economist does.

15A.3.5 Extending the First Welfare Theorem to Include All Rational Tastes

Before we move on to the limitations of the first welfare theorem, we need to note that while the assumption of quasilinear tastes will make policy analysis easier in some of the upcoming chapters, it is *not* a necessary condition for the result that competitive markets result in efficient output levels. Suppose, for instance, that the good x is normal. In this case, we would find the market equilibrium exactly as we did before: by adding up all the individual regular demand curves and finding where the market demand curve intersects with the market supply curve. In panel (b) of Graph 15.8, this results in the intersection of the market supply curve S^M with the market demand curve D^M at price P^A. The market demand curve is composed of individual demand curves such as the curve D^i in panel (a).

If tastes for good x are normal, we know that there exists an $MWTP$ curve for each consumer that intersects the individual's regular demand curve at the equilibrium price x from above; that is an $MWTP$ curve that is steeper than the demand curve. This is the $MWTP$ curve that is formed from the indifference curve that the individual finds themselves on in equilibrium, and it is plotted as $MWTP^i$ in panel (a) of the graph. These curves, just like the individual demand curves, can be added up and placed in the market picture in panel (b), and consumer surplus is now appropriately measured on this *aggregate MWTP* curve as the shaded dark brown area. Without assuming that individual income effects exactly offset each other, we cannot treat the market demand and aggregate *MWTP* curves as if they came from a single representative consumer. Notice that just as in the case where the demand and *MWTP* curves were the same under quasilinear tastes, it is still the case that each good that is produced has lower social marginal cost as represented by the supply curve than social marginal benefit as measured by the *MWTP* curve, and if any additional goods were produced, the marginal social value would fall below the *MSC*. Once again, the market produces where the total surplus in the *x* market is maximized, and the validity of the first welfare theorem is not contingent on any particular assumption about individual consumer tastes. In the absence of quasilinearity, we have to be careful if we want to determine the precise size of the consumer surplus, but the efficiency result remains.

Graph 15.8 The First Welfare Theorem With More General Tastes

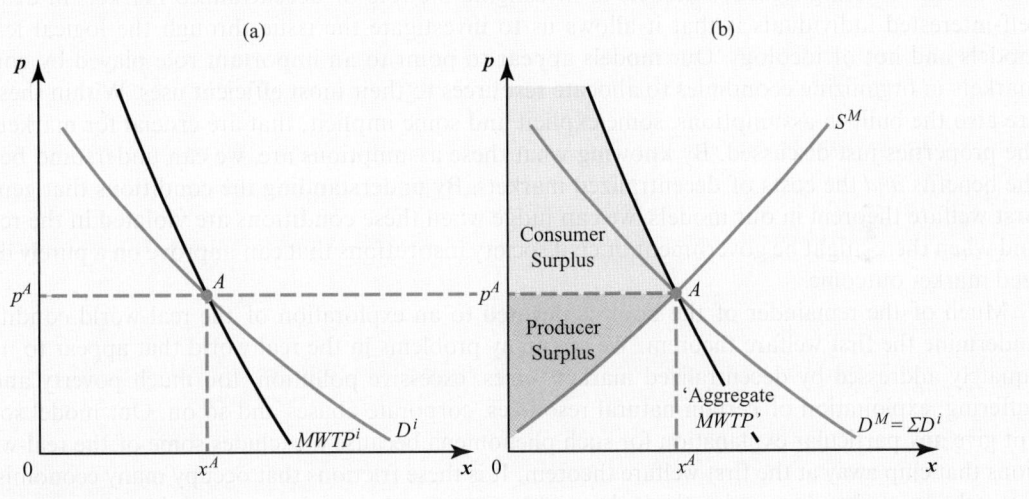

Exercise 15A.11

How would Graph 15.8 look if good *x* were an inferior good for all consumers?

Exercise 15A.12

True or False: If goods are normal, we will underestimate the consumer surplus if we measure it along the market demand curve, and if goods are inferior we will overestimate it.

There is, however, an important feature that is added by introducing income effects through tastes in ways that do not permit the market demand to be modelled by a representative consumer. In the absence of income effects, the BSP's choice of the overall output level of *x* remains the same regardless of how the BSP decides to distribute income across individuals. In the presence of income effects, the overall level of *x* production chosen by the BSP will depend on how other resources in the economy are distributed. If the BSP's ideal income distribution across individuals is different from the actual income distribution, the BSP may choose a different output level for *x* than the market will choose if tastes are not quasilinear in *x*.

They will do so not because the market's output level is inefficient; they will do so because they prefer a *different* efficient output level that satisfies the desire for a different distribution of overall resources in the economy. Markets still give rise to efficiency and the first welfare theorem still holds in the presence of income effects, but the market outcome may violate some notions of equity. The possible existence of different efficient allocations of resources, with some appearing more equitable than others, will be further discussed in Chapters 16 and 29. We will be able to show that the BSP could achieve their preferred outcome by redistributing income first and letting the market find the efficient level of x.

The first welfare theorem is quite general, extending well beyond the model we have illustrated thus far. For now, however, we will conclude by stating some of the limits of this theorem, and in the process we will set the stage for many of the remaining chapters in this book.

15A.4 Conditions Underlying the First Welfare Theorem

The benefit of using rigorous models to investigate the role of decentralized markets in dealing with self-interested individuals is that it allows us to investigate the issue through the logical lens of the models and not of ideology. Our models appear to point to an important role played by competitive markets in organizing economies to allocate resources to their most efficient uses. Within these models are also the built-in assumptions, some explicit and some implicit, that are crucial for markets to have the properties just discussed. By knowing what these assumptions are, we can understand better both the benefits *and* the costs of decentralized markets. By understanding the conditions that generate the first welfare theorem in our models, we can judge when these conditions are violated in the real world, and when there might be government or civil society institutions that can improve on a purely decentralized market outcome.

Much of the remainder of the book is devoted to an exploration of the real-world conditions that undermine the first welfare theorem. We see many problems in the real world that appear to not be adequately addressed by decentralized market forces: excessive pollution, too much poverty and human suffering, exploitation of certain natural resources, corporate abuses and so on. Our model so far does not give any particular explanation for such phenomena because it excludes some of the real-world frictions that chip away at the first welfare theorem. It is these frictions that occupy many economists whose research is aimed at discovering the real-world institutions that might act as a lubricant to permit decentralized markets to work with less friction and produce better results. We will mention these only briefly here and point to the upcoming chapters that deal with these issues more comprehensively.

15A.4.1 Policy Distortions of Prices The first implicit assumption we have made is that market prices operate as modelled, that they are permitted to form in such a way as to send an undistorted signal to the various actors in the market. A primary cause for this signal to become distorted lies in deliberate government policies such as taxes, price regulation, wage controls, subsidy programmes or, in some instances, the explicit prohibition of a market. Saying that such policies can distort market prices and therefore move the market away from the situation where it maximizes social surplus is, however, *not necessarily* the same as saying that we should not have these policies. There may be circumstances when policy makers are perfectly aware of the fact that price-distorting policies will shrink the total social surplus as we have measured it thus far, but nevertheless believe that some other sufficiently useful purpose is served by the policy. At other times, the loss in social surplus seems so stark, and the distortionary policy so contrary to its stated purpose once we consider the impact on markets, that it becomes difficult to believe policy makers truly thought that a sufficiently useful *social* purpose was served by the policy to justify its social cost. We will consider a number of common price-distorting policies in Chapters 18 to 20.

15A.4.2 Externalities, Social Costs and Property Rights In arguing that the *MSB* and *MSC* curves in Graph 15.7 are the same as the market demand and supply curves, we made a crucial assumption. The only individuals whose welfare is affected by the production of a particular unit of x are the producer and the consumer of that unit. This is not always the case. Consider, for instance, the greenhouse gases that are produced by firms in certain industries; many people not party to the production of these gases might be affected by this pollution. The *MSC* is, therefore, higher than the producers' costs that result in the market supply curve. Similarly, the consumption of certain goods, travelling in a polluting car, for instance, may affect others in ways that are not captured in demand or even $MWTP$ curves for cars. Whenever this is the case, there exists an *externality*, and whenever an externality exists, the intersection of MSC and MSB will be different from the intersection of market demand and supply. In the presence of externalities, the decentralized market does *not* produce the efficient quantity, and the market price signals sent to consumers and producers coordinate their behaviour in ways that do not maximize social surplus. We will discuss these issues in more detail in Chapters 21 and 27. In Chapter 21, we will also uncover explicitly the most important efficiency-enhancing role of governments; to ensure that property rights are well established and enforced so as to minimize the inefficiencies from externalities that arise when property is commonly owned.

15A.4.3 Asymmetric Information In addition to an absence of externalities, we have implicitly assumed that all economic actors have the same information about the relevant aspects of the market. Consumers and producers can look at good x and both fully know its uses and quality; employers can fully discern the qualification of workers and those selling used cars know just as much about the cars as the potential buyers. This is not always so, and when it isn't, new issues enter the analysis as more informed parties can use their information to take advantage of less well-informed parties. We will consider this in more detail in Chapter 22.

15A.4.4 Market Power We have assumed that economic actors – consumers, workers, financial planners and producers – are small relative to the market and that each economic actor takes their economic environment as exogenously given, with no one able to control prices in the economy. We have assumed that no one in the economy has *market power*, the power to influence the economic environment itself. When an industry is composed of a single or only a few firms, each firm may well be large enough to impact the economic environment in the industry. The same is true when one or only a few consumers make up all the demand for a particular good. The conclusions of the first welfare theorem do not necessarily hold when the assumption of competitive behaviour is relaxed. We have also not paid much attention to the surplus created by innovative activities that create new goods and new markets, and the role of the profit motive in generating new surplus rather than simply producing surplus within existing markets. We will deal with instances of this in more detail in Chapters 23 to 26.

15A.4.5 Efficiency Versus Alternative Social Objectives Finally, we have made an implicit assumption that attaining efficient outcomes is the most desirable objective for society. In some sense, this has some intuitive appeal. If we find a way of organizing society so that the total pie is as large as possible, there is more pie to go around, so why not get it to be as large as possible? Most of us care not only about the size of the pie but also about its distribution. If the pie is huge but only one person gets to eat it while everyone else starves, few of us would think we have reached a good society. The market not only maximizes the total pie under certain conditions but it also divides this pie between producers and consumers, firms and workers in ways that may not be as appealing to us as we might like. We will mention this concern at various times and return to an explicit treatment of considerations other than efficiency in Chapter 29.

| 15B | Equilibrium Welfare Analysis: Preliminaries and an Example |

15B.1 Consumer Surplus

Market demand functions cannot automatically be treated as if they had the same properties as individual demand functions; that is, as if they fit into a duality picture derived from a single set of rational tastes. For the special case of quasilinear tastes, however, we illustrated that we *can* treat market demand as if it had arisen from the optimization of rational and quasilinear tastes by a single representative consumer. We developed the intuition in Graph 15.1 that market demand has the properties of individual demand curves more generally as long as individual tastes are such that income can be redistributed among individual consumers with no overall change in demand; that is, with changes in individual demand resulting from such redistributions exactly offsetting one another.

15B.1.1 Representative Consumers Consider the example of the aggregated household demand for consumers A and B, and whether this household demand can be treated as if it had arisen from rational household tastes. Intuitively, we argued in Graph 15.1 that the household's demand can be treated as if it were an individual demand function if and only if the household's demand for each good is independent of who controls the money in the family. The change in B's demand for good x_i when their income changes must be exactly the same as the change in the demand when A's income changes *regardless of how income is initially divided.* Letting B's income be denoted by the superscript n and A's by the superscript m, this implies that:

$$\frac{\partial x_i^m}{\partial I^m} = \frac{\partial x_i^n}{\partial I^n} \quad \text{and} \quad \frac{\partial^2 x_i^m}{\partial (I^m)^2} = \frac{\partial^2 x_i^n}{\partial (I^n)^2} = 0. \tag{15.1}$$

The first derivative of A's and B's demands with respect to income must be the same in order for the changes in demand from income redistribution to offset one another, and the second derivative must be zero in order for changes to always offset one another regardless of where they start. In order for the second derivative of a demand function with respect to income to be zero, income cannot enter the function in any way other than linearly so that it drops out when we take the first derivative. With a little work, we can see that the demand functions must take the form:

$$x_i^m(p_1, p_2, I^m) = a_i^m(p_1, p_2) + I^m b_i(p_1, p_2),$$
$$x_i^n(p_1, p_2, I^n) = a_i^n(p_1, p_2) + I^n b_i(p_1, p_2), \tag{15.2}$$

where a_i^m denotes a function specific to good i and individual m while b denotes a function specific to good i but the same for all individuals.

Exercise 15B.1

Demonstrate that the conditions in equation (15.1) are satisfied for the demand functions in (15.2).

Exercise 15B.2

Can you see why equation (15.2) represents the most general way of writing demands that satisfy the conditions in equation (15.1)?

Demand functions of this type are known in microeconomics as satisfying the *Gorman Form*, and it is whenever individual demand functions are of the Gorman Form that aggregate demand functions can be treated as if they had arisen from the utility maximization of a representative consumer. This condition is often expressed in terms of conditions on the indirect utility function, with tastes for individual m that satisfy the Gorman Form leading to indirect utility functions of the form $v^m(p_1, p_2, I^m) = \alpha^m(p_1, p_2) + \beta(p_1, p_2)I^m$, where α and β are functions.

15B.1.2 The Special Case of Quasilinear Tastes In Section A, we focused on the special case of quasilinear tastes, demonstrating in Graph 15.2 that changes in individual demand for both x_1 and x_2 exactly offset one another as income is redistributed. Suppose that we know both A and B have tastes that are quasilinear in x_1, with A's tastes represented by the utility function $u^n(x_1, x_2) = v^n(x_1) + x_2$ and B's represented by $u^m(x_1, x_2) = v^m(x_1) + x_2$. From our work in earlier chapters, we know that both of our demand functions for x_1 are *not* a function of income, while our demand for x_2 is determined by the income left over after they purchase the amount of x_1 that does not depend on their income; that is:

$$x_1^m = x_1^m(p_1, p_2) \quad \text{and} \quad x_2^m = \frac{I^m}{p_2} - \frac{p_1 x_1^m(p_1, p_2)}{p_2}$$

$$x_1^n = x_1^n(p_1, p_2) \quad \text{and} \quad x_2^n = \frac{I^n}{p_2} - \frac{p_1 x_1^n(p_1, p_2)}{p_2}$$

(15.3)

Check for yourself that these demand functions satisfy the Gorman Form, and thus the first and second derivative conditions in equation (15.1). It is furthermore the case that the aggregate household demand takes the form it would take if it had been derived from a single quasilinear utility function.

Exercise 15B.3

What are B's household demand functions for x_1 and x_2 if A's and B's individual demands are those in equation (15.3)? Do the household demand functions also satisfy the Gorman Form?

15B.1.3 Aggregate Consumer Surplus We already know from our work in Chapter 10 that individual consumer surplus in the market for the good x can be measured as the area below the $MWTP$ or Hicksian or compensated demand curve down to the price where the relevant $MWTP$ curve is derived from the indifference curve that contains the consumption bundle the individual has chosen. This can be expressed mathematically using an integral as:

$$\text{Consumer surplus in } x_1 \text{ market} = \int_{p_1}^{\infty} h_1(p_1, p_2, u)dp,$$

(15.4)

where $h_1(p_1, p_2, u)$ is the compensated or Hicksian demand function and $\int_{p_1}^{\infty}$ is the integral of the function above p_1, which means the area underneath the function above the price p_1. In many cases, we might approximate this function with a strictly linear function, in which case consumer surplus can be calculated as the area of the triangle that is equivalent to this integral. When all individual tastes are quasilinear, we can replace the compensated demand function $h_1(p_1, p_2, u)$ with the uncompensated demand function $x_1(p_1, p_2, I)$ in equation (15.4).

When individual demands satisfy the Gorman Form, we know we can treat aggregate market demand as if it had arisen from a single representative consumer. Since quasilinear demand functions satisfy the Gorman Form, we can avoid having to calculate aggregate consumer surplus by going to all individual demand functions and adding up individual consumer surpluses. Instead, we can treat the *aggregate* demand function as if it had arisen from the optimization problem of a representative consumer whose tastes are quasilinear. Applying the formula in equation (15.4) with $h_1(p_1, p_2, u)$ replaced by the uncompensated aggregate demand function will give consumer surplus for the fictional representative consumer, which in turn is the same number we would get if we added up individual consumer surpluses.

In our example of the equilibrium we calculated in Chapter 14 and depicted graphically in Graph 14.12, for instance, the underlying individual tastes are assumed to be quasilinear, implying that individual demand curves are equivalent to $MWTP$ curves and that aggregate demand curves can be interpreted as if they had arisen from a single representative consumer with quasilinear tastes. In panel (a) of Graph 15.9, we replicate panel (b) from Graph 14.12 – the picture of market equilibrium with the numerical example we have been using. To this picture, we have added the labels (a), (b) and (c) to indicate areas, and our work in Part A of this chapter suggests that the dark brown area (*a*) is equal to consumer surplus and the dark blue area (*b*) is equal to producer surplus or profit.

Graph 15.9 $S^M(p) = 547192/p^{2/3}$ and $D^M(p) = 40000000/p^2$ from Graph 14.12

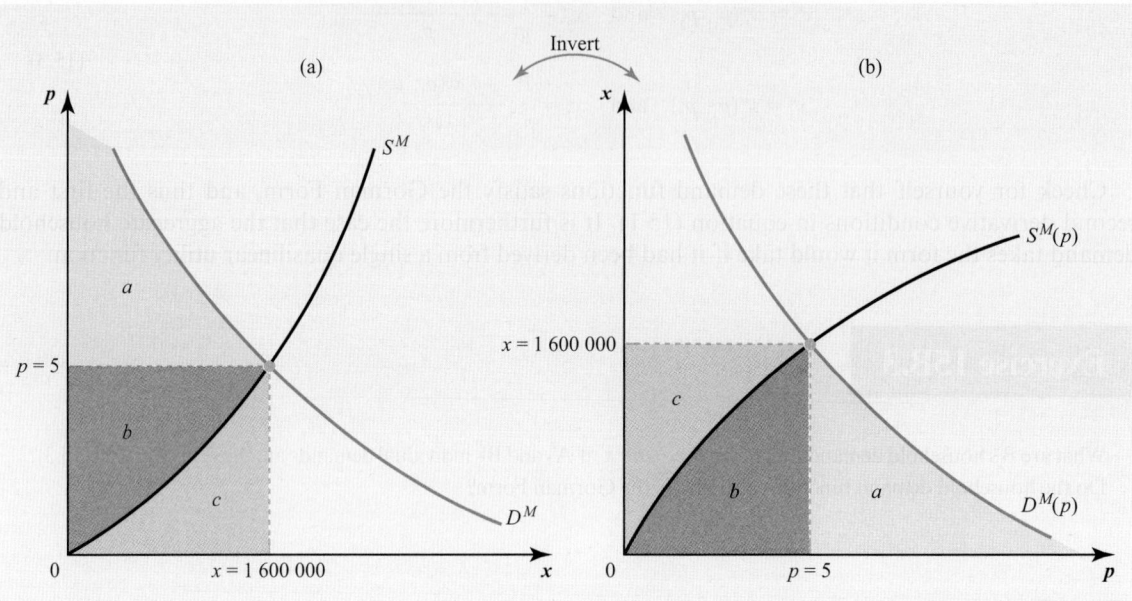

As noted in Chapter 14, however, this picture graphs the *inverse* of the relevant slices of the underlying demand and supply functions. Panel (b) of Graph 15.9 inverts panel (a) to get a picture of the actual slices of the demand and supply functions we have calculated mathematically. Area (*a*) now shows up as the area *underneath* the demand function beginning at the equilibrium price $p = 5$, or the integral identified in equation (15.4). For the numerical example we used in Chapter 14, the market demand function was $D^M(p) = 40000000/p^2$. Thus, if you are comfortable with the concept of computing an integral, consumer surplus can be calculated as:

$$\text{Consumer surplus} = \int_5^\infty \frac{40000000}{p^2} dp = 8000000. \tag{15.5}$$

15B.2 Producer Surplus

We have demonstrated in Graph 15.4 that profit or producer surplus can be measured as an area on individual as well as aggregate supply curves. In Graph 15.9, this is equivalent to area (*b*) in the two panels of the graph. Using the supply function in panel (b) as opposed to the inverse supply function in panel (a), we see that this is equivalent to the area *underneath* the supply function up to the market price measured either on the short-run supply function, for short-run producer surplus, or the long-run supply function for long-run producer surplus. Put into equations for a single firm, these are:

$$\text{Short-run producer surplus} = \int_0^p x_k(w, p)dp \quad \text{and}$$
$$\text{Long-run producer surplus} = \int_0^p x(w, r, p)dp, \tag{15.6}$$

where $x_k(\ell, p)$ and $x(\ell, r, p)$ are the short-run and long-run supply functions with capital assumed to be fixed at k^A in the short run. Since cost functions which make up supply functions can be aggregated into market supply functions, and since the market supply function can be interpreted as if it had arisen from a single representative firm, aggregate producer surplus can also be measured using the same formulas as those in equation (15.6), with individual supply functions replaced by aggregate market supply functions.

In the short-run equilibrium depicted graphically in Graph 15.9, for instance, we assumed an underlying production function of $f(\ell, k) = 20\ell^{2/5}k^{2/5}$ for each firm in the market, with each firm also incurring a recurring fixed licence fee of €1280 and a short-run fixed level of capital $k_A = 256$. Using equations in (13.31) and (13.33) from Chapter 13, we derived the following short- and long-run input demand and output supply functions for each of the firms:

$$\text{Short run: } x_{k^A=256}(p, w) = 3225\left(\frac{p}{w}\right)^{2/3} \text{ and } \ell_{k^A=256}(p, w) = 1290\left(\frac{p}{w}\right)^{5/3}$$

$$\text{Long run: } x(p, w, r) = 81920\frac{p^4}{wr^2}, \quad \ell(p, w, r) = \frac{(8p^5)}{w^3r^2} \text{ and } k(p, w, r) = \frac{(8p^5)}{w^2r^3}. \tag{15.7}$$

Exercise 15B.4

Given that the firms encounter a recurring fixed cost of €1280, which of the previous functions should actually be qualified to take account of this fixed cost?

When prices are $(p, w, r) = (5, 20, 10)$, we concluded in Chapter 14 that there are 1250 firms. At these prices, each firm produces 1280 units for an overall output level of 1 600 000 and industry revenue (at $p = 5$) of $1250(1280)(5) = €8 000 000$. In equation (14.11) of Chapter 14, we used this information to calculate the short-run market supply function at $w = 20$ as $S^M(p) = 547192p^{2/3}$. The long-run market supply curve, on the other hand, is horizontal at the lowest point of the firm AC curves, which happens at €5 in our example. Using the notion of an integral to calculate the area below a function, we can calculate short- and long-run producer surplus as:

$$\text{Short-run producer surplus} = \int_0^5 547192p^{2/3}dp = 4 800 000 \quad \text{and}$$

$$\text{Long-run producer surplus} = 0, \tag{15.8}$$

with zero long-run surplus arising from the fact that the long-run supply curve is horizontal at $p = 5$.

We can check to see that this is correct by calculating the short-run and long-run profits of each firm in equilibrium more directly – subtracting the appropriate economic costs from revenue – and adding these up across the number of firms that exist in equilibrium. Substituting prices $(p, w, r) = (5, 20, 10)$ into equations in (15.7), we get that each firm uses 128 units of labour and 256 units of capital to produce 1280 units of output. In the short run, the firm incurs a cost for labour equal to €2560 while earning revenue of €6400. Since the fixed licence fee and the cost of capital are not economic costs in the short run, each firm earns producer surplus equal to €3840, and since there are 1250 firms in equilibrium, the aggregate short-run producer surplus is €4 800 000 just as we calculated by taking the integral in equation (15.8). In the long run, each firm incurs an additional licence fee of €1280 and a cost for capital of €2560, which results in a long-run profit of €0 for each firm.

15B.3 The First Welfare Theorem

We can demonstrate the applicability of the first welfare theorem to the example we have used in Graph 15.9. To do this, we consider the optimization problem faced by the BSP from Section A.

In essence, we could view the BSP as both the representative consumer and producer who is simply attempting to maximize their own well-being. They know the long-run cost of producing x, which we have assumed in our example to be €5 per unit. This allows them to draw a social *production possibilities frontier*, which is a society-wide budget constraint that illustrates the trade-offs faced as more x is produced in terms of a composite good y. Since the composite good y is denominated in euros, 1 unit of x costs society 5 units of y, and the most y we could produce is equal to the total income I of all the consumers in the society.

If we now know a utility function $U(x, y)$ that can represent the representative consumer's tastes, we could write the BSP's problem of attempting to maximize social surplus in the world as:

$$\max_{x,\, y} \; U(x, y) \text{ subject to } I = 5x + y. \tag{15.9}$$

Exercise 15B.5

Draw the production possibility frontier previously described. How would it look differently if the long-run market supply curve slopes up? *Hint*: With an upward-sloping supply curve, society is facing an increasing cost of producing x, implying that the trade-off in the society-wide production possibility frontier must reflect that increasing cost.

It is possible to recover a utility function that would give rise to the demand function $D^M(p) = 40\,000\,000/p^2$ from our example in Chapter 14. For instance, check for yourself that the utility function $U(x, y) = 12\,649.11x^{1/2} + y$ accomplishes this. Solving the problem in equation (15.9) using this utility function for the BSP gives the solution that the BSP should produce $1\,600\,000$ units of x, which is the equilibrium quantity produced in the market.

Exercise 15B.6

Verify that this is the case.

Exercise 15B.7

One way to verify that the representative consumer's utility function is truly representative is to calculate the implied demand curve and see whether it is equal to the aggregate demand curve $D^M(p) = 40\,000\,000/p^2$ that we are trying to represent. Illustrate that this is the case for the utility function $U(x, y) = 12\,649.11x^{1/2} + y$.

End-of-Chapter Exercises

15.1† **Everyday Application:** *Labour-Saving Technologies.* Consider inventions such as washing machines or vacuum cleaners. Such inventions reduce the amount of time individuals have to spend on basic household chores and in essence increase their leisure endowments.

    A. Suppose that we wanted to determine the aggregate impact such labour-saving technologies will have on a particular labour market in which the wage is w.

        a. Draw a graph with leisure on the horizontal axis and consumption on the vertical and assume an initially low level of leisure endowment for worker A. For the prevailing wage w, indicate this worker's budget constraint and their optimal choice.

b. On the same graph, illustrate the optimal choice for a second worker B who has the same leisure endowment and the same wage w but chooses to work more.

c. Now suppose that a household labour-saving technology, such as a vacuum cleaner, is invented and both workers experience the same increase in their leisure endowment. If leisure is quasilinear for both workers, will there be any impact on the labour market?

d. Suppose instead that tastes for both workers are homothetic. Can you tell whether one of the workers will increase their labour supply by more than the other?

e. How does your answer suggest that workers in an economy cannot generally be modelled as a single representative worker even if they all face the same wage?

B. *Consider the problem of aggregating actors in an economy where we assume individuals have an exogenous income.

a. When the indirect utility for individual m can be written as $v^m(p_1, p_2, I^m) = \alpha^m(p_1, p_2) + \beta(p_1, p_2)I^m$, demands can be written as in equation (15.2). Can you demonstrate that this is correct by using Roy's Identity?

b. Now consider the case of workers who choose between consumption priced at 1, and leisure. Suppose they face the same wage w but different workers have different leisure endowments. Letting the two workers be superscripted by n and m, can you derive the form that the leisure demand equations $\ell^m(w, L^m)$ and $\ell^n(w, L^n)$ would have to take in order for redistributions of leisure endowments to not impact the overall amount of labour supplied by these workers together in the labour market?

c. Can you rewrite these in terms of labour supply equations $\ell^m(w, L^m)$ and $\ell^n(w, L^n)$?

d. Can you verify that these labour supply equations have the property that redistributions of leisure between the two workers do not affect overall labour supply?

15.2 **Business and Policy Application:** *Licence Fees and Surplus without Income Effects.* In previous chapters, we explored the impact of recurring licence fees on an industry's output and price. We now consider their impact on consumer and producer surplus.

A. Suppose that all firms in the fast food restaurant business face U-shaped average cost curves prior to the introduction of a recurring licence fee. The only output they produce is wraps. Suppose throughout that wraps are a quasilinear good for all consumers.

a. Assume that all firms are identical. Illustrate the long-run market equilibrium and indicate how large consumer and long-run producer surplus that is, profit, are in this industry.

b. Illustrate the change in the long-run market equilibrium that results from the introduction of a licence fee.

c. Suppose that the licence fee has not yet been introduced. In considering whether to impose the licence fee, the government attempts to ascertain the cost to consumers by asking a consumer advocacy group how much consumers would have to be compensated in cash in order to be made no worse off. Illustrate this amount as an area in your graph.

d. Suppose instead that the government asked the consumer group how much consumers would be willing to pay to avoid the licence fee. Would the answer change?

e. Finally, suppose the government simply calculated consumer surplus before and after the licence fee is imposed and subtracted the latter from the former. Would the government's conclusion of how much the licence fee costs consumers change?

f. What in your answers changes if, instead of all firms being identical, some firms had higher costs than others but all have U-shaped average cost curves?

B. Suppose that each firm's cost function is given by $C(w, r, x) = 0.047287w^{0.5}r^{0.5}x^{1.25} + F$ where F is a recurring fixed cost.

a. What is the long-run equilibrium price for wraps x as a function of F assuming wage $w = 20$ and rental rate $r = 10$?

b. Suppose that prior to the imposition of a licence fee, the firm's recurring fixed cost F was €1280. What is the pre-licence fee equilibrium price?

c. What happens to the long-run equilibrium price for wraps when a €1340 recurring licence fee is introduced?

d. Suppose that tastes for wraps x and a composite good y can be characterized by the utility function $u(x, y) = 20x^{0.5} + y$ for all 100 000 consumers in the market, and assume that all consumers have budgeted €100 for x and other goods y. How many wraps are sold before and after the imposition of the licence fee?

e. Derive the expenditure function for a consumer with these tastes.

f. *Use this expenditure function to answer the question in A(c).

g. *Use the expenditure function to answer the question in A(d).

h. **Take the integral of the demand function that gives you the consumer surplus before the licence fee and repeat this to get the integral of the consumer surplus after the licence fee is imposed.

i. How large is the change in consumer surplus from the price increase? Compare your answer with what you calculated in parts (f) and (g).

15.3† Business and Policy Application: *Licence Fees and Surplus with Income Effects.* In this exercise, assume the same set-up as in exercise 15.2 except that this time we will assume that wraps are a normal good for all consumers.

A. As in exercise 15.2, we'll consider the long-run impact of a licence fee for fast food restaurants on consumer surplus. In (a) and (b) of exercise 15.2, you should have concluded that the long-run price increases as a result of the licence fee.

a. Consider your graph from part (c) of exercise 15.2. Does the area you indicated over- or underestimate the amount consumers would have to be compensated in cash in order to accept the licence fee?

b. Does the area over- or underestimate the amount consumers are willing to pay to avoid the licence fee?

c. How would your answers to (a) and (b) differ if wraps were instead an inferior good for all consumers?

d. Do any of your conclusions depend on the assumption made explicitly in exercise 15.2 that all firms are identical?

B. Suppose that tastes by consumers are characterized by the utility function $u(x, y) = x^{0.5}y^{0.75}$ and that each consumer had €100 budgeted for wraps x and other goods y.

a. Calculate how many wraps each consumer consumes – and how much utility as measured by this utility function each consumer obtains – when the price of wraps is €5 and the price of other goods is €1.

b. Derive the expenditure function for a consumer with such tastes.

c. Suppose that the licence fee causes the price to increase to €5.77 as in exercise 15.2. How does your answer to (a) change?

d. *Using the expenditure function, calculate the amount the government would need to compensate each consumer in order for them to agree to the imposition of the licence fee.

e. *Calculate the amount that consumers would be willing to pay to avoid the licence fee.

f. **Suppose you used the demand curve to estimate the change in consumer surplus from the introduction of the licence fee. How would your estimate compare to your answers in (d) and (e)?

g. **Can you use integrals of compensated demand curves to arrive at your answers from (d) and (e)?

15.4 Policy Application: *Redistribution of Income without Income Effects.* Consider the problem a society faces if it wants to maximize efficiency while also ensuring that the overall distribution of happiness in the society satisfies some notion of equity.

A. Suppose that everyone in the economy has tastes over x and a composite good y, with all tastes quasilinear in x.

a. Does the market demand curve for x in such an economy depend on how income is distributed among individuals assuming no one ends up at a corner solution?

b. Suppose you are asked for advice by a government that has the dual objective of maximizing efficiency as well as ensuring some notion of equity. In particular, the government considers two possible proposals. Under proposal A, the government redistributes income from wealthier individuals to poorer individuals before allowing the market for x to operate. Under proposal B, on the other hand, the government allows the market for x to operate immediately and redistributes money from wealthy to poorer individuals after equilibrium has been reached in the market. Which would you recommend?

c. Suppose next that the government has been replaced by an omniscient social planner who does not rely on market processes but who shares the previous government's dual objective. Would this planner choose a different output level for x than is chosen under proposal A or proposal B in part (b)?

d. *True or False*: As long as money can be easily transferred between individuals, there is no tension in this economy between achieving many different notions of equity and achieving efficiency in the market for x.

e. To add some additional realism to the exercise, suppose that the government has to use distortionary taxes in order to redistribute income between individuals. Is it still the case that there is no trade-off between efficiency and different notions of equity?

B. Suppose there are two types of consumers. Consumer type 1 has utility function $u^1(x, y) = 50x^{1/2} + y$, and consumer type 2 has utility function $u^2(x, y) = 10x^{3/4} + y$. Assume that consumer type 1 has income of 800 and consumer type 2 has income of 1200.

a. Calculate the demand functions for x for each consumer type.

b. Calculate the aggregate demand function when there are 32000 of each consumer type.

c. Suppose that the market for x is a perfectly competitive market with identical firms that attain zero long-run profit when $p = 2.5$. Determine the long-run equilibrium output level in this industry.

d. How much x does each consumer type consume?

e. Suppose the government decides to redistribute income in such a way that after the redistribution, all consumers have equal income; that is, all consumers now have income of 1000. Will the equilibrium in the x market change? Will the consumption of x by any consumer change?

f. Suppose instead of a competitive market, a social planner determined how much x and how much y every consumer consumes. Assume that the social planner is concerned about both the absolute welfare of each consumer as well as the distribution of welfare across consumers, with more equal distribution being more desirable. Will the planner produce the same amount of x as the competitive market?

g. *True or False*: The social planner can achieve their desired outcome by allowing a competitive market in x to operate and simply transferring y across individuals to achieve the desired distribution of happiness in society.

h. Would anything in your analysis change if the market supply function were upward sloping?

i. Economists sometimes refer to economies in which all individuals have quasilinear tastes as transferable utility economies, which means that in economies like this, the government can transfer happiness from one person to another. Can you see why this is the case if we were using the utility functions as accurate measurements of happiness?

15.5† **Policy Application**: *Markets, Social Planners and Pollution*. One of the conditions we identified as important to the first welfare theorem is that there are no *externalities*. One of the most important externalities in the real world is pollution from production.

A. Suppose that we consider the production of some good x and assume that consumers have tastes over x and a composite good y where x is quasilinear.

a. Illustrate the market equilibrium in a graph with x on the horizontal and the price p of x on the vertical axis. Assume that the supply curve is upward sloping, either because you are considering the short run in the industry or because the industry is composed of firms that differ in their cost curves.

b. On your graph, indicate the consumer surplus and producer profit or producer surplus.

c. In the absence of externalities, why is the market equilibrium output level the same as the output level chosen by a social planner who wants to maximize social surplus?

d. Now suppose that for every unit of x that is produced, an amount of pollution that causes social damage of δ is emitted. If you wanted to illustrate not just the marginal cost of production as captured in supply curves but also the additional marginal cost of pollution that is not felt by producers, where would that social marginal cost curve lie in your graph?

e. In the absence of any non-market intervention, do firms have an incentive to think about the marginal cost of pollution? Will the market equilibrium change as a result of the fact that pollution is emitted in the production process?

f. Would the social planner who wishes to maximize social surplus take the marginal social cost of pollution into account? Illustrate in your graph the output quantity that this social planner would choose and compare it to the quantity the market would produce.

g. Redraw your graph with the following two curves: the demand curve and the marginal social cost curve that includes both the marginal costs of producers and the cost imposed on society by the pollution that is generated. Indicate on your graph the quantity x^* that the social planner wishes to produce as well as the quantity x^M that the market would produce. Can you identify in your graph an area that is equal to the deadweight loss that is produced by relying solely on the competitive market?

h. Explain how pollution-producing production processes can result in inefficient outcomes under perfect competition. How does your conclusion change if the government forces producers to pay δ in a per-unit tax?

B. Assume an aggregate demand function $X^D(p) = 250\,000/p^2$ from the presence of 10 000 consumers with tastes that can be represented by the utility function $u(x, y) = 10x^{0.5} + y$. Suppose that this accurately characterizes the demand side of the market in the current problem. Suppose further that the market supply curve is given by the equation $X^S(p) = 250\,000p$.

a. Derive the competitive equilibrium price and quantity produced in the market.

b. **Derive the size of consumer surplus and profit or producer surplus.

c. Consider a social planner who wants to maximize the social surplus. How would this planner arrive at the same output quantity as the market?

d. Now suppose that each unit of x that is produced results in a pollution cost to society of €0.61. What would be the market outcome in the absence of any non-market intervention?

e. Verify that when each unit of x results in €0.61 pollution cost, the social planner would choose $x = 160\,000$ as the optimal output quantity.

f. Calculate the total social cost of pollution under the competitive market outcome. How much is social surplus reduced from what it would be in the absence of pollution?

g. **Calculate the overall social surplus including the cost of pollution under the social planner's preferred outcome.

h. What deadweight loss is produced as a result of the market's overproduction?

15.6 **Policy Application:** *Anti-Price-Gauging Laws.* Governments sometimes interfere in markets by placing restrictions on the price that firms can charge. One common example of this is so-called anti-price-gauging laws that restrict profits for firms when sudden supply shocks hit particular markets.

A. Assume a severe storm disrupts the supply of oil to refineries in Scotland. Assume also that the Scottish government is able to enforce laws that prosecute fuel stations for raising prices as a result of natural disaster-induced drops in the supply of fuel.

a. On a graph with weekly litres of fuel on the horizontal and price per litre on the vertical, illustrate the result of a sudden leftward shift in the supply curve in the absence of any laws governing prices.

b. Suppose that fuel is a quasilinear good for consumers. Draw a graph similar to the one in part (a) but include only the post-storm supply curve as well as the unchanged demand curve. Illustrate consumer surplus and producer profit if price is allowed to settle to its equilibrium level.

c. Now consider the Scottish government prohibits price adjustments as a result of natural disaster-induced supply shocks. How much fuel will be supplied in Scotland? How much will be demanded?

d. Suppose that the limited amount of fuel is allocated at the pre-crisis price to those who are willing to pay the most for it. Illustrate the consumer surplus and producer profit.

e. On a separate graph, illustrate the total surplus achieved by a social planner who ensures that fuel is given to those who value it the most and sets the quantity of fuel at the same level as that traded in part (c). Is the social surplus different from what arises under the scenario in (d)?

f. Suppose that instead the social planner allocates the socially optimal amount of fuel. How much greater is the social surplus?

g. How does the total social surplus in (f) compare to what you concluded in (b) that the market would attain in the absence of anti-price-gauging laws?

h. *True or False*: By interfering with the price signal that communicates information about where fuel is most needed, anti-price-gauging laws have the effect of restricting the inflow of fuel to areas that most need it during times of supply disruptions.

B. **Suppose again that the aggregate demand function $X^D(p) = 250\,000/p^2$ arises from $10\,000$ local consumers of fuel with quasilinear tastes.

a. Suppose that the industry is in long-run equilibrium and that the short-run industry supply function in this long-run equilibrium is $X^S(p) = 3906.25p$. Calculate the equilibrium level of weekly local fuel consumption and the price per litre.

b. What is the size of the consumer surplus and short-run profit?

c. Next suppose that the storm-induced shift in supply moves the short-run supply function to $\overline{X}^S = 2000p$. Calculate the new short-run equilibrium price and output level.

d. What is the sum of consumer surplus and short-run profit if the market is allowed to adjust to the new short-run equilibrium?

e. Now suppose the Scottish government does not permit the price of fuel to rise above what you calculated in part (a). How much fuel will be supplied?

f. Assuming that the limited supply of fuel is bought by those who value it the most, calculate overall surplus, that is, consumer surplus and short-run profit under this policy.

g. How much surplus is lost as a result of the government policy to not permit price increases in times of disaster-induced supply shocks?

*conceptually challenging
**computationally challenging
†solutions in Study Guide

Chapter 16

General Equilibrium

Our analysis of competitive markets has focused on a single market. It has not treated the entire economy as an interrelated system in which there are equilibrium forces that cross markets, and for this reason the model is often called a *partial equilibrium model*. The simplicity of the model makes it a powerful tool for economists to develop insights about markets, and provides a convenient benchmark to think about economic forces that may distort markets.

The partial equilibrium model is, however, restrictive in a number of ways. A deviation from quasi-linearity in tastes creates complications for the simple introductory economics approach because of the emergence of income or wealth effects. In addition, we assume that the single market being analyzed is small relative to other markets, thus not impacting prices in those other markets. Often markets are fundamentally interrelated, with changes in one market spilling over into others through changes in input prices, through substitution effects as consumers switch between products and through the creation of wealth effects. *General equilibrium models* view the economy as a closed system of related markets, explicitly taking into account the effects that are assumed away in partial equilibrium analysis. Such models can be particularly important in policy analysis because policies represent institutional changes that affect many markets and create feedback effects that are ignored if we consider only a single market at a time.

Over the past 50 years, economists have developed a large number of increasingly sophisticated models of this general equilibrium kind, with different models making different simplifying assumptions depending on the particular application for which they are designed. The pioneers in this area were Kenneth Arrow (1921–), Gerard Debreu (1921–2004) and Lionel McKenzie (1919–2010). In 1972, Arrow was awarded the Nobel Prize in economics, followed by a 1983 Nobel award to Debreu. We will illustrate some examples and show how the first welfare theorem remains fully intact as we move away from the assumptions of the partial equilibrium model. Within these general equilibrium models, we can further illustrate some other important concepts: the second welfare theorem, a notion of stability of resource allocations known as the core, and the result that this core converges to what emerges through decentralized market forces. At the end of the chapter, we will discuss some more general examples of the importance of general equilibrium effects, examples that go beyond the analytic tools we can illustrate here.

16A   A Graphical Exposition of General Equilibrium

There are three basic economic activities that occur in a market economy: production, exchange and the consumption that results from these. Rich general equilibrium models in which large numbers of firms and consumers engage in economic activity have been developed mathematically with the basic tools we have introduced in this text, but some of the underlying concepts and ideas that emerge from these models can be illustrated in small examples that lend themselves to a graphical approach, with the same insights generalizing to a much richer setting. We will introduce these ideas in two steps.

16A.1 A Pure Exchange Economy

We begin with a *pure exchange economy* defined as *an economy in which there is no production and in which consumers are endowed with different bundles of goods.* This offers us the simplest possible setting in which to illustrate the basic insights and methods of general equilibrium theory.

The simplest version of an exchange economy is one with two consumers, X and Y, and two goods, say oranges and bananas. X has a basket with 10 oranges and 4 bananas, and Y a basket with 3 oranges and 6 bananas. X and Y, therefore, have a total of 13 oranges and 10 bananas to sustain them, and each is interested in exploring a trade that would make them both better off.

This simple economy is defined by (1) the individuals in the economy, (2) their tastes over goods, and (3) the endowments of goods that they own in the economy. If all X and Y do is consume their individual endowments, they can each get to a certain indifference curve on their indifference map. These indifference curves are illustrated in panels (a) and (b) of Graph 16.1, with the bundle E_2 denoting X's endowment bundle in panel (a) and the bundle E_1 denoting Y's endowment bundle in panel (b).

Graph 16.1 Deriving a Graphical Depiction of a Two-Person, Two-Good Exchange Economy

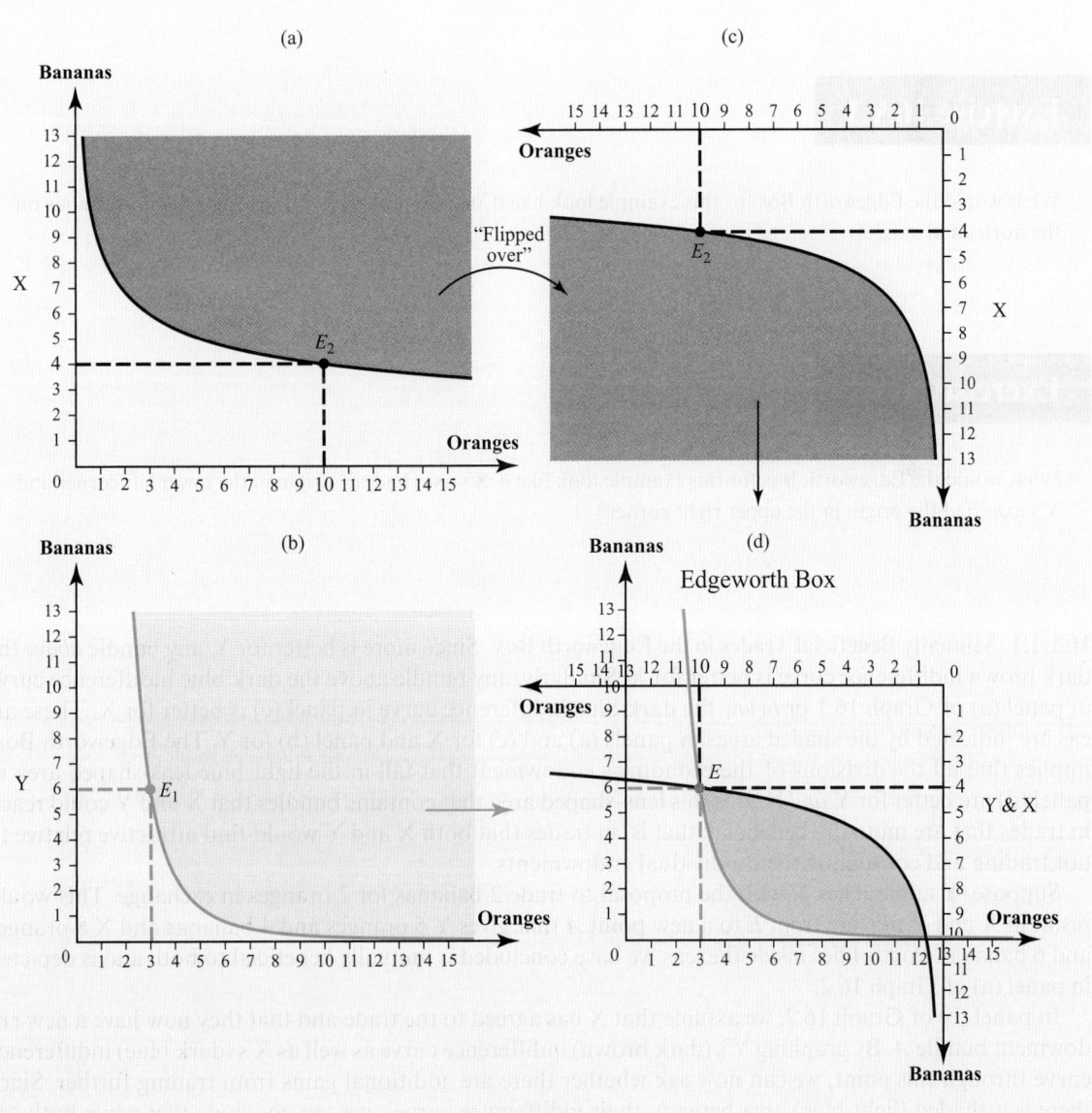

X and Y are now interested in exploring whether there are other feasible distributions of their joint endowment that could make them both better off and thus lead to a mutually beneficial trade.

It is not easy to see whether such trades are possible when X's and Y's situation are depicted separately as they are in panels (a) and (b). Economists, beginning with the 19th-century economist Francis Edgeworth (1845–1926), developed a graphical technique that allows us to see the fundamentals of this exchange economy within a single picture. In panel (c), we take the picture from panel (a) by the origin and flip it over so that the origin now lies on the upper right rather than the lower left corner. We replicate panel (b) in panel (d) and move the flipped graph in panel (c) on top of this graph in such a way that point E_2 lies on top of point E_1. Although points E_1 and E_2 now appear to be the same point, they remain distinct points with the relevant levels of oranges and bananas read off the axis with the origin at the lower left corner for Y and off the axis with the origin on the upper right corner for X.

The box in panel (d) of the graph is known as the *Edgeworth Box*. By moving point E_2 on top of point E_1, the width of the box is equal to 13 oranges and the height of the box to 10 bananas, with 13 oranges and 10 bananas representing the total endowment that X and Y jointly have. All the points inside the box represent different ways of dividing the total endowment in this economy between X and Y. The endowment point $E = E_1 = E_2$ represents one possible way of dividing the total endowment in the economy: 3 oranges and 6 bananas for Y and 10 oranges and 4 bananas for X.

Exercise 16A.1

What would the Edgeworth Box for this example look like if oranges appeared on the vertical and bananas on the horizontal axis?

Exercise 16A.2

What would the Edgeworth Box for this example look like if X's axes had the origin in the lower left corner and Y's axes had the origin in the upper right corner?

16A.1.1 Mutually Beneficial Trades in the Edgeworth Box Since more is better for Y, any bundle *above* the dark brown indifference curve is better for Y. Similarly, any bundle above the dark blue indifference curve in panel (a) of Graph 16.1 or *below* the dark blue indifference curve in panel (c) is better for X. These areas are indicated by the shaded areas in panels (a) and (c) for X and panel (b) for Y. The Edgeworth Box, implies that all the divisions of the economy's endowment that fall in the light blue lens-shaped area in panel (d) are better for Y *and* X. It is this lens-shaped area that contains bundles that X and Y could reach in trades that are mutually beneficial; that is, in trades that both X and Y would find attractive relative to not trading and consuming their individual endowments.

Suppose, Y approaches X with the proposal to trade 2 bananas for 2 oranges in exchange. This would result in X and Y moving from E to a new point A that gives Y 5 oranges and 4 bananas and X 8 oranges and 6 bananas. Point A lies inside the lens we have concluded is mutually beneficial to both and is depicted in panel (a) of Graph 16.2.

In panel (b) of Graph 16.2, we assume that X has agreed to the trade and that they now have a new endowment bundle A. By graphing Y's (dark brown) indifference curve as well as X's (dark blue) indifference curve through this point, we can now ask whether there are additional gains from trading further. Since there is a shaded (light blue) area between their indifference curves, we can conclude that while both are better off at A than they were at the original endowment E, there are additional gains from trade because whenever there are feasible bundles that lie *above* Y's indifference curve and *below* X's, they can both do better by trading more.

Graph 16.2 Exhausting Gains From Trade in the Edgeworth Box

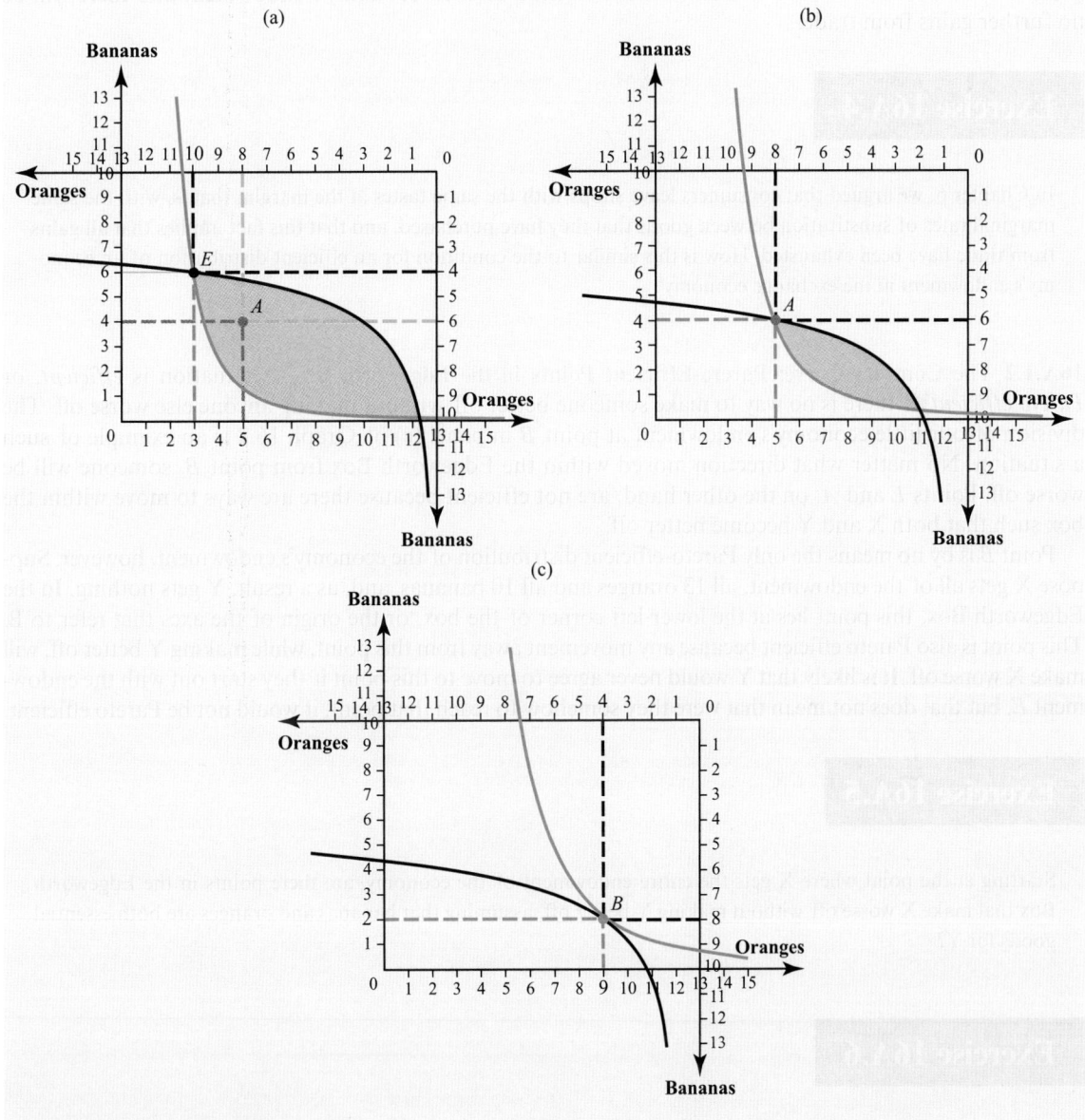

Exercise 16A.3

True or False: Starting at point A, any mutually beneficial trade will involve Y trading bananas for oranges, and any trade of bananas for oranges will be mutually beneficial. *Hint*: Part of the statement is true and part is false.

It is therefore reasonable to assume that X and Y will continue to trade until they reach a point in the Edgeworth Box that does *not* give rise to a lens-shaped area between their indifference curves through that point. Panel (c) of Graph 16.2 illustrates such a point: point *B* that contains 9 oranges and 2 bananas for Y and 4 oranges and 8 bananas for X. If they trade to the point *B* where Y has given up 4 bananas in exchange for 6 oranges from the original endowment *E*, we find that any further trade proposed will make either Y or X worse off. If they reach point *B* in the Edgeworth Box, they will have exhausted all gains from trade and have reached an efficient division of their economy's endowment and there will be no further gains from trade.

Exercise 16A.4

In Chapter 6, we argued that consumers leave shops with the same tastes at the margin, that is, with the same marginal rates of substitution between goods that they have purchased, and that this fact implies that all gains from trade have been exhausted. How is this similar to the condition for an efficient distribution of an economy's endowment in the exchange economy?

16A.1.2 The Contract Curve: Pareto-Efficient Points in the Edgeworth Box A situation is *efficient*, or *Pareto efficient*, if there is no way to make someone better off without making anyone else worse off. The division of our little economy's endowment at point *B* in panel (c) of Graph 16.2 is an example of such a situation. No matter what direction moved within the Edgeworth Box from point *B*, someone will be worse off. Points *E* and *A*, on the other hand, are not efficient because there are ways to move within the box such that both X and Y become better off.

Point *B* is by no means the only Pareto-efficient distribution of the economy's endowment, however. Suppose X gets all of the endowment, all 13 oranges and all 10 bananas, and, as a result, Y gets nothing. In the Edgeworth Box, this point lies at the lower left corner of the box, or the origin of the axes that refer to B. This point is also Pareto efficient because any movement away from this point, while making Y better off, will make X worse off. It is likely that Y would never agree to move to this point if they start out with the endowment *E*, but that does not mean that were they somehow to reach that point, it would not be Pareto efficient.

Exercise 16A.5

Starting at the point where X gets the entire endowment of the economy, are there points in the Edgeworth Box that make X worse off without making Y better off, assuming that bananas and oranges are both essential goods for Y?

Exercise 16A.6

Is the point on the upper right-hand corner of the Edgeworth Box Pareto efficient?

Exercise 16A.7*

If bananas and oranges are essential goods for both Y and X, can any points on the axes other than those at the upper right and lower left corners of the Edgeworth Box be Pareto efficient?

Now consider an arbitrary dark brown indifference curve for Y, such as that depicted in panel (a) of Graph 16.3. Let's start at a relatively low indifference curve such as the light brown curve for X, and ask if we can make them better off without pushing Y below the dark brown indifference curve we have picked. As long as there is a lens-shaped area between the dark brown curve and the light brown curve, the answer is yes, we can move to higher and higher indifference curves for X. This process stops when we reach the dark blue indifference curve in the graph, a curve that is just tangential to the dark brown curve at point C. Once we reach C, any higher indifference curve for X implies that Y will end up below the dark brown indifference curve.

Graph 16.3 The Contract Curve: Pareto-Efficient Allocations in the Edgeworth Box

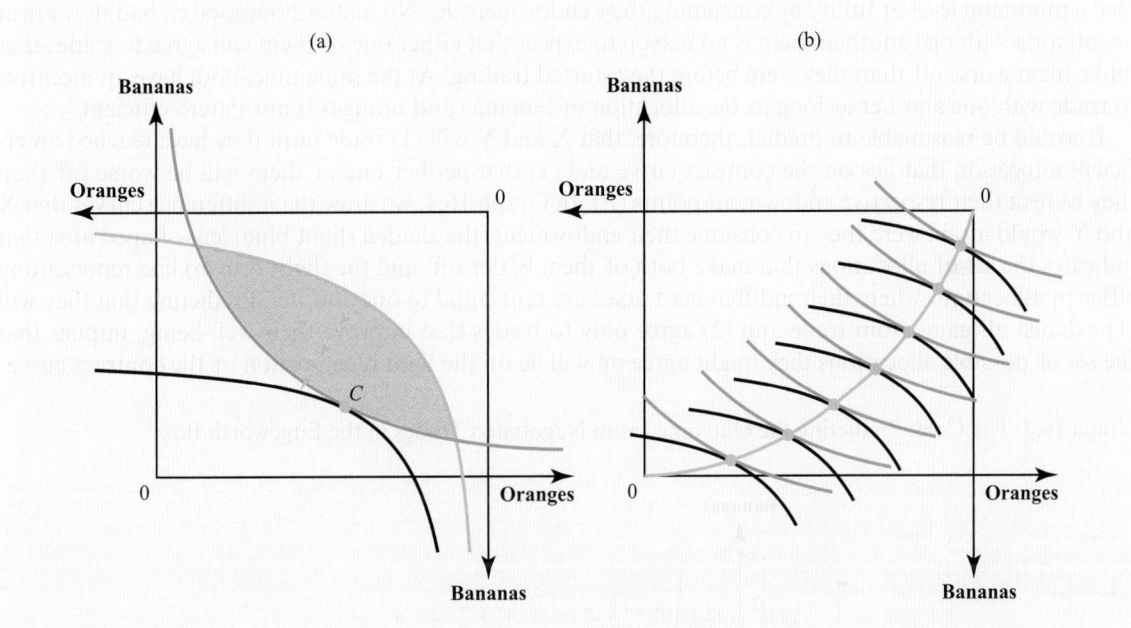

Point C represents another Pareto-efficient point, an allocation of the economy's endowment where it is not possible to make one better off without making the other worse off. We could have picked any other arbitrary indifference curve for Y and gone through exactly the same process to find a tangency with an indifference curve for X, thus again arriving at a Pareto-efficient allocation. Panel (b) of the graph illustrates that there is a whole range of Pareto-efficient points, beginning at the lower left corner of the Edgeworth Box and extending to the upper right corner. Points B in panel (c) of Graph 16.2 and C in panel (a) of Graph 16.3 are two examples of such points. Because it is reasonable to assume that regardless of where the initial endowment in the economy falls, individuals will find trades or contracts that lead to efficient allocations of the economy's endowment, *the entire set of Pareto-efficient allocations of the economy's endowment is called the contract curve.*

Exercise 16A.8*

What would the contract curve look like if bananas and oranges were perfect complements for both Y and X? *Hint*: It is an area rather than a curve. What if they were perfect complements for Y and perfect substitutes for X?

Exercise 16A.9*

What does the contract curve look like if bananas and oranges are perfect substitutes one-for-one for both Y and X? *Hint*: You should get a large area within the Edgeworth Box as a result.

16A.1.3 Mutually Beneficial Efficient Trades and the Core We have already noted that the mere fact a particular allocation of bananas and oranges is Pareto efficient does not imply that we would expect that allocation to emerge from mutually agreed upon trades by Y and X. Y knows that they can be guaranteed a minimum level of utility by consuming their endowment E_1, and similarly X knows they can be guaranteed a minimum level of utility by consuming their endowment E_2. No matter how good or bad they are at negotiating with one another, there is no reason to expect that either one of them will agree to trades that make them worse off than they were before they started trading. At the same time, both have an incentive to trade with one another as long as the allocation of bananas and oranges is not Pareto efficient.

It would be reasonable to predict, therefore, that X and Y will (1) trade until they have reached an efficient allocation that lies on the contract curve and (2) that neither one of them will be worse off than they were at their respective endowment points (E). In Graph 16.4, we draw the indifference curves that X and Y would attain were they to consume their endowment, the shaded (light blue) lens-shaped area that indicates the set of allocations that make both of them better off, and the (light brown) line representing efficient allocations where their indifference curves are tangential to one another. Predicting that they will (1) exhaust all gains from trade and (2) agree only to trades that improve their well-being, implies that the set of possible allocations they might agree on will lie on the light blue portion of the contract curve.

Graph 16.4 The Core: Predicting the Outcome From Negotiated Trades in the Edgeworth Box

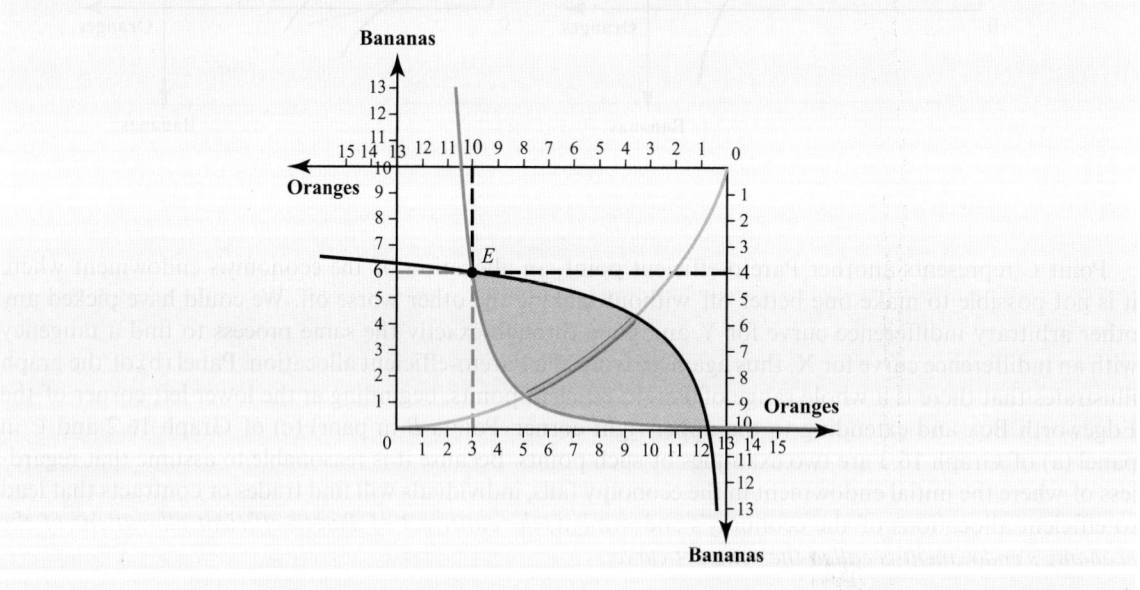

Without knowing more about their relative bargaining skills, it is difficult to say much beyond that. If X is the better negotiator, they might end up on the lower portion of the light blue segment where X ends up enjoying more of the gains from trade than Y does. If Y is incompetent at bargaining, X might convince Y to trade to the very lowest point on this light blue segment where Y ends up just as well off as they were at point E and X becomes much better off. Y's poor negotiating skills are sufficient to keep Y from agreeing to anything less than that.

This light blue segment on the contract curve is often referred to as the *core* of the two-person exchange economy. *An allocation lies in the core if and only if no subset of individuals in the economy can make themselves better off by trading between one another.* In our example of an exchange economy with only two individuals, this implies that for an allocation of the endowment to lie in the core, there is no way the two individuals can figure out a means for both to become better off. In the two-person case, the core is equivalent to the set of Pareto-efficient allocations that lies within the lens-shaped mutually beneficial region. When the economy is composed of more than two individuals, the core will typically be a subset of this (light blue) portion of the contract curve.

16A.1.4 Competitive Equilibrium in the Edgeworth Box Now suppose there is a third person in this economy, Z and Z agrees to spare X and Y the pain of negotiating with one another. Z proposes the following: they will try to find a set of prices for oranges and bananas such that Y will agree to sell Z some of their bananas and X will sell Z some of their oranges, and Z in turn will sell Y some of the oranges bought from X and sell them some of the bananas they bought from Y at those same prices. X and Y promise to take the prices Z quotes as given and trade based on those prices; that is, they agree to be price-takers. Z's problem, however, is that, since they have no bananas or oranges of their own, they have to find prices such that what Y is selling to Z is what X will agree to buy at and what Y is buying from Z is what X will agree to sell at. Z has to find prices such that demand for both goods is equal to supply.

Budget constraints, remember, arise when income is based solely on endowments and not on some exogenous money income. Since it is always possible, regardless of what prices are quoted, for Y to consume their endowment E_1 and not trade anything at those prices, E_1 will always lie on Y's budget constraint. The prices Z quotes determine the slope at which Y's budget line passes through point E_1. More precisely, the ratio $-p_1/p_2$, or the price of good 1 (oranges) *relative to* the price of good 2 (bananas), determines the slope of Y's budget through their endowment E_1. Since the *ratio* of prices is what matters when income is defined by an endowment, we can set the price of the good on the horizontal axis (oranges) to 1 and focus on the price of the good on the vertical axis (bananas). The good whose price is set to 1 is often referred to as the *numeraire* in general equilibrium models.

Graph 16.5 A Disequilibrium Price: Supply Is Not Equal to Demand

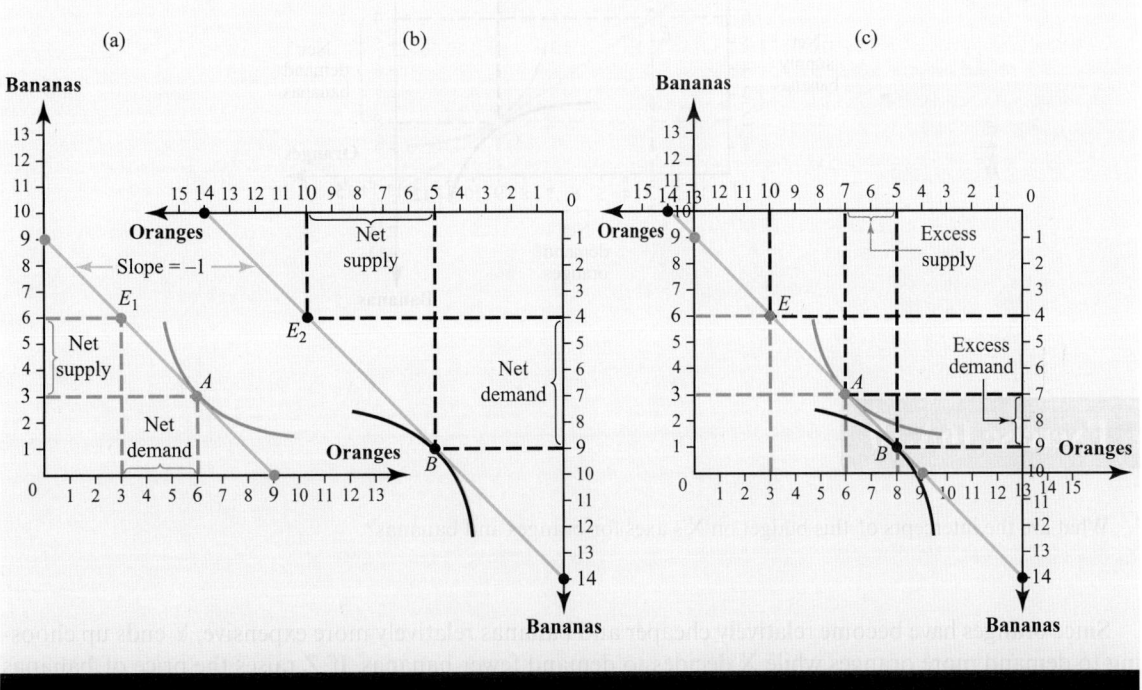

Go to MindTap to interact with this graph

Assume Z sets the price of bananas also equal to 1, making the ratio of prices 1. Z has set prices such that 1 orange can be traded for 1 banana. Panel (a) of Graph 16.5 above, illustrates the resulting budget constraint for Y, while panel (b) illustrates the budget constraint for X with their graph flipped over as it will appear in the Edgeworth Box. As a result, you notice that Y chooses *A* as their optimal consumption bundle on this budget, supplying 3 bananas to Z's 'store' and demanding 3 oranges. X, on the other hand, chooses *B* as their optimal point, supplying 5 oranges and demanding 5 bananas.

Note that X is supplying more oranges than Y is demanding from Z, and Y is supplying fewer bananas than X is demanding from Z. The prices Z has, cause an excess supply of oranges and an excess demand for bananas. This can be seen in the Edgeworth Box in panel (c) where X and Y choose different allocations of bananas and oranges at the prices Z has set. At the current prices, X and Y want to end up at different points in the Edgeworth Box, and there is no way for Z to make both of their wishes come true. Under the prices as specified, we are in disequilibrium.

The only way that supply will equal demand is if, at the prices Z quotes, X is willing to give up exactly as many oranges as Y wants to buy and Y is willing to give up exactly as many bananas as X is willing to buy. Since setting the price of bananas equal to the price of oranges, as we did in Graph 16.5, resulted in an excess supply of oranges and an excess demand for bananas, it would seem reasonable that Z has set the price of bananas too low relative to the price of oranges. If Z tries to raise the price of bananas to 1.5, leaving the price of oranges at 1, the resulting price ratio becomes 2/3, forming the budget constraint in the Edgeworth Box of Graph 16.6.

Graph 16.6 Competitive Equilibrium Prices: Supply Equals Demand

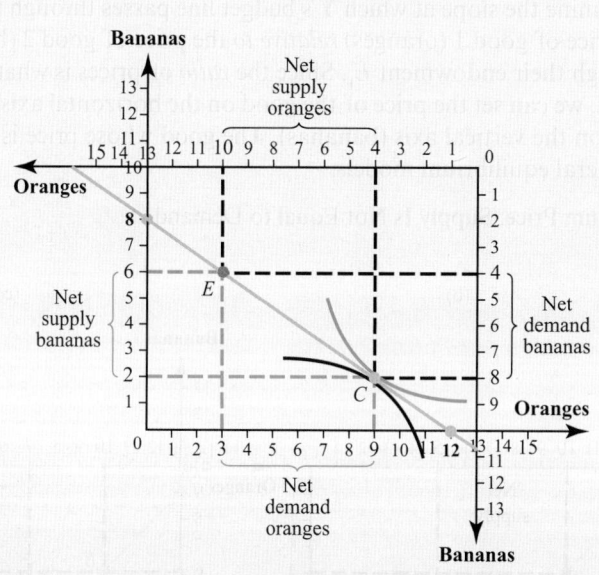

Exercise 16A.10

What are the intercepts of this budget on X's axes for oranges and bananas?

Since oranges have become relatively cheaper and bananas relatively more expensive, Y ends up choosing to demand more oranges while X decides to demand fewer bananas. If Z raises the price of bananas by just the right amount, this will result in the quantities demanded and supplied by X and Y to equal one another, which in turn results in both X and Y choosing the same point in the Edgeworth Box as their optimal point. This does not mean that they will consume identical bundles since X's consumption bundle is read off a different axis than Y's. In Graph 16.6, X sells 6 oranges earning €6 and buys 4 bananas for €6 while Y sells 4 bananas earning €6 and buys 6 oranges for €6. Demand equals supply and they end up choosing the allocation C. Z has successfully found a set of prices that result in both X and Y individually optimizing in such a way that they end up at C. Since these prices result in demand equalling supply when X and Y act as price-takers, they are *competitive equilibrium prices* for our economy.

Exercise 16A.11

Suppose both oranges and bananas are normal goods for both X and Y. Draw separate graphs for X and Y, with the initial budget constraint when the prices were both equal to 1 and the new budget constraint when the price of bananas is raised to 1.5. Illustrate, using substitution and wealth effects, why Y's demand for oranges will unambiguously increase and X's demand for bananas will unambiguously decrease. Can you say unambiguously what will happen to Y's demand for bananas and X's demand for oranges?

Exercise 16A.12

Suppose Z decided to leave the price of bananas at 1 and to change the price of oranges. What price for oranges would Z have to set in order to achieve the same equilibrium outcome?

Exercise 16A.13

Suppose Z sets the price of oranges equal to 2 instead of 1. What price for bananas will result in the same equilibrium outcome?

There is something artificial in this exercise. Why would individuals in a two-person economy ever be price-takers? In such a setting, it is much more reasonable to assume that the two individuals find their way to an efficient outcome through bargaining rather than assuming some fixed price. The only reason to restrict ourselves to a two-person exchange economy here is that it allows us to graph some basic intuitions and derive some fundamental results. This same intuition works for much larger economies in which there are many individuals who could reasonably be assumed to take prices as given since each is small relative to the economy.

We have implicitly assumed thus far that there exists only one competitive equilibrium in an exchange economy like the one composed of X and Y. For most of the mathematical examples that we would usually work with, this is in fact the case. There are instances where indifference maps for X and Y are such that more than one equilibrium is possible.

16A.2 The Fundamental Welfare Theorems and Other Results

Three basic results lie at the heart of general equilibrium theory, and an understanding of these is important in appreciating the role markets play, the limits they encounter and the degree to which non-market institutions can improve on market outcomes. The first is the *first welfare theorem* that provides conditions under which market outcomes are efficient. The second, known as the *second welfare theorem*, is in some sense the inverse of the first. It states that as long as the government can redistribute endowments in a lump sum way, any efficient allocation can in fact be a market equilibrium. If initial endowments result in an equilibrium that gives rise to unacceptable levels of inequality, for example in the presence of lump sum redistribution, the government can rely on markets to produce more equitable outcomes once it redistributes some endowments. Finally, it has been shown that as economies become large, the core of an economy shrinks down to just the set of market equilibrium outcomes, a result we will refer to as *core convergence*. This is perhaps the most abstract of the results, but it provides some real reason as to why we think the concept of a competitive market equilibrium is such a powerful one for predicting outcomes. Since it is reasonable to expect that individuals using their bargaining skills will trade with one another until they reach an allocation in the core, the result suggests that when individual bargaining power is diluted as many consumers enter an economy, the competitive equilibrium outcome is in fact the only one we should expect to arise. We will discuss each of these results in sequence.

16A.2.1 The First Welfare Theorem In the partial equilibrium model we investigated a single market at a time and derived the first welfare theorem, which states that under certain conditions, the competitive equilibrium in a market is efficient. In the general equilibrium model of an exchange economy, where we are analyzing equilibrium across several markets, such as the market for oranges and for bananas, the same theorem holds, again under the conditions outlined at the end of the previous chapter.

In the two-person, two-good exchange economy of the Edgeworth Box, the insight is illustrated in Graph 16.6. Since an equilibrium price results in the two consumers optimizing along their budgets at the same point in the Edgeworth Box, and since their indifference curves are tangential to identically sloped budget constraints, the indifference curves are tangential to one another. When an allocation in the Edgeworth Box is such that the indifference curves through that allocation are tangential to one another and do not give rise to a lens-shaped area in between the indifference curves, the allocation is Pareto efficient. This insight holds for exchange economies with many individuals and many goods as well, with the intuition virtually identical to what emerges from the simple Edgeworth Box.

Exercise 16A.14

True or False: When the first welfare theorem holds, competitive equilibria in an exchange economy result in allocations that lie on the contract curve but not necessarily in the core.

16A.2.2 The Second Welfare Theorem While the first welfare theorem contains remarkable insights, it does not imply that the allocation of goods that results from competitive market prices is good. Rather, the theorem tells us that under the conditions outlined in Chapter 15, the market allocation of goods will be efficient. As we have seen in our derivation of the contract curve, however, there are many different efficient allocations, and most of us would probably judge some of these to be more desirable than others. For instance, under many notions of equity or fairness, we might be disturbed if the allocation in the economy is such that one person gets almost everything while everyone else gets little to nothing, even if that allocation is Pareto efficient.

Thinking along these lines leads us to a second general equilibrium insight known as the *second welfare theorem*. This theorem is in some sense a mirror image of the first. It states that *any Pareto-efficient allocation can result from a competitive equilibrium as long as the initial endowments are redistributed appropriately.* Thus, while the first welfare theorem says that competitive equilibria are efficient, the second welfare theorem says that any efficient allocation can be a competitive equilibrium allocation *as long as the government can redistribute endowments without shrinking the economy in the process.*

The intuition for this is seen in the Edgeworth Box for two-person, two-good exchange economies. Assume that E in Graph 16.7 is the initial endowment point for this economy but that for some reason, we wanted to get the efficient allocation D to be the competitive equilibrium allocation. It should be clear that no set of prices for bananas and oranges could possibly result in X and Y trading from E to D; after all, the dark blue indifference curve that contains D lies *below* E, which implies that X would prefer to consume their initial endowment rather than agree to trade to D.

Graph 16.7 The Second Welfare Theorem

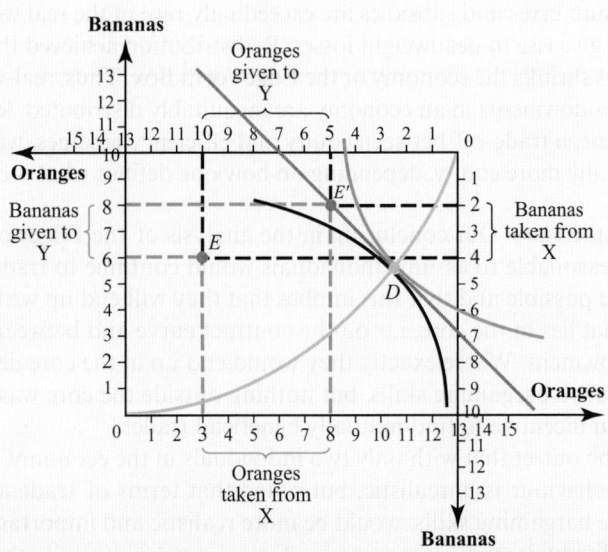

If D were to become an equilibrium allocation, it would have to be the case that we could draw a budget constraint into the Edgeworth Box such that this constraint passes through D and has exactly the slope of the dark brown and dark blue indifference curves at point D. The light blue line in Graph 16.7 satisfies these conditions and would therefore have to be the equilibrium budget constraint for X and Y in order for D to be an equilibrium allocation. Since budget lines always pass through endowment points, the only way this line can be a budget constraint for X and Y is if their endowment point lies on that line. For instance, were their initial endowment at E' rather than E, D would be an equilibrium allocation.

The second welfare theorem stated says that any efficient allocation can be an equilibrium allocation as long as the initial endowments are redistributed appropriately. In our example in Graph 16.7, one appropriate redistribution from the initial endowment E would be to redistribute 5 oranges and 2 bananas from X to Y, which would make the new endowment point E'.

Exercise 16A.15

Can you think of other redistributions of oranges and bananas that would be appropriate for ensuring that D is the competitive equilibrium outcome?

At first glance, this second welfare theorem seems very powerful because it appears to suggest that if we find the competitive market outcome inequitable, we can redistribute the endowments of individuals in the economy in a more equitable manner and allow the market to find a new equilibrium that will once again be efficient. The theorem implies that there is no trade-off between equity and efficiency, that we can achieve more equitable market outcomes through redistribution of endowments and rest assured that the market will preserve efficiency.

However, we need to be cautious in not reading too much into this first glance impression of what the second welfare theorem states. The hidden assumption in the theorem is that redistribution can be undertaken without cost, that we can redistribute without shrinking the size of the economy. The second welfare theorem assumes that lump sum redistribution – redistribution through the use of lump sum taxes and subsidies – is possible. However, lump sum taxes and subsidies are exceedingly rare in the real world, and almost all real-world taxes and subsidies give rise to deadweight losses. Redistribution achieved through real-world distortionary taxes and subsidies shrinks the economy or the Edgeworth Box. Thus, real-world redistributions will result in inefficiencies. If endowments in an economy are inequitably distributed, leading to an efficient but inequitable market outcome, a trade-off between equity and efficiency emerges, with redistribution leading to inefficiency but potentially more equity, depending on how one defines what is equitable.

16A.2.3 Equilibrium and the Core Our conclusion in the analysis of the Edgeworth Box exchange economy is that it would be reasonable to assume individuals would continue to trade until no further mutually beneficial trades were possible and that this implies that they will end up with some allocation of the economy's endowment that lies in the core, i.e. on the contract curve and between the indifference curves through the original endowment. Where exactly they would end up in the core depended on assumptions about the individuals' relative bargaining skills, but nothing outside the core was likely to last since individuals would still have an incentive to find mutually beneficial trades.

We acknowledged at the outset that with only two individuals in the economy, the assumption of competitive or price-taking behaviour is unrealistic, but noted that terms of trade arising from competitive prices, rather than relative bargaining skills, would be more realistic and important in general equilibrium economies with many individuals.

The core and the set of competitive equilibrium allocations in an exchange economy are related. The competitive equilibrium allocation *must* lie in the set of core allocations but that the latter is typically a much larger set than the former. What is not obvious from what we have done so far is that as an exchange economy gets larger, the set of core allocations shrinks; and as the size of the economy becomes really large, the core shrinks to just the set of competitive equilibrium allocations. Were we to predict who gets what in a large exchange economy by finding allocations that lie in the core of the economy, it would be the same exercise as finding the set of allocations that can be supported by competitive market prices. In large economies, only stable allocations in which no subgroup can find a way to make itself better off can arise as a competitive equilibrium, and no allocation that cannot arise as a competitive equilibrium has that stability property.

The intuition behind the result is that when there are only X and Y in the economy, Y has bargaining power because the only way X is ever going to be able to make a trade is to make it with Y. As we envision larger economies with other consumers like Y, X suddenly has options. If Y doesn't trade with X, X can find someone else similar to Y to trade with. The increasing competition from others like Y reduces Y's bargaining power. Similarly, as the economy gets larger there are others like X, and their bargaining power is decreasing for the same reason as Y's. What is remarkable is that the competition between Y and consumers like Y as they all try to make bargains without any reference to any prices, leads to the same outcome as if they were in a competitive equilibrium in which market prices, rather than competition with others in bargaining, governed everyone's behaviour.

Compare two countries that are identical in all ways except that in one there are shopping malls in which shops post their prices, with no haggling allowed or tolerated, and in the other the shops post no prices but each tries to get customers to bargain about the price. In the first country, we would predict that who gets what is determined by a competitive market process in which individual behaviour is guided by the posted prices. In the second country, we would predict that who gets what depends on the bargaining skills of individuals as everyone tries to haggle towards the best possible deal. If there are many similar shops in the mall, our results suggest that the competition between similar shops will lead to the same outcome as the price mechanism produces in the first country.

16A.3 A Simple Production Economy

Let us assume a simple economy with one individual, W, on an island without any provisions.

If W is going to survive, they will have to expend some effort to find food. Suppose W finds that the only food that grows on this island is bananas. We can now think of W as a producer and a consumer: they are a producer who uses labour to produce bananas, and a consumer who gives up leisure in order to be able to eat. It is the simplest possible economy that contains both a producer and a consumer. Such an example is used purely to illustrate a setting in which we can use graphs to provide insights that hold up in much more complicated economies.

16A.3.1 W Doing the Best They Can We can imagine W's search for bananas as being characterized by a set of feasible production plans inside a simple production frontier such as the one depicted in panel (a) of Graph 16.8. The only input into production is labour hours per week l on the horizontal axis, and the only output is the number of bananas harvested per week x on the vertical axis. We assume that the producer choice set ends at $\ell = 60$ and thus assume that W has a total leisure endowment of 60 hours per week.

Graph 16.8 W Choosing Their Optimal Bundle

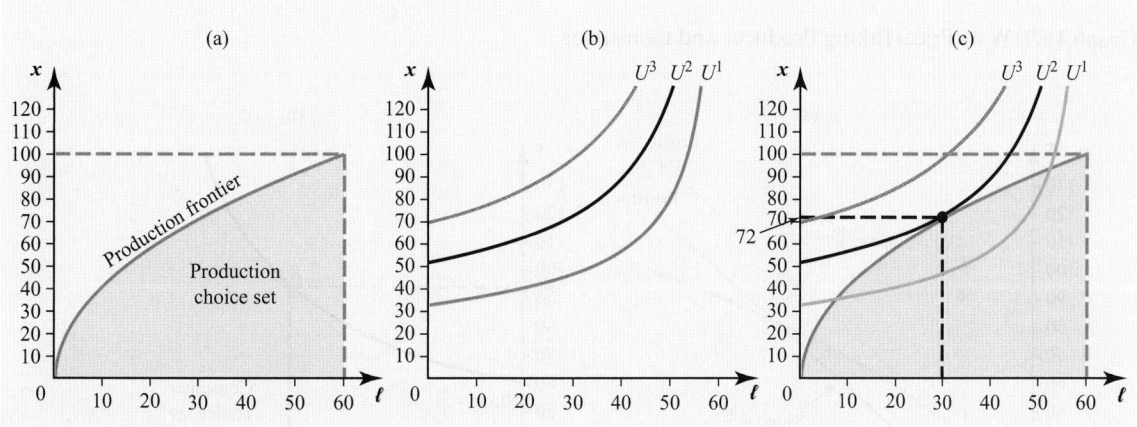

Exercise 16A.16

Does this production frontier exhibit increasing, decreasing or constant returns to scale? Is the marginal product of labour increasing, constant, or decreasing?

In panel (b) of Graph 16.8, we illustrate a set of indifference curves for W on a graph that again has labour hours on the horizontal and bananas on the vertical axis. Since we are illustrating these indifference curves with *labour* rather than *leisure* on the horizontal axis, W becomes better off as their consumption bundle shifts to the northwest of the graph, with less labour, i.e. more leisure, and more consumption.

Exercise 16A.17

As drawn, which of our usual assumptions about tastes – rationality, convexity, monotonicity or continuity – are violated?

Panel (c) of Graph 16.8 combines the first two panels to illustrate the optimal decision for W on this island. Once they reach the bundle that has them working 30 hours per week and consuming 72 bananas, they have reached the highest possible indifference curve that still contains at least 1 bundle that lies within their producer choice set.

16A.3.2 W with a Split Personality So far, there isn't much of a market here; W is choosing their optimal bundle from their choice set, with no one trading anything at any particular prices. Now imagine that W has a split personality, with part of them acting only as a profit-maximizing producer and part of them acting only as a utility-maximizing consumer. Assume further that both parts of W behave as price-takers, taking as given the price of labour w and the price of bananas p.

In panel (a) of Graph 16.9, we graph the producer's profit-maximization problem, with isoprofit lines representing the indifference curves for W as a producer. This is identical to the single-input production analysis of Chapter 11 where each isoprofit line corresponds to all production plans that yield a given level of profit. The intercept of an isoprofit is equal to the profit π, along that set of production plans divided by p, and the slope of each isoprofit is w/p. The profit-maximizing production plan X is one that hires 11 labour hours and produces 43 bananas per week.

Graph 16.9 W as Price-Taking Producer and Consumer

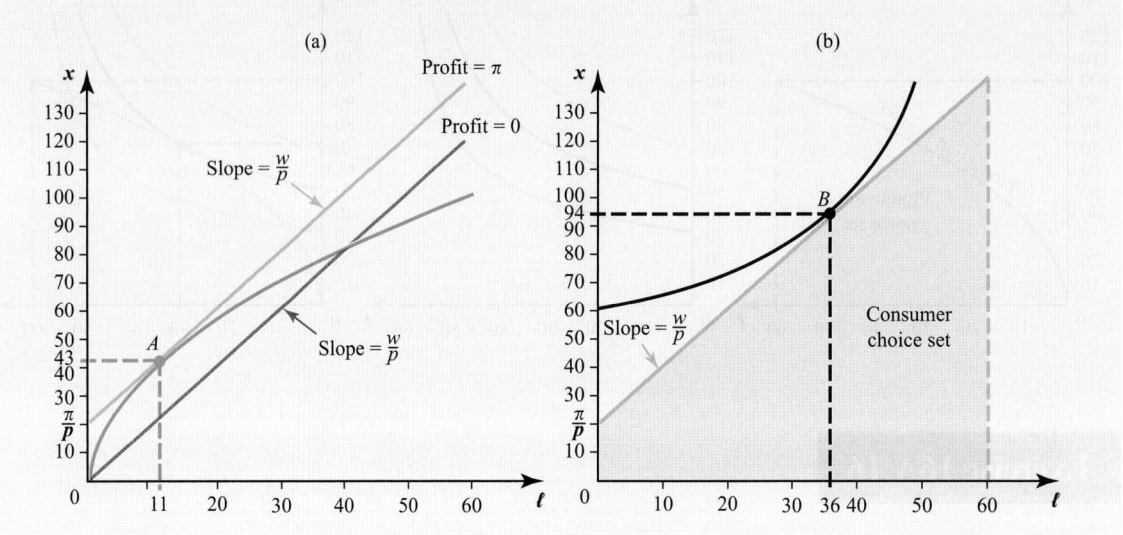

In panel (b) of the graph, we view the problem from the perspective of W as a consumer who faces the price p for bananas and the wage w per labour hour. In addition, to whatever extent the firm is producing profits π, we will assume that W, as the owner of the firm, takes that profit as part of the income they derive and can use for purchasing bananas, and we'll assume as we have done in previous chapters that W has a total endowment of 60 leisure hours per week they can potentially devote to earning income.

Even if W does not work at all, they will have the profits of the firm available for spending on bananas. For instance, if profits from the firm are €60 and the price of a banana is $p = 10$, W can purchase 6 bananas without expending any labour effort. The budget constraint starts at the intercept π/p. As W sells labour, they will earn a wage w with which they can buy additional bananas. They earn w for the first hour sold, which will permit them to buy w bananas if the price of a banana is €1 or w/p bananas if the price is given by p. Thus, the slope of W's budget, starting at the intercept π/p, is w/p, and their budget constraint ends when W has sold all 60 available leisure hours.

We can add the indifference curves from panel (b) of Graph 16.8 to panel (b) of Graph 16.9 to find the optimal consumption bundle B given this budget constraint: 36 hours of labour and 94 bananas per week.

16A.3.3 Disequilibrium and Equilibrium in the Simple Economy The two panels of Graph 16.9 show that the wage and price that are being taken as given by W as a producer and as a consumer are *not* equilibrium prices. As a producer, W wants to employ 11 hours of labour to produce 43 bananas per week, but as a consumer W wants to sell 36 hours of labour to consume 94 bananas per week. There is an *excess supply of labour* and an *excess demand for bananas* under this wage and price.

We can illustrate this disequilibrium in a single graph once we notice that the budget constraint in panel (b) of Graph 16.9 is identical to the optimal isoprofit line in panel (a). Moving the two panels on top of each other, we get panel (a) of Graph 16.10, with the producer choosing bundle A that is feasible and the consumer choosing bundle B that is not feasible in this economy. In order for this economy to be in equilibrium, p and w have to change such that the optimal production plan for the producer coincides with the optimal consumption plan for the consumer. Panel (b) illustrates a combination of w^* and p^* that results in such an equilibrium. Here, both the producer and the consumer, taking w^* and p^* as given, choose optimal plans (point C) that result in demand equalling supply in both the labour and output markets.

Graph 16.10 Disequilibrium and Equilibrium in the Simple Economy

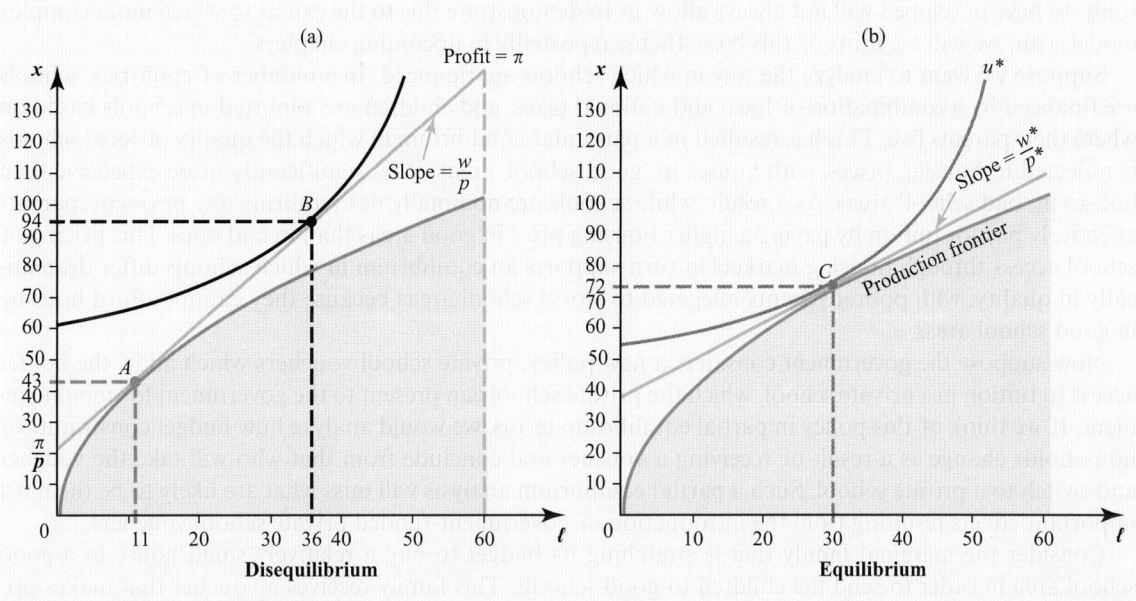

16A.3.4 First and Second Welfare Theorems

The first welfare theorem is a theorem that specifies the conditions under which a competitive equilibrium is Pareto efficient. In an economy with a single individual, Pareto efficiency means that the single individual is doing the best they can given their circumstances. In Section 16A.3.1, we illustrated how W would choose the best possible bundle available to them by finding the highest indifference curve that still contained a consumption bundle that was feasible in Graph 16.8. In panel (b) of Graph 16.10, on the other hand, we illustrated a competitive market equilibrium in which W maximizes profits as a producer and maximizes utility as a consumer, subject to market prices p^* and w^*. If we remove the isoprofit line, which doubles as the consumer budget constraint, in panel (b) of Graph 16.10, we are left with panel (c) of Graph 16.8 that illustrates how W does the best they can given their circumstances. *The competitive equilibrium in the simple economy is Pareto efficient* and the first welfare theorem holds. Similarly, we can see that the second welfare theorem holds in the simple economy. The second welfare theorem says that any Pareto optimum in an economy can be supported as an equilibrium. A Pareto optimum looks like panel (c) of Graph 16.8 with an indifference curve tangential to the production frontier. This means that we can fit a line that is tangential to both the production frontier and the optimal indifference curve, a line that defines a ratio w/p, which results in this optimum being an equilibrium as long as the producer and consumer both take w and p as given. The second welfare theorem is guaranteed to hold only if the producer choice set and tastes are convex. The same caveat applies to the second welfare theorem for exchange economies.

16A.4 General Equilibrium Analysis and Policy

Public policy is often all about making large institutional changes in an economy, changes that alter the budget constraints faced by consumers, the production constraints faced by producers, and/or the prices faced by both. The first welfare theorem suggests that such policy changes will generate inefficiencies unless there are already distortionary forces at work and the policy is designed to combat the impact of these forces.

There is also a more general lesson that emerges from taking a general equilibrium view of policy analysis. For example, taxes and subsidies change prices in particular markets. Sometimes, these changes happen in such a way that we can isolate a market and analyze it fruitfully without considering the general equilibrium in an economy; but often, even if a policy explicitly alters only a single price, individual decisions that follow spill over in important ways into other markets. This complicates policy analysis considerably, but economists have shown that the general equilibrium effects or the *unintended* consequences that follow from a policy change are frequently more important than the initial partial equilibrium effects or the *intended* consequences that a policy maker might have at the forefront of their mind. Although the tools we have developed will not always allow us to demonstrate this to the extent to which more complex models can, we will see hints of this basic theme repeatedly in upcoming chapters.

Suppose we want to analyze the way in which schools are financed. In a number of countries, schools are financed by a combination of local and national taxes, and children are admitted to schools based on where their parents live. This has resulted in a particular equilibrium in which the quality of local schools is reflected in housing prices, with houses in 'good school' areas often significantly more expensive than houses in 'bad school' areas. As a result, while schools are nominally not requiring any payment, parents effectively pay for tuition by paying a higher housing price in good areas than in bad ones. This pricing of school access through housing markets in turn supports an equilibrium in which schools differ dramatically in quality, with poorer parents relegated to worse school areas because they cannot afford housing in good school areas.

Now suppose the government considers a new policy: private school vouchers which allow the holder access to tuition in a private school, which the private school can present to the government for reimbursement. If we think of this policy in partial equilibrium terms, we would analyze how budget constraints of households change as a result of receiving a voucher and conclude from that who will take the voucher and switch to a private school. Such a partial equilibrium analysis will miss what are likely to be the most important effects resulting from the introduction of government-funded private school vouchers.

Consider the marginal family that is stretching its budget to buy a relatively small house in a good school area in order to send the children to good schools. This family receives a voucher that makes private schooling an option. If the family chooses to use the voucher, why would it continue to pay the high premium on housing in the good school district? This family could find cheaper housing in other areas now that it no longer cares about accessing the 'good' school in an area. Using the voucher for this family could result in a move to a house in another area, driving up demand for housing resulting in an increase in housing prices in other areas and a corresponding decrease in prices for houses in good school areas. This implies that those who own houses in other areas will see an increase in their wealth because their houses are worth more while those who own houses in good school areas will see a decline in their wealth as their housing prices fall. The introduction of private school vouchers, aimed at altering individual decisions about schooling, causes general equilibrium price effects in housing markets, which in turn cause wealth effects that alter decisions individuals make. Research on this suggests that most families will be impacted more by these general equilibrium changes in housing markets than by the change in school markets, which implies that an analysis of school vouchers that ignores general equilibrium effects will lead to incorrect predictions about who benefits and who is hurt by this policy. See, for instance, T. Nechyba, Mobility, Targeting and Private School Vouchers, *American Economic Review* 90, no. 1 (2000), 130–46.

Exercise 16A.18

In votes on referenda on school vouchers, researchers have found that renters vote differently from homeowners. Consider a renter and homeowner in a bad school area. Who do you think will be more likely to favour the introduction of school vouchers and who do you think will be more likely to be opposed?

Exercise 16A.19

How do you think the elderly who do not have children in school but who typically do own a home will vote differently on school vouchers depending on whether they currently live in a good or bad school area?

Exercise 16A.20

If you were considering opening up a private school following the introduction of private school vouchers, would you be more likely to open your school in poor or in wealthy areas?

Exercise 16A.21

Suppose two different voucher proposals were on the table. The first proposal limits eligibility for vouchers only to families below the poverty line, while the second limits eligibility to those families who live in bad school areas. Which policy is more likely to lead to general equilibrium effects in housing markets?

This is just one example of how policy analysis that focuses too narrowly on partial equilibrium effects can be misleading. At this point, a general lesson from our example is that after thinking through the partial equilibrium effects of a policy, we should ask carefully: are there other markets that are likely to be impacted in significant ways by this policy? If so, how are these effects likely to change our predictions?

16B   The Mathematics of Competitive General Equilibrium

General equilibrium theory is one of the more mathematical branches of modern economics, and we will only scratch the surface of a rich literature that evolved over the latter half of the 20th century. At its heart lie the basic insights developed intuitively in part A of this chapter – the nature of competitive equilibrium prices, the first and second welfare theorems and the idea that the core of an economy converges to the set of competitive equilibria if the economy becomes large. We will show in this section how the basic model of an exchange economy can be formalized for many individuals and many goods, and we will prove more formally the first welfare theorem. Our main focus will be on demonstrating how we can use the basic tools we learned so far to calculate an equilibrium in both an exchange economy and a simple economy.

16B.1 A Pure Exchange Economy

We defined an exchange economy as *an economy in which there is no production and in which consumers are endowed with different bundles of goods.* Formally, we can define an exchange economy as a collection of consumers with preferences and endowments. Suppose, for example, that the economy contains N consumers denoted by $n = 1, 2,..., N$, who choose between M goods denoted by $m = 1, 2,..., M$. An exchange economy is defined by:

$$(\{(e_1^n, e_2^n, ..., e_m^n)\}_{n=1}^N, \{u^n : \mathbb{R}^M \to \mathbb{R}^1\}_{n=1}^N), \tag{16.1}$$

where $(e_1^n, e_2^n, \ldots, e_m^n)$ gives the endowment of each of the M goods for individual n and $u^n : \mathbb{R}^M \to \mathbb{R}^1$ is individual n's utility function over the M goods. The notation $\{\}_{n=1}^N$ indicates that whatever appears in the curly brackets is listed for each of the N different consumers in the economy. We will let individuals appear as superscripts and goods as subscripts; thus e_m^n is read as 'individual n's endowment of good m'.

Returning to the example from Section 16A.1 of X and Y with oranges and bananas. In this case, $N = 2$ since there are only two consumers, and $M = 2$ since the only goods are oranges and bananas. In this example, Y is endowed with 3 oranges and 6 bananas while X is endowed with 10 oranges and 4 bananas. Letting oranges be denoted by x_1 and bananas by x_2, and letting Y be denoted by the superscript 1 and X by the superscript 2, we can denote their endowments as $(e_1^1, e_2^1) = (3, 6)$ and $(e_1^2, e_2^2) = (10, 4)$. Furthermore, their tastes are represented by a utility function $u^1 : \mathbb{R}^2 \to \mathbb{R}^1$ for Y and $u^2 : \mathbb{R}^2 \to \mathbb{R}^1$ for X, and in many of the graphs in Section 16A.1 we have implicitly assumed that $u^1(x_1, x_2) = x_1^{3/4} x_2^{1/4}$ and $u^2(x_1, x_2) = x_1^{1/4} x_2^{3/4}$.

The endowment point in such an economy is, as we have seen in the Edgeworth Box, only one possible way of dividing the economy's endowment between the individuals in the economy. Any other allocation of goods between the individuals in the economy is *feasible* as long as we are not allocating more of each good than what is available overall. For any good m, we can define the economy's overall endowment E_m by adding up all the individual endowments; that is:

$$E_m = e_m^1 + e_m^2 + \cdots + e_m^N. \tag{16.2}$$

We can define the *set of feasible allocations FA* in an exchange economy as:

$$FA = \{\{(x_1^n, x_2^n, \ldots, x_M^n)\}_{n=1}^N \in \mathbb{R}_+^{NM} \mid x_m^1 + x_m^2 + \cdots + x_m^N = E_m \text{ for all } m = 1, 2, \ldots, M\}. \tag{16.3}$$

The statement to the left of the '|' sign states that the allocation has to specify how much of each of the M goods each individual is allocated. Since there are M goods and N individuals, this implies that we have to specify NM quantities, and thus a point in $\mathbb{R}_+^{NM}$. The statement following the '|' sign indicates that the sum of what is given out for each of the M goods must be equal to the overall endowment of that good that is available in the economy. We can read the full statement in equation (16.3) as 'the set of feasible allocations of goods to individuals is such that the total amount of each good that is allocated between the individuals is equal to the economy's endowment of that good'. When $M = N = 2$ in our example, this set is equivalent to what we have drawn as the allocations in the Edgeworth Box and can be written formally as:

$$FA = \{(x_1^1, x_2^1, x_1^2, x_2^2) \in \mathbb{R}_+^4 \mid x_1^1 + x_1^2 = 13 \quad \text{and} \quad x_2^1 + x_2^2 = 10\}. \tag{16.4}$$

Exercise 16B.1

Can you see how the Edgeworth Box we drew in Section A contains all the allocations in this set?

Exercise 16B.2

True or False: The Edgeworth Box represents a graphical technique that allows us to graph in a two-dimensional picture points that lie in four dimensions.

16B.1.1 Mutually Beneficial Trades Before we engage in any trade, X and Y can already achieve some level of utility by consuming their endowments. We can refer to the level of utility that they can attain on their own as their *reservation utility*. In order for trade to be mutually beneficial, it must be that the division of the economy's endowment that emerges from trade gives X and Y at least their reservation utility. Letting individual n's reservation utility be denoted by U^n, we can calculate the appropriate reservation utility value by evaluating utility at the endowment:

$$U^n = u^n(e_1^n, e_2^n, \ldots, e_M^n). \qquad (16.5)$$

Exercise 16B.3

What are the reservation utilities for X and Y given the utility functions previously specified?

The set of allocations of the economy's endowment that is mutually beneficial for everyone in the economy, denoted MB, is the set of feasible allocations that give each consumer at least their reservation utility; that is:

$$MB = \{\{(x_1^n, x_2^n, \ldots, x_M^n)\}_{n=1}^N \in FA \mid u^n(x_1^n, x_2^n, \ldots, x_M^n) \geq U^n \text{ for all } n = 1, 2, \ldots, N\}. \qquad (16.6)$$

The statement to the left of the '|' sign states that the allocation has to be a feasible allocation, while the statement after the '|' sign states that given what each of the N individuals is given, it must be the case that everyone achieves at least their reservation utility. We can read the full statement in equation (16.6) as 'the set of mutually beneficial allocations is equal to the set of feasible allocations of goods to individuals such that each individual attains at least their reservation utility'. This is equivalent to the set of allocations in the lens-shaped area between the indifference curves that pass through the endowment point in an Edgeworth Box.

Exercise 16B.4

For the example of X and Y, write the set of mutually beneficial allocations in the form of equation (16.6). Can you see that the lens-shaped area identified in the Edgeworth Box in Graph 16.2 is equivalent to this set?

16B.1.2 The Contract Curve Not all mutually beneficial trades necessarily lead to a Pareto-efficient allocation, neither is it the case that all efficient allocations lie in the lens-shaped region of mutually beneficial trades. In Graph 16.2, for instance, X and Y initially trade from their endowment E to the new point A, but their indifference curves through point A still formed a lens-shaped area in which both could be made better off. Viewed from the initial endowment, point A was mutually beneficial but it was not efficient because both could be made better off. The allocation where X is given the entire endowment of the economy, on the other hand, is efficient because there is no way to make one better off without making the other worse off. At the same time, such an allocation is not mutually beneficial when viewed from X and Y's initial endowment.

To calculate the set of Pareto-efficient allocations – the *contract curve* – we have to find allocations in the Edgeworth Box where indifference curves are tangential to one another and thus no lens-shaped area of mutually beneficial trades is possible. We can define this set PE for the more general setting of N individuals and M goods as:

$$PE = \{\{(x_1^n, x_2^n, \ldots, x_M^n)\}_{n=1}^N \in FA \mid \text{there does not exist } \{(y_1^n, y_2^n, \ldots, y_M^n)\}_{n=1}^N \in FA$$
$$\text{where } u^n(y_1^n, y_2^n, \ldots, y_M^n) \geq u^n(x_1^n, x_2^n, \ldots, x_M^n) \text{ for all } n = 1, 2, \ldots, N$$
$$\text{and } u^n(y_1^n, y_2^n, \ldots, y_M^n) > u^n(x_1^n, x_2^n, \ldots, x_M^n) \text{ for some } n\}. \tag{16.7}$$

The statement to the left of the '|' sign states that the allocation has to be a feasible allocation. The statement following the left of the '|' sign states that there does not exist another feasible allocation that makes everyone at least as well off and at least one person better off.

Exercise 16B.5

Can you see that no allocation in the set PE of an Edgeworth Box could have indifference curves pass through it in a way that creates a lens-shaped area between them?

Using the example of X and Y with oranges and bananas, suppose that their tastes can be represented by the utility functions $u^1(x_1, x_2) = x_1^{3/4} x_2^{1/4}$ and $u^2(x_1, x_2) = x_1^{1/4} x_2^{3/4}$ and their endowments by $(e_1^1, e_2^1) = (3, 6)$ and $(e_1^2, e_2^2) = (10, 4)$. Within the Edgeworth Box, if a consumption bundle (x_1^1, x_2^1) is given to Y, it means that X received the remaining available goods; that is, $(x_1^2, x_2^2) = (13 - x_1^1, 10 - x_2^1)$, since the economy as a whole is endowed with 13 of the x_1 good and 10 of the x_2 good. A Pareto-efficient allocation occurs wherever their indifference curves are tangential to one another in the Edgeworth Box; that is, wherever Y's marginal rate of substitution $MRS^1(x_1^1, x_2^1)$ is equal to X's $MRS^2(13 - x_1^1, 10 - x_2^1)$. For the utility functions specified for X and Y, this tangency of their indifference curves implies that:

$$MRS^1(x_1^1, x_2^1) = \frac{3x_2^1}{x_1^1} = \frac{(10 - x_2^1)}{3(13 - x_1^1)} = MRS^2(13 - x_1^1, 10 - x_2^1). \tag{16.8}$$

Solving the middle part of expression (16.8) for x_2^1, we get:

$$x_2^1 = \frac{10x_1^1}{(117 - 8x_1^1)}. \tag{16.9}$$

This equation represents all Y's consumption bundles for oranges and bananas where their indifference curve is exactly tangential to X's in the Edgeworth Box. In other words, equation (16.9) is the contract curve identified in Graph 16.3. We can use this equation to define the set PE for this exchange economy as:

$$PE = \left\{(x_1^1, x_2^1, x_1^2, x_2^2) \in \mathbb{R}_+^4 \mid x_2^1 = \frac{10x_1^1}{(117 - 8x_1^1)}, x_1^2 = 13 - x_1^1 \text{ and } x_2^2 = 10 - x_2^1\right\}. \tag{16.10}$$

Exercise 16B.6

Verify that the contract curve we derived goes from one corner of the Edgeworth Box to the other.

Exercise 16B.7*

A different way to find the contract curve would be to maximize Y's utility subject to the constraint that X's utility is held constant at utility level u^* and that their consumption bundle is whatever is left over after Y has been given their consumption bundle. This problem can be written as:

$$\max_{x_1, x_2} x_1^{3/4} x_2^{1/4} \text{ subject to } u^* = (13 - x_1)^{1/4}(10 - x_2)^{3/4}$$

where we drop the superscripts given that all variables refer to Y's consumption. Demonstrate that this leads to the same solution as that derived in equation (16.9).

16B.1.3 The Core

The *core* of a two-person exchange economy was defined in Section A as the set of Pareto-efficient allocations that is also mutually beneficial given the endowments that individuals in the economy have. The core in the two-person case is the intersection of the set MB and PE; that is:

$$Core = MB \cap PE. \tag{16.11}$$

For the example of X and Y, we can define the core as the subset of the contract curve PE that contains allocations yielding utility above their reservation utilities. X and Y's reservation utilities are found by substituting their endowments (3, 6) and (10, 4) into their utility functions, which gives reservation utilities of $U^1 = 3^{3/4}6^{1/4} = 3.57$ and $U^2 = 10^{1/4}4^{3/4} = 5.03$. The core can be written as:

$$Core = \{(x_1^1, x_2^1, x_1^2, x_2^2) \in PE \,|\, (x_1^1)^{3/4}(x_2^1)^{1/4} \geq 3.57 \quad \text{and} \quad (x_1^2)^{1/4}(x_2^2)^{3/4} \geq 5.03\}. \tag{16.12}$$

This corresponds to the core allocations derived graphically in Graph 16.4. Note, however, that this definition of the core as the intersection of MB and PE holds only for the case of two-person exchange economies. More generally, the core is defined as the set of allocations under which no coalition of individuals can do better on their own. With only two individuals, this is equivalent to saying that an allocation lies in the core when the two individuals cannot reallocate goods such that both are better off, leaving us with the intersection of MB and PE. In the appendix, we will treat the more general case of how the core of an exchange economy evolves when there are more than two individuals in the economy.

16B.1.4 Competitive Equilibrium

In our development of consumer theory, we drew a distinction between models in which income was *exogenously* given and models where income arose *endogenously* as the consumer sold some endowment. When income is exogenously given, the uncompensated demand function for some good m took the form $x_m(p^1, p^2, ..., p_M, I)$ where p_m represents the price of good m and I represents the exogenous income. When income is derived endogenously from endowments, the I term is replaced by the market value of the consumer's endowment, or $p_1 e_1 + p_2 e_2 + \cdots + p_M e_M$. In a two-good exchange economy in which trade is governed by prices, for example, the demand for good m by individual n can be expressed as $x_m^n(p_1, p_2, (p_1 e_1^n + p_2 e_2^n))$. To cut down on notation, we will assume a two-good, two-person exchange economy for the rest of this section, but it is the case that everything we are doing can be written more generally with additional notation.

In equilibrium, the market prices for goods have to be such that supply is equal to demand. A consumer n becomes a *net supplier* of a good m if their demand at the market price is less than their endowment (i.e. $x_m^n(p_1, p_2, (p_1 e_1^n + p_2 e_2^n)) - e_m^n < 0$), and the consumer becomes a *net demander* if their demand is greater than their endowment (i.e. $x_m^n(p_1, p_2, (p_1 e_1^n + p_2 e_2^n)) - e_m^n > 0$). Supply is equal to demand whenever the amount supplied by net suppliers is cancelled out exactly by the amount demanded by net demanders.

X set of equilibrium prices for a two-person, two-good exchange economy can be defined as a set of prices (p_1, p_2) such that:

$$(x_1^1(p_1, p_2, (p_1e_1^1 + p_2e_2^1)) - e_1^1) + (x_1^2(p_1, p_2, (p_1e_1^2 + p_2e_2^2)) - e_1^2) = 0$$
$$(x_2^1(p_1, p_2, (p_1e_1^1 + p_2e_2^1)) - e_2^1) + (x_2^2(p_1, p_2, (p_1e_1^2 + p_2e_2^2)) - e_2^2) = 0. \tag{16.13}$$

Alternatively, we can rewrite this same condition for equilibrium prices by adding the endowment terms to both sides to get:

$$x_1^1(p_1, p_2, (p_1e_1^1 + p_2e_2^1)) + x_1^2(p_1, p_2, (p_1e_1^2 + p_2e_2^2)) = e_1^1 + e_1^2$$
$$x_2^1(p_1, p_2, (p_1e_1^1 + p_2e_2^1)) + x_2^2(p_1, p_2, (p_1e_1^2 + p_2e_2^2)) = e_2^1 + e_2^2; \tag{16.14}$$

that is, aggregate demand for each good on the left-hand side of the equations is equal to the aggregate endowment of that good on the right-hand side.

Let Y's endowment be $(e_1^1, e_2^1) = (3,6)$, X's endowment be $(e_1^2, e_2^2) = (10,4)$, and their tastes represented by the utility functions $u^1(x_1, x_2) = x_1^{3/4}x_2^{1/4}$ and $u^2(x_1, x_2) = x_1^{1/4}x_2^{3/4}$. Solving their optimization problems using the value of our endowments as their income, we get demands:

$$x_1^1(p_1, p_2) = \frac{3(3p_1 + 6p_2)}{4p_1} \quad \text{and} \quad x_2^1(p_1, p_2) = \frac{(3p_1 + 6p_2)}{4p_2}$$
$$x_1^2(p_1, p_2) = \frac{(10p_1 + 4p_2)}{4p_1} \quad \text{and} \quad x_2^2(p_1, p_2) = \frac{3(10p_1 + 4p_2)}{4p_2} \tag{16.15}$$

Exercise 16B.8

Verify that these are the correct demands for this problem.

We concluded in our discussion of the Edgeworth Box that a set of equilibrium prices in this exchange economy cannot be determined unless we normalize one of the prices because the budget constraints of each individual always go through the endowment point with slope $-p_1/p_2$. If we find one set of equilibrium prices that gives rise to the right slope to get both individuals to optimize at the same point in the Edgeworth Box, any other set of prices that gives rise to the same ratio of prices will also work. Thus, all we can do is determine the *relative prices* that can create an equilibrium.

Consider the first of the two equations in expression (16.15): demand equal to supply for good 1. Substituting in the relevant expressions from (16.16), we get:

$$\frac{3(3p_1 + 6p_2)}{4p_1} + \frac{(10p_1 + 4p_2)}{4p_1} = 3 + 10, \tag{16.16}$$

which reduces to:

$$p_2 = \frac{3}{2}p_1. \tag{16.17}$$

This implies that in order for the good 1 market to be in equilibrium, the price of good 2 has to be 1.5 times the price of good 1. Normalizing p_1 to be equal to 1, p_2 has to be equal to 3/2 in equilibrium.

Exercise 16B.9

Write down the equilibrium condition in the x_2 market from the second equation in expression (16.15) using the appropriate expressions from (16.16) and solve for the equilibrium price ratio. You should get the same answer.

To determine what X and Y will consume in equilibrium, we can substitute in the equilibrium prices $p_1 = 1$ and $p_2 = 3/2$ into the demand functions in expression (16.16) to get:

$$(x_1^1, x_2^1) = (9, 2) \quad \text{and} \quad (x_1^2, x_2^2) = (4, 8); \tag{16.18}$$

that is, Y ends up consuming 9 oranges and 2 bananas while X ends up consuming 4 oranges and 8 bananas in equilibrium, the equilibrium we depicted graphically in Graph 16.6.

The reason we can find only a price ratio and not precise prices without normalizing one of the prices first can be seen intuitively in our graphs of budget constraints with endowments in which the price ratio determines the slope of the budget and the endowment point determines its location in each consumer's optimization problem. Mathematically, this arises from the fact that *demand functions are homogeneous of degree 0 in prices*. As long as all prices rise by the same proportion, the consumer is just as well off because, while goods are more expensive, endowments are worth more. Thus, for any individual n and good m: $x_m^n(p_1, p_2, (p_1 e_1^n + p_2 e_2^n)) = x_m^n(tp_1, tp_2, (tp_1 e_1^n + tp_2 e_2^n))$ for any $t > 0$.

Exercise 16B.10

Demonstrate that the same equilibrium allocation of goods will arise if $p_1 = 2$ and p_2 is 1.5 times p_1; that is, $p_2 = 3$.

A *competitive equilibrium* for an exchange economy is defined as a set of prices and a set of allocations such that, at those prices, each individual in the economy will choose the equilibrium allocation and supply is equal to demand. Several technical issues related to competitive equilibria in exchange economies are not discussed here. One issue relates to the *existence* of such equilibria. The main condition that is required is that tastes are convex. A second issue relates to the *uniqueness* of equilibria. Under what condition is there only a single competitive equilibrium allocation? In general, there might be more than a single such equilibrium allocation. However, with the functional forms for utility that we use in this text, there will generally be a single equilibrium in our examples. Finally, economists have worried about conditions under which equilibria are *stable*. For examples in this text, the equilibrium is always stable.

Exercise 16B.11

Can you demonstrate that the equilibrium allocation we derived for X and Y lies in the core that we defined in equation (16.13)?

16B.1.5 Walras's Law In our calculation of the competitive equilibrium for the two-person, two-good economy, you might have wondered why it is that we do not need to solve the system of the two equations in expression (16.15) to solve for the equilibrium price ratio? Each of the two equilibrium equations individually yielded the same result. The reason for this is that we implicitly have a third equation that is a natural consequence of individuals optimizing.

We know that the budget constraint for each individual *binds* at the optimum; that is, at the optimum a consumer's indifference curve is tangential to the budget constraint. Mathematically, this can be stated for consumer n as $p_1 x_1^n + p_2 x_2^n = p_1 e_1^n + p_2 e_2^n$; spending on the left-hand side for consumer n is equal to income on the right-hand side. If this holds for each individual consumer, it also holds for the economy as a whole: *the aggregate budget constraint for the economy binds*. In the two-person, two-good economy, this aggregate budget constraint for the economy becomes:

$$p_1(x_1^1 + x_1^2) + p_2(x_2^1 + x_2^2) = p_1(e_1^1 + e_1^2) + p_2(e_2^1 + e_2^2). \tag{16.19}$$

The condition is known as *Walras's Law*, after Leon Walras (1834–1910), one of the earliest mathematical economists who built the initial foundations of general equilibrium theory and is considered by many as 'the father of general equilibrium theory'. (Walras also graphed demand functions with p on the horizontal and x on the vertical axis, the mathematically correct way, but the profession ignored him in that regard and continued graphing inverse demand functions as demand curves.) Since it follows directly from individual optimizing behaviour, it is implicit that when we write down the first equation in expression (16.15), the second equation will hold; demand equals supply in the good 1 market necessarily implies that demand equals supply in the good 2 market. It is for this reason that we can solve one of the two equations in expression (16.15) to solve for the equilibrium price ratio.

More generally, if we are dealing with an N-person, M-good exchange economy, we can write down M different demand equals supply equations such as those in expression (16.15), but because of Walras's Law, we only need to solve $(M-1)$ equations to find the relative prices for the M goods because if demand equals supply holds in $(M-1)$ markets, it necessarily holds in the last market.

16B.2 The Fundamental Welfare Theorems and Other Results

As in Section A of this chapter, we will now turn to some of the main results of general equilibrium theory that establish a benchmark for when we can think of market economies as efficient. These results include the first welfare theorem, the second welfare theorem and the core convergence theorem.

16B.2.1 The First Welfare Theorem We will now prove the first welfare theorem more formally using the notation developed thus far and will confine ourselves to the case of a two-person, two-good exchange economy to keep the notation to a minimum. The same logic can be used to demonstrate the first welfare theorem for an N-person, M-good exchange economy, although the notation gets a little more involved.

Assume that $\{p_1, p_2, x_1^1, x_2^1, x_1^2, x_2^2\}$ is a competitive equilibrium for an exchange economy defined by $\{e_1^1, e_2^1, e_1^2, e_2^2, u^1, u^2\}$, where u^1 and u^2 are utility functions that represent the two individuals' tastes. We will use what is known as a *proof by contradiction* (also known in Latin as *reductio ad absurdum*) to illustrate that the equilibrium allocation $(x_1^1, x_2^1, x_1^2, x_2^2)$ must be Pareto efficient. A proof by contradiction is a logical method of proving a statement to be true by assuming that it is not true and showing how that assumption leads to a logical contradiction. If we can show that assuming the statement to be untrue leads to a logical contradiction, we have shown that the statement must be true.

Suppose the equilibrium allocation $(x_1^1, x_2^1, x_1^2, x_2^2)$ is *not* efficient. This would imply that there must exist another feasible allocation of the economy's goods that makes no one worse off and at least one person better off. Let's call that allocation $(y_1^1, y_2^1, y_1^2, y_2^2)$. Assume that both individuals are better off under this allocation as opposed to the equilibrium allocation. Since each individual did the best they could at the equilibrium prices (p_1, p_2) to get to the equilibrium allocation, it must be that (y_1^1, y_2^1) is not affordable for individual 1 at the equilibrium prices and (y_1^2, y_2^2) is not affordable for individual 2 under those prices. Thus:

$$p_1 y_1^1 + p_2 y_2^1 > p_1 x_1^1 + p_2 x_2^1 \quad \text{and} \quad p_1 y_1^2 + p_2 y_2^2 > p_1 x_1^2 + p_2 x_2^2. \tag{16.20}$$

Adding each side of these inequalities together implies:

$$p_1(y_1^1 + y_1^2) + p_2(y_2^1 + y_2^2) > p_1(x_1^1 + x_1^2) + p_2(x_2^1 + x_2^2). \tag{16.21}$$

The right-hand side of this equation is the same as the left-hand side of equation (16.20), which is Walras's Law. Thus, equations (16.20) and (16.22) imply:

$$p_1(y_1^1 + y_1^2) + p_2(y_2^1 + y_2^2) > p_1(e_1^1 + e_1^2) + p_2(e_2^1 + e_2^2), \tag{16.22}$$

which can be rewritten as:

$$p_1(y_1^1 + y_1^2 - e_1^1 - e_1^2) + p_2(y_2^1 + y_2^2 - e_2^1 - e_2^2) > 0. \tag{16.23}$$

Since prices are positive, this implies that $(y_1^1 + y_1^2 - e_1^1 - e_1^2)$ or $(y_2^1 + y_2^2 - e_2^1 - e_2^2)$ or both are greater than zero, which in turn implies that $(y_1^1 + y_1^2) > (e_1^1 + e_1^2)$ and/or $(y_2^1 + y_2^2) > (e_2^1 + e_2^2)$. This further implies that the allocation $(y_1^1, y_2^1, y_1^2, y_2^2)$ is not feasible because it allocates more than the economy has of at least one of the goods. Assuming that there exists a feasible allocation $(y_1^1, y_2^1, y_1^2, y_2^2)$ that is preferred by everyone to the equilibrium allocation $(x_1^1, x_2^1, x_1^2, x_2^2)$ leads to a logical contradiction, which implies that there cannot be such a universally more preferred allocation. Thus, the equilibrium allocation $(x_1^1, x_2^1, x_1^2, x_2^2)$ must be efficient.

Exercise 16B.12*

In our proof, we began by assuming that there exists an allocation $(y_1^1, y_2^1, y_1^2, y_2^2)$ that is strictly preferred by everyone to $(x_1^1, x_2^1, x_1^2, x_2^2)$ and showed that there cannot be such an allocation within this economy. Can you see how the same logic also goes through if we assume that there exists an allocation $(z_1^1, z_2^1, z_1^2, z_2^2)$ that is strictly preferred by one of the individuals while leaving the other indifferent to $(x_1^1, x_2^1, x_1^2, x_2^2)$?

For the more complicated setting of N individuals and M goods, the same steps we just went through will lead to the conclusion that any allocation that is at least as good as the equilibrium for everyone and better for at least one person will similarly lead to the conclusion that this alternative allocation will not be feasible given the economy's endowment.

Exercise 16B.13*

Can you demonstrate that this is in fact the case for an N-person, M-good economy?

16B.2.2 The Second Welfare Theorem The formal proof of the second welfare theorem, which states that there always exists a redistribution of the economy's endowment such that any point on the contract curve can be supported as a competitive equilibrium after the redistribution, is somewhat more difficult. It assumes that tastes are convex, which the first welfare theorem does not require. We will forego a formal demonstration of this here, but the intuition is relatively straightforward. For example, one could redistribute the endowment so that it coincides with the Pareto-efficient allocation on the contract curve and demonstrate that there exists a set of prices such that each individual would choose to remain at this new endowment point. Any other endowment allocation on the budget line formed in this way would also work.

The first welfare theorem is powerful in that it tells us that there are conditions under which a competitive equilibrium is efficient. The second welfare theorem, as we discussed in Section A, is somewhat less powerful because it assumes that we can redistribute endowments without cost; that is, that there exist what we have previously called lump sum taxes that do not give rise to substitution effects. It furthermore assumes that we have enough information about the individuals in the economy to be able to redistribute in just the right way to get our preferred point on the contract curve to emerge as an equilibrium. Nevertheless, the second welfare theorem suggests that as long as redistribution of endowments is possible, competitive markets can be used to achieve a fairer equilibrium outcome than the one that might emerge from the initial distribution of endowments in an economy. The fact that we might think endowments are unfairly distributed does not imply that markets cannot still play an important efficiency role after redistribution has taken place.

16B.2.3 Equilibrium and the Core Once we are convinced of the first welfare theorem in an exchange economy, it implies that the competitive equilibrium of a two-person exchange economy must lie within the core of the economy. Remember that when the economy has only two consumers, the core is just the subset of the Pareto-efficient allocations that is mutually preferred by each individual to their endowment. The first welfare theorem guarantees that the competitive equilibrium is Pareto efficient. Furthermore, the logic of individual optimization implies that each individual willingly agrees to give up their endowment to move to the equilibrium allocation under the equilibrium prices. Each individual always has the option of not trading and consuming their endowment regardless of what the prices in the economy are. Therefore, it must be the case that the equilibrium allocation is at least as good for each individual as that individual's endowment. Thus, the equilibrium allocation lies in the Pareto-efficient set *PE*, i.e. on the contract curve, *and* is mutually agreed as better than the endowment allocation by all market participants. The logic in this paragraph holds for two-person exchange economies. In larger economies, the result that the equilibrium lies in the core still holds, but the logic behind the result is more involved. The reason for this is that the core is the set of allocations such that any *subgroup* in the economy cannot do better with their endowment by segregating from the larger economy. Subgroups in two-person economies are just individuals, which implies that the core requirement reduces to the requirement that each person cannot do better by going off on their own with their endowment.

The second result involving competitive equilibria and the core is that as an economy expands in the sense of having many individuals of each type, the core shrinks to the set of competitive equilibria. This is known as the *core convergence theorem* which is demonstrated in the appendix of this chapter. Since the set of core allocations is the set of allocations that might feasibly arise from bargaining by individuals and groups, the core convergence theorem tells us that when competition in bargaining becomes sufficiently intense because of the large number of consumers, each person's bargaining power is reduced sufficiently for the outcome of any bargaining process to become identical to the outcome of competitive behaviour in markets.

16B.3 A Simple Production Economy

In Section A, we illustrated graphically how we can think of a simple economy in which W is the only person choosing to use some of their leisure time to produce bananas.

16B.3.1 W Doing the Best They Can In Graph 16.8, we illustrated how W would arrive at their optimal consumption plan – the optimal amount of labour effort to expend in order to generate banana consumption – given their circumstances. Assume that the production frontier is defined by the production function:

$$x = f(\ell) = A\ell^\beta, \tag{16.24}$$

and suppose that W's tastes can be summarized by the utility function:

$$u(x, (L - \ell)) = x^\alpha (L - \ell)^{(1-\alpha)}. \tag{16.25}$$

We are denoting *labour hours* by ℓ but defining utility over leisure, which is the difference between a leisure endowment L and labour hours ℓ. The optimization problem is to maximize utility subject to the production constraint faced and can be written as:

$$\max_{x, \ell} x^\alpha (L - \ell)^{(1-\alpha)} \text{ subject to } x = A\ell^\beta. \tag{16.26}$$

Setting up the corresponding Lagrange function, taking first order conditions and solving these, we get:

$$\ell = \frac{\alpha\beta L}{1 - \alpha(1 - \beta)} \quad \text{and} \quad x = A\left(\frac{\alpha\beta L}{1 - \alpha(1 - \beta)}\right)^\beta. \tag{16.27}$$

Exercise 16B.14

Verify the results in equation (16.28).

In Graphs 16.8 to 16.10, we used these functional forms, with $A = 13.15$, $\beta = 0.5$, $\alpha = 2/3$ and $L = 60$. Substituting these into equation (16.28), we get the result that W would choose 30 hours of work and banana consumption of 72 as illustrated in Graph 16.9.

16B.3.2 W as Consumer and Producer We next considered a competitive economy in which W determines how many bananas to produce separately from how many they consume based on market prices for labour and bananas. As a producer, W takes the price of bananas p and the wage w as given and solves the profit-maximization problem:

$$\max_{x, \ell} px - w\ell \text{ subject to } x = f(\ell) = A\ell^\beta, \tag{16.28}$$

which can alternatively be written, by substituting the constraint into the objective function, as:

$$\max_\ell pA\ell^\beta - w\ell. \tag{16.29}$$

Solving this, we get optimal input demand ℓ^D for the profit-maximizing firm as:

$$\ell^D(w, p) = \left(\frac{\beta pA}{w}\right)^{1/(1-\beta)}, \tag{16.30}$$

and substituting this into the production function in equation (16.25), we get output supply:

$$x^S(w, p) = A\left(\frac{\beta p A}{w}\right)^{\beta/(1-\beta)}.$$

(16.31)

Exercise 16B.15

Verify that this is the correct solution.

The supply side of the labour market and the demand side of the banana market are determined by W's behaviour as a consumer. Since W owns the firm, they not only generate income by selling leisure but also receive the weekly profits of the firm. We can calculate these profits by subtracting labour costs $w\ell^D(w, p)$ from revenues $px^S(w, p)$ to get the profit function:

$$\pi(w, p) = (1 - \beta)(Ap)^{1/(1-\beta)}\left(\frac{\beta}{w}\right)^{\beta/(1-\beta)}.$$

(16.32)

The income W has as a consumer to spend on bananas is equal to $\pi(w, p)$ plus the labour income derived from giving up leisure. Assuming a total of L leisure hours are available per week, this allows us to write W's consumer utility maximization problem as:

$$\max_{x, \ell} u(x, (L - \ell)) = x^\alpha(L - \ell)^{(1-\alpha)} \text{ subject to } px = w\ell + \pi(w, p).$$

(16.33)

Solving this (which requires some tedious algebra), we can derive labour supply as:

$$\ell^S(w, p) = \alpha L - \frac{(1 - \alpha)\pi(w, p)}{w} = \alpha L - \frac{(1 - \alpha)(1 - \beta)}{\beta}\left(\frac{\beta p A}{w}\right)^{1/(1-\beta)},$$

(16.34)

and demand for bananas as:

$$x^D(w, p) = \frac{\alpha}{p}(wL + \pi(w, p)) = \frac{\alpha w}{p}\left(L + \frac{(1 - \beta)}{\beta}\left(\frac{\beta p A}{w}\right)^{1/(1-\beta)}\right).$$

(16.35)

Exercise 16B.16

Verify that these solutions for labour supply and banana demand are correct.

We have derived demand and supply equations for both the labour and the banana market. These presume that W behaves as a price-taker in both markets in both their roles as consumer and producer, and in general there is no reason to think that supply will equal demand for some arbitrarily chosen w and p. For example, in Graph 16.9, we illustrate a set of prices in the economy at which W will choose to produce 43 bananas per week using 11 labour hours (production plan B in the graph), but in their role as a consumer will demand 94 bananas and supply 36 hours of labour, consumption plan B in the graph. Check for yourself that this is the approximate outcome when $A = 13.15$, $\beta = 0.5$, $\alpha = 2/3$ and $L = 60$ and when the output price p is 10 and the wage is 20 as was assumed when drawing the graph. Note, these solutions are approximate. The actual solutions are 10.81 for labour demand, 43.23 for output supply, 36.40 for labour supply and 94.41 for output demand.

16B.3.3 Equilibrium in the Simple Economy

To calculate equilibrium prices for this simple economy, we have to ensure that demand is equal to supply in the labour and output markets. Since the two markets are related to one another, it should be intuitive that equilibrium in one of the markets necessarily implies that the other market is also in equilibrium, much as we found in the exchange economy. This is most easily seen in our graphical depiction of an equilibrium in Graph 16.10 where we illustrated how the optimal isoprofit line for the firm is also the budget constraint for the consumer, with the equilibrium arising from the simultaneous tangency of the isoprofit line and the optimal indifference curve with the production frontier.

By setting ℓ^D from equation (16.31) equal to ℓ^S from equation (16.35), we can solve for the equilibrium wage w^* in terms of the output price p. This gives us:

$$w^* = \beta A \left(\frac{1 - \alpha(1 - \beta)}{\alpha \beta L} \right)^{(1-\beta)} p. \tag{16.36}$$

Alternatively, we can solve for the equilibrium relationship between w and p in the banana market by setting x^S from equation (16.32) equal to x^D from equation (16.36) and, if we do the maths right, we get the same expression as we did by solving for equilibrium prices in the labour market.

Exercise 16B.17**

Verify that the same equilibrium relationship between prices and wages arises by solving $x^S = x^D$.

As in the case of exchange economies, we can only solve for the equilibrium price ratio, and any set of w and p that satisfies this ratio can support an equilibrium in the economy. For the values $A = 13.15$, $\beta = 0.5$, $\alpha = 2/3$ and $L = 60$ used in the graphs of Section A, equation (16.37) becomes:

$$w^* = 1.2004p \tag{16.37}$$

implying that any set of prices such that wage is approximately 1.2 times price will result in an equilibrium in the labour and banana market. For instance, if $p = 10$ and $w = 12$, you can verify that labour demand and supply will be equal to 30 hours per week and banana supply and demand will be 72 bananas per week. Similarly, you can verify that the same holds whether $p = 1$ and $w = 1.2$, or $p = 2$ and $w = 2.4$, subject to some small rounding error.

Exercise 16B.18

Can you tell from the graph of an equilibrium in Graph 16.10 that any combination of w and p that satisfies a particular ratio will generate the same equilibrium in the labour and banana markets?

Exercise 16B.19

Can you tell from the graph of an equilibrium in Graph 16.10 whether profit will be affected by different choices of w and p that satisfy the equilibrium ratio? Verify whether your intuition holds mathematically.

16B.3.4 Welfare Theorems in the Simple Economy We illustrated in Section A the intuition behind the first and second welfare theorems in the context of our simple economy and therefore won't add much more here. Note, however, that our mathematical example already illustrates this for the particular functional forms we have chosen. In particular, we solved in Section 16B.3.1 for the optimum, or the Pareto-efficient outcome, when we asked how W would choose to optimize in the absence of looking separately at production and consumption decisions. This resulted in the labour and banana consumption bundle described in equation (16.28), with $\ell = 30$ and $x = 72$ when $X = 13.15$, $\beta = 0.5$, $\alpha = 2/3$ and $L = 60$, as is the case for the graphs in Section A. Substituting the expression for w^* from equation (16.38) into the expression for labour demand ℓ^D from equation (16.31) or alternatively substituting w^* into the expression for labour supply ℓ^S from equation (16.35), we can derive the equilibrium labour supply and demand as:

$$\ell = \frac{\alpha\beta L}{1 - \alpha(1 - \beta)}, \tag{16.38}$$

which is what we concluded in equation (16.28) is the efficient level of labour. You can similarly verify that the equilibrium wage w^* results in the optimal level of banana consumption. Thus, the Pareto-efficient allocation in this problem is the same as the equilibrium allocation, and the equilibrium is the same as the Pareto optimum.

Exercise 16B.20

Demonstrate that the equilibrium banana consumption and production is equal to the optimal level of banana consumption.

Appendix Core Convergence

We have shown within this chapter that the competitive equilibrium of a two-person exchange economy lies inside the set of core allocations. We also stated a second result, that as exchange economies become large, the set of core allocations shrinks to the set of competitive equilibrium allocations. *In the limit, the set of core allocations is equivalent to the set of competitive equilibrium allocations*, a result known as *core convergence* or *core equivalence*.

A core allocation has the property that there is no way any individual *or any coalition of individuals* can improve their well-being by separating from the larger economy with their endowment. If we expect that individuals will always search for ways to make themselves better off, we would expect core allocations to be the ones that emerge in economies where voluntary trade between individuals is permitted. The core convergence result states that for large economies, the *only* set of allocations that we would expect to emerge are those that arise under trades governed by competitive prices.

We can begin to get some intuition for why the set of core allocations in an economy shrinks as the economy grows by beginning with a two-person, two-good exchange economy just like the ones we have discussed throughout the chapter. In Graph 16.11, point E represents the endowment of the two individuals, and the light brown indifference curves labelled U^1 and U^2 represent their reservation utility levels. The light brown curve connecting the two origins of the Edgeworth Box represents the contract curve, and the darkened region between points A and B represents the set of core allocations.

Graph 16.11 End Points of Core No Longer in the Core as the Economy Expands

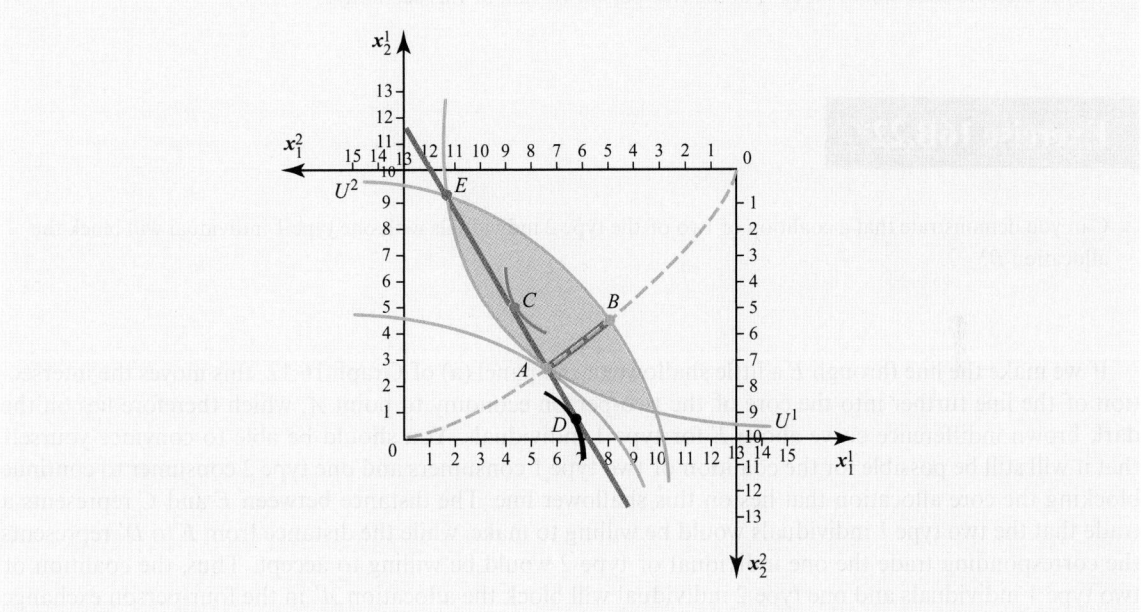

Now suppose that we replicate the economy; that is, we consider a four-person, two-good exchange economy in which we have two individuals of type 1 and two individuals of type 2. Individuals of the same type are assumed to have the same tastes and the same endowments. A core allocation in this replicated economy has to have the property that there does not exist a coalition of several individuals in the economy that can, by trading with one another, do better than the individuals under the core allocation.

We can now check whether a point like A, which is a core allocation in the two-person economy, is still a core allocation in the four-person replicated economy. Suppose allocation A is proposed, with each of the individuals getting the number of goods indicated by A as read off the relevant axes. Now suppose that as they consider whether to agree to move from E to A, the two type 1 individuals get together with one of the type 2 individuals to see if together they can make each other better off than they would be at A. For instance, starting at E, the type 1 individuals might propose terms of trade under which they give up 1 x_1 good for every 1 x_2 good they each receive. This implies that individual 2 would agree to accept 2 x_1 goods in exchange for 2 x_2 goods because there are 2 of type 1 and 1 of type 2. Any trade that is made under these terms implies that the new type 2 allocation after the trade is twice as far from E on the budget line that incorporates the proposed terms of trade as the new type 1 allocation.

Suppose that the subgroup composed of two type 1 and one type 2 individuals agrees to trade in such a way that type 1 individuals end up at C and the type 2 individual ends up at D, which is twice as far from E as C in Graph 16.11. This is logically possible for this three-person coalition; they are simply reallocating what they had at point E. But this means that the type 1 individuals will end up moving to the dark brown indifference curve while the one type 2 individual moves to the dark blue indifference curve; that is, all three individuals in the coalition are better off after trading with each other than they would be at point A. The allocation at point A is *not* in the core for the four-person economy even though it is in the core for the two-person economy. Economists would say that the coalition of two 'type 1' individuals and one 'type 2' individual *blocks* the proposed allocation A, and they would refer to this coalition as a *blocking coalition*.

Exercise 16B.21

Why is there no coalition to block A in the two-person version of this economy?

Exercise 16B.22*

Can you demonstrate that a coalition of two of the type 2 individuals with one type 1 individual will block the allocation B?

If we make the line through E a little shallower, as in panel (a) of Graph 16.12, this moves the intersection of the line further into the core of the two-person economy to point A, which therefore lies on the dark brown indifference curve above E for type 1 individuals. You should be able to convince yourself that it will still be possible for the coalition of two type 1 consumers and one type 2 consumer to continue blocking the core allocation that lies on this shallower line. The distance between E and C represents a trade that the two type 1 individuals would be willing to make, while the distance from E to D' represents the corresponding trade the one individual of type 2 would be willing to accept. Thus, the coalition of two type 1 individuals and one type 2 individual will block the allocation A' in the four-person exchange economy.

Graph 16.12 A Shrinking Core as the Economy Expands

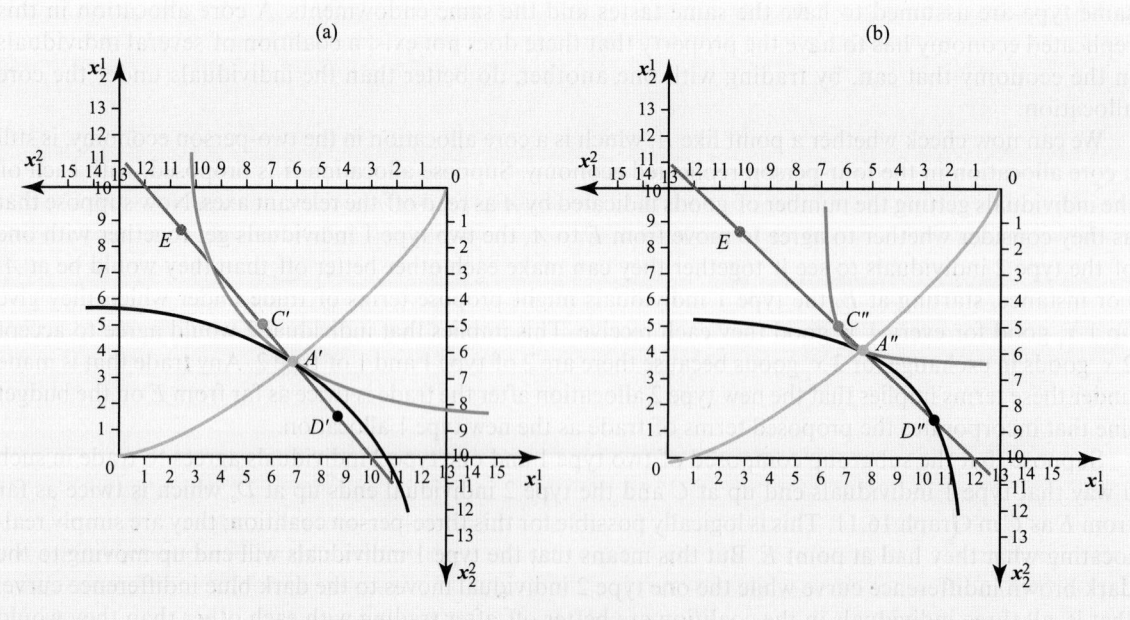

Exercise 16B.23*

Why must the distance between E and D' be twice the distance from E to C'?

If, however, the line becomes sufficiently shallow, it will no longer be possible for this coalition to block the two-person core allocation on that line. This is illustrated in panel (b) of Graph 16.12. Here, a trade from E to C leaves type 1 individuals just as well off as they are under the allocation A on the contract curve, and the corresponding trade from E to D for the type 2 individual leaves them also just as well off as under A. Any smaller trade would make the type 1 individuals worse off than at A, while any larger trade would make the type 2 individual worse off than at A. Thus, there are no trades from the two type 1 individuals to the one type 2 individual that will make anyone in the coalition better off without making someone else worse off, which implies that the coalition will no longer block A, and A is therefore in the core of the four-person exchange economy. The core is shrinking but not disappearing. In particular, the core is, as we have just shown, shrinking from below, and it is shrinking from above for analogous reasons.

Exercise 16B.24*

Demonstrate that the competitive equilibrium allocation must lie in the core of the replicated exchange economy.

As the economy is replicated further, with additional type 1 and type 2 individuals joining the economy, the number of possible blocking coalitions increases. The coalition previously discussed still exists, which implies that the core is no larger than it was when we had two consumers of each type. The increase in the number of other possible coalitions implies that further allocations that were previously in the core are blocked by some new coalition. You should be able to see, however, that the equilibrium allocation always remains in the core. While we won't demonstrate this formally here, the important result that can be proven rigorously is that as the economy becomes larger, the set of core allocations ultimately shrinks down to just the set of equilibrium allocations.

End-of-Chapter Exercises

16.1† Consider a two-person, two-good exchange economy in which person 1 is endowed with (e_1^1, e_2^1) and person 2 is endowed with (e_1^2, e_2^2) of the goods x_1 and x_2.

A. Assume that tastes are homothetic for both individuals.

a. Draw the Edgeworth Box for this economy, indicating on each axis the dimensions of the box.

b. The two individuals have identical tastes. Illustrate the contract curve, the set of all efficient allocations of the two goods.

c. *True or False*: Identical tastes in the Edgeworth Box imply that there are no mutually beneficial trades.

d. *The two individuals now have different but still homothetic tastes. *True or False*: The contract curve will lie to one side of the line that connects the lower left and upper right corners of the Edgeworth Box; that is, it will never cross this line inside the Edgeworth Box.

B. Let the tastes for individuals 1 and 2 be described by the utility functions $u^1 = x_1^\alpha x_2^{(1-\alpha)}$ and $u^2 = x_1^\beta x_2^{(1-\beta)}$, where α and β both lie between 0 and 1. Some of the following questions are notationally a little easier to keep track of if you also denote $E_1 = e_1^1 + e_1^2$ as the economy's endowment of x_1 and $E_2 = e_2^1 + e_2^2$ as the economy's endowment of x_2.

a. Let $\bar{x}_1$ denote the allocation of x_1 to individual 1, and let $\bar{x}_2$ denote the allocation of x_2 to individual 1. Use the fact that the remainder of the economy's endowment is allocated to individual 2 to denote individual 2's allocation as $(E_1 - \bar{x}_1)$ and $(E_2 - \bar{x}_2)$ for x_1 and x_2 respectively. Derive the contract curve in the form $\bar{x}_2 = x_2(\bar{x}_1)$; that is, with the allocation of x_2 to person 1 as a function of the allocation of x_1 to person 1.

b. Simplify your expression under the assumption that tastes are identical; that is, $\alpha = \beta$. What shape and location of the contract curve in the Edgeworth Box does this imply?

c. Next, suppose that $\alpha \neq \beta$. Verify that the contract curve extends from the lower left to the upper right corner of the Edgeworth Box.

d. Consider the slopes of the contract curve when $\bar{x}_1 = 0$ and when $\bar{x}_1 = E_1$. How do they compare to the slope of the line connecting the lower left and upper right corners of the Edgeworth Box if $\alpha > \beta$? What if $\alpha < \beta$?

e. Using what you have concluded, graph the shape of the contract curve for the case when $\alpha > \beta$ and for the case when $\alpha < \beta$.

f. Suppose that the utility function for the two individuals took the more general constant elasticity of substitution form $u = (ax_1^{-\rho} + (1-\alpha)x_2^{-\rho})^{-1/\rho}$. If the tastes for the two individuals are identical, does your answer to part (b) change?

16.2 Consider as in exercise 16.1 a two-person, two-good exchange economy in which person 1 is endowed with (e_1^1, e_2^1) and person 2 is endowed with (e_1^2, e_2^2) of the goods x_1 and x_2.

A. Tastes are homothetic and are also identical.

a. Draw the Edgeworth Box and place the endowment point to one side of the line connecting the lower left and upper right corners of the box.

b. Illustrate the contract curve, i.e. the set of efficient allocations you derived in exercise 16.1. Illustrate the set of mutually beneficial trades as well as the set of core allocations.

c. Why would we expect these two individuals to arrive at an allocation in the core by trading with one another?

d. Where does the competitive equilibrium lie in this case? Illustrate this by drawing the budget line that arises from equilibrium prices.

e. Does the equilibrium lie in the core?

f. Why would your prediction when the two individuals have different bargaining skills differ from this?

B. The tastes for individuals 1 and 2 can be described by the utility functions $u^1 = x_1^\alpha x_2^{(1-\alpha)}$ and $u^2 = x_1^\beta x_2^{(1-\beta)}$, where α and β both lie between 0 and 1.

a. Derive the demands for x_1 and x_2 by each of the two individuals as a function of prices p_1 and p_2, and as a function of their individual endowments.

b. Let p_1^* and p_2^* denote equilibrium prices. Derive the ratio p_2^*/p_1^*.

c. Find the equilibrium allocation in the economy – the amount of x_1 and x_2 that each individual will consume in the competitive equilibrium as a function of their endowments.

d. Now suppose tastes are the same for the two individuals ($\alpha = \beta$). From your answer in (c), derive the equilibrium allocation to person 1.

e. Does your answer to (d) satisfy the condition you derived in exercise 16.1B(b) for Pareto-efficient allocations, i.e. allocations on the contract curve? You should have derived the equation describing the contract curve as $\bar{x}_2(x_1) = (E_2/E_1)x_1$.

16.3† In this exercise, we explore some technical aspects of general equilibrium theory in exchange economies and simple economies. Unlike in other problems, parts A and B are applicable to both those focused on A-Section material and those focused on B-Section material. Although the insights are developed in simple examples, they apply more generally in much more complex models.

A. *The Role of Convexity in Exchange Economies.* In each of the following parts, suppose X and Y are the only individuals in the economy, and pick some arbitrary allocation E in the Edgeworth Box as their initial endowment. Assume throughout that Y's tastes are convex and that the contract curve is equal to the line connecting the lower left and upper right corners of the box.

   a. Begin with a depiction of an equilibrium. Can you introduce a non-convexity into Y's tastes such that the equilibrium disappears despite the fact that the contract curve remains unchanged?
   b. *True or False*: Existence of a competitive equilibrium in an exchange economy cannot be guaranteed if tastes are allowed to be non-convex.
   c. Suppose an equilibrium does exist even though X's tastes exhibit some non-convexity. *True or False*: The first welfare theorem holds even when tastes have non-convexities.
   d. *True or False*: The second welfare theorem holds even when tastes have non-convexities.

B. *The Role of Convexity in Simple Economies.* Consider a simple economy. Suppose throughout that there is a tangency between the worker's indifference curve and the production technology at some bundle *A*.

   a. Suppose first that the production technology gives rise to a convex production choice set. Illustrate an equilibrium when tastes are convex. Show that *A* may no longer be an equilibrium if you allow tastes to have non-convexities even if the indifference curve is still tangential to the production choice set at *A*.
   b. Next, suppose again that tastes are convex but now let the production choice set have non-convexities. Show again that *A* might no longer be an equilibrium even though the indifference curve and production choice set are tangential at *A*.
   c. *True or False*: A competitive equilibrium may not exist in a simple economy that has non-convexities in either tastes or production.
   d. *True or False*: The first welfare theorem holds even if there are non-convexities in tastes and/or production technologies.
   e. *True or False*: The second welfare theorem holds regardless of whether there are non-convexities in tastes or production.
   f. Based on what you have done in parts A and B, evaluate the following statement: 'Non-convexities may cause a non-existence of competitive equilibria in general equilibrium economies, but if an equilibrium exists, it results in an efficient allocation of resources. However, only in the absence of non-convexities can we conclude that there always exists some lump sum redistribution such that any efficient allocation can also be an equilibrium allocation'. Note: your conclusion on this holds well beyond the examples in this problem for reasons that are quite similar to the intuition developed here.

16.4 **Everyday Application:** *Children, Parents, Baby Booms and Baby Busts.* Economists often think of parents and children trading with one another across time. When children are young, parents take care of children; but when parents get old, children often come to take care of their parents. We will think of this in a two-period model in which children earn no income in period 1 and parents earn no income in period 2. For the purposes of this problem, we will assume that parents have no way to save in period 1 for the future and children have no way to borrow from the future when they are in period 1. Thus, parents and children have to rely on one another.

A. Suppose that during the periods when they earn income, i.e. period 1 for parents and period 2 for children, parents and children earn the same amount y. Suppose further that everyone has homothetic tastes with $MRS = -1$ when $c_1 = c_2$.

   a. Assume that there is one parent and one child. Illustrate an Edgeworth Box with current consumption c_1 on the horizontal and future consumption c_2 on the vertical axes. Indicate where the endowment allocation lies.
   b. Given that everyone has homothetic tastes and assuming that consumption now and in the future are not perfect substitutes, where does the region of mutually beneficial trades lie?
   c. Let p be the price of current consumption in terms of future consumption, and let the price of future consumption be normalized to 1. Illustrate a competitive equilibrium.
   d.*Suppose that there are now two identical children and one parent. Keep the Edgeworth Box the same dimensions as in (a). However, because there are now two children, every action on a child's part must be balanced by twice the opposite action from the one parent that is being modelled in the Edgeworth Box. Does the equilibrium price p^* go up or down? *Hint*: An equilibrium is now characterized by the parent moving twice as far on the equilibrium budget as each child.

e. *What happens to child consumption now and parent consumption in the future?

f. *Instead, suppose that there are two parents and one child. Again show what happens to the equilibrium price p^*.

g. *What happens to child consumption now and parent consumption in the future?

h. Would anything have changed in the original one-child, one-parent equilibrium had we assumed two children and two parents instead?

i. *While it might be unrealistic to apply a competitive model to a single family, we might interpret the model as representing generations that compete for current and future resources. Based on your analysis, will parents enjoy a better retirement if their children were part of a baby boom or a baby bust? Why?

j. *Will children be more spoiled if they are part of a baby boom or a baby bust?

k. *Consider two types of government spending: (1) spending on welfare benefits for the elderly, and (2) investments in a clean environment for future generations. When would this model predict whether the environment will do better: during baby booms or during baby busts? Why?

B. Suppose the set-up is as described in A and A(a), with $y = 100$, and let tastes be described by the utility function $u(c_1, c_2) = c_1 c_2$.

a. Is it true that given these tastes, the entire inside of the Edgeworth Box is equal to the area of mutually beneficial allocations relative to the endowment allocation?

b. Let p be defined as in A(c). Derive the parent and child demands for c_1 and c_2 as a function of p.

c. Derive the equilibrium price p^* in the case where there is one parent and one child.

d. What is the equilibrium allocation of consumption across time between parent and child?

e. Suppose there are two children and one parent. Repeat (c) and (d).

f. Suppose there are two parents and one child. Repeat (c) and (d).

g. Suppose there are two children and two parents. Repeat (c) and (d).

16.5† **Business Application:** *Valuing Land in Equilibrium.* Consider a simple economy with one worker who has preferences over leisure and consumption and one firm that uses a constant returns to scale production process with inputs land and labour.

A. Suppose that the worker owns the fixed supply of land that is available for production. Throughout the problem, normalize the price of output to 1.

a. Explain why we can normalize one of the three prices in this economy where the other two prices are the wage w and the land rental rate r.

b. Assuming the land can fetch a positive rent per unit, how much of it will the worker rent to the firm in equilibrium given their tastes are only over leisure and consumption?

c. Given your answer to (b), explain how we can think of the production frontier for the firm as a single-input production process that uses labour to produce output?

d. What returns to scale does this single-input production process have? Draw the production frontier in a graph with labour on the horizontal and output on the vertical axis.

e. What do the worker's indifference curves in this graph look like? Illustrate the worker's optimal bundle if the worker took the production frontier as their constraint.

f. Illustrate the budget for the worker and the isoprofit for the firm that lead both worker and firm to choose the bundle you identified in (e) as the optimum. What is the slope of this budget/isoprofit? Does the budget/isoprofit have a positive vertical intercept?

g. *In the text, we interpreted this intercept as profit that the worker gets as part of their income because the worker owns the firm. Here, however, the worker owns the land that the firm uses. Can you reinterpret this positive intercept in the context of this model, keeping in mind that the true underlying production frontier for the firm has constant returns to scale? If land had been normalized to 1 unit, where would you find the land rental rate r in your graph?

B. *Suppose that the worker's tastes can be represented by the utility function $u(x,(1 - \ell)) = x^\alpha(1 - \ell)^{(1-\alpha)}$, where x is consumption, ℓ is labour and where the leisure endowment is normalized to 1. Suppose further that the firm's production function is $f(y, \ell) = y^{0.5}\ell^{0.5}$ where y represents the number of acres of land rented by the firm and ℓ represents the labour hours employed.

a. Normalize the price of output to be equal to 1 for the remainder of the problem and let land rent and the wage be equal to r and w. Write down the firm's profit-maximization problem, taking into account that the firm has to employ both land and labour.

b. Take the first order conditions of the firm's profit-maximization problem. The worker gets no consumption value from their land and therefore will rent their whole unit of land to the firm. You can replace land in your first order conditions with 1 and solve each first order condition for ℓ and from this derive the relationship between w and r.

c. The worker earns income from their labour and from renting their land to the firm. Express the worker's budget constraint in terms of w and solve for the worker's labour supply function in terms of w.

d. Derive the equilibrium wage in your economy by setting labour supply equal to labour demand which you implicitly derived in (b) from one of your first order conditions.

e. What is the equilibrium rent of the land owned by the worker?

f. Now suppose we reformulate the problem slightly. Suppose the firm's production function is $f(y, \ell) = y^{(1-\beta)}\ell^{\beta}$, where y is land and ℓ is labour, and the worker's tastes can be represented by the utility function $u(x,(L - \ell)) = x^{\alpha}(L - \ell)^{(1-\alpha)}$, where L is the worker's leisure endowment. Compare this to the way we formulated the simple economy in the text. If land area is in fixed supply at 1 unit, what parameter in our formulation in the text must be set to 1 in order for our problem to be identical to the one in the text?

g. *True or False*: By turning land into a fixed input, we have turned the constant returns to scale production process into one of decreasing returns to scale.

h. Suppose that as in the earlier part of the problem, $\beta = 0.5$ and the worker's leisure endowment is again normalized to $L = 1$. Use the solution for the equilibrium wage in the text to derive the equilibrium wage now, again normalizing the output price to 1.

i. Use the profit function in equation (16.33) of the text to determine the profit of the firm given the equilibrium wage and given the parameter values used here. Compare this to the equilibrium land rent you derived in (e). Explain your result intuitively.

16.6 **Policy Application:** *Distortionary Taxes in General Equilibrium.* Consider a two-person exchange economy in which A own 200 units of x_1 and 100 units of x_2 while B owns 100 units of x_1 and 200 units of x_2.

A. Suppose A and B have identical homothetic tastes.

a. Draw the Edgeworth Box for this economy and indicate the endowment allocation E.

b. Normalize the price of good x_2 to 1. Illustrate the equilibrium price p^* for x_1 and the equilibrium allocation of goods in the absence of any taxes. Who buys and who sells x_1?

c. The government introduces a tax t levied on all transactions of x_1 and paid in terms of x_2. For instance, if one unit of x_1 is sold from A to B at price p, A will only get to keep $(p - t)$. Explain how this creates a kink in their budget constraints.

d. Suppose a post-tax equilibrium exists and that price increases for buyers and falls for sellers. In such an equilibrium, A will still be selling some quantity of x_1 to B. Can you explain why? How do the relevant portions of the budget constraints A and B face look in this new equilibrium, and where will they optimize?

e. When we discussed price changes with homothetic tastes in our development of consumer theory, we noted that there are often competing income or wealth and substitution effects. Are there such competing effects here relative to our consumption of x_1? If so, can we be sure that the quantity we trade *in equilibrium* will be less when t is introduced?

f. You should see that, in the new equilibrium, a portion of x_2 remains not allocated to anyone. This is the amount that is paid in taxes to the government. Draw a new Edgeworth Box that is adjusted on the x_2 axis to reflect the fact that some portion of x_2 is no longer allocated between the two individuals. Locate the equilibrium allocation point that you derived in your previous graph. Why is this point not efficient?

g. *True or False*: The deadweight loss from the distortionary tax on trades in x_1 results from the fact that their marginal rates of substitution are no longer equal to one another after the tax is imposed and *not* because the government raised revenues and thus lowered the amounts of x_2 consumed by them.

    h. *True or False*: While the post-tax equilibrium is not efficient, it does lie in the region of mutually beneficial trades.

    i. How would taxes that redistribute endowments as envisioned by the second welfare theorem be different from the price distorting tax analyzed in this problem?

B. Suppose A and B's tastes can be represented by the utility function $u(x_1, x_2) = x_1 x_2$. Let their endowments be specified as at the beginning of the problem.

    a. Derive their demand functions for x_1 and x_2 as functions of p – the price of x_1 when the price of x_2 is normalized to 1.

    b. Derive the equilibrium price p^* and the equilibrium allocation of goods.

    c. Now suppose the government introduces a tax t as specified in A(c). Given that A is the one that sells and B the one that buys x_1, how can you now rewrite their demand functions to account for t? *Hint*: There are two ways of doing this: either define p as the pre-tax price and let the relevant price for the buyer be $(p + t)$ or let p be defined as the post-tax price and let the relevant price for the seller be $(p - t)$.

    d. Derive the new equilibrium pre- and post-tax prices in terms of t. *Hint*: You should get to a point where you need to solve a quadratic equation using the quadratic formula that gives two answers. Of these two, the larger one is the correct answer for this problem.

    e. How much of each good do A and B consume if $t = 1$?

    f. How much revenue does the government raise if $t = 1$?

    g. Show that the equilibrium allocation under the tax is inefficient.

Chapter 17

Choice and Markets in the Presence of Risk

In our analysis so far, we have not considered the impact of risk on decision making. Sometimes the risks we face are personal such as dying in a car crash. Other times, the risk is financial, for example in purchasing an asset such as a house or a stock, we risk the value of the asset falling.

Where risk exists, there is a potential market for products that reduce the risk in the form of insurance, for example. In this chapter, we will use some of the tools we have already developed to extend our analysis of choice and markets to circumstances where risk is central to the concerns of the individual who is choosing. In much of the chapter, we will use the example of life insurance to illustrate a model that can be used to address all sorts of situations that involve risk. It will be a combination of tastes and constraints that will determine choice, with different individuals having different attitudes or tastes towards risk, and with prices in markets determining the options that individuals have for dealing with the risks they face. We will find that in the absence of distorting forces, competitive markets result in efficient outcomes. In Chapter 22, we will discover that markets that deal with risk often face, almost by definition, distortions arising from asymmetric information, and it is from these distortions that we will later see a role for non-market institutions to improve on market outcomes that involve risk.

17A	An Intuitive Model of Choice in the Presence of Risk

Whenever we face risk, we essentially face choices over gambles in which there are better and worse outcomes and we can't be sure which of the outcomes will ultimately materialize. Insurance offers a means of changing the gamble, improving the bad outcomes while giving something up in the good outcomes. The simplest cases to analyze are those where the only thing that matters about the outcomes is money. When we invest in the stock market, for instance, we care about how much of a return we will ultimately get on our investment. The degree to which the investment pays off determines the budget constraint we will face, but our tastes or indifference map over the goods we consume are unaffected by how well our stock portfolio is doing. When we consider investing in disability insurance, on the other hand, we probably care about a lot more than how much money we have depending on whether we become disabled or not; the disability itself, apart from its financial implications, is something that we probably have strong feelings about. When we think about the appropriate level of disability insurance, we face a situation in which our indifference map over the goods we consume may well depend on whether we are disabled or not.

We will begin with the simpler of the situations where risky choices involve only money, and refer to these types of situations as involving state-independent utility because our tastes or utility are independent of what state of the world we end up facing. We will outline a more complicated model in which

465

we evaluate consumption differently depending on what risky outcome happens. After investigating how individuals make choices in these models, we use the tools developed in Chapter 16 to investigate how competitive market equilibria emerge in situations involving risk. Finally, while we will develop many of these ideas in the context of life insurance markets, we will conclude Section A with a brief discussion of how the model can also deal with risk in financial markets.

17A.1 Risky Choices Involving Money

We begin with a model in which individual tastes over consumption are independent of what risky outcome we end up facing. The assumption is that the consumer uses the same rule for evaluating the value of consumption regardless of whether the good outcome or the bad outcome happens. While we will restrict ourselves to gambles in which there are only two possible outcomes, the model can in principle be extended to include a large number of possible outcomes.

17A.1.1 Utility and Expected Utility Suppose a husband, John and wife, Emma make a decision that Emma will specialize in earning income to support the household while John specializes in running the household. For John there is a risk – the decision that might leave him in a precarious financial position were anything to happen to Emma. For simplicity, let's suppose that there is a probability, δ, where $0 < \delta < 1$, that Emma will die and leave John with a significantly reduced standard of living and some chance $(1 - \delta)$ that she will live to continue supporting the household.

Assume that the only way Emma can contribute to John's well-being is through her income, how will John's well-being be affected by the introduction of the risk of premature death of Emma? In panel (a) of Graph 17.1, we begin with a model of a single-input production process where the input is John's consumption, labelled J_c and the output is John's utility (J_u). In this consumption/utility relationship, consumption exhibits *diminishing marginal product*, or *diminishing marginal utility* of consumption.

Graph 17.1 Relation of Utility to Consumption.

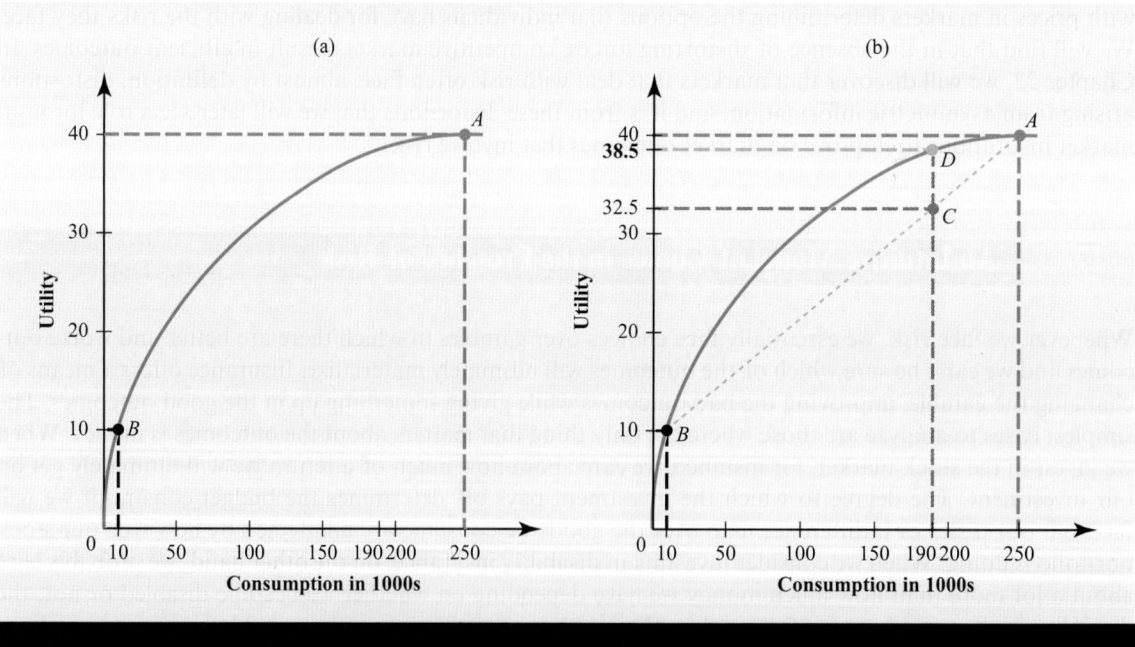

Go to MindTap to interact with this graph

Recall in Chapter 4 we noted that modern economists don't believe we can objectively measure utility in this way. Here, we are not assuming we can measure utility and marginal utility as panel (a) of Graph 17.1 seems to suggest. What we are doing is assuming something known as the *independence axiom* which is at the core of neoclassical models of risk. This assumption says the following: suppose there are three possible gambles you could play. You are offered the choice of either (A) playing Gamble 1 half the time and Gamble 3 half the time or (B) playing Gamble 2 half the time and Gamble 3 half the time. Our assumption is that if you prefer Gamble 1 to Gamble 2, you will prefer choice A to choice B. For example, you might be invited to a casino and offered the choice between (A) flipping a coin to determine if you will play roulette or slot machines and (B) flipping a coin to determine if you play poker or slot machines. The independence axiom says that if you like roulette better than poker, you will choose A over B.

Economists have shown that this basic axiom allows us to conclude that there exists a consumption/utility relationship, like the one we are graphing, that can be used as a *tool* to predict choice over risky gambles *without assuming that we have to interpret this relationship literally as objectively measuring utility*.

Exercise 17A.1

If the relationship depicted in panel (a) of Graph 17.1 were a single-input production function, would it have increasing, decreasing or constant returns to scale?

Assume Emma's financial position improves and her salary increases to €250 000 a year. If Emma died, however, the household will be left with just €10 000 in annual income from some savings that John will inherit. Suppose further, for illustration, that Emma is not very popular at work and that there is a 25 per cent chance that someone there will arrange for her early demise (i.e. $\delta = 0.25$), and, again for illustration, let's suppose John is looking ahead one year as he thinks about the risk he is taking by relying so heavily on Emma.

From John's perspective, he knows he can count on €250 000 in consumption with probability 0.75 and €10 000 in consumption with probability 0.25. His *expected consumption*, defined as the probability of the good outcome times €250 000 plus the probability of the bad outcome times €10 000, is €190 000. We will sometimes also refer to this as the *expected value* of the gamble he is taking.

Exercise 17A.2

Verify that John's expected household consumption is €190 000.

From panel (a) of Graph 17.1, we can also read off John's utility, as quantified by the consumption/utility relationship that we can use as a tool given the independence axiom, under each scenario. If Emma survives the year and earns €250 000, John's utility is read off A as 40, but if she dies and he is left with only €10 000, his utility is read off point B as only 10. Looking ahead towards next year, John's *expected utility* – defined as the probability of the good outcome times 40 plus the probability of the bad outcome times 10 – is 32.5.

The geometry of this is illustrated in panel (b) of Graph 17.1. The dashed line connecting A and B is the set of points in the graph that average points A and B using different weights. For example, the mid-point of this line takes the average of A and B. Point C, on the other hand, lies three-quarters of the way towards point A and thus represents the weighted average of A and B where A is given a weight of 0.75 and B is given a weight of 0.25. Point C places the same weight on the good and bad outcomes as John does given that he knows Emma has a 75 per cent chance of surviving the year, and it is at point C that we can read off John's expected utility of 32.5 on the vertical axis. The expected value of the gamble – €190 000 – is analogously read off the horizontal axis.

17A.1.2 Different Attitudes About Risk If we only had panel (a) of Graph 17.1 and looked to determine John's expected utility, you might have been tempted to calculate that his expected consumption is €190 000, and rely on the fact that John's utility of having €190 000 is 38.5 to answer the question. The problem with this reasoning is that John's utility of having €190 000 *with certainty* is 38.5, but what we really want to know is what his utility is of getting €250 000 with probability 0.75 and €10 000 with probability 0.25.

In panel (b) of Graph 17.1 and in our calculations, we find that John's expected utility from facing this risk, read off point C, is less than the utility he would get by receiving €190 000 with certainty, read off point D. The reason for this is that in drawing the relationship between income and utility as we have, we have implicitly assumed that John is *risk averse* and would prefer to have €190 000 with certainty, rather than face the risk of perhaps receiving a higher amount and perhaps receiving a lower amount even though in expectation he is receiving the same. *A risk-averse person's utility of the expected value of a gamble is always higher than the expected utility of the gamble.*

Different people have different attitudes towards risk, and not everyone may be as risk averse as John. In Graph 17.2, we illustrate three different cases, with panel (a) replicating the graph that we just developed for John and thus representing the case of a risk-averse person who prefers a sure thing to a gamble that has the same expected value but involves risk. In panel (b), we consider the case of *risk-neutral* tastes, or a person who is indifferent between a sure thing and a gamble with the same expected value; and in panel (c) we consider a person who is *risk loving* and would prefer to take a gamble rather than get the expected value of the gamble for sure.

Exercise 17A.3

What is the relationship between increasing, constant and decreasing marginal utility of consumption to risk-loving, risk-neutral and risk-averse tastes?

Exercise 17A.4

We said that a risk-averse person's utility of the expected value of a gamble is always higher than the expected utility of the gamble. How does this statement change for risk-neutral and risk-loving tastes?

If John's tastes were accurately graphed as in panel (b) of Graph 17.2, at point A', his utility of getting €250 000 is 40, while at point B' his utility of getting €10 000 is just 1.6. Given that he will attain utility of 40 with probability 0.75 and utility of 1.6 with probability 0.25, this implies his expected utility is 30.4.

Graph 17.2 Risk Aversion, Risk Neutrality and Risk Loving

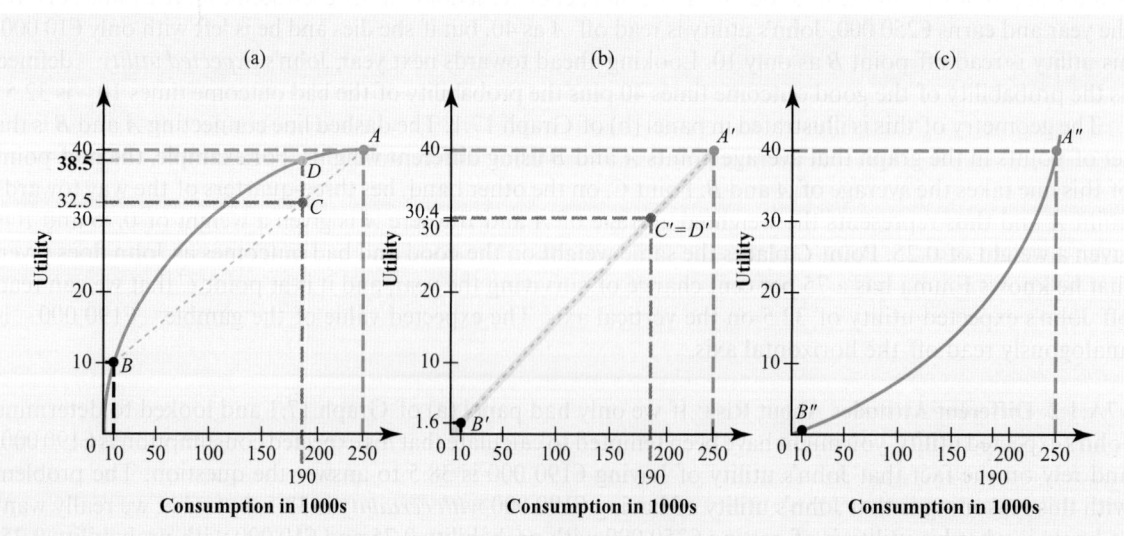

This is read off graphically at point C' on the line connecting points A' and B' three-quarters of the way towards point A', only now this line lies right on top of the consumption/utility relationship. Were we to ask how much utility John would get by receiving €190 000 with certainty, we would read this off at exactly the same point as 30.4. As the curvature of the consumption/utility relationship in the risk-averse case of panel (a) is reduced, point D comes closer and closer to point C, and when the consumption/utility relationship becomes linear, the two points overlap as they do in panel (b). In this case, John would be indifferent between getting €190 000 with certainty as opposed to facing the risk of getting €250 000 with probability 0.75 and €10 000 with probability 0.25. He does not care about the risk and only cares about the expected value of the gamble he is facing.

Exercise 17A.5

Illustrate that if tastes are as described in panel (c) of Graph 17.2, John prefers the risky gamble of getting €250 000 with probability 0.75 and €10 000 with probability 0.25 over the sure thing €190 000 with certainty that has the same expected value.

17A.1.3 The Certainty Equivalent and Risk Premium So far, we have shown that a risk-averse person who is asked to take a chance would prefer to get the expected value of the gamble for sure rather than have to face the risk of the gamble. In panel (a) of Graph 17.2, for instance, John would prefer to get €190 000 for sure rather than face a gamble that has an expected value of €190 000. Some people are more risk averse than others, which raises the question of how we might quantify the degree of risk aversion that we can compare across individuals, rather than just identifying some as risk averse and some as risk loving or risk neutral.

One way to do this is to begin by asking the following question: What's the least that has to be given to the person for sure in order for them to agree not to participate in the gamble at all? Put into the context of the gamble John takes on Emma, how much would we have to give him so that he would agree to run off and get neither €250 000 if Emma survives the year, nor €10 000 if she doesn't? In Graph 17.3, we answer this question by illustrating John's risk-averse tastes. We know from what we have done so far that we can read off his utility of taking the gamble at point C as 32.5. If we want to buy him out of this gamble, we would have to offer him an amount that makes him indifferent to facing the gamble; that is, an amount that will give him utility of 32.5. We can check to see how much consumption it would take to accomplish this by finding the point E where the dashed horizontal line at utility of 32.5 intersects the consumption/utility relationship. Point E lies at €115 000 on the consumption axis, which implies that John will get utility of 32.5 if he receives €115 000 with certainty. He would be indifferent between betting on Emma and receiving €115 000 without risk.

The lowest possible amount that someone is willing to take for sure in order not to participate in a gamble is called the *certainty equivalent of the gamble*. John's certainty equivalent of facing the gamble of getting €250 000 with probability 0.75 and €10 000 with probability 0.25 is, therefore, €115 000. The *risk premium* of a gamble is the difference between the expected value of a gamble and its certainty equivalent. John's risk premium is, therefore, €75 000, which represents the amount he is willing to sacrifice in expected value in order to eliminate the risk he faces.

Exercise 17A.6

What is the certainty equivalent and the risk premium for John if he had tastes that can be summarized as in panel (b) of Graph 17.2?

Graph 17.3 Certainty Equivalent and Risk Premium

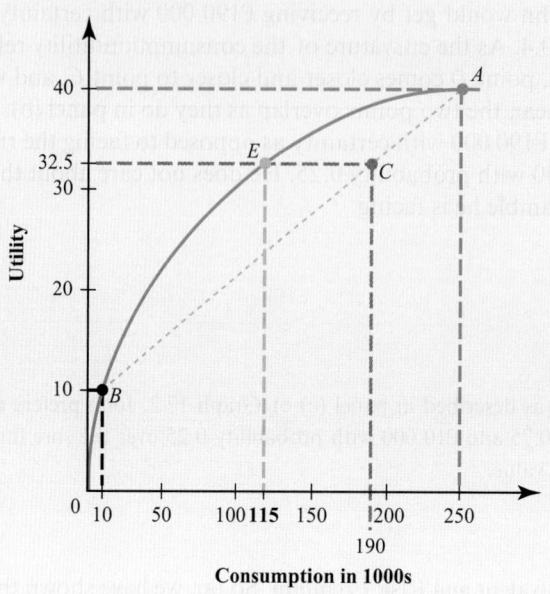

Exercise 17A.7

In panel (c) of Graph 17.2, is the risk premium positive or negative? Can you reconcile this with the fact that the tastes in this graph represent those of a risk lover?

Exercise 17A.8

True or False: As an individual becomes more risk averse, the certainty equivalent for a risky gamble will fall and the risk premium will rise.

17A.1.4 Actuarially Fair Insurance Markets Since John is risk averse, he might be interested in finding an arrangement under which he pays some amount to reduce or eliminate the risk that he faces. He might be interested in investing in life insurance on Emma. This is the point of insurance: to pay something up front in order to reduce risks faced.

An *insurance contract* or an *insurance policy* is composed of two parts: an *insurance premium* that the buyer agrees to pay before knowing what outcome they face, and an *insurance benefit* that the insured buyer is entitled to if they end up facing the bad outcome. For example, if John agrees to take out a €100 000 life insurance policy on Emma for a premium of €10 000, he in essence agrees to reduce his consumption if he faces the good outcome by €10 000 because he will have had to pay the €10 000 insurance premium without getting anything back from the insurance company, in exchange for increasing his consumption by €90 000 if he faces the bad outcome because, although he will have paid a €10 000 insurance premium, he will end up collecting a €100 000 insurance benefit from the policy.

Suppose that there is a competitive insurance industry that has full information about the risks that individuals face. For simplicity, suppose that many other consumers find themselves in a position similar to John's, and insurance companies compete for the business of these consumers. Assume that the risks are not correlated across individuals, which implies that in any given year, 25 per cent of those who are insured will be owed payments by an insurance company and 75 per cent will find themselves facing the good outcome and thus will not require payment from an insurance company.

Insurance companies might offer a variety of insurance contracts, some with high premiums and high benefits, others with lower premiums and lower benefits. Since each insurance company covers many consumers, it can be reasonably certain that it will have to pay benefits to 25 per cent of its customers while collecting the premium from all of them. An insurance company that offers a policy with benefit b and premium p to 100 customers will receive $100p$ in revenues and incur $25b$ in costs. Thus, if b is less than or equal to $4p$, the insurance company will make a profit, assuming it has negligible costs of collecting premiums and paying benefits. Under perfect competition, each insurance company will make zero profit, which implies that the long-run equilibrium insurance contract will have benefits that are four times as high as premiums. More generally, if the probability of the bad outcome is δ, $b = (p/\delta)$ in equilibrium.

Exercise 17A.9

Verify that the zero-profit relationship between b and p is as described in the previous sentence.

The type of insurance contract that we have just described is known as *actuarially fair*. An *actuarially fair insurance contract reduces the risk a consumer faces without changing the expected value of the gamble for which the consumer buys insurance.* In expectation, a consumer who buys an actuarially fair insurance policy pays an amount equal to what they receive back, which therefore causes the insurance company to make zero profit. As we will see shortly, such an actuarially fair life insurance contract in our example might, for instance, have a premium of €20 000 and a benefit of €80 000, or a premium of €40 000 and a benefit of €160 000, or a premium of €60 000 and a benefit of €240 000.

Suppose John purchases the first policy with a premium of €20 000 and a benefit of €80 000. This would imply that if Emma survives the year and earns €250 000, John will have only €230 000 left given that he had to pay the €20 000 premium. If Emma does not survive to earn the money, on the other hand, John would still have paid the €20 000 premium but would receive a benefit of €80 000, thus leaving him with €60 000 more than the €10 000 he would have had in the absence of insurance. By purchasing this policy, John would have a 0.75 probability of facing a good outcome with €230 000 and a 0.25 probability of facing a bad outcome with €70 000. His *expected consumption*, however, remains unchanged at €190 000. He has reduced his risk without changing his expected consumption level.

Exercise 17A.10

Verify that John's expected income is still €190 000 under this insurance policy.

Would John be interested in such an insurance policy? To analyze this, we can return again to the graph of his consumption/utility relationship and find his expected utility under this insurance policy. In panel (a) of Graph 17.4, we begin with point A indicating the relevant point under the good outcome and B indicating the relevant point under the bad outcome assuming John has bought no life insurance on Emma. If he buys the insurance policy with b = €80 000 and p = €20 000, the good outcome shifts to point A_1 while the bad outcome shifts to point B_1. We can read off John's expected utility under this insurance policy by drawing the line connecting points A_1 and B_1 and finding the utility level (36.5) associated with the point that lies three-quarters of the way towards point A_1 at the consumption level €190 000. Since John's expected utility without insurance is 32.5 and his expected utility with this insurance policy is 36.5, we can conclude that he would prefer to hold this insurance rather than no insurance at all. It should be intuitive that this is the case given John is risk averse. The actuarially fair insurance policy does not change the expected value (€190 000) of the gamble he faces, but it does reduce the risk.

Graph 17.4 Buying Actuarially Fair Insurance

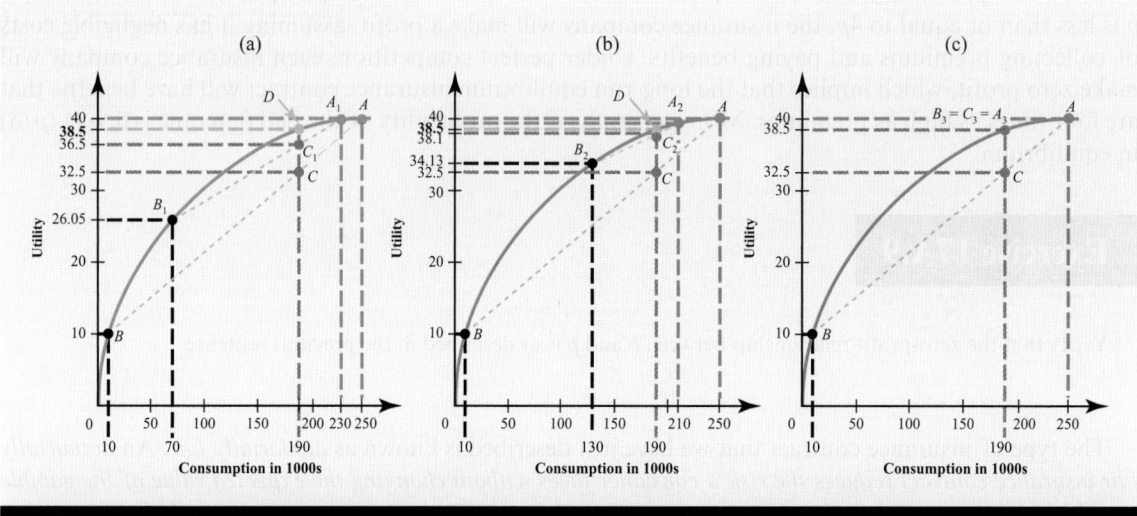

Go to MindTap to interact with this graph

Panel (b) of the graph illustrates points A_2 and B_2 associated with the good and bad outcomes under the second insurance policy that has a €40 000 premium and a €160 000 benefit. The €40 000 premium reduces John's consumption in the good outcome to €210 000, and the premium combined with the benefit raises his consumption in the bad outcome by €120 000 to €130 000. You can check that the expected value of John's situation remains unchanged, but this policy further reduces the risk John faces. We can read off the graph that John's expected utility under the second policy is 38.1, which is higher than under the first insurance policy where the expected utility was 36.5.

Finally, consider the third insurance policy that provides a benefit of €240 000 in exchange for a premium of €60 000. The premium would reduce John's consumption if Emma survived to €190 000, and the combination of the premium and the benefit would raise his consumption if she does not survive by €180 000, from €10 000 to €190 000. Under this policy, John is *fully insured* in the sense that he has eliminated all risk by equalizing the good and bad outcomes to exactly the expected value of the initial gamble he faced. His expected utility is the utility from having an income of €190 000 read off the consumption/utility relationship. Since this is higher than any of the other insurance contracts, we can conclude that he will choose to insure fully.

Exercise 17A.11

What are some examples of other actuarially fair insurance contracts that do not provide full insurance? Would each of these also earn zero profit for insurance companies? Can you see why none of them would ever be preferred to full insurance by John?

Exercise 17A.12*

Referring back to what you learned in Graph 17.3, what is John's consumer surplus if he fully insures in actuarially fair insurance markets?

Exercise 17A.13*

What actuarially fair insurance policy would a risk-loving consumer purchase? Can you illustrate your answer within the context of a graph that begins as in panel (c) of Graph 17.2? *Hint*: The benefit and premium levels will be negative.

Exercise 17A.14

True or False: A risk-neutral consumer will be indifferent between all actuarially fair insurance contracts.

17A.1.5 Actuarially Unfair Insurance Now suppose that the insurance policies John is offered are not actuarially fair; that is, John's expected consumption falls as he insures more heavily. Consider again three policies, the first with premium €20 000, the second with premium €40 000 and the third with premium €60 000. In the previous section, we saw that such policies would be actuarially fair if the benefit associated with each was four times as high as the premium: €80 000, €160 000 and €240 000. In order for these policies to be actuarially unfair, it must be the case that each has a benefit that is less than four times the premium. For instance, suppose that the benefits associated with these policies were €65 000, €100 000 and €122 000.

The three panels of Graph 17.5 illustrate the expected utility for these policies. Notice that the first policy in panel (a) gives John an expected consumption of €186 250, and the next two policies cause this expected consumption to fall to €175 000 and €160 500 respectively. The expected utility of the first insurance policy is read off as 35.75, three-quarters of the way towards point A_1 on the line connecting B_1 and A_1 at the expected consumption value of €186 250. Similarly, we can read the expected utility of the second and third policies in panels (b) and (c) as 36 and 35.5.

Each of the policies is therefore preferred to no insurance at all because each gives higher utility than 32.5. The insurance policy with premium €40 000 and benefit €100 000 yields the highest utility. When faced with these choices, John would choose not to buy the policy that comes closest to full insurance.

Exercise 17A.15

Verify the numbers on the horizontal axis of Graph 17.5.

This is an example of a more general result. *While we found in the previous section that risk-averse individuals will choose to fully insure when insurance markets are actuarially fair, this is not the case when insurance markets are actuarially unfair.*

Exercise 17A.16*

True or False: If firms in a perfectly competitive insurance industry face recurring fixed costs and marginal administration costs that are increasing, risk-averse individuals will not fully insure in equilibrium.

Exercise 17A.17*

Suppose only full insurance contracts were offered by the insurance industry; that is, only contracts that ensure that John will be equally well off financially regardless of what happens to Emma. What is the most actuarially unfair insurance contract that John would agree to buy? *Hint*: Refer back to Graph 17.3.

Graph 17.5 Actuarially Unfair Insurance

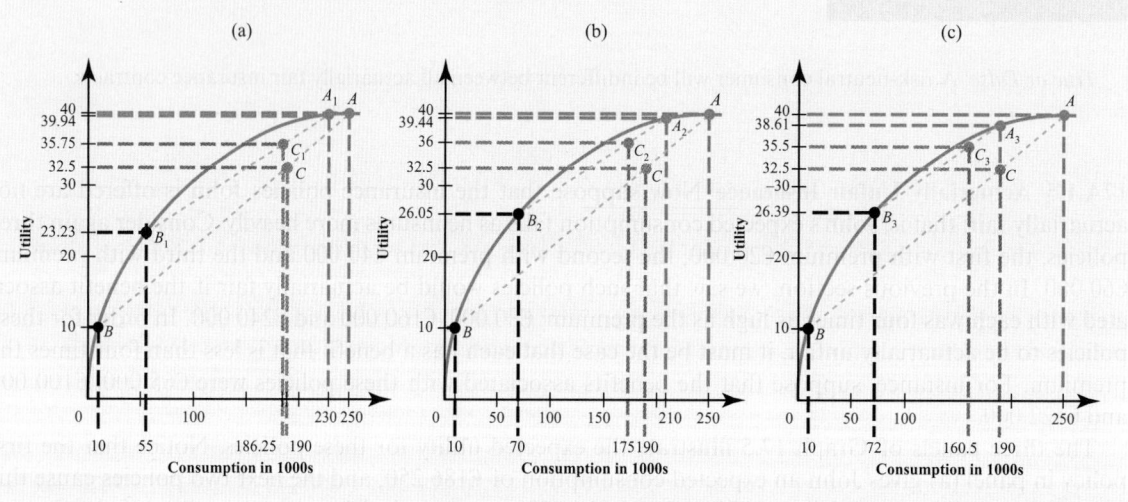

17A.2 Risky Choices Involving Multiple States of the World

Clearly the discussion so far has been unrealistic. We have assumed that all John cares about is money, with Emma's existence adding no utility to his consumption and her untimely death causing him no pain to detract from the pleasure of consumption. John and Emma might have a loving relationship in which each takes pleasure from the other's company. In the economist's language, we would say that life with Emma and life without her therefore represent two very different *states of the world* for John. In the good state when Emma is around, each euro of consumption means more than it does in the bad state when she is not around. John gets utility from consumption in part because they consume in each other's presence, and when they were not around, consumption or income means less to him. It is therefore not true that so long as John's income is the same in the two states of the world, he will be equally happy.

The example illustrates the limits of the simple model of the previous section, and it suggests that the model is useful only in some circumstances. For instance, if the gamble we are analyzing involves an investment opportunity that is risky, we may think the model is perfectly appropriate because nothing fundamentally changes, aside from income, when an investment pays off more or less. In circumstances where the cause of the bad state is itself undesirable and affects how we evaluate money, we need a more general model of choice in the presence of risk. This model contains the model discussed in the previous section as a special case but also permits a more realistic analysis of situations like John's decision to buy life insurance on Emma.

17A.2.1 Modelling Consumption in Different States of the World This more general model bears strong resemblance to the model of consumer choice in a two-good world when the consumer is endowed with different amounts of each good but has no other source of income. In panel (a) of Graph 17.6, we put consumption in the good state, denoted x_G on the horizontal axis, and consumption in the bad state denoted x_B on the vertical, in each case denominating consumption in thousands of euro units and thus implicitly assuming that consumption of goods can be modelled as a single composite good in each state. In the absence of insurance, John's consumption if Emma survives the year is €250 000, and his consumption if she does not survive is €10 000. This is illustrated by his endowment point E.

Graph 17.6 Consumption in Different States

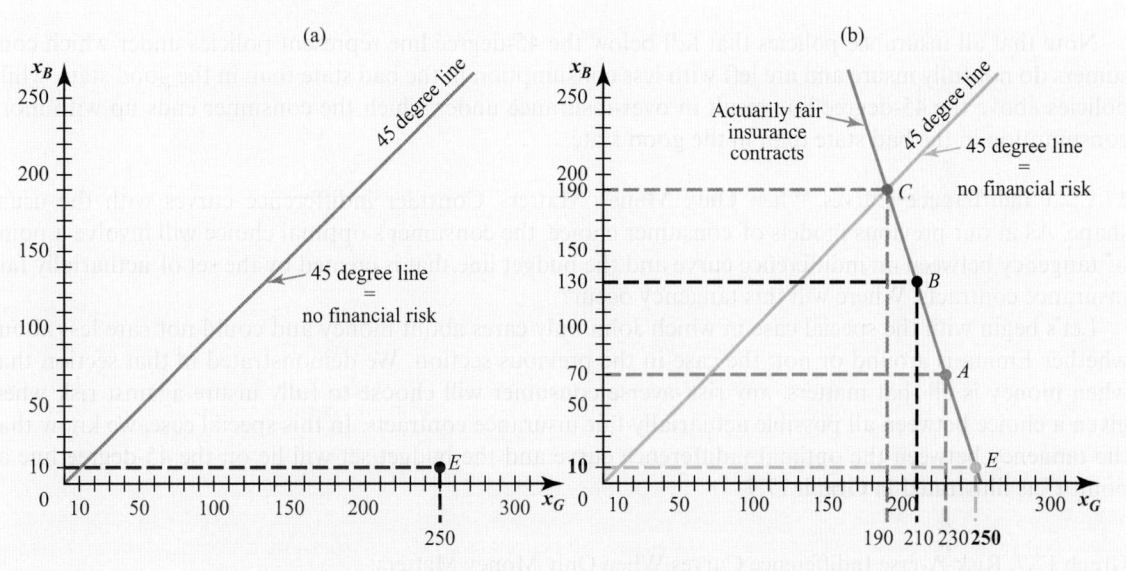

The 45-degree line in this graph represents points under which consumption in the good and bad states is equal, with points below the 45-degree line representing situations where consumption in the good state is higher than consumption in the bad state. Off the 45-degree line, the consumer faces financial risk that is absent on the 45-degree line. While the picture looks a lot like the pictures we are used to seeing in consumer theory, there is an important difference. When the two axes represent jeans and hoodies, a bundle represents a combination of jeans and hoodies that the consumer consumes; but when the axes represent consumption in the good and bad states, the consumer will never end up consuming both goods. Rather, they will consume at one level if the good state happens and at another if the bad state happens, but they don't know ahead of time which state they will face.

17A.2.2 Choice Sets Under Actuarially Fair Insurance We can now determine what John's choice set looks like when insurance markets offer actuarially fair insurance policies. Recall that such contracts leave the expected value of John's finances unchanged at €190 000, while increasing his consumption in the bad state and decreasing it in the good state. In order for the expected value of his consumption before he knows in which state he will find himself to remain unchanged, we have determined that the benefit offered by the insurance contract must be four times as high as the premium. For instance, we illustrated three such policies in the previous section: policy A with a premium of €20 000 and a benefit of €80 000, policy B with a premium of €40 000 and a benefit of €160 000, and policy C with a premium of €60 000 and a benefit of €240 000.

Under policy A, John's consumption in the good state will fall to €230 000 while his consumption in the bad state will rise to €70 000. Point A in panel (b) of Graph 17.6 illustrates this outcome. Similarly, points B and C correspond to the consumption levels John would attain in the good and bad states under policies B and C, with policy C representing full insurance that equalizes consumption in both states and removes all financial risk. There exists a number of other actuarially fair insurance contracts, with each having the feature that consumption in the bad state rises by €3 for every €1 paid in a premium. The line with slope −3 through E, A, B and C represents all possible actuarially fair insurance policies.

Exercise 17A.18

Why does consumption in the bad state rise only by three times the premium amount when actuarially fair insurance benefits are four times as high as the premium?

Note that all insurance policies that fall below the 45-degree line represent policies under which consumers do not fully insure and are left with less consumption in the bad state than in the good state, while policies above the 45-degree line result in over-insurance under which the consumer ends up with more consumption in the bad state than in the good state.

17A.2.3 Indifference Curves When Only Money Matters Consider indifference curves with the usual shape. As in our previous models of consumer choice, the consumer's optimal choice will involve a point of tangency between an indifference curve and the budget line that is created by the set of actuarially fair insurance contracts. Where will this tangency occur?

Let's begin with the special case in which John only cares about money and could not care less about whether Emma is around or not: the case in the previous section. We demonstrated in that section that when money is all that matters, any risk-averse consumer will choose to fully insure against risk when given a choice between all possible actuarially fair insurance contracts. In this special case, we know that the tangency between the optimal indifference curve and the budget set will lie on the 45-degree line at point C as illustrated in Graph 17.7.

Graph 17.7 Risk-Averse Indifference Curves When Only Money Matters

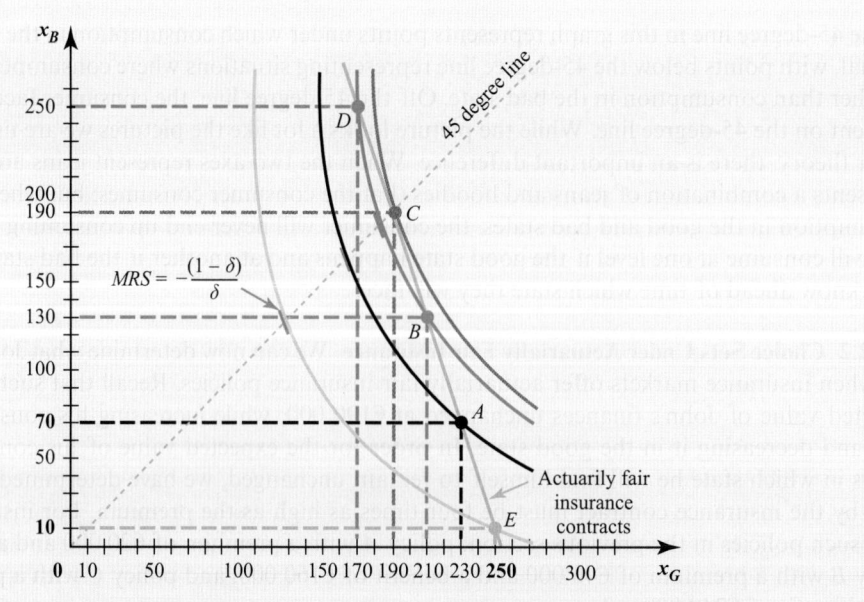

This implies that the marginal rate of substitution at point C, and similarly all along the 45-degree line, is equal to -3, the slope of the budget set created by the menu of actuarially fair insurance contracts. Adding indifference curves that go through points A, B and C, we see that John moves to higher and higher indifference curves as he purchases increasing levels of insurance up to the point where he is fully insured.

If the probability of the bad state is denoted by δ and the probability of the good state by $(1 - \delta)$, the slope of the budget constraint will be $-(1 - \delta)/\delta$. For the special case when there is no difference between the two states of the world, when only money matters, this implies that the marginal rate of substitution for the risk-averse consumer is also equal to $-(1 - \delta)/\delta$ along the 45-degree line.

Exercise 17A.19

Why is the slope of the budget constraint $-(1 - \delta)/\delta$?

Before leaving this special case, note the convexity property embedded in the usual shape of indifference curves has a particularly intuitive interpretation within this model. Convexity means that when we have extreme bundles like B and D that lie on the same indifference curve, an average of those bundles like C is preferred. Since the expected consumption level remains the same along the line through B, C and D, this implies that less risk (C) is better than more risk (B or D) so long as the expected value of the gamble remains unchanged; this is the definition of risk aversion. When indifference curves in this model satisfy convexity, the consumer is risk averse. In this extension of the model introduced in the previous section, the impression that we are in some way objectively measuring utility disappears, with no reference to marginal utility. What matters is the marginal rate of substitution which is not measured in utility units but expresses the willingness to trade consumption in one state for consumption in the other.

Exercise 17A.20

What would indifference curves look like for a risk-neutral consumer? What insurance policy would they purchase?

Exercise 17A.21

What would indifference curves look like for a risk-loving consumer? What insurance policy would they purchase?

Indifference curves for risk-averse consumers in this model look very much like the indifference curves over consumption bundles that we are used to seeing from models without risk, and the budget constraint formed by the set of actuarially fair insurance contracts also looks very much like our usual budget constraints. As we already mentioned, there is an important difference to keep in mind. In our previous consumer model without risk, a bundle (x_1, x_2) was a bundle of x_1 units of the first good *together with* x_2 units of the second good. A point (x_G, x_B) in our model with risk, on the other hand, represents two *separate* consumption levels that are *never* consumed together. In the good state, x_G is the quantity of consumption available, while in the bad state, x_B of the consumption good is available.

17A.2.4 Indifference Curves and Choices When the States Are Different We have established that if there is no inherent difference between the good and bad states aside from the different levels of income associated with each state, indifference curves for risk-averse consumers will have the usual convexity property and an *MRS* equal to $-(1 - \delta)/\delta$ along the 45-degree line. Now assume that the two states are inherently different, that money is not all that matters.

It is possible that consumption does not mean as much to John when Emma is not around. They may enjoy each other's company in different situations and if Emma was not around, John might search for new meaning elsewhere if it is no longer possible to consume with Emma. In that case, there is no reason for him to fully insure – to equalize his income in the good and bad states – even though he does not like risk. Because consumption is so much more meaningful with Emma around, he would not want to give up too much of it in order to insure greater consumption when she is not around.

In Graph 17.8, we depict what his optimal decision on life insurance might look like in this case. The endowment point is just as it was before, as is the set of actuarially fair insurance contracts that forms John's choice set. Unlike the case where only money mattered to John and where he chooses to fully insure where his budget constraint intersects the 45-degree line, we have now drawn an indifference curve tangent at point *A* where John purchases an €80 000 life insurance policy on Emma in exchange for a premium of €20 000, thus reducing his consumption in the good state to €230 000 and raising his consumption in the bad state to €70 000. While risk aversion implies full insurance in a state-independent model where only money matters, this illustrates that risk aversion is consistent with less than full insurance in the state-dependent model. *When we observe an individual not insuring fully, it may be because insurance markets are not actuarially fair and/or because the individual has state-dependent utility.*

Graph 17.8 Insurance Choice When Utility Is State-Dependent

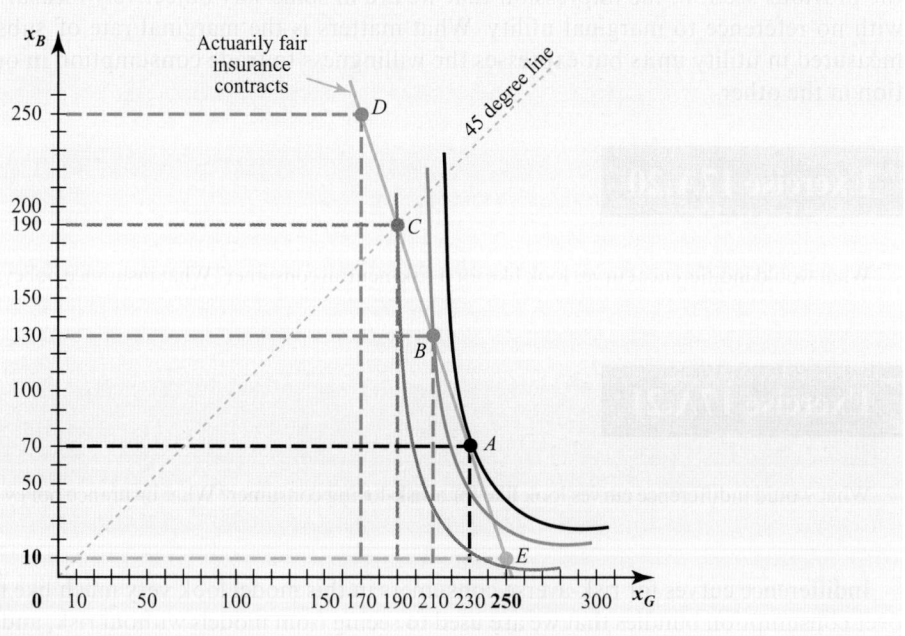

Exercise 17A.22

We concluded previously that when the two states are the same apart from the income level associated with each state, *MRS* $= -(1 - \delta)/\delta$ along the 45-degree line. In the case we just discussed, can you tell whether the *MRS* is greater or less than this along the 45-degree line?

Exercise 17A.23

Suppose John was actually depressed by Emma's presence and tolerates her solely for the income she generates. Because of this depression, consumption is not very meaningful in the good state when Emma is around, but if she was not around, he would be able to travel the world and truly enjoy life. Might this cause him to purchase more than full life insurance on Emma? How would you illustrate this in a graph?

Sports fans often bet on their favourite team. How can we explain this? If the fan agrees with the bookies on the odds of their team winning, we would have to assume that the fan is risk loving to explain their betting behaviour if money were all that mattered. By betting on the game, the sports fan is introducing risk without changing the expected level of consumption if they agree with the bookies on the odds of their team winning. For the true sports fan who despairs when their team does poorly and celebrates when their team wins, the state of the world is different depending on whether their favourite team wins or loses. Just as money might mean more to John when he can enjoy consuming it with Emma than when he has to consume in solitude, so money might mean more to the sports fan when their team wins and they go out to celebrate than when the team loses and all they want is to crawl into bed and cry themselves to sleep. The betting behaviour of the sports fan who bets on their own team might not be because of a love of risk but might be explained by the fact that the event that leads to them winning the bet also causes them to enter a very different state of the world where consumption means more.

Exercise 17A.24

Can you think of a different scenario in which it makes sense for the sports fan to bet against their own team?

17A.3 General Equilibrium With Uncertainty

We began by developing a model with the assumption that money is all that matters when individuals face risk and illustrate a second model in which the state of the world itself might matter in addition to the money associated with each state. The second model is more general than the first because the first model is a special case of the second. We will now conclude with a discussion of how these models relate to our insight in the first welfare theorem from other chapters that competitive markets will, under certain conditions, lead to efficient outcomes. As in the previous chapter, we will illustrate this for very simple economies that lend themselves to graphical representation, but the basic insights hold for much more general economies with many individuals and many goods.

17A.3.1 Efficiency Without Aggregate Risk Individuals X and Y are the only individuals on a deserted island. X owns half the island, and Y owns the other half, and in any given season, they might face rainy weather or drought. X's part of the island has a variety of banana plant that yields much more fruit in rainy conditions, and Y's has a variety that yields more fruit under drought conditions. There are, therefore, two states of the world, rain and drought, and banana endowments depend on which state occurs. For now, we'll assume that the total crop of bananas on the entire island is always the same, with the weather determining only where the bananas grow. This assumption implies that there is *no aggregate risk* because in the aggregate, the economy always produces the same regardless of which state occurs. Putting consumption in the rainy state on the horizontal axis and consumption in the drought state on the vertical, we can illustrate X's endowment in a graph similar to that of the previous section. Panel (a) of Graph 17.9 illustrates the point E^1, with e_r^1 bananas in the dry state and e_r^1 bananas in the rainy state, and u^1 represents the expected level of utility X can get by accepting the hand they are dealt by nature. We can illustrate Y's endowment E^2 in the same type of graph; Y's endowment will lie above the 45-degree line as in panel (b) of the graph. Illustrating both of these cases in a single Edgeworth Box, we get panel (c).

Exercise 17A.25

Which assumption in our example results in the square shape of this Edgeworth Box?

Panel (c) of Graph 17.9 looks like our usual Edgeworth Box, with the lens shape between the respective indifference curves suggesting that X and Y's situation is inefficient if they accept nature's outcome and eat their bananas when they grow them. Instead, they might wish to make a contract that specifies how many bananas X will give Y if the rainy state happens in exchange for some set of bananas Y will give X if they face the dry state. The terms of this contract can be denoted p_r/p_d, with this ratio telling us how much consumption in the drought state they can buy by giving up one banana in the rainy state. This is no different than the role prices play in forming budgets in the absence of risk and will therefore result in a budget line. X and Y will reach an efficient outcome when they have found contract terms such that both end up optimizing at the same point in the Edgeworth Box. Such a point must have the feature that their indifference curves in the Edgeworth Box have the same slope.

Graph 17.9 A Simple Economy With Risk

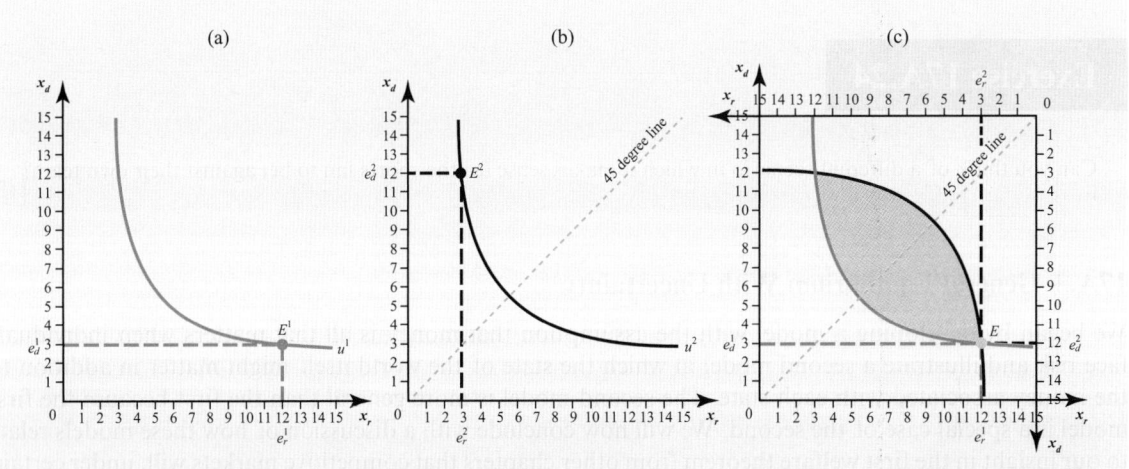

Assume X and Y's utilities are not state-dependent; they get just as much enjoyment from each banana whether it rains or shines. We know from our work in the previous section that along the 45-degree line, their indifference curves have marginal rates of substitution equal to the probability of the rainy state divided by the probability of the dry state. If the probability of drought is δ and the probability of rain is $(1 - \delta)$, this implies that $MRS^1 = MRS^2 = (1 - \delta)/\delta$ along the 45-degree line of the Edgeworth Box.

Exercise 17A.26

True or False: The 45-degree line is, in this case, the contract curve.

To find the competitive equilibrium terms p_r^*/p_d^* of the contract they will strike, we need to find terms that will create a budget line going through E with slope $-(1 - \delta)/\delta$; that is, $-p_r^*/p_d^* (-(1 - \delta)/\delta)$. This is illustrated in panel (a) of Graph 17.10, with any resulting equilibrium allocation A being efficient; the first welfare theorem holds. In the case of tastes that are not state-dependent, the equilibrium terms of X and Y's contract also have the feature that they are actuarially fair.

Graph 17.10 Equilibrium Contracts With No Aggregate Risk

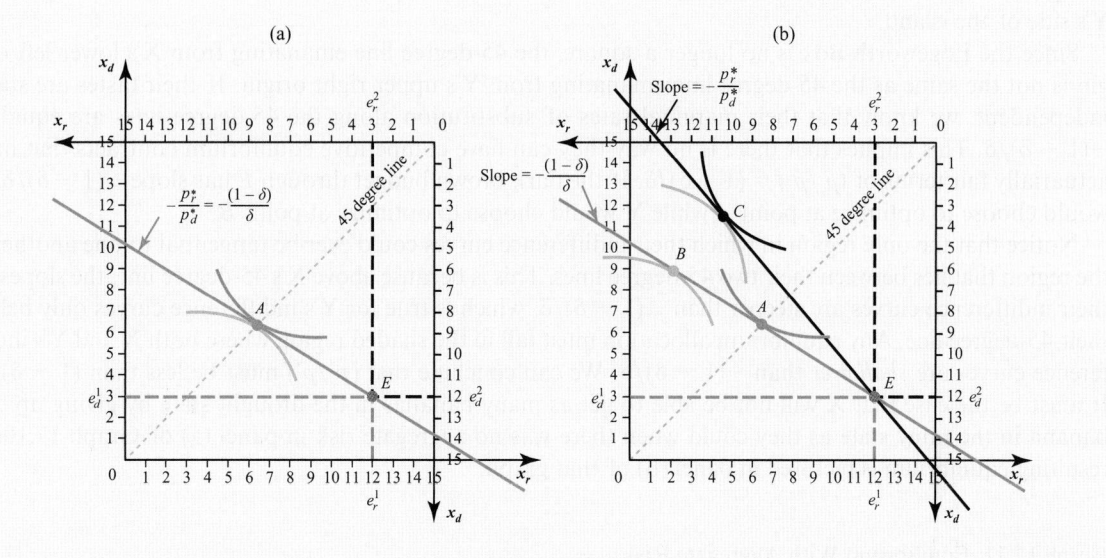

Next, suppose that X's tastes continue to be state-independent but Y places more value on consuming bananas when it rains than when it shines. Under the actuarially fair contract terms that give rise to budgets with slope $-(1-\delta)/\delta$, this would imply that X would choose to locate on the 45-degree line at A but Y would not. This is illustrated along the dashed dark brown budget in panel (b) of Graph 17.10 where Y would choose B, and it implies that these contract terms are no longer a competitive equilibrium. The equilibrium contract would now involve a ratio of prices p_r^*/p_d^* more favourable to X ($p_r^*/p_d^* > (1-\delta)/\delta$), and would result in an equilibrium allocation C above the 45-degree line as illustrated along the dark blue budget. Still, the first welfare theorem continues to hold.

Exercise 17A.27

What would the contract curve look like in this case?

Exercise 17A.28

Suppose Y liked bananas more when it rains than when it shines. Where would the equilibrium be?

Exercise 17A.29

Suppose Y was the one who had state-independent tastes and X was the one who values consuming bananas more when it shines than when it rains. Where would the equilibrium be?

17A.3.2 Introducing Aggregate Risk Now suppose that our little economy faces *aggregate risk* in addition to the *individual risk* X and Y face. In particular, suppose that the overall yield of bananas on their island is twice as large when it rains than when it shines. Panel (a) of Graph 17.11 illustrates the resulting Edgeworth Box, which is now twice as long as it is high because in the rainy state the economy produces twice as many bananas. Point E represents the endowment point, with e_r^1 and e_d^1 representing the bananas that grow on X's side of the island in the two states, and e_r^2 and e_d^2 representing the bananas that grow on Y's side of the island.

Since the Edgeworth Box is no longer a square, the 45-degree line emanating from X's lower left origin is not the same as the 45-degree line emanating from Y's upper right origin. If their tastes are state-independent, we know that their marginal rates of substitution along the 45-degree lines are equal to $-(1 - \delta)/\delta$. This implies that there is no way they can have competitive equilibrium contracts that have actuarially fair terms of $(p_r/p_d) = (1 - \delta)/\delta$. If the dark brown budget through E has slope $-(1 - \delta)/\delta$, X would choose to optimize at point A while Y would choose to optimize at point B.

Notice that the only region in which their indifference curves could ever be tangential to one another is the region that lies between their two 45-degree lines. This is because above X's 45-degree line, the slopes of their indifference curves are steeper than $-(1 - \delta)/\delta$, which is true for Y's indifference curves only below their 45-degree line. Any equilibrium allocation must fall in the shaded region where both X and Y's indifference curves are *shallower* than $-(1 - \delta)/\delta$. We can conclude that (p_r^*/p_d^*) must be less than $(1 - \delta)/\delta$. It must be the case that X will not be able to get as many bananas in the drought state by giving up one banana in the rainy state as they could when there was no aggregate risk in panel (a) of Graph 17.10. A resulting equilibrium is pictured in panel (b) of that graph.

Graph 17.11 Equilibrium With Aggregate Risk

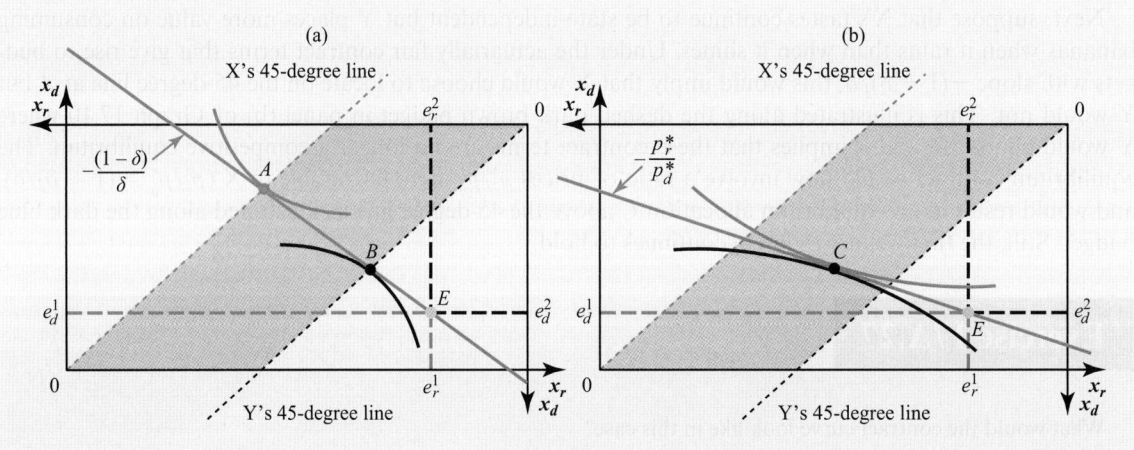

This result can be generalized as follows: *In the presence of aggregate risk, the good in the bad state is relatively more valuable the larger the aggregate risk.* We will see shortly how this relates to important themes in finance.

Exercise 17A.30

Given that there are more bananas in the aggregate in the rainy state of the world, consider an endowment that has relatively more bananas in the dry state and another that has relatively more bananas in the rainy state. If Y could choose their endowment, which endowment would they be more likely to want, assuming X and Y both have state-independent tastes and the overall endowments are not too different?

17A.3.3 Financial Asset Markets Much of our discussion of risk has centred around insurance markets since insurance is attempting to reduce the risks that life presents. Insurance markets are interesting for a number of reasons, some of which will not become clear until we get to the topic of asymmetric information in Chapter 22. Insurance markets are not the only markets that centre around attempts to deal with risk. Another important example arises in financial markets. When we look for places to invest money, we have different options such as government bonds that tend to have relatively low returns but also low risk, different types of stocks that tend to have higher average returns but also higher risk, and junk bonds that promise a really high return but also carry a high risk of losing all their value. Some investments have pro-cyclical returns, or high returns when the overall economy does well but low returns when the overall economy suffers, while other investments have counter-cyclical returns. Prices for all these assets are determined in a general equilibrium economy in which different types of investors with different levels of risk aversion and potentially state-dependent tastes, try to do the best they can, usually in the presence of aggregate risk.

In the simplest setting, you should be able to see how one can model such assets in ways similar to those we have described in this section. Assets have different returns in different states, and trading in assets changes the expected return on investments as well as the risk faced. Through trading in financial assets, investors can manage risk at prices determined from the sum total of the interactions of all investors. In the real world, most investors employ financial intermediaries who have over the past decades found new and innovative ways of managing risk in ways that can be modelled using this general framework. For our purposes, the important point is that in the absence of distortion that we have not at this point introduced in particular absent distortions because of asymmetric information, our analysis suggests that markets result in efficient outcomes when risk becomes part of the model.

Exercise 17A.31

In modelling equilibrium terms of trade that might emerge in financial markets, would you be likely to assume state-dependent or state-independent tastes?

Exercise 17A.32

Suppose the two states of the world are recessions and economic booms. If you put consumption in economic booms on the horizontal axis, will the height of the Edgeworth Box be larger or smaller than its width?

17B   The Mathematics of Choice in the Presence of Risk

Introducing the mathematics to go along with our graphs from Section A will illustrate some subtleties that are not immediately apparent from our intuitive treatment. We will see what is assumed and what is not assumed in expected utility theory, and illustrate with numerical examples some of the basic insights of the previous section.

17B.1 Utility and Expected Utility

In Section A, we began with an underlying consumption/utility relationship in Graph 17.1. We likened this to a single-input production process that takes consumption as an input and treats utility as an output, and illustrated how the shape of this function relates to the concept of risk aversion when John potentially faces a bad and a good outcome, x_B and x_G. We developed a more general model in which we illustrated indifference curves in a graph with x_G on the horizontal and x_B on the vertical axis. We will now see that it is really the indifference curves in this more general model, which allows for both state-independent and state-dependent utility, that represent tastes over risky gambles and that the underlying consumption/utility relationship is a by-product of modelling these indifference curves.

Suppose we are concerned about the case where John faces the possibility of low consumption x_B with probability δ and high consumption x_G with probability $(1 - \delta)$ depending on whether Emma survives. Initially, we'll assume that all John cares about is money and not whether Emma is around, aside from the implications this has on his consumption levels. We would like to represent John's tastes over the various possible combinations of x_G and x_B with a utility function $U(x_G, x_B)$ that gives rise to his indifference curves in a graph like Graph 17.7. As with any particular indifference map over pairs (x_G, x_B), there exist many utility functions that will give rise to that particular indifference map. John von Neumann (1903–1957) and Oskar Morgenstern (1902–1977), derived a condition under which *an underlying function* $u(x)$ *exists such that we can represent John's indifference map over pairs of* x_G *and* x_B *using a utility function that takes the form:*

$$U(x_G, x_B) = \delta u(x_B) + (1 - \delta)u(x_G); \tag{17.1}$$

that is, a utility function that is the expected utility *if we interpret the function* $u(x)$ *as measuring the utility of consumption.* As mentioned in Section A, the condition under which we can find such a function $u(x)$ is known as the *independence axiom*, explained in Appendix 1. It is not a very strong assumption, and we will take it as given much as we have taken as given the rationality axioms in our development of consumer theory in the absence of risk. At the same time, we should acknowledge that there are some famous paradoxes that appear to illustrate violations of the independence axiom, one of which is explored in Appendix 2. The utility function $U(x_G, x_B)$ that takes the expected utility form and represents a consumer's underlying indifference curves over risky gambles is often called a *von Neumann-Morgenstern expected utility function.*

The consumption/utility relationship in Graph 17.1 of Section A is the graph of such an underlying function $u(x)$; it is a graph of the utility function over consumption that allows us to write John's utility over risky gambles as an *expected utility.* This consumption/utility relationship is not some real underlying relationship between John's consumption level and his happiness. It is a mathematical function that permits us to represent his real preferences over risky gambles in the form of an expected utility function, $U(x_G, x_B)$. We do not have to assume that John actually has some internal production function for utility that allows him to measure his happiness in some quantifiable way as we sometimes appeared to be assuming in Section A. We have to assume that he has indifference curves over risky gambles such as those in Graph 17.7, just as we assumed that people have indifference curves over consumption bundles in our earlier development of consumer theory in the absence of risk.

Suppose that a function that allows us to represent John's tastes over gambles involving x_G (with probability $(1 - \delta)$) and x_B (with probability δ) with an expected utility function $U(x_G, x_B)$ is:

$$u(x) = 0.5 \ln x \tag{17.2}$$

Exercise 17B.1

Letting x denote consumption measured in thousands of euros, illustrate the approximate shape of John's consumption/utility relationship in the range from 1 to 250, interpreted as the range from €1000 to €250 000.

Exercise 17B.2

What does the graph of the utility function look like in the range of consumption between 0 and 1, corresponding to 0 to €1000?

Using the 'ruler' $u(x) = 0.5$ as a tool to measure utility, we can say that John's utility of consuming x_B is $u(x_B) = 0.5 \ln x_B$ and his utility of consuming x_G is $u(x_G) = 0.5 \ln x_G$. This does not mean that we think we are in any way objectively measuring John's happiness at consumption levels x_B and x_G, but we have chosen the ruler with which to measure his happiness in such a way that we can now express his utility of facing a particular gamble (x_G, x_B) (with probabilities $(1 - \delta, \delta)$) using the von Neumann-Morgenstern expected utility function:

$$U(x_G, x_B) = E(u) = \delta u(x_B) + (1 - \delta)u(x_G) = 0.5\delta \ln x_B + 0.5(1 - \delta) \ln x_G. \qquad (17.3)$$

Following our discussion in Section A, suppose that John's consumption is €250 000 if Emma survives and €10 000 if she does not survive. Expressing x in thousands of euros, $x_B = 10$ and $x_G = 250$. Suppose further that the probability Emma does not survive is 25 per cent; that is, $\delta = 0.25$. John's expected consumption level is therefore:

$$E(x) = \delta x_B + (1 - \delta)x_G = 0.25(10) + 0.75(250) = 190, \qquad (17.4)$$

and, using equation (17.3), his expected utility is:

$$E(u) = 0.5(0.25) \ln (10) + 0.5(0.75) \ln (250) \approx 2.358. \qquad (17.5)$$

Exercise 17B.3

What is the utility of receiving the expected income, denoted $u(E(x))$? Illustrate $E(x)$, $E(u)$ and $u(E(x))$ on a graph of equation (17.2).

Exercise 17B.4

True or False: If u is a concave function, $u(E(x))$ is larger than $E(u)$, and if u is a convex function, $u(E(x))$ is smaller than $E(u)$.

17B.1.1 Risk Aversion and Concavity of $u(x)$ In exercise 17B.3, you should have concluded that John's utility of receiving the expected value of the gamble he faces is approximately 2.624. Since we determined in equation (17.5) that his expected utility of facing the gamble is only 2.358, we know that he would prefer to collect 190 with certainty rather than take his chances and have 250 with probability of 0.75 but only 10 with probability 0.25. In other words, John would prefer to eliminate the risk of facing the gamble if he can keep the expected value of the gamble without risk. If a consumer prefers to reduce risk when offered the chance to do so without giving up consumption in expectation, we say that the consumer is *risk averse*.

Another way of saying the same thing is to say that *an individual is risk averse if and only if the utility of the expected value of the gamble is greater than the expected utility of the gamble*; that is, if and only if $u(E(x)) > U(x_G, x_B)$. This can be expanded to read:

$$u(\delta x_B + (1 - \delta)x_G) = u(E(x)) > U(x_G, x_B) = \delta u(x_B) + (1 - \delta)u(x_G). \tag{17.6}$$

Recall that a concave function can be defined as a function f such that, for all $x_1 \neq x_2$ and all δ between zero and 1:

$$f(\delta x_1 + (1 - \delta)x_2) > \delta f(x_1) + (1 - \delta)x_2. \tag{17.7}$$

Equation (17.6) defines risk aversion of tastes using the expected utility function and the appropriate function $u(x)$ that allows us to represent tastes with the expected utility form. Equation (17.7) defines concavity of a function. Looking at these side-by-side, you can see that equation (17.6) implies that the function $u(x)$ is concave. Thus, *if tastes over gambles involving x_B and x_G exhibit risk aversion, any function $u(x)$ that permits us to represent these tastes using an expected utility function $U(x_G, x_B)$ must be concave*. While our discussion in Section A may lead one to believe that risk aversion derives from the concavity of some underlying utility function $u(x)$, the real story is that an individual's risk aversion implies that any function $u(x)$ that allows us to represent such tastes with an expected utility function must be concave. We are not assuming concavity of $u(x)$ to get risk-averse tastes; we are deriving that $u(x)$ *must be* concave if underlying tastes over risky gambles exhibit risk aversion and u can be used to represent indifference curves over (x_G, x_B) in the expected utility form.

While it is at first confusing to keep in mind the difference between the expected utility $E(u)$ of a gamble and the utility of the expected value of the gamble $u(E(x))$, it is straightforward to show that the only way these can ever be the same is if $u(x)$ is linear. Suppose that $u(x) = \alpha x$:

$$E(u) = \delta \alpha x_B + (1 - \delta)\alpha x_G = \alpha(\delta x_B + (1 - \delta)x_G) = \alpha E(x) = (E(x)); \tag{17.8}$$

that is, John would be indifferent between accepting a risky gamble and the expected value of the gamble with certainty. This is the definition of *risk-neutral* tastes.

Exercise 17B.5

What would $E(u)$ and $u(E(x))$ be for John if his utility of consumption were given instead by the convex function $u(x) = x^2$? Illustrate your answer in a graph.

Exercise 17B.6

The convexity of a function f is defined analogously to concavity, with the inequality in equation (17.7) reversed. Can you show that tastes that exhibit risk seeking, as opposed to risk aversion, necessarily imply that any $u(x)$ used to define an expected utility function must be convex?

17B.1.2 Concavity of $u(x)$ and Convexity of Tastes So far, we have shown that if John's tastes exhibit risk aversion, any function $u(x)$ we use to measure his utility of consumption *must* be concave if we are to use it to represent his indifference curves over bundles of (x_G, x_B) using an expected utility function $U(x_G, x_B) = \delta u(x_B) + (1 - \delta)u(x_G)$. We can furthermore show that this in turn implies the convex shape of indifference curves that we concluded in Section A must be associated with risk aversion.

Recall that indifference curves exhibit the usual convexity property if averages are better than extremes. If a consumer is indifferent between two bundles, they would prefer any weighted average of the two bundles to either of the more extreme bundles they started with. In the context of our model of outcome bundles (x_G, x_B) suppose we begin with two such bundles, (x_G^1, x_B^1) and (x_G^2, x_B^2), over which the individual is indifferent; that is, two bundles such that:

$$U(x_G^1, x_B^1) = U(x_G^2, x_B^2) = \overline{U}. \tag{17.9}$$

Now consider a weighted average (x_G^3, x_B^3) of these two bundles of outcomes; that is, for some α that lies between 0 and 1, consider (x_G^3, x_B^3) such that:

$$x_G^3 = ax_G^2 + (1 - \alpha)x_G^1 \quad and \quad x_B^3 = ax_B^2 + (1 - \alpha)x_B^1. \tag{17.10}$$

By using the definition of the expected utility function $U(x_G, x_B)$ and the concavity of $u(x)$, we can conclude the following:

$$
\begin{aligned}
U(x_G^3, x_B^3) &= \delta u(x_B^3) + (1 - \alpha)u(x_G^3) \\
&= \delta u(\alpha x_B^2 + (1 - \alpha)x_B^1) + (1 - \delta)u(\alpha x_G^2 + (1 - \alpha)x_G^1) \\
&> \delta[\alpha u(x_B^2) + (1 - \alpha)u(x_B^1)] + (1 - \delta)[\alpha u(x_G^2) + (1 - \alpha)u(x_G^1)] \\
&= \alpha[\delta u(x_B^2) + (1 - \delta)u(x_G^2)] + (1 - \alpha)[\alpha u(x_B^1) + (1 - \delta)u(x_G^1)] \\
&= \alpha U(x_G^2, x_B^2) + (1 - \alpha)U(x_G^1, x_B^1) \\
&= \alpha \overline{U} + (1 - \alpha)\overline{U} = \overline{U}.
\end{aligned}
\tag{17.11}
$$

The first line substitutes the average bundle (x_G^3, x_B^3) into the expected utility function $U(x_G, x_B) = \delta u(x_B) + (1 - \delta)u(x_G)$; the second substitutes the equations from (17.10) for x_B^3 and x_G^3; the third inequality is a direct application of the definition of concavity of $u(x)$; the fourth rearranges terms; the fifth line derives from the fact that the terms in the parentheses in the fourth line are just the expected utilities of the original more extreme bundles; and the last line uses the fact that both the original bundles were on the same indifference curve $\overline{U}$. Taken together, we conclude that:

$$U(x_G^3, x_B^3) > \overline{U} = U(x_G^2, x_B^2) = U(x_G^1, x_B^1); \tag{17.12}$$

that is, the average bundle created from the more extreme bundles that lie on the same indifference curve is preferred to the more extreme bundles of outcomes. Thus, we have now shown that risk aversion implies concavity of $u(x)$ and concavity of $u(x)$ implies convexity of the indifference curves over pairs (x_G, x_B) of outcomes.

Exercise 17B.7*

Can you show in analogous steps that convexity of $u(x)$ must imply non-convexity of the indifference curves over outcome pairs (x_G, x_B)?

17B.1.3 Certainty Equivalents and Risk Premiums The *certainty equivalent* of a gamble is the minimum amount an individual would accept in order to give up participating in the gamble. For John, for instance, we calculated the expected utility of participating in the gamble of relying on Emma's income but facing the possibility of her not surviving to bring home an income as $U(250,10) = E(u) = 2.358$. To determine his certainty equivalent to facing this gamble, we need to find the value x_{ce} such that his utility of getting this amount is equal to the expected utility of facing the gamble; that is, we need to find for what value of x_{ce} the equation $u(x_{ce}) = 2.358$ holds. Using the function $u(x) = 0.5 \ln x$ as we have earlier, this implies we need to solve the equation $0.5 \ln x_{ce} = 2.358$ or, written slightly differently, $\ln x_{xe} = 2.358/0.5$, which solves to approximately $x_{ce} \approx 111.8$. Recall that the natural logarithm ln is defined with respect to base $e = 2.7182818$, and thus $x_{ce} = e^{2.358/0.5}$.

John would take an amount roughly equal to €111 800 in exchange for having Emma around and thus facing a 0.75 probability of a €250 000 income and a 0.25 probability of a €10 000 income. The *risk premium* of a gamble is defined as the difference between the expected value $(E(x))$ of the gamble and the certainty equivalent (x_{ce}) of the gamble. For our example, this is the difference between $E(x) = 190$ and $(x_{ce}) = 111.8$, or €78 200 euros.

Exercise 17B.8

Illustrate x_{ce} and the risk premium on a graph with John's utility function $u(x) = 0.5 \ln x$.

17B.1.4 Actuarially Fair Insurance Markets Now suppose John is offered a choice of different insurance contracts or policies. Such contracts are composed of two parts: an *insurance benefit b* that John receives in the event that Emma does not survive, and an *insurance premium p* that he has to pay prior to knowing whether or not she survives. Regardless of what happens to Emma, John has to pay p, which implies that his *net benefit* from buying insurance is $(b - p)$ in the event that she does not survive. Thus, his income if she survives will be $(x_G - p)$, and his income if she does not survive will be $(x_B + b - p)$.

Now suppose that the set of insurance contracts he is offered is the full set of *actuarially fair* policies; policies that reduce his risk without changing his expected income. In Section A, we argued that this would be the expected set of contracts that a competitive insurance industry with negligible costs would offer in equilibrium. Since, under any given contract (b, p) he gets a net payment of $(b - p)$ with probability δ but has to pay p with probability $(1 - \delta)$, his expected income will remain unchanged so long as $\delta(b - p) = (1 - \delta)p$, or, solving for b, as long as $b = p/\delta$. Thus, *an insurance contract (b, p) is actuarially fair if and only if $b = p/\delta$.*

We can ask which type of actuarially fair insurance policy John would choose if he could choose from a full set of policies, some with low premiums and low benefits, others with higher premiums and higher benefits. His expected utility from an actuarially fair policy (b, p) is:

$$U(x_G, x_B) = \delta u(x_B + b - p) + (1 - \delta)u(x_G - p) \text{ where } b = \frac{p}{\delta}, \quad (17.13)$$

or, substituting $b = p/\delta$,

$$U(x_G, x_B) = \delta u\left(x_B + \frac{(1-\delta)p}{\delta}\right) + (1 - \delta)u(x_G - p). \quad (17.14)$$

Choosing from a full set of actuarially fair insurance contracts involves John maximizing $U(x_G, x_B)$ from equation (17.14) by choosing the optimal premium p (and thus the optimal benefit $b = p/\delta$). When $u(x) = \alpha \ln x$, as in equation (17.2) where $\alpha = 0.5$, we can write this optimization problem as:

$$\max_{p} \delta\alpha \ \ln\left(x_{B} + \frac{(1-\delta)p}{\delta}\right) + (1-\delta)\alpha \ln (x_{G} - p). \qquad \text{(17.15)}$$

Taking the first derivative of the expression in (17.15), setting it to zero and solving for p, we get the optimal premium:

$$p^* = \delta(x_{G} - x_{B}) \qquad \text{(17.16)}$$

and, substituting this into the condition for actuarially fair insurance ($b = p/\delta$), the implied optimum insurance benefit:

$$b^* = x_{G} - x_{B} \qquad \text{(17.17)}$$

Exercise 17B.9

Verify the expressions for p^* and b^*.

In Section A, we concluded that when facing actuarially fair insurance markets, a risk-averse person in this model will always choose to fully insure, that is, to insure to the point where income is the same no matter what happens. Under the insurance policy (b^*, p^*), John's consumption is either ($x_{B} + b^* - p^*$) or ($x_{G} - p^*$) depending on whether Emma survives, and you can check that both these reduce to:

$$x = \delta x_{B} + (1 - \delta)x_{G}. \qquad \text{(17.18)}$$

For instance, when $x_{B} = 10$, $x_{G} = 250$ and $\delta = 0.25$, as in our life insurance example throughout this chapter, John's optimal insurance policy has him paying a premium of €60 000 in exchange for an insurance benefit of €240 000, which implies that whether Emma survives or not, John will have €190 000 available for consumption. He will choose the actuarially fair insurance contract that insures him fully against the risk of Emma's premature demise.

Exercise 17B.10

Even though we did not use the same underlying utility function as the one used to plot graphs in Section A, we have achieved the same result for the optimal actuarially fair insurance policy. Why is this?

17B.2 Risky Choices Involving Multiple States of the World

So far, we have illustrated a model in which John takes a gamble on two different states of the world: one with Emma in it, the other without her. The model presumes that aside from the income she generates, her presence in the world is entirely ornamental and has no direct impact on how John evaluates consumption. If consumption for John is more or less pleasurable when Emma is around than when she is not around, the two states of the world differ in ways that are not captured by the model in which the gamble John takes is solely about money.

17B.2.1 Modelling Consumption in Different States of the World Suppose that the state B of the world where Emma is no longer around differs from state G of the world where she is around, in the sense that John evaluates the benefits of consumption differently in the two states. This implies that the indifference curves over outcome bundles (x_G, x_B) will differ from the case where the state of the world was irrelevant to how John views consumption. An extension of von Neumann and Morgenstern's result implies that there will now exist two functions of x, $u_B(x)$ and $u_G(x)$, such that these indifference curves can be represented by an expected utility function of the form:

$$U(x_G, x_B) = \delta u_B(x_B) + (1 - \delta)u_G(x_G). \tag{17.19}$$

The only difference between this and our previous expected utility function is that the functions used to measure utility in the two different states of the world take on different forms, whereas before, when the state of the world was irrelevant to how John feels about consumption, a single function $u(x)$ was used in the expected utility function $U(x_G, x_B)$. State-dependent tastes can therefore be modelled as if John uses the function $u_G(x)$ to evaluate consumption in state G and $u_B(x)$ to evaluate consumption in state B. When tastes are state-independent, $u_G(x) = u_B(x)$, which is why the state-independent case is a special case of the state-dependent model.

Extending the model to the functional form for u that we used in the previous section, John might now have tastes such that $u_B(x) = \alpha \ln x$ and $u_G(x) = \beta \ln x$ can be used to formulate the expected utility function in equation (17.19). The expected utility function that represents his indifference curves over outcome pairs (x_G, x_B) becomes:

$$U(x_B, x_G) = \delta \alpha \ln x_B + (1 - \delta)\beta \ln x_G. \tag{17.20}$$

Exercise 17B.11

Derive the expression for the marginal rate of substitution for equation (17.20). Now suppose $\alpha = \beta$. What is the *MRS* along the 45-degree line on which $x_B = x_G$? Compare this to the result we derived graphically in Graph 17.7.

Exercise 17B.12

Can you see that the indifference curves generated by $U(x_G, x_B)$ in equation (17.20) are Cobb–Douglas? Write the function as a Cobb–Douglas function and derive the *MRS*. Does the property that must be true along the 45-degree line hold when tastes are not state-dependent?

Exercise 17B.13*

True or False: The expected utility function $U(x_G, x_B)$ can be transformed in all the ways that utility functions in consumer theory can usually be transformed without changing the underlying indifference curves, but such transformations will imply a loss of the expected utility form.

17B.2.2 Choice Sets Under Actuarially Fair Insurance Now that we know how indifference curves in the (x_G, x_B) space are formed, we can next ask how budget constraints arise when individuals have opportunities to insure against risk in an actuarially fair way. We can begin with the analogy to what we called the endowment point in our discussion of budgets in Chapter 3, which in our example is the point (e_G, e_B) that John faces in the absence of buying insurance. Letting consumption be denominated in thousands of euros, $(e_G, e_B) = (250,10)$ since John's consumption in the absence of insurance is €10 000 in state B and €250 000 in state G.

An insurance contract is a contract for which John pays a premium p regardless of what state he ends up facing in exchange for receiving a benefit b if state B occurs. As we discussed already, this contract is actuarially fair if and only if $b = p/\delta$. Beginning at the endowment point (e_G, e_B), this implies that for every euro John gives up in the state G, he will get $(1 - \delta)/\delta$ in state B; he will get a benefit of $1/\delta$ but still has to pay the €1 premium. His net benefit in state B is $((1/\delta) - 1)$, which can also be expressed as $(1 - \delta)/\delta$. The slope of the budget emanating from the point (e_G, e_B) is, therefore, $(-(1 - \delta)/\delta)$. Were John to pay a premium of e_G thus giving up all consumption in state G, he would receive a net benefit of $(1 - \delta)e_G/\delta$ in state B, which implies his overall consumption in state B, including his state B endowment e_B and net benefit from the insurance, would be $e_B + ((1 - \delta)e_G/\delta)$, which can be rewritten as $(\delta e_B + (1 - \delta)e_G)/\delta$. This is the vertical intercept of the budget line formed by the availability of actuarially fair insurance where we graph state B on the vertical axis to be consistent with our graphs from Section A.

We can use the intercept and slope we have just calculated to express the budget line arising from actuarially fair insurance as the equation:

$$x_B = \frac{\delta e_B + (1 - \delta)e_G}{\delta} - \frac{(1 - \delta)}{\delta}x_G, \qquad (17.21)$$

or, multiplying through by δ and collecting terms, as:

$$\delta e_B + (1 - \delta)e_G = \delta x_B + (1 - \delta)x_G. \qquad (17.22)$$

Exercise 17B.14

On a graph with x_G on the horizontal and x_B on the vertical axis, illustrate this budget constraint using values derived from the example of John's choices over insurance contracts. Compare it with panel (b) of Graph 17.6.

17B.2.3 Choice Over Actuarially Fair Insurance Contracts With tastes represented by the state-dependent expected utility function $U(x_G, x_B)$ as in equation (17.19) and budgets specified as in equation (17.22), we can write down the optimization problem that a consumer who faces a complete set of actuarially fair insurance contracts faces as:

$$\max_{x_G, x_B} U(x_G, x_B) = \delta u_B(x_B) + (1 - \delta)u_G(x_G)$$

$$\text{subject to } \delta e_B + (1-\delta)e_G = \delta x_B + (1 - \delta)x_G \qquad (17.23)$$

or, using the functional form for $U(x_G, x_B)$ from equation (17.20):

$$\max_{x_G, x_B} \delta\alpha \ln x_B + (1 - \delta)\beta \ln x_G \text{ subject to } \delta e_B + (1 - \delta)e_G = \delta x_B + (1 - \delta)x_G. \qquad (17.24)$$

Solving this we get:

$$x_B^* = \frac{\alpha(\delta e_B + (1 - \delta)e_G)}{\delta\alpha + (1 - \delta)\beta} \quad \text{and} \quad x_G^* = \frac{\beta(\delta e_B + (1 - \delta)e_G)}{\delta\alpha + (1 - \delta)\beta}. \tag{17.25}$$

Exercise 17B.15

Verify the result in equation (17.25).

We argued at the beginning of this section that the model in which only money matters is a special case of the model in which different states are associated with different ways in which consumption contributes to welfare. You can now see this in the context of our example by assuming that $\alpha = \beta$, which would make $u_G(x) = u_B(x)$. Replacing β with α in the equations for x_B^* and x_G^* we get:

$$x_B^* = \delta e_B + (1 - \delta)e_G = x_G^*. \tag{17.26}$$

When utility is not state-dependent, John will choose an actuarially fair insurance policy that equalizes his consumption in the good and bad states of the world.

Exercise 17B.16

Using the values of €10 and €250 as the consumption level John gets in state €10 and state €250 in the absence of insurance, what level of consumption does he get in each state when he chooses his optimal actuarially fair insurance policy assuming, as before, that state B occurs with probability 0.25 and state G occurs with probability 0.75?

Now suppose that $\beta > \alpha$, which implies that the marginal contribution of each euro to John's well-being is greater in state G when Emma is around than in state B when Emma is not. If we inspect the equations for x_B^* and x_G^*, this implies $x_B^* < x_G^*$ under John's optimal insurance contract. The reverse is true when $\alpha > \beta$.

Using the example we have employed throughout, with $e_B = 10$, $e_G = 250$ and $\delta = 0.25$, Table 17.1 gives the results for different ratios of α/β. Table 17.1 illustrates how insurance behaviour changes when utility is state-dependent, with the ratio α/β describing by how much utility of consumption differs in the two states. When $\alpha/\beta = 1$, utility is not state-dependent and the consumer fully insures. When $\alpha/\beta < 1$, consumption is more meaningful in state G, when John can consume with Emma, than in state B, and the first four rows of Table 17.1 illustrate different scenarios under which John will under-insure because of the state-dependence of his tastes. When $\alpha/\beta > 1$, on the other hand, consumption is more meaningful in state B when John is without Emma and can 'enjoy life', with the last four rows in Table 17.1 illustrating different scenarios under which John chooses to over-insure as a result of this type of state-dependence.

Exercise 17B.17**

Using an Excel spreadsheet, can you verify the numbers in Table 17.1?

Table 17.1 Over- and Under-Insurance

	Optimal Insurance Contracts When States Differ			
α/β	x	x_G	p	b
1/10	€24 516	€245 161	€4839	€19 355
1/4	€58 462	€233 846	€16 154	€164 615
1/2	€108 571	€217 143	€32 857	€131 429
3/4	€152 000	€202 667	€47 333	€189 333
1/1	€190 000	€190 000	€60 000	€240 000
4/3	€233 846	€175 385	€74 615	€298 462
2/1	€304 000	€152 000	€98 000	€392 000
4/1	€434 286	€108 571	€141 429	€565 714
10/1	€584 615	€58 462	€191 538	€766 154

Exercise 17B.18

Using a graph similar to Graph 17.8, illustrate the case of $\alpha/\beta = 1/4$ (row 2 in Table 17.1).

Exercise 17B.19

Using a graph similar to Graph 17.8, illustrate the case of $\alpha/\beta = 2/1$ (row 7 in Table 17.1).

17B.3 General Equilibrium With Risk

We have thus far introduced a model of risk in which we define different states of the world, and, to go along with each state, we defined a *state-contingent consumption level*. In principle, this could be extended to multiple types of consumption, with state-contingent consumption levels for each good specified in each of the states of the world. This is merely a matter of complicating the notation of the model and making it impossible to develop graphical versions, but it is important to keep in mind that what we are doing is much more general than may be initially apparent.

Insurance contracts represent particular ways of selling state-contingent consumption in one state in order to purchase state-contingent consumption in another. As noted at the end of Section A, other types of contracts, such as those involving investments in financial assets, can serve a similar purpose. We can model all of these types of markets as markets in *state-contingent assets*, in which individuals trade across states of the world at prices that are determined within the market. General equilibrium models of risk allow us to investigate how these prices are determined in equilibrium. As we saw in Section A, the mechanics of this are no different from those already developed in the previous chapter's treatment of exchange or Edgeworth Box economies.

We will mathematically illustrate the basic insights introduced intuitively in Section A by using a two-consumer model in which consumer utility can be state-dependent, in which consumers might differ in their beliefs about the *individual* risk that they face, and in which there might be *aggregate* risk for the whole economy. Each consumer is endowed with some consumption level in each state, with e_i^j representing consumer j's endowment of consumption in state i. Consumer 1's utility in states 1 and 2 is given by $u_1^1(x) = \alpha \ln x$ and $u_2^1(x) = (1 - \alpha) \ln x$, while consumer 2's utility in these states is given by $u_1^2(x) = \beta \ln x$ and $u_2^2(x) = (1 - \beta) \ln x$.

Exercise 17B.20

For what values of α and β is utility state-independent for each of these consumers?

Finally, we allow for the possibility that the two consumers have different beliefs about the likelihood of each of the two states actually transpiring, with consumer 1 placing probability δ on state 1 and consumer 2 placing probability γ on state 1. We write consumer 1's expected utility as:

$$U^1(x_1, x_2) = \delta\alpha \ln x_1 + (1 - \delta)(1 - \alpha) \ln x_2 \qquad (17.27)$$

and consumer 2's expected utility as:

$$U^2(x_1, x_2) = \gamma\beta \ln x_1 + (1 - \gamma)(1 - \beta) \ln x_2. \qquad (17.28)$$

Exercise 17B.21

Are we imposing any real restrictions by assuming that the utility weights placed on log consumption in the two states sum to one for each of the two consumers?

17B.3.1 Calculating Equilibrium Prices for State-Contingent Consumption Trades

In equilibrium, the terms of trade for changing consumption from one state into consumption in the other are determined by the price ratio (p_2/p_1) that specifies how much consumption in state 1 a consumer can get by giving up one unit of consumption in state 2. In order for this ratio to support an equilibrium, it must be the case that demand for each state-contingent consumption good is equal to supply in exactly the same way that this had to hold in our treatment of exchange economies in the previous chapter. The mathematics of calculating this equilibrium ratio is the same as it is for exchange economies without risk.

We can begin by solving each consumer's optimization problem given prices p_1 and p_2. For consumer 1, this can be written as:

$$\max_{x_1^1, x_2^1} \delta\alpha \ln x_1^1 + (1 - \delta)(1 - \alpha) \ln x_2^1 \text{ subject to } p_1 e_1^1 + p_2 e_2^1 = p_1 x_1^1 + p_2 x_2^1. \qquad (17.29)$$

Exercise 17B.22

How would you write the analogous optimization problem for individual 2?

Solving this and solving the analogous problem for consumer 2, we can derive each consumer's demand for x_1 as:

$$x_1^1(p_1, p_2) = \frac{\alpha\delta(p_1 e_1^1 + p_2 e_2^1)}{(\alpha\delta + (1 - \alpha)(1 - \delta))p_1} \text{ and } x_1^2(p_1, p_2) = \frac{\beta\gamma(p_1 e_1^2 + p_2 e_2^2)}{(\beta\gamma + (1 - \beta)(1 - \gamma))p_1}. \qquad (17.30)$$

In equilibrium, prices have to be such that demand is equal to supply, with demand given above and supply given by the sum of endowments in the economy. Demand equals supply in state 1 implies:

$$x_1^1(p_1 \, p_2) + x_1^2(p_1 \, p_2) = e_1^1 + e_1^2. \tag{17.31}$$

From our work in the previous chapter, and the intuition from the Edgeworth Box, we know that we can only calculate an equilibrium price *ratio* and that any two prices that satisfy that ratio will result in exactly the same equilibrium. We can therefore let $p_1^* = 1$ and solve for p_2^* by substituting the demands from (17.30) into equation (17.31). Some algebra gives us:

$$p_2^* = \frac{(1 - \alpha)(1 - \delta)(\beta\gamma + (1 - \beta)(1 - \gamma))e_1^1 + (1 - \beta)(1 - \gamma)(\alpha\delta + (1 - \alpha)(1 - \delta))e_1^2}{\alpha\delta(\beta\gamma + (1 - \beta)(1 - \gamma))e_2^1 + \beta\gamma(\alpha\delta + (1 - \alpha)(1 - \delta))e_2^2}. \tag{17.32}$$

Exercise 17B.23

Suppose that the overall endowment in the economy is the same in each of the two states (i.e. $e_1^1 + e_1^2 = e_2^1 + e_2^2$), that each consumer has state-independent utility, i.e. $\alpha = (1 - \alpha)$ and $\beta = (1 - \beta)$; and both consumers evaluate risk in the same way, i.e. $\delta = \gamma$. Can you demonstrate that equilibrium terms of trade will be actuarially fair; that is, $p_2^*/p_1^* = (1 - \delta)/\delta$?

Exercise 17B.24

For the scenario described in the previous exercise, can you use individual demand functions to illustrate that each consumer will choose to equalize consumption across the two states? Where in the Edgeworth Box does this imply the equilibrium falls?

Deriving the equilibrium price p_2^* while setting p_1^* to 1, is tedious, but the payoff is that we have a way to illustrate how the equilibrium changes as aggregate risk, the perception of individual risk, endowments and individual tastes change. In the following sections, we will therefore employ an Excel spreadsheet which specifies endowments, parameters in utility functions and levels of risk, and use equation (17.32) to calculate the equilibrium price. Finally, we can substitute equilibrium prices back into demand equation (17.30) to determine the equilibrium consumption levels for each consumer in each of the two states.

17B.3.2 General Equilibrium With Individual But No Aggregate Risk We begin with the case where the economy as a whole faces no aggregate risk and where the individuals in the economy agree on the likelihood of each of the two states arising. This is analogous to our example from Section A in which X and Y owned different parts of an island and each was aware of the likelihood of rain or drought; where the total level of banana production is the same regardless of whether it rains or not, but where the fraction of the banana crop that grows on their respective parts of the island does depend on weather conditions. No aggregate risk implies that $e_1^1 + e_1^2 = e_2^1 + e_2^2$, and each knowing the chance of rain and drought implies $\delta = \gamma$.

Exercise 17B.25

What is the shape of the Edgeworth Box representing an economy in which $e_1^1 + e_1^2 = e_2^1 + e_2^2$?

In exercise 17B.23, you were asked to make these assumptions and to assume in addition that utility for each of the two consumers is state-independent. You should have been able to demonstrate that this would result in an equilibrium price $p_2^* = (1 - \delta)/\delta$, and in exercise 17B.24 you should have concluded that this results in each individual fully insuring and the equilibrium falling on the 45-degree line in the Edgeworth Box as in panel (a) of Graph 17.10.

Now suppose that utility for our two consumers is state-dependent. Table 17.2 provides three sets of predictions about the nature of the resulting equilibrium. In each case, $\delta = 0.25 = \gamma$; that is, both individuals agree that the probability that they will face state 1 is 0.25 and the probability that they will face state 2 is 0.75. The endowments of the two individuals are symmetrically opposite, with $e_1^1 = 250$, $e_2^1 = 10$, $e_1^2 = 10$ and $e_2^2 = 250$. In the absence of trading state-contingent consumption, individual 1 ends up with a lot of consumption in state 1 but not in state 2, and the reverse is true for individual 2.

Table 17.2 $\delta = 0.25 = \gamma$, $e_1^1 = 250$, $e_2^1 = 10$, $e_1^2 = 10$ and $e_2^2 = 250$						
		Equilibrium With State-Dependent Utility				
α	β	p_2^*	x_1^1	x_2^1	x_1^2	x_2^2
0.50	0.25	7.15	80.36	33.74	179.64	226.26
0.50	0.50	3.00	70.00	70.00	190.00	190.00
0.50	0.75	1.51	66.27	131.69	193.73	128.31
0.75	0.75	1.00	130.00	130.00	130.00	130.00
0.75	0.60	1.49	132.45	88.86	127.55	171.14
0.75	0.40	2.64	138.20	52.35	121.80	207.65
0.75	0.25	4.47	147.33	32.99	112.67	227.01
0.25	0.25	9.00	34.00	34.00	226.00	226.00
0.25	0.40	5.02	30.02	53.82	229.98	206.18
0.25	0.60	2.75	27.75	90.91	232.25	169.09
0.25	0.75	1.83	26.83	132.26	233.17	127.74

The first three rows keep consumer 1's utility state-independent, with the middle row ($\alpha = \beta = 0.5$) representing the case where consumer 2's utility is state-independent as well and where, as a result, both consumers fully insure at the actuarially fair price $p_2^* = (1 - \delta)/\delta = 3$ We can tell that both fully insure because $x_1^1 = x_2^1$ and $x_1^2 = x_2^2$; that is, after trading state-contingent consumption, each individual ends up consuming the same regardless of which state they face.

Exercise 17B.26

Why do you think individual 1 ends up with less consumption than individual 2 once they fully insure?

The top row of Table 17.2 introduces state-dependent utility for individual 2, with that individual now placing less of a weight on state 1 consumption and more on state 2 consumption. The equilibrium price p_2^* now more than doubles, making it costlier to shift consumption from state 1 to state 2. As a result, individual 1, whose tastes we have not changed, keeps more of their consumption in state 1 and, therefore, under-insures. Individual 2 similarly under-insures because they do not care as much about consuming in state 1. The third row conducts the opposite simulation, with individual 1 now placing *more* weight on state 1 consumption. Individual 1, whose tastes we have still not changed, now over-insures because the equilibrium price of shifting consumption to state 2 has fallen by about half from the actuarially fair rate. Individual 2 similarly over-insures because they value state 1 consumption so much more.

Exercise 17B.27

Can you draw out the equilibrium in rows 1 and 3 of Table 17.2 in Edgeworth Boxes?

The second and third set of results in Table 17.2 illustrate cases where both consumers have state-dependent utility. The equilibrium price can differ greatly depending on the nature of the state-dependence of tastes and their relation to the distribution of endowments. In the first row of the second set of results, for instance, both individuals place heavy weight on state 1 consumption, resulting in a relatively low price p_2^* for shifting consumption from state 1 to state 2. Both individuals happen to be fully insuring, with individual 1 shifting a lot of consumption from state 1 to state 2 because it is cheap, and despite such a heavy utility weight on state 1 consumption, and individual 2 shifting a lot of consumption from state 2 to state 1 despite it being expensive because so much utility weight is placed on consuming in state 1. As individual 1 places less weight on state 1 consumption with β falling over the next three rows, the price p_2^* increases because state 2 consumption is in greater demand. Individual 1 reduces their state 2 consumption in favour of keeping more consumption in state 1 because of the higher price, and individual 2 increases their state 2 consumption despite the increase in price because it is becoming more desirable as β falls.

Exercise 17B.28*

Can you offer a similar intuitive explanation for the third set of results in Table 17.2?

17B.3.3 Introducing Differing Beliefs About Risk So far, we have assumed that both individuals hold the same beliefs about the probability of each state occurring; that is, $\delta = \gamma$. Now suppose that they hold different opinions about these probabilities. From looking at the equations for each consumer's expected utility, $U^1(x_1, x_2)$ and $U^2(x_1, x_2)$ in equations (17.27) and (17.28), it should be apparent that this will result in effects similar to those that arise when consumers place different value on each of the two states, i.e. when $\alpha \neq \beta$. For instance, the actual weight placed on state 1 in consumer 1's expected utility function U^1 is $\delta\alpha$ while the actual weight placed on state 1 in consumer 2's expected utility function U^2 is $\gamma\beta$. When their beliefs about the probability associated with state 1 are the same ($\delta = \gamma$), the only way consumer 1 will place less weight on state 1 is if $\alpha < \beta$, but the same difference in weights can arise if $\alpha = \beta$ and $\delta < \gamma$; that is, if consumer 1 believes state 1 is less likely to occur than consumer 2 believes.

Exercise 17B.29*

Suppose $\alpha = \beta = 0.25$. For what values of δ and γ will the equilibrium be the same as the one in the first row of Table 17.2? *Hint*: This is harder than it appears. In row 1 of the table, $\beta\gamma = 1/16$ and $(1 - \beta)(1 - \gamma) = 9/16$. Thus, the overall weight placed on state 2 is 9 times the weight placed on state 1. When you change β from 0.25 to 0.5, you need to make sure when you change γ that the overall weight placed on state 2 is again 9 times the weight placed on state 1.

Table 17.3 replicates Table 17.2 but now assumes state-independent utilities ($\alpha = \beta = 0.5$) and instead generates the same equilibria through different beliefs on the part of the two consumers.

Table 17.3 $\alpha = 0.5 = \beta$, $e_1^1 = 250$, $e_2^1 = 10$, $e_1^2 = 10$ and $e_2^2 = 250$

			State-Independent Utility With Differing Beliefs			
δ	γ	p_2^*	x_1^1	x_2^1	x_1^2	x_2^2
0.25	0.1000	7.15	80.36	33.74	179.64	226.26
0.25	0.2500	3.00	70.00	70.00	190.00	190.00
0.25	0.5000	1.51	66.27	131.69	193.73	128.31
0.50	0.5000	1.00	130.00	130.00	130.00	130.00
0.50	0.3333	1.49	132.45	88.86	127.55	171.14
0.50	0.1818	2.64	138.20	52.35	121.80	207.65
0.50	0.1000	4.47	147.33	32.99	112.67	227.01
0.10	0.1000	9.00	34.00	34.00	226.00	226.00
0.10	0.1818	5.02	30.02	53.82	229.98	206.18
0.10	0.3333	2.75	27.75	90.91	232.25	169.09
0.10	0.5000	1.83	26.83	132.26	233.17	127.74

17B.3.4 Introducing Aggregate Risk Finally, we can introduce aggregate risk by changing our assumption that the overall endowment in the economy is the same regardless of which state arises (i.e. $(e_1^1 + e_1^2 = e_2^1 + e_2^2)$. In the context of the example in Section A, rather than assuming that rain changes the distribution of banana production on the island, we can assume that rain increases or decreases the total banana crop, while also changing its relative distribution on the island.

If X has the land that does better with rain in state 1 and Y has the land that does better with drought in state 2, if there is no aggregate risk, X has to do as well under rain as Y does under drought. Our example so far has assumed that the endowment for consumer 1 (X, in this example) is $(e_1^1 = 250, e_2^1 = 10)$, and the endowment for consumer 2 (Y, in this example) is the mirror image $(e_1^2 = 10, e_2^2 = 250)$, which implies that the aggregate endowment in the economy is the same in the two states. Now suppose that only half as many bananas grow on the island during droughts as during rainy seasons, with X's endowment changing to $(e_1^1, e_2^1) = (250, 5)$ and Y's endowment changing to $(e_1^2, e_2^2) = (10, 125)$. This introduces aggregate risk because now the economy as a whole has 260 bananas in rainy seasons (state 1) and only 130 bananas during droughts (state 2). We'll assume in this example that that the probability of the rainy season occurring is 0.25 (i.e. $\delta = \gamma = 0.25$) and tastes are state-independent (i.e. $\alpha = \beta = 0.5$).

The resulting equilibrium is given in the first row of Table 17.4 and can be compared to the equilibrium without aggregate risk that is given in the second row. The price for trading state 1 consumption for state 2 consumption is higher as a result of the fact that the banana crop in state 2 has fallen by half, in row 1 relative to row 2. X's endowment is not much different in the two rows because most of it comes from the rainy season (state 1), but the increase in P_2^* causes X's consumption of bananas in the drought season (state 2) to fall by half. Y is similarly forced to cut back on consumption of bananas in the drought season because Y's crop has fallen.

Exercise 17B.30

Can you see from the demand equations why consumption in the rainy season remains unchanged?

Suppose next that a new fertilizer is discovered that quadruples banana output in drought seasons but has no impact on banana output in rainy seasons. The endowments now change to those in the third row of Table 17.4, and, because of the increased abundance of bananas in the drought season (state 2), the price of shifting consumption from state 1 to state 2 now falls. Both X and Y end up increasing banana consumption in the rainy season.

e¹₁	e¹₂	e²₁	e²₂	p*₂	x¹₁	x¹₂	x²₁	x²₂
				Table 17.4 $\alpha = 0.5 = \beta, \delta = 0.25 = \gamma$				
				Aggregate Risk With State Independence and Identical Beliefs				
250	5	10	125	6.00	70.00	35.00	190.00	95.00
250	10	10	250	3.00	70.00	70.00	190.00	190.00
250	20	10	500	1.50	70.00	140.00	190.00	380.00
250	10	5	125	5.67	76.67	40.59	178.33	94.41
250	10	10	250	3.00	70.00	70.00	190.00	190.00
250	10	20	500	1.59	66.47	125.56	203.53	384.44
125	5	10	250	1.59	33.24	62.68	101.76	192.22
250	10	10	250	3.00	70.00	70.00	190.00	190.00
500	20	10	250	5.67	153.33	81.18	356.67	188.82
250	10	250	10	75.00	250.00	10.00	250.00	10.00
250	10	130	130	8.14	82.86	30.53	297.14	109.47
250	10	10	250	3.00	70.00	70.00	190.00	190.00

Exercise 17B.31*

Can you depict the equilibria in rows 1 and 3 in two Edgeworth Boxes?

The second set of simulations in Table 17.4 keeps the productivity of X's land constant and varies solely Y's land productivity while still keeping Y's land relatively more productive in the drought season (state 2). As Y's land becomes more productive, the supply of bananas in the drought season increases relative to the supply of bananas in the rainy season, thus driving down the price of shifting consumption from the rainy season (state 1) to the drought season (state 2). Since the productivity of X's land remains unchanged, they are only affected through this change in P^*_2 and they substitute away from consumption in the rainy season and towards consumption in the drought season. Y, on the other hand, also becomes wealthier as their land becomes more productive, and they end up increasing consumption in both states. The results are also examples of the general principle introduced in Section A that *when there is aggregate risk, the terms of trade will be less favourable for consumers intending to trade consumption from the high aggregate output state to the low aggregate output state.* In the first row of the second set of simulations, the high output state is the rainy season (state 1) and as a result it is expensive to buy state-contingent consumption during droughts; that is, P^*_2 is high. These are not favourable terms of trade for X (individual 1) because they want to trade consumption in rainy seasons for consumption in dry seasons, but the terms are quite favourable to Y because they want to trade in the other direction. The reverse is true in the last row of the second set of simulations where the drought state, state 2, is the high productivity state.

Exercise 17B.32*

In the third set of results of Table 17.4, we hold Y's land productivity constant while varying X's. Can you make sense of the results?

In the last set of simulations, we again hold the productivity of X's land fixed and vary Y's land productivity, but this time we start initially with Y's land being identical to X's and alter the relative productivity during rainy and dry seasons in the direction of increasing productivity during droughts (state 2) and decreasing it during rain (state 1). When their land is identical, the equilibrium price is so high that neither X nor Y alters their consumption from their endowments and thus no insurance through trades in state-contingent commodities takes place. *Despite enormous aggregate risk, there is no way they can insure each other because their individual risk is the same.* This is an important insight. In order for insurance markets to enable individuals to protect one another against *individual risk*, risk cannot be so similarly distributed. It is not easy to insure fully against recessions because recessions hit the whole economy, but it is possible to insure against fire damage to homes because such damage does not hit everyone at once. As we increase Y's land productivity during drought seasons relative to rainy seasons, gains from trade across states emerge, for much the same reason as we can insure one another against fire damage.

Appendix 1 | Expected Utility and the Independence Axiom

Expected utility theory as developed in this chapter is based on an assumption that we mentioned only briefly in the chapter. This assumption is known as the *independence axiom*, and it builds the foundation to expected utility theory in much the same way as some of our assumptions about tastes in Chapter 4 built the foundation to choice theory in the absence of risk. Whenever individuals face risk, they are facing a gamble. Individuals have choices over which gamble to play, with institutions like insurance contracts offering ways of choosing gambles that are different from what nature has dealt. Choice in the presence of risk essentially involves choices over gambles that have different risks and expected values. Expected utility theory begins with the assumption that individuals have tastes or preferences over gambles in much the same way as they have tastes over consumption goods. In the chapter, we have illustrated these as indifference curves over outcome pairs (x_G, x_B), but we can take a further step back and think of them as preference relations. We will read a statement like '$G_1 \succsim G_2$' as Gamble 1 is preferred to or at least as good as Gamble 2 and a statement like $G_1 > G_2$ as Gamble 1 is strictly better than Gamble 2. The independence axiom is an assumption about individual preference relations over gambles.

Before we can state this assumption, we need to define what it means to mix two different gambles. Suppose that Gamble 1 places 0.60 probability on outcome 1 and 0.40 probability on outcome 2, while Gamble 2 places 0.20 probability on outcome 1 and 0.80 probability on outcome 2. If half the time an individual ends up playing Gamble 1 and half the time they end up playing Gamble 2, overall, they will reach outcome 1 with probability 0.60 half the time and with probability 0.20 half the time, for an overall probability 0.40 of reaching outcome 1. What we are doing is multiplying the probability of playing a particular gamble with the probability that outcome 1 is reached in that gamble. We do that for each gamble faced and add up the probabilities. For instance, in this case we find the probability of outcome 1 if we play Gamble 1 half the time and Gamble 2 half the time as $0.5(0.60) + 0.5(0.2) = 0.40$.

Exercise 17B.33

What is the probability of reaching outcome 2 if we play Gamble 1 half the time and Gamble 2 half the time?

In this case, we would say that we created a third gamble by averaging Gamble 1 and Gamble 2, and we would denote the new gamble as $(0.5G_1 + 0.5G_2)$. There are many ways to mix gambles by taking different *weighted* averages of the two gambles. For instance, if we place weight α (where $0 < \alpha < 1$) on Gamble 1, we would get a new gamble denoted as $(\alpha G_1 + (1 - \alpha)G_2)$.

Exercise 17B.34

What weights would have to be put on Gambles 1 and 2 in order for the mixed gamble to result in a 0.50 probability of reaching outcome 1 and a 0.50 probability of reaching outcome 2?

The independence axiom assumes the following. Suppose there are three gambles, G_1, G_2 and G_3:

$$G_1 \succsim G_2 \text{ if and only if } (\alpha G_1 + (1 - \alpha)G_3) \succsim (\alpha G_2 + (1 - \alpha)G_3). \qquad \textbf{(17.33)}$$

Gamble 1 is preferred to Gamble 2 if and only if a mixture of Gamble 1 with a third Gamble 3 is also preferred to the same mixture of Gamble 2 with Gamble 3. An individual's tastes over two gambles remain the same when those gambles are mixed with any other gamble, or an individual's tastes over two gambles are *independent* of what other gambles are mixed in, so long as they are mixed the same way.

This axiom has a lot of intuitive appeal. We can return to the example given in Section A. Suppose person A likes playing roulette better than playing poker. Suppose person B invites A to come to one of two game nights at a local casino and asks them to choose which night to come. On the first night, they flip a coin and play roulette if the coin comes up heads and slot machines if the coin comes up tails, and on the second night they will play poker if the coin comes up heads and slot machines if it comes up tails. If A likes roulette better than poker, A should come to the first night. The fact that there is a 50 per cent chance that A will end up playing slots on either night does not take anything away from the fact that the night with a chance at roulette should be better than the night with an equal chance at poker.

The following result forms the basis for using expected utility theory to analyze choice in the presence of risk. *If an individual's tastes over gambles satisfy the independence axiom, these tastes can be represented by an expected utility function.* So long as tastes over gambles satisfy the independence axiom, we will be able to find a function $u(x)$ over consumption such that we can represent indifference curves over outcome pairs (x_G, x_B) that happen with probabilities $((1 - \delta), \delta)$ with a von Neumann-Morgenstern expected utility function $U(x_G, x_B) = \delta u(x_B) + (1 - \delta)u(x_G)$ when tastes are not state-dependent. When tastes are state-dependent, an extension of the independence axiom will similarly imply that we can find functions $u_G(x)$ and $u_B(x)$ such that indifference curves over outcome pairs (x_G, x_B) that occur with probabilities $((1 - \delta), \delta)$ can be represented by an expected utility function $U(x_G, x_B) = \delta u_B(x_B) + (1 - \delta)u_G(x_G)$. The result extends to more than two outcome pairs. For instance, if there are three possible consumption outcomes – x_1, x_2 and x_3 – that will occur with probabilities δ_1, δ_2 and δ_3 respectively, we will be able to find a function $u(x)$, when tastes are state-independent, such that $U(x_1, x_2, x_3) = \delta_1 u(x_1) + \delta_2 u(x_2) + \delta_3 u(x_3)$. When tastes are state-dependent, we can find three u functions that will allow us to again express indifference curves with an expected utility function.

Appendix 2 | The Allais Paradox and Regret Theory

Almost since the conception of expected utility theory, certain paradoxical examples that violate the predictions of the theory have been studied, and, more recently, such examples have given rise to an interest in behavioural economics, a branch of economics that attempts to resolve such paradoxes by introducing principles from psychology and neurobiology into economic models.

The oldest and most famous of these paradoxes – dating back to at least 1953 – is known as the *Allais Paradox,* named after Maurice Allais (1911–2010) who was awarded the Nobel Prize in Economics in 1988 for his work on the theory of markets. Like other paradoxes, it deviates from the examples in this chapter in that it begins with three rather than two possible outcomes. Suppose, for instance, you are in a game show where the host presents you with three closed doors that appear identical. He tells you that behind one of the doors is a pot of €5 million, behind another door there is a pot of €1 million and behind a third door there is an empty pot.

You are asked to choose between two different games. Game 1 has a 100 per cent chance of you finding the door with €1 million behind it, while Game 2 has a 10 per cent chance of you finding the €5 million door, an 89 per cent chance of you finding the €1 million door and a 1 per cent chance of you finding the door with no money. Which option would you choose? It turns out that most people would choose to play Game 1.

Now suppose that you were instead asked to choose between two other games. Game 3 has an 11 per cent chance of you discovering the €1 million door and an 89 per cent chance of you discovering the door with no money. Game 4, on the other hand, has a 10 per cent chance of you finding the €5 million door and a 90 per cent chance of you finding the door with no money. Which would you choose now? Most people end up choosing to play Game 4 rather than Game 3.

It turns out, however, that it is not possible for an individual to behave in a way predicted by expected utility theory and choose Game 1 in the first case and Game 4 in the second. Suppose we have identified an underlying function $u(x)$ that permits us to represent a person's indifference curves over risky outcomes with an expected utility function, and suppose the utilities of getting €5 million, €1 million and €0 are denoted by this function $u(x)$, as u_5, u_1 and u_0 respectively. The expected utility of each game is the probability-weighted sum of the utility level associated with each outcome. If an individual chooses Game 1 over Game 2, it implies that their expected utility of Game 1 is greater than their expected utility of Game 2, or:

$$u_1 > 0.1u_5 + 0.89u_1 + 0.01u_0. \tag{17.34}$$

If you add $0.89u_0$ to both sides of this equation and subtract $0.89u_1$, equation (17.34) becomes:

$$0.11u_1 + 0.89u_0 > 0.1u_5 + 0.9u_0. \tag{17.35}$$

The left-hand side of equation (17.35) is the expected utility of Game 3, and the right-hand side the expected utility of Game 4. Thus, expected utility theory implies that anyone who chooses Game 1 over Game 2 should choose Game 3 over Game 4, yet the very people who choose Game 1 over Game 2 tend to choose Game 4 over Game 3. However reasonable the independence axiom that builds the foundation for expected utility theory is, it does not appear to hold for people who behave this way.

Exercise 17B.35*

Does the paradox still hold if people's tastes are state-dependent?

Examples like this have led some to develop what is known as *regret theory*. Perhaps the reason that Game 1 is preferred to Game 2 is that it is difficult for anyone to face the possibility of getting nothing when the individual could have had €1 million with certainty, even if getting nothing is a very low probability event. Looking ahead to the regret one would face, the individual might just go for the sure thing. When choosing between Games 3 and 4, on the other hand, there is a large probability of getting nothing in either game, so regret might be less of a factor, permitting individuals to go for the chance to have €5 million even though it increases the chance of having nothing slightly. This links closely to a concept known as probability weighting in the behavioural economics theory known as *prospect theory*.

An alternative view of the Allais Paradox is that we should not worry about its implications for real-world choices too much because the paradox arises only in examples where very small probability events are considered, such as the 1 per cent probability of getting nothing in Game 2.

End-of-Chapter Exercises

17.1† **A.** Suppose that there are two possible outcomes of a gamble. Under outcome A, you get €x_1 and under outcome B you get €x_2 where $x_2 > x_1$. Outcome A happens with probability $\delta = 0.5$ and outcome B happens with probability $(1 - \delta) = 0.5$.

a. Illustrate three different consumption/utility relationships: one that can be used to model risk-averse tastes over gambles, one for risk-neutral tastes and one for risk-loving tastes.

b. On each graph, illustrate your expected consumption on the horizontal axis and your expected utility of facing the gamble on the vertical. Which of these – expected consumption or expected utility – does not depend on your degree of risk aversion?

c. How does the expected utility of the gamble differ from the utility of the expected consumption level of the gamble in each graph?

d. Suppose you are made an offer $€\bar{x}$ to not face this gamble. Illustrate in each of your graphs where $\bar{x}$ would lie if it makes you just indifferent between taking $\bar{x}$ and staying to face the gamble.

e. Suppose you are offered some insurance; for every euro you agree to give another person if outcome A happens, that person will agree to give you y euros if outcome B happens. What's y if the deal they are offering you does not change the expected value of consumption for you?

f. What changes in your three graphs if you buy insurance of this kind, and how does it impact on your expected consumption level on the horizontal axis and the expected utility of the remaining gamble on the vertical?

B. Suppose we can use the function $u(x) = x^{\alpha}$ for the consumption/utility relationship that allows us to represent your indifference curves over risky outcomes using an expected utility function. Assume the rest of the set-up as described in A.

a. What value can α take if you are risk averse? What if you are risk neutral? What if you are risk loving?

b. Write down the equations for the expected consumption level as well as the expected utility from the gamble. Which one depends on α and why?

c. What's the equation for the utility of the expected consumption level?

d. Consider $\bar{x}$ as defined in A(d). What equation would you have to solve to find $\bar{x}$?

e. Suppose $\alpha = 1$. Solve for $\bar{x}$ and explain your result intuitively.

f. Suppose that instead of two outcomes, there are actually three possible outcomes: A, B and C, with associated consumption levels x_1, x_2 and x_3 occurring with probabilities δ_1, δ_2 and $(1 - \delta_1 - \delta_2)$. How would you write the expected utility of this gamble?

g. Suppose that u took the form:

$$u(x) = 0.1x^{0.5} - \left(\frac{x}{100\,000}\right)^{2.5} \qquad (17.36)$$

This is the equation that was used to arrive at most of the graphs in part A of the chapter, where X is expressed in thousands but substituted into the equation as its full value; that is, consumption of 200 in a graph represents $x = 200\,000$. Verify the numbers in Graphs 17.1 and 17.3. Note that the numbers in the graphs are rounded.

17.2 We have illustrated in several settings the role of actuarially fair insurance contracts (b, p), where b is the insurance benefit in the bad state and p is the insurance premium that has to be paid in either state. In this problem, we will discuss it in a slightly different way that we will later use in Chapter 22.

A. Consider again the example, covered extensively in the chapter, of John and life insurance on Emma. The probability of Emma dying is δ, and John's consumption if Emma doesn't die will be 10 and his consumption if she does die will be 250 in the absence of any life insurance.

a. Now suppose that John is offered a full set of actuarially fair insurance contracts. What does this imply for how p is related to δ and b?

b. On a graph with b on the horizontal axis and p on the vertical, illustrate the set of all actuarially fair insurance contracts.

c. Now think of what indifference curves in this picture must look like. First, which way must they slope given that John does not like to pay premiums but he does like benefits?

d. In which direction within the graph does John have to move to in order to become unambiguously better off?

e. We know John will fully insure if he is risk averse and his tastes are state-independent. What policy does that imply he will buy if $\delta = 0.25$?

f. Putting indifference curves into your graph from (b), what must they look like in order for John to choose the policy that you derived in (e).

g. What would his indifference map look like if he were risk neutral? What if he was risk loving?

B. Suppose $u(x) = \ln (x)$ allows us to write John's tastes over gambles using the expected utility function. John's income is 10 if Emma is not around and 250 if she is, and the probability of Emma not being around is δ.

a. Given his incomes in the good and bad state in the absence of insurance, use the expected utility function to arrive at his utility function over insurance policies (b, p)?

b. Derive the expression for the slope of an indifference curve in a graph with b on the horizontal and p on the vertical axis.

c. Suppose $\delta = 0.25$ and John has fully insured under policy $(b, p) = (240, 60)$. What is his MRS now?

d. How does your answer to (c) compare to the slope of the budget formed by mapping out all actuarially fair insurance policies as in A(b)? Explain in terms of a graph.

17.3† **Everyday Application:** *Venice and Regret.* Suppose that you can choose to participate in one of two gambles. In Gamble 1 you have a 99 per cent chance of winning a trip to Venice and a 1 per cent chance of winning tickets to a film about Venice; and in Gamble 2, you have a 99 per cent of winning the same trip to Venice and a 1 per cent chance of not winning anything.

A. Suppose you very much like Venice, and, were you to be asked to rank the three possible outcomes, you would rank the trip to Venice first, the tickets to the film about Venice second and having nothing third.

a. Assume that you can create a consumption index such that getting nothing is denoted as 0 consumption, getting the tickets to the film is $x_1 > 0$ and getting the trip is $x_2 > x_1$. Denote the expected value of Gamble 1 by $E(G_1)$ and the expected value of Gamble 2 by $E(G_2)$. Which is higher?

b. On a graph with x on the horizontal axis and utility on the vertical, illustrate a consumption/utility relationship that exhibits risk aversion.

c. In your graph, illustrate the expected utility you receive from Gamble 1 and from Gamble 2. Which gamble will you choose to participate in?

d. Next, suppose tastes are risk neutral instead. Redraw your graph and illustrate again which gamble you would choose. Be careful to accurately differentiate between the expected values of the two gambles.

e. It turns out, for reasons that become clearer in part B, that risk aversion or neutrality is irrelevant for how individuals whose behaviour is explained by expected utility theory will choose between these gambles. In a separate graph, illustrate the consumption/utility relationship again, but this time assume risk loving. Illustrate in the graph how your choice over the two gambles might still be the same as in parts (c) and (d). Can you think of why it in fact *has to be* the same?

f. It turns out that many people, when faced with a choice of these two gambles, end up choosing Gamble 2. Assuming that such people would rank the three outcomes the way we have, is there any way that such a choice can be explained using expected utility theory, taking as given that the choice implied by expected utility theory does not depend on risk aversion?

g. This example is known as *Machina's Paradox,* after Mark Machina (1954–), who first identified it. One explanation for the fact that many people choose Gamble 2 over Gamble 1 is that expected utility theory does not take into account *regret.* Can you think of how this might explain people's paradoxical choice of Gamble 2 over Gamble 1?

B. Assume again, as in part A, that individuals prefer a trip to Venice to the film ticket, and they prefer the film ticket to getting nothing. Furthermore, suppose there exists a function u that assigns u_2 as the utility of getting the trip, u_1 as the utility of getting the film ticket and u_0 as the utility of getting nothing, and suppose that this function u allows us to represent tastes over risky pairs of outcomes using an expected utility function.

a. What inequality defines the relationship between u_1 and u_0?

b. Multiply both sides of your inequality from (a) by 0.01, and add $0.99u_2$ to both sides. What inequality do you now have?

    c. Relate the inequality you derived in (b) to the expected utility of the two gambles in this example. What gamble does expected utility theory predict a person will choose, assuming the outcomes are ranked as we have ranked them?

    d. When we typically think of a gamble, we are thinking of different outcomes that will happen with different probabilities. We can also think of degenerate gambles; that is, gambles where one outcome happens with certainty. Define the following three such gambles: Gamble A results in the trip to Venice with probability of 100 per cent; Gamble B results in the film ticket with probability of 100 per cent; and Gamble C results in nothing with probability of 100 per cent. How are these degenerate gambles ranked by someone who prefers the trip to the ticket to nothing?

    e. Using the notion of *mixed gambles* introduced in Appendix 1, define Gambles 1 and 2 as mixed gambles over the degenerate gambles we have just defined in (d). Explain how the *independence axiom* from Appendix 1 implies that Gamble 1 must be preferred to Gamble 2.

    f. *True or False*: When individuals who rank the outcomes the way we have assumed choose Gamble 2 over Gamble 1, expected utility theory fails because the independence axiom is violated.

    g. Would the paradox disappear if we assumed state-dependent tastes?

17.4 **Business Application:** *Diversifying Risk along the Business Cycle.* Suppose you own a business that does well during economic expansions but not so well during recessions, which happen with probability δ. Let x_E denote your consumption level during expansions and let x_R denote your consumption level during recessions. Unless you do something to diversify risk, these consumption levels are $E = (e_E, e_R)$ where e_E is your income during expansions and e_R your income during recessions (with $e_E > e_R$). Your tastes over consumption are the same during recessions as during expansions and you are risk averse. For any asset purchases described here, assume that you pay for these assets from whatever income you have depending on whether the economy is in recession or expansion.

    A. *Suppose person A owns a financial firm that manages asset portfolios. All they care about as they manage their business is expected returns, and any asset they sell is characterized by (p, b_R, b_E) where p is how much they charge for 1 unit of the asset, b_R is how much the asset will pay you (as, say, dividends) during recessions, and b_E is how much the asset will pay you during expansions.

        a. Is someone like person A – who only cares about expected returns – risk averse, risk loving or risk neutral?

        b. Suppose that all the assets A offers have the feature that those who buy these assets experience no change in their expected consumption levels as a result of buying A's assets. Derive an equation that expresses the price p of A's assets in terms of δ, b_R and b_E.

        c. What happens to A's expected returns when they sell more or fewer of such assets?

        d. Suppose you buy 1 asset (p, b_R, b_E) that satisfies our equation from (b). How does your consumption during expansions and recessions change as a result?

        e. At what rate do assets of the kind A is offering allow you to transfer consumption opportunities from expansions to recessions? On a graph with x_E on the horizontal and x_R on the vertical axis, illustrate the budget line that the availability of such assets creates for you.

        f. Illustrate in your graph your optimal choice of assets.

    B. Overall output during recessions is smaller than during expansions. Suppose everyone is risk averse. Is it possible for us to all end up doing what you concluded you would do in (f)? Suppose that the function $u(x) = x^\alpha$ is such that we can express tastes over gambles using expected utility functions.

        a. If you have not already done so in part A, derive the expression $p(\delta, b_R, b_E)$ that relates the price of an asset to the probability of a recession δ, the dividend payment b_R during recessions, and the dividend payment b_E during economic expansions assuming that purchase of such assets keeps expected consumption levels unchanged.

        b. Suppose you purchase k units of the same asset (b_E, b_R), which is priced as you derived in part (a) and for which $(b_R - b_E) = y > 0$. Derive an expression for x_R defined as your consumption level during recessions, given your recession income level of e_R and assuming you purchase these assets. Derive similarly an expression for your consumption level x_E during economic expansions.

        c. Set up an expected utility maximization problem where you choose k – the number of such assets that you purchase. Solve for k.

d. How much will you consume during recessions and expansions?

e. For what values of α is your answer correct?

f. *True or False*: So long as assets that pay more dividends during recessions than expansions are available at actuarially fair prices, you will be able to fully insure against consumption shocks from business cycles.

g. Could you accomplish the same outcome by instead creating and selling assets with $(b_E > b_R)$?

17.5*† Business Application: *Diversifying Risk along the Business Cycle in General Equilibrium.* In exercise 17.4, we considered the case of person A trading assets that allow you to transfer consumption from good times to bad times. Suppose again that your income during economic expansions is e_E and your income during recessions is e_R, and that the probability of a recession is $\delta < 0.5$.

A. Also, suppose again that A's tastes are risk neutral while yours are risk averse and that $e_E > e_R$. A's consumption opportunity endowment, however, is the reverse of yours, with e_R equal to A's income during economic expansions and e_E equal to A's income during recessions.

a. Draw an Edgeworth Box representing the economy of you and A.

b. Illustrate the equilibrium in this economy. Will you do in equilibrium what we concluded you would do in exercise 17.4?

c. Next, suppose that there was a third person in our economy: your identical twin who shares your tastes and endowments. Suppose the terms of trade for transferring consumption in one state to the other remain unchanged, and suppose an equilibrium exists in which everyone ends up at an interior solution. Illustrate what this would look like, given that there are now two of you and only one of A. *Hint*: It should no longer be the case that our indifference curves within the box are tangential to one another because equilibrium now implies that two of your trades have to be exactly offset by one of A's.

d. Is anyone fully insured against consumption swings in the business cycle? Is everyone?

e. Now continue with the example but suppose that A's tastes, instead of being risk neutral, were also risk averse. Would the same terms of trade still produce an equilibrium?

f. How do the terms of trade now have to change to support an equilibrium when all are risk averse?

g. Will anyone be fully insured; that is, will anyone enjoy the same level of consumption during recessions as during expansions?

h. Relate your conclusion to the existence of aggregate risk in economies that experience expansions and recessions. Who would you rather be: A or you?

B. **Suppose that the function $u(x) = \ln x$ allows us to express your tastes over gambles as expected utilities. Also, suppose again that your income during expansions is e_E and your income during recessions is e_R, with $e_E > e_R$.

a. Let p_R be defined as the price of €1 of consumption in the event that a recession occurs and let p_E be the price of €1 of consumption in the event that an economic expansion occurs. Explain why $p_R = 1$ can be normalized and denote the price of €1 of consumption in the event of expansions as $p_E - p$.

b. Using these normalized prices, write down your budget constraint and your expected utility optimization problem.

c. Solve for your demand for x_R and x_E.

d. Repeat parts (b) and (c) for person A, assuming A shares your tastes but their income during *recessions* is e_E and their income during *expansions* is e_R, exactly the mirror image of your incomes over the business cycle.

e. Assuming you and A are the only ones in this economy, derive the equilibrium price, or terms of trade across the two states.

f. How much do you each consume during expansions and recessions at this equilibrium price?

g. Now suppose that there are two of you and only one of A in this economy. What happens to the equilibrium price?

h. Do you now consume less during recessions than during expansions? Does A?

17.6 **Policy Application:** *More Police or More Prisons? Enforcement Versus Deterrence.* Consider a person who is thinking about whether to engage in a life of crime. They know that if they get caught, they will be in prison and will sustain a consumption level of x_0, but if they do not get caught, they will be able to consume x_1, considerably above x_0.

A. Suppose that this person cares only about their consumption level, i.e. they have state-independent tastes.

    a. On a graph with consumption x on the horizontal axis and utility on the vertical, illustrate this person's consumption/utility relationship assuming they are risk averse.

    b. Suppose the probability δ of getting caught is 0.25. Illustrate the expected utility of choosing a life of crime. What if $\delta = 0.75$?

    c. Redraw the consumption/utility graph and suppose $\delta = 0.5$. Let $\bar{x}$ indicate the income this person would need to be able to make honestly in order for them to be indifferent between an honest living and a life of crime.

    d. Member of Parliament (MP) C believes the criminal justice system spends too much effort on identifying criminals but not enough effort on punishing them harshly. They propose an *increased deterrence policy* under which penalties for committing crimes are raised while less is spent on law enforcement. This implies a drop in both x_0 as well as δ. Suppose the expected consumption level for a person engaged in a life of crime remains unchanged under this policy. Will the person who was previously indifferent between an honest living and a life of crime still be indifferent?

    e. MP L believes we are treating criminals too harshly. They propose an *increased enforcement policy* that devotes more resources towards catching criminals but lowers the penalties that criminals face if caught. The policy thus increases x_0 as well as δ. Suppose that the expected consumption level of a person engaged in a life of crime is again unchanged under this policy. Will the person who was previously indifferent between an honest living and a life of crime still be indifferent?

    f. *True or False*: If criminals are risk averse, the increased deterrence policy is more effective at reducing crime than the increased enforcement policy.

    g. How would your answers change if criminals were risk loving?

B. Suppose that $x_0 = 20$ and $x_1 = 80$, where we can think of these values as being expressed in terms of thousands of euros, and the probability of getting caught is $\delta = 0.5$.

    a. What is the expected consumption level if the life of crime is chosen?

    b. Suppose the potential criminal's tastes over gambles can be expressed using an expected utility function that evaluates the utility of consumption as $u(x) = \ln(x)$. What is the person's expected utility from a life of crime?

    c. How does the expected utility compare with the utility of the expected value of consumption? Can you tell from this whether the criminal is risk averse?

    d. Consider the level of consumption this person could attain by not engaging in a life of crime. What level of consumption from an honest living would make the person be indifferent between a life of crime and an honest living? Denote this consumption level as $\bar{x}$.

    e. Now consider the *increased deterrence policy* described in A(d). In particular, suppose that the policy increases penalties to the point where x_0 falls to 5. How much can δ drop if the expected consumption level in a life of crime is to remain unchanged?

    f. What happens to $\bar{x}$ as a result of this increased deterrence policy?

    g. Now consider the *increased enforcement policy* described in A(e). In particular, suppose that δ is increased to 0.6. How much can x_0 increase in order for the expected consumption in a life of crime to remain unchanged?

    h. What happens to $\bar{x}$ as a result of this increased enforcement policy?

    i. Which policy is more effective at reducing crime assuming potential criminals are risk averse?

    j. Suppose that the function $u(x)$ that allows us to represent this individual's tastes over gambles with an expected utility function is $u(x) = x^2$. How do your answers change?

* conceptually challenging
** computationally challenging
† solutions in Study Guide

PART IV

Distortions of the Invisible Hand in Competitive Markets

Having built our models of individual choice in Parts 1 and 2 and illustrated how such individual choice can lead to competitive equilibria that are efficient in Part 3, we are now ready to investigate how the invisible hand of competitive markets can be distorted to cause inefficiencies. We have already mentioned that our first welfare theorem regarding the efficiency of the spontaneous order of markets is based on four sets of assumptions: first, prices are allowed to form without distortions; second, there are no externalities; third, there are no informational asymmetries that bestow informational advantages on one side of the market; and fourth, no one has market power.

In this part of the text, we will investigate what can go wrong in *competitive* markets; that is, in markets where no one has market power. We limit ourselves to competitive settings for now because all of the tools thus far have been developed under the assumption that individuals are small relative to the market and thus act as price-takers. In Part 5, we will develop new tools from game theory to tackle violations of the first welfare theorem that arise as a result of market power when individuals have an incentive to think strategically because they can impact the economic environment directly by shaping prices. Within competitive markets, inefficiencies can therefore arise from distortions of prices, typically caused by some government policy, the existence of externalities and the existence of informational asymmetries.

Chapter 18 begins with the most obvious and direct types of price distortions. For a variety of reasons, governments may choose to limit how high prices for particular goods may rise or how low prices are allowed to fall. Such policies, known as *price ceilings* and *price floors*, prohibit voluntary exchange at prices at which markets would otherwise trade.

In Chapter 19, we revisit *taxes* and *subsidies*, which are by far the most common ways in which market prices are distorted through policy. We have previously discussed in Chapter 10 how taxes cause substitution effects and create deadweight losses. Now that we have built models of markets, however, we can see more clearly how taxes and subsidies translate into price changes, whether consumers or producers are affected more depending on relative price elasticities, and which types of taxes and subsidies are likely to result in greater or lesser inefficiencies. We then turn in Chapter 20 to markets that extend across geographic regions or across time, markets that are connected through the activities of *exporters* and *speculators* who look for opportunities to buy low and sell high. Such activities have the effect of equalizing prices across regions and time, but sometimes governments interfere with this process by taxing trades across markets through *tariffs* or by imposing *quotas* that limit trade. We will see how such policies once again distort prices and cause inefficiencies, whether in goods markets where explicit trade is limited, or in labour markets where policies are often aimed at restricting worker or firm *migration*.

Chapter 21 introduces the topic of *externalities* – impacts of individual actions that affect others who are not participating in a given market transaction. Pollution generated in the production of goods is a prime example, but other types of externalities, both positive and negative, are pervasive in the real world. In Chapter 22, we turn to informational asymmetries that result in opportunities for the more informed parties in a market to take advantage of the less informed. When such informational asymmetries become sufficiently pronounced, entire markets might cease to exist since the less informed are too sceptical to engage in trades with the more informed. The phenomenon that leads to such problems for markets is known as *adverse selection*, with insurance markets providing a good example. The problem of informational asymmetries is not confined to insurance markets. One important example involves labour markets and, in particular, the emergence of racial and gender discrimination in such markets.

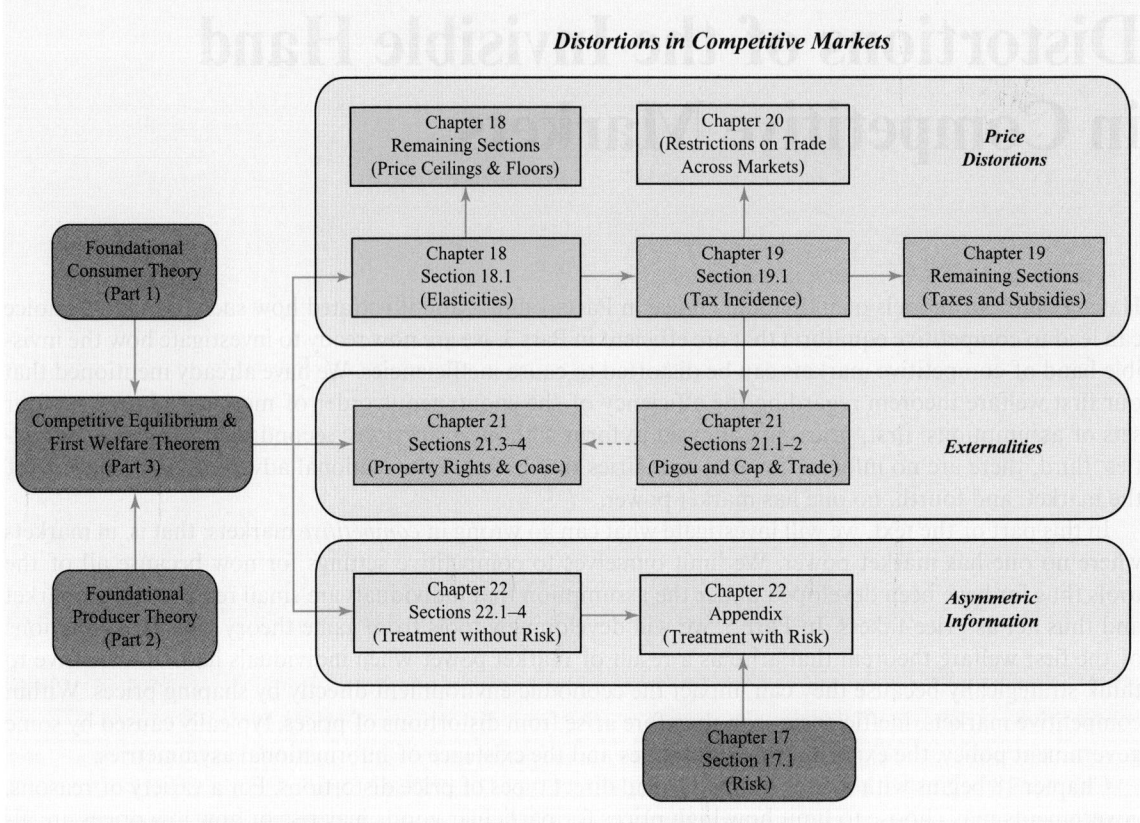

Chapter 18

Elasticities, Price-Distorting Policies and Non-Price Rationing

We have demonstrated in the last few chapters how prices form in competitive markets. Prices, we have argued, send important signals to all the relevant actors in an economy, allowing each individual actor to then choose how to behave in the market while ensuring that the market produces output at the lowest possible cost and channels it to those that value the output the most. In a world defined by scarcity, prices represent one way of *rationing* scarce resources, a way of determining who gets to consume what, how much everyone works, how much consumption will occur now as opposed to in the future and how much risk each individual faces.

We may not always like the way in which the competitive price system rations scarce goods. Maybe we do not like the fact that in an unregulated labour market, some individuals will be able to earn only very low wages, at least until they get more experience or acquire more skills or education. We may not like the fact that housing in some areas is so expensive as to preclude the poor from consuming it, or that innovations in agriculture are pushing aside the traditional small family farm. As a result, we often ask the government to tinker with the price system, to come up with ways of getting towards outcomes that we like better. Examples of this include minimum wage laws, price regulations, rent control and a variety of other policies aimed at improving in some way on the market outcome.

In the end, there may be good reasons why people disagree on the wisdom of such policies. Much of the disagreement comes from not understanding sufficiently the economics behind markets and policy interventions, and to the extent to which this is the cause of differing opinions, the economist has a role in clarifying the trade-offs involved. The most fundamental of these trade-offs rests on an understanding of the fact that in a world of scarcity, *something* will always lead to rationing of goods. There will always be some mechanism that determines who gets what goods and who is left out. Market prices represent one such rationing mechanism, and when we add other institutions in attempts to improve on market mechanisms, we will explicitly or implicitly add other rationing mechanisms on top of it. As some economists have put it, there is no 'free lunch', no magic wand that eliminates the problem of scarcity, at least not in the world we occupy.

The goal of this chapter is to use some commonly talked about policies that aim to improve on market outcomes to illustrate how such policies distort prices and thus change the rationing of scarce goods in the world. This is done most easily within the partial equilibrium model of Chapters 14 and 15. As we will see, the magnitude of the various impacts of price distortions will depend on the responsiveness of consumers and producers to price changes, on the *elasticity* of their behaviour. With some of the policies we discuss, it is the case that many economists end up on one side of the debate because they are persuaded that the *unintended consequences* of well-intentioned policies outweigh the intended benefits. The point here is not to argue for or against particular policies; rather, we will try to use the logic of our models to illustrate trade-offs that we should be aware of in these policy debates, and then everyone can decide for themselves whether what we have learned leads them to favour or oppose particular policies. By identifying the winners and losers from such policies, we will find that we can get a sense of why democratic political processes will sometimes implement certain policies over others, even if an economic analysis of those policies suggests that alternative policies should dominate.

18A   Interactions of Markets and Price-Distorting Policies

We begin our analysis of policy in competitive markets with two general classes of policies: those that aim to lower prices for the benefit of consumers, and those that aim to raise prices for the benefit of producers. Such policies can give rise to deadweight losses that can be quite large but they may also make some individuals in the economy better off while making others worse off. In this chapter, we will focus on providing a framework within which you can conduct policy analysis on your own.

Let's revisit our picture of a competitive market equilibrium to illustrate how the benefits of market interactions are distributed by the market process between producers and consumers, or workers and employers. To keep the analysis as simple as possible, focus on the special case where individual tastes are quasilinear in the good on which we are focusing. This will permit us to abstract away from the difference between marginal willingness to pay curves and demand curves and from general equilibrium considerations, and measure consumer and worker surpluses on output demand and labour supply curves.

18A.1 Elasticities and the Division of Surplus

Markets do more than just allocate scarce goods and services. They also determine how large a benefit from interacting in markets accrues to different economic actors without anyone controlling the process, as long as all economic actors are small.Consider the market demand and supply picture in panel (a) of Graph 18.1, developed in Chapter 15. Here we have the equilibrium price p^* emerging from the intersection of a demand and supply curve, and because we are assuming that tastes are quasilinear in the good x, we can interpret the demand curve as an aggregate marginal willingness to pay curve. The shaded areas representing consumer and producer surplus represent the aggregate size of consumer and producer surplus that emerges in this market. These areas represent how much of a benefit from the market interactions accrues to consumers and producers, or how total surplus in the market is divided among producers and consumers. Within each of these areas, there are some consumers and some producers who benefit relatively more; in particular, those consumers who value the good highly and those producers who can produce the good at very low cost.

Graph 18.1 Different Distributions of Consumer and Producer Surplus in a Market

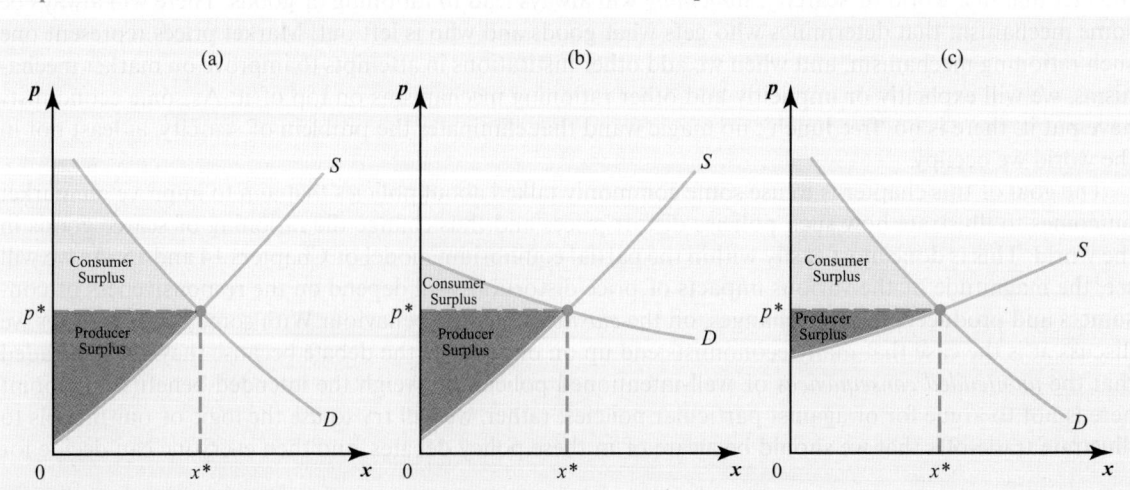

Panel (a) of Graph 18.1 illustrates a case where it appears that the overall social benefits created in this market are divided fairly evenly between consumers and producers. This is because of the particular way we have drawn these curves. Panels (b) and (c) illustrate how it is equally plausible that benefits are distributed very differently when demand and supply curves have different shapes. In panel (b), most of the benefits accrue to producers because the demand and marginal willingness to pay curve is relatively shallow, while in panel (c) the opposite is true because the demand curve is steep relative to the supply curve.

Exercise 18A.1

Knowing what you do from previous chapters, how would the social benefits from market interactions be distributed between producers and consumers in a long-run competitive equilibrium in which all producers face the same costs?

It would appear from Graph 18.1 that the relative division of society's surplus between consumers and producers depends on the relative slopes of demand and supply curves. This is correct, but economists have developed a somewhat better way of talking about this by using a concept known as price elasticity.

The problem with focusing solely on slopes of such curves is that slopes depend on the units we use to measure quantities on the horizontal and vertical axes. Do we measure prices, for instance, in euros or cents, in Swiss francs or the British pound? If the x good represents cola, do we measure it in cans, bottles or in litres? As we change these units, we change the slopes without changing the fundamental underlying economic content of the curves. *Elasticities* get around this by converting changes in behaviour from absolute changes to percentage changes.

18A.1.1 The Price Elasticity of Linear Demand Economists use the term elasticity to mean responsiveness. Elasticity refers to responsiveness in behaviour to changes in price or some other economic variable.

Consider first some extreme linear demand curves in Graph 18.2.

Graph 18.2 Perfectly Price Inelastic and Elastic Demand

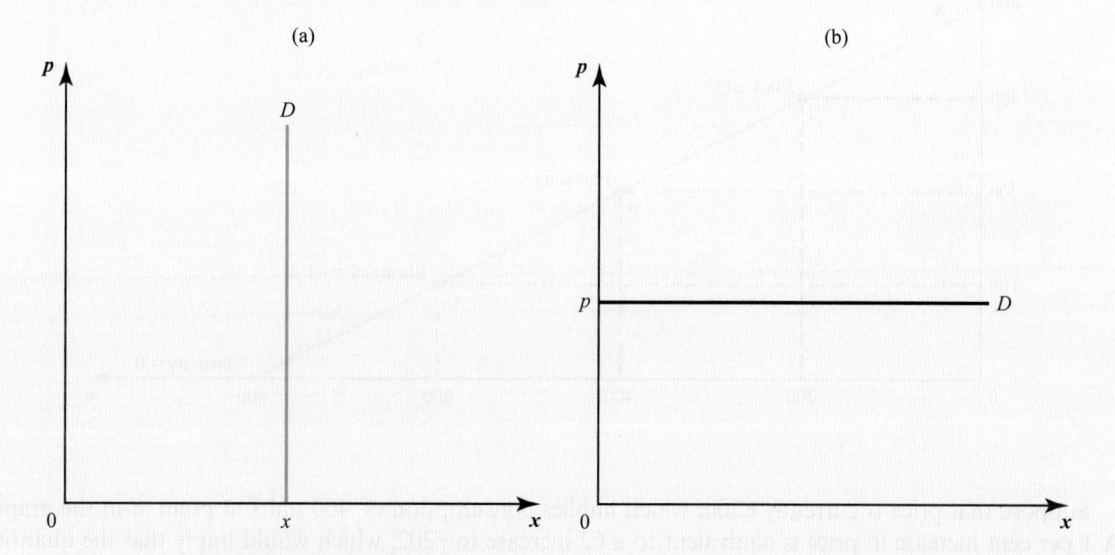

In panel (a), it does not matter what happens to the price of good x; the consumer will always buy exactly the same quantity. This is of course not an economic relationship that can persist for all levels of prices because it would imply that even as price goes to infinity the consumer would continue to purchase the same quantity of the good. Scarcity implies that eventually this demand curve must have a negative slope. Over the range of prices we have graphed, this consumer is extremely *unresponsive* to price changes, or we will say that the consumer's price elasticity of demand is zero and demand is *perfectly price inelastic*. In panel (b), on the other hand, even a miniscule increase in price from p will cause the consumer to no longer consume any of good x. Again, it can't be that this perfectly horizontal relationship between price and quantity persists forever because that would imply that the consumer is willing to buy an infinite amount of x at price p. Eventually, the demand curve must again have a negative slope. Over the range of quantity graphed in panel (b), this consumer is extremely responsive to increases in price. We will say that the consumer's price elasticity is minus infinity or their demand is *perfectly price elastic*.

Exercise 18A.2

True or False: If an individual consumer's demand curve is perfectly inelastic, the good is borderline between regular inferior and Giffen.

Real demand curves are not this extreme, and the concept of price elasticity becomes a little subtler along less extreme demand curves. Consider the particular linear demand curve in Graph 18.3. With the units we are using in the graph, this demand curve has a slope of $-1/2$ everywhere, indicating that whenever price goes up by €1, the quantity demanded falls by 2. Suppose we asked: With a 1 per cent change in price, how responsive is demand to a change in price?

Graph 18.3 Price Elasticity Along a Linear Demand Curve

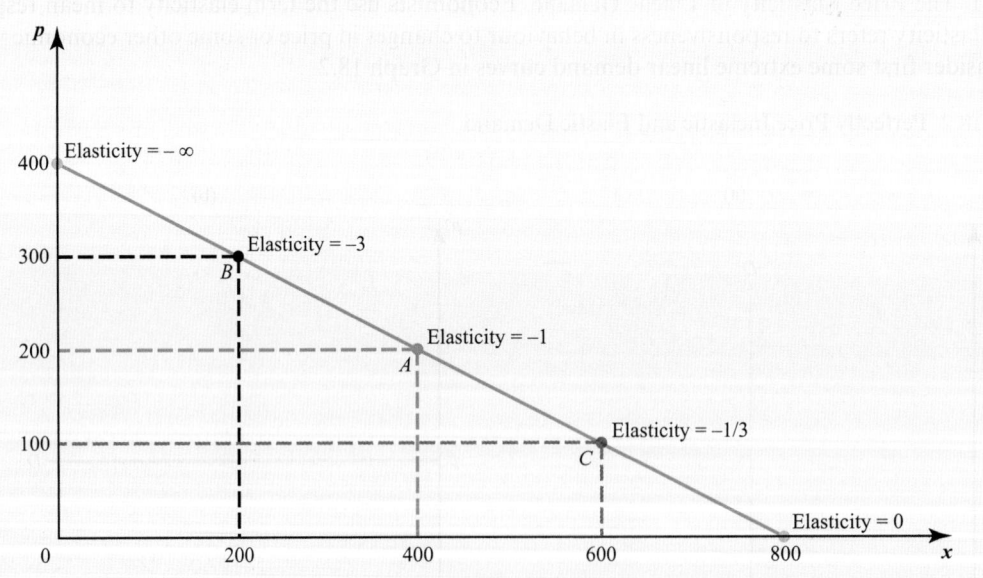

Suppose that price is currently €200, which implies consumption of 400 units at point A in the graph. A 1 per cent increase in price is equivalent to a €2 increase to €202, which would imply that the quantity demanded falls by 4 to 396. That is a 1 per cent drop in quantity from the original 400. When the price starts at 200, a 1 per cent change in the price leads to a 1 per cent change in the quantity demanded. If we had instead started at a price of €300 (point B), a 1 per cent increase in the price would be equal to a €3 increase, which would lead to a drop in the quantity demanded from 200 to 194, or a 3 per cent drop. Had we started at a price of €100, on the other hand, a 1 per cent increase in price would be equivalent to a €1 increase, leading to a drop in the quantity demanded from 600 to 598, or only a one-third of 1 per cent drop in quantity.

The *price elasticity of demand is defined as the percentage change in quantity resulting from a 1 per cent change in price*. Based on what we just calculated, the price elasticity of demand for the demand curve in Graph 18.3 is −1 at point A, −3 at point B and −1/3 at point C. While the absolute response to a €1 price change is the same at all of these points, in each case leading to a 2 unit drop in quantity, the *percentage change* in the quantity demanded differs depending on where along the demand curve we are measuring it. Because we are measuring price elasticity in percentage changes, it is immune to any change in the units we use to measure either quantity or price.

Exercise 18A.3

The price in Graph 18.3 is measured in euros. What would the demand curve look like if instead we measured price in terms of cents? Can you recalculate price elasticity at 200, 400 and 600 units of output and demonstrate that you get the same answers we just derived?

More generally, we can calculate approximate price elasticities for particular portions of demand curves whenever we are given at least two points on the demand curve. Suppose that we did not know the full demand curve in Graph 18.3 but only knew that consumers demand 600 units of x when price is €100 (point C) and 200 units of x when price is €300 (point B). We can then apply the following formula to calculate the approximate price elasticity at the midpoint between the two points you are given:

$$\text{Price elasticity at midpoint} = \frac{(\text{Change in } x)/(\text{Average } x)}{(\text{Change in } p)/(\text{Average } p)} = \frac{\Delta x/x_{avg}}{\Delta p/p_{avg}}. \quad (18.1)$$

In our example, this translates to:

$$\text{Price elasticity at } €200 = \frac{(600-200)/(400)}{(100-300)/(200)} = -1. \quad (18.2)$$

The negative sign indicates that quantity and price move in opposite directions as they do whenever demand curves slope down. Knowing that the price elasticity of demand is equal to −1 at a price of €200 means that when price is equal to €200, a 1 per cent increase in price leads to a 1 per cent decline in quantity, or alternatively, a 1 per cent decline in price leads to a 1 per cent increase in quantity. Notice that this is what we calculated when we knew the whole demand curve and calculated the elasticity of demand at point A at the price €200. The reason that the answer is *exactly* the same for our approximation formula is that the underlying demand curve is linear. The formula would give only an approximate answer whenever demand curves have curvature to them.

Exercise 18A.4

True or False: Unless a good is a Giffen good, price elasticity of demand is negative.

For any linear demand curve, the price elasticity of demand is −1 at the midpoint of the demand curve, less than −1 above the midpoint, and greater than −1 below the midpoint. The price elasticity of demand approaches zero as we approach the horizontal axis and minus infinity as we approach the vertical axis.

18A.1.2 Price Elasticity and Consumer Spending Whether a consumer *spends* more or less on consumption of a particular good when price increases depends on how responsive they are to changes in price. If they are relatively unresponsive, they may end up buying less of the good but still *spend more* than before because they pay a higher price for those units of the good they continue to buy. If, on the other hand, they are very responsive to the price change, they will end up buying sufficiently less so as to make their overall spending on the good decline despite the fact that each unit of the good costs more.

The impact of price changes on consumer spending depends on the price elasticity of demand. The three panels of Graph 18.4 replicate the linear demand curve we first graphed in Graph 18.3. In each panel, we consider an increase in the price of good x by €50, but in panel (a) the consumer finds themselves on the portion of their demand curve that has price elasticity between −1 and 0, in panel (b) they find themselves on the portion that has price elasticity of approximately −1, and in panel (c) they find themselves on the portion that has price elasticity of less than −1. Total spending at any given price is the price times the quantity consumed, or the rectangle formed by the vertical distance of the price and the horizontal distance of the quantity. The shaded dark brown area represents the decrease in spending that results from purchasing less of x as price increases, while the shaded dark blue area represents the increase in spending on those units of x that they continue to buy. The difference between the dark blue and dark brown areas is the increase in overall spending.

Graph 18.4 Price Elasticity and Changes in Consumer Spending

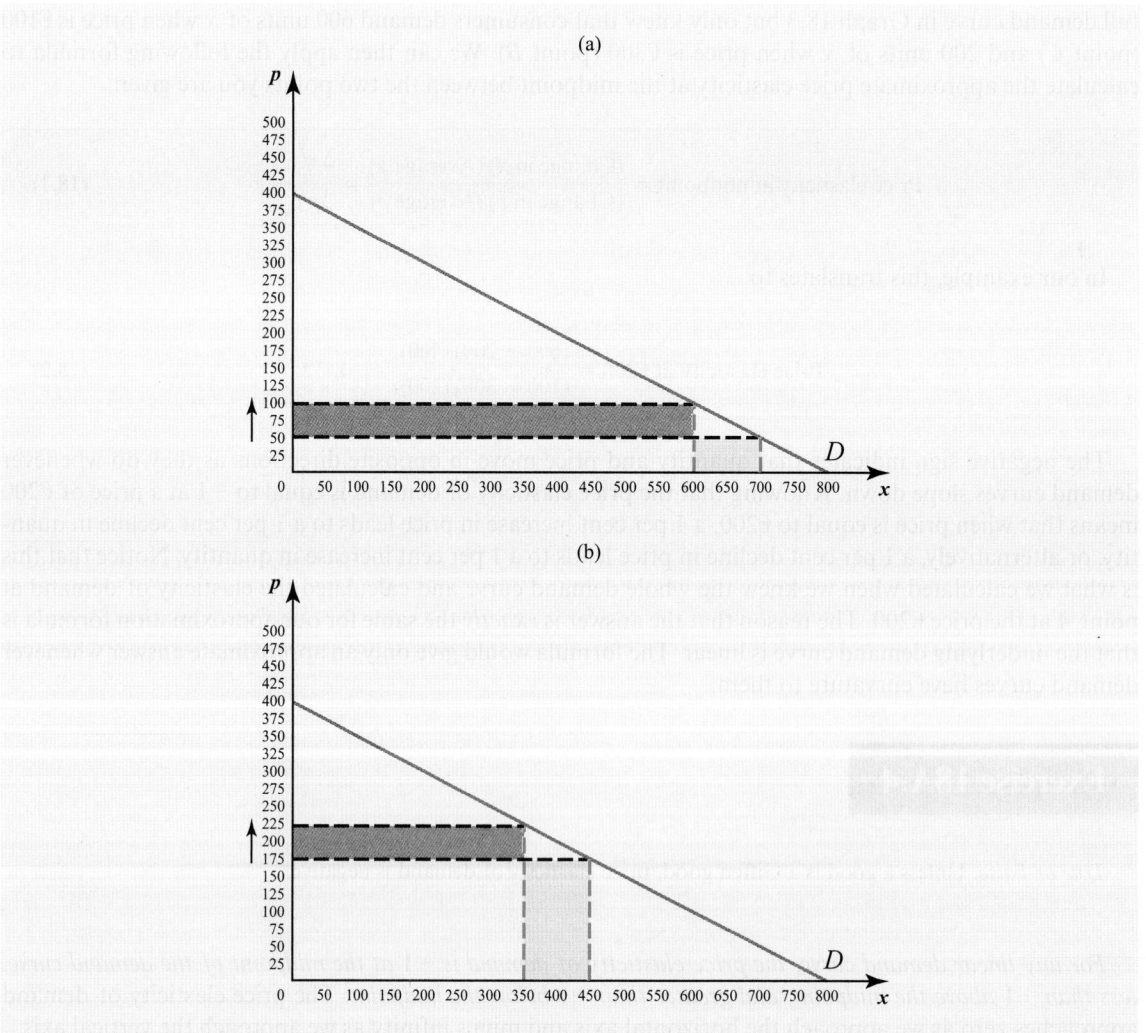

Graph 18.4 (continued)

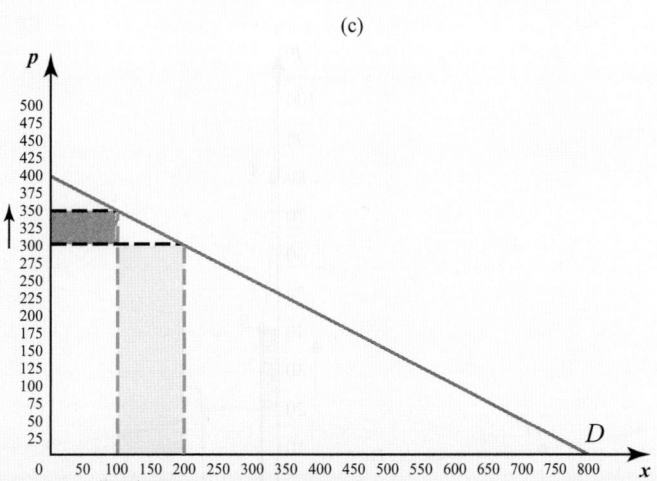

(c)

Notice that the two shaded areas are of equal size in panel (b), indicating no net change in spending, but the dark blue area is bigger than the dark brown area in panel (a), indicating a net increase in spending, while the reverse is true in panel (c), indicating a net decrease in spending. Given the numbers in the graph, a calculation of these areas confirms this.

Exercise 18A.5

Calculate the total spending the consumer undertakes at each of the two prices in panels (a) to (c) of Graph 18.4 and identify the magnitude and direction of the change in overall spending on good x.

We are finding that *consumer spending on a good increases with an increase in price when the price elasticity is between* -1 *and* 0, *stays the same when the price elasticity is* -1, *and decreases when the price elasticity is less than* -1. If quantity drops by 1 per cent whenever price increases by 1 per cent, the consumer buys 1 per cent fewer goods but pays 1 per cent more on those they buy, leaving overall spending constant. It follows that a larger drop in quantity demanded will cause spending to decline and a smaller drop will cause spending to increase. We say that *demand is relatively price inelastic* or relatively unresponsive to price changes *when the price elasticity lies between* -1 *and* 0, and *demand is relatively price elastic* or relatively responsive to price changes *when the price elasticity of demand is below* -1.

18A.1.3 Price Elasticities for Non-Linear Demand Curves Since price elasticity varies between 0 and negative infinity along linear demand curves that have the same negative slope everywhere, it is not surprising that price elasticity in general will be quite different at different points on demand curves more generally. We already illustrated two exceptions to this in Graph 18.2 where we illustrated demand curves that have price elasticity of 0 and minus infinity everywhere. A third example of a demand curve that has the same price elasticity everywhere is the demand curve depicted in panel (a) of Graph 18.5, which has price elasticity of -1 everywhere. At all the four points *A*, *B*, *C* and *D*, total consumer spending is €800. Such a demand curve is sometimes referred to as having the property of *unitary price elasticity*.

Graph 18.5 Constant Price Elastic Demand Curves

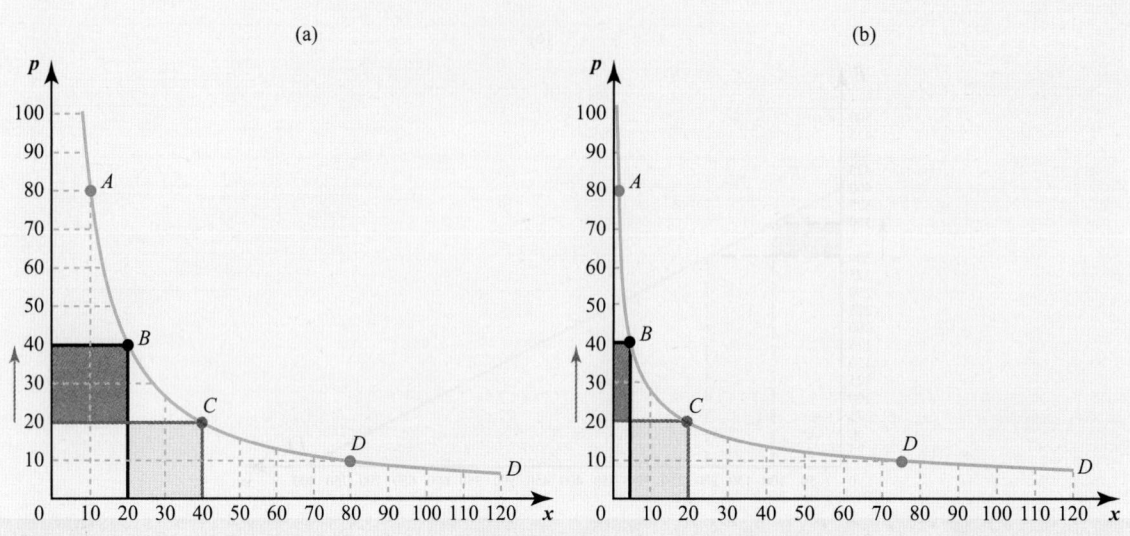

The set of constant elasticity demand curves is not limited to demand curves that have 0, minus infinity or −1 as the constant elasticity. The constant elasticity could be any negative number. For instance, panel (b) of the graph illustrates a demand curve with constant price elasticity of −2.

Exercise 18A.6

The diamond industry's marketing efforts have convinced many of the convention that an engagement ring should always cost the lucky groom exactly 3 months' salary. What does this imply about the price elasticity of demand for diamond size that the diamond industry is attempting to persuade us we should have?

18A.1.4 Other Elasticities Elasticities are measures of responsiveness to changes in economic variables. We have looked at the change in a consumer's demand for a good when that good's price changes. We can similarly define the responsiveness of a consumer's demand with respect to changes in other prices, and we refer to such measures as cross-price elasticities. We can also define income elasticities of demand, or how much the quantity demanded changes as income changes by 1 per cent.

Exercise 18A.7

Is the income elasticity of demand positive or negative? *Hint*: Does your answer depend on whether the good is inferior or normal?

Exercise 18A.8

What kind of good does x have to be in order for the demand for x to be perfectly income inelastic?

Exercise 18A.9

In a two-good model, is the cross-price elasticity of demand for good x_1 positive or negative if x_1 is a regular inferior good? *Hint*: Is the cross-price demand curve for good x_1 upward or downward sloping?

Consumers are not the only economic actors in an economy that respond to changes in economic variables. The responsiveness of *producers* to changes in prices can similarly be illustrated using the concept of price elasticity in exactly the same way using exactly the same formula. We begin by illustrating perfectly elastic and perfectly inelastic supply curves that would look exactly the same way as the perfectly elastic and inelastic demand curves in Graph 18.2. We can analyze the price elasticity of supply along a linear, upward-sloping supply curve, and find that the price elasticity in general will vary along such a curve. Unlike price elasticities of demand, when the underlying good is not a Giffen good, however, price elasticities of supply are positive numbers because an increase in price causes producers to produce *more* whereas it causes consumers to typically consume *less*.

Exercise 18A.10

Given what you learned in Chapter 13, is the price elasticity of supply for a competitive firm larger or smaller in the long run than in the short run?

Exercise 18A.11

Given what you learned in Chapter 14, what is the price elasticity of industry supply in the long run when all firms have identical costs?

Exercise 18A.12*

Suppose a supply curve is linear and starts at the origin. What is its price elasticity of supply?

Finally, we can consider the responsiveness of workers to changes in wages, or the responsiveness of savers to changes in interest rates. This gives us the concepts of wage elasticity of labour supply and interest rate elasticity of capital supply. We could similarly talk of concepts like wage elasticity of labour demand and rental rate elasticity of capital demand on the producer side.

Exercise 18A.13

If labour supply curves are backward bending in the sense that they are upward sloping for low wages and downward sloping for high wages, how does the wage elasticity of labour supply change as wage increases?

Exercise 18A.14

True or False: The wage elasticity of labour demand is always negative.

18A.2 Price Floors

We now investigate some common government policies that are aimed directly at altering the price used for trading between buyers and sellers in the market. One such policy involves the setting of a price floor. *A price floor is a minimum legal price the government mandates in a particular market, making all trades at prices below this price floor illegal.* Such a price floor will have no impact at all on the market if it is set below the equilibrium price because the market would automatically set a price above the floor with trading between buyers and sellers occurring at that market price. For instance, if the market price for door handles is €10 per pack and the government sets a price floor of €5, the policy has no impact since the market 'wants to' trade above €5 anyhow. It will, however, have an impact if the price floor is set *above* the equilibrium price because then the market price becomes illegal, with buyers and sellers forced to trade at a price above the price that would otherwise have arisen in the market.

As a result of the imposition of a price floor above the equilibrium price, a *surplus* of goods will emerge until some *non-price rationing* mechanism allocates the quantity of the good that is produced among the consumers who demand *less than* that quantity at the price floor. This is depicted in Graph 18.6 where the price floor p^f is set above the intersection of the market demand and market supply curve. Reading the quantity demanded x_d off the demand curve and the quantity supplied x_s off the supply curve, we see that $x_s > x_d$ at p^f. Because the government has interfered with the price mechanism that ensures $x_d = x_s$ at the equilibrium price p^*, producers are willing to supply more of the good at the higher price p^f than consumers are willing to buy at that price. The price floor has caused the market to enter a state of *disequilibrium*.

Graph 18.6 Disequilibrium Caused by a Price Floor

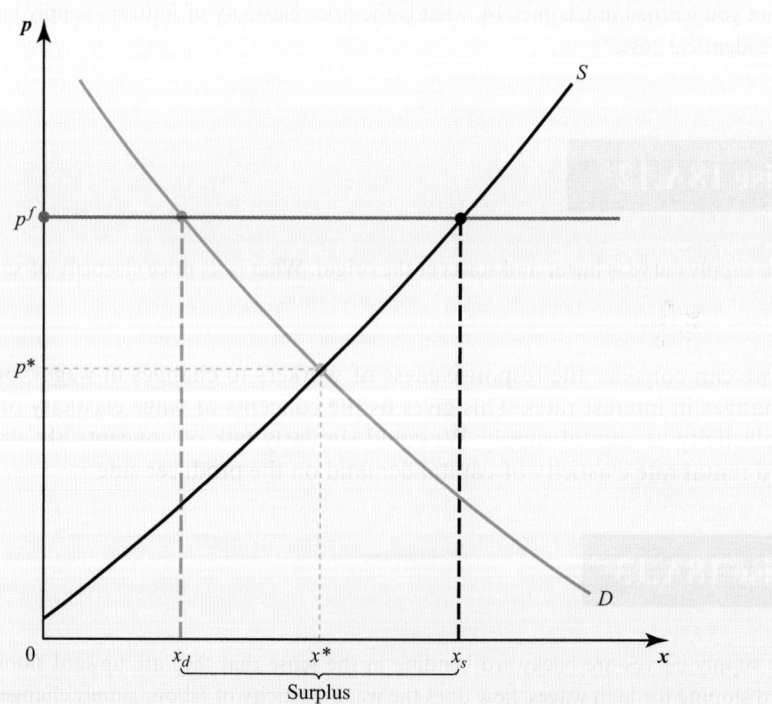

It cannot, however, be the case that suppliers will perpetually produce more than they can sell simply because the government has set a price above the equilibrium price. This would mean that producers are perpetually producing goods they cannot sell, which is inconsistent with the requirement that economic actors will do the best they can given their circumstances. Thus, *an equilibrium is not reached until some non-price mechanism emerges that ensures the quantity demanded is equal to the quantity supplied once again*. Such a mechanism could be constructed on purpose by a government that recognizes the disequilibrium caused by the imposition of the price floor, or, in the absence of government action, it will arise independently through some other form of non-price rationing that restores the market to a new equilibrium.

Exercise 18A.15

How does the size of the disequilibrium surplus change with the price elasticity of supply and demand?

18A.2.1 Non-Price Rationing in the Market Under Price Floors Consider the case where the government does not explicitly attempt to solve the disequilibrium created by the price floor. Given that producers now know that all producers together will attempt to sell more goods at the price floor than consumers demand, each individual producer has an incentive to expend additional effort attempting to convince consumers to buy from them. This additional effort represents an additional cost to producers, whether it takes the form of aggressive advertising or lobbying the government for special advantages that will cause consumers to purchase from one producer rather than from another. Whatever form the additional effort takes, the MC and AC curves for producers will shift up, which in turn causes the market supply curve to shift up until it intersects market demand at the quantity x_d. If producers in the market initially face different cost curves, we would expect those producers who face lower costs to be the ones who can most easily absorb the additional cost of expending effort to attract consumers, with other producers exiting the market.

Exercise 18A.16

Using the combination of industry and firm curves employed in Chapter 14, illustrate what happens to each firm's cost curves as a result of the imposition of a price floor.

Panel (a) of Graph 18.7 depicts a shift in market supply resulting from the shifts in individual cost curves, with the supply curve S representing the pre-price floor supply and S' the post-price floor market supply. Any less of a shift in the supply curve will still result in more being supplied than is demanded at the price floor, implying the market continues to be in disequilibrium with producers producing goods that they cannot sell. In the new equilibrium, it therefore has to be the case that costs shift up by the distance of the arrow in panel (a) of Graph 18.7, a distance equal to $(p^f - p')$. This is a new equilibrium because demand is once again equal to supply, with both producers and consumers once again doing the best they can given their changed circumstances. Consumers are buying bundles on their new budget constraints that incorporate the increase in price where their marginal willingness to pay, i.e. their MRS, is equal to the new price or where they are at a corner solution at which they no longer purchase x, while producers produce where the new price intersects with their new MC, or they exit the market altogether.

The reduction in market output depends not only on how high the government sets the price floor but also on the price elasticity of demand. In panel (b), for instance, the price floor is set exactly the same as in panel (a) but demand is depicted as more responsive to price – more price elastic – than in panel (a). As a result, x_d falls significantly more, causing more firms to exit the market as a substantially larger shift in supply is required to bring the market back to an equilibrium where producers do not produce a surplus quantity. In panel (c), on the other hand, demand is depicted as more price inelastic, resulting in a significantly smaller decrease in output in the market as producers do not have to expend as much effort to attract the remaining consumers.

Graph 18.7 Restoring Equilibrium Through Increased Costs for Producers

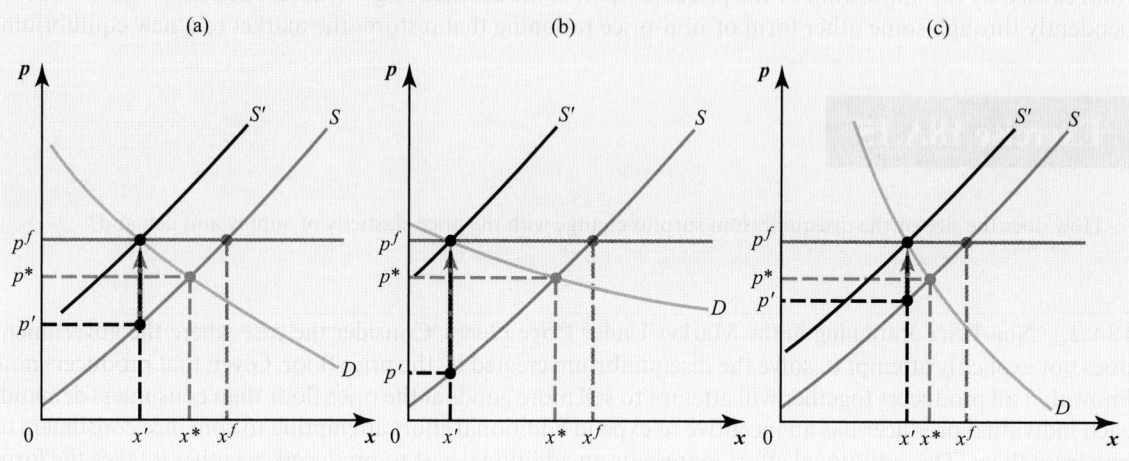

Exercise 18A.17

Depict the impact of a price floor on the quantity produced by the market when demand is perfectly price elastic. Repeat for the case when demand is perfectly price inelastic.

Exercise 18A.18

What is p' in long-run equilibrium when all firms face the same costs?

18A.2.2 Non-Price Rationing by Government Under Price Floors Alternatively, the government is often quite aware of the fact that setting price floors will result in reductions in market output and therefore accompanies price floor policies with additional government programmes to counteract the market's response. This has, for instance, been common in programs known as farm price supports, programmes under which the authorities, such as the European Union, not only sets a price floor for certain farm products but guarantees that it will purchase any surplus that producers cannot sell at the price floor.

When such a programme is implemented, producers no longer have an incentive to expend additional effort to attract consumers because they know they can always sell whatever remains to the government at the price p^f. As a result, the market supply curve does not shift, producers produce x_s in Graph 18.6, and consumers buy x_d. The difference between these two quantities is purchased by the authorities. Producers in the market do the best they can, as do consumers who will reduce how much they consume given the increased price, and a new equilibrium emerges in which $x_d < x_s$ while the government purchases the resulting surplus.

Exercise 18A.19

Would you expect any entry or exit of producers as a result of the imposition of a price floor when it is comple-mented by a government programme that guarantees surpluses will be purchased by the government at the price floor?

Exercise 18A.20

How will the amount that the government has to purchase change with price elasticities of demand and supply?

18A.2.3 Changes in Surplus and the Emergence of *DWL* From Price Floors By maintaining our assump-tion that consumer tastes are quasilinear in the good x, and demand curves can therefore be interpreted as marginal willingness to pay curves, we can analyze within the market supply and demand pictures how overall surplus in the market changes as a new equilibrium emerges under price floors. Graph 18.8 rep-licates Graph 18.6 but labels different areas within the graph to help identify the various surpluses that emerge under the two types of equilibria that may emerge under price floors. We begin by identifying the surpluses that exist in the absence of a price floor when x^* is produced in the market and sold at p^*. Con-sumer surplus is given by the area $(a + b + c)$ and producer surplus by the area $(d + e + f)$.

Graph 18.8 Changes in Costs and Surplus When Price Floors Are Imposed

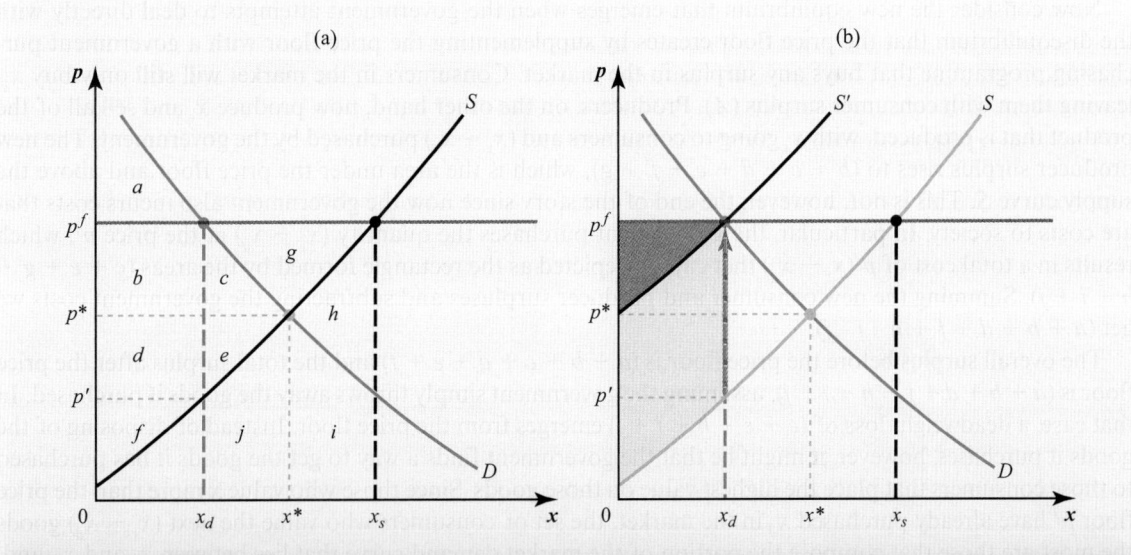

Go to MindTap to interact with this graph

Now consider the new equilibrium under the price floor when the government does not supplement the imposition of a price floor with any additional programmes and the supply curve therefore shifts as producers face higher costs when expending effort to attract the smaller number of consumers. Consum-ers will purchase only x_d, leaving them with a surplus of area (A). Without explicitly drawing in the shifted supply curve, it is a little trickier to see what happens to producer surplus, but once you see it, the picture is a lot more manageable without explicitly shifting the supply curve.

As illustrated in panel (a) of Graph 18.7 and again in panel (b) of Graph 18.8, the shift in supply is caused by an increase of $(p^f - p')$, i.e. the length of the arrow in marginal costs. In panel (b) of Graph 18.8, the shaded dark blue area represents the new producer surplus while the shaded dark brown area represents the additional costs that producers incur. We can find these same quantities in panel (a) without drawing in the new supply curve by recognizing that once we subtract the additional costs producers incur, they really receive a price p' for each of the goods they produce. By netting out the additional cost this way, we can measure the remaining marginal costs that have not changed because of the imposition of the price floor along the original supply curve. Area (f) is identical to the shaded dark blue area in panel (b), and area $(b + d)$ is equivalent to the shaded dark brown area in panel (b).

We have concluded that the sum of consumer and producer surplus shrinks from the initial $(a + b + c + d + e + f)$ to $(a + f)$. What happens to $(b + d)$, the increased costs faced by producers, depends on what exact form these costs take. For instance, it could be spent on advertising that provides little information to consumers and is thus socially wasteful, or it could represent transfers to individuals in the economy who benefit from receiving payment. It is therefore likely that some of $(b + d)$ is socially wasteful but some represents a transfer from producers to someone else in the economy. Area $(c + e)$, on the other hand, is unambiguously lost. Thus, the deadweight loss (DWL) from the imposition of the price floor and the resulting emergence of a new equilibrium is at least $(c + e)$ but may be as large as $(b + c + d + e)$.

Exercise 18A.21

How does the deadweight loss change as the price elasticity of demand changes?

Now consider the new equilibrium that emerges when the government attempts to deal directly with the disequilibrium that the price floor creates by supplementing the price floor with a government purchasing programme that buys any surplus in the market. Consumers in the market will still only buy x_d, leaving them with consumer surplus (A). Producers, on the other hand, now produce x_s and sell all of the product that is produced, with x_d going to consumers and $(x_s - x_d)$ purchased by the government. The new producer surplus rises to $(b + c + d + e + f + g)$, which is the area under the price floor and above the supply curve S. This is not, however, the end of the story since now the government also incurs costs that are costs to society. In particular, the government purchases the quantity $(x_s - x_d)$ at the price p^f, which results in a total cost of $p^f(x_s - x_d)$ that can be depicted as the rectangle formed by the areas $(c + e + g + h + i + j)$. Summing the new consumer and producer surpluses and subtracting the government costs we get $(a + b + d + f + h - i - j)$.

The overall surplus before the price floor is $(a + b + c + d + e + f)$ and the total surplus after the price floor is $(a + b + d + f - h - i - j)$, assuming the government simply throws away the goods it purchased. In that case, a deadweight loss of $(c + e + h + i + j)$ emerges from the price floor. Instead of disposing of the goods it purchases, however, it might be that the government finds a way to get the goods it has purchased to those consumers that place the highest value on those goods. Since those who value x more than the price floor p^f have already purchased x_d in the market, the set of consumers who value the next $(x_s - x_d)$ goods the most are those that compose the portion of the market demand curve that lies between x_d and x_s, and, since in our example we can interpret the demand curve as the marginal willingness to pay curve, the value these consumers place on the quantity of x the government has purchased can be read off the graph as the area below the demand curve between the quantities x_d and x_s. This area is given by $(c + e + i + j)$. If the government finds a way to get the goods it purchased to those who value them most rather than dispose of those goods, the government can recover $(c + e + i + j)$ in surplus. Subtracting this from the deadweight loss calculated when the government throws away the goods it purchased, we would then be left with a deadweight loss of area (h). Depending on how good the government is at getting the surplus it purchases to consumers who value x, the deadweight loss may therefore be as little as (h) or as high as $(c + e + h + i + j)$.

Exercise 18A.22

How does the deadweight loss change in size as the price elasticity of demand and supply changes?

A common example of a price floor is the minimum wage. The *minimum wage* is a price floor that has an impact on labour markets where the equilibrium wage falls below the minimum wage the government requires employers to pay to employees. Such labour markets are typically those involving relatively low skilled labour. Using the tools developed in this section, you can now analyze the impact of minimum wage laws on workers and producers in such labour markets.

18A.3 Price Ceilings

While price floors represent attempts by the government to impose prices above the equilibrium price, *price ceilings* are intended to place a cap on prices below the equilibrium price. More specifically, *price ceilings are legally mandated maximum prices*, with any trades made at prices above the price ceiling illegal. If the price ceiling is set above the equilibrium price, it will have no effect since the market would set the normal equilibrium price below the price ceiling. As a result, the price ceiling only has an effect on the equilibrium if it is set *below* the market equilibrium price.

Consider the case of a price ceiling set at p^c below the market equilibrium p^* in Graph 18.9. This price ceiling makes the initial equilibrium price p^* illegal and forces producers to exchange goods with consumers at the legal maximum price p^c. At that price, producers in the market are only willing to produce x_s, a quantity below x_d that consumers would like to purchase. As a result, a *shortage* emerges in the market, with $(x_d - x_s)$ more demanded than supplied. The market is in disequilibrium with less produced than is demanded.

Exercise 18A.23

How does the shortage that emerges in disequilibrium change as price elasticities of demand and supply change?

Graph 18.9 Disequilibrium When Price Ceilings Are Imposed

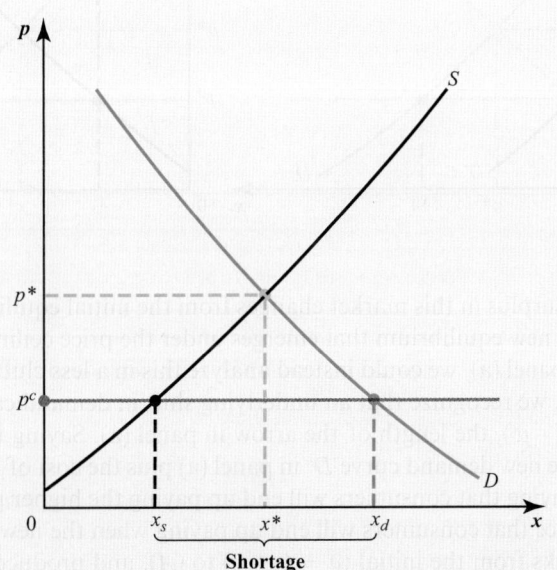

Whenever a shortage of goods emerges in disequilibrium, some form of non-price rationing must take the place of market price rationing to allocate the existing goods among consumers who want them. Non-price rationing can be the result of some deliberate mechanism designed by the government, or it can emerge without central direction. In either case, something or someone has to decide who gets the limited quantity of goods that is produced under the price ceiling, and a new equilibrium in which the quantity demanded is equal to the quantity supplied must emerge.

18A.3.1 Non-Price Rationing Under Price Ceilings In the case of surpluses generated by price floors, we said that producers will need to expend some additional effort to convince consumers to buy from them rather than from someone else. This caused the marginal costs of producers to increase, thus shifting the market supply curve until the new equilibrium was reached. In the case of shortages generated by price ceilings, on the other hand, consumers are the ones who will have to expend some additional effort since there are too few goods produced to meet demand. This additional effort will impose costs on consumers who, as a result, will have a lower marginal willingness to pay for each of the goods produced. This means that the demand curve will shift downwards as consumers take into account the additional cost of effort expended to get the limited quantity of goods produced. This effort may take a variety of forms, including standing in line, getting on waiting lists or even bribing producers or government officials to ensure that you are high enough up the waiting list to get the goods you would like.

Consider panel (a) of Graph 18.10. In order for the market to reach a new equilibrium in which all economic actors do the best they can given their economic circumstances, the initial demand curve D must shift downwards, as consumers expend effort, to the new demand curve D' where the quantity demanded is once again equal to the quantity supplied. The per-unit cost of the effort that is expended in the new equilibrium is equal to the vertical distance of the light blue arrow.

Graph 18.10 The Impact of Price Ceilings with Non-Price Rationing

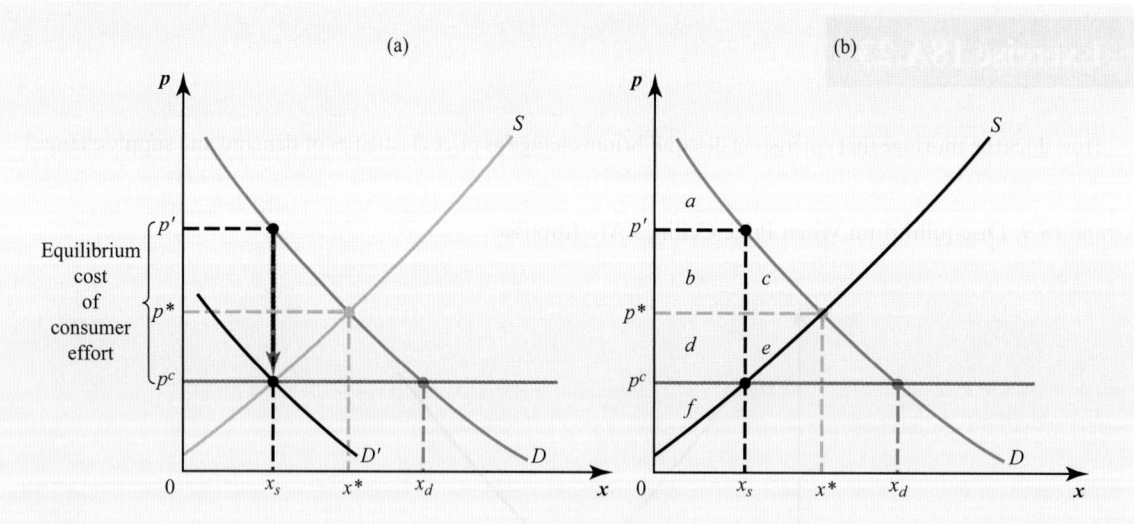

We can determine how surplus in this market changes from the initial equilibrium formed by the intersection of S and D and the new equilibrium that emerges under the price ceiling. Rather than shifting the demand curve as we do in panel (a), we could instead analyze this in a less cluttered graph such as the one depicted in panel (b). Here, we recognize that an underlying shift in demand causes consumers to have to expend effort that costs $(p' - p^c)$, the length of the arrow in panel (a). Saying that consumers will end up paying the price p^c along the new demand curve D' in panel (a) plus the cost of effort indicated by the light blue arrow is the same as saying that consumers will end up paying the higher price p' along their original demand curve. The real price that consumers will end up paying when the new equilibrium emerges is p'.

Consumer surplus shrinks from the initial $(a + b + c)$ to (A), and producer surplus shrinks from the initial $(d + e + f)$ to (f). Whether someone in the economy gets the area $(b + d)$ now depends on the exact nature of the non-price rationing that results in the new equilibrium. For instance, suppose that goods are allocated by individuals spending time standing in line. The cost of standing in line is of no benefit to anyone else in the economy and $(b + d)$ becomes a deadweight loss. If, on the other hand, side payments or bribes are permitted to ensure someone who really wants the goods gets them, the per-unit cost of the light blue arrow is a cost to the consumer but a benefit for whoever gets the bribe. In that case, the additional cost to the consumer is a benefit to someone else in the economy and thus not a deadweight loss. The area $(c + e)$, however, cannot be recovered by anyone in the economy because the goods that created this surplus are no longer produced. The overall deadweight loss from the price ceiling will lie between $(c + e)$ and $(b + c + d + e)$ depending on the precise form of non-price rationing that supports the new equilibrium. It is possible that the deadweight loss gets even larger than that if the non-price rationing mechanism is, for instance, waiting in line and it is not permitted that people can pay for someone else to wait in line for them. This can occur if those who have the highest marginal willingness to pay for good x also have a high opportunity cost of time and therefore are not willing to spend the time waiting in line, thus causing individuals whose marginal willingness to pay is lower to be the ones standing in line.

Exercise 18A.24

How does the size of deadweight losses from price ceilings vary with the price elasticities of demand and supply?

18A.3.2 Government Programmes to Address Shortages Under Price Ceilings It is also possible that the government introduces some programme designed explicitly to address the disequilibrium shortage that results from the imposition of a price ceiling. Governments might purchase goods that are traded at price ceilings on the world market, where there is no price ceiling, then sell them at the price ceiling to domestic consumers. Such a programme can introduce yet more additional deadweight losses.

In the case of price ceilings, however, it is more likely that the government designs some more explicit rationing mechanism that determines who gets the limited quantity of the goods that are produced. For instance, some countries have rent control programmes that set a price ceiling on rents that can be charged in the housing market. Often, the shortages that emerge under such programmes are addressed not only by rationing through the use of waiting lists but also through some explicit criteria that those who can get on the waiting lists have to satisfy. No such programme can alter the fact, however, that interference with the market price mechanism results in deadweight losses.

18A.3.3 Ethical Considerations in Some Markets With Price Ceilings of Zero There are also some interesting examples of price ceilings in markets that most non-economists don't think of as markets at all, examples where the government sets a price ceiling of zero. Consider, for instance, the market for kidneys. There are large numbers of individuals at any one time waiting for a donated kidney to replace their own kidneys that are failing as a result of some kidney disease. Some have advocated that the government should permit healthy individuals to sell one of their kidneys, since it is in most cases quite possible for someone to function with only a single kidney, and thus establish a market in kidneys that will save the lives of many through the increased quantity of those available. Others have advocated a system in which healthy individuals could sell the right to their kidneys to organizations who could channel those kidneys to those in need in the event that the healthy individual dies unexpectedly. Instead, the government has placed a price ceiling of zero in the kidney market, allowing individuals to donate a kidney but not to sell one. Since such a price ceiling leads to a shortage of kidneys, a complex, dynamically adjusting waiting list system has been developed to ration kidneys in the absence of a market, with those in need of a kidney moving up on the list as their own kidneys function less and less well. Many die every year because of the limited number of kidneys that are donated.

We raise this here merely to point out that while price ceilings inevitably create often significant deadweight losses from too little being supplied, they are sometimes motivated by concerns that some important consequences of eliminating price ceilings have been left out of our models or by deeper ethical considerations that lie well outside the sphere of competence of an economist. Some, for instance, fear there are negative externalities from allowing kidneys to be traded in a market – that allowing the sale of organs will cheapen the way we look at one another and cause us to treat one another badly in other spheres of life. Such negative externalities are violations of the first welfare theorem, violations that might indeed provide an efficiency case for only allowing donations of kidneys. Alternatively, philosophers can offer ethical arguments that while beyond the scope of this book, must also be considered in any proposals that would eliminate the price ceiling on kidneys.

Should individuals be permitted to sell their own organs? From an economist's perspective, if a market price were to emerge for kidneys, those who would sell their kidneys would disproportionately come from poor backgrounds where an additional €50 000 or even €10 000 that healthy kidneys might fetch in the market could be quite tempting. Is that bad given that real lives will be saved in the process? Again, all the economist can do is say how behaviour will change as institutions change, but it is left to us in our role as non-economists to make some of the deeper ethical judgments. Similar issues emerge in other areas, such as the sale of human eggs and sperm for reproductive purposes; the sale of frozen human embryos created in fertility clinics but no longer desired by the couples from whom they were derived; the sale of embryos for research; or explicit pricing in adoption markets for children.

18A.4 The Politics of Concentrated Benefits and Diffuse Costs

While sometimes there are clear ethical considerations that motivate the imposition of price ceilings, such as in the case of kidney markets that we have just discussed, in many cases such ethical considerations do not appear to be the main motivators of price floors and price ceilings in the real world, especially if the full impact of such policies is analyzed. Rather, there may be cases where such policies emerge as different interest groups capture a part of the political process and thereby gain surplus they otherwise would not gain in the market. We will treat this more explicitly in Chapter 28, but for now we introduce a way that some economists and political scientists have developed for thinking about why certain policies that create clear deadweight losses are implemented and others are not.

The basic idea is that in political processes that can be influenced by interest groups that expend effort to change policy, *it is easier for particular interest groups to be effective when the benefits of the policy are concentrated among a small number of individuals while the costs are diffused over a large number*. Consider, for instance, a farm price support system modelled along the lines of a price floor accompanied by a government purchasing programme that buys any surplus that is produced at the price floor. Who benefits from such a programme, and who pays the costs? The beneficiaries are relatively concentrated: farmers who will be able to sell more goods at higher prices, whether to consumers or the government, and perhaps some who will end up getting the products purchased by the government, if the government sells the products at a reduced price to them. The set of those paying the costs, on the other hand, includes essentially everyone: all those who purchase farm products, who now pay higher prices, and all taxpayers who must fund the additional purchases made by the government.

It may appear initially counterintuitive that when the beneficiaries of a policy include only a few and the losers from the policy include many, a democratic process is more likely to implement such a policy. If the policy-making process is impacted by interest group efforts, and if such efforts require interest groups to organize and lobby, it becomes much easier to organize the few who will benefit a lot from a policy than the many who will suffer a little bit. Food prices may be only slightly higher as a result of farm price support policies, causing all of us to pay just a little bit more while often not even being aware of why it is that we are paying more. It will not be easy to organize all of us, but it may be much easier to organize a small number of farmers who benefit a lot if the policy is put in place. The politics of concentrated benefits and diffuse costs can explain how policies that benefit a few by a lot but hurt many by a little can be implemented even when the sum total of all the costs is significantly larger than the sum total of all the benefits.

This points out a major challenge to policy makers. Whenever the sum total of benefits of a programme is outweighed by the sum total of the costs, it should in principle be possible to make everyone better off by eliminating the programme and compensating the beneficiaries of the programme. In other words, *whenever there is a deadweight loss from a policy, it should in principle be possible to eliminate the policy in such a way as to make some people better off without making anyone worse off, or even to do it so that everyone is better off.* Doing so, however, and then keeping the policy from coming back when interest groups organize once again to lobby, is often a difficult political challenge when benefits are concentrated and costs diffuse.

18A.5 A Note on General Equilibrium Considerations

Our analysis of price distortions in this chapter is entirely within a partial equilibrium framework where we are implicitly assuming that the effects of price ceilings and price floors in one market do not spill over into other markets. It is worth noting, however, that a fuller analysis of such policies would ask whether such spillovers are likely to happen, and if so, how this would change our analysis of the impact of the policy. An example might clarify how such general equilibrium considerations might be important.

Consider the minimum wage where the standard prediction is that the minimum wage will lead to a decline in employment in labour markets that are affected by it, a possible increase in surplus for minimum wage workers who remain employed, a decrease in surplus for those who lose their jobs as a result, and an increase in costs for firms that employ minimum wage workers. Some economists, however, have argued that a full analysis of the effects of minimum wage laws must include a general equilibrium analysis of how the increased costs faced by firms get translated into other price changes in the economy. It is often the case that minimum wage workers work in industries whose goods and services are disproportionately consumed by low-income households. Since costs increase disproportionately for such firms, prices of their products will tend to increase disproportionately. Some households may therefore benefit in the labour market from increased earnings only to turn around and face higher prices for the goods they purchase. It is obviously quite complex to trace all general equilibrium price effects from an increase in the minimum wage through the economy and then conclude something about who ultimately benefits by how much, but in some cases we will miss important economic effects of price-distorting policies unless we engage in such an analysis.

Exercise 18A.25*

Consider our simple economy from Chapter 16 and suppose that the economy is currently in equilibrium with wage w^* and price p^*. If the government requires that no wage lower than kw^* (with $k > 1$) be paid in this economy, what will happen in order for this economy to return to equilibrium?

18B   The Mathematics of Elasticities and Price Distortions

The mathematics of price elasticities involves a conversion of the elasticity formula to calculus notation.

18B.1 Elasticities

As we discussed in Section A, elasticities are measures of responsiveness of economic behaviour to some economic variable. When we use the term price elasticity of demand, for instance, we mean the responsiveness of demand to changes in price. When we say income elasticity of demand, we mean the responsiveness of demand to changes in income, and when we say cross-price elasticity of demand, we mean the responsiveness of demand for one good with respect to changes in the price of another good.

18B.1.1 The Price Elasticity of Demand In Section A, we gave the non-calculus-based formula for deriving price elasticity of demand (denoted as ε_d here) from two points on the demand curve as:

$$\varepsilon_d = \frac{\Delta x / x_{avg}}{\Delta p / p_{avg}} = \frac{\Delta x p_{avg}}{\Delta p x_{avg}} \tag{18.3}$$

In the special case of linear demand, this formula gives a precise estimate of the price elasticity at the midpoint between those used in the formula; but in cases where demand is not linear, it only gives an approximation. The precise formula for deriving the price elasticity of demand at a given point on the demand curve is calculated for small changes in price and quantity, which in calculus notation means a change of the 'Δs' in equation (18.3) to 'ds'; that is:

$$\varepsilon_d = \frac{dx}{dp}\frac{p}{x(p)}, \tag{18.4}$$

where the average variables in the approximation formula are replaced by the actual levels of these variables at the point with price p and quantity $x(p)$ at which we are trying to evaluate the price elasticity.

Consider the linear demand curve graphed in Graph 18.3, which is given by the equation $p = 400 - (1/2)x$ or, written in terms of x:

$$x(p) = 800 - 2p. \tag{18.5}$$

Taking the derivative $dx/dp(= -2)$ and substituting it into the formula for price elasticity, we get a general expression for the price elasticity as:

$$\varepsilon_d = -2\left(\frac{p}{800 - 2p}\right) = \frac{-p}{400 - p}, \tag{18.6}$$

where we have used the demand function $x = 800 - 2p$ in the denominator. This allows us to express the price elasticity as a function of price.

Exercise 18B.1

Could you also express the price elasticity as a function of only quantity? *Hint*: Think of replacing the numerator rather than the denominator.

When price is 300, this equation tells us that the price elasticity at $p = 300$ is -3; when price is 200, the equation gives us a price elasticity of -1; and when price is 100, it gives us a price elasticity of $-1/3$. These values are identical to the ones we derived for points B, A and C in Graph 18.3.

Exercise 18B.2

Using the formula for price elasticity derived in exercise 18B.1, verify that you get the same price elasticity for x equal to 200, 400 and 600 corresponding to points B, A and C in Graph 18.3.

We can also show formally now that *when demand curves are linear, price elasticity will be equal to exactly -1 at the midpoint of the demand curve*. Suppose the demand curve is given by $p = A - \alpha x$; on our graph of the linear demand curve, the price intercept is A and the slope is $-\alpha$. We can rewrite this as a function $x(p) = (A - p)/\alpha$, and, employing our price elasticity formula, this implies $e_d = -p(A - p)$. Setting e_d to -1, we can solve for the price at which price elasticity is equal to -1 as $p = A/2$; that is, the price halfway between the vertical intercept A and 0, or the midpoint of the demand curve.

18B.1.2 Price Elasticity and Consumer Spending We next argued in Section A that consumer spending increases as price rises when price elasticity lies between -1 and 0, and consumer spending decreases as price rises when price elasticity is less than -1.

Let the demand function take the general form $x(p)$. Demand functions are generally functions of all prices as well as income. In a model of M, different consumption goods, for instance the general expression of the demand function for good x_p takes the form $x_i(p_1, p_2, \ldots, p_M, I)$. By denoting the demand function for good x as $x(p)$, we are implicitly just looking at a slice of the more general demand function that holds all prices other than the price for x as well as income fixed. Total consumer spending on x is price times quantity, or $TS = px(p)$, and the change in consumer spending that results from a small increase in price is given by the derivative of TS with respect to price. Using the chain rule, this can be written as:

$$\frac{d(TS)}{dp} = x(p) + p\frac{dx}{dp}. \tag{18.7}$$

Whenever this expression is equal to zero, i.e. whenever $p(dx/dp) = -x(p)$, consumer spending does not change when price increases by a small amount. We can rewrite $p(dx/dp) = -x(p)$ as:

$$\frac{p}{x(p)}\frac{dx}{dp} = -1, \tag{18.8}$$

where the left-hand side is our formula for price elasticity ε_d. Thus, consumer spending remains unchanged with a small change in price whenever $\varepsilon_d = -1$.

Similarly, consumer spending will increase with a small increase in price whenever $p(dx/dp) > -x(p)$, or, dividing both sides by $x(p)$, whenever:

$$\frac{p}{x(p)}\frac{dx}{dp} = \varepsilon_d > -1. \tag{18.9}$$

When demand is *price inelastic* ($\varepsilon_d > -1$), consumer spending rises with an increase in price and falls with a decrease in price.

Exercise 18B.3*

Demonstrate that $\varepsilon_d < -1$ implies that consumer spending will fall with an increase in price and rise with a decrease in price.

18B.1.3 Demand Curves With Constant Price Elasticity For many types of tastes, the demand curves that result from individual optimizing behaviour have constant price elasticity throughout rather than price elasticities that vary along the demand curve. Consider, for instance, quasilinear tastes that can be represented by the utility function $u(x_1, x_2) = \alpha \ln x_1 + x_2$. You can check for yourself that the demand function for x_1 will have the form:

$$x_1(p_1, p_2) = \frac{\alpha p_2}{p_1}. \tag{18.10}$$

Using our formula for calculating price elasticity of demand εd, we get:

$$\varepsilon_d = \frac{dx_1}{dp_1}\left(\frac{p_1}{x_1(p_1, p_2)}\right) = \left(\frac{-\alpha p_2}{p_1^2}\right)\left(\frac{p_1}{\alpha p_2/p_1}\right) = -\left(\frac{\alpha p_2}{p_1^2}\right)\left(\frac{p_1^2}{\alpha p_2}\right) = -1. \tag{18.11}$$

Thus, the tastes captured by this utility function give rise to a *unitary elastic* demand curve for the quasilinear good x_1.

Exercise 18B.4

What is the price elasticity of demand for x_1 and x_2 when tastes are Cobb–Douglas; that is, when tastes can be represented by the utility function $u(x_1, x_2) = x_1^\alpha x_2^{(1-\alpha)}$? *Hint*: Recall that the demand functions in this case are $x_1(p_1, I) = \alpha I/p_1$ and $x_2(p_2, I) = (1 - \alpha)I/p_2$).

While unitary elastic demand curves are an example of demand curves that have the same elasticity throughout, it is also possible to have demand curves that have constant elasticity different from -1. Consider the quasilinear tastes represented by the utility function $u(x_1, x_2) = \alpha x_1^\beta + x_2$. The demand function for x_1 can be derived as:

$$x_1(p_1, p_2) = \left(\frac{\alpha\beta p_2}{p_1}\right)^{1/(1-\beta)}. \tag{18.12}$$

Applying the elasticity formula, we get that $\varepsilon_d = -1/(1 - \beta)$. For instance, if $\beta = 0.5$, the demand curve for x_1 has constant price elasticity of -2 throughout. Examples of demand curves with constant price elasticity of -1 and -2 are given in Graph 18.5.

18B.1.4 Other Price Elasticities Elasticities represent a general concept that can refer to any change in economic behaviour resulting from a change in some economic variable. The income elasticity of demand – or the percentage change in quantity demanded from a 1 per cent change in income – is given by:

$$\varepsilon_I = \frac{dx}{dI}\frac{I}{x(I)}, \tag{18.13}$$

and the cross-price elasticity of demand of x_i with respect to the price p_j of some other good x_j is given by:

$$\varepsilon_{x_i, p_j} = \frac{dx_i}{dp_j}\frac{p_j}{x_i(p_j)}. \tag{18.14}$$

Similarly, we can write the price elasticity of supply as:

$$\varepsilon_s = \frac{dx_s}{dp}\frac{p}{x_s(p)}. \tag{18.15}$$

Exercise 18B.5

Can you see from the expression for income elasticities that the sign of the elasticity will depend on whether the good x is normal or inferior?

Exercise 18B.6

Can you see that the sign of the cross-price elasticity depends on the slope of the cross-price demand curve?

18B.2 Calculating Equilibria Under Price Floors and Price Ceilings

Once we understand the graphs surrounding the impact of price floors and price ceilings, we can calculate the various components of these graphs as long as demand and supply curves are linear. In what follows, we will quickly illustrate this for one example. It does, however, become a little more challenging to do this when demand and supply curves are not linear. In essence, we will have to use integral calculus to derive consumer and producer surpluses rather than adding up geometric areas as we can do for linear demand and supply curves. For those of you comfortable with integral calculus, we will therefore provide a second example with non-linear demand curves. Our examples will deal with price floors.

18B.2.1 Price Floors and Ceilings When Demand and Supply Are Linear Suppose that the demand curve is $p = A - \alpha x_d$ and the supply curve is described by $p = B + \beta x_s$. These curves are illustrated in Graph 18.11, with intercepts and slopes labelled accordingly. Writing these equations in terms of quantities as functions of prices, the demand and supply functions are:

$$x_d(p) = \frac{A - p}{\alpha} \quad \text{and} \quad x_s(p) = \frac{p - B}{\beta}. \tag{18.16}$$

Graph 18.11 Linear Demand and Supply

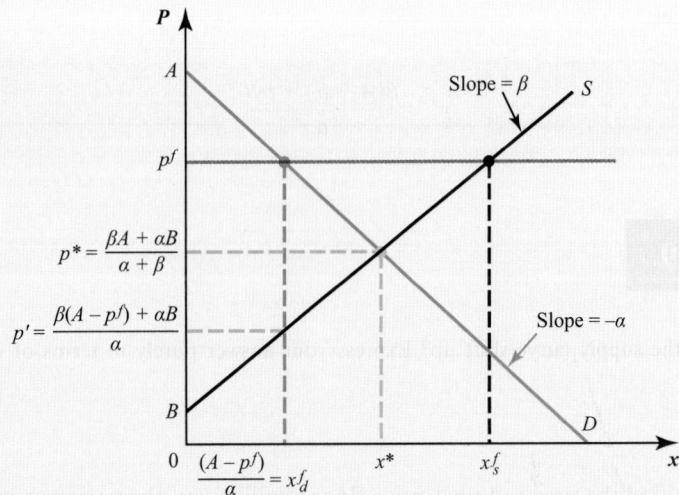

In equilibrium, in the absence of price distortions, $x_d(p) = x_s(p)$. Setting the two equations above equal to one another and solving for price, we get the equilibrium price p^*:

$$p^* = \frac{\beta A + \alpha B}{\alpha + \beta}.$$ (18.17)

Exercise 18B.7

Can you express x^* in Graph 18.11 in terms of the demand and supply parameters A, α, B and β?

Now suppose the government sets a *price floor* p^f above p^*. The quantity transacted in the market will then be determined by consumer demand at the higher price, and can be derived by substituting the price floor p^f into x_d to get $x_d(p^f) = (A - p^f)/\alpha$.

Exercise 18B.8

What is the surplus of x that exists in the initial disequilibrium?

From our work in Section A, we know that in the absence of any other programmes, producers will expend additional effort to sell their goods to the smaller number of consumers that are interested at the higher price. This additional effort is a cost to producers and thus shifts up the supply curve until it intersects the demand curve at p^f and at the quantity $(A - p^f)/\alpha$ demanded by consumers. The actual price p' that producers will receive net of the additional costs incurred in the new equilibrium has to satisfy the equation:

$$\frac{A - p^f}{\alpha} = \frac{p' - B}{\beta}.$$ (18.18)

Solving for p', we get:

$$p' = \frac{\beta(A - p^f) + \alpha B}{\alpha}.$$ (18.19)

Exercise 18B.9

By how much does the supply curve shift up? Express your answer purely in terms of demand and supply parameters and p^f.

Once we have identified the pre- and post-price floor equilibrium, the various consumer and producer surplus areas are calculated given the linear nature of demand and supply curves, since these areas are rectangles and squares. In Table 18.1, we put some numbers to this example by setting $A = 1000$, $B = 0$ and $\alpha = 10 = \beta$. As the price floor p^f increases, the quantity demanded and therefore the quantity transacted in the new equilibrium x_d^f falls, the price net of effort costs p' received by producers falls, as does consumer and producer surplus ($CS_{p'}$ and $PS_{p'}$). A lower and upper bound on how big the deadweight loss would be under each price floor is reported in the final columns, with the upper bound including the effort cost of producers.

Exercise 18B.10

Can you graphically illustrate why the lower and upper bounds of DWL ultimately converge as the price floor increases?

Exercise 18B.11

Can you express the total effort cost incurred by producers as a function of demand and supply parameters and p^f?

In the example of Table 18.1, demand and supply curves have the same slopes in absolute value, which accounts for the symmetry of the impact of price floors on producer and consumer surplus. Table 18.2 then reports the impact of a price floor of $p^f = €600$ for differently sloped demand and supply curves but with the pre-price floor equilibrium always having $p* = €500$ and $x* = 50$. In the first section of Table 18.2, the demand curve is unchanged, with intercept $A = 1000$ and slope $-\alpha = -10$, but the supply curve becomes shallower as the slope β falls while the intercept B is adjusted to keep the pre-price floor equilibrium unchanged. In the second part of Table 18.2, the supply curve is unchanged with intercept $B = 0$ and slope $\beta = 10$, while the slope α of the demand curve becomes shallower, and the intercept A is adjusted to keep the pre-price floor equilibrium unchanged. Finally, both demand and supply curves become shallower at the same time in the third part of Table 18.2.

Table 18.1 $A = 1000$, $B = 0$, $\alpha = \beta = 10$

			Equilibrium Under Price Floors With Linear Demand and Supply Curves					
p^f	x_d^f	P'	CS_{p*}	$CS_{p'}$	PS_{p*}	$PS_{p'}$	DWL_{low}	DWL_{high}
€500	50	€500	€12 500	€12 500	€12 500	€12 500	€0	€0
€600	40	€400	€12 500	€8000	€12 500	€8000	€1000	€9000
€700	30	€300	€12 500	€4500	€12 500	€4500	€4000	€16 000
€800	20	€200	€12 500	€2000	€12 500	€2000	€9000	€21 000
€900	10	€100	€12 500	€500	€12 500	€500	€16 000	€24 000
€1000	0	€0	€12 500	€0	€12 500	€0	€25 000	€25 000

Exercise 18B.12

For each of the three sections of Table 18.2, graphically illustrate the third row using the information in the table to label everything on the axes that you can label.

Table 18.2 Demand and Supply Parameters Set to Keep $p^* = 500$, $x^* = 50$, $p^f = 600$

Equilibrium Under Price Floors as Price Elasticities Change

$A = 1000$, $\alpha = 10$

β	B	x_d^f	CS_{p^*}	CS_{p^f}	PS_{p^*}	PS_{p^f}	DWL_{low}	DWL_{high}
10	0	40	€12 500	€8000	€12 500	€8000	€1000	€9000
8	100	40	€12 500	€8000	€10 000	€6400	€900	€8100
6	200	40	€12 500	€8000	€7500	€4800	€800	€7200
4	300	40	€12 500	€8000	€5000	€3200	€700	€6300
2	400	40	€12 500	€8000	€2500	€1600	€600	€5400
0	500	40	€12 500	€8000	€0	€0	€500	€4500

$B = 0$, $\beta = 10$

α	A	x_d^f	CS_{p^*}	CS_{p^f}	PS_{p^*}	PS_{p^f}	DWL_{low}	DWL_{high}
10	1000	40	€12 500	€8000	€12 500	€8000	€1000	€9000
8	900	37.50	€10 000	€5625	€12 500	€7031	€1406	€9844
6	800	33.33	€7500	€3333	€12 500	€5556	€2222	€11 111
4	700	25.00	€5000	€1250	€12 500	€3125	€4375	€13 125
2	600	0	€2500	€0	€12 500	€0	€15 000	€15 000

$B = 0 + \gamma$, $A = 1000 - \gamma$

$\alpha = \beta$	γ	x_d^f	CS_{p^*}	CS_{p^f}	PS_{p^*}	PS_{p^f}	DWL_{low}	DWL_{high}
10	0	40	€12 500	€8000	€12 500	€8000	€1000	€9000
8	100	37.50	€10 000	€5625	€10 000	€5625	€1250	€8750
6	200	33.33	€7500	€3333	€7500	€3333	€1667	€8333
4	300	25.00	€5000	€1250	€5000	€1250	€2500	€7500
2	400	0	€2500	€0	€2500	€0	€5000	€5000

Exercise 18B.13*

Why do the lower and upper bounds for *DWL* converge in the lower two sections of Table 18.2 but not in the top portion?

8B.2.2 Non-Linear Demands Calculating the impact of price ceilings and price floors when market demand and supply are not linear is quite similar to calculating these effects when the underlying functions are linear. The only exception is that we will have to employ integrals to precisely calculate consumer and producer surpluses. Consider the market demand and supply functions:

$$x_d(p) = \frac{40\,000\,000}{p^2} \text{ and } x_s(p) = 547\,192 p^{2/3}, \qquad (18.20)$$

which are identical to the demand and supply curves we worked with in Chapters 14 and 15 where demand was derived explicitly from quasilinear tastes and supply represents a short-run market supply curve derived from a particular production technology. These are graphed in panels (a) and (b) of Graph 18.12, with panel (a) graphing the inverse demand and supply functions and panel (b) graphing the actual functions.

Graph 18.12 Non-Linear Demand and Supply

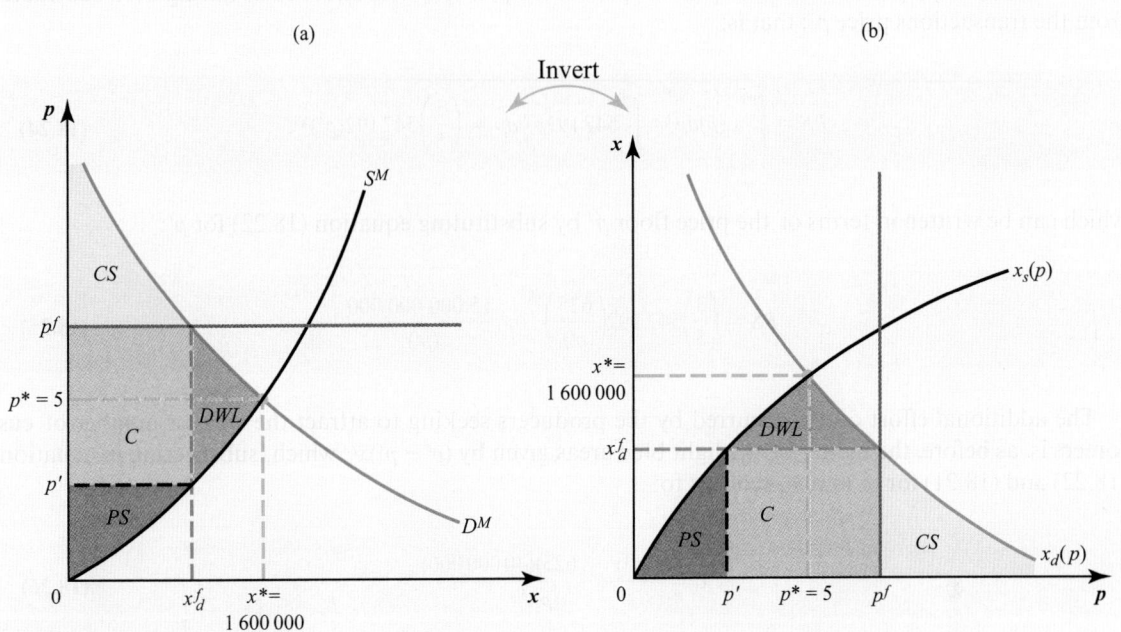

Exercise 18B.14

What is the price elasticity of demand? What is the price elasticity of supply?

You can verify again that the market equilibrium for these supply and demand functions is $p^* = €5$ and $x^* = 1\,600\,000$. Now suppose the government imposes a price floor of $p^f > €5$, indicated by the light blue horizontal line in panel (a) and the light blue vertical line in panel (b). The quantity transacted in the market will be determined by the reduced demand from consumers, with:

$$x_d(p^f) = \frac{40\,000\,000}{(p^f)^2}. \tag{18.21}$$

In order for producers to supply this quantity, their effective price p', taking into account their effort cost to get the smaller number of customers to pay attention, must satisfy the condition $x_d(p^f) = 547\,192(p')^{2/3}$. Substituting equation (18.21) into this condition and solving for p', we get:

$$p' = \frac{625}{(p^f)^3}. \tag{18.22}$$

In panel (b) of Graph 18.12, we can see that consumer surplus after the imposition of the price floor p^f is the dark brown area *underneath* the demand function $x_d(p)$ above p^f. Consumer surplus is:

$$CS = \int_{p^f}^{\infty} x_d(p)\,dp = \int_{p^f}^{\infty} \frac{40\,000\,000}{p^2}\,dp = \frac{40\,000\,000}{p^f}. \tag{18.23}$$

Producer surplus, on the other hand, can be seen in panel (b) of Graph 18.12 as the dark blue area *underneath* the supply function $x_s(p)$ up to the producer's price p', with effort costs having been subtracted from the transactions price p^f; that is:

$$PS = \int_0^{p'} x_s(p)dp = \int_0^{p'} 547\,192 p^{2/3}dp = \left(\frac{3}{5}\right)547\,192(p')^{5/3}, \qquad \textbf{(18.24)}$$

which can be written in terms of the price floor p^f by substituting equation (18.22) for p':

$$PS = \left(\frac{3}{5}\right)547\,192\left(\frac{625}{(p^f)^3}\right)^{5/3} \approx \frac{15\,000\,000\,000}{(p^f)^5}. \qquad \textbf{(18.25)}$$

The additional effort cost C incurred by the producers seeking to attract the smaller number of customers is, as before, the lighter of the light blue areas given by $(p^f - p')x_d^f$, which, substituting in equations (18.22) and (18.21) for p' and x_d^f, reduces to:

$$C = \frac{((p^f)^4 - 625)(40\,000\,000)}{(p^f)^5}. \qquad \textbf{(18.26)}$$

Finally, the deadweight loss has a lower bound and an upper bound, with actual deadweight loss depending on how much of C is lost as opposed to transferred. More specifically, deadweight loss might be as low as the darker of the light blue areas in Graph 18.12 or as large as the sum of both shades of the light blue areas.

Exercise 18B.15**

Can you derive the lower and upper bound of deadweight loss as a function of p^f?

Using the various equations we have just developed, Table 18.3 calculates equilibrium outcomes for different levels of the price floor p^f, with the first row illustrating the equilibrium when the price floor does not bind since it is equal to the competitive equilibrium price.

Table 18.3 All Values Other Than p^f and p' Are in 1000s

				Equilibrium Under Price Floors With Non-Linear Demand and Supply			
p^f	x_d^f	P'	CS	PS	C	DWL_{low}	DWL_{high}
€5	1600	€5.00	€8000	€4800	€0	€0	€0
€6	1111	€2.89	€6667	€1929	€3452	€753	€4204
€7	816	€1.82	€5714	€892	€4227	€1966	€6193
€8	625	€1.22	€5000	€458	€4237	€3105	€7342
€9	494	€0.86	€4444	€254	€4021	€4080	€8102
€10	400	€0.63	€4000	€150	€3750	€4900	€8650
€15	178	€0.19	€2667	€20	€2634	€7480	€10 114
€20	100	€0.08	€2000	€5	€1992	€8803	€10 795

End-of-Chapter Exercises

18.1† Consider a downward-sloping linear demand curve.

  A. In what follows, we will consider what happens to the price elasticity of demand as we approach the horizontal and vertical axes along the demand curve.

    a. Begin by drawing such a demand curve with constant negative slope. Then pick the point A on the demand curve that lies roughly three-quarters of the way down the demand curve. Illustrate the price and quantity demanded at that point.

    b. Next, suppose the price drops by half and illustrate the point B on the demand curve for that lower price level. Is the percentage change in quantity from A to B greater or smaller than the absolute value of the percentage change in price?

    c. Next, drop the price by half again and illustrate the point C on the demand curve for that new lower price. The percentage change in price from B to C is the same as it was from A to B. Is the same true for the percentage change in quantity?

    d. What do your answers imply about what is happening to the price elasticity of demand as we move down the demand curve?

    e. Can you see what will happen to the price elasticity of demand as we get closer and closer to the horizontal axis?

    f. Next, start at a point A' on the demand curve that lies only a quarter of the way down the demand curve. Illustrate the price and quantity demanded at that point. Then choose a point B' that has only half the consumption level as at A'. Is the percentage change in price from A' to B' greater or less than the absolute value of the percentage change in quantity?

    g. Now pick the point C' on the demand curve where the quantity demanded is half what it was at B'. The percentage change in quantity from A' to B' is the same as the percentage change from B' to C'. Is the same true of the percentage change in price?

    h. What do your answers imply about the price elasticity of demand as we move up the demand curve? What happens to the price elasticity as we keep repeating what we have done and get closer and closer to the vertical intercept?

  B. Consider the linear demand curve described by the equation $p = A - \alpha x$.

    a. Derive the price elasticity of demand for this demand curve.

    b. Take the limit of the price elasticity of demand as price approaches zero.

    c. Take the limit of the price elasticity as price approaches A.

18.2 In this exercise, we explore the concept of elasticity in contexts other than own-price elasticity of uncompensated demand. In cases where it matters, assume that there are only two goods.

  A. For each of the following, indicate whether the statement is true or false and explain your answer:

    a. The income elasticity of demand for goods is negative only for Giffen goods.

    b. If tastes are homothetic, the income elasticity of demand must be positive.

    c. If tastes are quasilinear in x, the income elasticity of demand for x is zero.

    d. If tastes are quasilinear in x_1, then the cross-price elasticity of demand for x_1 is positive.

    e. If tastes are homothetic, cross-price elasticities must be positive.

    f. The price elasticity of *compensated* demand is always negative.

    g. The more substitutable two goods are for one another, the greater the price elasticity of *compensated* demand is in absolute value.

  B. Consider the demand function $x = \alpha I/p$ that emerges from Cobb–Douglas tastes.

    a. Derive the income elasticity of demand and explain its sign.

    b. We know Cobb–Douglas tastes are homothetic. In what way is your answer to (a) a property of homothetic tastes?

    c. What is the cross-price elasticity of demand? Can you make sense of that?

    d. Without knowing the precise functional form that can describe tastes that are quasilinear in x, how can you show that the income elasticity of demand must be zero?

e. Consider the demand function $x_1(p_1, p_2) = (\alpha p_2/p_1)^\beta$. Derive the income and cross-price elasticities of demand.

f. Can you tell whether the tastes giving rise to this demand function are either quasilinear or homothetic?

18.3† In this exercise, treat the real interest rate r as identical to the rental rate on capital.

A. We will now consider the elasticity of savings and borrowing behaviour with respect to changes in the interest rate and other prices. Suppose that tastes over consumption now and in the future are homothetic, and further suppose that production frontiers that use labour and capital as inputs are homothetic. Can you tell whether the interest rate elasticity of savings or capital supply is positive or negative for someone who earns income now but not in the future?

a. Can you tell whether the interest rate elasticity of borrowing or capital demand is positive or negative for someone who earns no income now but will earn income in the future?

b. Is the interest rate elasticity of demand for capital by firms positive or negative?

c. Is the wage elasticity of demand for capital by firms positive or negative?

d. Is the output price elasticity of demand for capital positive or negative?

B. **Suppose that intertemporal tastes over consumption are Cobb–Douglas. Furthermore, suppose that production technologies, which take capital and labour as inputs, have decreasing returns to scale and are Cobb–Douglas.

a. Suppose that your income this period is e_1 and your income in the future is e_2. Set up your intertemporal utility maximization problem and derive your demand for consumption c_1 now.

b. Suppose all your income occurs now, i.e. $e_2 = 0$. What is your savings or capital supply function, and what is the interest rate elasticity of savings?

c. Suppose instead that all your income happens next period, i.e. $e_1 = 0$. What is the interest rate elasticity of borrowing or capital demand?

d. Next, derive the interest rate elasticity of capital demand by firms. Is it positive or negative?

e. Repeat this for the wage elasticity of capital demand as well as the output price elasticity of capital demand for firms.

18.4 **Business and Policy Application:** *Minimum Wage Laws.* Many countries prohibit employers from paying wages below some minimum level $\underline{w}$. This is an example of a price floor in the labour market, and the policy has an impact in a labour market as long as $\underline{w} > w^*$, where w^* is the equilibrium wage in the absence of policy-induced wage distortions.

A. Suppose $\underline{w}$ is indeed set above w^*, and suppose that labour supply slopes upwards.

a. Illustrate this labour market and the impact of the minimum wage law on employment.

b. Suppose that the disequilibrium unemployment caused by the minimum wage gives rise to more intense effort on the part of workers to find employment. Can you illustrate in your graph the equilibrium cost of the additional effort workers expend in securing employment?

c. If leisure were quasilinear and you could therefore measure worker surplus on the labour supply curve, what's the largest that deadweight loss from the minimum wage might become?

d. How is the decrease in employment caused by the minimum wage relative to the non-minimum wage employment level, related to the wage elasticity of labour demand? How is it related to the wage elasticity of labour supply?

e. Define unemployment as the difference between the number of people willing to work at a given wage and the number of people who can find work at that wage. How is the size of unemployment at the minimum wage affected by the wage elasticities of labour supply and demand?

f. *How is the equilibrium cost of effort exerted by workers to secure employment affected by the wage elasticities of labour demand and supply?

B. Suppose that labour demand is given by $\ell_D = (A/w)^\alpha$ and labour supply is given by $\ell_S = (Bw)^\beta$.

a. What is the wage elasticity of labour demand and labour supply?

b. What is the equilibrium wage in the absence of any distortions?

c. What is the equilibrium labour employment in the absence of any distortions?

d. Suppose $A = 24\,500$, $B = 500$ and $\alpha = \beta = 1$. Determine the equilibrium wage w^* and labour employment l^*.

e. Suppose that a minimum wage of €10 is imposed. What is the new employment level ℓ^A and the size of the drop in employment $(\ell^* - \ell^A)$?

f. How large is unemployment under this minimum wage, with unemployment U defined as the difference between the labour that seeks employment and the labour that is actually employed at the minimum wage?

g. If the new equilibrium is reached through workers expending increased effort in securing employment, what is the equilibrium effort cost c^*?

h. Create a table with w^*, ℓ^*, ℓ^A, $(\ell^* - \ell^A)$, U and c^* along the top. Then fill in the first row for the case you have just calculated; that is, the case where $A = 24\,500$, $B = 500$ and $\alpha = \beta = 1$.

i. Next, consider the case where $A = 11\,668$, $B = 500$, $\alpha = 1.1$ and $\beta = 1$. Fill in the second row of the table for this case and explain what is happening in terms of the change in wage elasticities.

j. Finally, consider the case where $A = 24\,500$, $B = 238.1$, $\alpha = 1$ and $\beta = 1.1$. Fill in the third row of the table for this case and again explain what is happening in terms of the change in wage elasticities.

18.5† **Business and Policy Application:** *Subsidizing Wheat through Price Floors.* Suppose the domestic demand and supply for wheat intersects at p^*, and suppose further that p^* also happens to be the world price for wheat. Since the domestic price is equal to the world price, there is no need for this country to either import or export wheat. Assume throughout that income effects do not play a significant role in the analysis of the wheat market.

A. Suppose the domestic government imposes a price floor $\bar{p}$ that is greater than p^* and it is able to keep imports of wheat from coming into the country.

a. Illustrate the disequilibrium shortage or surplus that results from the imposition of this price floor.

b. In the absence of anything else happening, how will an equilibrium be re-established and what will happen to producer and consumer surplus?

c. Next, suppose the government agrees to purchase any wheat that domestic producers cannot sell at the price floor. The government plans to sell the wheat it purchases on the world market, where its sales are sufficiently small to not affect the world price of wheat. Illustrate how an equilibrium will now be re-established, and determine the change in domestic consumer and producer surplus from this government programme.

d. What is the deadweight loss from the price floor with and without the government purchasing programme?

e. In implementing the purchasing programme, the government notices that it is not very good at getting wheat to the world market, and all of it spoils before it can be sold. How does the deadweight loss from the programme change depending on how successful the government is at selling the wheat on the world market?

f. Would either consumers or producers favour the price floor on wheat without any additional government programmes?

g. Who would favour the price floor combined with the government purchasing programme? Does their support depend on whether the government succeeds in selling the surplus wheat? Why might they succeed in the political process?

h. How does the deadweight loss from the price floor change with the price elasticity of demand and supply?

B. Suppose the domestic demand curve for tonnes of wheat is given by $p = 24 - 0.00000000225x$ while the domestic supply curve is given by $p = 1 + 0.00000000025x$. Suppose there are no income effects to worry about.

a. Calculate the equilibrium price p^* in the absence of any government interference. Assume henceforth that this is also the world price for a tonne of wheat.

b. What is the quantity of wheat produced and consumed domestically?

c. How much is the total social (consumer and producer) surplus in the domestic wheat market?

d. Next, suppose the government imposes a price floor of $\bar{p} = 3.5$ per tonne of wheat. What is the disequilibrium shortage or surplus of wheat?

e. In the absence of any other government programme, what is the highest possible surplus after the price floor is imposed, and what does this imply about the smallest possible size of the deadweight loss?

f. Suppose next that the government purchases any amount that wheat producers are willing to sell at the price floor $\bar{p}$ but cannot sell to domestic consumers. How much does the government have to buy?

g. What happens to consumer surplus? What about producer surplus?

h. What happens to total surplus assuming the government sells the wheat it buys on the world market at the price p^*?

i. How much does deadweight loss jump under just the price floor as well as when the government purchasing programme is added if $\bar{p} = 4$ instead of 3.5? What if it is 5?

18.6 **Policy Application:** *Kidney Markets.* A large number of patients who suffer from degenerative kidney disease ultimately require a new kidney in order to survive. Healthy individuals have two kidneys but usually can live a normal life with just a single kidney. Thus, kidneys lend themselves to live donations; that is, unlike an organ like the heart, the donor can donate the organ while alive, and live a healthy life with a high degree of likelihood. It is generally not permitted for healthy individuals to sell a kidney; kidneys can only be donated. In effect, this amounts to a price ceiling of zero for kidneys in the market for kidneys.

A. Consider the supply and demand for kidneys.

a. Illustrate the demand and supply curves in a graph with kidneys on the horizontal axis and the price of kidneys on the vertical. Given that there some people who choose to donate a kidney, make sure your graph reflects this.

b. Illustrate how the prohibition of kidney sales results in a shortage of kidneys.

c. In what sense would permitting the sale of kidneys eliminate this shortage? Does this imply that no one would die from degenerative kidney disease?

d. Suppose everyone has the same tastes but people differ in terms of their ability to generate income. What would this imply about how individuals of different income levels line up along the kidney supply curve in your graph? What does it imply in terms of who will sell kidneys?

e. How would patients who need a kidney line up along the demand curve relative to their income? Who would not get kidneys in equilibrium?

f. Illustrate in your graph the lowest that deadweight loss from prohibiting kidney sales might be, assuming that demand curves can be used to approximate marginal willingness to pay. *Hint:* The lowest possible deadweight loss occurs if those who receive donated kidneys under the price ceiling are also those that are willing to pay the most.

g. Does the fact that kidneys might be primarily sold by the poor, and disproportionately bought by well-off patients, change anything about our conclusion that imposing a price ceiling of zero in the kidney market is inefficient?

h. In the absence of ethical considerations that we are not modelling, should anyone object to a change in policy that permits kidney sales? Why do you think that opposition to kidney sales is so widespread?

i. Some people might be willing to sell organs – like their heart – that they cannot live without to provide financially for loved ones even if it means that the seller will die as a result. Assuming that everyone is purely rational, would our analysis of deadweight loss from prohibiting such sales be any different? Opposition to permitting such trade of vital organs is essentially universal. Might the reason for this also, in a less extreme way, be part of the reason we generally prohibit trade in kidneys?

B. Suppose the supply curve in the kidney market is $p = B + \beta x$.

a. What would have to be true in order for the phenomenon of kidney donations at zero price to emerge?

b. Would those who donate kidneys get positive surplus? How would you measure this, and how can you make intuitive sense of it?

* conceptually challenging
** computationally challenging
† solutions in Study Guide

Chapter 19

Distortionary Taxes and Subsidies

The most common government policies that distort market prices involve tax and subsidy policies rather than explicit regulatory policies aimed at setting prices directly such as price floors or ceilings. With national and local governments funded primarily through taxes, and with all government spending combined making up more than 40 per cent of most economies, tax policy becomes a particularly important area for understanding how price distortions impact welfare.

Because of the important role taxes play in most economies, we have already developed many of the concepts that are crucial to understanding tax policy in earlier chapters, particularly in the chapters leading up to and including Chapter 10. We already understand from this development that on the consumer, worker or saver side of markets, taxes result in deadweight losses or inefficiencies to the extent to which they give rise to *substitution effects*. Having added producers to the model, we are able to talk much more explicitly about how taxes affect economic behaviour *in equilibrium* when all sides of the market respond to changes in incentives. This makes it possible to become explicit about who is affected most by particular taxes – who ends up paying taxes in equilibrium and how this translates to welfare changes for consumers, producers and workers as well as society overall.

Note that in pointing out the logic behind the emergence of deadweight losses from taxation, the economist is not voicing opposition to taxes per se, but is identifying costs and benefits and leaving it up to others to judge whether particular policies with particular costs and benefits are good or bad. Taxes have hidden costs that policy makers should understand, and some taxes have greater hidden costs than others. Similarly, some taxes may appear to affect one group on the surface while in fact economic analysis suggests that they will actually affect a different group much more. Understanding issues of this kind is the point of this chapter, with later chapters identifying more clearly why we might need to use taxes despite their hidden costs. It is important to note that the inefficiencies from taxes and subsidies are identified here in a *competitive* setting in which *there are no other distortions*. We will see in upcoming chapters that in non-competitive settings or in the presence of other distortions, taxes and subsidies *may* become efficiency enhancing. Finally, we will develop the main ideas in this chapter within our partial equilibrium framework focusing on a single market, but at the end we will offer an example to illustrate how general equilibrium effects may also be important in many settings. This theme will then carry forward into Chapter 20.

19A Taxes and Subsidies in Competitive Markets

Almost all taxes change some opportunity costs in the economy. Many taxes distort some of the market prices that at least under certain circumstances, coordinate all sides of a market to an efficient outcome. As a result, almost all taxes when introduced into an efficient competitive economic environment, result in deadweight losses and are thus, to one degree or another, inefficient. Not all taxes are equally inefficient, neither do all taxes impact all groups in the same way. We begin our intuitive analysis of taxes with an analysis of who actually ends up paying taxes in equilibrium before we revisit the issue of deadweight loss and the potential for real-world taxes that might actually be efficient.

Taxes and subsidies are very similar in that both change the prices individuals face in an economy; we can think of subsidies as negative taxes. For instance, a government might impose a 10 per cent tax on every good that is sold in a market, or it might impose a 10 per cent subsidy. The 10 per cent tax will cause an increase in the price of the good sold in the market, while the 10 per cent subsidy will cause a decrease in the price. Taxes raise revenues for the government, while negative taxes (or subsidies) cause increases in government expenditures. Even when we do not explicitly treat taxes and subsidies separately in this chapter, you should always be able to conduct a particular economic analysis for both positive and negative taxes.

19A.1 Who Pays Taxes and Receives Subsidies?

Since there are always two sides to a market, buyers and sellers, a government that wants to tax the good sold in a market can in principle do so by writing many different types of tax laws. In particular, the government might write the law in such a way as to make the buyers be the ones that pay the tax, might write the law to make sellers send the tax payment to the government, or the government might do some combination of the two. For instance, in the case of National Insurance Contributions (NICs) in the UK, both employers and employees are required to pay a contribution.

19A.1.1 Statutory Versus Economic Incidence
It is of no consequence how the government writes tax laws, whether it requires the bulk of the tax to be paid by buyers or sellers. Economists use the term *statutory incidence of a tax* to refer to the way in which the legal or statutory obligation to pay a tax is phrased in tax laws. In the case of NICs, for instance, the statutory incidence of the tax falls on both employers and employees. We will distinguish this from the *economic incidence of a tax* by which we will mean how the tax burden is *actually* divided between buyers and sellers when a new equilibrium under the tax has emerged.

Consider a tax law that imposes a statutory incidence of a per-unit tax t on the producers of good x. For every unit of x that is produced, the firm producing it owes a tax of amount t. This raises the marginal cost of production by t, shifting up the MC and AC curves for each firm in the market. Since market supply in the short run is the combination of all MC curves above AC, this implies that the short-run market supply curve will shift up by t. Since the long-run market supply curve is determined by the lowest points of long-run AC curves, the long-run market supply curve will shift up by t. This shift in the market supply curve is illustrated in panel (a) of Graph 19.1 by the upward shift, equal to the vertical distance of the light blue arrow, of the market supply curve from the initial supply curve S to the new supply curve S'. This causes an increase in the market price from p^* to p', and it reduces the quantity of x transacted in the market from x^* to x'.

Exercise 19A.1

Will the increase in price from the tax be larger or smaller in the long run? *Hint:* How is the price elasticity of supply in the long run usually related to the price elasticity of supply in the short run?

Suppose that instead the government imposed the statutory incidence of an equally sized per-unit tax on consumers of x. In this case, costs would remain unchanged for producers, but each consumer who was previously willing to pay a price p will now only be willing to pay $(p - t)$ given that they know they must still send t per unit to the government. The demand curve will shift down by t, a distance indicated by the size of the light blue arrow in panel (b) of Graph 19.1, causing a new equilibrium to emerge at price p''. At first glance, it appears that panels (a) and (b) look quite different due to the different statutory incidence of the same per-unit tax.

Graph 19.1 Statutory Versus Economic Incidence of Taxes

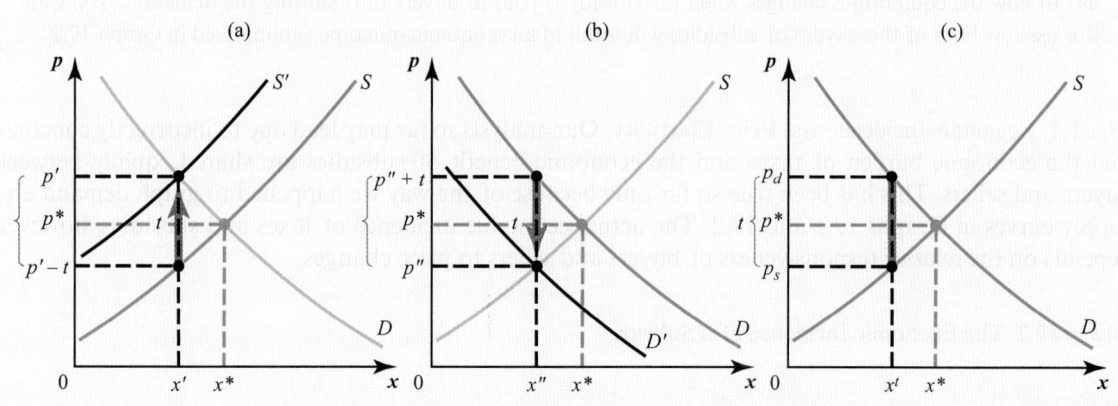

However, the two graphs actually end up being identical in the underlying predicted impact of the two taxes on buyers and sellers. In panel (a), good x is traded at price p' but sellers do not get to keep this price for each unit they sell. They still have to pay the government a tax t for each unit they sell, leaving them with a net-of-tax price $(p' - t)$ while buyers pay price p'. In panel (b), on the other hand, good x is traded at the lower price p'', but buyers still need to pay the tax t. Thus, buyers in panel (b) actually pay a price $(p'' + t)$ while sellers receive the lower price p''. *In both cases, sellers end up receiving a price that is exactly t below the price buyers pay, with the difference going to the government.*

Once we recognize this, we can graph the economic incidence of a tax *regardless of the statutory incidence* in a less complicated graph depicted in panel (c). Here, we insert a vertical line that is equal to the per-unit tax to the left of the pre-tax equilibrium and label the price read off the demand curve as p_d and the price read off the supply curve as p_s. Since the line segment in panel (c) has exactly the same height as the arrows in panels (a) and (b), it logically follows that p' in panel (a) is equal to p_d in panel (c) and p'' in panel (b) is equal to p_s in panel (c). The price p_d is the price paid by buyers after the tax is imposed, and p_s is the price received by sellers, with the difference t going to the government. Notice further that x^t in panel (c) is logically equal to x' and x'' in panels (a) and (b).

Exercise 19A.2

Using a pencil, redraw the graphs in panels (a) and (b) of Graph 19.1, but this time label which price buyers end up paying and sellers end up receiving, taking into account that sellers have to pay the tax in panel (a) and buyers have to pay the tax in panel (b). Then, erase the shifted curves in your two graphs. Do the two graphs now look identical to each other and to the graph in panel (c)?

Regardless of which way tax laws are phrased and who is legally responsible for paying a tax, the economic analysis of Graph 19.1 suggests that the economic incidence of the tax will always be the same. Buyers and sellers will share the burden of the tax, with buyers paying higher prices and sellers receiving lower prices than they did before the imposition of the tax. The same is true for negative taxes known as subsidies. Graph 19.2 illustrates the impact of a per-unit subsidy s, with the new price received by sellers p_s now higher than the new price paid by buyers p_d.

Exercise 19A.3

Illustrate how the equilibrium changes when the subsidy is paid to sellers, thus reducing their *MC*. Compare this to how the equilibrium changes when the subsidy is paid to buyers thus shifting the demand curve. Can you see how both of these types of subsidies will result in an economic outcome summarized in Graph 19.2?

19A.1.2 Economic Incidence and Price Elasticity Our analysis so far may lead one to incorrectly conclude that the economic burden of taxes and the economic benefit of subsidies are shared equally between buyers and sellers. This has been true so far only because of the way we happened to graph demand and supply curves in Graphs 19.1 and 19.2. The actual economic incidence of taxes and subsidies, however, depends on the relative responsiveness of buyers and sellers to price changes.

Graph 19.2 The Economic Incidence of a Subsidy

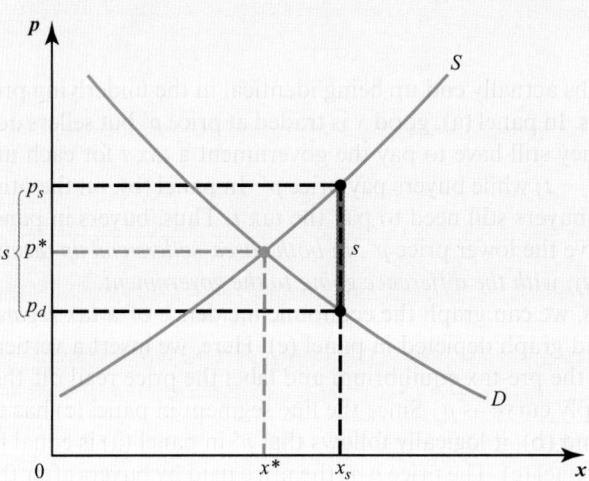

Consider, for instance, a tax on cigarettes. The evidence suggests that most smokers are relatively unresponsive to changes in the price of cigarettes and will continue to smoke roughly as much at higher prices as they do at lower prices. A tax imposed on cigarettes will therefore tend to primarily be passed onto consumers regardless of who is legally responsible for paying the tax. This is depicted in panel (a) of Graph 19.3 where demand is relatively price inelastic. A tax *t* will raise the price paid by buyers by a lot while lowering the price received by cigarette companies relatively little.

Now consider a tax on the sale of oil. Oil is, at least in the short run, in relatively fixed supply, leaving the oil market with a relatively steep supply curve. Panel (b) of Graph 19.3 illustrates that a tax will cause a sharp decline in the price received by sellers while causing only a small increase in the price paid by buyers. Thus, *the economic incidence of a tax falls disproportionately on those who are less responsive to price changes; that is, those whose behavioural response to price is more inelastic.*

Exercise 19A.4

In graphs with demand and supply curves similar to those in Graph 19.3, illustrate the economic impact on buyers and sellers of subsidies. How does the benefit of a subsidy relate to relative price elasticities?

Graph 19.3 Price Elasticities and the Relative Burden of Taxes on Buyers and Sellers

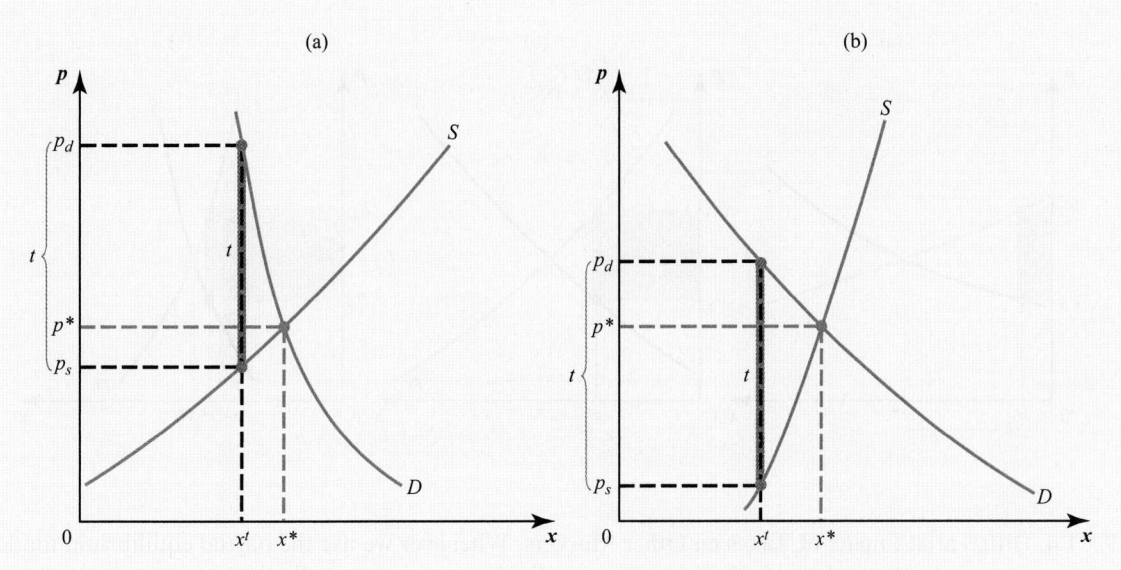

19A.1.3 The Impact of Taxes on Market Output and Tax Revenue Just as price elasticities determine who bears disproportionately more of the burden of a tax, or gains a disproportionate share of the benefit of a subsidy, price elasticities determine how much market output will respond to changes in taxes and consequently how much tax revenue will be raised. This is illustrated in Graph 19.4 where the impact on market output is illustrated for three different scenarios. In each panel of the graph, buyers and sellers are assumed to be similarly responsive to price changes, and the relative burden of a tax is therefore similar for both sides of the market. The size of the tax imposed in each of the panels is exactly the same. However, panel (a) of the graph begins with relatively price elastic market demand and supply curves that become increasingly more price inelastic in panels (b) and (c). As a result, market output drops a lot in panel (a), less in panel (b) and even less in panel (c). Thus, *as buyers and sellers become more unresponsive to price changes, taxes have a smaller impact on market output.*

Exercise 19A.5

Does the impact of subsidies on market output also rise with the price responsiveness of buyers and sellers?

In addition, each panel of Graph 19.4 illustrates the total tax revenue collected by the government using the same per-unit tax t as the shaded light blue areas. These areas are the vertical distance, which represents the per-unit tax rate, multiplied by the horizontal distance, which represents output after the tax is imposed. Note how tax revenue changes as demand and supply become more price inelastic. If consumers and producers are very responsive to price changes, their large response to a tax will undermine efforts to raise revenue.

Exercise 19A.6

Suppose the government has already imposed the taxes graphed in Graph 19.4 and is now considering raising this tax. Can you see in these graphs under what circumstances this would result in a decrease in overall tax revenues?

Graph 19.4 Taxes and Market Output as Economic Actors Become More Price Responsive

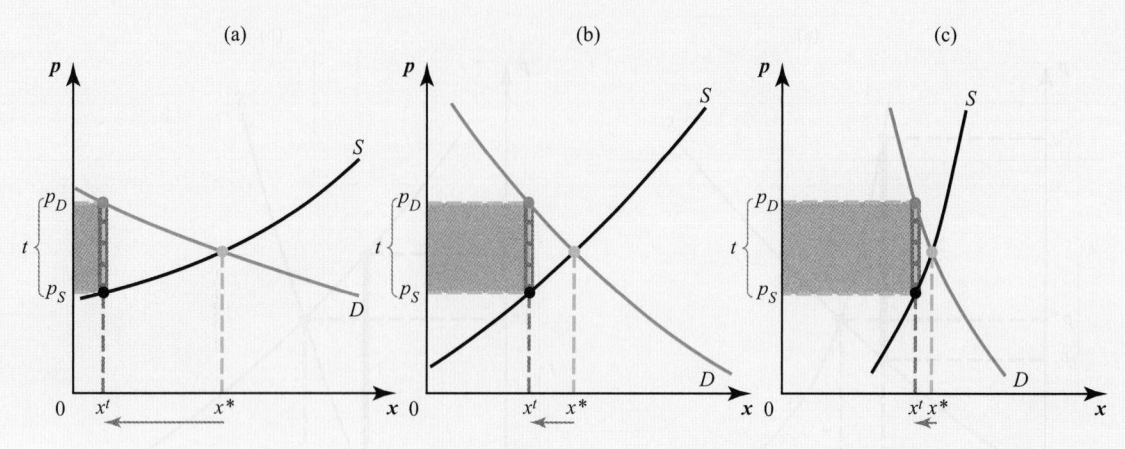

19A.1.4 Differential Impact of Taxes on Other Markets Whenever we use the partial equilibrium model that focuses on a single market in isolation, we are implicitly assuming that all other prices in the economy are moving in line and thus all other goods in the economy can be modelled as one big composite good. We are also treating our analysis of a tax change as if it occurred in an environment where other goods are not taxed. However, it is often the case that taxes imposed in one market impact other markets that are also taxed. For instance, suppose the government imposes a large tax on fuel. It is likely that markets for more-fuel-efficient cars are affected differently from markets for less-fuel-efficient cars, while markets for paperclips may not be impacted very much at all.

This creates further complications for tax policy analysts. If the government is already taxing car sales when it contemplates the imposition of a new tax on fuel, tax revenue in the market for fuel-efficient cars is likely to increase as a result of an increase in the tax on fuel as demand for such cars increases, while tax revenue is likely to decrease in markets for less-fuel-efficient cars where demand drops. When new taxes or increases in existing taxes are contemplated in economies that already have many pre-existing taxes, a full treatment of the economic impact of the new tax involves tracing the effect of the new tax through other markets that are affected. The secondary effects in these other markets may, in some cases, end up being of larger significance than the primary effect in the market for the taxed goods, which in turn can mean that a tax that looks good when analyzed in isolation looks bad in a fuller economic analysis. The reverse is, of course, also possible. An analysis of the types of effects hinted at is often referred to as *second-best analysis*. While we are implicitly assuming that our analysis starts in a first-best world of full efficiency, a second-best analysis starts with a model in which new taxes are introduced into a second-best world where there already exist tax distortions elsewhere.

Exercise 19A.7

Suppose the tax on fuel-efficient cars is low and the tax on fuel-inefficient cars is high. Is it likely that our partial equilibrium estimate of a tax on fuel will cause us to over- or underestimate the full impact on government revenues?

19A.2 Deadweight Loss From Taxation Revisited

Market demand and supply curves are full descriptions of predicted behavioural changes induced by price changes. As such, they are the appropriate tools with which to predict the economic incidence of taxes and subsidies; that is, how much prices paid by buyers and received by sellers will change, as well as the impact of such policies on market output. However, these are not necessarily the appropriate curves to use for an analysis of changes in welfare.

In particular, we know that consumer surplus and changes in consumer surplus can be measured as areas underneath marginal willingness to pay or compensated demand curves. Only when these curves are the same as regular, uncompensated demand curves can the market demand curves be used to measure consumer surplus. Recall that compensated and uncompensated demand curves are the same only when tastes for the underlying good are quasilinear. It is for this reason that we assumed quasilinear tastes in the previous chapter where we identified consumer surplus along uncompensated market demand curves. If we know that tastes for the underlying good are either normal or inferior, we have already demonstrated in Graph 10.9 how deadweight loss on the consumer side will be over- or underestimated if welfare changes are measured on uncompensated demand curves.

We begin our analysis of the full welfare impact on both buyers and sellers by initially once again assuming that tastes are quasilinear, and thus the market demand curve can be used to calculate consumer surplus in goods markets. We will then proceed to demonstrate cases in which quasilinearity is clearly the wrong assumption, and we will show how an analysis of welfare changes from taxation will necessarily lead to large policy mistakes if conducted as if tastes were indeed quasilinear.

19A.2.1 Deadweight Loss From Taxes and Subsidies When Tastes Are Quasilinear Graph 19.5 illustrates the economic effect of a tax t in panel (a) and of a subsidy s in panel (b) along the lines discussed in the previous section. Assuming for now that tastes are quasilinear and demand curves can therefore be interpreted as compensated demand curves, changes in consumer and producer surplus are identified much as we identified such changes in the previous chapter.

Graph 19.5 Deadweight Loss When Tastes Are Quasilinear

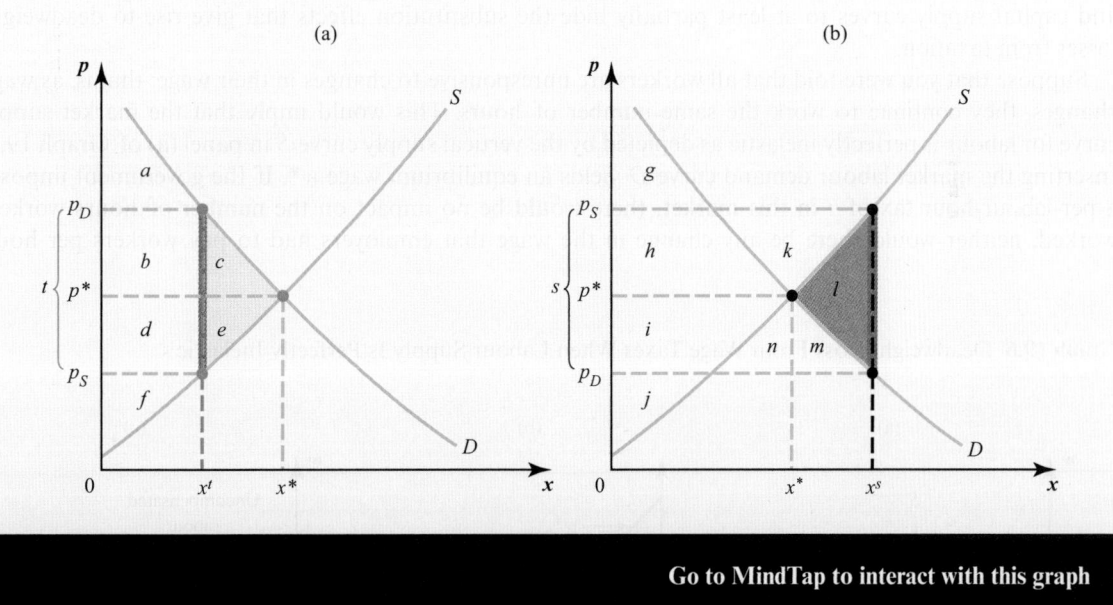

Go to MindTap to interact with this graph

In panel (a), an initial consumer surplus of $(a + b + c)$ shrinks to (a) as consumers face the higher after-tax price p_d while producer surplus shrinks from $(d + e + f)$ to (f) as producers face the lower after-tax price p_s. The government earns no tax revenue before the tax but gets area $(b + d)$ after it is imposed. The overall surplus in society therefore falls from the initial $(a + b + c + d + e + f)$ to an after-tax $(a + b + d + f)$, leaving us with a deadweight loss of $(c + e)$ represented by the shaded dark brown area in panel (a) of Graph 19.5.

For the subsidy in panel (b), on the other hand, both consumers and producers are better off after the subsidy, but the government incurs a cost that we also have to take into account. Consumer surplus rises from the initial $(g + h)$ to the final $(g + h + i + n + m)$ as consumers now face a lower price, while producer surplus rises from the initial $(i + j)$ to the final $(h + i + j + k)$ as producers now sell goods at a higher price. The joint surplus received by consumers and producers increases by $(h + i + k + m + n)$. The cost of the subsidy, however, is the per-unit subsidy rate times the number of units transacted, or (sx^s), which is represented by the area $(h + i + k + l + m + n)$. This implies that the increase in surplus for consumers and producers is (l) less than the cost of the subsidy, which in turn implies the area (l) in panel (b) of Graph 19.5 is the deadweight loss from the subsidy.

Once we know we can identify deadweight loss from taxation or subsidies as triangles to the left and right of the pure market equilibrium, we can see how the size of the deadweight loss is impacted by price elasticities of demand and supply. For instance, looking across the three panels of Graph 19.4, the deadweight loss triangle represented as the triangle next to the shaded rectangles shrinks as demand and supply become more price inelastic. In fact, were one of the two market curves completely price inelastic, the deadweight loss triangle would disappear entirely and the tax would be efficient. The same is true for deadweight losses from subsidies.

Remember that this analysis is valid only if the tastes for the underlying goods are quasilinear because only then are compensated and uncompensated demand curves the same. If we use uncompensated demand curves when goods are either inferior or normal, we will either over- or underestimate deadweight loss. Awareness of the difference between compensated and uncompensated curves becomes even more important as we analyze taxes in labour and capital markets where the way we have just illustrated deadweight loss is almost certainly incorrect.

19A.2.2 Deadweight Loss From Taxes in Labour and Capital Markets Most of the tax revenue raised by governments comes from taxation of income derived either from labour or from investments, i.e. savings. Such taxes alter the opportunity cost of leisure in the case of taxes on labour income, or the opportunity cost of consuming now or in the future in the case of taxation on savings. These taxes typically give rise to opposing wealth and substitution effects for labour or capital supply, thus causing uncompensated labour and capital supply curves to at least partially hide the substitution effects that give rise to deadweight losses from taxation.

Suppose that you were told that all workers are unresponsive to changes in their wage; that is, as wage changes, they continue to work the same number of hours. This would imply that the market supply curve for labour is perfectly inelastic as depicted by the vertical supply curve S in panel (a) of Graph 19.6. Inserting the market labour demand curve D yields an equilibrium wage w^*. If the government imposes a per-labour-hour tax of t in this market, there would be no impact on the number of hours workers worked, neither would there be any change in the wage that employers had to pay workers per hour.

Graph 19.6 Deadweight Loss From Wage Taxes When Labour Supply Is Perfectly Inelastic

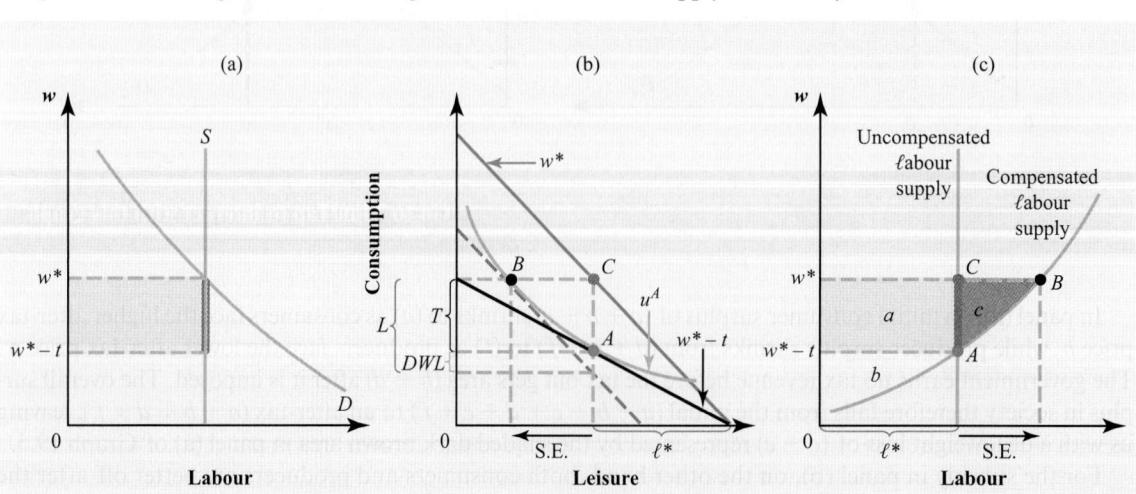

However, because of the inelasticity of labour supply, workers would end up bearing the entire burden of the tax and would receive an after-tax wage ($w^* - t$). The government would raise revenues equal to the dark brown shaded area in panel (a) of the graph. All of this is sound economic analysis using exactly the right market curves to predict the economic impact of the tax.

Notice that there is no triangle next to the box that indicates tax revenue, which might lead us to conclude that there is no deadweight loss. It is at this point that the market demand and supply curves become misleading because there is almost certainly a deadweight loss that is obscured in panel (a) of Graph 19.6. If there is a deadweight loss, it has to lie on the worker or supply side of the labour market since the wage rate paid by producers is unaffected by the tax.

Consider the underlying consumer choice picture that gives rise to individual labour supply curves and, when aggregated across all workers, to market labour supply. This picture is depicted in panel (b) of Graph 19.6 where leisure hours are on the horizontal and euros of consumption on the vertical axis. The entire economic incidence of the tax falls on workers in this case, as seen from panel (a), which implies that worker budget constraints shrink from the initial dark brown budget with slope $-w^*$ to the new dark blue budget with slope $-(w^* - t)$.

If workers are unresponsive to changes in wages, then the worker depicted in panel (b) of the graph will make the same leisure choice on the initial and the final budget. Panel (b) labels the after-tax choice as A and the before-tax choice as C, with C lying exactly above A due to the inelasticity of the worker's behaviour. When we add the indifference curve u^A, which makes point A optimal after the imposition of the tax, and introduce the light blue compensated budget that keeps utility at u^A but leaves the wage at the before-tax level, we see that the lack of change in worker behaviour is due to fully offsetting substitution and wealth effects.

The light blue compensated budget is equivalent to a lump sum tax that makes the worker just as well off at B as the wage tax does at point A. However, the lump sum tax raises revenue equal to the distance between the parallel dark brown and light blue budgets, while the wage tax raises revenue equal to the vertical distance between A and C. The lump sum tax raises revenue L while the wage tax raises only revenue T, implying a deadweight loss equal to the difference between the two quantities illustrated as DWL in the graph.

Why is there a deadweight loss in panel (b) for the individual worker we are modelling but no deadweight loss triangle in panel (a)? It is because deadweight losses on the worker side of the market arise only from substitution effects that are obscured by the counteracting wealth effect when uncompensated labour supply is derived as perfectly inelastic. Panel (c) presents the uncompensated and compensated labour supply curves for these workers within the same graph, illustrating a perfectly inelastic, uncompensated, labour supply curve but an upward sloping compensated labour supply that represents the change in labour choices for workers whose utility is kept at u^A. The former includes both the wealth and substitution effect, while the latter includes only the substitution effect, much as marginal willingness to pay – or compensated demand – curves for consumers only contain substitution effects.

Under the wage tax, the workers settle at point A in panel (c) of Graph 19.6 and receive a wage of ($w^* - t$). With worker surplus measured along the compensated supply curve, just as consumer surplus is measured along compensated demand curves, this gives an after-tax surplus of (b). Under the lump sum tax that leaves the workers just as well off, they would end up at point B earning a wage w^*. This would give them a worker surplus of ($a + b + c$), ($a + c$) greater than the surplus at point A. However, at point A the workers had already paid the wage tax (a), equal to the shaded dark brown area, in the form of a lower wage, while at point B we have not yet taken into account the fact that the workers have paid a lump sum tax that makes them just as happy as they would be at A. Since workers are equally happy at the two points as seen in panel (b) but have a surplus ($a + c$) greater at B than at A, it must be that the lump sum tax raises ($a + c$) in revenue. This leaves a difference (c) between the wage tax revenue and the lump sum tax revenue that both leave the workers equally well off, implying $DWL = c$.

Labour supply is not always perfectly inelastic and may even be downward sloping for some workers, but notice that the direction of the substitution effect always implies that the compensated labour supply curve is upward sloping. As a result, whether one can see it or not in a picture of market equilibrium in the labour market, wage taxes will have deadweight losses as long as there is any substitutability at all between leisure and consumption, which there almost certainly is.

Exercise 19A.8*

Illustrate, using an analogous set of steps to those just used as we worked our way through Graph 19.6, how wage subsidies are inefficient even when workers are completely unresponsive to changes in wages.

19A.2.3 Deadweight Losses From Subsidies in Labour or Capital Markets We can show a similar error that may arise when we use the uncompensated savings–interest rate relationship, which represents the supply curve for financial capital, to predict the welfare effect of savings subsidies. Consider the case where individuals are completely unresponsive to changes in the rate of return on savings – they always put the same amount into the savings account regardless of the interest rate. This gives a perfectly inelastic supply curve for capital as presented in panel (a) of Graph 19.7. When a subsidy for saving is now introduced, the entire benefit of the subsidy accrues to savers as their rate of return jumps from the initial equilibrium interest rate $r*$ to the new interest rate $(r* + s)$ that includes the per-unit subsidy s. If you have trouble seeing why this economic incidence of the subsidy emerges, try graphing the impact of a subsidy for the case where the supply curve is almost but not quite perfectly inelastic. Then make the supply curve increasingly inelastic until you see panel (a) of Graph 19.7 emerge. The shaded dark brown area is the cost incurred by the government, with no change in the capital saved given the inelastic response by savers.

Graph 19.7 Deadweight Loss From Subsidies for Saving When Saving Behaviour Is Perfectly Inelastic

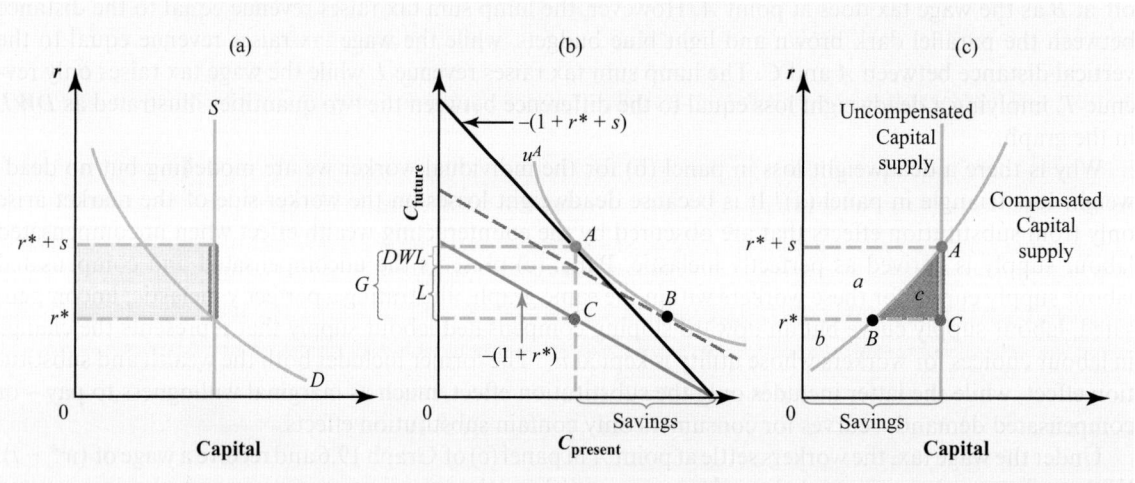

Once again it appears as if there is no deadweight loss triangle and the subsidy is therefore efficient. Again, this is not true because the capital supply curve obscures the very substitution effects that are responsible for the inefficiencies of subsidies. We can show this most easily by illustrating the case of a single saver who exhibits inelastic saving behaviour in panel (b) of the graph. The subsidy changes the budget from the original dark brown to the final dark blue, with A optimal after the subsidy and C optimal before, and with both bundles exhibiting exactly the same level of savings. Next, we can put in the indifference curve u^A that makes point A optimal after the subsidy raises the rate of return to savings, and we can put in the compensated light blue budget that results in the same utility as this saver gets at A but at the before-tax interest rate. The reason for the inelastic behavioural response for this worker is that the substitution effect is fully covered up by an equally large and opposite wealth effect.

It can also be seen in this graph that this subsidy is inefficient. The total government cost of paying the subsidy to this one saver can be measured as the vertical distance between A and C and is labelled G. At the same time, we can see from the difference between the dark brown and light blue budgets that a lump sum subsidy of L would make this individual exactly as well off as the distortionary subsidy that cost G. The difference between G and L is the deadweight loss for this one saver.

Translating points A, B and C to a graph with capital on the horizontal axis and the rate of return on the vertical, we can see what goes wrong when we try to find this deadweight loss in panel (a) of the graph. In panel (c) of the graph we illustrate the vertical uncompensated capital supply curve that is formed from points A and C in panel (b), but we also illustrate the *compensated* capital supply curve, derived from A and B in panel (b), that corresponds to the utility level u^4. Using this compensated curve, we can identify the saver surplus as $(a + b)$ under the distortionary subsidy and as just (b) under the lump sum subsidy at point B. Since this saver is equally happy at A and B, the lump sum subsidy at B must be equal to (a). The distortionary subsidy cost $(a + c)$, which is (c) more than the lump sum subsidy that made the saver just as well off. Thus, the DWL distance in panel (b) is analogous to the dark blue area (c) in panel (c).

19A.2.4 DWL and Revenue as Tax Rates Rise

In Chapter 10, we illustrated the idea that on the consumer side of the market, as tax rates rise by a factor of k, deadweight loss increases by approximately k^2. Now that we are familiar with the process by which taxes affect both the consumer and producer sides of the market, we can extend this intuition more generally.

Consider the market demand and supply curves in panel (a) of Graph 19.8, and to simplify the analysis assume that tastes for good x are quasilinear implying that the market demand curve is equivalent to the aggregate marginal willingness to pay curve. The market price in the absence of taxes is p^*. If a per-unit tax of t is imposed, the market output drops from x^* to x^1, with prices for consumers rising and prices for producers falling. The deadweight loss from this tax would be equivalent to the dark brown triangle, with half of the deadweight loss falling on the consumer side of the market and half falling on the producer side. If the tax is doubled to $2t$, this raises the price for consumers, decreases the price for producers, and leads to the output x^{2t}, with the deadweight loss increasing by the shaded dark blue area.

Graph 19.8 Deadweight Loss and Tax Revenue When Tastes Are Quasilinear

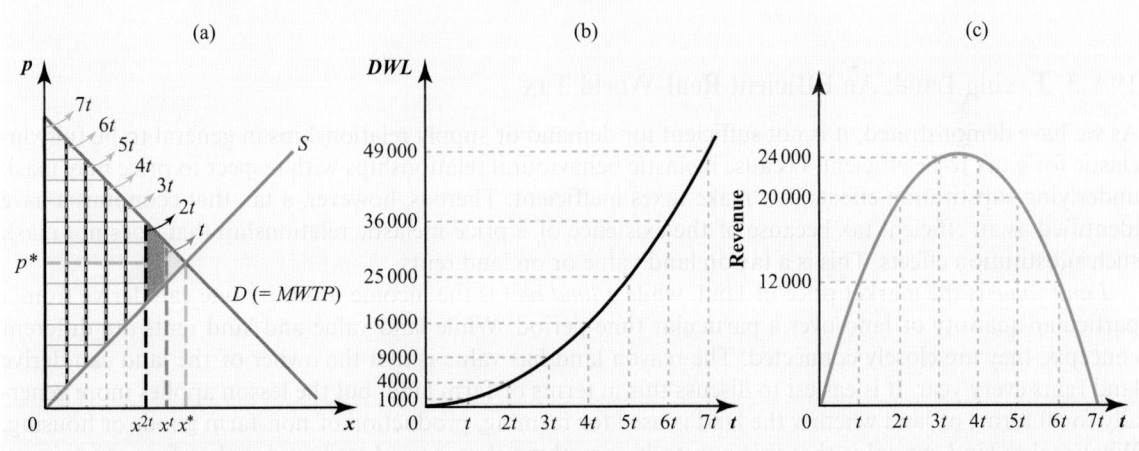

If each triangle, such as the two triangles that form the initial dark brown deadweight loss when the tax is t, is equal to €500, this implies that each square, such as the squares contained in the dark blue area, is equal to €1000. Adding these up, we find the deadweight loss associated with the initial tax t is €1000, while the deadweight loss associated with the tax $2t$ is €4000. A doubling of the tax leads to a quadrupling of the deadweight loss. We can keep increasing the tax to $3t$, $4t$, going all the way to $7t$, and by adding up the relevant deadweight loss areas, we can derive the relationship between the tax rate and the deadweight loss in panel (b) of Graph 19.8. The graph illustrates that it is still the case that with the linear demand and supply curves graphed in panel (a), deadweight loss rises by a factor of k^2 whenever the tax rate increases by a factor of k.

Exercise 19A.9

How large does deadweight loss get if the tax rate rises to $3t$? What if it rises to $4t$?

We can similarly trace out the tax revenue collected by the government as the tax increases. When the tax rate is set at t, the tax revenue is tx^t, which is equal to 12 squares in panel (a) or equivalent to €12 000 when each square represents €1000. Similarly, when the tax rate is $2t$, the tax revenue is $2tx^{2t}$ or €20 000. The relationship between the tax rate and tax revenue that emerges in panel (c) of the graph has an inverse U-shape, with tax revenue equal to zero when there is no tax and equal to zero once again when the tax becomes sufficiently high. This is another version of the *Laffer curve* that suggests governments will ultimately lose revenue if tax rates get too high.

While we are illustrating this in a stylized graph of linear demand and supply curves that lead to an equal sharing of economic tax incidence between consumers and producers, the intuitions are applicable more generally even if the precise relationship between tax rates, deadweight loss and tax revenue differs somewhat. As a result, the simple intuition emerging from these graphs has often led to the general advice from economists to governments that it is more efficient to levy low rates on large tax bases rather than high tax rates on small tax bases.

Exercise 19A.10

Illustrate the relationship between subsidy rates, the deadweight loss from a subsidy and the cost of the subsidy using the same initial graph of supply and demand as in panel (a) of Graph 19.8 in graphs analogous to panels (b) and (c).

19A.3 Taxing Land: An Efficient Real-World Tax

As we have demonstrated, it is not sufficient for demand or supply relationships in general to be fully inelastic for a tax to be efficient, because inelastic behavioural relationships with respect to price may mask underlying substitution effects that make taxes inefficient. There is, however, a tax that economists have identified as an efficient tax because of the existence of a price-inelastic relationship that does not mask such substitution effects. This is a tax on land value or on land rents.

Land value is the market price of land, while a *land rent* is the income or utility one can derive from a particular quantity of land over a particular time period. While land value and land rents are different concepts, they are closely connected. The reason land has value is that the owner of the land can derive land rents every year. It is easiest to discuss this in terms of farm land, but the lesson applies more generally to all forms of land whether the land is used for farming, production of non-farm goods or housing. What makes land special is that it is not itself something that is produced, and it therefore exists in essentially fixed supply.

19A.3.1 The Relationship Between Land Value and Land Rents Assume an individual buys 100 acres of farm land. They can derive annual income from this land by either producing potatoes directly or by renting it out to someone else who will produce potatoes. For it to be worth it to farm the land themselves, they have to receive compensation that covers the opportunity cost of time and the opportunity cost of the land that they will be using. The opportunity cost of their time is determined by what other market opportunities they have; perhaps their other alternative is teaching, which carries with it a certain level of compensation. The opportunity cost of using the land is the income that could derive from the land by renting it to someone else. How much the individual can rent the land for in the market depends on the quality of the land, and on how much someone else would be able to earn from it.

Assume the individual could rent the 100 acres in the market for €10 000 per year and their time is worth €100 000 per year. In order for them to farm the land themselves, they will have to be able to generate at least €110 000 in income, otherwise they are better off making €100 000 elsewhere and collecting €10 000 in rent. In equilibrium, only those who are relatively good at farming will end up making the choice to be farmers and the rest will do something else. If farming is a competitive industry, those who engage in farming will make zero profits and an amount equal to their opportunity cost of time plus the rent they have to pay for the land, whether they are paying it explicitly or whether they forego collecting rents from others if they own the land themselves.

The land itself produces an income stream of €10 000 per year: the annual land rent, which we will assume is collected at the end of each year. The *value* of the land, how much the individual could sell it for in the market, is based on not only this year's income stream but also all future income streams that can be produced from this land. In Chapter 3, we discussed how such future income streams are evaluated in the presence of interest rates. If, for instance, the annual interest rate is r, expressed in decimal form, then €10 000 one year from now is worth (€10 000/(1 + r)) and €10 000 n years from now is worth (€10 000/(1 + r)^n). The *value of land is the present discounted value of all future land rents*, or (€10 000/(1 + r)), from the rent derived a year from now for this year's rent, plus (€10 000/(1 + r)^2) from the rent derived two years from now, and so on. When all land rents into the future are added up in this way, the resulting land value is equal to (€10 000/r). More generally, land value LV is related to land rents, LR, according to the formula:

$$LV = \frac{LR}{(1 + r)} + \frac{LR}{(1 + r)^2} \cdots = \frac{LR}{r}. \tag{19.1}$$

9A.3.2 Taxation of Land Rents Now suppose that the government requires landowners to pay 50 per cent of their land rents as a tax. We will call this a 50 per cent land rent tax. Graph 19.9 illustrates the market for renting a particular type of land, say land of a particular quality in Germany. Such land is in fixed supply, which implies that the supply curve is completely inelastic. As a result, the economic incidence of the tax is fully on landowners who are renting the land to farmers or to themselves if they themselves are farming, with the annual rental value that landowners get to keep dropping by 50 per cent, while the rent paid by renters remains unchanged.

Graph 19.9 A 50 Per Cent Tax on Land Rents

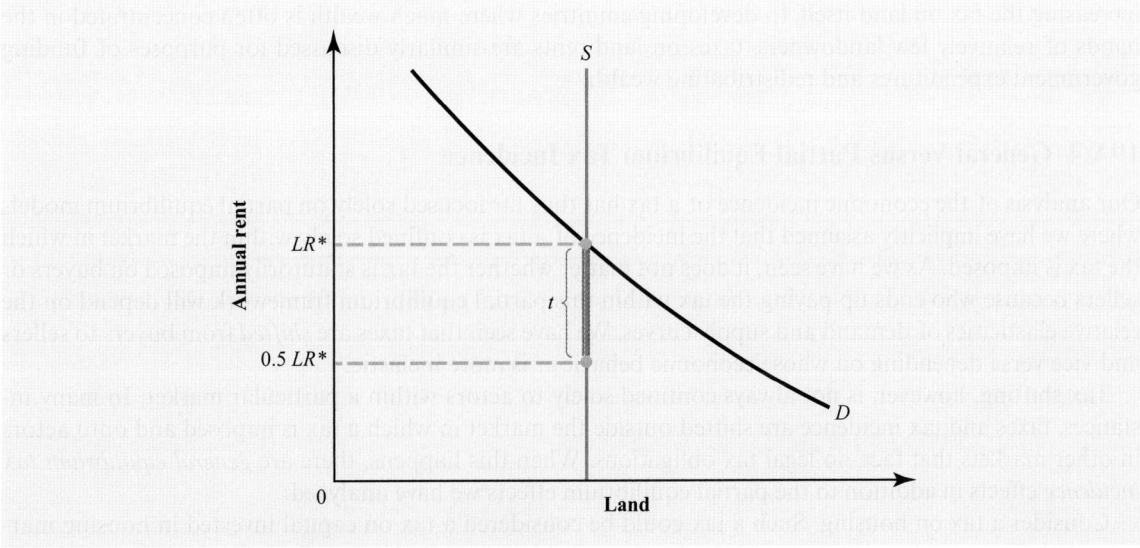

As the current owner of the land, the individual has no choice but to accept a lower, after-tax, rental price for their land. They may get very upset at this and try to sell the land instead, but remember that the value of land is equal to the present discounted value of all future land rents. Since all future, after-tax land rents have just fallen by 50 per cent, this implies that the value of the individual's land has just fallen from (LR^*/r) to $(0.5LR^*/r)$. The 50 per cent tax on land rents has caused the value of an asset owned to decline by 50 per cent, and the individual has no way to substitute with anything else and avoid the tax. If they continue to hold on to the land, they will make 50 per cent less on it every year, and if they decide to sell they will make 50 per cent less now and forego any future rents. In present value terms, they are equally well off whether they hold on to the land, whether they sell it or whether they hold on to it for a little while and then sell it.

You might think that perhaps they can make themselves better off by using the land for something else, but if the tax is truly on unimproved land rents, it is independent of what exactly is being done with the land because only the value of the unimproved land is taxed. Whether they use it for farming or for producing paperclips or for housing, a land rent tax still taxes the rental value of the land itself. There is nothing the individual can do to prevent paying this tax in one form or another, and thus no possibility for a substitution effect to emerge and make the tax inefficient. A tax on land rent is, therefore, a transfer of wealth from landowners to the government. Landowners are worse off, but the government captures all the wealth that landowners lost. It is in part for this reason that a writer by the name of Henry George (1839–1897), suggested over 100 years ago that all government expenditures should be financed by taxes on land rents. In fact, Henry George went even further and suggested that all land rents should be taxed at 100 per cent.

Exercise 19A.11

What would be the economic impact of a 100 per cent tax on land rents, levied on owners?

The proposal to tax land rents is a policy option that is increasingly considered in the United States by local governments that rely for much of their revenue on property taxes. Property taxes are not land rent taxes because they tax both land rents and the improvements on land, such as housing. To the extent that property taxes change the opportunity cost of improving land, such taxes may give rise to substitution effects that create inefficiencies by diverting capital away from housing and into other uses, and local governments can move towards more efficient taxes by lowering the tax on improvements on land and increasing the tax on land itself. In developing countries where much wealth is often concentrated in the hands of relatively few landowners, taxes on land rents are similarly discussed for purposes of funding government expenditures and redistributing wealth.

19A.4 General Versus Partial Equilibrium Tax Incidence

Our analysis of the economic incidence of a tax has thus far focused solely on partial equilibrium models where we have implicitly assumed that the incidence of a tax is confined solely within the market in which the tax is imposed. As we have seen, it does not matter whether the tax is statutorily imposed on buyers or sellers because who ends up paying the tax within this partial equilibrium framework will depend on the relative elasticities of demand and supply curves. We have seen that taxes are *shifted* from buyers to sellers and vice versa depending on whose economic behaviour is more inelastic.

Tax shifting, however, is not always confined solely to actors within a particular market. In many instances, taxes and tax incidence are shifted outside the market in which a tax is imposed and onto actors in other markets that face no legal tax obligations. When this happens, there are *general equilibrium tax incidence* effects in addition to the partial equilibrium effects we have analyzed.

Consider a tax on housing. Such a tax could be considered a tax on capital invested in housing markets, with investors bearing some of the burden of this tax as their rate of return on housing capital declines when the tax is imposed. Owners of capital have other options of where to invest their money. Prior to the imposition of a housing tax, it must be the case that the equilibrium rate of return on capital is the same for all forms of capital, at least to the extent to which other forms of capital have similar risk associated with it. If a tax on housing causes the after-tax rate of return on housing capital to decline, rational investors will shift away from investing in housing and towards investing in other forms of capital that now have a higher rate of return. An inward shift in housing capital supply will raise the after-tax rate of return on housing capital and cause an outward supply shift in other capital markets with a corresponding decline in the rate of return on non-housing capital. A new general equilibrium will be reached when the after-tax rate of return on housing capital is equal to the rate of return on non-housing capital. Some of the incidence of the housing tax is shifted away from owners of housing capital to owners of all capital.

We will see other examples of this in Chapter 20 where we will investigate the role of taxes imposed in one geographic region but not in another. As in the case of the housing tax where some of the incidence is shifted away from the housing market and towards other capital markets, we will see that taxes are also shifted from one region, where a tax is imposed, to another. Such general equilibrium effects of taxes can be extremely important and thus add a substantial layer of complexity to tax policy. *To the extent to which taxed inputs or goods are mobile across markets, the imposition of a tax in one market will generate general equilibrium tax incidence in other markets.* This is analogous to the role of price elasticity in determining tax incidence in a partial equilibrium model. Market actors who are more responsive bear less of the tax burden because they can shift that burden to actors who are less responsive. In the same way, market actors who are more mobile across markets are able to shift tax burdens to market actors that are less mobile across markets.

19B   The Mathematics of Taxes and Subsidies

In this section, we continue our exploration of tax incidence and deadweight loss from taxation. We begin with a general demonstration of the relationship between tax incidence and price elasticities, proving more formally that the degree to which market participants bear the burden of a tax increases in proportion to the relative inelasticity of their response to price changes. We continue by illustrating how deadweight losses are calculated, first for the quasilinear case and then, in an application to wage taxes, more generally. While tax incidence depends on uncompensated demand and supply curves, we will see once again that deadweight loss calculations depend on compensated curves. Finally, we conclude with a very simple example of tax incidence in a more general equilibrium setting where a tax on housing is shifted to other forms of capital when capital is mobile between different sectors in the economy.

19B.1 Tax Incidence and Price Elasticities

Consider the general case where demand is given by $x_d(p)$, supply is given by $x_s(p)$ and the pre-tax equilibrium has price p^* and quantity x^*. Now suppose a small tax t is introduced, to be paid by consumers for each unit of x that is purchased. This implies that the price p_d paid by buyers is t higher than the price p_s at which the good is purchased from suppliers; that is, $p_d = p_s + t$. Taking the differential of this, we get:

$$dp_d = dp_s + dt; \tag{19.2}$$

that is, the change in the consumer price p_d is equal to the change in the producer price p_s plus the change in t. In the new equilibrium, demand has to equal supply, with each evaluated at the relevant price; that is:

$$x_d(p_d) = x_s(p_s). \tag{19.3}$$

Taking the differential of this, we can write:

$$\frac{dx_d}{dp_d}dp_d = \frac{dx_s}{dp_s}dp_s \tag{19.4}$$

and substituting equation (19.2) into equation (19.4), this becomes:

$$\frac{dx_d}{dp_d}(dp_s + dt) = \frac{dx_s}{dp_s}dp_s. \tag{19.5}$$

Rearranging terms in this equation, we can write it as:

$$\left(\frac{dx_d}{dp_d} - \frac{dx_s}{dp_s}\right)dp_s = -\frac{dx_d}{dp_d}dt. \tag{19.6}$$

Before the tax is introduced, the equilibrium was at the intersection of supply and demand at p^* and x^*, which is a point on both the supply and demand curve. Multiplying equation (19.6) by p^*/x^*, it becomes:

$$\left(\frac{dx_d}{dp_d}\frac{p^*}{x^*} - \frac{dx_s}{dp_s}\frac{p^*}{x^*}\right)dp_s = -\frac{dx_d}{dp_d}\frac{p^*}{x^*}dt, \tag{19.7}$$

which contains several price elasticity terms evaluated at the pre-tax equilibrium. Rewriting the equation in terms of these price elasticities, it becomes:

$$(\varepsilon_d - \varepsilon_s)dp_s = -\varepsilon_d dt, \tag{19.8}$$

where ε_d is the price elasticity of demand and ε_s is the price elasticity of supply. Rearranging terms, we can also write this as:

$$\frac{dp_s}{dt} = -\frac{\varepsilon_d}{\varepsilon_d - \varepsilon_s}. \tag{19.9}$$

What does this tell us? Suppose that supply is perfectly inelastic with $\varepsilon_s = 0$. The equation says that $dp_s/dt = -1$ or $dp_s = -dt$; the producer's price adjusts by exactly the change in the tax, with the producers bearing the entire burden or incidence of the tax. If, on the other hand, demand is perfectly inelastic ($\varepsilon_d = 0$), $dp_s/dt = 0$ or $dp_s = 0$. The producer's price does not change and the producers bear none of the incidence of the tax. This conforms to the intuition we get from simple graphs. Finally, suppose that at the initial pre-tax equilibrium, consumers and producers were equally responsive to price changes with price elasticities of demand and supply equal to each other in absolute value, or $\varepsilon_s = -\varepsilon_d$. Substituting this into equation (19.9), we get $dp_s/dt = 0.5$ or $dp_s = 0.5dt$; producers bear half the incidence of the tax. The equation implies that *the incidence of the tax will fall disproportionately on the side of the market that is relatively less price elastic*, as we concluded intuitively in Graph 19.3.

Exercise 19B.1*

Demonstrate that whenever ε_d is less in absolute value than ε_s, consumers will bear more than half the incidence of the tax, and whenever the reverse is true, they will bear less than half the incidence of the tax.

THE MATHEMATICS OF TAXES AND SUBSIDIES

Exercise 19B.2*

Can you show that $dp_d/dt = \varepsilon_s/(\varepsilon_s - \varepsilon_d)$? *Hint*: Note that equation (19.2) implies $dp_d/dt = dp_s/dt + 1$.

Similar conclusions regarding the economic incidence of subsidies can be made for subsidies.

19B.2 Deadweight Loss From Taxation When Tastes Are Quasilinear

Tax incidence in a partial equilibrium model depends on the relative price elasticities of uncompensated demand and supply curves. Deadweight loss calculations, however, depend on elasticities of *compensated* demand and supply curves. As we know from our development of consumer theory, the difference between uncompensated and compensated relationships disappears when income effects disappear, and income effects disappear when tastes are quasilinear. We therefore begin our discussion of the mathematics of deadweight loss from taxation for the case when tastes are indeed quasilinear. We can do this by calculating areas under demand and supply curves, but we can also employ the expenditure function derived in Chapter 10 and thus avoid using integral calculus.

In the previous chapter, we demonstrated that when $u(x, y) = \alpha \ln x + y$, demand for the quasilinear good x is $x_d(p_x, p_y) = \alpha p_y/p_x$. You can also verify for yourself that the demand for y is given by $y_d(p_y, I) = (I - \alpha p_y)/p_y$. To focus on just good x within a partial equilibrium model, we can treat y as a composite good with $p_y = 1$, which allows us to write the demands for the two goods as:

$$x_d(p) = \frac{\alpha}{p} \quad \text{and} \quad y_d(I) = I - \alpha, \tag{19.10}$$

where p now denotes the price of good x.

Exercise 19B.3

What is the price elasticity of demand for x? What is the cross-price elasticity of demand for y?

Suppose that the demand side of the market for x can be modelled as arising from the optimization problem of a representative consumer with these tastes and some income level I. Suppose further that the supply side of the market can be represented by the supply curve $x_s = \beta p$.

Exercise 19B.4

What is the price elasticity of supply?

Setting supply equal to demand and solving for p, we get that the equilibrium price under no taxation is $p^* = (\alpha/\beta)^{1/2}$ and the equilibrium quantity transacted is $x^* = (\alpha\beta)^{1/2}$.

Now suppose the government imposes a per-unit tax t on producers, implying that producers will receive a price $(p_d - t)$ when consumers pay p_d. The new equilibrium requires that supply evaluated at the producer price equals demand evaluated at the consumer price; that is, $\beta(p_d - t) = \alpha/p_d$. Multiplying both sides of this equation by p_d and subtracting α, we get $\beta p_d^2 - \beta t p_d - \alpha = 0$, which, by the quadratic formula, implies a new equilibrium price paid by consumers of:

$$p_d = \frac{\beta t + \sqrt{(\beta t)^2 + 4\beta\alpha}}{2\beta} = \frac{t + \sqrt{t^2 + 4(\alpha/\beta)}}{2}, \tag{19.11}$$

with corresponding equilibrium price for producers, net of tax obligations of:

$$p_s = p_d - t = \frac{-t + \sqrt{t^2 + 4(\alpha/\beta)}}{2}. \tag{19.12}$$

Suppose that $\alpha = 1000$ and $\beta = 10$. The resulting demand and supply curves, and their inverses, are drawn in Graph 19.10, with before- and after-tax prices and quantities calculated using the previous equations and assuming $t = 10$. We know that since tastes for x are quasilinear, consumer surplus shrinks from the original area $(a + b + c)$ to just (a) while producer surplus shrinks from $(d + e + f)$ to just (f) while tax revenue grows from zero to area $(b + d)$, leaving a deadweight loss of $(c + e)$.

Graph 19.10 Welfare Changes with Quasilinear Demand

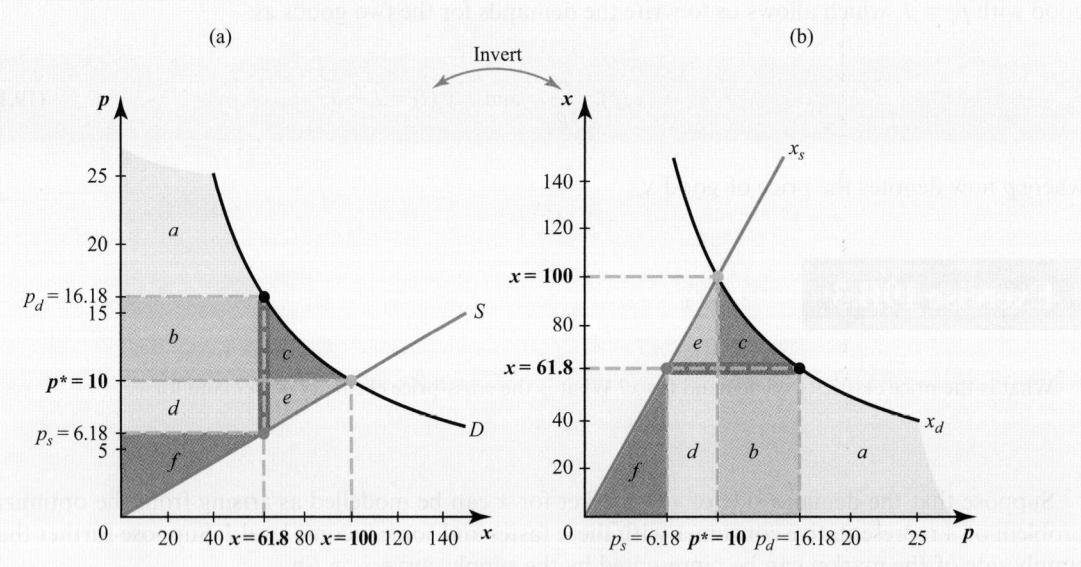

19B.2.1 Calculating Deadweight Loss Using Integrals Changes in consumer and producer surpluses can be derived using integrals to calculate the appropriate areas under the curves. Using the functions graphed in panel (b) of Graph 19.10, the change in consumer surplus $(b + c)$ is:

$$\Delta CS = \int_{p^*}^{p_d} x_d(p)dp = \int_{p^*}^{p_d} \frac{\alpha}{p}dp$$
$$= \alpha(\ln p_d - \ln p^*) = 1000(\ln(16.18) - \ln(10)) \approx 481 \tag{19.13}$$

and the change in producer surplus $(d + e)$ is:

$$\Delta PS = \int_{p_s}^{p^*} x_s(p)dp = \int_{p_s}^{p^*} (\beta p)dp = \frac{\beta}{2}((p^*)^2 - p_s^2) = 5(10^2 - 6.18^2) \approx 309. \tag{19.14}$$

Exercise 19B.5

Can you verify that our answer for ΔPS is correct by calculating the area of the rectangle (d) and the triangle (e) in Graph 19.10?

Summing the change in producer and consumer surplus, we get a total loss of surplus equal to approximately €790. The tax revenue collected by the government is equal to the €10 per-unit tax times the 61.8 units sold under the tax, or approximately €618. This gives us a deadweight loss of approximately €172.

19B.2.2 Calculating Deadweight Loss Using the Expenditure Function In Chapter 10, we also developed an alternative way of calculating the change in consumer surplus using the expenditure function. In particular, we concluded that the ΔCS (area $(b + c)$) is equal to the maximum lump sum tax the representative consumer would be willing to pay to avoid having the distortionary tax imposed. Substituting the demands $x_d(p)$ and $y_d(I)$ from equation (19.10) into the utility function $u(x, y) = \alpha \ln x + y$, we can derive the indirect utility function $V(p, I) = \alpha \ln (\alpha/p) + I - \alpha$. Because of the underlying quasilinearity in x, it does not matter in this case what income level we pick as long as it does not result in a corner solution. In our case, there is an interior solution as long as $I > \alpha$. Inverting this and replacing V with a utility value u, we can then get the expenditure function:

$$E(p, u) = u + \alpha - \alpha \ln \frac{\alpha}{p}. \tag{19.15}$$

Exercise 19B.6

Can you derive this expenditure function more directly through an expenditure minimization problem?

The representative consumer's utility under the distortionary tax is:

$$u_t = V(p_d, I) = \alpha \ln x_d(p_d) + y_d(I) = \alpha \ln \frac{\alpha}{p_d} + (I - \alpha), \tag{19.16}$$

and the expenditure necessary to reach that utility level u_t without distorting prices is:

$$\begin{aligned} E(p^*, u_t) &= u_t + \alpha - \alpha \ln \frac{\alpha}{p^*} = \alpha \left(\ln \frac{\alpha}{p_d} - \ln \frac{\alpha}{p^*} \right) + I \\ &= \alpha(\ln \alpha - \ln p_d - (\ln \alpha - \ln p^*)) + I = \alpha(\ln p^* - \ln p_d) + I \\ &= \alpha \ln \left(\frac{p^*}{p_d} \right) + I, \end{aligned} \tag{19.17}$$

where we use the property of logarithms that $(a/b) = \ln a - \ln b$.

Exercise 19B.7

Can you verify that the expenditure necessary to reach the after-tax utility at the pre-tax price is always less than or equal to I?

Exercise 19B.8

What has to be true for $E(p^*, u_t) = I$ to hold?

Finally, the maximum lump sum amount our representative consumer is willing to give up to avoid the distortionary tax, area $(b + c)$ in Graph 19.10, is the difference between the consumer's income and the expenditure necessary to get the consumer to their after-tax utility level at pre-tax prices $E(p^*, u)$; that is:

$$\Delta CS = I - E(p^*, u_t) = I - \left(\alpha \ln\left(\frac{p^*}{p_d}\right) + I \right)$$

$$= -\alpha \ln\left(\frac{p^*}{p_d}\right) = -1000 \ \ln\left(\frac{10}{16.18}\right) \approx 481.$$

(19.18)

Exercise 19B.9

Can you show that in general, before substituting in specific pre- and post-tax prices, equation (19.13), which we derived using integral calculus, and equation (19.18), which we derived using the expenditure function, yield identical results?

The representative consumer is therefore willing to pay €481 in a lump sum amount in order to avoid the tax. The consumer's share of tax revenue, however, is only €6.18(61.8) ≈ €382, implying a deadweight loss of approximately €99 on the consumer side of the market. On the producer side, we could similarly calculate profit before and after the tax and then compare the change in profit to the tax actually paid by producers. In our example, however, the supply curve is linear, and we can see in Graph 19.10 that the deadweight loss on the producer side is the triangle (e), which is $(100 - 61.8)(10 - 6.18)/2 \approx$ €73. Summing the deadweight losses from the two sides of the market, we get an overall deadweight loss of approximately €172, just as we did when we used integrals in the previous section.

Table 19.1 illustrates the impact of different levels of per-unit taxes for this example. Notice that as we have previously noted, deadweight loss increases at a significantly faster rate than the tax rate. However, because the price elasticity of demand is -1 everywhere, as you should have concluded in exercise 19B.3, no tax rate is ever high enough to fully shut down the market. In fact, given what we learned about the relationship between price elasticity of demand and consumer spending, we know that a price elasticity of -1 implies that consumers will always spend the same amount on their consumption of x regardless of price, which further implies that tax revenue always increases with higher tax rates.

Table 19.1 $x_d(p) = 1000/p, x_s(p) = 10p$							
			Welfare Changes From Per-Unit Tax				
t	P_d	P_s	$x_d = x_s$	ΔCS	ΔPS	Revenue	DWL
0	€10.00	€10.00	100.00	€0.00	€0.00	€0.00	€0.00
1	€10.51	€9.51	95.12	€49.98	€47.56	€95.12	€2.42
2	€11.05	€9.05	90.50	€99.83	€90.50	€181.00	€9.34
3	€11.61	€8.61	86.12	€149.44	€129.18	€258.36	€20.27
4	€12.20	€8.20	81.98	€198.69	€163.96	€327.92	€34.73
5	€12.81	€7.81	78.08	€247.47	€195.19	€390.39	€52.27
10	€16.18	€6.18	61.80	€481.21	€309.02	€618.08	€172.19
25	€28.51	€3.51	35.08	€1047.59	€438.48	€876.95	€609.12
50	€51.93	€1.93	19.26	€1647.23	€481.46	€962.91	€1165.76
100	€100.99	€0.99	9.90	€2312.44	€495.10	€990.20	€1817.34
1000	€1000.10	€0.10	1.00	€4605.27	€499.95	€999.90	€4105.32

Exercise 19B.10

Does the Laffer curve in this example have a peak? Why or why not?

When the tastes are not quasilinear, substitution effects will cause the compensated demand curve to differ from the uncompensated demand, implying that welfare changes and deadweight loss cannot be measured along the market demand curve. We will encounter this in the next section in our example of labour markets. In cases like this we can use the same expenditure function method developed here to calculate the change in consumer surplus.

19B.3 Deadweight Loss From Taxes in Labour and Capital Markets

Let's return to the example of workers with Cobb–Douglas tastes over leisure and consumption, as introduced in Chapter 9, represented by the utility function $u(c, \ell) = c^\alpha \ell^{(1-\alpha)}$. Given leisure endowment L, this implies demand for leisure and consumption of:

$$\ell = (1 - \alpha)L \quad \text{and} \quad c = \alpha w L. \tag{19.19}$$

Since labour supply is leisure endowment minus leisure consumption, this implies a perfectly inelastic labour supply function:

$$l_s = L - (1 - \alpha)L = \alpha L. \tag{19.20}$$

Exercise 19B.11

Verify that this labour supply function has zero wage elasticity of supply.

Suppose that a worker has 60 leisure hours per week ($L = 60$) and that $\alpha = 2/3$. The labour supply function implies that the worker will work 40 hours per week regardless of wage. If there are 1000 workers in this labour market, each having the same leisure endowment and the same tastes, this further implies a vertical market supply of labour at 60 000 hours per week. Suppose further that the market demand for labour is given by $l_d(w) = 25\,000\,000/w^2$. Setting this equal to the inelastic labour supply of 60 000, we can derive an equilibrium wage of $w^* = 25$.

Exercise 19B.12

What is the wage elasticity of labour demand?

19B.3.1 Calculating Deadweight Loss in the Labour Market

Now suppose a wage tax of €10 per labour hour is imposed as an additional cost on producers. Given the perfectly inelastic labour supply in this market, this drives the equilibrium wage down to €15, leaving producers entirely unaffected, given that they now pay a wage of €15 plus a €10 tax for a total of €25 per worker hour as before. We can focus entirely on the worker side of the market to determine deadweight loss from the tax.

Consider an individual worker who continues to work 40 hours per week under the lower wage. To determine the deadweight loss from the tax for this particular worker, we can ask the question: How much could we take from this worker in a lump sum way and leave them just as well off as they are when their wage drops from €25 to €15? Or, how much could we take in a lump sum way to make the worker just as well off as they are when their wage declines from w^* to $(w^* - t)$?

To answer this question, we first have to determine how happy the worker is under the tax t. Since the worker will always consume $(1 - \alpha)L$ in leisure, their consumption is given by $\alpha(w^* - t)L$. Substituting these values into their utility function, we get utility u_t under a tax t of:

$$u_t = (\alpha(w^* - t)L)^\alpha((1 - \alpha)L)^{(1-\alpha)} = \alpha^\alpha(1 - \alpha)^{(1-\alpha)}(w^* - t)^\alpha L. \tag{19.21}$$

Next, we have to determine how much expenditure would be necessary to achieve this utility level u_t if the wage were still w^*. The expenditure function emerges from the worker's expenditure minimization problem:

$$\min_{c, \ell} E = w\ell + c \text{ subject to } u_t = c^\alpha \ell^{(1-\alpha)}. \tag{19.22}$$

Solving this, we get the compensated leisure and consumption demands:

$$\ell^c(w) = \left(\frac{1 - \alpha}{\alpha w}\right)^\alpha u_t \quad \text{and} \quad c^c(w) = \left(\frac{\alpha w}{1 - \alpha}\right)^{(1-\alpha)} u_t, \tag{19.23}$$

and, substituting these back into $E = w\ell + c$, the expenditure function:

$$E(w, u_t) = \frac{w^{(1-\alpha)}u_t}{\alpha^\alpha(1 - \alpha)^{(1-\alpha)}}. \tag{19.24}$$

Exercise 19B.13

Verify this.

For instance, in our example of a worker with $\alpha = 2/3$ and $L = 60$ facing a tax that decreases their wage from $w^* = 25$ to $(w^* - t) = 15$, we can use equation (19.21) to calculate their after-tax utility as $u_t \approx 193.1$. Substituting this into equation (19.24), we get that the expenditure necessary to achieve this utility level in the absence of taxes is $E(w^*, u_t) \approx 1067.07$. Since the value of the worker's leisure endowment is €1500 (i.e. their leisure endowment of 60 hours times the wage of €25), this implies we could have raised approximately €432.93 from the worker in a lump sum way and kept them just as happy as they were under the €10 tax. Under the €10 wage tax, we raised only €400 from them, implying a deadweight loss of approximately €32.93. With 1000 workers in this market, the overall deadweight loss is, therefore, approximately €32 930.

We can then write the expression for deadweight loss per worker as:

$$DWL(t) = [w^*L - E(w^*, u_t)] - (tl_s(w - t)), \qquad (19.25)$$

where the term in brackets is the amount we could have raised in a lump sum way without making the worker worse off than they are under the tax and the term outside the brackets is the actual tax revenue from the wage tax.

Exercise 19B.14

Can you find in a graph such as panel (b) of Graph 19.6 the various numbers we have just calculated?

Table 19.2 illustrates the welfare and revenue effects of different levels of wage taxes for this example.

Table 19.2 $u(c, \ell) = c^\alpha \ell^{(1-\alpha)}$, $\alpha = 2/3$, $\ell = 60$

				Per-Worker Welfare Changes From Per-Hour Wage Tax				
t	(w^*-t)	$l_s(w^*-t)$	$l_s^c(w^*)$	u_t	$E(w^*, u_t)$	$\Delta Surplus$	$Revenue$	DWL
0	€25.00	40.00	40.00	271.44	€1500.00	€0.00	€0.00	€0.00
1	€24.00	40.00	40.53	264.15	€1459.73	€40.27	€40.00	€0.27
2	€23.00	40.00	41.08	256.76	€1418.89	€81.11	€80.00	€1.11
3	€22.00	40.00	41.63	249.27	€1377.46	€122.54	€120.00	€2.54
4	€21.00	40.00	42.19	241.66	€1335.40	€164.60	€160.00	€4.60
5	€20.00	40.00	42.76	233.92	€1292.66	€207.34	€200.00	€7.34
10	€15.00	40.00	45.77	193.10	€1067.07	€432.93	€400.00	€32.93
15	€10.00	40.00	49.14	147.36	€814.33	€685.67	€600.00	€85.67
20	€5.00	40.00	53.16	92.83	€512.99	€987.01	€800.00	€187.01
25	€0.00	40.00	60.00	0.00	€0.00	€1500.00	€1000.00	€500.00

19B.3.2 **Using Compensated Labour Supply to Calculate Deadweight Loss** In panel (c) of Graph 19.6, we argued that there was an alternative way of identifying deadweight loss as an area on the compensated labour supply curve.

Just as the uncompensated labour supply curve is the uncompensated leisure demand subtracted from the leisure endowment, the compensated labour supply curve l_s^c is the compensated leisure demand from equation (19.23) subtracted from leisure endowment L; that is:

$$l_s^c(w, u_t) = L - \ell^c(w) = L - \left(\frac{1-\alpha}{\alpha w}\right)^\alpha u_t.$$

(19.26)

In panel (b) of Graph 19.11, this function is graphed for $u_t = 193.1$, $L = 60$ and $\alpha = 2/3$ together with the inelastic uncompensated labour supply curve, and panel (a) graphs the inverses of these functions to facilitate comparison to Graph 19.6 where we first argued that deadweight loss can be measured on the compensated labour supply curve.

Graph 19.11 Deadweight Loss From a Wage Tax

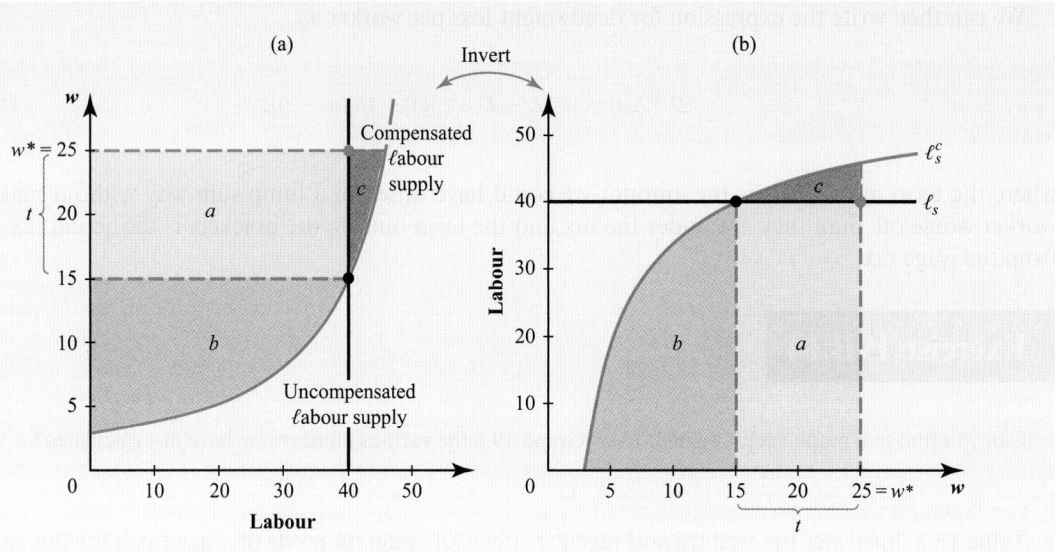

Areas under the compensated labour supply curve are defined by the integral:

$$\int l_s^c(w, u_t)dw = \left(Lw - \frac{w^{(1-\alpha)}u_t}{\alpha^\alpha(1-\alpha)^{(1-\alpha)}}\right),$$

(19.27)

which, when evaluated from w of 15 to 25 (with $u_t = 193.1$, $L = 60$ and $\alpha = 2/3$), gives area $(a + c)$ as:

$$\text{area } (a + c) = \int_{15}^{25} l_s^c(w, u_t)dw \approx 432.93.$$

(19.28)

Note that this is equal to the lump sum tax that would get the worker to the same utility level as the wage tax $t = 10$. Subtracting from that the actual tax revenue collected (area (a) in the graph), we again get deadweight loss of approximately €32.93 per worker, which is equal to area (c).

19B.3.3 DWL and Revenue as Tax Rates Rise In Graph 19.8, we illustrated for linear demand and supply curves the impact of raising tax rates on tax revenue and deadweight loss, under the assumption that un-compensated and compensated demand are equivalent. For tax revenue, we derived an inverted U-shape for the Laffer curve, indicating the existence of a tax rate that maximizes revenue. For deadweight loss, we argued that, as in earlier chapters, increasing a tax by a factor of k will often increase the deadweight loss by a factor of approximately k^2.

Consider the demand and supply functions given by $x_d(p) = (A - p)/\alpha$ and $x_s(p) = (p - B)/\beta$, and assume that there are no income effects. We can derive the equilibrium consumer price p_d and the equilibrium producer price $p_s = (p_d - t)$ as:

$$P_d = \frac{\beta A + \alpha B + \alpha t}{\alpha + \beta} \quad \text{and} \quad p_s = \frac{\beta A + \alpha B - \beta t}{\alpha + \beta}, \tag{19.29}$$

and the equilibrium quantity x_t as:

$$x_t = \frac{A - B - t}{\alpha + \beta}. \tag{19.30}$$

Exercise 19B.15

Verify these.

Tax revenue is the per-unit tax rate t times the quantity transacted x_t, which reduces to:

$$TR = \frac{(A - B)t - t^2}{\alpha + \beta}. \tag{19.31}$$

This is the functional form graphed in panel (b) of Graph 19.8, and it attains its peak when its derivative with respect to the tax rate is zero. You can verify for yourself that this occurs when $t = (A - B)/2$.

It is somewhat more tedious to derive the equation for deadweight loss, but if you are careful in the various algebra steps involved, you can verify that:

$$DWL(t) = \Delta CS + \Delta PS - TR = \frac{t^2}{2(\alpha + \beta)}. \tag{19.32}$$

Exercise 19B.16**

Verify the expression for deadweight loss. *Hint*: There are two ways of doing this: you can either take the appropriate integrals of the supply and demand functions evaluated over the appropriate ranges of prices, or you can add rectangles and triangles in a graph.

Thus, if a tax rate t is multiplied by k, the resulting deadweight loss will be k^2 the original deadweight loss; that is:

$$DWL(kt) = \frac{(kt)^2}{2(\alpha + \beta)} = k^2 \frac{t^2}{2(\alpha + \beta)} = k^2 DWL(t). \tag{19.33}$$

Both the Laffer curve and the result about increases in deadweight loss with increases in tax rates, therefore, arise straightforwardly in a partial equilibrium model with linear demand and supply curves, and these results form the basis for much intuition that guides tax policy. As we can see from our example in Table 19.1, however, these are only rules of thumb, and they do not necessarily arise the same way in all models. With unitary price elastic demand in Table 19.1, for instance, the Laffer curve does not attain a peak but only converges to a maximum tax revenue as the tax rate rises. This is a direct consequence of the unitary price elasticity of demand, which implies consumer spending on the taxed good never declines. In the real world, of course, it is unlikely that any demand curve truly has price elasticity of -1 regardless of how high the price goes, and we would therefore expect an eventual downward slope to the Laffer curve. Similarly, in Table 19.2, tax revenue for a wage tax continues to rise with the tax rate because of the perfectly inelastic labour supply curve.

You might also have noticed that deadweight loss in Table 19.1, while increasing at an increasing rate, does not increase in the same way as it does in the linear case. The rule of thumb that an increase in a tax rate by a factor k will lead to an increase in deadweight loss by a factor k^2 is therefore just that: a rule of thumb derived from the linear case. In Table 19.2, on the other hand, deadweight loss from multiplying the wage tax by a factor k increases by more than k^2. Even though the rule of thumb about the relationship between increases in tax rates and increases in deadweight losses does not hold precisely in all cases, it is typically the case that deadweight loss increases at an increasing rate as tax rates rise, leading to the common policy recommendation that it is more efficient to raise tax revenues through low tax rates on large tax bases rather than high tax rates on small tax bases.

19B.4 Taxing Land

We argued in Section A that a tax on land rents is one real-world tax that does not give rise to deadweight losses and is therefore efficient. The mathematics behind this was already explored somewhat in Section A.

19B.5 A Simple Example of General Equilibrium Tax Incidence

In Section A, we also briefly introduced the notion that tax burdens may not only be shifted between buyers and sellers within the taxed market, as in the partial equilibrium models of this chapter, but may also be shifted to actors outside the taxed market through general equilibrium effects. We mentioned in particular a tax on housing that leads to a reallocation of capital away from housing and into other uses, thereby reducing the rate of return to non-housing capital and thus shifting a portion of the tax burden to owners of non-housing capital.

We can illustrate the basic intuition behind this in a simple setting. Suppose we modelled owners of capital as a 'representative investor' who chooses to allocate K units of capital between the housing sector and all other sectors that make use of capital. Letting capital invested in housing be denoted by k_1 and capital invested in other uses by k_2, let's assume that the before-tax rate of return in the housing sector is determined by the production function $f_1(k_1) = \alpha k_1^{1/2}$, and the rate of return in the untaxed remaining sector is determined by the production function $f_2(k_2) = \beta k_2^{1/2}$. Suppose the government imposes a tax of t per cent on housing.

Our representative investor wants to maximize their total after-tax return by optimally choosing the allocation of their capital K across the two sectors. They want to solve the maximization problem:

$$\max_{k_1, k_2} (1 - t)f_1(k_1) + f_2(k_2) \text{ subject to } k_1 + k_2 = K. \tag{19.34}$$

The solution to this problem is:

$$k_1^* = \frac{(1 - t)^2\alpha^2 K}{(1 - t)^2\alpha^2 + \beta^2} \text{ and } k_2^* = \frac{\beta^2 K}{(1 - t)^2\alpha^2 + \beta^2}. \tag{19.35}$$

Table 19.3 demonstrates how the tax t on housing is partially shifted to other forms of capital when 1000 units of capital are available to the representative investor and when $\alpha = \beta = 100$, which implies that equal amounts are invested in housing and other forms of capital in the absence of taxes. The last column of Table 19.3 represents the marginal product of a unit of capital in the untaxed sector, and in equilibrium this has to be equal to the after-tax marginal product of a unit of capital in the taxed sector, which is reported in the second to last column. In the absence of taxes (first row), these marginal products are equal to 2.24. As the tax on housing is increased going down the table, this marginal product declines as capital is shifted out of the taxed sector, where its after-tax return is falling, and into the untaxed sector. Thus, even though the tax is imposed on housing, the burden of the tax falls equally on all capital. Implicitly, we are assuming that capital is perfectly mobile between sectors.

Table 19.3 $K = 1000$, $\alpha = \beta = 100$

Shifting of Housing Tax to Other Forms of Capital

t	k_1^*	k_2^*	$MP_1(k_1^*)$	$(1-t)MP_1(k_1^*)$	$MP_2(k_2^*)$
0	500.00	500.00	2.24	2.24	2.24
0.1	447.51	552.49	2.36	2.13	2.13
0.2	390.24	609.76	2.53	2.02	2.02
0.3	328.86	671.14	2.76	1.93	1.93
0.4	264.71	735.29	3.07	1.84	1.84
0.5	200.00	800.00	3.54	1.77	1.77
0.6	137.93	862.07	4.26	1.70	1.70
0.7	82.57	917.43	5.50	1.65	1.65
0.8	38.46	961.54	8.06	1.61	1.61
0.9	9.90	990.01	15.89	1.59	1.59

Exercise 19B.17

For $t = 0.5$, verify that the marginal product columns of Table 19.3 report the correct results.

Exercise 19B.18

If capital is sector-specific and cannot move from one use to another, would you still expect the housing tax to shift? Explain.

In addition to the degree of capital mobility between sectors, the degree to which owners of capital in other sectors are affected by a tax on housing also depends on the pre-tax size of the housing sector relative to the non-housing sector. In Table 19.3, we set values for the example so that the two sectors are initially of equal size. In Table 19.4, on the other hand, we keep α plus β at 200 but reduce the ratio of α/β below 1, which has the effect of reducing the housing sector relative to the non-housing sector. The final column of Table 19.4 reports the percentage drop in the marginal product of capital that results from a 50 per cent tax on housing.

Exercise 19B.19

Why is the relative size of the housing sector relevant for determining how much owners of capital in other sectors are affected by a tax on housing capital?

Table 19.4 $K = 1000$, $t = 0.5$, $\alpha + \beta = 200$

Tax Shifting Depends on Relative Size of Housing Sector

α/β	$(k_1/k_2)_{before}$	$(k_1/k_2)_{after}$	MP_{before}	MP_{after}	% Change
1	1.0000	0.2500	2.236	1.768	−26.471%
1/2	0.2500	0.0625	2.357	2.173	−8.466%
1/3	0.1111	0.2778	2.500	2.404	−3.972%
1/4	0.0625	0.0156	2.608	2.550	−2.275%
1/5	0.0400	0.0100	2.687	2.648	−1.473%
1/10	0.0100	0.0025	2.889	2.878	−0.373%
1/50	0.0004	0.0001	3.101	3.100	−0.015%

End-of-chapter Exercises

19.1† In our discussion of economic versus statutory incidence, the text has focused primarily on the incidence of taxes. This exercise explores analogous issues related to the incidence of benefits from subsidies.

    A. Consider a price subsidy for x in a partial equilibrium model of demand and supply in the market for x.

        a. Explain why it does not matter whether the government gives the per-unit subsidy s to consumers or producers.

        b. Consider the case where the slopes of demand and supply curves are roughly equal in absolute value at the no-subsidy equilibrium. What does this imply for the way in which the benefits of the subsidy are divided between consumers and producers?

        c. How does your answer change if the demand curve is steeper than the supply curve at the no-subsidy equilibrium?

        d. How does your answer change if the demand curve is shallower than the supply curve at the no-subsidy equilibrium?

        e. Can you state your general conclusion – using the language of price elasticities – on how much consumers will benefit relative to producers when price subsidies are introduced. How is this similar to our conclusions on tax incidence?

        f. Do any of your answers depend on whether the tastes for x are quasilinear?

    B. *In Section 19B.1, we derived the impact of a marginal per-unit tax on the price received by producers; that is, dp_s/dt.

        a. Repeat the analysis for the case of a per-unit subsidy and derive dp_s/ds where s is the per-unit subsidy.

        b. What is dp_d/ds?

        c. What do your results in (a) and (b) tell you about the economic incidence of a per-unit subsidy when the price elasticity of demand is zero? What about when the price elasticity of supply is zero?

        d. What does your analysis suggest about the economic incidence of the subsidy when the price elasticities of demand and supply are equal in absolute value, at the no-subsidy equilibrium?

        e. More generally, can you show which side of the market gets the greater benefit when the absolute value of the price elasticity of demand is less than the price elasticity of supply?

19.2 In the chapter, we discussed the deadweight loss from taxes on consumption goods when tastes are quasilinear in the taxed good, and we treated deadweight loss when tastes are not quasilinear for the case of wage taxes. In this exercise, we will consider deadweight losses from taxation on consumption goods when tastes are not quasilinear.

A. Suppose that x is a normal good for consumers.

    a. Draw the market demand and supply graph for x and illustrate the impact on prices for consumers and producers, and output levels when a per-unit tax t on x is introduced.

    b. Would your answer to (a) have been any different had we assumed that all consumers' tastes were quasilinear in x?

    c. On a consumer diagram with x on the horizontal and all other goods, denominated in euros on the vertical axes, illustrate the impact of the tax on a consumer's budget.

    d. In your graph from (c), illustrate the portion of deadweight loss that is due to this particular consumer.

    e. On a third graph, depict the demand curve for x for the consumer whose consumer diagram you graphed in (d). Then illustrate on this graph the same deadweight loss that you first illustrated in (d).

    f. Now return to your graph from (a). Illustrate where deadweight loss lies in this graph. How does it compare to the case where the original market demand curve arises from quasilinear tastes rather than the tastes we are analyzing in this exercise?

    g. *True or False*: We will overestimate the deadweight loss if we use market demand curves to measure changes in consumer surplus from taxation of normal goods.

B. Suppose that consumers all have Cobb–Douglas tastes that can be represented by the utility function $u(x, y) = x^\alpha y^{(1-\alpha)}$ and each consumer has income I. Assume throughout that the price of y is normalized to 1.

    a. Derive the uncompensated demand for x by a consumer.

    b. Suppose income is expressed in thousands of euros and each consumer has income $I = 2.5$, i.e. income of €2500. There are 1000 consumers in the market. What is the market demand function?

    c. Suppose market supply is given by $x_s = \beta p$. Derive the market equilibrium price and output level.

    d. Suppose $\alpha = 0.4$ and $\beta = 10$. Determine the equilibrium p_d, p_s and x_t when $t = 10$. How do these compare to what we calculated for the quasilinear tastes in Section 19B.2.1, where we assumed $\alpha = 1000$ and $\beta = 10$, as graphed in Graph 19.10?

    e. What is the before-tax and after-tax quantity transacted?

    f. If you used the market demand and supply curves to estimate deadweight loss, what would it be?

    g. Calculate the real deadweight loss in this case, and explain why it is different from in Section 19B.2.1 where market demand and supply curves were the same as here.

19.3† In the text, we discussed deadweight losses that arise from wage *taxes* even when labour supply is perfectly inelastic. We now consider wage *subsidies*.

A. Suppose that the current market wage is w^* and that labour supply for all workers is perfectly inelastic. The government agrees to pay employers a per-hour wage subsidy of €$_s$ for every worker hour they employ.

    a. Will employers get any benefit from this subsidy? Will employees?

    b. In a consumer diagram with leisure ℓ on the horizontal and consumption c on the vertical axes, illustrate the impact of the subsidy on worker budget constraints.

    c. Choose a bundle A that is optimal before the subsidy goes into effect. Locate the bundle that is optimal after the subsidy.

    d. Illustrate the size of the subsidy payment S as a vertical distance in the graph.

    e. Illustrate how much P we could have paid the worker in a lump sum way without distorting wages to make them just as well off as they are under the wage subsidy. Then locate the deadweight loss of the wage subsidy as a vertical distance in your graph.

    f. On a separate graph, illustrate the inelastic labour supply curve as well as the before- and after-subsidy points on that curve. Then illustrate the appropriate compensated labour supply curve on which to measure the deadweight loss. Explain where this deadweight loss lies in your graph.

g. *True or False*: As long as leisure and consumption are at least somewhat substitutable, compensated labour supply curves always slope up and wage subsidies that increase worker wages create deadweight losses.

B. Suppose that as in our treatment of wage taxes, tastes over consumption c and leisure ℓ can be represented by the utility function $u(c, \ell) = c^\alpha \ell^{(1-\alpha)}$ and that all workers have leisure endowment of L, and no other source of income. Suppose further that, again as in the text, the equilibrium wage in the absence of distortions is $w^* = 25$.

a. If the government offers an €11 per-hour wage subsidy for employers, how does this affect the wage costs for employers and the wages received by employees?

b. Assume henceforth that $\alpha = 0.5$. What is the utility level u_s attained by workers under the subsidy as a function of leisure endowment L?

c. *What is the least, in terms of leisure endowment L, we would need to give each worker in a lump sum way to get them to agree to give up the wage subsidy program?

d. *What is the per-worker deadweight loss in terms of leisure endowment L of the subsidy?

e. **Use the compensated labour supply curve to verify your answer.

19.4 **Business and Policy Application:** *Land Use Policies.* In most Western democracies, it is settled law that governments cannot simply confiscate land for public purposes. Such confiscation is labelled a 'taking', and even when the government has compelling reasons to take someone's property for public use, such as through compulsory purchase, it must compensate the landowner. While it is clear that a 'taking' has occurred when the government confiscates private land without compensation, constitutional lawyers disagree on how close the government has to come to literally confiscating private land before the action constitutes an unconstitutional 'taking'.

A. Any restriction that alters the way land would otherwise be used reduces the annual rental value of that land and, from the owner's perspective, can therefore be treated as a tax on rental value.

a. Explain why this statement is correct.

b. Suppose a land use regulation is equivalent from the owner's perspective to a tax of t per cent on land rents to be statutorily paid by landowners (where $0 < t < 1$). How does it affect the market value of the land?

c. Person X is about to buy an acre of land from you in order to build on it. Right before you both agree on a price, the government imposes a new zoning regulation that limits what X can do on the land. Who is definitively made worse off by this?

d. Suppose you own 1000 acres of land that is currently zoned for residential development. Then suppose the government determines that your land is home to a rare species of bat, and that it is in the public interest for no economic activity to take place on this land in order to protect this endangered species. From your perspective, what approximate tax rate on land rents that you collect is this regulation equivalent to? Do you think this is a 'taking'?

e. Suppose that instead of prohibiting all economic activity on your 1000 acres, the government reduces your ability to build residential housing on it to a single house. How does your answer change? What if it restricts housing development to 500 acres? Do you think this would be a 'taking'?

B. *Suppose that people gain utility from housing services h and other consumption x, with tastes described by the utility function $u(x, h) = \ln x + \ln h$. Consumption is denominated in euros with price therefore normalized to 1. Housing services, on the other hand, are derived from the production process $h = k^{0.5}L^\alpha$, where k stands for units of capital and L for acres of land. Suppose $0 < \alpha < 1$. Let the rental rate of capital be denoted by r, and assume each person has income of 1000.

a. Write down the utility maximization problem and solve for the demand function for land assuming a rental rate R for land.

b. Suppose your region consists of 100 000 individuals like this, and there are 25 000 acres of land available. What is the equilibrium rental rate per acre of land as a function of α?

c. Using your answers, derive the amount of land each person will consume.

d. Suppose the government imposes zoning regulations that reduce the coefficient α in the production function from 0.5 to 0.25. What happens to the equilibrium rental value of land?

e. Suppose that what you have calculated so far is the monthly rental value of land. What happens to the total value of an acre of land as a result of these zoning regulations assuming that people use a monthly interest rate of 0.5 per cent to discount the future?

f. Suppose that instead of lowering α from 0.5 to 0.25 through regulation, the government imposes a tax t on the market rental value of land and statutorily requires renters to pay. Thus, if the market land rental rate is R per acre, those using the land must pay tR on top of the rent R for every acre they use. Set up the renters' utility maximization problem, derive the demand for land and aggregate it over all 100 000 individuals. Then derive the equilibrium land rent per acre as a function of t, assuming $\alpha = 0.5$.

g. Does the amount of land consumed by each household change?

h. Suppose you own land that you rent out. What level of t makes you indifferent between the zoning regulation that drove α from 0.5 to 0.25 and the land rent tax that does not change α?

i. Suppose the government statutorily collected the land rent tax from the owner instead of from the renter. What would the tax rate then have to be set at to make the landowner indifferent between the zoning regulation and the tax?

19.5† Business and Policy Application: *Price Floors for Wheat: Is it a Tax or a Subsidy?*

A. For simplicity, assume that tastes are quasilinear in wheat.

a. We begin by considering a price floor without any additional government programme. Illustrate the equilibrium impact of such a price floor on the price of wheat paid by consumers as well as the price of wheat received by producers.

b. If you were to design a tax or subsidy policy that has the same impact as the standalone price floor, what would it be?

c. Consider the combination of a price floor and a government purchasing programme under which the government guarantee it will purchase any surplus wheat at the price floor and then sell it at a price sufficiently low for all of it to be bought. Illustrate the impact of this programme, including the deadweight loss.

d. If you were to design a tax or subsidy policy with the aim of achieving the same outcome for the marginal consumer and producer as the policy in (c), what would you propose?

e. Would your proposal result in the same level of consumer and producer surplus? Would it result in the same deadweight loss?

B. Suppose that the domestic demand curve for tonnes of wheat is given by $p = 24 - 0.00000000225x$ while the domestic supply curve is given by $p = 1 + 0.00000000025x$.

a. Suppose the government imposes a price ceiling of $\bar{p} = 3.5$. In the absence of any other programme, how much will consumers pay per tonne and how much will sellers keep per tonne after accounting for the additional marginal costs incurred by producers to compete for consumers?

b. If you wanted to replicate this same outcome using taxes or subsidies, what policy would you propose?

c. Suppose that the government supplemented its price floor from (a) with a government purchasing programme that buys all surplus wheat, and then sells it at the highest possible price at which all surplus wheat is bought. What is that price?

d. If you were to design a tax or subsidy policy that has the same impact on the marginal consumer and producer, what would it be?

13.6 Policy Application: *Rent Control: Is it a Tax or a Subsidy?* Consider rent control policies that impose a price ceiling in the housing rental market. The stated intent of such policies is often to make housing more affordable.

A. Begin by illustrating the impact of the rent control price ceiling on the price received by landlords and the eventual equilibrium price paid by renters.

a. Why is it not an equilibrium for the price ceiling to be the rent actually paid by renters?

b. If you wanted to implement a tax or subsidy policy that achieves the same outcome as the rent control policy, what policy would you propose?

    c. Could you credibly argue that the alternative policy you proposed in (b) was designed to make housing more affordable?

    d. If you did actually want to make housing more affordable, rather than trying to replicate the impact of rent control policies, would you choose a subsidy or a tax?

    e. Illustrate your proposal from (d) and show what would happen to the rental price received by landlords and the rents paid by renters. What happens to the number of housing units available for rent under your new policy?

    f. *True or False*: Policies that make housing more affordable must invariably increase the equilibrium quantity of housing, and rent control policies fail because they reduce the equilibrium quantity of housing while subsidies succeed for the opposite reason.

    g. *True or False*: Although rental subsidies succeed at the goal of making housing more affordable while rent control policies fail to do so, we cannot in general say that deadweight loss is greater or less under one policy rather than the other.

B. Suppose that the aggregate monthly demand curve is $p = 10\,000 - 0.01x$ while the supply curve is $p = 1000 + 0.002x$. For simplicity, suppose that there are no income effects.

    a. Calculate the equilibrium number of flats x^* and the equilibrium monthly rent p^* in the absence of any price distortions.

    b. Now consider the impact of a €1500 price ceiling. What housing tax or subsidy would result in the same economic impact?

    c. Suppose that you wanted to use tax/subsidy policies to actually reduce rents to €1500, the stated goal of the rent control policy. What policy would you implement?

    d. Consider the policies you derived in (b) and (c). Under which policy is the deadweight loss greater?

Chapter 20

Prices and Distortions Across Markets

Markets are considerably more complex than simply a place where buyers and sellers come together, compete with one another and trade goods at the prices that emerge in equilibrium. Markets involve goods being traded across geographic markets, from city to city, region to region and country to country. With decreasing transportation costs in growing sectors such as information technology, services are often performed in one country for customers across the world, and goods are traded as much across time as they are across space, with some purchasing now to sell in the future and others selling now what they bought in the past – or, as we will see, what they intend to buy in the future.

In each of these cases, we can think of trade as occurring both within and across markets. When goods are shipped between cities, we don't usually pay much attention to such trades, but when goods cross international boundaries, we refer to those that bring the goods into a country as *importers* and those that ship them out of a country as *exporters*. When someone buys in today's market with the intention of selling when price rises in the future, on the other hand, we refer to this person as a *speculator*. In this chapter we will demonstrate that exporters, importers and speculators can play an important efficiency role in markets. Policies that disturb this interconnection of markets disturb price signals that contain information that coordinates markets, and for this reason, such policies can cause deadweight losses.

This chapter therefore represents the third chapter investigating violations of the first welfare theorem due to government policy distorting prices, by investigating policies that interfere with prices that govern trade *across* interacting markets. This will require us to take a somewhat more general equilibrium view, something we began to hint at in Chapter 19 when we briefly discussed the shifting of tax burdens from taxed sectors, like housing, to untaxed markets, like non-housing capital, through capital mobility. We will see the same phenomenon here: a shifting of taxes across markets when a tax is imposed in only one of multiple markets that are connected by some form of mobility of goods or inputs.

20A   Exporters, Importers and Speculators

Just as market competition results in an equilibrium in which stores that are next to one another charge the same prices, competition across neighbouring *markets* results in the equalization of prices across these markets as long as trade between them is relatively costless. In the former case, this happens because consumers themselves will seek out lower prices and thus provide a disciplining force in the market. In the case of competition across markets, on the other hand, new economic actors that are neither producers nor consumers will emerge if prices differ, because when prices differ, money can be made by buying low and selling high, a process known as 'arbitrage'. We will see that these new economic actors impose the same kind of disciplining force across markets as consumers impose within markets.

20A.1 Buying Low and Selling High

Consider two markets for door handles, one in Switzerland and another in Germany, and suppose the market demand and supply curves of consumers and producers in these two markets are as depicted in Graph 20.1. If these markets operate in complete isolation, this would result in the quantity x^S produced and sold at a price p^S in Switzerland and the quantity x^G produced and sold at a price p^G in Germany. Suppose that on a trip an individual notices the difference in prices across these markets. The individual can see an opportunity to make money by buying door handles in Switzerland, where prices are low, and selling them in Germany, where prices are high. They can make money by *exporting* door handles from Switzerland and *importing* them to Germany.

Graph 20.1 Equilibrium Across Two Markets

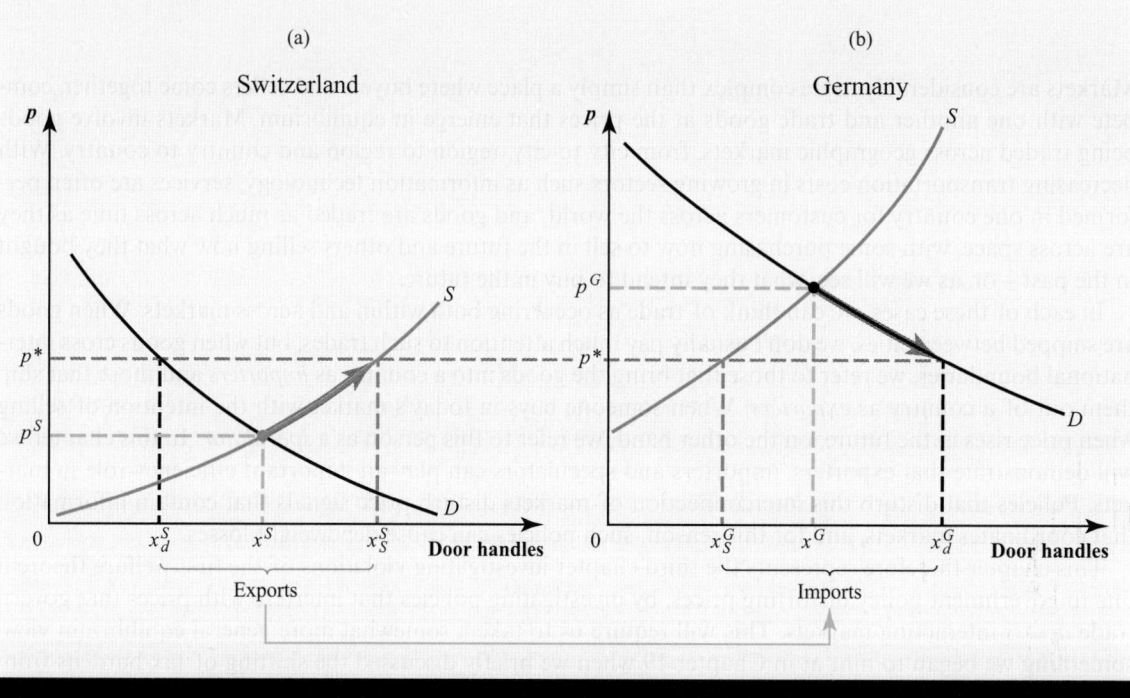

Go to MindTap to interact with this graph

It is unlikely that this individual is the only one who is in search of money-making opportunities. There are many in every economy who make it their business to find opportunities to buy low and sell high, and each one of them could find this same opportunity. Thus, exporters will go into the Switzerland market and shift the demand curve as they buy door handles, thus causing prices in Switzerland to rise. When they sell the same door handles in Germany, they will shift the supply curve, thus driving prices in Germany down. As long as there exist price differences that are larger than the cost of transporting the handles from one market to the other, this process will continue. If we abstract away from such transportation costs, the process of buying low and selling high will continue until prices are equal in the two markets, with the light blue arrows in the graphs indicating the shifts in equilibrium that result from the export of door handles from Switzerland to Germany. We are using the arrows to indicate how the equilibrium in each market changes as a result of changes in Swiss demand and German supply induced by exporters in order not to clutter the graph too much – and to keep in mind that demand by Swiss consumers is not shifting, neither is supply by Germans producers.

If we start in an initial equilibrium in which trade is not permitted between Switzerland and Germany, the opening up of trade between the markets will result in a new equilibrium in which the same price p^*

governs all trades in both Switzerland and Germany. This implies that producers in Switzerland will increase their production from x^S to x_s^S while consumers in Switzerland will lower their consumption from x^S to x_d^S as both face higher prices after trade is permitted than before. The dark brown difference between what is produced and what is consumed is exported to Germany, where consumers increase their consumption from x^G to x_d^G and producers decrease their production from x^G to x_s^G as both face lower prices than before. The dark blue difference between what is consumed and produced in Germany is what has been imported from Switzerland.

20A.1.1 Profits for Exporters and Importers

As we transition from the no-trade equilibrium to the trade equilibrium, exporters and importers are able to make economic profits by buying low and selling high. Notice that in the new equilibrium, the model suggests that exporters buy at the same price in Switzerland at which they sell in Germany. Why would they do this in equilibrium?

The answer is that the model gives us an approximation of the new equilibrium. Exporters and importers, just like everyone else in the world, face opportunity costs, which include the cost of their own time as well as the cost of shipping goods from one place to another. In equilibrium, they have to make enough to cover their opportunity costs. If they did not, they would be making negative economic, or subnormal profits, which tells us they could be doing better by undertaking another activity. Thus, prices will not fully equalize because some difference needs to remain to allow exporters and importers to cover their economic costs. However, the difference that remains will tend to be small in most markets given that exporters and importers ship large quantities of goods and therefore need only a tiny difference in price per unit to continue shipping goods from one place to another.

The fact that exporters and importers can make positive profits during the transition from a no-trade equilibrium to one with trade is consistent with our earlier work where producers often were able to make positive profits during the transition period from one equilibrium to another when economic conditions changed. This is the period over which entry and exit into an industry takes place, and it is that entry and exit that ultimately drives individual profits to zero. If the export/import business is also competitive in the sense that each economic actor in the business is small relative to the whole business, we know from what we have done previously that economic profits will be zero for each of them in the new equilibrium. As long as profits are positive, additional economic actors will enter the export/import business because they could be doing better here than in any other business.

For the purposes of our discussion, we will continue to illustrate an equilibrium with trade across regions as one in which the prices fully equalize as goods are exported from low-priced markets and imported into high-priced markets. We will do so with an implicit understanding that this is an approximation of the new equilibrium and that, in reality, prices might still differ slightly between markets as trade is unfolding.

20A.1.2 Winners and Losers From Trade Across Regions

Without doing much further analysis, it is already possible to identify the winners and losers by permitting trade across markets that were previously closed to one another. Consumers of door handles in Switzerland will be unhappy with the new equilibrium as they now have to pay higher prices than they did before. Producers in Switzerland, on the other hand, get to produce more at a higher price and therefore end up on the winning side. If all producers face the same costs, they would end up making zero profit once again in the new equilibrium. In that case, the long-run market supply curve would be perfectly elastic. Graph 20.1 implicitly assumes that producers face different costs, which results in an upward-sloping long-run supply curve. Similarly, consumers in Germany are better off as their prices drop, while producers in Germany are worse off as they face lower prices.

Exercise 20A.1

During the transition from the initial to the new equilibrium, which producers make positive profits and which might make negative long-run profits?

20A.1.3 Changes in Overall Surplus When Trade Is Permitted While we might indeed be quite interested in the changes in welfare for different groups, and while this almost certainly has an impact on the political decisions that are made about trade, the relevant issue from a pure efficiency perspective is whether trade makes the pie overall grow larger or smaller. Does trade across regions increase or decrease overall surplus?

To illustrate how surplus changes, it is easiest for us to assume that tastes over door handles are quasilinear because that allows us to interpret market demand curves as aggregate willingness to pay curves along which we can measure consumer surplus. The conclusion remains the same when tastes are not quasilinear, but the graphs would become more complex as we would have to introduce additional curves into the analysis.

Consider Graph 20.2, in which we replicate market demand and supply curves from Graph 20.1. In the absence of trade across the two regions, the initial consumer surplus in Switzerland is given by the area $(a + b)$, which is the area above the price paid by Swiss consumers up to their marginal willingness to pay curve. The initial producer surplus in Switzerland is given by area c, the area below the price received by producers down to their supply curve. Once trade has unfolded, consumer surplus shrinks to area a as consumers face higher prices, while producer surplus increases to area $(b + c + d)$. Thus, overall surplus in Switzerland increases by the dark brown area d because producer surplus increases more than consumer surplus shrinks. In Germany, on the other hand, consumer surplus increases from e to $(e + f + h)$, while producer surplus falls from $(f + g)$ to g. Thus, overall surplus in Germany also increases – by the dark blue area h – because in Germany consumers gain more than producers lose.

Graph 20.2 Changes in Surplus When Trade Is Permitted

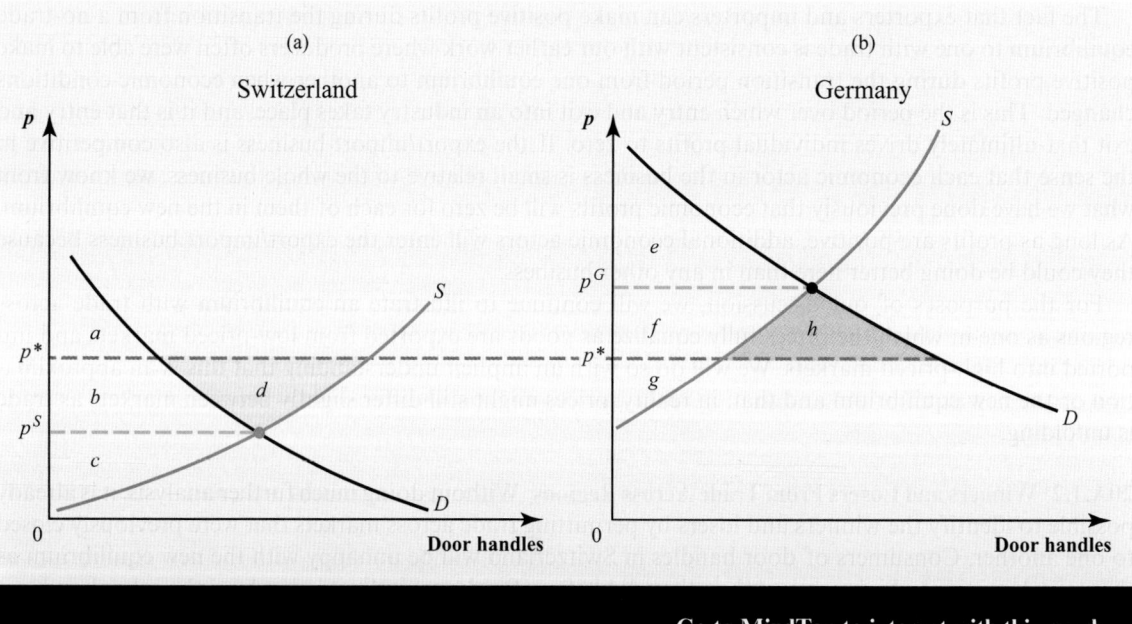

Go to MindTap to interact with this graph

The shaded areas in Graph 20.2 represent the equilibrium increase in overall surplus that is generated by the activities of exporters and importers across the two markets. Notice that nowhere in the analysis have we had to say anything about surplus for exporters and importers because we know that as long as the export/import industry is competitive, economic profit for exporters and importers will be zero. Trade makes both regions better off in the aggregate even though it causes some economic actors to be hurt (consumers in Switzerland and producers in Germany) while others benefit (producers in Switzerland and consumers in Germany). Because the overall surplus from trade increases, it is at least in principle possible to compensate the losers from trade with some of the gains from the winners of trade, thus leading to a potential for a unanimously shared improvement from the no-trade equilibrium to the new equilibrium.

20A.1.4 Restricting Trade and Price Gouging There is often heated debate over trade discussions, with one side arguing for the benefits of restricting trade and the other arguing for the benefits of allowing expanded trade. Since World War II, the world community has made enormous efforts to lower barriers to trade across countries, in large part because of the general recognition that, in the aggregate, all countries benefit from trade. At the same time, we have clearly seen in our analysis that lowering barriers to trade does produce winners and losers. For example, those who advocate restricting trade may do so because of a concern for those parties that are hurt when trade is expanded. While it is in principle possible to compensate those parties and still leave others better off, such compensation would have to involve additional efforts beyond just lowering trade barriers.

There are, however, cases where restrictions of trade by governments arise from an even deeper concern about the ethics of trade in particular circumstances. Consider, for instance, the change in economic circumstances for a particular region that emerges from a natural disaster. For example, suppose an earthquake hits central Italy and temporarily restricts the supply of drinkable water in that region. In the absence of trade, this shift in the supply curve for water in central Italy could dramatically raise water prices. Assume there are strict anti-price-gouging laws that prohibit those who have drinkable water from selling that water at a significantly higher price. Such laws, in effect, restrict trade because they keep individuals from taking advantage of the opportunity to buy water at low prices in northern Italy to sell it at high prices in central Italy. As a result, the price ceiling on water prices imposed by anti-price-gouging laws results in water shortages and the unfolding of some non-price rationing.

In the absence of anti-price-gouging laws, our economic analysis suggests that individuals would observe low prices for water in one place and high prices for water in another, and would therefore attempt to profit from this disequilibrium across markets by buying low and selling high. As we transition to a new equilibrium, this would imply that water is imported to central Italy, driving down the price of water while increasing the supply. The analysis predicts that this would happen solely because of the selfish motives of individuals who are trying to profit from the changed economic circumstances in central Italy, but it is precisely these selfish motives that would end up bringing water to areas that need it most desperately.

Many governments would not permit the market process from functioning in this way during times of crisis. Stiff penalties might be imposed on those who attempt to profit from the misfortune of others during such disasters despite the fact that this very profit motive might help resolve the water shortage and might thus alleviate suffering in the affected areas. As economists, we might wonder why we don't just allow markets to employ the selfish motives of individuals when we know that this will lead to more water being where it is required when it is needed most. As a human being, however, we might sympathize with the outrage that motivates the penalties on those who seek to profit from human suffering. Once again, the pure economic analysis may or may not be the most persuasive argument in the debate on price-gouging laws, but a recognition of the beneficial effects of market forces in such situations should be at least a part of the debate even if the desire to restrain self-interested behaviour ultimately outweighs the economic benefit from utilizing such self-interest for the common good.

20A.2 Restricting Trade Through Tariffs or Import Quotas

Often the debate about trade is not about whether or not to permit trade across countries but rather at what terms such trade will be permitted. The government has two options when contemplating restrictions, as opposed to the prohibition of trade. It can either use taxes on traded goods to limit the flow of goods across borders by affecting the price of such goods, or it can impose quantity restrictions that limit the volume of trade directly. In principle, taxes or quotas could be imposed on exports and imports, although in practice government policy is usually focused on imports. A tax levied on imports is called a *tariff*, while a quota restricting imports is called an *import quota*.

20A.2.1 Tariffs on Imports Since taxes on imports, or tariffs, raise revenue for the government, the imposition of such taxes could be motivated by a desire to raise revenues in order to cover government expenditures. The motivation for the imposition of tariffs rarely derives primarily from a desire to raise revenues and typically involves a desire to protect certain domestic industries from foreign competition. Regardless of the motivation, a tariff remains a tax, and our analysis of taxes thus far suggests that, to the extent that they distort a price signal in a competitive market, they lead to inefficiencies.

In the context of trade across countries, the main effect of a tax on imports is to restrict the activities of exporters and importers. While exporters and importers are often also producers of goods, it is convenient for the purposes of our analysis to treat them as if they were separate individuals. Economic actors are attempting to buy low and sell high, and the imposition of a tariff is essentially an imposition of an additional economic cost imposed on this activity. If such an economic actor sees an opportunity to buy at a low price in one country and sell the same good at a high price in a different country, they will be less able to take advantage of such an opportunity if, upon importing the good, they have to pay a significant tax for each unit of the good that is imported.

Suppose, for instance, that Switzerland and Germany are currently trading without any barriers to trade, and that Germany now imposes a per-unit tariff t on all door handles that are imported from Switzerland. Prior to the imposition of the tariff, prices for door handles in the two markets are equal because of the activity of exporters and importers who make zero profits in the trade equilibrium. This is what we illustrated in Graph 20.1, where consumers and producers in both markets faced the equilibrium price p^*, and this initial equilibrium is replicated in Graph 20.3.

Graph 20.3 The Imposition of a Tariff on Door Handles

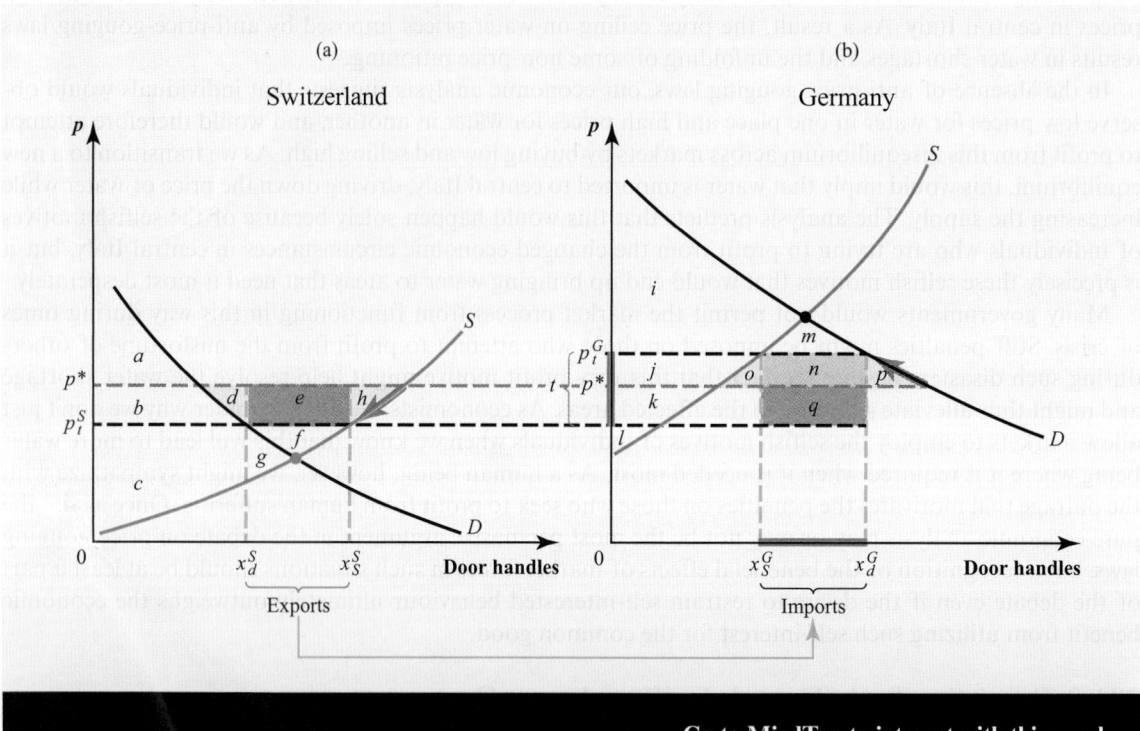

Go to MindTap to interact with this graph

When the tariff t is now imposed, exporters and importers no longer make zero profits because they have to pay this tax for each good that is imported. As a result, they will reduce the quantity they demand in Switzerland and the quantity they supply in Germany, thus causing prices in Switzerland to fall and prices in Germany to increase as the equilibrium moves down along the supply curve in Switzerland and up along the demand curve in Germany, as indicated by the light blue arrows. This process continues until exporters and importers once again make zero profit, and this in turn will happen once the price in Switzerland is t euros below the price in Germany. At that point, exporters and importers are able to buy at price p_t^S in Switzerland and sell at price p_t^G in Germany, with the difference covering the tax they owe for each good that they are importing. Understanding again that this is an approximation and that prices in the two regions will differ by a bit more for exporters and importers to be able to cover their other economic costs, we have reached a new equilibrium where exporters are making zero profits once again. In this new equilibrium, the quantity that is imported to Germany is the difference between what German producers manufacture (x_s^G) and what German consumers demand (x_d^G).

We can identify the winners and losers from the imposition of the tariff by looking at the new prices in Switzerland and Germany. Since prices fall in Switzerland, consumers there will be better off while producers will be worse off, and the reverse is true in Germany, where prices increase as a result of the tariff. To identify the deadweight loss from the tariff, we have to compare the change in overall surplus. Once again, the analysis is easiest if we assume that tastes for door handles are quasilinear, thus allowing us to measure consumer surplus along the market demand curve.

Consider the changes in surplus in Switzerland. Before the tariff, consumers and producers traded at price p^*, resulting in a consumer surplus of a and a producer surplus of $(b + c + d + e + f + g + h)$. Once the new equilibrium with the tariff has been reached, consumers and producers in Switzerland face the lower price p_t^S, giving rise to a consumer surplus of $(a + b)$ and a producer surplus of $(c + g + f)$. Total surplus shrinks by the shaded dark blue and dark brown areas $(d + e + h)$, which represents deadweight loss in Switzerland.

In Germany, on the other hand, prices rise as a result of the tariff, causing consumer surplus to shrink from $(i + j + m + n + o + p)$ to $(i + m)$ and producer surplus to rise from $(k + l)$ to $(k + l + j)$. Overall surplus among producers and consumers shrinks by the area $(n + o + p)$. Germany gets one additional benefit from the tariff: the tax revenue generated by the tariff. This tax revenue is equal to the tax rate times the quantity of imports, where the former is represented by the dark brown vertical distance on the vertical axis, i.e. the difference between the price in Switzerland and Germany, and the latter is represented by the dark blue horizontal distance on the horizontal axis. Multiplying these distances results in a tax revenue equal to $(n + q)$, the shaded light blue and dark blue areas. Thus, while consumers and producers jointly lose $(n + o + p)$, the government gains $(n + q)$, leaving Germany overall, better off by the area $(q - o - p)$.

Notice, however, that the dark blue areas in our two graphs are equal to one another. The area e in the Switzerland graph is equal to the area q in the Germany graph. Switzerland incurs a loss of $(d + e + h)$, whereas Germany benefits by $(q - o - p)$, which implies that Germany and Switzerland together lose $(d + h + o + p)$ because the benefit q in Germany is cancelled by the loss of e in Switzerland. The overall deadweight loss across Switzerland and Germany is equal to the shaded dark brown areas in the two graphs. This is summarized in Table 20.1.

Table 20.1 Welfare Effects From Tariffs

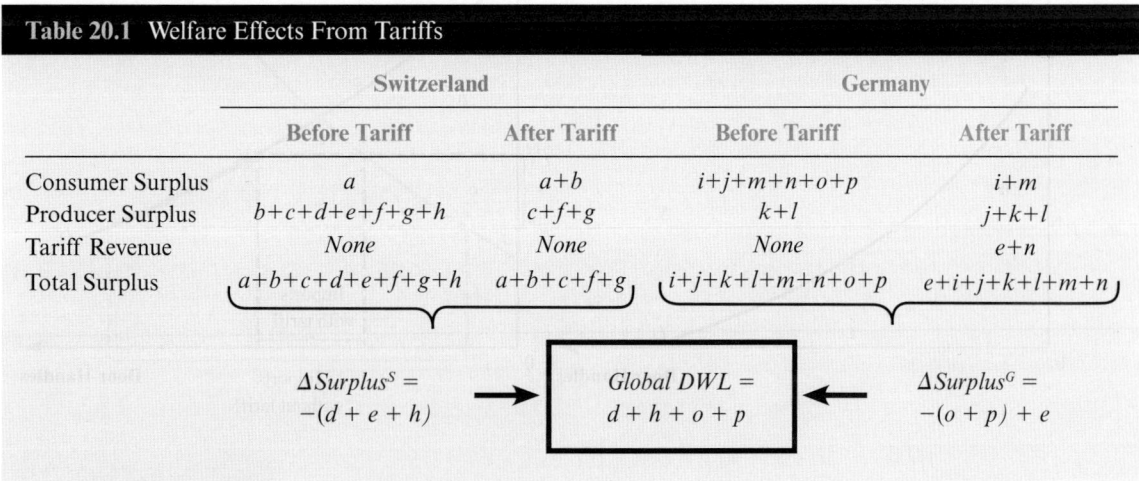

	Switzerland		Germany	
	Before Tariff	After Tariff	Before Tariff	After Tariff
Consumer Surplus	a	$a+b$	$i+j+m+n+o+p$	$i+m$
Producer Surplus	$b+c+d+e+f+g+h$	$c+f+g$	$k+l$	$j+k+l$
Tariff Revenue	*None*	*None*	*None*	$e+n$
Total Surplus	$a+b+c+d+e+f+g+h$	$a+b+c+f+g$	$i+j+k+l+m+n+o+p$	$e+i+j+k+l+m+n$

$\Delta Surplus^S =$
$-(d + e + h)$

$\longrightarrow$

Global DWL $=$
$d + h + o + p$

$\longleftarrow$

$\Delta Surplus^G =$
$-(o + p) + e$

Exercise 20A.2

In our treatment of taxes within a single market in Chapter 19, we concluded that a doubling of a tax results in approximately a quadrupling of the deadweight loss. Is the same true for tariffs?

20A.2.2 Passing the Burden of a Tariff to Other Regions As shown in Graph 20.3, Germany can benefit overall from the imposition of a tariff because it is shifting part of the burden of the tariff to Switzerland. We saw in Chapter 19 that tax burdens within a market are borne disproportionately by those whose economic behaviour is relatively price inelastic. It is for this reason that the extent to which Germany is able to pass part of the burden of the tariff to Switzerland depends on price elasticities. As a result, Germany as a whole will be able to benefit from imposing a tariff on imports from Switzerland only if the supply curve in Switzerland is sufficiently price inelastic.

To illustrate this, suppose that we conduct the same analysis as in Graph 20.3 but assume that the long-run supply curve in Switzerland is perfectly elastic, as it would be if all potential producers of door handles face the same cost curves. This is illustrated in Graph 20.4. Free trade, in this case, implies that the price in Switzerland under no trade is the same as the price p^* under trade because exporters can purchase any quantity they want at that price. This means that the price under free trade in Germany is also p^*, with the dark brown difference between x_d^G and x_s^G imported from Switzerland. When a tariff t is introduced, this raises the price in Germany by t to p_t^G while once again leaving the price in Switzerland unchanged. Although nothing changes in Switzerland in terms of consumer and producer surplus as a result of the tariff, consumer surplus in Germany falls from $(b + c + e + f + g + h)$ to $(b + e)$; producer surplus rises from d to $(c + d)$; and the government revenue rises from zero to g. Adding up all these benefits before and after the imposition of the tariff thus results in the conclusion that Germany by itself suffers a deadweight loss equal to the shaded area $(f + h)$. In fact, in this case Germany bears the entire deadweight loss that emerges from the imposition of the tariff across both regions, since no deadweight loss occurs in Switzerland.

Graph 20.4 A Tariff When Supply Is Perfectly Elastic in the Exporting Region

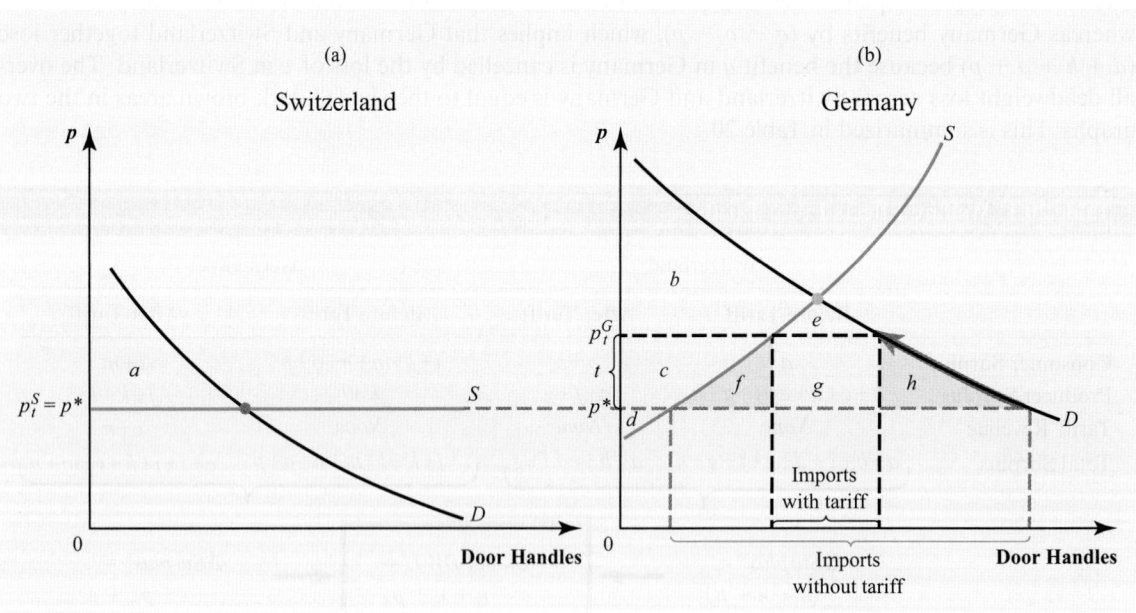

Thus, *Germany is more likely to suffer a loss in surplus from the imposition of a tariff as the supply curve in the market from which it is importing becomes more price elastic.* This is because *as Switzerland's supply curve becomes more price elastic, it becomes increasingly difficult to pass on a portion of the tariff to Swiss citizens.* Whether an exporting country's supply is relatively price elastic will depend in large measure on how large the country is relative to the importing country that is imposing the tariff. If the exporting country is large, imports to the tariff-imposing country will be small – implying that changes in demand from exporters will not be significant. Thus, we can rephrase our conclusion as follows: The smaller a country is, the less it is able to shift the burden of a tariff outside the country – and thus the more likely it is to suffer a loss in surplus from the imposition of a tariff.

20A.2.3 Trade Deals Between Regions or Countries We have shown in Graph 20.3 that there may be instances in which it is economically efficient *for a region* to impose tariffs on imports even if this causes deadweight loss across both regions combined. At the same time, if supply curves in the exporting region are sufficiently price elastic, the importing region will suffer a deadweight loss (Graph 20.4). Even when Germany can gain in overall surplus, however, the exporting region, Switzerland, loses more than the importing region, Germany, gains, which makes it possible at least in principle for the two regions to reach a trade agreement under which Switzerland compensates Germany for reducing or eliminating its tariffs. Thus, negotiated trade agreements between regions or countries can raise surplus for both regions or countries.

It is important to remember that all countries and regions are exporting as well as importing. Thus, while Switzerland may be exporting door handles to Germany, Germany may be exporting machine parts to Switzerland. This implies that while Germany might in principle benefit from the imposition of a tariff in the door handle market, Switzerland might similarly benefit from an imposition of tariffs on machine parts. Both tariffs, however, will be inefficient when Switzerland and Germany are considered simultaneously, and both countries will benefit from negotiated agreements that bring down multiple tariffs simultaneously. In practice, trade deals such as the North American Free Trade Agreement (NAFTA) and the European Union (EU) typically reduce many tariffs simultaneously.

20A.2.4 Import Quotas Unlike tariffs, which nominally permit any quantity of the import to enter a region, import quotas place a strict cap on how much of particular goods can be imported. The impact of import quotas on prices, however, is quite similar to the impact of tariffs.

Consider the example of Switzerland exporting door handles to Germany. Graph 20.5 begins with an initial equilibrium in which the two countries trade freely at the equilibrium price p^* as first illustrated in Graph 20.1. Now consider the case where Germany imposes an import quota q that is set below the number of imports of door handles that occur under free trade; were the import quota set above the current trade level, it would have no impact. In particular, suppose the quota is set at a quantity represented by the dark blue distance on the horizontal axis of the Germany graph.

Graph 20.5 The Imposition of an Import Quota

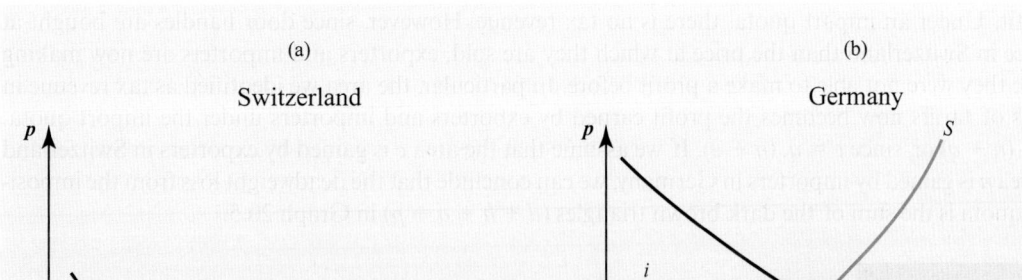

Exercise 20A.3

How would the analysis change if supply were perfectly elastic in both regions, with the supply curve lying at a higher price in Germany than in Switzerland?

Since market forces would ordinarily lead to imports greater than what is now permitted, we know that the full import quota will in fact be imported in the new equilibrium. Since this involves a lower quantity than before, exporters in Switzerland will reduce their demand for door handles, thus driving down prices in Switzerland. Similarly, importers in Germany will supply fewer door handles into the German market, thus driving up prices in Germany. In the new equilibrium, it must be the case that prices in Germany are such that consumers demand exactly q more goods than are supplied by German manufacturers, while prices in Switzerland are such that consumers in Switzerland demand exactly q less than is produced by Swiss manufacturers. This occurs at price p_q^G in Germany and price p_q^S in Switzerland. We can locate these prices in our graphs by inserting the horizontal (dark blue) distance q above the intersection of supply and demand in Switzerland and below that intersection in Germany.

Notice that just as in the case of tariffs, the new equilibrium results in a difference in prices between what is charged for door handles in Germany and in Switzerland. You should be able to convince yourself that *for every quota there exists a tariff that would have exactly the same impact on prices in Switzerland and Germany.* Since the impact of a quota on prices is exactly the same as the impact of a tariff on prices, consumer and producer surplus change in exactly the same way. From our work in Graph 20.3, which labels the areas in the graph with the same letters, we know that the joint consumer and producer surplus in Switzerland falls by $(d + e + h)$, while the joint producer and consumer surplus in Germany falls by $(n + o + p)$.

Exercise 20A.4

Identify separately consumer and producer surplus in both regions before and after the import quota, and check that the previous sentence is correct.

In the case of the tariff, we next need to consider the tax revenue that is raised under the tariff as another social benefit. Under an import quota, there is no tax revenue. However, since door handles are bought at a lower price in Switzerland than the price at which they are sold, exporters and importers are now making profit where they were not able to make a profit before. In particular, the area we identified as tax revenue in our analysis of tariffs now becomes the profit earned by exporters and importers under the import quota. This is area $(n + q)$ or, since $e = q$, $(n + e)$. If we assume that the area e is gained by exporters in Switzerland while the area n is gained by importers in Germany, we can conclude that the deadweight loss from the imposition of the quota is the sum of the dark brown triangles $(d + h + o + p)$ in Graph 20.5.

Exercise 20A.5

What is the economic effect of an import quota in Germany when the supply curve for door handles in Switzerland is perfectly elastic?

This analysis is not quite right in the sense that we have not yet explained how it is determined which exporters and importers now find themselves in the nice position of earning positive profits in equilibrium. Presumably, every exporter and importer would like to be in this game, which implies that exporters and importers will need to exercise additional effort, and thus incur additional costs, to be among those that operate under the import quota. To the extent to which such effort is socially wasteful, a portion of the areas e and n may in fact also be deadweight loss.

20A.3 Immigration Versus Outsourcing

We have thus far discussed trade solely in terms of *goods* being traded across countries, but trade can also occur in the labour market, and arguments relative to the impact of trade on labour often dominate the debate about free trade in general. Using the tools developed so far, we can now take a look at the economic issues related to this debate.

To focus our analysis, we will consider two ways in which labour might be traded across regions. In one case, firms in high-wage countries send a portion of the labour-intensive work abroad before shipping back the goods to be sold in the domestic market or elsewhere (outsourcing). It sounds like this might involve excessive transportation costs, but it has become common in many manufacturing sectors for firms to shift much of the labour-intensive portion of production abroad. It is even easier to do so for firms that are engaged in businesses such as telephone marketing or computer processing where direct-marketing phone calls can be made to a country directly from abroad or computer-processing results can be wired back to the country via the Internet.

In the second case, rather than production moving abroad to take advantage of low wages elsewhere, workers move to places where wages are high. Migration flows like this are obviously restricted by immigration laws, but one of the central debates in the European Union relates to the freedom of movement within the EU and perspectives on immigration was a significant factor in the decision by the UK to vote to leave the EU in 2016. Even in countries that are not joining common labour markets, such as the EU, temporary migration permits for guest workers from other countries are widely discussed, as are special visas for immigrants with special skills.

Throughout, we will implicitly be assuming that skill levels of workers, and thus worker productivity, is the same across countries. This is, of course, not generally true. It is important to keep this in mind, because our stark prediction that trade or immigration will erase wage differences depends on the artificial assumption of equal worker productivity across countries. In exercise 20.2, we will give an example of how the insights from this section change as differences in skill levels across countries are introduced.

20A.3.1 Outsourcing

Outsourcing labour-intensive parts of production is attractive to profit-maximizing firms that use labour that is relatively more expensive in the domestic market than it is in other countries. In order for outsourcing to emerge, wage rates across countries must differ. Consider an example in which a relatively high-wage country like the UK has production sectors that can benefit from employing workers in a relatively low-wage country like India. As we did in our example of trade in goods, we can begin with a state in which the labour markets are separate, with the UK market for a particular type of labour characterized by a high wage w^{UK} while the same market in India is characterized by a low wage w^I. This initial equilibrium in which the two labour markets function independently is depicted in Graph 20.6

Now suppose that outsourcing becomes an economically viable option for UK producers, and that the additional non-labour costs of outsourcing, like transportation of goods, are negligible. UK producers would demand less labour in the UK while increasing demand for labour in India. This creates downward pressure on wages in the UK labour market, through an inward shift in UK labour demand, while creating upward pressure on wages in India through an outward shift in India's labour demand, and if sufficiently many producers can make use of outsourcing, these pressures would continue until a new equilibrium emerges in which wages for this particular type of labour are equalized across the two countries at wage w^*. At this wage, UK producers demand L_d^{UK} hours of labour, but UK workers are willing to supply only L_s^{UK} hours, while Indian producers demand L_d^I and Indian workers supply L_s^I. A new equilibrium is reached when the dark brown difference in the hours of labour supplied and demanded in the UK is exactly equal to the dark blue difference in hours of labour demanded and supplied in India.

Outsourcing will generate winners and losers. Workers in the UK labour market experience falling wages, while workers in India experience rising wages, thus making workers in the UK worse off while making workers in India better off. The reverse is true for producers, with UK producers experiencing lower labour costs while Indian producers face increasing wages.

Graph 20.6 Outsourcing of Labour-Intensive Jobs from High- to Low-Wage Countries

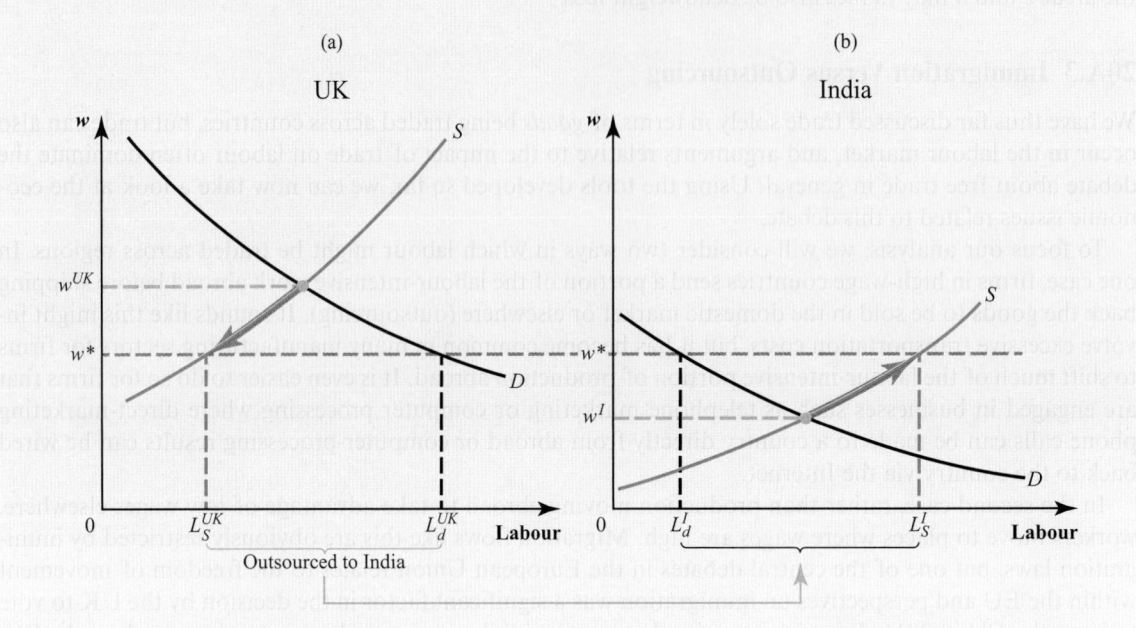

20A.3.2 **Immigration** Now consider the alternative way in which trade in labour may occur, with labour rather than production moving from one country to the other. Suppose that outsourcing is not an option but that workers can freely move across borders. Since production is not shifting from one country to another, labour demand will now remain constant in the two countries but labour supply will shift as workers in India immigrate to the UK to take advantage of higher wages. This increases the supply of labour in the UK and reduces the supply of labour in India, putting downward pressure on wages in the UK and upward pressure on wages in India. Assuming that migration of labour is relatively costless, such migration would continue until wages across the two labour markets are fully equalized at wage w^*, with the difference in the hours of labour demanded and supplied in the UK representing the number of hours provided in the UK by Indian workers who have immigrated to the UK. Similarly, the difference in labour supplied and labour demanded in India at the new wage w^* represents the hours of labour provided by Indian workers in the UK.

The process just described is depicted in Graph 20.7. Notice that this graph is almost exactly identical to Graph 20.6 for outsourcing. The only exception is that the downward pressure on wages in the UK and the simultaneous upward pressure on wages in India, represented by the light blue arrows, arise along supply curves under outsourcing and along demand curves under migration. This is because the pressures on market wages arise from shifts in labour demand in the two countries when firms move jobs, while pressures arise from shifts in labour supply in the two countries when workers themselves move between countries. The end effect, however, is exactly the same once the new equilibrium has been reached.

20A.3.3 **Moving Goods or Moving People?** In our example of a high-wage country competing with a low-wage country, we can characterize outsourcing as requiring the movement of goods, while immigration requires the movement of people. Outsourcing requires low barriers to trading goods, so that companies from the high-wage country can move operations to the low-wage country and transport goods back to the high-wage country, where they are disproportionately demanded. Immigration, on the other hand, requires low barriers to labour mobility so that workers can move where wages are high. Graphs 20.6 and 20.7 illustrate our model's prediction that both moving goods, as a result of outsourcing, and moving people, through migration of labour, have the same ultimate impact on wages because both mechanisms offer ways of integrating two labour markets. In both cases, people in the high-wage country in essence employ workers from the low-wage country to produce goods for them.

Graph 20.7 Migration from High- to Low-Wage Countries

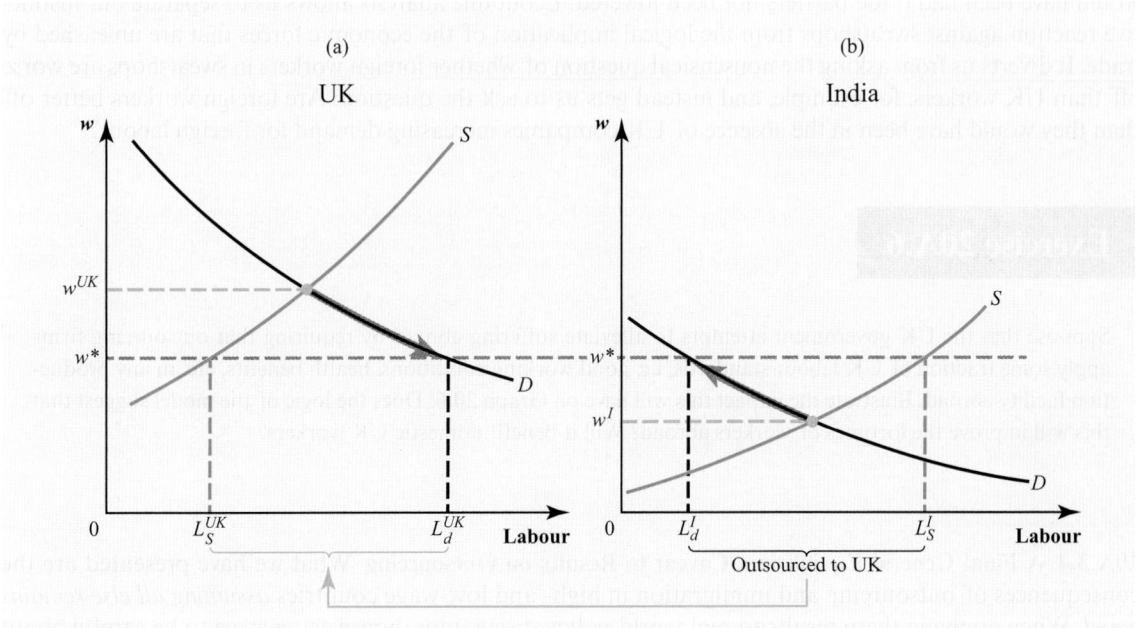

The difference between these two ways of integrating markets is that the workers from the low-wage country who are employed to produce for the high-wage country remain in their country of origin under outsourcing but physically move to the high-wage country under immigration. This may raise other concerns related to the integration of different cultures and languages in the host, i.e. the high-wage country. It may also raise issues of other potential government costs – workers who migrate have children who go to school, have health care needs, and so forth, but they also pay taxes. To what extent the net fiscal effect of immigration is positive or negative for the host country depends on a variety of other factors that are not raised when foreign labour is employed without migration through outsourcing. While there are important similarities between trade in goods and migration of labour, the difference between the two may explain the balance of trade and immigration policy that emerges in the real world.

Having said this, the reality is that both trade and migration, while increasing the overall surplus in all countries, brings with it winners and losers in both countries. The challenge for policy makers is to realize the increased overall surplus in such a way that those who are likely to lose from such policies are compensated through other policies that are implemented as barriers to trade are lowered. There are often debates about job retraining programmes at the same time as trade policy is discussed in high-wage countries, with policy makers seeking to find ways of retraining those workers who are adversely affected by trade. Our analysis suggests that since overall surplus increases with trade, it is at least in principle possible to make everyone better off by lowering barriers to trade and migration when such policies are implemented simultaneously.

From a more global perspective, of course, it is difficult to argue that high-wage countries should maintain barriers to trade and migration for the benefit of workers. While some workers in the affected labour markets in the UK will, in the absence of complementary policies, suffer losses in surplus, workers in India will experience gains. Those who are concerned with the suffering of people in less-developed countries might argue for increased trade and more open immigration laws precisely because such policies will raise the material well-being of those who are suffering the most in the world. At the same time, as trade barriers are lowered, we may be outraged by the working conditions and wages that workers in less-developed countries are experiencing even in those production facilities set up by companies that are outsourcing some of their labour-intensive production. Terms like 'sweatshops' have frequently been used to express such outrage, and it is argued that it is unethical to lower trade barriers that will result in firms setting up such sweatshops abroad. Nevertheless, the logic of economics gives the prediction that while worker conditions abroad may still be poor relative to what is expected in developed countries, they will be better than they otherwise would have been had trade barriers not been lowered. Economic analysis allows us to separate our instinctive reaction against sweatshops from the logical implication of the economic forces that are unleashed by trade. It diverts us from asking the nonsensical question of whether foreign workers in sweatshops are worse off than UK workers, for example, and instead gets us to ask the question: Are foreign workers better off than they would have been in the absence of UK companies increasing demand for foreign labour?

Exercise 20A.6

Suppose that the UK government attempts to alleviate suffering abroad by requiring that outsourcing firms apply some fraction of UK labour standards, i.e. good working conditions, health benefits, etc. in any production facility abroad. Illustrate the impact this will have on Graph 20.6. Does the logic of the model suggest that this will improve the fortunes of workers abroad? Will it benefit domestic UK workers?

20A.3.4 A Final General Equilibrium Caveat to Results on Outsourcing What we have presented are the consequences of outsourcing and immigration in high- and low-wage countries *assuming all else remains equal*. When applying these results to real-world policy discussions, however, we have to be careful about that assumption and would want to consider some general equilibrium changes in behaviour that might result from outsourcing. If UK firms save on labour costs, will they invest these savings in new innovations? Will these new innovations increase demand for other types of labour? Will these innovations result in lower production costs in other industries? Will the general decrease in production costs translate to cheaper consumption goods that in turn make real wages increase? If so, the overall impact of outsourcing or immigration on wages in the UK might well be more positive in the aggregate even as some sectors might experience decreased wages.

20A.4 Trading Across Time

All of our examples of trade thus far have involved trading across two markets at a given point in time, but trade in the real world also happens *across* time. Those who are looking for opportunities to buy low and sell high across markets may identify opportunities when the price of a particular good happens to be low right now while they anticipate that the price will rise in the future. This may permit them to purchase goods now, store them and then sell them in the future when price increases. Such behaviour is often referred to as speculation because it requires individuals to speculate that prices will rise in the future. In the real world, there are entire divisions of some firms that are occupied by market forecasters who try to identify such opportunities. Just as the impact of trade across regions has the effect of equalizing prices across regions at any given time, trade across time initiated by *speculators* can have the tendency to stabilize prices over time in markets that would otherwise experience price fluctuations.

We should not overemphasize this tendency, however, as there are circumstances under which trade across time – unlike trade across space – can lead to *less* stability. The important difference between trade *across space* and trade *across time* is that the former occurs in an environment of relative *certainty* while the latter may occur in an environment of relative *uncertainty*. Exporters and importers can see the difference in prices across regions and thus buy low and sell high at any given time, but speculators have to guess about price differences across time. When speculators are on average correct in their guesses, their behaviour will tend to have the stabilizing influence on prices across time that export/import behaviour has across space, but when speculators get it wrong, the same will not be true.

20A.4.1 Seasonal Demand for Fuel Consider the market for fuel in a country and let us assume that this market has predictable seasonal changes in consumer demand, with consumers demanding significantly more fuel in summer months due to holiday travel. We can model the fuel market at two points in time just as we modelled the door handle market at two points in space: in the spring and the summer. This is done in Graph 20.8, where the intersection of market demand and supply results in the relatively low fuel price p^{Spr} in the spring and the relatively high fuel price p^{Sum} in the summer in the absence of trade across time. An opportunity has arisen for someone to buy low and sell high as long as the costs of storing fuel in the meantime are relatively low. Suppose, for the purposes of illustration, that such storage costs are negligible. Speculators will purchase low-priced fuel in the spring and sell it in the summer, leading to increased demand in the spring and increased supply in the summer. This causes upward pressure on fuel prices in the spring and downward pressure in the summer as indicated by the light blue arrows, with the dark brown quantity indicated in the first graph stored for sale in the summer, and equal to the dark blue quantity in the summer graph. Just as in our analysis of trade across regions, prices are equalized through trade, with speculators ensuring that fuel is plentiful when it is most needed.

Graph 20.8 Speculation and the Price of Fuel

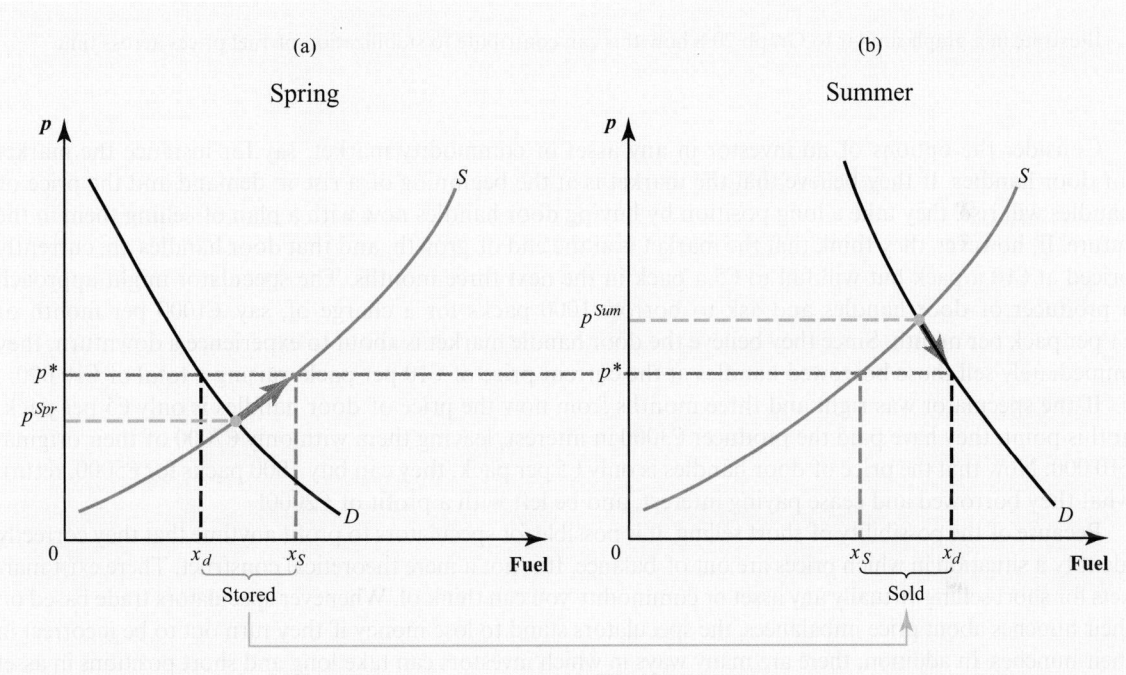

If fuel prices do rise as the summer months approach, it is an indication that the costs of storing fuel are in fact not negligible. As the summer months approach, more and more fuel gets stored away as it has to be held in storage for shorter and shorter periods of time. As consumer demand increases in the summer, speculators open their reserve to cash in, causing the price increase to come to an end just as people start their summer holidays.

Exercise 20A.7

Illustrate how Graph 20.8 changes as the cost to storing fuel is introduced. Can you see how price fluctuations across time will worsen as the cost of storing fuel increases?

20A.4.2 Long Versus Short Positions by Speculators In our previous example of speculators expecting fuel prices to increase, the speculator can make money by buying low now and selling high in the future. In financial markets, this type of speculation, which involves betting on prices rising and thus buying now, is known as *taking a long position* in the market. What if you notice a price that you think is high now and is likely to drop in the future? Can speculators play a role in equalizing prices in this case if they don't currently hold any of the good that is priced high?

As long as anyone in the economy is holding reserves of fuel that you think is currently priced too high, a speculator could ask to borrow some of their fuel reserves in exchange for some interest payment and sell it at the current high price. When the price falls, the speculator can buy an amount equal to that borrowed and return it to the person who had the reserves of fuel. The speculator is in essence selling high now and buying low in the future, as long as they are right about the price falling in the future. In financial markets, this is known as *selling short* or *taking a short position*.

Exercise 20A.8

Illustrate in a graph similar to Graph 20.8 how this can contribute to stabilization of fuel prices across time.

Consider the options of an investor in any asset or commodity market, say for instance the market for door handles. If they believe that the market is at the beginning of a rise in demand and the price of handles will rise, they take a long position by buying door handles now with a plan of selling them in the future. If, however, they think that the market is at the end of growth, and that door handles are currently priced at €10 a pack but will fall to €5 a pack in the next three months. The speculator might approach a producer of door handles and ask to borrow 1000 packs for a charge of, say, €1000 per month or €1 per pack per month. Since they believe the door handle market is about to experience a downturn, they immediately sell those borrowed handles at the current price of €10 per pack, raising a total of €10 000.

If the speculator was right and three months from now the price of door handles is only €5 per pack, at this point, they have paid the producer €3000 in interest, leaving them with only €7000 of their original €10 000. Now that the price of door handles is only €5 per pack, they can buy 1000 packs for €5000, return what they borrowed and cease paying interest, and be left with a profit of €2000!

Because of the possibility of short selling, it is possible for speculators to profit anytime that they correctly identify a situation in which prices are out of balance. It is not a mere theoretical construct. There exist markets for short selling virtually any asset or commodity you can think of. Whenever speculators trade based on their hunches about price imbalances, the speculators stand to lose money if they turn out to be incorrect in their hunches. In addition, there are many ways in which investors can take long and short positions in asset and commodities markets, and all we have done is to show the essence of each. You may, for example, have heard about *options*, which are *contracts giving the owner of the contract the right but not the obligation to buy or sell an asset or a commodity at a set price on or before a particular date*. A *call* option gives the owner of the option the right to buy, while a *put* option gives the owner a right to sell. Call options present another way to take a long position in the market, while put options are another way to take a short position.

Exercise 20A.9

Can you see why investors would want to hold a call option if they believe the price of the asset is likely to go up, and why they would want to hold a put option if they believe prices are likely to fall?

Note that, while our treatment suggests the behaviour of speculators will lead to stabilization of prices across time, there are real-world examples of financial bubbles, such as a significant increase in property values leading up to the 2008 financial crisis, in which speculator behaviour may have aggravated price instability.

20B   The Mathematics of Trading Across Markets

There is little new in the way of the underlying mathematics to the graphs in Section A. We will go through one exercise to illustrate how one sets up these kinds of problems mathematically. More in-depth treatments of trade across markets would involve an extension of our general equilibrium models, a topic that goes beyond the scope of this text.

20B.1 Trade, Tariffs and Quotas

Consider the case of linear demand and supply functions in two different countries, with local variables denoted by superscripts 1 and 2 for countries 1 and 2; that is:

$$x_d^1(p) = \frac{A - p}{\alpha} \quad \text{and} \quad x_s^1(p) = \frac{B + p}{\beta}, \tag{20.1}$$

for country 1 and:

$$x_d^2(p) = \frac{C - p}{\gamma} \quad \text{and} \quad x_s^2(p) = \frac{D + p}{\delta}, \tag{20.2}$$

for country 2.

    In the absence of trade across the two countries, equilibrium prices within each can be found by setting supply and demand within each country equal to one another and solving for price, giving:

$$p^1 = \frac{\beta A - \alpha B}{\alpha + \beta} \quad \text{and} \quad p^2 = \frac{\delta C - \gamma D}{\gamma + \delta}. \tag{20.3}$$

    If p^1 and p^2 are not equal to one another, trade between the regions should occur until prices are equalized. Suppose $p^2 > p^1$. In an equilibrium with trade, country 1 will export some amount X to country 2, causing demand in country 1 and supply in country 2 to increase by X; that is,

$$\tilde{x}_d^1(p) = \frac{A - p}{\alpha} + X \quad \text{and} \quad \tilde{x}_s^2(p) = \frac{D + p}{\delta} + X. \tag{20.4}$$

Letting $\tilde{x}_d^1(p) = x_s^1(p)$ and $x_d^2(p) = \tilde{x}_s^2(p)$ and solving for price in each country, we get:

$$\tilde{p}^1 = \frac{\beta A - \alpha B + \alpha \beta X}{\alpha + \beta} \quad \text{and} \quad \tilde{p}^2 = \frac{\delta C - \gamma D - \gamma \delta X}{\gamma + \delta}. \tag{20.5}$$

    The equilibrium level of exports X from country 1 to country 2 must equalize these two prices. Thus, setting setting $\tilde{p}^1 = \tilde{p}^2$ and solving for X, we get the equilibrium level of exports as:

$$X^* = \frac{(\alpha + \beta)(\delta C - \gamma D) - (\gamma + \delta)(\beta A - \alpha B)}{(\gamma + \delta)\alpha\beta + (\alpha + \beta)\gamma\delta}. \tag{20.6}$$

Exercise 20B.1

Can you verify that, when exports are X^*, prices in the two countries are equal?

Suppose that the importing country 2 imposes a per-unit tariff of t on all imports. Rather than than $\tilde{p}^1 = \tilde{p}^2$, the resulting equilibrium will have $\tilde{p}^1 = \tilde{p}^2 - t$. Solving this equation, the equilibrium level of exports under a tariff of t becomes:

$$X^*(t) = \frac{(\alpha + \beta)(\delta C - \gamma D) - (\gamma + \delta)(\beta A - \alpha B) - (\alpha + \beta)(\gamma + \delta)t}{(\gamma + \delta)\alpha\beta + (\alpha + \beta)\gamma\delta}. \tag{20.7}$$

Taking the derivative of $X^*(t)$ with respect to t, we get the decrease in exports from country 1 to country 2 for a 1 unit increase in the tariff t; that is,

$$\frac{dX^*(t)}{dt} = -\left(\frac{(\alpha + \beta)(\gamma + \delta)}{(\gamma + \delta)\alpha\beta + (\alpha + \beta)\gamma\delta}\right). \tag{20.8}$$

Now suppose that instead of a tariff, the government in country 2 imposed an import quota quota $\overline{X} < X^*$ The prices in the two countries will not equalize, with:

$$p^1(\overline{X}) = \frac{\beta A - \alpha B + \alpha\beta\overline{X}}{\alpha + \beta} \quad \text{and} \quad p^2(\overline{X}) = \frac{\delta C - \gamma D - \gamma\delta\overline{X}}{\gamma + \delta}. \tag{20.9}$$

Subtracting $p^1(\overline{X})$ from $p^2(\overline{X})$ tells us how much of a price difference between the two countries is created by the import quota $\overline{X}$, with:

$$p^2(\overline{X}) - p^1(\overline{X}) = \frac{\delta C - \gamma D}{\gamma + \delta} - \frac{\beta A - \alpha B}{\alpha + \beta} - \frac{((\gamma + \delta)\alpha\beta + (\alpha + \beta)\gamma\delta)\overline{X}}{(\alpha + \beta)(\gamma + \delta)}. \tag{20.10}$$

This can be rewritten in terms of the no-trade equilibrium prices p^1 and p^2 from equation (20.3) as:

$$p^2(\overline{X}) - p^1(\overline{X}) = p^2 - p^1 - \frac{((\gamma + \delta)\alpha\beta + (\alpha + \beta)\gamma\delta)\overline{X}}{(\alpha + \beta)(\gamma + \delta)}. \tag{20.11}$$

The difference between the prices in the two countries will shrink in proportion to the size of the import quota.

Exercise 20B.2

Can you demonstrate that a tariff $t = p^2(\overline{X}) - p^1(\overline{X})$ will result in the same level of exports from country 1 as the import quota $\overline{X}$ as well as the same equilibrium prices in the two countries?

20B.2 A Numerical Example

To add some numbers to this example, suppose that $A = 1000 = C$, $\alpha = \beta = 1 = \gamma = \delta$, $B = 0$ and $D = -400$. Demand and supply curves in the two countries are therefore identical except for the intercept term of the supply curves. Substituting these values into equation (20.3), we get $p^1 = 500$ and $p^2 = 700$, with resulting equilibrium quantities in the absence of trade $x^1 = 500$ and $x^2 = 300$. Substituting the appropriate values into equation (20.6), we get an equilibrium export level $X^* = 200$ under free trade, with the equations in (20.5) implying an equalized price under trade of $p^* = 600$.

Exercise 20B.3

Illustrate demand and supply curves in the two countries with price on the vertical axis and quantity on the horizontal axis. Label each intercept as well as the no-trade equilibrium prices and quantities. Illustrate the equilibrium under free trade.

Exercise 20B.4

Assuming that demand curves are also marginal willingness to pay curves, calculate the deadweight loss from prohibiting trade.

We could ask how trade is affected by different levels of tariffs and quotas. Suppose, for instance, that a per-unit tariff of €100 is imposed on all imports to region 2. Equation (20.7) tells us that exports will fall to 100.

Exercise 20B.5

Illustrate the impact of a €100 per-unit tariff on the equilibrium you have graphed in exercise 20B.3.

Exercise 20B.6

Assuming again that demand curves are marginal willingness to pay curves, what happens to surplus in countries 1 and 2 when considering each in isolation? What happens to overall deadweight loss when considering both countries jointly?

End-of-Chapter Exercises

20.1† In the text, we have argued that the burden of tariffs is shifted across markets in ways that are analogous to how tax burdens are shifted between consumers and producers.

    A. Consider two countries: country 1, in which product x would sell at p^1, and country 2, in which it would sell at p^2 in the absence of any trade between the countries. Suppose throughout that $p^2 > p^1$.

        a. Begin by illustrating the free trade equilibrium assuming negligible transportation costs.

        b. Illustrate how the imposition of an import tax or tariff of t per unit of x by country 2 changes the equilibrium.

        c. What in your answer to (b) would change if, instead of country 2 imposing a per-unit import tax of t, country 1 had imposed a per-unit *export* tax of the same amount t?

        d. In your graph, illustrate the economic incidence of the tax t on trade; that is, illustrate how much of the overall tax revenue is raised from country 1 and how much is raised from country 2.

e. How would your answer change if you made the supply curve in country 1 more elastic while keeping p^1 unchanged? What if you made the demand curve more price elastic?

f. We have noted that it does not matter whether a per-unit tax is imposed on producers or on consumers within a market – the economic impact will be the same. How is what you have found in this exercise analogous to this result?

g. If the supply curve in country 1 were perfectly inelastic, would any of the tariff be paid by country 2?

B. Now consider demand and supply functions $x_d^1(p) = (A - p)/\alpha$ and $x_s^1(p) = (B + p)/\beta$ for country 1 and $x_d^2(p) = (C - p)/\gamma$ and $x_s^2(p) = (D + p)/\delta$ for country 2 as in part B of the text.

a. Set up an Excel spreadsheet that calculates production and consumption levels in each country as a function of the demand and supply parameters A, B, α, β, C, D, γ and δ as well as the per-unit tariff t imposed by country 2. Would any of your spreadsheet differ if instead we analyzed a per-unit export tax in country 1?

b. Let $A = 1000 = C$, $\alpha = \beta = 1 = \gamma = \delta$, $B = 0$ and $D = -400$. Verify that you get the same result as what is reported in part B of the text for the same parameters when $t = 0$ and when $t = 100$.

c. Set up a table in which the rows correspond to scenarios where we change the parameters B and β from (49 500, 100) in the first row to (12 000, 25) (2000, 5), (500, 2), (0, 1), (−250, 0.5), (−375, 0.25), (−450, 0.1) and (−495, 0.1) in the next eight rows. Report in each row p^1 and x^1, which are the price and quantity in country 1 in the absence of trade; $p^* = \widetilde{p}^1 = \widetilde{p}^2$, which is the world price under free trade; X^*, which is the level of exports under free trade; $X^*(t)$, which is the level of exports when $t = 100$ is imposed; $\widetilde{p}^1(t)$ and $\widetilde{p}^2(t)$, which are the prices when a per-unit tariff of $t = 100$ is imposed; and the fraction k of the tariff that is shifted to country 1.

d. Explain what is happening as we move down the rows in your table.

e. Next, set up a table in which the rows correspond to scenarios where we change the parameters A and α from (50 500, 100) in the first row to (13 000, 25), (3000, 5), (1500, 2), (1000, 1), (750, 0.5), (625, 0.25), (550, 0.1) and (505, 0.01) in the next eight rows. Keep the remaining parameters as originally specified in (b). Report the same columns as you did in the table you constructed for part (c).

f. Are there any differences between your two tables? Explain.

20.2 The prediction that unrestricted trade causes a convergence of wages across the trading countries seems quite stark. Is it really the case that UK wages for example, will converge with the wages in the developing world if trade is unrestricted? We will consider this here.

A. Workers in the UK have significantly more *human capital* – education, skills, etc. – than workers in Bangladesh. As a result, workers in the UK have a higher marginal product of labour.

a. Begin by illustrating the UK and Bangladeshi labour markets side-by-side, with demand and supply in Bangladesh intersecting at a lower wage in the absence of trade and migration than in the UK.

b. Suppose workers in the UK are 20 times as productive per hour as workers in Bangladesh. To account for this, interpret the wage in your UK graph as the wage per hour and interpret the wage in Bangladesh as the wage per 20 hours of work. What will happen when trade between the UK and Bangladesh opens and UK companies outsource production?

c. Does your graph look any different from our outsourcing graphs in the text? Does it still imply that wages for UK workers will converge to wages of Bangladeshi workers?

d. *True or False*: In order for true convergence of wages to emerge from trade and outsourcing, countries in the developing world will have to first invest in schooling and other forms of human capital accumulation.

e. *True or False*: Under a full free trade regime across the world, differences in wages across countries will arise entirely from differences in skills and productivity levels of workers.

B. Consider the case where UK workers are k times as productive as Bangladeshi workers. Suppose labour demand and supply in Bangladesh are given by $l_d^B(w) = (A - w)/\alpha$ and $l_s^B(w) = (B + w)/\beta$, while labour supply in the UK is given by $l_s^{UK}(w) = (D + w)/\delta$. Since firms care about both wage costs as well as labour productivity, suppose that labour demand in the UK is given by $l_d^{UK}(w) = (C - (w/k))/\gamma$.

a. Derive the wage w^{UK} in the UK and the wage w^B in Bangladesh if there is no trade or migration.

b. Suppose trade between the UK and Bangladesh opens, and UK firms outsource some production to Bangladesh that used to take place in the UK. Suppose that the impact in labour markets is equivalent to immigration of X Bangladeshi workers to the UK. Determine the new wage $w^B(X)$ in Bangladesh and $w^{UK}(X)$ in the UK.

c. At the equilibrium level of migration X^*, what is the relationship between $w^{UK}(X^*)$ and $w^B(X^*)$?

d. Use this relationship to calculate the equilibrium level of migration that the outsourcing of UK production is equivalent to.

e. Suppose that $A = 16\,000$, $B = -1000$, $C = 160\,250$, $D = -10\,000$, $\alpha = 0.00018$, $\beta = 0.00002$, $\gamma = 0.0007$ and $\delta = 0.0002$. Suppose further that $k = 20$; that is, UK workers are 20 times as productive as Bangladeshi workers. What is w^B and w^{UK} in the absence of trade? What is the employment level in the UK and in Bangladesh?

f. When trade is opened up and we determine the migration level X^* that free trade is equivalent to, what is X^*?

g. What are the equilibrium wages in the UK and in Bangladesh in the new equilibrium? What are employment levels in the two countries?

20.3† **Business Application:** *Adaptive Expectations and Oil Price Instability.* Trading across time is similar to trading across space in that individuals find opportunities to buy low and sell high. Unlike the case where individuals trade across space, however, speculators who trade across time have to guess what future prices will be. If they guess correctly, they will introduce greater price stability over time, just as exporters equalize prices across regions. We now ask what might happen if this is not the case. More precisely, we will assume that individuals form *adaptive expectations*. Under such expectations, people expect prices in the future to mimic price patterns in the past.

A. Consider first the case of the oil industry. It takes some time to get additional capacity for oil production, so oil companies have to project where future oil prices will be to determine whether it is economically prudent to pay the large fixed costs of increasing their ability to pump more oil. They are, in essence, speculators trying to see whether to expend resources now to raise oil production in the future or whether to allow existing capacity to depreciate in anticipation of lower oil prices in the future.

a. Begin by drawing a demand and supply graph for oil, with linear supply steeper than linear demand, and label the equilibrium price as p^*.

b. Suppose that unexpected events have caused price to rise to p_1. Next, suppose that oil companies have adaptive expectations in the sense that they believe the future price will mirror the current price. Will they invest in additional capacity?

c. If the demand curve remains unchanged but the oil industry in the future produces an amount of oil equal to the level it would produce were the price to remain at p_1, indicate the actual price that would emerge in the future as p_2. *Hint:* After identifying how much the oil industry will produce on its supply curve at p_1, find what price will have to drop to in order for oil companies to be able to sell their new output level.

d. Suppose that firms have adaptive expectations and believe the price will now remain at p_2. If they adjust their capacity to this new reality and demand remains unchanged, what will happen to price in the next period? If you keep this going from period to period, will we eventually converge to p^*? This model is often referred to as the *Cobweb Model*. You might be able to see why if you begin to draw a horizontal line at p_1, then drop the line down to the demand curve, then draw a horizontal line at p_2 over to the supply curve, then connect it up to the demand curve where p_3 lies, etc.

e. Repeat (b) through (d), but this time do it for the case where demand is steeper than supply. How does your answer change?

f. How would your answer change if demand and supply were equally steep?

g. While this example offers a simple setting in which speculative behaviour can result in price fluctuations rather than price stability, economists are sceptical of such a simple explanation. To see why, imagine you are a speculator who is not an oil producer and you catch onto what's going on. What will you do? What will happen to the patterns of oil prices that you identified in the different scenarios?

B. The demand function for oil x is given by $x_d(p) = (A - p)/\alpha$ and the supply function by $x_s(p) = (B + p)/\beta$. Suppose throughout that $B = 0$ and $\beta = 0.00001$.

a. What is the equilibrium price p^* if $A = 80$ and $\alpha = 0.000006$?

b. Assume that some unexpected events led to a price of $p_1 = 75$, but the underlying fundamentals – supply and demand curves – remain unchanged. If oil suppliers expect the price to remain at €75 in period 2, how much will they produce in period 2? What will the actual price p_2 in period 2 be?

c. Suppose period 2 unfolds as you derived in part (b), and now oil suppliers expect prices to remain at p_2. How much will they produce in period 3? What will price p_3 be in period 3?

d. If the same process continues, what will the price be in period 10? In period 20?

e. Next, suppose instead that $A = 120$ and $\alpha = 0.000014$. What is the equilibrium price p^*?

f. Suppose that p_1 is unexpectedly 51 but the fundamentals of the economy remain unchanged. What are p_2 and p_3 as defined in (b) and (c) now? What about the prices in periods 10 and 11?

g. Finally, suppose that $A = 100$ and $\alpha = 0.00001$? What will be the price pattern over time if p_1 is unexpectedly 75? What if it is unexpectedly 51?

h. If you were a speculator of the type described in A(g), what would you do in period 2 in each of the three scenarios we have explored? What would be the result of your action?

20.4 Business Application: *The Risks of Short Selling.* Short selling can entail a lot more risk if the investor's guesses are wildly incorrect than taking the more conventional long position of buying and holding an asset.

A. Suppose oil currently sells for $50 a barrel. Consider two different investors. Ahmed thinks that oil prices will rise, and Amanda thinks they will fall. As a result, Ahmed will take a long position in the oil market, while Amanda will take a short position. Both of them have enough credit to borrow $10 000 in cash or an equivalent amount at current prices in oil. For purposes of this exercise, do not worry about any opportunity costs associated with the interest rate; simply assume an interest rate of 0 and suppose oil can be stored without cost.

a. Consider Ahmed first. How much will he have one year from now if he carries through with his strategy of investing all his money in oil and oil one year from now stands at $75 a barrel?

b. Now consider the worst-case scenario. A new energy source is found, and oil is no longer worth anything one year from now. Ahmed's guess about the future was wildly incorrect. How much has he lost?

c. Next, consider Amanda. How much will she have one year from now if she carries through with her strategy to sell oil short, if the price of oil one year from now stands at $25 a barrel?

d. Suppose instead that Amanda's prediction about the future was wildly incorrect and the price of oil stands at $100 a barrel next year. How much will she have lost if she leaves the oil market at that point?

e. Was the scenario in (d) the worst-case scenario for Amanda? Is there a limit to how much Amanda might lose by going short? Is there a limit to the losses that Ahmed might incur?

f. Can you explain intuitively, without referring to this example, why short selling entails inherently more risk for investors who are very wrong in their predictions than going long in the market does?

B. *Suppose more generally that a barrel of oil sells at price p_0 on the current spot market, which is defined as the market for oil that is currently being sold. Suppose further that you expect the price of a barrel of oil on the spot market n years from now to be p_n. Suppose the annual interest rate is r.

a. Write down an equation $\pi_n^L(p_0, p_n, r, q)$ that gives the profit, expressed in current dollars, from going long in the oil market for n years by buying q barrels of oil today?

b. How high does the ratio p_n/p_0 have to be to justify going long in the oil market in this way? Can you make intuitive sense of this?

c. Next, write down the equation for $\pi_n^S(p_0, p_n, r, q)$ that gives the profit from selling q barrels of oil short by borrowing them now and repaying them in n years? Assume that the person you are borrowing the oil from expects you to return $(1 + r)^n$ times as much oil; that is, they are charging the interest to be paid in terms of barrels of oil.

d. How high can p_n/p_0 be to still warrant a short selling strategy of this type? Can you make intuitive sense of this?

20.5*† Business Application: *Pricing Call and Put Options.* Contracts called call and put options are examples of somewhat more sophisticated ways in which one can take a short or long position in the market.

A. Suppose that the current price of oil is $50 a barrel. There are two types of contracts one can buy. The owner of contract 1 has the right to sell 200 barrels of oil at the current price of $50 a barrel one year from now. The owner of contract 2 has the right to buy 200 barrels of oil at the current price of $50 a barrel a year from now. Assume in this exercise that the annual interest rate is 5 per cent.

a. Suppose that Ahmed thinks the price of oil will rise while Amanda thinks it will fall. Consider Ahmed first and suppose he feels quite certain that oil will sell for $75 a barrel one year from now. What's the most he is willing to pay to buy contract 1? What is the most he is willing to pay to buy contract 2?

b. Next consider Amanda, who is quite certain that oil will be trading at $25 a barrel one year from now. What is the most that she is willing to pay for the two contracts?

c. Which contract allows a short position and which allows a long position in the oil futures market?

d. Suppose that contract 1 currently sells for $6000. What does that tell us about the market's collective prediction about the price of a barrel of oil one year from now?

e. Suppose instead that contract 2 currently sells for $6000. What does that tell us about the market's prediction of oil prices one year from now?

B. In part A, we considered only a single call or put option at a time. In reality, a much larger variety of such futures contracts can exist at any given time.

a. Suppose that a call option gives the owner the right to buy 200 barrels of oil at $50 one year from now. You observe that this futures contract is selling for $3000 in the market. What is the market's prediction about the price of oil one year from now? Assume again an interest rate of 5 per cent.

b. Suppose someone else has just posted another call option contract for sale. This one entitles the owner to buy 200 barrels of oil at a price of $43 one year from now. How much do you predict this contract will sell for given your answer to (a)?

c. A put option is posted for sale that allows the owner to sell 200 barrels of oil at a price of $71 one year from now. What do you think this option will be priced at by the market?

d. Let $P^C(\bar{p}, q, r, n)$ be the price of a call option to buy q barrels of oil n years from now at price $\bar{p}$ when the market interest rate is r and the market expectation of the actual price of oil n years from now is p. What is the equation that defines P^C?

e. Let $P^p(\bar{p}, q, r, n)$ be the price of a put option to sell q barrels of oil n years from now at price $\bar{p}$ when the market interest rate is r and the market expectation of the actual price of oil n years from now is p. What is the equation that defines P^p?

f. The price p at which oil actually sells at any given time is called the *spot price*. Illustrate what you have just found in a graph with the future spot price p on the horizontal axis and dollars on the vertical. First, graph the relationship of P^C to p, holding fixed $\bar{p}$, q, n and r. Label intercepts and slopes. Graph the same for P^p. Where must these intersect? Explain.

g. Illustrate the same thing in a second graph, except this time put the call or put price $\bar{P}$ on the horizontal axis. Where do the P^C and P^p lines now intersect? Explain.

20.6 **Policy Application:** *Trade Barriers against 'Unfair' Competition.* Some countries subsidize some of their industries heavily, which can lead domestic producers to lobby for tariffs against products from such industries. It is argued that countries with lower subsidies need to impose such tariffs to protect themselves from unfair foreign competition.

A. Suppose that initially the domestic demand and supply curves for steel intersect at the same price in Europe as in China.

a. Begin by illustrating this in side-by-side graphs.

b. Next, suppose China introduces a subsidy for each tonne of steel. Illustrate the impact this has on the price paid by buyers of steel in China before any trade with Europe emerges.

c. Suppose Europe does not introduce any tariffs on steel to counter the subsidy given in China. What will happen to steel prices in Europe? Why?

d. In your Europe graph, illustrate the change in consumer and producer surplus, and assume for simplicity that there are no income effects in the steel market. Are European steel producers rational when they lobby for steel tariffs in response to Chinese steel subsidies?

e. What happens to total surplus in Europe? On purely efficiency grounds, would you advocate for European tariffs in response to Chinese subsidies on steel?

f. Without pinpointing areas in the graph, do you think trade increases or reduces the deadweight loss from the subsidy in China?

g. How much of a tariff would Europe have to impose to eliminate any effect of the Chinese steel subsidies on European markets?

h. Suppose the steel industry is perfectly competitive in both China and Europe. *True or False*: The Chinese steel subsidy, if not followed by a European tariff on Chinese steel, would in the long run eliminate the European steel industry while at the same time increasing Europe's overall surplus.

B. Now consider demand and supply functions $x_d^1(p) = (A - p)/\alpha$ and $x_s^1(p) = (B + p)/\beta$ for China and $x_d^2(p) = (C - p)/\gamma$ and $x_s^2(p) = (D + p)/\delta$ for Europe. Let $\alpha = \gamma = 0.00006$, $\beta = \delta = 0.0001$, $A = C = 800$ and $B = D = 0$.

a. Calculate the prices and quantities in China and Europe in the absence of trade. Is there any reason for trade to emerge?

b. Suppose that China puts a €250 per tonne subsidy for steel in place. In the absence of any trade, what happens to the purchase price of a tonne of steel? What happens to the price received by sellers?

c. If there are no trade barriers in place, how much steel will now be exported from China to Europe? What will be the equilibrium price of steel in Europe?

d. How much of a tariff on steel would Europe have to impose to prevent the Chinese steel subsidy from affecting the European market for steel?

e. What is the deadweight loss in Europe of such a tariff, assuming no income effects?

Chapter 21

Externalities in Competitive Markets

You may have the impression that economists believe markets always and unambiguously result in efficient outcomes, with total surplus maximized when markets operate without interference from other institutions. If this were the case, there would be no efficiency role for non-market institutions in society, and their only justification would lie in concerns about the distribution of surplus, concerns about equity and fairness as these relate to the market allocation of scarce resources. While such equity issues do play an important role in justifying non-market institutions, including government, we now move on to investigate conditions under which non-market institutions are motivated by *efficiency* rather than equity concerns. The first condition we will look at is called *externalities*, and they arise whenever decisions of some parties in the market have a direct impact on others in ways that are not captured by market prices.

| 21A | The Problem of Externalities |

The essential feature of an externality is that either costs or benefits of production or consumption are directly imposed on non-market participants. Since non-market participants are neither demanders nor suppliers of goods, neither market demand nor market supply curves are affected by such externality costs or benefits. Thus, a competitive market composed of price-taking consumers and producers continues to produce in equilibrium where demand intersects supply. However, while the aggregate marginal willingness to pay curve still allows us to measure the benefits consumers receive from participating in markets and the supply curve still allows us to measure costs incurred by producers, there are now non-market participants who also incur benefits or costs. Thus, we can no longer simply use consumer and producer surplus to measure the net gains for society from the existence of markets. We have to include the externality costs and benefits that a competitive market ignores in our calculation of overall surplus.

In our analysis we will treat consumers and producers as separate *in their roles as consumers and producers* from their roles as individuals who may incur some damage or benefit from an externality. We generally lose nothing by making this assumption. Even if, for instance, a producer whose production causes pollution incurs health problems from pollution, no individual producer will take those costs into account in their production choices because, in competitive markets, each producer is so small relative to the market that their contribution to overall pollution is negligible. We will treat all producers as considering only their own production costs when making decisions and then lump them in separately with all economic actors who are hurt by the aggregate level of pollution produced by the industry. In other words, we will treat producers as individuals who consider their own cost of production when making supply decisions and then we will treat the part of that producer that is hurt by the overall level of pollution as a separate person.

21A.1 Production Externalities

Let's return to the example of an industry that produces door handles, but now we assume that the least-cost production process for producers involves the emission of greenhouse gases that contribute to environmental problems. Thus, in addition to the costs of production that are faced by each of the producers of door handles, costs of pollution are imposed on others in society. We will reconsider how many door handles would be produced by a social planner who knows all the relevant costs and benefits, and who seeks to maximize social surplus – how much production would take place if our omniscient and benevolent social planner (BSP) from Chapter 15 were to allocate resources. Our Chapter 15 analysis excluded production externalities like pollution, and we concluded that a BSP could do no better than the competitive market. We will see that this is no longer true when externalities become part of the analysis.

21A.1.1 A BSP Versus the Market In Graph 21.1, we begin with the market demand and supply graph for door handles in panel (a). Whether there are production externalities or not, the market will produce x^M at price p^M, with all consumers and all producers doing the best they can in equilibrium. Assuming tastes are quasilinear in door handles, consumers get the shaded dark brown area in surplus, while producers get the shaded dark blue area. If the production of door handles produces pollution, however, each door handle that is produced imposes a pollution cost on society, a cost that is borne neither by those who consume nor those who produce door handles.

Panel (b) of the graph inserts a light blue curve labelled SMC. This curve represents the *social marginal cost of producing* door handles. It includes the producers' marginal costs that are captured in the market supply curve, but it also includes the additional cost of pollution that is imposed on others. The social marginal cost curve must lie above the supply curve since it includes costs *in addition to* those incurred by producers. It may be that the SMC curve is parallel to the supply curve, implying a constant marginal cost of pollution for each door handle produced, or that it diverges from the supply curve, implying that each additional door handle results in a greater additional pollution cost than the last one. Regardless of how exactly it is related to supply, however, it is this curve that accurately reflects the society-wide cost of production.

Graph 21.1 Maximizing Social Surplus in the Presence of a Negative Production Externality

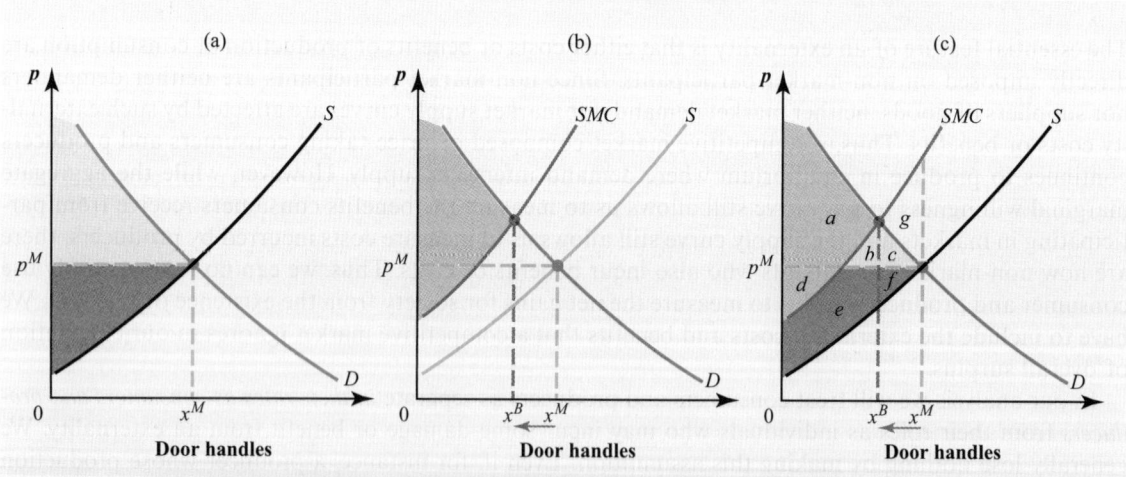

Go to MindTap to interact with this graph

As a result, our BSP would decide to continue to produce as long as the benefits from production as represented by the marginal willingness to pay of consumers outweighs the overall cost of additional production for society. The BSP would certainly produce the first door handle because there is some consumer to whom this is worth more than all the costs incurred by society as measured by SMC, and they would continue to produce until the light blue SMC crosses the dark brown marginal benefit curve. They would not, however, produce any more than that because once *SMC* is higher than the marginal willingness to pay of consumers, the society-wide cost of additional door handles is larger than the benefit. The BSP would choose to produce x^B, resulting in an overall surplus for society represented by the shaded light blue area.

Note that the social planner who seeks to maximize overall surplus will choose less production than will occur in the market. This implies that the market will produce an inefficiently high level of output in the absence of any non-market institutions that curtail production. This is clarified even further in panel (c) where we have labelled some areas in the graph that can now be used to calculate the deadweight loss society incurs under market production. Area $(a + b + c)$ is equal to the dark brown consumer surplus in panel (a), assuming the uncompensated demand is equal to marginal willingness to pay, while area $(d + e + f)$ is equal to the dark blue producer surplus from panel (a). Producers and consumers are, in their roles as producers and consumers, unaffected by the pollution and therefore receive the same surplus as if there were no pollution. However, we also know that in the presence of pollution, we have to take into account the overall cost of the pollution when the market quantity x^M is produced. That area is the difference between the costs incurred by producers and the costs as represented in the *SMC* curve, an area equal to $(b + c + e + f + g)$. Thus, we have to subtract that from consumer and producer surplus to get overall social surplus $(a + d - g)$ under market production. Under the BSP's allocation, on the other hand, society gets an overall surplus of $(a + d)$ equal to the light blue area in panel (b). The market therefore produces a deadweight loss equal to (g).

Exercise 21A.1

Suppose that the pollution emitted in the production of door handles is of a kind that has no harmful effects for humans but does have the benefit of killing the local midge population; that is, suppose the pollution is good rather than bad. Would the market produce more or less than the BSP?

Exercise 21A.2

Would anything fundamental change in our analysis if we let go of our implicit assumption that the aggregate demand curve is also equal to the aggregate marginal willingness to pay curve?

21A.1.2 Another Efficient Tax Our analysis thus far tells us that competitive markets will produce too much in the presence of negative pollution externalities. As a result, there exists the potential for government policy to enhance efficiency and thus reduce or eliminate the deadweight loss from market overproduction. We have seen in Chapter 19 that taxation of goods is one policy tool that can reduce market output. In the absence of externalities, this is inefficient because the market allocation of resources was efficient to begin with. Now, however, this reduction of an otherwise *inefficient* output level can reduce rather than increase deadweight loss.

Suppose we know both the market demand and supply curves as well as the optimal production level x^B that the BSP would choose. This information is depicted in panel (a) of Graph 21.2. We can determine the tax rate t required to reduce market output from x^M to x^B by letting t per unit be equal to the light blue vertical distance in the graph. As a result, buyers in the market would face the higher price p_B, while sellers would receive the lower price p_S with the difference between the two prices representing the payment t per unit in taxes. A tax such as this that is intended to reduce market output to its efficient quantity because of the presence of a negative production externality is called a *Pigouvian tax*, named after Arthur Cecil Pigou (1877–1959), a British economist and student of Alfred Marshall. Pigou developed the distinction between private and social marginal cost in his most influential work titled *Wealth and Welfare*.

Graph 21.2 An Efficient Pigouvian Tax

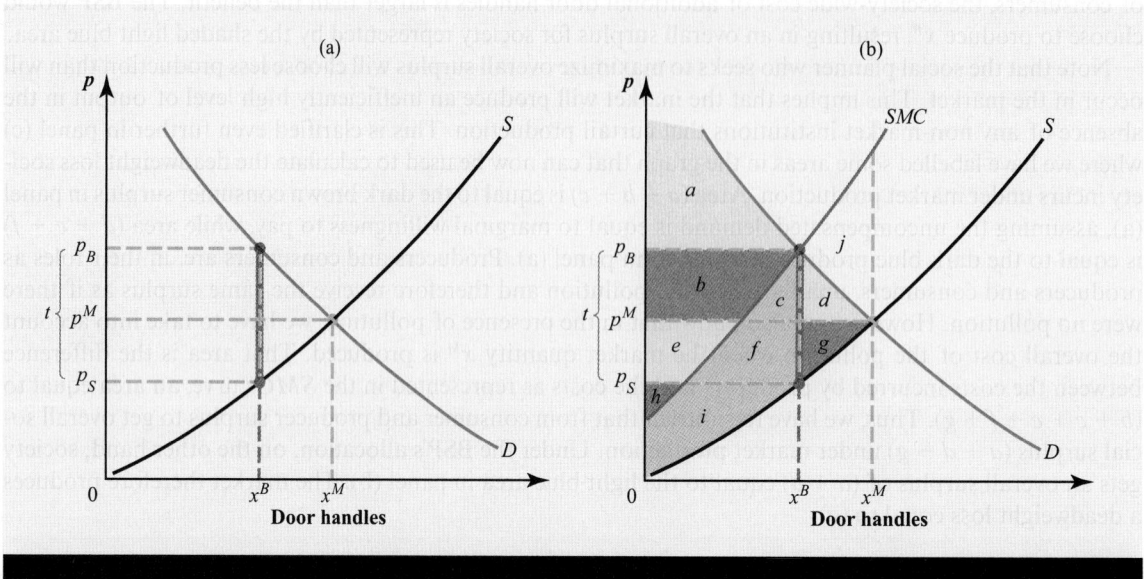

Go to MindTap to interact with this graph

In panel (b) of the graph, we can analyze more directly how this tax is efficient and the basic components of this analysis are summarized in Table 21.1. In the absence of the tax, the market produces output x^M at price p^M. You can check for yourself, in a way analogous to what we did in panel (c) of Graph 21.1, that the competitive market on its own will produce overall surplus equal to $(a + b + e + h - j)$, with the triangle (j) once again representing deadweight loss. Under the tax t, however, consumer surplus (a) and producer surplus ($h + i$) combine with a positive tax revenue ($b + c + e + f$) and a social cost from pollution ($c + f + i$) to produce an overall surplus ($a + b + e + h$). This is equal to the light blue maximum surplus achieved by the BSP in Graph 21.1 panel (b) and eliminates the deadweight loss (j). The reason we found taxes to be inefficient in Chapter 19 was that they distorted the price signal that coordinated efficient cooperation between producers and consumers but *in the presence of externalities, the price signal is already distorted* insofar as it does not efficiently coordinate production and consumption. The tax removes the distortion and causes the market to *internalize the externality*.

In order for the government to be able to impose an efficient Pigouvian tax t, it must however know the optimal quantity x^B it wants the market to reach *and* it must know the difference between the market demand and supply curve at that quantity; the government must know the *marginal social damage caused by pollution at the optimum quantity.* If it possesses this information, the government can achieve the maximum social surplus by setting the per-unit tax on output equal to this marginal social damage of pollution.

Table 21.1 The Welfare Effect of a Pigouvian Tax

	Without Tax	With Tax
Consumer Surplus	$a + b + c + d$	a
Producer Surplus	$e + f + g + h + i$	$h + i$
Pollution Damage	$-(c + d + f + g + i + j)$	$-(c + f + i)$
Tax Revenue	*None*	$b + c + e + f$
Total Surplus	$a + b + e + h - j$	$a + b + e + h$

Exercise 21A.3

What if the government only knows the marginal social damage of pollution at the equilibrium output level x^M and sets the tax rate equal to this quantity? Will this result in the optimal quantity being produced? If not, how do the *SMC* and the supply curve have to be related to one another in order for this method of setting the tax to work?

It may in principle not look too difficult for the government to gather sufficient information to implement a Pigouvian tax that causes markets to once again produce efficiently. However, suppose that there are now many different industries, each causing pollution. In order to set optimal Pigouvian taxes, the government now has to know this same information for each industry and set the per-unit tax in each industry, letting taxes vary across polluting industries as the marginal social damage of pollution at the optimum is different everywhere. This would result in a complex system of different Pigouvian taxes across all polluting industries. As technology changes, these rates would have to be continuously adjusted. Perhaps worst of all, unless the government adjusts Pigouvian taxes whenever firms find ways of reducing pollution on their own, individual firms in each industry would gain no benefit from applying pollution-abating technologies in their own firms because they would still face the same taxes. (It should be noted here that polluters may face two incentives for inventing new technologies – avoiding emissions with the old technology which may be associated with lower costs, and the benefits of reduced tax payments minus additional abatement costs. Both incentives must be compared with the costs of inventing.) While it may look easy in principle to impose Pigouvian taxes on output in polluting industries, it is much more difficult to do so in practice and to simultaneously encourage those industries for whom it is easy to reduce pollution to do so in ways other than simply cutting production due to the tax.

It is for this reason that economists have largely turned away from recommending Pigouvian taxes *on output* and have instead turned to alternatives that focus more directly on forcing producers to confront the trade-off between reducing pollution through less production or through the development of pollution-abating technologies, and paying for its social costs. This shift in focus has also been made possible by new technologies that allow governments to pinpoint who is producing pollution and thus to require polluters to pay for pollution directly. This can be done either through a *pollution tax*, as opposed to a Pigouvian tax on output, or through the design of market-based environmental policy.

Exercise 21A.4

In Chapter 18, we discussed the efficiency losses from government-mandated price ceilings or price floors. Could either of these policies be efficiency enhancing in the presence of pollution externalities, assuming the government has sufficient information to implement these policies?

21A.1.3 Market-Based Environmental Policy The most common market-based environmental policy works by the government determining an overall level of pollution of each kind that it finds acceptable and issuing pieces of paper that permit the owner to emit a certain quantity of different types of pollutants per time period. These pieces of paper, known as *pollution vouchers* or *tradable pollution permits*, represent the right to pollute by some amount. The government releases these rights, either by auctioning them off or by giving them to different firms in different industries. It does not matter which way the government uses to distribute such permits; the important feature for our analysis is that individuals who own such permits can sell them to others if they so choose and thus transfer the right to pollute to someone who is willing to pay more than it is worth to the original owner. The policy caps the overall pollution level by fixing the number of pollution permits and allows trade in permits to determine who uses them. For this reason, it has come to be known as a *cap-and-trade* policy.

Pollution vouchers have value to producers because they permit producers to emit pollution in their production process. At the same time, whenever a producer chooses to use such a voucher, they incur an economic or opportunity cost because they could have chosen to sell or rent the voucher to someone else instead. Each producer has to weigh the costs and benefits of using a pollution voucher, and each producer knows that they will have to use fewer vouchers the less they produce and the more they take advantage of pollution-abating technologies. Since some production processes lend themselves to pollution-abating technologies more easily than others, firms in some industries will have a greater demand for such vouchers than firms in other industries. As a result, by introducing pollution vouchers into an economy, and prohibiting the emission of pollution when firms do not own such vouchers, the government has created a new market: the market for pollution vouchers.

Exercise 21A.5

Explain how firms face a cost for pollution regardless of whether the government gives them tradable pollution vouchers or whether firms have to purchase these.

This market is depicted in Graph 21.3 where pollution vouchers appear on the horizontal axis and the price per voucher appears on the vertical. By introducing only a limited quantity of such vouchers, the government has set a perfectly inelastic supply at precisely the cap on overall pollution across all industries. Firms that emit pollution in their production processes are the demanders of such vouchers, with demand depending on how much pollution is involved in producing different types of goods and how easy it is for firms to find ways of reducing the pollution emitted in production. Those firms that find it difficult to reduce their pollution will be willing to pay more for the right to pollute than those that can easily put a filter on their chimneys. In equilibrium, pollution vouchers will sell at price p^*.

Graph 21.3 A Market for Pollution Vouchers

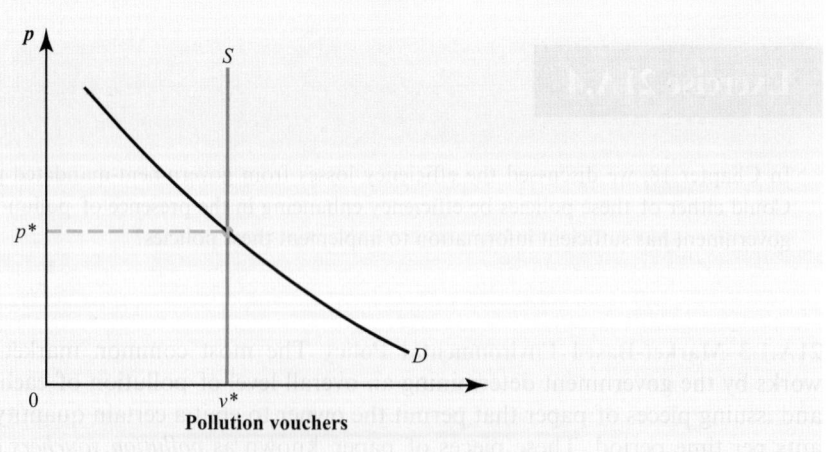

Assuming the government can monitor polluting industries effectively, which is becoming increasingly easy through the use of satellite technology, for example, a system of pollution vouchers achieves the following: it imposes a cost on polluters by requiring that they purchase sufficient pollution rights for the pollution they emit. This causes an upward shift in firm MC curves as pollution vouchers become an input into the production process and with it a shift in the market supply curve in polluting industries. Such a shift will result in less production of output in such polluting industries. Second, the system introduces an incentive for firms to search for, and invest in, pollution-abating technologies. As long as it costs less to reduce pollution from the firm than the pollution vouchers would cost, producers have an incentive to reduce emissions. Third, the system creates an incentive for new firms to arise and to independently invest in research and development of pollution-abating technologies because the system has increased the demand for such technologies in light of the fact that polluters now have to pay for the pollution they emit.

As a result, the system *achieves an overall reduction in pollution at the least social cost and without the government adjusting any policy to changing conditions.* The government does not have to be in the business of picking which industry reduces which type of pollution by how much, and it does not have to adjust those policies as pollution-abating technologies that are more applicable to some industries than to others, are produced. The government has to set an overall pollution target and print a corresponding quantity of pollution vouchers. The newly created pollution voucher market rations who gets the vouchers and who does not get them, with those for whom reductions in pollution are costliest, choosing to use vouchers and others choosing to reduce pollution cheaply. *Pollution vouchers are government interventions that harness the power of a newly created market to generate the information required to reduce pollution at the lowest possible cost without any further government interference.*

There is one final check on the system. While we have said thus far that polluters are the ones who will form the demand curve in the pollution voucher market, it is in principle possible to allow anyone at all to participate in that market. If, for instance, a group of deeply concerned citizens feels that the government is permitting too much pollution to be emitted into the air, they could pool resources and purchase some quantity of the vouchers, thus increasing the price, and raising the cost to polluting, while lowering the supply if they store away the pollution vouchers. Such groups face a difficult free-rider problem that they need to overcome, but if they can, they are able to impact the overall level of pollution without lobbying the government.

Exercise 21A.6

If the government, after creating the pollution voucher market, decides to tax the sale of pollution vouchers, will there be any further reduction in pollution?

While pollution vouchers offer a mechanism to reduce pollution to a target level in the least costly way, there is nothing in a pollution voucher system that guarantees that the socially optimal target for pollution is set to begin with. If the political process that determines this target is efficient, the target will be set optimally. Otherwise, the target might be too high or too low; all that the cap-and-trade system does is to get to the target in the least costly way.

21A.1.4 Pollution Taxes, Pigouvian Taxes and Cap-and-Trade While the idea of taxing *output* in polluting industries – as originally proposed by Pigou – has lost considerable favour among economists, the very technology that allows the establishment of markets in tradable pollution permits now enables governments to tax *pollution,* rather than output, directly. Taxing pollution directly has the same advantages over Pigouvian taxes that we have pointed out for cap-and-trade systems, and a per-unit-of-pollution tax is equivalent to establishing tradable pollution permits if the tax rate is set at the same level as the price per unit of pollution that emerges in cap-and-trade systems. Both systems provide incentives for firms to invest in pollution-abating technologies; neither requires governments to adjust industry tax rates as circumstances change, as is the case under Pigouvian taxes on output; overall pollution is reduced in the cheapest ways as firms for which it is easy to reduce pollution will do so rather than incur the cost of pollution by either paying a pollution tax or using pollution vouchers; and neither system automatically results in full efficiency unless the government has lots of information on what the efficient tax rate or the efficient number of pollution permits is.

Exercise 21A.7

Assume a politician advocates the cap-and-trade system over a carbon tax on the grounds that the carbon tax would be partially passed on to consumers in the form of higher prices. Another politician who also supports the cap-and-trade system corrects this assertion by suggesting that to whatever extent a carbon tax would be passed on to consumers, the same is true of costs of tradable permits under the cap-and-trade system. Who is right?

While pollution taxes and cap-and-trade systems are quite similar, environmental policy makers debate their relative merits. Some consider it important to set precise target levels for pollution, with cap-and-trade systems allowing an easy way of establishing such targets while letting the market for tradable permits determine the per-unit-of-pollution price required to implement the target. Others believe it is more important to specify the per-unit-of-pollution cost directly through a tax in order to allow firms to plan accordingly, leaving the level of pollution reduction to arise from firm responses to the tax. If the per-unit-of-pollution tax is set at the same rate as the per-unit-of-pollution price that emerges under a particular cap in a cap-and-trade system, the two policies have identical effects, but one gets there by being precise about the target pollution level up front while the other gets there by being precise about the per-unit-pollution cost up front.

A second issue that is raised in policy debates relates to politics and implementation. Some fear that a nationwide, or even worldwide, cap-and-trade system would involve excessive government bureaucracy to administer the various markets for different types of pollution vouchers, while others argue that administering pollution taxes would involve similar issues. In practice, however, there appears to be one important political reason for environmental policy makers to favour the cap-and-trade system, in that it has a built-in mechanism for overcoming concentrated opposition from industries that are particularly affected. Such industries would face increased marginal costs under both the pollution tax and the cap-and-trade system, but pollution vouchers could be given away for free to some industries in order to buy their political support. This involves a transfer of wealth in the form of pollution vouchers that can be traded without a change in the increased opportunity cost of emitting pollution. Under pollution taxes, one could similarly 'buy off' industry opposition through transfers of taxpayer money, but this appears to be politically more controversial.

Exercise 21A.8

Suppose that advocates of pollution taxes proposed a reduction in such taxes for key industries that would otherwise be opposed to the policy. How is this different from giving away pollution vouchers for free to such key industries in a cap-and-trade system?

Finally, to the extent to which the pollution problem to be addressed is global as in the case of greenhouse gases, rather than local as in the case of acid rain, policy makers may favour the cap-and-trade system as it permits the establishment of global markets in tradable pollution permits to achieve global reductions in pollution while allowing an initial establishment of country-specific caps through negotiated international agreements. Such a system does not enshrine country-specific caps because permits could be traded across national boundaries, but much as support from particular industries can be gained by giving some pollution permits away, international support for such agreements could be facilitated by initially allocating relatively more pollution permits to some countries than others.

Exercise 21A.9

Less-developed countries often point out that developed countries did not have to confront the fact that they caused a great deal of pollution during their periods of development, and thus suggest that developed countries should disproportionately incur the cost of reducing worldwide pollution now. Can you suggest a way for this to be incorporated into a global cap-and-trade system?

21A.2 Consumption Externalities

So far we have limited ourselves to externalities that have negative impacts on others, or what we have referred to as *negative externalities*. Externalities can, however, arise in production and consumption, and they can be positive or negative. We will now illustrate the impact of an externality on the consumer side, and, to differentiate it further from what we have done so far, we will consider a positive rather than a negative externality.

Suppose, for instance, that production of door handles entails no pollution whatsoever but, whenever a consumer purchases door handles, the world becomes a better place because it makes it easier for people to enter and leave buildings and ensures that doors are fully closed and thus help prevents the rapid spread of fire. This may sound silly because of the context of the example, but the essential nature of the argument is the same. In addition to the private benefits that consumers obtain directly from consumption, others in society benefit indirectly in ways that are not priced by the market.

21A.2.1 Positive Externalities from Consumption Graph 21.4 presents a series of graphs for positive externalities that is analogous to the series of graphs in Graph 21.1 for negative externalities. Panel (a) illustrates consumer and producer surplus along market supply and demand curves, under the assumption that demand can be interpreted as marginal willingness to pay. Panel (b) introduces a new curve called *SMB* or *social marginal benefit*. This curve includes all the benefits society gains from each unit of consumption. It therefore includes all the private benefits that consumers get and that are measured by the demand curve, plus it includes additional social benefits that are gained by others. As in the case of *SMC* and supply, *SMB* and demand can be related to each other in a variety of ways, but under positive externalities *SMB* must lie above demand or private marginal willingness to pay.

Graph 21.4 Underproduction in the Presence of a Positive Externality

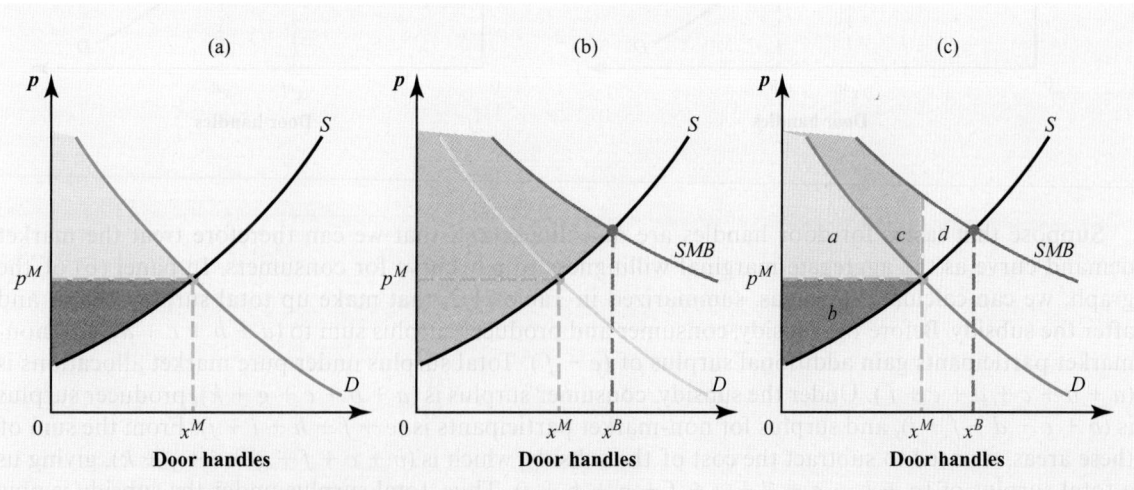

Our BSP would use this *SMB* to measure the marginal benefit of each door handle that is produced, while measuring the marginal cost along the supply curve in the absence of negative externalities. They

would choose the production level x^B in panel (b) of the graph, giving the shaded light blue area as overall social surplus. The market produces an inefficiently low quantity of a good that exhibits a positive consumption externality. We can derive the exact deadweight loss from the areas labelled in panel (c) of Graph 21.4. At the competitive market equilibrium, consumer surplus is area (a), equivalent to the dark brown area in panel (a), and producer surplus is area (b), equivalent to the dark blue area in panel (a). Since the market produces an output level x^M, the additional social benefit from the externality is given by area (c). The market achieves an overall social gain equal to area ($a + b + c$). Our BSP, on the other hand, achieves that *plus* area (d), implying that society incurs a deadweight loss of (d) in the absence of non-market institutions that induce additional production.

21A.2.2 Pigouvian Subsidies

Assume the government wants to raise output in the door handle market to x^B above the market quantity x^M. In panel (a) of Graph 21.5, this implies that the government can accomplish its goal by imposing a subsidy s equal to the light blue vertical distance, thus lowering the price for buyers to p_B and raising the price for sellers to p_S. The degree to which prices faced by buyers and sellers change depends on the relative price elasticities of market demand and supply curves. When such a subsidy is used to internalize a positive externality, it is known as a Pigouvian subsidy. As in the case of a Pigouvian tax, it can restore efficiency by removing the externality-induced distortion in market prices.

Graph 21.5 An Efficient Pigouvian Subsidy

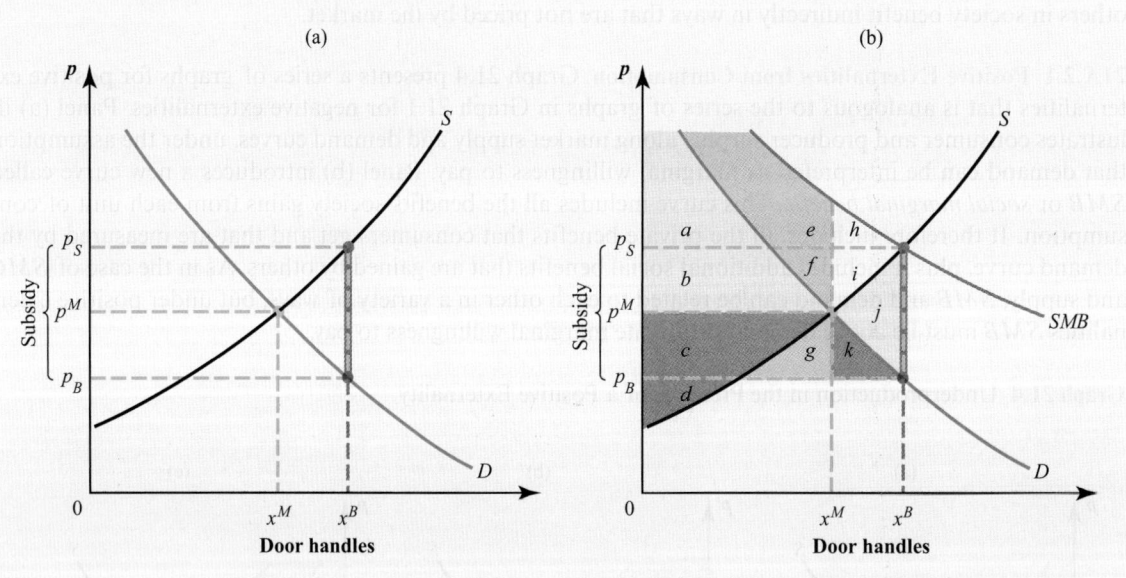

Suppose that tastes for door handles are quasilinear and that we can therefore treat the market demand curve as the aggregate marginal willingness to pay curve for consumers. In panel (b) of the graph, we can calculate the areas, summarized in Table 21.2, that make up total surplus before and after the subsidy. Before the subsidy, consumer and producer surplus sum to ($a + b + c + d$), and non-market participants gain additional surplus of ($e + f$). Total surplus under pure market allocations is ($a + b + c + d + e + f$). Under the subsidy, consumer surplus is ($a + b + c + g + k$), producer surplus is ($b + c + d + f + i$), and surplus for non-market participants is ($e + f + h + i + j$). From the sum of these areas, we need to subtract the cost of the subsidy, which is ($b + c + f + g + i + j + k$), giving us a total surplus of ($a + b + c + d + e + f + g + h + i$). Thus, total surplus under the subsidy is now equal to the light blue area in panel (b) of Graph 21.4, which we concluded was the maximum social gain possible, with the subsidy having eliminated the deadweight loss ($h + i$) that occurred under a pure-market allocation.

THE PROBLEM OF EXTERNALITIES | 609

Table 21.2 The Welfare Effect of a Pigouvian Subsidy

	Without Subsidy	With Subsidy
Consumer Surplus	$a + b$	$a + b + c + g + k$
Producer Surplus	$c + d$	$b + c + d + f + i$
Externality Benefit	$e + f$	$e + f + h + i + j$
Subsidy Cost	None	$-(b + c + f + g + i + j + k)$
Total Surplus	$a + b + c + d + e + f$	$a + b + d + e + f + h + i$

Exercise 21A.10

Suppose that, instead of generating positive consumption externalities, door handles impose negative consumption externalities by making it harder for some people to access buildings, especially those with certain disabilities. Can you see how such externalities can be modelled like negative production externalities?

21A.2.3 Charitable Giving, Government Policy and Civil Society In the case of the negative production externality of pollution, we illustrated how government could create a new market for pollution vouchers that can efficiently reduce pollution to some cap set by the government. In the case of positive consumption externalities, we can't offer a similar market-based policy that is currently under discussion, but we should note that the market outcome we have predicted in the model may not necessarily be the actual outcome if markets operate within the context of non-governmental and non-market institutions, i.e. *civil society*. This term does not have a clear definition and is often used to mean many different things. We will refer to an institution as a civil society institution whenever it is not clearly set up by the government and it does not operate strictly on the self-interested motives that generate explicit prices in markets. *Civil society institutions are the sets of interactions between individuals that occur outside the context of government and outside the context of explicit market prices.* Such institutions tend to arise as individuals try to use persuasion rather than the political process to address issues of concern that are not addressed in the market. The existence of positive consumption externalities offers an example because, as we have seen, it is a case when the market in the absence of non-market institutions produces too little of goods that are valued in society beyond their simple consumption value.

Many organizations spend substantial energy trying to make people aware of many social concerns in an attempt to persuade them to voluntarily contribute money or time to organized efforts aimed at addressing such concerns. For example, TV appeals for refugees from conflicts, organizations trying to provide water in drought-stricken areas, and so on. Efforts to appeal for charitable donations run into difficulties involving 'free riding' that we will address more explicitly in Chapter 27 and offer no guarantee of achieving a fully efficient outcome, but they appear to play an important role in many circumstances where positive externalities would make markets by themselves produce too little.

All three types of institutions that we have discussed – government, markets and civil society – face obstacles in achieving efficient outcomes. Markets will tend to under-produce in the presence of positive externalities and overproduce in the presence of negative externalities; governments may face difficulties in ascertaining the information necessary for implementing optimal outcomes through taxes or subsidies or other means, especially as circumstances within societies change, and in the face of political hurdles. Civil society efforts that rely on strictly voluntary engagement of non-market participants face difficulties in engaging those non-market participants fully as each will tend to rely on others to address the problem. Yet each appears to play a role in the real world.

Finally, just as the case of pollution vouchers represents an effort by government to engage market forces in finding efficient solutions to excessive pollution, government policies are often aimed at engaging civil society institutions more. The most obvious example of this can be found in the income tax policies of a number of countries, which offer tax deductions to individuals who voluntarily give to charitable causes, thus subsidizing such causes without the government making the explicit decision of which charities will end up engaging non-market participants. When the government faces too many hurdles in designing explicit subsidies for each industry that generates positive externalities, it can offer general subsidies aimed at reducing the hurdles faced by civil society organizations in finding non-market, non-governmental solutions.

Exercise 21A.11

In what sense does the tax-deducibility of charitable contributions represent another way of subsidizing charities?

Exercise 21A.12

In a progressive income tax system, with marginal tax rates increasing as income rises, are charities valued by high income people implicitly favoured over charities valued by low income people? Would the same be true if everyone could take a tax credit equal to some fraction k of their charitable contributions?

Exercise 21A.13

We did not explicitly discuss a role for civil society institutions in correcting market failures due to negative externalities. Can you think of any examples of such efforts in the real world?

21A.3 Externalities: Market Failure or Failure of Markets to Exist?

Thus far, we have seen that markets by themselves will produce inefficient quantities of goods that exhibit positive or negative consumption and production externalities. In the absence of government intervention, civil society efforts may contribute to greater efficiency. Alternatively, government policies can be designed to change market output directly, as in the case of Pigouvian taxes and subsidies, or to indirectly harness the advantages of market forces, as in the case of cap-and-trade policies, or civil society institutions, as in the case of the tax deductibility of charitable contributions to increase efficiency and lower deadweight losses. After we have explored more fully in the upcoming chapters the many hurdles faced by markets, governments and civil society institutions in implementing optimal outcomes for society, we will return in Chapter 30 of the book to a general approach for considering how we can ascertain the appropriate balance of markets, government and civil society depending on the particulars of the social problem that is to be solved.

In the meantime, we can see yet another efficiency-enhancing policy tool the government has at its disposal by exploring a little more deeply the fundamental problem created by the presence of externalities. We have seen that markets by themselves will tend to fail in the presence of externalities, and this has often led economists to refer to externalities as one of several potential *market failures*. In this section, we will see how this market failure arises because of the fact that whenever there is an externality generated in competitive markets, *we can trace the over or underproduction that arises from this externality to the lack of a market or the non-existence of a market somewhere else.*

21A.3.1 Pollution and Missing Markets Consider again the case of a market in which pollution is a by-product of production. The fundamental reason that a market will overproduce in this case, relative to the efficient quantity, is that producers are not forced to face the full costs they impose on societies when making production decisions. In particular, if the pollution that is generated is air pollution, the producer escapes paying for the input clean air that is used in the production process unless some mechanism, like Pigouvian taxes, pollution taxes or pollution vouchers, is implemented. Were there a market for each of the inputs used in production, including the input clean air, the producers would have to fully pay for all the costs they impose. *Air pollution therefore arises as a problem that keeps markets from producing efficiently because one of the inputs into production is not bought and sold.*

How could there be a market for clean air when no one owns the air and therefore no one can sell clean air to firms that use it in the production process? The conceptual point here is that the externality is a problem because we have not found a way to create a market in clean air. If there were such a market, and if all air was owned by different people, each user of clean air would have to pay for it as it is being used. Consumers of clean air, including producers who use clean air as an input, would have to pay for clean air just as firms have to pay for labour and capital. Such a market for clean air would therefore result in a market price that would, in the absence of any other externalities, result in maximum social surplus in the clean air market. As producers contemplate production that involves pollution, they would face a price for clean air, shifting their marginal cost curves up and thus shifting market supply up to be equal to the *SMC* of production rather than the marginal private cost that excludes the social cost of pollution. This would result in the efficient quantity of the pollution-generating output, with social surplus once again maximized purely by market forces.

In an abstract conceptual sense, the market failure generated by the presence of externalities can be traced to the failure of a market to exist. Does recognizing this get us any closer to solving the problem? In the case of pollution, it is that recognition that has led economists to come up with the proposal for creating markets in pollution vouchers. Pollution voucher markets are not the same as markets in clean air, but they represent an attempt to resolve a problem created by the non-existence of a market for clean air through the creation of a different type of market that can help. Recognizing the market failure generated by externalities as a failure of a market to exist can create the opportunity for innovative government interventions that may, at least in some cases, work better than other government solutions we might otherwise implement.

21A.3.2 The Tragedy of the Commons This insight points towards a huge role that governments more generally have to play in order for markets to function efficiently. Throughout our treatment of the efficiency of markets we made the implicit assumption that markets for all sorts of inputs such as labour and capital actually exist. Presuming that such markets exist presumes that individuals own resources that they can trade, and *this presumes that there is some mechanism in place that protects the property rights of owners of resources.* Firms cannot just take a worker's leisure and use it for labour inputs; they are required to persuade them to sell leisure to them by offering a wage that is considered sufficient. Similarly, they cannot just take an individual's savings or retirement account and use the money to buy labour, land and equipment; they have to pay for using their financial capital by paying interest or some alternative such as that devised under Islamic finance. All this requires a well-established *system of legally enforced property rights*, and such a system has in practice typically required government protection and a well-functioning court system to enforce property rights.

Externalities, as we have seen, arise when such property rights have not been established. Pollution is a problem because there does not exist a system of property rights to clean air that forces firms to pay for using clean air as an input into production. In effect, without some other institution in place, firms are able to take clean air for 'free' as they produce goods, something we do not permit for inputs like labour and capital. Were they to similarly be able to take leisure and capital, were there no legal system of property rights in those input markets, we would have even worse externality issues to deal with. Whenever a resource is not clearly owned by someone, it therefore becomes possible for economic actors to take those resources without incurring a cost, even though this imposes costs on society. It is a logical consequence that, if it is feasible for the government to establish a system of property rights in resources that are not currently owned by anyone, such government interference can create additional markets that reduce the problem of externalities by forcing market participants to face the true social cost of what they are doing.

For this reason, economists have come to refer to externality problems that arise from the non-existence of markets as the *Tragedy of the Commons*, the tragedy of *social losses that emerge when resources are commonly rather than privately owned*. We could say, for instance, that clean air is owned by everyone, but that means it is owned by no one in particular. It is argued that much human suffering in the world can be directly traced to societies not heeding the lessons of the Tragedy of the Commons. Entire societies have been set up in attempts to abolish private property and replace the mechanism of markets with some alternative mechanism. It takes only a quick glance at 20th-century history, for instance, to see how much societies that have protected private property and thus established markets, have economically thrived, while societies that have attempted to do the opposite have failed. A full understanding of externalities suggests that such societies failed because they created huge externalities by eliminating markets without finding an alternative government or civil society mechanism to generate social surplus. By not supporting markets, they have created large tragedies of the commons.

Exercise 21A.14

Large portions of the world's forests are publicly owned and not protected from exploitation. Identify the Tragedy of the Commons and the externalities associated with it that this creates.

Exercise 21A.15

Why do you think there is a problem of overfishing in the world's oceans?

21A.3.3 Congestion on Roads Economists estimate that the social cost of externalities in terms of the social cost of time wasted on congested roads rivals the social cost of environmental damage from pollution. Think of your own experiences being stuck in traffic. It is mind-numbing to be stuck in traffic even for short periods of time because the opportunity cost of our time is large. In some larger cities, commuters routinely spend significant amounts of time in precisely such a position.

The problem of congested roads is an example of a Tragedy of the Commons. Roads, by and large, are commonly or publicly owned, which is to say that they are not owned by anyone. As individuals get on the road, they may think about the cost of the journey, the cost of their time, the fuel used and the depreciation of their car. They may not, however, think about the cost they are imposing on everyone else who is also taking a trip. There is a negative externality each person imposes on everyone else who is on the road as each adds to the congestion. In the absence of a mechanism that makes people face the social cost of their private actions, they will tend to take too many trips, and we will be on the road at the wrong times. Each individual may consider that their own contribution to the congestion of the roads is minor, but every person together is causing the congestion problem that wastes billions of euros worth of time each week on the congested roads of cities throughout Europe and beyond. If one person's entry onto the road causes thousands of others to take even one more second to get to where they are going, that person is imposing a social cost on others without paying any attention to it.

Exercise 21A.16

Can you think of any other costs that people tend not to think about as they decide to get onto public roads?

Solutions for this particular Tragedy of the Commons are still evolving, and changes in technology are playing a large part in shaping these solutions just as new technologies that permit detection of pollution have shaped new environmental policies, such as pollution taxes and cap-and-trade systems. The difficulty in finding a way for individuals to internalize the social cost they are imposing on others on the road lies in the difficulty of establishing a market that will price that social cost. Economists have often proposed somewhat blunt policies falling into two general categories. First, taxes can be imposed on fuel that will raise the cost of driving and therefore reduce the amount of driving individuals will undertake; and second, when there are sufficiently many individuals in sufficiently dense geographic areas, governments can design public transportation systems like tram and underground systems that are expensive to build but that, once built, can offer attractive alternative means of transportations within cities.

The building of public transportation may alleviate congestion, but it does not in itself address the Tragedy of the Commons that remains on public roads, and it may create a different Tragedy of the Commons if public transportation is priced in such a way as to cause congestion in buses, tram systems and so on. Nevertheless, it has represented an important element of addressing crowding on roads in some urban areas. Taxation of fuel is appealing in that it does raise the cost of driving and brings it more into line with the social cost of individual decisions during peak traffic hours, but it also raises the cost of driving during off-peak hours when congestion is not a problem, thus creating deadweight losses during those hours just as it reduces deadweight losses during peak hours.

Exercise 21A.17

Are there other externality-based reasons to tax fuel?

In recent years, however, it has become possible to price driving on congested roads more directly through tolls. Before the advent of electronic equipment that has made this easier, such tolls have involved toll booths, which themselves can contribute to congestion around the booths as traffic slows down even as they keep individuals off the roads. As technology improves, however, we are beginning to see increasingly efficient mechanisms for tolls to be imposed, mechanisms that do not require individuals to stop, reach into their pockets and pay a toll-booth attendant. As a result, we are seeing cities increasingly use electronic tolls that can vary with the time of day that individuals choose to use roads. User fees in the form of tolls represent an attempt to make individuals face the social cost of driving during peak hours. At least in principle, such technology also permits the more direct establishment of markets in roads, in which road networks are privately owned and the use of the road is priced within markets. As technology and our understanding of the underlying causes of externalities on roads is changing, we therefore see the emergence of new ways for government policy to interact with markets to reduce the social costs of an important externality.

Exercise 21A.18

Some have argued against using tolls to address the congestion externality on the grounds that wealthier individuals will have no problem paying such tolls while the poor will. Is this a valid argument against the efficiency of using tolls?

21A.4 Smaller Externalities, the Courts and the Coase Theorem

We have thus far focused primarily on externalities that affect many individuals, such as pollution and congestion. Many of the externalities that we are most aware of in our daily lives are much less grand: the loud music from the room next to yours, the odour from the student who insists on sitting next to you in seminars but who also insists on showering infrequently, the insensitivity of the person on the train who talks loudly into their phone, or that baby that just stopped screaming only to have switched from an externality that affects the auditory nerve to one that affects our sense of smell. These are all negative externalities, but we could think of positive ones as well. A person smiling in the corridor at work may mean a few people a day might derive direct benefits from their cheerful disposition, or if someone opens the door for a colleague, which means that person's life might be just a bit better for that day by a kindly gesture. Externalities exist everywhere that people operate within close proximity to one another: in the workplace, in restaurants, in neighbourhoods. Sometimes these externalities cause people to take each other to court.

21A.4.1 The Case of the Shadow on Your Swimming Pool

Imagine that two people, Sam and Laura, live next to each other in peace and harmony. Laura then wins some money on the lottery and decides that she wants to extend her house. She draws up some plans to add an additional floor to her existing house. Normally, Sam would not care about this, but it turns out that the additional floor will cast a long shadow onto his property and in particular the area of the property that currently contains a beautiful and sunny swimming pool. Sam gets very upset that his swimming pool will suddenly be in the shade all the time, and so he goes to court to prevent the building plans. Sam argues that Laura is imposing a negative externality on him which she is not taking into account.

The court sees your point but wants to be careful and wants to assess whether it would or would not be efficient to build the addition to Laura's house despite the adverse effect this will have on Sam. The court might consider the extent of the enjoyment from the house extension for Laura in comparison to the loss Sam suffers from the shade on his swimming pool and vice versa. It might cost Sam very little to move to a different house and have someone who does not care about the shade on the swimming pool move into his house, thereby eliminating the externality. Maybe it would be easy for Laura to find a bigger house elsewhere and relatively costless for her to move. It's hard to tell without the court assessing a lot of details about the case, and one might argue that there isn't an easy way to judge this on a basis other than efficiency. After all, both are equally to blame for the existence of the externality. It would not exist if Laura were not trying to build an extension, but it also would not exist if Sam was not so insistent on having the sun shining on his pool!

21A.4.2 The Coase Theorem

Ronald Coase, an economist at the University of Chicago, came along and had a neat insight that might, under certain conditions, make the judge's life a lot easier and that relates directly to our observation. Ronald Coase (1910–2013) won the 1991 Nobel Prize in part for his contribution to the issue of externalities arising from a lack of fully specified property rights. His work led to what was termed the Coase Theorem, encapsulated in the article, 'The Problem of Social Cost' (*The Journal of Law and Economics* 3 (1960), 1–44). Coase thought that the reason Sam might take Laura to court is that they are confused about who has what property rights, and this ambiguity makes it difficult for people to come up with the optimal solution to their problems on our own. Suppose, for instance, Sam *knew* the judge would rule that Laura had the right to build regardless of the damage this does to him. Sam might invite Laura for coffee and ask if there is a way he could convince her not to build the extension. If the damage that is done to Sam is greater than the pleasure Laura gets from the extension – if it would be efficient for her not to build the extension – Sam might be willing to pay Laura an amount that will persuade her not to build the extension. Laura may find another way to extend her house, or perhaps she would move with the money Sam gives her to not build. If, on the other hand, Sam's pain from the extension is less in euro terms than Laura's pleasure – if it is efficient for her to build the extension – he would discover over coffee that he isn't willing to pay her enough to stop the extension. Sam may decide to suffer in a shaded pool, or perhaps move elsewhere. Note that once Sam *knows* that Laura has every right to build the addition, he has an incentive to find out whether he can pay her to stop, and once he finds out, he will ensure that the efficient outcome happens.

The same is true in the case where Laura knows that *Sam* has the property right; that is, that he has a right to block the extension. In that case, Laura has an incentive to invite Sam for coffee to persuade him to let her go ahead. If the extension means more to Laura than the pain it causes Sam, he will be willing to accept a payment that she is willing to pay in order to get him to drop his objections. If, on the other hand,

Laura's gain from the extension is less than his pain, she won't be willing to pay Sam enough to get him to stop his objections. If the initial property right rests with Sam, Laura is the one who has an incentive to work out whether her gain is greater than Sam's pain and in the process gets both to do what is efficient. Note that neither actually cares about efficiency, but once they know who has what rights, their private incentives make it in their interest to find the efficient outcome.

Exercise 21A.19

True or False: While it might not matter for efficiency which way the court rules, Laura and Sam nevertheless care about the outcome of its ruling.

No matter what the court decides, Laura and Sam will arrive at the efficient outcome; the most important thing is that the court needs to define the property rights so that they can have coffee and know what they are negotiating about.

21A.4.3 Bargaining, Transactions Costs and the Coase Theorem The Coase Theorem says it is *essential that* property rights be clearly defined in cases when there are negative externalities, but it is *not necessarily essential how* those rights are defined. Recall that we emphasized in the previous section that the absence of markets for the externality is the real underlying problem with externalities. Coase's argument is similar, except that he does not insist that we have to have a *competitive* market in the externality; all we need to do is establish who has what rights and let people solve the problem on their own by bargaining with one another. In our example of Laura and Sam, there is no hope of establishing a real competitive market, but they can clarify property rights sufficiently to give them an incentive to work out how to solve the externality problem.

Coase was not, however, naive, and he recognized that there might be barriers that keep people from getting together to bargain their way out of an externality problem once property rights are fully defined. These barriers are called *transactions costs*, and if they are sufficiently high, Laura and Sam might never have coffee to talk about how to proceed. If they can't stand each other's presence in the same room, there is a transactions cost to getting together, and when this is the case, the court's decision suddenly matters a great deal more. If the efficient outcome is for Laura to build her extension and the court rules in Sam's favour, these transactions costs would keep her from getting together with Sam to offer the payment necessary to let her proceed. Similarly, if the efficient outcome is for Laura not to build the extension and the court rules in her favour, transactions costs again keep them from getting together in order for Sam to offer the payment necessary not to build. Thus, in the presence of sufficiently high transactions costs, the court needs to assess what the efficient outcome is and rule accordingly so that it is not necessary for them to get together to solve the problem through side payments between them both. The full Coase Theorem can be stated as follows: *If transactions costs are sufficiently low, the efficient outcome will arise in the presence of externalities as long as property rights are sufficiently clear.*

The Coase Theorem offers a decentralized way out of externality problems as long as transactions costs are low, and transactions costs will tend to be lower the fewer individuals are affected by an externality. If it's just Laura and Sam arguing about the building of an extension that only affects the two of them, they might think that transactions costs are sufficiently low and will bargain their way to a solution if the assignment of property rights requires such bargaining. For this reason, we might not worry about all the everyday externalities that affect only small numbers of people. Chances are probably better that individuals themselves will work out the efficient outcome than that a government with limited information can dictate the efficient outcome. As long as people in small externality settings have reasonable expectations about how the law will treat externality issues if such issues were to be adjudicated in a court, such problems are best handled in the civil society in which people interact voluntarily outside the usual price-governed market setting.

Exercise 21A.20

Use the Coase Theorem to explain why the government probably does not need to get involved in the externality that arises when an individual plays music sufficiently loud that their neighbours are adversely affected, but it probably does need to get involved in addressing pollution that might lead to global warming.

21A.4.4 Bees and Honey: The Role of Markets and Civil Society The Coase Theorem applies to all types of externalities, positive or negative. So far, we have been sticking with the example of the negative externality of the shadow cast on Sam's pool by the extension to Laura's house. A classic example of *positive* externalities involves beekeepers and apple orchard owners. This externality was pointed out by the Nobel Prize winning economist James Meade (1907–1995), who argued in 1952 that Pigouvian subsidies were needed to remedy the problem. Although the example was originally given as motivation for Pigouvian subsidies, this is a case where Coase's insights, as well as our more general insights on markets and property rights, have held true in the real world, and there appears to be no need for further Pigouvian interventions.

Externalities in the case of bees and apple orchards abound. In order for apple trees to produce fruit, bees need to travel from tree to tree to carry pollen. In order for bees to produce honey, they need some blossoms to visit. Beekeepers that let their bees roam impose a positive externality on apple orchard growers who benefit from the cross-pollination services, and apple orchard growers bestow a positive externality on beekeepers by providing them with the means for apple honey production. Even if there was a way for markets to solve this problem in general, there is a second problem: bees have a way of not staying on the precise properties on which they are released. If one orchard owner hires cross-pollination services or invests in their own bees, the bees will cross into neighbouring orchards and provide services there, while also contributing to honey production.

In the absence of markets that can price all these externalities, our theory predicts that there would be too few bees on apple orchards, resulting in too little cross-pollination and too little honey. None of this is a surprise to beekeepers and orchard growers. Fairly sophisticated markets for beekeepers to release their bees on orchards have emerged spontaneously, markets that established themselves in an environment where government's only role has been to guarantee the integrity of contracts and thus the property rights that are defined in those contracts. The flowers on apple trees do not produce much honey, causing the externality to go almost entirely from beekeepers to apple orchard growers. Clover, on the other hand, produces tons of honey. Growers of clover produce a net-positive externality for beekeepers. While apple growers pay beekeepers to release their bees on the orchard, beekeepers pay clover growers for permitting them to release their bees on the clover farms. This is an example of competitive markets resolving an externality problem when property rights are well established.

Exercise 21A.21

In what sense do you think the relevant property rights in this case are in fact well established?

This does not, however, resolve the more local externalities between orchard owners. If one owner hires bee-services, those same bees can cross over into other orchards, benefitting those growers while also benefitting the beekeepers. Economist Steven Cheung has looked at this closely and he identifies a social custom that has emerged within the civil society, that is to say, outside the realm of explicit market-based transactions and outside the realm of government intervention. This has been dubbed 'the custom of the orchards', and takes the form of an implicit understanding among orchard owners in the same area that each owner will employ the same number of bee hives per acre as the other owners in the area. While the

Coase Theorem literally interpreted suggests that individuals will resolve these local externalities through bargaining, this illustrates another possible way for the theorem to unfold. Sometimes it is easier to converge on some local understanding of appropriate behaviour that can be sustained among small groups within the civil society rather than negotiate all the time about how many beehives everyone is going to hire this time around.

21B | The Mathematics of Externalities

We will begin our mathematical exploration of externalities in competitive markets with the example of a polluting industry in partial equilibrium. Using linear supply and demand curves, we can demonstrate how to calculate the optimal Pigouvian tax. We will explore how the establishment of pollution permit markets can in principle achieve the same efficiency gains as an optimally set Pigouvian tax and that there exists a cap-and-trade policy that is equivalent to any Pigouvian tax policy in the absence of pollution-abating technologies. In the presence of such technologies, we will suggest that pollution voucher markets as well as direct pollution taxes have an inherent advantage over Pigouvian output taxes. While we won't cover positive externalities and accompanying Pigouvian subsidies in detail, the mathematics is virtually identical to that underlying Pigouvian taxes.

We then turn to a more in-depth analysis of how externalities and the inefficiencies they give rise to are fundamentally problems of missing markets. In particular, we'll demonstrate how new markets can be defined in an exchange economy that contains consumption externalities and how establishment of these new markets should in principle resolve the inefficiency from externalities. We demonstrate this in an extension of our example of a two-person exchange economy before concluding with a discussion of the Coase Theorem.

21B.1 Production Externalities

Mathematically determining the extent of deadweight losses from pollution or to arrive at an optimal Pigouvian tax when using linear demand, supply and social marginal cost SMC curves, is relatively straightforward. We will assume for convenience that the uncompensated market demand curve is also the appropriate marginal willingness to pay curve along which to measure consumer surplus.

21B.1.1 BSP Versus the Market We begin with linear market demand and supply functions used in previous chapters:

$$x_d = \frac{A - p}{\alpha} \quad \text{and} \quad x_s = \frac{B + p}{\beta}, \tag{21.1}$$

The competitive market equilibrium is:

$$p^M = \frac{\beta A - \alpha B}{\alpha + \beta} \quad \text{and} \quad x^M = \frac{A + B}{\alpha + \beta}. \tag{21.2}$$

Now suppose that each unit of output x produces δ units of carbon dioxide pollution, and that the damage from this pollution increases quadratically with additional pollution dumped into the air. Assume the externality cost is given by $C_E(x) = (\delta x)^2$. The *marginal* externality cost for each unit of x is the derivative of $C_E(x)$ with respect to x, or $MC_E = 2\delta^2 x$. The inverse of the supply curve in equation (21.1) is the industry's marginal cost curve; that is, $MC_S = -B + \beta x$. Added together, these two curves make up the SMC curve:

$$SMC = -B + (\beta + 2\delta^2)x. \tag{21.3}$$

Exercise 21B.1

Suppose $A = 1000$, $\alpha = 1$, $\beta = 0.5$, $\delta = 0.5$ and $B = 0$. Illustrate the market demand and supply as well as the SMC curves in a graph with x on the horizontal axis.

The efficient or optimal output level x^{opt}, the output BSP would choose, occurs at the intersection of the SMC and the inverse demand curve $p = A - \alpha x$. Solving the equation $-B + (\beta + 2\delta^2)x = A - \alpha x$ for x, we get:

$$x^{opt} = \frac{A + B}{\alpha + \beta + 2\delta^2},$$

(21.4)

which is less than the competitive equilibrium quantity x_M in equation (21.2).

Exercise 21B.2

Suppose the pollution emitted is actually not harmful and kills the midge population in the area. The SMC of the pollution might be negative; that is, this kind of pollution might actually produce social benefits. Will the efficient quantity now be greater or less than the market quantity? Show this within the context of the example.

21B.1.2 The Efficient Pigouvian Tax

We can determine the optimal Pigouvian tax t^{opt} that will ensure that the market produces the efficient level of output. In order for consumers to want to buy x^{opt}, they must face a price p_d such that $x^{opt} = x_d(p_d) = (A - p_d)/\alpha$. Similarly, in order for producers to supply x^{opt} in equilibrium, they must face a price p_s such that $x^{opt} = x_s(p_s) = (B + p_s)/\beta$. Solving these equations and substituting in our solution for x^{opt} from equation (21.4), we get:

$$p_d = \frac{(\beta + 2\delta^2)A - \alpha B}{\alpha + \beta + 2\delta^2} \quad \text{and} \quad p_s = \frac{\beta A - (\alpha + 2\delta^2)B}{\alpha + \beta + 2\delta^2},$$

(21.5)

and subtracting p_s from p_d gives the optimal Pigouvian tax t^{opt} required to get this difference in consumer and producer prices; that is:

$$t^{opt} = p_d - p_s = \frac{2\delta^2(A + B)}{\alpha + \beta + 2\delta^2}.$$

(21.6)

Exercise 21B.3

Complete exercise 21B.1 by illustrating and labelling the Pigouvian tax for this example.

Exercise 21B.4

Using the graph from the previous exercise, calculate consumer surplus, producer surplus, the externality cost and overall surplus in the absence of the Pigouvian tax. Calculate these again under the Pigouvian tax, taking into account the tax revenue raised. What is the deadweight loss from not having the Pigouvian tax?

21B.1.3 Cap-and-Trade Assume that instead of imposing a tax t on output, the government requires that producers hold a pollution voucher for each unit of carbon dioxide emitted in the production process. Since every unit of output x produces δ units of pollution, a producer must hold δ pollution vouchers for every unit of output they produce. If the rental price of a voucher is r, this implies that the industry marginal cost goes from $(-B + \beta x)$ to:

$$MC = -B + \beta x + \delta r. \tag{21.7}$$

Exercise 21B.5

Illustrate how this shifts the supply curve in your graph where you assume $A = 1000$, $\alpha = 1$, $\beta = 0.5$, $\delta = 0.5$ and $B = 0$.

Setting this equal to the inverse demand curve, which is $p = A - \alpha x$, and solving for x, we get the new equilibrium quantity (given a voucher rental rate of r) as:

$$x^*(r) = \frac{A + B - \delta r}{\alpha + \beta}. \tag{21.8}$$

This equation and the graph you drew in exercise 21B.5 suggest that the market will produce less as long as the rental price of vouchers is greater than zero. This does not answer the question of how the rental price of vouchers is determined in the first place. This price is, as demonstrated in Graph 21.3, determined in the new market for pollution vouchers that the government creates when it limits the quantity of vouchers to some level V.

Every unit of output causes δ in pollution and thus requires δ pollution vouchers. In the absence of any new introduction of pollution-abating technologies, a total voucher level of V implies that the market will reduce its output to $(1/\delta)V$. Substituting this into equation (21.8) on the left-hand side and solving for r, we get the equilibrium rental price for vouchers given an overall supply of vouchers fixed at V as:

$$r(V) = \frac{\delta(A + B) - (\alpha + \beta)V}{\delta^2}. \tag{21.9}$$

If the government provides exactly enough vouchers to allow the market quantity $x^M = (A + B)/(\alpha + \beta)$ to be produced; that is, suppose the government sets $V = \delta(A + B)/(\alpha + \beta)$, and substituting this into equation (21.9), we get an equilibrium voucher price of zero: the voucher giving the producer the right to pollute ceases to be worth anything. For any level of V below this, equation (21.9) tells us we will have a positive rental price for vouchers.

We can relate this directly to Graph 21.3 in which we argued that firms will form a demand curve in the market for vouchers while the government will set a perfectly inelastic supply by setting a fixed voucher and thus a fixed pollution cap. Equation (21.9) *is* the demand curve or the inverse demand function for vouchers by polluting firms, and the inverse of this equation:

$$v(r) = \frac{\delta(A + B) - \delta^2 r}{\alpha + \beta}, \tag{21.10}$$

is the demand function that relates the rental price r to the quantity demanded by producers.

Exercise 21B.6

Verify that a voucher price of zero results in the market output according to this demand function.

Exercise 21B.7

Illustrate the demand curve for pollution vouchers and label its slope and intercept.

An alternative and perhaps more intuitive derivation of the demand for pollution vouchers gives the maximum amount that a firm is willing to pay to be allowed to produce one more unit of output depending on how much the firm thinks it can sell its output for and what the firm's other costs are. In panel (a) of Graph 21.6, for instance, if the government limited the quantity in the market to x_1, the marginal firm would be willing to pay an amount equal to the dark brown distance in order to produce because this is the difference between the marginal cost of production for this firm and the marginal willingness to pay for the output by the marginal consumer. If the government limited total output to x_2, the marginal firm would be willing to pay at most an amount equal to the dark blue distance.

Now assume we convert the units in which we measure x to voucher units, knowing that we will have to have δ vouchers for 1 unit of output x. The marginal benefit or inverse demand function when units are measured in terms of x is just the demand curve $MB = A - \alpha x$. If we now measure vouchers instead of output on the horizontal axis, the marginal benefit of the first unit is A/δ, giving a vertical intercept of A/δ for our new marginal benefit curve. The horizontal intercept of the original marginal benefit curve, on the other hand, has to change from A/α to $\delta A/\alpha$. From this, we can calculate the slope of the new marginal benefit curve as the negative vertical intercept divided by the horizontal intercept, or $(-(A/\delta)/(\delta A/\alpha)) = -\alpha/\delta^2$. The marginal benefit curve when output is expressed in voucher units is:

$$MB(v) = \frac{A}{\delta} - \frac{\alpha}{\delta^2}v = \frac{\delta A - \alpha v}{\delta^2}, \tag{21.11}$$

and, applying similar logic to the producers' marginal cost curve $MC = -B + \beta x$, the marginal cost curve when output is expressed in voucher units is:

$$MC(v) = \frac{-\delta B + \beta v}{\delta^2}. \tag{21.12}$$

Panel (b) of Graph 21.6 illustrates these marginal benefit and cost curves, which are equivalent to those in panel (a) except that the units on the horizontal axis are $1/\delta$ the units in panel (a).

Graph 21.6 Going from the Market for x to the Pollution Voucher Market

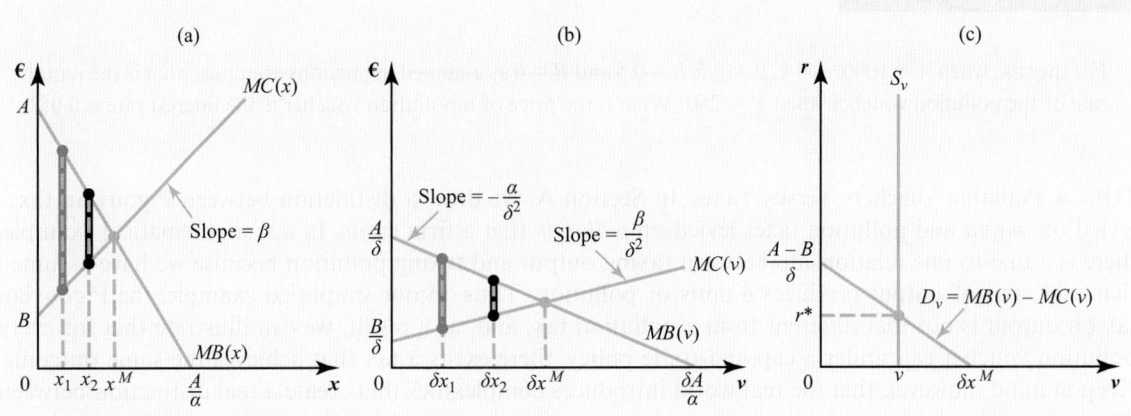

Exercise 21B.8

What is the relationship between the length of the dark brown and dark blue lines in panels (a) and (b)?

Exercise 21B.9

Implicitly, we are assuming $\delta = 2$ in panel (b) of Graph 21.6. How would this graph change if $\delta < 1$, that is, if each unit of output produces less than one unit of pollution?

The most that the marginal firm is willing to pay for a voucher is the difference between $MB(v)$ and $MC(v)$:

$$MB(v) - MC(v) = \frac{\delta(A + B) - (\alpha + \beta)v}{\delta^2},$$ (21.13)

exactly the expression for the voucher demand curve in equation (21.9). This function is graphed in panel (c) of Graph 21.6, and the equilibrium price r^* in the voucher market is determined by the intersection of this demand curve with the inelastic supply capped at V by the government or, mathematically, by substituting V for v in equation (21.13).

Exercise 21B.10

If $V = \delta x_2$, which distance in panels (a) or (b) of Graph 21.6 is equal to r^*?

Exercise 21B.11

For the case when $A = 1000$, $\alpha = 1$, $\beta = 0.5$, $\delta = 0.5$ and $B = 0$ as assumed in previous exercises, what is the rental rate of the pollution voucher when $V = 250$? What is the price of a pollution voucher if the interest rate is 0.05?

21B.1.4 Pollution Vouchers Versus Taxes In Section A, we drew a distinction between Pigouvian taxes levied on *output* and pollution taxes levied on *pollution* that a firm emits. In our mathematical example, there is a one-to-one relationship between taxing output and taxing pollution because we have assumed that each unit of output produces δ units of pollution. Thus, in our simplified example, the Pigouvian tax on output is not that different from a pollution tax, and, as a result, we can illustrate that for every pollution voucher cap under a cap-and-trade policy, there exists a tax that achieves the same outcome. Keep in mind, however, that the real world introduces complexities that create a real distinction between Pigouvian and pollution taxes, an issue we return to after demonstrating the equivalence of tax and cap-and-trade policies for our example.

Suppose the government knows the optimal level of output x^{opt} in equation (21.4) as well as the amount δ of pollution emitted by each unit of production. The information, combined with our knowledge of supply and demand curves, is sufficient to set the optimal voucher level at:

$$V^{opt} = \delta x^{opt} = \frac{\delta(A + B)}{\alpha + \beta + 2\delta^2}. \tag{21.14}$$

Substituting V^{opt} into equation (21.9), implies an equilibrium rental rate for vouchers of:

$$r^*(V^{opt}) = \frac{2\delta(A + B)}{\alpha + \beta + 2\delta^2}. \tag{21.15}$$

In order to produce one unit of output, we have to rent δ vouchers, implying that the marginal cost of production has increased by:

$$\delta r^*(V^{opt}) = \frac{2\delta^2(A + B)}{\alpha + \beta + 2\delta^2}. \tag{21.16}$$

Note that this is equal to the optimal Pigouvian tax t^{opt} derived in equation (21.6); that is:

$$t^{opt} = \delta r^*(V^{opt}). \tag{21.17}$$

As long as the government sets the number of pollution vouchers correctly, the market for these vouchers will result in a price equal to the tax the government would have liked to impose had it chosen to use a Pigouvian tax instead. As illustrated in Table 21.3, *for any tax imposed on outputs, there exists an equivalent voucher level that will result in a voucher rental rate that has the same impact on producers as the tax.*

Exercise 21B.12

Suppose the government simply gives away the pollution vouchers. Why is the deadweight loss the same under tax and cap-and-trade policies that satisfy $t = \delta r^*(V)$ even though one makes revenue for the government while the other does not?

Table 21.3 $A = 1\,000, \alpha = 1, \beta = 0.5, \delta = 0.5$, and $B = 0$

		Equivalent Tax and Pollution Voucher Policies			
t	V	$r''(V)$	x	x^{opt}	DWL
€0	333	€0	667	500	€27 778
€50	317	€100	633	500	€17 778
€100	300	€200	600	500	€10 000
€150	283	€300	567	500	€4444
€200	267	€400	533	500	€1111
€250	250	€500	500	500	€0
€300	233	€600	467	500	€1111
€350	217	€700	433	500	€4444
€400	200	€800	400	500	€10 000
€450	183	€900	367	500	€17 778
€500	167	€1000	333	500	€27 778

Exercise 21B.13

Illustrate on a graph where the deadweight loss falls when $t = 400$ in Table 21.3. What about when it falls at $t = 100$?

Our mathematical example obscures within its simplicity a difference between taxing output in polluting industries and taxing pollution emissions directly. This is because we illustrated the case of a single industry, ignoring the fact that many industries engage in pollution, *and* we have not introduced the potential for pollution-abating technologies to play a role. Even within a single industry, a Pigouvian tax on output differs from a pollution tax in that the latter allows firms to reduce their tax obligations by introducing pollution-abating technologies while the former does not unless it is constantly reassessed. The equivalence of a Pigouvian tax to a pollution tax within an industry only survives if we assume that the government will adjust the Pigouvian tax on output as firms introduce pollution-abating technologies. When considering pollution across industries, this is further complicated by the fact that industries will differ in terms of the ease with which they can introduce pollution-abating technologies, with any equivalence between Pigouvian taxes and pollution taxes, assuming that the government continuously adjusts Pigouvian per-unit taxes as pollution-abating technologies are introduced in different settings. The equivalence between cap-and-trade and pollution taxes, on the other hand, is robust to the introduction of such real-world complications.

21B.2 Consumption Externalities

The mathematics behind our graphical development of consumption externalities is almost identical to that behind production externalities. We now proceed to considering the problem of consumption externalities in a general equilibrium setting where we will be able to illustrate more precisely what we mean when we say that the presence of an externality necessarily implies the absence of a market that, if established, would eliminate the externality.

21B.3 Externalities and Missing Markets

The idea of using pollution voucher markets to solve the externality problems created by pollution is closely linked to a more general understanding of externalities as a problem of missing markets – a failure of markets to exist. The intuition behind this becomes clearer when we see how the missing markets could be defined and how pricing within those markets will lead those who emit externalities to face the costs or benefits they impose on others. Using our tools from Chapter 16, however, we can be a little more precise about what we mean by missing markets and how an establishment of those markets resolves the inefficiency from externalities under competition. We will do so here for the case of externalities in an exchange economy, but one could similarly illustrate this in an economy with production.

21B.3.1 Introducing Consumption Externalities Into an Exchange Economy Recall that an exchange economy is a set of consumers denoted $n = 1, 2, \ldots, N$ with each consumer characterized fully by their endowments of each of M different goods as well as their tastes summarized by utility functions defined over M goods (denoted $m = 1, 2, \ldots, M$). An exchange economy is given by:

$$(\{(e_1^n, e_2^n, \ldots, e_m^n)\}_{n=1}^N, \{u^n : \mathbb{R}^M \to \mathbb{R}^1\}_{n=1}^N). \tag{21.18}$$

If you are uncomfortable with this notation, please review the discussion surrounding expression (16.1) in Chapter 16. Because each consumer cares only about their own consumption of each of the goods, and because there are no other actors like producers, there is no externality in this exchange economy. *An externality in the absence of production arises when one consumer's consumption directly enters the utility function of another consumer.* In principle, such consumption externalities in an exchange economy could arise in every direction, with every consumer's consumption of each good entering every other consumer's utility function.

We could think of consumer M as consuming some of each of the M goods *and* being affected by their impression of each other consumer's consumption of each of the M goods. Suppose, for instance, that we let x_{ij}^n denote person n's impression of person j's consumption of good i. If x_{ij}^n enters person n's utility function, person j is generating a consumption externality when consuming good i. If each person's consumption of each good potentially enters each person's utility function, each person is in essence consuming NM different goods rather than M goods as before. For instance, if $N = 2$ and $M = 2$, consumer 1 consumes $(x_{11}^1, x_{21}^1, x_{12}^1, x_{22}^1)$.

Exercise 21B.14

Which two of these four goods represent the consumption levels x_1^1 and x_2^1 that exist for person 1 in an exchange economy without externalities?

We have therefore taken an economy with M goods and defined, for each person, NM goods that enter their utility function. The exchange economy defined in equation (21.18) can be rewritten with consumption externalities as:

$$(\{(e_1^n, e_2^n, \ldots, e_m^n)\}_{n=1}^N, \{u^n : \mathbb{R}^{NM} \to \mathbb{R}^1\}_{n=1}^N). \tag{21.19}$$

21B.3.2 The Missing Markets in an Exchange Economy With Externalities We have now introduced impressions of other individuals' consumption explicitly as new goods. This implies that we have implicitly introduced production into the exchange economy because *each time a consumer makes a decision to consume some of the M goods, they are producing $(N - 1)$ of these newly defined goods.* When an individual consumes good 1, they are producing an impression of their consumption of good 1 that now potentially enters everyone else's utility function. Our exchange economy has no markets that set prices for such goods and thus no market mechanism to govern the individual's production decisions.

Suppose, for instance, that person j's consumption of good i enters individual n's utility function in a positive way. In this case, person j is a producer of an output x_{ij}^n, an output that consumers like n would be willing to pay for but don't since there is no market and no price. Alternatively, suppose that x_{ij}^n enters person n's utility function negatively, implying consumer j emits a *negative* consumption externality by consuming good i. In this case, we can view consumer j as using x_{ij}^n as an *input* into the production of their own consumption of good i. Once again because there is no market for this input and thus no price, consumer j does not need to purchase the input x_{ij}^n when deciding how much of the good i to consume.

Exercise 21B.15

If there are two consumers and two goods, how many missing markets are there potentially? More generally, how many missing markets could there be when there are M goods and N consumers?

In some cases, externalities will take a form where the externality affects every consumer whereas in other cases the externality may affect only some consumers. Suppose, for instance, that consumer j is choosing good i that represents the number of car rides they take, and each car ride emits pollution that contributes to poor air quality. In that case, their car rides enter each consumer's utility function in the same quantity, even though different consumers will feel differently about how bad this externality is. In this example:

$$x_{ij}^n = x_{ij} \text{ for all } n \neq j; \tag{21.20}$$

that is, each individual other than j experiences the impact of j's car rides in the same quantity. In other cases, an externality is more local, affecting some individuals differently than others. For instance, if j chooses good i that represents music played in the garden, their immediate neighbours are affected more than more distant neighbours. In this case, x_{ij}^n will differ depending on the distance between individual j and n.

21B.3.3 **Introducing Property Rights and New Markets** In order to establish the new markets that can price the externality effects within this exchange economy, we have to begin by specifying a set of new property rights. If an individual's car rides cause pollution, do they have the right to pollute, or do others have the right not to have pollution inflicted on them? If they play loud music in their garden, do they have the right to do as much of this as they want to, or do others have the right to not be bothered by their music? For efficiency purposes, however, it turns out that what matters most is that property rights be established so that markets can form. For now, we will illustrate in a simple example how markets price externalities when markets are established, and we will return to a discussion of the extent to which it matters how property rights are assigned in Chapter 27.

One way to think of how property rights are established in the new markets is to extend the endowments for individuals to include endowments of the new goods. In this way, rights could be distributed in a variety of ways, although we will typically think of rights being established strictly one way or another; that is, either someone has the right to pollute or the victims of pollution have the right not to be bothered by pollution unless they sell their rights. Once we have established a system of property rights, we have arrived at an exchange economy that has more types of goods than before. None of the goods now appears in more than one utility function, which means there is technically no more externality in the economy with the expanded set of markets. Since we know that exchange economies without externalities are such that competitive equilibria are efficient regardless of how many goods and consumers there are in the economy, the establishment of these new markets leads to an economy in which competitive equilibria are efficient, with prices of the newly defined goods causing the emitters of externalities to take full account of the marginal social costs and benefits of their actions.

21B.3.4 A Numerical Example In Chapter 16, we worked through an example of a two-person, two-good exchange economy in which $(e_1^1, e_2^1) = (3, 6)$, $(e_1^2, e_2^2) = (10, 4)$, $u^1(x_1, x_2) = x_1^{3/4}x_2^{1/4}$, and $u^2(x_1, x_2) = x_1^{1/4}x_2^{3/4}$. Given that only each individual's own consumption appears in their utility function, this represents an exchange economy without externalities. Suppose now, however, that consumption of good 1 by individual 1 enters individual 2's utility function. Using our notation, this implies that the good x_{11}^2, individual 2's perception of individual 1's consumption of good 1, enters $u2$. To keep our notation in this example as simple as possible, let's define $x_3 = x_{11}^2$, and let individual 2's utility function be redefined as:

$$u^2(x_1, x_2, x_3) = x_1^{1/4}x_2^{3/4}x_3^{\gamma}. \tag{21.21}$$

Depending on whether γ is greater or less than zero, individual 1 is now imposing a positive or negative consumption externality on individual 2. When $\gamma = 0$, the example reduces to our example from Chapter 16 with no externality.

We can first ask what the competitive equilibrium of this exchange economy will be. In the absence of a market for x_3, however, nothing fundamental has changed from the way we calculated the equilibrium of this economy in Chapter 16. Individual 1 will maximize the same utility function subject to the same budget constraint as before and will thus have the same demand equations. Individual 2 will maximize the new utility function in equation (21.21) subject to the same constraints as before, but x_3^{γ} will cancel out as we solve for their demand equations, resulting in the same demands as in Chapter 16. With both individuals exhibiting the same demands, we get the same competitive equilibrium as before, with $p^2/p^1 = 3/2$, $(x_1^1, x_2^1) = (9, 2)$ and $(x_1^2, x_2^2) = (4, 8)$.

Exercise 21B.16

Verify that individual 2's demand functions for x_1 and x_2 are unchanged as a result of the inclusion of x_3 in their utility function.

Exercise 21B.17

Do you think the conclusion in exercise 21B.16 that demands for x_1 and x_2 do not change will hold regardless of what form the utility function takes?

Now suppose that a market is introduced for the good x_3 with price p_3. Let's begin by thinking of the externality as negative (i.e. $\gamma < 0$), and suppose that property rights are assigned such that individual 2 has the right not to experience the externality unless they agree voluntarily to do so. This implies that individual 1 will have to pay not only p_1 for each unit of x_1 they consume but also p_3 (since $x_1^1 = x_3$). The optimization problem for consumer 1 becomes:

$$\max_{x_1, x_2} u^1(x_1, x_2) = x_1^{\alpha}x_2^{(1-\alpha)} \text{ subject to } p_1e_1^1 + p_2e_2^1 = (p_1 + p_3)x_1 + p_2x_2. \tag{21.22}$$

Solving this we get:

$$x_1^1 = \frac{\alpha(p_1e_1^1 + p_2e_2^1)}{p_1 + p_3} \text{ and } x_2^1 = \frac{(1-\alpha)(p_1e_1^1 + p_2e_2^1)}{p_2}. \tag{21.23}$$

Individual 2, on the other hand, will receive p_3 for every unit of x_3 that individual 1 emits, but, since individual 2 is given the property rights to x_3, individual 2 chooses how much of x_3 to sell. The optimization problem for individual 2 becomes:

$$\max_{x_1, x_2, x_3} u^2(x_1, x_2, x_3) = x_1^\beta x_2^{(1-\beta)} x_3^\gamma \text{ subject to } p_1 e_1^2 + p_2 e_2^2 + p_3 x_3 = p_1 x_1 + p_2 x_2. \tag{21.24}$$

Solving this, we get:

$$x_1^2 = \frac{\beta(p_1 e_1^2 + p_2 e_2^2)}{(1+\gamma)p_1}, \ x_2^2 = \frac{(1-\beta)(p_1 e_1^2 + p_2 e_2^2)}{(1+\gamma)p_2}, \text{ and } x_3 = \frac{-\gamma(p_1 e_1^2 + p_2 e_2^2)}{(1+\gamma)p_3}. \tag{21.25}$$

Exercise 21B.18

Verify these demand functions. *Hint*: It becomes significantly easier algebraically to first take natural logs of the utility function.

Exercise 21B.19

Do the demand functions converge to those we derived in the absence of an externality as the externality approaches zero, i.e. as γ approaches zero?

We can now solve for equilibrium prices. As in Chapter 16, we will be able to solve only for *relative* prices and can therefore set one of the prices to 1. Suppose we set:

$$p_1 = 1. \tag{21.26}$$

Setting demand equal to supply in the market for good 2, that is, setting $x_2^1 + x_2^2 = e_2^1 + e_2^2$, we can solve for p_2 as:

$$p_2 = \frac{(1-\alpha)(1+\gamma)e_1^1 + (1-\beta)e_1^2}{\alpha(1+\gamma)e_2^1 + (\beta+\gamma)e_2^2}. \tag{21.27}$$

In addition, it must be true that demand is equal to supply in the x_3 market, where the amount of x_3 consumer 2 is willing to sell must be equal to the amount of x_1 that consumer 1 wants to consume; that is, $x_1^1 = x_3$. Solving this, we can get p_3 in terms of p_2 with p_1 again set to 1:

$$p_3 = \frac{-\gamma(e_1^2 + p_2 e_2^2)}{\alpha(1+\gamma)(e_1^1 + p_2 e_2^1) + \gamma(e_1^2 + p_2 e_2^2)}. \tag{21.28}$$

In Table 21.4, we calculate the competitive equilibrium prices and quantities when the market for good x_3 has been established. The table begins with negative values for γ, that is, with the case where individual 1's consumption of good 1 imposes a negative externality on individual 2. As we move down the table, the externality becomes less severe, with no externality when $\gamma = 0$. Finally, the table moves into positive values for γ, implying a positive externality on individual 2 from the consumption of good 1 by individual 1. Notice that p_3 is positive whenever the consumption externality is negative, implying that the presence of a negative externality results in individual 2 receiving compensation for suffering the negative effects of individual 1's consumption. When the externality becomes positive, p_3 becomes negative, implying that now individual 2 compensates individual 1 for the positive effect x_1^1 has on individual 2. Thus, *the establishment of the missing market results in individual 2 imposing a 'tax' on individual 1's consumption of good 1 when the externality is negative and a 'subsidy' when the externality is positive.*

Table 21.4 $\alpha = 3/4$, $\beta = 1/4$, $(e_1^1, e_2^1) = (3,6)$, $(e_1^2, e_2^2) = (10, 4)$

				Equilibrium With Missing Market Established			
γ	p_1	p_2	p_3	x_1^1	x_2^1	x_1^2	x_2^2
−0.4	€1.00	€3.79	€6.64	2.52	1.70	10.48	8.30
−0.3	€1.00	€2.72	€1.61	5.54	1.76	7.46	8.22
−0.2	€1.00	€2.13	€0.64	7.21	1.85	5.79	8.15
−0.1	€1.00	€1.76	€0.23	8.27	1.93	4.73	8.07
0.0	€1.00	€1.50	€0.00	9.00	2.00	4.00	8.00
0.1	€1.00	€1.31	−€0.15	9.54	2.07	3.46	7.93
0.2	€1.00	€1.17	−€0.25	9.94	2.14	3.06	7.86
0.3	€1.00	€1.05	−€0.32	10.27	2.21	2.73	7.79
0.4	€1.00	€0.96	−€0.38	10.53	2.28	2.47	7.72

Just as in Chapter 16, it would not be reasonable to expect market prices to govern exchange – either in the presence or in the absence of externalities – when there is literally only one individual on each side of the market. The two-person exchange economy provides a useful tool with which to illustrate how markets set prices in general equilibrium. The previous analysis continues to hold exactly the same way if we assume that there are many type 1 and many type 2 individuals when competitive price-taking behaviour becomes more realistic. For the two-person case we have the Coase Theorem to fall back on.

21B.4 Small Markets and the Coase Theorem

In Section A, we introduced the insight of Ronald Coase with respect to the types of externalities that make people mad enough to take each other to court. We gave the example of Laura building an extension to her house and Sam taking her to court because the extension would cast a shadow on his swimming pool. It is precisely in such small settings that, even if we established markets of the types we have discussed, there would not be much of a market since only one or a few people would be operating on each side of the market. While we can theoretically investigate what market prices would look like if they arose, it is more realistic to think of bargaining as the way in which externality issues would be resolved in such markets.

21B.4.1 Bargaining Under Complete and Incomplete Information Bargaining by definition does not happen in competitive settings, since in competitive settings each consumer and producer is a price-taker. We are therefore jumping a bit ahead of ourselves as we think about bargaining under the Coase Theorem. Laura and Sam are decidedly not price-takers during their coffee as they discuss the level of compensation that Sam has to offer Laura to stop building if the court ruled in his favour, or the level of compensation Laura will pay to let her build if the court ruled in his favour. We are jumping ahead because we are thinking of a strategic setting, one in which Laura and Sam have some real control over their economic environment.

Over the past few decades, economists, particularly game theorists, have arrived at a well-defined theory of bargaining, some of which was directly inspired by Coase's confidence that bargaining in an atmosphere in which property rights have been fully clarified will lead to efficient outcomes when externalities are involved. Some of that theory assumes that Laura and Sam have perfect information about each other's costs and benefits of the extension to the house. Under such circumstances, Coase appears to be on solid ground. The theory predicts that Laura and Sam will reach a bargain that will lead to the efficient outcome under the conditions envisioned by Coase. In cases where income or endowment effects are important, as when tastes are not quasilinear, we have to be slightly more careful because the efficient outcome may differ depending on how property rights are assigned. If the story told in Section A about how they will bargain their way to efficiency made sense, you have the basic intuition.

21B.4.2 Bargaining Under Incomplete Information In Section A, however, we implicitly assumed what we have just made explicit: that Laura and Sam *both* know what the costs are to Sam relative to him solving his shaded pool problem in other ways, of Laura extending her house in a way that casts a shadow on his swimming pool, and what the benefits are to her of building the extension in this way relative to other ways of solving her need for additional housing. Let's denote Sam's costs as c and Laura's benefit as b. Efficiency dictates that Laura goes ahead with her addition if $b > c$, and we argued that as long as property rights have been specified and transactions costs are low, the efficient outcome will happen.

Suppose that Sam is not sure what b is and Laura is not sure what c is. Sam has beliefs about b and Laura has beliefs about c. Let Laura's beliefs be represented by $0 \leq \rho(c) \leq 1$ for any $c > 0$, with $\rho(c)$ equal to the probability she places on Sam's costs being less than or equal to c. Similarly, let Sam's beliefs be represented by $0 \leq \delta(b) \leq 1$ for any $b > 0$, with $\delta(b)$ equal to the probability that he places on her benefits being less than or equal to b. Now suppose the court rules in Sam's favour; that is, he now has the right to a shadow-free pool and Laura cannot build her extension unless he agrees to it.

Laura offers Sam compensation based on her beliefs of what his costs are. To arrive at an offer Laura has to calculate the offer p that maximizes her expected payoff. Laura's expected payoff from any offer p is the probability that the offer will be accepted times the benefit she receives from having the offer accepted. For any offer p, she believes the probability that Sam's true costs are less than or equal to p is $\rho(p)$, which implies that she believes the probability of him accepting the offer is $\rho(p)$. The benefit received if the offer is accepted is Laura's benefit b from having the extension built minus the payment p she has to make to Sam; the benefit received if the offer is accepted is $(b - p)$. Laura solves the following optimization problem as she calculates her optimal offer given the beliefs she has:

$$\max_p \rho(p)(b - p). \tag{21.29}$$

Laura will not make an offer $p > b$, and Sam will not accept an offer $p < c$. Depending on what Laura's beliefs are, she may well make an offer p^* that maximizes her expected payoff but where $p^* < c$ even though $b > c$. Thus, depending on her beliefs about Sam's true underlying costs, the extension may not get built if the court rules in Sam's favour despite the fact that building the addition is efficient.

Exercise 21B.20

Suppose the court rules in Laura's favour instead. What optimization problem would need to be solved as Sam comes over to have coffee in order to offer Laura a payment for not building the extension? Can it be the case that the efficient outcome does not happen for certain beliefs δ Sam might have about Laura's true benefit from the extension?

Depending on how we define what we mean by transactions costs, we now may or may not have to amend the Coase Theorem. The theorem says that as long as property rights are sufficiently specified in the presence of externalities, the efficient outcome will occur from decentralized decisions if transactions costs are sufficiently low. As we have just seen, strategic bargaining between individuals who understand the assignment of property rights in the presence of externalities may not result in efficiency even when there are no transactions costs keeping the individuals from getting together and bargaining. The cost of obtaining information about the relative costs and benefits from the externality may in itself be considered a transactions cost, in which case we can leave the Coase Theorem as stated before.

Appendix	Fundamental Non-Convexities in the Presence of Externalities

In our treatment of how the establishment of missing markets can restore efficiency in the presence of externalities, we glanced over a technical problem that has become known as the problem of *fundamental non-convexities*. The essence of the problem is that suppose we reconsider our numerical example of an exchange economy with a negative consumption externality from consumer 1's consumption of good 1 as we did in the chapter. Suppose further that we take the assumption that consumer 2 has a right to not experience the externality and must be persuaded to sell that right by accepting payment in proportion to the externality that is emitted. We know that if the price p_3 is zero, consumer 2 will not sell any rights to consume good 1 to consumer 1 since consumer 2 would experience a negative externality without compensation. Now suppose that $p_3 > 0$ as in the equilibria we described in Table 21.4. What is to keep consumer 2 from wanting to sell an infinite number of rights to pollute, thus making an infinite income to spend on consumption of goods 1 and 2? If there is no limit on the number of rights that individual 2 can sell, a positive price will cause the consumer to want to sell an infinite quantity of x_3 while a non-positive price will cause them to want to sell zero. No matter what p_3 is set at, consumer 2 therefore prefers a corner solution. This is referred to as a fundamental non-convexity because it represents a non-convexity in the production set for pollution rights. The problem of fundamental non-convexities in externality markets was first pointed out by D. Starrett, 'Fundamental Nonconvexities in the Theory of Externalities' (*Journal of Economic Theory* 4 (1972), 180–199).

If consumer 2 will sell only zero or an infinite amount of x_3, no equilibrium in the x_3 market exists, and the establishment of the x_3 market with all rights assigned to the victim of the negative externality does not lead to a competitive equilibrium that eliminates the inefficiency from the externality. In order for the equilibria discussed in Table 21.4 to emerge, there *must* be some limit to the number of rights that consumer 2 can sell.

The solution to this fundamental non-convexity problem lies in finding ways of bounding the property rights in externality markets such that, for instance, victims of pollution cannot sell large or infinite amounts of these rights when the price is positive. While this is not easily done in the context of defining externality markets in the way that we have done in our exchange economy example, we have already shown how this can be done when rights are defined along the lines of pollution vouchers. Here, a limited number of these rights are allocated in the economy, thus eliminating the problem of fundamental non-convexities.

Exercise 21B.21

Why did our mathematical methods of solving for consumer 2's demand for x_3 not uncover this problem?

End-of-Chapter Exercises

21.1† Consider the case of a positive consumption externality.

A. Suppose throughout this exercise that demand and supply curves are linear, that demand curves are equal to marginal willingness to pay curves and that the additional social benefit from each consumption unit is k and is constant as consumption increases.

a. Draw two graphs with the same demand curve but one that has a fairly inelastic and one that has a fairly elastic supply curve. In which case is the market output closer to the optimal output?

b. Does the Pigouvian subsidy that would achieve the optimal output level differ across your two graphs in part (a)?

c. Draw two graphs with the same supply curve but one that has a fairly inelastic demand curve and one that has a fairly elastic demand curve. In which case is the market output closer to the optimal output?

    d. Does the Pigouvian subsidy that would achieve the optimal output level differ across your two graphs in part (c)?

    e. *True or False*: While the size of the Pigouvian subsidy does not vary as the slopes of demand and supply curves change, the level of underproduction increases as these curves become more elastic.

    f. In each of your graphs, indicate who benefits more from the Pigouvian subsidy: producers or consumers.

B. Suppose demand is given by $x_d = (A - p)/\alpha$ and supply is given by $x_s = (B + p)/\beta$.

    a. Derive the competitive equilibrium price and output level.

    b. Suppose that the marginal positive externality benefit is k per unit of output. What is the function for the social marginal benefit SMB curve?

    c. What is the optimal output level?

    d. What is the Pigouvian subsidy? Show the impact it has on prices paid by consumers and prices received by producers, and illustrate that it achieves the optimal outcome.

    e. Next, suppose that the total externality social benefit is given by $SB = (\delta x)^2$. Does the market outcome change? What about the optimal outcome?

    f. Derive the Pigouvian subsidy, and illustrate again that it achieves the social optimum.

21.2 The Coase Theorem is often applied in court cases where the parties seek to clarify who has the right to do what in the presence of externalities. Consider the case of the extension to Laura's house that casts a shadow on Sam's swimming pool. Suppose that Laura's benefit from the extension is b and the cost Sam incurs from the shadow is c. Suppose throughout this exercise that transactions costs are zero.

    A. In this part of the exercise, suppose that Laura and Sam both know what b and c are.

        a. If they both know b and c, why don't they get together and try to settle the matter over coffee rather than ending up in court?

        b. If the court also knows b and c, propose a sensible and efficient rule for it to use to adjudicate the case.

        c. Courts rarely have as much information as plaintiffs and defendants. It is therefore reasonable for the court to assume that it cannot easily ascertain b and c. Suppose it rules in Laura's favour. What does Coase predict will happen?

        d. What if it instead rules in Sam's favour?

        e. In what sense will the outcome always be the same as it was in part (b), and in what sense will it not?

    B. Next, assume that Laura knows b and Sam knows c, but she does not know c and Sam does not know b.

        a. Suppose the court rules in Sam's favour and Laura attempts to convince Sam to let her build the extension anyway. She makes an offer based on her belief that Sam's cost is less than $\bar{c}$ with probability $\rho(\bar{c}) = \bar{c}/\alpha$. What offer will she make?

        b. For what combinations of b and c will the outcome be inefficient?

        c. Suppose instead that the court ruled in Sam's favour. He visits Laura to convince her not to build the extension even though she now has the right to do so. He makes her an offer based on his belief that Laura's benefit from the extension is less than or equal to $\bar{b}$ with probability $\delta(\bar{b}) = \bar{b}/\beta$ What offer will Sam make?

        d. For what combinations of b and c will the outcome be inefficient?

        e. Explain how the cost of obtaining information might be considered a transactions cost, and the results you derived here are therefore consistent with the Coase Theorem.

21.3† Everyday Application: *Children's Toys and Gucci Products.* In most of our development of consumer theory, we have assumed that tastes are independent of what other people do. This is not true for some goods. For instance, children are notorious for valuing toys more if their friends also have them, which implies their marginal willingness to pay is higher the more prevalent the toys are in their peer group. Some consumers take pleasure out of consuming high value branded goods that few others have. Their marginal willingness to pay for these goods falls as more people in their peer group consume the same goods.

    A. The two examples we have cited are examples of positive and negative *network externalities*.

        a. Consider children's toys first. Suppose that for a given number N of peers, demand for some toy x is linear and downward sloping, but that an increase in the network of children, i.e. an increase in N, causes an upward parallel shift of the demand curve. Illustrate two demand curves corresponding to network size levels $N_1 < N_2$.

b. Suppose every child at most buys one of these toys, which are produced at constant marginal cost. For a combination of p and x to be an equilibrium, what must be true about x if the equilibrium lies on the demand curve for network size N_1?

c. Suppose you start in such an equilibrium and the marginal cost, and thus the price, drops. Economists distinguish between two types of effects: a *direct* effect that occurs along the demand curve for network size N_1 and a *bandwagon effect* that results from increased demand due to increased network size. Label your original equilibrium A, the temporary equilibrium before network externalities are taken into account as B, and your new equilibrium that incorporates both effects as C. Assume that this new equilibrium lies on the demand curve that corresponds to network size N_2.

d. How many toys are sold in equilibrium C? Connect A and C with a line labelled $\overline{D}$. Is $\overline{D}$ the true demand curve for this toy? Explain.

e. If you were a marketing manager with a limited budget for a children's toy company, would you spend your budget on aggressive advertising early as the product is rolled out or wait and spread it out? Explain.

f. Now consider consumers who like Gucci products more if few of their friends have them. For any given number of friends N that also have Gucci products, their demand curve is linear and downward sloping, but the intercept of their demand curve falls as N increases. Illustrate two demand curves for $N_1 < N_2$.

g. Assume for convenience that everyone buys at most one Gucci product. Identify an initial equilibrium A under which N_1 Gucci products are sold at some initial price p and a second equilibrium C at which N_2 Gucci products are sold at price $p' < p$. Can you again identify two effects: a *direct* effect analogous to the one you identified in (c) and a *snob effect* analogous to the bandwagon effect you identified for children's toys? How does the snob effect differ from the bandwagon effect?

h. *True or False*: Bandwagon effects make demand more price elastic while snob effects make demand less price elastic.

i. *Take an example of an upward-sloping demand curve for Gucci products, with the upward slope emerging from the fact that utility is increasing in the price of Gucci products. Might the demand that takes both the direct and snob effects into account also be upward sloping in the presence of the kinds of network externalities modelled here?

B. Consider the positive and negative network externalities previously described.

a. Consider first the case of a positive network externality such as the toy example. Suppose that, for a given network size N, the demand curve is given by $p = 25N^{1/2} - x$. Does this give rise to parallel linear demand curves for different levels of N, with higher N implying higher demand?

b. Assume that children buy at most one of this toy. Suppose we are currently in an equilibrium where $N = 400$. What must the price of x be?

c. Suppose the price drops to €24. Isolate the direct effect of the price change; that is, if child perception of N remained unchanged, what would happen to the consumption level of x?

d. Can you verify that the real equilibrium that includes the bandwagon effect will result in $x = N = 576$ when price falls to €24? How big is the direct effect relative to the bandwagon effect in this case?

e. Consider the negative network externality of the Gucci example. Suppose that given a network of size N, the market demand curve for Gucci products is $p = (1000/N^{1/2}) - x$. Does this give rise to parallel linear demand curves for different levels of N, with higher N implying lower demand?

f. Assume that no one buys more than one Gucci item. Suppose we are currently in equilibrium with $N = 25$. What must the price be?

g. Suppose the price drops to €65. Isolate the direct effect of the price change; that is, if people's perception of N remained unchanged, what would happen to the consumption level of x?

h. Can you verify that the real equilibrium that includes the snob effect will result in $x = N = 62$? How big is the direct effect relative to the snob effect in this case?

i. Although the demand curves for a fixed level of N are linear, can you sketch the demand curve that includes both direct and snob effects?

21.4 Business Application: *Fishing in the Commons.* We introduced the notion of the *Tragedy of the Commons* and found its source in the emergence of externalities when property rights are not well established. This exercise demonstrates the same idea in a slightly different way.

A. Consider a self-contained lake that is home to fish that are sold on the market at price p. Suppose the primary input into fishing this lake is nets that are rented at a weekly rate of r, and suppose the single input production frontier for fish has decreasing returns to scale.

    a. Draw a graph with fishing nets on the horizontal axis and fish on the vertical. Illustrate the marginal product of fishing nets.

    b. Recalling the relationship between marginal and average quantities, add the *average* product curve to your graph.

    c. If you own the lake, what is the relationship between the marginal product of fishing nets and prices (p, r) assuming you maximize profit?

    d. Illustrate the profit-maximizing quantity of nets n^* on your graph. On a graph below it that plots the production frontier for fish, illustrate the number of fish x^* that are brought to market.

    e. *Suppose you instead charge a weekly fee for every fishing net that fishermen bring to your lake. Does the number of fish produced and nets used change?

    f. Next, consider a nearby lake that is identical in every way except that it is publicly owned, with no one controlling who can come onto the lake to fish. Assuming all nets are used with the same intensity, each fishing net that is brought onto the lake can be expected to catch the *average* of the total weekly catch. Illustrate on your graphs how many nets $\bar{n}$ will be brought onto this lake and how many fish $\bar{x}$ this implies will be brought to market each week.

    g. Which lake yields more fish per week? Which lake is being harvested for fish efficiently?

    h. Suppose that what matters is not just the current crop of fish but also its implication for the future fish population of the lake. Explain how the privately owned lake is likely to house a relatively constant population of fish over time, while the publicly owned lake is likely to run out of fish as time passes.

    i. The trade in elephant tusks, or ivory, has decimated much of the elephant population in some parts of Africa but not in others, with hunters often slaughtering entire herds, removing the tusks and leaving the rest. In some parts of Africa, the land on which elephants roam is public property; in other parts it is privately owned with owners allowed to restrict access. Can you guess from our lake example what is different about the parts of Africa where elephant herds are stable compared with those parts where they are nearing extinction?

    j. Why do you think that wild buffalo in the American West are nearly extinct but domesticated cattle are plentiful in the same region?

B. Let n again denote the fishing nets used in the lake and assume that r is the weekly rental cost per net. The number of fish brought out of the lake per week is $x = f(n) = An^{\alpha}$ where $A > 0$ and $0 < \alpha < 1$, and fish sell on the market for p.

    a. Suppose you own the lake and you don't let anyone other than yourself fish. How many fish will you pull out each week assuming you maximize profit?

    b. Suppose instead you allow others to fish for a fee per net and you want to maximize your fees. Will more or fewer fish be pulled out each week?

    c. Next, consider the identical lake that has just been discovered near yours. This lake is publicly owned, and anyone who wishes to can fish there. How many fish per week will be pulled out from that lake?

    d. Suppose $A = 100$, $\alpha = 0.5$, $p = 10$ and $r = 20$. How many fish are harvested per week in (a), (b) and (c)? How many nets are used in each case?

    e. What is the weekly rental value of the lake? If we count all your costs, including the opportunity cost of owning the lake, how much weekly profit do you make if you are the only one to fish on your lake?

    f. How much profit including the opportunity cost of fishing on the lake yourself do you make if you allow others to fish on your lake for a per-net fee? How much profit do the fishers who pay the fee to fish on your lake make?

    g. How much profit do the fishers who fish on the publicly owned nearby lake make?

    h. If the government auctioned off the nearby lake, what price do you think it would fetch if the weekly interest rate is 0.12 per cent or 0.0012?

    i. If the government auctioned off the nearby lake with the condition that the same number of fish per week needs to be brought to market as before, what price would the lake fetch?

21.5† **Business and Policy Application:** *The Externality when Fishing in the Commons.* In exercise 21.4, we showed that free access to a fishing lake causes overfishing because fishers will continue to fish until the cost of inputs, i.e. fishing nets in our example, equals *average* rather than *marginal* revenue product.

    A. Suppose that the lake in exercise 21.4 is publicly owned.

        a. What is the externality that fishers impose on one another on this lake?

        b. Seeing the problem as one involving this externality, how would you go about setting a Pigouvian tax on fishing nets to remedy the problem? What information would you have to have to calculate this?

        c. Suppose instead that the lake is auctioned off to someone who charges per-net fees to fishers who would like to fish on the lake as in A(e) of exercise 21.4. How do you think the fees charged by a profit-maximizing lake owner compare to the optimal Pigouvian tax?

        d. Do you think it is easier for the government to collect the information necessary to impose a Pigouvian tax in part (b) or for a lake owner to collect the information necessary to impose the per-net fees in part (c)? Who has the stronger incentive to get the correct information?

        e. How would the price of the lake that the government collects in (c) compare to the tax revenues it raises in (b)?

        f. Suppose instead that the government tries to solve the externality problem by setting a limit on per-net fishing licences that fishers are now required to use when fishing on the public lake. If the government sets the optimal cap on licences and auctions these off, what will be the price per licence?

        g. What do each of the previous solutions to the Tragedy of the Commons share in common?

    B. *Let N denote the total number of fishing nets used by everyone and $X = f(N) = AN^\alpha$ the total catch per week. As in exercise 21.4, let r be the weekly rental cost per net, let p be the market price for fish and let $A > 0$ and $0 < \alpha < 1$.

        a. The lake is freely accessible to anyone who wants to fish. How much revenue does each individual fisher make when they use one net?

        b. What is the loss in revenue for everyone else who is fishing the lake when one fisher uses one more net?

        c. Suppose that each fisher took the loss of revenue to others into account in their own profit maximization problem when choosing how many nets n to bring. Write down this optimization problem. Would this solve the externality problem?

        d. A Pigouvian tax is optimally set to be equal to the marginal social damage an action causes when evaluated at the optimal market level of that action. Evaluate your answer to (b) at the optimal level of N to derive the optimal Pigouvian tax on nets.

        e. Suppose that all fishers just consider their own profit but that the government has imposed the Pigouvian per-net tax you derived in (d). Write down the fisher's optimization problem and illustrate its implications for the overall level of N. Does the Pigouvian tax achieve the efficient outcome?

        f. Suppose the government privatized the lake and allowed the owners to charge per-net fees. The owner might first, calculate the maximum profit not counting the rental value of the lake they would be able to make by fishing the lake themselves with the optimal number of nets, then set the fee per net at this profit divided by the number of nets they would have used. What per-net fee does this imply?

        g. Compare your answer to (f) with your answer to (d). Can you explain why the two are the same?

        h. Suppose $A = 100$, $\alpha = 0.5$, $p = 10$ and $r = 20$. What is the optimal Pigouvian per-net tax and the profit-maximizing per-net fee that an owner of the lake would charge?

21.6 Policy Application: *Social Norms and Private Actions.* When asked to explain our actions, we sometimes simply respond by saying 'it was the right thing to do'. This concept is one that is often formed by observing others, and the more we see others do the right thing, the more we believe it is in fact the right thing to do. In such cases, my action to do the right thing directly contributes to the social norm that partially governs the behaviour of others, and we therefore have an example of an externality.

A. Consider for instance the use of observably green technology, such as driving hybrid cars. Suppose there are two types of car-buyers: (1) a small minority of 'greens' for whom green technology is attractive regardless of what everyone else does and whose demand for green cars is therefore independent of how many others are using green cars; and (2) the large majority of 'means' who don't care that much about environmental issues but do care about being perceived as 'doing the right thing'.

   a. Draw a graph with the aggregate demand curve D_0 for the greens. Assume that green cars are competitively supplied at a market price p^*, and draw in a perfectly elastic supply curve for green cars at that price.

   b. There are two types of externalities in this problem. The first arises from the positive impact that green cars have on the environment. Suppose that the social marginal benefit associated with this externality is an amount k per green car and illustrate in your graph the efficient number of cars x_1 that this implies for greens. Illustrate the Pigouvian subsidy s that would eliminate the market inefficiency.

   c. The second externality emerges in this case from the formation of *social norms*, a form of *network externality*. Suppose that the more green cars the means see on the road, the more of them that become convinced it is the right thing to do to buy green cars even if they are somewhat less convenient right now. Suppose that the means' linear demand D_1 for green cars when x_1 green cars are on the road has vertical intercept below $(p^* - k)$. In a separate graph, illustrate D_1, and then illustrate a demand curve D_2 that corresponds to the demand for green cars by means when $x_2(>x_1)$ green cars are on the road. Might D_2 have an intercept above p^*?

   d. Does the subsidy in (b) have any impact on the behaviour of the means? In the absence of the network externality, is this efficient?

   e. How can raising the subsidy above the Pigouvian level have an impact far larger than one might initially think from the imposition of the original Pigouvian tax? If the network externalities are sufficiently strong, might one eventually be able to eliminate the subsidy altogether and see the majority of means use green cars anyway?

   f. Explain how the imposition of a larger initial subsidy has changed the social norm, which can then replace the subsidy as the primary force that leads people to drive green cars.

   g. Sometimes people advocate for so-called 'sin taxes', taxes on such goods as cigarettes or pornography. Explain what you would have to assume for such taxes to be justified on efficiency grounds in the absence of network externalities.

   h. How could sin taxes like this be justified as a means of maintaining social taboos and norms through network externalities?

B. Suppose you live in a city of 1.5 million potential car owners. The demand curves for green cars x for greens and means in the city are given by $x_g(p) = (D - p)/\delta$ and $x_m(p) = (A + BN^{1/2} - p)/\alpha$, where N is the number of green cars on the road and p is the price of a green car. Suppose throughout this exercise that $A = 5000$, $B = 100$, $D = 100\,000$, $\alpha = 0.1$ and $\delta = 5$.

   a. Let the car industry be perfectly competitive, with price for cars set to marginal cost. Suppose the marginal cost of a green car x is €25 000. How many cars are bought by greens?

   b. Explain how it is possible that no green cars are bought by means?

   c. Suppose that the purchase of a green car entails a positive externality worth €2500. For the case described in (a), what is the impact of a Pigouvian subsidy that internalizes this externality? Do you think it is likely that this subsidy will attract any of the 'means' market?

   d. Would your answer change if the subsidy were raised to €5000 per green car? What if it were raised to €7500 per green car?

   e. **Suppose that a subsidy of €7500 per green car is implemented, and suppose that the market adjusts to this in stages as follows: first, greens adjust their behaviour in period 0; then, in period

1 means purchase green cars based on their observation of the number of green cars on the road in period 0; from then on, in each period n, means adjust their demand based on their observation in period $(n-1)$. Create a table that shows the number of green cars x_g bought by greens and the number x_m bought by means in each period from period 1 to 20.

f. Explain what you see in your table in the context of network externalities and changing social norms.

g. *Now consider the same problem from a slightly different angle. Suppose that the number of green cars driven by greens is $\bar{x}$. Then the total number of green cars on the road is $N = \bar{x} + x_m$. Use this to derive the equation $p(x_m)$ of the demand *curve* for green cars by means, and illustrate its shape assuming $\bar{x} = 16\,000$.

h. Given that you can calculate $\bar{x}$ for different prices, what are the stable equilibria when $p = 25\,000$? What if $p = 22\,500$? What if $p = 17\,500$?

i. Explain now why the €2500 and €5000 subsidies would be expected to cause no change in behaviour by means while a €7500 subsidy would cause a dramatic change.

j. Compare your prediction for x_m when the subsidy is €7500 to the evolution of x_m in your table from part (e). Once we have converged to the new equilibrium, what would you predict will happen to x_m if the subsidy is reduced to €2500? What if it is eliminated entirely?

* conceptually challenging
** computationally challenging
† solutions in Study Guide

Chapter 22

Asymmetric Information in Competitive Markets

In this chapter, we will see another example of an economic force, other than externalities, that can result in the non-existence of certain markets, and in an inefficient allocation of scarce resources in existing markets. This economic force arises from certain types of information being distributed asymmetrically across potential market participants and relates closely to a particular type of externality that is generated in the process.

Information tends to be different for buyers and sellers, with buyers knowing about the tastes and economic circumstances that underlie their demand for a good and sellers knowing the costs of production that underlie their supply decisions. One of the great advantages of markets is that through the formation of market prices, such information is utilized in an efficient manner as the price sends a signal to buyers and sellers about how scarce goods should be allocated in the market. Information asymmetries that cause externality problems in markets, however, are different from diverse sets of knowledge about our own individual tastes and costs. They involve *hidden information that impacts others adversely* because the information can be used to take advantage of the person on the other side of the market.

Information asymmetries occur whenever buyers and sellers have different information regarding the nature of the product or service that is being traded or the true costs of providing that product or service. A common example of this occurs in insurance markets. If an individual approaches an insurance company about purchasing car insurance, that individual has inherently more information than the insurance company. In particular, they know more about their own driving behaviour, how often they speed, how many times they decide to drive through a red light, whether they use their mobile phone for texting while driving, whether they take the risk of driving while under the influence of alcohol or drugs, and so on. In particular, the individual also knows whether their driving behaviour will change as a result of being insured, for example, by driving more aggressively. This is information the insurance company would very much like to have in order to ascertain the likely cost of providing insurance to that individual. The more comprehensive the insurance cover, the more the individual might take risks which they now feel are covered by having insurance. For the insurance company, the greater risk means that it is more likely to have to pay out for claims. The individual also has every incentive to hide their tendency to risky behaviour in order to get a reasonable price for cover. If the insurance company cannot distinguish between people who are hiding information about their behaviour and careful drivers who want insurance but have nothing to hide, it may end up finding it impossible to provide insurance packages that careful drivers would be willing to buy. The problem of asymmetric information, and the associated problem of those with hidden information adversely selecting into insurance markets, can lead to missing markets.

Similar problems arise in other markets. In the used car market, for instance, the owner of a used car may have significantly more information about the quality of the car than potential buyers. In labour markets, workers know more about their real qualifications than employers may be able to ascertain.

In mortgage markets, potential homeowners may know more about their real ability to make mortgage payments in the future than the banks that lend the money. In pharmaceutical markets, drug companies may know much more about the real effectiveness of particular drugs than patients or even doctors. In financial markets, corporate officers know more about the true financial health of a corporation than the average shareholder. Each of these cases shares some of the characteristics of insurance markets in that one side of the market has inherently more information that is relevant for the market transaction than the other side, which may make the other side hesitate about entering a transaction. In each case there may exist other market mechanisms, civil society institutions or government policies that can alleviate the problems markets face in dealing with such information asymmetries.

22A Asymmetric Information and Efficiency

The presence of hidden information on one side of the market can bring about inefficiencies by generating a particular type of externality. In some cases, this will lead to the non-existence of markets that, if information were more generally available, would make everyone better off. In other cases, it will lead to market distortions in which we can see in principle how more information will lead to greater efficiency.

22A.1 Grade Insurance Markets

Let's begin with a hypothetical example. Suppose an individual, let's call her Anya, approaches your lecturer the day before the beginning of the semester and tells them she wants to sell 'grade insurance' in your cohort. Let's assume that students in the cohort receive a grade for their work over the year, in the range A to F. If a student wants to ensure that they get at least a grade x in the class, they can purchase insurance that guarantees them grade x as a minimum grade for a price p_x. Higher grade guarantees will carry with it a higher price. At the end of the semester, the lecturer and Anya will look at the legitimate grade distribution and particularly at the grades earned by those who bought insurance from her. If an earned grade falls below x for which a student bought insurance at the beginning of the semester, Anya has to pay the lecturer to overcome their scruples and raise the grade, with the size of the payment depending on how much the grade needs to be raised in order to get to the grade for which the student had bought insurance. If, on the other hand, a student who bought insurance for grade x actually earned a grade at or above x, no grade adjustment is necessary and no cost is incurred by Anya's grade insurance company; she gets to keep what the student paid without paying anything to the lecturer.

To make this example more concrete, let's suppose that the grade insurance business is perfectly competitive, which implies that each grade insurance company will end up making zero economic profit in equilibrium, and let's suppose that grades in your course are curved, prior to Anya paying off the lecturer to raise some grades, around a C, with 10 per cent of all students earning an A, 25 per cent earning a B, 30 per cent earning a C, 25 per cent earning a D and 10 per cent earning an F. Finally, assume that your lecturer's scruples are such that it costs a minimum of c for them to raise your grade by 1 letter grade, $2c$ to raise it by 2 letter grades and $3c$ to raise it 3 letter grades, etc.

22A.1.1 A-Insurance and the Adverse Selection Problem To focus on one particular problem that the grade insurance market faces, suppose first that only A-insurance can be offered and that student behaviour will be exactly the same whether or not a student has insurance. Students who buy insurance at the beginning of the semester study and work just as hard as they would have in the absence of having insurance. Students themselves have a pretty good idea whether they are likely to do well or poorly in the class, but as an outsider coming in, Anya doesn't know anything about any individual student and only knows the distribution of grades that will emerge at the end.

If everyone were forced to buy the A-insurance, it would not be difficult to determine the equilibrium insurance premium p_A, if we know that everyone in the grade insurance business makes zero profit in equilibrium. We would know that Anya would have to pay $4c$ for everyone in the 10 per cent of the class that earns an F, $3c$ for everyone in the 25 per cent of the class that earns a D, $2c$ for everyone in the

30 per cent of the class that earns a C, and c for everyone in the 25 per cent of the class that earns a B. The insurance premium would be:

$$p_A = 0.1(4c) + 0.25(3c) + 0.3(2c) + 0.25c = 2c. \tag{22.1}$$

The price of A-insurance would be determined by how much it takes to pay off your lecturer to raise a grade by one level. If that price is €100, the premium would be equal to €200 per student.

Exercise 22A.1

What would be the equilibrium insurance premium if, in a system that forced all students to buy insurance, the only insurance policy offered were one that guarantees a B? What if the only policy that were offered was one that guaranteed a C?

Suppose that not everyone is forced to buy a particular policy but it is left up to individual students. If it were reasonable to expect the set of students who choose to buy insurance to be a random sample of the class, the same logic we used earlier would result in exactly the same premium. It is true that this would involve some risk for the insurance company since a random sample will sometimes contain relatively more good students and other times relatively bad students, but if the insurance company sells many of these types of contracts in different cohorts, that risk would disappear. It seems likely that those students choosing to buy insurance will not represent a random sample, with students who are expecting an A being uninterested in purchasing insurance. If Anya charged the insurance premium in equation (22.1), she would lose money.

Assume that all students are willing to pay as much as $2c$ to raise their grade by one level and $0.5c$ for any additional increase in the grade by another level. An F student is willing to pay $2c$ to raise their grade to a D, $2.5c$ to raise their grade to a C, $3c$ to raise their grade to a B, and $3.5c$ to raise their grade to an A.

Exercise 22A.2

In an efficient allocation of grade insurance when only A-insurance is offered, who would have A-insurance? *Hint*: Compare the total cost of raising each student type's grade to the total benefit that this would yield for each student type.

Exercise 22A.3

If all types of insurance policies were available – A-insurance, B-insurance, etc. – who would have what type of insurance under efficiency? *Hint*: Compare the marginal cost of raising each student type's grade by each level to the marginal benefit of doing so.

This would imply that 90 per cent of the class would be willing to buy the A-insurance if it were offered at a premium of $2c$. Anya's insurance company, however, would now incur higher costs. If there were 100 students in the cohort, Anya would incur a cost of c for the 25 B students, a cost of $2c$ for the

30 C students, a cost of $3c$ for the 25 D students and a cost of $4c$ for the 10 F students, for an overall cost of $200c$ or an average cost of $2.22c$ for each of the 90 students that buy the insurance. In order for Anya to make zero profit, she now has to charge a premium of $2.22c$ for the A-insurance. At that price, the B students would no longer be willing to pay for the A-insurance because the price is above what they are willing to pay for a one-letter grade increase in their grade. This means that Anya would have to charge a premium of approximately $2.69c$ for the same insurance policy in order to break even if only C, D and F students bought her insurance.

Exercise 22A.4

Verify that Anya's break-even insurance premium for A-insurance would have to be approximately $2.69c$ if only the 65 C, D and F students bought the insurance.

The C students are no longer willing to pay for the insurance since they are willing to pay only $2.5c$ to raise their grade by two levels: $2c$ for the first level and $0.5c$ for the second. Thus, only D and F students are willing to pay $2.69c$ for Anya's A-insurance. If they are the only ones buying, Anya's premium has to go up to approximately $3.29c$ – sufficient to get only F students to be interested in the A-insurance, which would necessitate a premium of $4c$ that not even F students are willing to pay. If students are allowed to choose whether or not to buy A-insurance, Anya will not be able to sell any insurance in equilibrium if the students know what kind of students they are and she does not. This is an example of a more general problem known as the *adverse selection* problem that can arise in markets with asymmetric or hidden information.

As illustrated in Table 22.1, the adverse selection problem arises because each student has more information than Anya's insurance company about how much of a cost she will incur if she sells grade insurance. As a result, students will adversely select into buying insurance, with high-cost students more likely to demand insurance than low-cost students. It would be efficient for B and C students to hold A-insurance in our example, but neither does. It is efficient for B and C students to hold A-insurance when only A-insurance is an option, because the cost of raising their grades is c and $2c$ respectively, while their benefit from getting an A is $2c$ and $2.5c$ respectively. The benefit is equal to the cost for D students, and it is therefore efficient for them to have or not have insurance; F students benefit by $3.5c$ and cost $4c$. As in the case of the externalities in Chapter 21, the competitive equilibrium is inefficient. Even if students cannot perfectly predict what grade they will earn in the absence of insurance, they will have more information than Anya does about the probability that they will earn a good grade. Thus, even if students that end up earning an A in the absence of insurance are willing to buy insurance at the beginning of the semester, they will still be willing on average to pay less than those who end up with a worse grade. Because of the adverse selection problem, students who line up to buy insurance from Anya impose a negative externality in the market by raising the average cost of insurance and thus the premium she has to charge. Their decision to enter the market adversely impacts the other students. It is this negative externality that arises from asymmetric information, and it is because of the presence of this externality that a market equilibrium does not exist in our example.

Table 22.1 Unravelling of an Insurance Market

	All Students Buy	B, C, D & F Students Buy	C, D, F Students Buy	D & F Students Buy	F Students Buy
0-profit price	$2c$	$2.22c$	$2.69c$	$3.29c$	$4c$
	↓	↓	↓	↓	↓
	A students won't buy	B students won't buy	C students won't buy	D students won't buy	F students won't buy

Exercise 22A.5

Would Anya be able to sell A-insurance if students were always willing to pay $2c$ for every increase in their letter grade? Would the resulting equilibrium be efficient?

22A.1.2 Information, Adverse Selection and Statistical Discrimination We have seen how the asymmetry of information in the A-insurance market can lead to a non-existence of the insurance market due to the negative externality generated through adverse selection. To focus a little further on how asymmetric information causes this, we can consider how the equilibrium or lack thereof will change if Anya is able to obtain the information that we have so far assumed only students possess.

Suppose first that Anya can observe student transcripts at the beginning of the semester and, from them, she can perfectly infer what grade each student will make at the end of the semester in the absence of insurance. She could offer each student a menu of insurance policies and price them with that information in mind. For a B student, for instance, she could offer the A-insurance at a price of c, which the student would be more than willing to pay with Anya making zero profit. For C, D and F students, she could similarly price A-insurance at $2c$, $3c$ and $4c$ respectively, with C and D students willing to pay the price but F students unwilling, since such insurance is worth only $3.5c$ to them. We have thus restored the market for A-insurance by eliminating the informational asymmetry. We have furthermore done so in an *efficient* way, with insurance sold only to students whose willingness to pay is above the cost of the insurance product.

The real world, of course, is never that certain, and neither students nor Anya can perfectly predict what grade they will end up earning at the end of the term in the absence of insurance. Suppose that Anya observes from transcripts what grades a student has made on average and is able to classify students into A students, B students, C students and D students. Suppose she also knows by looking at the past performance of students in the course that A students earn an A 75 per cent of the time and a B 25 per cent of the time, and all other students earn a grade one level above their usual grade 25 per cent of the time, their usual grade 50 per cent of the time, and a grade below their usual grade 25 per cent of the time. Assuming that students have no more information than Anya does, she could offer the different insurance policies to each type of student at a premium that will result in an expected zero profit for her.

For instance, since Anya knows that she will incur a cost of c with 25 per cent probability for an A student, she can price an A-insurance policy for an A student at $0.25c$. Similarly, since she knows a B student who purchases an A-insurance will cost her nothing with 25 per cent probability, c with 50 per cent probability and $2c$ with 25 per cent probability, she can price an A-insurance for a B student at c. You can verify on your own that the equilibrium price for an A-insurance would again be $2c$ for a C student and $3c$ for a D student.

Exercise 22A.6

What would be the equilibrium price p_A^F for an F student if that student will earn an F with 75 per cent probability and a D with 25 per cent probability?

Notice that nothing has fundamentally changed if the grade outcome is uncertain *as long as it is equally uncertain from the student's perspective as it is from Anya's*. As long as the student has no more information than she does, whether that information involves uncertainty or not, no adverse selection problem will arise and an equilibrium price will emerge for A-insurance but will differ depending on what type of student is purchasing the insurance. When Anya has perfect information about each student and can perfectly predict the type of grade they will earn in the absence of insurance, she will discriminate based on the *individual* characteristics of the student. In the case where both Anya and the students are somewhat uncertain about what the semester will hold, however, she ends up discriminating based on the statistical evidence she has regarding the probabilities that a particular student will earn particular grades. Such price discrimination that is based on the underlying characteristics *of the group* to which an individual belongs is called *statistical discrimination*.

22A.1.3 The Moral Hazard Problem Throughout our discussion of the problems in our hypothetical *A*-insurance market, we have made the assumption that students will study just as hard and diligently if they have grade insurance as if they did not; but would they? Would the knowledge of the guarantee of a certain grade offered by Anya's insurance company cause some students to reduce their study efforts, stop attending lectures and seminars, and maybe even miss exams? Some students will study because they enjoy and value learning more than simply the grade they get on a piece of paper; others might study just as hard if there were no exams and no grades given. Students will vary in terms of how much value they place on the grade relative to the actual learning in a course, which implies that the degree to which students will change behaviour under grade insurance will differ across students. The problem of individuals changing behaviour in this way after entering a contract is known as the *moral hazard problem*, and it makes executing the contract more expensive for the other party to the contract.

If all students react the same to being insured, Anya can predict how much more they will cost her than they would if they continued to behave as if they were not insured. If, for instance, a random selection of half the class buys *A*-insurance, we calculated that a premium of $2c$ would make Anya's expected profit zero in the absence of moral hazard. If each of the students who bought insurance changes behaviour sufficiently to end up with one letter grade below where they would have ended up otherwise, Anya would have to charge a premium of $3c$ to have an expected profit of zero. The anticipation of moral hazard behaviour by those she insures implies she must charge more than she otherwise would, and it arises in insurance markets whenever individuals engage in riskier behaviour when insured.

If students differ in their change in behaviour once they have insurance, however, we have a bigger problem than higher insurance premiums *assuming students know themselves better than Anya knows them*. Once again, she would possess less information about the student than the student themselves possess, and this will *reinforce the adverse selection problem* that we discussed in the absence of moral hazard. Even if Anya could identify the *A*, *B*, *C*, *D* and *F* students from their transcripts and knew precisely what grade each would earn in the absence of insurance, she would have to worry about the fact that some of each type of student will exhibit greater moral hazard once they are insured than others. The *B* student that knows they can earn a *B* in the course and that they will work just as hard if insured will not, for instance, be willing to pay as much for *A*-insurance as the *B* student who knows they can enjoy leisure a whole lot more if they have *A*-insurance. Thus, students will adversely select into Anya's insurance pool based on the level of moral hazard they will exhibit once insured. As long as they know this information and she does not, we can get the same kind of unravelling of the insurance market we saw in our initial example of adverse selection.

Adverse selection causes problems for insurance companies because of the adverse externality that high-cost customers impose on low-cost customers as they drive up the price of insurance, and may cause insurance markets to no longer function in equilibrium. Moral hazard by itself, on the other hand, is a problem that insurance companies can, in our example, deal with through the pricing of premiums. However, if moral hazard creates informational asymmetries because insurance companies cannot identify how different individuals will engage in different levels of risky behaviour once insured, this creates another adverse selection problem that can once again undermine the existence of markets. Much has been written by economists about the optimal ways in which insurance companies, and others facing moral hazard problems on the other side of the market, can arrange contracts so as to minimize moral hazard behaviour. Although we will not develop this formally in this chapter, you can think of some possible conditions Anya's insurance company might place on those who buy grade insurance. For instance, she might require as part of the contract that your lecturer certifies at the end of the term that students who will benefit from owning grade insurance have in fact attended lectures, handed in assignments and taken exams. For now, we can note that to the extent to which insurance companies can find ways of minimizing moral hazard through contractual arrangements as they sell insurance, they limit the adverse selection problem that accompanies the existence of moral hazard.

22A.1.4 Less Extreme Equilibria With Adverse Selection The non-existence of markets due to adverse selection is an extreme manifestation of the problem of adverse selection, and not all markets that are subject to adverse selection will cease to exist entirely. Suppose, for instance, that your lecturer will not permit Anya to sell A-insurance but only agrees to let her sell insurance that guarantees a student will earn at least a B in the course. To make the example as simple as possible, let's assume that there is no moral hazard problem, that students know exactly what grade they will earn, that Anya has no information about any individual student and that it is prohibitively costly for her to gather any useful information on individual students.

We know that no A or B student would be interested in buying insurance. In a class of 100 students, only the 65 C, D and F students are therefore potential customers. If they all end up buying the insurance, Anya knows that she will incur a cost of c for the 30 C students, $2c$ for the 25 D students and $3c$ for the 10 F students. Her average cost per customer is $110c/65$ or approximately $1.69c$. Since students are willing to pay $2c$ for a one-level increase in their grade and $0.5c$ for each additional level increase, we know that C, D and F students would be willing to pay $2c$, $2.5c$ and $3c$ for B-insurance and thus are all willing to pay the break-even premium of $1.69c$. In this case, *the adverse selection problem is not sufficiently large to eliminate the equilibrium in the B-insurance market.*

Exercise 22A.7

Conditional on only B-insurance being allowed, is this equilibrium efficient?

Now suppose that student demand for grade insurance was slightly different. Suppose a student is willing to pay $1.5c$ for a one-level increase in their grade and c for each additional increase. This implies that C students would only be willing to pay $1.5c$ for B-insurance, less than the premium of $1.69c$ Anya has to charge to break even when all C, D and F students buy insurance. If she ends up providing B-insurance to only the 35 D and F students, she would have to charge a break-even premium of approximately $2.29c$. Since this is less than the value D and F students place on B-insurance, the equilibrium would involve 35 B-insurance policies sold to just those students. *The externality of adverse selection causes fewer policies to be sold, but an equilibrium still exists.*

Exercise 22A.8

Conditional on only B-insurance being allowed, is this equilibrium efficient?

The example can get a lot more complex if the lecturer allows her to sell all forms of insurance; that is, A-, B-, C- and D-insurance. If we assume that individuals are uncertain about exactly what grade they will get, and are willing to pay $1.5c$ to get their typical grade but only $0.5c$ more for each grade above their usual level, then in that case it is inefficient for anyone to buy insurance other than insurance to guarantee their usual grade. This is because the cost of insuring the usual grade is c, while the benefit is $1.5c$, but raising the grade each level above the usual is valued at only $0.5c$ but costs c. Adverse selection will result in inefficiency once again.

22A.1.5 Signals and Screens to Uncover Information We have shown how asymmetric information can cause problems in our grade insurance market. Good – or low-cost – students have an incentive to find ways of credibly revealing information to Anya's insurance company so that she can give them a better deal. Anya's insurance company has an incentive to invest in ways of uncovering information, by getting access to transcripts, interviewing students, etc. Students have an incentive to *signal* information to Anya and she has an incentive to *screen* the applicant pool. These signals and screens can be efficiency enhancing, but they can also be wasteful under different assumptions about the grade insurance market.

22A.2 Revealing Information Through Signals and Screens

Let's now move away from the artificial grade insurance market and consider the case for insurance more generally. While our treatment in this section can be applied to all types of insurance, we'll frame our discussion in terms of car insurance. Suppose that there are two types of potential consumers: high-cost consumers that are likely to have accidents, and low-cost consumers that drive safely and are less likely to call on insurance companies to pay for damages. We can think of car insurance for type 1 consumers carrying an expected marginal cost of MC^1 and car insurance for type 2 consumers carrying an expected marginal cost of MC^2, with $MC^1 > MC^2$. To make the example as simple as possible, let's suppose further that demand curves are equal to marginal willingness to pay curves and that the aggregate demand curve D^1 for type 1 consumers is the same as the aggregate demand curve D^2 for type 2 consumers.

Panel (a) of Graph 22.1 illustrates what the car insurance market would be like if there were only type 1 consumers, and panel (b) illustrates what it would be like if there were only type 2 consumers. In each case, we can predict how the competitive market would allocate resources, assuming there are no substantial recurring fixed costs to running insurance companies. In panel (a), the equilibrium price p^1 would cause consumers of type 1 to purchase x^1, the efficient quantity that maximizes social surplus. In panel (b), the equilibrium price p^2 would similarly cause type 2 consumers to buy x^2 insurance policies, once again allocating resources efficiently. If a competitive insurance industry can tell type 1 consumers apart from type 2 consumers, this is the outcome that will emerge, with all insurance policies priced at the marginal cost relevant for the type of consumer who is purchasing insurance.

Graph 22.1 Adverse Selection in Car Insurance Market

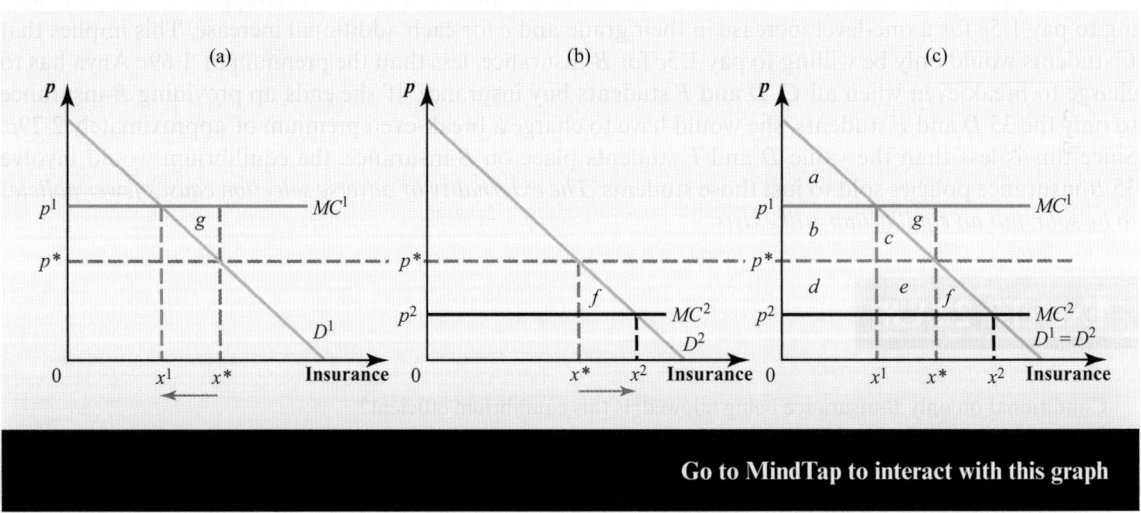

Go to MindTap to interact with this graph

Panel (c) of Graph 22.1 merges panels (a) and (b) into a single picture. If insurance companies can tell safe drivers apart from unsafe drivers, type 1 consumers will get consumer surplus equal to area (a) while consumers of type 2 will get consumer surplus equal to area ($a + b + c + d + e + f$). Since insurance firms are making zero profit, the overall social surplus would be equal to ($2a + b + c + d + e + f$).

22A.2.1 Deadweight Loss From Asymmetric Information
Now suppose that firms cannot distinguish between type 1 and type 2 drivers and thus cannot price car insurance based on the expected marginal cost of each consumer who walks through the door. The only information that firms have is that half of all drivers are of type 1 and half are of type 2. Each insurance company gets a random selection of drivers to insure and knows that half their customers are high cost and half are low cost. Under perfect competition that drives profits for insurance companies to zero, this implies that the single price charged for car insurance will lie halfway between MC^1 and MC^2 indicated by p^* in panel (c) of Graph 22.1.

Exercise 22A.9

Suppose the current market price for car insurance were less than p^*. What would happen under perfect competition with free entry and exit? What if instead the market price for car insurance were greater than p^*?

It can be seen that high-cost consumers will benefit from the information asymmetry we have introduced. Their price for car insurance drops from p^1 under full information to p^*. Consumers of type 2 will analogously be hurt by the informational asymmetry, seeing their price increase from p^2 to p^*. The fact that some consumers are better off and some are worse off does not, however, itself raise an efficiency problem. The efficiency problem emerges from the fact that *overall consumer surplus falls as a result of the informational asymmetry*.

In panel (c) of Graph 22.1, consumer surplus for type 1 consumers increases to $(a + b + c)$, while consumer surplus for type 2 consumers falls to $(a + b + c)$, giving us an overall surplus of $(2a + 2b + 2c)$. Note that area (b) is equal in size to area (d), which means we can rewrite this overall surplus as $(2a + b + 2c + d)$. Note further that the triangle (c) is equal in size to triangle (f), which means we can further rewrite the overall surplus as $(2a + b + c + d + f)$. Comparing this to the full information surplus of $(2a + b + c + d + e + f)$, we have lost area (e). This is the size of the deadweight loss from introducing asymmetric information that keeps firms from pricing insurance policies differently for consumers of type 1 and 2.

Area (g) is equal to half of area (e) and area (f) is equal to area (g), and thus also equal to half of area (e). The deadweight loss can equivalently be stated as area $(f + g)$. Panel (a) of the graph places area (g) into the graph for just consumers of type 1 where we originally said that consumers would buy x^1 insurance policies when they are priced at marginal cost. All the way up to x^1, the marginal benefit, as indicated by the demand curve, exceeds the marginal cost, and it is therefore efficient to provide policies up to x^1. For policies after x^1, however, the marginal cost of providing additional insurance policies exceeds the marginal benefit, making it inefficient to provide policies beyond x^1. When x^* policies are bought by type 1 consumers, the deadweight loss from this over-consumption of insurance is area (g). The reverse holds in panel (b) for low-cost consumers whose marginal benefit exceeds marginal cost until x^2 but who reduce their consumption to x^* under the uniform price p^*. Thus, consumers of type 2 are now under-consuming insurance, with the deadweight loss (f) emerging directly from this under-consumption.

Exercise 22A.10

True or False: The greater the difference between MC^1 and MC^2, the greater the deadweight loss from the introduction of asymmetric information.

Exercise 22A.11

Suppose that type 1 consumers valued car insurance more highly, implying D^1 lies above D^2. Can you illustrate a case where the introduction of asymmetric information causes type 2 consumers to no longer purchase any car insurance? What price would type 1 consumers pay?

Notice that the adverse selection problem in our car insurance market is very much like the problem we first encountered in the grade insurance market. Consumers that cost less to insure – safer drivers or better students – are driven out of the insurance market by rising premiums due to the adverse selection of consumers who cost more to insure. The result in Graph 22.1 is less extreme in the sense that not all low-cost consumers are driven out of the market and not all high-cost consumers come into the market, but the basic economic forces are the same.

22A.2.2 Screening Consumers The asymmetric information equilibrium in Graph 22.1, which is replicated in panel (a) of Graph 22.2, is called a *pooling equilibrium* because all consumer types end up in the same insurance pool with the same insurance contract, while the full information equilibrium in which the different types are charged based on their marginal cost is called a *separating equilibrium* because the types end up in separate insurance contracts. When asymmetric information leads to pooling of different types, however, it would be to the advantage of an insurance company to find a way of screening out high-cost customers and providing insurance to only low-cost types.

Graph 22.2 Insurance Companies Screening Drivers

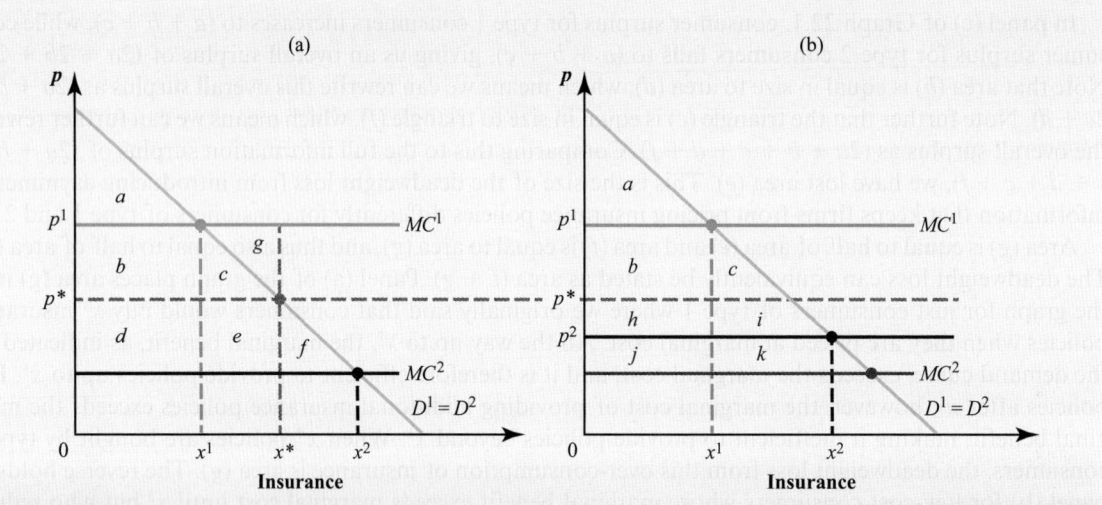

Go to MindTap to interact with this graph

Given that there is a demand for screening services that identify who the safe drivers are, we might imagine that a screening industry will form, a competitive industry that screens consumers and sells information to insurance companies. Suppose that this screening industry becomes very good at gathering information on consumers; so good, in fact, that the marginal cost of gathering information on any particular driver is virtually zero. In that case, competition in the screening industry will drive the price of screening services paid by insurance companies to zero. If the screening industry becomes very good at gathering information on drivers, information will be revealed to insurance companies at roughly zero cost. This leads us back to the full information separating equilibrium in which high-cost drivers are charged a price p^1 and low-cost drivers are charged p^2. The emergence of a screening industry that screens consumers at low cost restores the efficient equilibrium and recovers the deadweight loss from the pooling equilibrium.

Exercise 22A.12

How much do type 1 consumers lose? How much do type 2 consumers gain? What is the net effect on overall consumer surplus?

Now suppose that information is not all that easy to gather. In particular, suppose it costs q per driver to gather sufficient information to allow the screening firms to tell type 1 drivers apart from type 2 drivers. If insurance companies buy this information for all drivers that apply for policies, insurance companies will have to pass this screening cost on to consumers in order to maintain zero profits. They can't pass it on to type 1 consumers because if the price for high-cost insurance policies rose above p^1, a new insurance company could emerge and sell insurance at p^1 without incurring any screening cost. In order for insurance companies to make zero profit, they will have to price the policies of low-cost customers above MC^2 to pay for the screening price charged by the screening firms for both type 1 and type 2 consumers. Thus, the new separating equilibrium will have $p^1 = MC^1$ and $p^2 = MC^2 + \beta$ where $\beta > q$ and is sufficient to cover all the screening costs for both types of consumers.

Suppose that the screening cost q per driver is such that $\beta = (p^* - MC^2)$ is required in order for insurance companies to make zero profit in the separating equilibrium where they charge $p^1 = MC^1$ to type 1 consumers. This implies that $p^1 = p^*$; that is, the insurance premiums for low-cost drivers remain unchanged from the pooling equilibrium because of the screening cost. The premiums for high-cost drivers rises to MC^1 because insurance companies can now tell who the unsafe drivers are and thus will no longer insure them below marginal cost. In panel (a) of Graph 22.2, consumer surplus for type 1 drivers falls by $(b + c)$ from $(a + b + c)$ to (a), while consumer surplus for type 2 drivers remains unchanged. Overall consumer surplus falls by $(b + c)$, raising the deadweight loss that already existed in the initial pooling equilibrium. The cost of screening customers is paid to screening firms who make zero profit and thus is not a benefit to anyone. In panel (a) of Graph 22.2, this cost is equal to area $(d + e)$, which means that the increase in deadweight loss from moving to the separating equilibrium is $(b + c + d + e)$.

Exercise 22A.13

Why is the screening cost equal to area $(d + e)$?

Exercise 22A.14*

Why do firms in this case pay a screening cost that does not allow them to lower any premiums? *Hint*: Think about whether, given that everyone else pays for the screening costs and discovers who are the safe and unsafe drivers, an individual firm can do better by not discovering which of its potential customers are type 1 and which are type 2.

Thus, as screening costs rise, the move from a pooling equilibrium with asymmetric information to a separating equilibrium where the asymmetric information is eliminated through screening, becomes inefficient. This is because gathering information is itself costly to society, and someone will have to bear that cost. While the pooling equilibrium without screening gives rise to deadweight losses, these deadweight losses can be reduced through screening only if the cost of gathering information is relatively low.

Panel (b) of Graph 22.2 illustrates a less extreme case where the separating equilibrium price p^2 lies below the pooling equilibrium price p^* because screening costs are lower than previously assumed. Type 1 consumers still lose $(b + c)$ in consumer surplus as their premium rises to MC^1, but type 2 consumers now gain $(h + i)$ in consumer surplus. Overall consumer surplus changes by $(h + i - b - c)$. Screening costs are equal to $(j + k)$, implying an overall change in social surplus of $(h + i - b - c - j - k)$ as we move to the screening equilibrium. Note that as screening costs fall towards zero, $(j + k)$ approaches zero while $(h + i)$ approaches $(d + e + f)$. Since $(d + e + f)$ is unambiguously greater than $(b + c)$, overall surplus therefore increases for sufficiently low screening costs.

Exercise 22A.15

Could there be a screening-induced separating equilibrium in which p^2 is higher than p^*?

Exercise 22A.16

Would your analysis be any different if the insurance companies did the screening themselves rather than hiring firms in a separate industry to do it for them?

22A.2.3 Consumer Signals Assume that insurance companies find it too costly to screen consumers, and we are therefore in our pooling equilibrium where p^* is charged to all drivers. As we have already shown, this implies that low-cost drivers are paying too much, and high-cost drivers are paying too little. It is therefore in the interest of low-cost drivers to find a way to *signal* to insurance companies that they are a safe bet and, if they succeed in signalling their type, it becomes in the interests of high-cost types to falsely signal that they, too, are safe drivers. Whether a separating equilibrium can emerge in the insurance market through consumer signals depends on the cost of signalling your true type, as well as the cost of falsely signalling that you are a different type than you actually are.

Consider the extreme case where it is costless for type 2 drivers to signal that they are safe but it is very costly for type 1 drivers to falsely signal that they too are safe drivers. Because it is easy for type 2 drivers to reveal information that cannot easily be obscured by type 1 drivers, a full information separating equilibrium with insurance premiums $p^1 = MC^1$ and $p^2 = MC^2$ will emerge, and the deadweight loss from pooling will be eliminated through consumer signalling. If, on the other hand, it is equally costless for type 1 drivers to pretend to be type 2 drivers, this cannot happen, and we remain in the pooling equilibrium where no useful information is conveyed to the insurance companies.

Exercise 22A.17

True or False: When it is costless to tell the truth and very costly to lie, consumer signalling will unambiguously eliminate the inefficiency from adverse selection.

Now suppose that things get a little murkier in that it costs δ for type 2 consumers to signal that they are safe drivers and it costs γ for type 1 consumers to pretend to be safe drivers. If the industry is currently pooling all drivers into a single insurance contract with price p^*, type 2 drivers would be able to reduce their premiums to MC^2 if they can credibly signal that they are safe drivers thus each getting a benefit of $(p^* - MC^2)$. As long as $\delta < (p^* - MC^2)$, it therefore makes sense for a type 2 consumer who is currently paying p^* to absorb the cost of signalling their type and get their premium lowered to MC^2.

Suppose that the type 2 consumers successfully signal their type and induce a separating equilibrium where the industry charges MC^2 to type 2 consumers and MC^1 to type 1 consumers. The only way this can truly be an equilibrium is if it is too costly for the type 1 consumers to falsely signal that they, too, are safe drivers, and a type 1 consumer in a separating equilibrium would be willing to pay as much as $(MC^1 - MC^2)$, the difference between the low and high insurance premiums, to pretend to be a safe type. Thus, we can get a separating equilibrium if $\delta < (p^* - MC^2)$ and $\gamma > (MC^2 - MC^1)$; that is, if the signalling cost plus the low-cost insurance premium is less than the pooling insurance premium for safe drivers *and* the cost of lying is greater than the difference between the low- and high-cost insurance rates. Is this outcome necessarily efficient? Just as in the case of screening, the answer again depends on how high δ is, i.e. the cost of revealing information.

Exercise 22A.18

Suppose $\delta < (p^* - MC^2)$ and $\gamma > (MC^1 - MC^2)$. What is the increase in deadweight loss in going from the initial pooling equilibrium to the separating equilibrium?

Exercise 22A.19

True or False: If δ and γ are such that a separating equilibrium emerges from consumer signalling, the question of whether the resulting resolution of asymmetric information enhances efficiency rests only on the size of δ, not the size of γ.

Suppose $\delta < (p^* - MC^2)$ and $\gamma < (MC^1 - p^*)$; that is, the cost of truthfully signalling that you are a safe driver is less than the amount that safe drivers are overpaying in the initial pooling equilibrium *and* the cost of lying is less than the amount that unsafe drivers are underpaying. It is possible to get a *pooling equilibrium with signalling* where both types send signals that they are safe drivers, but because both types send these signals, no actual information is conveyed to the insurance companies that therefore continue to price all policies at p^*. Given that everyone is sending an 'I am safe' signal, not sending such a signal might be interpreted as you being 'unsafe', and thus everyone will send them because everyone else is sending them. This is of course unambiguously inefficient. Consumers are sending costly signals without revealing any actual information and thus without changing anything in the insurance industry.

Exercise 22A.20*

Is it possible under these conditions for there to also be a pooling equilibrium in which no one sends any signals? *Hint*: What would insurance companies have to believe in such an equilibrium if they did see someone holding up the 'I am safe' sign?

Exercise 22A.21*

Suppose $(p^* - MC^2) < \delta = \gamma < (MC^1 - p^*)$. Will there be a separating equilibrium?

Exercise 22A.22

Why is it possible for a signalling equilibrium to result in a pooling equilibrium in which no information is revealed, but it is not possible to have such a pooling equilibrium emerge when firms screen?

22A.2.4 Information Costs and Deadweight Losses Under Asymmetric Information Our example of car insurance has illustrated two fundamental points. First, as already shown in our grade insurance examples, the presence of asymmetric information may cause pooling equilibria in which behaviour is based on average characteristics rather than individual characteristics. This will lead to the emergence of deadweight losses as some will over-consume while others will under-consume relative to the efficient level or, if the problem is sufficiently severe, entire markets will cease to exist. Second, it may be possible for information asymmetries to be remedied through the revelation of information, either because the informed side of the market signals or because the uninformed side of the market screens. This only leads to greater efficiency if the cost of transmitting information is relatively low *and* if the information that is exchanged is actually informative and thus leads to a separating equilibrium. We now turn to a discussion of some of the most prevalent real-world situations in which asymmetric information plays an important role. As you will see, many of these have nothing to do with insurance even though they can be understood with the tools we have developed within the insurance context.

22A.3 Real-World Adverse Selection Problems

In our development of the basic demand and supply model of markets earlier in the book, we distinguished between three different types of markets: output markets in which consumers demand goods supplied by producers, labour markets in which producers demand labour supplied by workers, and financial markets in which producers demand capital from investors or savers. Asymmetric information can appear in any of these markets. We will point to three types of institutions that can ameliorate the externality problem created by adverse selection. New *markets*, like the screening firms in our car insurance example, might appear and facilitate the exchange of hidden information; non-market *civil society* institutions might play a similar role; or *government* policy might be crafted to address the problem. In many instances a combination of these approaches is utilized in the real world.

22A.3.1 Adverse Selection in Output Markets We have already discussed extensively the problems of adverse selection in one particular output market where the 'output' is insurance. In some insurance markets, there is much that insurance companies can observe about individuals, thus giving rise to a relatively small adverse selection problem, while in other insurance markets much remains hidden information. In the case of life insurance, for instance, the chances of a consumer using the insurance can be predicted reasonably well as long as the insurance company knows a few basics such as the consumer's age, gender, health condition, the level of alcohol consumption and whether or not the consumer smokes. While some consumers might behave more recklessly if their life is insured, giving rise to a moral hazard problem that can worsen adverse selection, most consumers probably will not change behaviour significantly just because their heirs will receive a payment if they die. Life insurance companies can therefore use relatively costless screens to categorize consumers into different risk types and price life insurance policies accordingly. As a result, we rarely hear of calls for government intervention in life insurance markets, with insurance providers employing actuaries who predict the probability of premature death for different types of consumers.

Exercise 22A.23

Another factor that lessens the adverse selection problem in life insurance markets is that the bulk of demand for life insurance comes from people who are young to middle-aged and not from the elderly. How does this matter?

In the case of unemployment insurance, on the other hand, markets may face considerably more difficulty in overcoming the adverse selection problem. As someone approaches an insurance company to inquire about unemployment insurance policies, it is difficult for the insurance company to tell whether the consumer is asking for this insurance because they know that they are about to be made redundant. Age or health exams do not provide a useful screen because the hidden knowledge is much more difficult to unearth. Consumers themselves may also not find easy ways to signal their type. It may therefore be the case that signalling and screening are too costly for widespread unemployment insurance markets to form without some non-market institution to spur such a market. Before governments became involved in insuring everyone, certain civil society institutions, for instance, utilized local knowledge of individual reputations to provide insurance within small communities where individual reputations were relatively well known. In most developed countries, such institutions disappeared when governments instituted mandatory unemployment insurance for everyone, using compulsory unemployment insurance taxes to fund the system. The justification for such a policy lies in the adverse selection problem that may be sufficiently severe for private markets and civil society institutions to offer too little insurance.

Exercise 22A.24

In our car insurance example, asymmetric information caused the market to create a pooling equilibrium in which some over-consumed and others under-consumed. Why might this not be the case in the unemployment insurance market where those with high demand are much more likely to be those with high probability of being made redundant? *Hint*: Can you imagine an unravelling of the market for reasons similar to what we explored in the grade insurance case?

Exercise 22A.25

Is mandatory participation in government unemployment insurance efficient, or do you think it might just be more efficient than market provision?

Insurance markets, however, are not the only output markets that might suffer from adverse selection problems. The *used car market*, for instance, is plagued by adverse selection, but this time the hidden information resides with the seller rather than the buyer. You may have heard that when you buy a new car, its value drops by several thousand euros the moment you drive it off the dealer's forecourt. Why? Because if you were to try to sell this car to someone else the week after you bought it, potential buyers would wonder whether you have discovered something about the car that is not observable to them and whether you might not be adversely selecting as a seller into the used car market. Consumers in the used car market can employ various screens to try to get to the potentially hidden information, screens such as taking the used car to a trusted mechanic who can give an independent *third-party certification* of quality. Or used car dealerships might offer *warranties* that signal to consumers the quality of the used car. Some brands of cars are known to have fewer problems, and so *brand names* can signal quality. *Brand names, warranties and third-party certifications* all represent ways that hidden information can be unearthed and at least partially overcome the adverse selection problem.

Exercise 22A.26

Consider used car dealerships in small towns. How might *reputation* play a role similar to brand names in addressing the asymmetric information problem?

In a world with increasingly complex products, the issue of product quality that is potentially hidden from consumers extends far beyond the used car market. The quality of much of what many people see in stores – from computers to televisions to kitchen appliances to over-the-counter medications – is difficult for them to evaluate. Warranties can signal quality, as can the brand names that have good reputations. Third-party certification groups such as the magazine *Which* have emerged. They routinely test products and *sell the information* in a separate market, through for instance, the *Which Consumer Reports* or website, and consumer advocacy groups outside the market provide similar services. Industry groups have often established *industry standards*, sometimes requiring third-party certification to ensure quality. While all these signals are costly and thus use some of society's resources, they nevertheless *can be* and often are socially beneficial if they are not too costly and if they lead to more widespread information that can overcome adverse selection externalities in markets. Some producers might be able, at least in the short run, to signal that their products are of higher quality than they actually are, expending wasteful effort to hide their true type in order to end up in a pooling equilibrium with high-quality producers. Thus, just as in the example of car insurance, signals may in some instances represent a socially wasteful use of resources aimed at deceiving rather than informing, or they may be too costly even when they result in a resolution of the information asymmetry.

Exercise 22A.27

What is *Which* analogous to in our discussion of car insurance?

Finally, as in insurance markets, the government often steps in as well. Cigarette packages contain dire warnings required by law, and electricians and gas installers have to have a licence to operate. We have to be careful in interpreting such government involvement as solely serving the purpose of reducing adverse selection. Our goal here, however, is not to sort out which of the various signals and screens aimed at adverse selection problems are good and which are bad, which truly raise social surplus and which are socially wasteful. There are a variety of market, civil society and government-supported signals, and screens in fact operate all around us.

22A.3.2. **The Special Case of Health Insurance** Our age and health status are excellent predictors of how much health care we will use in any given year – which implies that the health insurance market has straightforward screens it can employ to substantially reduce information asymmetries. Some countries will provide health care which is 'free' at the point of use while others require its citizens to take out insurance policies to cover their health care, should the need arise. Unregulated competitive health insurance markets will therefore charge substantially higher premiums to older and sicker individuals – so high, in fact, that health insurance often becomes unaffordable for those who might most likely want to take out such insurance. While a separating equilibrium from reductions in asymmetric information is typically efficiency enhancing, the prospect of those most in need of health care not being able to get it is not a pleasant one for many.

The typical efficiency argument for a separating equilibrium becomes problematic when we think of buying health insurance *across the life cycle* as opposed to as an annual event. This is because when it comes to health care, almost everyone starts as a low-cost consumer but, as we grow older, we become higher-cost consumers. While pooling everyone into a single insurance pool implies the young and healthy subsidize the old and sick *in any given year*, it also implies today's young are pooled with their future selves that are likely to get old and sick *over their life cycle*. If health insurance contracts were lifetime contracts as opposed to annual contracts, and if everyone behaved rationally, the young would rationally choose to pool with their future selves. Real-world health insurance contracts are not structured this way, and there is substantial evidence from behavioural economics that – even if they were – many would not approach such markets in a fully rational way when they are young and would thus find themselves unable to afford health insurance when they need health care later in life.

The adverse selection problem in health insurance markets arises from individuals making short-run choices in real time rather than long-run choices for the whole life cycle. Because insurance companies can easily screen for age and health status, health insurance becomes very costly for the old and less healthy when insurance companies are permitted to price-discriminate based on age and health status. If, on the other hand, insurance companies are not permitted to price-discriminate in this way, the young and healthy will tend to adversely select out of the market, causing premiums for those who most need health care to escalate much as grade insurance premiums at the beginning of the chapter escalated as better students selected out of the market. It is for these reasons, in addition to equity-based arguments, that governments tend to be heavily involved in health insurance markets.

Broadly speaking, three different approaches have emerged. In some countries like the United Kingdom the government owns most hospitals and employs most doctors and nurses while providing national health insurance to all citizens in a *single payer/single provider* system. In countries like Canada, on the other hand, the government provides national health insurance by acting as the *single payer* for health care that is delivered primarily through private hospitals, doctors and nurses. Finally, countries like Switzerland have *regulated insurance markets* with mandates and subsidies. Under such a system, insurance companies are not permitted or are severely limited in their ability to price-discriminate based on age or health status, but everyone is required to buy health insurance and the poor's premiums are subsidized. While these three general approaches differ greatly, they each respond to adverse selection by creating a single insurance pool that includes most or all citizens.

22A.3.3 Adverse Selection in Labour and Capital Markets There is only so much that an employer can ascertain about a potential employee before hiring them. The adverse selection problem in labour markets occurs when workers have hidden information about their own productivity. Education, work experience and letters of reference offer ways to signal information to employers, but workers with identical CVs may still be quite different on the job. Additional information might be signalled less formally in job interviews aimed at screening applicants. Depending on the cost of the signal relative to the benefit, such efforts may once again be socially productive in the sense that they convey true information, or socially wasteful if they signal false information or are too costly.

We are often led to believe, for instance, that more education is beneficial. This may be true if the only reason for someone to get more education is to truly increase productivity on the job and if the marginal benefit of additional education is greater than the marginal cost for the student. In some instances, education may serve as a signal masking the underlying productivity of a worker. If the cost of getting the signal of having attained a certain level of education is sufficiently low, low-productivity workers might get an education to end up in a pooling equilibrium with truly high-productivity workers. While this may make the unproductive worker better off, it dilutes the information of the signal and does not serve to convey the information that employers seek. The adverse selection problem is less severe if it is easy for firms to release workers who prove less productive than they initially appeared, but many laws and regulations as well as union protections for workers often make releasing workers costly for firms.

Exercise 22A.28

Which of the following possibilities makes it more likely that widespread university attendance is efficient: (1) universities primarily provide skills that raise marginal product or (2) universities primarily certify who has high marginal product?

The same issues arise in financial markets. Banks and mortgage companies have less information than those who apply for loans. Applicants therefore seek ways of signalling their creditworthiness and banks seek ways of screening applicants. In the past, when individuals moved less often and resided more within small communities, one's informal *reputation* was an important signal; if everyone knows someone is a liar and a cheat, there is not much point in lending them money. In today's world, such informal mechanisms are less effective, but other institutions have taken their place. Credit companies keep detailed records on anyone who has ever had a credit card or a loan or a bank account. A strong credit history provides a signal to a lender of reliability. As informal reputations became less effective, new markets formed, markets that gather and sell information about our creditworthiness. In many ways, a credit report has become a reputation in credit markets.

We face similar information problems when we try to decide where to invest our money. Companies try to get us to buy their stocks, and banks try to sell us various types of savings instruments with different risks and returns. Often, the places we consider investing have much more information about their true value than we do, and we therefore have to expend effort, or hire someone to expend effort on our behalf, to gather information that might be hidden. There exist many different financial advisers that specialize in gathering such information and selling it to us for a price or a commission, and non-profit institutions provide information on firms, often on websites accessible to potential investors. In addition, some governments have created their own oversight mechanisms, requiring financial disclosure statements by publicly traded companies and offering their seal of approval in terms of deposit insurance to banks. This, too, has been the source of much policy discussion – and new legislation in several countries – following the 2007–2009 financial crisis in which financial firms considered too big to fail took excessive risk knowing the government was likely to come to their rescue if needed. This is an example of moral hazard.

22A.4 Racial and Gender Discrimination

Many societies continue to struggle with overcoming social problems arising from the legacy of racial and gender discrimination. Such discrimination has deep historical roots, dating back to some of the darker periods in history when prejudice was endemic and often explicitly supported by government policy. Despite legislation that now outlaws such discrimination, studies continue to suggest instances when applicants for employment in labour markets or credit in financial markets are offered different wages or interest rates despite identical observable qualifications, with less favourable deals offered to women and those from ethnic minorities. Such discrimination may persist in markets *even when old prejudices have died out* if markets are characterized by asymmetric information of the type discussed throughout this chapter.

22A.4.1 **Statistical Discrimination and Gender** We have discussed how life insurance companies calculate the expected probability of premature death for individuals. Smokers, for instance, are required to pay higher life insurance premiums than non-smokers because, *on average*, smokers die earlier than non-smokers. At the same time, many of us know of people who smoked all their life and ended up living to a ripe old age. Smoking appears to be more damaging to some than to others, with some individuals being fortunate to have genes that protect them from the adverse consequences of smoking. Even if a person knows that their family tends to be able to smoke and still survive to an old age, insurance companies will discriminate against them in their pricing policies if they know that they smoke. Because they lack information on the individual probability of being affected by smoking, they discriminate *based on the statistical evidence on smokers as a group*; they engage in *statistical discrimination* because of the informational asymmetry that keeps them from knowing fully their individual characteristics.

This statistical discrimination against smokers in life insurance markets is similar to statistical discrimination *against men* in these markets. Women *on average* live longer than men, but a person whose family may be more pre-disposed to cancer or heart disease may be offered lower life insurance premiums. The same is true of young people in car insurance markets: a 22-year-old may be a much better driver than a 60-year-old, but because *on average* older people tend to have fewer accidents, the 22-year-old ends up having to pay a much higher car insurance premium than the 60-year-old. *Statistical discrimination – discrimination based on the average statistics of the demographic groups to which individuals belong –* is therefore economically rational in insurance markets that are characterized by asymmetric information.

Exercise 22A.29

What are we implicitly assuming about the costs of screening applicants in these markets?

While we may not see a big moral issue arising from such statistical discrimination in certain insurance markets, we might be considerably more disturbed when the same type of discrimination emerges in other markets. *On average*, for instance, women are more likely to exit the labour force for some period in order to raise children. This is not at all true for *some* women, and an increasing number of men are also taking larger responsibility for child rearing. Employers, however, have a difficult time identifying which women and men are *individually* more likely to exit the labour force for child rearing, but it is easy for them to identify whether employees or potential employees are men or women. As a result of this *asymmetric information*, employers may therefore use the underlying statistics of average behaviour by men and women to infer the likelihood that a particular employee will be with the company for a long period. As a result, they may *statistically discriminate* against female employees, offering them lower wages or less job training in anticipation of the greater likelihood that they will leave the company. From a purely economic perspective, this is no different from the insurance company statistically discriminating against a male and a female when applying for life insurance; because the company does not have full information, it uses the available statistical evidence to infer information that is true *on average* but may be false for any given individual. Just as in the case of life insurance, the discrimination that results in equilibrium may have nothing to do with companies inherently preferring one gender over another.

Exercise 22A.30

True or False: Statistical discrimination leads to equilibria that have both separating and pooling features.

22A.4.2 Gender Discrimination Based on Prejudice Versus Statistical Discrimination When we observe incidences of gender discrimination, it is difficult to know whether the discrimination arises from inherent prejudices or from economic considerations due to asymmetric information. *Discrimination based on prejudice is defined as discrimination that arises from tastes that inherently prefer one group over another*, while *statistical discrimination arises from asymmetric information*. Life insurance companies that charge lower premiums to women do not do so because they like women more than men; they do so because women *on average* live longer than men. Similarly, employers who discriminate against women in labour markets *may* be motivated solely by economic considerations rooted in asymmetric information. This is not to say that such discrimination may be due to more pernicious causes related to men on corporate boards feeling uncomfortable about allowing women more economic opportunities. The same logic that causes life insurance companies to discriminate in favour of women and against smokers may also lie behind *some* of the discrimination against women we might observe in labour markets. A better understanding of the root causes of discrimination may help us better formulate solutions that eliminate all forms of gender discrimination, including those based on prejudice.

Exercise 22A.31

Suppose schools invested more resources into gender sensitivity training in the hopes of lessening gender discrimination in the future. Would you recommend this if you knew that gender discrimination was purely a form of statistical discrimination?

Markets, for instance, tend to punish employers for discriminating based on prejudice. Suppose that companies *A* and *B* in a competitive market are identical in every way except for the fact that company *A* is governed by a corporate board that is prejudiced against working with women while company *B* is not. This implies that company *B* has a larger pool of talent to draw from and will be able to gain a competitive advantage over company *A* by employing qualified women. Both companies may operate in equilibrium, but the prejudiced company will earn lower euro profits because part of its 'profit' comes in the form of prejudiced corporate leaders getting utility from excluding women. Shareholders should prefer to invest in company B that makes more euro profits, which implies that the stock of company B will have a higher market value than the stock of company A. This presumes, of course, that not all shareholders are similarly prejudiced. In other instances, it may be that the market rewards taste-based discrimination if prejudice is widespread. For instance, if a town's population is prejudiced against migrant workers, a café might economically benefit from discriminating against migrant waiters in an attempt to attract prejudiced customers.

Consider a third company C that is just like company B, but suppose that C is willing to engage in statistical discrimination while B is not. If the labour market is characterized by asymmetric information and if women *on average* are more likely to leave the labour force to rear children, company C will engage in statistical discrimination that will likely make it more profitable. While the market thus tends to punish companies that engage in taste discrimination based on prejudice, it will *reward* companies that engage in statistical discrimination. Finally, suppose there exists a fourth company D that has developed an effective screening tool that can differentiate *individually* between applicants of both genders, between those that are likely to leave the labour force and those that are not. This company can, of course, do even better than company C by using its information and eliminate all forms of discrimination.

As societies consider ways of eliminating all forms of gender discrimination in labour markets, the appropriate strategies differ depending on what form the discrimination takes. Both taste discrimination due to prejudice and statistical discrimination due to asymmetric information can persist in markets, but markets tend to punish the former while rewarding the latter. Taste discrimination disappears as old prejudices disappear from people's tastes, but statistical discrimination persists as long as companies are economically rewarded when discriminating in the presence of asymmetric information. Statistical discrimination will tend to persist as long as underlying statistical differences between the genders persist unless other institutions are put in place to make statistical discrimination less profitable. If, for instance, men *on average* demand equal amounts of time away from the labour force in order to rear children, the root cause of statistical gender discrimination in labour markets disappears. Alternatively, some governments have instituted *mandatory* parental leave for both genders when children enter a household, some have focused on subsidizing child care to make it easier for women to return to the labour force, and some have instituted rigorous anti-discrimination laws that offset the rewards from statistical discrimination with government sanctions. Finally, there exists an incentive for companies, such as company D in our example, to consider more effective ways of differentiating between potential employees of both genders and for potential employees to signal whether they are likely to leave the labour force or not. The goal here is not to advocate one form of institutional solution over another but to suggest that there are a variety of government and non-government institutions that might emerge to address the asymmetric information problem that results in statistical gender discrimination in labour markets.

22A.4.3 Racial Discrimination Just as gender discrimination in labour markets can result from either inherent prejudice or from asymmetric information, persistent racial discrimination can have the same two root causes. We began our discussion of gender discrimination in the context of life insurance markets where insurance companies price-discriminate against men because of the higher *average* life expectancy of women. For a variety of complex reasons, South Asian men in the UK have shorter *average* life expectancy than white males. Gender discrimination in insurance markets, however, is legal, while racial discrimination is not. Thus, the statistical discrimination that would tend to make life insurance premiums higher for South Asian men is not permitted, causing insurance companies not to explicitly price-discriminate against South Asians as they do against white males. Even in the absence of legal barriers, the bad publicity from explicit racial discrimination in the pricing of life insurance premiums might be sufficient to keep this from happening as long as large numbers of potential customers would be offended by seeing insurance premium tables that have separate columns for different races. At the same time, it may well be the case that insurance companies practise a more discrete discrimination by being less aggressive in advertising their life insurance products to South Asian males.

Despite the legal barriers to racial discrimination and despite much progress over the past decades, however, it appears that such racial discrimination continues to persist in other markets. It becomes difficult to ascertain what fraction of the observed discrimination in those markets is due to taste discrimination based on prejudice as opposed to statistical discrimination based on asymmetric information. In the case of racial discrimination, such statistical discrimination may well be due to *average* differences between groups that emerge from the historical legacy of past and present racial discrimination elsewhere.

In many countries, where a child lives can determine the quality of the school they go to. Some areas will have schools that serve disproportionate numbers of ethnic minority children and children from poor and disadvantaged backgrounds, which, on average, perform systematically worse than schools in other areas. A variety of economic factors therefore continue to cause children from deprived backgrounds and those from ethnic minorities, on average, to attend under-performing schools than other children even as governments have attempted to put in place systems and processes to reduce disparities.

Now suppose that an employer is faced with identical CVs from two applicants, one from a student from an ethnic minority living in a deprived area and one from a white middle class student from an affluent area. For all the employer knows, the first applicant has many unobservable characteristics that will make them a much better employee than the second. The employer also knows that *on average*, children from schools in the deprived area have not had the same opportunity to gain skills as those from schools in affluent areas. The employer faces the same asymmetric information problem we have discussed throughout this chapter and will be tempted to *statistically discriminate* against the first applicant *even if they have no inherent prejudice.* Recognizing that it may thus be economically rational for them to discriminate does not imply moral approval for such discrimination. Whether discrimination in labour markets results from inherent prejudice or from asymmetric information, it is deeply disturbing to many of us. Recognizing that such discrimination can persist even in the absence of explicit taste discrimination suggests that market forces by themselves may be insufficient to stamp out racial discrimination when underlying *average* group differences arise from discrimination elsewhere. It furthermore suggests that even if all forms of racial discrimination were illegal, it is likely that subtle and difficult-to-detect racial discrimination may persist in markets as long as these markets are characterized by such asymmetric information.

In the short run, societies can combat such discrimination through a variety of civil society and government institutions. For instance, if a decline in inherent prejudice due to pernicious tastes leads to an increasing number of individuals placing explicit value on diversity, employers might overcome their temptation to statistically discriminate because their non-minority employees gain utility from knowing that they are working in a diverse environment and because their customers are offended if civil society advocacy groups advertise that a particular company has a homogeneous labour force. Alternatively, governments have instituted a variety of different forms of affirmative action policies to explicitly encourage more diverse work environments. In the long run, however, the temptation to engage in statistical discrimination of the kind we have raised here subsides only when more equal access to educational opportunities is offered to all irrespective of race and ethnicity. A society that successfully equalizes such opportunities will therefore eliminate the very statistical group differences that lead to informational asymmetries that cause statistical discrimination. The tendency of racial discrimination to persist in markets is therefore not fully eliminated until attitudes in people's tastes are non-discriminatory *and* opportunities for different groups are truly equal.

22B   Insurance Contracts With Two Risk Types

We deviate in this chapter from our usual practice of formalizing mathematically in Section B what we did intuitively in Section A. We will build a model of adverse selection directly on the topics related to insurance markets introduced in Chapter 17, models in which we considered a whole menu of actuarially fair insurance contracts ranging from no insurance to full insurance. The mathematical Sections 22B.1.2, 22B.2.2 and 22B.3.3 are put in separate subsections, allowing you to skip them if you'd prefer to focus on just the graphical exposition. While we will develop some new intuitions and insights with this model, we should note, however, that the car insurance model in the previous section could be reinterpreted to yield similar insights.

Assume that consumers face the possibility of a bad outcome in which their consumption is x_1 and the possibility of a good outcome in which their consumption is x_2. Suppose further that there are two consumer types, with consumers of type δ facing outcome x_1 with probability δ and outcome x_2 with probability $(1 - \delta)$ and consumers of type θ facing outcome x_1 with probability θ and outcome x_2 with probability $(1 - \theta)$. We will adopt the convention that $\delta < \theta$, implying that the δ types face less risk than the θ types. Otherwise, the two consumer types are identical in every way, with $x^1 < x^2$ the same for both types and with each type having the same underlying tastes, which we will assume throughout are independent of which state of the world occurs. We will assume that each individual's tastes over risky gambles can be expressed as an expected utility, and that each type knows the risks they face but that insurance companies do not necessarily know which type any given individual represents. In most of what follows, the insurance companies only know that a fraction γ of the population is of type δ and the remaining fraction $(1 - \gamma)$ is of type θ.

Recall that insurance companies offer contracts that are defined by an insurance premium p and an insurance benefit b. If a consumer purchases an insurance contract (p, b), their consumption in the good state falls to $(x^2 - p)$ while consumption in the bad state rises to $(x^1 + b - p)$. Since we assume that tastes over consumption are state-independent, each consumer type would choose to fully insure as long as they faced complete and actuarially fair insurance markets.

22B.1 Equilibrium Without Adverse Selection

If insurance companies were able to offer actuarially fair and thus zero-profit contracts to each type separately, these contracts could be graphed with the insurance benefit b on the horizontal and the insurance premium p on the vertical. Such contracts would have the feature that $p = \delta b$ for consumer type δ and $p = \theta b$ for consumer type θ.

Exercise 22B.1

Explain why such contracts are actuarially fair.

22B.1.1 A Graphical Depiction of Equilibrium Without Adverse Selection Panel (a) of Graph 22.3 does this for a consumer of type δ where $x_1 = 10$, $x_2 = 250$ and $\delta = 0.25$. Notice that this consumer becomes better off as they move southeast on the graph because moving southeast implies greater insurance benefits and lower insurance premiums. The graph also contains the line $p = \delta b$ that represents the menu of actuarially fair insurance contracts for this consumer type. Since tastes are state-independent in this example, our work in Chapter 17 implies that our risk-averse consumer will fully insure, purchasing a policy $(b, p) = (240, 60)$ at which their indifference curve must be tangential to the line representing their insurance options.

Graph 22.3 Equilibrium Insurance Policies in the Absence of Asymmetric Information

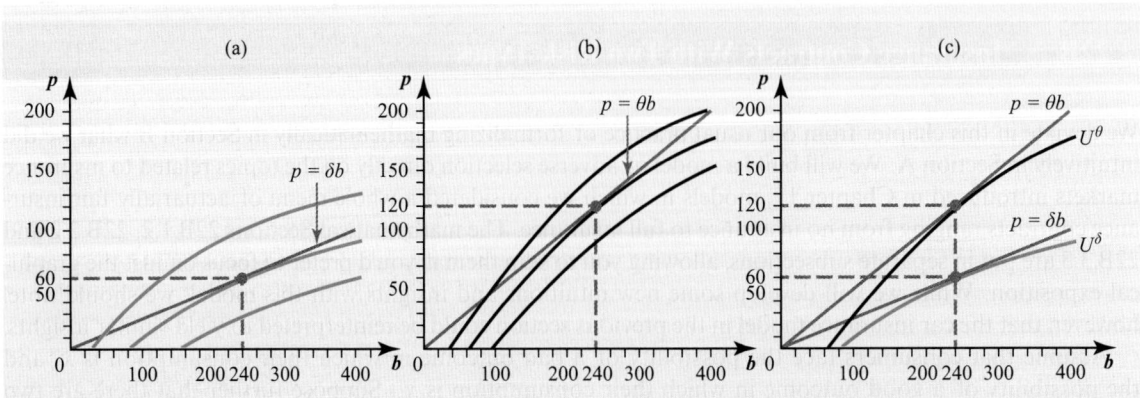

Exercise 22B.2

Why is $(b, p) = (240, 60)$ an insurance contract that provides full insurance to a δ type consumer?

Exercise 22B.3

What would indifference curves look like for risk-neutral consumers? What about risk-loving consumers?

Panel (b) of the graph illustrates the same for consumer type θ assuming that $\theta = 0.5$, that is, assuming that this consumer type is twice as likely to encounter the bad state. Risk aversion implies that the consumer will choose to fully insure when faced with a menu of actuarially fair insurance contracts, but such contracts are twice as expensive for type θ since the insurance company is twice as likely to have to pay out benefits.

Exercise 22B.4

Demonstrate that full insurance for type θ implies the same benefit level as for type δ.

If insurance companies can tell which consumer type they are facing when they enter an insurance contract, panel (c) depicts the competitive equilibrium in which the full insurance contract $(b^\delta, p^\delta) = (240, 60)$ is sold to type δ and the full insurance contract $(b^\theta, p^\theta) = (240, 120)$ is sold to type θ, with insurance companies earning zero profit. This equilibrium is efficient. There is no way to make anyone, consumers or firms, better off without making someone else worse off.

22B.1.2 **Calculating the Equilibrium Without Adverse Selection** Graph 22.3 and the remaining graphs in this chapter, assume that the state-independent utility of consumption can be described by the function $u(x) = \alpha \ln x$. This results in an *expected utility* from the insurance contract (b, p) for type δ of:

$$U^\delta(b, p) = \delta\alpha \ln (x_1 + b - p) + (1 - \delta)\alpha \ln (x_2 - p), \qquad (22.2)$$

and for type θ:

$$U^\theta(b, p) = \theta\alpha \ln (x_1 + b - p) + (1 - \theta)\alpha \ln (x_2 - p). \qquad (22.3)$$

If you have trouble seeing how we arrive at this as the expected utility, review the concepts in Chapter 17.

Exercise 22B.5

Are these consumer types risk averse?

If consumer type δ faces an actuarially fair menu of insurance contracts described by $p = \delta b$, they will choose (b, p) to maximize equation (22.2) subject to $p = \delta b$. Solving this problem results in an optimal choice of:

$$b = x_2 - x_1 \quad \text{and} \quad p = \delta(x_2 - x_1), \qquad (22.4)$$

which fully insures the consumer.

Exercise 22B.6

Set up the expected utility maximization problem for θ types and derive the optimal choice assuming they face an actuarially fair insurance menu.

Exercise 22B.7

How do these results relate to the values in Graph 22.3?

22B.2 Self-Selecting Separating Equilibria

Now suppose that insurance companies cannot tell the low-risk type δ consumers apart from high-risk type θ consumers unless some information is revealed through signalling or screening. In part A of the chapter, we investigated how consumers can send explicit signals to try to reveal their type and how firms can invest in screens that reveal information, and we implicitly assumed that such signals and screens could be bought at some cost. There is another way that consumers of insurance can identify themselves when multiple different insurance contracts are offered to all customers. They could choose different contracts depending on which risk type they are and thus *self-select* into different insurance pools. Firms may therefore want to design the set of contracts that are offered in such a way that consumers reveal their type through their actions. We could not investigate this possibility in our car insurance example of part A because we assumed there that the decision to insure was a discrete decision – either you bought insurance or you did not – and not one that involved choices over *how much* insurance to buy.

The full information equilibrium depicted in panel (c) of Graph 22.3 can no longer be an equilibrium when firms do not know who is what type. Under full information, there was no problem having insurance companies offer all actuarially fair insurance contracts $p = \delta b$ to δ types because they knew who the θ types were and could prevent them from buying insurance contracts intended for low-cost δ types. If insurance companies cannot tell who the high-cost types are, they can no longer offer all the $p = \delta b$ contracts because type θ consumers would end up buying one of those contracts rather than those intended for them. Insurance companies would make negative profits as they incur higher costs on type θ consumers while selling them low-cost insurance. In the absence of knowing who is what type, the insurance industry will therefore have to restrict what types of contracts it offers.

22B.2.1 A Graphical Exposition of Self-Selecting Separating Equilibrium We can ask which insurance contracts will *not* be offered in an equilibrium in which insurance companies achieve the outcome that individuals self-select into different insurance pools based on their risk types. First, note that it must be the case that high-risk types still get fully insured at actuarially fair rates in such an equilibrium. If this were not the case, there would be room for new insurance companies to enter and offer such actuarially fair full insurance to high-risk types. This implies that the insurance contracts that will be restricted are those for

low-risk types. Since those types face less risk, it is less costly for them to forego *some* insurance in order to be able to get a better deal on their insurance contract than they could if they chose from contracts intended for high-risk types. This opens the door for low-risk types to *signal* that they are in fact low-risk types by choosing an insurance contract that is actuarially fair for them but does not fully insure, with insurance companies not making actuarially fair full insurance available for low-risk types.

This is illustrated in panel (a) of Graph 22.4 where we again have two actuarially fair contract lines, one for high-risk θ types and another for low-risk δ types. The high-risk θ types optimize along the actuarially fair set of insurance contracts aimed at them, settling at the full insurance contract A. All the contracts that lie in the shaded area below $U\theta$, however, are preferred by high-risk types to their actuarially fair full insurance contract A. They would therefore much prefer to choose an insurance contract from the portion of the $p = \delta b$ line that lies within the shaded region, with any contract on that line to the right of B strictly preferred by them to A. Thus, if insurance companies want to induce high- and low-risk types to self-select into separate actuarially fair insurance contracts, they cannot offer any of the $p = \delta b$ contracts to the right of B.

Graph 22.4 Self-Selecting Separating Equilibrium With Asymmetric Information

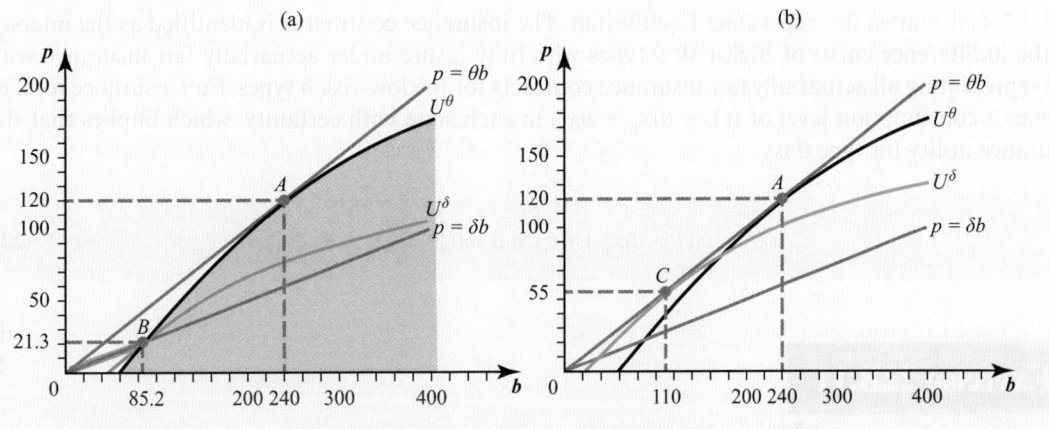

In a *separating equilibrium* in which risk types identify themselves through the insurance contracts that they purchase, the only actuarially fair insurance contracts that can be offered are those that are located on the bold portion of the $p = \delta b$ line in panel (a) of Graph 22.4. Of these, risk-averse consumers of type δ will demand only the contract represented by point B since all other contracts that are offered involve greater risk without a change in the expected value of the outcome.

Exercise 22B.8

Suppose insurance companies offer all actuarially fair insurance contracts to type θ. Can you identify in panel (b) of Graph 22.4 the area representing all insurance contracts that consumers of type δ would purchase rather than choosing from the menu of contracts aimed at type θ?

Exercise 22B.9

From the area of contracts identified in exercise 22B.8, can you identify the subset that insurance companies would be interested to offer assuming they are aware that high-risk types might try to get low-cost insurance?

Exercise 22B.10

From the contracts identified in exercise 22B.9, can you identify which of these contracts could not be offered in equilibrium when the insurance industry is perfectly competitive?

It can be seen that the competitive separating equilibrium in this example is inefficient. In particular, the competitive equilibrium in the absence of asymmetric information, depicted in panel (c) of Graph 22.3, has low-risk types δ with higher utility without anyone else doing worse, since high-risk θ types do equally well and firms make zero profits in either case. The inefficiency arises from the fact that there are *missing markets* – not all the actuarially fair insurance contracts for δ types are offered under asymmetric information. The missing markets arise from the adverse selection problem, that is, the problem that high-risk types would adversely select into the low-risk insurance market if the missing market for fuller insurance targeted at low-risk customers were to emerge.

22B.2.2 Calculating the Separating Equilibrium The insurance contract B is identified as the intersection of the indifference curve of high-risk θ types who fully insure under actuarially fair insurance with the line representing all actuarially fair insurance contracts for the low-risk δ types. Full insurance for a θ type implies a consumption level of $((1 - \theta)x_2 + \theta x_1)$ in each state with certainty, which implies that the full insurance utility for type θ is:

$$U_f^\theta = u((1 - \theta)x_2 + \theta x_1) = \alpha \ln((1 - \theta)x_2 + \theta x_1). \tag{22.5}$$

Exercise 22B.11

Can you verify that full insurance implies consumption of $((1 - \theta) x_2 + 0x_1)$?

The indifference curve that gives all combinations of b and p such that a θ type is indifferent to the full insurance outcome is given by all (b, p) under which their *expected* utility $U^\theta(b, p)$ is equal to U_f^θ from equation (22.5); that is,

$$U^\theta(b, p) = \alpha\theta \ln(x_1 + b - p) + \alpha(1 - \theta) \ln(x_2 - p)$$
$$= \alpha \ln((1 - \theta)x_2 + \theta x_1) = U_f^\theta. \tag{22.6}$$

We can cancel the δ terms and use the rules of logarithms to rewrite the middle part of this equation as:

$$(x_1 + b - p)^\theta (x_2 - p)^{(1-\theta)} = (1 - \theta)x_2 + \theta x_1, \tag{22.7}$$

which we can solve for b to get:

$$b = \left(\frac{(1 - \theta)x_2 + \theta x_1}{(x_2 - p)^{(1-\theta)}}\right)^{1/\theta} + p - x_1. \tag{22.8}$$

Although Graph 22.4 is not drawn using this precise function, this is the inverse of the equation for the dark blue indifference curve in panel (a) of Graph 22.4 when we substitute in $\theta = 10$, $x_2 = 250$ and $x_1 = 10$; that is, the equivalent to the dark blue indifference curve in our graph is described by the equation:

$$b = \left(\frac{(1 - 0.5)250 + 0.5(10)}{(250 - p)^{(1-0.5)}}\right)^{1/(0.5)} + p - 10 = \frac{130^2}{250 - p} + p - 10. \qquad (22.9)$$

Our logic told us that the highest actuarially fair insurance policy for the low-risk δ types that can exist in a separating equilibrium is given by the intersection of this indifference curve with the line $p = \delta b$ that represents the menu of all actuarially fair insurance contracts for low-risk types. Written in terms of b, this line is $b = p/\delta$ or $b = 4p$ when $\delta = 0.25$ as we assumed in our graph. The premium at point B in the graph is given by the intersection of equation (22.9) and the actuarially fair insurance menu $b = 4p$ represented by the lower light blue line in panel (a) of Graph 22.4. This means we need to solve the equation:

$$4p = \frac{130^2}{250 - p} + p - 10, \qquad (22.10)$$

which can be rewritten as:

$$3p^2 - 740p + 14\,400 = 0. \qquad (22.11)$$

Applying the quadratic formula, we get $p = 225.37$ and $p = 21.30$, which represent the two premiums at which the dark brown indifference curve crosses the lower light blue line in panel (a) of Graph 22.4. Point B in our graph lies at the lower of these premiums, with $p = 21.30$ and corresponding $b = 4p = 85.20$. In a competitive separating equilibrium, we therefore have two insurance contracts that are sold, $(b^\theta, p^\theta) = (240, 120)$ and $(b^\delta, p^\delta) = (85.2, 21.3)$, with high-risk θ types fully insuring under the former and low-risk δ types revealing their type by purchasing less than full insurance under the latter contract.

Exercise 22B.12

Can you show mathematically by evaluating utilities that this equilibrium is inefficient relative to the equilibrium identified in panel (c) of Graph 22.3?

Exercise 22B.13

True or False: Under perfect competition and assuming that insurance companies incur no costs other than the benefits they pay out, risk-averse individuals with state-independent tastes will fully insure in the absence of asymmetric information but may insure less than fully in its presence.

Exercise 22B.14

Can you verify the intercepts for point C in panel (b) of Graph 22.4?

Table 22.2 presents the equilibrium insurance contracts for low-risk δ types as the high-risk type becomes riskier, that is, as θ increases. For our particular example, low-risk types continue to find some insurance regardless of how risky the θ types are unless θ reaches 1, but low-risk types clearly purchase less insurance in separating equilibria as high-risk types become riskier. The externality from adverse selection increases in severity as high-risk types become riskier. In cases where insurance can only be sold in discrete units, such as cases like those in Section A where grade insurance was not continuous, low-risk types might be frozen out of the insurance market altogether.

Table 22.2 $\delta = 0.25$, $x_1 = 10$, $x_2 = 250$				
		Equilibrium Insurance for Low-Risk δ Types		
θ	p	b	$x_1 + b - p$	$x_2 - p$
0.25	60.00	240.00	190.00	190.00
0.33	31.05	124.20	102.10	219.30
0.50	21.30	85.20	73.90	228.70
0.75	12.19	48.76	46.57	237.81
0.90	5.77	23.08	27.31	244.23
0.99	0.68	2.70	12.03	249.32
1.00	0.00	0.00	10.00	250.00

Exercise 22B.15

Draw a graph, with b on the horizontal and p on the vertical axis, illustrating the separating equilibrium in row 4 of Table 22.2.

22B.3 Pooling Contracts With Asymmetric Information

In our treatment of self-selecting separating equilibria, we have implicitly assumed that insurance companies cannot earn positive profit by offering an insurance contract that attracts *both* high- and low-risk types into the same insurance pool. We will now explore how such a possibility might emerge, and how it might make the self-selecting equilibrium we have analyzed so far impossible to achieve. We will see that this possibility depends crucially on the number of high-risk types relative to the number of low-risk types in the economy.

Suppose an insurance company were to offer a contract that was more attractive for *both* risk types than the separating equilibrium contracts we previously identified. If a fraction γ of the population is of type δ, and the remaining fraction $(1 - \gamma)$ is of type θ, such an insurance company would expect on average to pay δb for the fraction γ of its customers that are low-risk types and θb to the fraction $(1 - \gamma)$ of its customers who are high-risk types. Thus, the insurance company would expect to make zero profits when:

$$p = \gamma \delta b + (1 - \gamma)\theta b = [\gamma \delta + (1 - \gamma)\theta]b. \tag{22.12}$$

22B.3.1 **Pooling Contracts That Eliminate Self-Selecting Separating Equilibria** Note that when $\gamma = 0$, this reduces to the equation $p = \theta b$ that defines the zero-profit line for high-risk types, and when $\gamma = 1$ it reduces to the zero-profit line for low-risk types. As γ increases from zero to 1, the zero-profit line from having both types buy the same policy rotates from the high-risk zero-profit line to the low-risk zero-profit line. In panel (a) of Graph 22.5, the zero-profit pooling line is depicted for the case where $\gamma = 0.5$, with this light blue line lying exactly midway between the zero-profit lines for the individual risk types.

Graph 22.5 A Pooling Equilibrium Does Not Exist

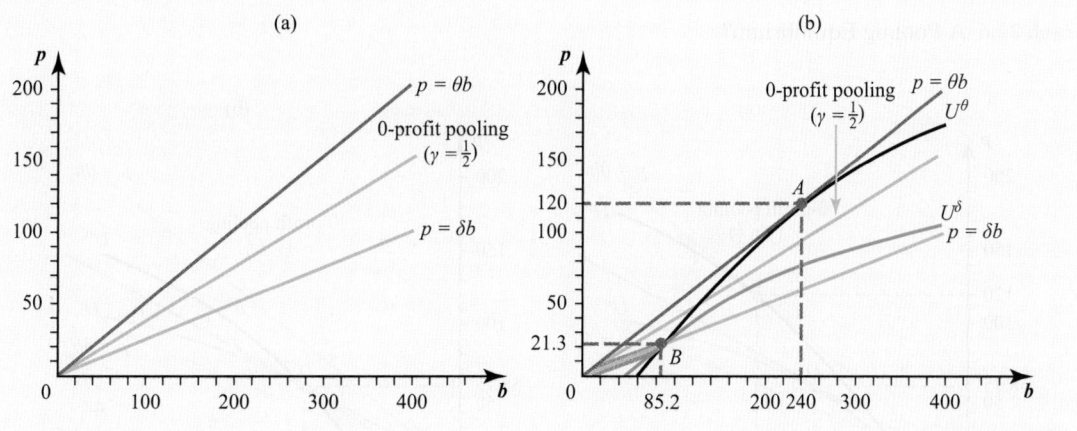

We can now think about the possibility of a pooling insurance contract that breaks the self-selection separating equilibrium in this example. Panel (b) of Graph 22.5 replicates panel (a) from Graph 22.4 and illustrates the contracts A and B that would be bought by types θ and δ in a separating equilibrium. In this case, the dark brown indifference curve for δ types that goes through contract B lies to the southeast of the light blue zero-profit pooling line, which implies that the low-risk δ types prefer to identify themselves as low-risk types by choosing the contract B over any possible zero-profit pooling contract. There is no pooling contract that would attract both risk types *and* result in non-negative profit for insurance companies when B is currently offered. The self-selecting separating equilibrium stands.

Now suppose that γ is equal to 2/3 instead of 1/2; that is, that 2/3 of the population was low risk and 1/3 of the population was high risk. What changes as a result in panel (b) of Graph 22.5? The zero-profit lines aimed at the two types individually are given by $p = \delta b$ and $p = \theta b$ and thus are unaffected by changes in γ. Similarly, the tastes of the two types are unchanged since individual tastes have nothing to do with how many others of each type there are in the economy, which implies the dark brown and dark blue indifference curves remain unchanged. The only thing that changes is the light blue line representing the possible pooling contracts that give insurance companies zero profit. In particular, as γ increases, this line becomes shallower without a change in the intercept, and as it becomes shallower, it will eventually cross the dark brown indifference curve for δ types.

Exercise 22B.16

Using equation (22.12), can you show that the last sentence is correct?

Panel (a) of Graph 22.6 illustrates the zero-profit pooling line for $\gamma = 2/3$, and it illustrates the dark brown indifference curve for δ types that is tangential to this line at point D. Point B, the best possible contract that would allow δ types to identify themselves without θ types wanting to imitate them, now lies slightly to the northwest of this indifference curve, implying that low-risk δ types would slightly prefer D even though this contract is not actuarially fair from their perspective. Similarly, θ types prefer D to the actuarially fair full insurance contract A; that is, while the contract D does not fully insure them, it represents terms that are better from their perspective than actuarial fairness. Thus, we have identified a contract D that is strictly preferred by both risk types to the contracts B and A in the previous separating equilibrium, and the same is true for contracts slightly to the northwest of D, which would result in positive profits for insurance companies. This makes it impossible to sustain the separating equilibrium we were able to sustain when γ was 0.5. By raising γ to $2/3$, we have made it sufficiently easy to find pooling contracts that everyone prefers. This becomes easier as γ increases further.

Graph 22.6 A Pooling Equilibrium?

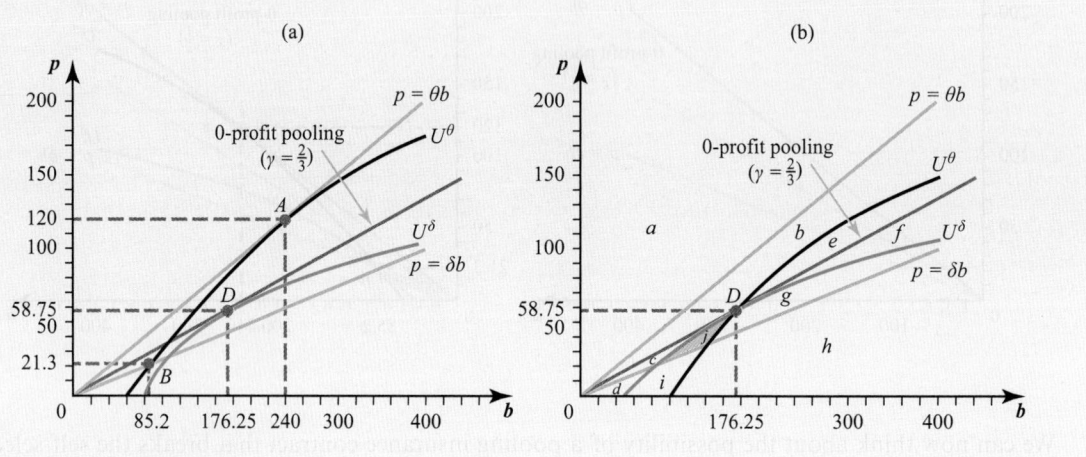

Exercise 22B.17

What is the expected value of consumption for θ types at point D? Is it higher or lower than under full insurance? Explain.

Exercise 22B.18

What is the expected value of consumption for δ types at point D? Is it higher or lower than the expected value of consumption without insurance? Explain.

22B.3.2 **Almost a Pooling Equilibrium** We have so far shown that the separating equilibrium breaks down when there are sufficiently many low-risk types relative to high-risk types in the economy, because this allows firms to offer pooling contracts that are both preferred to the separating equilibrium contracts by all types and result in positive profit. To check whether there exists a pooling *equilibrium*, however, is trickier. Not only would we have to identify a zero-profit contract, such as D in Graph 22.5 that breaks the separating equilibrium, but we would further need to demonstrate that no other contract could result in positive profits for a firm that offers such a contract when all other firms offer D.

Exercise 22B.19

Why must any potential pooling equilibrium contract D lie on the zero-profit pooling line?

Panel (b) of Graph 22.6 illustrates point D on the zero-profit pooling line but this time shows both the dark blue indifference curve for high-risk types and the dark brown indifference curve for low-risk types that contain point D. We can ask whether there exist insurance contracts in each of the areas, labelled by lower-case letters, that would earn an individual insurance company positive profits given that all other companies offer the contract D.

Note that all insurance contracts that fall in the regions (a), (b), (c) or (d) lie to the northeast of both the dark brown and dark blue indifference curves, and thus any company that offers a contract in those regions would attract no customers. Contracts that lie in the regions (e) and (f) lie to the northeast of the dark brown indifference curve and to the southeast of the dark blue indifference curve, which implies that such contracts would attract only high-risk θ types and thus yield negative profit given that all these contracts lie below the zero-profit line for high-risk types. Contracts that fall in the regions (g) and (h) lie to the southeast of both the dark brown and dark blue indifference curves, which implies they will attract both high and low-risk types. All such contracts lie below the zero-profit pooling line, which implies that an insurance company would earn negative profits when offering such contracts. This leaves regions (i) and (j) that lie to the southeast of the dark brown indifference curve and the northeast of the dark blue indifference curve, implying that such contracts would attract only low-risk δ types. Those contracts falling in region (i), however, lie below the zero-profit line for δ types and would thus earn negative profit.

We are left with only contracts in the shaded region (j) that could potentially earn positive profit for a firm that offers insurance contracts in this region while other companies all offer the policy D. Without some friction in the market, everyone offering policy D is therefore not a competitive equilibrium. However, there are several ways in which we might still have D emerge as a pooling equilibrium. First, it might be that there are some start-up costs to offering an insurance policy that are different from what the market offers, e.g. costs of advertising and alerting consumers about the new policy. If those costs are sufficiently high, it may well be that contracts in region (j) will not result in positive profits for individual insurance companies when all others are offering D. It might be that there is some search cost that consumers incur when looking for something other than the prevalent market policy, and if this cost is sufficiently high, the policies in region (j) might not lie to the southeast of the dark brown indifference curve once the search cost is taken into account.

If firms in the market adjust quickly to changing circumstances, it might be that firms who currently offer D know that as soon as they make a positive profit in region (j), other firms will offer policies closer to the zero-profit line $p = \delta b$ and will thus drive profits to zero. If the firms anticipate this, they may not offer policies in region (j). This, however, begins to get us into the area of strategic thinking on the part of firms, a topic for later chapters.

Exercise 22B.20*

Can you think of what would have to be true about how the dark brown and dark blue indifference curves relate to one another at D in order for the problematic area (j) to disappear? Explain why this would imply that D is a competitive equilibrium pooling contract.

Exercise 22B.21

For the case where $\gamma = \frac{1}{2}$ and where a pooling equilibrium therefore does not exist as shown in panel (b) of Graph 22.5, can you divide the set of possible insurance contracts into different regions and illustrate that no firm would have an incentive to offer any contracts other than those that are provided in the separating equilibrium?

22B.3.3 Calculating the Almost-Pooling Equilibrium From our graphical exposition, it is clear that a competitive pooling equilibrium can arise only if the optimal insurance contract for low-risk δ types from the set of zero-profit pooling contracts given in equation (22.12) yields greater utility for δ types than the insurance contract that allows δ types to separate from high-risk θ types. We can begin by calculating the optimal contract from the set of contracts (b, p) satisfying $p = [\gamma\delta + (1 - \gamma)\theta]b$; that is, we can solve the optimization problem:

$$\max_{b,p} U^\delta(b, p) = \alpha\delta \ln (x_1 + b - p) + \alpha(1 - \delta) \ln (x_2 - p) \text{ subject to}$$
$$p = [\gamma\delta + (1 - \gamma)\theta]b. \tag{22.13}$$

Solving this we get:

$$b = \frac{(1 - \delta)x_1}{\gamma\delta + (1 - \gamma)\theta - 1} + \frac{\delta x_2}{\gamma\delta + (1 - \gamma)\theta}, \tag{22.14}$$

and:

$$p = \frac{(\gamma\delta + (1 - \gamma)\theta)(1 - \delta)x_1}{\gamma\delta + (1 - \gamma)\theta - 1} + \delta x_2. \tag{22.15}$$

In panel (a) of Graph 22.6, we assumed $\gamma = 2/3$ (with $\delta = 0.25$, $\theta = 0.5$, $x_1 = 10$ and $x_2 = 250$). Substituting these into equations (22.14) and (22.15), we get $(b, p) = (176.25, 58.75)$ which is point D in the graph. Substituting these back into the utility function for δ types, we get utility of 5.1522α. Low-risk δ types could alternatively purchase the contract $(b, p) = (85.2, 21.3)$, represented by point B, that allows them to separate from high-risk types, but substituting this contract into the expected utility function for δ types gives utility of 5.1500α, which is just below what the same types can attain by pooling with high-risk types. Thus, δ individuals prefer D to B when $\gamma = 2/3$, and by implication for all $\gamma > 2/3$.

Exercise 22B.22

Can you demonstrate mathematically that θ types also prefer D to their separating contract A which has $(b, p) = (240, 120)$?

Exercise 22B.23

When $\gamma = 0.5$ as in Graph 22.5, equations (22.14) and (22.15) give $(b, p) = (154.67, 58)$. Can you demonstrate that the indifference curve containing this point lies below the indifference curve that δ types can attain by purchasing the contract B that allows them to separate?

Table 22.3 reports results for higher values of γ, with the insurance contract approaching that of actuarially fair full insurance for the low-risk δ types as the fraction of δ types in the population approaches 1.

Exercise 22B.24

Can you explain intuitively the change in pooling contracts as you move down Table 22.3? What happens to the problematic (j) region from our graph as we go down the table?

Table 22.3 $\delta = 0.25$, $\theta = 0.5$, $x_1 = 10$, $x_2 = 250$

	Pooling Contracts			
γ	p	b	$x_1 + b - p$	$x_2 - p$
2/3	58.75	176.25	127.50	191.25
0.80	59.29	197.62	148.33	190.71
0.85	59.47	206.86	157.39	190.52
0.90	59.66	216.93	167.27	190.34
0.95	59.83	227.93	178.10	190.17
1.00	60.00	240.00	190.00	190.00

22B.4 Non-Existence of a Competitive Equilibrium

In panel (b) of Graph 22.6, we gave an example of how competitive markets may have difficulty sustaining a pooling equilibrium when γ is sufficiently high such that a separating equilibrium does not exist. In particular, we illustrated for a particular set of indifference curves that unless there are some frictions that make it difficult for individual insurance companies in competitive markets to deviate from the commonly offered pooled insurance contract, there exists an incentive for firms to find contracts in the region denoted (j) that is preferred by low-risk types to the pooled contract D and that would earn the deviating firm a positive profit. None of the policies in the (j) region of the graph represent policies that can be sustained as an equilibrium either. Thus, if γ is sufficiently high to make the potential pooling preferable to separating for low-risk types, a competitive equilibrium may in fact not exist in this set-up. For other sets of indifference curves, such an equilibrium does exist, as you might have already worked out in within-chapter-exercise 22B.20.

How should we interpret such a non-existence of an equilibrium? It may lead us to conclude that insurance markets like this will shift back and forth, with firms moving policies around to attract customers, earning profits briefly before shifting policies again to adjust to changing market conditions. It may imply that markets will search for other ways – more explicit signals and screens – to separate different risk types into different insurance pools. As we have argued in Section A, there may be instances when firms can gain only noisy information that can lead to *statistical discrimination*. The insurance industry may also develop particular norms or industry standards that constrain the set of insurance contracts that can be offered. Alternatively, the government could, in principle, solve the non-existence or instability problem by offering a single insurance contract like D, and not permitting an insurance industry to operate in this market, or it could regulate the insurance market and mandate that only D is offered within that market. None of these solutions, however, will implement efficiency unless they find ways of costlessly revealing the asymmetric information to all parties and thus allowing the industry to reach the full information competitive equilibrium.

End-of-Chapter Exercises

22.1† Consider the example of grade insurance. Suppose students know whether they are typically A, B, C, D or F students, with A students having a 75 per cent chance of getting an A and a 25 per cent chance of getting a B; with B, C and D students having a 25 per cent chance of getting a grade above their usual, a 50 per cent chance of getting their usual grade and a 25 per cent chance of getting a grade below their usual; and with F students having a 25 per cent chance of getting a D and a 75 per cent chance of getting an F. Assume a bell-shaped grade distribution – that is, in the absence of grade insurance, 10 per cent of grades are A, 25 per cent are B, 30 per cent are C, 25 per cent are D and 10 per cent are F.

A. Suppose that grade insurance companies operate in a competitive market and incur a cost c for every level of grade that is changed for those holding an insurance policy. Assume that A to D students are willing to pay $1.5c$ to insure they get their usual grade and $0.5c$ for each grade level above the usual; F students are willing to pay $2c$ to get a D and $0.5c$ for each grade level above that.

    a. Suppose first that your lecturer allows Anya only to sell A-insurance in your classroom. Will she be able to sell any?

    b. Suppose next that your lecturer only allowed Anya to sell B-insurance. Would she be able to sell any?

    c. What if she were only allowed to sell C- or D-insurance?

    d. *If they were the only policies offered, could policies A and D attract customers in a competitive equilibrium at the same time? In equilibrium, who would buy which policy? *Hint*: Only C, D and F students buy insurance in equilibrium.

    e. *If they were the only policies offered, could policies A and C attract customers in a competitive equilibrium at the same time?

    f. *If they were the only policies offered, could policies B and D attract customers in a competitive equilibrium at the same time?

    g. Without doing any further analysis, do you think it is possible to have an equilibrium in which more than two insurance policies could attract customers?

    h. Are any of the equilibria you identified efficient? *Hint*: Consider the marginal cost and marginal benefit of each level of insurance above insuring that each student gets their typical grade.

  B. In A(d), you identified a particular equilibrium in which A- and D-insurance are sold when it was not possible to sell just A-insurance.

    a. How is this conceptually similar to the self-selecting separating equilibrium we introduced in Section B of the text?

    b. How is it different?

22.2 Suppose that everything in the grade insurance market is as described in exercise 22.1. Instead of taking the asymmetric information as fixed, we will now ask what can happen if students can transmit information. Assume throughout that no insurance company will sell A-insurance to students other than A students, B-insurance to students other than B students, etc. whenever they know what type students are.

  A. Suppose that a student can send an accurate signal to Anya about the type of student they are by expending effort that costs c. Furthermore, suppose that each student can signal that they are a better student than they actually are by expending additional effort c for each level above their true level. For instance, a C student can signal their true type by expending effort c but can falsely signal that they are a B student by expending effort $2c$ and that they are an A student by expending $3c$.

    a. Suppose everyone sends truthful signals to insurance companies and that insurance companies know the signals to be truthful. What will be the prices of A-insurance, B-insurance, C-insurance and D-insurance?

    b. How much surplus does each student type get, taking into account the cost c of sending the truthful signal?

    c. Now investigate whether this truth-telling can be part of a real equilibrium. Could B students get more surplus by sending a costlier false signal? Could C, D or F students?

    d. Would the equilibrium be any different if it was costless to tell the truth but it costs c to exaggerate the truth by each level? Assume F students would be willing to pay $1.5c$ for getting an F just as other students are willing to pay $1.5c$ to get their usual grade.

    e. Is the equilibrium in part (d) efficient? What about the equilibrium in part (c)? *Hint*: Think about the marginal cost and marginal benefit of providing more insurance to any type.

    f. Can you explain intuitively why signalling in this case addresses the problem faced by the insurance market?

  B. In Section B of the text, we considered the case of insurance policies (b, p) in an environment where the bad outcome in the absence of insurance is x_1 and the good outcome in the absence of insurance is x_2. We further assumed two risk types: δ types that face the bad outcome with probability δ and θ types that face the bad outcome with probability θ, where $\theta > \delta$.

    a. Suppose that both types are risk averse and have state-independent tastes. Show that, under actuarially fair insurance contracts, they will choose the same benefit level b but will pay different insurance premiums.

b. Suppose throughout the rest of the problem that insurance companies never sell more than full insurance; that is, they never sell policies with b higher than what you determined in (a). In Section B, we focused on self-selecting equilibria where insurance companies restrict the contracts they offer in order to get different types of consumers to self-select into different insurance policies. In Section A, as in part A of this question, we focused on explicit signals that consumers might be able to send to let insurance companies know what type they are. How much would a θ type be willing to pay to send a credible signal that they are a δ type if this would permit them access to the actuarially fair full insurance contract for δ types?

c. Suppose for the rest of the problem that $u(x) = \ln x$ is a function that permits us to represent everyone's tastes over gambles in the expected utility form. Let $x_1 = 10$, $x_2 = 250$, $\delta = 0.25$ and $\theta = 0.5$. Assume that we are currently in a self-selecting equilibrium of the type that was discussed in the text where not all actuarially fair policies are offered to δ types Recall from the text that in this separating equilibrium, δ types bought the insurance policy $(b, p) = (85.2, 21.3)$. While the u function in the text is multiplied by α, we showed that the indifference curves are immune to the value α takes, and so we lose nothing in this problem by setting it to 1. How much would a θ type be willing to pay to send a credible signal to an insurance company to let them know they are in fact a δ type?

d. Suppose we are currently in the separating equilibrium, but a new way of signalling your type has just been discovered. Let c_t be the cost of a signal that reveals your true type and let c_f be the cost of sending a false signal that you are a different type. For what ranges of c_t and c_f will the efficient allocation of insurance in this market be restored through consumer signalling?

e. Suppose c_t and c_f are within the ranges you specified in (d). Has efficiency been restored?

22.3† In exercise 22.2, we showed how an efficient equilibrium with a complete set of insurance markets can be re-established with truthful signalling of information by consumers. We now illustrate that signalling might not always accomplish this.

A. Begin by once again assuming the same set-up as in exercise 22.1. Suppose that it costs c to truthfully reveal who you are and $0.25c$ more for each level of exaggeration; that is, for a C student, it costs c to reveal that they are a C student, $1.25c$ to falsely signal that they are a B student, and $1.5c$ to falsely signal that they are an A student.

a. Begin by assuming that insurance companies are pricing A-, B-, C- and D-insurance competitively under the assumption that the signals they receive are truthful. Would any student wish to send false signals in this case?

b. *Could A-insurance be sold in equilibrium where premiums have to end up at zero-profit rates given who is buying insurance? *Hint*: Illustrate what happens to surplus for students as premiums adjust to reach the zero-profit level.

c. *Could B-insurance be sold in equilibrium? What about C- and D-insurance?

d. *Based on your answers to (b) and (c), can you explain why the equilibrium in this case is to have only D-insurance sold, and bought by both D and F students? Is it efficient?

e. Now suppose that the value students attach to grades is different. They would be willing to pay as much as $4c$ to guarantee their usual grade and $0.9c$ more for each level of grade above that. Suppose further that the cost of telling the truth about yourself is still c but the cost of exaggerating is $0.1c$ for each level of exaggeration about the truth. How much surplus does each student type get from signalling that they are an A student if A-insurance is priced at $2c$?

f. Suppose that insurance companies believe that any applicant for B-insurance is a random student from the population of B, C, D and F students; that any applicant for C-insurance is a random student from the population of C, D and F students; and any applicant for D-insurance is a random student from the population of D and F students. How would they competitively price B-, C- and D-insurance?

g. Suppose that, in addition, insurance companies do not sell insurance to students who did not send a signal as to what type they are. Under these assumptions, is it an equilibrium for everyone to signal that they are A students?

h. There are two sources of inefficiency in this equilibrium. Can you distinguish between them?

B. In exercise 22.2B, we introduced a new signalling technology that restored the efficient allocation of insurance from an initially inefficient allocation in a self-selecting separating equilibrium. Suppose that insurance companies believe anyone who does not send a signal that they are a δ type must be a θ type.

    a. Assume that c_f is below the range you calculated in B(d) of exercise 22.2. Can you describe a pooling equilibrium in which both types fully insure and both types send a signal that they are δ types?

    b. In order for this to be an equilibrium, why are the beliefs about what a non-signal would mean important? What would happen if companies believed that both types are equally likely not to signal?

    c. *True or False*: For an equilibrium like the one you described in part (a) to be an equilibrium, it matters what firms believe about events that never happen in equilibrium.

22.4   Assume again the basic set-up from exercise 22.1.

A. We will now investigate the role of firm *screens* as opposed to consumer signals.

    a. Suppose that an insurance company can *screen* students. More precisely, suppose an insurance company can, for a fee of c, obtain a student's transcript and thus know what type a student is. If insurance companies will only sell insurance of type i to students who have been screened as type i, what would be the equilibrium insurance premium for each insurance assuming perfect competition and no recurring fixed costs?

    b. Would each insurance type be offered and bought in equilibrium?

    c. How high would the cost of obtaining transcripts have to be in order for the insurance market to collapse?

    d. In the case of *signalling*, we had to consider the possibility of pooling equilibria in which the same insurance is sold to different types of students who care sufficiently for the higher grade to each be willing to pay the zero-profit premium as well as, for some, to pay the cost of falsely signalling their type. If insurance companies can *screen* for the relevant information, could it ever be the case, assuming that individuals care sufficiently much about higher grades, that several types will get the same insurance? *Hint*: Suppose an insurance company attempted to price a policy such that several types would get positive surplus by buying this policy. Does another insurance company have an incentive to compete away some of the potential customers for that policy?

    e. Does the separating equilibrium that results from screening of customers depend on how many of each different type are in the class, and what exactly the curve is that is imposed in the class?

    f. Suppose we currently have a market in which a large number of insurers sell the different insurance types at the zero-profit price after screening customers to make sure insurance of type i is only sold to type i. Now suppose a new insurance company enters the market and devises B-insurance for C students. Will the new company succeed in finding customers?

    g. Would your answer to (f) change if students are willing to pay $1.5c$ to insure their usual grade and c rather than $0.5c$ for each grade above the usual?

    h. *True or False*: When insurance companies screen, the same insurance policy will never be sold to different student types at the same price, but it may be the case that students of different types will insure for the same grade.

B. *Now consider the introduction of screening into the self-selection separating equilibrium of Section B of the text. Assume that consumption in the absence of insurance is 10 in the bad state and 250 in the good state and that δ types have a probability of 0.25 of reaching the bad state while θ types have a probability of 0.5 of reaching that state. Suppose further that individuals are risk averse and their tastes are state-independent.

    a. Instead of graphing b on the horizontal and p on the vertical axis, begin by graphing x_2 (consumption in the good state) on the horizontal and x_1 (consumption in the bad state) on the vertical. Indicate with an endowment point E where consumption would be in the absence of insurance.

    b. Illustrate the actuarially fair insurance contracts for the two types of consumers, and indicate the two insurance policies that are offered in a self-selection separating equilibrium.

    c. Suppose a screening industry emerges, an industry of firms that can identify what type an insurance applicant is for a cost of k per applicant. If an insurance firm gives applicants the option of paying

k as an application fee to enable the company to pay a screening firm for this information, would θ types pay it?

   d. What is the highest that k can be in order for δ types to agree to pay the fee? Illustrate this in your graph.

   e. The applicant's decision of whether to pay the fee is really a decision of whether to send a signal. How is this different from the type of signal we analyzed in exercise 22.3? In particular, why does θ's signalling behaviour matter in exercise 22.3 but not here?

   f. Suppose that instead of asking applicants to pay the screening fee, the insurance company paid to get the information from the screening firms for *all* applicants before determining the terms of the insurance contract they offered. Will the highest that k can be to change the self-selection separating equilibrium differ from what you concluded in part (d)?

   g. Will the insurance allocation be efficient if the screening industry ends up selling information to insurance firms?

22.5† **Everyday Application:** *Non-Random Selection Is Everywhere.* The problem in our initial discussion of *A*-grade insurance markets was that adverse selection led to non-randomness in the insurance pool: Although almost everyone was willing to pay the insurance premium that would have made zero expected profit for insurance companies with a randomly selected insurance pool, no one was willing to pay as higher-cost students adversely selected into the pool. This kind of *non-random selection* is, however, not confined to insurance markets but lies at the heart of much that we see around us.

A. Consider the following examples and describe the non-random selection that can cause observers to reach the wrong conclusion, just as insurance companies would charge the wrong premiums if they did not take into account the effect of non-random selection.

   a. Suppose we want to know the average weight of fish in a lake. You take out a boat and fish with a net that has 25cm holes. You fish all day, weigh the fish, take the average and report back.

   b. A TV report tells us the following: A recent study revealed that people who eat broccoli twice a week live an average of 6 years longer than people who do not. The reporter concludes that eating broccoli increases life expectancy.

   c. A cigarette company commissions a study on the impact of smoking on fitness. To compare the average fitness of smokers to that of non-smokers, they recruit smokers and non-smokers at a fitness centre. In particular, they recruit smokers from the aerobics programme and they recruit non-smokers from a weight-loss class. They find that smokers are more fit than non-smokers.

   d. From a sample of dentists that are provided with free dental products by the company that makes the toothbrushes, four out of five dentists recommend this particular toothbrush.

   e. When surveyed after one year of buying and using a facial cream, 95 per cent of women attest to its effectiveness at making their skin look younger.

   f. Children in private schools perform better than children in state schools. Thus, concludes an observer, private schools are better than state schools. Careful: the selection bias may go in either direction!

   g. A study compares the test scores of children from high-income and low-income households and demonstrates that children from high-income households score significantly higher than children from low-income households. An observer concludes that we can narrow this test score gap by redistributing income from high-income families to low-income families.

B. It is often said that the gold standard of social science research is to have a randomized experiment where some subjects are assigned to the treatment group while others are randomly assigned to the control group. Here is an example. A school voucher programme is limited to 1000 voucher participants, but 2000 families apply, with each having their child tested on a standard exam. The administrators of the programme randomly select 1000 families that get the voucher – or the treatment – and treat the remaining 1000 families as the control group. One year later, they test the children again and compare the change in average test scores of children from the two groups. They find that those who were randomly assigned to the treatment group have, on average, significantly higher test scores.

   a. Suppose that all 1000 children in each group participated in the testing that led to the computation of average score changes for each group. Would you be comfortable concluding that it was likely that access to the voucher programme *caused* an increase in student performance?

b. Suppose that only 800 students in each group participated in the testing at the end of the first year of the programme, but they were randomly selected within each group. Would your answer to (a) change if only the average change in test scores for these students were used?

c. Suppose that families had a choice in terms of whether to participate in the testing at the end of the year. Families in the treatment group were told that the only way they can continue using the voucher for another year is to have their child tested; and families in the control group were told that some new slots in the voucher programme would open up because some of the voucher families have dropped out of the programme, but the only way the families in the control group get another chance to be picked to receive a voucher is to have their child tested. In the treatment group, who do you think is more likely to self-select to have their child tested: families that had a good experience with their voucher, or families that had a bad experience?

d. In the control group, who do you think is more likely to self-select to have their child tested: families that had a good experience the previous year outside the voucher programme, or families that had a bad experience?

e. Suppose that 800 students from each group participated in the testing, but now you know about the incentives that families have for showing up to have their child tested. How does this affect your answer to (b)?

f. From a researcher's perspective, how can the non-random selection for testing be described as adverse selection that clouds what you can conclude from looking at average test score differences between the two groups? How is this example similar to part A(c)?

22.6 **Policy Application:** *Statistical Profiling in Random Car Searches.* The police sometimes engage in random searches of cars to look for illegal substances. When one looks at the data of who is actually searched, however, the pattern of searches often does not look random.

A. In what follows, assume that random searches have a deterrent effect; that is, the more likely someone believes they are going to be searched, the less likely they are to engage in transporting illegal substances.

a. Suppose first that it has been documented that, *all else being equal*, illegal substances are more likely to be transported in lorries than in passenger cars. If van owners are searched with the same probability as passenger car owners, the police will be more likely to find illegal substances when they randomly search a van than when they randomly search a passenger vehicle. If the objective by police is to find the most illegal substances given that they have limited resources and thus cannot search everyone, is it optimal for them to search randomly?

b. Suppose the police force decides to allocate its limited resources by searching vans with probability δ and passenger cars with probability γ where $\delta > \gamma$. After a few months of this policy, the police discover that they find on average 2.9 g of illegal substances per van search and 1.5 g of illegal substances per passenger vehicle. Given their limited resources, how would you advise the police to change their search policy in order to increase the amount of drugs found?

c. Given your answer to (b), what has to be true about the probability of finding illegal substances in vans and passenger cars *if* the search probabilities for the two types of vehicles are set optimally relative to the police's objective to find the most illegal substances?

d. If you observe that $\delta > \gamma$, can you conclude that the police are inherently biased against van owners? Why or why not?

e. What would have to be true about the average yield of illegal substances per search for the different types of vehicles for you to argue that the police were inherently biased against vans?

f. Could it be the case that $\delta > \gamma$ *and* the police show behaviour inherently biased against passenger cars?

g. We have used the emotionally neutral categories of vans and passenger vehicles. Now consider the more empirically relevant case of areas with a high proportion of ethnic minorities and areas with mostly indigenous population with the police often searching cars in the former with significantly higher probability than in the latter. Can you argue that such behaviour by the police is not inherently racist in the sense of being motivated by animosity against one group, but that instead it could be explained as a matter of *statistical discrimination* that maximizes the effectiveness of car searches in deterring the trafficking in illegal substances? What evidence might you look for to make your case?

B. Suppose that the police force has sufficient resources to conduct 100 car searches per day and that half of all vehicles are vans and half are passenger cars. The probability of finding an illegal substance in a van is $p_t(n_t) = 9/(90 + n_t)$ where n_t is the number of van searches conducted. The probability of finding an illegal substance in a passenger car is $p_c(n_c) = 1/(10 + n_c)$, where n_c is the number of car searches conducted.

   a. Suppose that the objective of the police is to maximize the number of illegal substances seized. Write down the optimization problem, with n_t and n_c as choice variables and the constraint that $n_t + n_c = 100$.
   b. According to the police's objective function, how many vans should be searched per day? How many passenger vehicles?
   c. If the police conduct searches as calculated in (b), what is the probability of seizing illegal substances in vans? What is the probability of seizing such substances in passenger cars?
   d. If the police search vans and cars at the rates you derived in (b), how many illegal substance seizures would on average occur every day?
   e. How many of each type of car would on average be searched each day if the police instead searched vehicles randomly?
   f. If the police conducted random searches, what would be the probability of finding illegal substances in each of the two vehicle types? How does this compare to your answer to (c)?
   g. How many illegal substance seizures per day would on average occur if the police conducted random searches instead of what you derived in (d)?
   h. Why is your answer to (d) different from your answer to (g)?
   i. Insurance companies charge higher insurance rates to young drivers than to middle-aged drivers. How is their behaviour similar to the behaviour by police who search vans more than passenger cars in (b)?

* conceptually challenging
** computationally challenging
† solutions in Study Guide

PART V

Distortions of the Invisible Hand From Strategic Decisions

In almost everything we have done so far, we have typically assumed that individual decision makers – whether consumers or workers or firms – are sufficiently small relative to the market that they cannot influence market prices, they are price takers. We could call such behaviour non-strategic because in a world where economic actors are so, there is no way to strategically alter their behaviour in order to change the general economic environment that is characterized by prices. This non-strategic or price-taking behaviour was fundamental to the first welfare theorem, a theorem that only holds in competitive price-taking settings assuming no price distortions, externalities or asymmetric information.

In Part 5, we turn to an analysis of *strategic behaviour* that arises in economic settings where individuals are not small relative to their economic environment and where their actions can therefore alter that environment. This takes us beyond the model of competitive markets and permits us to demonstrate how the efficiency prediction of the first welfare theorem ceases to hold when some individuals gain *market power*. If we can think of perfectly competitive markets as one extreme, we can think of perfect *monopoly* in which a single firm is the only one producing a particular good as the opposite extreme. Chapter 23 begins with this opposite extreme and illustrates how such concentrated market power typically leads to inefficiency.

Over the past 50 or so years, game theory has emerged in economics and other social sciences as the primary tool for thinking about strategic behaviour, and we consider this in Chapter 24. It models economic situations in the form of games in which players face incentives similar to those that individuals with market power face in the real world. The competitive model can be reframed as a game theory model in which individuals have no incentive to think strategically, but as the economic environment becomes less competitive, strategic considerations become increasingly important.

Chapters 25 and 26 consider market structures that fall in between the extremes of perfect competition and perfect monopoly, market structures where competitors with market power have to think about what others do before determining what the best course of action is. While different types of imperfect competition certainly represent the most obvious cases where strategic choices become important, there are other interesting topics that involve such strategic thinking. We will conclude Part 5 with two chapters that investigate such topics. In Chapter 27, we will return to the problem of externalities and focus attention on a special type of externality problem that arises when markets, civil society or government provides *public goods*. Chapter 28 concludes our discussion of strategic choices by looking inside the black box of democratic political processes.

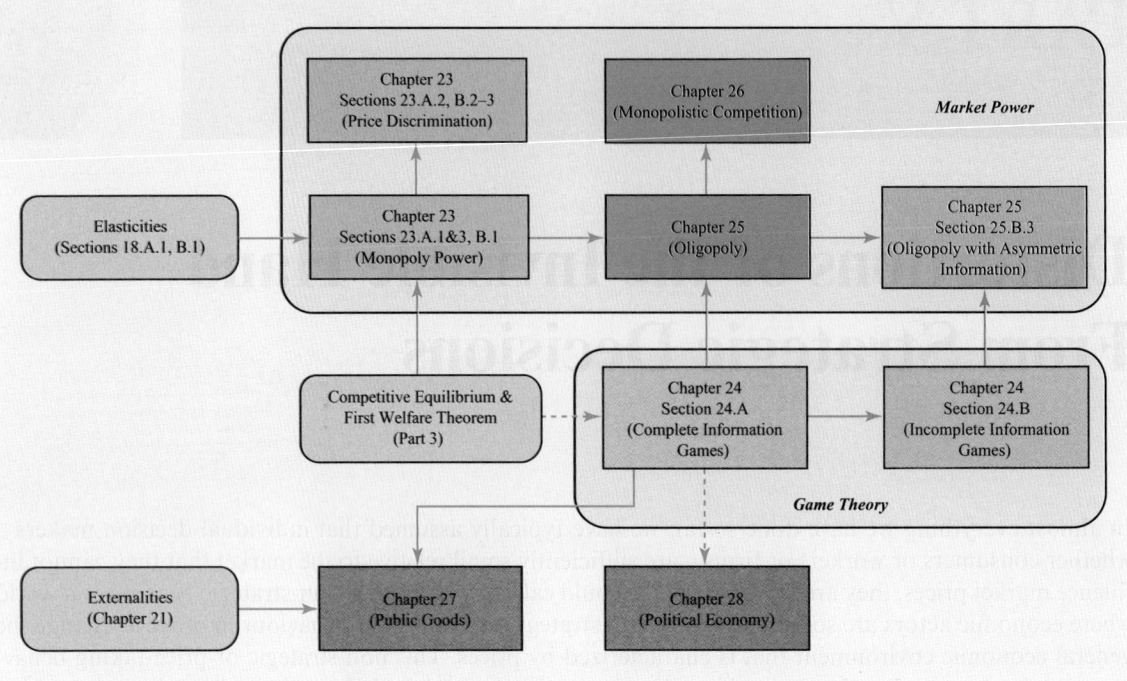

Chapter 23

Monopoly

Under perfect competition, we assumed that industries are composed of so many small firms that each firm has no impact on the economic environment in which decisions are made. As a result, individual firms in an industry take the market price as given as they determine how much to produce in order to maximize profits. In the case of a monopoly the firm must make a decision not only on how much to produce but also on what price to charge. There is, in the case of monopoly, no market to set the price. In this sense, the monopolist has some control over its economic environment that the competitive producer lacks.

While we will often talk about a monopoly as if it was a fixed concept, it is important to keep in mind that monopoly power comes in more and less concentrated doses. Under perfect competition, the demand that a firm faces for its product is perfectly elastic because of the existence of many firms that produce the same product at the market price. Whenever a firm faces a demand curve for its product that is not perfectly elastic, it has some market power. For example, a producer might produce a soft drink in a largely competitive market, but their soft drink is nevertheless a bit distinctive. In a sense, this soft drink is a separate product with a separate market, but in another sense it is part of a larger market in which other firms produce close but imperfect substitutes. The demand curve for the soft drink may not be perfectly elastic, which gives the producer some market power, but that power is limited by the fact that there are close substitutes in the larger soft drink market. If, on top of the existence of close substitutes, there is free entry into the soft-drink market, market power is limited even more.

In other settings there is less of an availability of substitutes for a particular firm's product. If there are market entry barriers that keep potential competitors from producing substitutes, the producer's monopoly power would be considerably more pronounced, and the demand for their product considerably less elastic. For now, we will treat monopolies as firms that face downward-sloping demand curves in an environment where barriers to entry keep other firms from entering to produce substitute goods. The stark model of monopoly in this chapter is an extreme model that rarely holds fully in the real world, but it gives us a good starting point to talk about market power, just as perfect competition gives us a useful starting point to talk about competition.

23A	Pricing Decisions by Monopolist

We begin our analysis of monopoly power by analyzing how the profit-maximizing condition of marginal revenue being equal to marginal cost translates into optimal firm decision making when a firm faces a downward-sloping demand curve. At first, we'll assume that the firm is restricted in its pricing policy in the sense that it can only set a single price per unit of output, a single price that is charged to every consumer. We proceed to think about how a monopoly might want to differentiate the price it charges to different consumers, and under what conditions that is possible. Finally, we consider the kinds of barriers to entry that might result in real-world monopolies, and how the nature of the barrier to entry might determine the extent to which we think monopoly power is a problem that requires government intervention.

The profit-maximization problem under the assumption that the competitive firm takes price as fixed and solves for the profit-maximizing production plan by finding the tangency between isoprofit curves with production frontiers no longer holds for monopolists because the method presumes a fixed price that the price-taking firm takes as given. The two-step profit-maximization method, sees the first step focusing solely on the cost side where firms attempt to minimize cost. This is the same for monopolists. The difference enters in the second step where we compare revenue to cost, with revenue for the monopolist depending on the price that the monopolist chooses rather than the price that is set by the market. We can therefore take everything we learned about *cost curves* – marginal costs, average costs, recurring fixed costs, etc. – and focus on the revenue side in analyzing monopoly decisions.

23A.1 Demand, Marginal Revenue and Profit

For competitive producers, price is the same as marginal revenue. The competitive producer knows they can sell any amount of the good they could feasibly produce at the market price. The marginal revenue received for each good produced is the price set by the interactions of producers and consumers in market equilibrium. The producer could choose to sell goods at a lower price, but that would not be profit maximizing. If, on the other hand, they try to sell goods at a price above the market price, consumers will shop at a competitor. *While the market demand curve in competitive markets is downward sloping, the demand curve for each competitive producer is perfectly elastic at the market price.*

For a monopolist, however, the market demand is the same as the firm's demand since the monopolist is the only producer in the market. As a result, the monopolist gets to choose a point on the market demand curve, which involves a simultaneous choice of how much to produce and how much to charge. When a monopolist decides to increase output, it faces the following trade-off: on the one hand, it can sell more goods to consumers, but on the other, it sells *all* goods at a lower price than before. Thus, as a monopolist increases output, marginal revenue is *not* equal to the price charged initially because it has to lower price in order to sell the additional output.

23A.1.1 Marginal Revenue Along a Market Demand Curve Suppose we consider a demand curve first illustrated in Graph 18.3 and replicated here as panel (a) in Graph 23.1.

Graph 23.1 Linear Demand and Marginal Revenue

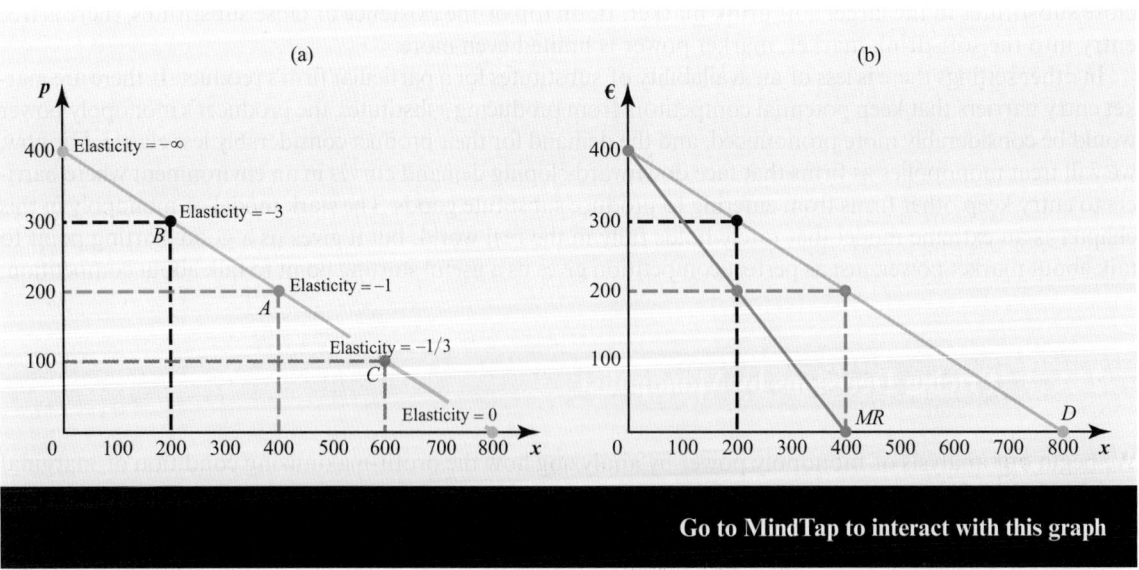

Go to MindTap to interact with this graph

The first unit produced by a monopolist facing such a demand can be sold for approximately €400. The marginal revenue for the first unit of output is approximately €400. Next, suppose the monopolist was currently producing 199 units of the output for €300.50 each. Were this monopolist to produce two additional units of output, it would have to lower price to €299.50 in order to sell all 201 goods. It experiences a €599 increase in total revenues from the 200th and 201st good, but simultaneously loses €1 on each of the first 199 goods produced. Marginal revenue from producing two additional units is therefore €400, or approximately €200 for each of the two units.

Next, suppose that the monopolist was producing 399 units and selling each at €200.50, and then considered producing two additional units. It would have to lower the price to €199.50 in order to sell the additional two units, earning an additional revenue of €399 on those units but losing €399 on the units previously produced because it had to lower the price by €1 for each of the 399 units. Marginal revenue from producing two additional units is 0.

The *marginal revenue curve* for this monopolist is depicted in panel (b) of Graph 23.1. It begins at the same point as the demand curve because the marginal revenue of the first good is approximately €400. When the monopolist is at approximately point *B* on the market demand curve, we demonstrated that marginal revenue from producing an additional unit is approximately €200, and when the monopolist is at approximately point *B* on the demand curve, marginal revenue from producing an additional unit is approximately 0. Connecting these gives us the dark brown line that shares the intercept of the demand curve but has twice the slope.

Exercise 23A.1

What is the marginal revenue of producing an additional good if the producer is at point *C* on the demand curve in Graph 23.1?

23A.1.2 Price Elasticity of Demand and Revenue Maximization Graph 23.1 shows that that marginal revenue is positive when price elasticity is below −1, becomes zero as the price elasticity of demand approaches −1 and becomes negative when price elasticity lies between −1, and 0. This implies that total revenue for the monopolist increases as it moves down the demand curve until it reaches the midpoint where price elasticity is equal to −1, and total revenue falls if it moves beyond that midpoint into the range of the demand curve where price elasticity is between −1 and 0. As a result, *the maximum revenue the monopolist can raise occurs at the midpoint of a linear demand curve where price elasticity is equal to −1.*

Exercise 23A.2

Where does *MR* lie when price elasticity falls between −1 and 0?

This is closely related to our discussion of consumer spending and price elasticity in Chapter18. In Graph 18.4, we illustrated that consumer spending rises with an increase in price along the inelastic portion of demand, while it falls with an increase in price along the elastic portion of demand. For the monopolist, consumer spending is the same as revenue. Thus, *if a monopolist finds themselves on the inelastic portion of demand, it knows it can increase revenue by raising the price. If, on the other hand, it finds itself on the elastic portion of demand, it can increase revenue by lowering price.* Consumer spending, and thus revenue, is therefore maximized when price elasticity of demand is −1.

Exercise 23A.3

Where does a monopolist maximize revenue if it faces a unitary elastic demand curve such as the one in Graph 18.5?

23A.1.3 Profit Maximization for a Monopolist We assume that monopolists aim to maximize *profit*, which is economic revenue minus economic costs. In order for us to see what combination of price and quantity a monopolist will choose, assuming it produces at all, we need to know marginal revenue *and* marginal cost.

Assume that the marginal cost of producing is zero, the monopolist's *MC* curve is a flat line that lies on the horizontal axis in panel (b) of Graph 23.1, intersecting the *MR* curve at 400 units of output. If the monopolist has no variable costs, maximizing revenue and maximizing profit is exactly the same thing, and so the monopolist would choose point *A* on the demand curve where price elasticity is equal to −1. By selling 400 units at €200 each, revenue and profit, not counting recurring fixed costs, is equal to €80 000. As long as recurring fixed costs are not larger than €80 000, the monopolist would choose to produce 400 units of output in both the short and the long run.

Exercise 23A.4

True or False: If recurring fixed costs are €40 000, the monopolist will earn €80 000 in short-run economic profit and €40 000 in long-run economic profit.

Next, suppose that the monopolist has the more common U-shaped *MC* curve depicted in panel (a) in Graph 23.2. If this monopolist produces a positive quantity, it will choose the quantity x^M where *MC* intersects *MR* and charge the price P^M that allows it to sell everything it is producing. As long as the short-run average variable cost at x^M is less than P^M, this implies the monopolist will produce in the short run, and as long as average long-run cost, including recurring fixed costs, at the quantity x^M lies below P^M, it will produce in the long run.

Exercise 23A.5

Suppose *MC* is equal to €200 for all quantities for a monopolist who faces a market demand curve of the type in Graph 23.1. At what point on the demand curve will it choose to produce?

Graph 23.2 Profit Maximization for a Monopolist

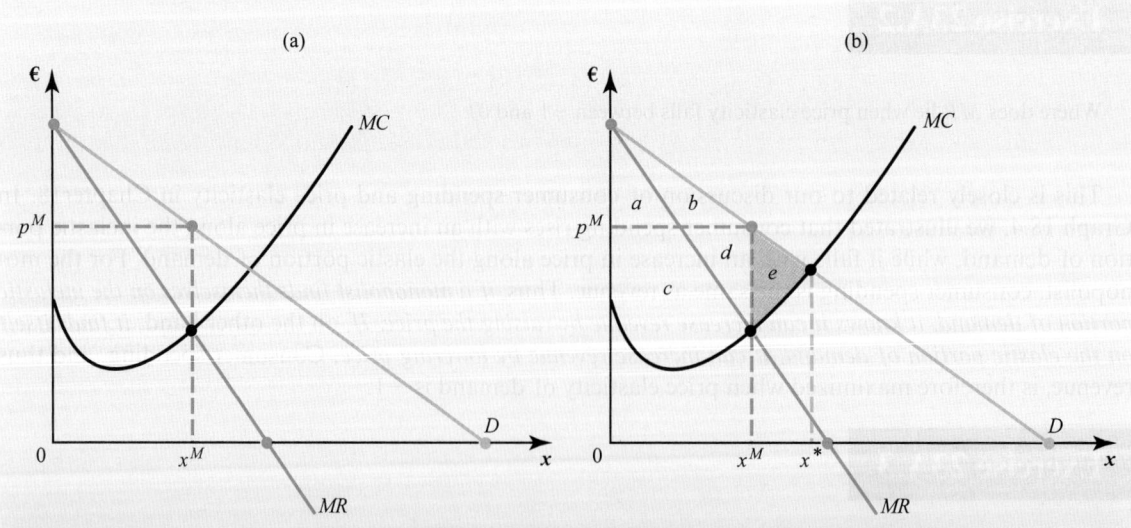

Go to MindTap to interact with this graph

The first thing to note is that *whenever MC is positive, a monopolist will choose to produce on the elastic part of demand*. This is because, for any positive *MC*, the intersection of *MC* and *MR* must lie to the left of the intercept of *MR* with the horizontal axis, which in turn occurs where price elasticity is equal to −1. If a monopolist finds itself on the inelastic portion of demand, it can raise revenue by increasing price and producing less. If producing costs something, this implies that whenever a monopolist is on the inelastic portion of demand, it can raise revenue *and* reduce costs by producing less and charging a higher price. As a result, it makes no sense for a monopolist to produce on the inelastic portion of demand.

Exercise 23A.6

Suppose a deep freeze causes the Spanish orange crop to be reduced by 50 per cent, which causes the price of oranges to increase. As a result, we observe that the total revenues of Spanish orange growers increases. Could the Spanish orange industry be a monopoly?

The concept of a supply curve we developed for competitive firms does not make any sense when we talk about monopolists. A supply curve illustrates the relationship between the price set by the market and the quantity of output produced by a profit-maximizing firm. A monopolist does not have a market that sets price; the monopolist sets the price. Thus, for any given demand curve and any technology that results in cost curves, the monopolist picks a *supply point*.

23A.1.4 Monopoly and Deadweight Loss We can see in Graph 23.2 that the profit-maximizing monopolist will produce an *inefficiently low quantity*. In panel (b) of the graph, consumer surplus assuming no income effects can be identified as area (*a* + *b*) and monopolist surplus in the short run, or in the absence of recurring fixed costs, as area (*c* + *d*). There are additional units of output that could be produced at a marginal cost below the value consumers place on that output. Such additional output could be produced all the way up to the intersection of *MC* and demand at output x^*, and additional surplus of (*e*) could be produced if a benevolent social planner rather than a monopolist were in charge of production. Area (*e*) is a *deadweight loss, which arises because the monopolist strategically restricts output in order to raise price to its profit-maximizing level*.

Notice that the deadweight loss does *not* arise because the monopolist makes a profit. Even if a social planner forced the monopolist to produce the quantity x^* and sell it at the appropriate price along the demand curve, the monopolist might make a profit; the profit just would not be as large as it is when the monopolist raises price to p^M and restricts output. The deadweight loss emerges from the fact that the monopolist is using its power to strategically restrict output in order to raise price. The monopolist's market power causes self-interest to come into conflict with the social good – at least when the social good is measured in efficiency terms – unless something else interferes and causes the monopolist to produce more.

Exercise 23A.7

Suppose that demand is as depicted in Graph 23.1 and *MC* = 0. What is the monopolist's profit-maximizing output level and what is the efficient output level? What if *MC* = 300?

Exercise 23A.8

True or False: Depending on the shape of the *MC* curve, the efficient output level might lie on the elastic or the inelastic portion of the demand curve.

Exercise 23A.9

True or False: In the presence of negative production externalities, a monopolist may produce the efficient quantity of output.

Exercise 23A.10

True or False: If demand were not equal to marginal willingness to pay due to the presence of income effects on the consumer side, the deadweight loss area may be larger or smaller but would nevertheless arise.

23A.1.5 Monopoly Rent-Seeking Behaviour and Deadweight Loss We have demonstrated that monopolists are able to achieve economic profits if they have secured monopoly power in some way. We have demonstrated that this economic profit comes at a social cost as the monopolist produces below the socially optimal level in order to raise price above marginal cost, and we have denoted that social cost as deadweight loss. The deadweight loss may be larger because firms may engage in socially wasteful activity in order to secure and maintain the monopoly power that gives it the opportunity to generate economic profits.

There are a variety of ways in which barriers to entry that lead to monopoly power can arise. One possibility is that monopoly power is granted through government intervention, with governments granting to a single firm the exclusive right to produce a certain product. In such circumstances, firms may compete for government favour, in the process expending resources on lobbying politicians. The maximum amount that a firm would be willing to invest in order to secure a government-granted monopoly is equal to the present discounted value of the future profits the firm can expect to make from exercising its monopoly power. It is conceivable that firms will expend resources equal to their monopoly profits in order to get the monopoly power, and it is similarly conceivable that many of these resources are spent in socially wasteful ways. This is referred to as *political rent seeking*. To the extent to which the resources spent on political rent seeking are socially wasteful, this would add to deadweight loss beyond what we have derived in our graphs thus far.

23A.2 Market Segmentation and Price Discrimination

So far, we have assumed that the monopolist is constrained in the sense that it can only charge a single price to all of its customers. This is the case when a monopolist cannot effectively differentiate between consumers and their marginal willingness to pay for its product, or when charging different prices to different consumers, a practice known as *price discrimination,* is illegal. Let us assume that price discrimination, is permitted *and* that the monopolist can *segment* the set of consumers into those who are willing to pay relatively more and those who are willing to pay relatively less. Even when a monopolist can segment the market into different types of consumers, it must also have some way of *preventing resale* to keep those consumers who purchase the product at a low price from selling to those who are being offered the same product at a higher price.

We will illustrate three different ways in which monopolists may price-discriminate under different circumstances. First, the case where monopolists can perfectly identify each consumer's demand and can offer each consumer a particular quantity at a particular overall price for that quantity. One way to achieve this is to charge each consumer both a fixed fee for the right to purchase and a per-unit price for each unit that is purchased, with both the fee and the per-unit price potentially differing across consumers. This is known as *perfect* or *first-degree price discrimination*. A case where the monopolist, while still being able to identify each consumer's demand perfectly, can offer different *per-unit prices* but no fixed fees to different customers who potentially want to buy multiple units of the good is called *imperfect* or *third-degree price discrimination*. Finally, the case where a monopolist knows that there are different types of consumers with different demands, but it does not know what type each particular consumer is and where the monopolist can construct price/quantity packages or combinations of fixed fees and per-unit prices that cause customers to reveal their type, is known as *second-degree price discrimination*.

23A.2.1 Perfect or First-Degree Price Discrimination Assume that the monopolist knows all of its customers extremely well and can perfectly ascertain each consumer's willingness to pay for its product. For example, assume Jan is an artist who has his own studio and gallery and is the only one who produces his unique type of art. He knows his customers personally and invites them individually to sip wine while viewing his art. To make the analysis as simple as possible, let's further suppose that each of Jan's clients will buy a single piece of art.

The demand curve for Jan's art is composed of many different individuals who each place a certain value on one of his pieces. As he produces his art, he can invite first the individual who places the most value on his art, and who sits at the very top of the demand curve that Jan faces. Suppose this individual places a value of €10 000 on Jan's art. In that case, he will charge that individual exactly €10 000. The second biggest fan might place a value of only €9900 on Jan's art. He can sell a piece of art to this individual for exactly €9900. Jan's marginal revenue for the first piece was €10 000, and the marginal revenue for the second piece was €9900. Since he can charge different prices to each of his clients, he can produce a second piece of art without foregoing any profit on the first piece. As a result, *the demand curve becomes his marginal revenue curve when he can price-discriminate perfectly* between all his clients.

Graph 23.3 illustrates the behaviour by a profit-maximizing producer who can perfectly price-discriminate in this way. Since demand is equal to MR, this producer chooses to produce x^M where MC intersects demand. No single price is charged because each consumer is charged exactly what they are willing to pay for each good along the market demand curve. Consumers therefore attain no surplus, and all the surplus, equal to the shaded area, accrues to the monopolist. In the process, the efficient quantity is supplied.

Graph 23.3 Perfect Price Discrimination

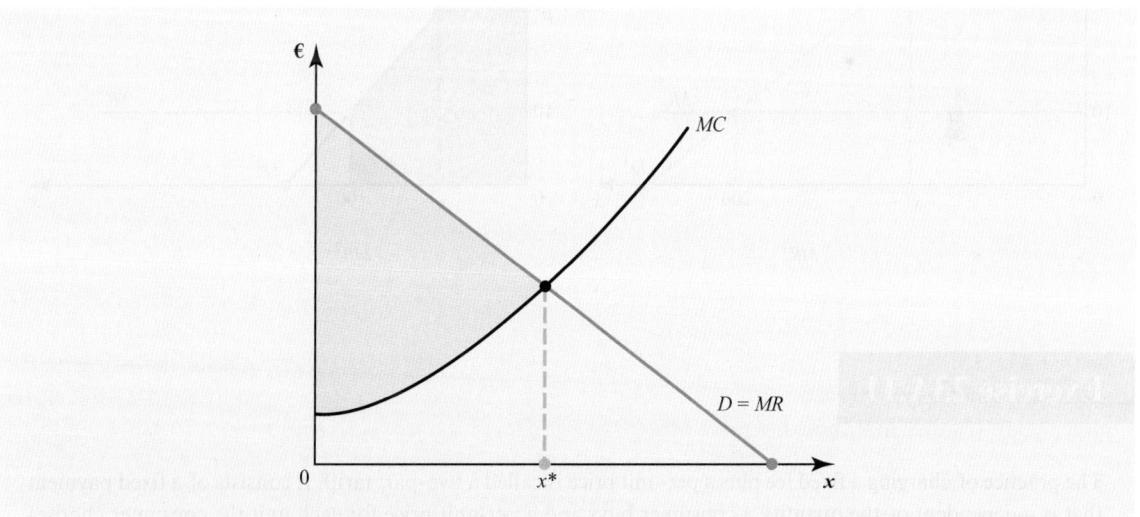

This form of *perfect price discrimination*, when extended to cases in which consumers might purchase multiple units and are thus charged their exact marginal willingness to pay for *each* unit they purchase, is also referred to as *first-degree price discrimination*. While it leads to an efficient quantity of output, it clearly leaves consumers worse off than the non-price-discriminating outcome in the previous section. This is because consumers now attain no consumer surplus while they do attain some consumer surplus, albeit at a lower output level, when there is no price discrimination. Efficiency is a statement about the maximum overall surplus and says nothing about whether the *distribution* of the surplus is desirable.

23A.2.2 Imperfect or Third-Degree Price Discrimination Perfect price discrimination assumes that a monopolist can not only identify perfectly each consumer type's demand but can also charge an amount that is exactly equal to each consumer's total willingness to pay. In our hypothetical example of Jan's art studio, we assumed that each consumer only demands one piece of art, implicitly assuming that the marginal value of the second piece is zero for each consumer. As a result, perfect price discrimination meant that Jan arrived at an individualized price equal to exactly each consumer's willingness to pay for one piece of art.

More generally, consumers have downward-sloping demand curves and thus place value on more than one unit of output. Consider, for instance, two types of consumers whose demands are given as D^1 and D^2 in panels (a) and (b) of Graph 23.4. Assume that the producer faces a constant marginal cost of €10 per unit of output. Under perfect price discrimination, the producer would sell 200 units of the output to type 1 consumers and 100 units of the output to type 2 consumers, and it would charge type 1 consumers the entire shaded dark brown area in panel (a) and type 2 consumers the entire shaded dark blue area in panel (b). When consumers place value on more than one good, perfect price discrimination implies that the monopolist will not charge a per-unit price but rather a single price for all the units sold to a consumer together or, equivalently, a fixed fee plus a per-unit price.

Graph 23.4 Imperfect, Third-Degree Price Discrimination

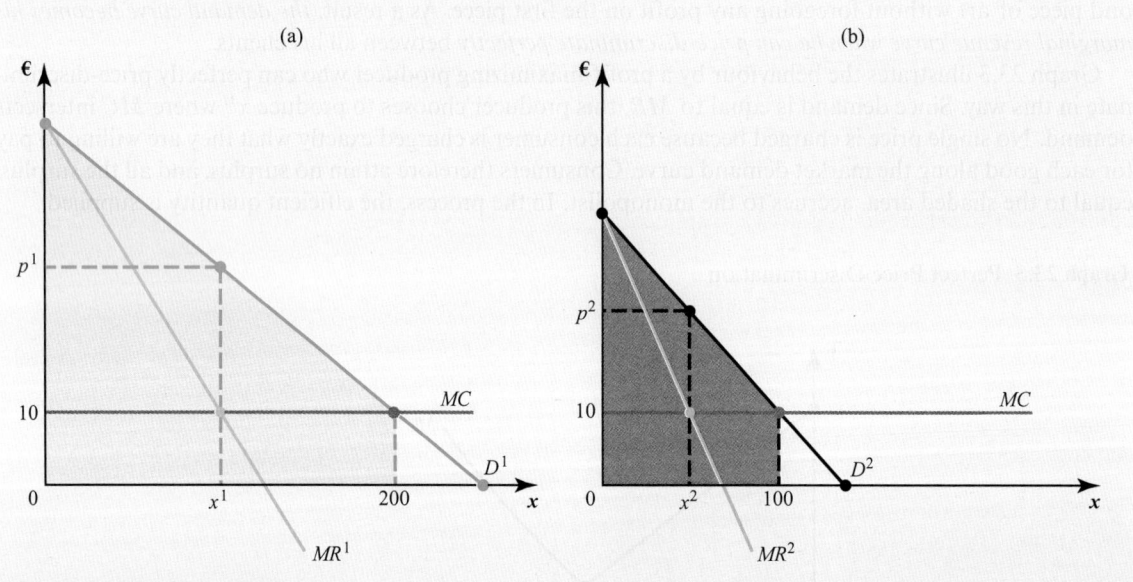

Exercise 23A.11

The practice of charging a fixed fee plus a per-unit price is called a two-part tariff. It consists of a fixed payment that is independent of the quantity a consumer buys and a per-unit price for each unit the consumer chooses to purchase. Can you identify in Graph 23.4 which portion would be the fixed payment and what would be the per-unit price for each of the two consumers if the two-part tariff is implemented by a perfectly price-discriminating monopolist?

In many situations, this seems rather unrealistic. Instead, it might be that a monopolist who can identify different types of consumers is restricted to charging a per-unit price for the goods, a price that can differ across different types of consumers but remains constant for any amount a particular consumer chooses to purchase. If this is the case, the monopolist can typically no longer perfectly price-discriminate in the sense of capturing all consumer surplus but will rather price-discriminate imperfectly. Such price discrimination is also known as *third-degree price discrimination*.

For our example in Graph 23.4, this would imply that the monopolist determines the marginal revenue curve for each of the two types of consumers and sets output where the constant MC intersects MR. This leads the monopolist to charge the price p^1 to type 1 consumers, with those consumers choosing to consume x^1 in panel (a). Similarly, a potentially different price p^2 would be charged to type 2 consumers who would consume x^2 in panel (b). Thus, when monopolists can charge a per-unit price that differs across identifiable consumer types, it will restrict output below what it would be under efficient first-degree price discrimination. As a result, a deadweight loss will arise under imperfect or third-degree price discrimination.

Exercise 23A.12

In our example of Jan running his art studio and selling to consumers who place value only on the first piece of art they purchase, is there a difference between first-and third-degree price discrimination? Explain.

While we know that deadweight loss will emerge under third-degree price discrimination, it is not clear whether eliminating the ability by the monopolist to price-discriminate in this way will lead to greater or less deadweight loss. If such price discrimination were deemed illegal, the monopolist would revert to charging a single price to all consumers, which would entail a lower price for the high demanders and a higher price for the low demanders. Conceivably, this uniform price could be such that low demanders will no longer consume *any* of the good, leading to the effective closing of the market in the low-demand consumer sector. The welfare losses sustained by low demanders combined with the reduction in profit for monopolists would have to be weighed against the welfare gains by high demanders. Depending on the types of demand the different consumers have, the elimination of third-degree price discrimination could lead to either a welfare improvement if the high demanders gain more than the low demanders and the monopolist lose, or an additional welfare loss if the low demanders and the monopolist lose more than the high demanders gain. Without knowing the specifics in any particular case of third-degree price discrimination, it is not possible to make a uniform efficiency-based policy recommendation on how to treat monopolists who engage in third-degree price discrimination.

Exercise 23A.13

Why do we not run into similar problems of ambiguity in thinking about the welfare effects of first-degree price discrimination?

23A.2.3 Non-Linear Pricing and Second-Degree Price Discrimination
Sometimes there are external signals that a firm can use to infer the type of consumer it is facing. Cinemas know that students will generally have different demands than adults in the labour force, and they may therefore offer student prices that are different from regular prices and not available to non-students. This is an example of third-degree price discrimination. In many real-world circumstances, firms do not have such external signals and therefore are unsure of what types of consumers they face at any given moment. It is often difficult to tell just by looking at someone whether that person is a high demander or a low demander, even if a firm knows how many high demanders there are relative to low demanders.

Even in such cases, however, the monopolist can try to find ways of increasing profit through market segmentation and strategic pricing. Since the monopolist cannot tell what type of consumer it is facing, it has to structure pricing in such a way as to give the incentive to consumers to self-identify who they are.

This involves the setting of *a single non-linear price schedule*, or *offering different quantities of the good at different prices*. Such a pricing strategy does not explicitly discriminate between different consumers because all consumers are offered the same price schedule for different quantities of the good. Consumers end up paying different average prices *based on their choices* once they see the non-linear price schedule the monopolist posts.

Assume that the monopolist knows it has two types of customers, just as in Graph 23.4, but it cannot tell in any particular instance which type of consumer has entered its shop; all it knows is that there is an equal number of both types of consumers in the economy. In panel (a) of Graph 23.5, we illustrate the dark brown type 1 demand curve D^1 and the dark blue type 2 demand curve D^2 within the same picture and again assume a constant marginal cost of €10 per unit of output. If the monopolist could price-discriminate perfectly, it would want to offer 200 units of output to type 1 consumers and charge the entire area under D^1 that is, €2000 + a + b + c. Similarly, it would want to offer 100 units of the output to type 2 consumers and charge the entire area under D^2 that is, €1000 + a. This would result in no consumer surplus and a surplus for the monopolist of $2a + b + c$ assuming there is one consumer of each type.

Graph 23.5 Second-Degree Price Discrimination

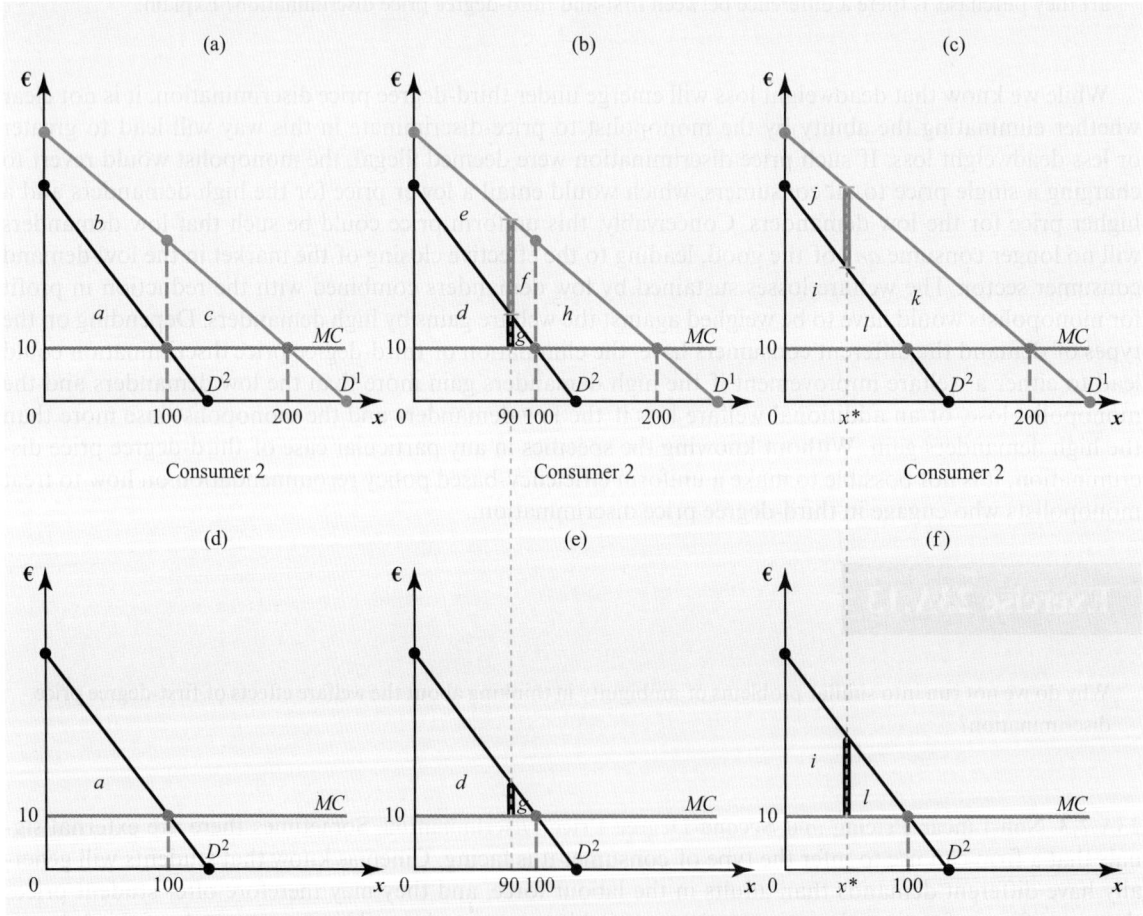

When the monopolist cannot tell which consumers are type 1 and which are type 2, it cannot implement this perfect price discrimination neither can it implement the third-degree price discrimination from Graph 23.4. This is because type 1 consumers now have an incentive to pretend to be type 2 consumers, purchase 100 units at the price €1000 + a, and get consumer surplus of (b). Were the monopolist to offer the 100 and 200 unit packages at the first-degree price-discriminating prices, it could look ahead and know that no one will pick the 200-unit package, leaving them with surplus of only ($2a$).

Exercise 23A.14

Why would the monopolist not be able to offer two per-unit prices as in Graph 23.4?

In order to induce type 1 consumers to behave differently from type 2 consumers, the monopolist must come up with a different set of price/quantity packages. For instance, the monopolist might continue to offer 100 units at the price €1000 + a, while reducing the price of 200 units to €2000 + a + b. This would equalize the surplus a type 1 consumer will get under the two packages, and knocking off even a cent more from the 200-unit package would therefore make it optimal for type 1 consumers to pick 200 units. As a result, the monopolist would be able to expect a surplus of $2a + c$, which is larger than the surplus of $(2a)$ it could expect under the previous price/quantity combinations.

Exercise 23A.15

In exercise 23A.12, we introduced the notion of a two-part tariff. Can you express the pricing suggested in the preceding paragraph in terms of two-part tariffs?

In panel (b) of Graph 23.5 and in the accompanying chart, however, we can see that the monopolist can do even better by making the package targeted at type 2 consumers less attractive in order to be able to charge more for the package containing 200 units. Consider, for instance, the scenario under which the monopolist offers a package with 90 units and another with 200 units. Type 2 consumers will be willing to buy the 90 units at a price of €900 + d but now the monopolist can charge €2000 + d + f + g + h for the 200-unit package, giving an overall surplus of $2d + f + g + h$. The surplus of $2a + c$ in panel (a) is the same as the surplus of $2d + 2g + h$ in panel (b), which implies that the monopolist's surplus has changed by $f - g$ as it switched from offering the 100-unit package to offering a 90-unit package instead. Area (f) is larger than area (g), so profit has increased.

Toward Second-Degree Price Discrimination

	With 100 Unit *Low-Demand* Package	With 90 Unit *Low-Demand* Package	
Profit from *Low-Demand* Type	$d + g$	d	Making the low-demand package less attractive increases profit by $(f - g)$.
Profit from *High-Demand* Type	$d + g + h$	$d + g + f + h$	
Total Profit	$2d + 2g + h$	$2d + g + f + h$	

Once the monopolist recognizes that it can earn higher profit by reducing the attractiveness of the package targeted at type 2 consumers, it can do even better. In panel (b) of the graph, the vertical dark blue distance represents the approximate loss in profit from type 2 consumers if the monopolist decreases the type 2 package by another unit from 90 to 89, while the vertical dark brown distance represents the approximate increase in profit from type 1 consumers that can now be charged a higher price for the 200-unit package. The monopolist can increase profit by reducing the type 2 package as long as the vertical dark blue distance is shorter than the vertical dark brown distance. A forward-looking monopolist would reduce the type 2 package to a quantity x^* where the two distances are equal to one another. This is represented in panel (c) of the graph.

Exercise 23A.16

What price will the profit-maximizing monopolist charge for x^* and for 200 units in panel (c) of Graph 23.5?

Exercise 23A.17

We have assumed in our example that there is an equal number of type 1 and type 2 consumers in the economy. How would our analysis change if the monopolist knew that there were twice as many type 1 consumers as type 2 consumers?

Exercise 23A.18

In Chapter 22, we analyzed situations in which there is asymmetric information between consumers and producers, as in the insurance market. Explain how the problems faced by an insurance company that does not know the risk types of its consumers are similar to the problem faced by the monopolist who is trying to second-degree price-discriminate?

This example is just one of many that might arise for a monopolist who seeks to price-discriminate between different customers whose type it cannot identify. In the real world, the packages offered to different types of consumers may also vary in ways that are related to quality and not just quantity. For instance, in the airline industry, fares for the same flights are often priced quite differently for business and leisure travellers, with business travellers facing fewer restrictions on when and how they can change their tickets.

23A.3 Barriers to Entry and Remedies for Inefficient Monopoly Behaviour

So far, we have assumed that a particular firm has a monopoly in the market for good x, but how does a firm get such monopoly status in the first place, and how does it hold onto it? *There must exist some barrier to entry* of new firms in order for a monopoly to be able to earn long-run positive profits. Such a barrier might emerge from the technological nature of production, or it may come about through legislation that limits or prohibits competition in some markets.

23A.3.1 Technological Barriers to Entry and Natural Monopolies In our discussion of perfectly competitive firms, we never considered the case of a firm that has increasing returns to scale for all output quantities. We focused on firms that may have increasing returns to scale in their production process for low levels of output but eventually face decreasing returns to scale as output increases. It is because of this assumption that MC and AC curves eventually sloped up. While we argued in Chapter 11 that the logic of scarcity requires that marginal product of each input eventually diminishes, there is no particular reason that the production process itself cannot have increasing returns to scale over very large ranges of inputs.

Assume the production process for good x always has increasing returns to scale. This implies that the MC curve is always downward sloping and always lies below AC, which further implies that any price-taking firm will either produce nothing at a particular price or will produce an infinite quantity of the good. In a world of scarcity, consumers will not demand an infinite quantity of the good at a positive price, which implies that the assumption of price-taking behaviour on the part of the firm is not reasonable under increasing returns to scale. It is for this reason that no competitive industry can have firms whose production process always has increasing returns to scale.

Similar logic applies when a production process has a large initial or a significant recurring fixed cost together with a constant marginal cost, a case that is illustrated in panel (a) of Graph 23.6. This can arise in many different contexts. For instance, a large investment in research and development may be required prior to the production of a vaccine, but once the research is complete, the vaccine can be produced easily at constant MC. Or a utility company might have to invest a large amount in laying electricity lines within a city in order to be able to provide electricity to everyone at a constant MC. Or a software company might work for years to produce a piece of software that can be offered at virtually no marginal cost by having customers download it from the internet.

A *natural monopoly* is defined as *a firm that faces an AC curve that declines at all output quantities*. This declining AC curve can be due to increasing returns to scale everywhere or due to the presence of a recurring fixed cost with constant marginal cost. In either case, we cannot identify a supply curve that is equal to the MC curve above AC because MC never lies above AC. It is therefore natural for a single firm to emerge as a monopoly.

Exercise 23A.19

Can you see in panel (a) of Graph 23.6 that a price-taking firm facing a downward-sloping AC curve would produce either no output or an infinite amount of the output depending on what the price is?

Exercise 23A.20

Suppose the technology is such that AC is U-shaped, but the upward-sloping part of the U-shape happens at an output level that is high relative to market demand. Can the same natural monopoly situation arise?

Panels (b) and (c) of Graph 23.6 add demand and MR curves to the cost curves from panel (a). In panel (b), demand is relatively high, and the usual profit-maximizing single price p^M, read off the demand curve at quantity x^M where MC and MR intersect, results in a positive profit for the monopoly firm assuming no recurring fixed costs. In panel (c), on the other hand, demand is relatively low, causing the monopoly to make a loss if it produced where MR intersects MC.

Graph 23.6 A Natural Monopoly

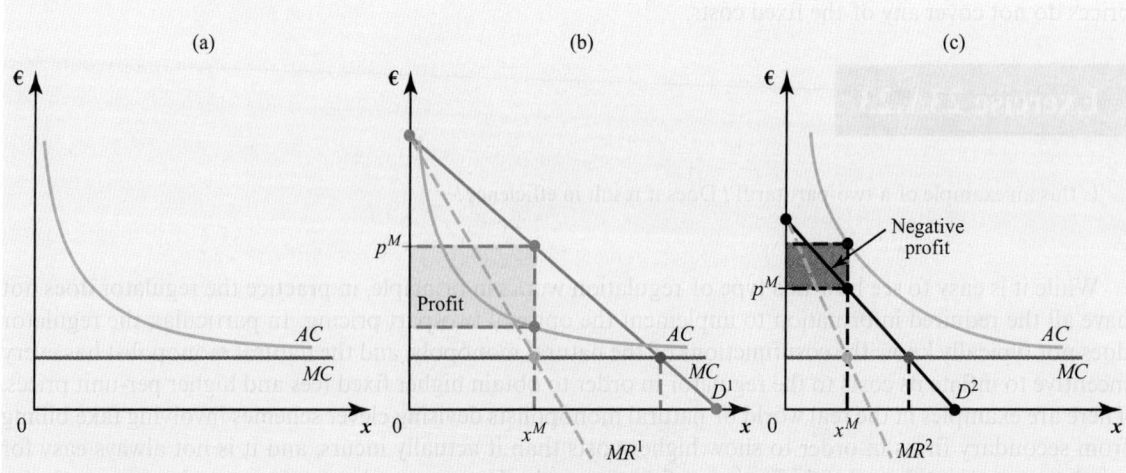

In order for a firm facing the situation in panel (c) to make a positive profit, it would have to price output differently, employing some variant of the price discrimination strategies discussed in the previous section. In the absence of being able to identify different consumer types, this implies that in order to produce, the firm would have to engage in a form of pricing that involves more than just a single per-unit price. The most common such strategy for natural monopolists in the absence of price regulation is to charge a fixed fee plus a per-unit price – a two-part tariff. In the case of utility companies, for instance, there might be a fixed service fee per month plus a price per unit of electricity consumed.

Because the technological constraints are such that multiple firms in such industries would entail higher per-unit costs, governments have often favoured *regulation* of natural monopolies over alternative policies to address the deadweight loss from monopoly pricing. Such regulation typically focuses on pricing policies that guarantee a fair market return for the natural monopolist while moving production closer to the socially optimal level. Given that the fixed cost is a sunk cost once the monopolist is operating, efficiency would require output where MC crosses the demand curve. Because AC lies above MC, forcing the natural monopolist to price the output at MC would imply negative profits for the monopolist.

Exercise 23A.21

In a graph similar to panel (b) of Graph 23.6, illustrate the negative profit that arises when the monopolist is forced to price at MC.

Exercise 23A.22

Suppose the fixed cost is a one-time fixed entry cost that is sufficiently large to result in a picture like panel (c). *True or False*: If the government pays the fixed cost for the firm, it will not have to regulate the firm in order to make sure the firm makes a profit, but the monopoly outcome will be inefficient.

If the monopolist faces high recurring fixed costs, regulators who attempt to achieve efficient output levels in natural monopolies might aim to set price at MC and allow monopolists to charge an additional fixed fee that each customer has to pay independent of the level of consumption. For instance, an electricity provider might charge a fixed connection fee and a per-unit price for each unit of electricity consumed, or a phone company might charge a fixed monthly fee plus a per minute charge for phone calls made. The fixed fees can be set in such a way as to make the natural monopoly profitable even though the per-unit prices do not cover any of the fixed costs.

Exercise 23A.23

Is this an example of a two-part tariff? Does it result in efficiency?

While it is easy to see how this type of regulation works in principle, in practice the regulator does not have all the required information to implement the optimal two-part pricing. In particular, the regulator does not typically know the cost functions of the natural monopoly, and the natural monopolist has every incentive to inflate its costs to the regulator in order to obtain higher fixed fees and higher per-unit prices. There are examples in the real world of natural monopolists devising clever schemes involving fake billing from secondary firms in order to show higher costs than it actually incurs, and it is not always easy for regulators to identify such falsifications of cost records. The monopolist furthermore has no particular incentive to find innovative ways of lowering costs through technological innovations even if it is perfectly honest in how it reports the costs actually incurred.

For some of these reasons, more recent policy approaches have made an effort to introduce competition into some industries that face these cost curves by having the government pay the fixed costs that cause AC curves to be downward sloping. In the utility industry, for instance, the government could lay and maintain the electricity lines to all the houses in a region and allow any utility company to use these lines in order to distribute electricity to individual houses. It is much like the government laying a system of roads that different haulage companies can use to deliver goods. With the fixed costs paid by the government, individual electricity suppliers have only variable costs, and thus flat or upward-sloping MC curves. It becomes possible for many different electricity providers to compete for households, with households choosing a provider based on quality of service and price.

Exercise 23A.24

Assume a private company is charged with laying all the infrastructure and charges competing electricity firms to use the electrical grid. How might this raise a different set of efficiency issues related to monopoly pricing? Would these issues still arise if the government auctioned off the right to build an electricity grid to a single private company?

23A.3.2 Legal Barriers to Entry Legal barriers might derive from general patent and copyright laws that grant the exclusive right to produce particular products for a certain number of years to those firms that were awarded the patent or copyright. The motivation behind such laws is not to encourage the formation of monopolies, but rather to provide incentives for innovations by ensuring that innovators can profit from their activities for some period.

Patent and copyright laws are not, however, the only legal barriers to entry. As we have seen, free entry in the absence of technological barriers tends to drive economic profits to zero. Thus, if a firm can successfully lobby the government to protect it from competitors, it will invest resources to accomplish this if the required resources are smaller than the present discounted value of the monopoly profits the firm can expect to earn if legal barriers to entry were erected. To the extent to which such lobbying involves socially wasteful activities, the deadweight loss from government-created monopolies may exceed the loss due to the decline in production that results under monopoly profit maximization.

Monopoly power has been granted by governments to a variety of firms throughout history. In the 15th and 16th centuries, for instance, the British Crown awarded exclusive rights to shipping companies to establish trade routes to the West Indies and other parts of the world. The UK government granted the exclusive right to collect and deliver letters to the Royal Mail, a monopoly which lasted for over 350 years and which ended in 2006. More recently, the UK government also granted exclusive rights to firms to operate certain rail franchises. In each of these cases, the firm that attained the exclusive rights to serve a particular market benefits from the government's entry barriers, and as a result it might have a vested interest in engaging in socially wasteful lobbying activities in order to retain its monopoly power.

23A.3.3 Restraining Monopoly Power While governments have been prime culprits of granting monopoly power to certain firms, the increasing awareness of potential social losses from the exercise of monopoly power has also led to government policies aimed at restraining monopolies. The question of when and under what circumstances government intervention is desirable is a complicated one. The tendency of monopolies to limit output in order to raise price has the clear deadweight loss implications that we have discussed. At the same time, patent protection of innovation may have led to the emergence of products that might otherwise never have seen the light of day, implying the creation of social surplus despite the fact that, at any given moment, more surplus could be gained by forcing monopolies to produce more. The existence of increasing returns to scale or high fixed costs in certain industries implies that natural monopolies may lower per-unit costs even as they attempt to use their monopoly status to raise price above marginal cost.

Some of the potential remedies that one might think of applying to monopolies are either ineffective or counter-productive. These include per-unit taxes and profit taxes. We have already noted that attempts to directly regulate the pricing of monopoly goods run into informational constraints because regulators typically do not know the real costs of firms and because such regulation would give little incentive for cost innovations by monopolies. This does not imply that regulation in some circumstances is not the appropriate policy, but it does imply that regulation is no panacea in all cases. In some instances, governments have forced the break-up of monopolies, and in other cases they have found ways of addressing the root causes of natural monopolies by disconnecting the fixed cost infrastructure from the marginal cost provision of services. Governments have furthermore actively blocked mergers of large companies that might have resulted in excessive monopoly power. Finally, there has been an increasing trend towards deregulation of industries where regulation itself such as in the airline industry in some countries created monopolies to begin with.

In many circumstances, however, the most effective tool for restraining monopoly power has little to do with direct government actions and more to do with the fact that when a monopoly does exercise its power to create profit, there is a powerful incentive for entrepreneurs to find new ways to challenge that monopoly power. A firm may, for instance, have captured a large portion of the market, perhaps for no other reason than being first and making early, strategically smart decisions as in the case of Microsoft and its Windows operating system. There is no doubt that such firms will use their monopoly power to their advantage, but they may also be more cognizant of the threat of competitors that may find ways of producing substitutes than our simple static models of monopoly behaviour predict. The more a firm exercises its monopoly power, the greater is the incentive for others to find ways of producing such substitutes, and a forward-looking monopolist should take that into account when setting current prices. Sometimes barriers to entry that may seem very strong at one time can fall quickly with new technological innovations, as, for instance, with the sudden emergence of mobile phone technology, internet calling and cable provision of telephone service that are challenging traditional phone companies. In such environments, governments can play an important role in ensuring that existing firms, such as traditional phone companies, do not successfully erect barriers of entry through legislation or regulation by prohibiting, for instance, internet providers from providing telephone services. Just as there exists a powerful incentive for innovators to find ways of breaking barriers to entry by existing firms, there is a similarly powerful incentive on the part of existing firms to find other ways of shoring up these barriers to entry in order to preserve market power.

Exercise 23A.25

In the 1970s when OPEC countries raised world prices for oil substantially by exercising their market power, the Saudi oil minister is said to have warned them: 'Remember, the Stone Age did not end because we ran out of stones'. Explain what he meant and how his words relate to constraints that monopolies face.

23B The Mathematics of Monopoly

From a mathematical point of view, monopolies engage in the same optimization problem that competitive firms undertake except that monopolies have additional choice variables. Both types of firms face some cost function that emerges from the cost minimization problem and tells them the total cost $c(x)$ of producing any quantity x. We should note at the outset that for much of this section we will assume that $dc(x)/dx = c$; that is, the firm faces a constant marginal cost.

Exercise 23B.1

Explain why the cost minimization problem in the firm's duality picture of Chapter 13 is identical for firms regardless of whether they are monopolies or perfect competitors.

A monopoly that is restricted to charging a single per-unit price solves the problem:

$$\max_{x,p} \pi = px - c(x) \text{ subject to } p \le p(x), \tag{23.1}$$

where the price the monopolist charges when trying to sell the quantity x cannot be greater than the price for that quantity given by the inverse demand function $p(x)$. The perfect competitor's problem could be written in exactly the same way, except that for the perfect competitor the inverse demand function is $p(x) = p^*$, where p^* is the market price. Thus, price ceases to be a choice variable when price is set by the competitive market, but it is a choice variable for a monopolist who faces a downward-sloping demand curve.

Since the monopolist will set price as high as it can while still selling all the goods produced, the inequality in equation (23.1) will bind; that is, $p = p(x)$. The monopolist's problem can therefore be rewritten as:

$$\max_{x} \pi = p(x)x - c(x). \tag{23.2}$$

Note that by choosing profit-maximizing optimal quantity x^M, the monopolist implicitly chooses the profit-maximizing price $p^M = p(x^M)$ once we have substituted the constraint into the objective function of the optimization problem. Because of the resulting one-to-one mapping from quantity to price, the monopolist's problem could alternatively be written as:

$$\max_{p} \pi = px(p) - c(x(p)), \tag{23.3}$$

where $x(p)$ is the market demand function as opposed to the inverse market demand function $p(x)$ in the previous problem. Whether we view the monopolist as choosing quantity as in equation (23.1) or price as in equation (23.3), the same monopoly quantity and price will emerge.

When a monopolist is not restricted to charging a single per-unit price, it has additional decisions to make as we have seen in our discussion of price discrimination in Section A. The exact nature of that choice problem depends on what the firm knows and what pricing strategies are available to the firm. If the firm can identify consumer types prior to consumption choices by consumers, first- and third-degree price discrimination become possible, assuming resale can be prevented, and if the firm only knows the distribution of consumer types in the population, second-degree price discrimination becomes possible. Different forms of such discrimination are restricted by the types of pricing schedules that firms are permitted to post. Fundamentally the firm is still just maximizing profit by making production choices and potentially by engaging in strategic price differentiation.

23B.1 Demand, Marginal Revenue and Profit

Suppose that the market demand facing a monopolist is of the form:

$$x(p) = A - \alpha p, \tag{23.4}$$

which gives rise to an inverse market demand:

$$p(x) = \frac{A}{\alpha} - \frac{1}{\alpha}x. \tag{23.5}$$

For consistency, we will use this market demand specification repeatedly, both in this chapter as well as in the following chapters that deal with other market structures within which firms might operate.

23B.1.1 Marginal Revenue and Price Elasticity For the monopolist, total revenue is equal to price times output, where price is determined by the inverse market demand or what we usually call the market demand curve; that is,

$$TR = p(x)x = \left(\frac{A}{\alpha} - \frac{1}{\alpha}x\right)x = \frac{A}{\alpha}x - \frac{1}{\alpha}x^2. \quad (23.6)$$

In Section A, we argued verbally that the marginal revenue curve for a monopolist has the same intercept as the demand curve but twice the slope. This is verified mathematically, with marginal revenue the derivative of TR with respect to output:

$$MR = \frac{dTR}{dx} = \frac{A}{\alpha} - \frac{2}{\alpha}x. \quad (23.7)$$

More generally, we can write the inverse demand function as $p(x)$ and total revenue as $TR = p(x)x$. Using this expression, we can differentiate TR with respect to x to get:

$$MR = p(x) + \frac{dp}{dx}x. \quad (23.8)$$

If we multiply the second term in equation (23.8) by $(p(x)/p(x))$. we can write the expression for MR as:

$$MR = p(x)\left(1 + \frac{dp}{dx}\frac{x}{p(x)}\right). \quad (23.9)$$

The price elasticity of demand for an inverse demand function $p(x)$ is given by $\varepsilon_D = (dx/dp)(p(x)/x)$, which is the inverse of the second term in parentheses in equation (23.9). Thus, we can write the expression for MR as:

$$MR = p(x)\left(1 + \frac{1}{\varepsilon_D}\right). \quad (23.10)$$

Suppose, for instance, that we are currently at the midpoint of a linear demand curve such as the one in panel (a) of Graph 23.1 where the price elasticity of demand is equal to -1. Equation (23.10) tells us that marginal revenue at that point is equal to 0, precisely as we derived in panel (b) of Graph 23.1.

Exercise 23B.2

Use equation (23.10) to verify the vertical intercept of the marginal revenue curve in panel (b) of Graph 23.1.

23B.1.2 Revenue Maximization In order to maximize total revenue TR, the monopolist would set MR equal to zero. Using equation (23.10) for MR, it follows that revenue is maximized when $\varepsilon_D = -1$. With the linear demand specified in equation (23.4), this implies an output level of $A/2$.

Exercise 23B.3

Set up a revenue maximization problem for the firm. Verify that this is indeed the revenue-maximizing output level and that at that output, $\varepsilon_D = -1$.

23B.1.3 Profit Maximization The monopolist's profit-maximization problem differs from revenue maximization in that costs are taken into account. This problem, already introduced at the beginning of this section, can be written as:

$$\max_{x} \pi = p(x)x - c(x), \tag{23.11}$$

where $c(x)$ is the total cost function that is derived from the production function. Taking first order conditions, we get:

$$MR = p(x) + \frac{dp}{dx}x = \frac{dc(x)}{dx} = MC. \tag{23.12}$$

Exercise 23B.4

Can you use equation (23.10) to now prove that as long as $MC > 0$, the monopolist will produce where $\varepsilon_D < -1$?

If market demand is linear as specified in equation (23.4) and $c(x) = cx$ our $MR = MC$ condition implies:

$$\frac{A}{\alpha} - \frac{2}{\alpha} = c, \tag{23.13}$$

which further implies a monopoly output x^M and price p^M of:

$$x^M = \frac{A - \alpha c}{2} \quad \text{and} \quad p^M = \frac{A + \alpha c}{2\alpha}. \tag{23.14}$$

Exercise 23B.5

Illustrate that profit maximization approaches revenue maximization as $MC = c$ approaches zero.

Exercise 23B.6

Verify for the example of our linear demand curve and constant marginal cost c that it does not matter whether the firm maximizes profit by choosing x or p as in the problems defined in equations (23.2) and (23.3).

23B.1.4 Constant-Elasticity Demand and Monopoly Mark-Ups Another way to write the optimal monopoly price emerges from substituting the elasticity-based expression for MR from equation (23.10) into the $MC = MR$ condition of equation (23.12):

$$p\left(1 + \frac{1}{\varepsilon_D}\right) = MC. \tag{23.15}$$

Rearranging terms, we get:

$$\frac{p - MC}{p} = \frac{-1}{\varepsilon_D}. \qquad (23.16)$$

The difference between price and MC, that is $(p - MC)$, is called the *monopoly mark-up* because it represents how much the monopolist marks up its price above marginal cost where we would expect competitive firms to produce. The left-hand side of equation (23.16) is called the *monopoly mark-up ratio*, which is the mark-up relative to the price charged by the monopolist. The mark-up ratio is also called the *Lerner Index*. Since the price elasticity term ε_D is negative, this cancels the negative sign on the right-hand side and makes the mark-up ratio itself positive.

Suppose that instead of facing a linear demand curve for which price elasticity differs at each point, a monopolist faces a constant-elasticity demand curve of the form $x = \alpha p^{-\varepsilon}$ for which the price elasticity of demand is $-\varepsilon$ everywhere. Equation (23.16) tells us that the monopolist's mark-up ratio is inversely proportional to the price elasticity of demand. This implies that the mark-up ratio and the mark-up itself approaches zero as the price elasticity of demand approaches minus infinity. As the price elasticity of demand approaches minus infinity, the monopolist faces a demand curve that increasingly looks like the demand curve a perfect competitor faces. When working with the family of constant-elasticity demand curves, the price elasticity of demand is therefore a measure of the degree of monopoly power that the firm actually has.

23B.2 Price Discrimination When Consumer Types Are Observed

In Section A of the chapter, we differentiated between three different types of price discrimination that monopolists might employ depending on what it knows about its consumers and the degree to which the monopolist can prevent consumers from undermining the price discrimination. In cases where monopolists can identify demand by each consumer, the firm can perfectly, or first-degree, price-discriminate and capture the consumers' entire surplus *as long as something prevents consumers from selling the goods to each other*. When monopolists are restricted to charging per-unit prices but are not restricted to charging the *same* per-unit price to all consumers whose demand it can again identify, we illustrated how it can employ third-degree price discrimination, again assuming that consumers cannot engage in resale. Finally, if monopolists know that different consumers have different demands, but cannot identify which consumer is which type, we saw that the firm can second-degree price-discriminate by designing non-linear price/quantity combinations that cause consumers to self-select into packages based on their type. We will begin in this section with the mathematically easier cases of first- and third-degree price discrimination where we assume that firms observe consumer types prior to setting pricing policies.

23B.2.1 Perfect or First-Degree Price Discrimination First-degree price discrimination implies that the firm will charge the consumer their marginal willingness to pay for each of the goods they purchase. Suppose that a monopolist faces a constant marginal cost MC, and let $p^c = MC$ represent the per-unit price we would expect under perfect competition. For a particular consumer n, let CS^n represent the consumer surplus p^c would receive under competitive pricing, with the consumer choosing to consume where p^c crosses their demand curve. D^n. One way to think of perfect price discrimination is to think of the monopolist as continuing to charge a per-unit price of p^c but supplementing this with a fixed fee that the consumer has to pay at the same time before they can purchase anything at all (thus avoiding a possible income effect which might occur if the fee is paid at a different time). Notice that this fixed fee is a sunk cost for the consumer once it is paid and therefore has no impact on the quantity the consumer will purchase once the fee is paid.

The only question for the consumer is whether they want to pay the fixed fee in order to be able to purchase from the monopolist. Since they expect a consumer surplus of CS^n when they face a per-unit price of p^c in the absence of a fixed fee, they will be willing to pay any fixed fee that is less than or equal to CS^n. The monopolist can therefore set a *two-part tariff*, with the overall payment p^n charged to consumer n equal to:

$$P^n(x) = CS^n + p^c x \qquad (23.17)$$

Under this two-part tariff, the monopolist has set a price policy for consumer n that will leave the consumer with no surplus, but results in the efficient level of consumption by consumer n. The fixed portion of the price policy is different for each type of consumer, which implies the monopolist must know each consumer's type in order to implement the first-degree price discrimination if consumers have different demands.

Exercise 23B.7

Illustrate graphically the two different parts of the two-part tariff in equation (23.17).

23B.2.2 Third-Degree Price Discrimination Suppose now that the monopolist is selling to two different distinct markets but is limited to charging per-unit prices in each market, and thus cannot implement a two-part tariff of the type in equation (23.17). With knowledge of the two inverse demand functions $p^1(x)$ and $p^2(x)$ for the two markets, the monopolist will try to maximize profit across the two markets by choosing how much to produce in each market and thus also how much to charge in each market; that is, the monopolist will solve the problem:

$$\max_{x^1,x^2} \pi = p^1(x^1)x^1 + p^2(x^2)x^2 - c(x^1 + x^2), \tag{23.18}$$

where c is the firm's total cost function. Taking first-order conditions, we get:

$$\frac{\partial \pi}{\partial x^1} = p^1(x^1) + \frac{dp^1}{dx^1}x^1 - \frac{dc}{dx} = 0,$$
$$\frac{\partial \pi}{\partial x^2} = p^2(x^2) + \frac{dp^2}{dx^2}x^2 - \frac{dc}{dx} = 0, \tag{23.19}$$

which can be rewritten as:

$$MR^1 = MC = MR^2, \tag{23.20}$$

where MR^1 is the marginal revenue function derived from the ith market's inverse demand function. Since we know from equation (23.10) how to write MR functions in price elasticity terms, we can write this as:

$$p^1\left(1 + \frac{1}{\varepsilon_{D^1}}\right) = MC = p^2\left(1 + \frac{1}{\varepsilon_{D^2}}\right), \tag{23.21}$$

which extends equation (23.15) to two separate markets, with the mark-up in each market reflecting the price elasticity in each market. This implies:

$$\frac{p^1}{p^2} = \frac{(\varepsilon_{D^2} + 1)\varepsilon_{D^1}}{(\varepsilon_{D^1} + 1)\varepsilon_{D^2}}. \tag{23.22}$$

Regardless of what the MC of production is, the price charged in one market *relative to* that charged in the other market depends only on the price elasticities of demand in the two markets when MC is constant.

If a monopoly faces constant marginal cost equal to c and the demand functions in two different markets are $x^1 = A - \alpha p$ and $x^2 = B - \beta p$, these demand functions give rise to inverse demand functions or demand curves:

$$p^1 = \frac{A - x^1}{\alpha} \text{ and } p^2 = \frac{B - x^2}{\beta}, \qquad (23.23)$$

and the first-order conditions requiring marginal revenue to be equal to marginal cost in both markets imply:

$$x^1 = \frac{A - \alpha c}{2} \text{ and } x^2 = \frac{B - \beta c}{2} \qquad (23.24)$$

and:

$$p^1 = \frac{A + \alpha c}{2\alpha} \text{ and } p^2 = \frac{B + \beta c}{2\beta}. \qquad (23.25)$$

Exercise 23B.8

Verify that equation (23.22) holds for this example. Evaluate the elasticities at the profit-maximizing output levels.

Exercise 23B.9*

True or False: The higher-priced market under third-degree price discrimination is more price inelastic.

As we noted in our Section A discussion of third-degree price discrimination, the welfare effect of eliminating such discrimination is ambiguous and requires an analysis of the gains by low-elasticity consumers relative to the losses by high-elasticity consumers and the monopolist.

23B.3 Discrimination When Consumer Types Are Not Observable

First- and third-degree price discrimination assume firms know the types of consumers they face. When they do not know the consumer types, but are only aware of the fraction of the population that falls into each category, the monopolist's problem becomes more difficult and involves more strategic considerations. In particular, since the monopolist has no external signal about the consumer types it is facing, it must design its pricing policy in such a way that consumers themselves choose to reveal what type they are through the types of purchases they make. All the various ways of thinking about monopoly pricing involve the firm choosing two-part tariffs of the form:

$$P^n(x) = F^n + p^n x \text{ for } n = 1,2. \qquad (23.26)$$

We can express each of the pricing strategies as separate two-part tariffs aimed at the two types of consumers. The difference in all these strategies is that in some cases we are restricting fixed charges F^n to be zero and in some cases we are restricting the monopolist to only a single pricing schedule. Table 23.1 illustrates this for the forms of price discrimination we have treated and those we are about to discuss. For instance, we began Section 23B.1 with a monopolist who was restricted to charging a single per-unit price to all consumers, effectively assuming $F^1 = F^2 = 0$ and $p^2 = p^1$ as in the first column of the table. Under first-degree price discrimination, on the other hand, we make no restrictions on the fixed and per-unit prices that the monopolist can use. Under third-degree price discrimination, no fixed fees are permitted, that is, $F^1 = F^2 = 0$ but no restrictions are placed on the per-unit prices the monopolist can charge. We will shortly revisit the case where no restrictions are placed on fixed fees or per-unit prices as in first-degree price discrimination, but under the informational constraint that the firm cannot observe consumer type prior to consumers making their purchasing decisions. This is second-degree price discrimination, represented in the last column of Table 23.1. We will build up to this full second-degree price discrimination by first considering the case where a firm does not observe consumer type and is restricted to posting a single two-part tariff rather than separate two-part tariffs aimed at different consumer types. This is represented in the second-to-last column in Table 23.1 and represents a case we did not treat in Section A of the chapter.

Table 23.1 F^n = Type n's Fixed Charge; p^n = Type n's Per-Unit Price

	Two-Part Tariff Restrictions for Different Forms of Price Discrimination				
	None	1st Degree	3rd Degree	Two-Part Tariff	2nd Degree
F^1	$= 0$		$= 0$		
F^2	$= 0$		$= 0$	$= F^1$	
p^1					
p^2	$= p^1$			$= p^1$	

To simplify the analysis to its essentials, we will also allow a single preference parameter to differentiate the different consumer types in this section. In particular, suppose that consumer n has tastes for the monopoly good x that can be represented by the utility function:

$$U^n = \theta_n u(x) - P(x), \qquad (23.27)$$

where $p(x)$ is the total charge for consuming quantity x. Differences in consumer tastes are captured by differences in the value of θ_n. Note that this is not the typical type of utility function we have worked with given that it is defined over only a single good. However, as we demonstrate in a short appendix, this type of reduced-form utility function can be justified as arising from preferences that are separable between other consumption and the good x when the overall spending on the good x represents only a small portion of the consumer's income. We demonstrate in the Appendix that we can assume identical underlying, separable preferences where consumers differ only in their income, and that the differences in the value of θ_n in the reduced form utility function above are related to underlying differences in consumer income.

23B.3.1 Second-Degree Price Discrimination With a Single Two-Part Tariff We begin our consideration of second-degree price discrimination with a restricted version that we did not discuss in Section A, a version in which the monopolist is limited to using a *single* two-part tariff for both consumer types rather than two different two-part tariffs aimed at the two different types. If the monopolist is so constrained, $p(x)$ has to take the form:

$$P(x) = F + px, \qquad (23.28)$$

where F is the fixed charge and p the per-unit price, with neither being superscripted by n since the same price schedule applies to both types. Maximizing consumer utility from equation (23.27) given the two-part tariff from equation (23.28) entails the simple optimization problem:

$$\max_x \theta_n u(x) - F - px, \tag{23.29}$$

and gives us the first-order condition:

$$\theta_n \frac{du(x)}{dx} = p. \tag{23.30}$$

The analysis becomes particularly clean if we assume the following functional form for $u(x)$:

$$u(x) = \frac{1 - (1 - x)^2}{2}, \tag{23.31}$$

which has a first derivative with respect to x that is $(1 - x)$. Substituting this into equation (23.30) and solving for x, we get the consumer's demand function as:

$$x^n(p) = \frac{\theta_n - p}{\theta_n}. \tag{23.32}$$

Notice that we have specified underlying preferences in such a way as to once again have linear demand curves of the form $x(p) = A - \alpha p$ where $A = 1$ and $\alpha = 1/\theta_n$.

Exercise 23B.10

Intuitively, why does the fixed charge F from the two-part tariff not show up in the demand function?

Exercise 23B.11

Derive the price charged to consumer n by a third-degree price-discriminating monopolist with constant marginal cost c.

In Graph 23.7, we depict the inverse of this demand function and illustrate the consumer surplus triangle CS^n that for a particular per-unit price p with $F = 0$, is of size:

$$CS^n(p) = \frac{(\theta_n - p)x^n(p)}{2} = \frac{(\theta_n - p)^2}{2\theta_n}. \tag{23.33}$$

Assume a monopolist faces two types of consumers, type 1 and type 2, with preference parameters θ_1 and θ_2 respectively and with $\theta_1 < \theta_2$. Suppose further that the monopolist knows that a fraction $\gamma < 1$ of the consumers are of type 1, with the remaining fraction $(1 - \gamma)$ made up of consumers of type 2. Finally, assume the monopolist faces a constant marginal cost of c. Whatever per-unit price the monopolist chooses, it has to respect the constraint that the lower demand consumer 1 will not choose to consume any of the good if the fixed charge F is set above $CS^1(p) = (\theta_1 - p)^2/(2\theta_1)$. This constraint is often referred to as the *individual rationality constraint.* For a given per-unit price p, the monopolist's optimal fixed charge is $CS^1(p)$.

Knowing this, the monopolist needs to determine the optimal per-unit charge in the two-part tariff. We can think of this is as a process in which the monopoly maximizes the expected profit from each encounter with a consumer, knowing the fractions of the consumer pool that fall into one type or the other. This expected profit takes the form:

$$E(\pi) = CS^1(p) + \gamma(p - c)x^1(p) + (1 - \gamma)(p - c)x^2(p) \tag{23.34}$$

Graph 23.7 Consumer n's Inverse Demand Function

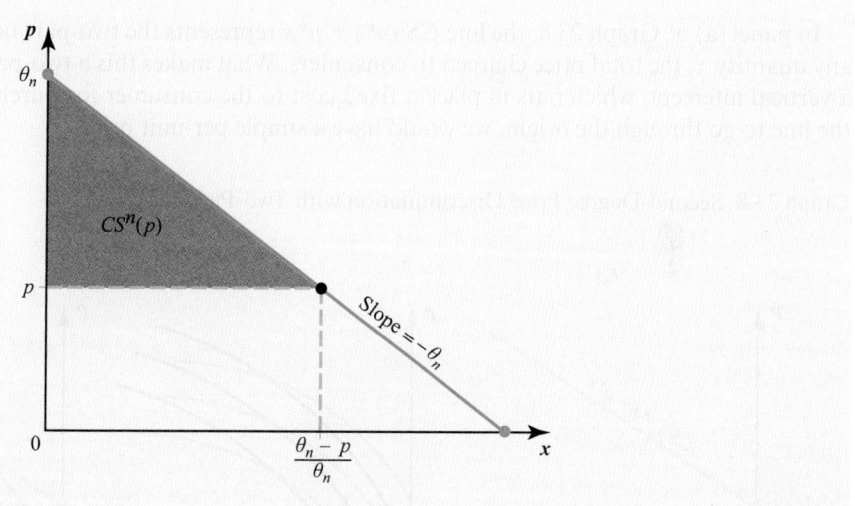

The $CS^1(p)$ term is the fixed charge that we have concluded the firm will set in its two-part tariff, a charge that will be paid by both types of consumers. Thus, the firm receives that amount for certain each time a customer shows up. With probability γ, the firm faces a consumer of type 1 who will purchase $x^1(p)$ at price p. When multiplied by the difference between price p and marginal cost c, we get the expected additional profit from facing this type of consumer. Similarly, with probability $(1 - \gamma)$ the firm will face a consumer of type 2 and with it an additional profit of $(p - c)x^2(p)$.

Substituting in for what we derived for $CS^1(p)$, $x^1(p)$ and $x^2(p)$ in equations (23.33) and (23.32) and rearranging terms, the expected profit can be expressed as:

$$E(\pi) = \frac{(\theta_1 - p)^2}{2\theta_1} + (p - c)\left[1 - \left(\frac{\gamma}{\theta_1} + \frac{(1 - \gamma)}{\theta_2}\right)p\right]. \tag{23.35}$$

Exercise 23B.12

Verify that this equation is correct.

The only choice variable for the monopolist in this expected profit equation is p. Thus, maximizing the expected profit subject to the implicit constraint that only a two-part tariff can be employed is maximizing

$E(\pi)$ by choosing p. Solving the first-order condition from this maximization problem for p, we get the optimal per-unit price p^*:

$$p^* = \frac{c(\gamma\theta_2 + (1 - \gamma)\theta_1)}{2(\gamma\theta_2 + (1 - \gamma)\theta_1) - \theta_2}. \tag{23.36}$$

Exercise 23B.13**

Verify that this equation is correct.

In panel (a) of Graph 23.8, the line $CS^1(p^*) + p^*x$ represents the two-part tariff $P(x)$ that indicates, for any quantity x, the total price charged to consumers. What makes this a two-part tariff is that the line has a vertical intercept, which puts in place a fixed cost to the consumer for purchasing from the firm. Were the line to go through the origin, we would have a simple per-unit price.

Graph 23.8 Second-Degree Price Discrimination with Two-Part Tariffs

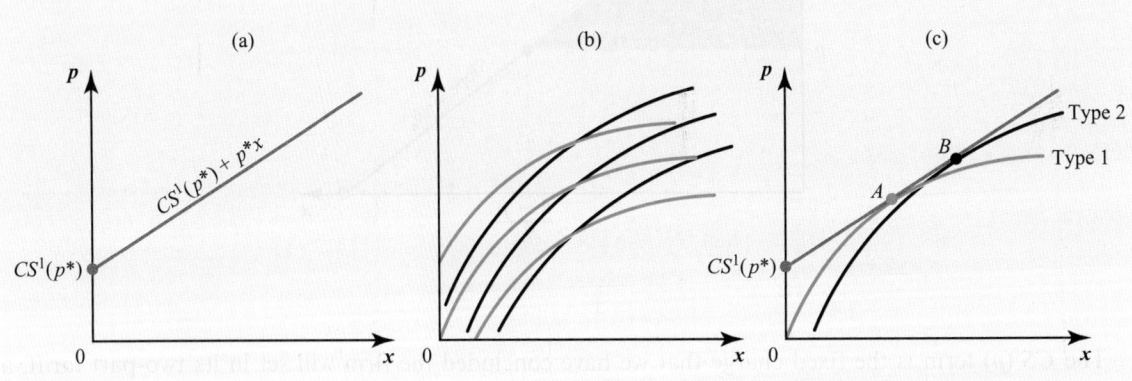

In panel (b) of the graph, we illustrate the shape of indifference curves for the two types of consumers, with the dark brown indifference curves representing type 1 and the dark blue indifference curves representing type 2. Consumers prefer to have more of x and less of P and thus become better off as they move towards indifference curves to the southeast of the graph.

Exercise 23B.14

Are these preferences convex?

Exercise 23B.15

Note that each set of dark brown and dark blue indifference curves cross once, with the dark blue indifference curve having a steeper slope at that point than the dark brown indifference curve. Can you give an intuitive explanation for this?

Finally, in panel (c) of the graph, we put indifference curves and the two-part tariff-induced constraint into a single graph to illustrate the consumers' optimal choices, with type 1 consumers optimizing at point *B* and type 2 consumers optimizing at point *A*. The optimal dark brown indifference curve for type 1 crosses the origin, which implies that type 1 consumers are as well off at point *A* as they are at point $(0,0)$ where they consume no *x* and pay no price. Consumers of type 1 attain zero consumer surplus at point *A* under the two-part tariff that has been set by the firm.

Exercise 23B.16

Given that you know how the firm constructed the two-part tariff, can you give an intuitive explanation for this?

While the firm that is implementing the two-part tariff does not know what type of consumer it faces prior to a consumption decision, the graph illustrates that the two-part tariff allows the firm to know what type of consumer it faced *after* the decision has been made. The firm has induced a separating equilibrium, with the consumer types signalling their type through their consumption choices.

23B.3.2 Second-Degree Price Discrimination More Generally In our definition of second-degree price discrimination, we did not limit the monopolist to using a *single* two-part tariff but allowed it to create price/quantity packages that in effect enabled it to charge different fixed fees and different per-unit prices. In order to reconcile our treatment here with the graphs we drew in Section A, particularly Graph 23.5, we can again consider the problem using demand curves rather than indifference curves. Panel (a) of Graph 23.9 illustrates the demand curves for type 1 (dark brown) and type 2 (dark blue) as well as the per-unit price p^* in the single two-part tariff just derived.

Graph 23.9 Two-Part Tariff Illustrated With Demand Curves

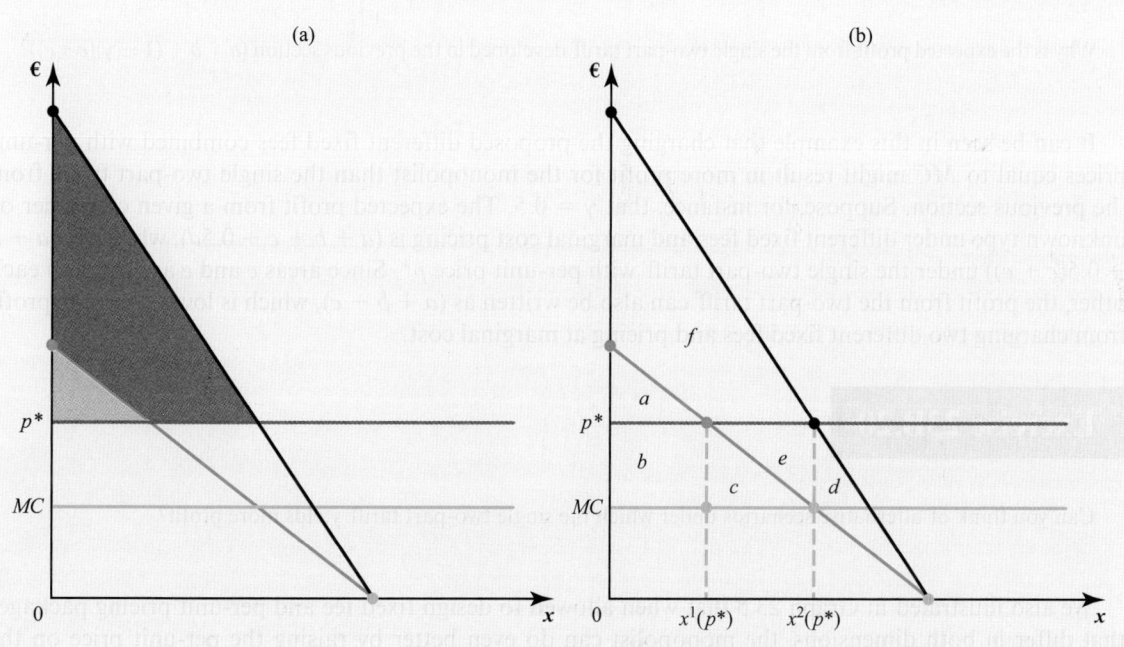

Exercise 23B.17

Explain why, for the preferences we have been working with, the two demand curves have the same horizontal intercept.

Since the monopolist in our example sets the fixed charge in the two-part tariff equal to the consumer surplus type 1 would get under only the per-unit price, the shaded dark brown area is equal to the fixed charge F. This implies zero consumer surplus for type 1 consumers and consumer surplus equal to the dark blue area for type 2 consumers.

We began our exploration of second-degree price discrimination in Section A, however, by proposing that the firm set a per-unit price at $MC = c$ instead of p^*, that it charge type 1 consumers the maximum possible fixed fee and that it charge type 2 consumers the highest possible fee that would still cause those consumers to behave differently from type 1 consumers. We replicate this in panel (b) of Graph 23.9 for the demand curves we are working with, taking the liberty of drawing these in a particular way so as to minimize the number of areas we have to keep track of. After setting per-unit price at MC, the firm charges a fee $F^1 = (a + b + c)$ to type 1 thereby capturing all of type 1's consumer surplus, and a fee $F^2 = (a + b + c + d)$ to type 2 consumers. The expected profit from a consumer of unknown type is $(a + b + c + (1 - \gamma)d)$ under this pricing policy, while it is $(a + b + (1 - \gamma)(c + e))$ under the single two-part tariff we calculated in the previous section.

Exercise 23B.18

Why is $F^2 = (a + b + c + d)$ the highest possible fixed fee the firm can charge to type 2 consumers given that it sets per-unit prices at MC and charges type 1 $F^1 = (a + b + c)$?

Exercise 23B.19

Why is the expected profit from the single two-part tariff developed in the previous section $(a + b + (1 - \gamma)(c + e))$?

It can be seen in this example that charging the proposed different fixed fees combined with per-unit prices equal to MC might result in more profit for the monopolist than the single two-part tariff from the previous section. Suppose, for instance, that $\gamma = 0.5$. The expected profit from a given consumer of unknown type under different fixed fees and marginal cost pricing is $(a + b + c + 0.5d)$, while it is $(a + b + 0.5(c + e))$ under the single two-part tariff with per-unit price p^*. Since areas c and e are equal to each other, the profit from the two-part tariff can also be written as $(a + b + c)$, which is lower than the profit from charging two different fixed fees and pricing at marginal cost.

Exercise 23B.20

Can you think of alternative scenarios under which the single two-part tariff yields more profit?

We also illustrated in Graph 23.5 that when allowed to design fixed fee and per-unit pricing packages that differ in both dimensions, the monopolist can do even better by raising the per-unit price on the low-demand consumer and thus increasing the fixed fee for the high-demand consumer. Complete freedom in designing pricing when faced with different consumer types results in high-demand consumers purchasing the socially optimal quantity but paying a higher fixed fee, and the lower demand consumers purchasing sub-optimal quantities and paying a lower fixed fee.

A potentially profit-maximizing level of second-degree price discrimination, analogous to what we derived in Section A, is pictured in Graph 23.10. It can be viewed as consisting of *two* separate two-part tariffs, with consumers free to choose which one to select. The two-part tariff targeted at low-demand consumers consists of a per-unit price $\bar{p}$ accompanied by a fixed fee equal to that consumer type's consumer surplus $CS^1(\bar{p})$ under the per-unit price $\bar{p}$. Under this two-part tariff, type 1 consumers will choose $x^1(\bar{p})$ and pay a total of:

$$P^1 = CS^1(\bar{p}) + \bar{p}x^1(\bar{p}), \tag{23.37}$$

which is equal to the shaded dark brown area in the graph plus the rectangle $cx^1(\bar{p})$ underneath the shaded dark brown area.

Graph 23.10 Optimal Second-Degree Price Discrimination Using Two-Part Tariffs

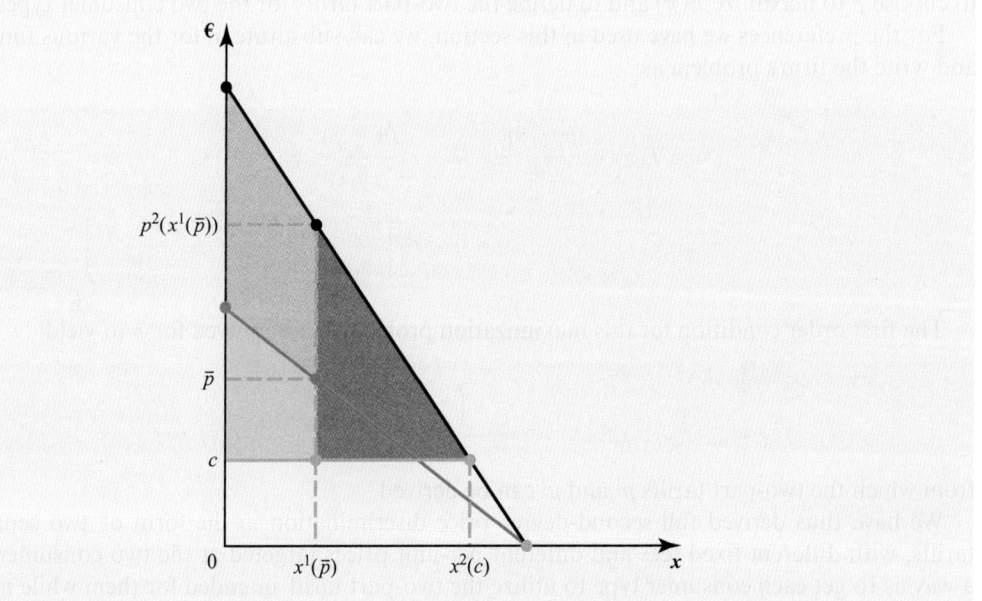

The tariff aimed at high-demand consumers, on the other hand, consists of a per-unit price c equal to marginal cost and the highest possible fixed fee that will keep type 2 consumers from taking the two-part tariff aimed at type 1 consumers. This will result in type 2 consumers purchasing the quantity $x^2(c)$, leaving them with consumer surplus equal to the shaded dark brown, light blue and dark blue areas in the absence of a fixed fee. Since type 2 consumers can obtain consumer surplus equal to the shaded light blue area by accepting the two-part tariff aimed at low-demand consumers, the most that the firm can charge in a fixed fee is equal to the shaded dark brown plus the shaded dark blue areas. The resulting two-part tariff P^2 aimed at type 2 consumers is given by:

$$P^2 = \left\{ \left[CS^1(\bar{p}) + (\bar{p} - c)x^1(\bar{p})\right] + \left[\frac{(p^2(x^1(\bar{p})) - c)(x^2(c) - x^1(\bar{p}))}{2}\right] \right\} + cx^2(c), \tag{23.38}$$

where the first bracketed term represents the shaded dark brown area and the second bracketed term represents the shaded dark blue area. This implies that the firm can expect profit of:

$$\pi^1(\bar{p}) = CS^1(\bar{p}) + (\bar{p} - c)x^1(\bar{p}), \tag{23.39}$$

from type 1 consumers and:

$$\pi^2(\bar{p}) = CS^1(\bar{p}) + (\bar{p} - c)x^1(\bar{p}) + \left[\frac{(p^2(x^1(\bar{p}) - c)(x^2(c) - x^1(\bar{p})))}{2} \right], \tag{23.40}$$

from type 2 consumers. The expected profit from encountering a consumer of unknown type is $E(\pi) = \gamma\pi^1(\bar{p}) + (1 - \gamma)\pi^2(\bar{p})$ or:

$$E(\pi) = CS^1(\bar{p}) + (\bar{p} - c)x^1(\bar{p}) + (1 - \gamma)\left[\frac{(p^2(x^1(\bar{p}) - c)(x^2(c) - x^1(\bar{p})))}{2} \right]. \tag{23.41}$$

The only variable in the expression for $E(\pi)$ that is under the control of the monopolist is the price $\bar{p}$, because the setting of $\bar{p}$ determines the fixed charges that can be levied on the two types of consumers and we already know that the per-unit price for type 2 consumers is c. Thus, the monopolist's problem is to choose $\bar{p}$ to maximize $E(\pi)$ and to define the two-part tariffs for the two consumer types accordingly.

For the preferences we have used in this section, we can substitute in for the various functions in $E(\pi)$ and write the firm's problem as:

$$\max_{\bar{p}} E(\pi) = \frac{(\theta_1 - \bar{p})^2}{2\theta_1} + (\bar{p} - c)\frac{(\theta_1 - \bar{p})}{\theta_1}$$
$$+ \frac{(1 - \gamma)}{2}\left[\frac{\theta_2\bar{p}}{\theta_1} - c \right]\left[\frac{(\theta_2 - c)}{\theta_2} - \frac{(\theta_1 - \bar{p})}{\theta_1} \right] \tag{23.42}$$

The first order condition for this maximization problem can be solved for $\bar{p}$ to yield:

$$\bar{p} = \left(\frac{\theta_1\gamma}{\theta_1 - (1 - \gamma)\theta_2} \right)c, \tag{23.43}$$

from which the two-part tariffs p^1 and p^2 can be derived.

We have thus derived full second-degree price discrimination in the form of two separate two-part tariffs, with different fixed fees and different per-unit prices targeted at the two consumer types in such a way as to get each consumer type to utilize the two-part tariff intended for them while maximizing the monopolist's profit, conditional on the monopolist not being able to a priori identify the consumer types.

There is one final caveat for the monopolist who is contemplating this pricing policy. If there are sufficiently many high-demand consumers, that is, if γ is sufficiently low, or if the high demanders have sufficiently greater demand than low demanders, that is, θ_2 is sufficiently above θ_1, it may be better for the monopolist to write off the type 1 market and set a single two-part tariff intended to extract the most possible surplus from type 2 consumers. This can be seen in Graph 23.10. Suppose, for instance, that $\gamma = 0.5$, implying an equal number of type 1 and type 2 consumers. By choosing second-degree price discrimination, the monopolist chooses to forego capturing the shaded light blue area in type 2's consumer surplus in exchange for instead getting the shaded dark brown area of type 1's consumer surplus. The alternative is for the firm to capture the light blue area of type 2's surplus and not offer anything that type 1 consumers would choose, thus foregoing the shaded dark brown area. Note that in our graph, the light blue area is larger than the dark brown area. Thus, with $\gamma = 0.5$, the monopolist is better off engaging in first-degree price discrimination with respect to type 2 consumers and not sell to type 1 consumers than to engage in second-degree price discrimination.

Exercise 23B.21

If the monopolist is restricted to offering a single two-part tariff rather than two separate tariffs intended for the two consumer types, are they more or less likely to forego second-degree price discrimination in favour of first-degree price discrimination with respect to the high-demand type?

23B.3.3 Comparing Different Monopoly Pricing: An Example We noted at the beginning of our discussion of second-degree price discrimination that we can think of each of the pricing strategies we have covered as different personalized two-part tariffs of the form $P^n(x) = F^n + P^n x$. Under some strategies, we assume fixed charges F^n to be zero; under others, we require them to be equal for the different consumer types, as summarized in Table 23.1. This gives a convenient way of comparing the different forms of price discrimination.

Table 23.2 undertakes this comparison for a particular example in which $\theta_1 = 100$, $\theta_2 = 150$, $\gamma = 0.5$ and the marginal cost $c = 25$. The first column begins by presenting the outcome of monopoly behaviour when no price discrimination takes place, with the next two columns presenting the outcome for first- and third-degree price discrimination where the firm knows each consumer's type, and the final two columns presenting the outcome when the firm does not know each consumer's type and is at first restricted to using a single two-part tariff and permitted to employ separate two-part tariffs aimed at the two consumer types. In each case, we begin with the fixed fees and the per-unit prices charged to the two consumer types and report the consumption levels, consumer surpluses and the firm's expected profit per consumer. The final row of the table sums the consumer surpluses and the firm's profit to arrive at the total surplus.

Table 23.2 $\theta_1 = 100$, $\theta_2 = 150$, $\gamma = 0.5$, $c = 25$

| | Different Forms of Monopoly Price Discrimination | | | | |
	None	1st Degree	3rd Degree	Two-Part Tariff	2nd Degree
F^1	€0	€28.13	€0	€23.63	€12.50
F^2	€0	€52.08	€0	€23.63	€33.33
P^1	€72.50	€25.00	€62.50	€31.25	€50.00
P^2	€72.50	€25.00	€87.50	€31.25	€25.00
x^1	0.2750	0.7500	0.3750	0.6875	0.5000
x^2	0.5167	0.8333	0.4167	0.7917	0.8333
CS^1	3.7813	0	7.0313	0	0
CS^2	20.0208	0	13.0208	23.3724	18.7500
$E(\pi)$	18.8021	40.1042	20.0521	28.2552	29.1667
TS	30.7031	40.1042	30.0781	39.9414	38.5417

First-degree price discrimination results in full efficiency, with the entire surplus accruing to the firm. It is therefore not surprising to see that the firm's profit and the total surplus are the largest under first-degree price discrimination, neither is it surprising that this is the least preferred outcome for consumers whose entire surplus is taken in fixed fees by the monopolist. It should also not be surprising that the firm's profit is the lowest when it is not permitted to engage in any price discrimination. We can see from Table 23.2 that the firm is most restricted in its pricing policy in that case, with no possibility of charging a fixed fee and no possibility of differentiating the per-unit price between the consumer types. These restrictions are lifted partially under third-degree price discrimination, resulting in higher firm profit, and fully lifted under first-degree price discrimination. It is therefore natural to expect the firm's profit from third-degree price discrimination to fall in between the no-discrimination and full first-degree discrimination scenarios.

In the case where firms can discriminate but do not know the consumer types, represented in the last two columns, it is again not surprising that the firm makes more profit than it does in the no-discrimination case, neither should it be surprising that firm profit is higher when the firm can charge two separate two-part tariffs in the last column than when it is restricted to a single two-part tariff in the second-to-last column. The only case that is theoretically ambiguous with respect to firm profit is the comparison between third-degree price discrimination and the two forms of second-degree price discrimination in the last two columns. For our particular example, it turns out that both forms of second-degree price discrimination result in greater profit than third-degree price discrimination, but for other examples the reverse could be true.

Exercise 23B.22

From looking at Table 23.2, it seems that the firm is unambiguously less restricted in its pricing under second-degree price discrimination than under third-degree price discrimination. How could it theoretically be the case that profit is higher under third-degree price discrimination?

We can summarize these implications in two sets of equations, with:

$$\pi(\text{None}) \le \pi(\text{Two-part tariff}) \le \pi(\text{2nd Degree}) \le \pi(\text{1st Degree}), \qquad (23.44)$$

comparing profit under the second-degree price discrimination scenarios to the extremes of no discrimination and perfect discrimination, and with:

$$\pi(\text{None}) \le \pi(\text{3rd Degree}) \le \pi(\text{1st Degree}), \qquad (23.45)$$

comparing third-degree price discrimination to these same extremes.

Exercise 23B.23*

Can you think of a scenario under which all the inequalities turn to equalities in equations (23.44) and (23.45)? *Hint:* Think of goods for which consumers demand only 1 unit.

Turning from profit to consumer surplus, we can derive the following implications for the low-demand consumers:

$$0 = CS^1(\text{1st Degree}) = CS^1(\text{Two-part tariff}) = CS^1(\text{2nd Degree})$$
$$\le CS^1(\text{None}) \le CS^1(\text{3rd Degree}). \qquad (23.46)$$

Exercise 23B.24

Can you give an intuitive explanation for why this has to hold?

For the high-demand consumers, however, the implications for consumer surplus are not nearly as unambiguous. We can definitively conclude that:

$$0 = CS^2 \text{ (1st Degree)} \leq CS^2 \text{ (3rd Degree)} \leq CS^2 \text{ (None)}, \tag{23.47}$$

and:

$$CS^2 \text{ (1st Degree)} \leq CS^2 \text{ (2nd Degree)} \leq CS^2 \text{ (Two-part tariff)}, \tag{23.48}$$

but we again cannot be certain about how consumer surplus for the high-demand type under no and third-degree price discrimination compares to consumer surplus under the two forms of second-degree price discrimination. In our example, third-degree price discrimination happens to be worse for high-demand consumers than either of the forms of second-degree price discrimination, but no discrimination is better than second-degree price discrimination.

The theoretical ambiguities with respect to profit and consumer surplus of high-demand consumers create theoretical uncertainty about the overall efficiency, or total surplus, under different monopoly behaviour. The only conclusions that hold regardless of the types of demand are that total surplus is largest under first-degree price discrimination. For instance, by changing γ in our example from 0.5 to 0.4, the ranking of total surplus changes from one in which second-degree price discrimination is more efficient than no discrimination which is more efficient than third-degree price discrimination, as illustrated in Table 23.2, to one where no discrimination is more efficient than third-degree price discrimination which is more efficient than second-degree price discrimination. It is therefore important from an efficiency-focused policy perspective to know as much as possible about underlying demands before intervening in monopoly pricing behaviour. Furthermore, it may be that policy makers are less concerned about monopoly profit and more concerned about consumer welfare, in which case overall surplus is not the relevant outcome to consider.

Exercise 23B.25

Can you think of any definitive policy implications if the goal of policy is to maximize consumer welfare with no regard to firm profit?

Exercise 23B.26

Explain all the zeros in Table 23.2.

Exercise 23B.27

In Table 23.1, we note that there are no restrictions on per-unit prices for the two consumer types under either first- or second-degree price discrimination, with firms being able to tell consumer types apart in the former case but not the latter. Yet in Table 23.2, the firm appears to be charging exactly the same per-unit prices to the two consumers under first-degree price discrimination when it can tell the consumers apart and *different* per-unit prices under second-degree price discrimination when the firm cannot tell the consumer types apart. Explain this intuitively.

Appendix | Deriving a Reduced-Form Utility Function From Separable Preferences

In Section 23B.3, we introduced what we called a reduced-form utility function representing preferences for the monopoly good x that took the form:

$$U^n = \theta_n u(x) - P(x), \tag{23.49}$$

where θ_n became our preference parameter that distinguished consumer types and $P(x)$ was the total charge to the consumer for consuming the quantity x of the monopoly good. We indicated at the time that this way of representing preferences for a single good can be derived from a more typical utility function over x and a composite good y. We furthermore indicated that one can assume consumers in fact have identical underlying preferences and that the parameter θ_n is a measure of consumer income, with consumer demands therefore differing solely because of underlying income differences. We will now illustrate this more fully.

Suppose that consumers have underlying preferences that can be represented by the utility function:

$$\overline{U}(x, y) = u(x) + v(y). \tag{23.50}$$

If spending on the monopoly good x represents a relatively small fraction of the consumer's income I, we can approximate this utility function by writing it as:

$$\overline{U}(x, I) \approx u(x) + v(I) - P(x)\frac{dv(I)}{dI}. \tag{23.51}$$

When we choose x to maximize $\overline{U}(x, I)$, the term $v(I)$ plays no role in the first-order conditions, leaving only the portion $(u(x) - P(x)dv(I)/dI)$ as relevant for the optimization problem. We can define $\theta = 1/dv(I)/dI$ and multiply this relevant portion of the utility function by θ to get:

$$\widetilde{U}(x, \theta) = \theta u(x) - P(x) \text{ with } \theta = \frac{1}{dv(I)/dI}. \tag{23.52}$$

The term θ is the inverse of the marginal utility of income. To the extent to which we place meaning in the concept of marginal utility of income, it is common to assume that marginal utility of income declines in income; that is, $dv(I)/dI < 0$. Since θ is the inverse of marginal utility of income, this implies that θ is increasing in income; that is, $d\theta/dI > 0$.

Suppose that we have two consumers with identical preferences that can be represented by the separable utility function in equation (23.50) but their incomes are $I_1 < I_2$, we can represent their preferences for purposes of determining demand for the monopoly good x by the equation:

$$U(x) = \theta_n u(x) - P(x) \text{ with } \theta_1 < \theta_2. \tag{23.53}$$

Thus, low-demand consumers will be those with less income than high-demand consumers. This implies that, for instance, under full second-degree price discrimination, lower-income consumers purchase the monopoly good at a higher per-unit price but are charged a lower fixed fee than high-demand consumers.

End-of-Chapter Exercises

23.1† The demand curve for a product x provided by a monopolist is given by $p = 90 - x$ and the monopolist's marginal cost curve is given by $MC = x$.

A. In this part, we will focus on a graphical analysis, and revisit this with maths in part B. It is not essential that you have done Section B of the chapter in order to do (a) to (d) of part B of this question.

a. Draw a graph with the demand and marginal cost curves.

b. Assuming that the monopolist can only charge a single per-unit price for x, where does the marginal revenue curve lie in your graph?

c. Illustrate the monopolist's profit-maximizing supply point.

d. In the absence of any recurring fixed costs, what area in your graph represents the monopolist's profit? There are actually two areas that can be used to represent profit. Can you find both?

e. Assuming that the demand curve is also the marginal willingness to pay curve, illustrate consumer surplus and deadweight loss.

f. Suppose that the monopolist has recurring fixed costs of an amount that causes its actual profit to be zero. Where in your graph would the average cost curve lie? In particular, how does this average cost curve relate to the demand curve?

g. In a new graph, illustrate again the demand, MR and MC curves. Illustrate the monopolist's average cost curve assuming the recurring fixed costs are half of what they were in part (f).

h. In your graph, illustrate where profit lies. *True or False*: Recurring fixed costs only determine *whether* a monopolist produces, not how much it produces.

B. Consider again the demand curve and MC curve as specified at the beginning of this exercise.

a. Derive the equation for the marginal revenue curve.

b. What is the profit-maximizing output level x^M? What is the profit-maximizing price p^M assuming that the monopolist can only charge a single per-unit price to all consumers?

c. In the absence of recurring fixed costs, what is the monopolist's profit?

d. What is consumer surplus and deadweight loss assuming that demand is equal to marginal willingness to pay?

e. What is the cost function if recurring fixed costs are sufficiently high to cause the monopolist's profit to be zero?

f. Use this cost function to set up the monopolist's optimization problem and verify your answers to (b).

g. Does the average cost curve relate to the demand curve as you concluded in part A(f)?

h. How does the profit-maximization problem change if the recurring fixed costs are half of what we assumed in part (e)? Does the solution to the problem change?

23.2 **Everyday and Business Application:** *Diamonds Are a Girl's Best Friend.* Historically, most of the diamond mines in the world have been controlled by a few companies and governments. Through clever marketing by diamond producers, many consumers have furthermore become convinced that 'diamonds are a girl's best friend' because 'diamonds are forever'. The marketing message is that the only way to show true love is to give a diamond engagement ring that costs the equivalent of three months' salary. We will refer to this throughout the exercise as 'the claim'.

A. For purposes of this question, assume that diamonds are only used for engagement rings, that there is no secondary market for engagement rings and that the diamond industry acts as a single monopoly.

a. Let x be the size of diamonds in carats. Draw a demand curve for x with the price per carat on the vertical axis, and make the shape of this demand curve roughly consistent with the claim at the beginning of the question.

b. If this claim is true, what is the price elasticity of demand for diamonds?

c. What price per carat would be consistent with the diamond monopoly maximizing its *revenues* assuming the claim accurately characterizes demand?

d. What price is consistent with *profit* maximization?

e. How large would the diamonds in engagement rings be if the marketing campaign to convince us of the claim at the beginning of the question was fully successful and if the diamond industry really has monopoly power?

f. *True or False*: By observing the actual size of diamonds in engagement rings, we can conclude that either the market campaign has not yet fully succeeded or the diamond industry is not really a monopoly.

B. Suppose that demand for diamond size is $x = (A/p)^{(1/(1-\beta))}$.

a. What value must β take in order for the claim to be correct?

b. How much *revenue* will the diamond monopoly earn if the claim holds? Does this depend on what price it sets?

c. Derive the marginal revenue function assuming the claim holds. Assuming $MC > 0$, does MR ever cross MC?

d. If $MC = 0$, how large a diamond size per engagement ring is consistent with profit maximization assuming the claim holds?

e. Suppose the diamond monopoly has recurring fixed costs that are sufficiently high to cause its profits to be zero. If marginal costs were zero, what would be the relationship between the demand curve and the average cost curve?

f. Suppose $\beta = 0.5$ and $MC = x$. What is the profit-maximizing diamond size now?

g. What if instead $\beta = -1$?

23.3† **Business and Policy Application:** *Labour Unions Exercising Market Power.* Labour unions use market power to raise wages for their members.

A. Consider a competitive industry in which workers have organized into a union that is now renegotiating the wages of its members with all the firms in the industry.

a. To keep the exercise reasonably simple, assume that each firm produces output by relying solely on labour input. How does each firm's labour demand curve emerge from its desire to maximize profit? Illustrate a single firm's labour demand curve with the number of workers on the horizontal axis. *Note*: Since these are competitive firms, this part has nothing to do with market power.

b. On a graph next to the one you have just drawn, illustrate the labour demand and supply curves for the industry as a whole prior to unionization.

c. Label the competitive wage w^* and use it to indicate in your first graph how many workers an individual firm hired before unionization.

d. *Suppose that the union that is negotiating with the firm in your graph is exercising its market power with the aim of maximizing the overall gain for its members. Suppose further that the union is sufficiently strong to be able to dictate an outcome. Explain how the union would go about choosing the wage in this firm and the size of its membership that will be employed by this firm. *Hint*: The union here is assumed to have monopoly power, and the marginal cost of a member is that member's competitive wage w^*.

e. If all firms in the industry are becoming unionized, what impact will this have on employment in this industry? Illustrate this in your market graph.

f. Suppose that those workers not chosen to be part of the union migrate to a non-unionized industry. What will be the impact on wages in the non-unionized sector?

B. *Suppose that each firm in the industry has the same technology described by the production function $f(\ell) = A\ell^\alpha$ with $\alpha < 1$, and suppose that there is some recurring fixed cost to operating in this industry.

a. Derive the labour demand curve for each firm.

b. Suppose that the competitive wage for workers of the skill level in this industry is w^*. Define the optimization problem that the labour union must solve if it wants to arrive at its optimal membership size and the optimal wage according to the objective defined in A(d). It may be more straightforward to set this up as a maximization problem with w rather than ℓ as the choice variable.

c. Solve for the union wage w^U that emerges if the union is able to use its market power to dictate the wage. What happens to employment in the firm?

    d. Can you verify your answer by instead finding *MR* and *MC* from the perspective of the union and setting these equal to one another?

    e. Given the fixed cost to operating in the industry, would you expect the number of firms in the industry to go up or down?

23.4* **Business and Policy Application:** *Monopsony: A Single Buyer in the Labour Market.* The text treated extensively the case where market power is concentrated on the *supply* side, but it could equally well be concentrated on the *demand* side. When a buyer has such market power, it is called a *monopsonist.* Suppose, for instance, the labour market in a modest-sized town is dominated by a single employer like a large factory. In such a setting, the dominant employer has the power to influence the wage just like a typical monopolist has the power to influence output prices.

A. Suppose that there is a single employer for some type of labour, and to simplify the analysis, suppose that the employer only uses labour in production. Assume throughout that the firm has to pay the same wage to all workers.

    a. Begin by drawing linear labour demand and supply curves assuming upward-sloping labour supply. Indicate the wage w^* that would be set if this were a competitive market and the efficient amount of labour ℓ^* that would be employed.

    b. Explain how we can interpret the labour demand curve as a marginal revenue curve for the firm. *Hint:* Remember that the labour demand curve is the marginal revenue product curve.

    c. How much does the first unit of labour cost? Where would you find the cost of hiring a second unit of labour if the firm could pay the second unit of labour more than the first?

    d. We are assuming that the firm has to pay all its workers the same wage; that is, it cannot wage discriminate. Does that imply that the marginal cost of hiring the second unit of labour is greater or less than it was in part (c)?

    e. How does the *monopsony* power of this firm in the labour market create a divergence between labour supply and the firm's marginal cost of labour, just as the *monopoly* power of a firm causes a divergence between the output demand curve and the firm's marginal revenue curve?

    f. Profit is maximized where $MR = MC$. Illustrate in your graph where marginal revenue crosses marginal cost. Will the firm hire more or fewer workers than a competitive market would if it had the same demand for labour as the monopsonist here?

    g. After a monopolist decides how much to produce, it prices the output at the highest possible level at which all the product can be sold. Similarly, after a monopsonist decides how much to buy, it will pay the lowest possible price that will permit it to buy this quantity. Can you illustrate in your graph the wage w^M that the dominant firm will pay workers?

    h. Suppose the government sets a minimum wage of w^* as defined in (a). Will this be efficiency enhancing?

    i. We gave the example of a modest-sized town with a dominant employer as a motivation for thinking about monopsonist firms in the labour market. As it becomes easier to move across cities, do you think it is more or less likely that the monopsony behaviour we have identified is of significance in the real world?

    j. Labour unions allow workers to create market power on the supply side of the labour market. Is there a potential efficiency case for the existence of labour unions in the presence of monopsony power by firms in the labour market? Would increased mobility of workers across cities strengthen or weaken this efficiency argument?

B. Suppose that the firm's production function is given by $f(\ell) = A\ell^\alpha$ (with $\alpha < 1$) and the labour supply curve is given by $w_s(\ell) = \beta\ell$.

    a. What is the efficient labour employment level ℓ^*? *Hint:* You should first calculate the marginal revenue product curve.

    b. At what wage w^* would this efficient labour supply occur?

    c. Define the firm's profit-maximization problem, keeping in mind that the wage the firm must pay depends on ℓ.

    d. Take the first order condition of the profit-maximization problem. Can you interpret this in terms of marginal revenue and marginal cost?

    e. How much labour ℓ^M does the monopsonist firm hire, and how does it compare to ℓ^*?

    f. What wage w^M does the firm pay, and how does it compare to w^*?

    g. Consider the more general case of a monopsonist firm with production function $f(\ell)$ facing a labour supply curve of $w(\ell)$. Derive the $MR = MC$ condition, which is the same as the condition that the marginal revenue product equals MC from the profit-maximization problem.

    h. Can you write the MC side of the equation in terms of the wage elasticity of labour supply?

    i. *True or False*: As the wage elasticity of labour supply increases, the monopsonist's decision approaches what we would expect under perfect competition.

23.5† **Business and Policy Application:** *Two Natural Monopolies: Microsoft versus Utility Companies.* We suggested in the text that there may be technological reasons for the barriers to entry required for the existence of a monopoly. In this exercise, we consider two examples.

    A. Microsoft and your local utilities company, such as electricity suppliers, have one thing in common: they both have high fixed costs with low variable costs. In the case of Microsoft, the fixed cost involves producing software which, once produced, can be reproduced cheaply. In the case of an electricity company, the fixed cost involves maintaining the infrastructure that distributes electricity to homes, with the actual delivery of that electricity costing relatively little if the infrastructure is in good shape.

      a. Draw a graph with low constant marginal costs and a downward-sloping demand curve. Add Microsoft's marginal revenue curve and indicate which point on the demand curve Microsoft will choose assuming that it is not worried about potential competitors. Draw a second and similar graph for the electricity company.

      b. There is one stark difference between Microsoft and the electricity company: Microsoft has not asked the government for help to allow it to operate but has instead been under strict scrutiny by governments around the world for potential abuse of its market power. Utility companies, on the other hand, have often asked for government aid in regulating prices in such a way that the companies can earn a reasonable profit. What is missing from your two graphs that can explain this difference?

      c. Put into words the problem in the two cases from a government's perspective assuming the government cares about efficiency.

      d. In the case of Microsoft, how can the granting of a copyright on the software explain the existence of the problem? How much is Microsoft willing to pay for this copyright?

      e. Now consider the problem in the electricity industry. How would setting a two-part tariff allow the electricity company to produce at zero profit? If properly structured, might its output level be efficient?

      f. Explain how the alternative of having the government lay and maintain the infrastructure on which electricity is delivered could address the same problem.

      g. What would be the analogous government intervention in the software industry, and why might you think that this was not a very good idea there? *Hint*: Think about innovation. Could you think of a way to offer a similar criticism regarding the proposal of having the government provide the infrastructure for electricity delivery?

    B. We did not develop the basic mathematics of natural monopolies in the text and therefore use the remainder of this exercise to do so. Suppose demand for x is characterized by the demand curve $p(x) = A - \alpha x$. Suppose further that x is produced by a monopolist whose cost function is $c(x) = B + \beta x$.

      a. Derive the monopolist's profit-maximizing supply point, that is, the price and quantity (p^M, x^M) under the implicit assumption of no price discrimination.

      b. At the output level x^M, what is the average cost paid by the monopolist?

      c. How high can fixed costs be and still permit the monopolist to make non-negative profit by choosing the supply point you calculated in (a)?

      d. How much is Microsoft willing to pay its lawyers to get copyright protection?

      e. Suppose Microsoft and the electricity company share the same demand function. They also share the same cost function except for the fixed cost B. Given our description of the problem faced by Microsoft versus the electricity company, whose B is higher?

    f. Suppose B for the electricity company is such that it cannot make a profit by behaving as you derived in (a) and suppose there are N households. Suggest a two-part tariff that will allow the electricity company to earn a zero profit while getting it to produce the efficient amount of electricity.

    g. Suppose the government were to build and maintain the infrastructure needed to deliver electricity to people's homes. It furthermore allows any electricity firm to use the infrastructure for a fee δ per unit of electricity that is shipped. Can the electricity industry be competitive in this case? What has to be true about the fee for using the infrastructure in order for this industry to produce the efficient level of electricity?

23.6 **Policy Application:** *Some Possible Remedies to the Monopoly Problem.* At least when our focus is on efficiency, the core problem with monopolies emanates from the monopolist's strategic under-production of output, not from the fact that monopolists make profits. Policy prescriptions to deal with monopolies are often based on the presumption that the problem is monopolies make excessive profits.

  A. Suppose the monopoly has marginal costs $MC = x$ and faces the demand curve $p = 90 - x$. Unless otherwise stated, assume there are no recurring fixed costs. In each of the policy proposals that follow, indicate the impact the policy would have on consumer welfare and deadweight loss.

    a. The government imposes a 50 per cent tax on all economic profits.

    b. The government imposes a per-unit tax t on x. It does not matter whether the tax is levied on production or consumption.

    c. The government sets a price ceiling equal to the intersection of MC and demand. *Hint*: How does this change the marginal revenue curve?

    d. The government subsidizes production of the monopoly good by s per unit.

    e. The government allows firms to engage in first-degree price discrimination.

    f. Which of these analyses might change if the firm also has recurring fixed costs?

    g. *True or False*: In the presence of distortions from market power, price distorting policies *can* be efficient.

  B. Suppose demand and marginal costs are as specified in part A. Unless otherwise stated, assume no recurring fixed costs.

    a. Determine the monopolist's optimal supply point assuming no price discrimination. Does it change when the government imposes a 50 per cent tax on economic profits?

    b. Suppose the government imposes a €6 per-unit tax on the production of x. Solve for the new profit-maximizing supply point.

    c. Is there a price ceiling at which the monopolist will produce the efficient output level?

    d. For what range of recurring fixed costs would the monopolist produce prior to the introduction of the policies in (a), (b) and (c), but not after their introduction?

    e. What is the profit-maximizing output level if the monopolist can perfectly price-discriminate?

    f. How high a per-unit subsidy would the government have to introduce in order for the monopolist to produce the efficient output level?

    g. For what range of recurring fixed costs does the monopolist not produce in the absence of a subsidy from part (f) but produces in the presence of the subsidy? If recurring fixed costs are in this range, will the monopolist produce the efficient quantity under the subsidy?

Chapter 24

Strategic Thinking and Game Theory

The case of monopolies is just one example of a large set of possible economic settings in which such deliberate – or strategic – thinking becomes important, and strategic considerations can become considerably more complex than those we encountered in Chapter 23.

Before we can proceed to a more general analysis of strategic behaviour, we have to develop some new tools. Known collectively as *game theory*, these tools find their roots in the pioneering work of John Nash (1928–2015) in the 1940s and 1950s and have become integrated into a variety of social sciences over the following decades. For economic situations in which strategic thinking matters, the game theory approach models the most salient features of such situations as a 'game' in which fictional players face incentives that are similar to those faced by the real-world actors in the underlying economic setting. In 1994, this approach received the full recognition of the economics community when John Nash and two succeeding game theorists, John Harsanyi (1920–2000) and Reinhard Selten (1930–), were awarded the Nobel Prize in Economics. Nash's compelling life story has since been immortalized in the film *A Beautiful Mind*.

While game theory opens the door to incorporating strategic thinking into economic models, the models still follow the same path that we have seen in our development of competitive markets. First, a model is defined; second, we analyze how individuals do the best they can within the context of the model; and finally, we investigate how an equilibrium emerges, an equilibrium in which we discover the economic environment that arises when everyone is doing the best they can *given what everyone else is doing.* The only difference from our competitive models is that there is now an incentive for individuals to strategically consider how their own behaviour impacts the equilibrium, a consideration that is absent when individuals are too small to have such an impact. Our goal in this chapter is to begin to appreciate how one can model equilibria that emerge from such strategic thinking in a systematic way. The exercises provide the opportunity to apply these models.

Before we begin we point out two basic distinctions between different types of games, distinctions that give rise to four types of games. In some settings, it is reasonable to assume that all economic actors that are modelled as players have *complete information*, meaning that all players know the economic benefits that all the other players will receive as the game unfolds in different ways. In other situations, economic actors do not have such complete information; that is, they do not fully know how other players fare as the game unfolds in different ways and therefore cannot as easily put themselves in their opponents' shoes. Such games are characterized by *incomplete information*. In an auction in which two people bid for a €100 note, for instance, both can be reasonably certain how much the other values the prize. In an auction where the same two people bid on a painting, they can't be sure how much the painting is valued by the other unless they know each other really well.

The second important distinction between games is whether all players in a game have to decide on the actions they will take at the same time or whether some players take actions before others do. We will call a game in which all players move at the same time *a simultaneous move game*, while we will call a game in which players move in sequence *a sequential move game*. In the latter, some players know at least a bit about how the other player is playing the game when the time comes to make a move. Simultaneous move games are sometimes referred to as *static*, while sequential move games are often called *dynamic*. The game Rock, Paper, Scissors for example, is a simultaneous move game, but the game of chess is a sequential move game.

Combining these two distinctions, we have four basic types of games summarized in Figure 24.1. These games become increasingly complex to analyze as one proceeds from left to right and from the top to the bottom row of the chart. Section A will focus solely on games of complete information, and Section B will extend our analysis to incomplete information games. Many games have both sequential and simultaneous stages, as we will see in our treatment of repeated simultaneous move games – games in which players meet repeatedly and, at each meeting, play a simultaneous move game. Similarly, we will see in Section B that some games have some players that have complete information and other players that have incomplete information. In such games, less informed individuals may attempt to gain information about the more informed players through their own strategic choices. We have already encountered examples in our treatment of asymmetric information where, for instance, insurance companies have less information than clients and in our treatment of second degree price-discriminating monopolists who had less information about what type of consumer they were dealing with than the consumers themselves.

Figure 24.1 Examples of Four Types of Games

	Simultaneous Moves	Sequential Moves
Complete Information	Rock, paper, scissors	Chess
Incomplete Information	Sealed bid art auction	Ascending bid art auction

24.A   Game Theory Under Complete Information

In this section, we will introduce the basics of game theory under complete information.

24A.1 Players, Actions, Sequence and Payoffs

We begin by defining the basic structure of complete information games. This structure is given by specifying who the players are, what actions they can take, in what sequence they move and what their payoffs are depending on the combination of moves made by the different players.

24A.1.1 Players and Actions Each of N different players in a given game is often permitted to take one of M possible *actions*. We will denote the set of possible actions for player n as a set $A^n = \{a_1^n, a_2^n, \ldots, a_M^n\}$. Often, the actions that different players of the game can take are the same for all players, in which case we can dispense with the superscript notation and denote the common set of possible actions for all players by the same set $A = \{a_1, a_2, \ldots, a_M\}$. Sometimes the set of possible actions will be continuous. For instance, it might be that a player n can choose any number on the interval $[0,1]$ as an action, in which case we denote the set of possible actions for player n as $A^n = [0,1]$.

Consider a simple game in which two individuals in a small town are the only ones that drive cars. They might choose to drive on the left side of the road or on the right side of the road. In this case, the two players have the same common set of actions $A = \{Left, Right\}$. Alternatively, we might have a game involving a single consumer and a single producer, where the producer can set a price between 0 and 100 for their product, and the consumer can decide to buy the product or not buy it. In that case, the set of actions available to the producer would be $A^p = [0,1]$ whereas the set of actions available to the consumer would be $A^c = \{Buy, Don't Buy\}$. Or an employer might offer either a high wage or a low wage to a worker, and the worker has the option of accepting or rejecting the offer, resulting in $A^e = \{High\ Wage,\ Low\ Wage\}$ and $A^w = \{Accept,\ Reject\}$.

Exercise 24A.1

In the case of employer and worker, which set of actions might be more appropriately modelled as continuous?

24A.1.2 Sequence of Actions A further feature of a game involves the *sequencing* of moves by the different players. In some cases, we might model an economic situation as one where all players have to decide what action to take *simultaneously*, while in other cases we might model a situation where some players will make *sequential* moves, with the actions of players who move early observable to the players who decide on their actions later on. The first is a *simultaneous move game*, while the second is a *sequential move game*. For instance, as two fuel station owners on opposite sides of a street come to work in the morning, they might face a simultaneous choice of what price to post as rush hour traffic is about to start. Alternatively, one fuel station owner might show up half an hour later to work, in which case they might be able to observe what their competitor has posted prior to deciding what they will post. *Players in a game are defined not only by the set of actions they have available to choose from but also by whether or not they are able to observe the other players' moves prior to determining their own.*

24A.1.3 The Payoff Matrix for a Simultaneous Move Game Once we have defined the set of possible actions and the sequence of moves for the relevant players in a game, we have to settle on what the consequences of different combinations of actions will be for each player. These consequences are referred to as *payoffs*, and the payoff for player n may depend on both their own action as well as the action(s) taken by others.

Exercise 24A.2*

Suppose that for every player n in a game, the payoffs for player n depend on player n's action as well as the sum of all the other players' actions, but no single other player has, alone, a perceptible influence on player n's payoff. Would such a game characterize a setting in which strategic thinking was important?

Payoffs for two-player, simultaneous move games in which both players have a discrete number of possible actions they can take are typically represented in a payoff matrix such as that depicted in Table 24.1.

Table 24.1 Payoffs in a Two-Player Simultaneous Move Game

		Player 2	
		a_1^2	a_2^2
Player 1	a_1^1	$u^1(a_1^1, a_1^2), u^2(a_1^1, a_1^2)$	$u^1(a_1^1, a_2^2), u^2(a_1^1, a_2^2)$
	a_2^1	$u^1(a_2^1, a_1^2), u^2(a_2^1, a_1^2)$	$u^1(a_2^1, a_2^2), u^2(a_2^1, a_2^2)$

In the game that is depicted, each player has two possible actions, with the actions for player 1 appearing on the left as a_1^1 and a_2^1 and actions for player 2 appearing at the top as a_1^2 and a_2^2. The payoffs for player 1 appear as either utility values or currencies in the matrix, (we will use euros) with $u^1(a_1^1, a_1^2)$ denoting the utility or euro payoff player 1 receives when both they and player 2 take action a_1, $u^1(a_1^1, a_1^2)$ denoting their payoff when they play action a_1 but their opponent plays action a_2, and so on. Similarly, player 2's payoffs appear as $u^2(a_1^1, a_1^2)$ when both players take action a_1, as $u^2(a_2^1, a_1^2)$ when player 1 takes action a_2 and they play a_1 and so forth.

Assume we again considered the simple game in which two individuals in a small town have to decide on which side of the road they should drive. In the end, neither individual cares much about which side of the road is ultimately chosen as long as their cars don't crash into each other when the two individuals choose different actions. The payoffs from this game might be represented in a payoff matrix such as the one depicted in Table 24.2 in which both individuals receive a payoff of 10 when they pick the same action but a payoff of 0 when they pick different actions.

Table 24.2 Driving on the Left or Right Side of the Road

		Player 2	
		Left	Right
Player 1	Left	10, 10	0, 0
	Right	0, 0	10, 10

Payoffs in games where players have a continuous set of possible actions, such as $A = [0,1]$, are represented in payoff *functions* that specify a player n's payoffs for any combination of actions taken by all the players. In a two-player game, we would find player n's payoff as a function $u^n(a^1, a^2)$ where u^n is a function that assigns a payoff value for n to any combination of player 1 and player 2 actions, both of which are drawn from the interval $[0,1]$ when $A = [0,1]$ for both players.

24A.1.4 Game Trees for Sequential Move Games Sequential move games are often represented in *game trees* that clearly specify the sequence of moves prior to indicating the payoff each player receives as different actions are taken. Graph 24.1 presents an example of such a game tree for the case where two players each have two possible actions to choose from, with player 1 moving before player 2.

Graph 24.1 Example of a Two-Player Sequential Move Game

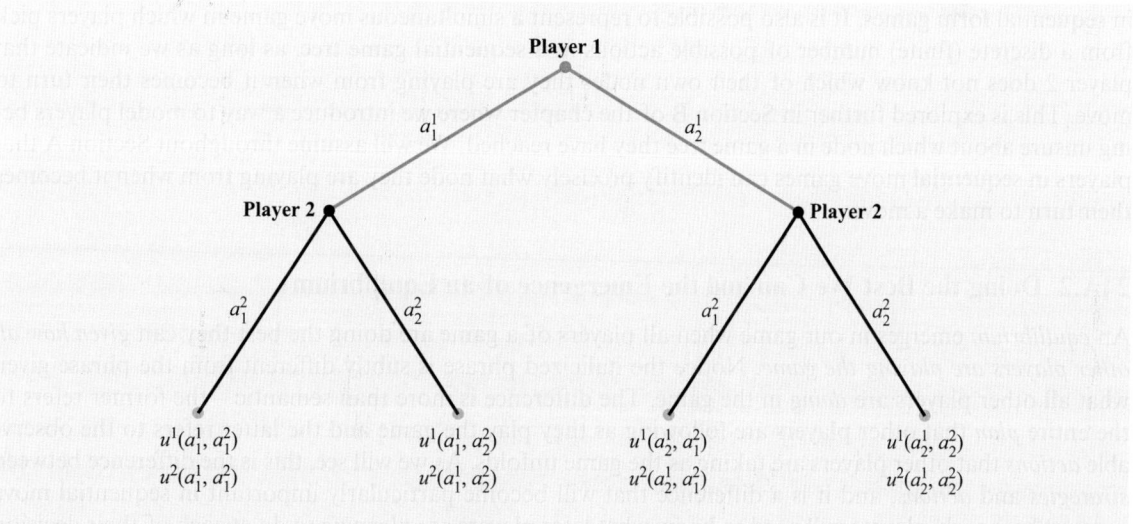

For player 2, two possible information nodes – or just *nodes* – emerge depending on which action player 1 has taken. If player 1 chooses action a_1, player 2 has sufficient information to know that they are making their decision at the left node, whereas if player 1 chooses action a_2, player 2 knows they are making their decision at the right node in the game tree. At the end of the game tree, the payoffs that result from each possible sequence of actions are indicated as utility values for each player.

Consider the same game as in Table 24.2 in which each player has a choice of driving on either the right or the left. Instead of assuming that the players choose simultaneously on which side of the road to drive, player 1 gets on the road first and player 2 gets to observe player 1's choice prior to making their own choice. Graph 24.2 displays the game tree for this sequential move game. The payoffs at the bottom of the game tree are the same as those we see in the payoff matrix in Table 24.2, with both players receiving a payoff of 10 if they choose the same side of the road and a payoff of 0 when they crash into each other because they chose different sides of the road.

Graph 24.2 Driving on the Left or Right Side of the Road with Sequential Moves

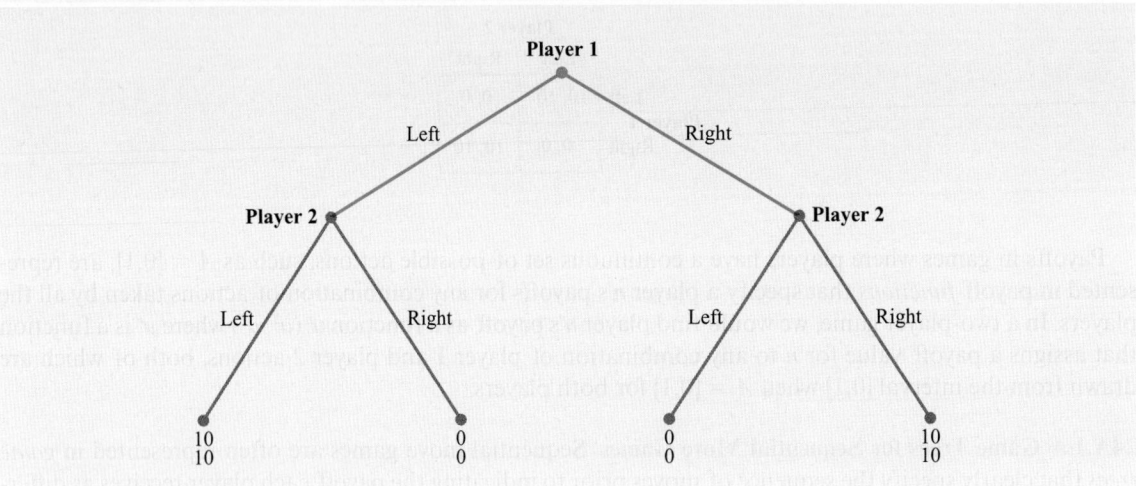

While game trees represent a very convenient way to present the structure of sequential move games in which each player picks from a discrete and finite number of possible actions, we will see that it is possible to also represent such games in payoff matrices once we have defined how *strategies* differ from *actions* in sequential form games. It is also possible to represent a simultaneous move game in which players pick from a discrete (finite) number of possible actions in a sequential game tree, as long as we indicate that player 2 does not know which of their own nodes they are playing from when it becomes their turn to move. This is explored further in Section B of the chapter where we introduce a way to model players being unsure about which node in a game tree they have reached. We will assume throughout Section A that players in sequential move games can identify precisely what node they are playing from when it becomes their turn to make a move.

24A.2 Doing the Best We Can and the Emergence of an Equilibrium

An *equilibrium* emerges in our game when all players of a game are doing the best they can *given how all other players are playing the game*. Notice the italicized phrase is subtly different from the phrase given what all other players are *doing* in the game. The difference is more than semantic – the former refers to the entire *plan* that other players are following as they play the game and the latter refers to the observable *actions* that other players are taking as the game unfolds. As we will see, this is the difference between *strategies* and *actions*, and it is a difference that will become particularly important in sequential move games where early players will need to know what later players are *planning* to do at each of their decision nodes in the game tree in order to know which action early on in the game has them doing the best they can. We will first define *strategies* as *plans of action* for each player, and we will say that an equilibrium has been reached when each player is playing a strategy that is the *best response* to the strategies played by the other player(s).

24A.2.1 **Strategies** Strategies are most straightforwardly defined in simultaneous move games in which all players have to choose a plan of action at the same time. Each player in such a game can either settle on a particular action to take or decide to play particular actions with some probability. A strategy that involves picking a particular action with probability 1 is called a *pure strategy*, while a strategy that places probabilities of less than 1 on more than one action is called a *mixed strategy*. In most of the chapter, we will focus only on pure strategies, but we will conclude Section A with an optional discussion of mixed strategies and their role in the development of game theory models. In fact, all strategies can be viewed as mixed strategies, with pure strategies being special cases that assign probability 0 to all but one action.

In sequential move games, strategies are a little more complicated because some players will already know what other players are doing when they decide on their own actions. Thus, a complete plan of action for a player other than the one who moves first involves a plan for what to do *at each possible node at which a player might find themselves in the game tree*. A pure strategy for player 2 in the game depicted in Graph 24.2, for instance, involves a plan for what to do in case player 1 has chosen the action *Left* and what to do if player 1 has chosen the action *Right*. Pure strategies in simultaneous move games involve picking one action, while pure strategies in sequential move games involve picking one action at each node in the game tree. Just as in simultaneous move games, a mixed strategy in a sequential setting involves playing different pure strategies with probabilities that sum to 1, but we will limit our discussion of mixed strategies to simultaneous move games.

When we restrict ourselves to considering pure strategies, player 2 in the game in Graph 24.2 has *four possible strategies even though they only have two possible actions available*. These strategies are:

Strategy 1: Always play *Left*.
Strategy 2: Always play *Right*.
Strategy 3: Play *Left* if player 1 plays *Left* and play *Right* if player 1 plays *Right*.
Strategy 4: Play *Right* if player 1 plays *Left* and play *Left* if player 1 plays *Right*.

We can denote these four strategies as (*Left, Left*), (*Right, Right*), (*Left, Right*) and (*Right, Left*), with the first action in each pair indicating the plan of action if player 2 ends up on the left node in the game tree and the second action in each pair indicating the plan of action if player 2 finds themself on the right node in the game tree.

Exercise 24A.3

True or False: In simultaneous move games, the number of pure strategies available to a player is necessarily equal to the number of actions a player has available.

Once we recognize that players who move later in the sequence within a sequential move game have more pure strategies than actions available to them, we can see how we can represent the structure of such games in payoff matrices rather than game trees. All we have to do is list the payoffs that each player will receive for each combination of pure *strategies*. For the game in which players choose the right or left side of the road sequentially, this implies that player 1 has only 2 pure strategies equal to the actions they are able to take, while player 2 has four pure strategies. The sequential move game represented in Graph 24.2 can also be represented in the payoff matrix in Table 24.3. Representing a game in a payoff matrix is often referred to as the game's *normal form*, whereas representing the game in a game tree is often referred to as the game's *extensive form*.

Exercise 24A.4

Verify that the payoffs listed in Table 24.3 are consistent with those given in the game tree of Graph 24.2.

24A.2.2 Pure Strategy Nash Equilibrium in Simultaneous Move Games John Nash was the first to formalize the notion of an equilibrium in games, and what we explore next has therefore come to be called a *Nash equilibrium*. The definition of such an equilibrium is best given in terms of best responses, where *a best response for player n to a set of strategies played by other players is a strategy that will result in the highest possible payoff for player n given the strategies played by others*. A *Nash equilibrium* is reached whenever *each player in the game is playing a best-response strategy relative to the strategies played by all other players*; that is, whenever everyone's plan is the best possible plan given the plans that all the others have adopted. In some cases, we will see that it is very clear what Nash equilibrium will emerge as individual players try to do the best they can given how others are playing the game. Sometimes, a single equilibrium will emerge, while other times multiple different equilibria are possible. Depending on the structure of the game, we will find instances when only pure strategies are employed in equilibrium, but many games also have mixed strategy equilibria. In games where there are no pure strategy equilibria, there generally exists a mixed strategy equilibrium. In the original investigation by Nash on the existence of Nash equilibria, it was proved that such equilibria generally exist as long as the equilibrium concept includes mixed strategies. In games in which there are multiple pure strategy equilibria, there generally also exist mixed-strategy equilibria.

Table 24.3 A Sequential Move Game Represented in a Payoff Matrix

		Player 2			
		(Left, Left)	(Right, Right)	(Left, Right)	(Right, Left)
Player 1	Left	10, 10	0, 0	10, 10	0, 0
	Right	0, 0	10, 10	10, 10	0, 0

Let's consider the game represented in the payoff matrix in Table 24.2. Player 1 is contemplating what pure strategy to play. If player 2 chooses to drive on the left side of the road, player 1 knows that they will get a payoff of 10 if they also choose the left side but will receive a payoff of 0 if they choose the right side. Their best response to player 2's strategy of playing *Left* is therefore to play *Left* as well. Similarly, if player 2 chooses the right side of the road, player 1's best response is to also choose *Right*. Player 1 will do the best they can if they mimic what player 2 does. Player 2 faces the same incentives.

We can look at each of the four possible outcomes and check to see if the outcome could be supported by Nash equilibrium strategies. The two outcomes that result in 0 payoff for each player cannot possibly be an equilibrium outcome because, if they find themselves crashing into each other as they are choosing different sides of the road, there is a way for player 1 to improve their fortunes by changing what they do. The two outcomes that result in payoffs of 10, on the other hand, can be equilibrium outcomes. Whenever one of them chooses *Left*, the other's best response is to also choose *Left*, and whenever one of them chooses *Right*, the best response of the other is to also choose *Right*. If they end up in the upper left corner of the payoff matrix, neither has an incentive to change what they are doing, implying that they have reached an equilibrium. The same holds for the lower right corner of the payoff matrix.

In this example, it is unclear whether both players driving on the right side or both driving on the left side will emerge as an equilibrium. In the real world, conventions arise and are often formalized in laws that ensure everyone knows which equilibrium is to be expected. In some societies, the convention of driving on the left side of the road has become the equilibrium, while in other societies the convention of driving on the right side has emerged. Games like this are sometimes called *coordination games* because the key for the players is to *coordinate* their actions to get to one of the possible pure strategy equilibria.

Exercise 24A.5

Are the two pure strategy Nash equilibria we have identified efficient?

It might appear at this point that an equilibrium will necessarily entail both sides achieving the maximum possible payoffs. If this were always the case, the first welfare theorem would still hold in the sense that decentralized decision making by individuals is resulting in efficient outcomes. This is not necessarily the case. Suppose we changed the payoff matrix in Table 24.2 by assuming that each has an innate preference for driving on the left side of the road and thus they only receive a payoff of 5 each if they end up driving on the right side. In this case, both players driving on the right side of the road is still an equilibrium of the game; if one chooses to play *Right*, it remains a best response for the other to also choose *Right. Games with multiple equilibria might therefore have some equilibria that are better for everyone than others*. In such cases, a role for non-market institutions emerges to try to get individuals to switch from the suboptimal equilibrium to the more efficient one.

24A.2.3 Dominant Strategy Equilibria in Simultaneous Move Games Even in games where there is a single pure strategy Nash equilibrium, however, there is no guarantee that the Nash equilibrium will achieve the maximum possible payoffs for the players. Consider the games defined by the payoff matrices in Tables 24.4 and 24.5. In the first game, a clear optimal strategy for each player is to always play the action *Up* because *regardless of what the other player does*, each individual player is better off playing *Up* rather than *Down*. This is an example of a game with a clear *dominant strategy, a strategy where a player always has the incentive to play a single action regardless of what the opponent does.* Even if you think your opponent will play the action *Down*, it is best for you to play *Up* because that will give you a payoff of 7 rather than 5. Since both players face the same incentives, a single pure strategy equilibrium emerges in which both players play *Up* and thus receive a payoff of 10. The game in Table 24.4 therefore unambiguously leads to an equilibrium in which both players receive the highest possible payoff; that is, the Nash equilibrium is efficient and is particularly compelling since it is both the only equilibrium *and* it involves each player playing a strategy that is the best for that player regardless of what the other player does.

Table 24.4 A Game with a Single Efficient Pure Strategy Nash Equilibrium

		Player 2 Up	Down
Player 1	Up	10, 10	7, 7
	Down	7, 7	5, 5

Exercise 24A.6

True or False: If a simultaneous move game gives rise to a dominant strategy for a player, that strategy is a best response for any strategy played by the other players.

Now consider the game in Table 24.5. If player 1 plays *Up*, player 2 will receive a payoff of 10 by also choosing *Up* and a payoff of 15 if player 2 chooses *Down*. Player 2's best response to player 1 playing *Up* is therefore to play *Down*. If, on the other hand, player 1 chooses to play *Down*, player 2 will receive a payoff of 0 if they play *Up* and a payoff of 5 if they play *Down*. Playing *Down* is also 2's best response to 1 playing *Down*. Playing *Down* is a *dominant strategy* for 2 because it is their best response to any strategy player 1 plays. Since player 1 faces the same incentives, they will both end up playing *Down*, resulting in the equilibrium outcome represented by the payoffs (5,5) in the lower right corner of the payoff matrix. Thus, *even though they would both prefer the payoffs (10,10) in the upper left corner of the matrix, the incentives in the game are such that both will end up in the lower right corner with payoffs (5,5)*. The unique Nash equilibrium of this game is therefore inefficient, and it is just as compelling an equilibrium as the one we found in Table 24.4 in that it is the only pure strategy equilibrium *and* it involves only dominant strategies.

Table 24.5	A Game With a Single Inefficient Pure Strategy Nash Equilibrium		
		Player 2	
		Up	Down
Player 1	Up	10, 10	0, 15
	Down	15, 0	5, 5

We will discuss this game – known as the 'Prisoner's Dilemma' – in more detail because it will represent an important game that can be used to analyze many economic situations in the real world. For now, however, it should be clear that we will be unable to come up with something analogous to the first welfare theorem derived for competitive economies when individual players have an incentive to be strategic in their decision making. We will not be able to say in general that equilibria that rely on decentralized decision making by individuals are always efficient in economic circumstances that can be modelled by game theory. Sometimes they are, and sometimes they are not.

Exercise 24A.7

Suppose that player 2 has payoffs as in Table 24.4, while player 1 has payoffs as in Table 24.5. Write out this payoff matrix. Is there a dominant strategy equilibrium? Is there a unique Nash equilibrium? If so, is it efficient?

Exercise 24A.8

Suppose both players' payoffs are as in Table 24.5 except that player 1's payoff when both players play *Up* is 20. Is there a dominant strategy equilibrium? Is there a unique Nash equilibrium? If so, is it efficient?

Exercise 24A.9

Suppose payoffs are as in exercise 24A.8 except that player 2's payoff from playing *Down* is 10 less than before regardless of what player 1 does. Is there a dominant strategy equilibrium? Is there a unique Nash equilibrium? If so, is it efficient?

24A.2.4 Nash Equilibrium in Sequential Move Games The notion of a Nash equilibrium can be straightforwardly applied in sequential move games if we represent the structure of such games within a payoff matrix in which we specify the set of payoffs for each combination of strategies. In Table 24.3 we depicted the structure of the game in which two players sequentially chose which side of the road to drive.

Exercise 24A.10

Can you find which strategies in the game depicted in Table 24.3 constitute a Nash equilibrium? *Hint*: You should be able to find four combinations of strategies that constitute Nash equilibria.

A slightly more interesting version of this game arises when we assume that the players have different innate preferences for driving on the left side of the road. Suppose that player 1 is from the UK and prefers driving on the left while player 2 is from Germany and prefers driving on the right. This results in a payoff of 10 for player 1 and a payoff of 5 for player 2 if they both choose *Left*, the reverse when they both choose *Right*, and payoffs of 0 for both when they choose different sides of the road. In the case when the players move simultaneously, this would result in two pure strategy equilibria: one in which both players drive on the left side of the road and one in which both players drive on the right side of the road.

When player 2 makes their choice after player 1 moves, the payoff matrix with strategies properly defined analogous to what we derived in Section 24A.2.1, is given in Table 24.6.

There are now several Nash equilibria in this sequential game, with the accompanying equilibrium outcomes shaded in Table 24.6. One of these equilibria involves player 1 playing *Right* and player 2 playing (*Right, Right*). Given that player 2 always plays *Right*, it is a best response for player 1 to play *Right*, and given that player 1 plays *Right*, player 2's (*Right, Right*) strategy is a best response. Thus, the outcome of both players driving on the right side of the road is possible in a Nash equilibrium in the sequential move game.

Exercise 24A.11

Is it also a Nash equilibrium for player 1 to play *Right* and player 2 to play (*Left, Right*)? If not, why was it a Nash equilibrium before when players were indifferent between coordinating on the left or the right side of the road?

In the case where player 1 gets to decide first which side of the road to pick, however, this equilibrium seems very counterintuitive. The only reason this is a Nash equilibrium is that player 2 is in effect threatening to drive on the right side of the road regardless of what player 1 chooses to do. This threat is fundamentally non-credible because player 1 knows that player 2 is better off driving on the left side of the road once they see that player 1 has chosen to drive on the left. For this reason, game theorists have developed a more refined notion of Nash equilibrium for sequential move games, a refinement that eliminates the possibility that non-credible threats are taken seriously in equilibrium. This refinement is known as *subgame perfection*.

24A.2.5 Subgame Perfect Equilibria in Sequential Move Games It is reasonable to assume that players who move early in a sequential move game will look down the game tree and determine what strategies by players that follow are *credible*, and that only credible strategies can emerge in an equilibrium. This implies that player 1 will look at each node in the game tree of the sequential move game to determine what is optimal for player 2. Player 1 can infer something about what player 2 plans to do once player 2 has observed the action of player 1.

Consider the game tree in Graph 24.3 that depicts the game represented in the payoff matrix in Table 24.6. Player 1 can now view each of the 2 nodes that player 2 could face as a separate *subgame* in which player 2 is the only player. If the left node is reached as a result of player 1 playing *Left*, it is optimal for player 2 to also play *Left*, which we indicate in the graph by highlighting this action. Thus, player 1 can infer that they will receive a payoff of 10 if they move *Left*. If the right node is reached as a result of player 1 playing *Right*, on the other hand, player 1 knows it will be optimal for player 2 to play *Right*, leading to a payoff of 5 for player 1. We indicate this in the graph by highlighting that action. In choosing between *Left* and *Right*, player 1 knows that they are choosing between a payoff of 10 and a payoff of 5 and will therefore choose to play *Left*. The only rational response for player 2 is to also play *Left*, which leads to a unique equilibrium in which both players drive on the left side of the road.

Graph 24.3 Game Tree for the Game Represented in Table 24.6

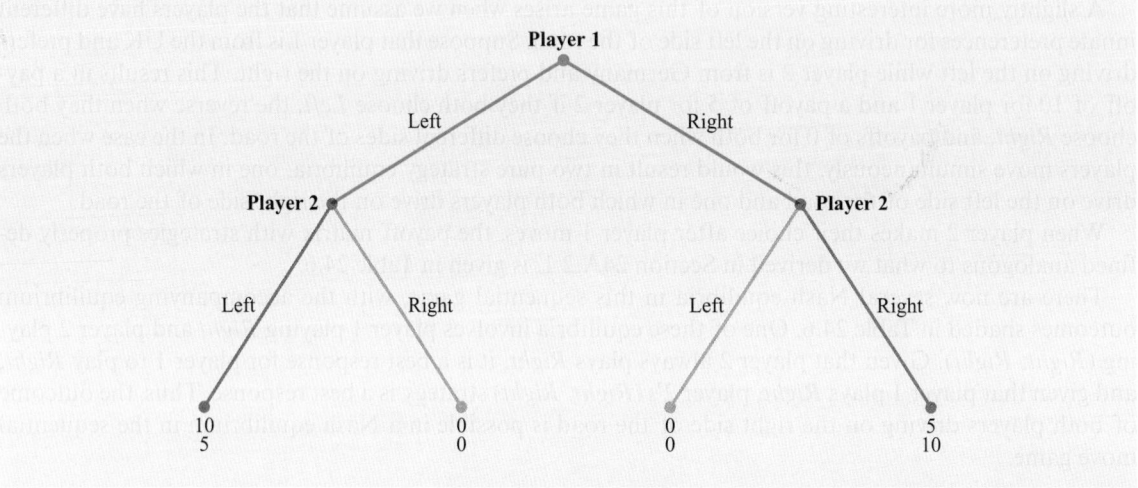

Table 24.6 The Sequential *Right/Left* Game with *Left* Preferred by Player 1 and *Right* Preferred by Player 2

		Player 2			
		(Left, Left)	(Right, Right)	(Left, Right)	(Right, Left)
Player 1	Left	**10, 5**	0, 0	**10, 5**	0, 0
	Right	0, 0	**5, 10**	5, 10	0, 0

While the outcome in which both players drive on the right side can therefore arise from a Nash equilibrium in which player 2 plays the strategy (*Right, Right*), this outcome cannot emerge as an equilibrium in which player 1 refuses to give into non-credible threats. The elimination of Nash equilibria that are supported by non-credible threats results in *subgame perfect equilibria*. The notion of subgame perfection is due to Reinhard Selten who was awarded the Nobel Prize together with John Nash. Subgame perfect equilibria can equivalently be defined as Nash equilibria under which the equilibrium strategies represent Nash equilibria *for every subgame* of the actual sequential game. In this game, the logic of subgame perfection implies that player 1 has a *first-mover advantage*. Player 1 gets their preferred outcome as long as they do not give into non-credible threats.

Exercise 24A.12

True or False: In sequential move games, all pure strategy subgame perfect equilibria are pure strategy Nash equilibria, but not all pure strategy Nash equilibria are subgame perfect.

Exercise 24A.13

What are the Nash equilibria and the subgame perfect equilibria if player 2 rather than player 1 gets to move first in this version of the game?

It is not the case that a *first mover* in a game will always get their way. Consider a firm that currently has a monopoly in a particular market, but worries about a potential second firm entering the market and competing. To keep the game simple, assume that the existing firm can set a *Low* or a *High* price for the product and that the potential firm can choose to *Enter* or *Not Enter* after observing the price set by the existing firm. Assume that the payoffs, or profits, in this game are as depicted in Graph 24.4.

Graph 24.4 Facing Potential Competition

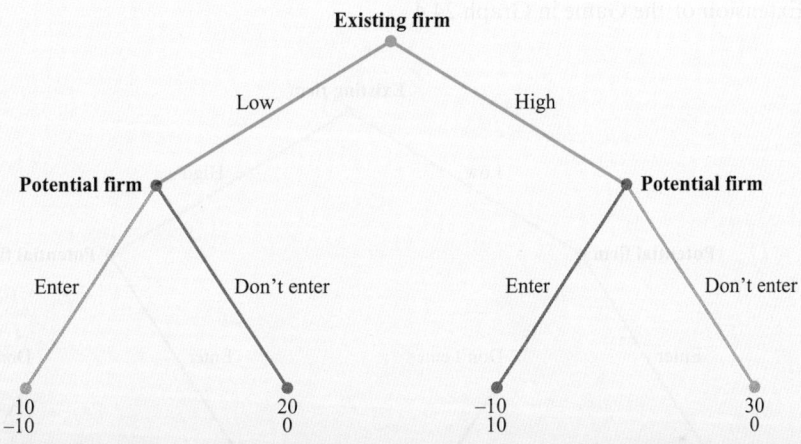

Go to MindTap to interact with this graph

If the potential firm does not enter, it receives a profit of 0, but if it enters, it earns a positive profit when the current price is high and a negative profit when the current price is low. The existing firm, on the other hand, earns the highest profit under a high price and no competition and the lowest profit if it announces a high price and the competitor enters and undercuts that price in order to steal customers. The existing firm looks down the game tree at each node faced by its potential competitor and determines what the competitor will do at each node. When price is set low by the existing firm, the competitor will not enter because they would make a profit of -10 by entering, but when price is set high, they will enter. In choosing between *Low* and *High*, the existing firm is choosing between a payoff of 20 and a payoff of -10 and will choose the low price in order to keep the potential firm from entering. This results in the subgame perfect equilibrium in which the existing firm sets a low price and the potential firm does not enter. Notice that in this case, the subgame perfect equilibrium does not result in the most preferred outcome for the first mover, and it is supported by a credible threat that the potential firm will enter if the price is set high by the existing firm.

Finally, we can note from the sequential move game in Graph 24.4 that just as we found in simultaneous move games, there is no guarantee that equilibria in game theory are efficient; that is, there is no general first welfare theorem. The efficient outcome from the perspective of the two players is the outcome that maximizes the sum of the profits or payoffs. In our example, that occurs when the existing firm earns a profit of 30 and faces no competition from potential entrants. At least as the game is specified in Graph 24.4, this is not a subgame perfect equilibrium. Rather, the subgame perfect equilibrium results in a profit of 20 for the existing firm and a profit of zero for the potential entrant. From the perspective of the two firms, a move to the outcome in which the existing firm gets to set a high price and the potential firm does not enter makes one player better off without making the other worse off, but it is not an outcome that can be sustained as an equilibrium in the game without some non-market institution altering the incentives of the game.

Exercise 24A.14

Suppose the game had a third stage in which the existing firm gets a chance to re-evaluate its price in the event that a new firm has entered the market. This would imply that the game tree in Graph 24.4 continues as depicted in Graph 24.5. What is the subgame perfect equilibrium in this case?

Graph 24.5 An Extension of the Game in Graph 24.4

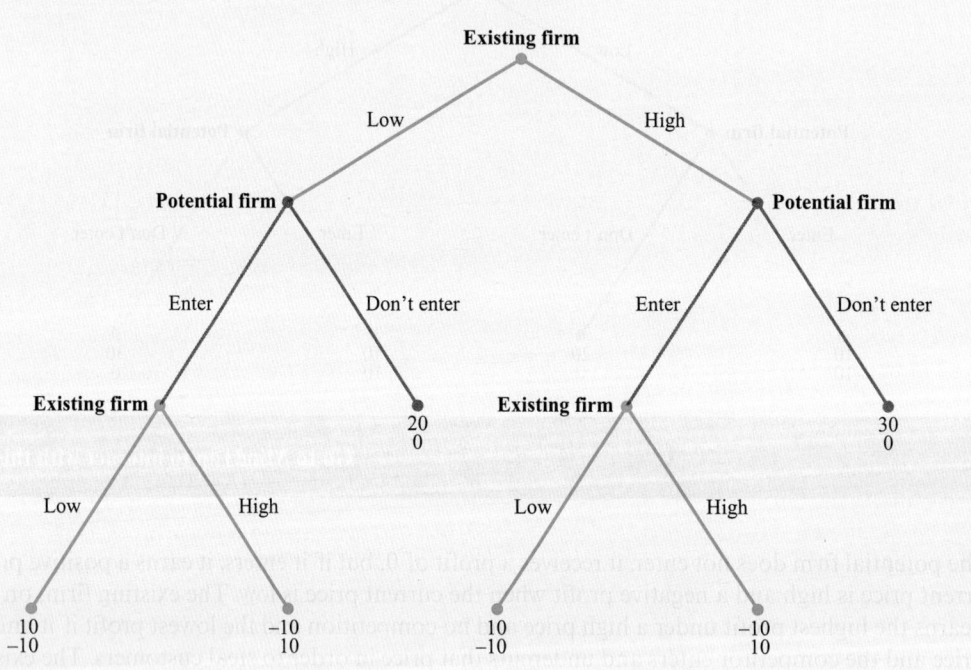

Exercise 24A.15

In our example in Graph 24.4, we say that the subgame perfect equilibrium is not efficient from the perspective of the two players. Could it be efficient from the perspective of society?

24A.2.6 Solving for Pure Strategy Nash and Subgame Perfect Equilibria It is useful to briefly review the method by which we solve for equilibria. *In the case of Nash equilibria in which two players have a finite number of actions to choose from, we start with the payoff matrix*, whether this represents a simultaneous move game or a sequential move game. Let's refer to the player whose strategies appear in the rows of the matrix as the row player and the player whose strategies appear in the columns of the matrix as the column player. To solve for pure strategy Nash equilibria, we start with the first strategy of the row player and ask which strategy or strategies the column player would play as a best response. For each of these best-response strategies by the column player, we ask whether the first-row strategy is a best response by the row player. When we find a case where the first-row strategy is a best response to one of the column player's best responses, we have identified a Nash equilibrium. Doing this for each row, we end up finding all the pure strategy Nash equilibria.

When the set of possible actions for players in a simultaneous move game are not finite, such as when the set A is a continuum like the line segment [0,1] from which the player can choose any point, we cannot use payoff matrices as just described because such matrices would have to specify the payoffs from an infinite number of combinations of actions. We will develop the method for solving such games explicitly in the next chapter. For now, note the logic of a strategy and an equilibrium remains the same; all we will do is define best-response functions that must intersect in an equilibrium. This is similar to how we solve games with discrete numbers of possible actions for mixed strategy equilibria in Section 24A.4.

In the case of subgame perfect Nash equilibria to sequential games in which players have a finite number of actions to choose from, *we have to start with the game tree rather than the payoff matrix of the game.* In particular, we start at the bottom of the game tree and ask which action is optimal at each node of the last player. These actions are the only actions that could be planned in a credible strategy for that player, and we assume that these are in fact the actions that would be played at the respective nodes. We move to the second-to-last player and ask which action at each of the player's nodes is optimal given that the player assumes the final player will play rationally at each of their nodes in the next stage. This allows us to identify the optimal actions for the second-to-last player, which can be taken as given by the third-to-last player. In this way, we can solve the game backwards to the top and derive the full set of subgame perfect equilibrium strategies. It is important to keep in mind, however, that the equilibrium is defined by best-response *strategies*, and not just by the path along which the game unfolds in equilibrium. The players' plans off the equilibrium path are often crucial to keeping other players on the equilibrium path. When some players have a continuum of possible actions they can choose from, we will see that the basic logic for solving such games will mirror that for games with a finite set of possible actions.

24A.3 The Prisoner's Dilemma

In Table 24.6, we illustrated a simultaneous move game in which each player has a dominant strategy, and in which the resulting Nash equilibrium is inefficient. This type of game is often referred to as the *Prisoner's Dilemma*, and it occupies a particularly important place in microeconomics because it so starkly illustrates how strategic behaviour can lead to outcomes that can be improved on through some type of non-market institution.

The name *Prisoner's Dilemma* has its origins in the 1950s when Albert Tucker (1905–1995), a mathematician and dissertation adviser to the young John Nash, attempted to find an accessible way of illustrating the basic incentives of the game with a story that made sense to psychology undergraduates at Stanford University, USA. The underlying game was already known at the time and played a significant role in the Rand Corporation's investigation of game theory as part of a government sponsored project to research incentives in global nuclear strategy. A police detective knows that two individuals they have in custody have committed armed robbery but they do not have enough evidence to convict them on anything other than a relatively minor charge of illegal possession of an offensive weapon. The detective puts them in separate rooms and tells each of them that they can choose to confess or deny the armed robbery. If one confesses and the other does not, the detective will let the confessor out on parole while using the testimony to go for the maximum sentence of 20 years in prison for the one that remains silent. If they both confess, they will each get a plea agreement that will put them in prison for five years. If neither confesses, all the detective can do is pursue the illegal weapons convictions and get them one-year prison sentences each.

Table 24.7 illustrates the payoff matrix that the detective has created for the two prisoners. Confessing is a dominant strategy for each of the players, implying a unique Nash equilibrium outcome in which both confess and get five-year prison terms. Both prisoners would have preferred the outcome in which they only go to prison for one year. This, however, would require both of them to deny the armed robbery, and this would require that each play a strategy that is not a best response; *regardless* of what the other prisoner does, each prisoner is better off confessing. From the perspective of the prisoners, the detective's game has set up incentives that will result in an inefficient outcome. It will also cause them to falsely confess if they happen to be innocent.

Exercise 24A.16

Why is this outcome inefficient from the perspective of the two players? Could it be efficient from the perspective of society?

Many economic circumstances have similar incentives. We may all wish to live in a society in which we smile and are courteous to one another. Smiling and being courteous requires effort, and so regardless of whether others smile and show courtesy, it might be a dominant strategy to individually behave impolitely. We may all want to live in a world in which we look out for our neighbours and provide them with help when they are in need, but helping others requires effort and it might just be a dominant strategy to not bother and just hope others will take care of it. Once you have internalized the incentive structure of the Prisoner's Dilemma game, you'll see these incentives all around you. We want to live in a world in which we cooperate with one another for the common good, but it is often in our self-interest not to cooperate and hope everyone else will. The fact that individuals inadvertently cooperate in competitive markets and maximize overall social surplus as illustrated by the first welfare theorem does not mean they cooperate purposefully when put in situations where they have an incentive to behave strategically.

An understanding of the incentives in Prisoner's Dilemma games means that observing a lack of cooperation in the world is not surprising. What is surprising is how much cooperation we actually do observe in the real world despite the predictions of the Prisoner's Dilemma. While it may not happen to the extent to which we would hope, we see neighbours helping one another, individuals holding open doors for strangers, charities successfully raising money to combat hunger and disease, and soldiers dying in battle to save another's life. We also see prisoners denying crimes when faced with the incentives in Table 24.7 and firms colluding to set prices even when it appears that they would individually benefit by producing more than their collusive agreement permits. In some sense, once we understand the Prisoner's Dilemma, the question becomes not 'Why don't we observe people cooperating more with one another?', but rather 'Why do we see any cooperation in many of these situations at all?'

Table 24.7 The Prisoner's Dilemma With Years in Prison as Payoffs

		Prisoner 2	
		Deny	Confess
Prisoner 1	Deny	1, 1	20, 0
	Confess	0, 20	5, 5

24A.3.1 Repeated Prisoner's Dilemma Games and the Unravelling of Cooperation One possible explanation for cooperation in the real world is that, at least in some circumstances, players run into each other repeatedly and therefore develop a cooperative relationship. It turns out, however, that repeated interaction in circumstances that can be described by the Prisoner's Dilemma is not enough for game theory to predict cooperation.

Exercise 24A.17

Why is this a Prisoner's Dilemma game?

Suppose two people face the payoffs in euro terms in Table 24.8 every time they meet. Assume player 1 and player 2 know that they will run into each other 100 times, and each time they will face the incentives in Table 24.8. This means they are now playing a *sequential move game* in the sense that they encounter each other after the first time, knowing what they did in previous encounters, but in each encounter they play a *simultaneous move game*. Subgame perfection requires that we start at the very bottom of the game tree that, in this case, consists of 100 different simultaneous move games. We can ask: What would we expect will happen when they encounter each other for the 100th, and last time?

Since they will know that they will not encounter each other again, it will be as if they played the game one time, with each facing a dominant strategy of not cooperating in that last encounter. When they meet each other the 99th time, it is not credible for either one to promise or threaten any action other than not cooperating in the 100th round. They will both know in the 99th round that they will not cooperate in the 100th round, but there is no particular reason to cooperate in the 99th round; once again, regardless of what player 2 does in the 99th round, player 1 will do better by not cooperating. They both realize when they play the 98th round that they will not cooperate in the 99th or 100th rounds, which, by the same logic, implies they won't cooperate in the 98th round or in any round before that. *The prediction from subgame perfection is that they will not cooperate in the Prisoner's Dilemma even if they know they will interact repeatedly n different times.* This holds true regardless how large *n* is assuming it is finite.

Notice what is going on in this argument for why cooperation will not arise even under repeated interactions. They might think that if they know they will run into each other 100 times, player 1 could say to player 2, 'Why don't we cooperate since we will run into each other repeatedly and we both know we'll be better off by cooperating?' Player 2 might trust that what player 1 said is true. Player 1 might even try a carrot-and-stick approach by telling player 2 that they will cooperate as long as player 2 cooperates, but if they see 2 not cooperating, 1 will punish player 2 and never cooperate again. The problem is that player 1's promise to cooperate is not credible because as player 2 looks down the game tree, they know 1 will not cooperate in the 100th round, which means that there is no incentive to cooperate in the 99th round, which means there is no incentive to cooperate in the 98th round, and so on.

Table 24.8 Another Prisoner's Dilemma With Payoffs in €s

		Player 2	
		Cooperate	Don't cooperate
Player 1	Cooperate	100, 100	0, 200
	Don't cooperate	200, 0	10, 10

Exercise 24A.18*

Does the same logic hold for any repeated simultaneous game in which the simultaneous game has a single pure strategy Nash equilibrium? Does subgame perfection require that players in such games always repeat the simultaneous game Nash equilibrium?

24A.3.2 Infinitely Repeated Games, Trigger Strategies and Cooperation The reason why cooperation un-ravels in the repeated Prisoner's Dilemma is that both players can look towards the last time they interact and work backwards to realize that there is no credible, that is subgame perfect, way of sustaining any cooperation. What if there were no 'last time'? What if the players keep running into each other without end? Or more realistically, what if they are never sure whether they'll run into each other again, but each time they run into each other they know there is a good chance they'll see each other again under similar circumstances?

Exercise 24A.19

True or False: In an infinitely repeated Prisoner's Dilemma game, every subgame of the sequential game is identical to the original game.

Before answering this question, we need to briefly address what the concept of subgame perfection means in the case of a game that has no end. So far, we have thought of subgame perfection as eliminating non-credible strategies by solving the game from the bottom up, but now there is no bottom! The basic idea of subgame perfection can, however, be expressed a little differently and in a way that allows us to apply it to infinitely repeated games. When we solve the game backwards in a finite sequential game, we are actually making sure that the Nash equilibrium is such that each *subgame* of the whole game – that is, each game that begins at one of the nodes in the game tree – is also in equilibrium. We are requiring that the subgames that are off-the-equilibrium path and are never reached still involve strategies that are best responses to each other in the hypothetical case that such subgames were reached. We can restate the concept of a subgame perfect equilibrium by defining it as follows: *A Nash equilibrium in a sequential move game of complete information is subgame perfect if all subgames of the sequential game, whether they are reached in equilibrium or not, also involve Nash equilibrium strategies.*

Now let's return to the question: What could be a subgame perfect equilibrium in a repeated Prisoner's Dilemma game in which there is no definitive end to the interactions? Robert Axelrod (1943–), a political scientist, has written a famous series of papers in which precisely this question was analyzed theoretically and experimentally. Consider the case in which two players meet repeatedly, and each time they meet they know that they will meet again with probability γ. At the beginning of their interactions, they decide on their strategies. A strategy for player 1 is a complete plan for what they will do each time they run into each other, a plan in which they can make their actions dependent on how they interacted in the past. Axelrod distinguished between two kinds of such plans or strategies they might adopt: those that are 'nice' and those that are 'not nice'. Nice strategies are those in which an individual will not stop cooperating first, while not nice strategies are those in which an individual is the first to stop cooperating.

Exercise 24A.20

True or False: If two players play nice strategies in the repeated Prisoner's Dilemma, they will always cooperate with one another every time they meet.

Suppose, for instance, player 1 plays a strategy in which they plan to cooperate the first time they see player 2 and plan to continue cooperating every time they see player 2 as long as all their previous interactions have been characterized by both cooperating. If at some point they do not cooperate, player 1 will punish player 2 by never cooperating again. One act of non-cooperation, according to this strategy, will trigger player 1's non-cooperation at every meeting thereafter, which is why this type of strategy is sometimes called a *trigger strategy*.

Exercise 24A.21

Explain why this type of trigger strategy is nice.

What is player 2's best response to this strategy? One possible best response might well be for them to play the same strategy, resulting in both always cooperating. This is because the cost of being punished with non-cooperation from now on is too high to justify the gain from not cooperating once while player 1 is still cooperating. Whether it's worth it to player 2 to cheat player 1 at their current encounter by not cooperating, despite knowing that player 1 will never cooperate again thereafter depends on two things: the probability γ that they will meet again and the degree to which player 2 discounts the future. If γ is sufficiently high and player 2 does not discount the future too much, they will value future cooperation more than the one-time payoff they could get by cheating at the present meeting.

Exercise 24A.22

Would player 2 playing 'Cooperate Always' also potentially be a best response for player 2 to player 1's trigger strategy? Would player 1's trigger strategy be a best response to player 2's 'Cooperate Always' strategy?

If player 2 playing the trigger strategy is a best response to player 1 playing this strategy, it is also a best response for player 1 to play this strategy if player 2 plays it. When both play this strategy, they will always cooperate with one another. It is certainly possible to have Nash equilibria in which cooperation is sustained in repeated relationships that are characterized by Prisoner's Dilemma incentives if those relationships have no clear end. Is such a Nash equilibrium subgame perfect? Given our restated definition of subgame perfection as involving only strategies that are Nash equilibrium strategies to every subgame, are the Nash equilibrium strategies proposed also Nash equilibrium strategies in every subgame of the infinitely repeated game? Every such subgame is an infinitely repeated game identical to the original game, but subgames have different histories of previous interactions between the two players that led up to them. Unlike the first time they meet, player 1 knows something about how player 2 is playing the game every time they meet thereafter, and player 2 knows something about how player 1 plays the game.

When they reach a particular subgame, there are two possible histories that have brought them there: either they have got there by always cooperating, or by not cooperating at some point. If they had always cooperated previously, given that they are playing their trigger strategies, they are starting this subgame in exactly the same way as they started the first time they interacted. They both cooperate and plan to continue cooperating unless one of them deviates at some point. If the proposed trigger strategy played by both was a Nash equilibrium to the original game, it must be a Nash equilibrium to this subgame. This leaves us to consider the off-the-equilibrium path case where cooperation broke down at some point in a previous meeting. In this case, their trigger strategies for the next subgame require both to 'Never Cooperate'. Given that player 2 will never cooperate, it is a best response for player 1 to never cooperate and the other way around. They are best responding to each other in this kind of a subgame, and they have shown that both playing the proposed trigger strategy represents a Nash equilibrium in every subgame of their infinitely repeated game. These strategies are therefore subgame perfect.

The threats required to sustain cooperation are credible in our example. As we demonstrate in the appendix, *anything between no cooperation and full cooperation* can be part of a subgame perfect equilibrium through similar trigger strategies in an infinitely repeated Prisoner's Dilemma. When Prisoner's Dilemma games are repeated infinitely, many possible subgame perfect equilibria emerge even though there is only a single subgame perfect equilibrium when such games are repeated a large but finite number of times.

Exercise 24A.23

Why can't the same type of trigger strategy sustain cooperation in a repeated Prisoner's Dilemma that has a definitive end?

Exercise 24A.24

If you model the decision about whether to be friendly to someone you run into as part of a Prisoner's Dilemma, why might you expect people in small towns to be friendlier than people in big cities?

24A.3.3 The Evolution of Cooperation and the Emergence of Tit-for-Tat Axelrod was interested in more than just demonstrating that cooperation could in principle emerge in repeated relationships – he wanted to know what kinds of strategies individuals might use to sustain such cooperation. The answer is far from obvious. Once relationships have no clear end, and cooperation in the repeated Prisoner's Dilemma does not unravel from the bottom, many different strategies, some sustaining cooperation and others not, can be part of a subgame perfect Nash equilibrium. Which will people actually choose?

To answer this question, Axelrod did several very clever experiments, outlined in *The Evolution of Cooperation* (New York: Basic Books, 1984). First, he asked the world's most eminent game theorists to submit strategies that they think might do well in repeated Prisoner's Dilemmas that have no definitive end. He placed no limit on how complex these strategies could be and included them all in a computer simulation in which different strategies encountered each other randomly. The strategy that consistently outperformed all others was remarkably simple and has become known as the *tit-for-tat strategy*.

Under the tit-for-tat strategy, a player begins at a first encounter with someone by cooperating and from then on mimics what the opposing player did at the last meeting. If the other player also cooperates, the tit-for-tat player will cooperate again next time. If the other player does not cooperate, the tit-for-tat player punishes them at the next meeting by not cooperating and will continue to not cooperate at each successive meeting unless the other player shows goodwill by cooperating at some point. If so, the tit-for-tat player will begin cooperating again.

Axelrod also took the same strategies submitted by game theorists and did another simulation in which strategies reproduced if they achieved high average payoffs and decreased in the population if they received relatively low payoffs. As the computer simulation continued, unsuccessful strategies would die out while successful strategies would increase in number. Eventually, he found only one strategy survived this evolutionary process and was left standing – tit-for-tat. Eventually Axelrod showed that strategies that were evolutionarily stable had to have properties similar to the tit-for-tat strategies. Strategies that would do well in evolutionary settings had to (1) attempt cooperation and sustain it if it is reciprocated, that is, the strategies have to be nice; (2) punish non-cooperation; but (3) leave the door open for forgiving non-cooperation if a player signals that they are ready to cooperate again.

24A.3.4 Sustaining Cooperation in Prisoner's Dilemmas Through Institutions It is possible for cooperation in Prisoner's Dilemma games to emerge if the same players meet repeatedly without any definitive end to the repetitions. Even in such settings, however, equilibria without cooperation are also possible, and in settings other than that, cooperation unravels under subgame perfection. There are, however, other ways in which market and non-market institutions might emerge to help sustain cooperation when the incentives in each interaction are themselves insufficient.

One possibility is for the individuals in a Prisoner's Dilemma to write a contract that imposes sufficient penalties for not cooperating. If there is a way to enforce the penalties, such a contract in essence changes the payoffs in the matrix to eliminate the Dilemma. The prisoners depicted in Table 24.6, for instance, might be part of a 'gang' that has the rule that those who cooperate with prosecutors will be severely punished. In joining the gang, individuals implicitly sign a contract that imposes penalties for not cooperating with the goals of the gang, that is, cooperating with prosecutors. Getting out of prison early loses some of its appeal if the prisoner knows they will be killed in some particularly gruesome way as soon as they are released.

Not all institutions that solve Prisoner's Dilemma problems are as sinister as a gang. Religious institutions might, for instance, persuade individuals that there are eternal benefits from cooperating, thus changing the way in which we evaluate the payoffs in a Prisoner's Dilemma because we get utility from the act of cooperating. Private fund-raisers have developed ways of personalizing our participation in large efforts to help the poor, and thus making us view the payoffs from helping others differently. Organizations that help poor children in developing countries offer the opportunity for individuals to sponsor particular children whose pictures and stories are shared with the donors. There is no particular reason to believe that the children whose pictures are sent to sponsors would not have been helped had the particular sponsor not decided to contribute to the organization, but the use of pictures personalizes the contribution in a way that appears to move people to give more.

In some cases, government policy can alter the payoffs in Prisoner's Dilemma games, sometimes achieving positive and sometimes achieving less desirable outcomes. If individuals face Prisoner's Dilemma incentives in their decision to give to charitable organizations, tax breaks for charitable contributions or other forms of more explicit government subsidies for giving to charitable causes might change behaviour in the direction of greater efficiency. At the same time, if large corporations in concentrated industries face Prisoner's Dilemma incentives when trying to collude on setting high prices, they might also look to government to act as the enforcer of their collusion.

24A.3.5 Sustaining Cooperation in Prisoner's Dilemmas Through Reputations Another way in which cooperation might emerge is if there is a way for individuals to credibly establish a reputation for cooperating. This is, however, far from trivial and requires the introduction of uncertainty on the part of one player with respect to the type of player they are facing in a finitely repeated setting. It requires the modelling of repeated interactions as sequential games of *incomplete* information, a topic we take up in Section B.

Exercise 24A.25

True or False: Whenever individuals find themselves in a Prisoner's Dilemma game, there is profit to be made if someone can determine a way to commit players to change their behaviour.

Exercise 24A.26

How might your answer to the previous exercise help explain why we see more cooperation in real-world Prisoner's Dilemma games than we expect from the incentives contained in the game?

24A.4 Mixed Strategies

The distinction between strategies and actions has been most apparent for the case of sequential games where a plan for the game is different for at least some players than just picking an action. In simultaneous move games, however, *pure strategies* have involved picking an action, but this is not true for *mixed strategies*.

Consider the following game. Two people, James and Abbie, are asked to put a one-euro coin on a table. If their coins match in the sense that they both have the same side of the coin showing, James ends up getting Abbie's coin. If, on the other hand, the coins do not match, i.e. one shows *Heads* and the other *Tails*, Abbie gets James' euro. This simple game, known as *matching coins*, is illustrated in Table 24.9.

In this game there is no pure strategy Nash equilibrium; James' best response to any move of Abbie's is to match it while Abbie's best response to any move of James is to contradict it. In such a game, there is no way to predict for sure what will happen because the very structure of the game prohibits such predictability. A common way to think of this formally is through the use of mixed strategies.

A *mixed strategy* for a player is a *probability distribution over the pure strategies*. Even though we will only explore mixed strategies for simultaneous move games, the same definition holds for sequential move games. James has two pure strategies in the matching coins game: *Heads* and *Tails*. A mixed strategy is a set of two probabilities $(\rho, 1 - \rho)$ such that $0 \le \rho \le 1$. If James decide to play the mixed strategy $(0.5, 0.5)$, it means that he will play *Heads* with probability 0.5 and *Tails* with probability 0.5. More generally, if a player has n different pure strategies available to them, a mixed strategy is a list of n probabilities $(\rho_1, \rho_2, \ldots, \rho_n)$ (with $\rho_i \ge 0$ for all $I = 5; 1, 2, \ldots, n$ and the sum of all ρ_i's equal to 1).

Table 24.9 Matching Coins

		Abbie	
		Heads	Tails
James	Heads	1, −1	−1, 1
	Tails	−1, 1	1, −1

Exercise 24A.27

It is always possible to write a pure strategy in the form of a mixed strategy with one probability set to 1 and the others set to zero. How would you write James' pure strategy of *Heads* in the form of a mixed strategy?

24A.4.1 Best Responses to Mixed Strategies Now suppose that James has some belief about the probability λ with which Abbie will play *Heads* and he is trying to determine how best to respond by setting his own probability ρ of playing *Heads*. James' goal is to match Abbie's coin. If James thinks $\lambda > 0.5$, he will do best by playing *Heads* all the time, that is, by setting $\rho = 1$. Similarly, if James thinks $\lambda < 0.5$, he should just play *Tails*, which implies setting $\rho = 0$. If James thinks Abbie is setting $\lambda = 0.5$, he could always play *Heads* (that is, $\rho = 1$) or always play *Tails* (that is, $\rho = 0$), and his expected payoff would be exactly the same in either case.

Exercise 24A.28

What would be James' expected payoff if he plays *Heads* all the time when Abbie plays the mixed strategy that places probability 0.5 of *Heads*?

If Abbie sets $\gamma = 0.5$, James could play any mixed strategy in between and get the same payoff. To see this, note that if Abbie ends up playing *Heads*, which she will do with probability 0.5, James will get her coin with probability ρ and will lose his coin with probability $(1 - \rho)$. In expectation, James will get $\rho - (1 - \rho) = (2\rho - 1)$ in the event that Abbie puts down *Heads*. If, on the other hand, she puts down *Tails*, which she will do half the time, James will win a coin with probability $(1 - \rho)$ and lose with probability ρ. In expectation, James will get $(1 - \rho) - \rho = (1 - 2\rho)$. His expected payoff from playing the mixed strategy that places probability ρ on *Heads* when he believes Abbie is playing a mixed strategy that places probability 0.5 on *Heads* is $0.5(2\rho - 1) + 0.5(1 - 2\rho) = 0$, exactly the same expected payoff as if he choses to always play *Heads* or always *Tails* when Abbie plays *Heads* with probability 0.5.

In panel (a) of Graph 24.6, we graph James' best-response mixed strategy to all possible mixed strategies Abbie might be playing. On the horizontal axis, we plot λ, which is the probability Abbie assigns to *Heads*, while on the vertical axis we plot ρ. For any $\lambda < 0.5$, James' best response is $\rho = 0$, and for any $\lambda > 0.5$, his best response is $\rho = 1$. Finally, for $\lambda = 0.5$, his best response can set ρ anywhere between 0 and 1.

Graph 24.6 Mixed Strategy Nash Equilibrium for Matching Coins

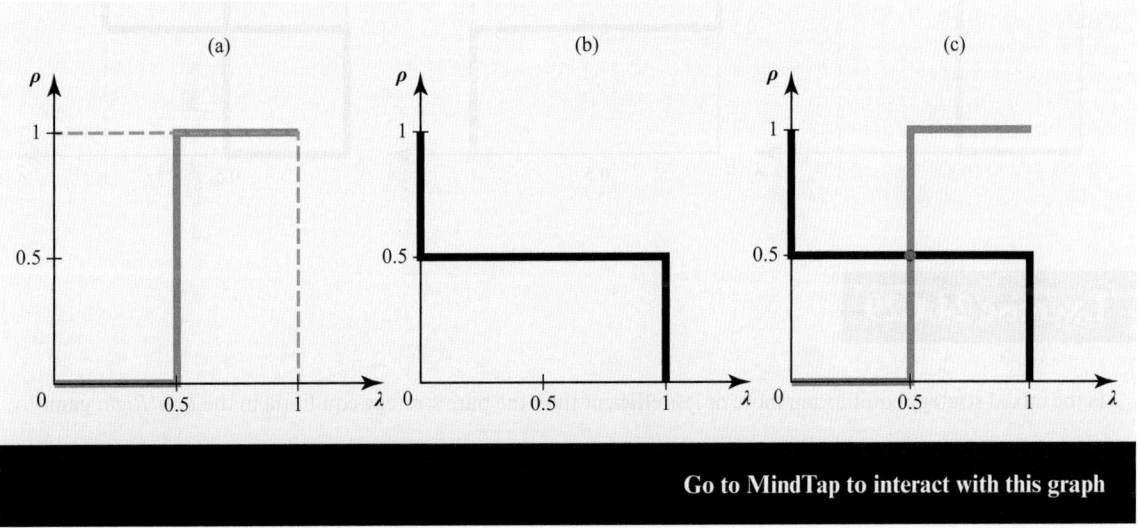

Go to MindTap to interact with this graph

Panel (b) does the same from Abbie's perspective, illustrating her best response in terms of setting λ to any possible ρ that James might set. Finally, we put the two panels together in panel (c) of the graph and note that their best responses intersect at $\lambda = \rho = 0.5$.

24A.4.2 Mixed Strategy Nash Equilibrium Recall that a Nash equilibrium requires each player to play a strategy that is a best response to the strategy played by the opposing player. This is no different for the case of mixed strategies. The only way James and Abbie are in a Nash equilibrium is if she is best responding to James' ρ when she sets λ just as James is best responding to Abbie's λ when he sets his ρ. The only time they are at a Nash equilibrium is if their best responses in panel (c) of Graph 24.6 intersect. In the matching coins game, there is only a single Nash equilibrium, one in which both play mixed strategies in which they place probability 0.5 on each of their two possible pure strategies.

The matching coins game is a natural game to use to motivate the notions of mixed strategies and mixed strategy equilibrium because the game does not give rise to any pure strategy equilibria. Even in games with pure strategy equilibria, there may exist separate mixed strategy equilibria. Consider, for instance, the *Left/Right* game pictured in Table 24.2. In Graph 24.7, we plot out the best responses for James and Abbie to different mixed strategies by the other. It turns out that James' best-response function in panel (a) looks exactly like the one plotted for him in the matching coins game. This is because he is trying to match Abbie's action in both games. Abbie's best response in panel (b) differs across the two games because she is trying to contradict James' action in the matching coins game while trying to match it in the *Left/Right* game. As a result, when putting the two best-response functions together in panel (c), they now intersect three times: at $\rho = \lambda = 0$, at $\rho = \lambda = 0.5$ and at $\rho = \lambda = 1$.

Two of the intersections of the best-response functions involve both playing one of their pure strategies with probability 1. These are the pure strategy Nash equilibria identified earlier. In addition, however, they have now discovered a third Nash equilibrium in mixed strategies, one in which both play each of their two possible pure strategies with probability 0.5.

Graph 24.7 Nash Equilibria for Left/Right Game From Table 24.2

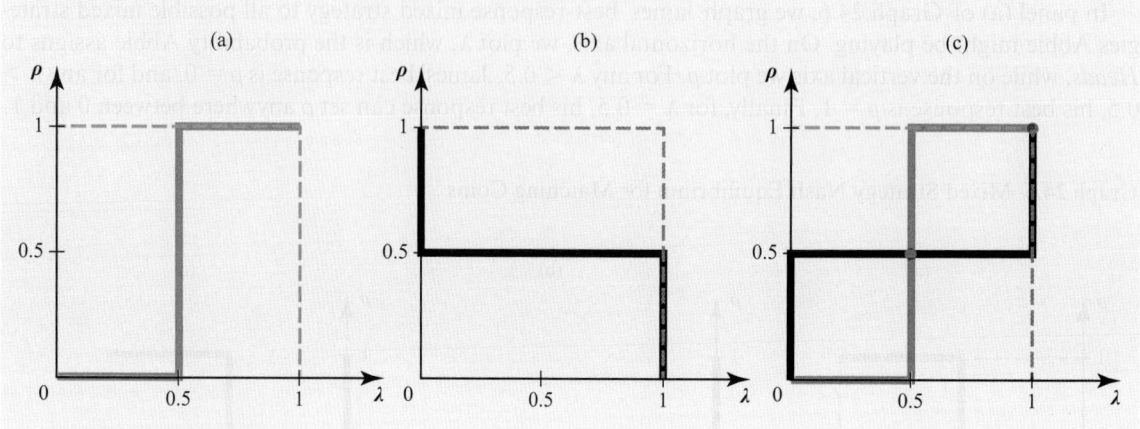

Exercise 24A.29

Is the mixed strategy equilibrium more or less efficient than the pure strategy equilibria in the *Left/Right* game?

Because of the particular payoff values chosen so far, the two mixed strategy equilibria found that both involve each player placing equal weight on each of their pure strategies. One can easily identify games where a mixed strategy equilibrium involves other weights. For instance, in the version of the left/right game in which the payoffs for both players choosing right are 5 rather than 10, the mixed strategy equilibrium involves $\rho = \lambda = 1/3$. We can also think of settings in which the two players will place different probabilities on their pure strategies, such as, for instance, when the payoff from both choosing left is 10 for player 1 but 5 for player 2 and the payoff from both choosing right is 5 for player 1 and 10 for player 2.

Exercise 24A.30*

Determine the mixed strategy Nash equilibrium for the game described in the previous sentence.

24A.4.3 A Quick Note on the Existence of Nash Equilibria John Nash proved in 1950 that all well-defined games have at least one Nash equilibrium. The proof makes use of fixed point theorems that are beyond the scope of this text, but the intuition for it is that in graphs plotting best-response functions to mixed strategies, each player's best-response function must cross the 45-degree line at some point, and this ensures that the two players' best-response functions must cross at least once, though not necessarily on the 45-degree line. When they cross, we have a Nash equilibrium. As we saw in the matching coins game, not all games have pure strategy equilibria. Similarly, the Prisoner's Dilemma is a game in which there does not exist a mixed strategy equilibrium and we are left with only the single pure strategy equilibrium. As a general rule, if there are no pure strategy equilibria in a game being analyzed, there is sure to be a mixed strategy equilibrium. If there is a single pure strategy equilibrium, there won't be a mixed strategy equilibrium to the same game. If there are two pure strategy equilibria, there will also be at least one mixed strategy equilibrium.

Exercise 24A.31

Plot the best-response functions to mixed strategies for the Prisoner's Dilemma game and illustrate that there exists only a single, pure strategy equilibrium.

24A.4.4 How Should We Interpret Mixed Strategies? The concept of a mixed strategy taken literally means that players just randomize over pure strategies in some fashion. There is another interpretation that many game theorists think makes more sense. In particular, it can be shown that if we change a game of complete information in which all the players know everyone's payoffs to a very similar game with just a little bit of incomplete information in which there is some uncertainty on the part of some players about the payoffs of other players, a mixed strategy equilibrium in the complete information game can be interpreted as a pure strategy Nash equilibrium in the incomplete information game. The mixing might arise from a little uncertainty about other players' payoffs.

24B | *Game Theory Under Incomplete Information

So far we have dealt only with complete information games. There are economically important situations in which players don't have such complete information. For example, consider a sealed bid auction in which two people, May and Ian, are bidding on a painting. May knows what the painting is worth to her, but she has no idea what it is worth to Ian. May, therefore, knows only her own payoff from winning the auction. Or think of two firms in an industry that is not perfectly competitive competing without knowing quite what costs the other is facing. Each firm will know its own profit under different output prices, but not the other firm's. We consider such games of incomplete information and will distinguish between simultaneous move games and sequential games. Games of incomplete information are also often called *Bayesian games*.

24B.1 Simultaneous Bayesian Games

When we introduced games of complete information, we specified the set of N players, their possible actions and the payoffs each player receives from different combinations of actions. In particular, we assumed that a player n could take an action from a set of possible actions denoted A^n. Player n's payoff was given by a function $u^n : \mathbb{R}^N \to \mathbb{R}^1$ that specifies a payoff value $u^n(a^1, a^2, \ldots, a^n)$ for all possible combinations of actions that the N players might take. In games of incomplete information, we similarly need to specify the set of N players and their possible actions A^n, but the payoffs are now no longer common knowledge. We therefore have to introduce *beliefs* on the part of players about other players' payoffs.

24B.1.1 Types and Beliefs This is typically accomplished by assuming that players could be one of several (or many) *types*, and that player n's payoff depends on their type t as well as on the set of actions $(a^1, a^2, \ldots, a^N)$ taken by everyone in the game. If a player n could be one of T different types, they now have T different possible payoff functions $(u_1^n, u_2^n, \ldots, u_T^n)$, with $u_t^n : \mathbb{R}^N \to \mathbb{R}^1$ giving the payoff $u_t^n(a^1, a^2, \ldots, a^N)$ when n is type t. We will assume that each player knows their own payoff function, which is equivalent to saying that each player knows their own type before they have to make a move in the game, but at least some players in the game only have *beliefs* about what type other players are. The set of types, as we will see in the following examples, could be a finite number of possible types or a continuum of types.

Beliefs are probability distributions that players have over the set of possible types that other players might be. Suppose there are two players, May and Ian, and each could be one of three types. If May knows her own type, there are three possible scenarios she is facing: Ian could be type 1, 2 or 3. May's beliefs about the game can be characterized by the probability distribution $(\rho 1, \rho 2, \rho 3)$, where $0 \leq \rho_i \leq 1$ for all i and $\sum_i^\rho \rho i = 1$. This means that May believes Ian is a type 1 player with probability ρ_1, a type 2 player with probability ρ_2 and a type 3 player with probability ρ_3. If there are three players and three possible types, May (as player 3) faces nine possible scenarios, assuming she knows her own type, with beliefs given by the probability distribution $(\rho_{11}, \rho_{12}, \rho_{13}, \rho_{21}, \rho_{22}, \rho_{23}, \rho_{31}, \rho_{32}, \rho_{33})$ where ρ_{ij} is the probability that the first player is of type i and the second player is of type j. If an opposing player can take on types from a continuous interval such as $T = [0,1]$, the probability distribution is given in terms of a function $\rho : T \to \mathbb{R}^1$, with $p(t)$ equal to the probability that the player is a type less than or equal to t.

Exercise 24B.1

If there are N players and T possible types, how many probabilities constitute May's beliefs about the other players in the game?

Note that this structure of beliefs as probability distributions makes it possible for some player n's payoffs to be known with certainty by everyone; the other players' beliefs would assign probability zero to player n being of a different type. We therefore do not require that everyone is equally uncertain about what type everyone else is in the game, but even if only one player is uncertain about another one's type, we will call this a Bayesian game of incomplete information.

24B.1.2 The Role of Nature It has become common to introduce into Bayesian games a non-strategic fictional player called 'Nature' that has no payoffs that moves prior to any other move. Thus, even simultaneous move Bayesian games have a sequential structure in the sense that Nature goes first and everyone else moves at the same time. The only role played by Nature is that it assigns a type to each player, with knowledge of one's own type becoming private information for each individual. In some games, Nature might also share some information about other players' types with some of the players, perhaps leaving some players more informed than others. Only if all information about player types were shared with everyone in the game would the game cease to be one of incomplete information. In this sense, we can think of games of complete information as a special case of games of incomplete information. The crucial assumption we will make throughout is that *all players know the probability distribution Nature uses to assign types to players, and each player is assigned their type independently of others.* All players in the game begin, prior to Nature moving, with the same initial beliefs about types.

24B.1.3 Strategies A strategy is a *complete* plan of action *prior to the beginning of the game.* In the case of simultaneous move games with complete information, this implies that a pure strategy for player n involves picking an action from the set A^n, but in the sequential move case, it means something more for those players that move later in the game. In a sequential game, a strategy involves specifying an action for each possible prior history of the game. In the two-player case, this means that player 2's strategy involves a plan for what to do for each possible action that player 1 might have taken in the first stage of the game, even if player 1 never chooses a particular action in equilibrium.

This is relevant for our discussion of simultaneous move Bayesian games because we have embedded the simultaneous moves that the players make into a sequential structure in which the fictional player Nature moves first. Since the game begins with Nature's move, and since a strategy is a complete plan for how to play the game prior to the beginning of the game, a strategy now involves each player settling on what action they will take *for each possible type Nature might assign to them.* By introducing the fictional player Nature as the first player in the game, we implicitly require that every actual player determines a plan for how to play the game *before finding out what type of player they are.*

At first glance, this may seem silly. After all, the player Nature is just a fiction, so why can't we just assume that each player will decide on a plan of action once they find out their type? Think of it this way: suppose Ian and May are in a simultaneous Bayesian game and May knows what type Nature has assigned to her. She wants to figure out what her best course of action is. In order to do that, she has to think about what Ian's strategy will be, and his strategy will depend on what he thinks May will do. Since only May knows her true type, Ian will have to use his beliefs to infer what May will do, which means he will need to think about what May would do depending on what type she is and appropriately weight each of the possibilities by the probability Ian's beliefs assign to May being a particular type. Ian has to be thinking about what May would do for each possible type that she could have been assigned. That in turn means that May needs to think about what she would have done had she been assigned another type because this goes into Ian's thinking about what he will do in the game.

A *strategy* in a simultaneous Bayesian game is therefore a plan of action for each possible type that a player might be assigned by Nature. If a player's type is drawn from the set of possible types T and this player can choose from actions in the set A, their strategy is a function $s: T \to A$, that is, a function that assigns to every possible type in T an action from A. Such a strategy might have a player choosing the same action regardless of what type they were assigned, or it might have the player choose a different action for each type they might be assigned. We will later refer to the first type of strategy as a *separating strategy* and the second as a *pooling strategy*. Regardless, however, it is important to remember that we will no more be able to find an equilibrium in a Bayesian game without fully specified strategies than we would be able to find an equilibrium in a sequential complete information game without specifying full strategies. Plans for what to do off-the-equilibrium path can, in either case, affect the nature of the equilibrium.

Exercise 24B.2

In what sense does the distinction between Nash and subgame perfect equilibrium illustrate how off-the-equilibrium path plans – that is, plans that are never executed in equilibrium – can be important?

24B.1.4 Bayesian Nash Equilibrium Once we have fully understood the set-up of a simultaneous move Bayesian game and its implications for what a strategy is for each player, the definition for a Nash equilibrium is exactly the same as it has always been, with one twist at the end: a *Bayesian Nash equilibrium* in a simultaneous move game of incomplete information occurs when each player's strategy is a best response to every other player's strategy *given the player's beliefs that are consistent with how the game is being played*.

The twist at the end, the part that extends the concept of a Nash equilibrium to incomplete information games, is important in simultaneous games because, as we have already noted, we assume that everyone knows the probabilities with which the player Nature assigns types to players in the stage of the game that precedes the simultaneous move game. Unless new information is revealed in the course of the game, which does not happen when the rest of the game is a simultaneous move game, each person's beliefs are therefore just the probabilities with which types are assigned. This will change in a sequential game of incomplete information where information may be revealed in the actions taken by players that move early in the game. In simultaneous move Bayesian games, having beliefs be consistent with how the game is being played means that equilibrium beliefs have to be consistent with how the player Nature plays the game.

Exercise 24B.3

Do you agree or disagree with the following statement: 'Both complete and incomplete information simultaneous move games can be modelled as games in which Nature moves first, but Nature plays only pure strategies in complete information games while it plays mixed strategies in incomplete information games'?

24B.1.5 A Simple Example Consider the two complete information games from exercises 24A.8 and 24A.9, which are depicted at the bottom of Graph 24.8. These games differ only in terms of player 2's payoffs, with payoffs for playing R being 10 more in the first game than in the second. In both games, player 2 has a dominant strategy, but player 1's best response will depend on player 2's strategy. In particular, player 1's best response to L is U, giving a payoff of 20 instead of 15, and their best response to R is D, giving a payoff of 5 instead of 0. Since player 1's payoffs are the same in both games, these best responses to strategies played by player 2 are the same in both games.

Graph 24.8 Incomplete Information About Player 2's Payoffs

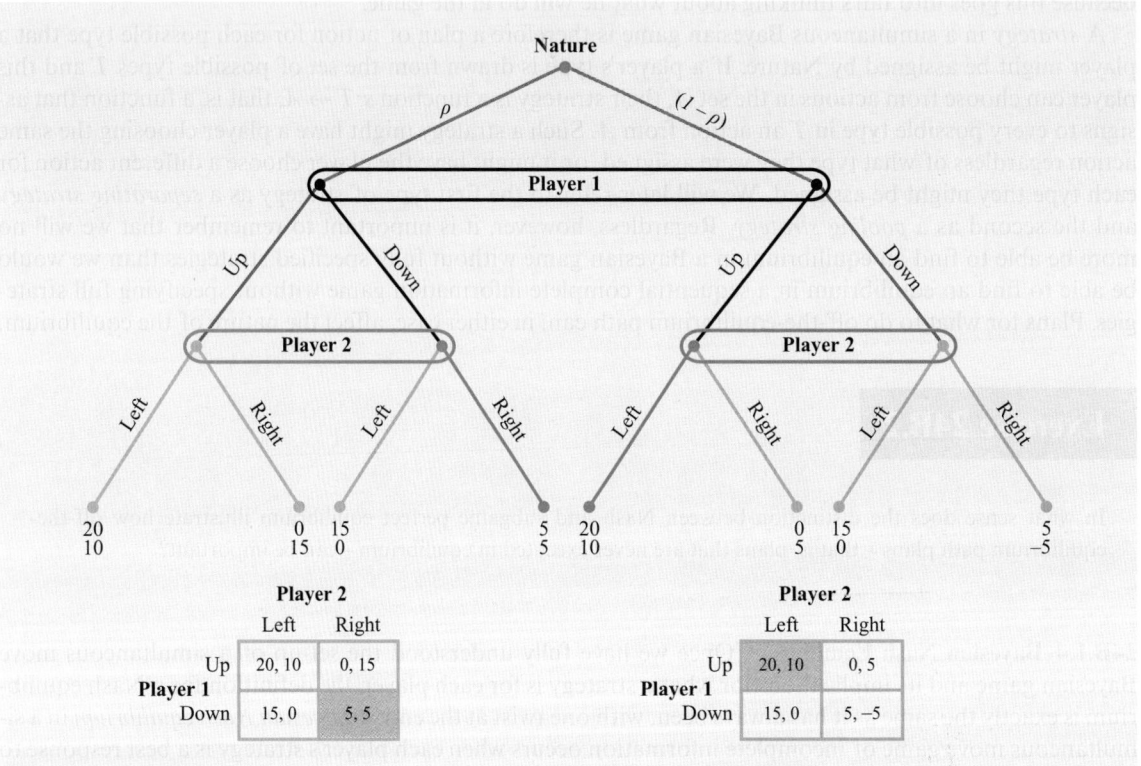

	Player 2	
	Left	Right
Up	20, 10	0, 15
Down	15, 0	5, 5

Player 1 (rows Up/Down)

	Player 2	
	Left	Right
Up	20, 10	0, 5
Down	15, 0	5, −5

Player 1 (rows Up/Down)

Exercise 24B.4

What is player 2's dominant strategy in each of the two games?

Now suppose that there is a probability ρ that player 2 will be of type I with payoffs as in the first game and a probability $(1 - \rho)$ that player 2 will be of type II with payoffs as in the second game. Player 2 knows what type they are before the game starts, but player 1 does not know what type they are facing in player 2. This is a simultaneous move Bayesian game in which player 2 could be one of two possible types. To model this, we introduce a third player – Nature – that moves before the simultaneous game begins, assigning type I to player 2 with probability ρ and type II with probability $(1 - \rho)$. If $\rho = 1$, the game is a complete information game in which player 1 plays a player 2 of type I; that is, the two players play the game captured by the payoff matrix in the bottom left of Graph 24.8. If $\rho = 0$, the game is similarly a complete information game, but this time player 1 plays a player 2 of type II; that is, the two players play the game captured by the payoff matrix on the bottom right of Graph 24.8. In the first case, player 1 would play D in equilibrium, and in the second case, they would play U. What will they play if $0 < \rho < 1$?

Exercise 24B.5

How can we be sure that player 1 will play D in equilibrium in the left-hand side game but U in the right-hand side game?

Before answering this question, we need to show how we can illustrate, using either a payoff matrix or a game tree, the kind of game we have just introduced. Note first that our two-player Bayesian game actually has three players once we introduce the fictional player Nature, and this makes it difficult to depict such a game in a payoff matrix. Second, note that this third player adds a sequential structure to the simultaneous game, which suggests that the resulting game might best be illustrated in a game tree. Such a tree would begin with Nature moving first, as is done in the game tree in Graph 24.8. If player 1 moves second in the tree, we have to find a way to indicate that player 1 does not know the outcome of Nature's move when it is their turn to play because Nature only reveals player 2's type to player 2. We do this by pulling both of player 1's nodes in the game tree – the left-hand node that results from Nature assigning type I to player 2 and the right-hand node that results from Nature assigning type II to player 2 – into a single *information set*. This is depicted in Graph 24.8 with the dark blue oval that contains both of these nodes, and it indicates that player 1 is uncertain about which of their two possible nodes they are playing from when it is time to make their move.

Exercise 24B.6

Since all players know the probabilities with which types are assigned, how would you characterize player 1's beliefs about which node they are playing from once the game reaches their information set?

Note that the two players play the complete information game depicted in the payoff matrix on the lower left of the graph if they are playing from player 1's left-hand side node, and they play the complete information game depicted in the payoff matrix on the lower right of the graph if they are playing from player 1's right-hand side node. In order for us to depict the Bayesian game that includes Nature's move in a game tree, we have to find a way to depict the complete information games from these payoff matrices in game tree format. In Section A, when we showed how a sequential game can be depicted in a payoff matrix, we hinted at the fact that it was possible to represent a simultaneous move complete information game in a game tree, but we postponed illustrating this as there was no particular need to do so at the time and because we were still missing a key ingredient – the concept of an *information set* – which we have just introduced.

Given this new tool, we have to make sure that the information sets over the nodes following Nature's move are such that no new information is conveyed through the actions of any player because all players following Nature's move are playing simultaneously. Thus, player 2 does not know whether player 1 moved *Up* or *Down*, which means both actions by player 1 must end in the same information set for player 2. We cannot allow player 2 to infer anything from the fact that player 1 has taken a particular action, because player 2 is acting at the same time as player 1 even though the game tree shows them making a decision further down the game tree. Player 2 *does* know whether Nature assigned type I or type II, and thus whether they are playing the left-hand side or the right-hand side game. As a result, the information sets for player 2 do not cross from one side of the tree to the other.

Exercise 24B.7

True or False: If we depict a simultaneous move complete information game in a game tree, each player only has one information set.

Exercise 24B.8

How would you depict the complete information game from either of the payoff matrices in the graph if you had player 2 rather than player 1 at the top of the game tree?

Notice that the game tree in Graph 24.8 fully captures all aspects of a simultaneous move Bayesian game; the actions that each player has available, the types that players might be assigned by Nature, the beliefs captured by the probability ρ and the payoffs for each player and type. Reading the game tree from the top down, we see that Nature begins by moving left with probability ρ and right with probability $(1 - \rho)$. We see from player 1's information set that player 1 cannot tell what Nature did when the time comes for them to choose between the actions *Up* and *Down*. We can furthermore note from player 2's two information sets that player 2 can never tell whether player 1 has decided to go *Up* or *Down* but they *can* tell whether Nature moved left or right.

Exercise 24B.9

You could also draw the game tree in Graph 24.8 with player 2 going first and player 1 going second. What do the information sets look like if you depict the game in this way?

While pure strategies in each of the games at the bottom of Graph 24.8 are actions, strategies in the Bayesian game depicted in the graph are now more complicated for player 2 *because they have to represent complete plans of action prior to the beginning of the game,* prior to Nature's move. Player 2's strategy must specify an action for each of their information sets; that is, for the case where Nature assigns them type I and for the case where Nature assigns them type II. Player 1, on the other hand, has only a single information set in the game, which implies that a pure strategy for player 1 is an action for that one information set.

Exercise 24B.10

True or False: Player 2 has four possible strategies while player 1 has two possible strategies.

Since each of the two simultaneous move games at the bottom of Graph 24.8 has a dominant strategy for player 2, we know that player 2 will play R if they are assigned type I and L if assigned type II. Player 1 knows this and knows that they are at the first node in their information set with probability ρ and at the second node with probability $(1 - \rho)$. This implies that their expected payoff from playing U is $0\rho + 20(1 - \rho)$ while their expected payoff from playing D is $5\rho + 15(1 - \rho)$. The former is larger than the latter as long as $\rho < 0.5$. Thus, if $\rho < 0.5$, player 1 will play U and if $\rho > 0.5$, they will play D. If $\rho = 0.5$, they are indifferent between their two possible actions and could play either.

Exercise 24B.11

How would the outcome be different if the two games at the bottom of Graph 24.8 were the games in Table 24.5 and exercise 24A.7 with player 2's actions labelled L and R instead of U and D?

24B.1.6 Sealed Bid Auctions One of the most common applications for simultaneous games of incomplete information is in the area of auctions. In a *sealed bid auction,* different players bid on the same item at the same time by submitting sealed bids, with none of the players knowing exactly what the item is worth to the other players. Consider such an auction in which the player who bids the most ends up getting the item and has to pay the price that they bid. This type of auction is called a *first-price sealed bid auction.*

Suppose, for instance, that Ian and May are bidding on a painting. May knows that the painting is worth t^m to her, and Ian knows that it is worth t^i to him. May does not know how much the painting is worth to Ian and Ian does not know how much it is worth to May. Assume that all they know is that for any potential bidder n, the private value t^n is drawn randomly and independently from the uniform distribution on the interval $[0,1]$. Assuming that individual valuations are drawn *independently* means that Ian cannot infer something about May's valuation of the painting from knowing his valuation. Assuming that the distribution is *uniform* means that each value on the interval $[0,1]$ is equally likely to be drawn. The set of possible types is $T = [0,1]$, and the probability that Nature assigns to a player a type t less than $\bar{t}$ (for any $0 \le \bar{t} \le 1$ is $\bar{t}$.

Exercise 24B.12

What is the probability that Nature assigns a type greater than $\bar{t}$ to a player?

Each player n has to choose an action a^n that is just their bid for the painting. If a player wins the auction, their payoff is their consumer surplus $(t^n - a^n)$. If a player loses the auction, on the other hand, they do not get the painting and do not have to pay anything, leaving them with a payoff of 0. Finally, we will assume that when both players bid the same amount, the auctioneer will flip a coin, which gives each player a 50 per cent chance of winning the auction and thus an expected payoff of $(t^n - a^n)/2$. We will, however, be able to ignore the possibility of ties in our example because they happen with probability zero.

Exercise 24B.13

What is the set of possible actions A for this game?

A *strategy* for each of the bidders in this auction has to be a complete plan of action for every possible type that a player might be assigned. A *type* in this game is determined by the valuation t^n that a player was assigned by Nature, which could lie anywhere on the continuum between 0 and 1. A strategy must be a function $s^n:[0,1] \to \mathbb{R}^1$ that specifies a bid for each possible value that a player might place on the painting. It is possible to formally demonstrate that such strategies in this setting will, in equilibrium, take on a linear form; that is, $S^n(t^n) = \alpha_n + \beta_n t^n$. Demonstrating this involves the use of differential equations and is beyond the scope of this text.

Suppose that Ian plays the strategy $S^i(t^i) = \alpha_i + \beta_i t^i$. May's best response to this strategy is to maximize her expected payoff, which is ignoring the possibility of a tie:

$$\max_{a^i} (t^i - a^i)\text{Prob}\{a^i > a_i + \beta_i t^i\}. \tag{24.1}$$

By rearranging the terms in the previous inequality, we can write the probability term as:

$$\text{Prob}\{a^i > a_i + \beta_i t^i\} = \text{Prob}\left\{t^i < \frac{a^m - a_i}{\beta_i}\right\}. \tag{24.2}$$

Recall that, given the underlying uniform probability distribution on the interval [0,1] with which Nature assigns types, the probability that $t^i < \bar{t}$ is $\bar{t}$, which implies:

$$\text{Prob}\left\{t^i < \frac{a^i - \alpha_i}{\beta_i}\right\} = \frac{a^i - \alpha_i}{\beta_i}. \tag{24.3}$$

We can rewrite equation (24.1) as:

$$\max_{a^m} (t^i - a^i)\frac{a^i - \alpha_i}{\beta_i}, \tag{24.4}$$

which solves to:

$$a^i = \frac{t^i + \alpha_i}{2}. \tag{24.5}$$

Exercise 24B.14

Verify that this is correct.

May's best response to Ian playing $s^i(t^i) = \alpha_i + \beta_i t^i$ is $s^m(t^m) = \alpha_m + \beta_m t^m$, where $\alpha_m = \alpha_i/2$ and $\beta = 1/2$. If May plays $s^m(t^m) = \alpha_m + \beta_m t^m$, the same steps imply that Ian's best response is $s^i(t^i) = \alpha_i + \beta_i t^i$ where $\alpha_i = \alpha_m/2$ and $\beta_i = \frac{1}{2}$; $\alpha_m = \alpha_i/2$ and $\alpha_i = \alpha_m/2$ can both hold only if $\alpha_m = \alpha_i = 0$, which implies that our equilibrium strategies are:

$$s^i(t^i) = \frac{t^i}{2} \text{ and } s^i(t^i) = \frac{t^i}{2}. \tag{24.6}$$

In equilibrium they will each bid half of the value that they attach to the painting.

Exercise 24B.15

Suppose that both bidders know how much each of them values the painting; that is, suppose the game was one of complete information. What would be the Nash equilibrium bidding behaviour? How does it differ from the incomplete information game?

This is a relatively simple auction setting, and there exist many different types of auctions and different economically relevant beliefs that might be introduced in different settings. Since the late 1990s, an extensive literature on auctions has developed, all based on game theoretic modelling of the underlying incentives. This literature has guided the design of large auctions, such as auctions for rights to harvest timber on government land or for rights to broadcast on particular frequencies. Many of these auctions, however, have a sequential structure that goes beyond the simultaneous Bayesian games we have defined so far.

24B.2 Sequential Bayesian Signalling Games

While we can think of economically interesting applications of simultaneous games of incomplete information, the set of potential applications of *sequential* games of incomplete information is much richer. Such games have the feature that some players not only have *private information* but, *through their actions in the early part of the game, they can reveal some, all or none of that information to the other players.* In the chapter on asymmetric information, we dealt with situations of this kind, where buyers had less information than sellers, as in the used car market, or workers had more information about their productivity than potential employers, or insurance clients had more information about their risk type than the insurance company. These instances of asymmetric information are precisely the kinds of economic situations that can be represented in sequential games of incomplete information, games in which the more informed party can *signal* something about themselves or in which the less informed party can set up incentives so as to extract information.

Just as we needed to extend the concept of Nash equilibrium to that of *subgame perfect* Nash equilibrium in the sequential complete information case, we now need to extend the concept of a Bayesian Nash equilibrium to that of a subgame *perfect* Bayesian Nash equilibrium in the sequential incomplete information case. We need to do so for the same reason as before: to eliminate implausible Nash equilibria that rely on non-credible behaviour off-the-equilibrium path. To do so, however, we will again *need to make beliefs, and not just strategies, part of the equilibrium.* We will need to specify what beliefs players hold on- *and* off-the-equilibrium path in order to be sure the equilibrium strategies are in fact part of an equilibrium, and we need to make sure that players *update their beliefs* from those they hold at the beginning of the game if new information is revealed by the actions taken early on in the game. We will return to these issues more formally after first illustrating them in concrete settings where we will use the logic of subgame perfection to find sensible equilibria in sequential Bayesian games. By the 'logic of subgame perfection', we mean attacking the sequential game from the bottom up as we did in the complete information games of Section A.

24B.2.1 Simple Signalling When Beliefs Don't Matter We will use one of the most common families of games of incomplete information to fix ideas. This family of games is known as *signalling games*, in which a person first finds out from Nature what type they are, and sends a signal to the other player before that other player takes an action that impacts both players. The signalling player initially has private information that they might choose to reveal before the other player makes a move.

The simplest such setting is one in which one player, whom we will call the *sender*, might be one of two possible types and can send one of two possible signals. The other player, the *receiver*, has to choose between two actions. Consider a sequential version of the simultaneous game we introduced in Graph 24.8. In that game, player 2 was one of two possible types, with their payoff depending on which type they were. To turn this game into a signalling game, player 2 would first find out their type, would be able to play the actions L or R before player 1, and *after observing player 2's signal*, gets a chance to undertake their action of either U or D. Thus, player 2 becomes the sender who signals through their choice of L or R, and player 1 becomes the receiver. A convenient way to represent the new structure of this game is given in Graph 24.9.

Unlike the game trees we have looked at so far, this tree begins in the centre with Nature revealing the sender's type, assigning type I with probability ρ and type II with probability $(1 - \rho)$. After finding out their type, the sender can play L or R going either left or right in the graph. The receiver only observes the sender's actions, not their type. Thus, the receiver's two nodes on the left, following L by the sender, are in the same information set as are the receiver's two nodes on the right following R by the sender. The person we called player 2 in the simultaneous version of the game gets the private information and thus moves *first* in the signalling game. As you compare payoffs in Graph 24.9 with those in Graph 24.8, keep in mind that the first payoff at each terminal point in the sequential game should therefore correspond to player 2's payoff in the previously graphed simultaneous game.

Graph 24.9 Turning the Simultaneous Game in Graph 24.8 Into a Signalling Game

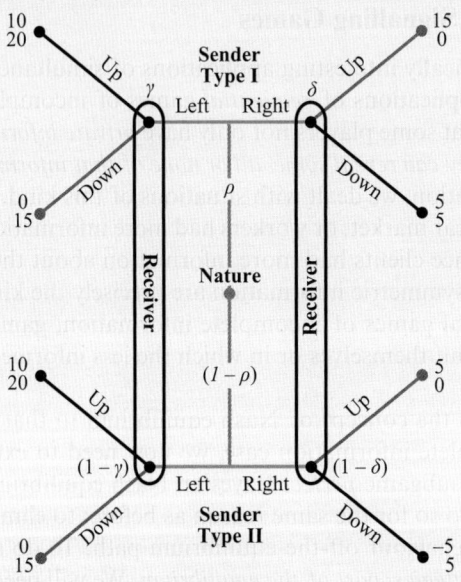

Exercise 24B.16

Check that the payoffs listed in Graph 24.9 correspond to the payoffs in Graph 24.8.

First, note that the receiver's subgame perfect strategy can be worked out in this game because once the receiver observes which action the sender has taken, they know exactly what they want to do even if they are uncertain about which of the nodes in their information set they have reached. If the sender plays L, the receiver's best response is U regardless of what type the sender is, and if the sender plays R, the receiver's best response is D, again regardless of the sender's type. This is indicated in the graph through the bold lines at each node for the receiver. The receiver's subgame perfect strategy therefore must be (U,D), where the first action indicates their plan if the sender plays L and the second indicates their plan if the sender plays R. Since this strategy is optimal for the receiver *regardless of what type the sender is*, beliefs do not play an important role in this game.

Next, let's consider the possible strategies that the sender could employ and recall that a strategy in a Bayesian game is a complete plan of action prior to the beginning of Nature's move. The sender has to have a plan for what to do depending on what type they turn out to be. The four possible pure strategies are: (L,L), (R,R), (L,R) and (R,L), where the first action in each pair corresponds to their plan if they turn out to be type I and the second action corresponds to their plan if they turn out to be type II. If they choose one of the two latter strategies, they will implicitly reveal their type to the receiver because they are taking a different action depending on which type they are. This is called a *separating strategy* because it involves separate observable actions depending on which type is assigned to the sender. The first two strategies, on the other hand, provide no information to the receiver beyond what the receiver already knows, that is, the probability that Nature assigns one type rather than the other. Such a strategy is called a *pooling strategy* because the different types of sender end up looking as if they came from the same pool. When there are more than two types, we might get hybrid strategies in which some types pool and some separate.

We can begin to look at each strategy for the sender and see if it could plausibly be part of an equilibrium. Suppose the sender plays (L,L). We have already determined that the receiver's optimal strategy is (U,D) regardless of whether the sender reveals any information through their strategy, and so (U,D) is a best response to (L,L). Now we have to check whether (L,L) is also a best response for the sender to the receiver's (U,D). Note that both sender types would do worse by switching to R given that the receiver would respond by playing D, with sender type I getting 5 rather than 10 and sender type II getting -5 rather than 10. Thus, (L,L) for the sender and (U,D) for the receiver are part of a subgame perfect equilibrium. It can also be seen that none of the other possible pure strategies for the sender could be a subgame perfect equilibrium because in each case at least one of the types of sender would have an incentive to deviate given that the receiver is playing (U,D).

Exercise 24B.17

Determine for each of the three remaining sender pure strategies why the strategy cannot be part of a subgame perfect equilibrium.

Exercise 24B.18

Suppose the -5 payoff in the lower right corner of the game tree were 0 instead. Would we still get the same subgame perfect equilibrium? Could (R,R) be part of a Nash equilibrium that is not subgame perfect?

Exercise 24B.19

Suppose that we changed the -5 payoff in Graph 24.9 to 20. Demonstrate that this would imply that only the separating strategy (L,R) can survive in equilibrium.

Since the equilibrium we have identified involves both sender types playing the same signal L, the receiver gets no information about the sender's type from observing the sender's action, and therefore the receiver cannot update their beliefs from those held at the beginning of the game when they knew that Nature would assign type I to the sender with probability ρ and type II with probability $(1 - \rho)$. These are the equilibrium beliefs for the receiver. In this game, the receiver's beliefs play no role because their response to either action on the part of the sender is clear cut and independent of their beliefs. This is not generally true in signalling games, and when it is not true, beliefs take on a much more critical role.

24B.2.2 Signalling Games Where Off-the-Equilibrium Path Beliefs Matter Now suppose we change the game in Graph 24.9 slightly by changing the payoff for the receiver in the upper right of the graph where type I sender plays R and the receiver plays U, from 0 to 10. This is depicted in Graph 24.10, and as a result of this change, the receiver's optimal action when they observe R from the sender is no longer the same irrespective of their beliefs about which node within their information set they occupy when choosing the action. The optimal receiver action after the sender plays R is U if the sender is of type I and D if the sender is of type II, as indicated through the bold lines in the graph. If the receiver observes L from the sender, they will still unambiguously play U.

Recall that we extended the concept of a Nash equilibrium to a subgame perfect Nash equilibrium by insisting that a Nash equilibrium in a sequential game also consists of a Nash equilibrium in each *subgame* of the sequential game. Subgames were defined as beginning at a particular node that had been reached in the game tree. The problem we now face is that such subgames may not be readily available in games of the type depicted in Graphs 24.9 and 24.10. When the receiver gets to move after receiving a signal from the sender, they do not find themselves at a particular node; rather, they are at an information set that contains two nodes, with some *belief* about which of the two nodes they might actually be playing from. Those beliefs now become important for determining what the best response for the receiver should be if they observe R.

Graph 24.10 Small Change to the Previous Game and Beliefs Matter

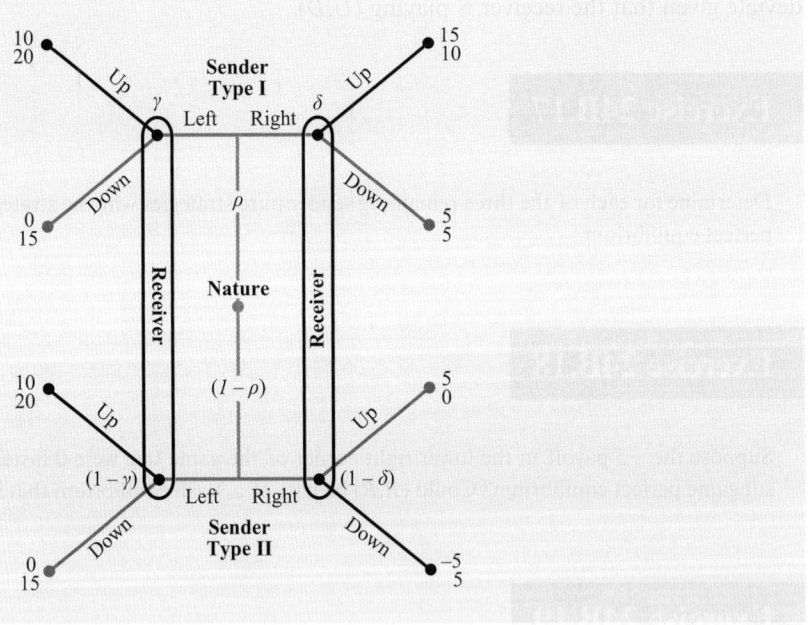

Exercise 24B.20

In the previous section, we talked about subgame perfect strategies in ways that we cannot do here. What is different?

Suppose the player's belief after observing R is that the sender is of type I with probability δ and of type II with probability $(1 - \delta)$. Their expected payoff from playing U is $10\delta + 0(1 - \delta)$, while the expected payoff from playing D is $5\delta + 5(1 - \delta) = 5$. The latter is greater than the former if $\delta < 0.5$, which implies that the receiver's best response to observing R is to play D *only if* their belief is that the sender is more likely to be of type II than of type I. The receiver will play U if they observe L regardless of what type they believe the sender to be, but they will play U after observing R only if they believe the sender is of type I with probability of at least 0.5. Otherwise, they will play D.

Now we can check to see if the pooling strategy (L,L) for the sender can still be part of an equilibrium. If the sender plays that strategy, we know that the receiver will play U, resulting in payoff (10,20) for the two players regardless of what type the sender is. Now we can ask whether either of the sender types could do better by playing R, and the answer depends on what the receiver would do if they ever saw a signal R. If (L,L) is indeed part of an equilibrium, the receiver will never see the signal R, but a full plan of action still requires them to have a plan in case they do see R, and we need to know what that plan is in order to be able to answer whether either of the sender types could do better by sending R rather than L. If the receiver were to plan U following a signal R, a type I sender would indeed be better off sending R rather than L, which in turn would imply that (L,L) cannot be part of an equilibrium. We concluded in the previous paragraph that the receiver will play U after observing R only if $\delta > 0.5$. In order for the pooling strategy (L,L) to be an equilibrium strategy, the receiver must believe that the sender is more likely to be type II if a signal R is observed. *The receiver's beliefs have to be appropriately specified as part of the pooling equilibrium.* We see in this example that beliefs off the equilibrium path can be critical for sustaining an equilibrium; that is, in the equilibrium $\{(L,L), (U,D)\}$ where $\delta < 0.5$, it matters what the receiver believes in the event that R is observed *even though R is not observed in equilibrium.*

Exercise 24B.21

There is no way for (R,R) to be an equilibrium sender strategy. Can you explain why?

We can also ask whether there is a *separating equilibrium* in this case; that is, an equilibrium that involves the sender playing either (L,R) or (R,L). Consider the strategy (L,R). Under this strategy, the receiver knows with certainty which type the sender is because different sender types play different actions observable to the receiver. As a result, the receiver will update their beliefs; that is, γ, the probability that the sender is type I if L is observed, is 1 and δ, the probability that the sender is of type I if R is observed, is 0. That means that the receiver will play U after observing L and D after observing R. Given this response by the receiver, a type I sender cannot do better by changing their signal to R because that would reduce their payoff from 10 to 5. A type II sender *can* get a higher payoff by switching from the signal R to L given the receiver's response. Thus, (L,R) cannot be part of an equilibrium.

Exercise 24B.22

How much higher a payoff would a type II sender get by switching their signal in this way?

Next, consider the other separating strategy: (R,L). If the sender plays this strategy, the receiver will know that the sender is of type I if they observe R (that is, $\delta = 1$), and they will know that the sender is of type II if they observe L (that is, $\gamma = 0$). Either way, their best response is to play U. For this to be an equilibrium, we have to make sure that neither of the two sender types could do better given that the receiver will always play U. If type I switched, their payoff would fall from 15 to 10, and if type II switched, their payoff would fall from 10 to 5. Neither type can benefit from deviating from the strategy (R,L), which means we have found a separating equilibrium $\{(R,L), (U,U)\}$ with equilibrium beliefs $\delta = 1$ and $\gamma = 0$.

The initial probability ρ with which Nature assigned types no longer matters because all information is revealed in the separating strategy played by the sender.

Exercise 24B.23*

For the game in Graph 24.10, we have found both a separating and a pooling equilibrium, but for the pooling equilibrium we needed to place a restriction on out-of-equilibrium beliefs. Do you find this restriction reasonable in this example? Note: this is far from a trivial question and it has concerned game theorists a great deal. After all, what does it mean for beliefs related to events that do not happen in equilibrium to be reasonable? An approach to this, known as the 'Intuitive Criterion' has been derived.

24B.2.3 Signalling Games Where Beliefs and Nature's Probabilities Matter In the previous example, we have seen that out-of-equilibrium beliefs on the part of the receiver might be critical to sustaining a pooling equilibrium, because those beliefs determine what action the receiver would take if one of the sender types were to deviate from the pooling strategy. Beliefs along the pooling equilibrium path, however, have not yet played a crucial role. This is because so far, we have had examples in which the optimal action from each node in the information set that is reached in the pooling equilibrium is the same.

Now suppose we change the game in Graph 24.10 a little more by changing the receiver's payoff from playing U when they face a type I sender who plays L from 20 to 10. This new game is depicted in Graph 24.11, with the optimal receiver actions from each node highlighted. Note that now we have a game in which the receiver's optimal action differs across the nodes in each of their two information sets.

First, we can begin with the receiver and ask which way they will play from each of their information sets. If they observe L and thus play from their left information set, their payoff from U is $10\gamma + 20(1 - \gamma) = 20 - 10\gamma$, while the payoff from D is $15\gamma + 15(1 - \gamma) = 15$. The former is larger than the latter as long as $\gamma < 0.5$, which means the receiver will play U following L if they believe the probability that the sender is of type I is less than 0.5 and D if they believe that the probability is greater than 0.5. Similarly, from what we did in the previous section, we know that the receiver will play U following R if $\delta > 0.5$ and D if $\delta < 0.5$.

Graph 24.11 Beliefs Matter Even More

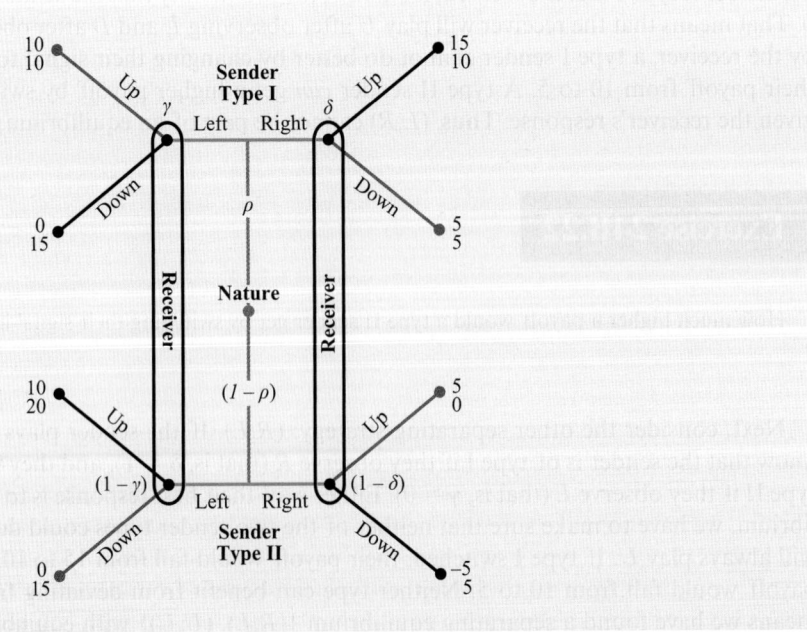

Next, we can begin with the pooling strategy (L,L) and see whether it can still be part of an equilibrium. The receiver's response would, as we just argued, depend on their belief γ, but if the two sender types both always play L, the receiver's belief about the probability that they are facing each type after observing L should be unaltered from what it was at the beginning of the game. Since we assume that all players know the probability ρ with which Nature assigns types, this means that, under the sender strategy (L,L), $\gamma = \rho$. Since we determined that the receiver will play U from their left information set if $\gamma < 0.5$, this means that we know they will play U under the pooling strategy (L,L) as long as $\rho < 0.5$ and D as long as $\rho > 0.5$. If the receiver were to play D, type I senders can make themselves better off by playing R since their payoff would be greater than 0 regardless of what the receiver planned in that event. So (L,L) cannot be a pooling equilibrium if $\rho > 0.5$, only if $\rho \le 0.5$.

Exercise 24B.24

What has to be true about δ in order for (L,L) to be an equilibrium pooling strategy when $\rho < 0.5$?

We can also check if the second pooling strategy (R,R) could be part of an equilibrium. If (R,R) is played, the sender again reveals nothing about themselves, which means that the receiver should not change their beliefs about what sender type they are facing if they observe R. Thus, $\delta = \rho$. Since the receiver will play U from their right information set if $\delta > 0.5$ and D if $\delta < 0.5$, we know they will play U if $\rho > 0.5$ and D if $\rho < 0.5$. If the receiver were to play D, type II senders can do better by deviating and playing L since both possible payoffs for them would be larger than -5, so (R,R) cannot be part of an equilibrium if $\rho < 0.5$.

To ensure that (R,R) can be an equilibrium pooling strategy with the receiver playing U after seeing R when $\rho > 0.5$, we need to make sure that type II senders can't do better by deviating. Since such senders would get a payoff of 5 under the proposed equilibrium, this means they can't think that the receiver would play U if they observed L since that would result in a payoff for type II players of 10. We concluded before that the receiver would in fact play D following L if they believed $\gamma > 0.5$. (R,R) and (D,U) are pooling equilibrium strategies as long as $\rho > 0.5$ and $\gamma > 0.5$. Since L is never played in this equilibrium, any belief γ is an out-of-equilibrium belief, and thus could take on any form including $\gamma > 0.5$. Despite the fact that L is not played in this pooling equilibrium, we can have an equilibrium only if the receiver thinks an L signal (that is never sent) is most likely indicative of a type I sender. We therefore have a pooling equilibrium $\{(R,R), (D,U)\}$ with beliefs $\delta = \rho > 0.5$ and $\gamma > 0.5$.

Finally, consider the separating equilibrium strategy (R,L). If the sender plays this strategy, the receiver will best respond by playing (U,U), which results in payoffs of 15 and 10 for type I and II senders respectively. Neither sender type can do better by deviating, which means we have found a separating equilibrium $\{(R,L), (U,U)\}$ with $\delta = 1$ and $\gamma = 0$, an equilibrium where the sender reveals their type and the receiver therefore knows with certainty which type the sender is by the time they have to choose an action.

Exercise 24B.25

Could the separating strategy (L,R) be part of an equilibrium in this case?

Exercise 24B.26*

Suppose that, in the game in Graph 24.10, we had changed the receiver's payoff from playing U when facing a sender of type II who plays left from 20 to 5 instead. Could there be a separating equilibrium in that game? Is there a pure strategy equilibrium for all values of ρ?

24B.2.4 Perfect Bayesian Nash Equilibria in Signalling and Other Games So far, we have talked through several different signalling games, illustrating the possibility of separating and pooling equilibria and demonstrating the role that beliefs play in supporting such equilibria. Given the intuition we have developed, we can now be more precise about what we mean by an equilibrium in a sequential game of incomplete information such as a signalling game.

Recall that a game of incomplete information (or a Bayesian game) has the following components:

1 actions for each player;
2 types for each player;
3 beliefs about other players' types; and
4 payoffs that depend on which types are actually in the game and what actions they take.

Furthermore, recall that we have assumed throughout that all players know the probabilities with which Nature assigns types to individuals, and that these probabilities therefore form everyone's initial beliefs. In simultaneous move games, those initial beliefs are the same throughout the game since no new information about other players' types is revealed before an action has to be taken. In sequential move games, individuals will *update their beliefs* if actions by others reveal new information.

We have seen such updating of beliefs in the signal game when we considered separating strategies by the sender. In that case, the sender fully revealed their type through the signals they sent, allowing the receiver to update their beliefs. In the case where the sender did not reveal additional information because of the use of a pooling strategy, no updating had to be done once the receiver reached their information set, leaving them with the same beliefs they had at the beginning of the game. Off-the-equilibrium path, we did not restrict the receiver's beliefs because it is not clear how one forms beliefs in circumstances that happen with zero probability. We did hint in one of the exercises, however, that game theorists have developed reasonable restrictions (that are beyond the scope of this text) on such out-of-equilibrium beliefs.

More generally, updating of beliefs in sequential Bayesian games satisfies what is known as *Bayes rule*. Bayes rule in the context of sequential Bayesian games means the following: suppose that a particular information set I contains nodes $N_1, N_2, \ldots, N_k$, with $P(N_i)$ giving the probability that node Ni is reached (and the probability of the information set I being reached therefore equal to $\sum_{i=1}^{k} P(N_i)$. Suppose that as the game progresses, the information set I is actually reached. The updated probability that N_i has been reached *given that the information set I has been reached* is:

$$P(N_i|I) = \frac{P(N_i)}{P(I)}. \qquad \textbf{(24.7)}$$

Suppose, for instance, that player 1 in a game moves first and has three available actions: a_1, a_2 and a_3. Suppose player 1 is playing a mixed strategy that places equal weight of 1/4 on a_1 and a_2 and 1/2 on a_3, and suppose that player 2 can tell whether player 1 has played a_1 but cannot tell the difference between player 1 having played a_2 and a_3. Thus, player 2 has two information sets $I_1 = \{a_1\}$ and $I_2 = \{a_2, a_3\}$. Now suppose that player 2 faces a decision after reaching information set I_2; that is, suppose player 2 knows that player 1 did not play a_1. According to Bayes rule, player 2 now believes that player 1 has played actions a_2 and a_3 with probabilities 1/3 and 2/3 because:

$$P(a_2|I_2) = \frac{P(a_2)}{P(I_2)} = \frac{1/4}{3/4} = \frac{1}{3} \text{ and } P(a_3|I_2) = \frac{P(a_3)}{P(I_2)} = \frac{1/2}{3/4} = \frac{2}{3}, \qquad \textbf{(24.8)}$$

with $P(a_1|I_2) = 0$. If, on the other hand, player 2 reaches information set I_1, Bayes rule says the updated probabilities are $P(a_1|I_1) = \frac{1/4}{1/4} = 1$ and $P(a_1|I_2) = P(a_3|I_1) = 0$.

Note that implicitly we have applied Bayes rule a number of times as we updated beliefs in our signalling games. Suppose the sender played a pooling strategy L, thus taking the receiver to the information set on the left of our game trees with probability 1. Let's denote that information set as I_L, which contains two nodes defined by whether the sender was a type I or a type II. To make the upcoming notation a bit easier to read, let's denote type I as T_1 and type II as T_2. The receiver knows that Nature, at the beginning of the game, assigned T_1 to the sender with probability ρ and T_2 with probability $(1 - \rho)$. If the sender plays a pooling strategy that results in the receiver making decisions from the information set I_L, Bayes rule implies that the receiver should have beliefs $P(T_1|I_L) = P(T_1)/P(I_L) = \rho/1 = \rho$ and $P(T_2|I_L) = P(T_2)/P(I_L) = (1 - \rho)/1 = (1 - \rho)$. Since the sender's pooling strategy adds no information, no updating of beliefs occurs. Under a separating strategy where the sender plays L if type I and R if type II, Bayes rule implies $P(T_1|I_L) = P(T_1)/P(I_L) = \rho/\rho = 1$, $P(T_2|I_R) = P(T_2)/P(I_R) = (1 - \rho)/(1 - \rho) = 1$ and $P(T_2|I_L) = 0 = P(T_1|I_R)$.

Exercise 24B.27

If the sender plays a pooling strategy (L,L), why is the receiver's belief about nodes in the information set I_R undefined according to Bayes rule?

Earlier, we said a Bayesian Nash equilibrium occurs when each player's strategy is a best response to every other player's strategy *given the player's beliefs that are consistent with how the game is being played*. We can now extend this formally to say that in a sequential Bayesian game, a *subgame perfect Bayesian Nash equilibrium* is a Bayesian Nash equilibrium in which all the strategies and beliefs in all subgames that begin at each information set also constitute a Bayesian Nash equilibrium for each 'subgame'. We are putting *subgame* in inverted commas here because subgames are usually defined as beginning at one node. For this reason, the equilibrium concept we are now defining is usually referred to as a perfect rather than subgame perfect Bayesian Nash equilibrium. This is analogous to the relationship between Nash equilibria and subgame perfect Nash equilibria in a complete information game, where subgame perfection in sequential settings required all subgames to be in equilibrium as well and thus eliminated Nash equilibria that relied on non-credible strategies down the game tree. The difference in sequential Bayesian games is that at least some 'subgames' now begin with information sets that contain more than a single node, and this in turn requires the specification of beliefs.

All such beliefs have to be consistent with how the game is played, which meant that all players shared beliefs consistent with Nature's probabilities in our initial simultaneous move game where no new information could arise for players to update their beliefs. In a sequential setting, however, it means that beliefs have to be updated using Bayes rule wherever it applies, beginning with initial beliefs consistent with the probabilities employed by Nature. Bayes rule applies at information sets that are reached with positive probability under the equilibrium strategies. At information sets that are reached with probability 0, however, Bayes rule does not apply and beliefs are therefore unrestricted, which is not the same as saying they can remain *unspecified*. In order to sustain an equilibrium, these off-the-equilibrium-path beliefs have to be structured so as to make the equilibrium strategies best responses to one another in all subgames that are not reached.

Exercise 24B.28

Is every Bayesian Nash equilibrium also a perfect Bayesian Nash equilibrium? Is every perfect Bayesian Nash equilibrium also a Bayesian Nash equilibrium? Explain.

Exercise 24B.29

True or False: When a game tree is such that all information sets are single nodes, then subgame perfect Nash equilibrium is the same as perfect Bayesian Nash equilibrium.

24B.3 Reputations in Finitely Repeated Prisoner's Dilemmas

In Section A of this chapter, we placed a lot of emphasis on the Prisoner's Dilemma because it is a game that has particular relevance in many economic settings. We solved the simultaneous Prisoner's Dilemma and found that there exists a single Nash equilibrium that involves both parties in the game choosing not to cooperate with one another *despite the fact that the cooperative outcome is preferred by both to the non-cooperative outcome*. We also found that if two players face each other repeatedly a finite number of times, the only subgame perfect Nash equilibrium involves a lack of cooperation in every stage of the repeated game. We noted that in experimental settings as well as in many real-world settings, we see significantly more cooperation than what the model predicts, and we discovered a way to think about repeated Prisoner's Dilemma games in which the players are uncertain about whether they will meet again each time that they meet or in which players expect to interact an infinite number of times. In such a setting, we argued, it is plausible that cooperation can emerge, and we show in the appendix that anything between no cooperation and full cooperation can in fact emerge in infinitely repeated Prisoner's Dilemma games assuming players do not discount the future too heavily.

This set of results is, in some ways, quite odd. In finitely repeated Prisoner's Dilemma games, not the slightest bit of cooperation can emerge under subgame perfection, while in the infinitely repeated game, or a game in which individuals are uncertain about whether they will meet again but think it sufficiently likely each time, all levels of cooperation can be sustained under subgame perfection. In some sense, one model seems to predict too little cooperation; the other potentially predicts too much.

We will now introduce a Bayesian element to repeated Prisoner's Dilemma games in which players are uncertain about what type they face and not about whether they will interact again. What we will find is that the introduction of uncertainty of a certain kind can result in equilibrium cooperation even in finitely repeated Prisoner's Dilemma settings. In particular, we will see that the introduction of uncertainty on the part of one player about the type of player they are facing opens the possibility for the opposing player to establish a 'reputation' for cooperation, a reputation that will cause cooperation to persist for some time even among rational players in finitely repeated Prisoner's Dilemmas.

24B.3.1 Introducing the Possibility of a Tit-for-Tat Player Suppose that Nature moves before the beginning of a finitely repeated Prisoner's Dilemma game involving two players, player 1 and player 2, and suppose that the payoffs in each stage of this game after Nature moves are as in Table 24.10. Nature's move determines 1's type, assigning them with probability ρ the tit-for-tat type t_1 and with probability $(1 - \rho)$ the rational player type t_2. If 1 is assigned the tit-for-tat type, they will play the tit-for-tat strategy, begin by playing C and then mimic for the rest of the game the last action played by the opposing player in the previous period. If, on the other hand 1 is assigned the rational player type, they maximize their own utility as we have assumed throughout. As in our signalling games, we assume that 1 learns their own type at the beginning of the game but 2 does not.

This is a little different than previous incomplete information introduced into our Bayesian games in which Nature assigned different *payoffs* to different types. Here, Nature is rather assigning 1 a particular strategy (tit-for-tat) with probability ρ, thus removing choice about the strategy that they adopt in the event that they are assigned this type. One could argue that we are assuming Nature is making 1 'irrational' with probability ρ, but irrational in a particular way. One could also model this more in line with our previous models as a change in payoffs for the first type such that tit-for-tat is the optimal strategy. For instance, we could assume that there is a chance that 1 was raised to believe tit-for-tat is the correct moral path in life, that they are deeply committed to this path and that they would suffer greatly if they chose a different path.

24B.3.2 Considering a Twice-Repeated Prisoner's Dilemma Game Assume that the players know they are going to play the Prisoner's Dilemma twice and, to keep things as simple as possible, they do not discount the future. From earlier discussion, we know that a typical rational player will choose D the second time they play. If 1 ends up being a t_2 rational player, they know this when they play the first time and will therefore choose D each time the players meet. If 1 is a t_1 type, they have no choice and will play the tit-for-tat strategy. This leaves an open question for player 2. Should they play C the first time they meet in the hope of 1 being a tit-for-tat type, which would mean 2 could get the cooperative payoff 10 the first time they meet *and* get 15 the second time they meet by playing D when the tit-for-tat type will play C? Playing C followed by D gives 2 a combined payoff across the two periods of 25 if they face a tit-for-tat type, but it gives a payoff of only 5 if they end up facing 1 as a rational t_2. Playing C first followed by D gives 2 an *expected* payoff of $25\rho + 5(1 - \rho) = 20\rho + 5$, while 2's *expected* payoff from playing D both periods is $10\rho + 10$.

Table 24.10 Prisoner's Dilemma

		Player 2	
		Cooperate	Don't cooperate
Player 1	Cooperate	10, 10	0, 15
	Don't cooperate	15, 0	**5, 5**

Exercise 24B.30

Verify the last sentence.

Player 2's expected payoff from playing C followed by D is larger than their expected payoff from playing D always if $\rho > 0.5$. If 1 is more likely to be a tit-for-tat player than a rational t_2 player, the perfect Bayesian Nash equilibrium has 2 playing (C,D), with 1 playing (C,C) if 1 is a tit-for-tat player and (D,D) if they are not.

Exercise 24B.31

What are the beliefs that support this as a perfect Bayesian equilibrium?

24B.3.3 Considering a Thrice-Repeated Prisoner's Dilemma Game Now suppose that the players know at the beginning that they are going to play the game three times and suppose that $\rho > 0.5$. Player 1 learns at the very beginning whether they are a tit-for-tat player or not, but 2 learns it only if 1 chooses to reveal it by violating the tit-for-tat strategy when 1 is a type t_2.

Suppose that 1 learns they are t_2 and thus does not have to play the tit-for-tat strategy. If 1 plays D in the first game, they will have revealed to 2 that they are not a tit-for-tat type, and Bayesian updating of 2's beliefs will imply that 2 now places probability 1 on player 1 being a t_2 type by the time they begin the second game. Knowing that, it will be best for 2 to play D in the second and third game. If, on the other hand, 1 plays C in the first game after finding out that 1 is a t_2 type, they are at this point acting as if they were a tit-for-tat player by beginning the game with a pooling strategy. Bayes rule tells us that 2 has no information to update their beliefs about what type 1 is, which means they enter game 2 with the same information that they had at the beginning of the twice-repeated game just analyzed. This implies that if 2 also played C in the first round, the beginning of game 2 is identical to the Twice-Repeated Prisoner's Dilemma and our previous analysis holds for the rest of the game. If both players cooperate in the first stage, they know that 2 will play C followed by D in the second and third game while 1 will play C for the rest of the game if they are a tit-for-tat type and D for the rest of the game if they are not. If 2 observes 1 playing D in the first stage, however, they will plan to play D for the rest of the game. The question we now want to think about is whether the following strategies are part of a perfect Bayesian Nash equilibrium:

Strategy for 1 if they are type t_2: Play C in the first game and D in the second and third games.

Strategy for 2: Play C in the first game. If 2 observes 1 also playing D in the first game, play C in the second game. Otherwise, play D in the second game. Finally, play D in the last game.

Exercise 24B.32

Verify that if the players play these strategies, 2's expected payoff will be $35\rho + 15(1 - \rho) = 20\rho + 15$, and 1's payoff as a t_2 type will be 30.

Suppose, that 1 plays this strategy. Can 2 do better by playing D in the first game? Since the players know that 2 will do best playing D in the third that is, the last game, 2 will play either $D - D - D$ or $D - C - D$ over the three games if they choose D in the first stage. By playing $D - D - D$, 2's payoffs will be $15 + 5 + 5 = 25$ if they face a tit-for-tat t_1 type who will mimic their D's in the second and third games, exactly the same as if they faced a rational t_2 type who plays the suggested equilibrium strategy $C - D - D$. Player 2's expected payoff from playing $D - D - D$ is 25. By playing $D - C - D$, on the other hand, 2 will get payoffs $15 + 0 + 15 = 30$ if they face a tit-for-tat t_1 opponent who will respond with $C - D - D$, and payoffs $15 + 0 + 5 = 20$ if they face a rational t_2 opponent, giving expected payoff $30\rho + 20(1 - \rho) = 20 + 10\rho$ from playing $D - C - D$. Since we are assuming $\rho > 0.5$ throughout, 2's expected payoff from $D - D - D$ (that is, 25) falls short of their expected payoff from $D - C - D$ (that is, $20 + 10\rho$), implying that *if 2 were to deviate from playing C in the first stage, they would play $D - C - D$*. Player 2's payoff from playing the suggested equilibrium strategy is $20\rho + 15$, which exceeds their expected payoff from the deviation $D - C - D$ given that $\rho > 0.5$. The suggested equilibrium strategy is therefore a best response to the t_2 strategy suggested for 1 given that there is a probability $\rho > 0.5$ that 1 is a tit-for-tat player.

Next, we can check if 1 has an incentive to deviate from the proposed strategy. We know from our work on the twice-repeated game that if 1 does not deviate in the first stage by playing D, they cannot benefit from deviating in the second and third stage by playing C since the game starting in the second stage is identical to the twice-repeated game if both players play C in the first stage. The only question is if 1 can benefit by playing D rather than C in the first stage, thereby revealing in the first game that they are a t_2. If 1 does so, they will get a payoff of 15 in the first game followed by payoffs of 5 in the next two stages for a total payoff of 25. By playing the proposed strategy, 1's payoff is 30. They cannot benefit from deviating from the proposed strategy, which means the proposed strategy is a best response to 2's proposed strategy.

We have demonstrated that 2's suggested strategy is a best response to 1's and 1's is a best response to 2's. In the thrice-repeated Prisoner's Dilemma, both players cooperating in the first game can therefore emerge as part of a perfect Bayesian Nash equilibrium as long as the probability of 1 being a tit-for-tat player is sufficiently high. The reason for this is that it is now in 1's interest as a rational player to try to establish a reputation for being a tit-for-tat player or, more generally, for being a cooperative player in order to get 2 to cooperate with them for a while.

24B.3.4 *N*-Times Repeated Prisoner's Dilemma and The Role of Reputations If we are trying to show that a perfect Bayesian Nash equilibrium exists for *N*-Times Repeated Prisoner's Dilemma games with players cooperating up to some point in the game, then such an equilibrium with early cooperation will also exist for an $(N + 1)$-Times Repeated Prisoner's Dilemma. By demonstrating that player 1 and player 2 (as a t_2 type) might choose to cooperate in the first game of a Thrice-Repeated Prisoner's Dilemma if the probability of 1 being a tit-for-tat player is high enough, we have picked an unlikely game for which to demonstrate our result. As N becomes larger, cooperation in the early part of the game becomes easier to sustain and can emerge for smaller probabilities of 1 being a tit-for-tat player. For large but finite N, this probability can get very close to zero, meaning that we will observe cooperation in Finitely Repeated Prisoner's Dilemma games even if there is only a small chance that one of the players is a tit-for-tat player.

It is furthermore the case that for the payoffs in the game of Table 24.10, there is a perfect Bayesian Nash equilibrium under which cooperation will persist between player 2 and player 1 when 1 is a type t_2 player in all games prior to the second-to-last game in an N-Times Repeated Prisoner's Dilemma as long as $\rho > 0.5$. For a sufficiently high probability that one of the players is a tit-for-tat player, cooperation in an N-Times Repeated Prisoner's Dilemma can persist for long periods, $(N - 2)$ periods to be exact. Such cooperation will persist for a shorter period as ρ falls.

Thinking through this problem, the results for the N-Times Repeated Prisoner's Dilemma may seem intuitive, but it takes a little doing to prove formally. We will therefore forego formal proofs and note that we have, using the concept of perfect Bayesian Nash equilibrium, arrived at one possible explanation for why we see cooperation in finitely repeated settings when subgame perfection suggests that such cooperation should not occur among rational players. That explanation essentially says that in environments where there is some uncertainty about the type of opponents that players face, players like 1 may want to establish a *reputation* for being cooperative in order to sustain cooperation over some period of time.

| Appendix | Infinitely Repeated Games and the Folk Theorem |

Consider the Prisoner's Dilemma in Table 24.5, which is depicted in panel (a) of Graph 24.12 with the actions relabelled C for Cooperate and D for Don't Cooperate.

Graph 24.12 Average Payoffs Under Infinite Repetition of the Prisoner's Dilemma

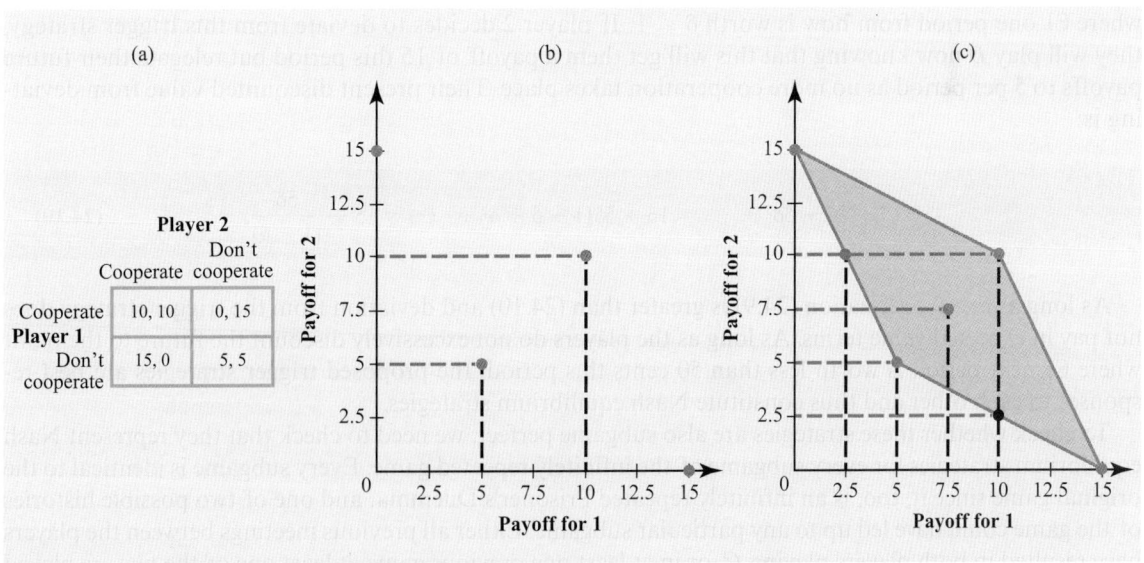

The four possible payoff combinations are graphed in panel (b). Each of these is of course a possible *average* per-period payoff in the infinitely repeated game if the two players were to always play the actions that lead to those payoffs in the simultaneous game. By alternating different combinations of actions in different stages of the sequential game, other combinations of average payoffs per game become possible. For instance, if players alternated between both playing C and both playing D, they would alternate between payoffs of 5 and 10, thus getting an average payoff of 7.5 each. If they alternated between both playing C and player 1 playing D while player 2 plays C, player 1 would get an average payoff of 10 while player 2 would get an average payoff of 2.5.

Exercise 24B.33

Propose a way that average payoffs could be 5 for player 1 and 12.5 for player 2.

It can be seen that, by combining different ways of playing the game in different periods, *any* payoff combination in the light blue shaded region in panel (c) of the graph can arise in the infinitely repeated game as the *average* payoffs for the two players. The question we would like to turn to now is which of these average payoff combinations could arise in a subgame perfect Nash equilibrium?

We begin by showing, as we did earlier in the chapter, that the fully cooperative average payoff outcome (10,10) can emerge under subgame perfection and then we will discuss how the same logic can lead to many other average equilibrium payoffs.

Suppose each player in the game plays what we previously called a *trigger strategy* of the following kind. Play C in the first stage of the infinitely repeated game and continue to do so as long as both players cooperated in all previous stages; otherwise, play D. We can first check that these are best responses to one another. Suppose player 1 plays this strategy. If player 2 also plays the same strategy, they will receive a payoff of 10 in every stage of the game. Recall that, for $0 < \delta < 1$, $1 + \delta + \delta^2 + \cdots = 1/(1 - \delta)$, which implies that the present discounted value of receiving a payoff of 10 in every period from now on is:

$$10 + 10\delta + 10\delta^2 + \cdots = \frac{10}{(1 - \delta)}, \qquad (24.9)$$

where €1 one period from now is worth $\delta < 1$. If player 2 decides to deviate from this trigger strategy, they will play D now knowing that this will get them a payoff of 15 this period but relegate their future payoffs to 5 per period as no more cooperation takes place. Their present discounted value from deviating is:

$$15 + 5\delta + 5\delta^2 + \cdots = 15 + 5\delta(1 + \delta + \delta^2 + \cdots) = 15 + \frac{5\delta}{(1 - \delta)}. \qquad (24.10)$$

As long as $\delta > 0.5$, equation (24.9) is greater than (24.10) and deviation from the trigger strategy does not pay in expected value terms. As long as the players do not excessively discount the future to the point where €1 next period is worth less than 50 cents this period, the proposed trigger strategies are best responses to each other and thus constitute Nash equilibrium strategies.

To check whether these strategies are also subgame perfect, we need to check that they represent Nash equilibrium strategies for every subgame of the infinitely repeated game. Every subgame is identical to the original game since it, too, is an infinitely repeated Prisoner's Dilemma, and one of two possible histories of the game could have led up to any particular subgame. Either all previous meetings between the players have resulted in both players playing C, or in at least one previous game at least one of the players played D. In the first case, we are still playing the same trigger strategy in the subgame, which is identical to the original game for which we already demonstrated these trigger strategies to be a Nash equilibrium. In the second case, we are playing the strategy Always D. Given the other player i plays this strategy, it is a best response for player j to do the same, and so again we have a Nash equilibrium in the subgame. We can therefore conclude that the proposed trigger strategies are subgame perfect, and they result in full cooperation with average per-period payoffs of 10 for each player.

The *Folk Theorem*, however, says more than this; not only is full cooperation possible through the use of the particular trigger strategy we specified, but partial cooperation is also possible. By *partial cooperation*, we mean sequences of equilibrium actions that result in payoffs for the two players that give more than the non-cooperative average payoff of 5 to each player. This corresponds to the average payoff combinations that lie in the light blue shaded region in Graph 24.13.

It can be seen how any of these payoffs could emerge in a subgame perfect Nash equilibrium of the infinitely repeated game. Pick any payoff combination in the shaded area of Graph 24.13. By definition, these payoffs are greater than what a player could get under non-cooperation. Determine the sequence of actions necessary to ensure the average payoff combination chosen and define a trigger strategy that says: 'Play this sequence as long as the other player plays their part; otherwise switch forever to *D*'. You should be able to see that as long as δ is sufficiently close to 1, and we therefore do not discount the future too much, it is a subgame perfect equilibrium for both players to play this trigger strategy.

Graph 24.13 The Folk Theorem for the Infinitely Repeated Prisoner's Dilemma

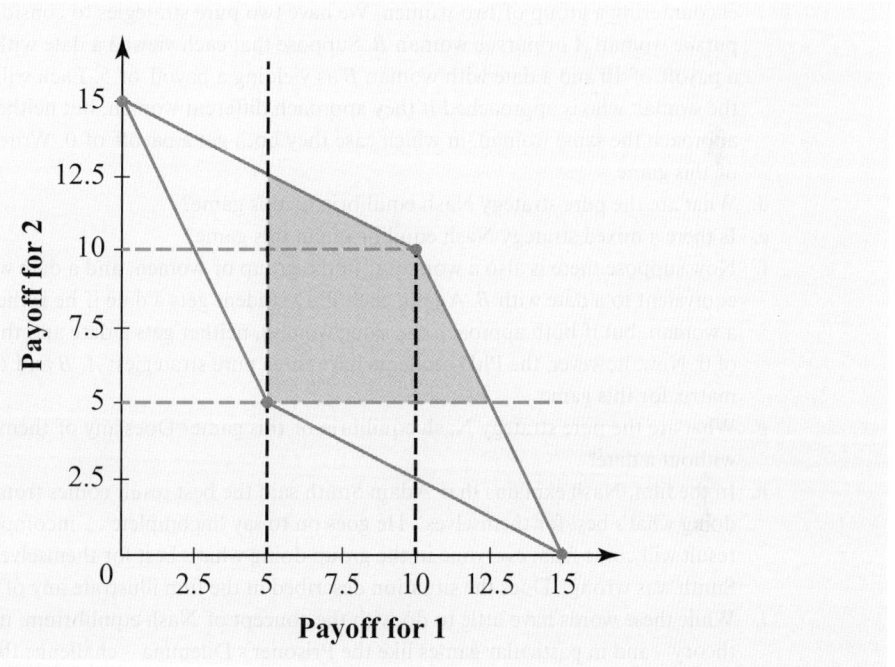

You should also see that similar logic can be extended to games other than the Prisoner's Dilemma where average payoffs above any simultaneous Nash equilibrium payoffs can arise under subgame perfection through the use of similar trigger strategies. Thus, the Folk Theorem is considerably more general than applying to repeated Prisoner's Dilemmas, and in fact it has been extended in ways that will become relevant when we discuss oligopoly behaviour in Chapter 25.

End-of-Chapter Exercises

24.1† In the Hollywood film *A Beautiful Mind*, Russell Crowe plays John Nash, who developed the Nash equilibrium concept in his PhD thesis at Princeton University, USA. In one of the early scenes of the film, Nash finds himself in a bar with three of his fellow male mathematics PhD students when a group of five women enters the bar. The attention of the PhD students is focused on one of the women, with each of the four PhD students expressing interest in asking her out. One of Nash's fellow students reminds the others of Adam Smith's insight that pursuit of self-interest in competition with others results in the socially best outcome, but Nash, in what appears to be a flash of insight, claims 'Adam Smith needs revision'.

A. In the film, John Nash explains that none of them will end up with the woman they are all attracted to if they all compete for her because they will block each other as they compete, and that furthermore they will not be able to go out with the other women in the group thereafter because none of them will agree to a date once they know they are at best everyone's second choice. Instead, he proposes, they should all ignore the woman they are initially attracted to and instead ask the others out. It's the only way they will get a date. He quickly rushes off to write his thesis, with the film implying that he had just discovered the concept of Nash equilibrium.

   a. If each of the PhD students were to play the strategy John Nash suggests, each one selects a woman other than the one they are all attracted to. Could this in fact be a pure strategy Nash equilibrium?

   b. Is it possible that any pure strategy Nash equilibrium could result in no one pursuing the woman they are all attracted to?

   c. Suppose we simplified the example to one in which it was only Nash and one other student encountering a group of two women. We have two pure strategies to consider for each PhD student: pursue woman A or pursue woman B. Suppose that each viewed a date with woman A as yielding a payoff of 10 and a date with woman B as yielding a payoff of 5. Each will in fact get a date with the woman who is approached *if* they approach different women, but neither will get a date if they approach the same woman, in which case they both get a payoff of 0. Write down the payoff matrix of this game.

   d. What are the pure strategy Nash equilibria of this game?

   e. Is there a mixed strategy Nash equilibrium in this game?

   f. Now suppose there is also a woman C in the group of women, and a date with C is viewed as equivalent to a date with B. Again, each PhD student gets a date if he is the only one approaching a woman, but if both approach the same woman, neither gets a date and thus both get a payoff of 0. Now, however, the PhD students have three pure strategies: A, B and C. Write down the payoff matrix for this game.

   g. What are the pure strategy Nash equilibria of this game? Does any of them involve woman A leaving without a date?

   h. In the film, Nash explains that 'Adam Smith said the best result comes from everyone in the group doing what's best for themselves'. He goes on to say 'incomplete ... incomplete ... because the best result will come from everyone in the group doing what's best for themselves *and* the group ... Adam Smith was wrong'. Does the situation described in the film illustrate any of this?

   i. While these words have little to do with the concept of Nash equilibrium, in what way does game theory – and in particular games like the Prisoner's Dilemma – challenge the inference one might draw from Adam Smith that self-interest achieves the best outcome for the group?

B. Consider the two-player game described in part A(c).

   a. Suppose that the players move sequentially, with player 1 choosing A or B first and player 2 making his choice after observing player 1's choice. What is the subgame perfect Nash equilibrium?

   b. Is there a Nash equilibrium in which player 2 goes out with woman A? If so, is there a non-credible threat that is needed to sustain this as an equilibrium?

   c. Consider again the simultaneous move game from A(c). Draw a game tree for this simultaneous move game, with player 1's decision on the top. *Hint*: Use the appropriate information set for player 2 to keep this game a simultaneous move game. Can you state different beliefs for player 2 when player 2 gets to their information set such that the equilibria you derived in A(d) and A(e) arise?

   d. Continue to assume that both players get payoff of 0 if they approach the same woman. As before, player 1 gets a payoff of 10 if they are the only one to approach woman A and a payoff of 5 if they are the only one to approach woman B. Player 2 might be one of two possible types. If they are type 1, they have the same tastes as player 1, but if they are type 2, they get a payoff of only 5 if they are the only one to approach woman A and a payoff of 10 if they are the only one to approach woman *B*. Prior to the beginning of the game, Nature assigns type 1 to player 2 with probability δ and thus assigns type 2 to player 2 with probability $(1 - \delta)$. Graph the game tree for this game, using information sets to connect nodes where appropriate.

e. What are the pure strategy equilibria in this game? Does it matter what value δ takes?

24.2 Everyday Application: *Splitting the Pot.* Suppose two players are asked to split €100 in a way that is agreeable to both.

A. The structure for the game is as follows: player 1 moves first, and they are asked to state some number between 0 and 100. This number represents their offer to player 2; that is, the amount player 1 offers for player 2 to keep, with player 1 keeping the rest. If player 1 says 30, they are offering player 2 a split of the €100 that gives €70 to player 1 and €30 to player 2. After an offer has been made by player 1, player 2 chooses from two possible actions: either accept the offer or reject it. If player 2 accepts, the €100 is split in the way proposed by player 1; if player 2 rejects, neither player gets anything. A game like this is often referred to as an *ultimatum game*.

   a. What are the subgame perfect equilibria in this game assuming that player 1 is restricted to making their offer in integer terms; that is, assuming that player 1 has to state a whole number.

   b. Now suppose that offers can be made to the cent; that is, offers like €31.24 are acceptable. How does that change the subgame perfect equilibria? What if we assumed euros could be divided into arbitrarily small quantities, that is fractions of cents?

   c. It turns out that there are at most two subgame perfect equilibria to this game and only one if euros are assumed to be fully divisible, but there is a very large number of Nash equilibria regardless of exactly how player 1 can phrase their offer and an infinite number when euros are assumed fully divisible. Can you, for instance, derive Nash equilibrium strategies that result in player 2 walking away with €80? Why is this not subgame perfect?

   d. This game has been played in experimental settings in many cultures, and while the average amount that is offered differs somewhat between cultures, it usually falls between €25 and €50, with players often rejecting offers below that. One possible explanation for this is that individuals across different cultures have somewhat different notions of fairness, and that they get utility from standing up for what's fair. Suppose player 2 is willing to pay €30 to stand up to injustice of any kind, and anything other than a 50-50 split is considered by player 2 to be unjust. What is now the subgame perfect equilibrium if euros are viewed as infinitely divisible? What additional subgame perfect equilibrium arises if offers can only be made in integer amounts?

   e. Suppose instead that player 2 is outraged at unfair outcomes in direct proportion to how far the outcome is removed from the fair outcome, with the utility player 2 gets from rejecting an unfair offer equal to the difference between the amount offered and the fair amount. Suppose player 2 believes the fair outcome is splitting the €100 equally. Thus, if the player faces an offer $x < 50$, the utility they get from rejecting the offer is $(50 - x)$. What are the subgame perfect equilibria of this game now under the assumption of infinitely divisible euros and under the assumption of offers having to be made in integer terms?

B. Consider the same game as that outlined in A and suppose Ahmed is the one who splits the €100 and Sima the one who decides to accept or reject. Ahmed thinks there is a pretty good chance that Sima is the epitome of a rational human being who cares only about walking away with the most they can from the game. Ahmed doesn't know Sima that well, and thinks there is some chance ρ that she is a self-righteous moralist who will reject any offer that is worse for her than a 50-50 split. Assume throughout that euros can be split into infinitesimal parts.

   a. Structure this game as an incomplete information game.

   b. There are two types of pure strategy equilibria to this game depending on what value ρ takes. What are they?

   c. How would your answer change if Sima, as a self-righteous moralist, which she is with probability ρ, rejects all offers that leave her with less than €10?

   d. What if it's only less than €1 that is rejected by self-righteous moralists?

   e. What have we implicitly assumed about risk aversion?

24.3† Everyday and Business Application: *Auctions.* Many items are sold not in markets but in auctions where bidders do not know how much others value the object that is up for auction. We will analyze a straightforward setting like this here, which technically means we are analyzing for much of this exercise an incomplete information game of the type covered in Section B of the chapter. The underlying logic of the exercise is, however, sufficiently transparent for you to be able to attempt the exercise even if you have not read Section B of the chapter. Consider the following, known as a *second-price sealed bid auction*. In this kind of auction, all people who are interested in an item x submit sealed bids simultaneously. The person whose bid is the highest gets the item x at a price equal to the second highest bid.

A. Suppose there are n different bidders who have different marginal willingness to pay for the item x. Player i's marginal willingness to pay for x is denoted by vi. Suppose initially that this is a complete information game; that is, everyone knows everyone's marginal willingness to pay for the item that is auctioned.

   a. Is it a Nash equilibrium in this auction for each player i to bid v_i?

   b. Suppose individual j has the highest marginal willingness to pay. Is it a Nash equilibrium for all players other than j to bid zero and player j to bid v_j?

   c. Can you think of another Nash equilibrium to this auction?

   d. Suppose that players are not actually sure about the marginal willingness to pay of all the other players, only about their own. Can you think of why the Nash equilibrium in which all players bid their marginal willingness to pay is now the most compelling Nash equilibrium?

   e. Now consider a *sequential first-price auction* in which an auctioneer keeps increasing the price of x in small increments and any potential bidder signals to the auctioneer if they are willing to pay that price. Assume that the signal from bidders to auctioneer is not observable by other bidders. The auction ends when only a single bidder signals a willingness to pay the price, and the winner buys the item x for the price equal to their winning bid. Assuming the increments the auctioneer uses to raise the price during the auction are sufficiently small, approximately what will each player's final bid be?

   f. In equilibrium, approximately what price will the winner of the sequential auction pay?

   g. *True or False*: The outcome of the second-price sealed bid auction is approximately equivalent to the outcome of the sequential first-price auction.

B. Assume a department head of an economics department in a university annually decides how to assign graduate students to faculty to provide teaching and research support. Students are paid a stipend by the department, but their services were free to the faculty member to whom they were assigned.

   a. Under this system, faculty complains perpetually of a teaching assistant shortage. Why do you think this is?

   b. Assume the system is replaced with the following: aside from some key assignments of graduate students as teaching assistants (TAs) to large courses, the department head no longer assigns any students to faculty. Instead, they ask faculty to submit euro bids for the right to match with a graduate student. If the university department has N graduate students available, the department head takes the top N bids, lets those faculty know they had qualified for the right to match with a student and let the matches take place with students and faculty seeking each other out to create matches. Every faculty member who had a successful bid is charged to their research account a price equal to the lowest winning bid, which we call the market price. Assume there is a large number of faculty, should any individual faculty member think that their bid would appreciably impact the market price?

   c. In an annual e-mail to faculty at the beginning of the auction for rights to match with students, the department head includes the following line: 'For those of you who are not game theorists, please note that it is a dominant strategy for you to bid the actual value you place on the right to match with a student'. Do you agree or disagree with this statement? Why?

   d. Would it surprise you to discover that the department head does not receive any complaints that there was a TA shortage? Why or why not?

   e. Why do you think the department head called the lowest winning bid the market price? Can you think of several ways in which the allocation of students to faculty might have become more efficient as a result of the implementation of the new way of allocating students?

24.4 **Business Application:** *Monopoly and Price Discrimination.* In Chapter 23, we discussed first, second and third degree price discrimination by a monopolist. Such pricing decisions are strategic choices that can be modelled using game theory, which we proceed to do here. Assume throughout that the monopolist can keep consumers who buy at low prices from selling to those who are offered high prices.

A. Suppose a monopolist faces two types of consumers: a high demand consumer and a low demand consumer. Suppose further that the monopolist can tell which consumer has low demand and which has high demand; that is, the consumer types are observable to the monopolist.

   a. Model the pricing decisions by the monopolist as a set of sequential games with different consumer types.
   b. Suppose the monopolist can construct any set of two-part tariffs, that is, a per-unit price plus fixed fee for different packages. What is the subgame perfect equilibrium of your games?
   c. *True or False*: First-degree price discrimination emerges in the subgame perfect equilibrium but not in other Nash equilibria of the game.
   d. How is this analysis similar to the game in exercise 24.2?
   e. Next, suppose that the monopolist cannot charge a fixed fee but only a per-unit price, but it can set different per-unit prices for different consumer types. What is the subgame perfect equilibrium of your games now?

B. Next, suppose that the monopolist is unable to observe the consumer type but knows that a fraction ρ in the population are low demand types and a fraction $(1 - \rho)$ are high demand types. Assume that firms can offer any set of price/quantity combinations.

   a. Model the price-setting decision by the monopolist as a game of incomplete information?
   b. What is the perfect Bayesian equilibrium of this game in the context of concepts discussed in Chapter 23? Explain.

24.5† **Everyday, Business and Policy Application:** *Education as a Signal.* In Chapter 22, we briefly discussed the signalling role of education; the fact that part of the reason many people get more education is not to learn more but rather to signal high productivity to potential employers in the hopes of getting a higher wage offer. We return to this in part B of this exercise in the context of an incomplete information game built on concepts from Section B of the chapter, but first consider the lack of a role for signalling in a complete information game. Throughout, suppose that there are two types of workers, type 1 workers with low productivity and type 2 workers with high productivity, with a fraction δ of all workers being type 2 and a fraction $(1 - \delta)$ being type 1. Both types can earn education by expending effort, but it costs type 1 workers e to get education level $e > 0$, while it costs type 2 workers only $e/2$. An employer gets profit $(2 - w)$ if they employ a type 2 worker at wage w and $(1 - w)$ if they employ a type 1 worker at wage w. Employers get zero profit if they do not employ a worker. We assume that the worker decides in stage 1 how much education to get; in stage 2, they approach two competing employers who decide simultaneously how much of a wage w to offer; and finally, in stage 3, they decide which wage offer to accept.

A. Suppose that worker productivity is directly observable by employers; that is, firms can tell who is a type 1 and who is a type 2 worker by just looking at them.

   a. Solving this game backwards, what strategy will the worker employ in stage 3 when choosing between wage offers?
   b. Given that firms know what will happen in stage 3, what wage will they offer to each of the two types in the simultaneous move game of stage 2 assuming that they best respond to one another? *Hint*: Ask yourself if the two employers could offer two different wages to the same worker type, and, if not, how competition between them impacts the wage that they will offer in equilibrium.
   c. Note that we have assumed worker productivity is not influenced by the level of education e chosen by a worker in stage 1. Is there any way that the level of e can have any impact on the wage offers that a worker gets in equilibrium?
   d. Would the wages offered by the two employers be any different if the employers moved in sequence, with employer 2 being able to observe the wage offer from employer 1 before the worker chooses an offer?
   e. What level of e will the two worker types get in any subgame perfect equilibrium?

     f. *True or False*: If education does not contribute to worker productivity and firms can directly observe the productivity level of job applicants, workers will not expend effort to get education, at least not for the purpose of getting a good wage offer.

B. Now suppose that employers cannot tell the productivity level of workers directly; all they know is the fraction δ of workers that have high productivity and the education level e of job applicants.

     a. Will workers behave any differently in stage 3 than they did in part A of the exercise?

     b. Suppose that there is a *separating equilibrium* in which type 2 workers get education $\bar{e}$ that differs from the education level type 1 workers get, and thus firms can identify the productivity level of job applicants by observing their education level. What level of education must type 1 workers be getting in such a separating equilibrium?

     c. What wages will the competing firms offer to the two types of workers? State their complete strategies and the beliefs that support these.

     d. Given your answers so far, what values could $\bar{e}$ take in this separating equilibrium? Assuming $\bar{e}$ falls in this range, specify the separating perfect Bayesian Nash equilibrium, including the strategies used by workers and employers as well as the full beliefs necessary to support the equilibrium.

     e. Next, suppose instead that the equilibrium is a *pooling equilibrium*; that is, an equilibrium in which all workers get the same level of education $\bar{e}$ and firms therefore cannot infer anything about the productivity of a job applicant. Will the strategy in stage 3 be any different than it has been?

     f. Assuming that every job applicant is type 2 with probability δ and type 1 with probability $(1 - \delta)$, what wage offers will firms make in stage 2?

     g. What levels of education $\bar{e}$ could in fact occur in such a perfect Bayesian pooling equilibrium? Assuming $\bar{e}$ falls in this range, specify the pooling perfect Bayesian Nash equilibrium, including the strategies used by workers and employers as well as the full beliefs necessary to support the equilibrium.

     h. Could there be an education level $\bar{e}$ that high productivity workers get in a separating equilibrium and that all workers get in a pooling equilibrium?

     i. What happens to the pooling wage relative to the highest possible wage in a separating equilibrium as δ approaches 1? Does this make sense?

24.6 Policy Application: *Some Prisoner's Dilemmas.* We mentioned in this chapter that the incentives of the Prisoner's Dilemma appear frequently in real-world situations.

A. In each of the following, explain how these are Prisoner's Dilemmas and suggest a potential solution that might address the incentive problems identified in such games.

     a. A lecturer teaches the topic of Prisoner's Dilemmas in large classes that also meet in smaller sections once a week. The lecturer sometimes offers the following extra exercise which gives some grade payoff: Every student is given 10 points. Each student has to decide how many of these points to donate to a section account and convey this to the lecturer privately. Each student's payoff is a number of extra grade points equal to the number of points they did *not* donate to their section *plus* twice the average contribution to the section account by students registered in their section. For instance, if a student donates 4 points to their section and the average student in the section donated 3 points, this student's payoff would be 12 extra grade credit points: 6 because the student only donated 4 of their 10 points, and 6 because they get twice the average donated in their section.

     b. People get in their cars without thinking about the impact they have on other drivers on the road, and at certain predictable times, this results in congestion problems on roads.

     c. Everyone in your community would love to see some really great community fireworks on the next New Year's Eve, but somehow no fireworks ever happen in your community.

     d. People like downloading pirated music for free, but would like to have artists continue to produce lots of great music.

     e. Small business owners would like to keep their businesses open during business hours and not on evenings and weekends. In some countries, they have successfully lobbied the government to force them to close in the evening and at the weekends.

B. In Chapter 21, we introduced the *Coase Theorem*, and we mentioned in Section 21A.4.4 the example of bee keeping on apple orchards. Apple trees, it turns out, don't produce much honey when frequented by bees, but bees are essential for cross-pollination.

    a. In an area with lots of apple orchards, each owner of an orchard has to ensure that there are sufficient numbers of bees to visit the trees and do the necessary cross-pollination. Bees cannot easily be kept to just one orchard, which implies that an orchard owner who maintains a bee hive is also providing some cross-pollination services to neighbouring orchards. In what sense do orchard owners face a Prisoner's Dilemma?

    b. How does the Coase Theorem suggest that orchard owners deal with this problem?

    c. We mentioned in Chapter 21 that some have documented a 'custom of the orchards', an implicit understanding among orchard owners that each will employ the same number of bee hives per acre as the other owners in the area. How might such a custom be an equilibrium outcome in a repeated game with indefinite end?

* conceptually challenging
** computationally challenging
† solutions in Study Guide

Chapter 25

Oligopoly

The models of perfect competition and monopoly which we have covered so far represent polar opposites and are useful because they allow us to develop intuition about important economic forces in the real world. At the same time, few markets in the real world really fall on either of these extreme poles, and so we can now turn to some market structures that fall in between.

The first of these is the case of *oligopoly*. An oligopoly is a market structure in which a small number of firms is collectively isolated from outside competition by some form of barrier to entry. We will assume in this chapter's analysis of oligopoly that the firms produce the same identical product. Were the firms in the oligopoly to combine into a single firm, they would therefore become a monopoly. Were the barriers to entry to disappear, on the other hand, the oligopoly would turn into a competitive market as new firms would join as long as positive profits could be made.

Since there are only a few firms in an oligopoly, a firm's decision about how much to produce will have an impact on the price the other firms can charge, or the decision about what price to set may determine what price others will set. Firms within an oligopoly therefore find themselves in a *strategic* setting, a setting in which their decisions have a direct impact on the economic environment in which they operate.

25A | Competition and Collusion in Oligopolies

While we could think of oligopolies with more than two firms, we will focus here primarily on the case where two firms operate within the oligopoly market structure sometimes called a duopoly. The basic insights extend to cases where there are more than two firms in the oligopoly, but as the number of firms gets large, the oligopoly becomes more and more like a perfectly competitive market structure. We will also simplify our analysis by assuming that the two firms are identical in the sense of facing identical cost structures and that the marginal cost of production is constant.

We will use the following example: two firms, Fibretech and SpiralMedia, have the exclusive right to sell broadband services. The buyers of broadband services are those who provide the actual supply to houses and businesses and meet once a year to make their purchases from Fibretech and SpiralMedia. The two firms, therefore, have to determine their strategy for selling their product at these meetings.

The firms in this oligopoly essentially have two choices to make: (1) how much to produce and (2) how much to charge. If it is relatively easy to duplicate contracts at the meetings, the firms might decide to post a price at their booth and produce the contracts as needed. In this case, *price* is the strategic variable that is being set prior to getting to the meetings as the firms advertise to the attendees to try to get them to come to their booth. Alternatively, it might be that the firms have to produce the contracts before they get to the meetings because it's not possible to produce them on the spot as needed. In that case, *quantity* is the strategic variable since the firms have to decide how many contracts to bring prior to getting to the meetings, leaving them free to vary the price depending on how many buyers want to buy contracts at the meetings. Whether price or quantity is the right strategic variable to think about depends on the circumstances faced by the firms in an oligopoly, on what we will call the economic setting in which the firms operate. We will therefore develop two types of models: models of *quantity competition* and models of *price competition*.

The other feature of oligopoly models is an assumption that firms in an oligopoly make their strategic decision *simultaneously* or *sequentially*. It might take Fibretech longer to get its advertising materials together and end up posting its price after SpiralMedia, or maybe Fibretech only has the capacity to produce a certain quantity of contracts before SpiralMedia. We can employ the concept of Nash equilibrium for the case of simultaneous decision making while we use the concept of subgame perfect Nash equilibrium in the case of sequential decisions. Sometimes, as we will see, it matters who moves first.

We will begin with price competition and move to quantity competition, each time considering both the simultaneous and the sequential case. In the case of price competition, we will see that the sequential and simultaneous versions of the model give the same prediction, but this is not the case for quantity competition. This results in the three types of models illustrated in Table 25.1 and which we will introduce sequentially. We will also see that strategic choices by dominant firms in a market may be aimed at deterring the entry of a competitor in cases where some entry of new firms is possible, and throughout we will see that oligopolistic firms could in principle do better by combining forces and behaving like a single monopoly. Following our discussion of oligopoly price and quantity competition, we will therefore consider the circumstances under which oligopoly firms might succeed in forming *cartels* that behave like monopolies by eliminating competition between the firms in the oligopoly.

Table 25.1 Timing of Decisions

Strategic Variable	Simultaneous	Sequential
Price	Bertrand Model	
Quantity	Cournot Model	Stackelberg Model

25A.1 Oligopoly Price or Bertrand Competition

Competition between oligopoly firms that strategically set price rather than quantity is often referred to as *Bertrand competition* after the French mathematician Joseph Louis Francois Bertrand (1822–1900). Bertrand took issue with another French mathematician, Antoine Augustin Cournot (1801–1877), whose work on quantity competition had suggested that oligopolies would price goods somewhere between where price would fall under perfect competition and perfect monopoly. Bertrand came up with a quite different and striking conclusion: he suggested that Cournot had focused on the wrong strategic variable – quantity – and that his result goes away when firms instead compete on price. In particular, Bertrand argued that such price competition will result in a price analogous to what we would expect to emerge under perfect competition (price equal to marginal cost) even if only two firms are competing with one another.

25A.1.1 Simultaneous Strategic Decisions About Price Bertrand's logic can be seen in a model with two identical firms that make decisions simultaneously and face a constant marginal cost of production with no recurring fixed cost. Assume our two firms face no fixed costs and can adjust the quantity of contracts produced on the spot at the buyer meetings. They therefore decide to advertise a *price* and produce whatever quantity is demanded by consumers at that price. As they think about announcing a price, they have to think about what price the other might announce and how consumers might react to different price combinations. If the firms announce different prices, consumers will go to the firm that announced the lower price, and the other firm won't be able to sell anything.

Fibretech, for example, would therefore want to avoid two scenarios. First, it will not want to set a price that is so low that it would result in negative profits if it managed to attract consumers at that price. Since we are assuming no recurring fixed costs and constant marginal costs, this means it will not want to set a price below marginal cost. Second, assuming SpiralMedia similarly won't set a price below marginal cost, Fibretech will not want to set a price higher than what SpiralMedia sets because it will not get any customers. Whatever price SpiralMedia sets, it cannot be a best response for Fibretech to set a higher price or a price below marginal cost. The same is true for SpiralMedia, which means that in any Nash equilibrium in which both do the best they can given the strategy played by the other, they will charge identical prices that do not fall below marginal cost.

We can go further; suppose that the price announced by both is above marginal cost. Fibretech is not playing a best response because, given that SpiralMedia has announced a price above marginal cost, it can do better by charging a price just below that and getting all the customers. The only time this is not true is if both firms are announcing a price equal to marginal cost. Given that SpiralMedia is charging this price, Fibretech can do no better by charging a lower price, which would result in negative profit, or a higher price, which would result in it getting no customers. The same is true for SpiralMedia given that Fibretech is charging a price equal to marginal cost. By each announcing a price equal to marginal cost, they are both playing best-response strategies to the other, and the outcome is a Nash equilibrium.

Exercise 25A.1

Can you see how this is the only possible Nash equilibrium? Is it a dominant strategy Nash equilibrium?

Exercise 25A.2

Is there a single Nash equilibrium if more than two firms engage in Bertrand competition within an oligopoly?

25A.1.2 Using Best-Response Functions to Verify Bertrand's Logic We will now develop a tool that will be useful throughout our discussion of oligopoly: best-response functions. These functions are plots of the best response of one player to particular strategic choices by the other. They are useful when players have a continuum of possible actions they can take in a simultaneous move game rather than a discrete number of actions as in most of our game theory development in Chapter 24. When best-response functions for both players are plotted on the same graph, they can help us identify the Nash equilibria.

Consider panel (a) of Graph 25.1. On the horizontal axis, we plot p_1, the price set by Fibretech, and on the vertical axis we plot p_2 the price charged by SpiralMedia. We plot SpiralMedia's *best responses* to different prices Fibretech might announce. We already know that SpiralMedia will never want to set a price below marginal cost (MC), and if Fibretech were to ever set a price below MC, any $p_2 > p_1$ would be a best response for SpiralMedia since it would result in it not selling anything and letting Fibretech get all the business. For the purposes of our graph, we can let SpiralMedia's best response to $p_1 < MC$ be $p_2 = MC$. If Fibretech announces a price p_1 above MC, we know that SpiralMedia will want to charge a price just below p_1 to get all consumers away from Fibretech's booth. Thus, for $p_1 > MC$, SpiralMedia's best response is $p_2 = p_1 - \epsilon$ where ϵ is a small number close to zero. Since $p_1 = p_2$ on the 45-degree line in the graph, this means that SpiralMedia's best response in panel (a) will lie just below the 45-degree line for $p_1 > MC$.

In panel (b) of Graph 25.1, we do the same for Fibretech, only now p_2 on the vertical axis is taken as given by Fibretech, and it finds its best response to different levels of p_2. If SpiralMedia sets its price below MC, Fibretech's best response can be taken to be $p_1 = MC$, and if SpiralMedia sets its price p_2 above MC, Fibretech's best response is $p_1 = p_2 - \epsilon$ which lies just above the 45-degree line.

Graph 25.1 Best-Response Functions for Simultaneous Bertrand Competition

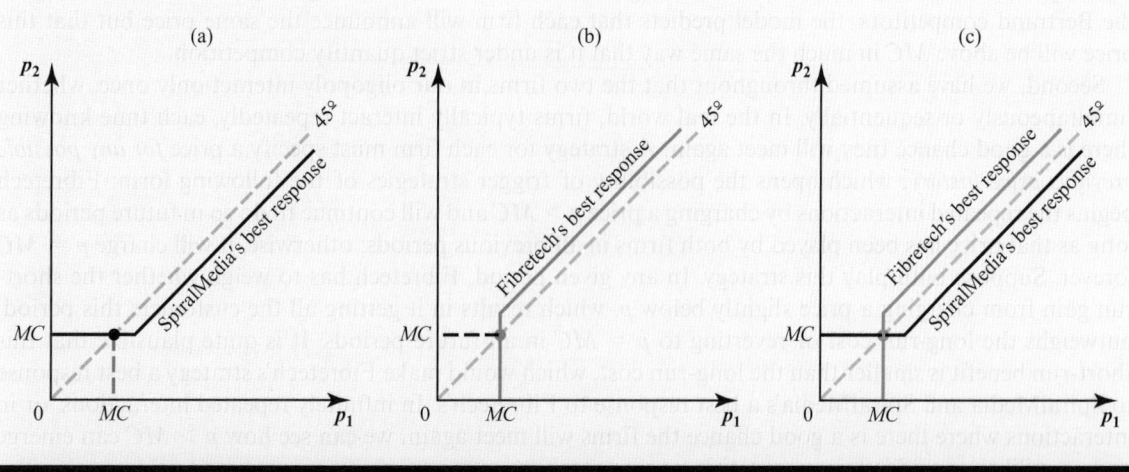

Go to MindTap to interact with this graph

We defined a Nash equilibrium in Chapter 24 as a set of strategies for each player that are best responses to each other. In order for an equilibrium to emerge in our price setting model, *Fibretech's price has to be a best response to SpiralMedia's price, and SpiralMedia's price has to be a best response to Fibretech's price*. When we put the two best-response functions onto the same graph in panel (c), the equilibrium happens where the two best response functions intersect. This happens at $p_1 = p_2 = MC$, just as we derived intuitively.

25A.1.3 Sequential Strategic Decisions About Price In the real world, it is often the case that one firm has to make a decision about its strategic variable before the other, with the second firm being able to observe the first firm's decision when its turn to act comes. As we argued in our chapter on game theory, sometimes this makes a big difference, with the first mover gaining an advantage or disadvantage from having to declare its intentions in advance of the second mover. This is not, however, the case for our two firms engaging in Bertrand competition.

Suppose Fibretech moves first and SpiralMedia gets to observe Fibretech's advertised price before it advertises its own. Remember that in such *sequential* settings, subgame perfection requires that Fibretech will have to think through what SpiralMedia will do before any action it announces. Our previous discussion already tells us the answer: SpiralMedia will choose a price just below p_1 whenever $p_1 > MC$, leaving Fibretech with no consumers. Since Fibretech will not choose a price below MC, this implies that it will set $p_1 = MC$ and SpiralMedia will follow suit, with the two firms splitting the market by charging prices exactly equal to MC.

Exercise 25A.3

How would you think about subgame perfect equilibria under sequential Bertrand competition with three firms where firm 1 moves first, firm 2 moves second and firm 3 moves third?

25A.1.4 Real-World Caveats to Bertrand's Price Competition Result There are several real-world considerations that considerably weaken the Bertrand prediction regarding price competition in oligopolies, and here we will briefly mention some of them.

First, the pure Bertrand model assumes that firms are able to produce *any* quantity demanded at the price that they announce. This might be true in some markets but typically does not hold. As a result, real-world firms have to set some capacity of production as they think about announcing a price, and this capacity choice introduces *quantity* as a strategic variable. In cases where capacity choices are binding on the Bertrand competitors, the model predicts that each firm will announce the same price but that this price will be above MC in much the same way that it is under strict quantity competition.

Second, we have assumed throughout that the two firms in our oligopoly interact only once, whether simultaneously or sequentially. In the real world, firms typically interact repeatedly, each time knowing there is a good chance they will meet again. A strategy for each firm must specify a price *for any possible previous price history*, which opens the possibility of trigger strategies of the following form: Fibretech begins the repeated interactions by charging a price $p > MC$ and will continue to do so in future periods as long as that price has been played by both firms in all previous periods; otherwise, it will charge $p = MC$ forever. Suppose both play this strategy. In any given period, Fibretech has to weigh whether the short-run gain from charging a price slightly below p, which results in it getting all the customers this period, outweighs the long-run cost of reverting to $p = MC$ in all future periods. It is quite plausible that this short-run benefit is smaller than the long-run cost, which would make Fibretech's strategy a best response to SpiralMedia and SpiralMedia's a best response to Fibretech's. In infinitely repeated interactions, or in interactions where there is a good chance the firms will meet again, we can see how $p > MC$ can emerge as an equilibrium under price competition.

Exercise 25A.4

Suppose the two firms know that they will encounter each other n times and never again thereafter. Can $p > MC$ still be part of a subgame perfect equilibrium in this case assuming they engage in pure price competition?

Finally, Bertrand assumed that firms are restricted to producing *identical* products. If we allow for the possibility that consumers differ somewhat in their tastes for broadband services, the firms might decide to produce slightly different levels of service, and through such product differentiation become able to charge $p > MC$. This is because consumers who have a strong preference for one level of service will still buy from Fibretech, for example, at a somewhat higher price, and similarly those with a preference for another level of service will continue to buy SpiralMedia's at a somewhat higher price. Product differentiation therefore also introduces the possibility of $p > MC$ emerging under price competition.

25A.2 Oligopoly Quantity Competition

The implicit assumption that underlies Bertrand competition is that firms can easily adjust quantity once they set price. In our example, we assumed that both firms can produce the required contracts on the spot at the buyer meetings. As we just mentioned, many firms have to set capacity for their production and, once they have done so, cannot easily deviate from this in terms of how much they will produce. It might be hard for the firms to set up contract writing facilities at their booth at the meetings, which means they will have to produce contracts ahead of time and bring them with them to their booths. In such circumstances, it is more reasonable to assume that firms choose capacity or quantity first and sell what they produce at the highest price they can get. This is the scenario that Cournot had in mind when he investigated competition between oligopolistic firms, and it is the scenario we turn to study next. As we will see, this model, known as the *Cournot model*, has very different implications regarding the equilibrium price at which oligopolistic firms produce. As in the previous section, we will continue by assuming that firms in our oligopoly are identical and face constant MC.

25A.2.1 *Simultaneous* Strategic Decisions About Quantity: Cournot Competition
We continue to use best-response functions to see what Nash equilibrium will emerge when two firms in an oligopoly choose capacity simultaneously. In panel (a) of Graph 25.2, we begin by considering SpiralMedia's best response to different quantities x_1 set by Fibretech. If Fibretech sets $x_1 = 0$, SpiralMedia would know that it will have a monopoly on contracts at the buyer meetings. From our work in Chapter 23, we can determine the

optimal quantity for SpiralMedia by solving the monopoly problem. This is depicted in panel (b) of the graph where D is the market demand curve and MR is SpiralMedia's monopoly's marginal revenue curve that has the same intercept as D but twice the slope. SpiralMedia would produce the monopoly quantity x^M where $MR = MC$ and charge the monopoly price p^M. The quantity x^M therefore becomes its best response to $x_1 = 0$ and determines the intercept of its best-response function in panel (a).

Graph 25.2 The Best-Response Function for SpiralMedia Under Simultaneous Cournot Competition

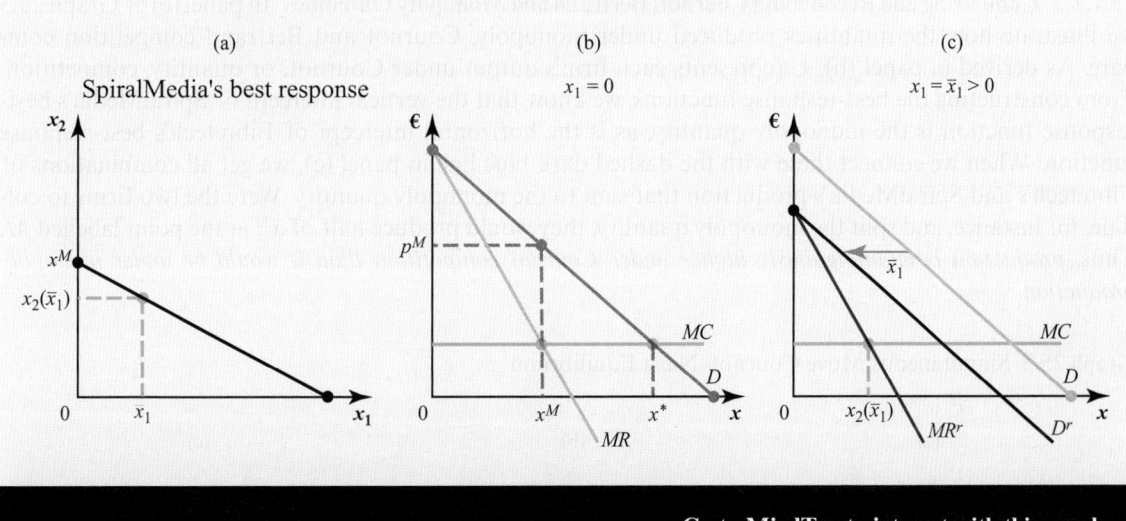

Go to MindTap to interact with this graph

Now suppose Fibretech sets $x_1 = \bar{x}_1 > 0$. SpiralMedia knows that it no longer faces the entire market demand curve because Fibretech has committed to filling $\bar{x}_1$ of the market demand. SpiralMedia now faces a demand curve that is equal to the market demand curve D *minus* $\bar{x}_1$, and it is this *residual demand curve* that tells it how much it will be able to charge given what the other firm is already producing. In panel (c) of Graph 25.2, we therefore shift the demand D by $\bar{x}_1$ to get the new residual demand D^r that remains given that Fibretech will satisfy a portion of market demand. From this, we can calculate the residual marginal revenue curve MR^r that now applies to SpiralMedia. SpiralMedia maximizes profit where marginal revenue equals marginal cost; that is, $MR^r = MC$. This results in a new optimal quantity *given* $\bar{x}_1$ – denoted $x^2(\bar{x}_1)$ – which in turn becomes its best response to Fibretech having set $x_1 = \bar{x}_1$. Note that $x^2(\bar{x}_1)$ necessarily lies below x^M; that is, SpiralMedia's best-response quantity decreases as x_1 increases. We can imagine doing this for all possible quantities of x_1 to get the full best-response function for SpiralMedia as depicted in panel (a).

Exercise 25A.5

Can you identify in panel (b) of Graph 25.2 the quantity that corresponds to the horizontal intercept of Spiral-Media's best-response function in panel (a)?

Exercise 25A.6

What is the slope of the best-response function in panel (a) of Graph 25.2? *Hint*: Use your answer to exercise 25A.5 to arrive at your answer here.

We do what we did for Bertrand competition by putting the best-response functions of the two firms together into one graph to see where they intersect. Since our two firms are identical, Fibretech's best-response function can be similarly derived. This is done in panel (a) of Graph 25.3, which is just the mirror image of the best-response function for SpiralMedia that we derived in the previous graph. The two best-response functions intersect at $x_1 = x_2 = x^C$ in panel (b), with x^C the Cournot–Nash equilibrium output for each of our firms in the oligopoly.

25A.2.2 Comparing and Reconciling Cournot, Bertrand and Monopoly Outcomes In panel (c) of Graph 25.3 we illustrate how the quantities produced under monopoly, Cournot and Bertrand competition compare. As derived in panel (b), C represents each firm's output under Cournot, or quantity, competition. From constructing the best-response functions, we know that the vertical intercept of SpiralMedia's best-response function is the monopoly quantity, as is the horizontal intercept of Fibretech's best-response function. When we connect these with the dashed dark blue line in panel (c), we get all combinations of Fibretech's and SpiralMedia's production that sum to the monopoly quantity. Were the two firms to collude, for instance, and split the monopoly quantity, they would produce half of x^M at the point labelled M. Thus, *production is unambiguously higher under Cournot competition than it would be under monopoly production.*

Graph 25.3 Simultaneous Move Cournot–Nash Equilibrium

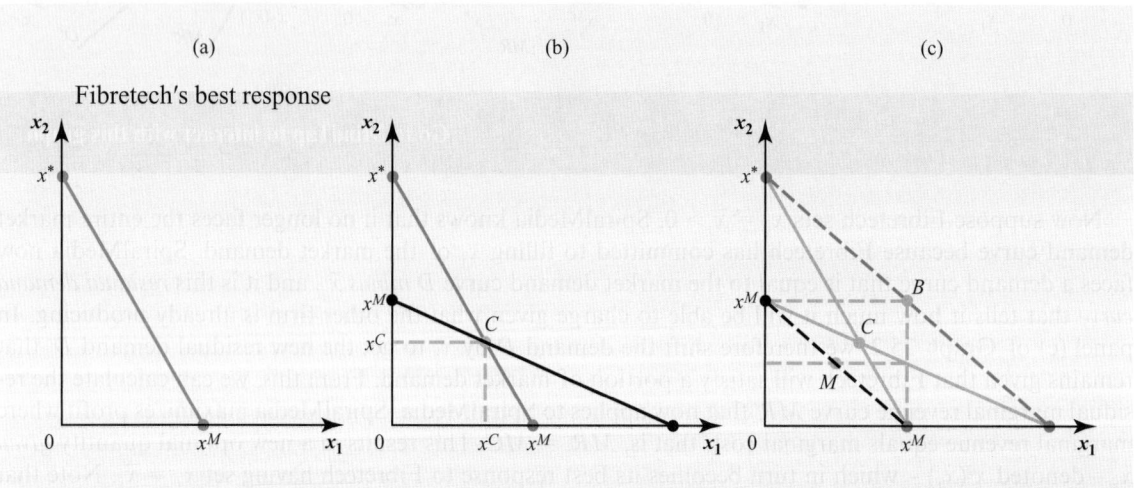

We can also see how Cournot production compares to Bertrand production. We know that Bertrand or price competition results in both firms charging a price equal to MC. At such a price, market demand will be equal to x^* in panel (b) of Graph 25.2. Now suppose that under Cournot competition, SpiralMedia determines its best response to Fibretech setting its quantity to x^*. This would imply that SpiralMedia's residual demand is equal to D shifted inward by x^*, leaving it with a residual demand curve that has a vertical intercept at MC. Thus any output that SpiralMedia would produce *given that Fibretech is producing x^** would have to be sold at a price below MC, which implies SpiralMedia's best response is to produce $x_2 = 0$. This further implies that SpiralMedia's best-response function reaches zero at $x_1 = x^* = 2x^M$; that is, the horizontal intercept of SpiralMedia's best-response function lies at x^*. Since the two firms are identical, the same is true for Fibretech's vertical intercept.

If we connect the horizontal intercept of Fibretech's best-response function with the vertical intercept of SpiralMedia's best-response function with the dashed dark brown line in panel (c), we get all the different ways in which the two firms could split production and produce x^*, the quantity that would be sold when $p = MC$, as happens under Bertrand competition. Assuming that when both firms charge the Bertrand price of $p = MC$, the two firms split overall output, each firm would produce half of x^* as indicated at point B in the graph. Thus, *Bertrand competition leads to unambiguously higher output than Cournot competition.*

Exercise 25A.7

Which type of behaviour under simultaneous decision making within an oligopoly results in greater social surplus: quantity or price competition?

Exercise 25A.8

True or False: Under Bertrand competition, $x_1^B = x_2^B = x^M$.

The dramatic difference between Bertrand and Cournot competition seems quite strange, and it is not easy to choose between the two models on intuitive grounds. On the one hand, it seems that firms in the real world often set prices when they are not in perfectly competitive settings, and this seems to speak in favour of the Bertrand model. On the other, the Bertrand prediction of price being set equal to MC even when only two firms are competing seems a stretch, which speaks in favour of the Cournot model. This model not only arrives at the intuitively reasonable prediction that price falls between the monopoly and the competitive level when there are only two firms, but it also predicts, as we will show in Section B, that oligopoly prices converge to competitive prices as the number of firms in the oligopoly becomes large. As a result, much work has been done by economists to reconcile these models of oligopoly competition.

One of the most revealing results, which we have already mentioned in our discussion of Bertrand competition, is suppose that firms really do set prices as the Bertrand model assumes but that they set capacities for production which sounds a lot like the quantity setting of the Cournot model before announcing prices. Under plausible conditions, it has been shown that this Bertrand equilibrium outcome of price competition results in Cournot quantities and prices. This was demonstrated by D. Kreps and J. Scheinkman, Quantity Precommitment and Bertrand Competition Yield Cournot Outcomes, *RAND Journal of Economics* 14 (1983), 326–37. Economists have therefore often come to view oligopoly competition as guided in the long run by production capacity competition as envisioned by Cournot equilibrated through price competition as envisioned by Bertrand in the short run when capacities are fixed. Both models appear to have their place, and both play important roles in how we think of oligopoly competition.

25A.2.3 *Sequential* **Strategic Decisions About Quantity: The Stackelberg Model** Under Bertrand competition, we concluded that it does not matter whether firms determine their price simultaneously or sequentially; in either case, firms end up charging $p = MC$ in equilibrium. The same is not true for quantity competition.

The sequential quantity competition model is known as the *Stackelberg model*, named after Heinrich Freiherr von Stackelberg (1905–1946), a German economist. In the model, the firm designated to move first is called the *Stackelberg leader* while the firm that moves second is called the *Stackelberg follower*. In sequential move games, we concluded in Chapter 24 that non-credible threats are eliminated by restricting ourselves to Nash equilibria that are subgame perfect; that is, to equilibria in which early movers look forward and determine the best responses by their opponents later on in the game. When it decides how much capacity to set, the Stackelberg leader will take into account the entire best-response function of the follower because that function tells the leader exactly how the follower will respond once it finds out how much the leader will be producing. Thus, rather than guessing about the quantity the opposing firm will set, as is the case under simultaneous quantity competition, the leader now has the luxury of *inducing* how much the follower will set by its own actions in the first stage.

Suppose that SpiralMedia is the follower and Fibretech is the leader. Fibretech already knows Spiral-Media's best-response function for any quantity that it might set; we derived this in panel (a) of Graph 25.2, which we now replicate in panel (a) of Graph 25.4. In deciding how much capacity to set, Fibretech has to determine its residual demand curve *given SpiralMedia's best-response function. This residual demand* *curve tells Fibretech what price it can expect to be able to charge depending on how much it produces given that it knows how much SpiralMedia will produce once SpiralMedia observes Fibretech's level of output.* For any output level $x_1 \geq x^*$ for instance, SpiralMedia's best response is not to produce, which implies that Fibretech knows it will own the light brown market demand curve if it chooses to produce above x^*. Thus, Fibretech's residual demand – the demand curve that tells it what price to expect based on how much it produces – is equal to the light brown market demand for quantities greater than x^*.

If Fibretech sets capacity below x^*, however, it knows that SpiralMedia will produce along its best-response function once it finds out how much capacity Fibretech sets. To arrive at Fibretech's residual demand, it therefore has to subtract the quantity that it knows SpiralMedia will produce for any $x_1 < x^*$. If it sets capacity close to x^*, SpiralMedia will choose to produce relatively little, but as x_1 falls, SpiralMedia's best-response quantity rises and reaches x^M, the monopoly quantity, when $x_1 = 0$. Fibretech's residual demand curve D^r therefore begins at the monopoly price p^M which would emerge if it sets $x_1 = 0$, and reaches the market demand curve D when it crosses MC.

Graph 25.4 Stackelberg Equilibrium

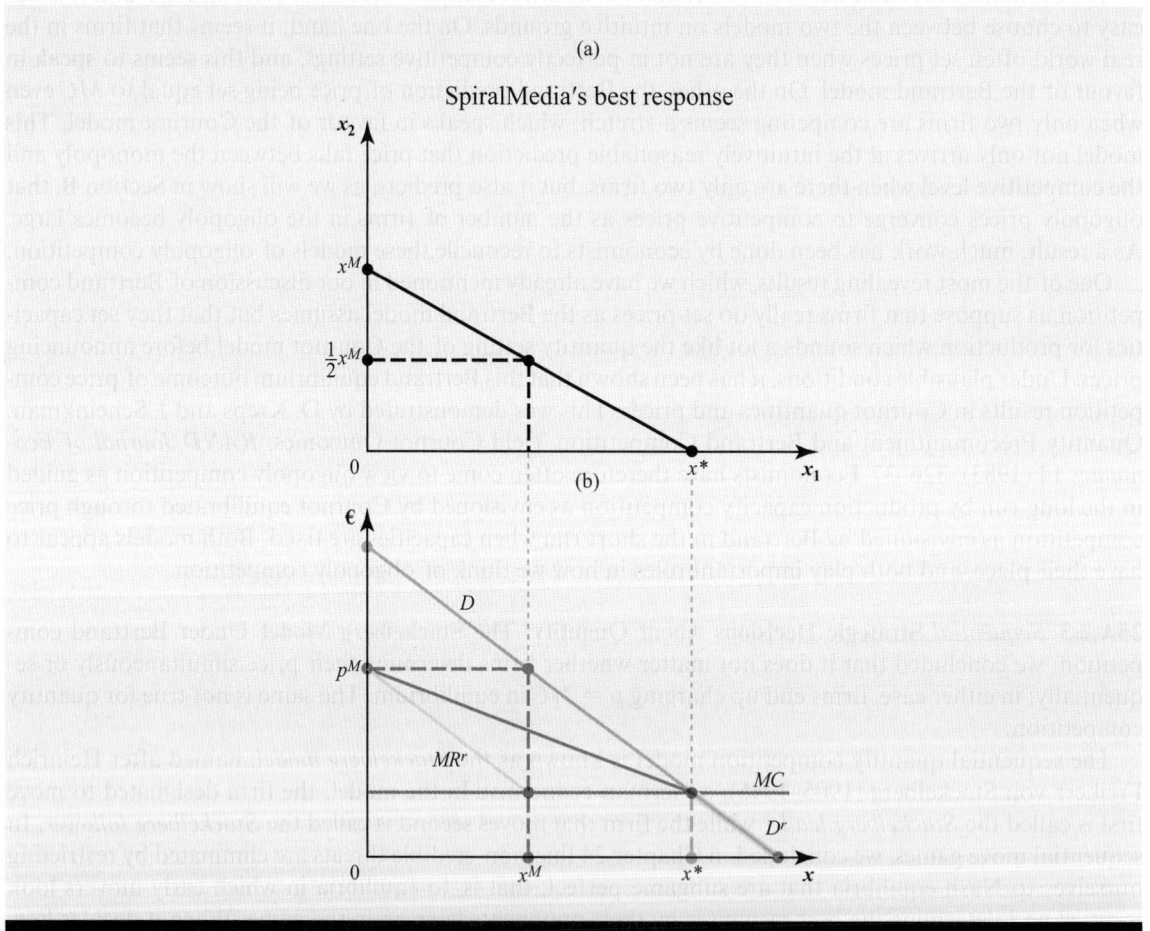

Go to MindTap to interact with this graph

Having identified Fibretech's residual demand, we can now identify Fibretech's optimal capacity; plot out the MR^r curve that corresponds to D^r and find its intersection with MC. Because all the relationships are linear, this intersection occurs at half the distance between x^* and 0, which happens to be the monopoly quantity x^M. Thus, the Stackelberg leader, Fibretech, will set $x_1 = x^M$, and the Stackelberg follower will produce half this amount as read off its best-response function. Given what Fibretech as the leader has done in the first stage, SpiralMedia as the follower is doing the best it can, and given its predictable output decisions in the second stage, as summarized in its best-response function, Fibretech has done the best it can. We have reached a subgame perfect equilibrium.

Exercise 25A.9

Determine the Stackelberg price in terms of p^M – the price a monopolist would charge – and MC.

Adding this outcome to our predicted outputs for Bertrand, Cournot and monopoly settings from Graph 25.3, we can see that the Stackelberg quantity competition results in greater overall output than simultaneous Cournot competition but less overall output than Bertrand price competition.

Exercise 25A.10

Where is the predicted Stackelberg outcome in panel (c) of Graph 25.3?

25A.2.4 The Difference Between Sequential and Simultaneous Quantity Competition We can now step back a little and ask why the Stackelberg model differs fundamentally from the Cournot model. Why, for instance, doesn't Fibretech threaten to act like a Stackelberg leader when it and SpiralMedia are competing simultaneously?

Suppose both set quantity simultaneously before they arrive at the buyer meetings, but Fibretech calls SpiralMedia ahead of time and tells it that it will produce the Stackelberg leader quantity and thus expects SpiralMedia to best respond by producing the Stackelberg follower quantity. Would SpiralMedia have any reason to believe Fibretech when it threatens to do this? The answer is that SpiralMedia should not take Fibretech's threat seriously. If it thought that Fibretech guessed SpiralMedia would produce $x^M/2$, Fibretech's best response, according to its best-response function in Graph 25.3, would be to produce less than x^M. This can be seen in panel (c) of the graph where the horizontal dashed light brown line that passes through M at an output level of $x^M/2$ for SpiralMedia crosses Fibretech's best-response function to the left of x^M. SpiralMedia's best response to Fibretech producing less than x^M would be to produce more than $x^M/2$. Fibretech's threat to produce x^M is therefore not credible when it tries to bully SpiralMedia over the phone.

When the game assumes a sequential structure, however, the threat becomes real because SpiralMedia *knows* how much Fibretech has produced by the time that it has to decide how much to produce. It's no longer an idle threat for Fibretech to say it will produce the Stackelberg leader quantity; it has just done so. Now it is a best response for SpiralMedia to produce the Stackelberg follower quantity, and given that it will do so it is best for Fibretech to have produced the Stackelberg leader quantity. It is the sequential structure of the game that results in the difference in equilibrium behaviour, and without that sequential structure, there is no way for Fibretech to credibly threaten to do anything other than produce the Cournot quantity. The sequential structure of the game gives the Stackelberg leader a first mover advantage.

25A.3 Incumbent Firms, Fixed Entry Costs and Entry Deterrence

The insight that the sequential structure of the oligopoly quantity competition changes the outcome of that competition can get us to think of other ways in which sequential decision making might matter. An important point is the case in which one firm is the *incumbent firm* that currently has the whole market, but is threatened by a second firm that might potentially enter the market and turn its structure from a monopoly into an oligopoly. Is there anything the incumbent firm can do to prevent the potential entrant from coming into the market? The answer depends on two factors: (1) how costly it is for the potential entrant to actually enter the market and begin production, and (2) the extent to which the incumbent firm can credibly threaten the potential entrant.

25A.3.1 Case 1: Incumbent Quantity Choice Follows Entrant Choice Suppose the potential entrant has to pay a one-time fixed entry cost FC to begin production. Now consider the case in which the potential entrant makes its decision on whether to enter the market before either firm makes a choice about how much to produce. Panels (a) and (b) in Graph 25.5 picture two such scenarios. In both panels, SpiralMedia first decides whether or not to enter, and if it does not enter, Fibretech sets its quantity x_1. If SpiralMedia does enter, the firms are assumed to choose their production quantities simultaneously in panel (a) and sequentially in panel (b).

Recall that we solve games of this kind from the bottom up to find subgame perfect equilibria. If SpiralMedia does not enter, we know that Fibretech will optimize by producing the monopoly quantity and thus will make the monopoly profit π^M while SpiralMedia will make zero profit. If SpiralMedia enters, on the other hand, the two firms will engage in simultaneous Cournot competition in panel (a), with each firm making the Cournot profit π^C but with SpiralMedia paying the fixed entry cost FC. Spiral-Media, therefore, looks ahead and makes its entry decision based on whether or not $(\pi^C - FC)$ is greater than zero. As long as the profit from producing the Cournot quantity at the Cournot price is greater than the fixed cost of entering, SpiralMedia will enter the market. Similarly, in panel (b), SpiralMedia knows that it will be a Stackelberg follower if it enters, and so it will enter as long as the profit π^{SF} from producing the Stackelberg follower quantity at the Stackelberg price is greater than the fixed cost of entering.

Exercise 25A.11

True or False: Once the entrant has paid the fixed entry cost, this cost becomes a sunk cost and is therefore irrelevant to the choice of how much to produce.

Exercise 25A.12

Is the smallest fixed cost of entering that will prevent SpiralMedia from coming into the market greater in panel (a) or in panel (b)?

Notice that in neither of these cases can the incumbent firm (Fibretech) do anything to affect SpiralMedia's entry decision, because the entry decision happens before quantities are set. This implies that SpiralMedia's entry decision is entirely dependent on the size of the fixed entry cost FC. The problem from Fibretech's perspective is once again that there is no way it can credibly threaten SpiralMedia, a problem that can disappear if Fibretech gets to *commit* to an output quantity *before* SpiralMedia makes its entry decision.

25A.3.2 Case 2: Entry Choice Follows Incumbent Quantity Choice Now consider the sequence pictured in panel (c) of Graph 25.5 where the incumbent (Fibretech) chooses its quantity x_1 before the potential entrant (SpiralMedia) makes its decision on whether to enter the market and produce. We can solve the resulting game from the bottom up, beginning with the case in which SpiralMedia has decided to enter the market. SpiralMedia's optimal quantity is given by its best-response function derived in Graph 25.2 to the quantity set by Fibretech, which is known to SpiralMedia at the time it makes its quantity decision. Fibretech knows SpiralMedia's best-response function, which implies that *if* SpiralMedia *enters the market*, Fibretech is a Stackelberg leader. Thus, if SpiralMedia enters, the equilibrium payoffs are the Stackelberg profits, π^{SL} and π^{SF}, minus the fixed entry cost for SpiralMedia.

The incumbent firm, however, would very much like to remain the only firm in the market. The only way to persuade SpiralMedia to stay out of the incumbent's monopoly market is for the incumbent to ensure that SpiralMedia cannot make a positive profit by entering. The only way to do that is to commit to producing a quantity that is sufficiently large to ensure the resulting price will keep SpiralMedia from wanting to come into the market. Whether it is possible for Fibretech to do this and thereby make a profit higher than that of a Stackelberg leader depends on just how big the fixed entry cost FC is for SpiralMedia.

Graph 25.5 Possible Sequences of Entry and Quantity Choices

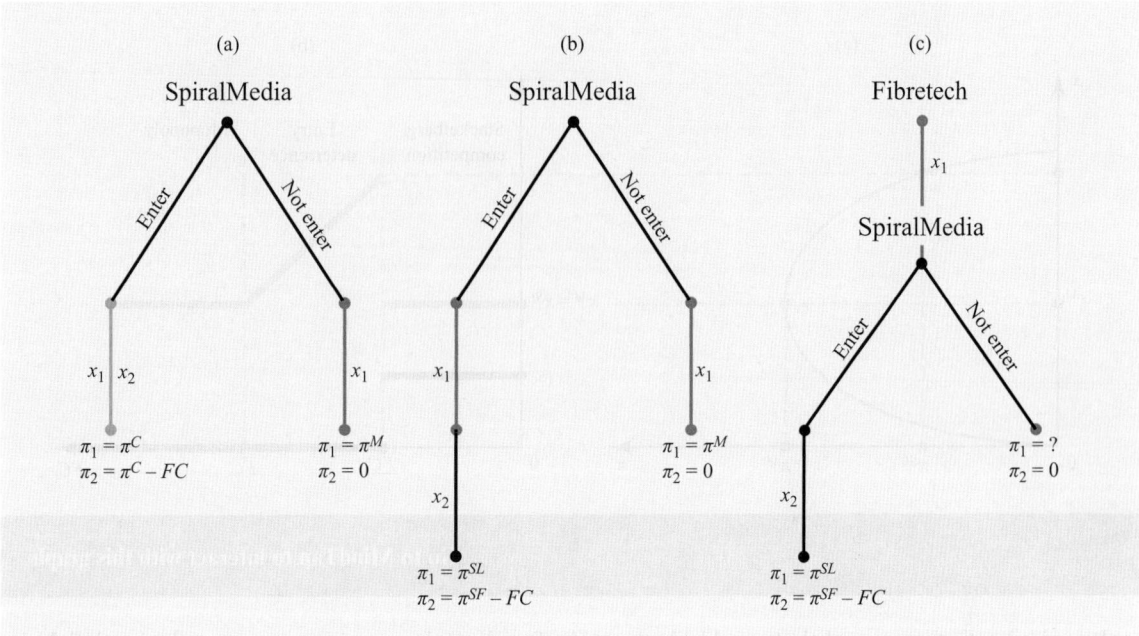

This is illustrated in the two panels of Graph 25.6. In panel (a), we plot the profit that the incumbent can expect from different output levels *if it remains the only firm in the market*. The highest possible profit occurs at the monopoly quantity x^M, which, as we have seen, is also the Stackelberg leader quantity x^{SL}. *If the fixed entry cost is very high*, the incumbent can produce x^M and rest assured in its monopoly given that it is too costly for any potential entrant to enter the market. This is illustrated in panel (b) where, for $FC \geq \overline{FC}$ Fibretech produces x^M, as indicated by the dark brown line while SpiralMedia stays out of the market and thus produces zero, as indicated by the dark blue line. *If the fixed entry cost is very low*, on the other hand, there is little that Fibretech can do to keep the entrant out of the market, and so Fibretech produces the Stackelberg leader quantity x^{SL} and accepts SpiralMedia's production of the Stackelberg follower quantity x^{SF}. This is illustrated in panel (b) for $FC \leq \overline{FC}$.

The interesting case of *entry deterrence* arises for fixed entry costs between $\underline{FC}$ and $\overline{FC}$. Suppose, for instance, that FC is just below $\overline{FC}$; that is, that SpiralMedia would make a slightly positive profit by entering if Fibretech behaved like a Stackelberg leader and produced x^{SL}. If Fibretech produces just a little more than x^{SL}, this will ensure that SpiralMedia can no longer make a positive profit by entering. The incumbent firm can *deter entry* by producing above x^{SL}. While this will mean that Fibretech's profit falls below the monopoly profit, it is preferable to engaging in Stackelberg competition with SpiralMedia, in which case Fibretech would only get π^{SL}. As the fixed entry cost falls, it becomes harder and harder for Fibretech to do this, necessitating higher and higher levels of output to deter entry. It's worth it as long as the incumbent's profit remains above the Stackelberg leader profit π^{SL}. Thus, the highest quantity that Fibretech would ever be willing to produce to deter entry, x^{ED}_{max}, is the quantity that will ensure π^{SL}. When fixed entry costs fall below $\underline{FC}$, it is too costly for the incumbent to deter entry, and Fibretech reverts back to producing the Stackelberg leader quantity.

This is a more rigorous treatment of an idea raised in Chapter 23 when we discussed the possibility that a monopoly might be restrained in its behaviour and might produce more than the monopoly quantity if it feels threatened by potential competitors. Notice that, if it could, the incumbent firm would like to reduce its output back to the monopoly quantity x^M once it has successfully deterred an entrant, but the only way that deterrence could succeed is if the incumbent was able to *commit* to not doing so by setting output prior to SpiralMedia's entry decision. It is this commitment that made the threat to the entrant credible; were it possible to go back on the commitment, the threat would not be credible and entry could not be deterred. In the real world, incumbent firms can make such credible commitments by raising observable production capacity, in forms like factory size, above the monopoly level.

Graph 25.6 Setting Quantity to Deter Entry

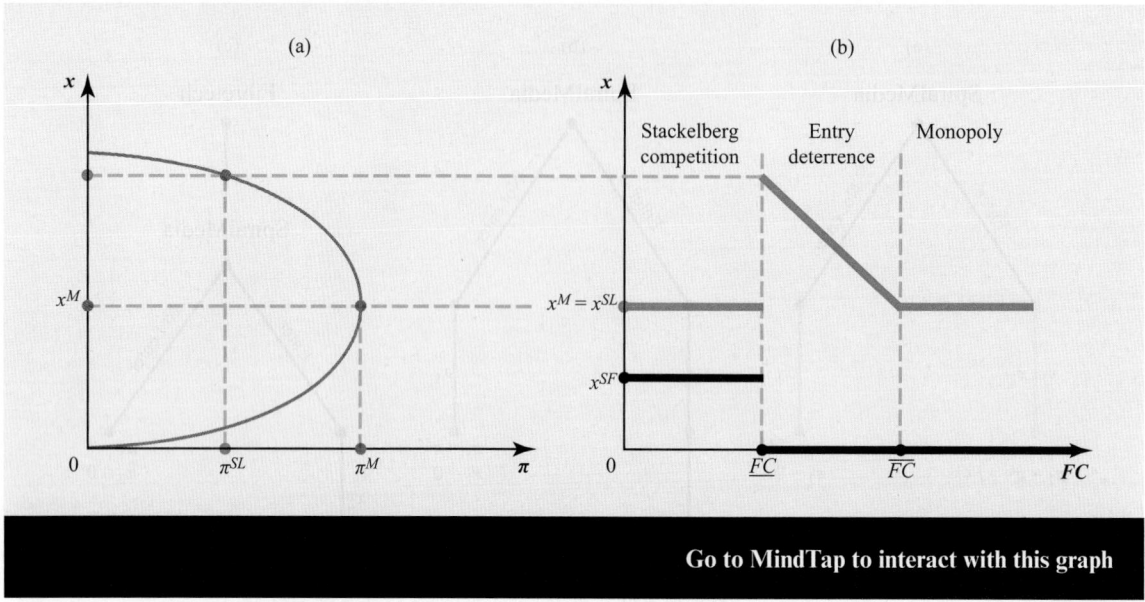

Go to MindTap to interact with this graph

It is similar to the general that would like to strike fear into the opposing army on the battlefield by telling them that his army will fight to the death. Of course, just saying 'We will fight to the death' is not credible – anyone can *say* it. The general might cross a bridge into the battlefield and burn the bridge down, thus cutting off any possibility of retreat. This would certainly make the threat to fight to the death more credible, just as the incumbent firm's threat to increase production to prevent entry becomes credible when the firm actually does it and thus cuts off any possibility of retreat.

25A.4 Collusion, Cartels and Prisoner's Dilemmas

So far, we have assumed that the two firms will act as competitors within the oligopoly, strategically competing on either price or quantity decisions. Now suppose instead that Fibretech calls SpiralMedia before the buyer meetings and say: 'Why don't we stop competing with each other and instead combine forces to see if we can't do better by coordinating what we do?'

Logically, both firms should be able to do better if they don't compete. If they could act like one firm that has a monopoly, they would be able to do at least as well as they can do if they compete by producing the same quantity as they do under oligopoly competition. We know from panel (c) of Graph 25.3 that as a monopoly they would produce less than they do under Cournot, Stackelberg or Bertrand competition. Their joint profit would therefore be higher if they could find a way of splitting monopoly production and charging a higher price than it would be under any competitive outcome that results in a price below the monopoly price. They, therefore, have an incentive to find a way to collude instead of compete.

25A.4.1 Collusion and Cartels A *cartel* is a collusive agreement between firms in an oligopoly to restrict output to raise price above what it would be under oligopoly competition. The most famous cartel is the Organization of Petroleum Exporting Countries (OPEC), which is composed of countries that produce a large portion of the world's oil supply. Oil ministers from OPEC countries routinely meet to set production quotas for each of the countries. Their claim is to aim for a stable world price of oil, but what they have typically aimed for is a high world price for oil. The emergence of new technologies involving shale oil, particularly in the United States, has in recent years reduced fixed entry costs into the oil market. As a result, OPEC appears to be engaged in aggressive entry deterrence – which has in turn limited its ability to set a high world price for oil.

Suppose our two firms are currently engaged in Cournot competition, with each producing x^C as depicted in panel (b) of Graph 25.3. To do better, they have to calculate the monopoly output level x^M and agree to each limit their own production to half of that. This would allow them to sell their product at the buyer meetings at the monopoly price p^M, with each making half the profit they would if their individual firm was the sole monopoly but more profit than they are making as Cournot competitors. The same cartel agreement would make each better off if they currently engaged in Bertrand competition.

Exercise 25A.13*

How might the cartel agreement have to differ if they were currently engaged in Stackelberg competition? *Hint*: Think about how the cartel profit compares to the Stackelberg profits for both firms, and use the Stackelberg price determined in exercise 25A.9 along the way.

25A.4.2 A Prisoner's Dilemma: The Incentive of Cartel Members to Cheat Suppose that both firms enter a collusive cartel agreement and decide to each produce half of x^M in order to maximize their joint profit. It is certainly in their interests to sign such an agreement, but is it optimal for them to stick to their agreement as they prepare to come to the buyer meeting?

Suppose Fibretech believes SpiralMedia will stick to the agreement. We can ask what it would gain from producing one additional contract above the quota set in the cartel. In panel (a) of Graph 25.7, we assume that the firms have agreed to behave as a single monopolist, jointly producing x^M, which allows them to sell all their contracts at price p^M. Were they, as a monopoly, to produce one more contract, they would have to drop the price in order to sell the larger quantity. This would result in a loss of profit equal to the dark blue area since they can no longer sell the initial x^M goods at the price p^M. It would also result in an increase in profit equal to the dark brown area since they get to sell one more contract. For a monopoly, the quantity x^M is profit maximizing because the dark blue area is slightly larger than the dark brown area; that is, monopoly profit would fall if they produced one more contract.

Now think about the question of whether to produce one more contract from the perspective of one of the members of the cartel that has agreed to behave as a single monopolist. In the cartel agreement, the firms agreed that Fibretech would produce half of the monopoly output level x^M and SpiralMedia would produce the other half. If SpiralMedia produces one more contract, it will lose only half the dark blue area in profit from having to accept a price slightly lower than p^M for the half of x^M it is producing under the cartel agreement, but it would get all of the dark brown area in additional profit from the additional unit it produces. Since the dark blue area is only slightly larger than the dark brown area, half of the dark blue area is certainly smaller than all of the dark brown area in the graph, which means *SpiralMedia's profit will increase if it cheats* and produces one more contract than it agreed to in the cartel.

Panel (b) looks at this in another way and asks not only whether it would be in SpiralMedia's best interest to produce one unit of output beyond the cartel agreement but *how much* more it would want to produce assuming it believes that Fibretech will stick to the agreement to produce only half of x^M. The residual demand D^r that SpiralMedia would face given that Fibretech produces $x_1 = 0.5x^M$ is equal to the market demand D minus $0.5x^M$, which intersects MC at the quantity $1.5x^M$. The corresponding residual marginal revenue curve MR^r has twice the slope and intersects MC at $0.75x^M$, implying that it would be optimal for SpiralMedia to produce $0.75x^M$ rather than $0.5x^M$ as called for in the cartel agreement. If SpiralMedia believes Fibretech will produce $0.5x^M$, its best response is to produce $0.75x^M$.

Exercise 25A.14

Can you verify the last sentence by just looking at the best-response functions we derived earlier in Graph 25.2?

If SpiralMedia calculates that it is in its best interest to cheat on the cartel agreement, chances are that Fibretech will also arrive at the same conclusion. This means that unless the firms can find a way to enforce the cartel agreement, the cartel will unravel as each firm cheats. If each knows that the other will cheat, we are back to Cournot competition and both will end up behaving as if there was no cartel agreement at all.

Graph 25.7 The Incentive to Cheat on a Cartel Agreement

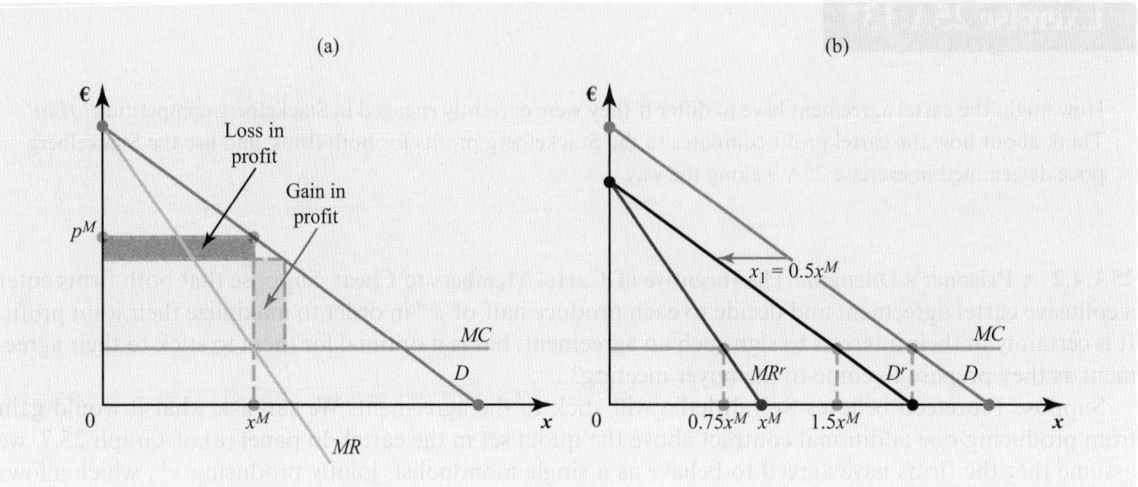

In terms of the game theory language, the firms face a classic Prisoner's Dilemma. Both would be better off colluding and producing in accordance with the agreement than they would be by competing against one another either in Bertrand or Cournot competition, but both have a strong incentive to cheat on the agreement whether the other party cheats or not and bring more contracts to the buyer meetings than promised. As noted in our discussion of Prisoner's Dilemmas, these types of games do not result in the optimal outcome for the two players unless the players can find a way to enforce the agreement. Inconveniently for us, cartel agreements are usually, but not always, illegal.

Exercise 25A.15

The Prisoner's Dilemma the firms face as they try to maintain a cartel agreement works towards making both worse off. How does it look from the perspective of society at large?

While the Prisoners' Dilemma incentives of cartel members undermine cartel agreements, there are real-world examples of cartel agreements that have lasted for long periods. They may not always be successful at maintaining exactly monopoly output, but they often do restrict output beyond what Cournot competition would predict. This raises the question of how firms can overcome the Prisoner's Dilemma incentives that would, if unchecked, lead to a full unravelling of a cartel.

We can think of two possible ways of accomplishing this. First, firms might find ways of hiring an outside party to enforce the cartel, just as our two prisoners in the classic Prisoner's Dilemma might do by joining a gang that enforces silence when the prisoners are interrogated by the prosecutor. Second, in our discussion of repeated Prisoner's Dilemmas in Chapter 24, we found that if the game is repeated an infinite number of times or, more realistically, if the players know that there is a decent chance that they will meet again each time that they meet, cooperation in the Prisoner's Dilemma can emerge as part of a subgame perfect equilibrium strategy.

25A.4.3 Enforcing Cartel Agreements Through Government Protection In 1933, in the midst of the Great Depression, the United States Congress passed the National Industrial Recovery Act (NIRA) at the urging of newly inaugurated President Franklin D. Roosevelt who proclaimed it 'the most important and far-reaching' legislation 'ever enacted by the American Congress'. The Act represented a stark departure from laissez-faire attitudes towards industry, envisioning a more planned economy in which industrial leaders would coordinate production and prices to 'foster fair competition', with compliance enforced by the newly created National Recovery Administration. In essence, the Act legalized cartels in major manufacturing sectors, thus putting the force of law behind oligopolists' efforts to set price and quantity within particular markets. It generally received strong support from large corporations, but was opposed by smaller firms. The NIRA was an example of how oligopolists can employ the government as an enforcer of cartel agreements to limit quantity and raise price. Less than two years after its enactment, the US Supreme Court unanimously declared the portion of the NIRA that established cartels as unconstitutional.

Exercise 25A.16

Why would oligopolists who cannot voluntarily sustain cartel agreements want to have such agreements enforced?

While this large-scale establishment of cartels vanished in the United States with the demise of the NIRA, similar legislation often governs industry in other countries. There continues to be more modest attempts to establish cartels through government action, typically with the stated purpose of benefiting the 'general welfare' but with the actual consequence of restricting quantity and raising price. In some cases, it is generally recognized that the purpose of government sponsored cartels is to limit competition in order to raise price. Few, for instance, would argue that this is not the prime mission of OPEC, which meets frequently to set production quotas for each of its 13 member countries. Yet one would not be able to tell this from OPEC's official mission statement, which states: 'OPEC's mission is to coordinate and unify the petroleum policies of Member Countries and to ensure the stabilization of oil prices in order to secure an efficient, economic and regular supply of petroleum to consumers, a steady income to producers and a fair return on capital to those investing in the petroleum industry'. The words sound similar to those used to advocate for the NIRA in 1933 and continue to be similar to those articulated whenever government enforcement for cartel agreements is sought by firms.

25A.4.4 Self-Enforcing Cartel Agreements in Repeated Oligopoly Interactions Alternatively, we can turn to the case where oligopolists that seek to establish a cartel agreement know that they will meet repeatedly. From our game theory chapter, we know that this is not sufficient for cooperation to emerge. If the firms know they will interact repeatedly but that this interaction will end at some definitive point in the future, subgame perfection leads to an unravelling of cooperation from the bottom of the repeated game tree upwards. The firms know that in their final interaction, neither will have an incentive to stick by the cartel agreement. That, however, means that in the second-to-last period, there will also be no incentive to cooperate since there is no credible way to punish non-cooperation in the final interaction. That means that there is no way to enforce cooperation in the third-to-last interaction given that both firms know that non-cooperation will take place in the last two periods. By the same logic, cooperation cannot emerge in any period.

The real world is rarely quite as definitive as setting up a finitely repeated set of interactions with a clear end-point. Firms will know that they are likely to interact again each time that they meet, and we can therefore treat such interactions as infinitely repeated. As we saw in our discussion of repeated Prisoner's Dilemmas in Chapter 24, this removes the unravelling feature of finitely repeated games because there is no definitive final interaction, and it opens the possibility to simple trigger strategies under which firms begin by complying with the cartel agreement, continue to do so as long as everyone complies in previous interactions, and revert to oligopoly competition if someone deviates from the agreement. Such strategies can sustain cartel cooperation as long as the immediate payoff from violating the cartel agreement is not sufficiently large to overcome the long-run loss from the disappearance of the cartel and the reversion to oligopoly competition.

Real-world strategies of this type are complicated by the fact that firms might not be able to tell for sure whether another firm has violated the agreement. For instance, suppose that oil producers cannot observe how much oil is produced by any given company but they can only see the price that oil sells for in the market. Suppose further that oil price in any given period depends on both the overall quantity of oil supplied by the oligopoly firms *and* unpredictable and unobservable demand shocks to the oil market. If a firm observes an unexpectedly low price in a given period, it might be because a member of the cartel has cheated and has produced more oil than the agreement specified, but it might also be because of an adverse demand shock in the oil market. Firms in such markets may find it difficult to be certain about whether cartel members are cheating and run the risk of misinterpreting an unexpectedly low price as a sign of cheating. Economists have introduced such complicating factors into economic models of oligopolies and cartels, and it becomes plausible to observe equilibria in which cartel agreements break down and re-emerge in repeated oligopoly interactions. This corresponds well to observed cartel behaviours in some industries.

Exercise 25A.17

In circumstances where firms are not certain about demand conditions in any given period, why might a more forgiving trigger strategy like tit-for-tat that allows for the re-emergence of cooperation be better than the extreme trigger strategy that forever punishes perceived non-cooperation in one period?

25B   The Mathematics of Oligopoly

Throughout most of this section, we will assume that firms face a constant marginal cost $MC = c$ with no recurring fixed costs, and that the market demand for the oligopoly good x is linear and of the form:

$$x = A - \alpha p. \tag{25.1}$$

Note that, under our current assumptions, were the oligopoly to function as a single monopoly, we know from our work in Chapter 23 (equation (23.14)) that, assuming no price discrimination, the firm would produce the monopoly quantity x^M and sell it at the monopoly price p^M where:

$$x^M = \frac{A - \alpha c}{2} \quad \text{and} \quad p^M = \frac{A + \alpha c}{2\alpha}. \tag{25.2}$$

Exercise 25B.1

Verify x^M and p^M in equation (25.2).

25B.1 Bertrand Competition

Bertrand competition, whether simultaneous or sequential, will result in both firms setting price equal to MC. To determine the overall Bertrand oligopoly output level, we substitute $MC = c$ for price in the market demand function to get the joint output level $x = A - \alpha c$. Assuming that consumers will come to our two firms in equal numbers when they charge the same price, this implies Bertrand output levels for the two firms of:

$$x_1^B = x_2^B = \frac{A - \alpha c}{2} \tag{25.3}$$

sold at the Bertrand price of $p^B = c$. For the linear demand and constant MC model we are using, the Bertrand model predicts that *each* of the two firms will produce the quantity that a single monopolist would choose to produce on its own, because the competitive quantity is twice the monopoly quantity.

The Bertrand model becomes more interesting when firms can differentiate their products; that is, when firms are not producing identical products but are still part of an oligopoly.

25B.2 Quantity Competition: Cournot and Stackelberg

25B.2.1 Cournot Competition To calculate the best quantity response functions for the two firms in the oligopoly described in part A, we begin by calculating Fibretech's *residual demand given it assumes SpiralMedia produces $\bar{x}_2$*. If the market demand is given by equation (25.1), Fibretech's residual demand if SpiralMedia produces $\bar{x}_2$ is:

$$x_1^r = A - \alpha p - \bar{x}_2. \tag{25.4}$$

To make this analogous to the residual demand curve graphed in panel (c) of Graph 25.2, we need to put it in the form of an inverse demand function:

$$p_1^r = \left(\frac{A - \bar{x}_2}{\alpha}\right) - \left(\frac{1}{\alpha}\right)x_1. \tag{25.5}$$

Exercise 25B.2

Verify that p_1^r is the correct inverse demand function.

The marginal revenue curve for any linear inverse demand function is itself a linear function with the same intercept as the inverse demand function but twice the slope; that is, the relevant marginal revenue function for Fibretech given it assumes SpiralMedia will produce $\bar{x}_2$ is:

$$MR_1^r = \left(\frac{A - \bar{x}_2}{\alpha}\right) - \left(\frac{2}{\alpha}\right)x_1. \tag{25.6}$$

Exercise 25B.3

Derive this MR function using calculus.

Given this residual marginal revenue for Fibretech, it can determine the optimal quantity to produce assuming it thinks SpiralMedia is producing $\bar{x}_2$ by setting equation (25.6) equal to marginal cost $MC = c$. Solving this for x_1, we get:

$$x_1 = \frac{A - \bar{x}_2 - \alpha c}{2}. \tag{25.7}$$

Because the two firms are identical, SpiralMedia's best response to thinking that Fibretech produces some quantity $\bar{x}_1$ is symmetric. For any quantity x_1 that Fibretech is producing, we can now write down the best response for SpiralMedia in terms of x_1, and for any quantity of x_2 that SpiralMedia is producing, we can write down Fibretech's best response in terms of x_2. This gives us the best-response functions $x_1(x_2)$ and $x_2(x_1)$ as:

$$x_1(x_2) = \frac{A - x_2 - \alpha c}{2} \quad \text{and} \quad x_2(x_1) = \frac{A - x_1 - \alpha c}{2}. \tag{25.8}$$

In a Nash equilibrium, the quantity $\bar{x}_2$ that Fibretech predicts SpiralMedia will be producing has to be SpiralMedia's best response to what Fibretech is producing; that is, $\bar{x}_2 = x_2(x_1)$. We can therefore substitute $x_2(x_1)$ into our expression for $x_1(x_2)$ and solve for x_1, which gives us the Cournot output level for Fibretech as:

$$x_1^c = \frac{A - \alpha c}{3}. \tag{25.9}$$

Because our two firms are identical, SpiralMedia's Nash equilibrium quantity should be the same.

Exercise 25B.4

Verify that this is correct.

Exercise 25B.5

Verify that these quantities are in fact the Nash equilibrium quantities; that is, show that given SpiralMedia produces this amount, it is best for Fibretech to do the same, and given that Fibretech produces this amount, it is best for SpiralMedia to do the same.

Note that this implies that together the firms will produce $2(A - \alpha c)/3$, which is larger than the monopoly quantity $(A - \alpha c)/2$ derived in equation (25.2) and smaller than the competitive and Bertrand quantities $(A - \alpha c)$.

Exercise 25B.6

How does the monopoly price p^M derived in equation (25.2) compare to the price that will emerge in the Cournot equilibrium? How does it compare to the Bertrand price?

25B.2.2 Cournot Competition With More Than Two Firms We can also demonstrate how Cournot competition changes as the number of firms increases. Suppose that the inverse market demand function is $p(x)$ and that all firms have the same cost function $c(xi)$ that gives the total cost of production as a function of the firm's production level xi. Suppose there are N firms in the oligopoly, and let's denote the output levels of all firms other than firm i as $x_{-i} = (x_1, x_2, \ldots, x_{i-1}, x_{i+1}, \ldots, x_N)$. Firm i's profit-maximization problem given $\bar{x}_{-i}$ is:

$$\max_{x_i} \pi_i = p(x_i, \bar{x}_{-i})x_i - c(x_i) \\ = p(\bar{x}_1 + \bar{x}_2 + \cdots + \bar{x}_{i-1} + x_i + \bar{x}_{i+1} + \cdots + \bar{x}_N)x_i - c(x_i). \tag{25.10}$$

The first-order condition:

$$\frac{dp(x_i,\overline{x}_{-i})}{dx}x_i + p(x_i,\overline{x}_{-i}) - \frac{dc(x_i)}{dx_i} = 0 \tag{25.11}$$

can be written as:

$$MR_i = \frac{dp(x_i,\overline{x}_{-i})}{dx}x_i + p(x_i,\overline{x}_{-i}) = \frac{dc(x_i)}{dx_i} = MC_i. \tag{25.12}$$

We can express the MR_i as:

$$MR_i = p\left(1 + \frac{dp}{dx}\frac{x_i}{p}\right). \tag{25.13}$$

Since we are assuming all firms are identical, in equilibrium they will produce the same quantity. This means that $Nx_i = x$, and this in turn means we can write the MR_i equation as:

$$MR_i = p\left(1 + \frac{dp}{dx}\frac{x_i}{p}\frac{N}{N}\right) = p\left(1 + \frac{dp}{dx}\frac{x}{p}\frac{1}{N}\right) = p\left(1 + \frac{1}{N\varepsilon_D}\right), \tag{25.14}$$

where $\varepsilon_D = (dx/dp)(p/x)$ is the price elasticity of market demand. Using this as the expression for MR_i, and recognizing that in equilibrium marginal costs will be the same for all our firms even though we are allowing MC to be non-constant by expressing costs as $c(x)$, we can write equation (25.12) as:

$$MR_i = p\left(1 + \frac{1}{N\varepsilon_D}\right) = MC. \tag{25.15}$$

As N becomes large, this implies that price approaches MC just as it does under perfect competition. Thus, as oligopolies with identical firms become large, Cournot competition approaches perfect competition as well as Bertrand competition.

Exercise 25B.7

Can you make a case for why the Cournot model gives intuitively more plausible predictions than the Bertrand model for oligopolies in which identical firms produce identical goods?

25B.2.3 Stackelberg Competition Now suppose we return to our linear demand and constant MC example and suppose that we set quantity sequentially, with Fibretech being the Stackelberg leader and SpiralMedia being the Stackelberg follower. Subgame perfection requires that Fibretech calculates what SpiralMedia's optimal response will be for any x_1 it might set in the first stage of the game. This is Spiral-Media's best-response function, which we already calculated in equation (25.8) to be:

$$x_2(x_1) = \frac{A - x_1 - \alpha c}{2}. \tag{25.16}$$

Fibretech can determine the residual demand for its goods by subtracting what it knows SpiralMedia will produce from the market demand:

$$x'_1 = A - \alpha p - x_2(x_1) = A - \alpha p - \frac{A - x_1 - \alpha c}{2}. \tag{25.17}$$

To derive the inverse residual demand curve Dr that we graphed in panel (b) of Graph 25.4, we solve this for p to get:

$$p'_1 = \frac{A + \alpha c}{2\alpha} - \frac{1}{2\alpha}x_1. \tag{25.18}$$

Exercise 25B.8

Verify that this is the correct inverse residual demand function for Fibretech.

Exercise 25B.9

In panel (b) of Graph 25.4, the residual demand curve has a kink at the level of MC. Verify that the function we previously derived meets the market demand curve at $p = MC$. How would you fully characterize the residual demand curve mathematically taking into account the fact that it is kinked?

From p'_1 we can now derive Fibretech's residual marginal revenue curve by recognizing that it will have the same intercept but twice the slope:

$$MR'_1 = \frac{A + \alpha c}{2\alpha} - \frac{1}{\alpha}x_1. \tag{25.19}$$

We can set this equal to $MC = c$ and solve for Fibretech's optimal Stackelberg leader (SL) quantity:

$$x_1^{SL} = \frac{A - \alpha c}{2}. \tag{25.20}$$

Given this output level for Fibretech, SpiralMedia's best-response function implies the optimal Stackelberg follower (SF) quantity of:

$$x_2^{SF} = \frac{A - \alpha c}{4}. \tag{25.21}$$

Exercise 25B.10

How does the overall level of Stackelberg output relate to the monopoly quantity and the Cournot quantity? What is more efficient in this setting from society's vantage point: Cournot or Stackelberg competition?

Exercise 25B.11

What will be the output price under Stackelberg competition, and how does this relate to the Cournot and monopoly prices?

Exercise 25B.12

Can you draw a graph analogous to panel (c) of Graph 25.3, indicating the monopoly outcome assuming the two firms would split the monopoly output level, the Cournot outcome, the Stackelberg outcome and the Bertrand outcome? Label all the points.

25B.3 Oligopoly Competition With Asymmetric Information

So far we have assumed that firms always know the costs of other firms, but this is not generally true in the real world. Suppose, for instance, we have a relatively new oligopoly, with Fibretech having lost its monopoly status given the successful entry of SpiralMedia into the industry. It might be reasonable to assume that Fibretech's costs are well known given its history as a monopolist, but SpiralMedia's costs might not be known. Or suppose that it is known that SpiralMedia invented a new manufacturing process but it is not yet known how costly that process is. Either of these scenarios results in an oligopoly in which SpiralMedia knows Fibretech's costs but Fibretech does not know SpiralMedia's costs. We now have asymmetrically informed firms and thus one player (Fibretech) with incomplete information. The resulting oligopoly quantity-setting game is an example of a simultaneous Bayesian game.

Suppose that the oligopoly faces the same market demand $x = A - \alpha p$, with inverse market demand of $p = (A/\alpha) - x/\alpha$. In a two-firm oligopoly, this inverse demand can be written as $p = (A - x_1 - x_2)/\alpha$, with x_i indicating firm i's production level. Fibretech is assumed to have MC of c as before, but SpiralMedia might either have high MCs of c^H or low MCs of c^L, with $c^H > c^L$. The high-cost type in SpiralMedia occurs with probability ρ while the low-cost type occurs with probability $(1 - \rho)$. SpiralMedia knows its type but Fibretech only has beliefs about its type based on the probability with which each type occurs. We will consider Cournot competition in this setting.

Intuitively, SpiralMedia will produce a different level of output depending on whether its costs are high or low. A strategy for SpiralMedia involves settling on a quantity depending on whether the firm is a high- or a low-cost type (remember that a simultaneous Bayesian game involves Nature assigning types first, and a strategy for each player therefore involves a plan of action for each possible type that might be assigned). Fibretech does not have the luxury of setting its quantity with the knowledge of SpiralMedia's cost structure; it has to settle on a single quantity given its beliefs about the likelihood of SpiralMedia being a high-cost rather than low-cost type. Fibretech needs to solve the optimization problem:

$$\max_{x_1}\left[\rho\left(\frac{A - x_1 - x_2^H}{\alpha} - c\right)x_1 + (1 - \rho)\left(\frac{A - x_1 - x_2^L}{\alpha} - c\right)x_1\right], \quad (25.22)$$

where x_2^H and x_2^L are the SpiralMedia production levels of high- and low-cost types. Depending on which type i SpiralMedia is assigned by Nature, it solves the optimization problem:

$$\max_{x_2^i}\left(\frac{A - x_1 - x_2^i}{\alpha} - c^i\right)x_2^i. \quad (25.23)$$

The first-order condition of the optimization problem in (25.22) solves to:

$$x_1 = \frac{A - \alpha c - \rho x_2^H - (1 - \rho)x_2^L}{2} \tag{25.24}$$

for Fibretech, and the first-order conditions for the optimization problems for the two types in (25.23) for SpiralMedia solve to:

$$x_2^H = \frac{A - x_1 - \alpha c^H}{2} \text{ and } x_2^L = \frac{A - x_1 - \alpha c^L}{2}. \tag{25.25}$$

Exercise 25B.13

Show that the first-order condition for Fibretech approaches an expression similar to the first-order condition for each of the SpiralMedia types as Fibretech's uncertainty diminishes; that is, as ρ approaches 0 or 1.

Substituting the first-order conditions for SpiralMedia into equation (25.24) and solving for x_1, we get Fibretech's optimal quantity x_1^* as:

$$x_1^* = \frac{A - 2\alpha c + \alpha(\rho c^H + (1 - \rho)c^L)}{3}. \tag{25.26}$$

Now suppose that Fibretech actually knew SpiralMedia's type. This would imply that it would produce $(A - 2\alpha c + \alpha c^H)/3$ if it knew it was facing a high-cost firm and $(A - 2\alpha c + \alpha c^L)/3$ if it knew it was facing a low-cost firm. Since it does not know what type it is facing, Fibretech produces a quantity in between these, thus producing less than it would under complete information when it faces a high-cost opponent and more when it faces a low-cost opponent.

SpiralMedia has an informational advantage and will try to use that to its advantage. Suppose, for instance, it has high MCs of c^H. Substituting Fibretech's output level from equation (25.26) into x_2^H in expression (25.25), we can solve for the output level of SpiralMedia when it has high costs. This gives us:

$$x_2^{H*} = \frac{2A + 2\alpha c - \alpha(3 + \rho)c^H - \alpha(1 - \rho)c^L}{6}, \tag{25.27}$$

which, by adding and subtracting $\alpha\rho c^H$, can be written as:

$$x_2^{H*} = \frac{A + \alpha c - 2\alpha c^H}{3} + \frac{\alpha(1 - \rho)}{6}(c^H - c^L). \tag{25.28}$$

In the absence of informational asymmetries, the high-cost SpiralMedia would produce only the first term in this expression, which implies that it will produce *more* than it would under complete information when it knows it has high costs but its opponent does not. We just saw that Fibretech will produce *less* than it would under complete information when it faces a high-cost opponent. SpiralMedia is therefore using its informational advantage to its advantage.

We can similarly solve for x_2^{L*} to get:

$$x_2^{L*} = \frac{A + \alpha c - 2\alpha c^L}{3} - \frac{\alpha\rho}{6}(c^H - c^L), \tag{25.29}$$

and we can now see that SpiralMedia will produce *less* than it would under complete information when it knows it is a low-cost type, allowing Fibretech to produce more.

Exercise 25B.14**

Verify the last equation.

Exercise 25B.15*

Can you tell whether the Cournot price will be higher or lower under this type of asymmetric information than it would be under complete information? *Hint*: For both the case of a high-cost and a low-cost type, can you see if overall production is higher or lower in the absence of asymmetric information?

Exercise 25B.16*

Suppose the two firms engage in price (Bertrand) competition, and suppose $c > c^H$. What price do you expect will emerge?

Exercise 25B.17*

Suppose again the two firms engage in price (Bertrand) rather than quantity competition, and suppose $c^L < c < c^H$. This case is easier to analyze if we assume sequential Bertrand competition, with Fibretech setting its price first and SpiralMedia setting it after it observes p_1 and after it finds out its cost type. What equilibrium prices would you expect? Does your answer change with ρ?

25B.4 Fixed Entry Costs and Entry Deterrence

We showed in Section 25A.3 that for particular fixed costs of entry, it is possible for an incumbent firm to deter entry by a new firm *if the incumbent firm is able to set quantity prior to the potential entrant's entry decision*. Given our previous work, we can now show exactly the range of fixed costs for which the intuition we developed in part A is correct. Recall that the sequence of moves required for entry deterrence has the incumbent firm setting quantity first, followed by an entry and quantity decision by the potential entrant. That sequence is pictured in panel (c) of Graph 25.5.

We begin by asking how high fixed entry costs FC would have to be in order for the incumbent firm to not have to worry about challenges from an entrant. Suppose Fibretech produces the monopoly quantity x^M in equation (25.2), which we have shown is equal to the Stackelberg leader quantity x^{SL} in equation (25.20) under our linear assumptions about demand and costs. The best SpiralMedia could do if it did enter is to produce the Stackelberg follower quantity x^{SF} in equation (25.21) and to sell that quantity at the Stackelberg price, which you should have calculated in exercise 25B.11 to be:

$$p^S = \frac{A + 3\alpha c}{4\alpha}. \tag{25.30}$$

The profit π_2 for SpiralMedia from entering is equal to revenue minus the cost of production minus the fixed cost of entry FC:

$$\pi_2 = p^S x^{SF} - cx^{SF} - FC = \frac{(A - \alpha c)^2}{16\alpha} - FC. \tag{25.31}$$

Exercise 25B.18

Verify that this equation is correct.

We can conclude that as long as $FC > (A - \alpha c)^2/16\alpha$, the profit from entering is negative if the incumbent firm is producing the monopoly output level and so SpiralMedia would choose not to enter. Fibretech would produce x^M without feeling the threat of competition from the potential entrant. In terms of the notation in panel (b) of Graph 25.6, this implies:

$$\overline{FC} = \frac{(A - \alpha c)^2}{16\alpha}. \tag{25.32}$$

Next, we can ask at what fixed entry cost the incumbent firm would be better off accepting the Stackelberg outcome rather than attempting to raise quantity to keep the entrant from coming into the market. To answer this, we first have to determine, for any given FC, how much Fibretech would have to produce to keep SpiralMedia from entering. Whatever x_1 is produced, SpiralMedia will respond, if it enters, by producing according to its best-response function $x_2(x_1)$ in equation (25.8). This allows us to calculate the price that Fibretech can expect to emerge for any quantity x_1 conditional on SpiralMedia entering the market:

$$p(x_1) = \frac{A}{\alpha} - \frac{x_1 + x_2(x_1)}{\alpha} = \frac{A - x_1 + \alpha c}{2\alpha}. \tag{25.33}$$

Exercise 25B.19

Verify that this derivation of $p(x_1)$ is correct.

SpiralMedia will enter if $(p(x_1 + x_2(x_1) - cx_2(x_1)) > FC$. Substituting in for $x_2(x_1)$ and $p(x_1)$, this implies SpiralMedia will enter as long as:

$$\frac{(A - x_1 - \alpha c)^2}{4\alpha} > FC. \tag{25.34}$$

Exercise 25B.20

Verify that this derivation is correct.

Fibretech is in full control of what x_1 will be when SpiralMedia has to make its entry decision, which implies that Fibretech has to make sure the inequality in (25.34) goes in the other direction if it wants to keep SpiralMedia out. Fibretech therefore has to solve:

$$\frac{(A - x_1 - \alpha c)^2}{4\alpha} \le FC \tag{25.35}$$

for x_1. Doing so, we get the minimum output for Fibretech to deter SpiralMedia from entering as:

$$x_1^{ED} = A - \alpha c - 2(\alpha FC)^{1/2}. \tag{25.36}$$

When fixed entry costs are below $\overline{FC} = (A - \alpha c)^2/(16\alpha)$, the incumbent firm now has a choice. It can either produce the *entrance deterrent quantity* x_1^{ED} and keep SpiralMedia from entering, or it can produce the *Stackelberg leader quantity* and accept SpiralMedia's competition. If the incumbent settles into Stackelberg leadership and accepts SpiralMedia's entry, its profit π_1^{SL} will be:

$$\pi_1^{SL} = \frac{(A - \alpha c)^2}{8\alpha}. \tag{25.37}$$

Exercise 25B.21

Verify that this is correct. Does it make sense that profit for the Stackelberg leader is exactly twice the profit of the Stackelberg follower which we calculated in equation (25.31) when $FC = 0$?

The profit from producing a quantity x as the sole producer in the market graphed in panel (a) of Graph 25.6 is:

$$\pi = (p(x) - c)x = \left(\frac{A - x}{\alpha} - c\right)x = \left(\frac{A - x - \alpha c}{\alpha}\right)x. \tag{25.38}$$

Since the incumbent can always just decide to be a Stackelberg leader, the most it is ever willing to produce to deter entry is an amount that sets equations (25.37) and (25.38) equal. Doing so and solving for x using the quadratic formula, we get the highest quantity that would ever be produced to deter entry as:

$$x_{max}^{ED} = \frac{(2 + 2^{1/2})(A - \alpha c)}{4}. \tag{25.39}$$

Note that the quadratic formula gives two solutions for x. However, one of these is less than the Stackelberg leader quantity and we can therefore discard that solution as economically irrelevant.

Exercise 25B.22

As noted, the quadratic formula also gives a second solution, namely $x = (2 - 2^{1/2})(A - \alpha c)/4$. Can you locate this solution in panel (a) of Graph 25.6?

Setting this equal to equation (25.36), we can calculate the lowest fixed cost $\underline{FC}$ at which entry deterrence is still optimal for Fibretech as:

$$\underline{FC} = \left(\frac{(2 - 2^{1/2})(A - \alpha c)}{8} \right)^2. \tag{25.40}$$

Thus, if the fixed entry cost falls below $\underline{FC}$, the incumbent firm will make no effort to deter SpiralMedia from entering, and the two firms play the Stackelberg game. If the fixed entry cost falls between $\underline{FC}$ and $\overline{FC}$ from equation (25.32), the incumbent firm will raise its output to x_1^{ED} from equation (25.36) and will thereby successfully deter SpiralMedia from entering the market. Finally, if the fixed entry cost is higher than $\overline{FC}$, the incumbent can safely produce the monopoly quantity x^M without worrying about SpiralMedia entering.

25B.5 Dynamic Collusion and Cartels

We will briefly illustrate mathematically the temptation by members of cartels to cheat on cartel agreements before illustrating how dynamic collusion can nevertheless emerge under the right conditions.

25B.5.1 The Temptation to Cheat on a One-Period Cartel Agreement
Continuing with the assumption that market demand is given by $x = A - \alpha p$, we have already calculated that a monopolist facing this market demand will produce $x^M = (A - \alpha c)/2$ and sell at $p^M = (A + \alpha c)/2\alpha$. Two identical firms in an oligopoly facing the same market demand would therefore maximize their joint profit if they agree to each produce half the monopoly quantity; that is, $x_i^{Cartel} = x^M/2 = (A + \alpha c)/4$. If both parties to a cartel agreement abide by the agreement, this implies that profit for each cartel member i would be:

$$\pi_i^{Cartel} = (p^M - c)\frac{x^M}{2} = \left(\frac{A + \alpha c}{2\alpha} - c \right)\frac{A - \alpha c}{4} = \frac{(A - \alpha c)^2}{8\alpha}. \tag{25.41}$$

Now suppose that firms i and j have entered such a cartel agreement but firm i, rather than blindly following the agreement, asks itself if it could produce a different quantity and do better. If firm j sticks by the agreement to produce $x^M/2$, this means firm i would choose x_i to solve:

$$\max_{x_i} \pi_i = \left(\frac{A - (x^M/2) - x_i}{\alpha} - c \right)x_i = \left(\frac{3(A - \alpha c) - 4x_i}{4\alpha} \right)x_i. \tag{25.42}$$

Solving the first-order condition, we can calculate the optimal quantity for firm i conditional on firm j sticking by the cartel agreement. Denoting this quantity as x_i^D,

$$x_i^D = \frac{3(A - \alpha c)}{8}, \tag{25.43}$$

which is 50 per cent greater than half the monopoly quantity assigned to firm i in the cartel agreement. The profit from deviating, π_i^D, conditional on firm π_j^D not deviating from the cartel agreement can be calculated to be:

$$\pi_i^D = \frac{9(A - \alpha c)^2}{64\alpha}. \tag{25.44}$$

Exercise 25B.23

Verify π_i^D. Is it unambiguously larger than π_i^{Cartel}?

25B.5.2 Collusion in Finitely Repeated Oligopoly Quantity Setting It can be concluded from what we just derived that unless there is some outside enforcement mechanism that can get the two firms to abide by the cartel agreement, it is not possible to sustain the agreement in equilibrium once the firms meet. The two firms are caught in a classic Prisoner's Dilemma. They both know that an enforced cartel agreement makes both of them better off, but without enforcement, it is rational for both of them to cheat. The equilibrium continues to be the Cournot equilibrium despite the cartel agreement. This does not change when the firms interact repeatedly a finite number of times since cooperation of repeated Prisoner's Dilemma games unravels from the bottom up under subgame perfection.

As we noted in Section A, however, there are many real-world instances of collusion in oligopolies, which cast doubt on the real-world relevance of the result that collusion cannot arise under subgame perfection in finitely repeated oligopoly interactions. We already discussed in Section A some of the real-world considerations that might be responsible for instances of firm collusion despite this theoretical result. It may, for instance, be that firms found a way to enforce their cartel agreement, perhaps by employing government in some fashion. Or it may be the case that there is a Bayesian dimension to the game that we have not considered. For instance, there may be firms that will always play tit-for-tat even if it is not in their best interests to do so, and that Fibretech might be uncertain about whether it is playing such an opponent. We have shown that even if the probability of encountering an irrational tit-for-tat opponent is small, the mere possibility that one of the players might be such an opponent may be enough for rational players to want to establish a reputation for cooperating. Or it may be the case that firms are uncertain about whether they will interact again, which in essence turns the finitely repeated game into one that can be modelled like a game of infinitely repeated interactions.

25B.5.3 Infinitely Repeated Oligopoly Interactions The unravelling of cooperation in finitely repeated Prisoner's Dilemmas is due to the fact that there is a definitive end to the interactions of the players. In the real world, we rarely know when the last time will be that we interact with someone, and so it might be with firms in an oligopoly. We could model this directly as a probability that firms will interact again when they find themselves interacting. Or we can model the game as an infinitely repeated game in which the firms discount the future. We will do the latter here, assuming that €1 next period is worth €δ this period, where $\delta < 1$. Recall that this means a stream of income of y per period starting this period is worth $y/(1 - \delta)$, and a stream of income of y per period starting next period is worth $\delta y/(1 - \delta)$.

Assuming firms do not discount the future too much, collusion between firms in an oligopoly can emerge in infinitely repeated settings. One possibility is that players employ trigger strategies, strategies that presume cooperation initially but that trigger eternal non-cooperation if non-cooperation ever enters the game. In the context of oligopolies in cartel agreements that assign to each of two identical firms half of the monopoly output in each period, such a strategy would be: 'produce $(x^M/2)$ in the first period; every period thereafter, produce $(x^M/2)$ if everyone in previous periods has stuck by the cartel agreement, but produce the Cournot quantity x^C otherwise'. One instance of non-cooperation therefore triggers the Cournot equilibrium from then on.

Such a trigger strategy, if adopted by both players, is a subgame perfect equilibrium of the infinitely repeated oligopoly game as long as one of the firms cannot make enough additional profit immediately by deviating this period to compensate for the loss of cartel profits in the future. When firm i considers whether to deviate, it knows that it can get π_i^D from equation (25.44) this period at the cost of settling for the Cournot profit π_i^C for every period thereafter; that is, deviating results in profit of $\pi_i^D + \delta\pi_i^C/(1 - \delta)$. Not deviating, on the other hand, implies a profit of π^{Cartel} from equation (25.42) every period starting now or, in present value terms, $\pi^{Cartel}/(1-\delta)$. Deviating from the trigger strategy, therefore, does not pay as long as:

$$\frac{\pi_i^{Cartel}}{(1-\delta)} > \pi_i^D + \frac{\delta\pi_i^C}{(1-\delta)}. \tag{25.45}$$

We calculated in equation (25.9) the Cournot quantity to be $x^C = (A - \alpha c)/3$, and in exercise 25.6(B) you should have derived the Cournot price as $p^C = (A + 2\alpha c)/3\alpha$. This implies a Cournot profit for each firm of $\pi_i^C = (A - \alpha c)^2/(9\alpha)$.

Exercise 25B.24

Verify that this is the correct per-period profit in the Cournot equilibrium.

Substituting the relevant quantities into the inequality (25.45), we get:

$$\frac{(A - \alpha c)^2}{8\alpha(1-\delta)} > \frac{9(A - \alpha c)^2}{64\alpha} + \frac{\delta(A - \alpha c)^2}{9\alpha(1-\delta)}. \tag{25.46}$$

Solving for α, we get that:

$$\delta > \frac{9}{17} \approx 0.53. \tag{25.47}$$

Thus, as long as €1 next period is worth more than €0.53 this period, neither firm will want to deviate from the proposed trigger strategy, which implies the two firms will collude in accordance with their cartel agreement.

This is, as our discussion of the Folk Theorem in the appendix to Chapter 24 illustrated, not the only way to sustain collusion in infinitely repeated oligopoly games. Furthermore, in a world where there is less certainty than we have assumed here, the trigger strategy we proposed here seems far too severe since it eternally punishes deviations. Consider a world in which firms in an oligopoly cannot observe the output of other firms, but only see what the equilibrium price turned out to be in every period. In a two-firm oligopoly, this is enough to infer the other firm's output, but only if firms know market demand perfectly. If there is some uncertainty in each period about what exactly market demand looks like – if there are unobservable market demand shocks – it becomes more difficult to know whether an unexpectedly low price was due to unexpectedly low market demand in a given period or whether it was due to the other firm cheating on its cartel agreement. A number of economists have investigated such settings closely and have concluded that more forgiving trigger strategies are likely to be optimal from the cartel's perspective, strategies where a price below some level triggers punishment for some period but eventually collusion is restored. Our only point here is that when firms interact without knowing that their interactions will end at some point, collusion may well be sustainable despite the incentives to deviate from cartel agreements in finitely repeated games.

End-of-Chapter Exercises

25.1*† We have demonstrated the equilibrium that emerges when two oligopolists compete on price when there are no fixed costs and marginal costs are constant. In this exercise, continue to assume that firms compete solely on price and can produce whatever quantity they want.

A. We now explore what happens as we change some of these assumptions. Maintain the assumptions we made in the text and change only those referred to in each part of the exercise. Assume throughout that costs are never so high that no production will take place in equilibrium, and suppose throughout that price is the strategic variable.

    a. First, suppose both firms paid a fixed cost to get into the market. Does this change the prediction that firms will set $p = MC$?

    b. Suppose instead that there is a recurring fixed cost FC for each firm. Consider first the sequential case where firm 1 sets its price first and firm 2 follows assuming that one of the options for both firms is to not produce and not pay the recurring fixed cost. What is the subgame perfect equilibrium? If you get stuck, there is a hint in part (f).

    c. Consider the same costs as in (b). Can both firms produce in equilibrium when they move simultaneously?

    d. What is the simultaneous move Nash equilibrium? There are actually two.

    e. *True or False*: The introduction of a recurring fixed cost into the Bertrand model results in $p = AC$ instead of $p = MC$.

    f. You should have concluded that the recurring fixed cost version of the Bertrand model leads to a single firm in the oligopoly producing. Given how this firm prices the output, is this outcome efficient, or would it be more efficient for both firms to produce?

    g. Suppose next that in addition to a recurring fixed cost, the marginal cost curve for each firm is upward sloping. Assume that the recurring fixed cost is sufficiently high to cause AC to cross MC to the right of the demand curve. Using logic similar to what you have used thus far in this exercise, can you again identify the subgame perfect equilibrium of the sequential Bertrand game as well as the simultaneous move pure strategy Nash equilibria?

B. Suppose that demand is given by $x(p) = 100 - 0.1p$ and firm costs are given by $c(x) = FC + 5x^2$.

    a. Assume that $FC = 11\,985$. Derive the equilibrium output x^B and price p^B in this industry under Bertrand competition.

    b. What is the highest recurring fixed cost FC that would sustain at least one firm producing in this industry? *Hint*: When you get to a point where you have to apply the quadratic formula, you can infer the answer from the term in the square root.

25.2 In exercise 25.1, we checked how the Bertrand conclusions that flow from viewing *price* as the strategic variable hold up when we change some of our assumptions about fixed and marginal costs. We now do the same for the case where we view *quantity* as the strategic variable in the simultaneous move Cournot model.

A. Maintain all the assumptions in the text unless you are asked to specifically change some of them.

    a. First, suppose both firms paid a fixed cost to get into the market. Does this change the predictions of the Cournot model?

    b. Let x^C denote the Cournot equilibrium quantities produced by each of two firms in the oligopoly as derived under the assumptions in the text. Suppose that there is a recurring fixed cost FC for each firm and FC does not have to be paid if the firm does not produce. Assuming that both firms would still make non-negative profit by each producing xC, will the presence of FC no longer make this a Nash equilibrium?

    c. Can you illustrate your conclusion from (b) in a graph with best-response functions that give rise to a single pure strategy Nash equilibrium with both firms producing x^C? *Hint*: You should convince yourself that the best-response functions are the same as before for low quantities of the opponent's production, but at some output level for the opponent, jump to 0 output as a best response.

    d. Can you illustrate a case where FC is such that both firms producing x^C is one of three different pure strategy Nash equilibria?

    e. Can you illustrate a case where FC is sufficiently high such that both firms producing x^C is no longer a Nash equilibrium? What are the two Nash equilibria in this case?

    f. *True or False*: With sufficiently high recurring fixed costs, the Cournot model suggests that only a single firm will produce and act as a monopoly.

g. Suppose that instead of a recurring fixed cost, the marginal cost for each firm was linear and upward sloping, with the marginal cost of the first unit the same as the constant marginal cost assumed in the text. Without working this out in detail, what do you think happens to the best-response functions, and how will this affect the output quantities in the Cournot equilibrium?

B. Suppose that both firms in the oligopoly have the cost function $c(x) = FC + (cx^2/2)$, with demand given by $x(p) = A - \alpha p$.

a. Derive the best-response function $x_1(x_2)$ of firm 1's output given firm 2's output as well as $x_2(x_1)$.

b. Assuming that both firms producing is a pure strategy Nash equilibrium, derive the Cournot equilibrium output levels.

c. What is the equilibrium price?

d. Suppose that $A = 100$, $c = 10$ and $\alpha = 0.1$. What is the equilibrium output and price in this industry, assuming $FC = 0$?

e. How high can FC go with this remaining as the unique equilibrium?

f. How high can FC go without altering the fact that this is at least one of the Nash equilibria?

g. For what range of FC is there no pure strategy equilibrium in which both firms produce but two equilibria in which only one firm produces?

h. What happens if FC lies above the range you calculated in (g)?

25.3† In exercise 25.2, we considered *quantity* competition in the simultaneous Cournot setting. We now turn to the sequential Stackelberg version of the same problem.

A. Suppose that firm 1 decides its quantity first and firm 2 follows after observing x_1. Assume initially that there are no recurring fixed costs and that marginal cost is constant as in the text.

a. Suppose that both firms have a recurring $FC = 0$ that does not have to be paid if the firm chooses not to produce. Will the Stackelberg equilibrium derived in the text change for low levels of FC?

b. Is there a range of FC under which firm 1 can strategically produce in a way that keeps firm 2 from producing?

c. At what FC does firm 1 not have to worry about firm 2?

d. Could FC be so high that no one produces?

e. Suppose instead (that is suppose again $FC = 0$) that the firms have linear, upward-sloping MC curves, with MC for the first output unit equal to what the constant MC was in the text. Can you guess how the Stackelberg equilibrium will change?

f. Will firm 1 be able to engage in entry deterrence to keep firm 2 from producing?

B. *Consider again the demand function $x(p) = 100 - 0.1p$ and the cost function $c(x) = FC + 5x^2$ as you did in exercise 25.1 and implicitly in the latter portion of exercise 25.2.

a. Suppose first that $FC = 0$. Derive firm 2's best-response function to observing firm 1's output level x_1.

b. What output level will firm 1 choose?

c. What output level does that imply firm 2 will choose?

d. What is the equilibrium Stackelberg price?

e. Now suppose there is a recurring fixed cost $FC > 0$. Given that firm 1 has an incentive to keep firm 2 out of the market, what is the highest FC that will keep firm 2 producing a positive output level?

f. What is the lowest FC at which firm 1 does not have to engage in strategic entry deterrence to keep firm 2 out of the market?

g. What is the lowest FC at which neither firm will produce?

h. Characterize the equilibrium in this case for the range of FC from 0 to 20 000.

25.4* Business Application: *Quitting Time: When to Exit a Declining Industry.* We illustrated in the text the strategic issues that arise for a monopolist who is threatened by a potential entrant into the market. In this exercise, suppose instead that an industry is in decline in the sense that demand for its output is decreasing over time. Suppose there are only two firms left: a large firm L and a small firm S.

A. Since our focus is on the decision of whether or not to exit, we will assume that each firm i has fixed capacity k^i at which it produces output in any period in which it is still in business; that is, if a firm i produces, it produces $x = k_i$. Since L is larger than S, we assume $k^L > k^S$. The output produced is produced at constant marginal cost $MC = c$. Assume throughout that once a firm has exited the industry, it can never produce in this industry again.

   a. Since demand is falling over time, the price that can be charged when the two firms together produce some output quantity $\overline{x}$ declines with time; that is, $p_1(\overline{x}) > p_2(\overline{x}) > p_3(\overline{x}) > \cdots$ where subscripts indicate the time periods $t = 1, 2, 3$. If firm i is the only firm remaining in period t, what is its profit π_t^i? What if both firms are still producing in period t?

   b. Let t^i denote the last period in which demand is sufficiently high for firm i to be profitable, that is to make profit greater than or equal to zero, if it were the only firm in the market. Assuming they are in fact different, which is greater: t^L or t^S?

   c. What are the two firms' subgame perfect strategies beginning in period $(t^S + 1)$?

   d. What are the two firms' subgame perfect strategies in periods $(t^L + 1)$ to t^S?

   e. Suppose both firms are still in business at the beginning of period t^L before firms make their decision of whether to exit. Could both of them producing in this period be part of a subgame perfect equilibrium? If not, which of the two firms must exit?

   f. Suppose both firms are still in business at the beginning of period $(t^L - 1)$ before exit decisions are made. Under what condition will both firms stay? What has to be true for one of them to exit, and if one of them exits, which one will it be?

   g. Let $\overline{t}$ denote the last period in which $(p_t(k^S + k^L) - c) \geq 0$. Describe what happens in a subgame perfect equilibrium, beginning in period $t = 1$, as time goes by, that is, as $\overline{t}$, t^L and t^S pass. Is there ever a time when price rises as the industry declines?

   h. Suppose that the small firm has no access to credit markets and therefore is unable to take on any debt. If the large firm knows this, how will this change the subgame perfect equilibrium? *True or False*: Although the small firm will not need to access credit markets to be the last firm in the industry, it will be forced out of the market before the large firm exits if it does not have access to credit markets.

   i. How does price now evolve differently in the declining industry when the small firm cannot access credit markets?

B. Suppose $c = 10$ $k^L = 20$, $k^S = 10$ and $p^t(\overline{x}) = 50.5 - 2t - \overline{x}$ until price is zero.

   a. How does this example represent a declining industry?

   b. Calculate t^S, t^L and $\overline{t}$ as defined in part A of the exercise.

   c. Derive the evolution of output price as the industry declines.

   d. How does your answer change when firm S has the credit constraint described in A(h)?

   e. How would your answer change if the large rather than the small firm had this credit constraint?

   f. Suppose firm S can only go into debt for n time periods. Let $\overline{n}$ be the smallest n for which the subgame perfect equilibrium without credit constraints holds, with $n < \overline{n}$ implying the change in equilibrium you described in part A(h). What is $\overline{n}$? Assume no discounting.

   g. If $n < \overline{n}$, how will output price evolve as the industry declines?

Note: This exercise is derived from Martin J. Osborne, *An Introduction to Game Theory* (New York: Oxford University Press, 2004).

25.5† **Business Application:** *Financing a Strategic Investment under Quantity Competition.* Suppose you own a firm that has invented a patented product that grants you monopoly power. Patents only last for a fixed period of time, as does the monopoly power associated with the patent. Suppose you are nearing the end of your patent and you have the choice of investing in research that will result in a patented technology that reduces the marginal cost of producing your product.

A. The demand for your product is linear and downward sloping and your current constant marginal cost is *MC*. There is one potential competitor who faces the same constant *MC*. Neither of you currently faces any fixed costs, and the competitor observes your output before they decide whether and how much to produce.

    a. If this is the state of things when the patent runs out, will you change your output level? What happens to your profit?

    b. Suppose you can develop an improved production process that lowers your marginal cost to *MC′* < *MC*. Once developed, you will have a patent on this technology, implying that your competitor cannot adopt it. You would finance the fixed cost of this new technology with a payment plan that results in a recurring fixed cost *FC* for the life of the patent. If you do this, what do you think will happen to your output?

    c. If *MC′* is relatively close to *MC*, will you be able to keep your competitor out? In this case, might it still be worth it to invest in the technology?

    d. If the technology reduces marginal costs by a lot, might it be that you can keep your competitor from producing? If so, what will happen to output price?

    e. Do you think that investments like this – intended to deter production by a competitor – are efficiency enhancing?

    f. Suppose the potential competitor could also invest in this technology. Might there be circumstances under which your firm will invest and your competitor does not?

B. *Suppose again that demand is given by $x = A - \alpha p$, that there are currently no fixed costs, that all firms face a constant marginal cost c and that you are about to face a competitor because your patent on the good you produce is running out.

    a. What will happen to your output level if you simply engage in the competition by producing first? What will happen to your profit?

    b. If you lower your marginal cost to $c' < c$ by taking on a recurring fixed cost *FC*, what will be your profit assuming that your competitor still produces?

    c. Suppose that $A = 1000$, $c = 40$ and $\alpha = 10$. What is the highest *FC* can be for you to decide to go ahead with the investment if the new marginal cost is $c' < c$ and assuming the competitor cannot get the same technology? Denote this $\overline{FC}_1(c')$.

    d. Now consider the competitor. Suppose they see that firm 1 has invested in the technology and thus lowered its marginal cost to c'. Firm 2 finds out that the patent on firm 1's technology has been revoked, making it possible for firm 2 to also adopt the technology at a recurring fixed cost *FC*. What is the highest *FC* at which firm 2 will adopt the technology in equilibrium? Denote this $\overline{FC}_2$.

    e. Suppose $c' = 20$. For what range of *FC* will firm 1 adopt and firm 2 not adopt the technology even if it is permitted to do so?

25.6 **Policy Application: *Subsidizing an Oligopoly*.** It is common in many countries for governments to subsidize the production of goods in certain large oligopolistic industries. Common examples include the aircraft and car industries.

A. Suppose that a two-firm oligopoly faces a linear, downward-sloping demand curve, with each firm facing the same constant marginal cost and no recurring fixed cost.

    a. If the intent of the subsidy is to get the industry to produce the efficient output level, what should be the subsidy for Bertrand competitors?

    b. *How would your answer to (a) change if each firm faced a recurring fixed cost?

    c. What happens as a result of the subsidy to best-response functions for firms that are setting quantity rather than price? How does this impact the Cournot equilibrium?

    d. How would you expect this to impact the Stackelberg equilibrium?

e. Suppose policy makers can either subsidize quantity-setting oligopoly firms to get them to produce the efficient quantity or invest in lowering barriers to entry into the industry so that the industry becomes competitive. Discuss how you would approach the trade-offs involved in choosing one policy over the other.

f. How would your answer be affected if you knew that it was difficult for the government to gather information on firm costs?

g. Suppose there are recurring fixed costs that are sufficiently high for only one firm to produce under quantity competition. Might the subsidy result in the entry of a second firm?

B. Suppose demand is given by $x(p) = A - \alpha p$, that all firms face constant marginal cost c, and that there are no recurring fixed costs.

a. If the government introduces a per-unit subsidy $s < c$, what happens to the marginal costs for each firm?

b. How do monopoly, Bertrand, Cournot and Stackelberg equilibria change as a result of the subsidy?

c. **Suppose $A = 1000$, $c = 40$ and $s = 15$. What is the economic incidence of the subsidy in each economic environment; that is, what fraction of the subsidy is passed on to consumers and what fraction is retained by producers?

d. **How would your answer to (c) change if the government instead imposed a per-unit tax $t = 15$?

e. How much of a tax or subsidy has to be set to get the efficient level of output under each of the four market conditions?

f. Suppose you are advising the government on policy and you have two choices. Either you subsidize the firms in the oligopoly, or you lower the barriers to entry that keep the industry from being perfectly competitive. For each of the four market conditions, determine what cost you would be willing to have the government incur to make the industry competitive rather than subsidize it.

g. *Suppose that pollution was produced in this industry, emitting a constant level of pollution per unit of output, with a cost of b per unit of output imposed on individuals outside the market. How large would b have to be under each of the market conditions in order for the outcome to be efficient without any government intervention?

* conceptually challenging
** computationally challenging
† solutions in Study Guide

Chapter 26

Product Differentiation and Innovation in Markets

In discussing different market structures, we have assumed that there is such a thing as the market for the good that is being discussed. This has made markets appear to be quite *static* in the sense that something in the past has led up to the existence of certain markets for certain well-defined goods, but nothing is currently happening to change this. All that is happening is that different market structures satisfy existing consumer demand in one way or another, dividing total potential surplus between consumers, producers and possibly deadweight loss. In this static world, firms are relegated to producing goods that someone else invented at some point, making sure to not waste any resources in the process, while looking for some strategic pricing advantage from which to profit.

The real world appears to be constantly changing, with firms attempting to get an edge by finding new and better technologies for production, by changing features of existing products and inventing new ones, and by altering the image of products through aggressive marketing and advertising. The real world is *dynamic*, constantly changing and adapting to new circumstances. Firms often do not take as given that their choice is to produce or not to produce some combination of existing goods; they try to differentiate what they do and innovate towards creating new markets in which they can meet consumer demand more effectively while also establishing just a bit of market power from which to profit. It is to this process of *product differentiation* and *innovation* that we now turn. Much of our exploration of product differentiation will be in the context of the Bertrand price-setting model. This is one way to resolve the 'Bertrand Paradox' – the prediction of the simple Bertrand model that as we go from a single firm to two firms, price competition immediately implies perfectly competitive behaviour. While the idea that firms compete on price is both intuitive and powerful, it does not predict well in the simplest setting of the previous chapter. With the introduction of product differentiation, however, the intuitive idea gains predictive power and allows us to think about many real-world markets.

As we develop the underlying ideas of this chapter, we will find this to be a second way to fill the gap between the extremes of perfect competition and perfect monopoly. By merging product differentiation into the Bertrand model and allowing barriers to entry to be less extreme, we will now develop the model of *monopolistic competition*. We will see that price gradually converges to the competitive price, this time as entry barriers gradually fall. We will thus have found a way to bridge the gap between the more extreme models with both a quantity setting and a price-setting framework. Which of these is the better model will depend on the underlying economic realities in real-world industries, with the approach developed in this chapter particularly applicable to industries that experience ongoing innovation.

26A | Differentiated Products and Innovation

We will first look at the implications of moving away from the assumption that oligopolists are producing identical products and instead assume that oligopoly firms produce differentiated products in an attempt to lessen price competition.

26A.1 Differentiated Tastes in Oligopoly Markets

Despite its extreme prediction of fierce price competition, the Bertrand model prediction of price equalling marginal cost under price competition changes when products are differentiated. At the same time, the Bertrand model often seems more intuitive than the Cournot model in terms of how it defines the strategic variables for firms in oligopolies. Is it really the case that firms set quantities and wait for prices to emerge once all the firms in the oligopoly have brought their goods to market, or is it that, at least sometimes, firms advertise prices and meet demand through production? When Apple unveiled the MacBook Pro, it immediately advertised a price from which it did not deviate over the coming year. It produced and shipped MacBook Pro computers as demand revealed itself in different parts of the country. Apple did not produce a quantity just to sit back and wait for a price to emerge; it set the price the moment it unveiled the computer.

The Bertrand model is not as silly in its predictions once we allow firms to differentiate their products, as Apple certainly does, due to differentiated consumer tastes. It is in part for this reason that the model continues to play a large role in economics, not because its initial prediction of price equal to MC is taken seriously, but because it is intuitively more plausible in many settings that firms set prices for products while trying to differentiate them from the products of competitors. Such product differentiation only makes sense, however, if consumer tastes are also differentiated.

26A.1.1 Differentiated Tastes for Coke and Pepsi
In blind taste tests many people cannot tell the difference between Coke and Pepsi. However, most consumers purport to express a preference for one over the other; most consumers, therefore, do not view Coke and Pepsi as the same product, although most do consider them substitutes to an extent. One way to think of an oligopoly like the soft drink industry where differentiated products are produced is to think of demand for Coke as dependent on both the price of Coke and the price of Pepsi, with demand for Coke rising as the price of Coke falls *and as the price of Pepsi rises*. Specifying demand in this way leads to Bertrand competition in which the prices charged by the oligopolistic firms are above marginal cost.

If Coke and Pepsi were identical in the minds of all consumers, everyone would always buy from the lower-priced producer, which in turn drives prices down to MC as Bertrand predicted. If some consumers prefer Coke to Pepsi when they are equally priced, Coke will not lose all of its market share if it charges a price above Pepsi's. It may well be the case that some consumers will purchase Coke at $p > MC$ even if Pepsi hands its soft drinks out for nothing. The fact that Coke and Pepsi are different in the eyes of consumers implies that demand does not shift so radically as the price of Coke rises above the price of Pepsi, making room for producers to raise price above MC.

Exercise 26A.1

True or False: Suppose that Coke knows it has positive consumer demand if it sets $p = MC$, it must be the case that Coke will price above MC.

26A.1.2 Modelling Choice of Product Characteristics
In markets where producers engage in price competition but where they can differentiate their products because of differentiated consumer tastes, we see a more complicated oligopoly setting because both price and product characteristics become strategic variables. During our discussion of Coke and Pepsi, we have not yet made this leap because we have taken it as given that Coke and Pepsi produce somewhat different products but have not yet thought about how they came to choose the product characteristics to begin with. To make our analysis of product characteristic choice in an environment of price competition more tractable, we will develop a new model to deal with this complication and will illustrate how product differentiation emerges within oligopolies as firms attempt to soften the harsh price competition envisioned by Bertrand.

We begin with a setting in which products vary in terms of one characteristic that can take on a value on the interval from 0 to 1. Firms will choose where on this interval to locate their product, and how much to differentiate their products from one another. We will also assume that each consumer demands only one good in this market, and that consumers are characterized by an 'ideal point' on the interval [0, 1]. Thus, a consumer $n \in [0, 1]$ is defined as a consumer whose ideal product has the characteristic n. If the consumer ends up consuming a product with characteristic $y \neq n$, we will assume that the consumer incurs a cost in addition to the price they pay for the product, with that additional cost increasing the further away n is from y. We will also assume that consumer ideal points are equally spread, i.e. *uniformly distributed* across the interval [0, 1].

This type of model of product differentiation is called the *Hotelling model* and is useful in analyzing product differentiation for oligopolies with two firms. The model originated with Harold Hotelling (1895–1973), a mathematical statistician and economic theorist. Panel (a) of Graph 26.1 represents the set of possible product characteristics, as well as the set of possible ideal points for consumers, for this model. Panel (b) of Graph 26.1 represents an alternative way of modelling product characteristics along a circle rather than a line, a model developed by Steven Salop, 'Monopolistic Competition with Outside Goods', *Bell Journal of Economics* 10 (1979), 141–56. This way of representing the possible product characteristics is more useful as we consider markets with more than two firms as well as markets in which firms can enter after paying a fixed entry cost. The basic idea, however, is similar to the Hotelling model in that product characteristics can fall anywhere along the circle, as can consumer ideal points, with a consumer n once again paying a cost in addition to the price of the product that increases as the distance along the circle between the characteristic of the good y and their ideal point n increases. Note that in panel (a) there are better and worse places to locate in the sense that more consumers are close to the firm at the centre than at the extremes. In panel (b), on the other hand, no particular point on the circle is better or worse in this sense as long as consumer ideal points are distributed uniformly around the circle.

Graph 26.1 Two Ways of Representing Product Characteristics

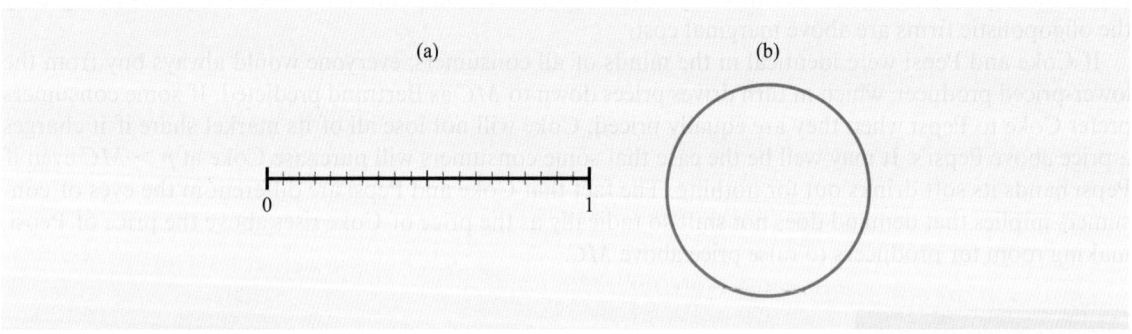

Exercise 26A.2

We have said that under product differentiation we would expect the quantity of Coke that is demanded to be affected by both the price of Coke and the price of Pepsi. Can you see how the models of product differentiation result in firms facing precisely this kind of demand when they locate at different points in the product characteristics interval or circle?

26A.2 The Hotelling Model of Oligopoly Product Differentiation

Suppose that there is a single characteristic of the good that can be differentiated, perhaps the sweetness of the soft drink, and we think of this characteristic as ranging from 0 to 1 as in panel (a) of Graph 26.1. Suppose further that consumers have ideal points along that interval, with each consumer attempting to get a soft drink that is as close as possible to their ideal point. Assume that consumer ideal points are uniformly distributed along the interval [0, 1] and that each consumer demands just one unit of the good. While this is not the most natural assumption in the soft drink market, the assumption becomes more natural in markets such as cars or computers in which most consumers only purchase one unit at a time. We can ask how much product differentiation we should expect by two firms that can each choose to produce a product that has a sweetness characteristic somewhere on that interval.

26A.2.1 Product Differentiation in the Absence of Price Competition

Assume the soft drink industry is regulated and the two firms are required to charge some fixed price $p \geq MC$, and are therefore not permitted to engage in price competition. Suppose the only strategic variable is the product characteristic that can fall between 0 and 1 and that price is not a strategic variable at all. We can derive each firm's best response to the other firm's product characteristic. If Coke sets its product characteristic y_1 below 0.5, Pepsi's best response is to choose a product characteristic $y_2 = y_2 + \epsilon$ where ϵ is small enough so that there exists no consumer with ideal point between y_1 and y_2. This way, Pepsi captures all consumers to the right of $y_1 < 0.5$; and since consumers are uniformly distributed along the interval [0, 1], this implies Pepsi gets more than half the market. The reverse is true if Coke sets $y_1 > 0.5$; Pepsi's best response is to choose $y_2 = y_1 - \epsilon$ where ϵ is again small enough so that no consumer's ideal point falls between y_2 and y_1. Finally, suppose Coke sets $y_1 = 0.5$. Pepsi would get less than half the market if it set y_2 below or above y_1, which means that as long as we can assume the two firms will split the market equally when $y_1 = y_2$, Pepsi's best response to $y_1 = 0.5$ is to set $y_2 = 0.5$.

Panel (a) of Graph 26.2 plots this best-response function for firm 2 (Pepsi), with:

- $y_2 = y_1 + \epsilon < 0.5$ if $y_1 < 0.5$,
- $y_2 = y_1 - \epsilon > 0.5$ if $y_1 > 0.5$ and
- $y_2 = y_1 = 0.5$ if $y_1 = 0.5$.

Coke's best response to Pepsi's choice of y_2 is similarly derived and plotted in dark brown in panel (b) of the graph with Pepsi's best response in dark blue. The two best-response functions intersect at 0.5, implying a unique Nash equilibrium in which both firms set their product characteristic to exactly 0.5. *In the absence of price competition, the model predicts that there will be no product differentiation.*

Graph 26.2 Best-Response Product Differentiation Without Price Competition

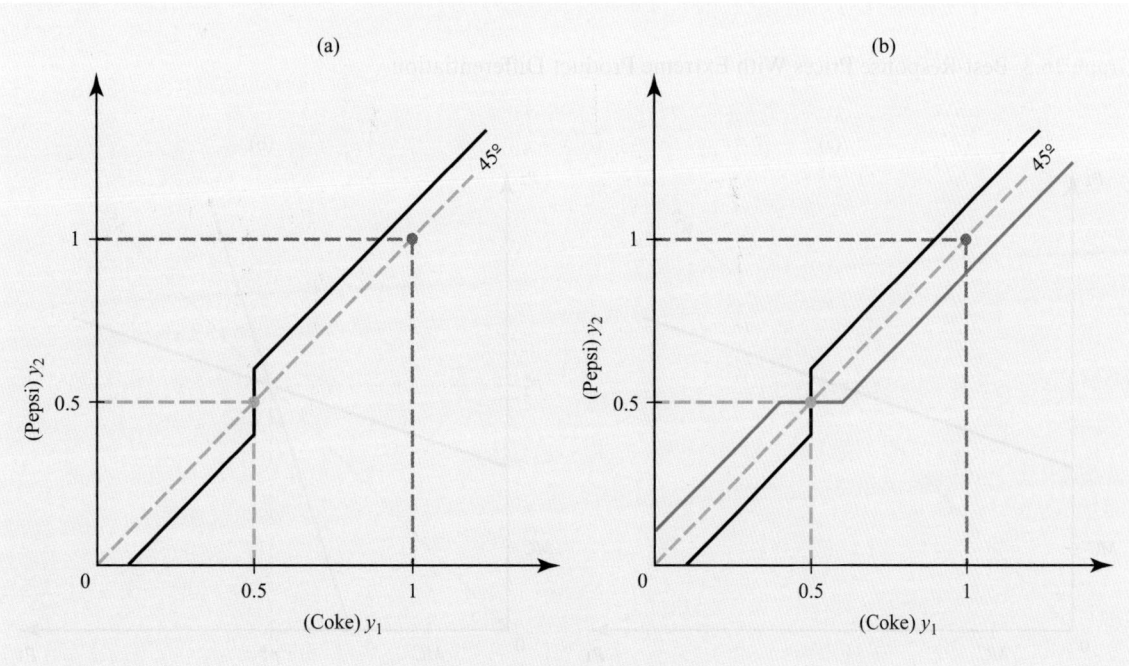

Exercise 26A.3

Would the equilibrium outcome be different if one firm announced its product characteristic prior to the other one having to do so?

26A.2.2 The Impact of Product Differentiation on Bertrand Price Competition Looking at a different example, suppose now that two firms have chosen extreme product differentiation, with firm 1 locating at $y_1 = 0$ and firm 2 at $y_2 = 1$. We can ask what impact this will have on the nature of Bertrand price competition between the two firms.

We are thinking about what the best-response functions for each firm will be to actions taken by the other firm. Unlike in the previous section where price was fixed and product characteristics were the strategic variables, we now have a situation where product characteristics are fixed (with $y_1 = 0$ and $y_2 = 1$) and prices become the strategic variables. We begin in panel (a) of Graph 26.3 by plotting firm 1's price on the horizontal axis and firm 2's price on the vertical. We ask what the best price response for firm 2 might be for different prices chosen by firm 1.

Suppose that firm 1 sets its price to 0. It might well be the case that there are still consumers whose ideal point lies close to 1 and who would prefer to purchase from firm 2 at a price above MC rather than get a good with worse characteristics from firm 1 for free. Assuming consumer preferences distinguish sufficiently between the two product characteristics, firm 2's best price response to $P_1 = 0$ might therefore have an intercept as shown in panel (a). Furthermore, as firm 1 increases its price, firm 2 will be able to also increase its price and retain consumers. Thus, firm 2's best-response function must have a positive slope.

Exercise 26A.4

Suppose the demand for firm 2's output is zero for any p_2 at or above MC when firm 1 sets price p_1 to zero. Furthermore, suppose that demand for firm 2's output becomes positive at $p_2 = MC$ when firm 1 sets a price $\bar{p}$ that lies between 0 and MC. What would firm 2's best-response function look like?

Graph 26.3 Best-Response Prices With Extreme Product Differentiation

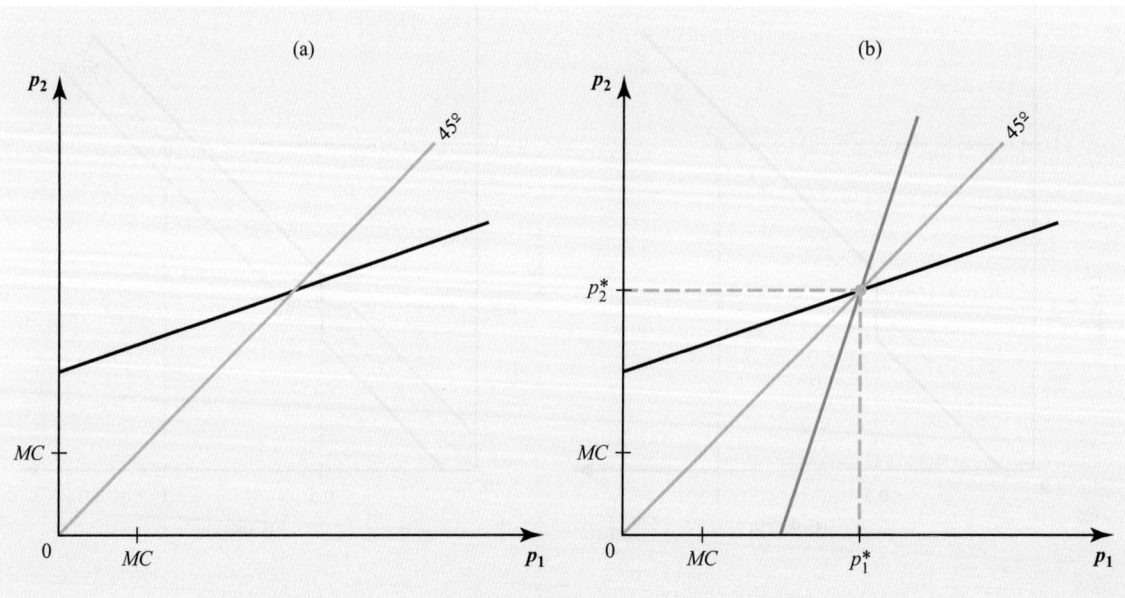

The problem is symmetric for firm 1, and its best-response function is plotted in dark brown in panel (b) of the graph. In equilibrium, each firm's price must be a best response to the other firm's price, which occurs when the dark brown and dark blue best-response functions intersect. Because of the symmetry of the two firms, that intersection must lie on the 45-degree line, with both firms in equilibrium charging equal prices for their differentiated goods. These prices now lie above MC; that is, above the prices predicted by the Bertrand price competition model when products are not differentiated.

Exercise 26A.5

Consider the case described in exercise 26A.4 and assume the two firms are symmetric relative to one another. Will it still be the case that $p > MC$? Can you see how decreasing product differentiation in the minds of consumers will lead to a result that approaches $p = MC$? *Hint*: As $\bar{p}$ gets closer to MC, product differentiation diminishes.

We have demonstrated that, under maximal product differentiation on the Hotelling line, firm profits will be higher than under no product differentiation, thus giving firms an incentive to differentiate their products from one another when they are engaged in price competition. In Graph 26.2, on the other hand, we illustrated that there is no incentive to differentiate products in the absence of price competition. The incentive for product differentiation arises directly from price competition, *because strategic product differentiation allows the oligopoly firms to soften the price competition they face and thus retain some market power*.

26A.2.3 **Choosing Product Characteristics *and* Prices Strategically** We have not, at this point, analyzed the full game that oligopolistic firms in the Hotelling model face. A reasonable way of specifying such a game is in two stages. In the first stage, firms choose product characteristics, and in the second stage, they set prices knowing the product characteristics that each has chosen in the first stage. Such a game therefore consists of two simultaneous games, one in which product characteristics are the strategic variable and another in which prices are the strategic variable. The games are played sequentially. Subgame perfection requires that we solve the simultaneous price-setting game first for any set of product characteristics (y_1, y_2) chosen in the first stage, and we solve the first stage product characteristics game with each firm knowing how pairs of product characteristics translate into prices and profits in the second stage.

The equilibrium of this sequential game of product characteristic and price setting depends on the underlying characteristics of the game and is therefore somewhat complicated to solve without using mathematics extensively. In Section B, we will specify an intuitive model of consumer tastes over product characteristics and will demonstrate that, when consumer ideal points are uniformly distributed along the interval [0, 1], firms will choose maximal product differentiation ($y_1 = 0$, $y_2 = 1$) in anticipation of minimizing price competition in the second stage. While this may be technically difficult to demonstrate formally, it seems more intuitive once we realize how product differentiation allows both firms to charge higher prices.

26A.2.4 **Going From the Hotelling Model to the Real World** The Hotelling model illustrates how oligopolists have an incentive to strategically differentiate their products to soften Bertrand price competition. At the same time, the model tends to predict extreme or maximal product differentiation, with firms locating at the extreme ends of the product characteristic interval [0, 1]. While the intuition that product differentiation can be strategically used to reduce price competition in oligopolies is quite appealing and of real-world significance, there do exist real-world forces that inhibit maximal differentiation of the type predicted by the Hotelling model. First, we illustrated that the incentive for product differentiation disappears when price competition is eliminated. If, for instance, prices within oligopolies are regulated by governments, firms have no incentive to engage in product differentiation. This has been true in the past in certain heavily regulated industries such as the airline industry prior to deregulation. A potential cost from government attempts to regulate prices within oligopolies is the loss of product differentiation within the regulated industry, a cost that becomes more severe the more diverse consumer tastes are. A related cost of price regulation is a decreased incentive on the part of oligopolists to innovate further in order to achieve even greater product differentiation.

Second, the Hotelling model assumes that consumer tastes or ideal points are uniformly distributed along the product characteristic interval. Often, however, it might be much more reasonable to assume that consumer tastes are clustered around the middle of that interval, with most consumers having in-between ideal points and fewer consumers having more extreme tastes. Introducing such distributions of consumer tastes into the Hotelling model introduces a force against extreme product differentiation because, while firms want to soften price competition through differentiation, they also would like to locate their product characteristics where there is relatively more demand. As a result, one can construct Hotelling models in which strategic product differentiation is balanced against clustering of demand on particular product characteristics, with firms still differentiating their products (that is, $y_1 < y_2$) but doing so in a less extreme way than we might otherwise predict (that is, $0 < y_1$ and $y_2 < 1$).

Third, when we think of product differentiation as spatial differentiation in terms of where firms physically locate within, say, a city, it may be that firms gain other benefits from being near one another. For instance, in some markets consumers might have to invest a great deal of time searching over the different goods that are offered and thus are more likely to shop in places where multiple firms have settled. A firm might therefore gain a sufficient advantage from locating near another firm because of increased consumer demand from such clustering, which outweighs the hardening of price competition that such a location entails. This can be seen in the case of car dealerships that may locate near one another. Or there may be other externalities between firms that foster clustering. When high-tech firms locate near one another, for instance, they may have access to a more qualified pool of workers who in turn share important information that helps the individual firms.

26A.3 Entry Into Differentiated Product Markets

The Hotelling model is useful for thinking about product differentiation in oligopolies with two firms, and it helps illustrate the incentive to differentiate products in order to avoid the intense price competition of the simple Bertrand model. The model becomes less useful as we think about competition between more than two firms and as we think about how the number of firms in an oligopoly arises when product differentiation is possible. We now turn to the second model of product differentiation introduced in panel (b) of Graph 26.1, a model in which product characteristics lie on a circle that we can normalize to have circumference of 1.

Suppose that firms can enter this market by paying a fixed set-up cost FC and that once they have paid this cost, they face a constant marginal cost of production. The existence of a fixed cost is the only barrier to entry, and firms will enter this market as long as profit once in the market is sufficient to cover the fixed set-up cost. We will continue to assume that consumer ideal points are uniformly distributed around the circle that represents different product characteristics. We also assume that consumers pay in addition to the price they are charged for a product a cost that increases with the distance between their ideal point and the actual product characteristic y that is produced by the firm from which the consumers purchase. A consumer with ideal point n on the circle will purchase from the firm whose product characteristic y lies closest to n assuming all firms charge equal prices.

We can consider the following two-stage game, which involves two sequentially played simultaneous games. In stage 1, a large number of potential firms decide whether to pay the fixed cost FC to enter this market, and in stage 2 the firms that chose to enter in stage 1 strategically choose an output price knowing where on the circle they as well as all their competitors have located their product characteristic. Since this is a sequential game, subgame perfection requires that we solve the game beginning in stage 2 by determining what prices the firms will charge given the outcome of stage 1. We proceed to stage 1, with firms choosing whether to enter the market knowing what prices will emerge in stage 2 for different entry decisions. Since all the firms are identical prior to making their product characteristic choice, it is reasonable to assume that in any equilibrium, those firms that enter in stage 1 will choose to locate their product characteristics at equal distances from one another along the circle that represents all possible product characteristics. We will operate under this assumption as we begin by thinking about price setting in stage 2.

26A.3.1 Stage 2: Strategic Price Setting Suppose N firms entered in the first stage and are now located at equal distances from one another along the product characteristic circle. The second stage of the game begins with an oligopoly that has N firms producing differentiated products as they engage in Bertrand price competition. The Hotelling model suggests that such product differentiation softens price competition, and that the equilibrium price that emerges under Bertrand competition will lie above MC when firms produce differentiated products.

Since all the N firms face the same constant MC and are located at equal distances from one another, in equilibrium we should expect them to end up choosing the same price. Each firm's best price response function to the price charged by all other firms will be identical to every other firm's best price response function. We will formally derive these in Section B, but the prediction that emerges from the formal analysis is that for a given number of equally spaced firms N, each firm will choose the same price $p^*(N)$ in the Bertrand equilibrium, with $p^*(N) > MC$ as long as N is finite. Furthermore, the larger the number of firms that entered in stage 1, the closer $p^*(N)$ will get to MC, with price converging to MC as the number of firms becomes large and product differentiation between neighbouring firms diminishes.

Exercise 26A.6

If there is no first-stage entry decision and the number of firms is fixed as in an oligopoly with barriers to entry, can you see how this represents the full equilibrium of the game?

This conforms to our intuition from the Hotelling model, i.e. the greater the product differentiation between any two adjacent firms, the more this will soften Bertrand price competition. As the number of firms that enter in the first stage increases, firms will necessarily be closer to one another on the product characteristic circle. While N can be large, in equilibrium each firm actually only faces two competitors: those adjacent to the firm on both sides of the product characteristic circle. When these competitors are nearer to one another as N increases, the relevant competitors are producing products more similar to one another, with the firms facing greater price competition due to less product differentiation with their direct competitors. This greater price competition results in lower prices.

26A.3.2 Stage 1: The Entry Decision The number of firms, however, is only fixed in the second stage because it emerges from the entry decisions of potential firms in the first stage. We thought about the price-setting stage among a fixed number of firms first only because subgame perfection requires that firms contemplate their entry decision without taking seriously non-credible threats by other firms about prices they might charge in the second stage. Entry decisions are therefore made with credible expectations about prices that will emerge under price competition once firms have committed to entering by paying the fixed entry cost FC.

Since we are assuming that this fixed entry cost is the only barrier to entry, it must be the case that in equilibrium firms enter as long as expected profits, given credible equilibrium pricing expectations once a firm has entered, are at least as high as the fixed entry cost. The equilibrium number of firms N^* that emerges in stage 1 is a number sufficient to drive the profit from entering, which includes fixed entry costs, to zero. The equilibrium number will stop just short of the number of firms that would make the profit from entering negative.

Exercise 26A.7

In the context of this model, why is the last sentence slightly more correct than the second to last sentence in the previous paragraph?

It is the case that the higher the fixed entry cost, the smaller will be the equilibrium number of firms, and the smaller the equilibrium number of firms going into stage 2, the higher will be the price charged by firms that enter. On the other hand, lower fixed entry costs imply more firms will enter in stage 1, which in turn implies prices will be lower, and as fixed costs fall to zero, the number of firms becomes large and price converges to MC as one would expect in a model of perfect competition with no barriers to entry.

Exercise 26A.8

True or False: As long as the fixed entry cost $FC > 0$, firms in the industry will make positive profits while firms outside the industry would make negative profits by entering the industry.

The circle model of product differentiation allows us to fully fill in the gap between perfect competition and monopoly through the use of industry fixed entry costs. For very high fixed costs, we only have a single firm entering; that is, we have a monopoly. As fixed costs fall, we may still only have one firm, but it will begin to lower its price as it engages in strategic entry deterrence. At some point, fixed entry costs fall sufficiently for strategic entry deterrence to no longer be worthwhile, and a second firm enters on the opposite side of the circle. We now have a Bertrand model with differentiated products, with each firm using price as its strategic variable and each firm setting price above MC as illustrated first in Graph 26.3. As fixed entry costs fall further, we get increasing numbers of firms with market power declining, until fixed entry costs disappear entirely and we have a perfectly competitive industry with no barriers to entry.

Exercise 26A.9

True or False: While we needed a model of product differentiation to allow for Bertrand competition to be able to fully fill the gap between perfect competition and monopoly, we do not need anything in addition to what we introduced in Chapter 25 to do the same for Cournot competition.

26A.4 Monopolistic Competition and Innovation

In our discussion of firm entry followed by price competition in a market characterized by product differentiation along a circle of possible product characteristics, we have seen the emergence of a possible market structure in which firms have some market power which allows them to set $p > MC$, but new firms cannot enter and earn positive profits. Existing firms for which the fixed entry cost has become a sunk cost make positive profits from pricing above MC, but potential entrants for which fixed entry costs are still real economic costs would make negative profits if they chose to enter. The simultaneous existence of positive economic profits for firms and a lack of entry of new firms is therefore quite plausible in the presence of fixed entry costs.

This idea is one that predates game theoretic models of product differentiation and is credited to the American economist Edward Chamberlin (1899–1967) and the British economist Joan Robinson (1903–1983) who simultaneously (and independently) worked on the topic. Their work in many ways gave rise to the economics of imperfect competition. In the absence of game theory, however, economists thought about the issue a bit differently and in ways that link to our previous discussion of monopoly. Their model of *monopolistic competition* also allows us to tell a story of dynamic innovation even if it does not itself capture this directly.

26A.4.1 Fixed Costs and Average Cost Pricing Suppose a firm i is one of many that produces in a market like the circle model, in which each producer is producing a somewhat different output and fixed entry costs are keeping new firms from entering. Think, for example, of your most recent trip down the super-market aisle that contains breakfast cereals or shampoos or toilet paper. There are a large number of different cereals or shampoos or toilet paper varieties, each differing only slightly from the other. Or think of restaurants in larger cities, each providing a menu a bit different from the others. Many consumers have tastes that distinguish between these goods, which gives rise to downward-sloping demand curves for each of the types of goods that is produced despite the fact that they are close substitutes.

We can illustrate firm i's output and pricing decision, assuming no price discrimination, exactly as we did at the beginning of our discussion of monopoly. This is because each firm in such a market has some monopoly power since it faces a downward-sloping demand curve. In panel (a) of Graph 26.4, D^i represents firm i's demand curve and MR^i is the marginal revenue curve derived from D^i. When profit is defined as the difference between total revenue and variable cost, it can be seen in panel (a) as the shaded area.

Exercise 26A.10

Where in panel (a) of Graph 26.4 is the firm's total revenue given that it charges p^i? Where is its variable cost given that it produces x^i?

Graph 26.4 Zero Profit for a Monopoly That Sets $p = AC$

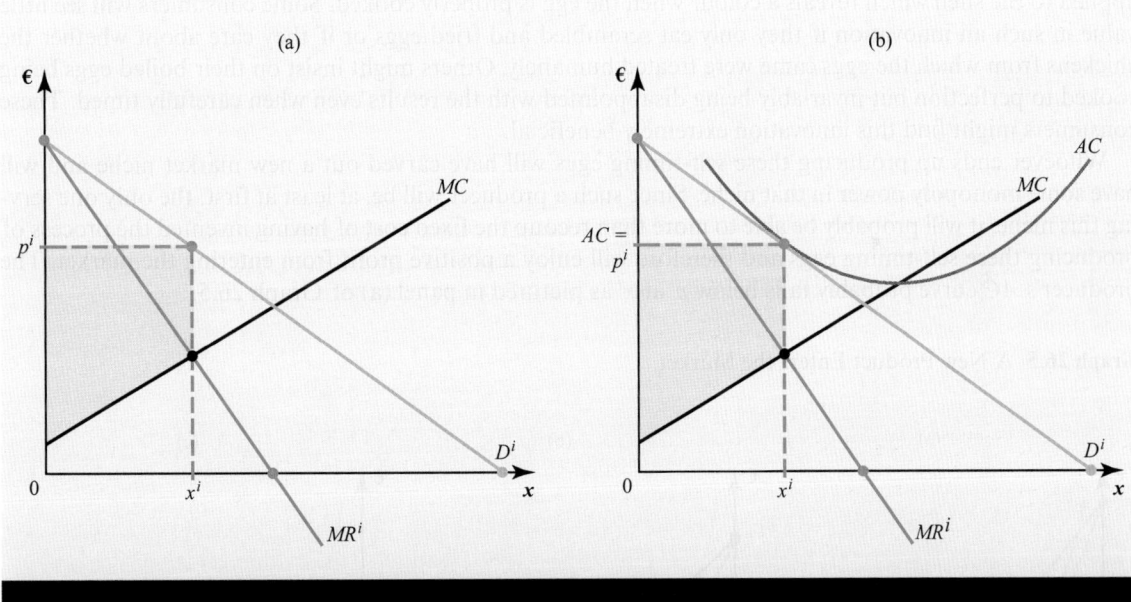

Go to MindTap to interact with this graph

In monopolistically competitive markets, however, firms enter as long as the profit *from entering* is positive, and they stop entering when profit from entering becomes negative. In order for firm i to operate in equilibrium, it must be that its profit as depicted in panel (a) is roughly offset by the fixed entry cost faced by potential entrants. This is because, just as in our circle model, such fixed costs are real economic costs for entrants and thus feature in the calculation of the expected profit *from entering* the market for those who currently are outside the market. For potential entrants, the relevant definition of profit is total revenue minus variable cost *minus fixed cost*, and in equilibrium it must be that this profit is approximately equal to zero. That means that in equilibrium it must be that the total revenue minus variable cost is approximately equal to the fixed entry cost.

In panel (b) of the graph, we illustrate the circumstance under which this is true. The graph is identical to that in panel (a) in every way except that we have now added the marginally entering firm's average total cost curve, which includes variable and fixed cost, as AC. When this curve is tangential to D^i at p^i, the *total* cost including fixed entry cost is equal to the revenue the firm makes when it enters. This can be seen as recognizing that total cost is average cost times output, $AC \times x^i$, while total revenue is price times output, $p^i \times x^i$. Since $p^i = AC$ when the average cost curve is tangential to D^i at p^i, revenue is equal to total cost.

Exercise 26A.11

True or False: With economic profit appropriately defined for each firm, the profit of firms in the industry is positive while the profit of a firm outside the industry would be zero or negative if it entered the monopolistically competitive market in equilibrium.

26A.4.2 A Story of Innovation in Monopolistically Competitive Markets Consider innovation in the egg market. The market already has some product differentiation, with some producers selling only brown eggs, some selling larger eggs, some selling eggs from farm raised chickens, some selling eggs from chickens fed with only organically grown grain, and so on. There is a new innovation that involves a treatment of eggs such that the egg itself tells you as you boil it when it is a perfectly soft-boiled egg with the yolks soft and the whites solid and when it has turned into a perfectly hard-boiled egg. An invisible ink logo is applied to the shell which reveals a colour when the egg is properly cooked. Some consumers will see little value in such an innovation if they only eat scrambled and fried eggs or if they care about whether the chickens from which the eggs came were treated humanely. Others might insist on their boiled eggs being cooked to perfection but invariably being disappointed with the results even when carefully timed. These consumers might find this innovation extremely beneficial.

Whoever ends up producing these self-timing eggs will have carved out a new market niche and will have some monopoly power in that niche. Since such a producer will be, at least at first, the only one serving this niche, it will probably be able to more than recoup the fixed cost of having invented the process of producing these self-timing eggs and therefore will enjoy a positive profit from entering the market. The producer's AC curve probably falls below p^i at x^i as pictured in panel (a) of Graph 26.5.

Graph 26.5 A New Product Enters the Market

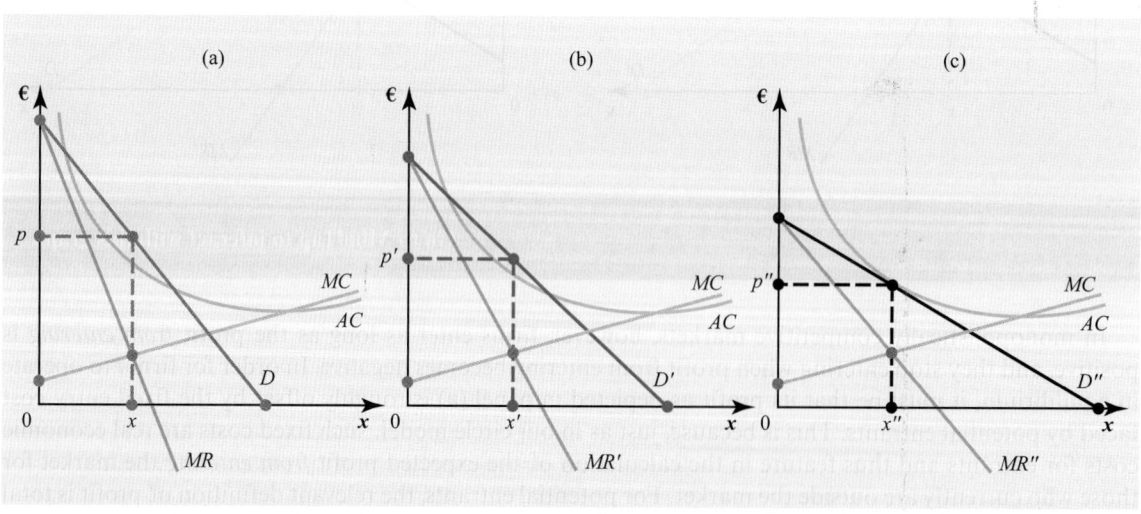

Given that there is free entry in monopolistic markets, aside from the fact that entrants have to pay a fixed entry cost, it cannot be that this is where the story ends. Perhaps the self-timing egg company is protected in the short run from competitors because the firm obtained a patent that keeps others from imitating the product, and perhaps this slows down the process by which new firms will challenge the self-timing egg company. If this egg really works, other potential firms that see the opportunity for profit will find other production processes that will achieve similar products or will perhaps innovate in other ways.

What will change for the self-timing egg firm as other firms find ways of challenging it? The firm's costs are what they are in the absence of other innovations, so the cost curves probably won't move. What will change, however, is the demand faced by the firm when new entrants chip away at demand as they produce competing products. In particular, it would be reasonable to assume that both the intercept and the slope of D in panel (a) of Graph 26.5 will change, with the intercept falling as even the most enthusiastic consumers are willing to pay less for the self-timing egg and the slope becoming shallower as all consumers become more price sensitive. This process should continue as long as the profit from entering is greater than zero and should stop when the profit from entering becomes zero.

In panel (b) of Graph 26.5, the erosion of the self-timing egg company's market power has begun as demand has changed to D' resulting in a lower price p' and a lower per-unit profit where profit is defined to include fixed costs. In panel (c), the process has run its course, with D'' now tangential to AC at the profit-maximizing quantity a'' and with per-unit profit, where profit is defined to include fixed costs, reaching zero. The innovation of the self-timing egg introduced disequilibrium into the monopolistically competitive egg market in panel (a) by generating the opportunity for new firms to make positive profit from entering or for existing firms changing their egg production to take advantage of additional profit opportunities. The transition to panel (c) through panel (b) represents the process by which equilibrium in the monopolistically competitive egg market re-emerges, ending in a market in which existing firms make positive profits that don't count fixed, or sunk, costs, but potential entrants cannot make positive profits from entering in the absence of new innovations.

Exercise 26A.12

The innovation discussed above was in terms of product characteristics and thus impacted demand. Can you tell the same kind of story where a firm innovates in a way that reduces its costs?

26A.4.3 Patents and Copyrights Companies that throw monopolistically competitive markets into disequilibrium through their innovations are often able to slow the process of reaching a new equilibrium by gaining patent or copyright protection that keeps other firms from imitating the innovation for some period of time. As we mentioned in our chapter on monopoly, such government-granted patents and copyrights represent one way in which governments erect temporary barriers to entry that establish temporary monopolies.

We have noted some scepticism about the value of government-erected barriers to entry in earlier chapters where it can be the case that such barriers are inefficient and generate socially wasteful lobbying by firms that are attempting to strengthen their monopoly power. Copyright and patent laws are in many circumstances in a very different category, with such laws emerging over time as a way of fostering innovation that becomes the primary way of generating new and larger social surplus in the long run. There is some debate on whether the market requires such incentives for innovation or might innovate effectively without it, but a considerable fraction of economists take the view that patent and copyright protections can play an important role in fostering innovation.

One can look at our picture of a monopolistically competitive firm in equilibrium as in panel (b) of Graph 26.4 and panel (c) of Graph 26.5, however, and come to a very different conclusion. Each firm in such an equilibrium is producing a quantity below the intersection of demand and MC, which implies that in principle the firm could be forced to generate additional social surplus by increasing production and lowering price. The firm is, after all, a monopoly even as it operates in a competitive environment in which its equilibrium profit including fixed costs is held to zero through competition. The equilibrium picture does not, in this case, tell the full story.

Imagine, for instance, that a new drug has come on the market and that this drug is considerably more effective than existing drugs at treating a particular disease for some patients. By granting the pharmaceutical company a patent on this drug, it is granted some monopoly power, and this will result in a level of production that looks suboptimal in our graphs. The pressure to tell the firm it has to lower price and increase output in order to treat more patients whose benefits from using the drug outweigh the marginal cost of producing it might be considerable. If this is done, there might be a lowering of the incentive for firms to engage in innovations that lead to new and better drugs because such firms would reasonably expect that they will similarly be forced into lower profits than they can obtain under patent protection. As a result, patent and copyright laws attempt to strike a balance between (1) providing an incentive for new innovations through the establishment of monopoly power for n years and (2) the underproduction that takes place during those n years in the absence of other innovations that supersede the initial innovation. Increasing n provides greater incentives for innovations but also increases the period of time during which too little of the good is produced. As a result, there must exist some n between zero, where no patent is granted, and infinity, where the patent protection lasts forever, that makes the trade-off in an optimal way. Some recent work on patents and innovation suggests that the patent laws that have evolved over time do a pretty good job of striking the right balance by setting n in the range of 14 to 20 years. Not everyone, however, agrees, with some proposing that n could be set much closer to zero without any appreciable decline in product innovation.

Exercise 26A.13

Many of the advocates for lowering n in patent laws draw on the burst of innovation in open source software communities. Can you see why?

26A.4.4 Innovation in Real-World Markets The concept of equilibrium is useful in providing a benchmark towards which the market is striving in the absence of new changes. We also know that markets never actually reach a stable equilibrium from which they no longer deviate because they are subject to new variables constantly entering the mix. This is the case in many of the most interesting real-world markets in which innovation plays an important role.

The software industry, for instance, is made up of many producers who are constantly attempting to gain an edge in an intensely competitive environment by producing the next software package that will bring just a bit more market power. New firms come out with new software that chips away at demand for existing software, and existing firms find new innovations to their products that chip away at the demand for products produced by competitors. In terms of our model, these firms are constantly engaged in ways of trying to get their demand curves to have higher intercepts and steeper slopes to get more market power, but competitors and new firms are doing the same thing. The software market is not in a static equilibrium in which an existing set of firms produce an existing set of products, with potential new firms unable to make positive profits from entering. The market is, from a static perspective, in disequilibrium as new innovations move demand curves for each firm's products and some firms gain temporary market power while others are left behind. Successful firms in this dynamic environment are those that keep innovating and thus keep finding better ways of meeting consumer demand or lower cost ways of producing existing products.

There are markets that are considerably more mature and stable, in which the likely gains from innovation are small and which have settled into a state that resembles our static equilibrium models much more. Some of these are perfectly competitive, with each firm producing essentially the same product and pricing at MC as our perfectly competitive model predicts. Semi-skimmed milk, for example, is semi-skimmed milk, and most of us cannot tell the difference between different semi-skimmed milk regardless of which company produces it. Other markets are monopolistically competitive with little new innovation to disturb the static equilibrium. Cereal comes in many different forms and shapes, with limited prospect for innovation disturbing the equilibrium, at least to the extent to which parents can keep children from thinking that a picture of a current TV favourite on the cereal box makes for a truly different product worthy of special attention. Other markets might be more appropriately characterized as relatively stable oligopolies with high fixed entry costs and some product differentiation. Only a handful of companies are producing cars, and these differ in the features they offer consumers. Innovation does take place, and sometimes these innovations, such as the development of driverless vehicles, are quite dramatic and might truly disturb the static equilibrium our models predict. Other times the innovations are, perhaps, sufficiently minor to allow us to continue to think of the industry as being in a roughly stable equilibrium.

All markets, as we have seen, add to human welfare, at least as economists think of welfare, by producing social surplus – sometimes at efficient levels and at other times not – for consumers, workers and owners of firms. Mature markets that have reached a state that can be approximated by our static equilibrium models do so in a way in which a constant amount of surplus is produced. Markets that are characterized by innovations, however, add *additional* surplus through the creation of new products that change the way we live. For example, the development of compact discs in the mid-1980s presented a different way to listen to music than cassettes that degrade or LPs that can easily be scratched or 8-track cartridges which consumers never really took to. Now many people will forego CDs in favour of listening to music in digital format and can carry thousands of songs on a smart phone or stream their music via the Internet. Because of innovation, people can now carry more high quality music in their pockets than people used to be able to listen to in a lifetime. New medical innovations are extending lives while improving the quality of life; new ways of transporting goods allow people to experience aspects of the world they could previously only experience through costly travelling; the internet is constantly creating new ways of accessing information previously contained only in distant libraries.

The point is to illustrate the powerful force that innovation represents in the real world, and to further point out that our equilibrium models of different market structures suffer from not really being able to capture this innovative process very well. We are good at finding ways of representing stable equilibria that have emerged in mature industries with low marginal gains from innovation, but we need to think beyond the static models to understand less mature industries with large marginal gains from innovation. Well-managed firms in mature industries maintain surplus generated by previous innovations, but innovative entrepreneurial firms generate new ways of producing surplus, both now and in the future.

26A.5 Advertising and Marketing

So far, we have always assumed that consumers are aware of the types of goods offered in the market and the prices that firms are charging for those goods. We have also assumed that consumers understand how they themselves feel about the physical characteristics of goods that they consider consuming. When these assumptions are violated, firms have reason to think about not only producing goods but also engaging in advertising and marketing.

We can distinguish between two views of advertising – *informational advertising* and *image marketing*. The informational advertising view emerges from the economist's typical assumption that consumers are rational but may lack information. The image marketing view finds its roots more in psychology where consumer rationality is called into question and the possibility of firms manipulating the irrational aspect of consumers by altering the image of the product rather than the product itself becomes a real possibility. Drawing this distinction of views as one arising from the economist's and the other arising from the psychologist's perspective is not to say that there are not economists who take the psychology view of advertising. Famous and highly regarded economists such as Paul Samuelson (1915–2009), one of the first winners of the Nobel Prize in Economics, and John Kenneth Galbraith (1908–2006), one of the most influential economists and public intellectuals of the 20th century, have taken the latter view. The image marketing view of advertising fits well into this chapter because it views advertising as a way for firms to create artificial product differentiation when the products themselves are really not all that different.

26A.5.1 Informational Advertising Suppose that consumers are rational in the sense that they have complete and transitive preferences over differentiated goods, but that they do not have perfect information about the prices and the types of goods that are offered by firms. Without introducing a formal model, we can see how advertising under these assumptions might play a socially useful purpose. In the absence of such advertising, firms enjoy protection from competition to the extent to which some consumers are unaware of the existence of competitors or the prices charged by competitors. If advertising is prohibited, as it is for goods like cigarettes in some countries, the market is less competitive than it could be and thus leaves firms with more market power than they otherwise would have. Such market power can result in deadweight losses as firms restrict output to raise price.

When advertising is permitted in such markets, individual firms have an incentive to advertise because, regardless of what other firms do, a firm will gain more customers if it makes sure more consumers know about its products and prices. If each firm individually has an incentive to engage in informative advertising, all firms will do so and, in the end, they will split the market in roughly the same proportion as in the absence of advertising, only now they face more competition because consumers are more aware of competitors' products. The advertising itself is costly and therefore gets incorporated into prices, but it is quite conceivable in many circumstances that the upward pressure on prices from increased costs will be outweighed by the downward pressure from increased competition. *Informational advertising of this kind can, at least in principle, generate additional social surplus.* Formal models have confirmed this, with some predicting that the equilibrium amount of advertising in such settings is socially optimal as we will see in a special case discussed in Section B.

Exercise 26A.14

Consider an oligopoly with consumers being only partially aware of each firm's products and prices, and suppose that firms in the oligopoly decide to engage in informational advertising. In what sense might they be facing a Prisoner's Dilemma?

Exercise 26A.15

Suppose you hear that an industry group is attempting to persuade the government to ban advertising in its industry. Given your answer to exercise 26A.13, might you be suspicious of the industry group's motives?

26A.5.2 Image Marketing: Advertising as a Means to Manipulate Preferences Now suppose that advertising is not used to convey information but to manipulate preferences by shaping the image of what we consider the real underlying product. While we have just seen that informational advertising can increase competition in markets that are not perfectly competitive, the alternative of image marketing can do the reverse: restrain competition in markets that are quite competitive. For this reason, those who believe this is the correct view of advertising generally believe it is socially wasteful.

The logic behind their argument is straightforward. Suppose firms in a particular industry face intense competition. Perhaps the industry is perfectly competitive, or perhaps it consists of only two firms that are engaged in fierce Bertrand price competition with undifferentiated products. Each firm in such settings has an incentive to set its goods apart from the crowd through product differentiation. In the rest of the chapter, we have assumed that such product differentiation means actually producing a product with different characteristics. A firm might instead find it more cost effective if consumers exhibit some irrationality to artificially differentiate its product by shaping its image rather than changing its underlying characteristics. Cereal companies are famous for this in their marketing to children. Take the same cereal and package it in a box that has the latest craze on it, and it becomes a lot more desirable. The product inside the box has not changed but the way that the relevant consumers feel about the cereal has been artificially altered. In the process, the cereal company has gained some market power as it has deputized an army of children to pester their parents to buy its product even at a higher price. Social losses arise from both the decrease in competition and the cost incurred by the cereal company to engage in this form of advertising.

Many economists might argue that they can see how this form of advertising leaves the actual product unchanged while increasing market power and creating socially wasteful advertising expenditures. On the other hand, some would recognize that this view assumes they know better than the consumers what the product actually is. It could be argued that the product *has* changed in the eyes of children who suddenly want it. These children care about not only the type of cereal inside the box but also the box itself. By taking the view that a different design on the box does not change the product unless the cereal itself is different, we are taking the paternalistic view that what is on the cereal box *should not* change the way children feel about the product. Some economists have a tendency to respect consumer sovereignty in the sense of accepting consumer tastes without making value judgments.

If we carry the economist's respect for consumer sovereignty to its extreme, the distinction between informational advertising and advertising intended to manipulate preferences largely disappears. Consider two different ways in which a cereal company might differentiate its product. First, the company might increase the amount of raisins in the cereal, thus altering the physical characteristics of the cereal itself, and it might launch an informational advertising campaign that informs consumers that its cereal now has two scoops of raisins rather than one. Second, the company might instead put a Marvel comics character on its cereal box and advertise that its product now displays this popular character. Both advertising campaigns provide information about a change in the product to consumers, with the product defined as the cereal inside the box under the first campaign and as the combination of the cereal and the box in the other. Saying that the latter conveys no useful information while the former does is the same as saying that we take the position that the box itself is not a legitimate product characteristic for consumers to consider in their decision process while the quantity of raisins is. Both advertising campaigns will succeed only to the extent to which consumers themselves believe the emphasized product characteristics are legitimate to consider in decision making. If no one cares about raisins in cereal but many people care about the appearance of the cereal box, consumers are saying that the box is an important characteristic for them while the raisins are not. If we take this less paternalistic view about what product characteristics are legitimate means for product differentiation, we should place social value on the enthusiastic reception the character on the box generates in children. If so, it is far from obvious that advertising that shapes the image of the cereal is necessarily more socially wasteful than advertising that informs consumers of the fact that the cereal now has two rather than one scoop of raisins in it.

The distinction between informational advertising and image marketing is blurred and involves normative judgment calls about what should be. The study of image marketing has recently become important in behavioural economics which attempts to blend traditional economic modelling with insights from psychology and neuroscience.

26A.5.3 Distinguishing Informational Advertising From Image Marketing in the Real World To the extent to which we acknowledge a difference between informational advertising and image marketing, is there a way to tell what kind of advertising is actually taking place? Consider what we typically see advertised in newspapers versus that advertised on television. In local newspaper advertisements, shops may advertise that they have particular products at particular prices. This conveys real information to consumers on which they will sometimes act. Knowing that a local shop is selling a particular digital camera and offering it at an attractive price tells the consumer something useful, particularly if the same newspaper has an advert from another shop in the area of the same product being sold at a higher price. Much of newspaper advertising appears to have at least some informational content for consumers who cannot possibly be aware of all the choices they have in their local market.

Now consider the typical television advertisement. These adverts rarely give any information about price, but other adverts tell consumers about products such as Coke and Pepsi that they are familiar with already. What possible reason is there for Coke to advertise its product, without announcing any new price or some new Coke variety, unless it is to shape the image of Coke in a way that makes the consumer more likely to choose it over Pepsi? Does knowing that a high profile celebrity drinks Coke or Pepsi make any difference to the way Coke and Pepsi tastes, or does it convey any useful information about the taste of Coke and Pepsi, particularly when consumers are aware that they are paid handsomely to appear in the commercial?

Coke and Pepsi ads on television might be argued to represent a clear case that the purpose of the adverts is primarily to shape the image of the product that people consume, whereas newspaper adverts might more easily fall into the informational advertising category. There are the cases that lie in between, with information and image being melded by creative marketing firms. What if a high profile sports star has agreed to say on TV that they like a particular athletic shoe, after getting paid millions to do so, and that part of their contract is that they will wear that shoe in all the games or events they take part in? It can be argued that there is image marketing in such instances, but also some real information being conveyed since the sports star presumably would not agree easily to wear a shoe that handicaps their performance in competition. As is often the case in the real world, our abstract categories of, in this case, informational advertising and image marketing often flow together in practice.

26B   Mathematical Modelling of Differentiated Product Markets

26B.1 Differentiated Products in Oligopoly Markets

In Section A, we discussed the example of Coke and Pepsi, which, in the minds of many consumers, are sufficiently differentiated products that they prefer one over the other all else being equal, while at the same time being willing to substitute one for the other if the prices are sufficiently different. When Coke and Pepsi serve a similar market but nevertheless are somewhat distinct goods in the minds of consumers, the demand for each of the two products depends on both the price for Coke and the price for Pepsi. We can represent the demand for good x_i by $x_i(p_i, p_j)$ if there are two firms in the oligopoly. Firm I, which produces x_i, will have to take p_j as given when it selects its price p_i to solve the optimization problem:

$$\max_{p_i} \pi_i = (p_i - c)x_i(p_i, p_j), \tag{26.1}$$

where c represents constant marginal cost of production. Suppose firm i sets $p_i = c$. If the resulting demand for its goods, $x_i(c, p_j)$, is greater than zero, we know that it can do better by setting a price higher than marginal cost. This is because we know the firm's profit will be zero if $p_i = c$ but strictly higher, assuming $x_i(p_i, p_j)$ is continuously downward sloping in p_i, if price is raised just a bit above marginal cost.

To make things a bit more concrete, suppose that Coke and Pepsi face demands for their products that take the form:

$$x_i = A - \alpha p_i + \beta p_j \text{ where } \alpha > \beta. \tag{26.2}$$

Exercise 26B.1

Can you think of why it is reasonable to assume $\alpha > \beta$?

Demand for Coke falls as Coke increases its price but rises if Pepsi increases its price, and similarly, the demand for Pepsi falls as the price of Pepsi increases but rises as the price of Coke increases. Each firm faces a profit-maximization problem of the form:

$$\max_{p_i} \pi_i = (p_i - c)(A - \alpha p_i + \beta p_j). \tag{26.3}$$

Solving the first-order conditions for p_i, we get firm i's best-response function given p_j,

$$p_i(p_j) = \frac{A + \alpha c + \beta p_j}{2\alpha}. \tag{26.4}$$

since the two firms are symmetric, firm j's best response to p_i, $p_j(p_i)$ is the same with i and j in equation (26.4) reversed.

Exercise 26B.2

Suppose $P_j = 0$. Interpret the resulting best price response for firm i in light of what we derived as the optimal monopoly quantity and price when $x = A - \alpha p$.

Substituting $p_j(p_i)$ into $p_i(p_j)$ and solving for p_i, we get:

$$p_1^* = \frac{A + \alpha c}{2\alpha - \beta} = p_j^*, \tag{26.5}$$

which is larger than marginal cost c as long as $c < A/(\alpha - \beta)$.

Exercise 26B.3

Before going to our concrete example, we argued that Bertrand competition will lead to prices above marginal cost when $x_i(c, p_j) > 0$. In our example, we find that in equilibrium $p > c = MC$ as long as $c < A/(\alpha - \beta)$. Can you reconcile the general conclusion with the conclusion from the example?

26B.2 Hotelling's Model With Quadratic Costs

We have shown that price competition in oligopolies does not reach the initially predicted ferocity that leads to prices being equal to marginal cost when products produced by the firms in the oligopoly are differentiated. In light of this, it may be more realistic to model oligopolists who engage in price competition as having two strategic variables: price and product characteristics. The model we began to develop in Section A for this purpose is the Hotelling model that is aimed at investigating precisely such situations.

Recall that this model assumes product characteristics y could take on any value in the interval $[0, 1]$ and that each consumer $n \in [0, 1]$ had some ideal product characteristic n. Suppose that the cost a consumer n pays for consuming the product with characteristic y is $\alpha(n - y)^2$ in addition to the price the consumer has to pay for the product, and that the cost a consumer incurs for consuming away from their ideal product is quadratic in the distance of the product from their ideal point. We will now ask what equilibrium to expect in a two-stage game in which two firms simultaneously choose their product characteristics y_1 and y_2 followed by a second stage in which they simultaneously choose the product prices p_1 and p_2 knowing the product characteristics that were chosen in the first stage.

Note that demand for each firm's output can be calculated for any combination of prices and product characteristics by identifying the consumer $\bar{n}$ who is indifferent between purchasing from firm 1 and firm 2, with everyone to the left of $\bar{n}$ purchasing from the firm whose product characteristic lies to the left of $\bar{n}$ and everyone to the right of $\bar{n}$ purchasing from the other firm. Suppose, for instance, that $y_1 \leq y_2$. The consumer $\bar{n}$ who is indifferent between the firms is that consumer for whom the effective price of purchasing from firm 1 is equal to their effective price of purchasing from firm 2; that is, $\bar{n}$ is such that:

$$p_1 + \alpha(\bar{n} - y_1)^2 = p_2 + \alpha(\bar{n} - y_2)^2, \tag{26.6}$$

which we can solve to get:

$$\bar{n} = \frac{(p_2 - p_1) + \alpha(y_2^2 - y_1^2)}{2\alpha(y_2 - y_1)} = \frac{y_2 + y_1}{2} + \frac{(p_2 - p_1)}{2\alpha(y_2 - y_1)}. \tag{26.7}$$

Since everyone in the interval $[0, \bar{n}]$ will consume from firm 1, expression (26.7) also represents the fraction of consumer demand that goes to firm 1. Adding y_1 and subtracting $2y_1/2$ from the right-hand side, we can rewrite this as:

$$D^1(p_1, p_2, y_1, y_2) = y_1 + \frac{y_2 - y_1}{2} + \frac{(p_2 - p_1)}{2\alpha(y_2 - y_1)} \tag{26.8}$$

with the remaining demand $(1 - \bar{n})$ from interval $[\bar{n}, 1]$ equal to demand for firm 2's output. After some algebraic manipulation similar to what we did to derive D^1, we can write demand for firm 2's output as:

$$D^2(p_1, p_2, y_1, y_2) = 1 - \bar{n} = (1 - y_2) + \frac{y_2 - y_1}{2} + \frac{(p_1 - p_2)}{2\alpha(y_2 - y_1)}. \tag{26.9}$$

Exercise 26B.4

Derive the right-hand side of equation (26.9).

26B.2.1 Stage 2: Setting Prices Given Product Characteristics To solve for the subgame perfect equilibrium, we begin in the second stage when firms already know the product characteristic chosen by each firm in the first stage. Let these product characteristics be denoted by y_1 and y_2 respectively, and without loss of generality, assume that $y_1 \leq y_2$. In the simultaneous price-setting game of the second stage, we need to calculate the best-response functions for each firm to the price set by the other firm. To calculate firm 1's best price response function to prices set by firm 2, for instance, we need to choose p_1 to maximize firm 1's profit $\pi^1 = (p_1 - c)D^1(p_1, p_2, y_1, y_2)$, where c is constant marginal cost and where p_2, y_2 and y_1 are taken as fixed by the firm. Substituting equation (26.8) in for D^1, we can write the problem as:

$$\max_{p_1} (p_1 - c)\left(y_1 + \frac{y_2 - y_1}{2} + \frac{(p_2 - p_1)}{2\alpha(y_2 - y_1)}\right). \tag{26.10}$$

Solving the first-order condition for this problem, we get firm 1's best-response function:

$$p_1(p_2) = \frac{p_2}{2} + \frac{c + \alpha(y_2^2 - y_1^2)}{2}. \tag{26.11}$$

Going through the same steps for firm 2, we can similarly derive firm 2's best-response function to p_1 as:

$$p_2(p_1) = \frac{p_1}{2} + \frac{c - \alpha(y_2^2 - y_1^2) + 2\alpha(y_2 - y_1)}{2}. \tag{26.12}$$

Exercise 26B.5

Set up firm 2's optimization problem and verify the best-response function $p_2(p_2)$.

In order for the price-setting game to be in equilibrium, these best-response functions have to intersect. Substituting equation (26.12) into (26.11), we can solve for the equilibrium price for firm 1:

$$p_1^*(y_1, y_2) = c + \alpha\left(\frac{y_2^2 - y_1^2 + 2(y_2 - y_1)}{3}\right), \tag{26.13}$$

and substituting this into equation (26.12) we get the equilibrium price for firm 2:

$$p_2^*(y_1, y_2) = c + \alpha\left(\frac{y_1^2 - y_2^2 + 4(y_2 - y_1)}{3}\right), \tag{26.14}$$

26B.2.2 Stage 1: Selecting Product Characteristics In stage 1 of the game, firms know the prices that will emerge in stage 2 conditional on the product characteristics that are set in stage 1. Firm 1 thus chooses y_1 taking as given firm 2's choice of y_2 as well as $P_1^*(y_1, y_2)$ and $P_2^*(y_1, y_2)$ that will result in stage 2 of the game. To obtain firm 1's subgame perfect best-response function in stage 1, we solve:

$$\max_{y_1} \pi^1 = (p_1^*(y_1, y_2) - c)D^1(y_1; y_2, p_1^*(y_1, y_2), p_2^*(y_1, y_2)), \tag{26.15}$$

which can, given equation (26.8), be written as:

$$\max_{y_1} \pi^1 = (p_1^*(y_1, y_2) - c)\left[y_1 + \frac{y_2 - y_1}{2} + \frac{(p_2^*(y_1, y_2) - p_1^*(y_1, y_2))}{2\alpha(y_2 - y_1)}\right]. \tag{26.16}$$

An implicit constraint given the model we have defined is that $0 \le y_1 \le y_2 \le 1$, and this constraint complicates the mechanics of undertaking the optimization problem because of the presence of inequality constraints that make our usual Lagrange method inapplicable. An Excel spreadsheet can be set up and used to calculate different profits for firm 1 depending on the level of y_2 and what choice firm 1 makes regarding y_2. This is done in Table 26.1 where, for different levels of $y_2 \geq 0.5$ in the top row, the profit firm 1 makes for different choices of y_1 is given. (We do not have to consider the cases for $y_2 < 0.5$ since we have assumed $y_1 \leq y_2$ and that is not compatible with $y_2 < 0.5$.)

Exercise 26B.6

Explain the last sentence in parentheses.

Table 26.1 Firm 1's Profit When $c = 5$, $\alpha = 10$ (Assuming $y_1 \leq y_2$)

Setting Product Characteristics in First Stage

y_1	$y_2 = 0.5$	$y_2 = 0.6$	$y_2 = 0.7$	$y_2 = 0.8$	$y_2 = 0.9$	$y_2 = 1.0$
1.0						0.0000
0.9					0.0000	0.8450
0.8				0.0000	0.7606	1.6044
0.7			0.0000	0.6806	1.4400	2.2817
0.6		0.0000	0.6050	1.2844	2.0417	2.8800
0.5	0.0000	0.5339	1.1378	1.8150	2.5689	3.4028
0.4	0.4672	1.0000	1.6017	2.2756	3.0250	3.8533
0.3	0.8711	1.4017	2.0000	2.6694	3.4133	4.2350
0.2	1.2150	1.7422	2.3361	3.0000	3.7372	4.5511
0.1	1.5022	2.0250	2.6133	3.2706	4.0000	4.8050
0.0	1.7361	2.2533	2.8350	3.4844	4.2050	5.0000

Since firm 1's only choice variable in stage 1 is its own product characteristic y_1 we can trace out firm 1's best-response function in stage 1 of the game by looking down each column to see where firm 1 makes its highest profit. What can be seen is that regardless of what product characteristic y_2 is chosen by firm 2, firm 1 best responds by choosing $y_1 = 0$. Were we to trace out a symmetric table for firm 2's profits given choices of y_1 by firm 1, we would similarly find that firm 2's best response, given that we are assuming $y_1 \leq y_1$, is always to set $y_2 = 1$. Thus, the equilibrium product characteristics that emerge are characterized by *maximal product differentiation*; the two firms choose to select product characteristics that are as far apart as possible because they know that this will serve to minimize price competition in the second stage.

Exercise 26B.7

Suppose we do not restrict y_1 to be less than y_2. Given what we have done, can you plot the two firms' best-response functions to the product characteristics chosen by the other firm and illustrate the stage 1 pure strategy equilibria? How many such equilibria are there? *Hint*: Once the restriction that $y_1 \leq y_2$ is removed, there are two pure strategy equilibria.

Now that we know that the firms choose $y_1 = 0$ and $y_2 = 1$ in the first stage, we can substitute these into equations (26.13) and (26.14) to calculate the equilibrium prices that emerge as:

$$p_1^* = p_2^* = c + \alpha. \tag{26.17}$$

Recall the only place α enters the problem: it defines how large a cost $\alpha(n - y)^2$, in addition to price, a consumer pays when consuming a product that is not their ideal. As α goes to zero, the cost consumers incur from not consuming their ideal disappears, as does the firms' ability to make profit from differentiating their products. As α increases, on the other hand, consumers care more about being close to their ideal point, and firms are able to take advantage of this through product differentiation that allows them to charge price above marginal cost.

Exercise 26B.8

Can you plot the two firms' best-response functions in stage 2 of the game given that $y_1 = 0$ and $y_2 = 1$ were chosen in the first stage? Label slopes and intercepts. Are these prices the same for the two pure strategy equilibria in stage 1 that you identified in exercise 26B.7?

26B.2.3 **Comparing Oligopoly Product Innovation to Optimal Differentiation** In the Hotelling model with quadratic costs of deviating from the ideal product characteristic for consumers, we can ask how the oligopoly equilibrium compares to what a social planner would do if they were limited to only selecting two product characteristics to be produced. Note that quadratic costs of the type we have modelled imply that the *marginal* cost of deviating from a consumer's ideal point is increasing with distance from the ideal point. This implies that the optimal level of product differentiation minimizes the *average* distance between consumers' ideal points and their closest product characteristics, which allow us to determine the optimal level of product differentiation when consumer ideal points are uniformly distributed along the interval [0, 1].

In particular, the social planner will minimize this *average* distance by locating product characteristics. This is done when the social planner locates product characteristics halfway in between the midpoint and the extremes of the interval [0, 1] to both sides of the midpoint; that is, when the social planner sets $y_1 = 0.25$ and $y_2 = 0.75$. To see how this is more efficient than the equilibrium outcome, compare the situation where $(y_1, y_2) = (0, 1)$ to the situation where $(y_1, y_2) = (0.25, 0.75)$ assuming there exists a consumer at every point in the interval [0, 1]. In both cases, consumers in the interval [0, 0.5] buy from firm 1 and consumers in the interval [0.5, 1] buy from firm 2, with consumer 0.5 indifferent between the two firms, but the overall cost incurred by consumers is lower when there is less than extreme product differentiation. In what follows, we use an integral to illustrate this.

When $(y_1, y_2) = (0, 1)$ consumer $n \in [0, 0.5]$ incurs a cost αn^2 when shopping at $y_1 = 0$. Since the first and second halves of the [0, 1] interval are symmetric, we can derive the overall cost incurred by consumers when $(y_1, y_2) = (0, 1)$ as:

$$2\int_0^{0.5} \alpha n^2 dn = \frac{\alpha}{12}. \tag{26.18}$$

When $(y_1, y_2) = (0.25, 0.75)$, on the other hand, consumers in the interval [0, 0.25] incur costs symmetric to consumers in each of the other three quarters of the [0, 1] interval, implying that we can express the total cost to consumers as:

$$4\int_0^{0.25} \alpha n^2 dn = \frac{\alpha}{48}. \tag{26.19}$$

The oligopolists engage in socially *excessive product differentiation* because they strategically use product differentiation to dampen price competition.

Exercise 26B.9

Suppose that instead of being quadratic as we have modelled them here, the cost that consumer n pays for consuming a product with characteristic $y \neq n$ is linear; that is, suppose that this cost is $\alpha|n - y|$ where $|n - y|$ represents the distance between y and n. If the two oligopolists engage in maximal product differentiation, that is, $y_1 = 0$ and $y_2 = 1$, is that product differentiation still socially excessive? Note that in this exercise we are *assuming* that firms still choose $y_1 = 0$ and $y_2 = 1$ in the first stage. This is not an equilibrium under the linear cost model. The reason we assumed quadratic costs is because under the linear cost model there does not exist a pure strategy equilibrium but only a mixed strategy equilibrium.

26B.3 Firm Entry and Product Differentiation

The Hotelling model works well for thinking about competition between two firms in an oligopoly when such firms have the opportunity to engage in product differentiation. Many markets in the real world are not oligopolistic because there are no strict barriers to entry of potential firms, only a fixed entry cost. We now turn towards considering such markets and will assume that the only barrier to entry that exists is a fixed set-up cost FC. Once that cost is paid, it is a sunk cost, but potential entrants consider this cost as they determine whether it is worth entering a particular market in which product differentiation is possible.

We assume that consumers have different tastes as represented by different ideal points in terms of a product characteristic. However, once we proceed to cases where there might be more than two firms, it is more natural to define the product characteristic space in such a way that there is no natural advantage to any particular location within that space. The line segment $[0, 1]$ in the Hotelling model does not satisfy this requirement since locations near the centre naturally grant more access to consumers than locations at the extremes. For this reason, we now define product characteristics to lie on a circle and assume, without loss of generality, that the circumference of the circle is 1 as first illustrated in panel (b) Graph 26.1.

As in Section A, we can think of the following two-stage game. In the first stage, potential firms that face a fixed entry cost of FC and a marginal production cost of c decide whether or not to enter. It seems reasonable to assume that the firms that enter will locate along the circle of product characteristics equally distant from one another, and we therefore assume this from the start rather than modelling both the entry decision and the location decision on the circle. This is actually not a trivial matter. A fuller game might consist of three stages in which firms first decide *whether* to enter the market, decide *where* to locate in terms of product characteristics and finally decide what price to charge. In the second stage, firms strategically choose the price they charge for their product knowing where within the product characteristic circle all competitors have located. As in the Hotelling model, we will make the further simplifying assumption that consumers whose ideal points are uniformly distributed around the circle are only interested in purchasing a single unit of the good. We will assume that the effective price that consumers pay for a good is equal to the price that is charged plus a linear function of the distance of the consumer's ideal point from the product's characteristic; that is, the effective price for a consumer with ideal point n consuming from a firm with product characteristic y_1 that charges p_i is $p_i + \alpha|n - y_i|$ where $|n - y_i|$ represents the distance along the circle between n and y_i. This is in contrast to our treatment of the Hotelling model where we assumed quadratic costs of consuming away from one's ideal point.

26B.3.1 Stage 2: Setting Prices In order to determine the equilibrium prices that emerge once the number of firms and their locations have been determined in stage 1, we need to specify the demand for a firm's product as a function of the price it sets. In equilibrium, it will have to be the case that all firms charge the same price. Consider firm i's best response to all other firms charging a price p, and consider firm j that is adjacent on the circle to firm i in terms of product characteristics. A consumer whose ideal point $\bar{n}$ lies between y_i and y_j is indifferent between consuming from firm i and firm j if its effective price is the same for products from the two firms; that is, if:

$$p_i + \alpha|\bar{n} - y_i| = p + \alpha|y_j - \bar{n}|. \tag{26.20}$$

Suppose we let, without loss of generality, $y_i = 0$. If there are N firms in the market and all neighbouring firms are equally distant from one another along the circle with circumference 1, $y_j = 1/N$. Substituting this into equation (26.20), the equation becomes:

$$p_i + \alpha\bar{n} = p + \alpha\left(\frac{1}{N} - \bar{n}\right). \tag{26.21}$$

Solving this for $\bar{n}$, we get:

$$\bar{n} = \frac{p - p_i}{2\alpha} + \frac{1}{2N}. \tag{26.22}$$

Thus, given firm i's choice of p_i and given all other firms choose p, all consumers whose ideal points along the circle are located between y_i and $\bar{n}$ will consume from firm i. Because of the symmetry along the circle, the same is true for consumers whose ideal point lies to the other side of y, which implies that demand for firm i's output is $2\bar{n}$; that is:

$$D^i(p_i, p) = 2\bar{n} = \frac{p - p_i}{\alpha} + \frac{1}{N}. \tag{26.23}$$

To determine firm i's best-response price to other firms choosing p, we have to solve the problem:

$$\max_{p_i} \pi^i = (p_i - c)D^i(p_i, p) = (p_i - c)\left(\frac{p - p_i}{\alpha} + \frac{1}{N}\right). \tag{26.24}$$

Exercise 26B.10

Why does the fixed entry cost FC not enter this problem? If you did include it in the definition of profit, would it make any difference?

Taking the first-order condition and solving for p_i, we get firm i's best-response function to other firms charging p as:

$$p_i(p) = \frac{p + c}{2} + \frac{\alpha}{2N}. \tag{26.25}$$

Exercise 26B.11

Verify $p_i(p)$.

In equilibrium, all firms have to be best responding to each other, with $p_i(p) = p$. Thus, substituting p for $p_i(p)$ and solving for p, we get the equilibrium price:

$$p^*(N) = c + \frac{\alpha}{N}. \qquad (26.26)$$

Firms will charge prices above marginal cost in the price competition stage, with the mark-up proportional to the degree to which consumers care about consuming near their ideal point, that is α, and inversely proportional to the number of firms in the market. As the number of firms gets large, the mark-up goes to zero and firms charge price equal to MC, and as consumers lose the taste for product differentiation by α going to zero, firms engage in the usual Bertrand competition that drives price to MC.

26B.3.2 Stage 1: Firm Entry Decisions Knowing what prices $p^*(N)$ to expect in the second stage, firms decide in the first stage whether or not to enter the market. Firms will enter as long as the profit from entering including fixed entry cost FC is not negative, which implies that entry should drive profit including fixed entry costs to zero. Thus, the equilibrium number of firms that enter in the first stage is such that each firm makes zero profit when fixed costs are included in the profit calculation; that is, for every firm i that enters:

$$\pi^i = (p^* - c)\, D^i\, (p^*, p^*) - FC = 0. \qquad (26.27)$$

With demand D^i from equation (26.23) collapsing to $1/N$ when p_i is set equal to all other firms' prices, we can substitute p^* from equation (26.26) into this profit function and write the zero profit condition as:

$$\left(c + \frac{\alpha}{N} - c\right)\frac{1}{N} - FC = 0, \qquad (26.28)$$

which implies that the equilibrium number of entering firms N^* is:

$$N^* = \left(\frac{\alpha}{FC}\right)^{1/2}, \qquad (26.29)$$

and the equilibrium price from the second stage of the game becomes:

$$p^* = c + (\alpha FC)^{1/2}. \qquad (26.30)$$

Exercise 26B.12

Verify p^* and N^*.

In equilibrium, we expect the number of firms to increase as the fixed entry cost falls and as consumers care more about consuming close to their ideal point that is, as α increases. Furthermore, the mark-up above marginal cost will increase as consumers care more about being close to their ideal point and as fixed entry costs go up. If fixed entry costs disappear, all barriers to entry have been removed and the market becomes perfectly competitive. The result is what our perfectly competitive model predicts: a large number of small firms, each charging $p = MC$. As described in Section A, this circle model allows us to fully fill in the gap between perfect monopoly and perfect competition when price is the strategic variable for firms in the industry.

26B.3.3 Comparing the Number of Firms to the Optimal As in the Hotelling model, we predict that firms will engage in strategic product differentiation. We found in the Hotelling model that in the case of two oligopolistic firms differentiating their products, we predict socially excessive product differentiation, with a social planner, who is restricted to using only two firms, producing products that are more similar to one another than what occurs in equilibrium. In the case of differentiated firm entry as analyzed in this section, it is similarly true that a socially excessive degree of product differentiation emerges, but this time because too many firms enter the market.

To demonstrate this, we need to ask what our benevolent social planner would want to consider as they choose the number of firms for this industry. First, the planner would consider the fact that a fixed cost FC has to be paid for every one of the firms that enters the market, for a total of $N(FC)$ in fixed costs when the number of firms is set to N. Second, they would want to consider the cost consumers incur from not consuming their ideal product. When there are N firms equally spaced on our circle of product characteristics, each firm serves a fraction $1/N$ of customers, half of whom will come from the firm's 'left' and half from the firm's 'right'. Since we have normalized the circumference of the circle to 1, this implies that the furthest a customer's ideal point will lie from their firm's product y_i is $1/(2N)$ and the closest is 0, with the *average* customer's ideal point lying $1/(4N)$ from y_i. The same is true for customers to the right of y_i. In choosing N, the social planner therefore sets the average cost for consumers at $\alpha/(4N)$ since we have assumed a consumer's cost is α times the distance from their ideal point. When we assume that there is a consumer located at every point on the circle of circumference 1, this implies we have normalized the population size to 1, and thus the total cost to consumers from not consuming at their ideal points is just this average cost of $\alpha/(4N)$. Taking these two factors – the consumer costs and the fixed costs of setting up firms – into account, the social planner who seeks to find the efficient number of firms faces the problem:

$$\min_{N}\left(N(FC) + \frac{\alpha}{4N} \right), \qquad (26.31)$$

which solves to:

$$N^{opt} = \frac{1}{2}\left(\frac{\alpha}{FC} \right)^{1/2}. \qquad (26.32)$$

Note that this is exactly half of what equation (26.29) tells us the actual number of firms N^* will be in equilibrium. Only when fixed costs approach zero and the market becomes perfectly competitive with the number of firms approaching infinity does the social planner solution N^{opt} approach the market solution N^*. We therefore have another model where market power leads to a violation of the first welfare theorem, and the elimination of market power through the elimination of the fixed entry cost implies the first welfare theorem holds under the perfectly competitive conditions that arise from free entry. From a practical standpoint, it is not clear how much policy relevance this has since governments are far from omniscient social planners. However, if governments impose additional fixed costs to entry, such as the costs involved in obtaining copyright or patent protections, such costs might move the market closer to the social optimum.

Exercise 26B.13

In both the Hotelling case and the circle model, we have assumed for convenience that each consumer always just consumes one good from the firm that produces a product closest to their ideal. How does this assumption alleviate us from having to consider the price of output in our efficiency analysis even though we know that firms end up pricing above MC?

26B.4 Monopolistic Competition and Product Diversity

The model of monopolistic competition outlined in Section A is useful in that it helped us tell a story about innovation and product differentiation in a quasi-formal way. As we mentioned at the time, the model dates back to the 1930s and represents an early attempt to model market structures in which firms have market power and set $p > MC$, but no potential entrant can make positive profits by entering because of fixed costs of entry.

More recently, monopolistic competition has received a more modern treatment that will be the focus of this section. Different models of monopolistic competition have been developed over the past few decades. The model described here is due to Avinash Dixit (1944–) and Joseph Stiglitz (1943–) as well as Michael Spence (1943–). Stiglitz and Spence have both won the Nobel Prize in Economics, albeit primarily for their contributions to the economics of asymmetric information and not the work we are featuring here. It differs somewhat from the models in the previous two sections where we began by defining a set of possible product characteristics either along an interval of a line or along a circle on which firms choose to locate their product. In those models, we could talk about the degree of product differentiation between two products as the distance between the product characteristics, and we assumed that consumers can only choose one of the products and will choose the one whose product characteristic is closest to their ideal point. In many markets, consumers actually do not choose just one product type, but rather have a taste for product diversity. Think, for instance, of restaurants. Few of us go to the same restaurant every time we go out, but instead prefer areas with lots of different restaurants we can frequent over time. Product differentiation in such a market cannot really be modelled with the tools we have explored thus far since those tools assumed each consumer will always pick their 'favourite' restaurant.

The model we will present next therefore departs from the assumption that consumers consume only one good and thus choose the one that is closest to their ideal. Rather, we will model consumers as becoming better off the more choices within a market (like restaurants) they have. They will choose to spread their consumption in the differentiated product market across the different types of products offered. A firm i is assumed to produce a single type of product, denoted y_i, and all we will say is that this product is different but somewhat substitutable with other products y_j produced by other firms in the same market. Firm i might, for instance, offer Northern Italian food, while firm j might offer Chinese food. We will abstract away from degrees of product differentiation between two products in the same market and instead consider the entire market as more diversified the more firms it contains. As in the previous sections, we continue to assume that there are many potential firms that could in principle enter the market, but that entry entails payment of a fixed entry cost FC.

26B.4.1 Consumer Preferences for Diversified Products We will denote all the products in the market for y by y_i, with i denoting the firm that produces y_i. Our working assumption will be that the number of firms in the y market is N, and we will find out exactly what N will be in equilibrium. We will also assume that there are many other goods that consumers consume, goods outside the differentiated product market y, and we will represent these with a single composite good x denominated in euro units. Finally, we will assume that we can represent the consumer side of the economy with a representative consumer whose preferences can be captured by a utility function of the form:

$$u\left((x, v(y_1, \ldots, y_N))\right) = u(x, [y_1^{-\rho} + y_2^{-\rho} + \cdots + y_N^{-\rho}]^{-1/\rho}) = u\left(x, \left[\sum_{i=1}^{N} y_i^{-\rho}\right]^{-1/\rho}\right), \qquad (26.33)$$

where $-1 < P < 0$. Functions of this form, which can also be defined using integrals instead of summation signs, are often called *Dixit-Stiglitz utility* functions. You may recall from our consumer theory work that a utility function of the form $v(y_1, y_2, \ldots, y_N) = [y_1^{-p} + y_2^{-p} + \cdots + y_N^{-p}]^{-1/p}$ represents preferences over the y goods that exhibit constant elasticity of substitution (CES) and that the elasticity of substitution σ is given by $\sigma = 1/(1 + p)$. We have therefore constructed preferences in such a way that there exists a CES subutility function v over the y goods, and by restricting p to lie between -1 and 0, we are assuming that the elasticity of substitution of that subutility function lies between ∞ and 1. An infinite elasticity of substitution represents goods that are perfect substitutes, while an elasticity of substitution of 1 represents Cobb–Douglas preferences. We are purposefully restricting the complementarity of the y goods because we are attempting to model a differentiated product market y in which the products are relatively substitutable.

Some of what we will demonstrate will be true for any utility function that takes the form in equation (26.33), but to make the analysis more concrete, we will now work with the following special case:

$$u(x, v(y_1, y_2, \ldots, y_N)) = x^\alpha \left(\left[\sum_{i=1}^{N} y_i^{-p} \right]^{-1/p} \right)^{(1-\alpha)} = x^\alpha \left(\sum_{i=1}^{N} y_i^{-p} \right)^{-(1-\alpha)/p}. \tag{26.34}$$

From the first way in which this equation is written, it can be seen that a CES subutility is embedded over the y goods into a Cobb–Douglas specification, with x taken to the power α and the CES subutility to the power $(1 - \alpha)$.

Exercise 26B.14

What is the elasticity of substitution between x and the subutility over the y goods?

Cobb–Douglas preferences have the feature that when the exponents sum to 1, these exponents represent the share of the consumer's budget that will be spent on the good. Thus, if $\alpha = 0.9$, we know that the consumer will spend €$0.9I$ on the composite x good and €$0.1I$ on all of the y goods together, with I denoting the representative consumer's exogenous income. Furthermore, since each of the y_i goods enters exactly the same way into the subutility function for y goods, the consumer will divide their consumption on the y goods equally among all available N alternatives if these alternatives are equally priced at price $\overline{P}$. Thus, the consumer would choose:

$$x = \alpha I \quad \text{and} \quad y_i = \frac{(1-\alpha)I}{\overline{p}N} \text{(for all } i\text{)}, \tag{26.35}$$

which would give utility:

$$u = (\alpha I)^\alpha \left[N \left(\frac{(1-\alpha)I}{\overline{p}N} \right)^{-p} \right]^{-(1-\alpha)/p} = (\alpha I)^\alpha N^{-(1-\alpha)(1+p)/p} \left[\frac{(1-\alpha)I}{\overline{p}} \right]^{(1-\alpha)}. \tag{26.36}$$

Differentiating this with respect to N gives:

$$\frac{\partial u}{\partial N} = \frac{-(1-\alpha)(1+p)}{p} (\alpha I)^\alpha N^{-[(1-\alpha)(1+p)+p]/p} \left[\frac{(1-\alpha)I}{\overline{p}} \right]^{(1-\alpha)}, \tag{26.37}$$

which is greater than zero when $-1 < p < 0$ as we have assumed. Thus, consumer utility increases as y good expenditures are spread across more differentiated products.

To get a sense of the magnitude of the potential importance of product diversity in this model, Table 26.2 illustrates the impact on the representative consumer's utility as N goes up when we assume that consumers in this market have disposable income of €1 billion, $\alpha = 0.9$ which implies consumers will spend 10 per cent of their income in the differentiated product market and the price charged by each firm in the differentiated product market is $\overline{P} = 100$. In addition, we assume an elasticity of substitution across the y goods of 2 by setting $\rho = -0.5$.

The first row in the table sets the number of differentiated firms N, with the second row deriving the implied number of output units of y, the representative consumer purchases given a price of 100, and given the consumer devotes 10 per cent of their income to all the y goods together. The third row calculates the subutility in the y good market, and the fourth row presents the overall utility for the representative consumer. Finally, the last row derives the percentage reduction in overall income that the consumer would be willing to accept in exchange for the increased diversity in the y market from the baseline case of no product variation when $N = 1$ in the first column. Despite the fact that the representative consumer continues to spend only 10 per cent of income in the y market, the mere increase in the diversity of offerings in that market is worth a lot to this consumer. In particular, the consumer is willing to give up over 20 per cent of income to have 10 firms rather than 1 firm in the y market, 37 per cent to have 100 firms rather than 1 firm, 50 per cent to have 1000 firms rather than 1 firm, and 60 per cent to have 10 000 firms rather than 1 firm. Frequenting many restaurants makes the consumer better off than frequenting only a few even if their overall budget for going to restaurants is the same in both cases.

Table 26.2 $\alpha = 0.9, \rho = -0.5, I = $ €1 billion, $\overline{P} = 100$

Utility as N Changes

N	1	10	100	1000	10 000
y_i (in 10 000s)	10 000	1000	100	10	1
$(v(y_1, ..., y_N))^{(1-\alpha)}$	3.981	5.012	6.310	7.943	10.000
$u(x, y_1, ..., y_N))$ (in millions)	455.85	573.88	722.47	909.53	1145.03
% Equivalent Income	100%	79.43%	63.10%	50.12%	39.81%

26B.4.2 Utility Maximization and Demand The representative consumer faces a budget constraint:

$$x + p_1 y_1 + p_2 y_2 + \cdots + p_N y_N = x + \sum_{i=1}^{N} p_i y_i = I, \tag{26.38}$$

where I represents the representative consumer's exogenous income. We can write the consumer's utility maximization problem as an unconstrained optimization problem in which they choose only the y goods if we assume that the remaining income goes towards the x good by solving equation (26.38) for x and substituting it into the utility function. The resulting optimization problem for the representative consumer can be written as:

$$\max_{y_1, y_2, ..., y_N} u = \left(I - \sum p_i y_i\right)^\alpha \left(\sum y_i^{-\rho}\right)^{-(1-\alpha)/\rho} \tag{26.39}$$

where we have simplified notation a bit by taking it as given that the summations are from $i = 1$ to N. The problem becomes easier to solve if we take a positive monotone transformation of u by taking natural logs, thus rewriting u as $\overline{u}$ in the form:

$$\bar{u} = \alpha \ln\left(I - \sum p_i y_i\right) - \frac{(1-\alpha)}{\rho} \ln\left(\sum y_i^{-\rho}\right). \tag{26.40}$$

The first-order conditions for the resulting optimization problem set the partial derivatives of u with respect to each y_j to zero; that is:

$$\frac{-\alpha p_j}{I - \sum p_i y_i} + \frac{(1-\alpha)\rho y_j^{-(\rho+1)}}{\rho \sum y_i^{-\rho}} = 0 \quad \text{for all} \quad j = 1, 2, \ldots, N. \tag{26.41}$$

We can re-arrange this as:

$$y_j = \left[\frac{(1-\alpha)(I - \sum p_i y_i)}{\alpha \sum y_i^{-\rho}}\right]^{1/(\rho+1)} p_j^{-1/(\rho+1)}. \tag{26.42}$$

Because we are assuming that N is large, y_j has no major impact on the value of the terms in the summation signs, which allows us to approximate equation (26.42) as:

$$y_j(p_j) \approx \beta p_j^{-1/(\rho+1)} \quad \text{where} \quad \beta = \left[\frac{(1-\alpha)(I - \sum p_i y_i)}{\alpha \sum y_i^{-\rho}}\right]^{1/(\rho+1)} \tag{26.43}$$

which represents the representative consumer's approximate demand for good y_j as a function of p_j.

Exercise 26B.15

Demonstrate that the price elasticity of demand for y_j is $-1/(\rho + 1)$.

26B.4.3 Firm Pricing Recall that each of the goods in the y market is produced by a single firm, which means that firm j knows that the demand for *its* output is given by equation (26.43). When determining what price to charge, firm j therefore solves the problem:

$$\max_{p_j} \pi^j = (p_j - c)y_j(p_j) \approx (p_j - c)\beta p_j^{-1/(\rho+1)}. \tag{26.44}$$

Exercise 26B.16

Why do fixed entry costs not enter this problem?

Taking first-order conditions by setting the partial derivative of π^j with respect to p_j to zero, we can solve for p_j charged by firm j for output y_j as:

$$p_j = -\frac{c}{\rho}. \tag{26.45}$$

Recall that we have assumed the y goods are relatively substitutable by assuming $-1 < p < 0$, which implies that p_j in the previous equation is positive and $p_j > c$. Firms therefore charge above marginal cost but as the elasticity of substitution goes to ∞, that is, as p approaches -1, price approaches marginal cost. This complies well with the intuition developed earlier in this chapter that as product differentiation goes to zero with the y goods becoming perfect substitutes, price competition becomes more intense and approaches the undifferentiated products Bertrand result of price equal to marginal cost.

Since each of the firms in the y market faces a similar problem, this price is the price that is charged by all firms in the market; that is, the equilibrium price p^* is:

$$p^* = p_1 = p_2 = \cdots = p_N = -\frac{c}{\rho}. \tag{26.46}$$

26B.4.4 Firm Entry Equilibrium In equilibrium it must be the case that no potential entrant could enter the y market and make a positive profit, and no firm would have entered the market had that meant it made negative profit by entering. The profit from entering the market, which includes the fixed entry cost FC, must be zero even though, once in the market, firms make positive profits because entry costs have become sunk costs. In representative consumer models of this kind, it is typically assumed that the representative consumer is also the owner of all the firms in the economy and thus derives income from firm profits. Since firm profits are zero, however, we can conveniently ignore firm profits as a source of consumer income in the consumer's optimization problem.

This zero entry profit condition can be written as:

$$(p^* - c)y_i = \left(-\frac{c}{\rho} - c\right)y_i = -\left(\frac{1+\rho}{\rho}\right)cy_i = FC, \tag{26.47}$$

which implies that in full equilibrium,

$$y_i = \frac{-\rho}{1+\rho}\left(\frac{FC}{c}\right) = y^* \quad \text{for all} \quad i = 1, 2, \ldots, N. \tag{26.48}$$

The zero profit condition that emerges from entry of firms into the y market implies that firms must supply y^* in the full equilibrium in which there is no further incentive for firms to enter the market. Since we are restricting p to lie between 0 and -1, the term $-p/(1 + p)$ lies between 0 as p approaches 0, and ∞ as p approaches -1. Each firm in the y market produces a positive quantity, with production increasing (1) as the y goods become more substitutable for consumers that is, as p moves from 0 to -1; (2) as fixed entry cost FC increases; and (3) as marginal production costs c decrease.

Exercise 26B.17

Can you give an intuitive explanation for each of the three factors that causes firm output in the y market to increase?

If y^* is produced by each firm and sold at p^* in equilibrium, it must also be the case that the representative consumer demands exactly y^* at p^* for each of the y goods produced in equilibrium. It must be that demand is equal to supply.

The consumer demand in equation (26.42) for each of the y goods was derived from the consumer's optimization problem and thus has to satisfy the first-order condition of that problem in equation (26.41). Since all firms charge the same price p^* and produce the same quantity y^*, we can replace all the p_i and y_i terms in that first-order condition by p^* and y^*. This allows us to simplify the summation terms, with:

$$\sum p_i y_i = Np^* y^* \quad \text{and} \quad \sum y_i^{-\rho} = Ny^{*-\rho}. \tag{26.49}$$

Replacing these summations and substituting in p^* for the remaining p_j terms and y^* for the remaining y_j terms, the first-order condition (26.41) simplifies to:

$$\frac{\alpha p^*}{I - Np^* y^*} = \frac{(1-\alpha)}{Ny^*}, \tag{26.50}$$

which can be solved to yield:

$$N = \frac{(1-\alpha)I}{p^* y^*}. \tag{26.51}$$

Substituting equations (26.46) and (26.48) in for p^* and y^*, this gives us the equilibrium number of firms in the market:

$$N^* = \frac{(1-\alpha)(1+\rho)I}{FC}. \tag{26.52}$$

Thus, once we determined the equilibrium prices p^* charged by firms from the firm optimization problem that takes the consumer's approximate demand function $y_j(p_j)$ as given, we used this to determine the equilibrium quantity y^* produced by each firm by making sure that the zero entry profit condition holds. To ensure that demand is equal to supply, we substituted these into the first-order condition from the consumer problem to solve for the equilibrium number of firms, N^*.

The number of firms in the y market, and thus the amount of product diversity, increases (1) as consumers place more value on y goods, that is, as $(1-\alpha)$ increases; (2) as the y goods become less substitutable, that is, as ρ moves from -1 to 0; (3) as disposable income I increases; and (4) as the fixed entry cost FC falls.

Exercise 26B.18

Can you give an intuitive explanation for each of the four factors that increase product diversity in the y market?

A final observation about the model before we look at a brief example is that you may have noticed that only ρ and the cost parameters c and FC enter the expressions for y^* and p^*. This suggests that these might be independent of the Cobb–Douglas functional form we assumed and might hold for the more general utility function with CES subutility for the y goods we introduced at the beginning of our discussion of monopolistic competition. This is correct. The equilibrium number of firms N^* that we calculated does, however, depend on the Cobb–Douglas specification, although the basic intuitions it brings to light are more general.

26B.4.5 An Example Suppose, for instance, that the y goods represent tables served in restaurants in a city and that consumers in the city have €1 billion in disposable income to allocate between other consumption and eating out in restaurants. Suppose further that we know our consumers spend 10 per cent of disposable income on eating out. We know from our work with Cobb–Douglas preferences that when the Cobb–Douglas exponents sum to 1, the exponent on each good represents the share of a consumer's budget that will be allocated to consumption of that good. Thus, knowing that consumers will spend 10 per cent of their disposable income on eating out means that $(1 - \alpha) = 0.1$, or $\alpha = 0.9$, in the utility function in equation (26.34). On the firm side, suppose that it costs €100 000 to set up a restaurant and that the marginal cost of serving an average table in a restaurant is €100; that is, suppose $FC = €100\,000$ and $c = €100$.

Table 26.3 uses the equations derived to calculate the monopolistically competitive equilibrium under different assumptions about the elasticity of substitution between restaurants. In particular, the first row assumes different values of p that are translated into elasticity of substitution values σ in the second row, where we know from our understanding of CES utility functions that $\sigma = 1/(1 + p)$. The remaining rows report the resulting values for the equilibrium price p^* charged per table in each restaurant, the equilibrium number of tables y^* served in each restaurant, and the equilibrium number of restaurants N^* in the city.

Exercise 26B.19

Verify the values for the column $\rho = -0.5$ in Table 26.3.

Exercise 26B.20

What values in the Table 26.3 change if consumer income rises? What if consumers develop more of a taste for eating out; that is, what if α falls? What if the fixed cost of setting up restaurants increases?

This model of monopolistic competition, with consumer preferences that include a taste for diversity, has come to play an important role in the area of urban economics in which economists attempt to understand the characteristics of modern cities. An understanding of cities requires some appreciation of why it is that people might, all else being equal, want to live towards the centre of cities and why, in equilibrium, only some choose to actually live there. One way to think of this is to think of consumers as wanting, all else being equal, to consume the greater diversity of products that can be offered in geographically dense areas, with people who live further away from dense areas having less access to diversified product markets because of, say, fewer restaurants in suburbs, and having to pay a commuting cost to gain access to products offered in the city. Such models will predict that land prices fall with distance away from the diversified product market in the city, with people trading off more land and housing consumption in the suburbs against less access to diversified consumption possibilities like restaurants. Of course there are other factors that are important as well, such as access to better schools or lower crime rates that may exist in more rural areas. Combining these factors with models of tastes for product diversity can help explain why people might pay higher housing prices to live in cities until they have children, at which time they might choose to move to the suburbs to get access to better schools and larger houses while decreasing the number of times they go out to restaurants.

Table 26.3 $\alpha = 0.9$, $I = €1$ billion, $FC = 100\,000$, $c = 100$					
Equilibrium Prices, Quantities and Number of Firms					
ρ	−0.05	−0.25	−0.50	−0.75	−0.95
σ	1.05	1.33	2.00	4.00	20.00
p^*	€2000.00	€400.00	€200.00	€133.33	€105.26
y^*	52.63	333.33	1000.00	3000.00	19 000.00
N^*	950.00	750.00	500.00	250.00	50.00

26B.5 Advertising and Marketing

In Section 26A.5, we distinguished between two types of advertising that we called informational advertising and image marketing.

26B.5.1 Informational Advertising
Let us consider the simplest possible setting in which to think about informational advertising. Suppose that a market is perfectly competitive with many identical firms producing the same undifferentiated product x at marginal cost c in the absence of any fixed costs. Suppose further that there are n consumers who are also identical, with each willing to pay up to $s > c$ for one unit of x but less than c for any additional units. Since no firm will sell below marginal cost c, this implies that each consumer will demand exactly one unit of x as long as price p is less than s. In the absence of any informational constraints on the part of consumers, the competitive equilibrium in this market would have firms setting price equal to marginal cost and each consumer purchasing one unit of x.

Exercise 26B.21

What is the equilibrium if $s < c$? What if $s = c$?

Suppose that consumers are unaware of the existence of firms and their prices unless they receive an advert in the mail that informs them that a particular firm is producing x and selling at p. Suppose further that firms can send out any number of advertisements randomly to consumers, with each costing c_a. Given that there are n consumers in the market, the probability that any given advert will reach a particular consumer t is therefore equal to $1/n$.

A consumer will not purchase any x if they do not receive an advert from the firm because without an advert, the consumer is unaware that the product is available. If the consumer receives one advert, they will buy from that firm at the firm's price as long as $p \leq s$. If the consumer receives multiple adverts, they will purchase from the lowest priced firm, again assuming that this firm charges a price below s. Since it is pointless for firms to send out adverts announcing prices above s, we know that all adverts will announce prices no higher than s, and since firms would lose money at prices below marginal cost plus the cost of sending the advert, we know that no firm will announce a price below $c + c_a$. Thus, any price p featured in an advert will satisfy:

$$c + c_a \leq p \leq s, \tag{26.53}$$

which means, for the problem to remain interesting, $s > c + c_a$.

Exercise 26B.22

What is the equilibrium if $c \leq s < c + c_a$?

We can now reason our way to what must emerge in equilibrium assuming the existence of a large number of firms as we have done and a large number of consumers. Since there are no barriers to entry into this market, it must mean that all firms expect to make zero profit. The only way in which a firm can make a sale is to advertise, but advertising is no guarantee that a sale will be made since the consumer who receives the advert might have received an advert from another firm that advertised a lower price. Let $x(p)$ denote the probability that an advert announcing price p results in the consumer purchasing the product at that price from the advertising firm. The expected revenue from sending out an advert announcing p is $(p - c)x(p)$, while the cost of sending out the advert is c_a. The only way that expected profits are zero as the free entry assumption implies must hold in equilibrium is if the expected profit from each advert that is sent out is zero, that is, if:

$$(p - c)x^*(p) - c_a = 0, \qquad (26.54)$$

where $x^*(p)$ is the equilibrium probability that an advert announcing p will result in a sale. Notice that $x(p)$ looks a lot like a downward-sloping demand function. It tells us for any given price that might appear in an advert how likely it is that the consumer will respond to receiving the advert by buying the advertised good. The lower the advertised price, the higher the probability of a sale; that is, $dx(p)/dp < 0$.

The interesting conclusion that follows is that there is no particular reason to expect a single price to appear on every advert that is sent out. Higher priced adverts have a lower probability of resulting in a sale, but a higher profit if they do result in a sale. We would expect many prices that satisfy expression (26.53) to appear on adverts with free entry of firms ensuring that the expected profit from each advert remains at zero. For instance, even when a firm sends out an advert with $p = s$, there is some probability $x(s)$ that the receiving consumer did not receive any other adverts and will therefore purchase from the firm. From the zero profit condition (26.54), we know that in the free entry equilibrium it must be that:

$$x^*(s) = \frac{c_a}{s - c}. \qquad (26.55)$$

No matter how many adverts are sent by firms, there is always a chance that a particular consumer will not receive an advert since all are sent out randomly. If that probability is greater than $x^*(s)$, a firm could enter and make a positive expected profit by sending out an advert that announces price $p = s$. Thus, in equilibrium, the probability that a given consumer does not receive an advert and therefore does not consume x is equal to $x^*(s)$; that is, in equilibrium:

$$\text{(Probability that a consumer does not consume } x) = \frac{c_a}{s - c}. \qquad (26.56)$$

We have arrived at a market in which firms price above marginal cost but end up making zero expected profit because of the cost of informing consumers of the existence of their products. The competitive market takes on the characteristics of a monopolistically competitive market because of the need to convey information through costly advertising.

We can ask how the equilibrium outcome under this monopolistic competition relates to the efficient outcome that a social planner would dictate if the planner faced the same constraint of having to inform consumers of the existence of products through the same form of advertising. The planner does not have to bother with thinking about prices; they can give the product to the consumer who has been made aware of its existence due to the receipt of an advert. The planner will therefore keep sending out adverts as long as the cost of sending them out is no greater than the probability that the recipient has not yet received an advert times the social surplus that would be gained by getting the good to a consumer who does not yet have one. This social gain is $(s - c)$, and the cost of sending the advert is c_a. Let the probability that an advert reaches a consumer who has not yet received an advert be $p(a)$, where a is the number of adverts that have already gone out. The planner keeps sending adverts until $p(a)(s - c) = c_a$, or until:

$$P(a) = \frac{c_a}{s - c}. \tag{26.57}$$

Notice that $p(a)$ is exactly equal to the probability that a consumer will not be reached by an advert under monopolistic competition as derived in equation (26.56)! The social planner therefore chooses an amount of advertising that results in the same probability that a given consumer will not be informed of the existence of the product x, thus leaving exactly as many consumers without x as the monopolistically competitive market. *We have illustrated a model in which informational advertising results in the socially optimal level of information being conveyed through advertising.* While this is not a general first welfare theorem for informational advertising because the result does not hold in other types of plausible models, it makes the case that informational advertising *can* be socially optimal and certainly does convey socially useful information.

Exercise 26B.23

Suppose the social planner decides to sell goods at $p = c$. Is consumer surplus the same in the market with advertising as under this social planner's solution? If not, how is overall surplus the same?

One final note. In Section 26A.5, we discussed informational advertising in the context of a market where consumers are aware of some but not all firms and where the emergence of advertising creates increased awareness of competitors and thus increases competition. We could build this into a model such as the one presented here by assuming that consumers initially know of one firm which, in the absence of advertising, has market power. This would result in the intuitions from Section 26A.5; that is, advertising would lead to greater competition as consumers become aware of competitors, with firms themselves potentially preferring a ban on advertising.

26B.5.2 Image Marketing The idea behind image marketing is at once easy and difficult to grasp. From a gut-level perspective, it can be envisaged how adverts might seek to shape the image of the product, not the product itself. At the same time, if consumers respond to this image marketing, there is something that they value in what the firm is doing; there is something about the association of, say, a high profile sports star endorsing Coke that makes at least some consumers think of Coke as more differentiated from, say, Pepsi. It's not all that clear that the product itself has not changed when it is viewed as consisting of not only what's in the can. Economists do not have a comparative advantage in modelling something of this kind but we can try to do a bit just to illustrate how such image marketing might in fact be socially wasteful.

Suppose we think back to the Hotelling model and suppose that now the interval [0, 1] does not represent true product differentiation but rather marketing-induced product differentiation in the minds of consumers. In particular, let's assume exactly as in our Hotelling model that consumers are spread uniformly along the interval [0, 1] and demand only a single unit of y output as long as they receive non-negative surplus from doing so. As in our previous treatment of the Hotelling model, consumer $n \in [0, 1]$ incurs a utility cost of $\alpha(n - y)^2$ for consuming a product $y \in [0, 1]$, except now we will make α a function of the level of advertising taking place in the industry; that is, $\alpha = f(a_1, a_2)$ where a_i represents units of advertising purchased by firm i. If we choose f such that $f(0, 0) = 0$, we have defined a model in which firms' products are perfectly substitutable in the absence of advertising, with consumer n incurring no utility loss from consuming a good $y \neq n$.

Now consider a three-stage game. In the first stage, each firm chooses its level of advertising a_i, which it can purchase at a per-unit cost of c_a. At the conclusion of the first stage, the parameter α that indicates the degree to which consumers care about a product's location on the [0, 1] interval relative to their ideal points will have been determined, with $\alpha = f(a_1, a_2)$. In the second stage, the firms choose their locations y_1 and y_2 on the [0, 1] interval, and in the final stage they engage in price competition and set their prices p_1 and p_2.

Subgame perfection requires us to begin in stage 3 and work backwards. From our work in Section 26B.2, we already know that equilibrium prices in stage 3, equation (26.17), will take the form:

$$p_1 = p_2 = c + \alpha, \tag{26.58}$$

where c is again the marginal production cost. Since α is determined solely from the advertising choices in stage 1, we can write this as:

$$p_1 = p_2 = p(a_1, a_2) = c + f(a_1, a_2). \tag{26.59}$$

We also know from our work in Section 26B.2 that as soon as $\alpha > 0$, the firms will locate their products at $y_1 = 0$ and $y_2 = 1$ in stage 2. If $\alpha = 0$, that is, in the absence of advertising in the first stage, it does not matter to the firms where they locate their outputs since consumers view all locations on the interval [0, 1] as perfectly substitutable.

All that remains is to consider what will take place in the first stage of the game. To make our example concrete, suppose that the technology for differentiating products through advertising requires both firms to advertise their image differences and takes the Cobb–Douglas form:

$$\alpha = f(a_1, a_2) = a_1^{1/3} a_2^{1/3}. \tag{26.60}$$

Firm i will choose its level of advertising a_i taking as given firm j's advertising choice a_j, solving the problem:

$$\max_{a_i} \pi^i = (p(a_1, a_2) - c)\frac{1}{2} - c_a a_i, \tag{26.61}$$

where the per-unit profit $(p(a_1, a_2) - c)$ is multiplied by $1/2$ because the two firms will each get half the consumers in equilibrium assuming all consumers still purchase the good in equilibrium, and where $c_a a_i$ is the cost of advertising incurred by the firm. The solution to the first-order condition for this problem is:

$$a_i(a_j) = \frac{a_j^{1/2}}{6^{3/2} c_a^{3/2}} = \left(\frac{a_j}{216 c_a^3}\right)^{1/2}. \tag{26.62}$$

Exercise 26B.24

Verify that this best-response function is correct.

This is firm i's best response to firm j's advertising level a_j. Since the two firms are identical, their best-response functions are symmetric and we can solve for the equilibrium level of advertising:

$$a^* = a_1^* - a_2^* = \frac{1}{216_a^3},$$

(26.63)

which implies an equilibrium level of image differentiation of:

$$a^* = f(a_1^*, a_2^*) = \left(\frac{1}{216c_a^3}\right)^{1/3}\left(\frac{1}{216c_a^3}\right)^{1/3} = \frac{1}{36c_a^2},$$

(26.64)

Exercise 26B.25

Can you determine whether firms are making positive profits in equilibrium? What happens as the cost of image advertising gets large? What happens as it approaches zero? Can you make sense of this within the context of the model?

The firms engage in strategic image marketing in the first stage in order to position their otherwise identical products at different ends of the interval [0, 1], with the intent of softening price competition and raising profits. In the absence of such image marketing, there is nothing in the model to prevent fierce Bertrand price competition, with price ending at marginal cost and profits being zero. While profits increase as price rises above marginal cost, consumer welfare falls both because consumers pay higher prices and because consumers incur utility losses when $\alpha > 0$. The higher prices paid by consumers are, in this model, transfers from consumers to firms and thus carry no efficiency losses since we are assuming that consumers always end up buying 1 unit of the good. The utility loss benefits no one, and the advertising costs incurred by firms are similarly socially wasteful. This is precisely the result predicted by sceptics of image marketing.

The inefficiency result is also an artefact of the modelling. To be more precise, we can change the model slightly, get exactly the same equilibrium prediction about behaviour but the reverse prediction about welfare. Suppose we assume that consumer n incurs a utility change of $\gamma\alpha - \alpha(n - y)^2$ when they consume a good of type y, with $\gamma \geq 0$. The model above is just a special case of this where $\gamma = 0$ and a deviation from a consumer's ideal point therefore entails a pure utility loss of $\alpha(n - y)^2$. Assuming $\gamma > 0$ is equivalent to assuming that image marketing makes y goods more attractive by adding $\gamma\alpha$ to the utility of consuming the good while also imposing a utility cost on n to the extent to which n is far from y. If $\gamma > 1/4$, the utility gain from image marketing is at least as large as the utility loss as long as the distance $|n - y|$ is no greater than 1/2 which, in an equilibrium in which the two firms locate at $y_1 = 0$ and $y_2 = 1$, is the case for all consumers.

Allowing γ to be greater than 0, however, changes nothing in terms of the equilibrium behaviour of firms and consumers. Firms will still set prices as in equation (26.59) in the third stage of the game, will still choose $y_1 = 0$ and $y_2 = 1$ as long as $\alpha > 0$, and will still choose equilibrium advertising levels of a^* as derived in equation (26.63). This is because what matters for firm pricing is not the absolute utility level that all consumers get from consuming one y good, which is what is affected when $\gamma > 0$, but rather the degree to which the products have been differentiated. This differentiation drives the softening of price competition, the location choice on the interval [0, 1], and the optimal advertising levels. Similarly, consumers will still shop at firm 1 if $n < 0.5$ and at firm 2 if $n > 0.5$ because their decision depends on where they can get *more* utility, not whether all y locations have become more attractive.

While equilibrium *behaviour* is therefore independent of the value of $\gamma \geq 0$, the welfare predictions of the model are not. With γ sufficiently high and the cost of advertising c_a sufficiently low, we can generate a scenario under which image marketing is welfare enhancing. Since the behavioural predictions of the welfare enhancing scenario are exactly the same as the behavioural predictions of the welfare loss scenario, it's not possible to use behavioural observations to differentiate between the two, at least not within this model. In such a case, welfare analysis makes little sense even when behavioural predictions do. Our model tells us that at least under our particular assumptions, image marketing decreases price competition and raises firm profits, but it cannot tell us whether this raises or lowers social welfare.

This is illustrated in Table 26.4 where different equilibrium variables are calculated for increasing values of γ when we assume $c = 1$ and $c_a = 0.1$. The first four variables – equilibrium advertising levels (a^*), product image differentiation (α), prices (p^*) and firm profits (π^i) – are all unchanged as γ increases. The table reports the overall utility change induced by advertising across all consumers, with the utility change from the price increase above marginal cost not counted since it is merely a transfer to firms without efficiency loss. When added to the total cost of advertising, we get the social gain or loss from advertising in the last row. As can be seen, increasing γ changes the welfare implications of image advertising, with larger γ entailing lower social costs or, for sufficiently large γ, net social benefits.

Table 26.4 $c = 1$, $c_a = 0.1$					
Welfare From Image Marketing as γ Changes					
γ	**0**	**0.1**	**0.25**	**0.5**	**1**
a^*	4.623	4.623	4.623	4.623	4.623
α^*	2.778	2.778	2.778	2.778	2.778
p^*	3.778	3.778	3.778	3.778	3.778
π^i	0.926	0.926	0.926	0.926	0.926
Utility Change	−0.232	0.046	0.463	1.157	2.546
Total Ad. Cost	0.926	0.926	0.926	0.926	0.926
Social Gain (Loss)	(1.157)	(0.880)	(0.463)	0.231	1.620

End-of-Chapter Exercises

26.1† We introduced the topic of differentiated products in a simple two-firm Bertrand price-setting model in which each firm's demand increases with the price of the other firm's output. The specific context we investigated was that of imperfect substitutes.

A. Assume throughout that demand for each firm's good is positive at $p = MC$ even if the other firm sets its price to 0. Suppose further that firms face constant MC and no fixed costs.

a. Suppose that instead of substitutes, the goods produced by the two firms are complements; that is, suppose that an increase in firm j's price causes a decrease rather than an increase in the demand for firm i's good. How would Graph 26.3 change assuming both firms end up producing in equilibrium?

b. What would the inbetween case look like in this graph; that is, what would the best-response functions look like if the price of firm j's product had no influence on the demand for firm i's product?

c. Suppose our three cases – the case of substitutes (covered in the text), of complements (covered in (a)), and of the inbetween case (covered in (b)) – share the following feature in common: when $p_j = 0$, it is a best response for firm i to set $p_i = \bar{P} > MC$. How does $\bar{P}$ relate to what we would have called the monopoly price in Chapter 23?

d. Compare the equilibrium price and output levels in the three cases assuming both firms produce in each case.

e. In which of the three cases might it be that there is no equilibrium in which both firms produce?

B. Consider identical firms 1 and 2, and suppose that the demand for firm i's output is given by $x_i(p_i, p_j) = A - p_i - \beta p_j$. Assume marginal cost is a constant c and there are no fixed costs.

a. What range of values correspond to goods x_i and x_j being substitutes, complements and inbetween goods as defined in part A of the exercise.

b. Derive the best-response functions. What are the intercepts and slopes?

c. Are the slopes of the best-response functions positive or negative? What does your answer depend on?

d. What is the equilibrium price in terms of A, α, b and c. Confirm your answer to A(d).

e. Under what conditions will only one firm produce when the two goods are relatively complementary?

26.2 **Business and Policy Application:** *Mergers and Competition Policy in Related Product Markets.* In exercise 26.1, we investigated different ways in which the markets for good x_i produced by firm i, and good x_j produced by firm j may be related to each other under price competition. We now investigate the incentives for firms to merge into a single firm in such environments, and the level of concern that this might raise among competition regulators.

A. One way to think about firms that compete in related markets is to think of the externality they each impose on the other as they set price. For instance, if the two firms produce relatively substitutable goods as described in (a), firm 1 provides a positive externality to firm 2 when it raises p_1 because it raises firm 2's demand when it raises its own price.

a. Suppose that two firms produce goods that are relatively substitutable in the sense that when the price of one firm's good goes up, this increases the demand for the other firm's good. If these two firms merged, would you expect the resulting monopoly firm to charge higher or lower prices for the goods previously produced by the competing firms? Think of the externality that is not being taken into account by the two firms as they compete.

b. Next, suppose that the two firms produce goods that are relatively complementary in the sense that an increase in the price of one firm's good *decreases* the demand for the other firm's good. How is the externality now different?

c. When the two firms in (b) merge, would you now expect price to increase or decrease?

d. If you were a competition regulator, which merger would you be worried about: the one in (a) or the one in (c)?

e. Suppose that instead the firms were producing goods in unrelated markets with the price of one firm not affecting the demand for the goods produced by the other firm. What would you expect to happen to price if the two firms merge?

f. Why are the positive externalities we encountered in this exercise good for society?

B. Suppose we have two firms, firm 1 and 2, competing on price. The demand for firm i is given by $x_i(p_i, p_j) = 1000 - 10p_i + \beta p_j$.

a. Calculate the equilibrium price p^* as a function of β.

b. Suppose that the two firms merged into one firm that now maximized overall profit. Derive the prices for the two goods in terms of β that the new monopolist will charge, keeping in mind that the monopolist now solves a single optimization problem to set the two prices. Given the symmetry of the demands, you should get that the monopolist will charge the same price for both goods.

c. Create the following table: let the first row set different values for β ranging from -7.5 to $+7.5$ in 2.5 increments. Derive the equilibrium price for each β when the two firms compete and report it in the second row. In a third row, calculate the price charged by the monopoly that results from the merging of the two firms for each value of β.

d. Do your results confirm your intuition from part A of the exercise? If so, how?

e. Why would firms merge if, as a result, they end up charging a lower price for both goods than they were able to charge individually?

f. Add two rows to your table, calculating first the profit that the two firms together make in the competitive oligopoly equilibrium and the profit that the firms make as a monopoly following a merger. Are the results consistent with your answer to (e)?

26.3*† **Business Application:** *Advertising as Quality Signal.* In the text, we have discussed two possible motives for advertising, one focused on providing information, about the availability of goods or the prices of goods, and another focused on shaping the image of the product. Another possible motive might be for high quality firms to signal that they produce high quality goods to consumers who cannot tell the difference prior to consuming a good. Consider the following game that captures this. In each of two periods, firms get to set a price and consumers get to decide whether or not to buy the good. In the first period, consumers do not know if a firm is producing high or low quality goods; all they observe is the prices set by firms and whether or not firms have advertised. If a consumer buys from a firm in the first period, the consumer experiences the quality of the firm's product and thus knows whether the firm is a high or low quality firm when they make a decision of whether to buy from this firm in the second period. Assume throughout that a consumer who does not buy from a firm in the first period exits the game and does not proceed to the second period.

A. Notice that firms and consumers play a sequential game in each period, with firms offering a price first and consumers choosing whether or not to buy. In the first period, firms also have the option to advertise in an attempt to persuade consumers of the product's value.

a. Consider the second period first. Given that the only way a consumer enters the second period is if they bought from the firm in the first period, and given that they operate with the benefit of having experienced the good's quality, would any firm choose to advertise in the second period if it could?

b. Suppose that both firms incur a marginal cost of MC for producing their goods. High quality firms produce goods that are valued at $v_h > MC$ by consumers and low quality firms produce goods that are valued at $v_\ell > MC$, with $v_h > v\ell$. In any subgame perfect equilibrium, what prices will each firm charge in the second period, and what will consumer strategies be given they decide whether to buy after observing prices?

c. Now consider period 1. If consumers believe that firms that advertise are high quality firms and firms that don't advertise are low quality firms, what is their subgame perfect strategy in period 1 after they observe prices and whether a firm has advertised?

d. What is the highest cost a_h per output unit of advertising that a high quality firm would be willing to undertake if it thought that consumers would interpret this as the firm producing a high quality good?

e. What is the highest cost a_ℓ that a low quality firm would be willing to incur if it thought this would fool consumers into thinking that it produced high quality goods when in fact it produces low quality goods?

f. Consider a level of advertising that costs a^*. For what levels of a^* do you think that it is an equilibrium for high quality firms to advertise and low quality firms to not advertise?

g. Given the information asymmetry between consumers and firms in period 1, might it be efficient for such advertising to take place?

h. We often see firms sponsor sporting events, and it is difficult to explain such sponsorships as informational advertising in the way we discussed such advertising in the text. Why? How can the model in this exercise nevertheless be rationalized as informational advertising rather than image marketing?

B. Suppose that a firm is a high quality firm h with probability δ and a low quality firm ℓ with probability $(1-\delta)$. Firm h produces an output of quality that is valued by consumers at 4, while firm ℓ produces an output of quality 1 that is valued by consumers at 1, and both incur a marginal cost equal to 1 per unit of output produced. Assume no fixed costs.

a. Derive the level of a^* of advertising as defined in part A that could take place in equilibrium.

b. What is the most efficient of the possible equilibria in which high quality firms advertise but low quality firms do not advertise?

c. Do your answers thus far depend on δ?

d. The equilibria you have identified so far are *separating equilibria* because the two types of firms behave differently in equilibrium, thus allowing consumers to learn from observing advertising whether or not a firm is producing a high or low quality good. Consider now whether both firms choosing (p, a), and firms thus playing a *pooling* strategy, could be part of an equilibrium. Why is period 2 largely irrelevant for thinking about this?

e. If the firms play the pooling strategy (p, a), what is the consumer's expected payoff from buying in period 1? In terms of δ, what does this imply is the highest price p that could be part of the pooling equilibrium?

f. Suppose consumers believe a firm to be a low quality firm if it deviates from the pooling strategy. If one of the firms has an incentive to deviate from the pooling strategy, which one would it be? What does this imply about the lowest that p can be relative to a in order for (p, a) to be part of a pooling equilibrium?

g. Using your answers from (b) and (c), determine the range of p in terms of δ and a such that (p, a) can be part of a Bayesian Nash pooling equilibrium.

h. What equilibrium beliefs do consumers hold in such a pooling equilibrium when they have to decide whether or not to buy in period 1? What out-of-equilibrium beliefs support the equilibrium?

i. Can advertising in a pooling equilibrium ever be efficient?

26.4 **Business Application:** *Deterring Entry of Another Car Company.* Suppose that there are currently two car companies that form an oligopoly in which each faces constant marginal costs. Their strategic variables are price and product characteristics.

A. Use the Hotelling model to frame your approach to this exercise and suppose that the two firms have maximally differentiated their products, with company 1 selecting characteristic 0 and company 2 selecting characteristic 1 from the set of all possible product characteristics [0, 1].

a. Explain why such maximal product differentiation might be the equilibrium outcome in this model.

b. Next, suppose a new car company plans to enter the market and chooses 0.5 as its product characteristic, and suppose existing companies can no longer vary their product characteristics. If the new company enters in this way, what happens to car prices? In what way can we view this as two distinct Hotelling models?

c. How much profit would the new company make relative to the original two?

d. Suppose that the existing companies announce their prices prior to the new company making its decision on whether or not to enter. Suppose further that the existing companies agree to announce the same price. If the new company has to pay a fixed cost prior to starting production, do you think there is a range of fixed costs such that companies 1 and 2 can strategically deter entry?

e. What determines the range of fixed costs under which the existing companies will successfully deter entry?

f. If the existing companies had foreseen the potential of a new entrant who locates at 0.5, do you think they would have been as likely to engage in maximum product differentiation in order to soften price competition between each other?

g. We have assumed throughout that the entrant would locate at 0.5. Why might this be the optimal location for the entrant?

B. Consider the version of Hotelling's model from Section 26B.2 and suppose that two oligopolistic car companies, protected by government regulations on how many firms can be in the car industry, have settled at the equilibrium product characteristics of 0 and 1 on the interval [0, 1]. Suppose further that $\alpha = 12\,000$ and $c = 10\,000$ and assume throughout that car companies cannot change their product characteristics once they have chosen them.

a. What prices are the two companies charging? How much profit are they making given that they do not incur any fixed costs and given that we have normalized the population size to 1?

b. Now suppose that the government has granted permission to a third company to enter the car market at 0.5. The company needs to pay a fixed cost FC to enter. If the third company enters, we can now consider the intervals [0, 0.5] and [0.5, 1] separately and treat each of these as a separate Hotelling model. Derive $D^1(p_1, p_3)$. Derive $D^3(p_1, p_3)$ taking care to note that the relevant interval is now [0, 0.5] rather than [0, 1].

c. Determine the best-response functions $p_1(p_3)$ and $p_3(p_1)$. Calculate the equilibrium price.

d. How much profit will the three companies make not counting the FC that any of them had to pay to get into the market?

e. If company 3 makes its decision of whether to enter and what price to set at the same time as companies 1 and 2 make their pricing decisions, what is the highest FC that will still be consistent with the new car company entering?

f. Suppose instead that companies 1 and 2 can commit to a price before company 3 decides whether to enter. Suppose further that companies 1 and 2 collude to deter entry and agree to announce the same price prior to company 3's decision. What is the most that companies 1 and 2 would be willing to lower price to in order to prevent entry?

g. What is the lowest FC that would now be consistent with company 3 not entering? (Be careful to consider firm 3's best price response and the implications for market share.)

26.5† **Business and Policy Application:** *The Software Industry.* When personal computers first came onto the scene, the task of writing software was considerably more difficult than it is today. Over the following decades, consumer demand for software increased as personal computers became prevalent in more and more homes and businesses at the same time as it became easier to write software. Thus, the industry has been one of expanding demand and decreasing fixed entry costs.

A. In this part of the exercise, analyze the evolution of the software industry using the monopolistic competition model from Section 26A.4 as well as insights from our earlier oligopoly models.

a. Begin with the case where the first firm enters as a monopoly, that is, the case where it has just become barely profitable to produce software. Illustrate this in a graph with a linear downward-sloping demand curve, a constant MC curve and a fixed entry cost.

b. Suppose that marginal costs remain constant throughout the problem. In a separate graph, illustrate how an increase in demand impacts the profits of the monopoly and how a simultaneous decrease in fixed entry costs alters the potential profit from entering the industry.

c. Given the possibility of strategic entry deterrence, what might the monopolist do to forestall entry of new firms?

d. Suppose the time comes when strategic entry deterrence is no longer profitable and a second firm enters. Would you expect the entering firm to produce the same software as the existing firm? Would you expect both firms to make a profit at this point?

e. As the industry expands, would you expect strategic entry deterrence to play a larger or smaller role? In what sense is the industry never in equilibrium?

f. What happens to profit for firms in the software market as the industry expands? What would the graph look like for each firm in the industry if the industry reaches equilibrium?

g. If you were a competition regulator charged with either looking out for consumers or maximizing efficiency, why might you not want to interfere in this industry despite the presence of market power? What dangers would you worry about if policy makers suggested price regulation to mute market power?

h. In what sense does the emergence of open source software further weaken the case for regulation of the software industry? In what sense does this undermine the case for long-lasting copyrights on software?

B. In this part of the exercise, use the model of monopolistic competition from Section 26B.4. Let disposable income I be €100 billion, $\rho = -0.5$ and marginal cost $c = 10$.

a. What is the assumed elasticity of substitution between software products?

b. Explain how increasing demand in the model can be viewed as either increasing I or decreasing α. Will either of these change the price that is charged in the market? Explain.

c. We noted in part A of the exercise that fixed entry costs in the software industry have been declining. Can that explain falling software prices within this model?

d. *True or False*: As long as the elasticity of substitution between software products remains unchanged, the only factor that could explain declining software prices in this model is declining marginal cost. Can you think of real-world changes in the software industry that might be consistent with this?

e. Now consider how increases in demand and decreases in costs translate to the equilibrium number of software firms. Suppose $\alpha = 0.998$ initially. What fraction of income does this imply is spent on software products? How many firms does this model predict will exist in equilibrium under the parameters of this model, assuming fixed entry costs are €100 million? What happens to the number of firms as FC falls to €10 million, €1 million and €100 000?

f. Suppose that FC is €1 000 000. What happens as α falls from 0.998 to 0.99 in 0.002 increments as demand for software expands through changes in representative tastes when more consumers have computers?

g. Suppose FC is €1 000 000 and $\alpha = 0.99$. What happens if demand increases because income increases by 10 per cent?

26.6 **Policy Application**: *To Tax or Not to Tax Advertising*. In the text, we discussed two different views of advertising. One arises primarily from an economist's perspective, while the other emerges primarily from a psychologist's. The nature of public policy towards the advertising industry will depend on which view of advertising one takes.

A. Consider the two views: *informational advertising* and *image marketing*.

a. In what sense does information advertising potentially address a market condition that represents a violation of the first welfare theorem?

b. In what sense does image marketing result in potentially negative externalities? Might it result in positive externalities?

c. If you wanted to make an efficiency case for taxing advertising, how would you do it? What if you wanted to make an efficiency case for subsidizing it?

d. Suppose a public interest group lobbies for regulatory limits on the amount of advertising that can be conducted. Explain how this might serve the interests of firms.

B. Consider the three-stage image marketing model in Section 26B.6 but assume that $f(a_1, a_2) = a_1^{1/2} + a_2^{1/2}$. Suppose further that the cost for consumer n from consuming y is $\alpha(n - y)^2 - \gamma\alpha$, with $\gamma = 0$ unless otherwise stated.

a. Solving the game backwards in order to find subgame perfect equilibria, does anything change in stages 2 and 3 of the game?

b. What would be the advertising levels chosen by each firm?

c. Suppose the two firms can collude on the amount of advertising each undertakes but the rest of the game remains the same. Would they choose different levels of a_1 and a_2?

d. For what level of $\gamma = \overline{\gamma}$ is there no efficiency case for either subsidizing or taxing advertising? What if $\gamma > \overline{\gamma}$? What if $\gamma < \overline{\gamma}$?

e. Is there any way to come to a conclusion about the level of γ from observing consumer and firm behaviour?

* conceptually challenging
** computationally challenging
† solutions in Study Guide

Chapter 27

Public Goods

A *public good* is a good that can be consumed by more than one individual at a time, while a *private good* is a good that can be consumed by only a single individual. If a consumer buys a sandwich, they can take a bite or they can let someone else take a bite, but both cannot take the same bite. The sandwich bite is what economists call *rivalrous*, and this rivalry is what characterizes private goods. If a person sets off fireworks in their garden, on the other hand, other people can enjoy the same fireworks display without either taking away from the enjoyment of the other. The fireworks display is what economists call *non-rivalrous*, and this non-rivalry is what characterizes public goods. This gives rise to particular kinds of *externalities* because the person setting off the fireworks might not consider the benefits others get from the fireworks display as they decide how big to make them. In our discussion of public goods, we return to a topic partially covered in Chapter 21, but we do so now with the benefit of some game theory tools from Chapter 24.

While we will often consider the extreme cases of non-rivalry and rivalry, we should start by pointing out that it is actually more appropriate to think of goods as lying somewhere on a continuum between complete rivalry and complete non-rivalry. Complete non-rivalry would mean that we can keep adding additional consumers, and no matter how many we add, each new consumer can enjoy the same level of the good without taking away from the enjoyment of others. National defence is a good example of such an extreme. The national defence system of a country protects the entire population, and as new immigrants join the population or as new citizens are born, these additional 'consumers' can enjoy the same level of protection that current citizens enjoy without making current citizens less safe from external threats. If a city's population increases, it will need to get more police officers to keep public safety constant, which means that local public safety is not as non-rivalrous as national defence. A small group of people can probably enjoy the same large swimming pool without taking away from each other's enjoyment, but as more people join, things will get crowded and enjoyment falls when new consumers come on board.

The degree of non-rivalry characterizes the degree to which we think of a good as being a public good. The sandwich bite is on one extreme end of the spectrum, with even one other person crowding consumption to a point where it is no longer meaningful. National defence might be on the other extreme, with no limit to the number of people who can be protected by the same national security umbrella without crowding the protection enjoyed by everyone else. There are all the inbetween goods, goods that can be consumed by more than one person at a time but that are subject to crowding in the sense that, at least at some point, each individual's enjoyment of the public good falls when more people consume it. Within the class of public goods, there are of course those that are quite *local*, like a local swimming pool, and some that allow consumption over a wider geographic area, like national defence or reductions in greenhouse gas emissions. The former are sometimes referred to as *local public goods*, and these, like local public safety, in turn are typically, though not always, subject to some crowding within the area in which they are provided.

While the degree of rivalry of a good is one dimension along which we can distinguish between different goods, the geographic reach of non-rivalrous goods is another dimension, it will become important for us to distinguish between goods based on whether we can *exclude others* from consuming the good. If exclusion is possible, it is in principle, and often in practice, the case that firms can charge consumers for their consumption of public goods and consumers can decide, much as they do for private goods, whether it's worth it to pay the price of admission. If the good is non-excludable, that option is not typically available. Firms are much more likely to provide excludable public goods than they are non-excludable public goods.

Table 27.1 illustrates four stylized types of goods that emerge from distinguishing goods along the dimensions of rivalry and excludability. So far, we have almost always assumed that goods are rivalrous, and thus we have dealt almost exclusively with *private goods* from the first column of the table. Usually the private goods we dealt with were excludable, with consumers who were not willing to pay for such goods priced out of the market. In Chapter 21, however, we discussed the case of private rivalrous goods to which multiple people have access. Such goods included wood in a public forest or fish in the ocean, goods not owned by anyone, goods that are part of the commons. We illustrated that lack of ownership or property rights of such private goods can result in the Tragedy of the Commons, where individuals overuse the private good as they do not consider the impact their actions have on others who also wish to make use of the good. Overconsumption resulted from the non-excludability of private goods in the commons.

The second column in the table shows public goods that are at least to some extent non-rivalrous. When consumers cannot easily be excluded from consumption of such public goods as in the case of national defence or garden fireworks, we will call them *public goods* or, if their consumption is limited to small geographic areas, *local public goods*. Such public goods might be 'pure' in the sense that new consumers can always engage in consumption without taking away from the consumption of current consumers, i.e. national defence and fireworks, or they can be subject to crowding, i.e. public safety in cities and public swimming pools. When there exists a mechanism for excluding consumers such as in the case of the swimming pool, we will sometimes refer to such goods as *club* goods. The real world is much richer than this table suggests because there are many cases in between the extremes, but this categorization will become useful as we think about different ways in which goods can be provided by markets, governments and civil society.

Table 27.1 Different Kinds of Public and Private Goods

	Types of Goods	
	Rivalrous (Private)	Non-Rivalrous (Public)
Excludable	(Pure) Private Good	Club Good
Non-Excludable	Common (Private) Good	Public (or Local Public) Good

27A.1 Public Goods and Their Externalities

We will begin with the case of fully non-rivalrous goods in the absence of excludability, or what we just referred to as pure public goods in Table 27.1.

27A.1 Public Goods and the Free-Rider Problem

In panel (a) of Graph 27.1, we replicate panel (a) from Graph 14.1. In that graph, we illustrated how we add up individual demand curves in the case of a private good. Since private goods are rivalrous and can be consumed by only one person, this addition of demand curves was horizontal in nature; for every additional consumer, we added that consumer's demand at each price level to the previous demand curves. Public goods are different because they are non-rivalrous; that is, they can be consumed by more than one person at a time. To derive the aggregate marginal willingness to pay for one unit of the public good, we have to add how much that good is worth to the first consumer to how much it is worth to the second consumer and so on. When tastes are quasilinear, we can equivalently say that this amounts to adding demand curves vertically. This is done in panel (b) of Graph 27.1.

Graph 27.1 Aggregate Demand Curves for Private and Public Goods

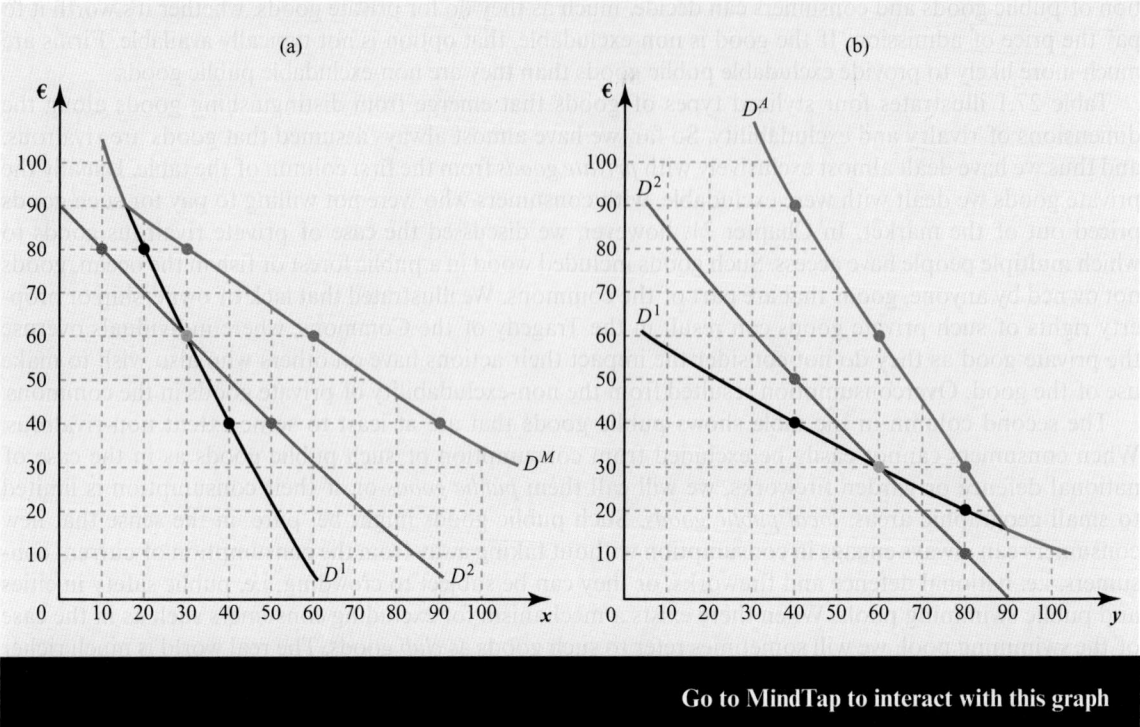

Go to MindTap to interact with this graph

27A.1.1 The Optimal Level of Public Goods Now suppose that the good on the horizontal axis can be produced at constant marginal cost. In the private good case, the efficient level of production occurs where marginal cost intersects the aggregate or market demand curve D^M in panel (a) of Graph 27.1 as we showed in Chapter 15. At that intersection point, it was the case that each consumer's marginal willingness to pay was equal to the marginal cost of production, and when the private good represented a composite good denominated in euro units, this is equivalent to saying that each consumer's marginal rate of substitution (MRS) was equal to the marginal cost of production.

Now consider a public good that can similarly be produced at constant marginal cost. It is still the case that efficiency requires that the good be produced as long as the marginal benefit of the good is greater than the marginal cost, but now all the consumers who consume the same public good are receiving a marginal benefit from doing so. To say that the efficient level of production of the public good occurs where marginal benefit is equal to marginal cost is the same as saying that production occurs where the *sum* of the marginal benefits of all consumers equals the marginal cost. In a sense, the same is true in the private goods case, except there the sum of the marginal benefits is only the marginal benefit of a single consumer since no good can be consumed by more than one person.

Exercise 27A.1

True or False: The efficient level of public good production therefore occurs where marginal cost crosses the aggregate demand for public goods as drawn in panel (b) of Graph 27.1.

Exercise 27A.2*

Can you explain how there is a single efficient level of the public good when tastes for public goods are quasi-linear, but there are multiple levels of efficient public good provision when this is not the case? *Hint*: Consider how redistributing income in a lump-sum way affects demand in one case but not the other.

There is another way we can derive this optimality condition for public good production. Remember that a situation is Pareto optimal or efficient if there is no way to change the situation and make some people better off without making anyone else worse off. Suppose that we consider the case of two consumers with preferences over a composite private good x and a public good y and with private good endowments e_1 and e_2. Assume that there exists a concave production technology that converts private goods x into public goods y. We can depict the trade-offs that our society of two individuals faces with the light blue production possibilities frontier in panel (a) of Graph 27.2 where the two consumers could have only private consumption equal to $e_1 + e_2$ on the vertical axis, or they could devote some of their private goods to producing a public good that they can both consume. A concave production technology implies that relatively little private good is needed to produce the first units of the public good, but that it takes increasingly more private goods to produce each additional unit of the public good. As a result, the trade-off that emerges takes on the shape depicted in the graph, with an initially shallow slope that becomes increasingly steep as more public goods are produced. The slope of this graph represents the number of x units required to produce one more unit of y, or the negative marginal cost $(-MC_y)$ in terms of x goods for producing another unit of public good.

Exercise 27A.3

Does this production technology exhibit increasing or decreasing returns to scale?

Exercise 27A.4

What would the relationship in Graph 27.2 look like if the technology had the opposite returns to scale as you have just concluded?

In panel (b) of the graph, we pick some indifference curve for consumer 2 and place it onto the graph of the production possibilities frontier. The slope of an indifference curve is the *MRS*, the amount of x consumer 2 would be willing to give up in order to get one more unit of y. Another way of expressing this is that the slope of the indifference curve is minus consumer 2's marginal benefit $(-MB_2)$ of one more unit of y expressed in terms of x.

Now let's see how high an indifference curve we could get for consumer 1 assuming we make consumer 2 no worse off than the indifference curve $\bar{u}_2$. If we were to produce $\underline{y}$ in panel (b) of the graph, we would have to give all remaining x goods to consumer 2 just to keep them at the indifference curve $\bar{u}_2$, leaving no x goods to give to consumer 1. The same is true were we to produce $\bar{y}$. For public good levels in between $\underline{y}$ and $\bar{y}$, we would have some x goods left over to give to consumer 1. Panel (c) of Graph 27.2 plots the amount of x that is left over for consumer 1 for each level of y good production between $\underline{y}$ and $\bar{y}$.

Graph 27.2 Optimal Provision of Public Goods

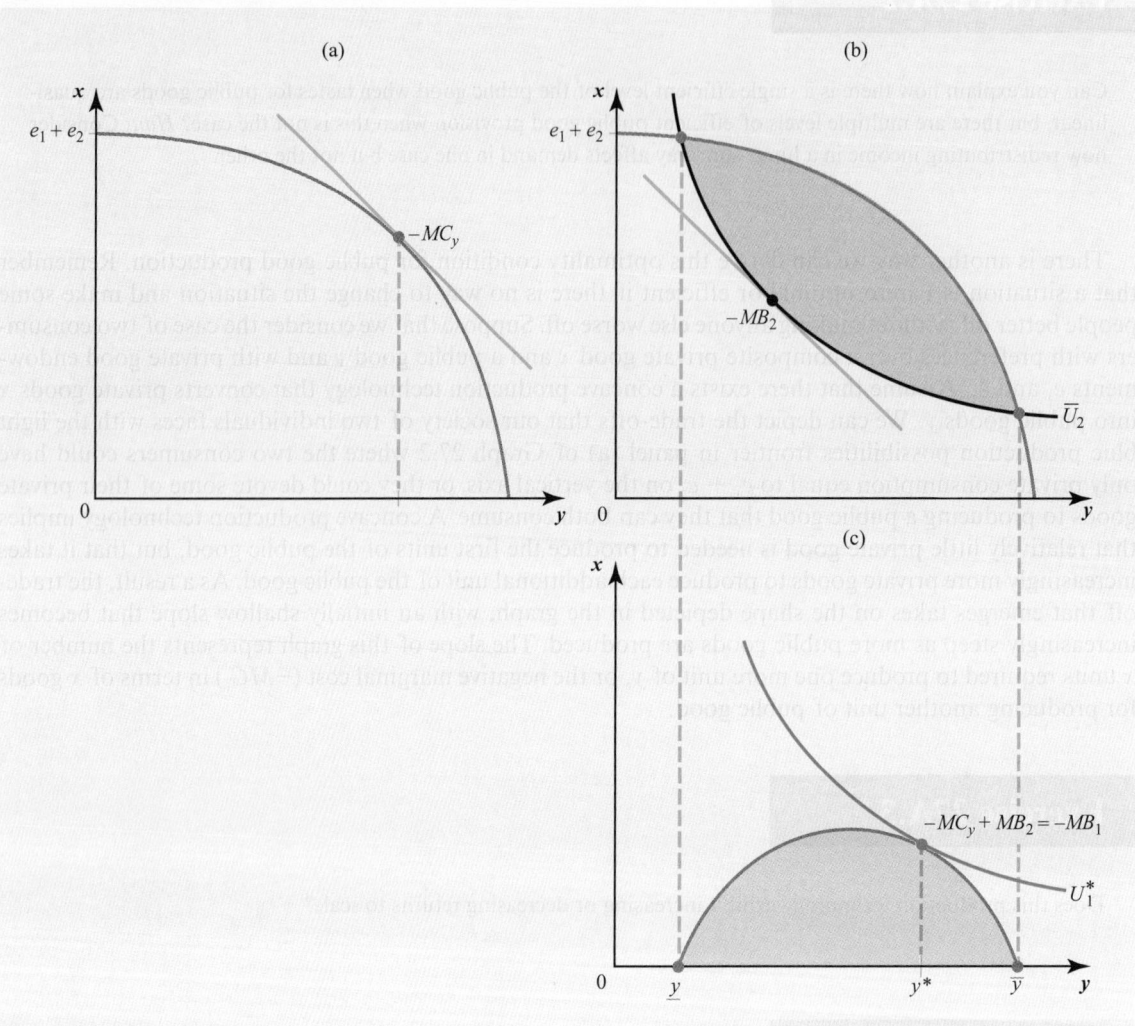

(a)

(b)

(c)

Exercise 27A.5

Why must the shaded areas in panels (b) and (c) of Graph 27.2 be equal to one another?

Panel (c) of the graph shows how high an indifference curve for consumer 1 can be attained assuming consumer 2 is held to indifference curve $\bar{u}_2$. We have to find the highest indifference curve for consumer 1 that still contains at least one point of the shaded set of possible (x, y) levels we have derived, leading to a public good level y^* at which the indifference curve u_1^* is tangential to the boundary of the shaded set in panel (c). This boundary of the shaded set is the production possibility frontier minus the indifference curve $\bar{u}_2$, which implies that the slope of the boundary of the shaded set is the difference between the slopes of the production possibilities frontier and the indifference curve $\bar{u}_2$; that is, $-MC_y - (-MB2) = -MC_y + MB_2$. At the tangency that occurs when public goods are set at y^*, this slope equals the slope of the indifference curve u_1^*, which implies that $-MB_1 = -MC_y + MB_2$. Subtracting MC_y from both sides of this equation and adding MB_1, we therefore get that $MB_1 + MB_2 = MC_y$.

The only thing that seems arbitrary about what we just did is that we just picked some indifference curve for consumer 2. Notice that the reasoning does not depend on what indifference curve for consumer 2 we pick in panel (b) as long as some shaded area remains. No matter what feasible indifference curve for consumer 2 is chosen, finding the public good level that ensures consumer 1 cannot be made better off without making consumer 2 worse off implies picking y such that $MB_1 + MB_2 = MC_y$. *Of the many possible Pareto-optimal solutions we can think of as we vary $\bar{u}_2$, all of them share in common that the public good level is set so that the sum of marginal benefits of the public good equals the marginal cost of producing the public good.* This is in contrast to the efficiency condition for private goods where, assuming all consumers are at an interior solution, *each* individual MB_i equals the marginal cost.

Exercise 27A.6*

Is there any reason to think that y^*, the optimal level of the public good, will be the same regardless of what indifference curve for consumer 2 we choose to start with? How does your answer change when tastes are quasi-linear in the public good? And how does this relate to your answer to exercise 27A.2?

27A.1.2 Decentralized Provision of Fireworks

Consider the case of two neighbouring families planning fireworks from their gardens on New Year's Eve. The resulting fireworks are a public good. One family's enjoyment as they glance up into the evening sky does not take away from the neighbouring family's enjoyment, and each family will get to enjoy the fireworks each sets off. It might be sensible for the two families to get together and pool their resources in order to arrive at the Pareto-optimal level of fireworks y^*, which, as just derived, implies that y^* would be set such that the sum of their marginal benefits equals the marginal cost of launching an additional firework. Instead, they go about their business and determine the number of fireworks they set off independently of one another knowing that the other is also doing so.

To estimate how many fireworks will be launched by each family, we have to look at the Nash equilibrium of the game being played as they try to anticipate how many fireworks the other will launch. In a Nash equilibrium, family A's level of firework production must be a best response to family B's and vice versa. We begin by thinking about family A's best response to any quantity of fireworks family B might set off.

If family A thought family B was not going to set off any fireworks, i.e. $y_2 = 0$, they would invest in their own fireworks until the marginal cost of launching one more firework is equal to the marginal benefit they receive; that is, they will set $y_1(0)$ such that $MB_1 = MC$. If A thinks B will produce some quantity $\bar{y}_2$, they will have to rethink how many fireworks they set off, because they know they already get to enjoy $\bar{y}_2 > 0$ of family B's fireworks. Family B purchasing fireworks is a lot like family A having additional disposable income, because they could now enjoy their fireworks and spend all their income on private goods. If all goods are normal goods, the additional income family A now has will be split between all goods, which means they will not spend all the effective additional income on the public good. While family A will end up *consuming* more fireworks if B buys some, they will *purchase* less themselves.

Exercise 27A.7

In a graph with y on the horizontal axis and a composite private good x on the vertical, illustrate family A's budget constraint assuming that $\bar{y}_2 = 0$. How does this budget constraint change when $\bar{y}_2 > 0$? Show that if tastes are homothetic, family A will end up consuming more y when $\bar{y}_2 > 0$ but will themselves purchase less y. Does this hold whenever y and x are both normal goods? Does it hold if y is an inferior good?

In panel (a) of Graph 27.3, we can illustrate family A's best-response function to different values of y_2 that B might choose on a graph with y_2 on the horizontal axis and y_1 on the vertical. Our reasoning implies that this best-response function has a positive intercept $y_1(0)$ when y_2, i.e. A will purchase fireworks until $MB_1 = MC$ but a negative slope, i.e. as y_2 increases, family A buys fewer fireworks. In panel (b), we put B's best-response function on top of A's assuming that they are just like A, with the two best-response functions therefore crossing on the 45-degree line. That intersection represents the levels of fireworks (y_1^{eq}, y_2^{eq}) that both families will buy in equilibrium when both best respond to the other's actions.

Graph 27.3 Private Provision of Public Goods

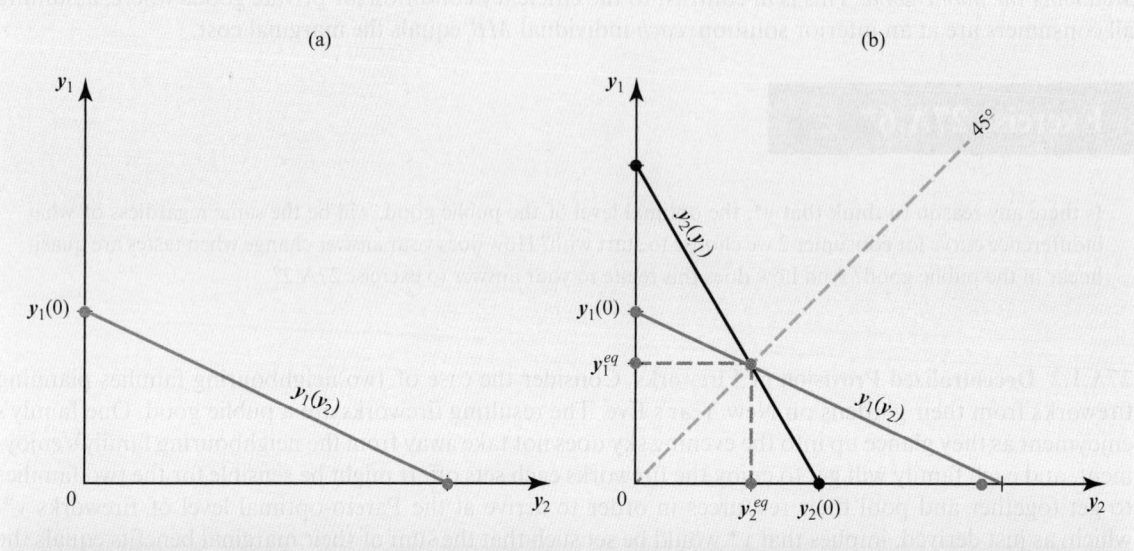

Go to MindTap to interact with this graph

Exercise 27A.8

If both families have identical tastes but A has more income than B, would the equilibrium fall above, on or below the 45-degree line assuming all goods are normal goods?

We can now ask if the total quantity of fireworks $y^{eq} = y_1^{eq} + y_2^{eq}$ is efficient. In equilibrium, family A is doing the best it can if, given that family B is purchasing y_2^{eq}, it continues to buy fireworks as long as A's own marginal benefit of additional fireworks is greater than the MC; that is, A would stop when $MB_1 = MC$. Since B also gets a benefit from the fireworks A sets off in their garden, this implies that A stops buying fireworks when $MB_1 + MB_2 > MC$, which implies that the equilibrium quantity of fireworks is less than the efficient quantity y^* for which we concluded before $MB_1 + MB_2 = MC$. Thus, $y^{eq} < y^*$; in equilibrium, the families are producing an inefficiently low quantity of fireworks.

The intuition for the result is that when A makes their choice on how many fireworks to buy, they are generating a *positive externality* for family B but family A has no incentive to take that into account. The same is true for family B. Because the two families have no incentive to take into account the benefits they are producing for others, they will underconsume fireworks. This is often referred to as the *free-rider problem*. Each family is free riding on the public good produced by the other.

27A.1.3 The Free-Rider Problem: Another Prisoner's Dilemma This free-rider problem is another example of a Prisoner's Dilemma. Both families could have got together before buying fireworks and agreed to split the cost of buying the optimal quantity of fireworks. Instead, they acted independently and did not explicitly cooperate. Even if they had chosen to coordinate beforehand and agreed to each buy their share of the optimal quantity of fireworks, they would not have an incentive to actually abide by their agreement regardless of what they thought the other was doing. This is because their private incentive is to behave in accordance with their best-response functions in Graph 27.3, setting private marginal benefit equal to the marginal cost they incur. In order to sustain cooperation when they prepare to buy, they need a mechanism to enforce their agreement. The families' incentives are like those of the oligopolists who make a cartel agreement in Chapter 25; abiding by the agreement would make them both better off than if they go it alone, but if there is no one to make sure they abide by the agreement, it is in their individual incentive to cheat.

In the fireworks example, we might be able to imagine an enforcement mechanism. One family buys the optimal number of fireworks and the other pays half the bill. They get together in one of their gardens and set off all the fireworks. Even in the absence of being so explicit about enforcing the agreement, they might think it's enough for them to know that they are likely to be neighbours for a long time and that they will keep having occasions to cooperate on the fireworks they set off. As we have seen in Chapter 24, introducing the likelihood that they will interact repeatedly, without knowing a definitive end to the game, can be enough for them to sustain cooperation in repeated interactions.

More generally there are many circumstances involving public goods where it is unlikely that it will be so easy to arrive at ways of overcoming the incentives of the one-shot Prisoner's Dilemma. Many public goods involve many players, and it is difficult for large numbers of players to cooperate the way that two families might when they prepare fireworks for an event. Not only is it more difficult to enforce cooperation but the incentives to free ride on the contributions of others get worse the more 'others' there are. We all benefit from investments in cancer research, but Cancer Research UK, for example, cannot easily get us all to consider the larger social benefits of cancer research when it appeals to individuals to contribute to the cause. We all benefit from an effective police force that keeps us relatively safe, but it's not easy to see how the police can walk around and collect the optimal level of donations for its worthwhile work. For this reason, we often look to non-market institutions like governments to bring our private incentives in line with socially desirable levels of investments in public goods.

27A.2 Solving the Prisoner's Dilemma Through Government Policy

As we have already seen in previous chapters, governments are often employed as non-market institutions that enforce ways out of Prisoner's Dilemmas. There are at least two possible avenues for governments to do so. First, in many cases, governments take on the responsibility of providing public goods and use the power to tax individuals to finance those goods. Second, in some cases, governments does not directly provide public goods but instead subsidizes private consumption of public goods. Each can, assuming governments have sufficient information, result in optimal levels of public good provision.

27A.2.1 Government Provision and Crowd-Out Perhaps the most straightforward solution to the public goods/free-rider problem is for the government to provide the public good directly. This happens in most countries for goods such as national defence or the establishment of an internal police force. The argument for government provision of public goods has also been used to justify income redistribution programmes in most Western democracies where it is assumed that most citizens place some value on making sure the least well off are taken care of to some extent. Assuming that this is the case, contributions to the alleviation of poverty are contributions to a public good because everyone who cares about the issue benefits from less poverty.

When governments do not know exactly what the optimal level of a particular good is and thus do not fund the optimal level, or alternatively, if political processes are not efficient and do not result in optimal economic decision making, a particular issue called *crowd-out* may arise. Consider government financing for public radio. In some countries government finances part of the cost of operating public radio stations, but radio stations attempt to get listeners to add private contributions on top of the funds received from the government. The government is, as a result, just one of many contributors to the provision of the public good public radio, and public radio listeners will presumably think about their own level of voluntary contribution in light of how much others are giving, with others including the government's contribution.

The resulting game is not unlike the game in which two families are trying to decide how much to contribute to their local fireworks except that now there is just another player called the government. We derived in the previous section an individual's best-response function in such a game as a function of how much others are giving to the public good, and noted that as others give more, each individual's best response is to give less. When the government contributes to a public good such as public radio that also relies on private contributions, game theory predicts that private contributions will decline as government contributions increase; government contributions to the public good crowd out private contributions. As we will see more formally in Section B, if the government taxes individuals in order to finance its contribution to a public good, the model would predict that individuals who are giving to the public good will reduce their contributions by exactly the amount that the government has taken from them in order to finance the same public good. Thus, as long as individuals are giving on their own, we would expect increased government contributions to be offset by decreases in private contributions.

Exercise 27A.9

True or False: If everyone is currently giving to a public good, including the government, this model would predict that the government's involvement has not done anything to alleviate the inefficiency of private provision of public goods.

In the case of public radio, not every taxpayer is also giving voluntarily to public radio stations. The tax revenues raised for public radio from individuals who are not giving do not result in decreased private contributions since those individuals are already at a corner solution where they do not give anything to public radio. In part, for this reason, we do not see government contributions to public goods in the real world accompanied by euro-for-euro decreases in private contributions. In the case of public radio, it appears that an increase of €1 in government contributions is accompanied by a decrease in the range of 10 to 20 cents in private contributions. (See Bruce Kingma, 'An Accurate Measurement of the Crowd-out Effect, Income Effect, and Price Effect for Charitable Contributions', *Journal of Political Economy* 97, no. 5 (1989), 1197–207.)

Exercise 27A.10

Could it be that an increase of government support for a public good causes someone who previously chose to give to that public good to cease giving? How would such a person's best-response function look?

27A.2.2 Government Provision Under Distortionary Taxes Another real-world problem governments face is that governments are rarely able to use non-distortionary taxes to raise revenues. If a government does find a non-distortionary or efficient tax that generates no deadweight loss, it would be optimal for it to provide the public good level y^* at which the sum of individual marginal benefits is equal to the marginal cost of providing the public good. If distortionary taxes have to be used in order to raise revenues for public good provision, the social marginal cost of government provision is higher than the cost of producing the public good because each euro in tax revenues raised is accompanied by a deadweight loss. The optimal level of government-provided public goods decreases the more distortionary the taxes used to finance public goods become.

Exercise 27A.11

Given what we have learned about the rate at which deadweight loss increases as tax rates rise, what would you expect to happen to the optimal level of government provision of a particular public good as the number of public goods financed by government increases?

Exercise 27A.12

If a particular public good is subject to some partial crowd-out when governments contribute to its provision, might it be optimal for the government not to contribute to the public good in the presence of distortionary taxation?

27A.2.3 Subsidies for Voluntary Giving An alternative policy to government provision of a public good involves the government subsidizing the private production of the good. This, too, should be intuitive as soon as we recognize the free-rider problem as arising from the presence of a positive externality. In our treatment of externalities, we illustrated that the underprovision of goods due to positive externalities can be corrected through Pigouvian subsidies.

Suppose, for instance, that the local government recognizes that families keep falling victim to Prisoner's Dilemma incentives when they are planning their New Year's Eve fireworks display. The local government decides to make it cheaper for each to buy fireworks by paying for some portion s of each firework they purchase. Both families will still be playing the same game they did before, except that their best-response functions will now shift up. Remember that family A's best response to any public good level y_2 that family B purchases is determined by the condition that A's marginal benefit from the last unit of public good they purchase will be equal to the marginal cost of making the purchase. If the government pays for a portion of each firework A buys, their marginal cost falls, which implies they will purchase more fireworks for any expectation they have of y_2 than they did before. Graph 27.4 illustrates how both families' best-response functions and thus the Nash equilibrium change as the subsidy increases from panel (a) to (c). In panel (a), there is no subsidy and each family purchases substantially less than the efficient quantity y^*. In panel (b), a modest subsidy shifts their purchases closer to the efficient level and in panel (c) the subsidy is exactly the size it needs to be in order for both to purchase half the efficient quantity and together, purchase y^*.

Exercise 27A.13

In Section B, we show mathematically that the optimal subsidy will involve the government paying for half the cost of the fireworks if both families have the same preferences. By thinking about the size of the externality or how much of the total benefit is not taken into account by an individual consumer, does this make intuitive sense?

Exercise 27A.14

Could the government induce production of the efficient level of fireworks if it only subsidized the purchases of one of the consumers?

Graph 27.4 The Changing Nash Equilibrium Under Subsidies

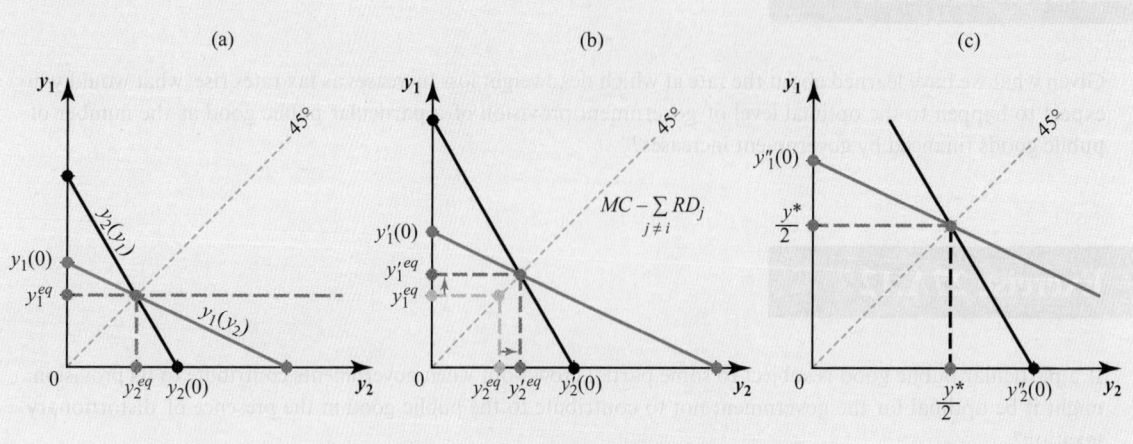

In the real world, the most common way in which governments fund private giving for public goods is through tax deductions. Many governments, for example, allow individuals to give to charitable institutions and not pay taxes on the amount that they give to such institutions. If an individual gives €100 of their income to a cancer charity, they get to deduct this from the income on which they would otherwise have to pay taxes. If the marginal income tax rate is 30 per cent, the individual has a choice of either paying €30 of the €100 in income taxes and spending the remaining €70 on goods they like to consume, or they can give €100 to the cancer charity. Giving €100 to the charity costs them only €70 in private consumption. By making charitable contributions tax deductible, the government has subsidized contributions by 30 per cent.

Exercise 27A.15

True or False: Under an income tax that has increasing marginal tax rates as income goes up, the rich get a bigger per-euro subsidy for charitable giving than the poor when charitable giving is tax deductible.

Exercise 27A.16

If the only way to finance the subsidy for private giving is through distortionary taxation, would you expect the optimal subsidy to be larger or smaller than if the subsidy could be financed through efficient lump-sum taxes?

27A.3 Solving the Prisoner's Dilemma by Establishing Markets

In Chapter 21, we saw that, at a fundamental level, the market failure that arises from the existence of externalities is really a failure of markets to exist. We argued that, hypothetically, if sufficient numbers of markets were established, the externality would disappear and with its disappearance, the first welfare theorem would reappear. We will therefore investigate the extent to which we can think of markets as a possible solution to the public goods problem.

We could apply this at a purely abstract level to our fireworks example. The fundamental public goods and free-rider problem emerges from the fact that when family *A consumes* fireworks, they are also *producing* fireworks consumption for family *B*. There is no market that prices the production of fireworks consumption for family *B*; that is, there is no price that *B* has to pay *A* when family *A* produces something that family *B* values. As a result, family *A* does not take into consideration the benefit that *B* receives from their fireworks. There is a positive externality, which is the same as saying there is a missing market for goods that are being produced as family *A* makes their consumption decision. It is not clear how the missing market could be established for family *A*'s fireworks production, neither would there be much of a market with only two consumers involved. The point is not to argue that such markets could generally be established, but neither does the difficulty of establishing the abstract missing markets mean that we cannot consider some form of market solution to the problem, as we saw in the example of negative pollution externalities and pollution voucher markets.

We therefore want to think about the conditions under which decentralized market provision of public goods *could* emerge if certain types of markets were appropriately set up. In order for us to have any chance of public goods being provided in such a decentralized market setting, it would seem that at the very least we have to assume that consumption of the public good is *excludable*; that is, we would have to assume that the producer of the public good can keep people from consuming the good if they do not pay what the producer demands. This does not take away from the *non-rivalry* of the good; that is, the public good can still be consumed by multiple people at the same time. For instance, a large swimming pool can be enjoyed by a large number of families at the same time, but the provider of the swimming pool can keep people out if they don't pay an entrance fee.

Exercise 27A.17

Can you think of other goods that are non-rivalrous at least to some extent but also excludable?

27A.3.1 Lindahl Price Discrimination and the Incentive to Lie Decentralized market exchanges are governed by prices, and in our typical competitive equilibrium, this means that everyone faces the same market price and each consumer gets to choose their optimal quantity at that price. *Same price, different quantities.* Now let's ask how a market for a typical pure public good would have to look. A pure public good is a good that all consumers can consume at the very same time in the same quantity. In a market for public goods, individuals would consume the same quantity of the public good. In order for that quantity to be something the consumer actually chooses given their budget constraint, different consumers would have to face different prices. *Different prices, same quantity*, which is the opposite of the decentralized market equilibrium for private goods.

Consider the case of fireworks and suppose that a producer of fireworks displays owns a sufficiently large land area such that the only way to see the fireworks is to step onto the producer's land. Suppose further that the producer has put up barbed wire around their land with, just to be mean, a sufficiently strong electrical current flowing through the wire to instantly knock any potential trespasser unconscious. The only way to step onto the land is to go through an entrance booth at which the producer can charge individuals an entry fee.

Now suppose the producer knows each consumer's demand curve for the intensity of firework displays, and can determine the optimal number of fireworks y^* to launch into the air during a particular show. Recall that we can calculate y^* by adding the demands vertically and finding where the resulting aggregate demand curve intersects marginal cost. The producer of fireworks can determine *individualized prices* for each consumer such that each consumer would choose y^* as part of their optimal consumption bundle at their own individual price. The individualized price for consumer i would be their marginal benefit of the public good y^*, and since the marginal benefits sum to marginal cost at y^*, the individualized prices sum to marginal cost.

Exercise 27A.18

Illustrate, using a graph of two different demand curves for two different consumers, how a producer would calculate y^* and what prices they would charge to each individual in order to get them to choose y^* as their most preferred bundle.

Exercise 27A.19

Does the producer collect enough revenues under such individualized pricing to cover marginal costs?

The resulting equilibrium would be one in which a single producer of the public good charges *different prices* to consumers in such a way that each consumer chooses the *same quantity* of the public good. This is the public good analogue to the private good competitive equilibrium, and it is known as a *Lindahl equilibrium*, named after Erik Lindahl (1891–1960), a Swedish economist who first proposed the idea in 1919. The prices that emerge in this equilibrium are known as *Lindahl prices*. Note that it involves *price discrimination* by the producer, with higher prices charged to consumers that have greater demand for the public good. In order to implement the price discrimination, the producer has to know the demands or preferences of individual consumers, and therein lies the problem with the Lindahl equilibrium.

Since an individual knows that the price they will be charged as they enter the land on which they can view the fireworks is directly related to the producer's impression of their tastes for fireworks, the individual has every incentive to play down how much they like fireworks. The individual has an incentive to lie about their preferences. That incentive increases the more people are lining up to get onto the land from which the fireworks can be enjoyed. If only two individuals are the only ones to see the fireworks, they face a trade-off when deciding how much to lie about their enthusiasm for fireworks. On the one hand, any lie will reduce the number of fireworks that will be launched because it will affect the calculation of y^*, but, on the other, the individual will not have to pay as much to get in if they lie. They lie a little bit but won't claim that they don't care about fireworks at all. If, however, there are 10 000 people lined up to get onto the land from which the fireworks display can be enjoyed, they are suddenly only one of many. This means that the impact of the individual's lie on y^* becomes very small, but the impact of their lie on the price they'll get charged continues to be big. As the number of consumers goes up, the incentive to lie increases. *Unless producers of public goods already know a lot about the preferences of their consumers*, a Lindahl equilibrium under which consumers choose the optimal quantity of the public good at individualized prices cannot emerge.

Exercise 27A.20

Consider the entrance fees to cinemas on days when not every seat fills up. If it is generally true that older people and students have lower demand for watching new releases in cinemas, can you explain entrance discounts for the elderly and for students as an attempt at Lindahl pricing?

One could argue that private goods markets also face such incentive problems; that is, when individuals negotiate over the price they will pay you for a litre of milk, they also have an incentive to pretend that the milk is not worth that much to them so that the producer gives it to them at a lower price. That's true, but the difference is that an individual's incentive to lie about their tastes for milk get weaker and weaker the more milk consumers there are because if they claim to not like milk that much, the seller will go to someone that isn't such a pain. Thus, in private goods markets, the incentive to misrepresent preferences disappears as the market becomes large, while in public goods markets that incentive gets bigger and bigger the larger the market. It may not have occurred to you to try to tell the local supermarket that you really don't care for milk that much in order to get a better price, but if you were told that your taxes will increase the more you say you like national defence but the increased tax payments from you will have little perceptible impact on the level of national defence, you'd probably pretend to be a pacifist. In Chapter 16, we argued that the concept of a competitive equilibrium becomes compelling once we realize that the set of stable allocations in the world, formalized in the concept of the core set of allocations, converges to the set of competitive equilibrium allocations as an economy becomes large. It can be shown that the opposite is true for public goods economies. As the economy becomes large, the set of core allocations explodes far beyond just the allocations that could be supported in a Lindahl equilibrium. The reason for this is closely related to the reason why the incentive to misrepresent one's preferences increases as the economy gets large.

27A.3.2 Clubs, Local Public Goods Markets and Voting with Feet The concept of a Lindahl equilibrium, while academically interesting, is of limited real-world usefulness given the necessity for producers to know consumer preferences that consumers themselves have every incentive to misrepresent. That does not, however, mean that other forms of market forces might not play an important role in shaping the kinds and varieties of *excludable* public goods we can choose. Homeowners' associations offer public security, swimming pools and golf courses; a variety of clubs offer access to public spaces to paying customers; and local governments of all kinds offer a variety of public services. The goods offered by such institutions are not pure public goods that are fully non-rivalrous, but each can still be consumed by multiple consumers at the same time. In each case, market forces play an important role.

This was pointed out by Charles Tiebout (1924–1968) in the 1950s and has given rise to one of the largest academic literatures in all of economics. Tiebout proposed a simple and intuitive hypothesis: when there are goods that are neither fully rivalrous nor fully non-rivalrous, and when there exists a mechanism for excluding consumers who do not pay the required fee for using the good, one can derive conditions under which multiple providers of such goods will compete in a market-like setting and provide efficient levels of the goods. Tiebout was thinking of local communities as being the providers, with local public services restricted to those who reside within the boundaries of local communities. Just as different shopping centres provide different varieties of shops and different levels of characteristics such as lighting in parking areas, a private security force to protect the shopping centre, etc. that consumers might care about, we can think of different communities providing different mixes of public services with different mixes of local fees and taxes for residents of those communities. Just as shopping centres compete with one another for customers who will decide to frequent one shopping centre more than others, communities compete for residents. Successful shopping centres find sufficient numbers of consumers with similar tastes to create a sufficiently large clientele, as do successful communities.

To the extent to which there is enough competition between shopping centres, each will make roughly zero profits in equilibrium and consumers can choose from the optimal number of different centres to find those that most closely match their tastes given their budgets. To the extent to which there is sufficient competition between local communities, such communities similarly offer a variety of bundles of goods and services for consumers to choose from, with each community's choices disciplined by competitive market forces. In the case of communities, *land* serves as the exclusionary device since only those who own or rent land and housing in a particular community have access to the public services offered. Such communities could be privately operated as are, for instance, homeowners' associations. Even when local governments are operated through political processes, politicians have to confront market pressures to ensure that the mix of public services and local taxes attracts a sufficient clientele of local residents.

Exercise 27A.21

Why do consumers not face the same incentive to lie about their tastes in such a Tiebout equilibrium as they do in a Lindahl equilibrium?

Clubs that are not tied to land offer another application of Tiebout's insight. For instance, one can think of churches as clubs providing public goods such as religious services, with churches competing for parishioners who have different tastes for the types of music, sermons and denominational affiliations that are offered. While churches typically do not charge an entrance fee, they find other ways of enforcing expectations about contributing to the church in financial and non-financial ways. Or one can think of private schools that offer a service that has at least some public goods characteristics, with such schools competing on both the types of curricula they offer and the level of tuition they charge. Or we can think of private operators of swimming pools and health clubs who charge for uses of their somewhat non-rivalrous goods and compete with others that do the same.

As with many economic theories, the insights rarely hold perfectly in the real world but they do play an important role in the bigger picture of how public goods are provided. For now, our main point is just that in speaking as if there were a crass distinction between private goods and public goods, we are implicitly ignoring a whole set of important goods that lie in between the extremes, and the inbetween cases are often provided by a rich combination of civil society, market and government actions.

27A.3.3 The Lighthouse: Another Look at Excludability and Market Provision

In our discussion of market provision of public goods, we have placed some emphasis on the importance of excludability of public goods if such goods are to be provided through market forces. After all, if a provider cannot exclude those who attempt to free ride, how can the provider ever expect to collect sufficient revenues to provide anything close to the optimal level of the public good?

There is much truth in the intuitive insight that providers other than governments that can use taxes must find ways to finance public goods, and that this typically involves some mechanism for excluding non-payers. We sometimes underestimate the extent to which providers might find creative ways of doing this. In a famous article, Ronald Coase studied the particularly revealing case of lighthouses in the 18th century. Until Coase's case study, the lighthouse was often given as a motivating example in textbooks to illustrate the difficulty of providing a vital public good without the government doing so directly. Before the invention of the current navigational technologies used on ships, lighthouses played a pivotal role in guiding ships safely along dangerous shores where, in the absence of the guidance offered by lighthouses, ships could easily run aground. The services offered by lighthouses are classically non-rivalrous; no matter how many ships are safely guided towards the shores by a lighthouse, additional ships can similarly make use of the light that is emitted. Economists writing about the problem of providing lighthouses could not see an easy way for private lighthouse operators to exclude those who did not pay.

Coase looked to see how lighthouses were actually provided in many instances, and what he found was that private providers had found ways of financing lighthouses by charging those who benefited most from them. It turns out that providers *bundled* the public good provided by the lighthouses with private goods, in particular the rights to dock a ship in the harbour to which the lighthouses guided ships. The light dues that funded lighthouses across England, Scotland and Wales were collected by customs officials in ports, which created the effective bundling of port use to use of lighthouses. While it is true that lighthouses offered additional positive externalities to ships that used the light to navigate the shore without docking in the harbour, it appears that these externalities were small relative to the benefits that could be priced for those who used the local harbours. While the British government played a role in the protection of property rights and the collection of light fees, it was not necessary to have the government directly provide lighthouses.

Exercise 27A.22

Can you think of the provision of free access to gyms in housing complexes in a way that is analogous to Coase's findings about lighthouses?

27A.4 Civil Society and the Free-Rider Problem

When we introduced the Prisoner's Dilemma, we pointed out that the model's prediction of complete non-cooperation is often contradicted by experimental and real-world evidence. In the real world, people do not seem to free ride nearly as much as the model predicts. As a result, the model does not successfully predict the *level* of voluntary contributions to public goods that we observe in the world. Neither does the model make sense of the *distribution* of charitable giving; nor, to be more precise, can the model make sense of the fact that the same person is often observed to give to *many* different charities.

To think of this in another way, to one extent or another, most of us care about large public goods such as finding cures for diseases, alleviating poverty, saving the environment and so on. Aside from people like Bill Gates, most of us have modest resources to contribute to solving these very large problems. As we contemplate how much and to whom to give, the rational course of action would be to find the public good that we care about most and where we think our contribution can have the biggest impact. We should give the entire amount that we decide to devote to charitable purposes to one *and only one* cause. Suppose, for example, an individual cares most about poor children in the developing world and wants to make as much of a difference there as they can. Once they have given €1000 or €10 000 to that effort, it is hard for them to think that they have now made enough of a difference in alleviating poverty in the developing world to move on to contribute their next euro to a different public good, say Alzheimer's research or meningitis research. The individual is too small a part of the world for their contribution to make a large enough marginal impact in the area they care about most to think they have solved that problem sufficiently to move on to the next one.

In most cases, we actually see individuals giving their time and money to multiple causes. A model of giving that assumes we only take into account the difference our giving makes in the world cannot rationalize this behaviour. When people give to multiple causes, there must be something else that explains this pattern, just as there must be something else that explains why we give as much as we do. That something else often has to do with the way that civil society institutions persuade us to give. In some instances, we might be seeing the Coase Theorem at work, and in other cases, civil society institutions persuade us that we get *private* benefits in addition to the *public* benefit from our giving. In this section, we'll further explore these ways in which the civil society engages, and why it sometimes succeeds so much more than at other times. Finally, civil society institutions might design creative incentive schemes that overcome the Prisoner's Dilemma incentives.

27A.4.1 Small Public Goods and the Coase Theorem In Chapter 21, we introduced the Coase Theorem in the broader context of externalities, and we illustrated Coase's argument that as long as property rights are sufficiently well defined and transactions costs are sufficiently low, decentralized bargaining would result in optimal outcomes. We developed the theorem for the case of negative externalities, but the same argument holds for positive externalities such as those produced by public goods.

Consider again the fireworks scenario. In this case, the property rights are pretty settled. Family *B* has the right to enjoy family *A*'s fireworks without paying for them and vice versa. If *A* takes *B* to court to demand compensation for the enjoyment family *B* gets from *A*'s fireworks, the court will probably dismiss the case out of hand. Family *A*, therefore, has an incentive to go to *B*'s house to discuss the whole fireworks issue and to see if they can find a way for family *B* to contribute so that they can jointly find a way out of the little Prisoner's Dilemma. If transactions costs, including the costs of enforcing an agreement, are sufficiently low, they should be able to solve their dilemma.

This might help explain why people often voluntarily provide for multiple public goods in their immediate vicinity, especially when combining our understanding of the Coase Theorem with the intuitions from the game theory chapter that suggest cooperation between players with Prisoner's Dilemma incentives can emerge in settings where the players interact repeatedly and each time believe there is a good chance they will meet again. It cannot get us very far towards explaining why people give to larger public goods the way they do: to museums, universities, hospitals and perhaps even economics departments.

27A.4.2 Private Benefits From Public Giving: The Warm Glow Effect An individual might give finds to support Alzheimer's research not only because they believe that their donation will have a positive marginal impact on the probability that a cure will be found but also because they might have some personal experience with the disease through a family member. In such cases, economists say that the donor is deriving a *warm glow* from giving to a public good. The donor gets a *private benefit* from their public giving. To the extent to which our purpose for giving to charitable causes fulfils a private need, we do not encounter the free-rider problem anymore than we do when we think of that same individual's 'contribution' to buying their lunch. While the free-rider problem is still present to the degree to which Alzheimer's research is a public good, it is counteracted by the private benefit the donor receives from making a donation to a charity. The more charities such as that for Alzheimer's get people to view donations as associated with personal motives rather than contributing to the big public good of finding a cure, the smaller is the free-rider problem that remains to be overcome.

Some charitable organizations deliberately manufacture such reasons in the way they market themselves. In a previous chapter, we mentioned the case of relief organizations that help poor families and communities in developing countries. Some of these agencies advertise that with a monthly contribution of €20, you can change a *particular* child's life. Not only that, the organization will match donors with a particular child and establish contact with the family, send you pictures and yearly updates, and so on. It seems highly unlikely that such organizations will actually stop helping a particular family if you stop sending funds, which means that your contribution is actually a contribution to a larger public good of alleviating poverty in the developing world. By framing their fundraising efforts in a way that personalizes contributions, the organizations in essence attempt to convert what is a fairly abstract public good to a concrete private good: helping one particular family that you end up caring about. It is an example of image marketing in which the organization changes the image of what it is asking you to contribute to in order to make it more likely that you will view your contribution as a private rather than a public good.

Exercise 27A.23

Explain how it is rational for a person to give to both relieving poverty in the developing world and to Alzheimer's research in the presence of warm glow but not in its absence.

Non-profit organizations can make use of image marketing just as for-profit firms do, except that we tend to think of successful image marketing that leads to greater charitable giving as a socially positive outcome given that it helps individuals overcome Prisoner's Dilemma incentives. Churches appeal to a sense that we are working towards a reward in the next life as we give 'selflessly' in this life; local relief organizations offer individuals a chance to build meaningful relationships as they volunteer to build houses for the homeless; and universities put names of large donors on buildings to give a private reward for giving to a public good. There is nothing in any of these efforts to guarantee an optimal level of public goods provision within the civil society, but all of them appear to succeed in overcoming Prisoner's Dilemma incentives to some extent through providing contributors with a warm glow from giving.

Exercise 27A.24

Can you use the warm glow effect to explain why government contributions to public goods do not fully crowd out private contributions?

27A.4.3 Civil Society, Warm Glows and Tipping Points There are the occasional episodes in history when very large public goods appear to emerge quite spontaneously from civil society interactions outside government or market mechanisms. Large social movements such as the civil rights marches in the 1960s in the United States when white and black Americans gave up their time, often at considerable risk, to demand social change, is one example. Similarly, the Solidarity movement in Poland that laid the foundation for the fall of the Iron Curtain in Eastern Europe, and the demonstration of 'people power' that drove dictators in places like the Philippines into exile. Such large social movements often aim at social change that affects us all, and as such they represent attempts to provide large public goods like more democracy, more human rights, etc. Most of our models would suggest that such movements are unlikely to gain much momentum because the larger they get, the deeper the free-rider problem they encounter. Does it really make sense for an individual to miss work or a day with family to go to a rally in which millions are already participating? Is there any chance that an individual's contribution to the rally will make any difference whatsoever?

Under some circumstances, individuals seem to be willing to risk almost anything to be a part of such movements, and on occasion, such movements have established public goods such as greater civil rights quite successfully without and often in spite of government action or inaction. One theory that explains such phenomena is based on an assumption that we derive increased private benefits from participating in such movements the more of our friends that participate. Someone who feels really strongly about a particular issue might start standing on a street corner, and most of the time that's pretty much where it ends. Maybe a few others who feel strongly about the issue show some support and stand there with them. Sometimes, as others join, yet more join and the movement builds into an avalanche that can't be stopped. At a critical point, such movements cross a tipping point where they gain a self-perpetuating momentum, while movements that don't cross the tipping point quickly fizzle out and become remembered as quaint fads.

Suppose individuals in some group like a church congregation differ in their demand for a public good y, like helping the poor, but all individuals receive a greater warm glow from giving to the public good the more others gave in the previous period, where you can think of a period as a day or a week or a month, depending on the application. Such models tend to have at least two pure strategy Nash equilibria. In one equilibrium, few people contribute and, because so few people contribute, most people do not get much of a warm glow from contributing. In a second equilibrium, most people contribute and, because so many contribute, people get substantial warm glow from contributing. Social entrepreneurs therefore often have the challenge of starting in a low contribution equilibrium and finding ways of getting sufficiently many individuals energized to cross a tipping point that takes them to the high contribution equilibrium. They must first find those who are most deeply committed and hope that such individuals have sufficient social contacts with others who care less about the public good at hand but who care more as the number of other people engaged in the movement increases.

Exercise 27A.25*

Suppose an individual's warm glow from demonstrating on the streets for some worthy cause depends on how much you demonstrate on the streets and vice versa. Letting the fraction of time spent demonstrating go from 0 to 1, suppose that the individual does not get enough of a warm glow from demonstrating unless you spend at least half your time on the streets, and you feel similarly about your warm glow and the individual's participation. Illustrate the best-response functions to each other's time on the streets. Where are the two stable, pure strategy Nash equilibria, and where is the tipping point?

27A.5 Preference Revelation Mechanisms

The problem of providing public goods optimally could be easily solved if we knew people's preferences for public goods. We would have to add up individual demands and find where the aggregate demand for public goods crosses the marginal cost of providing such goods. We could also implement Lindahl prices for public goods, which would ensure that individuals are charged appropriately for the marginal benefits they receive from the optimal level of public goods we provide. As we saw in our discussion of Lindahl pricing, we face a fundamental underlying problem in that individuals typically have an incentive to misrepresent their preferences for public goods if their contributions to the public good are linked to their stated preferences for public goods. Economists have thought hard about how to overcome this problem, and they have proposed mechanisms that take into account this incentive problem. The general study of creating mechanisms that provide individuals with the incentive to truthfully reveal private information like their preferences for public goods is called *mechanism design*.

The fundamental problem faced by mechanism designers is that the designer would have a clear idea of what they would like to do if they could magically know people's preferences. Since they do not know those preferences, they need to come up with an incentive scheme that makes it in people's best interests to tell the mechanism designer their true preferences. This scheme has to be such that individuals think it is in their best interests to reveal information truthfully as they take into account what the mechanism designer will do with the information they collect. In the public goods context, the mechanism designer would like to know people's preferences over public goods in order to implement the optimal public goods level. What they need to do is define 'messages' that individuals can send and that contain the information they need to determine optimal public good provision, and they need to define a method by which they use these messages to determine how much public good to produce. That method in turn needs to have the property that it provides individuals with the incentive to send true messages about their tastes for public goods.

Exercise 27A.26

Suppose you have a piece of art that you would like to give to the person who values it the most, but you do not know people's tastes. Explain how a second-price sealed bid auction represents a mechanism that accomplishes this while eliciting truthful messages from all interested parties.

27A.5.1 A Simple Example of a Mechanism Suppose two people live at the end of a cul-de-sac that currently has no streetlight. At night it gets very dark in front of their houses and they approach the local government about putting up a light. The local government would like to help but only if the value that both place on the streetlight actually exceeds the cost of the €1000 it takes to put it up. The two individuals do their best to use artful prose to verbalize their deep desire to have light, punctuated by an occasional reference to their phobias of darkness. The local government knows they have every incentive to exaggerate their desire for light and fear of the dark in order to get taxpayers to fund the light on their street. The local government, therefore, needs to work out a way for the two individuals to reveal their true desires.

The head of environmental services at the local government proposes the following. To begin with, they split the €1000 cost in two and ask each individual to pay the council €500. They then ask both people to tell them how much value above or below €500 they each place on the streetlight. The head of environmental services is asking for a message that is a number, which could be negative if the two people want to tell them they place less than €500 value on the light, or positive if they want to tell them they place more than €500 of value on the light. Let's denote the message that both people send as m_1 and m_2 respectively. The local council will only build the light if they indicate the value the two place on the light is at least €1000. Since the messages they send are messages about how much each values the light *above €500*, this means the local council will only build the streetlight if $m_1 + m_2 \geq 0$. The head of environmental services furthermore tells both people that if the local council ends up building the streetlight, they will refund person 1 an amount equal to the message m_1 that person 2 sent while refunding person 2 an amount equal to the message m_2 that person 1 sent. If person 2 sends a message $m_2 > 0$, person 1 will get a partial refund, but if person 2 sends a message $m_1 < 0$, person 1 will have to pay for the amount $(-m_1)$. If, on the other hand, the local council does not build the streetlight because $m_1 + m_2 < 0$, the head of environmental services will refund their €500 payments.

The local council has set up a simultaneous move message sending game in which each person now has to decide what message to send about their true underlying preference for the streetlight. Let v_1 and v_2 denote both people's true valuation of the light above €500. If the light is built, person 2 will get their true value v_1 from enjoying the streetlight beyond the €500 payment they have made, plus they will get a payment from the council equal to m_2 if $m_2 > 0$ or they will have to make a payment equal to $(-m_2)$ if $m_2 < 0$. Person 2's total payoff if the streetlight is built is therefore $(v_1 + m_2)$, while person 2's total payoff if the streetlight is not built is 0 since their €500 will be refunded.

At the time person 2 decides what m_1 message to send to the head of environmental services, they do not know what m_2 message person 1 is sending. It may be that $-m_2 \leq v_1$ or it may be that $-m_2 > v_1$. If $-m_2 \leq v_1$, we can add m_2 to both sides of the inequality and get $v_1 + m_2 \geq 0$. Thus, if person 2 sends a truthful message of $m_1 = v_1$, $m_1 + m_2 \geq 0$, the streetlight will be built. Person 2's resulting payoff is $v_1 + m_2 \geq 0$, which is at least as good as getting a payoff of 0 that would occur if they sent a false message that caused the light not to be built. If $-m_2 \leq v_1$, person 2 should send a truthful message $m_1 = v_1$. Now suppose the other scenario is true; that is, $-m_2 > v_1$. If, under that scenario, person 2 again sent a truthful message $m_1 = v_1$, then $m_1 + m_2 < 0$, the streetlight does not get built, and they get a payoff of 0. If person 2 instead sent a false message that is high enough to get the streetlight built, their payoff will be $v_1 + m_2 < 0$, so again it's best to send the truthful message $m_1 = v_1$. *Regardless of what message m_2 person 1 sends, it is person 2's best strategy to send a truthful message about their own preferences.* Truth telling in this game is a dominant strategy. Since person 1 faces the same incentives as person 2, they will both send truthful messages and the streetlight gets built only if they value the light more than what it costs.

If there are $N > 2$ people at the end of the cul-de-sac, the local council can design analogous mechanisms that will similarly result in truth telling. Instead of beginning with a charge of €500 for each person, the council would instead charge each person €1000/N at the beginning and build the light only if the sum of the messages is at least zero. It would refund to each person an amount equal to the sum of the other people's messages.

Exercise 27A.27*

Suppose three people lived at the end of the cul-de-sac and suppose the head of environmental services proposes the same mechanism except that they now ask person 2 for a €333.33 payment at the start instead of €500 and they are told (as player 1) that they will get a refund equal to $m_2 + m_3$ if $(m_1 + m_2 + m_3) \geq 0$ and the light is built. Otherwise, they just get their €333.33 back and no light is built. Can you show that truth telling is again a dominant strategy for person 2?

27A.5.2 Truth Telling Mechanisms and Their Problems We have given a simple example of a mechanism in which the local government elicits the necessary information to determine whether a public good should be built. The trick for doing this was that the payoff to each of the people does not depend on the message they send except to the extent that each person's message might be pivotal in determining whether or not the public good is provided. Remember, person 2's payoff was constructed to be equal to $v_1 + m_2$ if the streetlight is built and 0 otherwise. Nowhere in their payoff does their own message m_1 appear; it only matters in the sense that it enters the council's decision on whether to put up the streetlight. All they had to think about was whether it made sense to tell the truth knowing that this would determine whether the streetlight is built, and in making that decision the council forced them to consider the messages sent by others about how much they value the streetlight. The mechanism designed forces person 2 to consider in their own decision how much others value the streetlight by making a payment to them that equalled the sum of how much above €500 other people said they valued the light.

The typical public goods decision is not *whether* to provide a public good but also *how much* of the public good to provide. Governments, for instance, have to decide how many police resources to provide to ensure public safety, and how much to spend on national defence.

A second problem with our simple mechanism is that it will generally not yield sufficient revenues to fund the public good. Thus, while the mechanism elicits truthful information for the city to determine whether to invest in the public good, it does not provide sufficient funds for actually paying the cost.

Exercise 27A.28

Can you think of a case where our simple mechanism generates sufficient revenues to pay for the streetlight?

Exercise 27A.29

Can you think of a case where the mechanism results in an outcome under which the council needs to come up with more money than the cost of the streetlight in order to implement the mechanism?

More generally it turns out that preference revelation mechanisms cannot implement and fund fully efficient outcomes if our goal is to have truth telling be a *dominant strategy* Nash equilibrium, but they can do so if we only require truth telling to be a Nash equilibrium strategy. For now, the main point to take away from our discussion is that we *can* think of mechanisms to elicit truthful information about public goods preferences and thereby overcome the incentive to misrepresent preferences in order to free ride on others. However, such mechanisms come at a cost that might make it difficult to implement them in many circumstances. Such mechanisms have only been used on rare occasions to provide public goods.

27A.5.3 Mechanism Design More Generally Not all mechanisms have as their goal to provide public goods. There are many circumstances where some parties have more relevant information than others that would like to acquire some of that information. In such cases, mechanisms can be designed to get individuals to reveal private information knowing what will happen once that information is revealed. Economists, for instance, have had major roles in designing mechanisms by which large public holdings are auctioned in ways that reveal the private valuations by bidders for the public holdings. Economists have also designed mechanisms that, in the absence of market prices, result in optimal matches between buyers and sellers.

27B   The Mathematics of Public Goods

We begin our mathematical treatment of public goods in Section 27B.1 by illustrating the basic necessary condition for public good quantities to be optimal. While we do this for a general case with many consumers, we introduce an example involving two consumers with well-defined and identical preferences, and we will use this example throughout to illustrate the mathematics behind the intuitions developed in Section A. As in our intuitive development of the material, we will demonstrate the free-rider problem as an outgrowth of the presence of positive externalities that individuals generally do not take into account unless their choices are tempered by non-market institutions.

27B.1 Public Goods and the Free-Rider Problem

Public goods give rise to externalities, and we already know from earlier chapters that decentralized market behaviour in the presence of externalities often does not result in efficient outcomes. We begin by deriving the necessary condition for optimality of public goods, that the sum of marginal benefits must equal the marginal cost of producing the public good. We proceed to illustrate the free-rider problem that keeps decentralized market behaviour from being efficient.

27B.1.1 The Efficient Level of Public Goods Suppose x represents a composite private good and y represents the public good. There are N consumers in the economy, with $u^n(x_n, y)$ representing the nth consumer's preferences over their consumption of the composite private good x_n and the public good. Suppose

THE MATHEMATICS OF PUBLIC GOODS

further that f represents the technology for producing y from the composite good; that is, suppose $y = f(x)$. Finally, suppose that the total available level of private good in the absence of public goods production is X.

We are interested in deriving the necessary conditions that have to be satisfied for us to produce an efficient public good level y^*. For a situation to be efficient, we have to set y^* such that nothing can be changed to make one consumer better off without making some consumers worse off. We can calculate this by choosing the consumption levels $(x_1, x_2,..., x_N)$ and y to maximize one consumer's utility subject to holding the others fixed at some arbitrary level and subject to the constraint that $y = f(x - \Sigma x_n)$.

Exercise 27B.1

Explain the constraint $y = f(x - \Sigma x_n)$.

To cut down on notation as we write down this optimization problem formally, we can define a function $g(\Sigma x_n, y) = y - f(X - \Sigma x_n)$ and set up the optimization problem to derive the necessary conditions for an efficient public good level y^* as:

$$\max_{(x_1,...,x_N,y)} u^1(x_1, y) \text{ subject to } u^n(x_n, y) = \bar{u}^n \text{ for all } n = 2, \ldots, N \text{ and } g\left(\sum_{n=1}^{N} x_n, y\right) = 0. \tag{27.1}$$

The Lagrange function for this optimization problem is:

$$\mathcal{L} = u^1(x_1, y) + \sum_{n=2}^{N} \lambda_n(\bar{u}^n - u^n(x_n, y)) + \lambda_1 g\left(\sum_{n=1}^{N} x_n, y\right), \tag{27.2}$$

where $(\lambda_2,..., \lambda_N)$ are the Lagrange multipliers for the constraints that hold utility levels for consumers 2 through N fixed and λ_1 is the Lagrange multiplier for the production constraint. To get first-order conditions, we differentiate $\mathcal{L}$ with respect to each of the choice variables to get:

$$\frac{\partial \mathcal{L}}{\partial x_1} = \frac{\partial u^1}{\partial x_1} + \lambda_1 \frac{\partial g}{\partial x} = 0$$

$$\frac{\partial \mathcal{L}}{\partial x_n} = -\lambda_n \frac{\partial u^n}{\partial x_n} + \lambda_1 \frac{\partial g}{\partial x} = 0 \text{ for all } n = 2,...,N \tag{27.3}$$

$$\frac{\partial \mathcal{L}}{\partial y} = \frac{\partial u^1}{\partial y} - \sum_{n=2}^{N} \lambda_n \frac{\partial u^n}{\partial y} + \lambda_1 \frac{\partial g}{\partial y} = 0,$$

where we can express $\partial g/\partial x_i$ as $\partial g/\partial x$ since marginal increases in any x_i have the same impact on the first argument of the g function. The first of the first-order conditions can be written as $\partial u^1/\partial x_1 = -\lambda_1 \partial g/\partial x$. We can divide the first term of the third first-order condition by $\partial u^1/\partial x_1$ and the remaining terms by $-\lambda_1 \partial g/\partial x$. Subtracting the resulting last term from both sides, the last first-order condition becomes:

$$\frac{\partial u^1/\partial y}{\partial u^1/\partial x_1} + \sum_{n=2}^{N} \frac{\lambda_n}{\lambda_1} \frac{\partial u^n/\partial y}{\partial g/\partial x} = \frac{\partial g/\partial y}{\partial g/\partial x}. \tag{27.4}$$

The second set of first-order conditions can be rewritten as:

$$\frac{\lambda_n}{\lambda_1} = \frac{\partial g/\partial x}{\partial u^n/\partial x_n} \text{ for all } n = 2,\ldots,N, \tag{27.5}$$

which, when substituted for λ_n/λ_1 in equation (27.4), yields:

$$\frac{\partial u^1/\partial y}{\partial u^1/\partial x_1} + \sum_{n=2}^{N} \frac{\partial u^n/\partial y}{\partial u^n/\partial x_n} = \frac{\partial g/\partial y}{\partial g/\partial x}. \tag{27.6}$$

The first term in this equation can be brought into the summation in the second term, and the resulting equation can be inverted and multiplied by -1 to yield:

$$\sum_{n=1}^{N} -\frac{\partial u^n/\partial x_n}{\partial u^n/\partial y} = -\frac{\partial g/\partial x}{\partial g/\partial y}. \tag{27.7}$$

Notice that the left-hand side of the equation is the sum of the marginal rates of substitution for all the consumers in the economy, or the sum of the marginal benefits expressed in euros since we are interpreting x as a euro-denominated composite good. The right-hand side of the equation can be simplified given that g was defined as $g(\Sigma x_n, y) = y - f(X - \Sigma x_n)$, with $\partial g/\partial y = 1$ and $\partial g/\partial x = \partial f/\partial x$. The right-hand side simplifies to $\partial f/\partial x$, which is just the marginal cost in terms of x of producing one more unit of y. Equation (27.7) can be written as:

$$\sum_{n=1}^{N} MB_y^n = MC_y; \tag{27.8}$$

that is, the sum of the marginal benefits of the public good must be equal to the marginal cost of producing it. The optimality condition for public goods is often referred to as the Samuelsonian optimality conditions because of their original formal derivation by Paul Samuelson (1915–2009).

27B.1.2 An Example To make this more concrete in the context of an example we will continue to use in other parts of this section, suppose that we have an economy of two consumers who have identical Cobb–Douglas preferences that can be represented by the utility function:

$$u^n(x_n, y) = x_n^\alpha y^{(1-\alpha)}. \tag{27.9}$$

Suppose further a simple production technology $y = f(x) = x$ that permits us to produce 1 unit of the public good from 1 unit of the composite private good, and suppose the only resources we have are the incomes of the two consumers, I_1 and I_2.

To find the efficient level of the public good y^*, we can calculate this by choosing x_1, x_2 and y to maximize one consumer's utility subject to holding the other's fixed at some arbitrary indifference curve $\bar{u}$ and subject to the constraint that only the consumers' incomes can be used to fund the public good; that is, we can solve the optimization problem:

$$\max_{x_1, x_2, y} u^1(x_1, y) \text{ subject to } u^2(x_2, y) = \bar{u} \text{ and } y = (I_1 + I_2 - x_1 - x_2). \tag{27.10}$$

It is easier to solve this by taking natural logarithms of the utility function and substituting $y = (I_1 + I_2 - x_1 - x_2)$ into the utility functions for y. We can write the optimization problem as:

$$\max_{x_1, x_2} \alpha \ln x_1 + (1 - \alpha) \ln (I_1 + I_2 - x_1 - x_2) \text{ subject to}$$
$$\alpha \ln x_2 + (1 - \alpha) \ln (I_1 + I_2 - x_1 - x_2) = \bar{u}. \tag{27.11}$$

Solving the two first-order conditions, we get:

$$x_1 + x_2 = \alpha(I_1 + I_2) \tag{27.12}$$

which implies:

$$y^* = I_1 + I_2 - x_1 - x_2 = (I_1 + I_2) - \alpha(I_1 + I_2) = (1 - \alpha)(I_1 + I_2) \tag{27.13}$$

Exercise 27B.2

Verify the outcome of this optimization problem. *Hint*: Solve the first two first-order conditions for λ and use your answer to derive the equation for $(x_1 + x_2)$.

We can also check that this is the optimal quantity of the public good by adding up demand curves. We know that Cobb–Douglas preferences represented by $u(x, y) = x^\alpha y^{(1 - \alpha)}$ give rise to demand curves for y of the form $y = (a - \alpha)I/p$. Writing this as an inverse demand curve, consumer n's demand is $p = (1 - \alpha)I_n/y$. If we consider two consumers with identical preferences but different incomes, the vertical sum of these is:

$$\frac{(1 - \alpha)I_1}{y} + \frac{(1 - \alpha)I_2}{y} = \frac{(1 - \alpha)(I_1 + I_2)}{y} \tag{27.14}$$

When the production technology for y takes the form $y = f(x) = x$, the marginal cost of producing 1 additional unit of y is $c = 1$. Thus, a social planner who is interested in providing the efficient level of the public good would produce y as long as equation (27.14) is greater than marginal cost and would stop when:

$$\frac{(1 - \alpha)(I_1 + I_2)}{y} = 1. \tag{27.15}$$

Solving for y, we again get the optimal level of public goods as:

$$y^* = (1 - \alpha)(I_1 + I_2) \tag{27.16}$$

Exercise 27B.3

What is y^* if there are N rather than 2 consumers of the type described in our example, i.e. with the same Cobb–Douglas tastes but different incomes? What if everyone's income is also the same?

27B.1.3 Decentralized Provision of Public Goods Suppose we now continue with our example and we ask the two consumers to voluntarily contribute to the provision of the public good. In other words, suppose we asked each consumer n to decide on a contribution z_n of their income with each consumer knowing that the public good y will be a function of their joint contributions such that:

$$Y(z_1, z_2) = z_1 + z_2 \tag{27.17}$$

The consumers are engaged in a simultaneous-move game in which they both choose their individual contributions taking the other's contribution as given. To determine consumer 1's best-response function to consumer 2 contributing z_2, consumer 1 would solve the problem:

$$\max_{x_1, z_1} u^1(x_1, y) \text{ such that } I_1 = x_1 + p_1 z_1 \text{ and } y = z_1 + z_2, \tag{27.18}$$

where we have implicitly assumed that the price of x is 1 since x is a euro-denominated composite good. We have also assumed a 'price' P_n for contributing to the public good, where P_n is equal to 1 if no one is subsidizing the contributions of individuals. We are including the possibility of subsidies in preparation for discussing government subsidies of private giving.

Exercise 27B.4

Explain why $p_1 = p_2 = 1$ for both consumers in the absence of subsidies for giving to the public good.

Substituting $y = (z_1 + z_2)$ for y and $x_1 = I_1 - p_1 z_1$ for x_1 into the logarithmic transformation of the Cobb–Douglas utility function from equation (27.9), the problem becomes:

$$\max_{z_1} \alpha \ln (I_1 - p_1 z_1) + (1 - \alpha) \ln (z_1 + z_2), \tag{27.19}$$

where the first-order condition now just involves taking the derivative of the utility function with respect to z_1. Solving this first-order condition gives consumer 1's best-response function to z_2 as:

$$z_1(z_2) = \frac{(1 - \alpha)I_1}{p_1} - \alpha z_2, \tag{27.20}$$

and doing the same for consumer 2 we can similarly get consumer 2's best-response function to z_1 as:

$$z_2(z_1) = \frac{(1 - \alpha)I_2}{p_2} - \alpha z_1. \tag{27.21}$$

Exercise 27B.5

Draw the best-response functions for the two individuals in a graph similar to Graph 27.3. Label intercepts and slopes.

In a Nash equilibrium to this game, each consumer has to be best responding to the other. Substituting equation (27.21) for z_2 in equation (27.20), we can solve for consumer 1's equilibrium contribution as:

$$z_1^{eq} = \frac{I_1 p_2 - \alpha I_2 p_1}{(1 + \alpha)p_1 p_2} \qquad (27.22)$$

and substituting this back into equation (27.21), we get consumer 2's equilibrium contribution as:

$$z_2^{eq} = \frac{I_2 p_1 - \alpha I_1 p_2}{(1 + \alpha)p_1 p_2}. \qquad (27.23)$$

The sum of the individual contributions, and thus the equilibrium level of the public good under voluntary giving y^v, is therefore:

$$y^v(p_1, p_2) = z_1^{eq} + z_1^{eq} = \frac{(1 - \alpha)(I_1 p_2 + I_2 p_1)}{(1 + \alpha)p_1 p_2}. \qquad (27.24)$$

If the consumers do not receive any subsidy to give to the public good, this implies $p_1 = p_2 = 1$. Equation (27.24) simplifies to:

$$y^v(\text{no subsidy}) = \frac{(1 - \alpha)(I_1 + I_2)}{(1 + \alpha)} < (1 - \alpha)(I_1 + I_2) = y^*, \qquad (27.25)$$

where the inequality holds for all $\alpha > 0$. As long as consumers place at least some value on private good consumption, the voluntary contributions result in less than the optimal quantity of the public good as each consumer free rides on the contributions of the other.

Exercise 27B.6

Why do private contributions to the public good result in the optimal level of the public good when $\alpha = 0$?

Exercise 27B.7

Consider the equilibrium public good level as a fraction of the optimal public good level. In our example, what is the lowest this fraction can become, and what is the critical variable?

It can be seen how this underprovision of public goods under voluntary giving will continue, and get worse as the number of consumers increases. Suppose, for instance, that everyone is identical in every way, both in terms of their Cobb–Douglas preferences and in terms of their income, and that there is no subsidy for private giving to charity. Now instead of two people there are N people. In a symmetric equilibrium in which all the identical players play the same strategy, we can simplify equation (27.20) to:

$$z = (1 - \alpha)I - \alpha(N - 1)z, \qquad (27.26)$$

where $(N - 1)z$ is the contribution by all $(N - 1)$ players other than the one whose best-response function we are working with. Solving this for z, we get:

$$z^{eq} = \frac{(1 - \alpha)I}{1 + \alpha(N - 1)},$$ (27.27)

and the resulting equilibrium level of public good y^{eq} is equal to Nz^{eq} or:

$$y^{eq} = \frac{N(1 - \alpha)I}{1 + \alpha(N - 1)}.$$ (27.28)

In exercise 27B.3, you should have derived the optimal level of the public good for the N-person case as $y^* = N(1 - \alpha)I$, which means we can rewrite equation (27.28) as:

$$y^{eq} = \frac{y^*}{1 + \alpha(N - 1)}.$$ (27.29)

An increase in the number of consumers, N, of the public good increases the denominator of the right-hand side of this equation, which means that as N increases, the equilibrium quantity of the public good will be a decreasing fraction of the optimal quantity. *The free-rider problem gets worse as the number of consumers of the public good increases.*

Table 27.2 demonstrates this dramatically for the case where all consumers have income $I = 1000$ and $\alpha = 0.5$. The last row of the table reports the equilibrium public good level as a fraction of the optimal public good level. This is 1 when there is only a single consumer in the first column and there does not exist a free-rider problem. It falls quickly as we add consumers, already reaching 0.02 at $N = 100$.

Table 27.2 $I - 1000, \alpha - 0.5$

	Free Riding as Population Increases					
	$N = 1$	$N = 2$	$N = 5$	$N = 10$	$N = 25$	$N = 100$
y^{eq}	500	666.67	833.33	909.09	961.54	990.10
y^*	500	1000	2500	5000	12 500	50 000
y^{eq}/y^*	1.000	0.667	0.333	0.182	0.077	0.020

Exercise 27B.8

As N gets larger, what do y^* and y^{eq} converge to for the example in Table 27.2? What does the equilibrium level of public good as a fraction of the optimal level converge to?

27B.2 Direct Government Policies to Address Free Riding

As in Section A, we'll consider two direct approaches a government might take to the public goods problem. First, it may itself provide the public good, and second it may use subsidies to make it cheaper for individuals to give to public goods. To result in optimal levels of the public good, both approaches require knowledge of consumer preferences.

27B.2.1 Government Provision and Crowd-Out We have already seen how an efficiency-focused government would calculate the optimal level of public goods. Now suppose the government, either because it does not have sufficient information about preferences or because the political process is not efficient, decides to fund some amount g of the public good rather than the optimal quantity y^*, and suppose it funds this through a proportional income tax t. Since income is assumed to be exogenous and not the result of an explicit labour-leisure choice, such a tax would have no deadweight loss in our example. In order to raise sufficient revenues to fund g, it must be that $t(I_1 + I_2) = g$ or, rearranging terms:

$$t = \frac{g}{(I_1 + I_2)}. \tag{27.30}$$

Exercise 27B.9

Can you explain in more detail why the tax in this case is efficient?

Each consumer n has to determine how much z_n to give to the public good themselves *given that the government is contributing g*. Consumer 1 takes as given consumer 2's contribution z_2 as well as the government contribution g, which changes the optimization problem in equation (27.19) to:

$$\max_{z_1} \alpha \ln((1 - t)I_1 - p_1 z_1) + (1 - \alpha) \ln (z_1 + z_2 + g), \tag{27.31}$$

or, substituting in for t:

$$\max_{z_1} \alpha \ln\left(\frac{(I_1 + I_2 - g)I_1}{I_1 + I_2} - p_1 z_1\right) + (1 - \alpha) \ln (z_1 + z_2 + g). \tag{27.32}$$

Solving the first-order condition for z_1, we get consumer 1's best response to (z_2, g) as:

$$z_1(z_2, g) = \frac{(1 - \alpha)I_1(I_1 + I_2 - g)}{(I_1 + I_2)p_1} - \alpha(z_2 + g). \tag{27.33}$$

Similarly, consumer 2's best response to (z_1, g) is:

$$z_2(z_1, g) = \frac{(1 - \alpha)I_2(I_1 + I_2 - g)}{(I_1 + I_2)p_2} - \alpha(z_1 + g). \tag{27.34}$$

Exercise 27B.10

Demonstrate that these best-response functions converge to those in equations (27.20) and (27.21) as g goes to zero.

Substituting consumer 2's best-response function into consumer 1's and solving for z_1, we get consumer 1's equilibrium contribution to the public good as a function of the government's contribution:

$$z_1^{eq}(g) = \frac{(I_1 + I_2 - g)(I_1p_2 - \alpha I_2p_1)}{(1 + \alpha)(I_1 + I_2)p_1p_2} - \frac{\alpha g}{(1 + \alpha)},$$ (27.35)

with consumer 2's equilibrium contribution coming to:

$$z_2^{eq}(g) = \frac{(I_1 + I_2 - g)(I_2p_1 - \alpha I_1p_2)}{(1 + \alpha)(I_1 + I_2)p_1p_2} - \frac{\alpha g}{(1 + \alpha)}.$$ (27.36)

Adding these individual contributions to the government's, we get the equilibrium public good level $y^{eq}(g)$ as:

$$
\begin{aligned}
y^{eq}(g) &= z_1^{eq}(g) + z_2^{eq}(g) + g \\
&= \frac{(1 - \alpha)(I_1p_2 + I_2p_1)}{(1 + \alpha)p_1p_2} - g\left[\frac{(1 - \alpha)(I_1p_2 + I_2p_1)}{(1 + \alpha)(I_1 + I_2)p_1p_2} + \frac{2\alpha}{1 + \alpha}\right] + g \\
&= y^v + g - g\left[\frac{(1 - \alpha)(I_1p_2 + I_2p_1)}{(1 + \alpha)(I_1 + I_2)p_1p_2} + \frac{2\alpha}{1 + \alpha}\right],
\end{aligned}
$$ (27.37)

where y^v is our previous voluntary contribution level in the absence of government contributions from equation (27.29). When the government contributes €1 to the public good, private contributions decline by an amount equal to the bracketed term in the equation. Government contributions to the public good crowd out private contributions euro-for-euro if the bracketed term is equal to 1, which occurs when $p_1 = p_2 = 1$. When the government is not subsidizing private contributions to the public good and €1 in contributions costs €1, government contributions to the public good fully crowd out private contributions.

Our perfect crowd-out result holds, however, only to the extent to which consumers are giving to the public good when the government increases its contribution. If a consumer is at a corner solution where they do not give, the consumer remains at that corner solution as government contributions rise. Consider, for instance, the case where the two consumers have identical incomes I and where the government is not subsidizing individual contributions (i.e. $p_1 = p_2 = 1$). Equations (27.35) and (27.36) become:

$$z^{eq}(g) = \frac{(1 - \alpha)I}{1 + \alpha} - \frac{g}{2}.$$ (27.38)

This implies that individual contributions are zero when:

$$g = \frac{2(1 - \alpha)I}{1 + \alpha},$$ (27.39)

and for government contributions larger than this, there is no crowd-out.

Exercise 27B.11

Can you tell if there is any crowd-out for the last euro spent by the government if the government provides the optimal level of the public good in this case?

27B.2.2 Tax and Subsidy Policies to Encourage Voluntary Giving Finally, suppose that the government wanted to offer a subsidy s to reduce the effective price that individuals have to pay in order to contribute to the public good. They may do so directly or, as we discussed in Section A, by making charitable contributions tax deductible. In order to finance this subsidy, the government imposes a tax t on income, and since income is assumed to be exogenous, such a tax would be efficient. By choosing a policy (t, s), the government reduces consumer n's income to $(1 - t)I_n$ and their price for contributing to the public good to $(1 - s)$. Substituting these new prices and incomes under policy (t, s) into equation (27.24), we can write the total amount of giving to the public good as:

$$y^v(t, s) = \frac{(1 - \alpha)[(1 - t)I_1(1 - s) + (1 - t)I_2(1 - s)]}{(1 + \alpha)(1 - s)^2}$$

$$= \frac{(1 - \alpha)(1 - t)(I_1 + I_2)}{(1 + \alpha)(1 - s)}. \tag{27.40}$$

The government can't just pick any combination of t and s because tax revenues have to be sufficient to pay the subsidy. If the government wants to set subsidies to induce the efficient level of the public good $y^* = (1 - \alpha)(I_1 + I_2)$, it knows it must raise revenues equal to $sy^* = s(1 - \alpha)(I_1 + I_2)$. Its revenues are $t(I_1 + I_2)$, which implies that for a subsidy s that achieves the optimum level of public good y^*, the government needs to set t such that:

$$t(I_1 + I_2) = s(1 - \alpha)(I_1 + I_2) \tag{27.41}$$

which simplifies to $t = s(1 - \alpha)$. Substituting this into equation (27.40), we can write the level of giving as a function of s, assuming the government balances its budget and sets $t = s(1 - \alpha)$; that is:

$$y^v(s) = \frac{(1 - \alpha)(1 - s(1 - \alpha))(I_1 + I_2)}{(1 + \alpha)(1 - s)}. \tag{27.42}$$

To ensure the optimal level of contributions to the public good, it must be that $y^v(s) = y^*$, or:

$$\frac{(1 - \alpha)(1 - s(1 - \alpha))(I_1 + I_2)}{(1 + \alpha)(1 - s)} = (1 - \alpha)(I_1 + I_2). \tag{27.43}$$

With a little algebra, this solves to $s = 1/2$. Thus, the optimal combination of an income tax and a subsidy for giving to the public good is:

$$(t^*, s^*) = \left(\frac{1 - \alpha}{2}, \frac{1}{2}\right). \tag{27.44}$$

Exercise 27B.12

Can you offer an intuitive explanation for why $s^* = 1/2$? How would you expect this to change as the number of consumers increases?

Exercise 27B.13

We previously concluded that the optimal level of the public good is $(1 - \alpha)(I_1 + I_2)$. Can you use our solutions for s^* and t^* to show that this level is achieved through the voluntary contributions of the two individuals when the policy (s^*, t^*) is implemented?

27B.3 Establishing Markets for Public Goods

If we knew individual demands for public goods, we have seen that it would be possible to derive the optimal public good quantity; and, as we saw in Section A, it would also be possible to derive personalized prices for different consumers, prices under which consumers would choose the optimal public good level that is simultaneously chosen by others at their personalized prices as well. This notion of an equilibrium, called a Lindahl equilibrium, is the public good analogue to a competitive private good equilibrium. It is, in some sense, the mirror image of our notion of a competitive equilibrium where everyone faces the same prices and chooses different quantities, because in a Lindahl equilibrium everyone chooses the same quantities at different prices.

27B.3.1 Lindahl Pricing and Markets for Public Good Externalities
Suppose a firm is producing the public good and selling it to consumer n at p_n. The problem is that the firm can only produce a single quantity of y that will be consumed by all consumers, and so it looks for individualized prices such that (1) all consumers would choose to purchase the quantity y that is produced at their individualized prices and (2) the producer covers their costs. In order for the result to be efficient, it must further be the case that the quantity produced and demanded by each consumer is y^*.

Given the production function $y = f(x) = x$, the producer faces a constant marginal cost $c = 1$ for each unit of y they produce. Thus, to satisfy the condition that the producer's costs are covered in the absence of fixed costs, it has to be the case that:

$$p_1 + p_2 = 1. \tag{27.45}$$

We know from our work with Cobb–Douglas preferences that consumers will allocate a fraction of their income to each consumption good, with that fraction being equal to the exponent that accompanies that good in the utility function. Thus, we know that demand for y by consumer n is:

$$y_n = \frac{(1 - \alpha)I_n}{p_n}. \tag{27.46}$$

The price p^* that will induce consumer n to purchase the optimal public good quantity $y^* = (1 - \alpha)(I_1 + I_2)$ can therefore be determined by solving:

$$(1 - \alpha)(I_1 + I_2) = \frac{(1 - \alpha)I_n}{p_n} \tag{27.47}$$

for p_n. This gives us:

$$p_n^* = \frac{I_n}{I_1 + I_2}. \tag{27.48}$$

With each consumer being charged this price, the sum of the prices is 1 thus satisfying condition (27.45) and each consumer chooses $y^* = (1 - \alpha)(I_1 + I_2)$.

Exercise 27B.14

What do you think p_n will be in the N-person case if everyone shares the same Cobb–Douglas tastes? What if they also all have the same income level?

27B.3.2 Local Public and Club Goods An alternative market solution to local public goods provision involves, as we discussed in Section A, having clubs or local communities compete for customers or residents when public goods are excludable. Under certain conditions this results in competition that is analogous to our notion of a competitive equilibrium, with individuals choosing clubs and communities much as they choose supermarkets and shopping centres. The Tiebout literature that explores these intuitions is vast, and a detailed mathematical exploration of the properties of Tiebout models is beyond the scope of this text.

27B.4 Civil Society and the Free-Rider Problem

We noted in Section A that if all we care about is the overall level of the public good but not how that level was arrived at, we should almost never be observed to contribute to more than a single charity. Our contributions to charities are almost always small relative to the size of the public good that is being funded. This means that the marginal impact of our contribution is unlikely to cause a sufficiently large change in the overall public good to warrant switching charities.

Suppose there are three charities called a, b and c, and before an individual makes a donation, they have already received total contributions of Y_a, Y_b and Y_c. As the individual considers where to place their contribution, they have come to some judgment about how much these charities add in value to the world, and they can represent this judgment by a function $F(Y_a, Y_b, Y_c)$. If person X has an amount D to donate, they will want to donate in a way that maximizes the impact they have on the world based on their judgment F; that is, they would like to solve the problem:

$$\max_{y_a, y_b, y_c} F(Y_a + y_a, Y_b + y_b, Y_c + y_c) \text{ subject to } D = y_a + y_b + y_c, \tag{27.49}$$

where y_i is X's contribution to charity i. When D is small relative to each Y_i, the only way that X will arrive at an interior solution where $y_i > 0$ for $i = a, b, c$ is if, prior to their contributions,

$$\frac{\partial F}{\partial Y_a} = \frac{\partial F}{\partial Y_b} = \frac{\partial F}{\partial Y_c}. \tag{27.50}$$

In that case, X needs to make sure that they balance their contributions so that this equation continues to hold *after* they have contributed. If $\partial F/\partial Y_a$ is greater than $\partial F/\partial Y_b$ and $\partial F/\partial Y_c$, X will solve their optimization problem (27.49) by setting $y_a = D$ and $y_b = y_c = 0$, since it is unlikely that X's relatively small contribution lowers $\partial F/\partial Y_a$ in any perceptible way. Notice that to the extent to which X is uncertain about the marginal impact their contributions will have across charities, this is part of the F function that captures their judgments about where their contributions will have their largest impact, and so uncertainty does not undo the argument that people should give only to a single charity if they care only about the impact their contribution has on the world.

Exercise 27B.15

What is different for Bill Gates that might make him rationally contribute to multiple charities?

Exercise 27B.16

Suppose X only gives to small local charities. In what way might they be like Bill Gates and give rationally to more than one?

Exercise 27B.17

Can you explain why it is rational to diversify a private investment portfolio in the presence of risk and uncertainty but the same argument does not hold for diversifying charitable giving?

Given how often we see individuals give relatively small amounts to many charities, and given that individuals give more than a pure free-rider model would predict, we consider how our predictions change as individuals gain both public and private benefits from giving. Unlike in the analogous section in part A of this chapter, we will forego another discussion of the Coase Theorem and instead proceed directly to incorporating a warm glow effect into our model of voluntary giving.

27B.4.1 Public Goods and the Warm Glow Effect Suppose that consumers care about their individual contribution itself; that is, suppose consumers get a warm glow from giving to the public good in addition to knowing that the overall public good level is higher as a result of their contributions. We could represent preferences with the Cobb–Douglas utility function:

$$u^n(x_n, y, z_n) = x_n^\alpha y^\beta z_n^\gamma = x_n^\alpha \left(z_n + \sum_{j \neq n} z_j \right)^\beta z_n^\gamma, \tag{27.51}$$

where the public good y is the sum of all individual contributions. Consumer n's individual contribution z_n enters the utility function twice: once because it contributes to the overall public good level and again because the individual derives utility from donating to the public good. As the number of consumers increases, the impact of n's marginal contribution to y diminishes giving rise to a worsening free-rider problem, but the warm glow effect remains unchanged because it is, in essence, a private good.

Consider an example in which there are N consumers that are identical both in their incomes I and their preferences that can be represented as in equation (27.51). Since all individuals are identical, they will contribute identical amounts z to the public good in equilibrium. Taking everyone else's contribution as given, we can determine how much z_1 individual 1 will give to the public good by solving the problem:

$$\max_{z_1} \alpha \ln (I - z_1) + \beta \ln(z_1 + (N - 1)z) + \gamma \ln z_1, \tag{27.52}$$

where we have incorporated the individual's budget constraint by expressing $x_1 = I - z_1$ and we have taken the log of the utility function in equation (27.51) to make the derivation of the first order condition a bit less messy. The first order condition after rearranging a few terms can be written as:

$$(\alpha + \beta + \gamma)z_1^2 + (\alpha + \gamma)(N - 1)zz_1 = (\beta + \gamma)Iz_1 + \gamma(N - 1)Iz. \tag{27.53}$$

Solving this for z_1 would give individual 1's best response to everyone else giving z to the public good. We know that in equilibrium $z_1 = z$, and so we can substitute this into the first order condition and solve for z to get the equilibrium level of contribution by every individual as:

$$z^{eq} = \frac{(\beta + \gamma N)I}{\beta + (\alpha + \gamma)N}. \tag{27.54}$$

If you were a social planner choosing z, assuming you constrain yourself to choosing each individual's contribution to be the same as everyone else's, you would set:

$$z^* = \frac{(\beta + \gamma)I}{\alpha + \beta + \gamma}. \tag{27.55}$$

Exercise 27B.18

Verify our derivation of z^{eq} and z^*. Demonstrate that z^{eq} converges to z^* as β goes to zero. Can you make intuitive sense of this?

In Table 27.3, we can illustrate how the equilibrium public good level compares to the optimum as population increases. This is similar to our exercise in Table 27.2, where we assumed no warm glow from giving and saw the free-rider problem at work. In both cases, we are setting the exponent on the private good x equal to the exponent on the public good y, but now we are permitting γ, which was implicitly set to zero in Table 27.2, to be greater than zero to introduce a warm glow effect. Notice that the previous prediction that free riding will drive private contributions to zero as population increases now no longer holds because of the private benefit that individuals get from contributing.

Table 27.3 $I = 1000, \alpha = 0.4, \beta = 0.4, \gamma = 0.2$						
	\multicolumn{6}{c}{Warm Glow Free Riding as Population Increases}					
	$N = 1$	$N = 2$	$N = 5$	$N = 10$	$N = 25$	$N = 100$
y^{eq}	600	1000	2059	3750	8 766	33 775
y^*	600	1200	3000	6000	15 000	60 000
y^{eq}/y^*	1.000	0.833	0.686	0.625	0.584	0.563

27B.4.2 **Marketing Public Goods** Civil society institutions that request voluntary contributions clearly attempt to appeal to the warm glow that many of us get when we give to a cause we consider worthwhile. Such institutions may furthermore market their activities in ways that facilitate such a warm glow effect. Consider our example from Section A of an international relief agency that assists poor families in the developing world. The alleviation of suffering in developing countries is a public good to the extent that all of us care about it to some degree, and it is a huge public good with huge free-rider problems because it enters so many utility functions. Suppose that the agency can make us think of our individual contributions to this public good as a private good by matching us to specific families that we, and only we, if we believe the marketing, are helping. We can think of this as the marketing branch of our civil society institution telling us to forget about β in our utility function and focus on γ. In the Cobb–Douglas example we have been working with where we can think of the exponents as summing to 1, relief agencies – even if they cannot change how much we care about our own private consumption of x, and thus cannot alter α as a fraction of the sum of all the exponents – might be able to persuade us that γ is large relative to β.

How much does this help? Consider the example in Table 27.4. Here, we assume that there are 10 000 identical individuals considering a gift to a public good y. We set $\alpha = 0.4$ and ($\beta + \gamma = 0.6$) and ask how each individual's gift will change as the share of ($\beta + \gamma$) that is a warm glow increases, i.e. as γ increases relative to β. The impact is quite dramatic. If each of us considers our contribution solely to the extent to which it adds to y, we give 15 cents. If the charitable organization can get us to view even a small portion of what we are giving as a private good, our contributions go up significantly, and they continue going up the more successful the marketing department is in the charitable organization. The total funding for our charity is given in the second row of the table. The warm glow effect can help alleviate the free-rider problem by getting individuals to view their contributions as providing both public and private benefits. However, the effect will never fully overcome the free-rider problem unless we converge to the extreme case considered in exercise 27B.18.

Table 27.4 $I = 1000$, $N = 10\,000$, $\alpha = 0.4$, $\beta + \gamma = 0.6$

	Individual and Total Private Giving With Increasing Warm Glow						
	$\gamma = 0$	$\gamma = 0.1$	$\gamma = 0.2$	$\gamma = 0.3$	$\gamma = 0.4$	$\gamma = 0.5$	$\gamma = 0.6$
z^{eq}	€0.15	€200.08	€333.38	€428.60	€500.01	€555.56	€600.00
y^{eq}	€1500	€2 000 800	€3 333 800	€4 286 000	€5 000 100	€5 555 600	€6 000 000

27B.4.3 Civil Society and Tipping Points
Now suppose that instead of deriving some warm glow from knowing that we are contributing to a public good, the size of that warm glow is related to how many of our friends are also giving to the public good. In particular, suppose that the Cobb–Douglas exponent γ depends on the contribution z by others such that:

$$\gamma(z) = \delta_1 + \delta_2 \frac{z}{I}. \tag{27.56}$$

Substituting this into the first-order condition in equation (27.53), we could again solve for the equilibrium private contribution levels. As you do this, however, you will notice that it has become more difficult to solve for z^{eq} and that we would have to apply the quadratic formula to solve for two rather than one solutions: a low z^{eq}_{low} and a high z^{eq}_{high}.

Substituting $\gamma(z)$ into equation (27.54) and cross-multiplying, we get:

$$\beta z + \alpha N z + \gamma(z)N z = \beta I + \gamma(z)NI, \tag{27.57}$$

and replacing $\gamma(z)$ with $\delta_1 + \delta_2(z/I)$, we get after some more rearranging of terms:

$$\frac{\delta_2 N}{I}z^2 + (\beta - (\delta_2 - \alpha - \delta_1)N)z - (\beta + \delta_1 N)I = 0. \tag{27.58}$$

It is to this expression that the quadratic formula can be applied.

Some parameter choices for δ_1 and δ_2 will make both of these solutions feasible, which implies that we have two different Nash equilibria. Furthermore, since the equilibrium contributions shape preferences by influencing γ, the two equilibria result in different preferences depending on which equilibrium we reach.

In Table 27.5, we calculate the low and high equilibrium contributions for different values of δ_2 to illustrate how different the multiple equilibria in such settings can be. The values of the remaining parameters in the model are reported in the table. Take the middle column where $\delta_2 = 1$ as an example. In the low contributions equilibrium, we contribute not even 3 per cent of what we contribute in the high contribution equilibrium. This is because in the low contributions equilibrium, γ when α, β and γ are normalized to sum to 1, is 0.0084, or essentially zero. Thus, we barely derive a private benefit from giving because we all give so little, and we are essentially just playing the standard free-rider game. In the high contributions equilibrium, on the other hand, the same normalized γ is 0.422, with each deriving substantial private benefit from public giving.

Table 27.5 $I = 1000$, $N = 10\,000$, $\alpha = 0.4$, $\beta = 0.4$, $\delta_1 = -0.01$

Multiple Equilibria When Warm Glow is Endogenous

	$\delta_2 = 0.6$	$\delta_2 = 0.8$	$\delta_2 = 1.0$	$\delta_2 = 1.2$	$\delta_2 = 1.4$	$\delta_2 = 1.6$
z_{low}^{eq}	€56.59	€25.57	€16.79	€12.53	€10.00	€8.32
z_{high}^{eq}	€293.34	€486.88	€593.17	€662.44	€711.40	€747.90

Exercise 27B.19*

Suppose $\delta_2 = 1$. Using $\delta_1 = -0.01$ and the values z_{low}^{eq} and z_{high}^{eq} in Table 27.5, derive the implied level of γ in the two equilibria. Note that these will not match the ones discussed in the text because the table does not normalize all exponents in the utility function to sum to 1. Using the parameters for I, N, α and β provided in the table, employ equation (27.54) to verify z_{low}^{eq} as well as z_{high}^{eq}.

Nothing in the game theory that we have learned makes one of these equilibria more or less plausible than the other. They are two different ways in which individuals might coordinate their behaviour if they value their own contribution to public goods more when their friends are also contributing. If a civil society institution finds itself in a low contribution equilibrium, it might find ways to get individuals to coordinate on the high contribution equilibrium instead. If it can get sufficiently many individuals to temporarily deviate from their low contribution, this makes it more attractive for others to follow suit. The magnitude of the deviations matters a great deal because if deviations are not sufficiently large, individuals are likely to fall back into the low contributions equilibrium. If the institution can induce sufficiently large deviations, we can cross a tipping point where the critical mass has changed their contributions and the natural tendency is now to fall into the high contribution equilibrium.

27B.5 Preference Revelation Mechanisms

Individuals typically have an incentive to misrepresent their preferences for public goods if their contributions to the public good are linked to their stated preferences for public goods. Economists have proposed mechanisms that take into account this incentive problem. We will begin by introducing the general concept of *mechanism design* and will illustrate a more general example of a mechanism than the one introduced in Section A under which individuals reveal their true preferences for public goods to the institution that requests such information.

27B.5.1 Mechanism Design Suppose that A denotes the set of possible outcomes that we may wish to attain, and let $\{\succsim\}$ denote the set of possible preferences that individuals might have over these outcomes. For instance, in the public goods case, A might denote different levels of public goods and different ways of funding them. An institution like the government might have in mind some function $f:\{\succsim\}^N \rightarrow A$ that would translate the preferences of the N different individuals in the population into the best outcome from A according to some criteria captured by the function f. For instance, in the public goods case, the government might wish to implement the efficient level of public goods that depends on the preferences that people have in the population. If the government knew all the preferences in the population, it could do this.

Instead, however, the government needs to request the information about preferences from individuals in the form of messages that individuals can send to the government. Let M denote the set of possible messages that individuals are allowed to convey to the government. The government needs to take all the messages it collects and translate these into an outcome from A; that is, it needs to define a function $g : M^N \rightarrow A$. A *mechanism* is the combination of the definition of the types of messages that individuals are permitted to send and the manner in which the messages are translated into outcomes; that is, a mechanism is the combination (M, g).

The challenge for the mechanism designer is to define M and g such that the outcome that emerges from the messages sent by individuals is the same as the one the government would have chosen had it been able to observe preferences directly and used the function f to pick outcomes. The mechanism involves truth telling if the equilibrium strategy of individuals is to send messages that truthfully reveal the relevant information about their preferences needed by the government *given that individuals know the function g* that the government uses to translate messages into outcomes. The mechanism is said to *implement f* if the outcomes that emerge through the application of g to the equilibrium messages sent by individuals are the same outcomes that would have emerged if f could have been applied directly to the true preferences individuals have. This is depicted graphically in Graph 27.5 where, rather than being able to directly observe $\{\succsim\}^N$ and implement f to choose a social outcome from A, a mechanism (M,g) is set up to create a message game in which each player chooses what message to send given that messages are translated to outcomes through g.

Graph 27.5 Designing a Mechanism

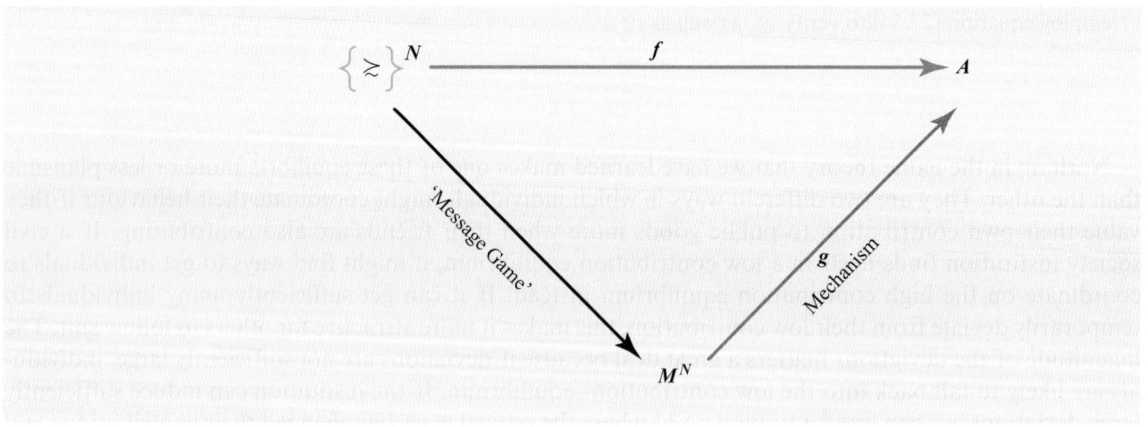

27B.5.2 The Groves–Clarke Mechanism for Public Goods Suppose that we consider a world in which N different individuals would benefit from the provision of a public good y that can be produced at constant marginal cost MC. Our objective f is to provide the efficient public good level and raise revenues to pay for the cost of doing so. In order to determine the optimal public good quantity y^*, we need to know individual demands for y, but we typically do not know what these demands are. We therefore need to have the N individuals report their demands by defining a set of possible messages M that they can send, and devise a scheme g by which we are going to settle on a public good level and a payment to be paid by each of the individuals. The *Groves–Clarke mechanism* is one such mechanism that has been proposed. The mechanism is named after Theodore Groves (1942–) and Edward Clarke (1939–2013) who separately developed different versions in the late 1960s and early 1970s. William Vickerey (1914–1996) is often credited with having hinted at a similar mechanism in his earlier work on auctions, and some therefore refer to the mechanism as the Vickery–Groves–Clarke mechanism.

The mechanism proceeds as follows, with (1) defining M and (2) and (3) together defining $g : M^N \rightarrow A$:

(1) First, individuals are asked to reveal their inverse demands for the public good, with each individual i revealing $RD_i(y)$. Such a revealed demand curve is depicted in panel (a) of Graph 27.6 for consumer i. The set of possible messages M is therefore the set of possible downward-sloping demand curves.

Graph 27.6 The Groves–Clarke Mechanism

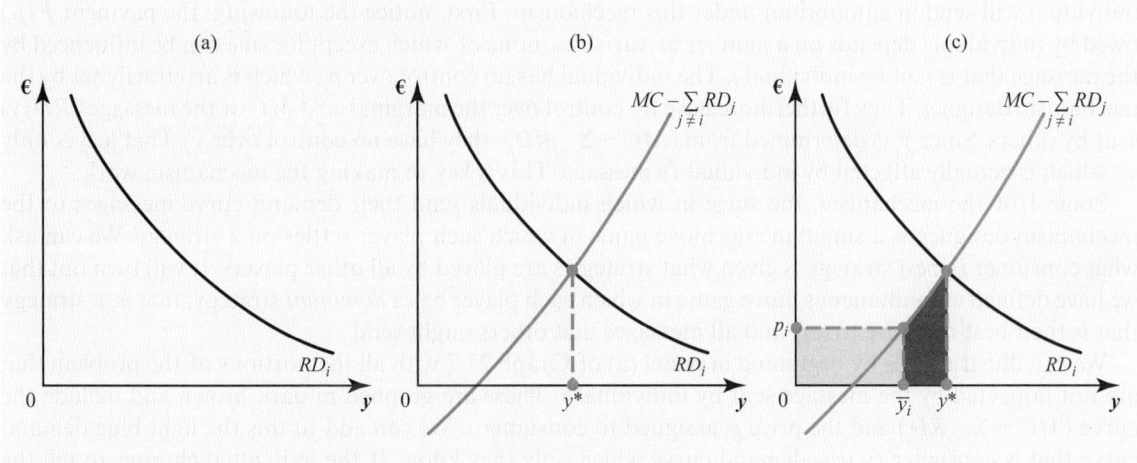

(2) The institution that implements the mechanism determines y^* as if the revealed demands were people's actual demands. The RD_i curves are added up, and y^* is set so that the vertical sum of revealed demands is equal to the marginal cost MC of producing the public good; that is:

$$\sum_{i=1}^{N} RD_i(y^*) = MC. \tag{27.59}$$

(3) Each individual is assigned a price p_i in some arbitrary way that has no relation to what individuals revealed, with the only restriction that the sum of the individual p_i's equals the marginal cost MC; that is, $\Sigma p_i = MC$. For each individual i, a quantity $\bar{y}_i$ is defined such that $p_i = [MC - \Sigma_{j \neq i} RD_j(y)]$ and the total payment p_i charged to individual i is set to:

$$P_i(p_i) = p_i \bar{y}_i + \int_{\bar{y}_i}^{y^*} \left(MC - \sum_{j \neq i} RD_j(y) \right) dy. \tag{27.60}$$

Graph 27.6 clarifies exactly what the mechanism proposes. In panel (a), we plot the revealed demand curve RD_i from consumer i, which is the message sent in step (1). In panel (b), we add to this graph the curve $(MC - \Sigma_{j \neq i} RD_j)$. At the intersection of these two curves, $(MC - \Sigma_{j \neq i} RD_j) = RD_i$, which implies that equation (27.59) is satisfied and we have located y^*. Finally, in panel (c) we determine the payment owed by consumer i. First, we find where $p_i = [MC - \Sigma_{j \neq i} RD_j(y)]$ to define $\bar{y}_i$. The payment owed by i consists of the two parts in equation (27.60): the part $p_i \bar{y}_i$ is equal to the shaded dark brown area, while the remainder is the dark blue area underneath the $(MC - \Sigma_{j \neq i} RD_j(y))$ function between $\bar{y}_i$ and y^*. The total payment $P_i(p_i)$ owed by consumer i is the sum of the dark brown and dark blue areas.

Panel (c) of Graph 27.6 assumes that $\bar{y}_i < y^*$, but it could be that we assigned a high enough p_i to individual i such that the reverse holds. In that case, the integral in equation (27.60) is negative, which implies that consumer i would face a payment that is less than $p_i \bar{y}_i$.

Exercise 27B.20

Illustrate in a graph similar to Graph 27.6 what the payment $P_i(p_i)$ for this individual would be if p_i is sufficiently high such that $\bar{y}_i > y^*$.

27B.5.3 Equilibrium Messages in the Groves–Clarke Mechanism We can now ask what messages each individual will send in equilibrium under this mechanism. First, notice the following: the payment $P_i(p_i)$ owed by individual i depends on a number of variables, none of which except for one can be influenced by the message that is sent by individual i. The individual has no control over p_i, which is arbitrarily set by the mechanism designer. They furthermore have no control over the marginal cost MC or the messages $RD_j(y)$ sent by others. Since $\bar{y}_i$ is determined from $(MC - \Sigma_{j \neq i} RD_j)$, they have no control over $\bar{y}_i$. That leaves only y^* which is actually affected by individual i's message. This is key to making the mechanism work.

Stage 1 of the mechanism, the stage in which individuals send their demand curve messages to the mechanism designer, is a simultaneous move game in which each player settles on a strategy. We can ask what consumer i's best strategy is given what strategies are played by all other players. It will turn out that we have defined a simultaneous move game in which each player has a *dominant* strategy; that is, a strategy that is their best response to any and all messages that others might send.

We can illustrate this by beginning in panel (a) of Graph 27.7 with all the portions of the problem that are not impacted by the message sent by individual i. These are graphed in dark brown and include the curve $(MC - \Sigma_{j \neq i} RD_j)$ and the price p_i assigned to consumer i. We can add to this the light blue demand curve that is consumer i's *true* demand curve which only they know. If the individual chooses to tell the truth and reports this as their message, the outcome will be that y^t will be produced, with consumer i charged the shaded dark brown and dark blue area.

In panels (b) and (c), we consider how consumer i will fare if they under- or over-report their demand for the public good. Consider first the case where they report the dark blue curve $RD_i^u(y)$ in panel (b). The charge they will incur will be equal to the area $(d + e + f)$ rather than the area $(b + c + d + e + f)$ that they would incur if they told the truth. Thus, by under-reporting their true demand for the public good, they will save $(b + c)$. At the same time, their under-reporting will cause the public good quantity that is produced to fall from y^t to y^u. If we use their light blue true demand as their marginal willingness to pay curve, we can conclude that this reduction in the public good will cause them to lose area $(a + b + c)$ in value from the lower public good output. While they would save $(b + c)$ in payments, they would lose the equivalent of $(a + b + c)$ in value from the reduced public good, leaving them worse off by area (a). Under-reporting their demand for the public good is therefore counterproductive.

Graph 27.7 Truth Telling is Optimal

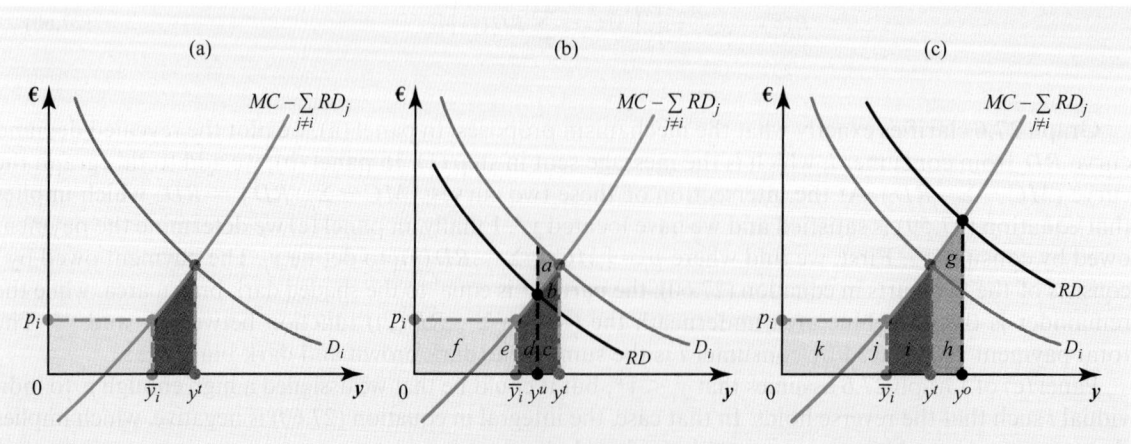

In panel (c), we do the analogous exercise for considering whether it might be in the consumer's interest to over-report their demand for the public good by reporting RD_i^o. This will increase the payment they owe from $(i + j + k)$ under truth telling to $(g + h + I + j + k)$ when the consumer over-reports their demand, thus increasing their payment by $(g + h)$. The additional value from the increase in the public good from y^t under truth telling to y^o when over-reporting is only h. Thus, sending the message RD_i^o rather than the truth results in a loss of (g). Over-reporting is therefore also counterproductive.

Exercise 27B.21

In Graph 27.7, we considered the case in which $\bar{y}_i < y^t$. Repeat the analysis to show that over- and under-reporting is similarly counterproductive when p_i is sufficiently high to cause $\bar{y}_i > y^t$.

Since none of our reasoning has assumed anything about whether individuals other than i are reporting their demands truthfully, we can conclude that it is a dominant strategy for consumer i to report their demand for the public good truthfully. The same reasoning applies to all consumers, implying that *truth telling is a dominant strategy equilibrium* under the Groves–Clarke mechanism. This in turn implies that the mechanism will produce the optimal level y^* of the public good.

27B.5.4 Feasibility of the Groves–Clarke Mechanism While we now know that individuals, when faced with the incentives of the Groves–Clarke mechanism, will report their demands for public goods truthfully, the mechanism will not be feasible unless it raises sufficient revenues TR for the mechanism designer to actually pay for the total cost which is equal to $TC = MCy^*$ in the absence of fixed costs of the public good output level y^* that emerges. We can illustrate that this is the case.

For each of the individuals affected by the mechanism, one of three scenarios will arise depending on what p_i the individual was assigned: (1) $\bar{y}_i < y^*$, (2) $\bar{y}_i = y^*$ or (3) $\bar{y}_i > y^*$. These three cases are graphed in the three panels of Graph 27.8.

Graph 27.8 Revenues Exceed Costs Under the Groves–Clarke Mechanism

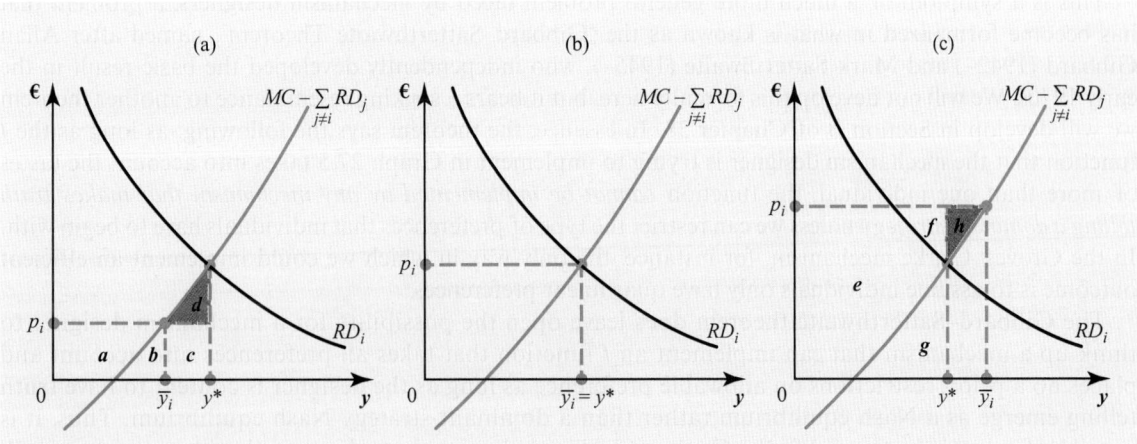

In panel (a), $\bar{y}_i < y^*$, which results in $P_i(p_i)$ that is equal to the area $(a + b + c + d)$. This area could be divided into an area $p_i y^* = (a + b + c)$ plus the remaining shaded triangle (d). In panel (c), $\bar{y}_i > y^*$, which results in $P_i(p_i) = (e + f + g + h)$, and this area can similarly be divided into $p_i y^* = (e + f + g)$ plus the shaded area (h). In both cases, we know that we will collect $p_i y^*$ plus some additional revenue. Only in panel (b) where $\bar{y}_i = y^*$ is the payment $P_i(p_i)$ exactly equal to $p_i y^*$. The total revenue TR we collect from all consumers is at least $\Sigma p_i y^*$, and since $\Sigma p_i = MC$, we can conclude that:

$$TR \geq \sum_{i=1}^{N} p_i y^* = MCy^* = TC. \qquad (27.61)$$

We can furthermore see from Graph 27.8 that the only way in which the inequality in the equation becomes an equality, that is, the only way that total revenues will exactly equal total costs, is if the prices happened to be assigned in such a way that $\bar{y}_i = y^*$ for all individuals as illustrated in panel (b) of the graph. In that special case, the prices we have assigned are like real prices in the sense that individuals pay exactly price times quantity for the public good. In that special case, it is true that all individuals would choose the optimal public good level y^* under the per-unit prices they were assigned. In other words, in that special case, p_i is the Lindahl price for all consumers and we have implemented a Lindahl equilibrium. Of course, this could only happen accidentally under the Groves–Clarke mechanism because the p_i's are assigned arbitrarily without knowledge of the underlying demands by individuals.

27B.5.5 A Fundamental Problem in Mechanism Design Our conclusion that the Groves–Clarke mechanism will almost always raise revenues that exceed the cost of providing the optimal level of the public good creates a problem: what do we do with the excess revenue? Remember that we are trying to implement an efficient solution to the public goods problem, which means that throwing away the excess revenue cannot be the answer. If we were to throw away the excess revenue, we could easily think of a way of making someone better off without making anyone else worse off. Just give the excess revenue back to one or some or all of the consumers; but that creates another problem. If we return the excess revenues, we would create income effects for consumers unless tastes are quasilinear, which would mean that we would alter the optimal level of the public good. Giving back the excess revenue alters y^*, which means our whole previous analysis is thrown out the window. For this reason, the Groves–Clarke mechanism can only implement an efficient outcome under the special assumption that individual preferences are quasilinear, a rather strong assumption to make about preferences we know nothing about at the beginning of the mechanism. If preferences were quasilinear in the public good, we could return all the excess revenues to individuals without changing y^*.

This is a symptom of a much more general problem faced by mechanism designers, a problem that has become formalized in what is known as the 'Gibbard–Satterthwaite Theorem', named after Allan Gibbard (1942–) and Mark Satterthwaite (1945–), who independently developed the basic result in the early 1970s. We will not develop this formally here, but it bears a striking resemblance to another theorem we will develop in Section B of Chapter 28. In essence, the theorem says the following: as long as the f function that the mechanism designer is trying to implement in Graph 27.5 takes into account the tastes of more than one individual, the function *cannot be implemented by any mechanism that makes truth telling a dominant strategy* unless we can restrict the type of preferences that individuals have to begin with. In the Groves–Clarke mechanism, for instance, the only way in which we could implement an efficient outcome is to assume individuals only have quasilinear preferences.

The Gibbard–Satterthwaite theorem does leave open the possibility for a mechanism designer to think up a mechanism that can implement an f function that takes all preferences into account and places no a priori restrictions on allowable preference as long as the designer is content to have truth telling emerge as a Nash equilibrium rather than a dominant strategy Nash equilibrium. Thus, it is possible, for instance, to modify the Groves–Clarke mechanism in such a way that there exists a truth telling Nash equilibrium that results in the optimal provision of public goods with total revenues exactly equalling total costs. Such mechanisms have been derived, and some of them are quite simple in terms of the messages they ask consumers to send. Some have even been implemented in the real world. The most famous such mechanism was developed in Theodore Groves and John Ledyard, 'Optimal Allocation of Public Goods: A Solution to the "Free Rider" Problem', *Econometrica* 45 (1977), 783–810.

End-of-Chapter Exercises

27.1† We discussed in the text the basic externality problem faced when we rely on private giving to public projects. In this exercise, we consider how this changes as the number of people involved increases.

A. Suppose that there are N individuals who consume a public good.

   a. Begin with the best-response function in panel (a) of Graph 27.3; that is, the best response of one person's giving to another person's giving when $N = 2$. Draw the 45-degree line into your graph of this best-response function.

   b. Now suppose that all N individuals are the same, just as we assumed the two individuals in Graph 27.3 are the same. Given the symmetry of the problem in terms of everyone being identical, how must the contributions of each person relate to one another in equilibrium?

   c. In your graph, replace y_2, the giving by person 2, with y and let y be the giving that each person other than person 1 undertakes assuming they all give the same amount. As N increases, what happens to the best-response function for person 1? Explain, and relate your answer to the free-rider problem.

   d. Given your answers to (b) and (c), what happens to person 1's equilibrium contribution as N increases? *Hint*: Where on the best-response function will the equilibrium contribution lie?

   e. When $N = 2$, how much of the overall benefit from their contribution is individual 1 taking into account as they determine their level of giving? How does this change when N increases to 3 and 4? How does it change as N gets very large?

   f. What does your answer imply for the level of subsidy s that is necessary to get people to contribute to the efficient level of the public good as N increases? Define s as the level of subsidy that will cause a €1 contribution to the public good to cost the individual only €$(1 - s)$.

   g. Explain how, as N becomes large, the optimal subsidy policy becomes pretty much equivalent to the government providing the public good.

B. In Section 27B.2.2, we considered how two individuals respond to having the government subsidize their voluntary giving to the production of a public good. Suppose again that individuals have preferences that are captured by the utility function $u(x, y) = x^\alpha y^{(1 - \alpha)}$, where x is euros worth of private consumption and y is euros spent on the public good. All individuals have income I, and the public good is financed by private contributions denoted z_n for individual n. The government subsidizes private contributions at a rate of $s \leq 1$ and finances this with a tax t on income.

   a. Suppose there are N individuals. What is the efficient level of public good funding?

   b. Since individuals are identical, the Nash equilibrium response to any policy (t,s) will be symmetric; that is, all individuals end up giving the same in equilibrium. Suppose all individuals other than n give z. Derive the best-response function $z_n(t, s, z)$ for individual n. As in the text, this is most easily done by defining n's optimization as an unconstrained optimization problem with only z_n as the choice variable and the Cobb–Douglas utility function written in log form.

   c. Use your answer to (b) to derive the equilibrium level of individual private giving $z^{eq}(t, s)$. How does it vary with N?

   d. What is the equilibrium quantity of the public good for policy (t, s)?

   e. For the policy (t, s) to result in the optimal level of public good funding, what has to be the relationship between t and s if the government is to cover the cost of the subsidy with the tax revenues it raises?

   f. Substitute your expression for t from (e) into your answer to (d). Determine what level of s is necessary in order for private giving to result in the efficient level of output you determined in (a).

   g. Derive the optimal policy (t^*, s^*) that results in efficient levels of public good provision through voluntary giving. What is the optimal policy when $N = 2$? Your answer should be equal to what we calculated for the two-person case in Section 27B.2.2. What if $N = 3$ and $N = 4$?

   h. Can you explain s^* when N is 2, 3 and 4 in terms of how the externality changes as N increases? Does s^* for $N = 1$ make intuitive sense?

   i. What does this optimal policy converge to as N becomes large? Interpret what this means.

27.2* In exercise 27.1, we extended our analysis of subsidized voluntary giving from 2 to N people. In the process, we assumed the government would set t to cover its costs, and that individuals would take t as given when they make their decision on how much to give. We now explore how the strategic setting changes when individuals predict how their giving will translate into taxes.

A. Consider again the case where N identical people enjoy the public good.

    a. First, suppose $N = 2$ and suppose the government subsidizes private giving at a rate of s. If individual n gives y_n to the public good, what fraction of the resulting tax to cover the subsidy on their giving will they have to pay?

    b. Compare the case where the individual does not take the tax effect of their giving into account to the case where they do. What would you expect to happen to n's best-response function for giving to the public good in the former case relative to the latter case? In which case would you expect the equilibrium response to a subsidy s to be greater?

    c. Explain the following true statement: when $N = 2$, a subsidy s in the case where individuals do not take the balanced-budget tax consequence of a subsidy into account will have the same impact as a subsidy $2s$ in the case where they do.

    d. Given your answer to (c), and given that the optimal subsidy level when $N = 2$ in exercise 27.1 was 0.5, what do you think s would have to be to achieve the efficient level of the public good now that individuals think about balanced-budget tax consequences?

    e. Next suppose N is very large. Explain why it is now a good approximation to assume that individual n takes t as given when they choose their contribution level to the public good as they did in exercise 27.1.

    f. *True or False*: The efficient level of the subsidy is the same when $N = 2$ as when N is very large if individuals take into account the tax implication of increasing their giving to the subsidized public good.

    g. Finally, suppose we start with $N = 2$ and raise N. What happens to the degree to which n's giving decisions impact on n's tax obligations as N increases? What happens to the size of the free-rider problem as N increases? In what sense do these introduce offsetting forces as we think about the equilibrium level of private contributions?

B. Consider the same set-up as in exercise 27.1, but now suppose that each individual assumes the government will balance its budget and therefore anticipates the impact their giving has on the tax rate t when the subsidy s is greater than zero.

    a. The problem is again symmetric in the sense that all individuals are the same, so in equilibrium, all individuals will end up giving the same amount to the public good. Suppose all $(N-1)$ individuals other than n give z when the subsidy is s. Express the budget-balancing tax rate as a function of s assuming person n gives z_n while everyone else gives z.

    b. Individual n knows that their after-tax income will be $(1-t)I$ while their cost of giving z_n is $(1-s)z_n$. Using your answer from (a), express individual n's private good consumption as a function of s and z_n given everyone else gives z.

    c. Set up the utility maximization problem for individual n to determine their best response giving function given that everyone else gives z. Solve for z_n as a function of z and y. The problem is easiest to solve if it is set up as an unconstrained optimization problem with only z_1 as the choice variable, and with utility expressed as the log of the Cobb–Douglas functional form.

    d. Use the fact that z_n has to be equal to z in equilibrium to solve for the equilibrium individual contribution z^{eq} as a function of s. You should be able to simplify the denominator of your expression to $(1 + \alpha(N-1)(1-s))$.

    e. If everyone gave an equal share of the efficient level of the public good funding, how much would each person contribute? Use this to derive the optimal level of s. Does it depend on N?

    f. *True or False*: When individuals take into account the tax implications of government-subsidized private giving, the optimal subsidy rate is the same regardless of N and equal to what it is when N gets large for the case when people do not consider the impact of subsidized giving on tax rates as explored in exercise 27.1.

27.3† **Everyday Application:** *Sandwiches, Chess Clubs, Cinemas and Fireworks.* While we often treat public and private goods as distinct concepts, many goods actually lie in between the extremes because of crowding.

A. We can think of the level of crowding as determining the optimal group size for consumption of the good, with optimal group size in turn locating the good on the continuum between purely private and purely public goods.

    a. One way to model different types of goods is in terms of the marginal cost and marginal benefit of admitting additional group members to enjoy the good. Begin by considering a bite of your lunch sandwich. What is the marginal benefit of admitting a second person to the consumption of this bite? What is therefore the optimal group size, and how does this relate to our conception of the sandwich bite as a private good?

    b. Next, consider a chess club. Draw a graph with group size N on the horizontal axis and euros on the vertical. With additional members, you'll have to get more chessboards, with the marginal cost of additional members plausibly being flat. The marginal benefit of additional members might initially be increasing, but if the club gets too large, it becomes impersonal and not much fun. Draw the marginal benefit and marginal cost curves and indicate the optimal group size. In what way is the chess club not a pure public good?

    c. Consider the same exercise with respect to a cinema that has N seats but you could add additional people by having them sit or stand in the aisles. Each customer adds to the mess and thus the clean-up cost. What might the marginal cost and benefit curves now look like?

    d. Repeat the exercise for fireworks.

    e. Which of these do you think the market and/or civil society can provide relatively efficiently, and which might require some government assistance?

    f. Why do you think firework displays are often provided by local governments, but some theme parks are able to put on fireworks every night without government help?

B. Consider in this part of the exercise only crowding on the cost side, with the cost of providing some discrete public good given by the function $c(N) = FC + \alpha N^\beta$ with $\alpha > 0$ and $\beta \geq 0$. Assume throughout that there is no crowding in consumption of the public good.

    a. Derive the marginal cost of admitting additional customers. In order for there to be crowding in production, how large must β be?

    b. Find the group membership at the lowest point of the average cost function. How does this relate to optimal group size when group size is sufficiently small for multiple providers to be in the market?

    c. What is the relationship between α, β and FC for purely private goods?

    d. Suppose that the good is a purely public good. What value of α could make this so? If $\alpha > 0$, what value of β might make this so?

    e. How does α affect optimal group size? What about FC and β? Interpret your answer.

27.4 **Everyday, Business and Policy Application:** *Competitive Local Public and Club Good Production.* In exercise 27.3, we considered some ways in which we could differentiate between goods that lie in between the extremes of pure private and pure public goods.

A. Consider the case where there is a recurring fixed cost FC to producing the public good y, and the marginal cost of producing the same level of y is increasing in the group size N because of crowding.

    a. Consider again a graph with N, the group size, on the horizontal and euros on the vertical. Graph the average and marginal cost of providing a given level of y as N increases.

    b. Suppose that the lowest point of the average curve you have drawn occurs at N^*, with N^* greater than 1 but significantly less than the population size. If the good is excludable, what would you expect the admissions price to be in long-run competitive equilibrium if firms or clubs that provide the good can freely enter and/or exit?

    c. You have so far considered the case of firms producing a given level of y. Suppose next that firms could choose lower levels of y (smaller swimming pools, schools with larger class sizes, etc.) that carry lower recurring fixed costs. If people have different demands for y, what would you expect to happen in equilibrium as firms compete?

    d. Suppose instead that the public good is not excludable in the usual sense, but rather that it is a good that can be consumed only by those who live within a certain distance of where the good is produced. Consider, for instance, a state school. How does the shape of the average cost curve you have drawn determine the optimal community size where communities provide the public good?

e. Local communities often use property taxes to finance their public good production. If households of different types are free to buy houses of different size and value, why might higher income households that buy larger homes be worried about lower income households free riding?

f. Many communities impose zoning regulations that require houses and land plots to be of some minimum size. Can you explain the motivation for such exclusionary zoning in light of the concern over free riding?

g. If local public goods are such that optimal group size is sufficiently small to result in a very competitive environment in which communities compete for residents, how might the practice of exclusionary zoning result in very homogeneous communities; that is, in communities where households are very similar to one another and live in very similar types of houses?

h. Suppose that a court rules that even wealthy communities must set aside some fraction of their land for low income housing. How would you expect the prices of low income houses in relatively wealthy communities that provide high levels of local public goods to compare to the prices of identical houses in low income communities? How would you expect the average income of those residing in identical low income housing to compare across these different communities?

i. *True or False*: The insights from this exercise suggest that local community competition might result in efficient provision of local public goods, but they also raise the equity concern that the poor will have less access to certain local public goods such as good state schools.

B. Consider the cost function $c(N) = FC + \alpha N^\beta$ with $\alpha > 0$ and $\beta \geq 0$ as we did in exercise 27.3.

a. In the case of competitive firms providing this excludable public good, calculate the long-run equilibrium admission price you would expect to emerge.

b. Consider a town in which, at any given time, 23 500 people are interested in going to the cinema. Suppose the per auditorium/screen costs of a cinema are characterized by the functions in this problem, with $FC = 900$, $\alpha = 0.5$ and $\beta = 1.5$. Determine the optimal auditorium capacity N^*, the equilibrium price per ticket p^* and the equilibrium number of screens.

c. Suppose instead that a spatially constrained public good is provided by local communities that fund the public good production through a property tax. Economic theorists have shown that if we assume it is relatively easy to move from one community to another, an equilibrium may not exist unless communities find a way of excluding those who might attempt to free ride. Can you explain the intuition for this?

d. Would the practice of being able to set a minimum income level for community members establish a way for an equilibrium to emerge? How does the practice of exclusionary zoning as defined in part A of the exercise accomplish the same thing?

e. In the extreme, a model with exclusionary zoning might result in complete self-selection of household types into communities, with everyone within a community being identical to everyone else. How does the property tax in this case mimic a per-capita user fee for the public good?

f. *Can you argue that, in light of your answer to A(g), the same might be true if zoning regulations are not uniformly the same within a community?

27.5† **Business Application:** *The Marketing Challenge for Social Entrepreneurs.* Social entrepreneurs are entrepreneurs who use their talents to advance social causes that are typically linked to the provision of some type of public good. Their challenge within the civil society is, in part, to motivate individuals to give sufficient funding to the projects that are being advanced. Aside from lobbying for government aid, we can think of two general ways in which social entrepreneurs might succeed in increasing the funding for their organizations. Both involve marketing: one aimed at increasing the number of individuals who are aware of the public good and thus to increase the donor pool, the other aimed at persuading people that they get something real out of giving to the cause.

A. We can think of the social entrepreneur as using their labour as an input into two different single-input production processes: one aimed at increasing the pool of donors, the other aimed at persuading current donors of the benefits they get from becoming more engaged.

a. Suppose that both production processes have decreasing returns to scale. What does this imply for the marginal revenue product of each production process?

b. If the social entrepreneur allocates their time optimally, how will their marginal revenue product of labour in the two production processes be related to one another?

c. Another way to view the social entrepreneur's problem is that they have a fixed labour time allotment L that forms a time budget constraint. Graph such a budget constraint, with ℓ_1, the time allocated to increasing the donor pool on the horizontal axis, and ℓ_2, the time allocated to persuading existing donors, on the vertical.

d. What do the isoquants for the two-input production process look like? Can you interpret these as the social entrepreneur's indifference curves?

e. Illustrate how the social entrepreneur will optimize in this graph. Can you interpret your result as identical to the one you derived in (b)?

f. Within the context of our discussion of warm glow effects from giving, can you interpret ℓ_2 as effort that goes into persuading individuals that public goods have private benefits?

g. How might you reinterpret this model as one applying to a politician or a 'political entrepreneur' who chooses between allocating campaign resources to mass mailings versus political rallies?

h. We discussed in the text that sometimes there is a role for tipping points in efforts to get individuals engaged in public causes. If the social entrepreneur attempts to pass such a tipping point, how might their strategy change as the fundraising effort progresses?

B. Suppose that the two production processes introduced in part A are $f_1(\ell_1)$ and $f_2(\ell_2)$, with $df_i/d\ell_i < 0$ for $i = 1, 2$ and with 'output' in each process defined as euros raised.

a. Assuming the entrepreneur has L hours to allocate, set up their optimization problem. Can you demonstrate your conclusion from A(b)?

b. Suppose $f_1(\ell_1) = A \ln \ell_1$ and $f_2(\ell_2) = B \ln \ell_2$ with both A and B greater than 0. Derive the optimal ℓ_1 and ℓ_2.

c. In equation (27.54), we determined the individual equilibrium contribution in the presence of a warm glow effect. Suppose that this represents the equilibrium contribution level for the donors that the social entrepreneur works with, and suppose $I = 1000$, $\alpha = 0.4$ and $\beta = 0.6$. In the absence of any efforts on the part of the entrepreneur, $N = 1000$ and $\gamma = 0.01$. How much will the entrepreneur raise without putting in any effort?

d. **Next, suppose that $N(\ell_2) = 1000(1 + \ell_2^{1/2})$, and $\gamma(\ell_2) = 0.01(1 + \ell_2^{1/2})$, and suppose that the entrepreneur has a total of 1000 hours to devote to the fundraising effort. Assume that they will devote all 1000 hours to the effort, with ℓ_2 therefore equal to $(1000 - \ell_1)$. Create a table with ℓ_1 in the first column ranging from 0 to 1000 in 100 hour increments. Calculate the implied level of ℓ_2, N and γ in the next three columns, and report the equilibrium level of individual contributions z^{eq} and the equilibrium overall funds raised y^{eq} in the last two columns. This is easier to do using a spreadsheet.

e. Approximately how would you recommend that the entrepreneur split their time between recruiting more donors and working with existing donors?

f. **Suppose all the parameters of the problem remain the same except for the following: $\gamma = 0.01(1 + \ell_2^{0.5} + 0.001N^{1.1})$. By modifying the spreadsheet that you used to create the table in part (d), can you determine the optimal number of hours the entrepreneur should put into their two fundraising activities now? How much will they raise?

27.6 **Policy Application:** *Do Anti-Poverty Efforts Provide a Public Good?* There are many equity- or fairness-based arguments for government engagement in anti-poverty programmes, and for general government redistribution programmes. Is there an efficiency case to be made for government programmes that redistribute income? One such possibility lies in viewing government anti-poverty efforts as a public good, but whether this is a credible argument depends on how we think contributions to anti-poverty efforts enter people's tastes.

A. Suppose there is a set, A, of individuals that contribute to anti-poverty programmes and a different set, B, of individuals that receive income transfers from such programmes and suppose that everyone in the population is in one of these two sets.

a. In considering whether there is an efficiency case to be made for government intervention in anti-poverty efforts, do we have to consider the increased welfare of those who receive income transfers?

b. How would the individuals who give to anti-poverty programmes have to view such programmes in order for there to be no externality to private giving?

c. If your answer to (b) is how individuals view anti-poverty efforts, are anti-poverty efforts efficient in the absence of government intervention? If the government introduced anti-poverty programmes funded through taxes on those who are privately giving to such efforts already, to what extent would you expect the government programmes to crowd out private efforts?

d. How would individuals have to view their contributions to anti-poverty programmes in order for such programmes to be pure public goods?

e. If the conditions in (d) hold, why is there an efficiency case for government redistribution programmes?

f. If government redistribution programmes are funded through taxes on the individuals who are voluntarily giving to anti-poverty programmes, why might the government's programme have to be large in order to accomplish anything?

g. How does your answer to (f) change if there is a third set of individuals that neither give to anti-poverty programmes nor benefit from them but would be taxed together with those who are privately giving to anti-poverty programmes to finance government redistribution programmes?

h. Some argue that private anti-poverty programmes are inherently more effective because civil society anti-poverty programmes make use of information that government programmes cannot reach. As a result, the argument goes, civil society anti-poverty efforts achieve a greater increase in welfare for the poor for every euro spent than government redistributive programmes. If this is indeed the case, discuss the trade-offs this raises as one thinks about optimal government involvement in anti-poverty efforts.

B. Denote individual n's private good consumption as x_n, the government contribution to anti-poverty efforts as g and individual n's contribution to anti-poverty efforts as z_n. Let individual n's tastes be defined as $u^n(x_n, y, z_n) = x_n^\alpha y^\beta z_n^\gamma$. Assume that anti-poverty efforts are pure transfers of money to the poor.

a. What has to be true for anti-poverty efforts to be strictly private goods?

b. What has to be true for anti-poverty efforts to be pure public goods?

c. Suppose the condition you derived in (a) applies and maintain this assumption until you get to part (g). Suppose further that there are N individuals who have different income levels, with n's income denoted I_n. Will private anti-poverty efforts be funded efficiently when $g = 0$? What will be the equilibrium level of private funding for anti-poverty programmes when $g = 0$ as N gets large?

d. If the government increases g without raising taxes, will private contributions to anti-poverty efforts be affected assuming still that the condition derived in (a) holds? *Hint*: How does the individual's optimization problem change?

e. Suppose the government instead levies a proportional tax t on all income and uses the funds solely to fund g. How much private funding for anti-poverty programmes will this government intervention crowd out? By how much will overall contributions to anti-poverty programmes including the government's contribution change? Consider again the impact on the individual's optimization problem.

f. Can this government intervention in anti-poverty efforts be justified on efficiency grounds?

g. Suppose instead that the condition you derived in (b) holds. To simplify the analysis, suppose that the N people who care about anti-poverty programmes all have the same income level I as well as the same preferences. What is the equilibrium level of funding for anti-poverty programmes when $g = 0$?

h. What happens to overall funding, both public and private, when the government increases g without changing taxes?

i. If the government instead imposes a proportional income tax t and uses the revenues solely to fund g, what happens to overall funding of anti-poverty efforts, assuming the N individuals still give positive contributions in equilibrium?

j. Under what condition will the balanced-budget (t, g) government programme raise the overall funding level for anti-poverty programmes?

*conceptually challenging
**computationally challenging
†solutions in Study Guide

Chapter 28

Governments and Politics

Throughout this book, we have treated individuals, whether they be consumers or workers or firms, as doing the best they can given their circumstances. What is best was typically interpreted as a subjective judgment of the individual, although we have assumed that firms view maximizing their profits as best. On a few occasions when we found particular real-world policies to be inefficient and sometimes inequitable, we hinted that we might want to look at politicians in the same way; that is, we might want to forego idealistic notions of democratic politicians implementing 'the will of the people' and rather take a more realistic view of the incentives that guide political behaviour.

In this chapter, that is precisely what we will do. The motivation for this arises from a famous result by Ken Arrow, an analytic proof of the proposition that, in a sense, there is generally no such thing as 'the will of the people'. I realize that may sound a bit odd, but it is absolutely true. What Arrow showed, and what we will demonstrate formally in part B of this chapter, is that democratic processes of aggregating voter preferences generally do not result in a rational social preference order that could be called the will of the people where social alternatives can be clearly ranked from best to worst. Rather, democratic processes tend to result in social preference rankings that make it possible for politicians, especially those who can set the agenda on which voting takes place, to manipulate the process to their own advantage.

For this reason, economists and political scientists have studied different types of political institutions extensively over the past few decades and have focused on the incentives contained in particular political institutions that shape the outcome of government policy in democratic societies. Some such institutions make it more difficult for politicians to manipulate the process; others make it easier. No matter how well-designed the institution, democracy is a messy business. *There is no first welfare theorem for politicians*; political competition in democratic institutions does not generally result in efficient outcomes. This is important to realize for economists who give policy advice. Just like markets and civil society, institutions face problems and so do governments. Which part of society, if any, should get involved in solving problems depends in part on which faces the fewest problems in implementing what we would like to ideally see happen.

We will depart in this chapter from our usual practice of having part A sections roughly correspond to part B sections. The main ideas of political economy introduced here are not particularly mathematically intensive and can be presented in an intuitive and graphical framework. The exception to this is an exposition of *Arrow's Theorem*, which involves a bit of mathematical notation and formal reasoning. We will therefore leave the full development of Arrow's Theorem as the main task of Section B of the chapter.

28A	The Economic Way of Thinking About Politics

It is important to understand a little about where Arrow was coming from and how his sweeping theorem has shaped the way we think of government policy formation. For centuries, political philosophers had spoken in terms of phrases such as the will of the people, and it was often taken for granted that political outcomes are expressions of this will. What, Arrow asked, do we mean when we use such phrases? Do such phrases even make sense?

It may be thought that the will of the people comprises the political processes that aggregate individual preferences over outcomes we all care about: taxes, public goods, regulations on private property, nuclear power, war and peace, abortion, stem cell research, civil liberties, religious freedom and so on. We refer to the aggregate preferences that shape political outcomes as the will of the people. That is exactly what Arrow had in mind. He viewed democratic processes as ways in which societies attempt to aggregate the preferences of their citizens so that the aggregated or social preferences that emerge can be used to make decisions and trade-offs on the important issues of our time. Different democratic processes, however, might lead to different ways in which individual preferences are aggregated to form social preferences, which implies that different democratic processes might lead to different wills of the same people. Arrow wanted to ask what kinds of social preferences, what kinds of wills of the people, we might expect to see emerge from democratic processes.

What he found was both startling and depressing, and it gave rise to a whole new branch of economics that intersects with political science. If we think of the social preferences that *should* emerge from a democratic process as preferences that respect a minimal level of democracy, that do not violate unanimously held views and that cannot be manipulated by politicians that control the political agenda, *we are out of luck*. There is no such general democratic process! There is, in a very real way, no such thing as the will of the people. When we speak collectively as 'we', there is, in a very real sense, no such thing. While we certainly make decisions through political institutions, those decisions are not, Arrow's Theorem implies, guided by anything that can be called social preferences or a will of the people.

Arrow's intention was not, however, to argue against democracy; quite the opposite, it was to get us to begin thinking seriously about how some democratic institutions are better than others and how democracy can be made to work better if we understand it better. What comes out of democratic political processes, Arrow demonstrated, not only depends on precisely how these processes are designed and have evolved but it also often depends a lot on who within politics shapes the agenda over which a subset of citizens vote, and how much the political institutions constrain that person from abusing their power. We can construct examples where the powers of this agenda setter approach those of a dictator despite all appearances of truly underlying democratic processes. We will also give examples of political institutions, some formal and some informal, that have emerged to restrain political agenda setters. In short, Arrow made the case for the study of political institutions, because political institutions and their incentives matter when there is no will of the people that is magically revealed as we go to the polls to vote.

We will describe in this chapter some of the ways in which political institutions matter and how we cannot in general expect democratic political institutions to necessarily result in policies that advance any particular goal consistently, whether that goal be economic efficiency, social equity of some kind, or making sure that flowers bloom everywhere all the time. In the process, it is hoped you will discover some of the ways in which we can think of political actors in much the same way as we have thought of consumers and producers: as actors with preferences trying to do the best they can given their circumstances.

28A.1 Agenda Setting and Manipulation of Policy

We will begin our discussion of political institutions in some simple settings. First, we will look at how a voting equilibrium can emerge when the set of issues we vote on can be neatly lined up on a single dimension. We can think of this as a single-dimensional issue, such as how much we would like to spend on local schools given that we have to raise the required revenues through a proportional tax. Political scientists also use such a single-dimensional issue space as a reduced form of representing preferences over more complicated sets of issues, with bundles of policies lined up from the political right to the political left. When we can think of the relevant issue as lying on such a single dimension, we can derive conditions on voter preferences that result in an equilibrium that bears a striking resemblance to the Hotelling model in the absence of price differentiation as introduced in Chapter 26. We will see how quickly a role for an agenda setter emerges as the underlying model is tweaked slightly, either in terms of the voter preferences that we consider or in terms of the dimensionality of the issue space.

28A.1.1 Single-Dimensional Politics and the Median Voter Theorem Consider the following example. Suppose there is a local referendum on school spending, and that for the moment there exists no such thing as private schools. Every family therefore has to send its children to local schools. Suppose further that spending is all that matters in schools, that every voter has one school-aged child, and that families have preferences over school spending y and a composite private good x. Finally, assume families understand that higher school spending has to be financed through a tax, and that any increase in y results in proportionately less x.

In panel (a) of Graph 28.1, we illustrate the trade-off a particular voter i faces between y and x, a trade-off that looks exactly like our usual budget constraint. What is different is that the slope of the budget constraint is not determined by the relative price of y, but rather by tax payments that the consumer has to make to finance more y. Furthermore, the consumer does not actually get to choose their most preferred bundle, but is one of many who votes in an election that will determine the bundle they get to consume.

Graph 28.1 Single-Peaked Preferences Over School Spending

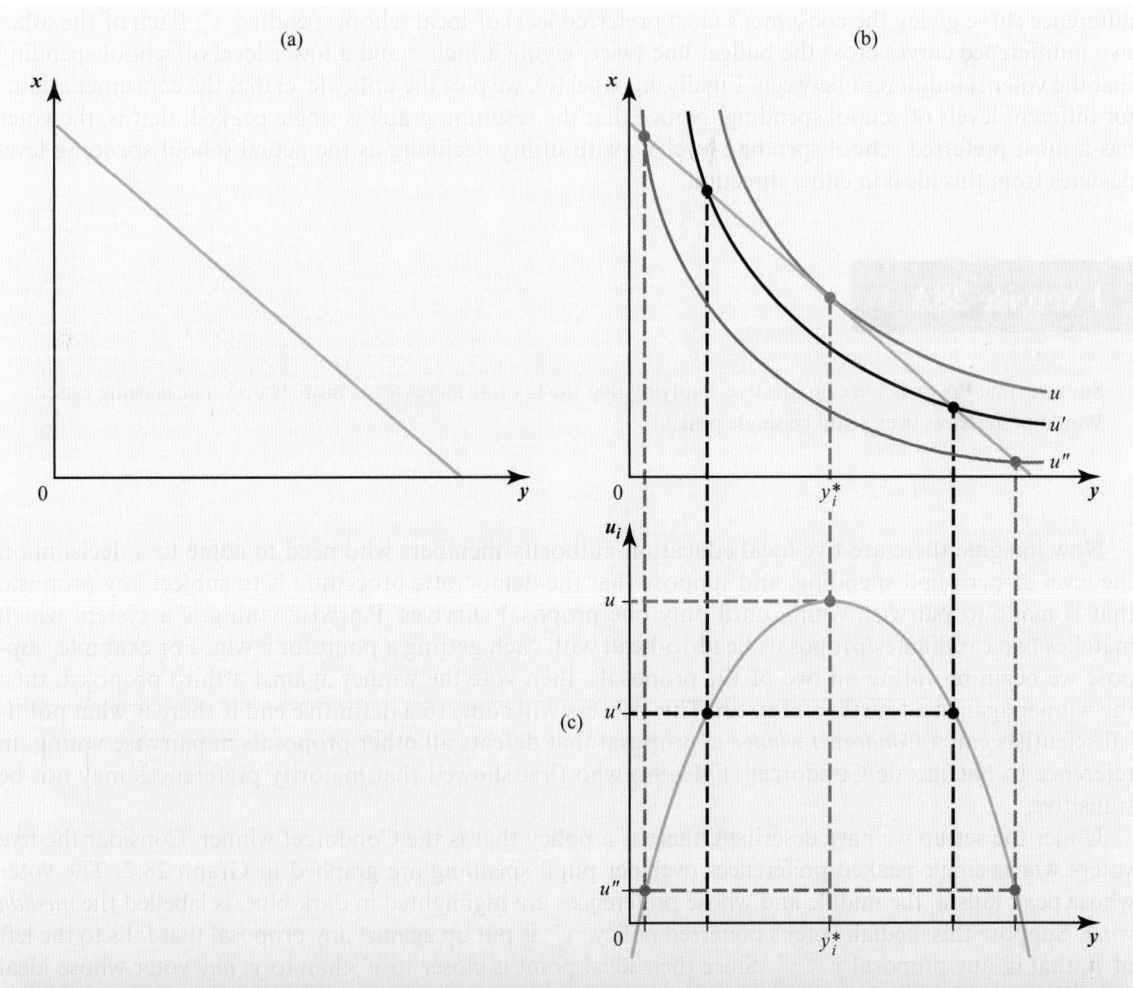

Go to MindTap to interact with this graph

Exercise 28A.1

Suppose y is defined as per pupil spending in local schools. If there are N different taxpayers and an equal number of school children, and if all taxpayers share the financing of local schools equally, what is the slope of this budget line?

Exercise 28A.2

Suppose instead that y is defined as the overall spending in local schools. What is the slope of the budget line under the same conditions as described in exercise 28A.1?

In panel (b) of the graph, we illustrate three indifference curves for our voter, with the dark brown indifference curve giving the consumer's most preferred level of local school spending y_i^*. Each of the other two indifference curves cross the budget line twice, giving a higher and a lower level of school spending that the voter is indifferent between. Finally, in panel (c), we plot the utility level that the consumer attains for different levels of school spending. Notice that the resulting graph is single peaked; that is, the voter has a most preferred school spending level y_i^*, with utility declining as the actual school spending level deviates from this ideal in either direction.

Exercise 28A.3

Suppose that tax rates were progressive, implying that the tax rate increases as more tax revenue is being raised. Would preferences over y still be single peaked?

Now imagine there are five local education authority members who need to come to a decision on the level of per pupil spending, and suppose that the democratic procedure is to subject any proposal that is made to pairwise voting until only one proposal survives. Pairwise voting is a system which matches two candidates/proposals head-to-head with each getting a point for a win. For example, suppose we begin by voting on two of the proposals, then vote the winner against a third proposal, then the winner against a fourth, and so on. This process will come to a definitive end if there is what political scientists call a *Condorcet winner*: a proposal that defeats all other proposals in pairwise voting, in reference to Nicolas de Condorcet (1743–94) who first showed that majority preferences may not be transitive.

Under the set-up we have described, there is a policy that is the Condorcet winner. Consider the five voters whose single-peaked preferences over per pupil spending are graphed in Graph 28.2. The voter whose peak falls in the middle and whose preferences are highlighted in dark blue, is labelled the *median voter*. Suppose this median voter's preferred policy, y_m^*, is put up against any proposal that falls to the left of it, that is, any proposal $y < y_m^*$. Since their ideal point is closer to y_m^* than to y, *any* voter whose ideal point lies to the right of y_m^* will prefer y_m^* to such a y. Thus, voters 4 and 5 will join the median voter in defeating any such proposal. Similarly, any proposal $y' > y_m^*$, will be defeated by voters 1 and 2 together with the median voter when put up against y_m^*. Thus, there does not exist any policy proposal that can beat y_m^*, which makes y_m^* the Condorcet winner.

Graph 28.2 The Median Voter Theorem

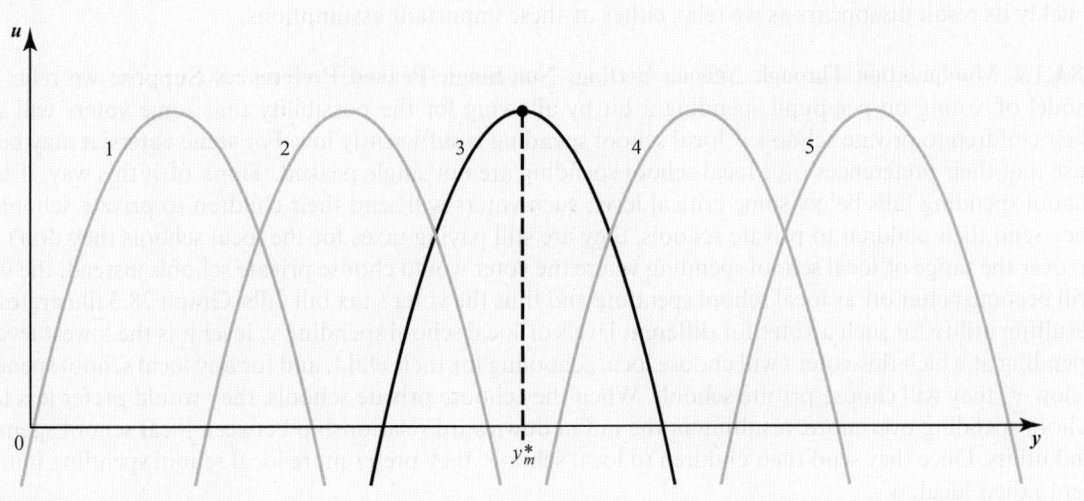

Exercise 28A.4

In the graph, we have depicted all the single-peaked preferences as having the same shape and differing only in the placement of the ideal point. Would the same Condorcet winner arise under single-peaked preferences that differ in their shapes but not the horizontal location of ideal points?

The result we just derived for five voters holds for any odd number of voters, no matter how many there are. For instance, we could model a presidential election in a country as a contest between two candidates that position themselves along an ideological spectrum that ranges from extreme left to extreme right. Large numbers of voters vote in presidential elections, and we could approximate that large number with a continuum of consumers whose ideal points are distributed across that spectrum, with each voter becoming worse off the further the elected president's ideological stance is from the voter's. We can ask where we think the candidates will position themselves, and the model predicts that if either candidate positions themselves at any point other than the median voter's ideal point, the other candidate can defeat the candidate by picking the median voter's position. In equilibrium, we would therefore expect the candidates to both cater to the median voter.

Exercise 28A.5

Can you see how this equilibrium prediction conforms to the equilibrium in the Hotelling model when firms are restricted to charging the same output price and where the ideological spectrum is replaced by product differentiation?

The insight from our model thus far can be summarized in what is known as the *Median Voter Theorem*: as long as the issues that are voted on fall on a single-dimensional spectrum and as long as voters have single-peaked preferences over that spectrum, majority rule over pairwise alternatives will result in the election of the median voter's ideal point. Notice the two important caveats in the statement of this theorem: voter preferences over the issues have to be *single peaked* and the issue space has to be *single-dimensional*. In the next two sections, we will see just how sensitive the median voter theorem is and how quickly its result disappears as we relax either of these important assumptions.

28A.1.2 Manipulation Through Agenda Setting: Non-Single-Peaked Preferences Suppose we relax our model of voting on per pupil spending a bit by allowing for the possibility that some voters will send their children to private schools if local school spending is sufficiently low. For some voters, it may be the case that their preferences over local school spending are not single peaked. Think of it this way: if local school spending falls below some critical level, such voters will send their children to private schools. If they send their children to private schools, they are still paying taxes for the local schools they don't use, so over the range of local school spending where the voter would choose private schools instead, the voter will become better off as local school spending and thus the voter's tax bill falls. Graph 28.3 illustrates the resulting utility for such a voter for different levels of local school spending y: level $\underline{y}_i$ is the lowest level of spending at which this voter i will choose local schooling for their child, and for any local school spending below $\underline{y}_i$, they will choose private schools. When they choose private schools, they would prefer less local school spending over more, resulting in the initial downward relationship between local school spending and utility. Once they send their children to local schools, they prefer more local school spending until we get to their ideal: y_i^*.

This is an example of non-single-peaked preferences over a single-dimensional issue. The example is given to illustrate that such preferences are quite plausible even in simple settings where there is only a single issue that is being voted on. We'll see next that this implies that no Condorcet winner might exist; that is, that there does not exist a per pupil spending level that can defeat any alternative proposal someone might make.

Graph 28.3 Non-Single-Peaked Preferences Over Public School Spending

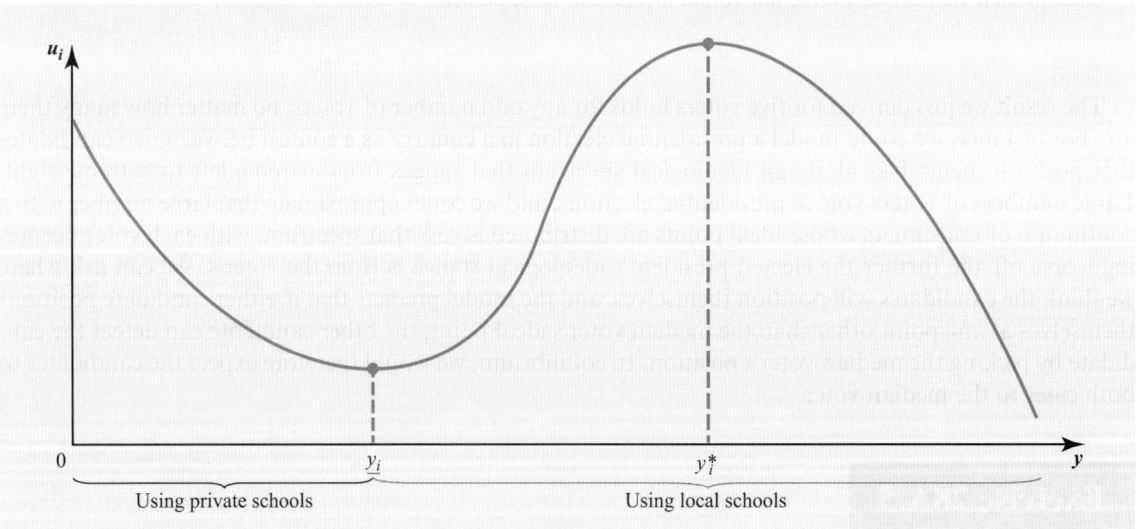

Suppose we have three spending levels that are being considered, with $y_1 < y_2 < y_3$. Assume there are three voters whose preferences are given by:

> Voter 1: y_1 preferred to y_2 preferred to y_3
>
> Voter 2: y_2 preferred to y_3 preferred to y_1 (28.1)
>
> Voter 3: y_3 preferred to y_1 preferred to y_2

Exercise 28A.6

Which of these voters has single-peaked preferences over local school spending?

Now consider what happens as we put different proposals against one another to see which one would win a majority of votes. In putting y_1 against y_2, we can see from the voter preferences that voters 1 and 3 will vote for y_1, thus defeating y_2. In putting y_2 against y_3, voters 1 and 2 will vote for y_2, thus defeating y_3. Finally, in putting y_3 against y_1, voters 2 and 3 will vote for y_3, thus defeating y_1. This gives the following result under majority rule:

$$y_1 \text{ defeats } y_2 \text{ defeats } y_3 \text{ defeats } y_1 \qquad\qquad (28.2)$$

There is no Condorcet winner because each of the three proposals is defeated by one of the others in a pairwise contest. In Arrow's words, social preferences in this case are not rational because they violate transitivity, and when transitivity is violated, it is difficult to make decisions. There is no will of the people because the people keep defeating each proposal. In our example, we could easily end up in an endless cycle of votes with no conclusion unless *someone* figures out a rule for how the voting will stop.

We will call that someone an *agenda setter*. The agenda setter might be one of the voters, or they might have no vote at all. They do have the job of determining how majority rule voting will be implemented and at what point the voting stops and a decision is made. Graph 28.4 illustrates the three natural voting agendas that such an agenda setter might implement. In panel (a), a decision is first made between y_1 and y_2, and the winning proposal is put up against y_3. Whatever proposal wins the second vote is the one that is implemented. The agendas in panels (b) and (c) differ in terms of which pair is voted on first, but all three agendas are fully governed by majority rule throughout.

Graph 28.4 Three Possible Voting Agendas

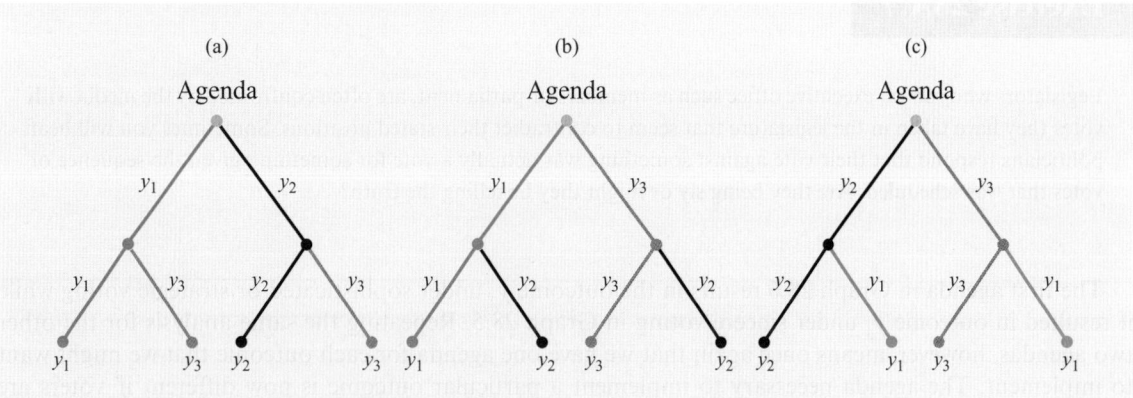

We can look at each of the three agendas and see what outcome will result from majority voting. In Graph 28.5, we replicate the three agendas but this time indicate in bold how each of the votes will turn out given what we concluded in expression (28.2). Notice that whoever sets the agenda determines the choice that is made *without even necessarily having a vote to cast themselves*. This is the issue with majority rule social preferences when such preferences violate transitivity. The intransitivity makes majority voting subject to manipulation by agenda setters because no Condorcet winner exists. When there is no coherent will of the people, it may be that the result of majority rule is the will of the agenda setter.

It might be considered that voters must be naive to let an agenda setter manipulate them in this way, and that may be correct. However, even when voters are not naive, the agenda setter in our example can still get their way. Consider the same three agendas, replicated again in Graph 28.6. This time, let's assume that our three voters are sophisticated; that is, let's assume voters look down the voting tree to see what will happen later as they vote in the first vote. In panel (a) of the graph, we highlight what will be the outcome in the second vote from each of the two possible nodes in the voting tree. If the first node is reached and y_1 is put up against y_3, we know y_3 will win, and if the second node is reached and y_2 is put up against y_3, we know y_2 will win. Thus, a sophisticated voter that looks ahead to the second vote under the agenda (a) knows that a vote that is framed as a vote of y_1 against y_2 is really a vote of y_3 against y_2, and if the voters are sophisticated, this will mean that y_2 will win the first vote. The crucial voter in this case is voter 1. If they vote their sincere preferences naively, they would vote for y_1 in the first vote since y_1 is their most preferred outcome. When voter 1 thinks in a sophisticated way, they realize that a vote for y_1 is really a vote for y_3 since y_1 will lose against y_3 in the next vote. Thus, since y_3 is their least preferred outcome, they will vote strategically for y_2 against y_1 despite y_1 being their most preferred policy.

Graph 28.5 Voting Outcomes Under the Three Agendas

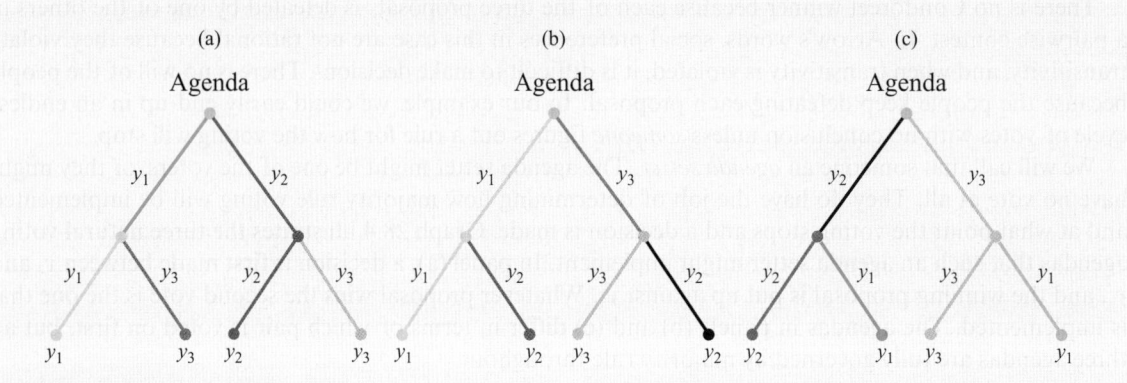

Exercise 28A.7

Legislators who run for executive office such as members of parliament, are often confronted by the media with votes they have taken in the legislature that seem to contradict their stated positions. Sometimes you will hear politicians respond that their vote against something was actually a vote for something given the sequence of votes that was scheduled. Are they being sly or might they be telling the truth?

The first agenda in Graph 28.6 results in the outcome y_2 under sophisticated or strategic voting while it resulted in outcome y_3 under sincere voting in Graph 28.5. Repeating the same analysis for the other two agendas, however, means once again that we have one agenda for each outcome that we might want to implement. The agenda necessary to implement a particular outcome is now different if voters are strategic than if they are naive, but the agenda setter can still get any outcome they want by manipulating the agenda.

This is the underlying reason why it matters so much which political party controls the key legislature chamber in a country because the party in the majority gets to set the broad agenda. This is generally well understood by most people who follow politics. What is less appreciated is that within many parliaments there are important committees whose chair gets to choose sequences of votes within committees, and in some cases, determine the rules under which legislative proposals come to the house for votes and amendments. Such agenda-setting powers are important because they influence outcomes, and they are important even though committee chairs often do not themselves vote on proposals.

Graph 28.6 Agenda Setting Under Sophisticated Voting

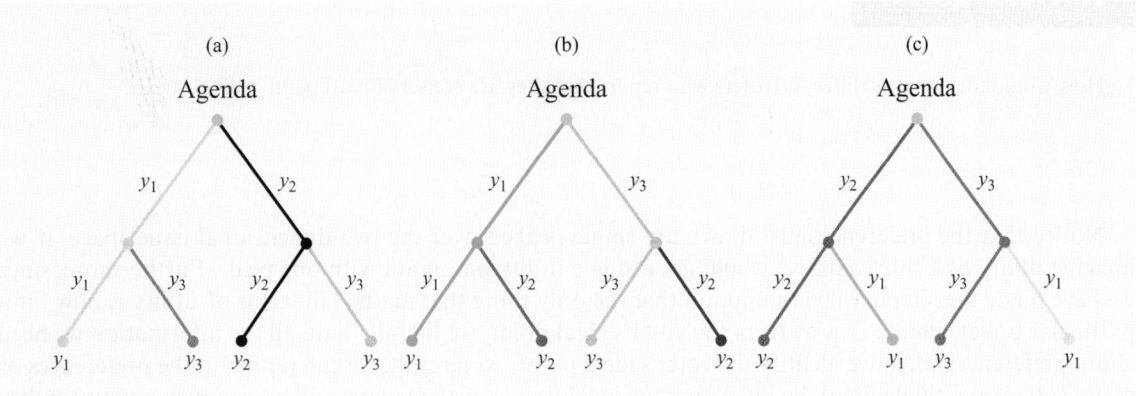

28A.1.3 Multidimensional Politics and the Anything-Can-Happen Theorem

The median voter theorem that guarantees a Condorcet winner required (1) single-peaked preferences over (2) a single-dimensional issue space. We have just seen what happens when preferences are not single peaked: we lose the guarantee of a Condorcet winner and with that loss introduce power for non-voting agenda setters. The same happens, in an even more dramatic way, when we allow the issue space to be multidimensional.

Suppose, for instance, that there are two general government budget priorities to set: domestic spending y and military spending z. In panel (a) of Graph 28.7, we illustrate this on a graph with domestic spending on the horizontal axis and military spending on the vertical. We can think of an individual voter i's preferences within this two-dimensional issue space. Such a voter understands that taxes have to be paid at least at some point to finance government spending of any kind, and so the voter's preferences cannot satisfy the more is better assumption for all levels of y and z. Eventually, the cost of paying additional taxes is too high to want more spending. So somewhere in the (y, z) space, our voter has an ideal point that is their most preferred. No matter which direction away from this ideal point we move in our two-dimensional issue space, our voter will become worse off. For simplicity, we can for instance assume that how much worse off they will be depends solely on the distance of a (y, z) bundle away from the voter's ideal bundle (y_i^*, z_i^*). This allows us to draw circles around the voter's ideal point, with each circle representing an indifference curve and with utility decreasing as the circles get bigger.

Graph 28.7 Two-Dimensional Issue Spaces

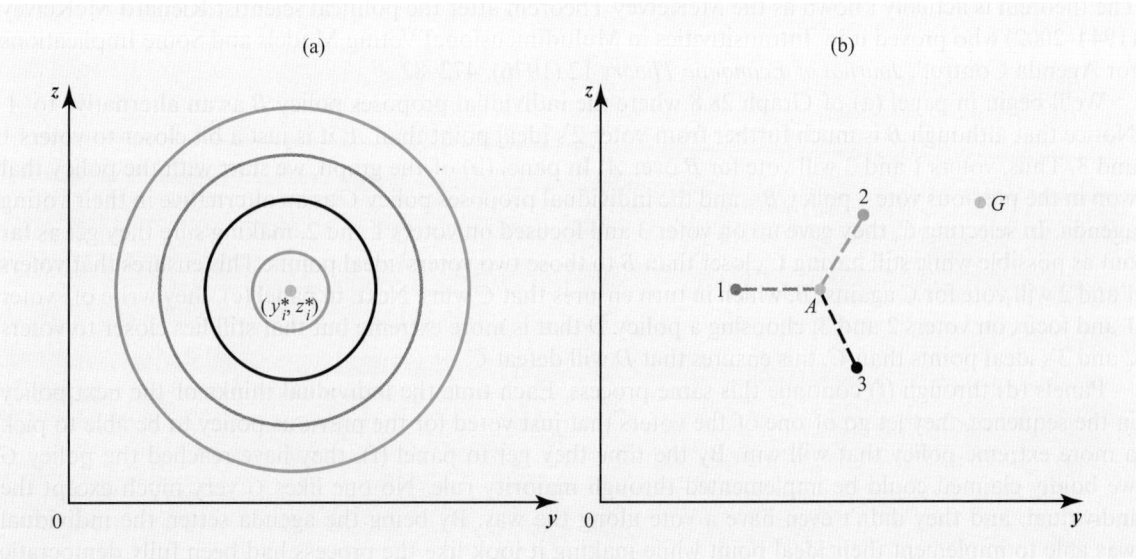

Exercise 28A.8

How would ideal points differ for voters who report that they are conservative, liberal or libertarian?

Notice that the preferences just drawn are single peaked over the two-dimensional issue space. If we imagine utility as a third axis, we would get a single utility mountain with one peak. Furthermore, since we have made the simplifying assumption that the only thing that matters in terms of utility is how far a particular policy bundle is away from the voter's ideal point, we literally have all the information we need about preferences when we identify the voter's ideal point. As a result, we can represent the preferences of many voters on a single graph by indicating the ideal points of the voters, and we can pick any two policy bundles and check which way each of the voters will vote depending on how far the two bundles are from each voter's ideal point.

For instance, in panel (b) of Graph 28.7, we illustrate three voters by drawing three different ideal points labelled 1, 2 and 3. In the same graph, we illustrate a policy labelled *A*. From each ideal point, we draw a dashed line to the proposal, and we will know that for any proposal *B* that is put up against proposal *A* in a vote, each voter will vote for *B* if and only if the distance from that voter's ideal point to *B* is smaller than the distance from the ideal point to *A*. It's immediately clear that there are many policies that could not win against *A* because *A* is so centrally located relative to the voters' ideal points. For instance, policy *G* over to the upper right of the graph would go down to unanimous defeat if put up against *A*.

Consider, however, this bold claim: suppose an individual was put in charge of designing an agenda, a sequence of pairwise votes where the winning proposal goes on to face the next proposal in the sequence. They could get the extreme policy *G* to be the outcome of a majority rule process with these three voters voting to implement *G* rather than *A*. The individual can get *any* policy in the two-dimensional issue space to be an outcome of a thoughtfully designed agenda that begins with a vote of *A* against some other policy. More than that, the individual can start with *any* policy at the beginning of the sequence of votes, and can construct a sequence to get to *any* other policy.

We won't prove this formally here, but we will show how to get from *A* to *G* when all voters would unanimously send *G* down to defeat if we voted *A* against *G*. For our purposes, we will assume that voters vote sincerely, as they would be likely to do if there were many voters of each type. From this example you should see how the general theorem, which we will call the 'Anything-Can-Happen theorem', must be true. The theorem is actually known as the McKelvey Theorem after the political scientist Richard McKelvey (1944–2002) who proved it in 'Intransitivities in Multidimensional Voting Models and Some Implications for Agenda Control', *Journal of Economic Theory* 12 (1976), 472–82.

We'll begin in panel (a) of Graph 28.8 where the individual proposes policy *B* as an alternative to *A*. Notice that although *B* is much further from voter 2's ideal point than *A*, it is just a bit closer to voters 1 and 3. Thus, voters 1 and 3 will vote for *B* over *A*. In panel (b) of the graph, we start with the policy that won in the previous vote – policy *B* – and the individual proposes policy *C* as an alternative in their voting agenda. In selecting *C*, they gave up on voter 3 and focused on voters 1 and 2, making sure they get as far out as possible while still having *C* closer than *B* to those two voters' ideal points. This ensures that voters 1 and 2 will vote for *C* against *B*, which in turn ensures that *C* wins. Next, in panel (c), they write off voter 1 and focus on voters 2 and 3, choosing a policy *D* that is more extreme but that still lies closer to voters 2 and 3's ideal points than *C*; this ensures that *D* will defeat *C*.

Panels (d) through (f) continue this same process. Each time the individual thinks of the next policy in the sequence, they let go of one of the voters that just voted for the previous policy to be able to pick a more extreme policy that will win. By the time they get to panel (f), they have reached the policy *G* we boldly claimed could be implemented through majority rule. No one likes *G* very much except the individual, and they didn't even have a vote along the way. By being the agenda setter, the individual was able to implement their ideal point while making it look like the process had been fully democratic throughout. They could have kept the outward spiralling of policies going and got to even more extreme policies if they had wanted.

Exercise 28A.9

Can you explain how panels (d) to (f) complete the argument that G can be implemented through a sequence of pairwise votes?

Graph 28.8 The 'Anything-Can-Happen' Theorem

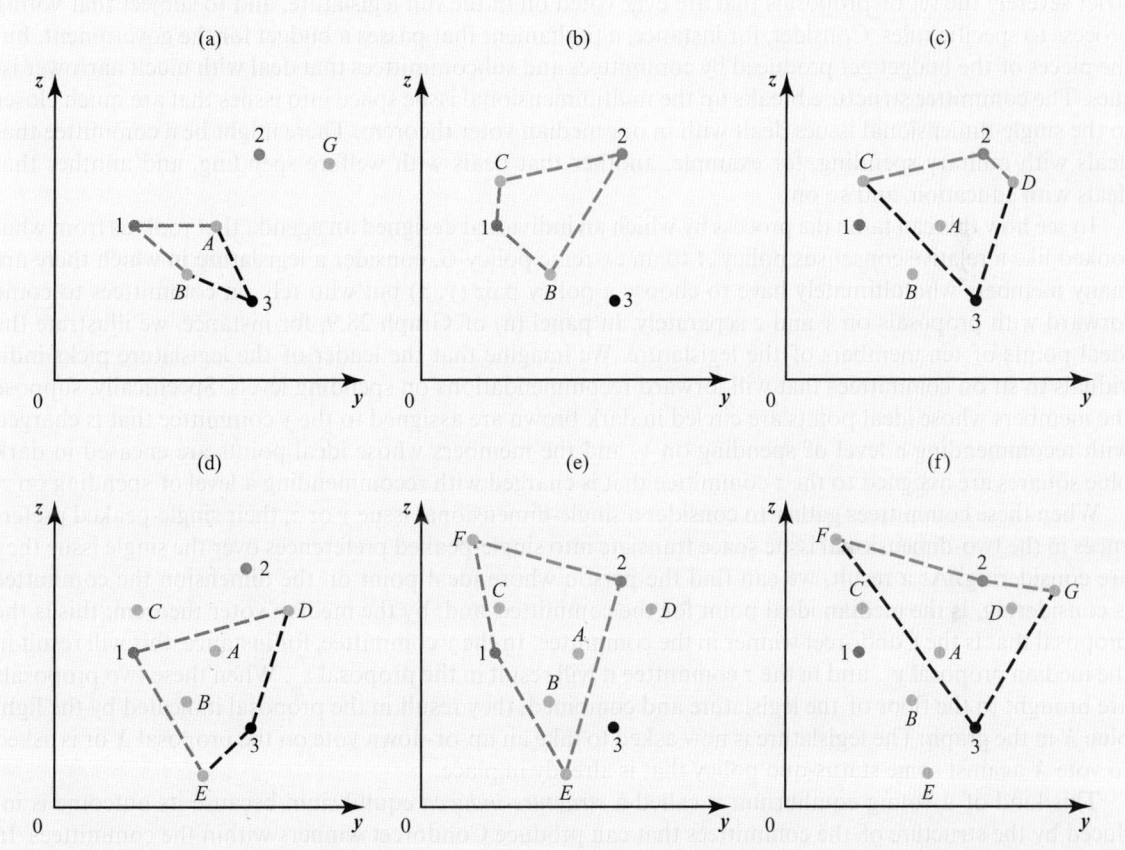

The result is remarkable. It says that when issues get complicated and can't just be modelled along a single dimension, agenda setters almost always control everything given that voter preferences do not add up to a coherent will of the people. We will shortly see how political institutions, rules and customs constrain this power of the agenda setter. If you doubt that agenda setters can in principle do what we have just done in Graph 28.8, refer to a fascinating account of how one of the founding fathers of experimental economics did precisely that in his flight club. To cut a long story short, he was put in charge of designing a democratic agenda that would lead to an expression of the will of the club members in selecting a new fleet of aircraft for the flight club to purchase. Understanding that there was probably no such thing as the will of the club members, Charles Plott set off to design an agenda that would implement a very particular outcome he determined in advance, and he proceeded to document exactly how successful he was in getting the club membership to democratically decide to implement what he determined he wanted at the beginning.

28A.2 Institutional Restraints on Policy Manipulation

The world is, of course, not as chaotic as all that. Agenda setters cannot just get anything they want, and they themselves must first get into the position of being able to shape the political agenda, which might mean that their preferences might not be as extreme as the individual in our previous example. Neither would a political system that does not find ways of constraining what agenda setters can dictate be among the more successful. It would therefore not be surprising if a combination of deliberate institutional design with the evolution of institutional features that proved worthwhile has led to a considerable taming of the chaos that could in principle emerge under majority rule voting. We will now consider two particular types of political institutions that tend to play important roles in democratic legislative processes.

28A.2.1 Structure-Induced Voting Equilibria: Breaking Up Complex Issues

One of the ways in which real-world legislative bodies deal with the potential chaos that can arise under democratic processes is to restrict severely the set of proposals that are ever voted on in the full legislature, and to subject that voting process to specific rules. Consider, for instance, a parliament that passes a budget for the government, but the pieces of the budget get produced by committees and subcommittees that deal with much narrower issues. The committee structure breaks up the multidimensional issue space into issues that are much closer to the single-dimensional issues dealt with in our median voter theorem. There might be a committee that deals with military spending, for example, another that deals with welfare spending, and another that deals with education, and so on.

To see how this can tame the process by which an individual designed an agenda that took us from what looked like a relative consensus policy A to an extreme policy G, consider a legislature in which there are many members who ultimately have to choose a policy pair (y, z) but who rely on committees to come forward with proposals on y and z separately. In panel (a) of Graph 28.9, for instance, we illustrate the ideal points of ten members of the legislature. We imagine that the leader of the legislature picks individuals to sit on committees that will forward recommendations on spending levels. Specifically, suppose the members whose ideal points are circled in dark brown are assigned to the y committee that is charged with recommending a level of spending on y, and the members whose ideal points are encased in dark blue squares are assigned to the z committee that is charged with recommending a level of spending on z.

When these committees gather to consider a single-dimensional issue y or z, their single-peaked preferences in the two-dimensional issue space translate into single-peaked preferences over the single issue they are considering. As a result, we can find the person whose ideal point on the dimension the committee is considering, is the median ideal point for the committee, and, by the median voter theorem, this is the proposal that is the Condorcet winner in the committee. In the y committee, for instance, this will result in the median proposal y_m, and in the z committee it will result in the proposal z_m. When these two proposals are brought to the floor of the legislature and combined, they result in the proposal indicated by the light blue X in the graph. The legislature is now asked to take an up-or-down vote on the proposal X or is asked to vote X against some status-quo policy that is already in place.

This kind of a voting equilibrium is called a *structure-induced* equilibrium because its outcome is induced by the structure of the committees that can produce Condorcet winners within the committees. In panel (a) of our graph, the process results in a proposal that appears to lie very much towards the middle of where all the individual ideal points are for members of the legislature. This is an artefact of the way we assigned members to committees. In panel (b) of the graph, we have reassigned the same members differently between the two committees. The resulting light blue proposal X' is more extreme than that produced in panel (a), containing more of y and more of z. Thus, by altering the committee assignments, the agenda setter in the legislature still has quite a bit of influence on how the final proposal looks.

Exercise 28A.10

How would you assign the members to committees if you wanted to get less spending on y and z than we did in panel (a) of Graph 28.9? What if you wanted more of y but less of z?

Graph 28.9 Structure-Induced Voting Equilibria

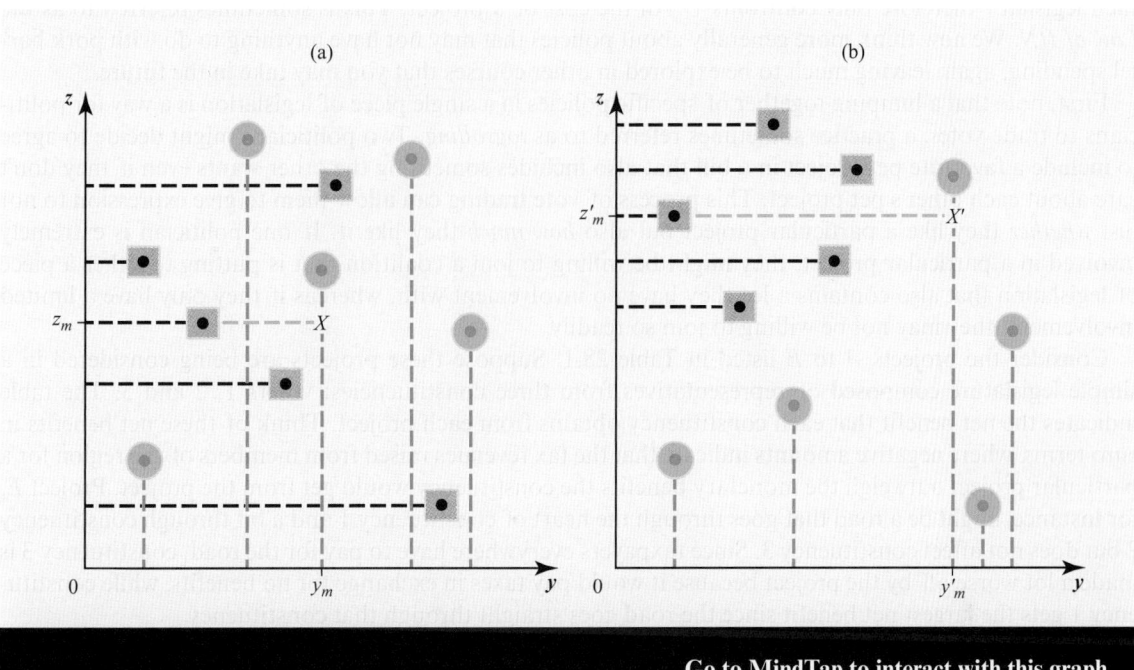

Go to MindTap to interact with this graph

Notice that agenda setting now takes a different form. The leader of the legislature might not be able to cleverly construct sequences of votes like we did in the last section, but they can influence the outcome in the legislature by cleverly choosing committee memberships. While this agenda setter retains a great deal of control over the ultimate outcome of the legislative process, you should also notice that the committee system limits how extreme an outcome can arise under democratic voting. In particular, if you found the smallest convex set of policies that contains all the members' ideal points, the policy produced by the committee system has to lie within that set. This was not true in Graph 28.8, where G lies far outside this set.

Committees in legislative bodies have arisen over time as such bodies have tried to figure out procedures that work. They are, in many ways, informal institutions that have emerged rather than having been explicitly designed. Similar institutions, like the rules that govern legislative debate and the rules that can be applied to limit the kinds of amendments that members can offer to bills that reach the floor of the legislature, have emerged and are rarely altered directly. Other institutions have been more deliberately designed. A number of political systems split the legislature into two separate bodies in part to have these institutions put a check on each other. Many countries also relegate some issues to local government control. Sometimes the political process asks voters to vote directly on single issues, such as when referenda are placed in front of voters. All these mechanisms – those that have been formally designed and those that have evolved over time – in part accomplish the task of imposing structure on democratic voting, with that structure helping to determine what outcomes ultimately emerge.

The political economy literature on how different structures under which voting happens result in different outcomes is vast, too vast for us to even begin to crack it here. The main lesson from what we have done is that when issues of any complexity require political solutions, any voting process will be subject to manipulation by agenda setters, but structured voting can lessen the degree to which such manipulation can result in extreme outcomes.

28A.2.2 Expressing Intensity of Preferences: Vote Trading and Reciprocity In real-world legislatures, politicians often find ways of lumping together different issues into single pieces of legislation that receive an up-or-down vote. This can relate to spending on special projects targeted at a legislator's constituency, and is referred to as *pork barrel spending*. Such spending is often inefficient for reasons that find their roots in the Tragedy of the Commons, with inefficiency rising as the number of constituencies N increases and each legislator therefore only confronts $1/N$th the cost of a project. This is sometimes referred to as the *Law of 1/N*. We now think more generally about policies that may not have anything to do with pork barrel spending, again leaving much to be explored in other courses that you may take in the future.

First, note that a lumping together of specific policies in a single piece of legislation is a way for politicians to trade votes, a practice sometimes referred to as *logrolling*. Two politicians might decide to agree to include a favourite pet project in a bill that also includes something the other wants even if they don't care about each other's pet project. This process of vote trading can allow them to give expression to not just *whether* they like a particular project but also *how much* they like it. If one politician is extremely involved in a particular project, they might be willing to join a coalition that is putting together a piece of legislation that also contains a lot they have no involvement with, whereas if they only have a limited involvement, they may not be willing to join so readily.

Consider the projects A to E listed in Table 28.1. Suppose these projects are being considered in a simple legislature composed of representatives from three constituencies: voters 1, 2 and 3. The table indicates the net benefit that each constituency obtains from each project. Think of these net benefits in euro terms, where negative amounts indicate that the tax revenues raised from members of the region for a particular project outweigh the monetary benefits the constituency would get from the project. Project E, for instance, might be a road that goes through the heart of constituency 1 and a bit through constituency 2 but does not affect constituency 3. Since taxpayers everywhere have to pay for the road, constituency 3 is made a lot worse off by the project because it would pay taxes in exchange for no benefits, while constituency 1 gets the largest net benefit since the road goes straight through that constituency.

Suppose that only A and B were on the agenda. Neither project could receive a majority of votes since only one voter would vote for each of the projects. Voters 1 and 2 can form a coalition and put the two projects into a single piece of legislation that is voted up or down. This bundled legislation will receive yes votes from voters 1 and 2, and as a bundle the two projects can therefore be implemented through majority rule. Voters 1 and 2 have, in effect, traded votes, with voter 1 agreeing to trade their vote for project A in exchange for voter 2 trading their vote for project B.

Table 28.1 Net Benefit of Five Projects for Three Voters

	Vote Trading				
	A	B	C	D	E
Voter 1	−1	3	0	−1	3
Voter 2	3	−1	−4	3	−1
Voter 3	−1	−1	2	−3	−3
Net Social Benefit	1	1	−2	−1	−1

In this case, the outcome is efficient since the net benefit across the three constituencies of each of the projects is positive. Vote trading has overcome an otherwise inefficient outcome of having two projects that create net social benefits defeated individually. There is no guarantee that vote trading will result in the implementation of efficient projects. Consider projects D and E whose net benefits are identical to those of D and E for voters 1 and 2 but not for voter 3. For the same reasons as before, D and E cannot be implemented through majority rule unless vote trading occurs and the two projects are bundled. Now the overall net benefit of both projects is negative, which implies that vote trading would result in the building of inefficient projects.

As in the previous sections, whoever exercises control over the agenda of what can be lumped together also exercises a great deal of power. Suppose, for instance, that projects A and B are currently under consideration and voter 3 suddenly becomes committee chair in charge of setting the agenda of what will be considered by the committee. By introducing C onto the agenda, the new chair will ensure that the coalition between voters 1 and 2 is broken up and that voter 1 will instead enter a coalition with them to implement projects B and C. The outcome is less efficient: project C has negative net social benefits while project A does not, but the new committee chair likes C and not B.

Bundling different projects into a single piece of legislation is one possible way for legislators to trade votes and thereby implement projects that could not be implemented on their own. There are also other ways for legislators to accomplish this. One such way is through the development of a 'norm of reciprocity' that, in essence, is an understood longer-run agreement between legislators encapsulated by the phrase 'I'll scratch your back if you'll scratch mine'. Since legislators understand that they will interact repeatedly, such norms can easily develop, with voter 1 comfortable voting for project B knowing that this will mean voter 2 will 'owe them a favour' and will therefore vote for project A when it comes up for a vote. Thus, even when projects are not explicitly bundled, implicit bundling may well emerge.

28A.3 Rent Seeking, Political Competition and Government as Leviathan

The study of political economy has evolved in different schools since the 1960s, with different assumptions guiding the development of these different schools and how they view democratic political competition and efficiency. The crucial concern of these schools revolves around the degree to which politicians are able to seek rents for themselves through the political process. Rent-seeking politicians have goals of their own that conflict with the goals of voters. They view the political process as a means to attain something equivalent to profit. They are, in some sense, no different than profit maximizing firms. In the case of competitive firms, we have found that competition can reduce, or in the extreme case eliminate, the potential for firms to make profits. It is natural to ask whether political competition can serve a function similar to market competition, driving political rents to zero just as market competition drives firm profits to zero.

This question is a bit different from what we have analyzed so far. In the previous sections of this chapter, we have assumed that politicians have preferences over policy outcomes and we have seen that in the absence of a Condorcet winner, those who control the political agenda have a great deal of power to shape the policy outcomes to those that conform with their own preferences. To the extent to which the agenda setter is not necessarily concerned about economic efficiency, policy outcomes that are shaped by the agenda setter may therefore deviate substantially from economic efficiency. We now ask a related question: Suppose that the politicians' preferences include preferences for political rents, which could be the satisfaction of seeing one's preferred, and quite possibly inefficient, policies implemented, or it could involve more personal rents such as plush offices, excessively large staffs to supervise, big projects bearing the names of the politician, and so on.

One school of political economy, known as the Chicago School, comes to the conclusion that political competition can serve the same purpose as market competition. Without going into great detail, the intuition for this conclusion can be seen from the simple Bertrand model in our study of oligopolies. In that model, even when only two firms competed, they ended up charging a price equal to marginal cost. Similarly, the Chicago School argues, political candidates that compete for votes will be forced to compete by lowering the rents they can obtain once elected, and just as profits fall to zero under Bertrand competition, so political rents fall to zero under political competition.

Another school of political economy, known as the Public Choice School, is considerably more sceptical that such Bertrand-like competition can effectively restrain political rents. The analogy to our study of Bertrand competition for oligopolistic firms again becomes useful to see the reasons for this scepticism. We found that the Bertrand result is quite crucially dependent on the assumption that firms are producing the same or perfectly substitutable products. As soon as we allowed for product differentiation in Chapter 26, Bertrand competition did *not* imply price being competed to marginal cost, with such product differentiation therefore opening the door for positive profits. In exactly the same way, the Chicago efficiency result for political competition holds only if candidates are viewed as perfect substitutes. Just as firms can strategically differentiate their products, political candidates can strategically differentiate themselves along, for instance, ideological lines or party affiliation, and this combined with barriers to entry into the political market place opens the door for political rents. Under Bertrand competition, it has to furthermore be the case that consumers are aware of the different producers' products, and unawareness can result in positive profits. Similarly, in the political process, consumers might not be aware of certain issues that have only a marginal impact on their well-being, opening the door for politicians to seek political rents in those areas. In this section, we will therefore briefly discuss a few of the insights that have emerged from this Public Choice School. The Public Choice School is most closely identified with 1986 Nobel Laureate James Buchanan (1919–2013).

28A.3.1 Interest Groups: The Politics of Concentrated Benefits and Diffuse Costs In some of our discussions of government policies, starting with our discussion of price ceilings and price floors in Chapter 18, we have already asked how economically inefficient policies appear to survive the political process. If price ceilings and price floors create more harm than benefit, how can they be sustained by democratic institutions? If trade on balance produces social surplus, why is it so politically difficult to lower trade barriers? In our previous discussions, we found an answer in a recognition that often the costs and benefits of policies are not evenly distributed. This insight came squarely from the Public Choice School we have just introduced.

Our basic argument in earlier chapters has been that *when benefits of a policy are concentrated* and *costs are diffuse*, it is more likely that political interest groups representing those who benefit from the policy will succeed in their attempt to influence policy. Underlying this argument is the assumption that it is costly to organize political interest groups. If this were not the case, those who lose from the policy would pool their resources to compete against those who win in the political arena, and if those who lose stand to lose more than those who gain stand to gain, one would expect them to be able to succeed in that arena. If it is sufficiently costly to organize a diffuse 100 million consumers of milk against milk price support policies, it may well be that the concentrated beneficiaries of such policies – a few large dairy farmers, for instance – will apply intense political pressure that does not meet very much of an opposition. Self-interested politicians who need the political and financial support of motivated constituencies will find it easy to listen to and accept money from concentrated beneficiaries, secure in their knowledge that the costs of the policy are spread across many consumers who are only partially aware of those costs and who are sufficiently large in number to not be able to organize effectively.

Exercise 28A.11

Relate the idea of concentrated benefits and diffuse costs to the free-rider problem faced by interest groups that represent beneficiaries and victims of policies.

You might notice that this argument is, in some way, similar to Coase's argument about decentralized solutions to externalities. Coase emphasized transactions costs. If those were sufficiently low, parties to externalities could resolve externalities as long as property rights were established. If political interest groups play a role in policy making, we might similarly expect efficient policies as long as the transactions costs of organizing such interest groups are low. If such costs are high, as they are in many circumstances, policies with concentrated benefits and diffuse costs are likely to win even if such policies produce net social losses.

28A.3.2 Regulatory Capture The Public Choice School's insights on the role of concentrated benefits and diffuse costs extends beyond the process of policy *making* to the process of policy *implementation*. Legislatures write broad policies that are implemented by agencies that are charged to interpret such policies in specific instances.

Since government agencies are institutions that are not disciplined by market competition, they are natural places where rent-seeking individuals might look to advance careers. In principle, they are overseen by democratic institutions both on the legislative and the executive sides of the government, but they are also subject to political pressure from those institutions and from outside individuals who have a large stake in what the agencies do. Whether indirectly through politicians that exert pressure on regulatory agencies, or whether directly through lobbying of the regulatory agency itself, the voice of concentrated beneficiaries is likely to outweigh the voice of more diffuse constituencies that bear the cost.

This, too, is something we have hinted at before, as in our treatment of regulating monopolies or oligopolies. The intent of legislation that creates regulatory agencies to oversee oligopolistic industries is typically to enhance consumer welfare by limiting anti-competitive behaviour in the industry. Consumers are the diffuse group that bears the cost of anti-competitive behaviour in industry and reaps the benefit of reducing such anti-competitive behaviour. Oligopolistic firms, on the other hand, reap concentrated benefits from anti-competitive behaviour and bear concentrated costs of limits to such behaviour. Those with the most to gain from being heard in the process of policy implementation by the regulating agency, therefore, are the oligopolists themselves. Public choice theory raises the possibility that such agencies will be 'captured' by those whose behaviour is to be regulated, and that regulations in practice are shaped in accordance with the wishes of the regulated. In public choice theory, this is referred to as *regulatory capture*.

28A.3.3 Self-Perpetuating Bureaucracy as Concentrated Beneficiary Milton Friedman, one of the best known economists of the 20th century and a deep sceptic of government, once said that a government programme epitomizes the closest thing to eternal life on earth. This succinctly captures another insight from public choice theory that once a government programme is established, a bureaucracy typically accompanies the programme, and individuals in that bureaucracy have an interest in keeping and expanding the programme because this keeps and expands career opportunities for these individuals. This is fine if the programme works, but if it does not work, there is nevertheless a powerful constituency that becomes a concentrated beneficiary. Those in the bureaucracy are likely to lobby for additional funding because it benefits them, and they are a concentrated group that can easily organize to make the case. The public choice theory of concentrated benefits and diffuse costs suggests that government bureaucracies will become inefficiently large and will perpetuate programmes even if they do not meet the initial expectations of legislators.

28A.3.4 Constitutions and Government Competition to Restrain Leviathan While we have only given some brief descriptions of how public choice theory predicts that political processes will lead to inefficient policy, it should be clear even from this brief description of public choice insights that this theory also predicts the emergence of a government that is inefficiently large. Some have dubbed this the Leviathan model of government, in reference to Hebrew images of large and typically malevolent monsters. Few public choice theories would argue that government should be dispensed with – rather, they, just like Arrow, are interested in institutional constraints on democratic governments – constraints that will restrain the Leviathan and make government more benevolent.

We have already mentioned some such institutional constraints in our discussion of multidimensional voting. While the Chicago School of political economy relies on democratic competition to restrain Leviathan, public choice theorists typically emphasize two further checks on democratic processes: (1) broad constitutional constraints that limit the scope of government and (2) the fostering of intergovernmental competition. Note that both of these emphases follow from the Public Choice School's identification of channels that lead to inefficiently large and self-perpetuating government activity, activity that emerges from the hypothesized disproportionate emphasis on concentrated beneficiaries of policies over the diffuse costs imposed on society at large.

28B	**An Exposition of Arrow's Impossibility Theorem**

While the Public Choice School that we have just discussed finds its roots in the writings of political philosophers of centuries ago, much of the more micro-foundational modelling of political institutions and processes originates with Arrow's Theorem that we have mentioned throughout. One of the criticisms often levied against the Public Choice School is that it has not fully linked to these microeconomic foundations and has relied on more informal insights on government behaviour. Over the last few decades, however, these different strands of political economy have increasingly merged, with those inspired by Arrow's Theorem increasingly taking up the challenge of adding micro-foundations to the insights of modern public choice theory. As a result, an understanding of Arrow's insight is increasingly important.

As we mentioned in the introduction, Arrow's Theorem directly challenges us to use microeconomics to think about political processes and to identify how different political institutions yield different policy outcomes. This would not be necessary if it were the case that democracy itself gives expression to a well-defined set of social preferences. Since Arrow demonstrates that such well-defined social preferences do not in general exist, he implicitly is giving us a roadmap for what kinds of trade-offs we face in modelling political institutions, and what kinds of trade-offs democratic institutions must make. Arrow tells us that politics matters, that the details of political institutions matter and that we cannot assume democratic institutions will give rise to outcomes that satisfy any particular social goal like economic efficiency.

Given the importance of Arrow's Theorem in the development of political economy, we therefore devote this section of the chapter to a full exposition of the theorem. That exposition begins with the concept of a *social choice function*, a function that translates individual preferences into aggregate social preferences over outcomes that political institutions are asked to decide. As we will see, Arrow's basic question asks whether we can expect particular social choice functions to emerge from democratic processes. He demonstrates that the functions that can emerge under democracy are functions that are subject to manipulation by those who can shape the agenda within political institutions, and that the type of institution will have every bit as much to do with the outcomes we should expect from democratic voting as with the underlying preferences of the voters.

28B.1 Social Choice Functions and the Axiomatic Approach

A *social choice function* is a function f that aggregates individual preferences over social outcomes to a single preference ordering. Let $\{\succsim\}$ denote the set of possible preference relations over a set of possible social outcomes A, and let $N = \{1, 2, \ldots, N\}$ denote the set of N individuals affected by those social outcomes. A social choice function takes the form $f: \{\succsim\}^N \to \{\succsim\}$ translating any profile of individual preferences $\{\succsim^n\}_{n=1}^N = \{\succsim^1, \succsim^2, \ldots, \succsim^N\}$ into a single preference, ordering $\succsim$.

Arrow took what is known as an *axiomatic* approach. This approach begins by specifying a set of axioms that a social choice function f should satisfy to facilitate social decision making. It investigates how much the set of all possible social choice functions is narrowed down by these axioms. In everything we do in the following sections, we will assume that there are at least two individuals and at least three possible social states, but everything we derive holds for any finite number of individuals and social states larger than that.

28B.2 Arrow's Five Axioms

Arrow began by defining five basic axioms that he thought would be sensible for any social choice function to satisfy. The first three are quite basic and require that social choice functions do not restrict individual preferences, that they respect unanimity and that they contain at least some minimal element of democracy. The last two axioms are intended to prohibit the democratic process that is represented by the social choice function from being capable of being manipulated by those who control the agenda.

28B.2.1 The Universal Domain Axiom Arrow's starting point is that we cannot dictate to individuals how they feel about social outcomes, which means that we must permit them to have whatever preferences they actually have. We may not like their individual preferences, and we may not pay that much attention to some of them in our social choice function, but we have to let people have the preferences they come with. The only restriction we will permit is that individual preferences must make sense, which, in the language we used in developing consumer preferences at the beginning of the book, means that the individual preference relations $\succsim^n$ are complete and transitive or 'rational'. We want the *domain* $\{\succsim\}^N$ of the social choice function $f: \{\succsim\}^N \to \{\succsim\}$ to universally admit all combinations of rational individual preferences. For this reason, we will refer to this axiom as *universal domain* and denote it as UD.

28B.2.2 The Pareto Unanimity Axiom The second requirement Arrow had for social choice functions is that unanimously held views are respected when social decisions are made. Thus, if an alternative $x \in A$ is preferred by *everyone* to an alternative $y \in A$, the social preference ordering should rank x above Y. If $x \succsim^n y$ for all $n = 1, 2, \ldots, N$, then $x \succsim y$ for $\succsim = f(\succsim^1, \succsim^2, \ldots, \succsim^N)$. Notice that under most preference profiles that actually occur in populations, this axiom would impose no restrictions on the actual outcome of the social choice process because it is presumably rare that *everyone* agrees one thing is better than another. All the axiom says is that *if* everyone happens to like one thing better than another, the outcome of a social choice process ought to agree with that preference ordering. Arrow originally called this the Pareto Axiom, but since it is not the same as Pareto Optimality, we will call it the *Pareto Unanimity* axiom and denote it as PU.

Exercise 28B.1

How does Pareto Optimality as a concept differ from Pareto Unanimity?

28B.2.3 The No-Dictatorship Axiom Arrow was fundamentally interested in *democratic* social choice processes; that is, social choice processes where the preferences of more than one person matter. It is natural for him to posit as one of his axioms that the social choice function should not be dictatorial. His definition of a dictator is a definition of a quite powerful dictator, which differs from our usual conception of a dictator as someone who controls many but not all things. For this reason, the kind of dictator that Arrow is attempting to prohibit from social choice processes is known as an *Arrow Dictator*.

An individual is an Arrow Dictator if, *for every pair* (x, y) of social states, *whenever* everyone else prefers x to y and they are the only one to disagree, the social choice function sides with them in opposition to everyone else. More formally, n is an Arrow Dictator if, for all $x \in A$ and all $y \in A$, whenever $x \succsim^j y$ for all $j \neq n$ and $y \succsim^n x$, the social preference ordering $\succsim = f(\succsim^1, \succsim^2, \ldots, \succsim^N,)$ is such that $y \succsim x$. The *No Dictatorship* axiom, denoted as ND, states that no individual in society should have such power over the social choice process; that is, the social choice function f should not permit one individual to *always* get their way *whenever* they are a minority of one. Note that the axiom is not violated if there is an individual who *almost always* gets their way when they are a minority of one. It just does not allow for an individual to *always* get their way.

Exercise 28B.2

In Section A, we developed the median voter theorem that says that when voters' preferences over a single-dimensional issue are single peaked, the outcome under majority rule is the outcome preferred by the median voter. If we define that social choice function to be majority rule, does this make the median voter an Arrow Dictator under that rule?

Exercise 28B.3

Is the agenda setter in Graph 28.5 an Arrow Dictator? Is the agenda setter in our discussion of the Anything-Can-Happen theorem an Arrow Dictator?

28B.2.4 The Rationality (R) Axiom When we introduced the concept of preferences in consumer theory, we insisted that completeness and transitivity were quite necessary properties to make much headway in analyzing consumer choice, because without them, it is not clear that a best consumption bundle is well defined. Completeness meant that when confronted with two consumption bundles, a consumer must be able to tell us which one they prefer or whether they are indifferent. Transitivity meant that the consumer could not like bundle x better than y, bundle y better than z *and* bundle z better than x. If this were violated, the consumer could end up in an endless cycle, choosing x over y, y over z, z over x, and so forth and thus never actually be able to make a decision. We lumped the properties of completeness and transitivity together and called it rationality.

Arrow insists that this basic rationality property must also hold for social preferences. As we have seen in Section A, if it does not, as may be the case under majority rule when preferences over a single-dimensional issue are not single peaked, the door is opened for an agenda setter to manipulate the outcome of the social choice process to fit with their own ideal. We therefore require that the social choice function f has the property that for *all* rational preference profiles $\{\succsim^n\}_{n=1}^N$ that might emerge in the population, the social preferences $\succsim = f(\{\succsim^n\}_{n=1}^N)$ must be rational; that is, they must satisfy completeness and transitivity. We will call this property *rationality* and denote it as R.

28B.2.5 The Independence of Irrelevant Alternatives Axiom

Of the five axioms specified by Arrow, the last is the least understood and the most controversial. Suppose that for a particular preference profile in the population the social choice process results in social preferences that pick x over y. It must be the case that the same social choice process results in social preferences that will still pick x over y for all other individual preference profiles that maintain individual rankings of x and y as they were in the original preference profile of the population. When society chooses between x and y, individual preferences over x and y should be what matters, and not individual preferences over other pairs of social outcomes. This ensures that an agenda setter cannot influence social preferences over x and y by adding a social state that is irrelevant for a choice over x and y to what is contained in the set of possible social states A. Note that it does not mean that x is chosen by society as the best outcome regardless of what other alternatives are considered in the set of possible alternatives A; it merely says that when confronted with a choice solely between x and y, it does not matter what other alternatives are in the set A. It is analogous to saying that consumers should feel the same way about two different consumption bundles that they are asked to compare regardless of what other consumption bundles are in the consumer's budget set.

We can state the axiom as follows: suppose f is such that when individual preferences take the form $\{\succsim^n\}_{n=1}^N$, the social preference ordering $\succsim = f(\{\succsim^n\}_{n=1}^N)$ results in $x \succsim y$. *For all* individual preference profiles $\{\succsim'^n\}_{n=1}^N$ where $x \succsim'^n y$ if and only if $x \succsim^n y$, it must be that the new social preferences $\succsim' = f(\{\succsim'^n\}_{n=1}^N)$ result in $x \succsim' y$. When this holds, we will say that the social choice over x and y is *independent* of all other alternatives that are *irrelevant* for the choice between x and y. When this holds for all pairs of social states, we will say that the *Independence of Irrelevant Alternatives* axiom, denoted as IIA, is satisfied by the social choice process f.

28B.3 Decisiveness of Coalitions

As we work our way towards the result that no social choice function f exists that satisfies all five of Arrow's axioms, it becomes useful to define a concept known as the *decisiveness* of a coalition of individuals. A *coalition* D is a subset of the set of all individuals; that is, $D \subseteq N$. You should think of D as just a set of individuals, not individuals with fixed preferences. We will define a coalition D to be *decisive over the pair* (x, y) *under the social choice function* f if the members of the coalition together have the powers of an Arrow Dictator with respect to the pair (x, y) of social states. In other words, we will say that the members of D are decisive over (x, y) if, *whenever* they all prefer y to x *and* everyone outside the coalition prefers x to y or if the reverse holds, the coalition's preferences are those respected by the social choice rule f.

We will formalize this notion in two steps. First, we will formally define the limited notion of decisiveness of a coalition, decisiveness over a pair of social states. We define a more sweeping version of the concept, full decisiveness over all pairs of social states. While these will seem quite different concepts of the power that a coalition has, we will demonstrate the surprising fact that under any social choice function f that satisfies Arrow's axioms, it must be the case that if a coalition is decisive over a pair of social states, it is decisive over *all* pairs of social states. Notice that if a coalition D is composed of only a single member and is decisive over all pairs of social states, the single member of that coalition is an Arrow Dictator.

28B.3.1 Limited and Full Decisiveness of Coalitions We now state our two different notions of the decisiveness of a coalition under a social choice function f more precisely. First, suppose there exist two social states, $x \in A$ and $y \in A$, and suppose we have a social choice function f that has the property that for some $D \subseteq A$,

$$x \succsim^i y \,\forall i \in D \quad \text{and} \quad y \succsim^j x \,\forall j \notin D \Rightarrow x \succsim y \tag{28.3}$$

and:

$$y \succsim^i x \,\forall i \in D \quad \text{and} \quad x \succsim^j y \,\forall j \notin D \Rightarrow y \succsim x, \tag{28.4}$$

where $\succsim = f(\{\succsim^n\}_{n=1}^N)$ and where the $\forall$ symbol means 'for all' and the $\Rightarrow$ symbol means 'implies'. We have a coalition D for which it is the case that members of the coalition get their choice of x over y under the social choice process f, whenever the members of the coalition unanimously agree on their ranking of the pair (x, y) and everyone else disagrees. We will say that such a coalition D is *decisive over (x, y) under f*.

This initial definition of decisiveness of a coalition is *limited* to just a pair of social states. When a coalition is decisive over *all* possible pairs of social states in A under the social choice process f, we will say that the coalition is *fully decisive under f*. Any coalition that is fully decisive is by definition decisive over a pair (x, y), but it does not logically follow that limited decisiveness over a pair of social states implies full decisiveness over all possible pairs. It turns out, however, that limited decisiveness *does* imply full decisiveness when f is assumed to satisfy all five of Arrow's axioms, a proposition we will show next to be true.

28B.3.2 Limited Decisiveness Implies Full Decisiveness Under Arrow's Axioms Suppose that under some social choice function f that satisfies all five of Arrow's axioms a coalition $D \subseteq N$ is decisive over a pair (x, y) from the set of all possible social states A. The UD axiom implies that the individuals should be able to have any set of rational preferences over the social states in A. Suppose that individual preferences $\{\succsim^n\}_{n=1}^N)$ happen to result in preference orderings over alternatives x, y and z such that:

$$x \succsim^i y \succsim^i z \,\forall i \in D$$
$$y \succsim^j z \succsim^j x \cdot \forall j \notin D. \tag{28.5}$$

Given that D is decisive over the pair (x, y), it must be the case that the social preference ordering $\succsim = f(\{\succsim^n\}_{n=1}^N)$ picks x over y; that is,

$$x \succsim y. \tag{28.6}$$

Exercise 28B.4

Explain why this conclusion follows from the definition of the decisiveness over (x, y) of the coalition D.

Furthermore, since f satisfies the PU axiom, it also must be the case that the social preference ordering chooses y over z since everyone agrees y is better than z; that is,

$$PU \Rightarrow y \succsim z. \tag{28.7}$$

Given conclusions (28.6) and (28.7), the R axiom implies that the social preference ordering chooses x over z; that is,

$$R \Rightarrow x \succsim z. \tag{28.8}$$

This means that the members of the coalition D appear to be decisive over the pair (x, y) as well. Only members of D prefer x to z, and everyone else prefers x to z, and we have just concluded that the social preference ordering sides with members of D. Furthermore, the IIA axiom implies that this social preference ordering over x and z is independent of how people feel about y, which means that the position of y in the individual preference orderings in (28.5) can be switched around without affecting the conclusion $x \succsim z$. Thus, *whenever* the members of D prefer x to z and everyone else prefers x to z, the social preference ordering will choose x over z.

Exercise 28B.5*

By changing the individual preference orderings in (28.5) and proceeding through similar steps, can you show that it is similarly true that whenever members of D prefer z over x and everyone else disagrees, the social preference ordering that arises from f must pick z over x as well?

The same reasoning holds for any other social state that appears in the set of possible social states A. Thus, we conclude that *if a coalition D is decisive over a pair of social states under f, it must be decisive over all social states under f if f satisfies Arrow's five axioms.*

28B.4 Proving Arrow's Theorem

We are now ready to demonstrate Arrow's Theorem that no social choice function f can simultaneously satisfy all five of Arrow's axioms. The proof is a *proof by contradiction*. Such a proof begins by assuming that the theorem is false, that there *does* exist a social choice function f that satisfies Arrow's five axioms. It uses these axioms to show that the assumption that such a function f exists leads to a logical contradiction and therefore cannot be true.

28B.4.1 ND $\Rightarrow$ A Decisive Coalition Exists
One of Arrow's axioms is the ND axiom. Recall that this axiom rules out the existence of an Arrow Dictator under the social choice function f; that is, it rules out the existence of a single individual who always gets their way in the social preference ordering whenever they are a minority of one. Let's define a coalition D that consists of everyone in N other than one person; for instance, let $D = \{2, 3, \ldots, N\}$ where we have just left out individual 1. Since individual 1 cannot be an Arrow Dictator, there is at least one pair of social states over which individual 1 does not get their way in the social preference ordering when they feel one way and everyone else feels the opposite. Let that pair of social states be denoted (x, y). Technically, the ND axiom only requires a single instance of a preference ordering under which individual 1 is in a minority of one and does not get their way. The IIA axiom implies that if this single instance involves the pair (x, y), individual 1 will not get their way for *any* set of individual preferences where individual 1 feels one way about the pair (x, y) and everyone else disagrees, with the individual preference orderings over other alternatives relative to x and y irrelevant to the social ordering over this pair.

From the previous section, we know that limited decisiveness over a pair of social states actually implies full decisiveness of that coalition over all pairs of social states when the other Arrow axioms are satisfied. Thus, given that our coalition $D = \{2, 3, \ldots, N\}$ is decisive over (x, y), it is also decisive over all other pairs in A.

Exercise 28B.6

This reasoning implies that every coalition of everyone but one person must be decisive. How can it be that both $D = \{2, 3, \ldots, N\}$ and $D' = \{1, 2, 3, \ldots, N-1\}$ can be decisive?

28B.4.2 UD, PU, R and IIA $\Rightarrow$ Decisive Coalitions Contain Smaller Decisive Coalitions Since we now know that a decisive coalition must always exist under a social choice function that satisfies Arrow's axioms, let's begin with such a coalition $D \subset N$ where D contains at least two members, since ND rules out a single person being decisive. Now let's partition D into two subsets of individuals; that is, $B \subset D$ and $C \subset D$ such that $B \cup C = D$ and $B \cup C = \emptyset$. The UD axiom implies that we are not restricting individual preferences, which means that preferences could be such that:

$$x \gtrsim^i y \gtrsim^i z \,\forall\, i \in B$$
$$z \gtrsim^j x \gtrsim^j y \,\forall\, j \in C \tag{28.9}$$
$$y \gtrsim^k z \gtrsim^k x \,\forall\, k \notin D.$$

Since we assume that the social preference ordering that arises from f is complete, it must be that the pair y and z is ranked. So, either $z > y$ or $y \gtrsim z$.

If $z > y$, the social choice rule is siding with members of the coalition C in a case where only members of C prefer z to y and everyone else disagrees. By the IIA axiom, that social preference ordering is preserved for *all* other individual preference profiles under which the pairwise orderings over y and z remain unchanged. Thus, in *every* case in which members of C prefer z to y and everyone else disagrees, the coalition C gets its way; that is, coalition C is decisive over the pair (y, z), which, because of our result that limited decisiveness implies full decisiveness under Arrow's axioms, implies that coalition C is fully decisive.

Now suppose instead that $y \gtrsim z$; that is, the social choice function chooses y over z under the preference profile in (28.9). Since we started with the assumption that D is decisive, we also know that $x \gtrsim y$ since everyone in D prefers x to y and everyone outside D disagrees. The transitivity requirement in the R axiom implies that $x \gtrsim z$. This means that in the social ranking of x relative to z, the social choice function is siding with members of the coalition B against everyone else, and the IIA axiom implies that this will hold for all other individual preference orderings that maintain individual rankings over the pair (x, y). Thus, *whenever* members of B prefer x over z and everyone else disagrees, members of B get their way. Thus, the coalition B is decisive over the pair (x, z), which, because of our result that limited decisiveness implies full decisiveness under Arrow's axioms, implies that coalition B is fully decisive.

Notice what we have just concluded. Beginning with a decisive coalition D, which we know exists given the ND axiom, we split that coalition into two and found that one way or another, one of the two sub-coalitions will be decisive. Thus, as long as D contains at least two members, *any decisive coalition D under f that satisfies Arrow's axioms can be divided into smaller sub-coalitions with one of those sub-coalitions again being decisive.*

28B.4.3 Proving Arrow's Theorem We have now basically finished with our proof of Arrow's Theorem. We began by assuming that we have a social choice function f that satisfies all five of Arrow's axioms. We showed that this implies there exists a coalition $D \subset N$ that is fully decisive. We showed that as long as this coalition contains at least two members, it can be divided into two sub-coalitions, with one of these being fully decisive. As long as that sub-coalition once again contains at least two members, it can by the same reasoning be further divided into two sub-coalitions, with one of these once again being fully decisive. We can keep doing this, and sooner or later we will end up with a decisive coalition that only has a single member. When we reach that point, we will have ended up with an Arrow Dictator, a single individual who, whenever they are a minority of one, gets their preferences respected by the social preference ranking. That contradicts our assumption that the social choice function f satisfies Arrow's five axioms. Since assuming that such a social choice function exists leads to a logical contradiction, we can conclude that such a function does not exist.

This allows us to state Arrow's Theorem formally in two different ways. The first phrases the result as a negative one.

Arrow's Impossibility Theorem: In a world in which there are at least two individuals and at least three social states to choose from, there does not exist a social choice process that satisfies UD, ND, PU, R and IIA.

Alternatively, we can rephrase the theorem as a positive result.

Arrow's Possibility Theorem: In a world in which there are at least two individuals and at least three social states to choose from, there exists a social choice process that satisfies UD, PU, R and IIA. However, that social choice process violates ND and therefore results in an Arrow Dictator.

End-of-Chapter Exercises

28.1† In the text, we discussed two main conditions under which the median voter's favoured policy is also the Condorcet winner.

A. Review the definition of a *Condorcet winner*.

    a. What are the two conditions under which we can predict that the median voter's position is such a Condorcet winner?

    b. Implicitly, we have assumed an odd number of voters such that there exists a single median voter. Can you predict a range of possible policies that cannot be beaten in pairwise elections when there is an even number of voters and the conditions of the median voter theorem are otherwise satisfied?

    c. Suppose that the issue space is two-dimensional, as in the case where we have to choose spending levels on military and domestic priorities. Consider the following special case: all voters have ideal points that lie on a downward-sloping line in the two-dimensional space, and voters become worse off as the distance between their ideal point and the actual policy increases. Is there a Condorcet winner in this case?

    d. Revisit the Anything-Can-Happen theorem in the text. Suppose that the current policy A in our two-dimensional policy space is equal to the ideal point of the median voter along the line on which all ideal points lie. If you are an agenda setter and you can set up a sequence of pairwise votes, which other policies could you implement assuming the first vote in the sequence needs to put up a policy against A?

    e. In our discussion of the Anything-Can-Happen theorem, we raised the possibility of single-issue committees as a mechanism for disciplining the political process and limiting the set of proposals that can come up for a vote in a full legislature. Is such a structure necessary in our special case of ideal points falling on the same line in the two-dimensional policy space?

    f. In the more general case where we allow ideal points to lie anywhere, the agenda setter still has some control over what policy alternative gets constructed in a structure-induced equilibrium in which single-issue committees play a role. In real-world legislatures, the ability of the agenda setter to name members of committees is often constrained by seniority rules that have emerged over time; that is, rules that give certain rights to committee assignments based on the length of service of a legislator. Can we think of such rules or norms as further constraining the Anything-Can-Happen chaos of democratic decision making?

B. Consider a simple example of how single-peaked and non-single-peaked tastes over policy might naturally emerge in a case where there is only a single-dimensional issue. A voter has preferences that can be represented by the utility function $u(x, y) = xy$ where x is private consumption and y is a public good. The only contributor to y is the government, which employs a proportional tax rate t. Suppose $y = \delta t$.

    a. Suppose an individual has income I. Write their utility as a function of t, δ and I.

    b. What shape does this function have with respect to the policy variable t?

    c. At what t does this function reach its maximum?

    d. Suppose that an individual with income I can purchase a perfect substitute to y on the private market at a price of 1 per unit. Determine, as a function of I, at what level of t an individual will be indifferent between purchasing the private substitute and consuming the public good.

    e. What does this imply for the real shape of the individual's preferences over the policy variable t, assuming $\delta > I/4$?

28.2 Everyday Application: *To Enter or Not to Enter the Race.* Suppose there are three possible candidates who might run for government, and each has to decide whether or not to enter the race. Assume the electorate's ideal points can be defined by the Hotelling line from Chapter 26; that is, the ideal points are uniformly distributed on the interval $[0, 1]$.

    A. Let π_i denote the probability that candidate i will win the election. Suppose that the payoff to a candidate jumping into the race is $(\pi_i - c)$ where c is the cost of running a campaign.

        a. How high must the probability of getting elected be for a candidate to get into the race?

        b. Consider the following model: in stage 1, three potential candidates decide simultaneously whether or not to get into the race and pay the cost c. In stage 2, they take positions on the Hotelling line, with voters then choosing in an election where the candidate who gets the most votes wins. *True or False*: If there is a Nash equilibrium in stage 2 of the game, it must be that the probability of winning is the same for each candidate that entered the race in stage 1.

        c. Suppose there is a Nash equilibrium in stage 2 regardless of how many of the three candidates entered in stage 1. What determines whether there will be one, two or three candidates running in the election?

        d. Suppose that the probability of winning in stage 2 is a function of the number of candidates who are running as well as the amount spent in the campaign, with candidates able to choose different levels of c when they enter in stage 1 but facing an increasing marginal cost $p(c)$ for raising campaign funds. The payoff for a candidate is therefore now $(\pi_i - p(c))$. In particular, suppose the following: campaign spending matters only in cases where an election run solely on issues would lead to a tie in the sense that each candidate would win with equal probability. In that case, whoever spent the most wins the election. What might you expect the possible equilibria in stage 1 where entry and campaign spending are determined simultaneously to look like?

        e. Suppose the incumbent is one of the potential candidates, and they decide whether to enter the race and how much to spend first. Can you in this case see a role for strategic entry deterrence similar to what we developed for monopolists who are threatened by a potential entrant?

        f. With the marginal cost of raising additional funds to build up a campaign war chest increasing, might the incumbent still allow entry of another candidate?

    B. Consider the existence of a Nash equilibrium in stage 2.

        a. What are two possible ways in which three candidates might take positions in the second stage of our game such that your conclusion in A(b) holds?

        b. Can either of these be an equilibrium under the conditions specified in part A?

        c. Suppose that instead of voter ideal points being uniformly distributed on the Hotelling line, one-third of all voters hold the median voter position with the remaining two-thirds uniformly distributed on the Hotelling line. How does your conclusion about the existence of a stage 2 Nash equilibrium with three candidates change? Does your conclusion from A(c) still hold?

28.3*† Everyday Application: *Citizen Candidates.* Whenever we have modelled political candidates who stand for election, we have assumed that they care only about winning and are perfectly content to change their position in whatever way maximizes the probability of winning. Now consider a different way of thinking about political candidates. Suppose that the citizens again have uniformly distributed ideal points on the Hotelling line $[0, 1]$. Before any election is held, each citizen has to decide whether to pay the cost $c > 0$ to run as a candidate, with the payoff from probability π of winning the election equal to $(\pi - c)$.

    A. Assume candidates cannot change their position from their ideal point, and citizens who do not become candidates get payoff equal to minus the distance of the winning candidate position x^* to their own on [0, 1]. The highest attainable payoff for a non-candidate is therefore 0. Candidates who lose get the same payoff as citizens who do not run, except that they also incur cost c from having run.

a. For what range of c is the following an equilibrium: a citizen with the median position 0.5 is the only candidate to enter the race and thus wins.

b. How high does c have to be for the following to be a possible equilibrium: a citizen with position 0.25 enters the race as the only candidate and therefore wins. How high must c be for an equilibrium to have a citizen with position 0 be the only candidate to run and thus win?

c. For what range of c will it be an equilibrium for two candidates with position 0.5 to compete in the election?

d. For what range of c is it an equilibrium for two candidates with positions 0.25 and 0.75 to compete?

e. For what range of c is it an equilibrium for two candidates with positions 0 and 1 to compete?

B. Consider the same set-up as in part A.

a. Let $x \in [0, 0.5]$. For what range of c is it an equilibrium for a citizen with position x to be the only candidate to run for office? Is your answer consistent with what you derived for A(b)?

b. For what range of c is it an equilibrium for two candidates to compete, one taking position x and the other taking the position $(1 - x)$? Is your answer consistent with your answers to A(d) and A(e)?

c. Let ϵ be arbitrarily close to zero. For what range of c will two candidates with positions $(0.5 - \epsilon)$ and $(0.5 + \epsilon)$ be able to run against one another in equilibrium? What does this range converge to as ϵ converges to zero?

d. How does the range you calculated in (c) compare to the range of c that makes it possible for two candidates with position 0.5 to run against one another in equilibrium as derived in A(c)?

28.4 **Business and Policy Application:** *Voting with Points.* Jean-Charles de Borda (1733–99), a contemporary of Condorcet in France, argued for a democratic system that deviates from our usual conception of majority rule. The system works as follows: suppose there are M proposals; each voter is asked to rank these, with the proposal ranked first by a voter given M points, the one ranked second given $(M - 1)$ points, and so on. The points given to each proposal are summed across all voters, and the top N proposals are chosen, where N might be as low as 1. This voting method, known as the *Borda Count*, is used in a variety of corporate and academic settings as well as some political elections in countries around the world.

A. Suppose there are five voters denoted 1 to 5, and there are five possible projects $\{A, B, C, D, E\}$ to be ranked. Voters 1 to 3 rank the projects in alphabetical sequence with A ranked highest. Voter 4 ranks C highest, followed by D, E, B and finally A. Voter 5 ranks E highest, followed by C, D, B and finally A.

a. How does the Borda Count rank these? If only one can be implemented, which one will it be?

b. Suppose option D was withdrawn from consideration before the vote in which voters rank the options. How does the Borda Count now rank the remaining projects? If only one can be implemented, which one will it be?

c. What if both D and E are withdrawn?

d. Suppose an individual gets to decide which projects will be considered by the group and the group allows them to use their discretion to eliminate projects that clearly do not have widespread support. Will the individual be able to manipulate the outcome of the Borda Count by strategically picking which projects to leave off?

B. Arrow's Theorem tells us that any non-dictatorial social choice function must violate at least one of his remaining four axioms.

a. Do you think the Borda Count violates Pareto Unanimity? What about Universal Domain or Rationality?

b. In what way do your results from part A of the exercise tell us something about whether the Borda Count violates the Independence of Irrelevant Alternatives (IIA) axiom?

c. Derive again the Borda Count ranking of the five projects in part A given the voter preferences as described.

d. Suppose voter 4 changed their mind and now ranks B second and D fourth rather than the other way around. Suppose further that voter 5 similarly switches the position of B and D in their preference ordering and now ranks B third and D fourth. If a social choice function satisfies IIA, which social rankings cannot be affected by this change in preferences?

e. How does the social ordering of the projects change under the Borda Count? Does the Borda Count violate IIA?

28.5† **Policy Application:** *Interest Groups, Transactions Costs and Vote Buying.* Suppose that a legislature has to vote for one of two mutually exclusive proposals: proposal A or B. Two interest groups are willing to spend money on getting their preferred proposal implemented, with interest group 1 willing to pay up to y^A to get A implemented and interest group 2 willing to pay up to y^B to get proposal B passed. Both interest groups get payoff of zero if the opposing group's project gets implemented. Legislators care first and foremost about campaign contributions and will vote for the proposal whose supporters contributed more money, but they have a weak preference for project B in the sense that they will vote for B if they received equal amounts from both interest groups.

A. To simplify the analysis, suppose that there are only three legislators. Suppose further that interest group 1 makes its contribution first, followed by interest group 2.

a. If $y^A = y^B$, will any campaign contributions be made in a subgame-perfect equilibrium?

b. Suppose $1.5y^B > y^A > y^B$. Does your answer to (a) change?

c. Suppose $y^A > 1.5y^B$. What is the subgame-perfect equilibrium now?

d. Suppose that project B is extending milk price support programmes while project A is eliminating such programmes, and suppose that $y^A > 1.5y^B$ because milk price support programmes are inefficient. Interest group 1 represents milk consumers and interest group 2 represents milk producers. Which interest group do you think will find it easier to mobilize its members to give the necessary funds to buy votes in the legislature?

e. Suppose $y^A > 3y^B$. It costs interest group 2 exactly €1 for every euro in contributions to a legislator, but, because of the transactions costs of organizing its members, it costs interest group 1 an amount €c per €1 contributed to a legislator. How high does c need to be for the inefficient project to be passed?

f. How might the free-rider problem be part of the transactions costs that affect interest group 1 disproportionately?

B. Consider the problem faced by the interest groups in light of results derived in Chapter 27. In particular, suppose that all members of interest group A have tastes $u^A(x, y) = x^{\alpha}y^{(1-\alpha)}$ where x is private consumption and y is a function of the likelihood that project A is implemented. Members of interest group B similarly have tastes $u^B(x, y) = x^{\beta}y^{(1-\beta)}$ where y is a function of the likelihood that project B is implemented. Suppose that interest groups have successfully persuaded members to believe y is equal to the sum of their contributions to the interest group. Everyone has income I, and there are N^A members of interest group 1 and N^B members of interest group 2.

a. What is the equilibrium level of contributions to the two interest groups?

b. Suppose again that B is a renewal of an inefficient government programme with concentrated benefits and diffuse costs and A is the elimination of the programme. What does this imply about the relationship between N^A and N^B? What does it imply about the relationship between α and β?

c. Suppose $N^A = 10\ 000$, $N^B = 6$, $I = 1000$, $\alpha = 0.8$ and $\beta = 0.6$. How much will each interest group raise? How does your answer change if N^A is 100 000 instead? What if it is 1 000 000?

d. Suppose that β is also 0.8, and thus equal to α. If the vote-buying process is as described in part A, will legislation B pass even though there are 1 000 000 members of interest group 1 and only 6 in interest group 2?

e. Finally, suppose that there is only a single beneficiary of B. How much will they contribute when $\beta = 0.8$? What if $\beta = 0.6$? Within this example, can even one concentrated beneficiary stop a project that benefits no one other than them?

28.6 **Policy Application:** *Government Competition, Leviathan and Benevolence.* Suppose governments can spend taxpayer resources on both public goods that have social benefits and political rents that are private benefits for government officials. To the extent to which governments emphasize the latter over the former, we have called them Leviathan, and this exercise investigates to what extent competition between governments can restrain this Leviathan. To the extent to which governments emphasize the former, we will call them benevolent. In part B of the exercise, we consider competition between such benevolent governments.

A. Consider a collection N of local governments that can employ local property taxes to fund public goods and local political rents. Suppose that local governments are pure Leviathans; that is, they seek only political rents. For simplicity, suppose also that all households are identical.

a. Begin with a demand and supply for housing graph for one community. If a local Leviathan government is a political monopolist in the sense that it faces no competitive pressures from other communities, how would it go about setting the tax rate that maximizes its rents?

b. Now consider the case where households are fully mobile across jurisdictional boundaries and thus choose to live where their utility is highest. In equilibrium, how must utility in any jurisdiction i be related to utility in any other jurisdiction j?

c. Suppose that the property tax is zero in all communities. Consider community i's Leviathan mayor. If they raise t_i above zero and use the revenues only for political rents, what will have to be true about housing prices in community i after the tax is imposed relative to before it is imposed? Can you demonstrate how this comes about? *Hint:* Consider the competitive pressure from household mobility.

d. *True or False:* As long as housing supply is not perfectly elastic, the Leviathan mayor in part (c) will be able to raise property taxes to fund political rents.

e. Now consider all local governments setting some tax rate t and using revenues for political rents. If t is very low, can a single community's Leviathan's mayor benefit from raising their tax rate? If t is very high, can a single Leviathan mayor benefit from lowering their tax rate?

f. Use your answer to (e) to argue that there must exist some level of Leviathan taxation across competing communities that will be a Nash equilibrium.

g. Evaluate the following statement: 'Unless housing supply is perfectly elastic, government competition between Leviathan governments is not sufficient to eliminate political rents, but it restrains the ability of Leviathan government to amass such rents'.

h. *True or False:* To the extent to which government behaviour is characterized by rent seeking, greater competition between governments enhances efficiency.

B. Next, consider the opposite type of government, that is, one that is benevolent and raises taxes only to the extent to which it can find worthwhile public goods to finance. Suppose again that there are N such governments that use a local property tax to fund local public goods, and suppose that all public benefits from such public goods are contained within each government's jurisdictional boundaries.

a. Begin, as in A(a), by assuming that there is mobility of consumers across jurisdictions and thus no government faces any competitive pressures. Will they produce the efficient level of local public goods?

b. Next, consider the competitive case. If the projects funded by local governments are truly local public goods, in what sense are taxes imposed by benevolent governments offset by benefits received?

c. Suppose governments are charging low tax rates that result in inefficiently low levels of public goods. If community i raises its tax rate and provides more public goods, will population increase or decrease in community i? Will housing prices go up or down?

d. Consider an equilibrium with benevolent local governments providing efficient levels of local public goods. Can any government raise property values by raising or lowering taxes? *True or False*: Property value maximizing local governments behave like benevolent local governments.

e. Suppose next that local property taxes are paid by both households and firms, but only households benefit from local public goods like schools. If firms are mobile, in what sense does community i's decision to tax the property of firms give rise to a positive externality for other communities?

f. What does your answer to (e) imply about the spending levels by benevolent local governments as competitive pressures increase in environments such as those described in (e)?

*conceptually challenging
**computationally challenging
† solutions in Study Guide

PART VI

Considering How to Make the World a Better Place

We have organized virtually all our discussion so far around the first welfare theorem, a result that tells us precisely the conditions under which markets can be expected to achieve an efficient outcome and thus implicitly outlines the set of real-world conditions under which markets require fine-tuning by civil society or government institutions if economic efficiency is our goal. In the process, we have also seen the fundamental challenges faced by each of the three sets of institutions in society. For *markets*, these challenges are captured by violations of the conditions that underlie the first welfare theorem. We have also seen that *civil society institutions* are often plagued by the free-rider problem and its associated Prisoner's Dilemma incentives, and *governments* face informational constraints as well as the difficulty of aggregating citizen preferences into coherent social preferences through democratic institutions that are almost always subject to manipulation by those who control some aspects of the agenda.

In Chapter 29 we consider the limits of neoclassical microeconomics and its primary focus on efficiency. We will find two sources of such limits. First, psychologists have compiled a set of anomalies to economic predictions, anomalies in the sense that people's observed behaviour in the laboratory and/or the real world departs from the predictions that emerge from models such as those we have developed throughout the text. This has given rise to the field of *behavioural economics* in which researchers adapt the ways in which we have modelled preferences and constraints to account for systematic psychological biases that appear to be important in some types of decisions we make.

This leads us to the branch of economics known as *normative economics* as distinguished from positive economics that has framed most of our previous chapters. To the extent to which we have implicitly assumed that efficiency is good in previous chapters, we have already taken a particular normative position, but one we have repeatedly pointed out is probably in need of further elaboration.

Chapter 29

What Is Good? Challenges From Psychology and Philosophy

As we mentioned at the outset of this text, the human being is considerably more complex than the simplified models used by economists, but the purpose of the models is not to fully represent what it means to be human. The purpose is to predict and understand individual as well as aggregate behaviour and, in many cases, to find ways of improving human welfare as a result of our increased understanding. There is, however, a considerable leap from modelling behaviour well to knowing what is good for us. If the model does not incorporate all the complexities of who we are, is it useful as we move from considering what is to what is good?

We have implicitly attempted to do just that in modest ways throughout the text, using notions of consumer surplus and profit to arrive at concepts like deadweight loss and efficiency-enhancing policy. The first welfare theorem has offered us a framework on which to consider how individual incentives might deviate from social goals, particularly when those goals centre on achieving outcomes that exploit all possible efficiency gains. Economics is not the only discipline that thinks about human *welfare*, and human welfare may well mean more than is captured by the definitions of surplus that emerge from within the very models we readily admit are almost grotesque in the simplicity with which they treat the human condition. It is furthermore not the only discipline to investigate human *behaviour*, with psychology in particular exposing a number of ways in which such behaviour might, under certain circumstances, deviate from what economic models would predict. Philosophers think about the human condition in much deeper ways, ways that we will see interact with normative economics. In thinking about the question: 'What is good?', we therefore consider in this chapter how our views might be influenced by insights from other disciplines.

In some of our chapters, we have already done a little of that, as, for example, in our considerations of how cooperation in Prisoner's Dilemmas may emerge for reasons having to do with how we sometimes bring each other along to reach tipping points in the presence of network effects. Social norms of ideas like fairness might cause us to engage in behaviour that might seem against our immediate self-interest while reinforcing our valued identity of standing up for what is right. Some of these topics cross not only into the area of psychology but also of sociology, with economists now more frequently than ever collaborating with sociologists on various topics of mutual interest.

We will now consider some intersections of economics and two particular disciplines more directly with the aim of illustrating some of the complexities of moving from what is to what is good while hopefully bringing a bit of clarity to the possible limits of neoclassical economics. We will touch on intersections between economics and psychology, asking whether insights from psychology can in some circumstances not only improve the predictive power of our models but also change the way we think about what is good in markets, civil society and government policy. We will investigate the intersection of economics with philosophy, asking once again how positive models can help us formulate answers to the question: 'What is good?'

926

29A   Who Are We Really, and What Is It All About?

The point of this chapter is not to give an answer to the question: 'What is good?' in the way we might expect to have an answer to the question 'What will people do when the price of fuel doubles?' It is to provide some lenses through which one might tackle this normative question in light of the positive theory and results that form the core of microeconomics. A tilting of economic models towards psychology will suggest that some scenarios that the economist might instinctively conclude are not good might be viewed differently when insights from psychology are incorporated into our positive models of behaviour.

29A.1 Psychology and Behavioural Economics

Much of the criticism levelled against neoclassical microeconomics comes from perceptions of conflicts between the discipline of economics and the discipline of psychology, and the often mistaken notion that economists believe everyone is always rational and selfish in particularly stark ways. While tension between the disciplines is undeniable, recent years have also seen increasing synergies between them, synergies that have formed the basis for the new subfield of *behavioural economics* in which insights from psychology are incorporated into economic models and the even newer subfield of *neuroeconomics* in which neuroscientists and economists jointly investigate how the physiology of the brain impacts decision making under different circumstances.

The impetus for much of this cross-disciplinary collaboration stems from widespread documentations of behavioural anomalies – systematic ways in which observed human behaviour appears to depart from economic predictions in some circumstances. As evidence on such anomalies became empirically compelling, behavioural economists began to explore how psychology-based modifications of traditional neoclassical economic assumptions might lead to new models that better predicted behaviour. This is not without controversy among economists, some of whom believe that the motivating anomalies can just as easily be rationalized through more careful economic modelling that does not borrow from psychology. Competing models, some drawing more on psychology and others relying primarily on expanded neoclassical assumptions, continue to be tested to see which better fit the available data as the debate on the degree to which economics and psychology need one another continues. We will not settle this debate here, but merely present some of the main anomalies and the most compelling behavioural explanations for them in this section.

Before proceeding, we should note that the subfield of behavioural economics is understood differently in different quarters, which is not unexpected given that the merging of economics and psychology is a relatively recent phenomenon. Some scholars who see themselves as behavioural economists specialize in documenting examples of anomalies within laboratory settings where people are observed as they make decisions in controlled settings. Such scholars are therefore also practitioners of another relatively recent subfield known as *experimental economics*. Obtaining experimental data through controlled laboratory experiments does not, however, come as naturally to most economists as it does to psychologists, with many economists arguing that the settings can seem artificial and withdrawn from the richness in which real-world decisions are made, that they frequently don't permit the kind of learning that happens in the real world, and that they so often rely on a very peculiar group (undergraduates) as subjects. There is considerable evidence that not all experimental results are robust to repetitions and learning. Some experimental evidence, repeatedly replicated under different conditions, is so compelling that it has had an impact on our discipline, usually because we see echoes of the same phenomena in data from the real world. We should nevertheless keep in mind, however, that experiments in and of themselves are not what define behavioural economics even if experimental results have often clarified how new features might be usefully included in existing economic models by behavioural economists.

While we will make some occasional reference to experiments, the real meat of behavioural economics for our purposes lies in the conceptual paths it has opened and the ways in which it has allowed us to modify some of our previous models to help explain *real-world* phenomena that are otherwise difficult to reconcile with economic analysis. Behavioural economics *does not* require that we let go of the fundamental approach that ties together all of microeconomics – that people try to do the best they can given their circumstances. Instead, it highlights for us aspects of what is best and what kinds of circumstances might matter. It helps us think more carefully about features of tastes and constraints that might be important and that we would probably neglect without the prodding from psychologists.

29A.1.1 Present-Biased Preferences and Self-Control Problems Most smokers plan to quit at some point in the future and believe they will quit even though they find it too costly to quit today. We plan to start exercising and eat better – next year. We have every intention of saving more for retirement as we drag home that big-screen TV we just charged to a credit card. After staying up several nights in a row to cram for end of semester exams, you vow not to let that happen again during the next exam session, but first you decide you need a little time to blow off some steam and get away from studying. These are all examples of behaviour that suggests *time-inconsistent* preferences, the kinds of preferences that make us think something in the future will be worthwhile but, without any change other than the passage of time, we change our mind when the future comes. Such behaviour suggests that there is something special about the present – the here and now – and because the future invariably becomes the present with the passage of time, the future will become similarly special when it arrives. Such *present-bias* leads to *preference reversals* that are of no particular surprise to psychologists who have long studied human *self-control problems*. They *are* unexpected when viewed through the lens of the standard microeconomist's model of time-consistent intertemporal choice, the kind of choice where people end up doing what they plan to do unless circumstances change.

Consider a simple example in which we suppose that €1 in period $(t + 1)$ is always worth €δ < €1 to you in period t. You are currently in period 0 and are thinking about what you will do in period 1 when you can take an action like studying or not smoking or saving that will cost you c but will get you a benefit b in period 2. Looking ahead from period 0, your present discounted value of c one period later is δc and your present discounted value of b in two periods is $\delta(\delta)b = \delta^2 b$. You'll look ahead and conclude that the costly action in period 1 is worth taking as long as $\delta c < \delta^2 b$, which reduces to $c < \delta b$. When period 1 comes and you actually have to undertake the costly action, you will incur a cost c now and get a benefit b one period later, with the present discounted value of b one period from now equal to δb. You will take the action next period as long as $c < \delta b$. Your view of the action one period in the future is the same as your view when period 1 comes, because we have not assumed that there is anything special about the present that will cause you to change your mind when the future becomes the present. Your tastes are therefore fully *time consistent*, with your decision rule as to whether or not to invest in period 1 the same when you look ahead from period 0 as when you face the actual choice in period 1. This is illustrated in the first row of Table 29.1.

Assume that the way we evaluate costs and benefits is a bit different. Instead of evaluating €1 next period as worth €δ and €1 two periods from now as €δ^2, we value the €1 next period at €$\beta\delta$ and the €1 two periods from now at €$\beta\delta^2$. Let's revisit our decision of whether to undertake an action that costs c in period 1 but yields benefit b in period 2. As we think about our decision today in period 0, we will value c one period from now at $\beta\delta c$ and b two periods from now at $\beta\delta^2 b$, and we will forecast the action in period 1 to be worthwhile as long as $\beta\delta c < \beta\delta^2 b$, which reduces to $c < \delta b$ just as it did before. This is illustrated as the first entry under $t = 0$ for the beta-delta model in Table 29.1. Now consider what happens when we actually have to undertake the costly action as we find ourselves in period 1, when period 1 has become the present. We now face an immediate cost of c and value the benefit b next period at $\beta\delta b$, implying that we will undertake the action as long as $c < \beta\delta$. If $\beta \neq 1$, our decision rule has changed as the future became the present. If $\beta < 1$, this implies that we might look from period 0 towards period 1 and think the investment worthwhile, but when period 1 rolls around, we may end up concluding that the investment isn't actually such a good idea after all. That's time inconsistent.

Exercise 29A.1

Suppose $c = 100$, $b = 125$, $\delta = 0.95$ and $\beta = 0.8$. What is the expected value of undertaking the investment c in period 1 when viewed from $t = 0$? What is it when viewed from $t = 1$?

This model, known as the *beta-delta model*, has been adapted from similar models used to explain animal behaviour since the mid-1900s and is now used by behavioural economists to explain the many empirical findings of individual self-control problems. The model is most closely associated with the Harvard economist David Laibson (1966–). His beta-delta model is also known as a model of *quasi-hyperbolic discounting*. It is different from the neoclassical model of intertemporal choice only in the term β, with β appearing before the usual δ discount terms. Since it appears as β in front of δ as well as δ^2, it drops out when we think about trade-offs that are fully contained in the future as you can see in the first row of Table 29.1 where we are merely contemplating whether we should undertake the investment in period 1 from our vantage point of period 0. When the future becomes the present, β matters because the model has incorporated the idea that there is always something special about the present moment. *The beta-delta model of time preference changes the way we think about the present versus the future, not the way we think about the future versus the more distant future.*

Table 29.1 Conditions for Investing c at $t = 1$ to Get b at $t = 2$

	Preference Reversals	
	$t = 0$	$t = 1$
δ Model	$c + \delta b > 0$	$c + \delta b > 0$
$\beta - \delta$ Model	$c + \delta b > 0$	$c + \beta\delta b > 0$

Exercise 29A.2

When psychologists offer people the choice of €50 today or €100 next year, they tend to pick the €50 immediately. When the same people are offered the choice of €50 five years from now or €100 six years from now, they usually pick the €100. Explain how this does not fit into the usual model of intertemporal choice, but it does fit into the modified model in the previous paragraph.

One of the dangers of introducing a present-biased model of this kind is that students often misinterpret the model as giving expression to *impatience* rather than present-bias. Someone is impatient if they place a lot more value on consuming now than consuming in the future, which means they discount the future a lot and will end up investing less and eating more now than someone who is more patient. *There is nothing time-inconsistent about impatience.* If you are really impatient, you will look forward to period 1 and know that you will not want to pay c to get b one period later unless b is very large relative to c, and that is precisely what you'll actually decide when period 1 becomes the present. A time-inconsistency problem arises when you plan to do something in the future and, without anything other than time changing, you can't stick to your plan as the future becomes the present. This inability to stick by what we plan is, in the beta-delta model, caused by present-bias that follows individuals through time whether they are patient or not, and it is what defines the self-control problem that we are trying to get at.

Table 29.2 illustrates this distinction between impatience and present-bias. In the first section of the table, we show how much larger the period 2 benefit b has to be than the period 1 investment cost c in order for the investment to be judged worthwhile. We assume that $\delta = 1/1.05 \approx 0.952$; that is, generally you view €1 in period $(t + 1)$ as equivalent to about €0.95 in period t. We also assume that you might be present-biased by considering different potential values of β listed in the very top row. Your future plans are unaffected by the inclusion of β in the way you discount, so when you are in period 0 and you look forward, only the δ discount parameter matters. This implies you will think the investment *will be* worthwhile as long as $(b/c) > 1.05$ as indicated in the row labelled Future Plan at $t = 0$. When $\beta = 1$, the beta-delta model introduces no bias and thus the decision rule at $t = 1$ remains to undertake the investment as long as $(b/c) > 1.05$. When $\beta < 1$, we have present-bias. For instance, the table tells us that $\beta = 0.5$ implies that when we have to make the decision of whether to invest, we will suddenly require $(b/c) > 2.1$ to get us to give up c now to get b next period, even though we had initially planned to go through with the investment as long as $(b/c) > 1.05$. In a sense, $\beta = 0.5$ implies we suddenly become impatient in terms of trading off the present for the future when $t = 1$ rolls around, even though we expected to be relatively patient in period 1 when we were looking forward from period 0.

The second part of Table 29.2 derives the δ that would be necessary if β were set to 1 to arrive at the same decision rule at $t = 1$ as the present-biased preferences in the first part. For instance, $\delta = 0.476$ gives us the same decision rule as the present-biased rule when $\beta = 0.5$. The difference is that when $\delta = 0.476$, we know we are impatient and we are OK with that in the sense that our future actions will not contradict our current plans. As a result, our future plan at time 0 is the same as our actual decision rule at time 1 for any level of impatience. When the same decision rule emerges from $\beta = 0.5$ in the top part of the table, we disagree at time $t = 1$ with the plans we had made at time $t = 0$.

Table 29.2 Ratio of b to c Necessary to Justify the Investment

Present-Bias Versus Impatience							
Time-Inconsistent Beta-Delta Model of Present-Bias (with $\delta = 1/1.05$)							
β	0.50	0.75	0.90	0.95	1.00	1.05	1.10
Future Plan at $t = 0$	1.050	1.050	1.050	1.050	1.050	1.050	1.050
Present-Bias at $t = 1$	2.100	1.400	1.167	1.105	1.050	1.000	0.955
Equivalent δ in Time-Consistent Model of Impatience (with $\beta = 1$)							
δ	0.476	0.714	0.857	0.905	0.952	1.000	1.047
Future Plan at $t = 0$	2.100	1.400	1.167	1.105	1.050	1.000	0.955
Decision Rule at $t = 1$	2.100	1.400	1.167	1.105	1.050	1.000	0.955

Exercise 29A.3

What does it mean for β to be greater than 1 in the beta-delta model?

Exercise 29A.4

Consider again the example in exercise 29A.2. Suppose $\delta = 1/1.05 \approx 0.952$. What is the highest level of β that could lead to the choices in the example? What would δ have to be now if $\beta = 1$ to lead to the present choice, and why does this not help us explain the dual result described in the example?

We might ask what implications such a model has for how we think about what is good with respect to markets, civil society and government policy. Some might, for instance, be concerned that impatience causes individuals to underinvest and overconsume, with many philosophers, for instance, seeing no moral justification for anyone discounting the future. Patience is therefore sometimes seen as a moral virtue, though not one easily forced on people. It takes a relatively paternalistic, or patronizing, form of government to use concerns over people's impatience as a basis for a policy that will force individuals to invest more when they would prefer to consume. From an efficiency standpoint, such a policy would be the opposite of a Pareto improvement, with some people being made worse off as judged by themselves while others who would have been patient without being forced were made no better off. Properly functioning credit markets may constrain the extent to which individuals can act on their impatience by lending only up to a point, but at the same time such markets are also interested in selling now rather than later and thus benefit from consumer impatience. However, a whole host of civil society institutions – parents, families, churches – are engaged in attempting to persuade us to adopt a longer-time horizon, to think about tomorrow as we make decisions today, and it seems plausible that such institutions might have a great deal of impact on how individuals make voluntary trade-offs over time. To the extent to which patience is a virtue, it is often within the civil society that the virtue is fostered, and perhaps a failure of the civil society if impatience gets out of hand.

Present-biased preferences and the accompanying self-control problems raise a different set of issues. Individuals who are aware of their self-control problems will search for ways of overcoming these, ways of binding themselves in the future so as to avoid the temptation to undo their own plans when the future becomes the present. If you know you have a problem with sticking to your plans, you would be willing to expend resources to fix the problem, to invest in what economists call *commitment devices* that force you to take actions in the future, actions that you rationally predict your future self will not want to take even though your present self wants the future self to do so. In Homer's famous Greek classic *Odyssey*, the hero's ten-year voyage home from the Trojan War takes him past the land of the Sirens whose intoxicating song is known to lure the toughest of warriors into a deadly trap. Odysseus wants to hear the Sirens' song but also does not want to fall under their spell and into their trap. He understands, however, that once he hears the song, he will not have the self-control to keep himself away. He therefore designs a commitment device, asking his shipmates to bind him to the ship's mast while plugging their own ears so that they can hear neither the song nor Odysseus's pleading commands to unbind him. His self-control awareness keeps him from giving in to the present-bias he knows he will have in the future, and the commitment device keeps him from giving in to the temptation he knows is coming.

We have our own ways of constructing commitment devices when we find ourselves in positions analogous to Odysseus. You might commit to your partner that you will stop smoking in the hopes that their disappointment in you when they smell smoke will keep you from violating your commitment. You might start a monthly savings plan that penalizes you for not making regular deposits or bind your retirement savings in a pension plan that penalizes you for early withdrawals. Perhaps you ask your lecturers to give you deadlines rather than trusting that you will pace yourself as an exam approaches. Many people ceremoniously cut up their credit cards following their latest buying binge so as not to be tempted to abuse them again. They invest their savings in illiquid assets, assets that they cannot easily sell when the itch to consume hits. The self-aware addict might take one more dose of cocaine but seek help from an agency that will help them break the habit, or we might ask a colleague in the workplace to throw away the rest of the cake someone has brought in to avoid the temptation of going back for more. For those who are searching for commitment devices to discipline their future selves, we find many examples of such devices – some sold in the market, some volunteered within the civil society and some designed by government. Leaving more options open is no longer the optimal strategy for those who believe they can't handle it, and limiting options therefore becomes desirable from the self-aware individual's perspective just as Odysseus was wise to bind himself to the ship's mast and not leave all options open.

Exercise 29A.5

Many people buy health club memberships only never to use them. Yet they hold on to them and continue paying their monthly fees for long periods of time. How can the purchase of such memberships be explained, and what does the fact that individuals hold on to their memberships without using them tell us about their awareness of how they are making decisions?

Exercise 29A.6

Some financial advisers recommend that people choose 15-year mortgages with higher monthly payments rather than 30-year mortgages with lower monthly payments even if the interest rates on both mortgages are the same and even if the 30-year mortgages allow people to pre-pay and thus pay them off in 15 years if they want to. How does this make sense from a behavioural economist's perspective when it makes less sense when viewed through a traditional economic model?

Exercise 29A.7

In the period prior to the 2007 housing crisis in the US, it was relatively easy for people to refinance their homes. If people choose 15-year rather than 30-year mortgages as a savings commitment device as suggested in exercise 29A.6, might the ready option to refinance have made self-aware but present-biased people worse off?

It is probably unreasonable to think that everyone who has self-control problems fully perceives themselves to have such problems. In some instances, it may be that institutions like markets don't have the right incentives to make people aware of their problem. 'Another drink? Why certainly', the bar person might say as they feed the addiction of their alcoholic client, just as the electronics store will gladly supply you with yet another set of gadgets on your credit card which is virtually at its limit. At first glance, it may seem that government intervention to assist the unaware reflects the same paternalism we sensed in government attempts to make us more virtuous by getting us to behave less impatiently, and some social commentators have therefore been highly sceptical of drawing policy inferences from the results of behavioural economists who work on present-bias. Many behavioural economists, however, argue for much less threatening types of policy interventions, interventions we will refer to as *libertarian paternalism*, which is a form of paternalism that does not presume the government knows best but rather sets up some 'nudges' that will get those with self-control problems to do what is ultimately in their best interests as judged by themselves while imposing no costs of great significance on those that have no such problems. The term 'nudge' is borrowed from the title of a book on behavioural economics (Richard Thaler (the 2016 Nobel Prize Winner) and Cass Sunstein, *Nudge*, New Haven, CT: Yale University Press, 2008). We will conclude the section on behavioural economics with some examples of such policies after covering a few other major insights from the intersection of economics and psychology that have a bearing on what such policies might look like.

29A.1.2 Reference Dependent Preferences, Loss Aversion and Endowment Effects It is often the case that the demand for tickets for sporting or entertainment events exceeds the available supply. In some cases, lotteries are used to determine the ultimate recipients of tickets. In the United States, Dan Ariely, a psychologist in the business school at Duke University, decided to call up students who had won the lottery for basketball tickets at the university's stadium to try to negotiate a price at which the winners might be willing to sell their tickets. He also called the losers from the lottery who were just as enthusiastic about Duke basketball as the winners and had shown this by jumping through all the same hoops to see how much they'd be willing to pay to buy tickets. His claim is that the winners were willing to sell their tickets for an average of about $1400 while the losers were willing to pay only about $170 to get a ticket.

Exercise 29A.8*

True or False: If individual tastes are quasilinear in basketball tickets, the prices people are willing to accept should be identical to the prices they are willing to pay.

The randomness with which students were selected into winners and losers suggests that we should be able to assume that their preferences and economic circumstances are on average roughly the same. If we assume this, the only difference between them is that winners have a basketball ticket and losers do not. The only difference between the two is a relatively modest wealth effect, so modest that we would think it should not amount to much of a difference between the marginal willingness to pay on the part of the losers and the marginal willingness to accept on the part of the winners. It is therefore virtually impossible to explain the actual result found by Ariely with the tools of standard neoclassical economics, and this failure of our typical model points to a wider class of phenomena uncovered by psychologists and brought into economics by behavioural economists.

As it turns out, people sometimes seem to evaluate options not in an absolute sense but rather in comparison to a *reference point* that is often but not always related to their current endowment. This and related insights are closely associated with a theory known as *prospect theory* developed by the psychologists Daniel Kahneman (1934–) and Amos Tversky (1937–1996). Our decisions are, as a result, sometimes *reference dependent*. In our example, for instance, suppose two students are identical except that student 1 is a loser in the basketball lottery and achieves utility level u_1 on their indifference map, and student 2 is a winner who achieves utility level $u_2 > u_1$. When called about either selling or buying a ticket, the two students formulate their response with their endowment of a ticket or no ticket as a reference point. This means that student 2 will view selling the ticket as the loss of a ticket whereas student 1 views buying the ticket as the gain of a ticket. Nothing yet is keeping us from expecting them to come up with roughly similar prices. There is another feature of tastes, however, that psychologists have found sometimes matters, which is that when we evaluate gains and losses relative to a reference point, we tend to place more weight on losses than on gains. Thus, when student 2 views selling the ticket as the loss of a ticket, this loss is psychologically more painful than the gain is pleasurable for student 1 who is considering buying a ticket, even though the ticket was worth exactly the same to both of them when they first started the process of attempting to secure a ticket.

This second insight is known as *loss aversion*, and together with the insight that we evaluate gains and losses relative to a reference point, it can help to explain what behavioural economists call the *endowment effect* or sometimes the *status quo effect*. This effect essentially says that there is something about *ownership* or the *status quo* that matters in ways not captured by our neoclassical model. We tend to place greater value on what we own after we take ownership than before, and we seem attached to the status quo of our current situation. This can change some of the insights from our initial development of consumer theory where consumers appear to form particular psychological attachments that seem to give rise to such endowment effects. These endowment and status quo effects, which show up in lots of psychology experiments, can help explain why the students who won the right to attend a basketball game could not easily be made to give it up, even though identical students who did not have a ticket were not willing to pay all that much to get the right to attend the game. It seems likely that if endowment effects are real, we might expect them to be particularly important when the endowment involves something in which our emotions get tied up, such as our home or the prospect of seeing our team beat their fierce rivals.

The concept of loss aversion can also make sense of one of the most frustrating things that people do, frustrating, that is, from an economist's perspective, which is that no matter how much we preach at people, there are times when they behave as if sunk costs were true economic costs. Consider an example we gave earlier in the text that of paying for a cinema ticket and discovering within the first few minutes that the film is terrible. How often have you not walked out of the film and instead suffered through it just because you paid to get in? Perhaps the reason is that you made your decision to stay with respect to a reference point – the fact that you owned a ticket – from which admitting a loss is psychologically painful.

Exercise 29A.9

Consider a situation where an individual makes a special trip to a library in order to return a book that would otherwise be overdue when they could have waited till the next day and returned the book on their way to work.

The late fee is €1. If this person is contacted on a night when they did not have a book due with special information that there was €1 hidden behind one of the books on the library shelf, and that they can be virtually assured of getting the euro if they visit the library now, they would never think it worth it to take that special trip for €1. Can you explain the individual's behaviour using reference-based preferences with loss aversion?

There are many other implications that emerge from reference-based decision making, some of which – in particular those related to risk – we will touch on in Section B. There are certainly implications for how an awareness of such decision making might change some of our conclusions about what is good. If we are indeed willing to give up more to avoid losses than we are to achieve gains, for instance taxing wealth – that is, taxing things that people own – might be considerably worse from an efficiency perspective than taxing income, even though a standard model might suggest the opposite. When taxing income, it might be better to withhold taxes from an employee's salary so that they never take ownership of the pre-tax income, rather than asking them to pay taxes all at once at the end of the year once they have already experienced the pre-tax income. Bankruptcy laws that are comparatively lenient in terms of allowing people to keep their homes might find some genuine justification. It might alter the way we think about the possible macroeconomic trade-off between smoothing business cycles and fostering growth.

Exercise 29A.10

In his book *Predictably Irrational*, Dan Ariely suggests (incorrectly, it turns out) that taxing fuel may not have much impact on long-run fuel consumption because, he hypothesizes, people will adjust their reference point and thus will respond primarily in the short run and not that much in the long run. This is exactly the opposite prediction that a neoclassical economist would make. Can you see how he arrives at his prediction?

Reference-based decision making can also, however, raise some deeper ethical issues when the reference point is not your own endowment, but rather your neighbour's consumption. As we will see in our section on the happiness literature, some behavioural economists have argued that this is precisely how we evaluate our own position in life, not in an absolute sense, i.e. not 'How well am I doing?' but rather in a relative sense, i.e. 'Am I doing better than my friend?' Such a view of human nature is sometimes argued to call for dramatically egalitarian policies, policies that aim to minimize the difference between people, quite possibly at the cost of dramatically reducing everyone's standard of living because of the incentive issues such policies would raise. Few economists take this view, perhaps because we are quite persuaded that human welfare is more likely to be affected by absolute rather than relative factors, or perhaps because there is something unseemly about basing large-scale social policy on what amounts to people's envy of one another.

29A.1.3 Some Neglected Constraints: Framing, Bounded Rationality and More Suppose you are very environmentally conscious and you are given Options 1, 2 and 3 as in Table 29.3. Assuming that each car would be driven the same number of kilometres for the next few years, which option would you pick to maximize the positive impact of less pollution on the environment? Next suppose you were give options A, B and C in the same table. Which one would you choose now?

You may have noted that option 1 is identical to option A, option 2 is identical to option B and option 3 is identical to option C. Both sets of options give you information on the fuel efficiency of the initial cars and the ones that would replace them, but the first set of options *framed* the choice in terms of kilometres per litre whereas the second framed it in terms of litres per 1000 kilometres. The information is the same, but it sounds very different. *Framing* matters in terms of what choices we make, a fact long understood by advertisers and the psychologists who help advertisers manipulate us.

Exercise 29A.11

Explain how the two sets of options are equivalent.

Table 29.3 Framing: An Example

Suppose our goal is to reduce consumption of fuel: Which option would we choose?

Option 1:	Replace an 8 KPL car with a 10 KPL car	
Option 2:	Replace a 25 KPL car with a 40 KPL car	Most people would instinctively pick Option 3
Option 3:	Replace a 50 KPL car with a 100 KPL car	

What about the following?

Option A:	Replace car that uses 125 litres with one that uses 100 litres per 1000 kilometres	
Option B:	Replace car that uses 40 litres with one that uses 25 litres per 1000 kilometres	Now, most people would pick Option A.
Option C:	Replace car that uses 20 litres with one that uses 10 litres per 1000 kilometres	

There are lots of reasons framing matters. In some cases, it matters because our *bounded rationality*, our limited capacity to absorb and process information, has led us to use simple rules of thumb or *heuristics* instead of really thinking through problems. Such heuristics may respond differently depending on how something is framed, and they may well have evolved over long periods of time to help us solve problems more easily and more effectively. As the world has changed and is changing more rapidly than it used to, some evolutionarily effective rules may now be poor in instances for which they were never intended.

In other cases, psychologists have discovered systematic ways in which we trip ourselves up even in circumstances that require only limited maths, such as not recognizing the equivalence between kilometres per litre and its inverse, litres per kilometre. In others, psychologists have discovered systematic ways in which individuals have difficulty internalizing some basics about probabilities of random events, and that framing impact has literally nothing to do with computational limitations and, in the words of Kahneman and Tversky, 'resemble perceptual illusions'. For instance, unscrupulous pollsters who are willing to get polling data to say whatever the client wants know a bit about how to frame polling questions to cause people to answer in one or the other direction. It may well be the case that certain types of decisions are impacted by emotions that find their roots in our complex brain chemistry, a subject that is taken seriously in the collaboration of neuroscientists with economists.

In instances where framing matters, we may see a role for markets, civil society and government to structure institutions in ways that minimize systematic errors. If, for instance, we indeed understand fuel efficiency better when phrased in terms of litres per kilometre rather than kilometres per litre, such an awareness might lead car companies, consumer advocacy groups or government to be proactive in reframing how fuel efficiency data on different vehicles is presented to consumers. In instances where firms are able to lead consumers into making systematic and profit-maximizing errors through marketing and advertising, there may be a role for government to reframe the issue, as perhaps governments worldwide have done by placing scary pictures and apocalyptic warnings on cigarette packets. There may once again be a role for libertarian paternalism, of which the scary pictures on cigarette packets might just be one example.

29A.1.4 Libertarian Paternalism Behavioural economics is not foremost about people making mistakes; it's about people exhibiting *systematic biases* that emerge from how the preferences and constraints have been shaped by psychological factors. It becomes tempting to fix the biases through policy, which almost instantly invites the question: If human decisions are meaningfully shaped by these biases, why would we not expect human beings who make policy to be similarly shaped by such biases as they legislate and implement such policies? Isn't there something obnoxiously paternalistic in a policy maker telling us they will now force us to do something we don't want to do because they want to protect us from our biases? To many behavioural economists and to many who have casually watched the development of the field, the policy implications are subtler and less paternalistic. We will illustrate with an example.

Consider the case of present-biased individuals who can't carry through on their plans to save for retirement. To the extent to which they are aware of their self-control problem, they might, as we have mentioned, find commitment devices, but perhaps they are only partially or not at all aware of the problem. Heavy-handed paternalism might lead us to legislating forced savings plans, while libertarian paternalism might involve a nudge to get people to consider regular monthly saving as their reference point.

Consider the following: businesses offer their employees the opportunity to save for retirement through tax-advantaged pension plans that deduct some percentage of the employees' salary and contribute the deducted amount into a retirement plan. Participation in these plans is entirely voluntary, but some businesses enrol employees automatically while giving them an option to discontinue their automatic payroll deductions and opt out of the plan, and other businesses do not enrol employees unless the employee requests it. In both cases, changing from the default policy requires little more than a phone call, which means that it really should not matter whether the default is for the business to enrol its employees or not *but it does matter – a lot*. People who are automatically enrolled in such pension plans are much more likely to stay in those plans than people who are not automatically enrolled are likely to enrol. Libertarian paternalism in the face of evidence on present-biased and reference-based savings decisions would suggest automatic enrolment of everyone into retirement programmes, thereby improving the welfare of those with self-control problems who also make reference-based decisions while imposing virtually no cost on those who make decisions in a more conventional way and might want to opt out.

Exercise 29A.12

How can reference-based preferences explain the empirical facts on enrolments in retirement programmes?

Note the difference between the type of heavy-handed paternalism that attempts to enforce the virtue of patience and this example of libertarian paternalism. In the former case, the object of the paternalism is to correct impatience, and in so doing it makes impatient people worse off while not impacting those that are already patient. It might also, of course, lead some who have self-control problems to save, but this form of paternalism offers no real path for a nuanced use of information that distinguishes between the merely impatient and the present-biased. The libertarian paternalism in our example allows for much more subtlety while minimizing the chances that anyone is seriously hurt by the policy. It is most effective if present-biased and reference-biased decision making are correlated, which would imply that those in greatest need of a mechanism to get them to save more are the very ones who will view the automatic enrolment in a pension plan as a relevant reference point that will keep them enrolled. It also allows the impatient who operate without reference bias to opt out and to indulge their impatient whims without interfering with their time-consistent plans to live a life full of impatience. Rather than imposing virtue, libertarian paternalism attempts to nudge people towards solutions they may not themselves be aware of while keeping costs low for those who require no help.

29A.2 Happiness: The Social Sciences Versus the Humanities

While they may not always agree on the degree to which neoclassical assumptions of microeconomics require tweaking, both traditional and behavioural economists share the same underlying approach that we think that we can best *predict* behaviour by assuming that people always try to do the best they can given their circumstances. What they might consider best may be subject to psychological biases, and their constraints may extend beyond economic constraints to cognitive constraints and framing biases, but in the end we still view individuals as optimizers. The thing they are optimizing is something we call 'utility', which is usually interpreted to mean happiness. The extent to which utility is the same as what most people call happiness is a somewhat open question among economists. Gary Becker (1930–2014), the 1992 recipient of the Nobel Prize in Economics, has for instance argued that what people call happiness might more appropriately be viewed as something analogous to a commodity that plays a role in determining an individual's utility but is not itself the entirety of what makes up utility. As such, it would be possible for someone who is fully rational to be observed undertaking an action that optimizes their utility while at the same time reporting that the action made them less happy as they trade off happiness against other contributors to utility. For instance, couples frequently report declines in happiness when they have children while also affirming that they made the right decision to have children. There are two ways in which we can view this thing called happiness that we think people are trying to soak in. The first defines happiness as whatever thing motivates people into action, as a work-horse of sorts that helps us understand why people do what they do. In the absence of distinguishing between utility and happiness, this work-horse definition of happiness is what is captured in what we have called tastes that confront constraints to shape the *behaviour* that we can actually observe, study and predict. We can quite confidently say that more money makes people happy because they seem to jump into action to pursue it. The economic model, whatever we think about how much to include psychological biases, predicts well in many circumstances precisely because positive economists – that is, economists who seek to predict behaviour – deliberately do not try to define a deeper meaning of happiness beyond this work-horse definition. It is a shallow view of happiness, but one whose purpose is quite deliberately not deep.

Yet this does not mean that there isn't some deeper view of happiness, a view deeper even than distinguishing between utility and happiness. Such a deeper view is often found in the humanities where attempts are made in all sorts of ways to reconcile the various aspects of the human being, attempts that sometimes give rise to puzzling but quite possibly true statements like money doesn't make you happy. If we are ultimately to address the question of what is good, it is difficult to not at some point confront that deeper meaning of happiness for which the positive economist legitimately has little use in their pursuit of good behavioural predictions.

We will return to a brief pedestrian discussion of this deeper view of happiness in Section 29A.2.3 after touching on some findings from a relatively recent social science happiness literature that tries to at least come to terms with what conditions people associate with the state of being happy at particular instances in time. This literature uses combinations of surveys and psychological indicators to arrive at measures of happiness, measures that throughout this book we have shied away from, given the modern economist's typical position that happiness is not objectively measurable even if individuals can subjectively experience it. Despite the economist's instinct against cardinal or measurable utility and in favour of ordinal utility that merely requires people to tell us what is better and what is worse, economists have recently collaborated with other social scientists in this literature that some have labelled *happiness economics*.

29A.2.1 The Social Science Happiness Literature Given our maintained position that all we need is some ordinal notion of preferences and not a cardinal – or measurable – happiness scale to predict behaviour, it is far from clear that the economist's work-horse notion of happiness is what is measured in data sets that contain a happiness index. At the same time, it is unlikely that the happiness measure in such data sets is what philosophers mean by some deeper meaning of happiness. It is therefore not entirely clear how to interpret empirical findings on how happiness quantitatively relates to various types of societal and personal indicators of well-being. Still, the results are intriguing and informative for those striving to move from the question of what is to the question of what is good. Early on in this literature, two apparently contradictory findings came to be known as the *Easterlin Paradox* named after Richard Easterlin (1926–), an economist who first raised it in 1974.

The first finding was that *within* countries at any given time, the marginal impact of greater income on happiness is positive but diminishes as income increases. While it is especially true that more money makes people happier at low levels of income, this is increasingly less true although it is never false as income rises. In terms of language that we have conspicuously avoided throughout this text, we can equivalently say that these findings suggest a positive but diminishing marginal utility of income and consumption.

Exercise 29A.13

Explain the last sentence.

Exercise 29A.14

Consider the notion of compensating differentials in labour markets – wage differences that emerge because some jobs are inherently less pleasurable or involve more risk, factors that in equilibrium will be reflected in wages. How might the existence of such compensating differentials bias researchers into finding the marginal utility of income to be diminishing when it actually is not?

This first finding is not particularly surprising to economists; more, it seems, is indeed better even if getting more makes less of a difference the more we have. The Easterlin Paradox, however, emerges from the second set of findings that there appeared to be relatively little relationship between average happiness and average incomes *across* countries except for the very poorest; and there appeared to be similarly little relationship between average happiness and average income *within countries over time* as average income increases. Thus, it isn't clear that people in richer countries are necessarily happier than those in somewhat poorer countries, neither does it appear that the older generation is all that much happier than their grandparents' generation whose material standard of living was less than a third of what they enjoy. In light of our discussion of reference-based preferences in the previous section, a behavioural economics explanation of these seemingly contradictory findings is that happiness above basic subsistence levels is primarily driven by *relative income* considerations and not by *absolute income* levels.

Exercise 29A.15

Explain how reference-based preferences can provide such an explanation for the two sets of findings.

Exercise 29A.16

If the reference-based preference explanation for the Easterlin Paradox is correct, how would this imply that we are all caught up in a big Prisoner's Dilemma?

Recent work has cast some doubt on the second set of findings in the Easterlin puzzle and thus on the extent to which there is a puzzle. The Easterlin Paradox therefore remains an issue of some debate in economic literature. There is, however, wide consensus that happiness as measured in the happiness literature is certainly not *only* produced by either absolute or relative income or consumption. Rather, reported happiness is also driven in large part by factors such as feelings of security, connectedness to social networks of friends and family, being good at something and being relatively healthy. The typical economic model that bases the bulk of its emphasis on happiness from material consumption certainly seems to result in many good predictions. Its work-horse definition of happiness cannot easily be viewed as the entire answer to the question 'What is happiness?' This may not be any more surprising to most economists than it is to most 'normal' people, even as economists find the work-horse model of happiness an extremely useful tool for predicting human behaviour in a wide variety of settings.

29A.2.2 Why Does Work-Horse Happiness Predict Behaviour? With evidence that our work-horse definition of happiness does not get to the heart of the complexity of what the good life is all about, why does the work-horse model predict so well? If the happiness literature had concluded that money doesn't make us happy, we'd have a serious puzzle on our hands. As it stands, however, the literature says that ultimately there are many aspects of life – friends, family, and so on – that matter, and that money appears not as important in producing happiness as these other aspects of life. Money *does* matter, and whether it matters in an absolute or relative sense is not as crucial for the question of why the work-horse model predicts well. In either case, an individual would *act as if* money mattered for their happiness. If material consumption matters *somewhat* in the empirical happiness literature but is modelled as essentially being the *only* thing that matters in most of economics, one is still left with a bit of a disconnect between the predictive power of economics and the importance of so much that we typically don't consider in our models.

If it is true that the work-horse definition of happiness predicts too well, psychologists have come up with one possible explanation, though add there are others as well. It seems that our brain remembers the past in a systematically biased way, and we use this information to determine what to do next. When we strive to get the money together to buy that shiny new car, for instance, we anticipate great utility from ultimately getting the car, with that anticipation motivating us to get there. When we do get there and begin to drive that new car, we often end up disappointed in the sense that the experience does not provide nearly as much pleasure as we thought it would. When we are asked a year or two later about what it was like to finally get that new car, we report a level of pleasure commensurate with our anticipation of getting the car, not the level we actually enjoyed. Thus, our brain tells us that getting more stuff like the new car will be really great because we remember how great it was to get that new car by remembering how great we *thought* it would be to get it! We act as if more makes us happy, thus making the positive economist's predictions so accurate even if we aren't becoming all that much happier as we get more.

Exercise 29A.17

Suppose we consider our brain as the outcome of an evolutionary process aimed at maximizing the survival of our species. How might this be consistent with the memory bias we have just discussed?

Exercise 29A.18

In what sense do you think this memory bias might work in the opposite direction as present-bias discussed earlier?

This might also help to explain why we insist on doing things that happiness researchers suggest make us downright miserable. For instance, one of the most robust findings of the happiness literature in psychology is that having children makes us less happy, with marital bliss maximized just before the arrival of children in the household and never quite recovering until they leave the nest, assuming the marriage has survived that long. How is it that most of us still have children, and even more puzzling, why is it that we wax on retrospectively about how wonderful a thing that was? Psychologists might suggest that the same memory bias is at play. We remember our children fondly when they aren't around or have left home, but what we are actually remembering is our anticipation of how wonderful it would be to have children rather than the actual experience.

29A.2.3 The Matrix, Philosophy and the Deeper Meaning of Life

This deeper aspect to the question of what is happiness is something the positive economist, behavioural or traditional, never has to confront. Philosophers often confront the question head on by posing the following hypothetical that was loosely adapted as the premise for the Hollywood film *The Matrix*. Imagine being confronted with the following offer: you can step into your lecturer's office and be hooked up to a machine that will remove your consciousness from this world and instead stimulate your brain into experiencing a much better world, one in which your desires are quickly met, one in which the machine provides conditions under which you will achieve substantially more utility than you can ever hope to achieve in the world we occupy. Suppose further that once you are hooked up to this machine, you will live out the rest of your life in this artificial world, but all your experiences will feel just as real as they do in this world. You will not know that you are anywhere other than the real world, but everything will be so much better than it is here. Do you accept the offer?

If we take the positive economist's work-horse definition of happiness or the more expanded version from the social science happiness literature literally, it is hard to see why you wouldn't. The machine offers you more of this kind of happiness that explains so much of your behaviour than you could ever attain in life, and happiness or utility is what we presume you maximize. The potential discomfort from knowing that you are entering an imaginary world for the few minutes it takes to hook you up to the machine can't possibly be so great as to cause you to give up such a life of bliss. Since this is a hypothetical thought experiment, we can even dispense with these few minutes and suppose that the machine is instantly hooked up to you. Still, most people say quite definitively that they would not agree to be hooked up to the machine, not even if it takes only a second to hook them up, not even if the machine has been proven 100 per cent flawless and there is no chance that it might ever malfunction.

This thought experiment is meant to point out that there must be something deeper than our work-horse definition of happiness that we crave, that there is more to the good life than a happy life, even one that expands the notion of happiness to the various components of factors that the happiness literature tells us matter. Even if the desire to achieve such happiness or utility can explain our actions, as positive economists attempt to argue it does to a remarkable extent, the fact that there is more to life than experiencing happiness suggests that we will miss something important if we rely solely on the utility ruler that helps us predict to fully evaluate whether social outcomes are good. The good life may not coincide perfectly with the happy life even if the happy life is what motivates much of the behaviour that is the subject of the analysis of social scientists including economists.

This is not a book on philosophy but, as we now turn to the topic of normative economics, it is difficult to fully avoid the questions philosophers think about when they ask what constitutes the 'good'. Still, all we can do here is raise these deeper questions because economists ultimately aren't in any special position to answer them in a satisfactory way. The main point of raising the questions is to suggest that some humility might be in order as we take an economist's, or even a broader social scientist's, predictive models towards a complete picture of defining what is good. Some economists might argue that the economist's framework is quite fundamental to coming to an answer, but it is almost certainly not sufficient in and of itself.

Having raised such a need for humility, we nevertheless now resort to simplified models as we consider the interaction of economics with a limited set of different philosophical approaches to answering the question 'What is good?'

29A.3 Evaluating Distributions of Outcomes: Philosophy and Normative Economics

We can agree to disagree about whether we think that happiness – or utility – can be measured in some meaningful way, or the extent to which individuals are fully rational in the traditional sense or instead riddled with psychological baggage that causes persistent mistakes. None of that, however, has to keep us from engaging in the philosophical question of how we would evaluate different distributions of utility in society if we were able to do so. Some of what we call normative economics does precisely that and, in the process, permits economists to engage in larger philosophical debates about what is good at an admittedly abstract level. We will begin with a discussion of this abstract debate while linking it to some of the micro foundations we developed earlier in the text in ways that are common in normative economics.

We will also ask what other normative measures we can bring to discussions of policy when such measures need to be based on an assumption that we cannot actually measure utility in practice. This, too, is a part of normative economics, albeit one that is much more loosely tied to philosophy. Both the abstract and the more concrete discussions in this section share one fundamental premise: that what matters in thinking about what is good is the outcomes or consequences that result from how institutions within society are set up. Whether these are outcomes we can actually measure such as income or consumption, or outcomes we may not be able to measure such as utility, the focus is on how distributions and levels of outcomes relate to how we think about the good in society. The underlying approach, therefore, is what philosophers might call *consequentialist*, which means entirely focused on outcomes rather than processes. It is not the only approach nor necessarily the most common among philosophers, but it is the approach most commonly employed in normative economics. In Section 29A.4, we will briefly discuss an alternative that is implicitly also advocated by many economists, although it might be at least in part for consequentialist reasons.

29A.3.1 Utility Possibility Frontiers A *utility possibility set* is a description of all the possible combinations of utilities for individuals that could be achieved in an economy. If there is truth in the notion of diminishing marginal utility of income, as suggested by the happiness literature, we might expect the boundary of the utility possibility set – known as the *utility possibility frontier* – to take on the general shape depicted in panel (b) of Graph 29.1 for cases where we consider a society made up of only two individuals. Notice that in drawing such a utility possibility frontier, we implicitly assume there are ways of converting individual 2's utility u_2 into individual 1's utility u_1 and vice versa, but that it becomes increasingly difficult to convert person 2's utility into u_1 the higher u_1 becomes. Diminishing marginal utility of income would get us this result if the means by which we convert utility across people is through redistribution of income.

Exercise 29A.19

Suppose the marginal utility of income is constant and we can costlessly redistribute income across individuals. What would that imply for the shape of the utility possibility frontier?

If you have read about Edgeworth Boxes in Chapter 16, we can illustrate how utility possibility frontiers arise from the set of Pareto efficient allocations in a typical neoclassical depiction of an exchange economy. In panel (b) of Graph 16.3, we traced out what we called the *contract curve* for such an economy – the set of Pareto efficient allocations. In panel (a) of Graph 29.1, we illustrate such a contract curve, but this time we add utility numbers to some of the indifference curves. In panel (b) of Graph 29.1, we translate the three highlighted points on the contract curve to a graph that has the utility of individual 1 on the horizontal axis and the utility of individual 2 on the vertical. By doing this for each of the possible points on the contract curve, we derive the utility possibility frontier that forms the boundary of the *utility possibility set*. All combinations of utilities in this set up to and including the frontier are possible in this Edgeworth Box economy, but combinations of utilities outside this set are not possible.

Exercise 29A.20

True or False: Every allocation on the contract curve in panel (a) of Graph 29.1 translates to a point on the utility possibility frontier in panel (b).

Graph 29.1 Deriving the Utility Possibility Frontier From an Edgeworth Box

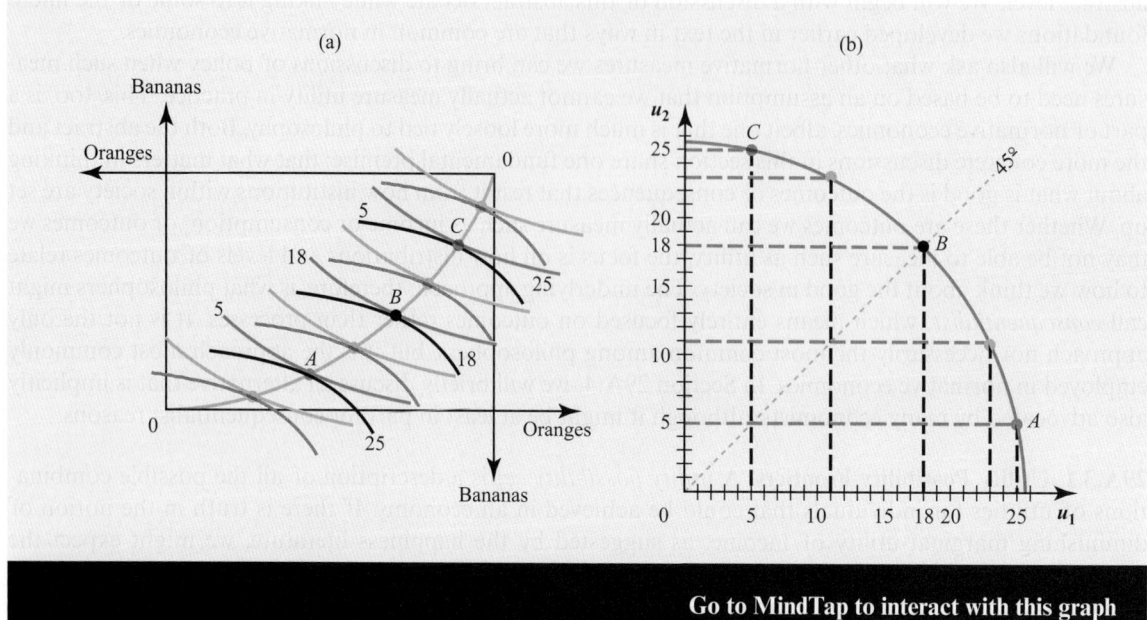

Go to MindTap to interact with this graph

Now notice that there exists a logical relationship between the utility allocations on the utility possibility frontier and the set of efficient outcomes. Points on the utility possibility frontier are such that there is no way to move to the northeast in the graph and still remain within the utility possibility frontier; that is, there is no way to make both people better off. There is similarly no way to move straight up or straight to the right, and thus no way to make one person better off without making anyone else worse off. By definition, the points on the utility possibility *frontier* represent the set of efficient outcomes for our little two-person society. As we have pointed out before, it is, for instance, efficient to give everything to one person or the other, but it is also efficient to have them share resources in ways such that there are no further gains from trade. Points inside the utility possibility set are inefficient because from such points it is possible to move to the northeast within the utility possibility set and thus make everyone better off.

It is unlikely that a consequentialist approach to deciding what is good within this framework will lead us to choose a point other than one that is located on the efficient utility possibility frontier. Were we to choose a point inside the frontier, we would need to conclude that it is best not to make everyone better off. This explains our heavy focus on efficiency because efficiency is a *necessary* condition for an optimal outcome under virtually any consequentialist normative approach. It is not, however, a *sufficient condition* for an optimal outcome because we might prefer some outcomes on the utility possibility frontier over others.

29A.3.2 First-Best and Second-Best Utility Possibility Frontiers The utility possibility frontier derived in Graph 29.1 plotted the utility allocations associated with all possible efficient outcomes in an economy. We paid no attention to whether it is actually *possible* to reach all of these allocations. Within the typical neoclassical economics model, we know that *as long as the government can use non-distortionary lump sum taxes to redistribute across individuals*, all efficient allocations are indeed feasible equilibrium outcomes for some redistributive government policy. In Chapter 16, we referred to this as the second welfare theorem. We also know from our treatment of taxes throughout the text that real-world governments rarely have access to lump sum taxes, but must instead rely on distortionary taxes that create deadweight losses. Under distortionary taxation, the utility possibility frontier that is *in principle* possible under lump sum taxes is no longer possible *in practice*.

We can think of lump sum taxes as a first-best redistributive tool for the government, and we can call the utility possibility frontier that emerges from applications of lump sum redistribution as the *first-best utility possibility frontier*. When the government must instead choose from distortionary taxes, we will refer to the best resulting utility possibility frontier as a *second-best utility possibility frontier*. We can similarly distinguish between first-best and second-best notions of efficiency, in each case referring to the utility allocations along the relevant utility possibility frontier.

Suppose, for instance, that individual 1 is initially endowed with everything in the economy. If nothing is done, we would be at the lower right-hand corner of our first-best utility possibility frontier. Now suppose we imagine the government using distortionary taxes to transfer wealth from individual 1 to individual 2. In panel (a) of Graph 29.2, we illustrate a possible (light blue) second-best utility possibility frontier and compare it with the (dark brown) first-best frontier taken from panel (b) of Graph 29.1. As distortionary taxes are imposed on individual 1, the deadweight loss from taxation results in the second-best utility possibility frontier lying inside the first-best utility possibility set, with the distance between the first- and second-best frontiers increasing as the tax and its associated deadweight loss increases.

Exercise 29A.21

Suppose that initial wealth was more equally distributed. Illustrate how the first- and second-best utility possibilities would be related to one another. What point do they share in common?

Panel (b) of Graph 29.2 illustrates an even more dramatic possibility. Think back to our development of the Laffer Curve in Chapter 8, a curve that illustrates the impact on labour tax revenues from a tax on wages. We concluded that as the tax on wages increases, there comes a point at which individuals would choose to no longer work. If we imagine individual 1 as the worker and individual 2 as someone unable to work and unable to consume unless they receive some transfer, we could imagine the second-best utility possibility frontier in panel (b) emerging. As taxes are levied initially on individual 1, there is some deadweight loss but not enough to keep us from being able to transfer some consumption to individual 2. As the tax on individual 1 increases, there comes a point at which increasing the tax further will reduce how much we raise from them, and thus reduce how much we can transfer to individual 2. From that point forward, both individuals become worse off as the wage tax increases.

Graph 29.2 First-Best and Second-Best Utility Possibility Frontiers

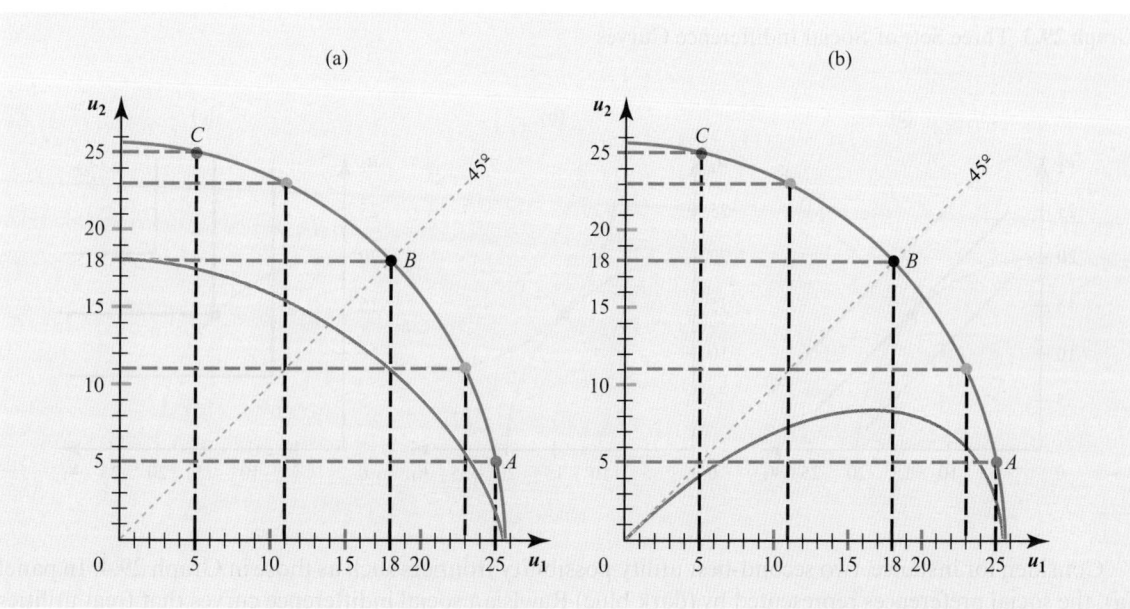

29A.3.3 Using Social Indifference Curves to Choose What is Best Before we can ask which allocation is best, we have to define a way to measure which allocations are better and which are worse. If all we care about is first-best efficiency, all the points on the first-best utility possibility frontier are best since they are all efficient. It might be argued that points that lie towards the middle of the first-best utility possibility frontier are better than points that lie towards the ends. This may be because people probably think that equality is also a value we should care about.

If panel (b) of Graph 29.1 had goods rather than utilities on the axes and the utility possibility frontier were a budget constraint for a consumer, we would already know how to think about what is better and what is worse. We would define the preferences of the individual who is trying to do the best they can, preferences like those for perfect complements or perfect substitutes or something in between. Now, however, we are trying to define social preferences over utility bundles rather than personal preferences over consumption bundles, and we would like to define these preferences in line with some ethical criterion.

Suppose that we thought of individual utilities as perfectly substitutable much like we thought of Coke and Pepsi as perfectly substitutable when we analyzed consumer preferences. Our social preferences would be such that they give rise to social indifference curves that are straight lines with slope -1. Such social indifference maps are often called *Benthamite social preferences* named after the 19th-century utilitarian philosopher Jeremy Bentham (1748–1832), who advocated the greatest good for the greatest number of people. Suppose instead that we thought of individual utilities as perfect complements, for example sugar and tea for some people. In that case, our social indifference curves would take on L-shapes with the corners of the L along the 45-degree line. Such social indifference maps are often referred to as *Rawlsian social preferences* after the 20th-century philosopher John Rawls (1921–2002). Or we could think of degrees of substitutability between these extremes, giving rise to social indifference curves that lie in between those of Benthamite straight lines and Rawlsian L-shapes. Graph 29.3 illustrates how we can choose the best allocation of utilities using different social indifference curves.

For the particular example illustrated in Graph 29.3, it turns out that each of our sets of social indifference curves picks out the exact same point on the utility possibility frontier. This is because we have assumed that both the utility possibility frontier and the social indifference curves are symmetrical, meaning that if we draw a 45-degree line, both the indifference curves and the utility possibility frontier below the 45-degree line are mirror images of the indifference curves and the utility possibility frontier above the 45-degree line. As we will argue in the next section, it is often natural to assume that social indifference curves are symmetrical in this way because that implies that all individuals are treated equally by the ethical criterion we are choosing to evaluate social outcomes. As we have already seen in our development of second-best utility possibility frontiers, it is far from obvious why we should assume that utility possibility frontiers are generally symmetrical.

Graph 29.3 Three Sets of Social Indifference Curves

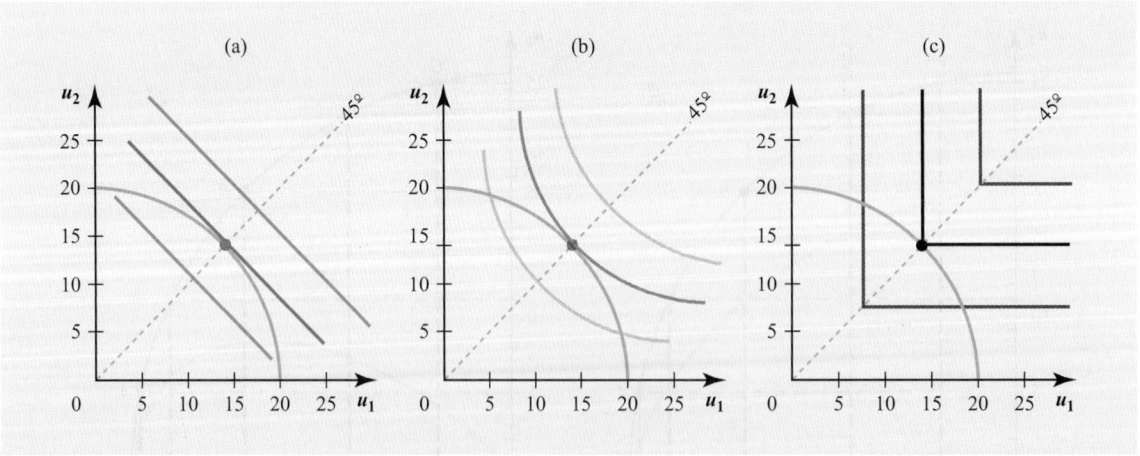

Consider, for instance, two second-best utility possibility frontiers such as those in Graph 29.4. In panel (a), the social preferences represented by (dark blue) Rawlsian social indifference curves that treat utilities as perfect complements result in point *A* being optimal, while the social preferences represented by (dark brown) Benthamite social indifference curves that treat utilities as perfect substitutes result in point *B* being optimal. Panel (b) of Graph 29.4 further illustrates how when second-best taxation is used for redistribution, the optimal outcome can lie off the 45-degree line even when utilities are perfect complements in the social indifference curves. The disappearance of the symmetry of the first-best utility possibility frontier due to second-best taxation creates a divergence of what we consider optimal depending on how we feel about the relative substitutability of individual utilities.

Graph 29.4 Choosing What Is Best With Second-Best Utility Possibility Frontiers

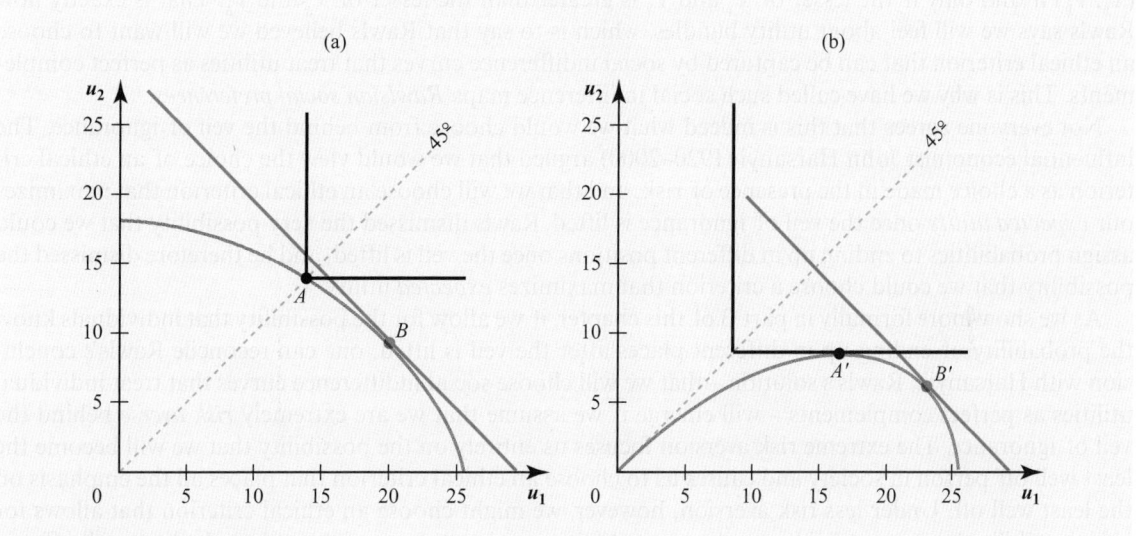

Exercise 29A.22

True or False: Symmetrical social preferences that view utilities as somewhat substitutable – that is, social preferences that give rise to indifference curves between the extremes of perfect complements and perfect substitutes – would result in optimal allocations that lie between *A* and *B* in panel (a) of Graph 29.4.

29A.3.4 Choosing Social Indifference Curves From Behind a Veil of Ignorance Given that different social indifference curves give different answers to what is best, how are we to choose the set of social indifference curves that should guide our policy choices? Given what we know from Arrow's Theorem, we cannot say that social preferences are those that emerge from democratic political processes because Arrow's Theorem tells us that democratic processes do not give rise to well-defined social preferences. Rather, the question is fundamentally an ethical question, and the answer therefore involves taking a philosophical stand on what *should* matter to us.

One conceptual approach that philosophers have developed to help us think through this issue is that of imagining that we have to choose an ethical criterion prior to knowing what position in society we actually occupy. Imagine that we are taken out of this world and placed behind a 'veil of ignorance' that conceals from us who we are in this world. Behind this veil, in a place that philosophers call the original position, we do not know whether we are born to rich or poor parents, whether we like Coke or Pepsi, whether we are clever or not so clever, beautiful or not, and so on. All we know is the various places that will exist in the world, any one of which we might actually end up occupying. In placing ourselves behind this veil, would we be able to agree on some ethical criterion that should guide how we will agree to evaluate social outcomes once we are born?

In his famous work *A Theory of Justice* (1971), John Rawls argues that we will choose a very particular answer from this position of ignorance – that we will find ourselves desiring a society that maximizes the welfare of the least well off individual. This would imply that in comparing different social outcomes, we will say that outcome A is better than outcome B if and only if the least well off individual under A is better off than the least well off individual under B. Notice that this is analogous to how a consumer who considers x and y perfect complements evaluates bundles of x and y. If x is tea and y is sugar, the individual cares only about how many drinkable beverages they have, and if they have 10 teas and 5 sugars, they only have 5 drinkable beverages. Bundle $A = (x_A, y_A)$ for such a consumer is better than bundle $A = (x_B, y_B)$ if and only if the lesser of x_A and y_A is greater than the lesser of x_B and y_B. That is exactly how Rawls says we will feel about utility bundles, which is to say that Rawls believed we will want to choose an ethical criterion that can be captured by social indifference curves that treat utilities as perfect complements. This is why we have called such social indifference maps *Rawlsian social preferences*.

Not everyone agrees that this is indeed what we would choose from behind the veil of ignorance. The influential economist John Harsanyi (1920–2000) argued that we would view the choice of an ethical criterion as a choice made in the presence of risk, and that we will choose an ethical criterion that maximizes our *expected utility* once the veil of ignorance is lifted. Rawls dismissed the very possibility that we could assign probabilities to ending up in different positions once the veil is lifted, and he therefore dismissed the possibility that we could choose a criterion that maximizes *expected* utility.

As we show more formally in part B of this chapter, if we allow for the possibility that individuals know the probability of ending up in different places after the veil is lifted, one can reconcile Rawls's conclusion with Harsanyi's. Rawls's solution – that we will choose social indifference curves that treat individual utilities as perfect complements – will emerge if we assume that we are extremely *risk averse* behind the veil of ignorance. The extreme risk aversion focuses us entirely on the possibility that we will become the least well off person in society and causes us to choose an ethical criterion that places all the emphasis on the least well off. Under less risk aversion, however, we might choose an ethical criterion that allows for substitutability between individual utility, accepting some risk that we might end up the least well off and worse off than under Rawls's criterion in exchange for higher utility if we end up not being so unlucky.

It seems that the conceptual device of imagining a veil of ignorance behind which an ethical criterion is chosen does *not* result in unanimous agreement among philosophers (or economists) about the types of social indifference curves that should guide our ethical judgments about what is good. There are, however, some areas on which there is agreement. First, it seems likely that we would agree to choose a point *on* at least the second-best utility possibility frontier, not a point that lies inside the utility possibility set. Furthermore, if the utility possibility frontier takes on a second-best shape such as that in panel (b) of Graph 29.2, it seems likely that we will *not* choose a point on the upward-sloping part of the frontier, at least not unless we allow envy to enter the calculation. We would almost certainly choose an ethical criterion that satisfies at least some notion of efficiency, even if it is a second-best notion of efficiency that accepts some deadweight losses from redistributive taxation. Second, it seems unlikely that not knowing who we will be in society, we would choose social indifference curves that would value the utility combination (u_a, u_b) more or less than the utility combination (u_b, u_a). Since the individual does not know if they will be individual 1 or individual 2, they will choose an ethical criterion that treats individuals 1 and 2 *symmetrically*.

29A.3.5 From Unmeasurable Utility to Measurable Outcomes Although practitioners in the happiness literature may disagree, most economists would still argue that it is difficult if not impossible to ever arrive at objective measures of utility. This difficulty limits the degree to which we can actually use the philosophical insights discussed thus far to guide actual evaluation of policy. If one is inclined to make ethical judgments that go beyond efficiency in evaluating outcomes from alternative institutional arrangements, one has to look for measurable outcomes on which to base these judgments. Personal income and consumption are two possible candidates for such measurable outcomes.

Rather than putting individual utilities on the axes of our graphs, we could put individual incomes on the axes, and we could define social indifference maps over income bundles just as we defined social indifference curves over utility bundles. Treating income as perfectly substitutable across individuals would imply that we have social preferences that cause us to choose policies that maximize *total* income in society. Treating individual incomes as perfect complements, on the other hand, would imply Rawlsian social preferences that cause us to maximize the income of the lowest income individual in society; we could again define many social preferences that fall in between these extremes.

Exercise 29A.23

Suppose that government income redistribution programmes cause no change in behaviour. *True or False*: The Rawlsian social indifference curves would imply full redistribution of income; that is, full income equality after redistribution.

Exercise 29A.24

Now suppose that government redistribution programmes cause changes in behaviour such as those predicted by the Laffer Curve from Chapter 8. Can you argue that Rawlsian social indifference curves would now imply less than full redistribution; that is, some income inequality would remain after the Rawlsian redistribution programme has been implemented?

Even this approach, despite now being fully based on observable outcomes, is often too involved to make certain kinds of real-world comparisons between institutional arrangements. As a result, economists have developed alternative tools to capture the degree of inequality that arises under different circumstances. A full description of these is beyond the scope of this text, and so we offer just one common example known as the *Gini coefficient*.

In Graph 29.5, we illustrate how this Gini coefficient is calculated.

Graph 29.5 Lorenz Curves

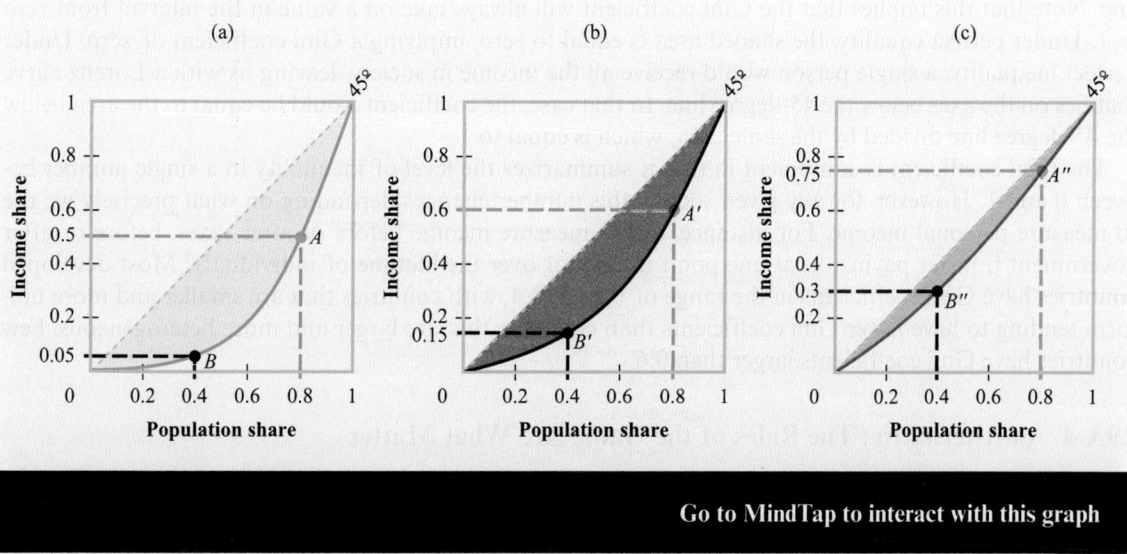

Go to MindTap to interact with this graph

The horizontal axis of each of the panels has the cumulative share of individuals from lowest to highest income. For instance, 0.4 on this axis represents the person who has a level of income such that 40 per cent of the population is poorer and 60 per cent is richer. The vertical axis, on the other hand, has the cumulative share of income earned, or the fraction of the society's income that accrues to the different segments of society. For instance, point B in panel (a) indicates that the poorest 40 per cent of the population earn just 5 per cent of the total income in society. Point A indicates that the poorest 80 per cent earn 50 per cent of total income, or the top 20 per cent earn half of all income. For any distribution of income in a society, we can therefore plot such a relationship, which is called the *Lorenz curve*.

Complete equality of income would imply that the poorest individuals earn the same percentage of total income as the richest. Thus, the poorest 5 per cent would earn 5 per cent of total income, the poorest 25 per cent would earn 25 per cent of total income, and the poorest 75 per cent would earn 75 per cent. This implies that full equality would result in a Lorenz curve that lies exactly on the 45-degree line. The sequence of panels in Graph 29.5 begins with a relatively unequal income distribution and moves towards greater equality.

Exercise 29A.25

Can the relationship in these graphs ever cross the 45-degree line?

Exercise 29A.26

Using the points analogous to A and B from panel (a) in Graph 29.5, show how panels (b) and (c) represent an increasingly equal income distribution.

The Gini coefficient, named after the Italian statistician Corrado Gini (1884–1965), is defined as the shaded area between the Lorenz curve and the 45-degree line divided by the area underneath the 45-degree line. Note that this implies that the Gini coefficient will always take on a value in the interval from zero to 1. Under perfect equality, the shaded area is equal to zero, implying a Gini coefficient of zero. Under perfect inequality, a single person would receive all the income in society, leaving us with a Lorenz curve that lies on the axes below the 45-degree line. In that case, the coefficient would be equal to the area below the 45-degree line divided by the same area, which is equal to 1.

The Gini coefficient is convenient in that it summarizes the level of inequality in a single number between 0 and 1. However, for any given society this number changes depending on what precisely we use to measure personal income. For instance, do we measure income before or after taxes, before or after government transfer payments, at one point in time or over the lifetime of individuals? Most developed countries have Gini coefficients in the range of 0.25 to 0.4, with countries that are smaller and more uniform tending to have lower Gini coefficients than countries that are larger and more heterogeneous. Few countries have Gini coefficients larger than 0.6.

29A.4 An Alternative: The Rules of the Game Are What Matter

We introduced the previous section by pointing out that we were initially focused solely on the consequences or outcomes of different institutions, which gave rise to a purely consequentialist approach to thinking about what is good. This is the most common way in which economists tend to think of normative questions. We are good at predicting consequences of institutional incentives using the positive economics we have developed throughout the text, and those consequences form the basis for how most economists think about the desirability of different policies.

Not all economists take this view, however. Part of the reason for this is the recognition that in the absence of objective measures of utility that allow for interpersonal utility comparisons, the consequentialist approach loses some of its natural appeal. If we think of measurable outcomes as those that enter social welfare functions, outcomes such as income or consumption, we are implicitly making much more fundamental normative judgments than if we were able to use the more abstract utility-based approach. Individuals with a love for teaching, for instance, might choose lower paying careers in education because they derive more utility from the combination of teaching and the accompanying salary than they would from higher paying jobs that carry with them less personal satisfaction. By using individual income or measurable consumption as the basis for thinking about equity, we miss the non-pecuniary benefits society offers to teachers. Should it really violate our sense of equity if a teacher makes less money than an engineer even if they are equally happy?

The philosopher Robert Nozick (1938–2002), in response to Rawls's *A Theory of Justice*, defended a different approach that is now embraced by some economists. Nozick argued that you cannot judge whether an observed distribution of income is just by observing the distribution; rather, you have to know how the distribution came about. If the starting point was just, he viewed the distribution of income or wealth or utility that emerges from that starting point as also just as long as the distribution was brought about by free exchange between consenting adults. If an individual chooses to have less income because they love teaching and teachers don't get paid as much in the market, this does not take away from the justness of the observed distribution because the person voluntarily chooses to trade off income with teaching satisfaction.

What mattered to Nozick is not how equal or unequal the current distribution of resources in a society is; the Gini coefficient is not relevant because it is a summary index of consequences that arose from choices made by people who started at some starting point. The questions that need to be answered to determine whether a society is just are: (1) was the starting point just and (2) did people freely choose their path from that point forward? If the starting point was just, and if the rules of the game were such that choices were made voluntarily and freely, there is nothing more to be gleaned from observing the outcome. You may notice that this perspective tends to lead to a decidedly libertarian view of government in society, government as an enforcer of contracts and property rights that allow individuals to engage in free and voluntary exchange.

Exercise 29A.27

Under what conditions would Nozick's just society lead to efficient outcomes?

The libertarian conclusion on the role of government presumes that the starting point was just to begin with. This raises the question of what we mean by the starting point and what conclusions we would draw about the role of government if we judge that starting point to be unjust. Uniform access to quality education, for instance, would seem to many as a necessary condition for the starting point to be truly just, but if parental incomes are vastly unequal, it is unlikely that children from different backgrounds really start at positions that are equitably distributed unless non-market institutions ensure access to education that is largely independent of parental income. Nozick's emphasis on starting points may therefore lead to more egalitarian policy prescriptions than might be apparent at first, although the nature of such policies would be more focused on ensuring equal opportunity rather than equal outcomes.

It is likely that economists who take the Nozick non-consequentialist position often do so in part for consequentialist reasons because they conclude from the first welfare theorem that the voluntary exchange in markets is the primary means through which welfare gains arise in a competitive economy. One might be a consequentialist in the sense that one takes consequences, rather than starting points and fair rules, as the basis for making moral judgments about what is good, but at the same time one believes that ensuring equitable starting points and allowing voluntary exchange to govern the end point is the best means to obtaining good consequences. In that sense, the views articulated by Rawls and Nozick might be at least partially reconciled.

29B	Some Tools in the Search for What Is Good

In Section A, we have tried to present some challenges to the material covered in the previous chapters in light of the larger question of how one might take some of the insights of this text and move from the positive question 'what is?' to the normative question 'what is good?' We'll make no attempt in Section B to replicate this overview, but we instead go into somewhat greater depth in particular dimensions.

29B.1 Probing Deeper Into Aspects of Behavioural Economics

We begin with the challenges economists face from the field of psychology. Behavioural economists do not dispense with the basic underlying framework used throughout this book and premised on the assertion that individuals try to do the best they can given their circumstances. Motivated by behavioural anomalies that are not easily explained within the standard microeconomics approach, they find ways of modelling tastes and circumstances with insights from psychology in mind. While it is often the case that there are other ways of tweaking standard models to bring their predictions in line with these empirical anomalies, behavioural economics sometimes offers the simplest and intuitively most compelling mechanisms. We focused in Section A especially on present-bias and reference-based decision making, and we now return to these topics in somewhat greater depth.

29B.1.1 Time-Inconsistent Tastes and Present-Bias
In Section A, we raised the fact that some individuals appear to have present-biased preferences that lead to self-control problems. One way to explain this is that such individuals discount the immediate future more heavily than the more distant future, thus searching for immediate gratification now while intending to invest for the future in the future. If preferences are truly present-biased, they will be so again in future presents, resulting in more search for immediate gratification combined with intentions to invest for the future in the yet-to-come future.

The model we introduced was the beta-delta model, a model in which trade-offs between costs and benefits between future periods are made just as they are in standard economic models. Trade-offs between future periods and the present are made with a bias towards consuming benefits in the present and postponing costs to the future. Crucially, the assumption is that the increased discounting of the future from the present is not just a phenomenon linked to the particular period in which we find ourselves but is linked to the idea of present that moves forward in time and thus changes future discount rates as the future becomes the present.

Extending the beta-delta model to more than three periods is trivial in that it only involves multiplying *all* δ discount terms by β. If we consider an investment project that costs c in t periods but will create benefit b in $(t + n)$ periods, we would conclude that the investment will be worth undertaking as long as $\beta\delta^t c < \beta\delta^{t(t+n)}$ or $c < \delta^n b$. When period t becomes period 0 and the future present has arrived, we will want to undertake the project only if $c < \beta\delta^n b$, which is a different rule than we had planned on using unless $\beta = 1$. Thus, just as in the three-period case, the beta-delta model introduces no bias between future periods, only a bias between now and any future period.

In Section A, we mentioned the danger of confusing the concept of *impatience* in the standard model of discounting with the idea of *present-bias* in the beta-delta model. A second danger is that many believe the model differs from the standard neoclassical model in that it permits discount rates to change. This is not so, with changing discount rates being neither problematic for the standard approach nor giving rise to time-inconsistent decision rules. To be sure, economists often assume constant discounting, but they do so more as a matter of convenience than necessity, not because changing discount rates will somehow give rise to time inconsistencies.

For instance, a person can plan to discount the future more as they get older, and as they look ahead and try to guess whether some investment will be worthwhile when they are 55, for example, they will come up with exactly the same decision rule as the one they will end up following when they are 55 *as long as the discount rates actually follow the pattern that they anticipate as the future becomes the present.* More generally, suppose that this person considers at time $t = 0$ an investment c in period t that results in a benefit b in period $(t + n)$, and suppose that they view €1 in period i as equivalent to €δ in period $(i + 1)$, with no restriction on how δ_i relates to δ_j for periods $i \neq j$. Looking ahead from period 0, they will think the investment in period t worthwhile as long as:

$$\delta_1\delta_2...\delta_t c < (\delta_1\delta_2...\delta_t)\delta_{t+1}\delta_{t+2}...\delta_{t+n}b \qquad (29.1)$$

which simplifies to:

$$c < \delta_{t+1}\delta_{t+2}...\delta_{t+n}b. \qquad (29.2)$$

The latter is the same as the decision rule they will use to determine whether the investment is worthwhile when they get to period t and actually have to pull the trigger on making or not making the investment c. *Time-consistent choice does not require constant discounting.* The key is that the different values of δ are attached to time periods defined in an absolute sense; that is, each subscript might refer to a specific calendar year or a specific age that they will be in that period, and they are not defined in a relative sense that would imply δ_t is always the relevant discount term t periods from now. t refers to a point in time is referred to as t as we allow discount terms to vary, not to a period of delay from the present moment.

In the same way, the beta-delta model does not require a single δ and can be governed by different δ's across *absolute* time as long as β continues to play the same role as before. With deltas as specified, we will get the same result as before – that is, the decision rule in equation (29.2) – as we contemplate an investment in the future, but we will get a less patient decision rule once t rolls around and becomes the present.

Exercise 29B.1

Demonstrate that the last sentence is true.

The beta-delta model does not add time-varying discount rates to economics; rather, it brings into economics the psychologist's idea that our discounting rule is present-biased, and thus alters our anticipated discount rates as the future becomes the present. It is one simple way to model self-control problems, one that has considerable intuitive appeal.

Exercise 29B.2

In exercise 29A.2, we implicitly assumed that δ is constant over time. Would allowing for the possible change in δ over time allow for the standard model to explain what we previously concluded only the beta-delta model could explain?

Finally, it is worth mentioning that the beta-delta model is also known as a model of *quasi-hyperbolic discounting* because it is a tractable simplification of a previously employed hyperbolic discounting model in which the present-bias is not as discrete as it is in the beta-delta model. The beta-delta model assumes that we don't change at all how future periods are traded off against one another, only how the future is being traded off against the present. More general hyperbolic discounting models soften this discreteness in difference between how the future is treated relative to the present versus how the more distant future is treated relative to the more immediate future. As a result, some models of hyperbolic discounting allow the bias to extend beyond the immediate present. In the end, however, it is often most convenient to focus on the simplest of all models that captures what we are after, and the beta-delta model is therefore frequently employed over less tractable hyperbolic discounting models for precisely this reason.

29B.1.2 Reference Points, Risk and Prospect Theory We mentioned in Section A the idea of reference points and the related notion of loss aversion that arises when we find that incurring losses is particularly difficult psychologically. The underlying theory, known as *prospect theory*, first put forward by Amos Tverski (1937–1996) and Daniel Kahneman (1934–), is actually more general than this and deals in particular with how people confront risk in many situations where the standard neoclassical approach does not predict well.

Suppose you face a gamble in which you will get a payoff of x_1 with probability δ and x_2 with probability $(1 - \delta)$. Prospect theory says that you will evaluate this gamble using the function:

$$\pi(\delta)u(x_1 - r) + \pi(1 - \delta)u(x_2 - r), \tag{29.3}$$

where r is a reference point and π is a function that transforms the real underlying probabilities with which the two events are likely to occur. Notice that our standard expected utility formulation of gambles is contained within this equation as a special case, with $\pi(\delta) = \delta$, $\pi(1 - \delta) = (1 - \delta)$, and $r = 0$.

Exercise 29B.3

Explain the last sentence.

For any $r \neq 0$, this formulation of utility in the presence of risk instantly becomes *reference dependent*. The phenomenon of *loss aversion* as described in Section A comes about if the utility function u is kinked at the reference point, with losses from the reference point weighted more heavily than gains. For instance, if the reference point is $r = 1000$ and $(x_1, x_2) = (800, 1200)$, x_1 is interpreted as a loss while x_2 is interpreted as a gain. Under loss aversion, $-u(-200) > u(200)$. These are the two types of effects that we mentioned in Section A.

Exercise 29B.4

In one set of experiments, individuals were asked how much they would be willing to pay to participate in a gamble in which they receive €8 when a coin comes up heads but owe €5 if it comes up tails. Close to two-thirds were not willing to pay anything, which can be explained in the standard expected utility framework only if we are willing to assume a level of risk aversion that is roughly equivalent to such individuals never leaving their house for fear of all the risks they will encounter. Can you rationalize the results of the experiment for a risk-averse individual using only the parts of prospect theory that incorporate reference bias and loss aversion?

Our formulation here, however, allows for two additional effects that appear to be important in at least some settings. First, Tversky and Kahneman hypothesized that the utility function used to evaluate equation (29.3) is concave over gains and convex over losses, giving rise to *diminishing sensitivity* of outcomes as we move further from the reference point. Consider again $r = 1000$ and $(x_1, x_2) = (800,1200)$ and compare it to the outcome pair $(x_1', x_2') = (600,1400)$. Diminishing sensitivity implies that this doubling of the distance away from the reference point affects the individual less in either direction than the initial deviation from the reference point.

To clarify this further, consider a famous experiment that starts with subjects randomly assigned to two different groups. Individuals in Group 1 are given €1000 as they enter the room while individuals in Group 2 are given €2000. In each group, individuals can choose between one of two options as outlined in Table 29.4. The *A* option involves no risk and has individuals leaving the experiment with €1500, with those in Group 1 receiving an additional €500 on top of the €1000 they initially received, while those in Group 2 have to give up €500 of the €2000 they initially received. The *B* option, on the other hand, involves risk, giving individuals in both groups a 50 per cent chance of walking away with €2000 and a 50 per cent chance of leaving with only €1000. It turns out that 84 per cent in Group 1 but only 31 per cent in Group 2 chose the safer *A* option.

Table 29.4 An Experiment to Illustrate Prospect Theory	
Group 1	**Group 2**
Subjects given €1000 as they enter the room.	Subjects given €2000 as they enter the room.
Option 1A: Get €500 more and leave the experiment.	Option 2A: Give up €500 and leave the experiment.
Option 1B: Accept a gamble where a coin toss results in an additional €1000 if the coin comes up heads and nothing more if it comes up tails.	Option 2B: Accept a gamble where a coin toss results in a loss of €1000 if the coin comes up heads and nothing if it comes up tails.

In panel (a) of Graph 29.6, we illustrate why our standard expected utility theory from Chapter 17 cannot rationalize what happens in this experiment. In the graph, we model a utility/consumption relationship that allows us to express a risk-averse individual's utility from taking gambles as an expected utility. Options 1*B* and 2*B* are identical in that the subject in each case faces an equal chance of being able to consume €1000 plus whatever other income x they have and consuming €2000 plus whatever other income x they have. Options 1*A* and 2*A* are similarly identical in the sense that the subjects in both cases leave the experiment with €1500 more consumption than they could get before the experiment. Expected utility theory therefore predicts that $u_{1A} = u_{2A}$ and $u_{1B} = u_{2B}$, implying that approximately the same number of subjects in the two groups should pick option *A* over option *B* when subjects are randomly assigned to both groups, but a lot more people in Group 1 end up doing so than in Group 2.

Exercise 29B.5

Demonstrate that the same conclusion – that is, that $u_{1A} = u_{2A}$ and $u_{1B} = u_{2B}$ – arises when tastes are risk loving. How are the options ranked differently by each group relative to risk aversion?

Panels (b) and (c) of Graph 29.6 illustrate how prospect theory can rationalize the outcome of the experiment *if the subjects use the amount of money they are handed at the outset as a reference point* against which to compare alternatives. Those in Group 1 get €1000 as they walk into the experiment, and thus the reference point r is €1000 as in panel (b). Those in Group 2, on the other hand, are handed €2000 as they walk into the experiment, and thus r = €2000 for them. In Group 1, everything that follows is interpreted as a gain, and thus is evaluated by the dark brown portion of the *u* function that lies to the right of r in panel (b) where the function is concave. In Group 2, on the other hand, everything that follows is interpreted as a loss, and thus is evaluated on the dark blue portion of the *u* function that lies to the left of r in panel (c) where the function is convex. Note that the shape of the function on both sides of the reference point exhibits diminishing sensitivity. As a result, you can see that $u_{1B} < u_{1A}$, implying that prospect theory predicts individuals in Group 1 will choose the safe *A* option. In panel (c), $u_{2A} < u_{2B}$, implying that the theory predicts individuals in Group 2 will choose the riskier *B* option instead. Notice that prospect theory therefore implies *risk aversion when people evaluate gains and risk loving when they evaluate losses*.

Graph 29.6 Prospect Theory Versus Standard Expected Utility Theory

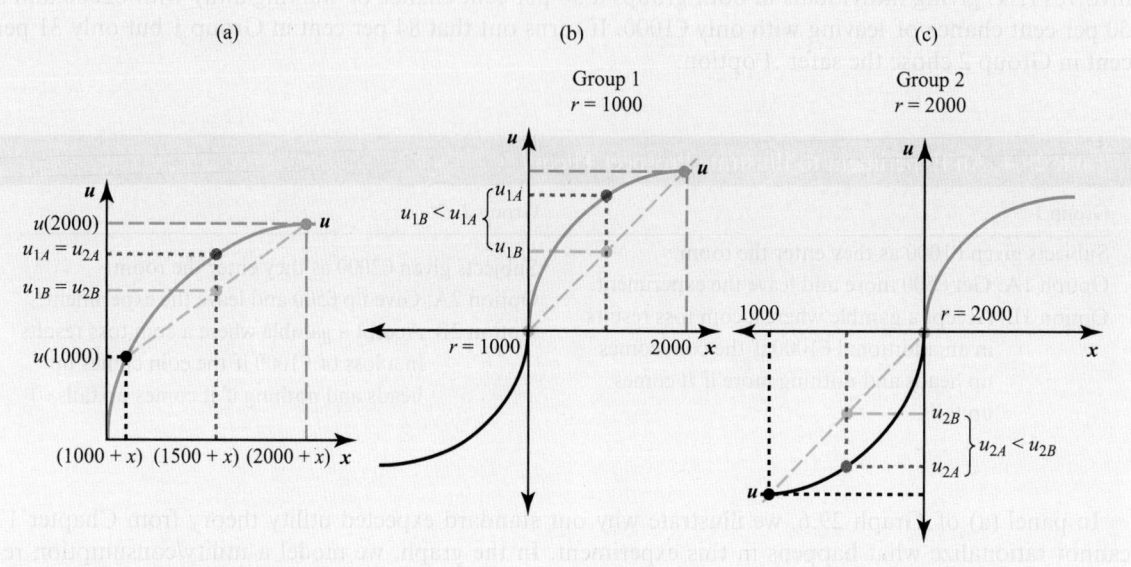

Exercise 29B.6

Can you explain how *diminishing sensitivity* gives rise to the switch between risk loving and risk aversion at the reference point?

The second additional effect allowed for in equation (29.3) is known as *probability weighting*. This arises because the equation suggests that individuals might not consider the actual probabilities of events, i.e. δ and $(1 - \delta)$, but rather some transformation π of these probabilities, with experimental and empirical evidence suggesting that π overweights small probabilities and underweights large probabilities. This offers an immediate possible explanation for how otherwise risk-averse people who buy insurance against all sorts of risks in their lives go out and buy lottery tickets that offer them a tiny probability of winning a large amount with an expected payoff that is negative. It may also help explain why individuals appear to consistently choose to pay substantially higher than actuarially fair insurance for small and relatively low-probability risks like small losses in homeowner's insurance policies.

Exercise 29B.7

Explain how probability weighting can make sense of the fact that risk-averse individuals play in lotteries. How can it explain purchases of insurance against small, low-probability risks when insurance policies are priced far from actuarially fair?

29B.2 Normative Economics When Consequences Matter

In Section A, we referred to different ways in which economists and philosophers might approach normative economics in the abstract and in practice, with the most common approach used by economists taking on a highly *consequentialist* flavour. Economists typically believe that the normative answer to what is good will depend a great deal on the positive answer to the question what is or what will be. Thus, knowing the consequences of different options we choose from will assist us in deciding which option is good and which isn't. In the abstract treatment of such an approach to normative economics, we can assume that we know the utility consequences of different options for different individuals and use a *social welfare function* that acts as a utility function over utility allocations to choose what is good. Thus, the social welfare function embodies within it normative or ethical judgments about distributional issues within societies, with some social welfare functions being more egalitarian in their focus on equality and some more utilitarian in their focus on overall societal utility.

We will leave some of the more practical concerns raised in Section A, such as measurement of happiness, largely untouched here and instead illustrate some of the basics of this approach to normative economics. We will, however, focus towards the end of the chapter on the Rawlsian assertion that were we to be able to choose from behind a veil of ignorance, we would tend to choose a society governed by Rawlsian social welfare functions and will present an economist's approach to the assertion and a challenge to it.

29B.2.1 First-Best and Second-Best Utility Possibility Frontiers

In Section A, we derived utility possibility frontiers from the contract curve in an exchange economy and distinguished between first-best and second-best utility possibility frontiers, with the former assuming the availability of efficient redistributive taxation while the latter constrains governments to using distortionary taxes. We illustrate here an example of how first- and second-best frontiers differ.

Suppose that consumer 1 is endowed with one normalized unit of leisure time, any fraction of which can be turned into an equal amount of private consumption through labour effort at a wage normalized to 1. Thus, if ℓ denotes their leisure consumption, their private good consumption c_1 in the absence of taxation is $(1 - \ell)$. Suppose further that individual 2 is not able to work and thus unable to earn an income. The only way that individual 2 can thus consume $c_2 > 0$ is if the government redistributes resources from individual 1 to individual 2. Assume the utility functions are given by:

$$u_1 = 2c_1^{1/2}\ell^{1/2} \text{ and } u_2 = c_2. \tag{29.4}$$

Consider first the case of an efficient lump sum tax that is used to redistribute a fraction T of consumer 1's endowment. Under such a non-distortionary tax, individual 1's endowment therefore shrinks from 1 to $(1 - T)$, and their consumption now becomes $(1 - T - \ell)$. We can solve for consumer 1's optimizing choice of leisure and consumption as $\ell^* = (1 - T)/2$ and $c_1^* = (1 - T)/2$, with consumer 2 receiving the lump sum transfer T and thus consuming $c_2 = T = u_2$. Substituting ℓ^* and c_1^* into consumer 1's utility function and substituting $u_2 = T$, we get:

$$u_1 = 2\left(\frac{(1 - T)}{2}\right)^{1/2}\left(\frac{(1 - T)}{2}\right)^{1/2} = (1 - T) = 1 - u_2, \tag{29.5}$$

which gives us the linear first-best utility possibility frontier $u_1 = 1 - u_2$.

Exercise 29B.8

Verify the derivation of this first-best utility possibility frontier.

Exercise 29B.9*

In Section A, we suggested that the shape of the utility possibility frontier has something to do with our assumptions about the marginal utility of income. Can you apply this insight here to explain the linear utility possibility frontier in our example?

Next, suppose instead that the government uses a distortionary tax t levied on individual 1's earnings $(1 - \ell)$. Depending on individual 1's leisure choice ℓ, the consumption levels for our two individuals will be:

$$c_1 = (1 - t)(1 - \ell) \text{ and } c_2 = t(1 - \ell). \tag{29.6}$$

Solving individual 1's utility maximization problem, we get their optimal choice as $\ell^* = 1/2$ and $c_1^* = (1 - t)/2$, with individual 2 receiving $c_2 = t(1 - \ell^*) = t/2$. Substituting ℓ^* and c_1^* into consumer 1's utility function, we conclude:

$$u_1 = 2\left(\frac{(1 - t)}{2}\right)^{1/2}\left(\frac{1}{2}\right)^{1/2} = (1 - t)^{1/2}. \tag{29.7}$$

With $c_1 = t/2$, we have $u_2 = t/2$ and can therefore substitute $t = 2u_2$ into our expression for u_1 to get the second-best utility possibility frontier $u_1 = (1 - 2u_2)^{1/2}$.

When we now solve our first- and second-best utility possibility frontiers for u_2, we can also express them as:

$$\text{First-Best Utility Possibility Frontier:} \quad u_2 = 1 - u_1$$

$$\text{Second-Best Utility Possibility Frontier:} \quad u_2 = \frac{1 - u_1^2}{2}. \tag{29.8}$$

Exercise 29B.10

Verify the derivation of the second-best utility possibility frontier.

Exercise 29B.11

Can you graph these two utility possibility frontiers and explain their relationship intuitively?

29B.2.2 Social Welfare Functions A social welfare function is the social planner's utility function over the two consumers' utility levels; that is, it is a function W that has u_1 and u_2 instead of the usual two consumption goods as its arguments. Such a function might, for instance, take the Cobb–Douglas form:

$$W = u_1^\alpha u_2^{(1 - \alpha)} \tag{29.9}$$

and the social planner's problem would be to maximize this function subject to the utility possibility constraint. In the case of our first-best constraint, the planner's problem would be:

$$\max_{u_1, u_2} \ W = u_1^\alpha u_2^{(1-\alpha)} \text{ subject to } u_2 = 1 - u_1, \tag{29.10}$$

which, when solved in the usual way, gives us the first-best optimum of:

$$u_1^{FB} = \alpha \text{ and } u_2^{FB} = (1 - \alpha). \tag{29.11}$$

If the social planner can only use the distortionary tax t, their problem is instead:

$$\max_{u_1, u_2} \ W = u_1^\alpha u_2^{(1-\alpha)} \text{ subject to } u_2 = \frac{1 - u_1^2}{2} \tag{29.12}$$

and the solution to this problem is:

$$u_1^{SB} = \left(\frac{\alpha}{2 - \alpha} \right)^{1/2} \text{ and } u_2^{SB} = \frac{1 - \alpha}{2 - \alpha}. \tag{29.13}$$

Exercise 29B.12

Verify these solutions for the different social welfare functions.

Table 29.5 First- and Second-Best Social Welfare Maxima

Cobb–Douglas Social Welfare Function $W = u_1^\alpha u_2^{(1-\alpha)}$

α	0.00	0.25	0.50	0.75	1.00
First-Best u_1	0.000	0.250	0.500	0.750	1.000
Second-Best u_1	0.000	0.378	0.577	0.775	1.000
First-Best u_2	1.000	0.750	0.500	0.250	0.000
Second-Best u_2	0.500	0.429	0.333	0.200	0.000

In Table 29.5, we calculate the first- and second-best utility levels for different α values in the social welfare function, where α is the relative weight the social welfare function places on individual 1's utility. When $\alpha = 0$, for instance, no weight is placed on u_1, implying that the optimum will be zero utility for individual 1, and this holds in both the first- and second-best case. Note that u_2 is only half as large in the second-best case as in the first-best case, a direct consequence of the fact that the second-best utility possibility frontier has a u_2 intercept half as large as the first-best utility possibility frontier. When $\alpha = 1$, on the other hand, the entire social weight is placed on individual 1, who ends up getting all the utility. Now, however, the first- and second-best cases are identical because the social optimum in both cases requires no redistribution and thus no distortionary tax in the second-best case. In between these extreme values of α, consumer 1 always gets more utility under the second-best case and consumer 2 gets less because the social planner will not redistribute as much when the tax is distortionary.

Exercise 29B.13

We have implicitly assumed that we can measure individual utilities in order to construct first- and second-best utility possibility frontiers. Suppose instead that we can only measure consumption. What would the first- and second-best consumption possibilities frontiers look like for our example?

Exercise 29B.14

Might a government that derives the first- and second-best consumption possibilities frontiers from exercise 29B.13 mistakenly think that there is no efficiency loss from redistribution? How does your conclusion illustrate our conclusion from earlier chapters that deadweight loss from labour taxes cannot be derived by looking at uncompensated labour supply curves?

Exercise 29B.15

If a government used the second-best consumption possibility frontier as if it were the appropriate utility possibility frontier, would it redistribute too much or too little relative to what it would do if it could measure utilities?

29B.2.3 Rawls Versus Bentham There is, of course, no particular reason to assume a Cobb–Douglas functional form for the social welfare function that gives expression to the ethical criterion we are using to choose socially optimal outcomes from efficient outcomes. For instance, we know from our development of utility functions in Chapter 5 that the Cobb–Douglas specification of utility is a special case of the more general constant elasticity of substitution specification, with perfect complements and perfect substitutes as the two most extreme special cases. In Section A, we similarly introduced the Rawlsian notion of social indifference curves that treat individual utility levels as prefect complements and would thus give rise to a *Rawlsian social welfare function* of the form:

$$W = \min\{u_1, u_2\}. \tag{29.14}$$

We also explored the opposite extreme of social indifference curves that treat individual utilities as perfect substitutes. The social welfare function that gives rise to such indifference curves is known as the *Benthamite social welfare function* and takes the form:

$$W = u_1 + u_2. \tag{29.15}$$

Since the Rawlsian social welfare function has indifference curves with right angles along the 45-degree line, we know that the social optimum will lie at the intersection of the 45-degree line and the utility possibility frontier as long as the utility possibility frontier is always downward sloping, which occurs at $u_1 = u_2 = 0.5$ in our first-best example and at $u_1 = u_2 \approx 0.414$ in our second-best example. Alternatively, we can consider the social optimum under the Benthamite function that gives rise to linear indifference curves with slope equal to -1. Since our example has a first-best utility possibility frontier that is also linear with slope -1, all utility allocations on the first-best frontier sum to the same total utility value and are thus all optimal according to this Benthamite social welfare function. In our second-best case, however, the only way to attain this much utility involves no distortionary redistribution, and thus the Benthamite social welfare function would choose the allocation $(u_1, u_2) = (1, 0)$ in the second-best case.

Exercise 29B.16

Can you draw the first- and second-best utility possibility frontiers and indicate how you would graphically arrive at the same results?

Exercise 29B.17

We concluded that the Benthamite, Rawlsian and Cobb–Douglas social welfare function with $\alpha = 0.5$ all agree that the first-best utility allocation $u_1 = u_2 = 0.5$ is optimal, but we also found that they quite dramatically disagree on what the second-best utility allocation is. Explain why.

29B.2.4 Risk Aversion Behind the Veil of Ignorance In Section A, we concluded our more abstract treatment of consequentialist normative economics with a discussion of how one might go about choosing the ethical criterion that should shape our social welfare function. Imagine again, as we discussed at more length in Section A, that you are asked to think about this criterion for social welfare from the original position behind the veil of ignorance. You know you will eventually assume one of N possible identities, each with probability $1/N$. There are A possible social states, with social state a giving composite good consumption x_a^n to individual n. Furthermore, if you end up as individual n, you will be endowed with utility function $u^n: \mathbb{R} \to \mathbb{R}$. Thus, under state a you will receive utility $u^n(x_a^n) = u_a^n$.

We mentioned that Rawls in essence argued that the Rawlsian social welfare function would be chosen by anyone from behind the veil of ignorance, while the economist Harsanyi argued that which social welfare function is chosen would depend on our assumptions about risk aversion behind the veil. We will now show that Harsanyi's approach results in the Rawlsian social welfare function only if risk aversion is infinite, and that less extreme forms of risk aversion would lead to less extreme social welfare functions. As noted in Section A, Rawls rejected this approach on the grounds that the probabilities one would need to know behind the veil in order to use expected utility theory cannot be assumed to be knowable behind the veil. In framing the problem in the previous paragraph, however, we have ignored this objection and have assigned probability $1/N$ to each position that might eventually be occupied by a person once they leave the veil of ignorance behind.

When viewed from the perspective of the model of choice in the presence of risk, the rational way for an individual to evaluate the desirability of a particular social state $a \in A$ is to consider their *expected utility* given by:

$$U(a) = \sum_{n=1}^{N} \frac{1}{N} u_a^n = \frac{1}{N} \sum_{n=1}^{N} u_a^n. \tag{29.16}$$

Thus, they would evaluate alternative a as better than b if and only if $U(a) > U(b)$, which, if we multiply each side by N, is equivalent to:

$$\sum_{n=1}^{N} u_a^n > \sum_{n=1}^{N} u_b^n. \tag{29.17}$$

This is the utilitarian criterion of the Benthamite social welfare function; all that matters is the sum of the utilities of the individuals, with their preferred social welfare function V expressed as:

$$V(a) = \sum_{n=1}^{N} u_a^n. \tag{29.18}$$

At this point, it seems that our derivation of social welfare functions from the original position does not permit a role for risk aversion. Might it not be that behind the veil of ignorance an individual would want to think about the risk that they might end up as the least well off individual, as suggested by Rawls?

Recall that risk aversion in the expected utility framework requires the u functions to be concave. We can incorporate a role for risk aversion into the analysis by incorporating it directly into the N utility functions that are summed in equation (29.18). Suppose we write n's utility as $v^n(x) = (-u^n(x))^{-\rho}$. As long as $\rho > 0$, this is a positive monotone transformation of u^n.

Exercise 29B.18

Verify that this is a positive monotone transformation.

Note that, as ρ increases, the curvature of the utility function v^n increases, implying that risk aversion is increasing in the parameter ρ, which results in infinite risk aversion as ρ approaches infinity. Equation (29.18) becomes:

$$\overline{V}(a) = \sum_{n=1}^{N} v^n(x_a^n) = - \sum_{n=1}^{N} (u_a^n)^{-\rho}. \tag{29.19}$$

The ordering of social states given by $\overline{V}$ does not change if we subject $\overline{V}$ itself to a positive monotone transformation. Thus, we can express the same utilitarian criterion as:

$$W(a) = (-\overline{V}(a))^{-1/\rho} = \left(\sum_{n=1}^{N} (u_a^n)^{-\rho} \right)^{-1/\rho}. \tag{29.20}$$

Exercise 29B.19

How is what we have just done a positive monotone transformation?

Notice that we now have a social welfare function that has the constant elasticity of substitution (CES) form, with elasticity of substitution $\sigma = 1/(1 + \rho)$. We know from our work with CES utility functions that σ approaches 0 as ρ approaches ∞. As ρ approaches ∞, the social welfare indifference curves approach those of perfect complements. Thus, extreme risk aversion at the individual level results in the Rawlsian social welfare function that treats individual utilities as perfect complements, thus ensuring that use of such a social welfare function will result in maximizing the welfare of the least well off person in society. The Rawlsian social welfare function can be viewed as a special case of the utilitarian criterion, one that assumes infinite risk aversion as individuals choose a social welfare function from the original position.

This has a certain intuitive appeal if we indeed think (as Rawls did not) that one can use the expected utility framework to think about what social welfare function would be chosen by individuals from behind the veil of ignorance. If such individuals exhibit extreme risk aversion, they will care only about the risk of being the least well off person and will thus choose a social welfare function that minimizes that risk. That social welfare function is the one that Rawls argued we would all choose from behind the veil of ignorance. Thus, if we believe we would indeed be extremely risk averse behind the veil, Rawls is right from the perspective of expected utility theory.

End-of-Chapter Exercises

29.1† Recall the *Allais Paradox*. Suppose there are three closed doors with €5 million, €1 million and €0 behind them. You are first offered a choice between Gamble 1 (*G1*) that will reveal the €1 million door with certainty and Gamble 2 (*G2*) that will open the €5 million door with probability 0.1, the €1 million door with probability 0.89 and the €0 door with probability 0.01. You get to keep whatever is behind the door that is revealed. You are offered the following choice instead: either Gamble 3 (*G3*) that reveals the €1 million door with probability 0.11 and the €0 door with probability 0.89, or Gamble 4 (*G4*) that opens the €5 million door with probability 0.1 and the €0 door with probability 0.9.

  A. It turns out that most people will pick *G1* over *G2* and *G4* over *G3*.

   a. Why is this set of choices inconsistent with standard expected utility theory?
   b. Suppose that people use reference-based preferences to evaluate outcomes when making their choice between gambles. Why might the most reasonable reference point in the choice between *G1* and *G2* be €1 million while the most reasonable reference point in the choice between *G3* and *G4* is €0?
   c. Can you explain how such reference-based preferences might explain the Allais paradox?

  B. Suppose that individuals' reference-based tastes can be described by $u(x, r) = (x - r)^{0.5}$ when $x \geq r$ and by $v(x, r) = -(r - x)^{0.75}$ when $x < r$ where x is the euro value of the outcome and r is the reference point.

   a. Consider the case where the reference points are as described in A(b). What are the utility values associated with the three outcomes when the choice is between *G1* and *G2*? What are they when the choice is between *G3* and *G4*?
   b. Which gamble would be chosen by someone with such preferences in each of the two choices? How does this compare to the choices people actually make?
   c. Show that the Allais paradox would arise if the reference point were always €0 rather than what you assumed in your resolution to the Allais paradox.
   d. We mentioned in the text that prospect theory also allows for the possibility of probability weighting. If people overestimate what low probabilities mean, could this also help explain the Allais paradox?

29.2 * Everyday Application: *Reference Points, Happiness and Envy.* The stylized results from the happiness literature suggest that happiness, at least as reported on surveys, is reference based in the sense that people evaluate how happy they are not exclusively based on how much they have, but, at least in part, based on how much they have *relative* to everyone else in their proximity.

  A. This form of reference-based taste differs from what we encounter in other settings in the sense that the reference point is typically something internal to the individual, such as the individual's current endowment.

   a. Explain how one might interpret the combination of the two empirical claims cited in the text as evidence of such reference-based determinants of happiness. The two empirical claims are: (1) within countries, happiness is increasing with income; and (2) excluding countries and times of extreme poverty, there appears to be little relationship between average happiness and average income across countries or across time.
   b. Suppose we have a situation where we have to allocate a fixed amount of money between two individuals. Individual 1 has reference-based preferences, with their happiness increasing only in

their own consumption but decreasing in individual 2's consumption. Individual 2, on the other hand, has the usual preferences, with their happiness increasing only in their own consumption. In what sense is individual 1 driven in part by envy while individual 2 is not?

c. Suppose utility for individual 2 is equal to euros of consumption and utility for individual 1 is euros of own consumption minus some fraction α of euros of individual 2's consumption. Begin by drawing the utility possibility frontier for the case where $\alpha = 0$. Show how the utility possibility frontier changes as α increases.

d. *True or False*: When $\alpha = 0$, equal division of resources between the two individuals is socially optimal for any social indifference map that is symmetrical across the 45-degree line, including the Rawlsian, the Benthamite and any that fall in between these extremes.

e. Now consider the utility possibility frontier when $\alpha > 0$. How will the Rawlsian and Benthamite social indifference maps now give different optimal divisions of resources? What about inbetween social indifference maps that are symmetric across the 45-degree line?

f. For an equal allocation of utilities when $\alpha > 0$, will resources also be equally allocated?

g. *True or False*: Envy is rewarded by each of our social indifference maps, but it is increasingly more rewarded as we move from the Rawlsian to the Benthamite extreme.

h. Can you explain how many might feel discomfort in incorporating such reference-based preferences as a foundation for normative analysis of redistribution?

B. Let x indicate individual 1's consumption in euros and let y indicate individual 2's consumption in euros. Suppose that individual 1's utility is given by $u_1(x, y) = x - \alpha y$ and individual 2's utility is given by $u_2(x, y) = y - \beta x$.

a. If the overall level of consumption to be divided between these two individuals is I, set up the optimization problem that maximizes individual 2's utility subject to individual 1 attaining utility u_1 and subject to the overall resource constraint.

b. Solve for the allocation (x, y) as a function of u_1; that is, solve for the optimal allocation of I between the two individuals given that individual 1 gets utility u_1. *Hint*: You do not need to solve your optimization problem from (a) because the two constraints by themselves determine the solution to the problem.

c. Solve for the utility possibility frontier $u_2(u_1, I)$; that is, a function giving the utility individual 2 can get as a function of u_1 and I as well as the α and β parameters.

d. Consider the special case in which $\alpha = 0.5$ and $\beta = 0$. Which of the two individuals now has reference-based preferences, and in what way can you characterize these as being driven by some degree of envy?

e. What allocation of utilities and resources will be chosen if the ethical standard determining the distribution of resources is encompassed in the Benthamite social welfare function $W = u_1 + u_2$? Does the same division of resources hold for any combination of $\alpha > \beta$?

f. Repeat for the case of $\alpha = 0.5$ and $\beta = 0$, using the Cobb–Douglas social welfare function $W = u_1^{\delta} u_2^{(1-\delta)}$, and using the Rawlsian social welfare function $W = \min\{u_1, u_2\}$.

g. Does your conclusion from A(g) hold?

29.3† **Everyday Application:** *Framing the Options: Praying while Smoking, and Fighting Pandemics*. By framing options for people in particular ways, we can sometimes get them to choose what we'd like them to choose. One such instance is when tastes are reference based.

A. When first introducing the topic of framing, we sometimes tell the story of two priests who wanted their bishop's permission to smoke while praying. The first asked the bishop if it would be permissible for them to smoke when praying. The second asked for permission if, during those moments of weakness when they smoke, it might be permissible for them to say a prayer.

a. The bishop said definitely not to one of the priests and of course, to the other. Can you guess which priest got which answer?

b. How can reference-based preferences on the part of the bishop explain the different responses to what amounts to the same question as to whether or not one can smoke during prayer?

B. Suppose that a local outbreak of a rare disease will, unless something is done, result in 600 deaths. There are two mutually exclusive emergency plans that can be put into place. Under plan A, 200 people will be saved, while under plan B, there is a one-third chance that all 600 people will be saved and a two-thirds chance that none of them will be saved. When presented with this choice, an overwhelming majority of people choose A over B.

   a. Do people exhibit risk aversion or risk-seeking preferences when making this choice?
   b. There is a different way to frame the same two programmes. Under plan C, 400 people will die, and under plan D, there is a one-third chance that no one will die and a two-thirds chance that 600 people will die. Explain how options A and C are identical and how options B and D are identical.
   c. Would someone have to be risk seeking or risk averse when choosing D over C?
   d. Can you use prospect theory to explain the fact that people prefer A to B and D to C? Draw a graph to explain your answer.

29.4 **Business Application:** *The Equity Premium Puzzle.* Investments in equities like shares yield substantially higher returns than investments in bonds. By itself, this is no surprise because shares are riskier than bonds. What is a surprise when viewed through the usual model of risk is the *size* of the premium that equities provide to investors. In a typical year, for instance, bonds might give investors a safe rate of return of 2 per cent while shares might give a return of between 6 per cent and 8 per cent. Economists who have tried to explain this equity premium in terms of risk aversion have concluded that the level of risk aversion necessary to explain the premium is far beyond what anyone can take seriously. Risk aversion alone therefore cannot explain the equity premium, which raises an anomaly known as the *equity premium puzzle*.

A. Consider the equity premium puzzle through the lens of reference-based preferences. In particular, suppose you are investing €1000 and you know you can get a 2 per cent return on this over 1 year by investing your money in bonds. Alternatively, you can invest the €1000 in a stock and expect to lose €100 with probability 0.1 and gain €100 with probability 0.9.

   a. What is the expected rate of return from a stock investment? What does this imply is the equity premium?
   b. Suppose you thought that investors had reference-based preferences. What do you think their reference point might be when comparing the two investments?
   c. Can you use the concept of loss aversion to explain how behavioural economics might have an explanation for the equity premium puzzle?
   d. *In your explanation in (c), you might have thought of the investor as having a one-year horizon. Suppose investors are in it for the long run, facing a 10 per cent chance of a loss on their shares each year. Do you think your behavioural economics explanation that relies on reference-based preferences and loss aversion can still explain the equity premium puzzle?

B. *Consider prospect theory that you implicitly used in part A a little more closely. Suppose that an investor bases their decision on a one-year investment horizon and evaluates risky gambles relative to a reference point that is equal to the amount they invest. Suppose they invest €1000, which becomes their reference point. If invested in risk-free bonds, the €1000 will be worth €1022.54, one year from now. If they invest the same amount in stocks, their investment will be worth €900 with probability 0.12 and €1100 with probability 0.88. The utility of any amount x is evaluated using the function:

$$u(x, r) = 100(x - r) - 0.5(x - r)^2 \text{ if } x \geq r \text{ and}$$
$$= 400(x - r) + 2(x - r)^2 \text{ if } < r, \qquad (29.21)$$

where r is the reference point, and the utility of a gamble that results in x_1 with probability δ and x_2 with probability $(1 - \delta)$ is given by $U = \delta u(x_1, r) + (1 - \delta)u(x_2, r)$.

   a. We discussed four features of prospect theory in the text: (1) reference-dependence, (2) loss aversion, (3) diminishing sensitivity and (4) probability weighting. Which of these are we modelling here, and which are we not?

    b. What is the expected return on investing €1000 in shares? What is the equity premium?

    c. What utility will this investor get from investing €1000 in bonds?

    d. What utility will they get from investing €1000 in stocks?

    e. If this is a typical investor, is the equity premium explained by our version of prospect theory?

    f. Suppose you are a young investor who is investing for retirement in 30 years. For all practical purposes, you can in this case be almost certain that an investment in shares will result in an average rate of return equal to the expected rate of return. Recalculate the average annual utility from investing €1000 in bonds versus investing €1000 in stocks for such an investor.

    g. If all investors were like this young investor, could our prospect theory still explain the equity premium puzzle?

29.5† **Policy Application:** *First- and Second-Best Rawlsian Income Redistribution.* Most governments raise tax revenues from higher income individuals and distribute them to lower income individuals in an attempt to achieve a more equal distribution of consumption. Such governments face a trade-off that emerges from the competing goals of achieving greater consumption equality while minimizing deadweight losses from taxation.

  A. Consider in this exercise a government with Rawlsian goals; that is, the goal of making the least well off individual the most well off. If the government does not have access to information about people's utilities, it may choose instead to treat people's consumption levels as if these represented utility values. Thus, instead of social indifference curves over utility allocations, the government would use social indifference curves over consumption allocations.

    a. Suppose individual 1 has income I_1 and individual 2 has income I_2, with $I_1 > I_2$. Draw the consumption possibilities frontier assuming that the government can costlessly redistribute income between the individuals. Indicate on your graph the consumption allocation that exists in the absence of government redistribution and in the absence of any voluntary charitable efforts.

    b. What consumption allocation on this possibilities frontier would a Rawlsian government choose?

    c. Now illustrate how the consumption possibilities frontier changes if the government uses an inefficient tax system. Suppose the inefficiency takes the following form: as the tax rate on the rich increases, consumption of the rich decreases as if the tax system were efficient, but the deadweight loss increases at an increasing rate as the tax rate rises, with this loss reducing the amount available for distribution to the poor.

    d. Illustrate how a Rawlsian government might now not choose to equalize consumption levels between the rich and the poor.

    e. Suppose that income differences arise in part from compensating differentials in the labour market; that is, suppose that higher income people make more money in part because they undertake unpleasant activities such as travelling a lot for their job and working long hours. If the government's real goal is to apply its social welfare function to utility allocations instead of consumption allocations, how might the Rawlsian social welfare function applied to consumption allocations lead to excessive redistribution?

    f. Suppose instead that the marginal utility of consumption diminishes as consumption increases. Would the application of the Rawlsian goal to consumption distributions now lead to a tax rate that is too high or too low?

  B. Suppose again that there are two individuals: one who makes an income I_1 and the other who makes only I_2, where $I_1 > I_2$. Assume that the government would like to redistribute income but does not have information on individual utilities. Thus, instead of applying a social welfare function to choose a utility allocation, the government applies a social welfare function to choose consumption allocations directly. The function it uses is the Rawlsian social welfare function $W = \min\{c_1, c_2\}$.

    a. Give an example of a utility function $u(c)$ that would make this equivalent to a social welfare function that chooses utility allocations. What has to be true about the marginal utility of consumption?

    b. Suppose that the government uses an income tax t charged to the rich and transfers the revenues to the poor. Suppose first that this income tax is a lump sum tax; that is, it raises revenues without deadweight loss. What tax rate t would the government choose?

c. Suppose next that the income tax used by the government is not a lump sum tax. For a tax rate $t < 1$, it is able to transfer the amount $(tI_1 - (KtI_1)^2)$ to individual 2. If the government wants to maximize the amount of transfer it can make, what tax rate will it choose?

d. Suppose $I_1 =$ €200 000 and $I_2 =$ €10 000. What is the government's first-best income tax rate when it can tax individual 1's income without any deadweight loss?

e. Consider next the second-best case and suppose $k = 0.0025$. For the same two income levels as in (d), what is the government's second-best income tax rate given that the tax system gives rise to the deadweight losses modelled in (c)?

f. How much consumption does each of the two individuals undertake under the first-best outcome? How about under the second-best outcome?

29.6 **Policy Application:** *Confirmation Bias, Politics, Research and Last-Minute Studying.* Individuals have lots of assumptions about the way the world works, assumptions that help frame how they make decisions. These assumptions are often challenged or confirmed by empirical evidence. However, psychologists who have analyzed how people change their assumptions about the world suggest that we tend to seek out evidence that confirms our assumptions and ignore evidence that contradicts our assumptions. This phenomenon is known as *confirmation bias*, and one of the early experiments uncovering this bias is described in part B.

A. Over the past few decades, there has been a vast increase in the number of sources that individuals can use to inform themselves about what is going on in the world. For instance, most individuals used to rely on their local newspaper and the evening newscast on TV. Today, on the other hand, there are lots of news channels people can choose from throughout the day, and an increasing number of people rely on news from internet sources.

a. Many observers of public discourse have suggested that the assumptions individuals bring to policy discussions are now often more diametrically opposed than in the past, with different camps often no longer able to hold civil dialogue because they so fundamentally disagree about the underlying facts. If this is true, how can this be explained by the increased number of news and opinion outlets?

b. Assume that in the past, opinion polls often suggested that public disapproval of a president or prime minister was in the single digits, but more recently, a president or prime minister is considered as doing well if their disapproval ratings are in the 20 per cent to 30 per cent range. Can confirmation bias in the more recent news environment explain this?

c. Assume that a government passes a law that establishes a Fairness Doctrine rule. This rule requires news outlets, particularly on radio and TV, to present opposing viewpoints. Part of the reason for the law was that there was a limited number of news outlets, and thus the Fairness Doctrine was required to allow people to get alternative points of view so that they could form informed opinions. Following the expansion of news outlets on the internet, the government relaxes the rule and allows news outlets to present news and opinions in any way they see fit. Increased competition now leads to competing news outlets in virtually all markets, and automatically allows individuals to gather alternative viewpoints to form their own opinions. Some groups in this society are now arguing for a reinstatement of the Fairness Doctrine while others view it as a violation of free speech and free competition of ideas in the product-differentiated marketplace. Can you argue both sides of this issue?

d. Some have observed an increase in the number of people who believe in a variety of conspiracy theories, theories such as the 9/11 attack being orchestrated by the United States government. How might this be explained in light of the fact that most individuals find evidence against such theories conclusive?

e. Empirical social scientists often do econometric regression analysis on real-world data to ascertain the direction and magnitude of people's responses to different policies. As computational analysis has become less costly, such researchers are now able to run literally tens of thousands of different regressions, using combinations of different variables and empirical specifications, whereas in the past they have had to limit themselves to a few regressions. Suppose that researchers have prior beliefs about what an empirical investigation might show. How might you view statistically significant empirical results reported in research papers more sceptically as a result of knowing about confirmation bias?

    f. In the final hours before an exam, students often study intensely by scanning their notes and focusing on key terms that they have highlighted. Some students find that this dramatically increases their sense of being prepared for the exam, but find that they do not do nearly as well in the exam as they had thought they would given their last-minute studying. Can you explain this using the idea of confirmation bias?

B. The following experiment, first conducted in the early 1960s, is an illustration of confirmation bias. Suppose that you are given the following sequence of numbers: 2–4–6. You are told that this sequence conforms with a particular rule that was used to generate the sequence and are asked to work out what the underlying rule is. To do so, you can generate your own three-number sequences and ask the experimenter for feedback on whether your sequence also conforms with the underlying rule. You can do this as often as you need to until you are certain you know what the underlying rule is, at which time you tell the experimenter your conclusion.

    a. Suppose that when you first see the 2–4–6 sequence, you recognize it as a sequence of even numbers and believe that the underlying rule probably requires the even numbers. What is an example of a sequence that you might use to test this assumption if you have confirmation bias?

    b. What sequence of numbers might you propose to test your assumption if you did not have confirmation bias and were open to your assumption being incorrect?

    c. The underlying rule was simple. In order to comply with the rule, it had to be an ascending sequence. Very few subjects correctly identified this rule, instead very confidently concluding that the rule was much more complex. The experimenters concluded that people consistently derived an incorrect rule because they gave examples that would confirm their assumptions rather than attempt to *falsify* them. A sequence intended to falsify an assumption would be one that violates the assumption. How is this consistent with your answers to (a) and (b)?

* conceptually challenging
** computationally challenging
† solutions in Study Guide

Chapter 30

Balancing Government, Civil Society and Markets

Do safer cars necessarily result in fewer traffic deaths? Is it sensible to subsidize shale gas exploration in an effort to make the UK less dependent on unstable regions of the world? Would outlawing live Christmas trees help to reduce deforestation? Should we impose laws against price gouging? Is boycotting companies that use cheap labour abroad a good way to express our outrage at the dismal working conditions in those countries? Would it be better for workers to require their employers to pay their social security taxes like National Insurance Contributions in the UK, rather than taxing the workers directly? Should we tax the sales by monopolies so that these companies don't earn such outrageous profits?

We began with this paragraph in Chapter 1, where we suggested that the economist's instinctive answers may differ from the answers given by many non-economists. Safer cars *might* lead to more deaths if we end up driving more recklessly as a result of knowing that we are less likely to get hurt in an accident. Subsidizing shale gas won't make the UK much less dependent on unstable regions in the world since oil is sold in a world market, and what ultimately matters is the world price of oil, which is determined only in part by UK oil production. Outlawing live Christmas trees might cause a reduction in forests grown precisely for the purpose of growing Christmas trees, and interfering with competitive prices will lead to non-price rationing that may in fact impose larger costs on the very individuals we aim to protect with price-gouging laws. Boycotting companies that use cheap labour abroad reduces foreign demand for low-wage workers, thereby depressing their wages. It should really not matter who pays social security taxes – employers or employees – since the economic incidence of such taxes depends on elasticities of labour supply and demand, not on how politicians write laws. Taxing the sales of monopolies will only make the inefficiency of monopoly pricing worse because it will increase already inflated consumer prices.

These are just a few examples of how an economist's perspective on the world differs not because economists are strange or ideologically driven, but rather because economists have internalized intuitions about how individual optimizing choices aggregate to result in the economic environments we see. It is these intuitions that form a basis for how economists and non-economists alike might develop a framework that allows a reasoned debate on what role we ideally envision for markets, civil society and government.

30A   Resolvable Versus Unresolvable Differences

This in no way implies, however, that everyone will agree on the right balance between these different institutions in society. We bring to the table different assumptions about the way the world works as well as different systems of values and beliefs on what is good. To the extent to which our disagreements are driven by assumptions about the way the world works, the positive economist and more generally, the positive social scientist, can be of great assistance as they bring their tool kit to an empirical investigation that can clarify which of our assumptions are correct and which are mistaken. The more we can agree on the underlying assumptions, the less we will typically disagree on what is desirable. In the end we might still disagree because we take different philosophical positions on points that have nothing to do with empirically falsifiable assumptions. While philosophers can help by clarifying our thinking, it seems unlikely that they will get us all to agree on what is good. In some instances, we may end up having to agree to disagree.

For instance, suppose two people disagree on what is good because one operates under the assumption that people are by and large rational in their decision making (as modelled by economists), and the second operates under the assumption that we are riddled with psychological biases that are pervasive and large in magnitude as suggested by many psychologists. This type of disagreement about assumptions can in principle be resolved through empirical testing, and if both people are open to the possibility that not all of their assumptions are true, empirical social science research will help us resolve some of the disagreements. This book is not one that develops the means by which we can undertake such empirical investigations. For our purposes, however, it is enough to recognize that differences in opinion can at least in principle be resolved to the extent to which such differences are rooted in assumptions that can be tested with real-world data. The biggest obstacle to resolving such differences might actually lie in a tendency by human beings to seek only evidence that confirms their assumptions to the exclusion of evidence that contradicts them, so-called confirmatory bias.

Suppose instead that disagreements about what is good arise from different philosophical positions that stand in at least partial contradiction to one another. Person 2 might believe that justice is rooted in a respect for natural rights and that such deference to natural rights prohibits any type of forced redistribution of income. Person 1, on the other hand, might be a Rawlsian utilitarian, convinced that justice requires society to be ordered in such a way as to make the least well off as well off as possible. If the utilitarian consequences of the natural rights position turn out to be in less conflict with person 2's Rawlsian ideal than is immediately apparent, both may still end up converging somewhat by learning from positive social science. Economists have, for instance, demonstrated the power of decentralized markets to generate large social surplus. Generating such surplus is important for utilitarians even if Rawlsian redistribution occurs alongside it. The enforcement of contracts and property rights required for decentralized markets to generate surplus is precisely what natural law philosophy might tell us a good society should do. Positive economics – knowing about what is – therefore creates common ground where we might not have seen any in its absence, but it is unlikely that it will remove all differences. The Rawlsian among us will always view property rights as a means to the end of a society in which the least fortunate do as well as possible, while the natural rights advocate will see the rights themselves as the end. The former is therefore willing to violate what the latter considers untouchable, and there is nothing the positive economist can really add to resolve that particular conflict.

30B   The Three-Legged Stool

To what extent can the material covered in this text help identify which of our differences are resolvable and which are the types of differences on which we will ultimately have to agree to disagree? Is there a bigger picture framework that emerges, or is it all just a mishmash of models that don't sum to more than their parts?

While much of the focus of the text has been on what markets do well and what they don't do so well, we have emphasized throughout that markets never operate in a vacuum. In fact, markets rely on the protection of contracts and property rights or else are subject to the Tragedy of the Commons, and as a result there is a role for non-market institutions on whose foundations market transactions rest. While there are certainly anarchist theories about how such protections can in principle exist without governments, we can think of few if any modern examples where this has ever been accomplished. Governments are defined by their claim to have an exclusive right to initiate the use of force, whether through taxation or regulation that are both backed by mechanisms to punish those who do not comply. We similarly know of no society that has existed without institutions that are governed neither by governments nor by market prices, institutions like families, which exist in a complex web of voluntary associations we have referred to as the civil society. Neither can we think of examples of societies where market forces have not played a role, even if sometimes operating within a 'shadow market' that functions outside the legal framework.

It can be concluded from all this that it is probably a fair statement to say the following: Virtually everyone agrees that the institutions that make up what we call society involve a mix of markets, civil society and government, a three-legged stool, so to speak, on which all activities in the society unfold. The question is not *whether* markets, civil society and government have a role to play; it is rather a question of what the appropriate sphere for each should be in a society that optimally balances these to achieve whatever aims we have set. While economics has a limited set of insights to contribute to what the *aims* should be, it has a lot to say about what trade-offs we face as we think of the appropriate balance between the three legs of our stool.

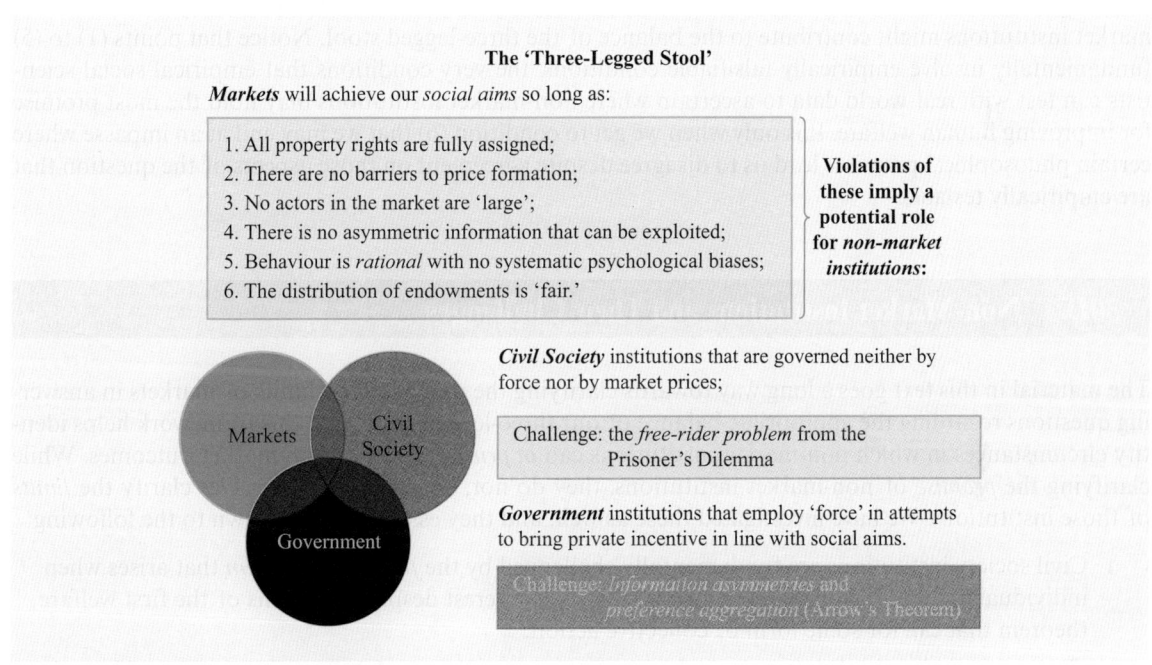

The 'Three-Legged Stool'

Markets will achieve our *social aims* so long as:

1. All property rights are fully assigned;
2. There are no barriers to price formation;
3. No actors in the market are 'large';
4. There is no asymmetric information that can be exploited;
5. Behaviour is *rational* with no systematic psychological biases;
6. The distribution of endowments is 'fair.'

Violations of these imply a potential role for *non-market institutions*:

Civil Society institutions that are governed neither by force nor by market prices;

Challenge: the *free-rider problem* from the Prisoner's Dilemma

Government institutions that employ 'force' in attempts to bring private incentive in line with social aims.

Challenge: *Information asymmetries* and *preference aggregation* (Arrow's Theorem)

Markets · Civil Society · Government

30C Combining the First Welfare Theorem With Other Insights

Our insights begin with the first welfare theorem that forms the underlying connection between all the various subfields in microeconomics. The theorem is important because it precisely delineates the admittedly unrealistic conditions for markets to operate in an efficient way, assuming that individuals are not subject to psychological biases in decision making. Were the world truly characterized by these conditions, the only question that would remain is whether non-market interventions are necessary to achieve a better *distribution* of outcomes than what markets achieve or, alternatively, whether the initial allocation of endowments is sufficiently just to permit us not to worry about tinkering with the efficient outcome that markets produce. We can combine the insights of the first welfare theorem with concerns from psychology and issues related to equity or fairness to arrive at the ideal conditions under which markets would achieve our social aims. In a nutshell, these are:

1 All property rights are clear and enforced, with all externalities, including those related to public goods, therefore internalized.

2 There are no barriers to market prices governing production and exchange.

3 No actors in the market are large enough to be able to exercise market power.

4 No actors are asymmetrically informed in ways that allow them to use this informational advantage to exploit those who are less informed.

5 Everyone is rational in the sense that everyone aims to do the best they can given their circumstances, with neither preferences nor the interpretation of circumstances subject to systematic psychological biases.

6 Depending on one's philosophical approach, either the initial distribution of endowments is judged to be fair, or the outcomes produced by markets satisfy our ethical criterion for distributional goals.

The psychology- and philosophy-based concerns in points (5) and (6) do not fall by the wayside when we recognize that conditions (1) to (4) often do not hold; they only add to the possible ways in which non-market institutions might contribute to the balance of the three-legged stool. Notice that points (1) to (5) fundamentally involve empirically falsifiable conditions, the very conditions that empirical social scientists can test with real-world data to ascertain where non-market institutions may hold the most promise for improving human welfare. It is only when we get to condition (6) that we may end at an impasse where certain philosophical premises lead us to disagree despite agreement on those aspects of the question that are empirically testable.

30D   Non-Market Institutions and Their Challenges

The material in this text goes a long way towards clarifying the promises and limits of markets in answering questions regarding the appropriate balance of our three-legged stool, and this framework helps identify circumstances in which non-market institutions can *in principle* improve on market outcomes. While clarifying the *promise* of non-market institutions, they do not, however, by themselves clarify the *limits* of those institutions. We have investigated these as well, and they essentially boil down to the following:

1 Civil society institutions are fundamentally challenged by the *free-rider problem* that arises when individuals cannot be forced to go against their self-interest despite violations of the first welfare theorem that call for some form of collective action.

2 Governments face both *informational asymmetries* as well as *preference aggregation problems* that result in a different kind of *strategic power* as they employ force to alter human behaviour.

The free-rider problem faced by civil society efforts arises from the fact that civil society institutions, unlike governments, cannot employ the use of force and must therefore rely on persuasion, and this links closely to the externality issues we uncovered in our development of the first welfare theorem. This suggests that voluntary efforts by civil society groups result in Prisoner's Dilemma incentives that will tend to cause such groups to insufficiently mobilize individuals who maximize their self-interested aims. While such institutions are often in possession of considerably more information than governments that seek to address the same problems, the Prisoner's Dilemma incentives result in a lack of the resources necessary to adequately meet the challenges they identify. These are challenges that are not impossible to overcome, with much evidence suggesting that civil society organizations like families and community groups fill gaps that link closely to aspects of human needs not easily included in standard neoclassical economics models. This opens the possibility for civil society institutions to play effective roles when these are not excessively undermined by either market or government forces. The free-rider problem remains a challenge that itself may require non-civil society institutions. Government support of such institutions may take a variety of forms, each intended to address the underlying externality problem that is present in civil society engagements.

Just like markets and civil society institutions, governments confront two challenges of their own. Even if they are made up of entirely benevolent policy makers, they often lack sufficient information to correct market failures or civil society failures without introducing distortions and unintended consequences that may create problems greater than the ones they seek to correct. One advantage of markets and, to at least some extent, civil society institutions, arises precisely from the more efficient use of individual knowledge that these can make to solve problems. Even if informational asymmetries posed no difficulties for governments, we have found that in the absence of benevolent dictators, democratic governments give rise to institutions that invariably create strategic power for concentrated interest groups and agenda setters whose aims may diverge from those we seek to implement. The challenge is to arrive at a role for government that provides ways for the use of force to achieve desirable social outcomes without that very force being strategically abused by concentrated power within governments. None of this is to suggest that governments cannot play important roles in enhancing social welfare; it only suggests that the mere presence of market failures and civil society failures no more implies an immediate role for government than a recognition of government failure implies no role for government.

30E | Spontaneous Order Outside the Market

There is, however, one final insight that a careful study of markets provides for those genuinely concerned about finding the appropriate balance for markets, civil society and government. In our initial development of the first welfare theorem, we noted how order can arise spontaneously from the self-interested engagements of individuals who possess no more information than what is naturally contained within each of them. This idea of a *spontaneous order*, while far from suggesting a perfect order, is not one that is limited solely to market interactions. It may, therefore, lead us to think differently than we otherwise would about *how* interactions between governments, civil society and markets ought to be structured.

Consider, for instance, the evolution of law, an idea that most of us instinctively associate with the laws that are written down in our constitutions and the various legislations and statutes that are written down by the political institutions set up by those constitutions. It naturally comes as a surprise to many that most of the law that governs many societies is not derived from laws that were at some point written down, just as most of the products produced in the market are not the result of conscious planning by the thousands of market participants that did the best they could given their limited information and circumstances. Much of what happens in European or British courtrooms is based on *common law*, a complex system of rules that has spontaneously emerged over centuries as different courts laid out basic principles that when judged to work well, were adopted by other courts to evolve into precedents that became universally accepted. Much as the Apple Corporation stumbled on the iPod or a car company first thought of the minivan only to see these ideas revolutionize the way we listen to music or shuttle around our children, innovations in the law were often driven by solutions to the needs of the moment that, when successful, were replicated by others. The same can be said of the evolution of *language* which, particularly in the English language, is rarely centrally directed but rather adapts to new needs and circumstances as societies change. At the same time, just as many crazy inventions in the marketplace quickly fizzle out and some language innovations turn out to be short-lived fads, certain rules made in courts end up producing bad unintended outcomes and thus never make it into the common law that is more or less universally accepted at least in societies based on common law principles.

Or consider our discussion of structure induced political equilibria, equilibria that discipline the chaos that can arise under democratic decision making through rules and conventions that are written down nowhere but accepted as nearly sacred where they are used. Many constitutions do not say anything about setting up committees that produce legislation to be considered by parliaments, neither is there anything in some constitutions about filibuster rules (filibustering is the deliberate extension of debate over legislation to delay its passage or to force it 'out of time') that state whether certain legislative houses have the power to declare legislation 'unconstitutional'. While most constitutions lay out a basic framework in which decisions are to be made, it leaves much to be determined by the spontaneous order that would shape the processes by which government actually functions. There is no guarantee that any one of these processes is good in some abstract sense any more than there is a guarantee that markets invent only good products, or the common law never gets us stuck in antiquated ways of thinking or language fads of the moment have any positive lasting impact. By recognizing the often surprising roles played by spontaneous orders that *can* emerge from the bottom up, we begin to see the usefulness of being open to allowing institutions to change from within as circumstances change.

In our discussion of public goods, we also touched on market-like mechanisms that can discipline governments, communities or clubs to be less rent-seeking and more responsive to constituent needs than might be apparent at first, much as competition between firms limits the extent to which firms can strategically manipulate price to achieve economic profit. The Tiebout model of competing governments, most appropriately applied to local rather than national competition, suggests an admittedly imperfect spontaneous order as citizen choice of where to live impacts what local governments do; and the possibility of excluding from consumption those who do not contribute to some forms of public goods opens up ways for market-like competition between firms and clubs that meet a variety of human needs. Once again, the idea of a spontaneous order is potentially powerful in helping us understand the purely empirical question of what sorts of failures that arise in abstract models may be ameliorated by institutions that emerge or compete within the real-world complexities that we actually face. Models are helpful in clarifying our thinking on where the problems might lie, but they are sometimes limiting if we cannot take insights from one model to the next to see how larger forces shape the societies we are analyzing and seeking to improve.

We have also seen how an appreciation of markets giving rise to spontaneous orders can shape policies that rather than mandating solutions, create a set of incentives to unleash entrepreneurial efforts aimed at achieving ends that markets themselves would otherwise have no incentive to address. In our treatment of pollution, for instance, we compared top-down approaches of regulation and some forms of Pigouvian taxation to examples of pollution voucher systems that create a role for market participants to determine where pollution is most efficiently reduced while providing incentives for new firms to innovate less polluting production processes. Economists therefore often find themselves favouring policies that create the right incentives rather than those that presume governments can obtain the necessary information *and* discipline themselves to use this information in ways that directly implement desirable outcomes. This economist-bias towards decentralized solutions based on incentives emerges precisely from an intuitive appreciation of how spontaneous orders can, within the appropriate institutional setting, make use of information and unleash entrepreneurial efforts.

There may be instances in which we cannot immediately see how civil society institutions can overcome the free-rider problem that can in principle cripple the civil society, and yet we see in many places a rich fabric of such institutions succeeding in all sorts of surprising ways. As we emphasized from the beginning in our discussion of the Prisoner's Dilemma, people seem to cooperate more in voluntary ways that appear to run against their narrow self-interest than we would predict in a simple economic model, with ideas like fairness and identity, tipping points and the warm glow from altruism adding to strictly rational forces of trigger strategies and punishment mechanisms that operate in complex ways. Social entrepreneurs often use such insights, some of which are rooted in the very psychological biases that create issues for the first welfare theorem, in effective ways to mobilize the civil society, and successful efforts there can be replicated just as they are elsewhere in governments and markets. Here, too, one can see possibilities for spontaneous orders that might be unnecessarily disturbed by attempts to discipline civil society or market failures without an appreciation of the larger forces at work.

30F A Beginning, Not An End

If a single course or a single textbook claims to offer all the answers, you should probably be suspicious. The world is too complex, and the underlying trade-offs we face, individually and as a society, are too intricate for simple answers that are often more rooted in ideological pre-suppositions and subject to confirmation biases that keep us from considering evidence that challenges our assumptions. The hope is that this text is a beginning, not an end – a beginning to thinking more clearly about the world around us while being open to challenges that can allow us to change our mind. So many of our heated debates result in little more than shouting matches because we skip steps, cling to presumptions without considering alternatives and develop the hubris of knowing the answer before coming to terms with the question. Reasoned debate, and reasoned acceptance of differences, can be found only if we discipline ourselves through the use of devices like those that we have tried to develop in the chapters of this text. It also typically results in more nuanced views of the world, views that shy away from corner solutions in which we emphasize one aspect of a problem to the exclusion of all others.

Ultimately, we would not be economists if we were not fundamentally convinced about the value that the economist's lens can bring to a fuller understanding of the world in which we live. Equally, we might not be sure if we would qualify as human beings if we did not also believe that all answers never rest in one lens. The challenge for anyone who begins the study of economics or any other discipline that aims to understand the human condition, is to ultimately synthesize its insights into a bigger picture, and it is the hope that this book offers a useful set of tools to do just that.

Glossary

The italics in the glossary indicate that the term is defined elsewhere in the glossary.

A

actuarially fair insurance Insurance contracts that reduce risk without changing expected values (and earn *zero profit* for insurance companies that serve a random selection of the population).

adverse selection The *asymmetric information* problem that causes higher cost customers to 'adversely select' into the market or, alternatively, that causes low quality suppliers to 'adversely select' into the market.

agenda setting The sequencing of votes and procedures that govern the process by which democratic institutions choose social outcomes.

aggregate risk Risk that impacts groups rather than randomly impacting individuals; as, for instance, the risk of economic recessions.

antitrust economics Subfield of economics that investigates the impact of government regulation and legal rulings on anticompetitive behaviour by firms.

asymmetric information Circumstances in which buyers and sellers do not share the same information relevant to the transaction they are entering into.

average cost *Cost* divided by output.

average expenditure *Expenditure* divided by output.

average variable cost *Variable cost* divided by output.

B

bandwagon effect A form of *network externality* under which individuals value an item more as consumption of the item by others increases.

barriers to entry A *fixed cost* incurred by a firm if it chooses to enter a market; if sufficiently high, it may prevent market entry by new firms.

battle of the sexes A type of *coordination game* in which two players want to engage in the same activity (rather than engaging in different activities), but they differ over the activity on which they wish to coordinate.

Bayes rule A rule for updating *beliefs* as new information is revealed.

Bayesian Nash equilibrium A *Nash equilibrium* extended to *incomplete information games* in which *beliefs* become part of the equilibrium.

behavioural economics A branch of economics that incorporates insights from psychology into economic models.

beliefs In *game theory*, a probability distribution over the possible types an opposing player might be.

Benthamite social preferences A normative metric for evaluating outcomes by ranking them according to the sum of all individual outcomes; all individuals are given equal weight.

Bertrand competition Strategic competition (by firms) in which firms view price as the strategic variable.

best-response function A *function* that mathematically summarizes the *best response strategies* to all possible strategies taken by others in a game.

best-response strategy In *game theory*, an individual's *strategy* that results in the highest possible payoff given the strategies played by others in the game.

beta-delta model A (*behavioural economics*) model of *present-biased* preferences.

binary relations Mathematical relations that rank pairs of alternatives.

bounded rationality The assumption that individuals are cognitively limited in terms of how much they can compute; often leads to the prediction of the use of 'rules of thumb' in complex choice environments.

budget constraint (or budget line) The set of possible alternatives that are affordable when the entire budget is used, i.e. the boundary of the *budget set*.

budget (or choice) set The set of possible alternatives that are affordable.

C

call option A contract that gives the holder the option of buying some quantity in the future at a predetermined price.

cap-and-trade A policy that caps the overall amount of pollution and requires polluters to purchase *tradable pollution permits* (also called pollution vouchers).

capital A variety of non-labour inputs into production, including financial capital and physical capital (plant and equipment).

cartel A group of firms that form an agreement to collude (either on price or quantity) in order to raise profit, e.g. OPEC.

certainty equivalent The amount x that would make someone who faces a risky *gamble* indifferent between participating in the gamble versus accepting x.

choice set The set of feasible alternatives.

choice variables The variables that can be chosen (rather than being taken as given) in a constrained or unconstrained *optimization problem*.

circumstances The constraints faced by someone who has to make a choice.

civil society Formal and informal institutions that facilitate cooperation without primarily relying on either prices or government coercion.

club goods *Non-rivalrous*, *excludable* goods, i.e. excludable *public goods*.

Coase Theorem The theorem that states that *externalities* will be fully internalized by the affected parties so long as *transactions costs* are low and property rights are clearly assigned.

Cobb–Douglas function $f(x_1, x_2) = x_1^\alpha x_2^\beta$ (where x_1 and x_2 are consumption goods when f is a *utility function* and production inputs when f is a *production function*).

collusion Explicit or implicit cooperation by firms in order to restrict quantity and raise price.

compensated budget A (typically) hypothetical budget that following a price change provides a consumer with just enough income to reach the pre-price change *indifference curve*.

compensated demand A consumer's demand holding utility constant, i.e. a consumer's demand under the assumption that, as prices change, the consumer will always receive just enough income to attain the same *indifference curve*.

compensated supply (of labour or capital) A worker's (or saver's) supply of labour (or capital) assuming utility remains unchanged as prices (i.e. wages and interest rates) change.

competitive equilibrium Prices and resource allocations in which no consumer or firm has an incentive to change what they are doing given the prevailing prices (assuming everyone is small relative to the market).

complements Goods that tend to be consumed together by consumers, or inputs that tend to be used together in production.

complete information games Games in which the payoffs of all players are known by all players.

complete tastes Tastes that enable individuals to rank all pairs of alternatives in terms of relative desirability.

composite good An artificial or hypothetical good that takes the place of 'all other consumption'; usually denominated in 'euros or pounds of other consumption', with price therefore set to 1 by definition.

compound interest The interest in future periods on interest earned this period.

concave functions A function f such that $f(\alpha x + (1 - \alpha)y) \geq \alpha f(x) + (1 - \alpha)f(y)$; in producer theory, concave *production functions* give rise to convex *producer choice sets*.

conditional input demand A cost-minimizing firm's demand for an input (at given input prices) conditional on producing a certain fixed level of output.

constant cost industry A perfectly competitive industry with no *barriers to entry* and identical firms—with a horizontal long-run industry demand curve.

constant elasticity of substitution (CES) Utility or production functions with the same *elasticity of substitution* between goods (or inputs) at all goods (or input) bundles.

constant returns to scale Production technologies under which a *t*-fold increase in all inputs results in a *t*-fold increase in output (when no inputs are wasted).

constrained optimization problem A mathematical problem in which some function is maximized subject to *constraints*.

constraint A limit on the choice set; for consumers, the constraint is typically formed by prices and incomes (or endowments); for firms the constraint is typically the technology that limits which production plans are technologically feasible.

consumer surplus The difference between what a consumer would have been willing to pay and what they had to pay for the quantity of a good that they purchase.

continuous tastes Tastes that are not subject to 'sudden jumps'.

contract curve The set of *Pareto efficient* allocations of goods in general equilibrium *exchange economies*.

convex combination The weighted average of two bundles (of goods or inputs).

convex production sets *Convex sets* of feasible *production plans* that emerge from decreasing (or constant) *returns to scale* production processes (represented by *concave production functions*).

convex set A set of points for which it is the case that any *convex combination* of two points within the set also lies within the set.

convex tastes Tastes under which the *convex combination* of equally preferred bundles is more desirable (or at least no worse) than the 'extreme' bundles; the set of bundles that are preferred to a bundle is a *convex set* when tastes are convex.

coordination games Games with multiple pure strategy *Nash equilibria* in which players choose the same strategy.

core The set of allocations (of goods) in general equilibrium *exchange economies* such that no coalition of individuals could do better on their own; in two-person exchange economies, this is equivalent to the set of *Pareto efficient* allocations that are mutually preferred to the initial endowments by both players.

corner solution A solution to an *optimization problem* in which zero quantity of at least one of the *choice variables* is chosen.

cost What is given up when a particular activity is chosen; also called *opportunity cost* or *economic cost*.

cost minimization The act of producing a given output level at the minimum economic cost possible (given input prices and given technological constraints).

Cournot competition Strategic competition (by firms) in which firms view quantity as the strategic variable.

cross-price demand curve The curve that relates demand for one good to the price of another good.

crowd-out The tendency of an increase in government spending on a project to lower private contributions for the same project.

D

deadweight loss A loss in social surplus resulting from a violation of the *first welfare theorem*'s conditions.

decentralized market equilibrium Perfectly competitive equilibrium when everyone is a *price taker*.

decreasing cost industries Industries with downward-sloping long-run industry supply curves.

decreasing returns to scale Production technologies under which a *t*-fold increase in all inputs results in less than a *t*-fold increase in output (when no inputs are wasted).

demand function Function that gives the quantity demanded as a function of the economic circumstances (i.e. prices and incomes) faced by the demander.

diffuse costs Costs spread across large numbers of individuals such that the cost for each individual is small.

diminishing marginal product *Marginal product* (of an input in production) that falls as more of the input is hired (holding all other inputs fixed).

diminishing marginal rate of substitution Property of convex tastes that results in individuals being increasingly less willing to substitute good x for good y the more y they already have.

diminishing sensitivity The hypothesis (in *prospect theory*) that individuals become less sensitive to marginal gains and losses the further these occur from their reference point.

diminishing technical rate of substitution The property of production processes that implies it becomes increasingly difficult to substitute one input for another and keep output constant.

discounting Valuing €1 in the future at less than €1 now.

disequilibrium An economic environment in which everyone is not doing the best they can given the circumstances they face.

distortionary Usually refers to a policy that alters prices and thus the opportunity costs faced by individuals.

Dixit-Stiglitz utility function A particular utility function that models utility increasing as the variety of available products increases.

dominant strategy A *strategy* that is a *best response* to all possible strategies played by others.

duality The connection between *utility maximization* and *expenditure minimization* (for consumers) and between *profit maximization* and *cost minimization* (for producers).

duopoly An *oligopoly* composed of two firms.

E

Easterlin paradox The finding that happiness increases with income within countries but not across countries.

econometrics The subfield in economics that investigates how to employ statistical techniques to test economic models.

economic costs *Opportunity costs.*

economically efficient production Cost minimizing production, i.e. production of output at the lowest possible economic cost.

economics of education Subfield of economics that deals with incentive issues related to the provision of primary, secondary and higher education.

Edgeworth box A graphical way of representing a two-person, two-good *exchange economy*.

efficient A situation that cannot be changed in a way that would make some people better off without making anyone worse off; same as *Pareto efficient*.

elasticity The percentage change in behaviour resulting from a 1 per cent change in some aspect of the economic environment.

elasticity of substitution The percentage change in the ratio of goods resulting from a 1 per cent change in the marginal rate of substitution along an *indifference curve*.

endogenous Arising from within the system, e.g. budgets that emerge from the sale of *endowments* at market prices.

endowment Assets that can be sold to generate income for consumption.

Engel curve *Income demand curve.*

entrepreneurial skill Innovative or managerial skills that are often in fixed supply within a firm even as other inputs can change.

entry deterrence The strategic setting of output or price by a firm in an attempt to deter entry of a competing firm into the market.

envelope theorem Mathematical theorem used in the derivation of *Hotelling's Lemma*, *Shephard's Lemma* and *Roy's Identity*.

equilibrium An economic environment in which everyone is doing the best they can given the circumstances they face (and given what others are doing).

equity premium puzzle The empirical observation of high risk-based returns that are difficult to justify with typical models of risk aversion.

essential goods Goods without which utility from consuming other goods would be the same as the utility of consuming nothing.

exchange economy An economy in which individuals trade existing goods but no new goods are produced.

excludability The property of private goods whose consumption can be restricted to only those who pay a price for consuming.

exit price The output price at which a firm will choose to exit a competitive market.

exogenous Given from outside the system, e.g. budgets that are fixed at some currency value independent of other economic variables.

expected utility The probability-weighted average of utilities associated with the outcomes of a *gamble*.

expected utility theory The theory that the utility over *gambles* can be expressed as an *expected utility*.

expected value The probability-weighted average of the outcomes of a *gamble*.

expenditure (or expense) The financial outlays of a firm including *economic costs* and *sunk costs*.

expenditure function In consumer theory, the function that gives, for any set of prices and utility level u, the minimum income necessary to attain u.

expenditure minimization problem Finding the minimum expenditure necessary to attain a particular indifference curve at given prices; also results in *Hicksian demand curves* (or *compensated demand curves*).

experimental economics Subfield of economics that tests economic models through controlled experiments.

exporters Individuals who buy in low priced regions and ship goods to high priced regions in order to make a profit.

extensive form A way of illustrating games using a *game tree*.

externalities The positive or negative impact that individual decisions have on others besides those specifically involved in a market transaction.

F

financial economics Subfield of economics that investigates financial markets.

first-degree price discrimination Perfect *price discrimination* under which monopolists can identify consumer types, prevent resale and vary prices across consumers as well as for different units sold to one consumer.

first-mover advantage Sequential move strategic settings in which players who move early can gain an advantage.

first-order conditions In a mathematical optimization problem, the first derivative conditions that represent the *necessary conditions* for a solution to be an optimum.

first-price auction An auction in which the winner pays the highest bid for the auctioned item.

first welfare theorem The theorem that states that resource allocations in an economy are *efficient* so long as there are no price distortions, no *externality*, no *asymmetric information* and no *market power*.

fixed cost An economic cost that remains unchanged regardless of how much output is produced.

fixed expenditure An expense that is independent of how much is produced and includes a *sunk cost*.

fixed input An input that cannot be varied by the firm (usually in the *short run*).

folk theorem In *game theory*, the theorem that illustrates that a wide range of possible equilibrium outcomes can occur in infinitely *repeated games*.

framing In *behavioural economics*, the observation that decisions can be impacted by the way that salient features of the decision are presented to the chooser.

free-rider problem The efficiency problem that emerges in settings where individuals have an incentive to not contribute in some way but rather rely on the contributions of others.

functions Mathematical rules that assign numbers (typically on the real line) to points.

fundamental non-convexities *Non-convexities* that arise in the creation of property rights markets aimed at solving *externality* problems.

G

gains from trade Increases in welfare for both parties when individuals choose to engage in voluntary trade.

gambler's fallacy When people erroneously believe that once a randomly generated event has occurred, it is less likely to occur again.

gambles A way to model choice involving risk when individuals know that different outcomes might happen with some probability.

game theory Subfield of economics that develops tools for investigating strategic decision making.

game tree A way of representing games in the form of a 'tree' that lays out decision nodes and outcomes.

general equilibrium models Models that take into account the interaction of markets as prices are formed.

generalized CES production function The *constant elasticity of substitution (CES) function* generalized to include a parameter specifying *returns to scale*.

Gibbard–Satterthwaite Theorem Theorem that proves the impossibility of designing a mechanism that can implement a function with truth telling as the *dominant strategy*.

Giffen goods *Inferior goods* with sufficiently small *substitution effects* relative to *income effects* such that the own price demand curve slopes up.

Gini coefficient Measure of inequality derived from the *Lorenz curve* (usually applied to income or wealth inequality).

Gorman form The form preferences must take in order for groups of consumers to behave as if they were a single *representative consumer*.

Groves–Clarke mechanism A mechanism designed to implement the efficient level of a *public good* when preferences are only known to individuals.

H

head tax A tax that is levied on everyone (who has a head) equally; example of a *lump sum tax*.

health economics Subfield of economics that deals with issues related to the health care sector.

Henry George Theorem A theorem illustrating the efficiency of land taxes.

Hicksian demand *Compensated demand*, i.e. the demand for a good holding utility constant (and assuming enough income is made available to always reach that utility level).

homogeneous function A function $f(x, y)$ such that $f(tx, ty) = t^k f(x, y)$ (which is then homogeneous of degree k).

homothetic producer choice set A *producer choice set* whose map of *isoquants* has the property that the *technical rate of substitution* depends only on the ratio of inputs (and is thus the same along any ray from the origin).

homothetic tastes Tastes whose map of *indifference curves* has the property that the *marginal rate of substitution* depends only on the ratio of goods (and is thus the same along any ray from the origin).

hot-hand fallacy Occurs when people erroneously believe that a randomly generated event is more likely to occur again if it has just been observed to have occurred multiple times.

Hotelling model A two-firm model of product differentiation along a line of possible product characteristics.

Hotelling's Lemma The derivative of the *profit function* with respect to output price is equal to the supply function; and the derivative of the *profit function* with respect to input price is the negative of the input demand function.

hyperbolic discounting In *behavioural economics*, a model of *discounting* that incorporates *present* (and near-present) *bias* and leads to *time inconsistent* choices.

I

image marketing Advertising aimed at altering the image rather than providing information on the quality or price of a product.

impatience Intertemporal decisions characterized by heavy *discounting* of the future.

import quota A legal maximum of how much of a particular good can be imported.

importers Individuals who have bought elsewhere at a low price and bring products into a high-priced region in order to sell them at a profit.

income demand curve Curve that illustrates the relationship between the quantity of a good that is demanded with income; also known as an *Engel curve*.

income effect The change in consumption behaviour resulting from a change in income.

income elasticity of demand The percentage change in the quantity demanded that results from a 1 per cent change in income.

incomplete information games Games in which players do not know the payoffs of all other players.

increasing cost industries Competitive industries for which the *long-run* industry supply curve is upward sloping.

increasing returns to scale Production technologies under which a t-fold increase in all inputs results in more than a t-fold increase in output (when no inputs are wasted).

incumbent firm A firm that is already operating in an industry for which there is a large *fixed cost* of entry.

independence axiom The assumption that underlies *expected utility theory*; states that if a gamble is preferred to another gamble, then the preference ordering does not change when both gambles are mixed with the same third gamble.

indifference curve A set of consumption bundles that a consumer is indifferent between.

indifference map A map of *indifference curves* that represents a person's tastes.

indirect utility function The function that tells us, for any set of economic circumstances, how much utility a person will attain (assuming the person maximizes utility).

industrial organization Subfield of economics that investigates competition in different types of industry structures.

inefficient A situation that can be changed in such a way as to make some individuals better off without making anyone worse off.

inferior good A good whose consumption increases as income falls (and falls as income increases).

information set The set of decision nodes that an individual knows has been reached along a *game tree*.

informational advertising Advertising that is aimed at providing information about the quality or price of a product.

innovation The search for new products or for improvements in existing products.

insurance A contract that reduces risk by increasing consumption in the 'bad' outcome while lowering consumption in the 'good' outcome.

interest rate The price of using financial capital.

interior solution A solution (to an optimization problem) that has strictly positive values for all choice variables.

intertemporal budget A budget illustrating consumption trade-offs across time.

isocost curve A set of input bundles that all cost the same (given current input prices).

isoprofit curve A set of *production plans* that all result in the same *profit* (given the current input and output prices).

isoquant A set of input bundles that all result in the same level of output (given the current technological constraint).

L

labour demand The demand for labour by firms (as a function of input prices).

labour economics Subfield of economics that deals with issues related to labour supply and demand (and related issues).

labour supply The supply of labour by workers (who trade off consumption and leisure).

Laffer curve Curve illustrating the relationship between tax rates and tax revenues.

Lagrange function A function composed of the *objective function* and (λ times) the *constraint* set to zero, used in mathematical *optimization problems*.

Lagrange multiplier The λ term in the Lagrange function.

land rent The rental price of a unit of land.

land value The market price of land, equal to the present discounted value of all future land rents.

law and economics Subfield of economics dealing with the intersection of law and economics.

law of 1/N In political science, a rule of thumb predicting the degree of inefficiency of a marginal public project (voted on in legislatures) as a function of the number N of legislators.

law of diminishing marginal product The fact that for any real-world production process, the *marginal product* of every input must at some point decline.

leisure Discretionary time not spent working.

Lerner index A monopolist's mark-up (i.e. price minus marginal cost) divided by price.

Leviathan government A government that maximizes political rents rather than social goals (such as efficiency).

lexicographic tastes An example of tastes that satisfy all our five basic assumptions except for continuity.

libertarian paternalism In *behavioural economics*, the idea that default choices should be set to overcome psychological biases while allowing individuals to choose differently.

Lindahl equilibrium An equilibrium concept in which individuals pay personalized prices for *public goods* such that their decentralized choices lead to *efficient* public good provision.

Lindahl prices Individualized prices that result in a *Lindahl equilibrium*.

local non-satiation A property of tastes that assumes there always exists an alternate consumption bundle close to the one currently consumed such that the consumer would prefer that alternate bundle.

local public finance Subfield in economics that studies the formation and functioning of local governments and clubs.

local public goods Locally non-*rivalrous* and non-*excludable* public goods.

logrolling Legislative deal making in which legislators agree to vote for each other's favourite *pork barrel projects*.

long run For firms, the period over which all inputs become variable; for industries, the period over which exit/entry of firms is possible.

Lorenz curve A curve relating the percentiles of the population to percentiles of income or wealth; used to calculate the *Gini coefficient*.

loss aversion In *prospect theory*, people's tendency to prefer avoiding losses to acquiring gains.

lump sum tax A non-*distortionary* tax, payment of which cannot be avoided through a change in behaviour.

luxury good A good whose consumption as a percentage of income increases as income increases.

M

macroeconomics Subfield in economics that deals with the determination of economic aggregates such as unemployment, inflation and growth.

marginal Refers to 'one additional' or 'the last' of some economic variable.

marginal cost The change in cost from one additional unit of output; or, equivalently, the change in cost from the last unit of output produced.

marginal rate of substitution The rate at which a consumer is willing to trade one good for another; also, the negative slope of an *indifference curve*.

marginal revenue The change in revenue from producing (and selling) one more unit of output, or, equivalently, the change in revenue from the last unit.

marginal technical rate of substitution See *technical rate of substitution*.

marginal utility The change in utility from one more unit of a good; or, equivalently, the change in utility from the last unit of a good.

marginal willingness to pay The willingness to pay for one more (or for the last) unit of a consumption good.

market A structure that permits buyers and sellers to trade.

market power The power to influence price.

mark-up Price minus *marginal cost*.

Marshallian demand *Uncompensated demand* that gives the quantity demanded as a function of prices and income (or wealth).

Marshallian consumer surplus The area above price up to the Marshallian demand curve.

matching pennies A *zero-sum game* in which one player attempts to mimic the other while the other player attempts not to mimic the first player.

McKelvey Theorem Theorem illustrating that, in general, sequences of pairwise majority rule votes can lead to even the most extreme outcomes.

mechanism design Subfield of economics that develops mechanisms to allocate scarce resources in the absence of market prices.

median voter theorem Theorem that predicts the median voter's most preferred policy will be implemented under majority rule if the issue space is single-dimensional and preferences are *single-peaked*.

minimum wage A *price floor*, or minimum legal price, in the labour market.

mixed gambles *Gambles* that result from gambling over gambles.

mixed strategy In *game theory*, strategies that place non-zero probability on more than one *pure strategy*.

monopolistic competition A market structure with relatively low (but non-zero) barriers to entry and (usually) some product differentiation.

monopoly Market structure with a single firm and high barriers to entry; the firm therefore has *market power*.

monopsony *Market power* on the demand side.

monotonic tastes Tastes under which more is better than (or at least as good as) less.

moral hazard The tendency to change behaviour after entering a contract, particularly one that reduces risk.

N

Nash equilibrium In *game theory*, equilibrium in which all players play a strategy that is a *best response* to the strategies played by all other players.

natural monopoly A *monopoly* that is protected from competition by barriers to entry that arise from the nature of the production process that gives rise to declining *average cost* (either because of high *fixed costs* or *increasing returns to scale* over large quantities).

necessary conditions Conditions that must be satisfied for something (usually an optimum, in our case) to be true.

necessity A good whose consumption as a percentage of income falls as income increases.

network externality The effect that one consumer's consumption decision has on the value of a product to others.

neuroeconomics Subfield that lies at the intersection of economics and neuroscience.

neutral goods Goods that neither raise nor lower utility.

non-convexity A property of sets under which one can find two points in the set such that the line connecting those points lies at least partially outside the set.

non-credible threats In *game theory*, threats that will not be carried out by rational players.

non-excludability The impossibility of excluding non-paying consumers from consuming certain goods.

non-price rationing Rationing mechanisms to allocate scarce resources when prices are distorted.

non-rivalry Property of *public goods* that can be consumed by more than one person at the same time.

norm of reciprocity A *social norm* that is encapsulated by the saying 'I'll scratch your back if you scratch mine'.

normal form In *game theory*, a representation of a game in a *payoff matrix* (rather than a *game tree*).

normal good A good that is consumed in greater amounts as income increases.

normative economics Subfield of economics that intersects with philosophy in that it asks 'what is good'.

numeraire In general equilibrium models, the good that is assigned a price of 1.

O

objective function The function that is being maximized or minimized in a mathematical *optimization problem*.

oligopoly Market structure in which several large firms compete in the presence of *barriers to entry* that keep other firms out of the market.

opportunity cost What someone gives up by undertaking an activity; also called *economic cost* or just cost.

optimization problem A problem in which some variables are chosen in order to maximize or minimize a function.

optimizing Doing the best one can (given the circumstances).

order-preserving function (or transformation) A *function* that preserves the ranking of numbers assigned to points.

outsourcing The practice of producing goods in low-wage markets while selling them in high-wage markets.

own-price demand curves Curves relating the quantity of a good demanded to that good's price (holding all else equal).

P

Pareto efficient Same as *efficient*.

Pareto optimal Same as *Pareto efficient*.

partial equilibrium model A model in which one market is analyzed in isolation.

patent A legal *barrier to entry* established to allow an innovating firm to operate without the threat of entry from other firms for a limited amount of time.

payoff matrix In two-player games, a matrix that provides each player's payoff for all combination of *strategies*.

perfect Bayesian (Nash) equilibrium In *incomplete information games*, a set of *strategies* and *beliefs* such that each player's strategy is a best response to all other players' strategies given the player's beliefs.

perfect complements Goods that produce utility only if consumed together.

perfect price discrimination *First degree price discrimination*.

perfect substitutes Goods that are completely substitutable for one another from the consumer's perspective.

perfectly competitive industry Market structure in which many small firms produce identical products and each acts as a *price taker*.

Pigouvian subsidy A *subsidy* designed to internalize a positive *externality*.

Pigouvian tax A tax designed to internalize a negative *externality*.

political economy Subfield that lies at the intersection of political science and economics in that it investigates the economics of political behaviour.

pooling contracts In insurance markets, when different risk types buy the same insurance contract.

pooling equilibrium In *incomplete information games*, equilibrium in which some players play *pooling strategies*; in insurance markets, equilibrium with pooling contracts.

pooling strategy In *incomplete information games*, strategies in which individuals play the same way regardless of what type they are.

pork barrel spending Government spending targeted at one legislator's region but paid for by everyone.

positive economics Branch of economics whose purpose is to predict behaviour and its equilibrium consequences.

positive monotone transformation Same as *order preserving transformation*.

preference revelation mechanism A mechanism designed to get individuals to reveal their true preferences (often for *public goods*).

present-bias In *intertemporal* decision making, a psychological bias that always treats the 'present' as unique; captured in the *beta-delta model*.

price ceiling A maximum legal price.

price discrimination The practice of charging different prices to different individuals for the same product.

price elasticity The percentage change in quantity from a 1 per cent change in price.

price floor A minimum legal price.

price subsidy A *subsidy* that lowers the price for consumers.

price-taking Non-strategic behaviour resulting from individuals rationally treating prices as given (because the individuals are too small relative to the market to impact the prices through their decisions).

price-gouging A popular term used to denote moral outrage at the charging of high prices during periods of supply disruptions.

Prisoner's Dilemma In *game theory*, a game in which not cooperating is a *dominant strategy* even though all players would be better off if they all cooperated.

private goods Goods characterized by *rivalry* and *excludability*.

probability weighting In *prospect theory*, the tendency of individuals to overweight small probabilities and underweight large probabilities as they make decisions.

producer choice set The set of *production plans* that are technologically feasible.

producer surplus The amount a producer would be willing to pay to operate in a market, i.e. economic *profit*.

product differentiation The practice of differentiating one's product in order to soften competition (and raise *profit*).

production frontier The boundary of the *producer choice set*, i.e. the production plans that are technologically feasible and that do not waste inputs.

production function Mathematical characterization of the *production frontier*.

production plan A list of inputs and outputs.

production possibilities frontier In a two-good model, a depiction of the highest possible quantity of one good that can be produced given how much of the second good is produced.

profit The difference between economic revenue and economic cost; also called *producer surplus*.

profit function The function that gives profit for any set of input and output prices (assuming profit-maximizing behaviour by the firm).

profit maximization The act of finding the *production plan* that yields the largest possible *profit* given the technological and economic *constraints* faced by a firm.

proof by contradiction A logical proof that begins by presuming that a statement is false and then illustrates that this presumption leads to a contradiction, which then implies that the statement is in fact true.

prospect theory A *behavioural economics* model of choice in the presence of risk that introduces psychological biases that are at odds with traditional *expected utility theory*.

public economics Subfield of economics that investigates taxation and government expenditures; also known as public finance.

public goods Goods that are characterized by *non-rivalry* (and often, but not always, *non-excludability*).

pure strategy In *game theory*, a *strategy* that plays an action with probability 1 at each *information set*.

put option A contract that gives the holder the option of selling some quantity in the future at a predetermined price.

Q

quasi-hyperbolic discounting A special case of *hyperbolic discounting* captured by the *beta-delta model*.

quasi-concave function A *function* whose level curves give rise to convex *upper-contour sets*.

quasilinear tastes Tastes under which the *marginal rate of substitution* is independent of the quantity of one of the goods in the consumption bundle; tastes that do not give rise to *income effects*.

R

rational tastes Tastes that are *complete* and *transitive*.

rationing Any process that allocates scarce resources.

Rawlsian social preferences An ethical rule that favours mechanisms that maximize the welfare of the least well off person.

Rawlsian social welfare function A function that represents *Rawlsian social preferences*.

real income In microeconomics, typically means utility constant income; in macroeconomics (and sometimes in microeconomics) it means inflation-adjusted income.

reference-dependent preferences In *behavioural economics*, preferences that evaluate choices relative to a status quo or reference point.

regular inferior goods *Inferior goods* that are not *Giffen goods*.

regulatory capture The tendency of regulators to be responsive to interests of those who are being regulated.

rent control A *price ceiling* in the housing rental market.

rental rate The price for use of *capital* (or land).

repeated game A game that is played repeatedly, with players observing the outcome of all previous interactions.

representative consumer A hypothetical consumer used to model the behaviour of a group of consumers.

representative producer A hypothetical producer used to model the behaviour of a group of producers.

reservation utility Utility that is obtainable for an individual in the absence of trading, usually from consumption of the *endowment*.

returns to scale Property of production technologies describing how output responds to proportional increases in all inputs.

risk aversion The willingness to pay positive amounts in order to reduce risk while not changing the expected outcome, i.e. tastes where the *certainty equivalent* is less than the *expected value* of a gamble.

risk neutral Indifference between gambles that have the same expected outcome but different levels of risk.

risk premium The difference between the *expected value* of a gamble and the *certainty equivalent*.

rivalry The feature of *private goods* that they can be consumed by only one person.

Roy's identity The mathematical relationship that allows one to derive output demand from *indirect utility functions*.

S

saving The difference between current income and current consumption.

screening In the presence of *asymmetric information*, the practice of expending effort to ascertain information about the individual (or firm) on the other side of a market transaction.

sealed bid auction Auctions in which bids are submitted at the same time without other bidders knowing any of the bids.

second-best analysis Economic analysis that investigates what happens when one or more efficiency conditions cannot be satisfied.

second-degree price discrimination *Price discrimination* when firms cannot identify consumer marginal willingness to pay and thus structure non-linear price schedules to induce consumers to reveal their type in a *separating equilibrium*.

second-order condition Sufficient condition for a solution (derived from *first order conditions*) to an *optimization problem* to be optimal.

second-price auction Auction in which the winner pays the second highest bid for the item.

second welfare theorem The theorem that states that any *efficient* allocation of resources in an economy can be achieved through a decentralized market process so long as governments can engage in *lump sum taxation* and redistribution.

secondary market A market in which goods previously obtained elsewhere are offered for sale.

separating equilibrium In *incomplete information games*, equilibrium in which all types of players play different strategies (thus revealing information); in insurance markets, equilibrium in which different insurance contracts are sold to different risk types.

separating strategy In *incomplete information games*, strategies in which individuals play differently depending on what type they are.

sequential move game A game in which players play in sequence, with later players observing at least some of what previous players have done.

Shephard's Lemma In consumer theory, the derivative of the *expenditure function* with respect to output price is equal to the *Hicksian demand* function; in producer theory, the derivative of the *cost function* with respect to input price is equal to the *conditional input demand* function.

short run For firms, usually the period over which some inputs are fixed; for industries, the period over which exit/entry of firms is not possible.

shut-down price The output price at which a firm will choose to stop producing in the *short run*.

signalling In the presence of *asymmetric information*, the practice of expending effort to provide information about oneself to the individual (or firm) on the other side of a market transaction.

signalling games Games in which players with private information can reveal their type by adopting particular strategies.

simple exchange economy A *general equilibrium* model of a single individual who acts as both a price taking producer and consumer.

simultaneous move games Games in which all players choose their action simultaneously.

single-crossing property Property of classes of tastes that implies indifference curves from two different *indifference maps* only cross once.

single-peaked preferences In *political economy* models, tastes that have a most preferred bundle, with utility decreasing in the distance from that bundle.

Slutsky equation The equation that decomposes the consumer response to a price change into the portion that is due to the *income effect* and the portion that is due to the *substitution effect*.

Slutsky substitution The change in behaviour from a price change when the individual is compensated so that they can still afford the original bundle.

snob effect A *network externality* that causes individuals to place a higher value on a good the fewer others who also consume that good.

social choice function A function that ranks different social states.

social entrepreneurs Entrepreneurs who aim to innovate in non-profit sectors to achieve social change.

social indifference curves Indifference curves over utility (or income or wealth) allocations across individuals.

social marginal benefit The sum of all marginal benefits resulting from an action.

social marginal cost The sum of all marginal costs resulting from an action.

social norms Behavioural expectations that are largely shared within the *civil society*.

social planner A hypothetical individual who is in possession of all information and allocates resources with the aim of maximizing some social goal.

social welfare function A *function* that ranks different utility (or income or wealth) allocations.

speculation The attempt to make money by trading across time.

speculator One who engages in *speculation*.

split-rate tax A property tax that levies a higher rate on building structures than on land.

spontaneous order An order that emerges without central planning.

spot market The market in which goods currently trade.

spot price The price in the *spot market*.

Stackelberg competition Strategic competition (by firms) in which firms view quantity as the strategic variable and firms move sequentially.

state-contingent assets Assets that become available if a particular state of the world materializes.

state-contingent consumption Consumption that is contingent on a particular state of the world materializing.

state-dependent tastes (or utility) *Expected utility* in the presence of risk, with different functions required to measure utility in different states of the world.

state-independent tastes (or utility) *Expected utility* in the presence of risk, with a single function used to measure utility in different states of the world.

statistical discrimination Discrimination that results from *asymmetric information* where the less informed party uses group averages to infer individual characteristics; a form of stereotyping.

status quo effect In *prospect theory*, the tendency of the status quo being used to evaluate changes in circumstances.

statutory tax incidence The legal incidence of tax obligations as written in tax laws (or statutes).

Stone–Geary utility function A utility function that incorporates subsistence levels of consumption below which utility is not defined.

strategy In *game theory*, a player's complete plan of action prior to the beginning of the game.

structure-induced voting equilibrium A voting equilibrium that emerges from institutional restrictions that limit what can be voted on and how.

subgame Any part of a sequential game that begins at an *information set* consisting of a single node and includes the rest of the game tree from there on, with all information sets following the initial node required to be fully contained in the subgame.

subgame perfect equilibrium A *Nash equilibrium* that does not rely on any *noncredible threats* (and thus is also a Nash equilibrium in all *subgames*).

subsidy Government financial assistance that may take the form of a cash payment and/or a *price subsidy*.

substitutability The degree to which consumption goods can be substituted for one another without changing utility, or inputs can be substituted for one another without changing output.

substitution effect In consumer theory, the portion of a response (to a price change) that is due solely to the change in *opportunity costs*; in producer theory, the change in input bundles that a *cost-minimizing* producer undertakes in response to input price changes (while keeping output constant).

sufficient conditions Conditions that, if satisfied, guarantee that something is true (usually an optimum derived from *first-order conditions*, in our case).

sunk cost An expense that is unaffected by the economic choice at hand.

supply curve A graph that relates quantity supplied to price.

supply function A function that for any economic environment, gives the amount that will be supplied.

T

tariff A tax on imports.

tastes A ranking of consumption bundles, also called preferences.

tax base The value of the activities that are subject to a tax.

tax credit An amount that can be deducted from a taxpayer's tax obligation prior to tax payment being made.

tax deduction An amount that can be deducted from a person's taxable income that is used to calculate the person's tax obligation.

tax incidence The analysis of how the burden of a tax is distributed between individuals.

tax-deferred savings Savings that are not subject to taxation until withdrawn for consumption (usually in retirement).

technical rate of substitution The rate at which inputs can be substituted for one another in production without changing output; also, the slope of *isoquants*; sometimes referred to as marginal technical rate of substitution.

technologically efficient production Production that does not waste inputs.

third-degree price discrimination *Price discrimination* in which monopolists can identify consumer marginal willingness to pay and can charge different per-unit prices to different consumers.

Tiebout model Model of *local public finance* in which residents choose locations by taking into account the mix of local taxes and services.

time inconsistency Intertemporal decisions in which individuals plan for the future in ways that they do not stick to as the future becomes the present.

tipping point A critical mass of engagement in an activity by individuals such that the activity turns from one undertaken in an initial equilibrium by only a few to one undertaken in a new equilibrium by many due to the presence of *network externalities*.

tit-for-tat strategy In repeated *Prisoner's Dilemma games*, the strategy that begins by cooperating and then always mimics the opponent's action from the last interaction.

total cost The sum of all economic costs.

total expenditure The sum of all expenses, including *sunk costs*.

tradable pollution permits Legal permits (in a *cap-and-trade* system) that entitle the holder to engage in a specified amount of pollution or to sell that right to someone else.

tragedy of the commons The overuse of commonly held resources due to the *free-rider problem*.

transactions cost The cost (other than the price paid) incurred by the parties to an economic exchange.

transitive tastes Tastes such that bundle A being preferred to B and B being preferred to C implies that A is preferred to C.

trigger strategy In *repeated games*, a *strategy* under which punishments in future interactions are triggered by an opponent's behaviour.

two-part tariffs Non-linear prices under which consumers are charged a fixed fee as well as a per-unit price.

U

uncompensated demand The demand for a good when the individual is not compensated for price changes; same as *Marshallian demand*.

unconstrained optimization problem An *optimization problem* that is not subject to a *constraint*, sometimes because the constraint has been substituted into the *objective function*.

upper contour set The set of points above the level curve of a function.

urban economics Subfield of economics that investigates the functioning of cities.

usury laws Laws that place *price ceilings* on interest rates.

utility function A function that represents *tastes* by ranking consumption bundles.

utility maximization The act of choosing from the *consumer choice set* the consumption bundle that yields the highest level of utility.

utility possibility frontier In a two-consumer model, a depiction of the highest possible utility attainable by one individual given how much utility is attained by the second individual.

utility possibility set The *utility possibility frontier* and all utility allocations below this frontier.

utils Hypothetical measurement unit for utility.

V

variable cost Cost that changes as the quantity produced changes.

veil of ignorance Hypothetical idea of a veil behind which individuals are imagined to choose social systems without knowing their own particular circumstances in life.

Von Neumann–Morgenstern expected utility Same as *expected utility*.

W

wage For firms, the price of labour; for workers, the opportunity cost of leisure.

Walras's law In *general equilibrium* theory, the result that permits us to conclude that supply is equal to demand in the nth market if supply is equal to demand in all other $(n-1)$ markets.

warm glow effect The utility one gets from the act of charitable giving (apart from the utility from the difference that is made by the charitable gift).

wealth effect In models with *endogenous* budgets, the change in behaviour (from a price change) that is due to the implicit change in wealth rather than the change in *opportunity costs*.

Z

zero profit Level of profit expected in *perfectly competitive industries* in the *long run;* implies a firm is doing as well as it could in its next best alternative activity.

zero-sum game Game in which the winners' winnings are exactly equal to the losers' losses.

Index